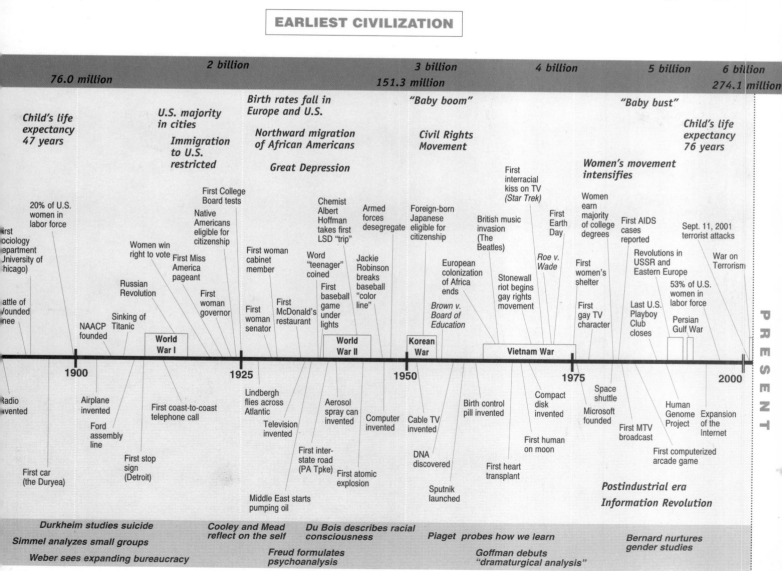 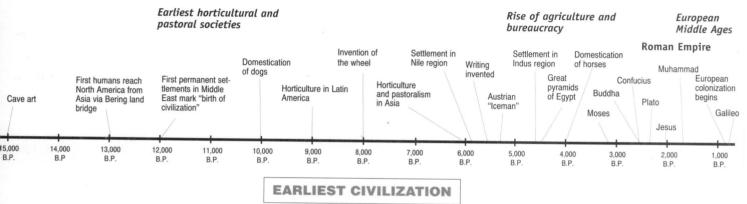

what we call civilization is relatively recent indeed, with the first permanent settlements occurring in the Middle East a scant 12,000 years ago. But the written record of our species' existence extends back only half this long, to the time humans invented writing and first farmed with animal-driven plows some 5,000 years B.P.

Sociology came into being in the wake of the many changes to society wrought by the Industrial Revolution over

the last few centuries—, _____ary perspective. The lower time line provides a close-up look at the events and trends that have defined The Modern Era, most of which are discussed in this text. Innovations in technology are charted in the beige panel below the line and provide a useful backdrop for viewing the milestones of social progress highlighted in the blue panel above the line. Major contributions to the development of sociological thought are traced along the very bottom of this time line.

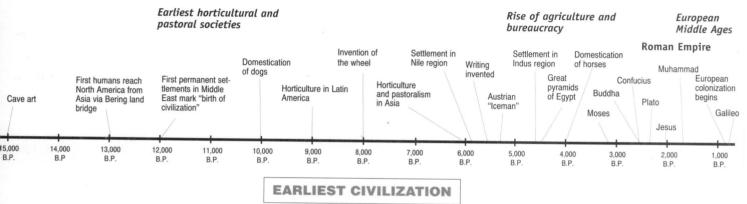

Earliest horticultural and pastoral societies

Rise of agriculture and bureaucracy

European Middle Ages

Roman Empire

Cave art

First humans reach North America from Asia via Bering land bridge

First permanent settlements in Middle East mark "birth of civilization"

Domestication of dogs

Horticulture in Latin America

Invention of the wheel

Horticulture and pastoralism in Asia

Settlement in Nile region

Writing invented

Austrian "Iceman"

Settlement in Indus region

Great pyramids of Egypt

Domestication of horses

Muhammad

Confucius

Buddha

Moses

Plato

Jesus

European colonization begins

Galileo

| 15,000 B.P. | 14,000 B.P | 13,000 B.P. | 12,000 B.P. | 11,000 B.P. | 10,000 B.P. | 9,000 B.P. | 8,000 B.P. | 7,000 B.P. | 6,000 B.P. | 5,000 B.P. | 4,000 B.P. | 3,000 B.P. | 2,000 B.P. | 1,000 B.P. |

EARLIEST CIVILIZATION

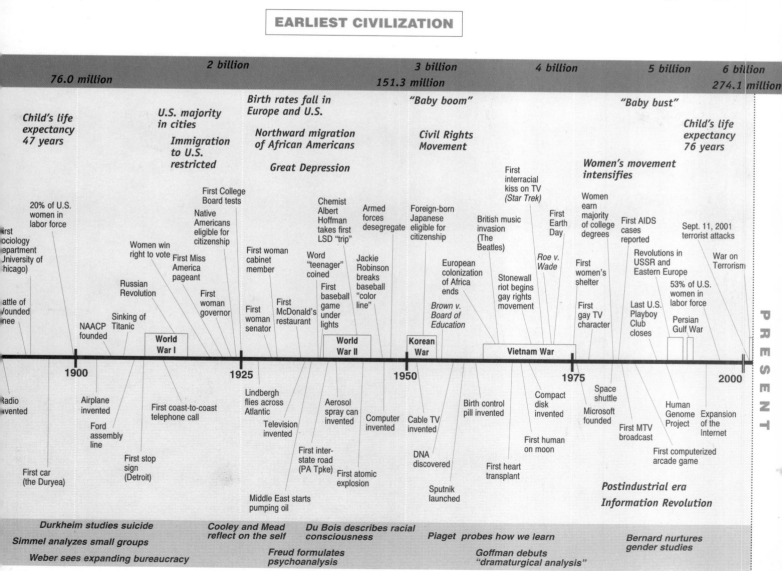

2 billion — 3 billion — 4 billion — 5 billion — 6 billion

76.0 million — *151.3 million* — *274.1 million*

Child's life expectancy 47 years

U.S. majority in cities

Immigration to U.S. restricted

Birth rates fall in Europe and U.S.

Northward migration of African Americans

Great Depression

"Baby boom"

Civil Rights Movement

"Baby bust"

Child's life expectancy 76 years

Women's movement intensifies

First sociology department (University of Chicago)

20% of U.S. women in labor force

Battle of Wounded Knee

Women win right to vote

First Miss America pageant

Russian Revolution

NAACP founded

Sinking of Titanic

First College Board tests

Native Americans eligible for citizenship

First woman governor

First woman senator

First woman cabinet member

First McDonald's restaurant

Chemist Albert Hoffman takes first LSD "trip"

Word "teenager" coined

First baseball game under lights

Armed forces desegregate

Jackie Robinson breaks baseball "color line"

Foreign-born Japanese eligible for citizenship

European colonization of Africa ends

Brown v. Board of Education

First interracial kiss on TV (Star Trek)

British music invasion (The Beatles)

Stonewall riot begins gay rights movement

First Earth Day

Roe v. Wade

Women earn majority of college degrees

First women's shelter

First gay TV character

First AIDS cases reported

Revolutions in USSR and Eastern Europe

Last U.S. Playboy Club closes

Persian Gulf War

Sept. 11, 2001 terrorist attacks

53% of U.S. women in labor force

War on Terrorism

World War I

World War II

Korean War

Vietnam War

| 1900 | 1925 | 1950 | 1975 | 2000 |

Radio invented

First car (the Duryea)

Airplane invented

Ford assembly line

First stop sign (Detroit)

First coast-to-coast telephone call

Lindbergh flies across Atlantic

Television invented

First interstate road (PA Tpke)

Middle East starts pumping oil

Aerosol spray can invented

First atomic explosion

Computer invented

Cable TV invented

DNA discovered

Sputnik launched

Birth control pill invented

First heart transplant

First human on moon

Compact disk invented

Space shuttle

Microsoft founded

First MTV broadcast

First computerized arcade game

Human Genome Project

Expansion of the Internet

Postindustrial era

Information Revolution

P R E S E N T

Durkheim studies suicide

Simmel analyzes small groups

Weber sees expanding bureaucracy

Cooley and Mead reflect on the self

Freud formulates psychoanalysis

Du Bois describes racial consciousness

Piaget probes how we learn

Goffman debuts "dramaturgical analysis"

Bernard nurtures gender studies

SOCIOLOGY

This book is offered to teachers of sociology in the hope that it will help our students understand their place in today's society and in tomorrow's world.

Jan J. Macionis

SOCIOLOGY

NINTH EDITION

John J. Macionis

Kenyon College

Prentice
Hall

Upper Saddle River, New Jersey 07458

Senior Acquisitions Editor: Christopher DeJohn
AVP, Publisher: Nancy Roberts
Editor in Chief of Development: Susanna Lesan
Development Editor: Harriett Prentiss
VP, Director of Production and Manufacturing: Barbara Kittle
Production Editor: Barbara Reilly
Copyeditors: Carol Peschke, Amy Macionis
Proofreader: Karen Bosch
Editorial Assistant: Christina Scalia
Prepress and Manufacturing Manager: Nick Sklitsis
Prepress and Manufacturing Buyer: Mary Ann Gloriande
Director of Marketing: Beth Mejia
Marketing Assistant: Anne Marie Fritzky
Creative Design Director: Leslie Osher
Art Director: Nancy Wells
Interior and Cover Designer: Laura Gardner

Line Art Manager: Guy Ruggiero
Line Art Illustrations: Lithokraft II
Maps: Carto-Graphics
Director, Image Resource Center: Melinda Reo
Interior Image Specialist: Beth Boyd-Brenzel
Manager, Rights and Permissions: Kay Dellosa
Permissions Coordinator: Debra Hewitson
Photo Researcher: Barbara Salz
Cover Coordinator: Kim Marsden
Cover Art: Bourbon Street Jazz Bars by Franklin McMahon,
    © Franklin McMahon/Corbis.
Senior Media Editor: John J. Jordan
Media Production Project Manager: Maurice Murdock
Media Project Producer: Steve Gagliostro
Media Producers: Matthew Krack, Bill Norris
Media Manager: Lynn Pearlman

This book was set in 10/11 Janson by Lithokraft II,
and was printed and bound by Von Hoffman Press, Inc.
The cover was printed by Phoenix Color Corp.

© 2003, 2001, 1999, 1997, 1995, 1993, 1991, 1989, 1987 by Pearson Education, Inc.
Upper Saddle River, New Jersey 07458

For permission to use copyrighted material, grateful
acknowledgment is made to the copyright holders listed
on pages 682–83, which is considered an extension of this
copyright page.

Printed in the United States of America
10 9 8 7 6 5 4 3 2 1

STUDENT ISBN 0-13-097763-2
AIE ISBN 0-13-098814-6

Pearson Education LTD., London
Pearson Education Australia PTY, Limited, Sydney
Pearson Education Singapore, Pte. Ltd
Pearson Education North Asia Ltd, Hong Kong
Pearson Education Canada, Ltd, Toronto
Pearson Educación de Mexico, S.A. de C.V.
Pearson Education—Japan, Tokyo
Pearson Education Malaysia, Pte. Ltd
Pearson Education, Upper Saddle River, New Jersey

Printed on Recycled Paper

BRIEF CONTENTS

TABLE OF CONTENTS

cyber.scope PART II
HOW NEW TECHNOLOGY IS
CHANGING OUR WAY OF LIFE   244

PART V
SOCIAL CHANGE

cyber.scope PART V
NEW INFORMATION TECHNOLOGY
AND SOCIAL CHANGE   648

BOXES

APPLYING SOCIOLOGY

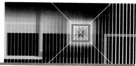

DIVERSITY: RACE, CLASS, AND GENDER

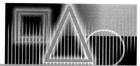

CRITICAL THINKING

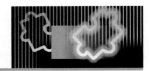

GLOBAL SOCIOLOGY

FEATURE ESSAYS

NEW INFORMATION TECHNOLOGY AND SOCIETY

 cyber.scope

MAPS

GLOBAL MAPS: WINDOW ON THE WORLD

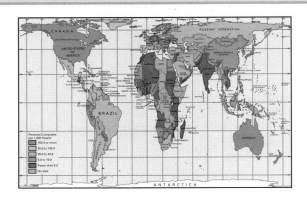

NATIONAL MAPS: SEEING OURSELVES

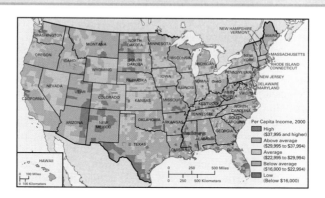

PREFACE

The final manuscript of this book was just about complete when the tragic events of September 11, 2001, took place. Rarely does the news of one day so change everyone's lives. There is little doubt that terrorism will leave its mark on life in the United States and elsewhere for years to come as our concern for security prompts us to reexamine so many dimensions of our everyday lives.

More generally, these events force us to confront the question of what kind of world we live in and what kind of world we want for ourselves and for our children. It is here that readers of this book will discover the importance of the discipline of sociology.

The daily e-mail I receive from students in the United States and around the world stands as testimony to the power of sociology to help people understand their world and, often, to transform people. Indeed, the material in this text was recently used in a presentation to the U.S. Supreme Court (*Falvo v. Owasso Ind. School District*, 2001). All instructors know well the deep satisfaction that comes from making a difference in the lives of our students. There is no greater reward for our work, and, in my case, no better reason for striving for ever-better revisions of *Sociology*, which, along with the briefer *Society: The Basics*, stands out as the discipline's most popular text.

I hope you will find *Sociology* to be authoritative, comprehensive, stimulating, and—as so many students testify—plain fun to read. In addition to the book, every new copy of *Sociology, Ninth Edition*, comes with a second learning tool, a CD-ROM that provides a number of short video selections that illustrate major concepts, ideas, and theories. Included on the CD-ROM is a series of "author's tip" videos—one for each chapter—that focuses on key chapter themes. Finally, the third part of the learning package that is available free with each new book is access to a full-featured Web site at http://www.prenhall.com/macionis From the main page, simply click on the cover of the text and select a chapter; you will find chapter summaries, learning objectives, suggested essay questions and paper topics, and multiple-choice and true-false questions prepared by the author of the text. As the student completes these tests, the server immediately grades them and points out exactly where the student needs more study. Also at this Web site, faculty will find a full complement of teaching resources, including Power Point slides for download and the Prentice Hall syllabus manager system that allows an instructor to post a course syllabus to the Internet without having to learn hypertext markup language (HTML).

Textbook, CD-ROM, and Web site: A three-part, multimedia package that is the foundation for sound learning in this new information age. We invite you to examine all three!

ORGANIZATION OF THIS TEXT

Part I of the textbook and the CD-ROM introduces the foundations of sociology. Underlying the discipline is the *sociological perspective*—the focus of Chapter 1, which explains how this invigorating point of view brings the world to life in a new and instructive way. Chapter 2 spotlights *sociological investigation*, or the "doing of sociology." This chapter explains the scientific, interpretive, and critical orientations of the discipline, and illustrates major research strategies with actual, well-known sociological work.

Part II surveys the foundations of social life. Chapter 3 focuses on the central concept of *culture*, emphasizing the cultural diversity that makes up our society and our world. The focus of Chapter 4 is the concept of *society*, presenting four time-honored models for understanding the structure and dynamics of social organization. This unique chapter provides introductory students with the background to understand the ideas of important thinkers—including Karl Marx, Max Weber, and Emile Durkheim, as well as Gerhard Lenski—that appear in subsequent chapters. Chapter 5 turns to *socialization*, exploring how we gain our humanity as we learn to participate in society. Chapter 6 provides a micro-level look at the patterns of *social interaction* that make up our everyday lives. Chapter 7 offers full-chapter coverage of *groups and organizations*, explaining the importance of group life and investigating how and why large organizations have come to dominate our way of life. Chapter 8 explains how the operation of society generates both *deviance and conformity*, and also surveys the operation of the criminal justice system. Chapter 9 explains the social foundations of *human sexuality*. This chapter surveys sexual patterns in the United States and also explores variations in sexual practices through history and around the world today.

Part III offers unparalleled discussion of social inequality, beginning with three chapters on *social stratification*. Chapter 10 introduces major concepts and presents theoretical explanations of social inequality. This chapter richly illustrates historical changes in stratification and how patterns of inequality vary in today's world. Chapter 11 surveys *social inequality in the United States*, confronting common perceptions of inequality and assessing how well they square with research findings. Chapter 12 extends the analysis with a look at *global stratification*, revealing the disparities in wealth and power that separate rich and poor nations. Both Chapters 11 and 12 pay special attention to how global developments affect stratification in the United States just as they explore our society's role in global inequality. Chapter 13, *gender stratification*, explains how gender is a central element in social stratification in the United States as it is worldwide. *Race and ethnicity*, additional important dimensions of social inequality that often intersect differences based on class and gender, are detailed in Chapter 14. *Aging and the elderly*, a topic of increasing concern to "graying" societies such as our own, is addressed in Chapter 15.

Part IV includes a full chapter on each social institution. Leading off is Chapter 16, *the economy and work*, because most sociologists recognize the economy as having the greatest impact on all other institutions. This chapter traces the rise and fall of industrial production in the United States, the emergence of a global economy, and explains what such transformations mean for the U.S. labor force. Chapter 17, *politics and government*, analyzes the distribution of power in U.S. society as well as surveying political systems around the world. In addition, this chapter includes discussion of the U.S. military, the threat of war, and an expanded discussion of terrorism as a new form of war in the twenty-first century. Chapter 18, *family*, explains the central importance of families to social organization, and underscores the diversity of family life both here and in other societies. Chapter 19, *religion*, addresses the timeless human search for ultimate purpose and meaning, introduces major world religions, and explains how religious beliefs are linked to other dimensions of social life. Chapter 20, *education*, analyzes the expansion of schooling in industrial and postindustrial societies. Here again, schooling in the United States comes to life through contrasts with educational patterns in other countries. Chapter 21, *health and medicine*, reveals health to be a social issue just as much as it is a matter of biological processes. This chapter traces the historical emergence of scientific medicine, analyzes current medical issues and alternative approaches, and compares U.S. patterns to those found in other countries.

Part V examines important dimensions of global social change. Chapter 22 highlights the powerful impact of *population growth* and *urbanization* in the United States and throughout the world with special attention to the *natural environment*. Chapter 23 explores forms of *collective behavior* and explains how people seek or resist social change by joining *social movements*. Chapter 24 concludes the text with an overview of *social*

change that contrasts *traditional, modern, and postmodern societies*. This chapter rounds out the text by explaining how and why world societies change and critically analyzing the benefits and liabilities of traditional, modern, and postmodern ways of life.

CONTINUITY: ESTABLISHED FEATURES OF *SOCIOLOGY*

Everyone knows that introductory sociology texts have some things in common; but differences run deep. The extraordinary success of *Sociology* and *Society: The Basics*, which are far and away the most widely adopted texts by sociologists across North America, results from a combination of the following distinctive features.

The best writing style. Most important, this text offers a writing style widely praised by students and faculty alike as elegant and inviting. *Sociology* is an enjoyable text that encourages students to read—even beyond their assignments. No one says it better than the students themselves, whose recent e-mail includes testimonials such as these:

> Thanks for writing such a brilliant book. It has sparked my sociological imagination. This was the first textbook that I have ever read completely and enjoyed. From the moment that I picked the book up I started reading nonstop.

> I have read four chapters ahead; it's like a good novel I can't put down! I just wanted to say thank you.

> Your book is extremely well written and very interesting. I find myself reading it for pleasure, something I have never done with college texts. It is going to be the only collegiate textbook that I ever keep simply to read on my own. I am also thinking of picking up sociology as my minor due to the fact that I have enjoyed the class as well as the text so much. Your writing has my highest praise and utmost appreciation.

> I am taking a Sociology 101 class using *Sociology*, a book that I have told my professor is the best textbook that I have ever seen, bar none. I've told her as well that I will be more than happy to take more sociology classes as long as there is a Macionis text to go with them.

> I am fascinated by the contents of this textbook. In contrast to texts in my other classes, I actually

enjoy reading *Sociology*. Thank you for such a thought-provoking, well-written textbook.

I absolutely love your sociology text! It is a wonderful book. This is by far the best textbook I have ever used. The CD-ROM has been very helpful and informative. I had no idea that I would love sociology so much!

A global perspective. *Sociology* has taken a leading role in expanding the horizons of our discipline beyond the United States. *Sociology* was the first text to mainstream global content, introduce global maps, and offer coverage of global topics such as stratification and the environment. No wonder this text has been adapted and translated in many languages for use all over the world. Each chapter explores global social diversity as well as explaining why social trends in the United States—from musical tastes to the pace of airport security to the growing disparity of income—are influenced by what happens elsewhere.

A focus on national diversity. *Sociology* invites students from all social backgrounds to discover a fresh and exciting way to see the world and to understand themselves. Readers will find in this text the diversity of U.S. society—people of African, Asian, Middle Eastern, European, and Latino ancestry as well as women and men of various class positions, in all parts of the country, and at all points in the life course. An independent survey of all introductory books gave this text top marks for mainstreaming race and ethnicity (Stone, 1996).

Emphasis on critical thinking. Critical-thinking skills include the ability to challenge common assumptions by formulating questions, identify and weigh appropriate evidence, and reach reasoned conclusions. This text not only teaches but encourages students to discover on their own.

The broadest coverage so instructors can choose. No other text matches *Sociology*'s twenty-four chapter coverage of the field. We offer such breadth—at no greater cost—knowing that few instructors will assign every chapter, but with the goal of supporting instructors as they choose exactly what they wish to teach.

Engaging and instructive chapter openings. One of the most popular features of *Sociology* is the engaging vignettes that begin each chapter. These openings—for instance, using the tragic sinking of the *Titanic* to illustrate the life and death consequences of social inequality, or the story of Linda Brown to explore racial inequality in the United States, or Utah's recent prosecution of Tom Green for polygamy to describe our ideas about

the family—spark the interest of readers as they introduce important themes. This revision retains eleven of the best chapter-opening vignettes found in earlier editions and offers thirteen new ones as well.

Inclusive focus on women and men. Beyond devoting two full chapters to the important concepts of sex and gender, *Sociology* mainstreams gender into *every* chapter, showing how the topic at hand affects women and men differently and explaining how gender operates as a basic dimension of social organization.

Theoretically clear and balanced. *Sociology, Ninth Edition*, makes theory easy. Chapter 1 introduces the discipline's major theoretical approaches, which are used in all the chapters that follow. The text highlights not only the social-conflict, structural-functional, and symbolic-interaction paradigms, but incorporates feminist theory, social-exchange analysis, ethnomethodology, cultural ecology, and sociobiology.

Chapter 4—unique to this text—provides students with an easy-to-understand introduction to important social theorists *before* they encounter their work in later chapters. The ideas of Max Weber, Karl Marx, and Emile Durkheim, as well as Gerhard Lenski's historical overview of human societies, appear in distinct sections that instructors may assign together or refer to separately at different points in the course.

Recent research and the latest data. *Sociology, Ninth Edition*, blends classic sociological statements with the latest research as reported in the leading publications in the field. Some 250 new studies inform this revision, and about half of the 1500 pieces of research cited throughout the book were published since 1995. From chapter to chapter, the text's statistical data are the most recent available and include the results of Census 2000.

Learning aids. This text has many features to help students learn. In each chapter, **key concepts** are identified by boldfaced type, and following each appears *a precise, italicized definition*. A list of key concepts with their definitions appears at the end of each chapter, and a complete **Glossary** is found at the end of the book. Each chapter also contains a numbered **Summary** and four **Critical-Thinking Questions** that help students review material and assess their understanding. Following these are a number of **Applications and Exercises**, which provide students with activities to do on or near the campus. Each chapter also includes an annotated list of worthwhile **Sites to See** on the Internet.

Outstanding images: photography and fine art. This book offers the finest and most extensive program of photography and artwork available in any sociology textbook. The ninth edition of *Sociology* displays about 100 examples of fine art as well as more than 250 color photographs—more than in any other text. Each of these images is carefully selected by the author and appears with an insightful caption. Moreover, both photographs and artwork present people of various social backgrounds and historical periods. For example, alongside art by well-known Europeans such as Vincent Van Gogh and U.S. artists including George Tooker, this edition has paintings by celebrated African American artists Jacob Lawrence and Henry Ossawa Tanner, outstanding Latino artist Diego Rivera, and the engaging Australian painter and feminist Sally Swain.

Thought-provoking theme boxes. Although boxed material is common to introductory texts, *Sociology, Ninth Edition*, provides a wealth of uncommonly good boxes. Each chapter typically contains four boxes, which fall into five types that amplify central themes of the text. **Global Sociology** boxes provoke readers to think about their own way of life by examining the fascinating social diversity that characterizes our world. **Diversity: Race, Class, and Gender** boxes focus on multicultural issues and amplify the voices of women and people of color. **Applying Sociology** boxes show the value of the sociological perspective to understanding the world around us. **Critical Thinking** boxes teach students to ask sociological questions about their surroundings and help them evaluate important controversial issues. Each Critical Thinking box is followed by three "What do you think?" questions. **Controversy & Debate** boxes complete each chapter by presenting several points of view on an issue of contemporary importance. The three "Continue the debate" questions that conclude each box are sure to stimulate spirited class discussion.

Sociology, Ninth Edition, contains ninety-four boxes in all. Fourteen of them are new to this edition and many more are revised and updated. A complete list of the boxes in this text can be found following the table of contents.

An unparalleled program of sixty-seven global and national maps. This is the text that pioneered the use of global and national maps. Windows on the World global maps—thirty-two in all and including eleven new ones—are truly sociological maps offering a comparative look at the number of children typically born to women, income disparity, favored languages and religions, the extent of prostitution, permitted marriage forms, the practice of female genital mutilation, the degree of political freedom, the incidence of HIV infection, and a host of other issues. The global maps use the non-Eurocentric projection devised by cartographer Arno Peters that accurately portrays the relative size of all the continents. A complete listing of the Window on the World global maps follows the table of contents.

Seeing Ourselves national maps—thirty-five in all with four new and many updated for this edition—help to illuminate the social diversity of the United States. Most of these maps offer a close-up look at all 3,014 U.S. counties, highlighting suicide rates, per capita income, labor force participation, college attendance, the prevalence of interracial marriage, most widespread religious affiliation, teen pregnancy rates, and, as measures of popular culture, where people play golf or where households prefer wine or drink beer. Each national map includes an explanatory caption that poses several questions to stimulate students' thinking about social forces. A complete list of the Seeing Ourselves national maps follows the table of contents.

INNOVATION: CHANGES IN THE NINTH EDITION

Each new edition of *Sociology* has broken new ground, one reason that the popularity of this text and its brief version keeps rising. A revision raises high expectations, but, after several years of planning and hard work, we are pleased to offer what we believe is the best revision yet. Here is a brief overview of the innovations that define *Sociology, Ninth Edition*.

Keeping up with the field. As surprising as it may seem, some textbooks fail to reflect new work in the field, making few references to sociology journals and taking little notice of new books. In preparing this revision, I have reviewed new publications—including *American Journal of Sociology, American Sociological Review, Rural Sociology, Social Forces, Sociological Focus, Sociological Forum, Society, The Public Interest, Social Problems, Population Bulletin, Teaching Sociology, Contemporary Sociology*, and *Social Science Quarterly*—as well as popular press publications that keep us abreast of current trends and events.

Improved high-tech! For this edition, the CD-ROM includes a video library, presenting short clips that illustrate important concepts and ideas. This video material, drawn from the video library of ABC News, takes learning to a whole new level.

Students buying new copies of *Sociology, Ninth Edition*, will have open access to an updated Web site at http://www.prenhall.com/macionis Begin by clicking on the cover of this book and follow the easy-to-use menus. At the site, students will find a full range of study materials including computer-graded practice tests. Faculty will find a resource bank including Power Point slides for download and software that allows instructors to put a course syllabus on the Internet without having to know anything about HTML. In addition, all users of this book are invited to make use of videos, biographies, and dozens of links found at the author's personal Web site at http://www.TheSociologyPage.com or http://www.macionis.com

Linking technology to the text. At four or five points in each chapter, the text directs students to visit carefully selected Web sites. These sites provide biographical material about sociologists, useful data, or information about an organization that deals with the topic at hand.

More coverage of rural issues. Although most of the population of the United States lives in urban places, most of our country's counties are rural. Therefore, this revision pays special attention not only to urban social patterns but also to rural issues. Examples of this rural focus include a comparative analysis of rural and urban poverty and homelessness in Chapter 11; discussion of women in coal mining in Chapter 13; a discussion of the aging of U.S. farmers in Chapter 15; a new diversity box in Chapter 17 on the rural-urban divide in U.S. politics; and a discussion of the "rural rebound" in Chapter 22, as well as more photographs and artwork that reflect rural life. In addition, we have recently added *Rural Sociology* to the list of journals that provide new research reported in this text.

New maps! The only way to improve our colorful maps is be sure they are as up to date as possible. This edition features sixty-seven global and national maps, fifteen of them new to this edition.

New chapter-opening vignettes. This revision keeps the best of the popular chapter-opening vignettes and adds thirteen new ones; overall, more than half of the openings are new to this edition.

Many new boxes. A total of ninety-four boxes supports five themes of the text: Global Sociology, Diversity: Race, Class, and Gender, Critical Thinking, Applying Sociology, and, focusing on social policy, Controversy &

Debate. Many boxes are revised and updated; fourteen boxes are new to this edition.

The latest statistical data. Instructors count on this text for including the very latest statistical data. The ninth edition comes through again, making use of data from the Internet as well as conventional bound publications of various government agencies and private organizations. The author and Carol A. Singer, a professional government documents librarian at Bowling Green State University (Ohio), have worked together to ensure that the newest statistics are used throughout the text—in many cases for 2000 and even for 2001. These data include reported results of Census 2000. In addition, readers will find 250 new research citations as well as references to many familiar current events to peak their interest.

New topics. The ninth edition of *Sociology* is thoroughly updated with new and expanded discussions in every chapter. Here is a listing, by chapter, of some of the new material:

• **Chapter 1 The Sociological Perspective**: A new chapter opening explores how and why U.S. children are deeply involved in sports; in addition, a new global map highlights the number of children born to women around the world.

• **Chapter 2 Sociological Investigation**: New material includes new end-of-chapter learning ideas and several new Web sites noted throughout the chapter.

• **Chapter 3 Culture**: A new chapter opening describes the visit of members of the Andean Q'ero society to New York City; find an update on the "culture of victimization" thesis, a new journal entry on visiting Disney World, new links to the author's videos on travel and cultural relativism, and a new Global Sociology box comparing the dominant cultures of the United States and Canada.

• **Chapter 4 Society**: There is an update on classic theorists' view of the Information Revolution as well as links to online biographies of sociology's founders.

• **Chapter 5 Socialization**: Find an update on how the violent content in television programming and video games affects young children; a Web link provides a complete chapter on the sociology of the mass media; a new Diversity: Race, Class, and Gender box examines how race and ethnicity affect the personal development of high-school students.

• **Chapter 6 Social Interaction in Everyday Life**: A new national map shows where people are and are not likely to be avid golfers; find updates on reality construction and the sociology of humor (including a few new jokes).

• **Chapter 7 Groups and Organizations**: A new global snapshot highlights arts-related organizations in selected countries; there is an update on McDonaldization as well as new data on the share of incumbents who held their congressional seats in the 2000 elections, discussion of using social networks to find jobs by gender, race, and ethnicity, an update on gender and management positions in the United States, and new material on the controversy surrounding computers, large organizations, and personal privacy.

• **Chapter 8 Deviance**: A new national map shows the risk of violent crime for all U.S. counties; there are updates on U.S. crime rates and a fresh look at the rising debate over capital punishment.

• **Chapter 9 Sexuality**: A new chapter opening illustrates the problems of acceptance faced by transgender individuals; there are updates on U.S. attitudes about sexual practices and a new global map shows the use of contraception around the world.

• **Chapter 10 Social Stratification**: Find an update on the unequal distribution of wealth in the United States; a new global snapshot shows that income inequality is greater in the United States than in high-income European nations.

• **Chapter 11 Social Class in the United States**: A new chapter opening looks at a case of high-flying executive pay; a new national map shows average income for all counties across the United States; we've added a new discussion of rural homelessness and updated statistics on income, wealth, and poverty.

• **Chapter 12 Global Stratification**: A new chapter opening notes natural disasters that are all too common in low-income nations; find new data showing which countries now fall into high-, middle-, and low-income categories as well as a new figure that charts the world's increasing income inequality.

• **Chapter 13 Gender Stratification**: The chapter includes two new global maps illustrating women's power and the practice of female genital mutilation in global perspective; there are updates on the share of women in various job categories, including new data on the number of women in top corporate positions; new statistics show the latest gaps in earnings between women and men and between various racial and ethnic categories; new Web links take readers to recent government reports concerning gender.

• **Chapter 14 Race and Ethnicity**: A new journal entry points out racial and ethnic stratification in everyday life; find Census 2000 data for various racial and ethnic categories as well as updates on income and other measures of social standing by race and ethnicity; there is more on the social construction of ethnicity as well as race, and the intersection of these variables with class and gender.

• **Chapter 15 Aging and the Elderly**: A new chapter opening looks at the role of middle-aged people caring for aging parents; new data show the advancing average age of U.S. farmers and give updates on income for all categories of elderly

people in the United States; a number of new Web sites provide access to recent data and analysis of issues related to aging.

• **Chapter 16 The Economy and Work**: A new chapter opener illustrates the power of technology to change the character of work; a new global map shows the share of the labor force in service sector jobs for world nations; the chapter offers new data (which may surprise you) on the relative importance of the three economic sectors in high-, middle-, and low-income nations; new data on the U.S. labor force highlight the increasing share of minorities.

• **Chapter 17 Politics and Government**: Updates the 2000 elections, including a new national map showing the county-by-county results of the presidential race; a new Diversity: Race, Class, and Gender box explains the rural-urban divide in U.S. politics; there is extensive coverage of terrorism and the events of September 11, 2001, including an analysis of terrorism as a new form of "asymmetrical" war.

• **Chapter 18 Family**: A new opening profiles the "plural marriage" of Tom Green and his conviction for bigamy; updates are provided on all family trends including singlehood, divorce, single parenting, and cohabitation as well as family data from Census 2000.

• **Chapter 19 Religion**: Did you know that the number of Muslims in the United States exceeds the number of Episcopalians, Presbyterians, or Jews? Find the most recent data, as well as an update on the ordination of women; there is also a new section on the search for spirituality in postdenominational U.S. society.

• **Chapter 20 Education**: A new chapter opening highlights the far better performance on proficiency tests by children living in high-income communities compared to those from low-income areas; find updates on educational statistics as well as a new discussion of the U.S. teacher shortage.

• **Chapter 21 Health and Medicine**: This chapter offers an update on the share of minority physicians in the United States as well as a new statistical profile of the health of the U.S. population; there is expanded discussion of health care policy in Canada.

• **Chapter 22 Population, Urbanization, and Environment**: Find a new chapter opening as well as a new section describing the "rural rebound" trend; a new Diversity: Race, Class, and Gender box uses Census 2000 to highlight the minority majority in half the nation's largest 100 cities; there are updates on all U.S. demographic data and more on "critical demography."

• **Chapter 23 Collective Behavior and Social Movements**: A new chapter opening describes the massive demonstration at the 1999 meeting of the World Trade Organization in Seattle; there is also a new discussion of moral panics, including the widespread fear in the wake of the events of September 11, 2001.

- **Chapter 24 Social Change: Traditional, Modern, and Postmodern Societies**: A new chapter opening highlights the lives of two families who resided in the same New York City apartment a century apart; a new table provides a snapshot of change in the United States across the twentieth century; a new journal entry describes the appearance of mass society and an updated figure shows support for science in selected nations around the world.

A WORD ABOUT LANGUAGE

This text's commitment to representing the social diversity of the United States and the world carries with it the responsibility to use language thoughtfully. In most cases, we prefer the terms *African American* and *person of color* to the word *black*. We use the terms *Hispanic* and *Latino* to refer to people of Spanish descent. Most tables and figures refer to "Hispanics" because this is the term the Census Bureau uses when collecting statistical data about our population.

Students should realize, however, that many individuals do not describe themselves using these terms. Although the term "Hispanic" is commonly used in the eastern part of the United States, and "Latino" and the feminine form "Latina" are widely heard in the West, across the United States people of Spanish descent identify with a particular ancestral nation, whether it be Argentina, Mexico, some other Latin American country, or Spain or Portugal in Europe.

The same holds for Asian Americans. Although this term is a useful shorthand in sociological analysis, most people of Asian descent think of themselves in terms of a specific country of origin (say, Japan, the Philippines, Taiwan, or Vietnam).

In this text, the term "Native American" refers to all the inhabitants of the Americas (including the Hawaiian Islands) whose ancestors lived here prior to the arrival of Europeans. Here again, however, most people in this broad category identify with their historical society (for example, Cherokee, Hopi, or Zuni). The term "American Indian" designates only those Native Americans who live in the continental United States, not including Native peoples living in Alaska or Hawaii.

Learning to think globally also leads us to use language carefully. This text avoids the word "American"—which literally designates two continents—to refer to just the United States. For example, referring to this country, the term "U.S. economy" is more correct than the "American economy." This convention may seem a small point, but it implies the significant recognition that we in this country represent only one society (albeit a very important one) in the Americas.

SUPPLEMENTS

Sociology, Ninth Edition, is the heart of an unprecedented multimedia learning package that includes a wide range of proven instructional aids as well as several new ones. As the author of the text, I maintain a keen interest in all the supplements to ensure their quality and integration with the text. The supplements for this revision have been thoroughly updated, improved, and expanded. Also, many of them are now available for easy download at http://www.prenhall.com/sociology_central

FOR THE INSTRUCTOR

Annotated Instructor's Edition. The AIE is a complete student text annotated by the author on every page. Annotations—which have been thoroughly revised for this edition—have won praise from instructors for enriching class presentations. Margin notes include summaries of research findings, statistics from the United States or other nations, insightful quotations, information highlighting patterns of social diversity in the United States, and high-quality survey data from the National Opinion Research Center's (NORC) *General Social Survey* and *World Values Survey* data from the Inter-university Consortium for Political and Social Research (CPSR).

Data File. This is the "instructor's manual" that is of interest even to those who have never used one before. The *Data File* provides far more than detailed chapter outlines and discussion questions; it contains statistical profiles of the United States and other nations, summaries of important developments, and significant research and supplemental lecture material for every chapter of the text. The *Data File* is available in Windows format as well as the traditional print version.

Test Item File. A revised test item file prepared by John Macionis is available in both printed and computerized forms. The file contains 2400 items—100 per chapter—in multiple-choice, true/false, and essay formats. Questions are identified as simple "recall" items or more complex inferential issues, and answers to all questions are page referenced to the text. Prentice Hall Custom Test is a test generator designed to allow the creation of personalized exams. It is available in Windows and Macintosh formats. Prentice Hall also provides a test preparation service to users of this text that is as easy as a call to our toll-free 800 number. Please contact your Prentice Hall representative for this number.

Film/Video Guide: Prentice Hall Introductory Sociology, Sixth Edition. Keyed to the chapters of this text, this guide describes more than 300 films and videos appropriate for classroom viewing. It also provides summaries, discussion questions, and rental sources for each film and video.

ABCNEWS **ABC News/Prentice Hall Video Library for Sociology.** Few will dispute that video is the most dynamic supplement you can use to enhance a classroom presentation. However, the quality of the video material and how well it relates to your course still make all the difference. Prentice Hall and ABC News are working together to bring to you the best and most comprehensive video ancillaries available in the college market.

Through its wide variety of award-winning programs—*Nightline, This Week, World News Tonight,* and *20/20*—ABC offers a resource for feature and documentary-style videos related to the chapters in *Sociology, Ninth Edition.* The programs have high production quality, present substantial content, and are hosted by well-versed, well-known anchors.

The authors and editors of Prentice Hall have carefully selected videos on topics that complement *Sociology, Ninth Edition,* and have included notes on how to use them in the classroom. An excellent instructor's guide carefully and completely integrates the videos into your lecture. The guide has a synopsis of each video that shows its relation to the chapter and discussion questions to help students focus on how concepts and theories apply to real-life situations.

Volume I: Social Stratification (0-13-466228-8)
Volume II: Marriage/Families (0-13-209537-8)
Volume III: Race/Ethnic Relations (0-13-458506-2)
Volume IV: Criminology (0-13-375163-5)
Volume V: Social Problems (0-13-437823-7)
Volume VI: Intro to Sociology I (0-13-095066-1)
Volume VII: Intro to Sociology II (0-13-095060-2)
Volume VIII: Intro to Sociology III (0-13-095773-9)
Volume IX: Social Problems (0-13-095774-7)
Volume X: Marriage/Families II (0-13-095775-5)
Volume XI: Race and Ethnic Relations II (0-13-021134-6)
Volume XII: Institutions (0-13-021133-8)
Volume XIII: Introductory Sociology IV (0-13-018507-8)
Volume XIV: Introductory Sociology V (0-13-018509-4)

Prentice Hall Introductory Sociology PowerPoint™ Transparencies. Created by Roger J. Eich of Hawkeye Community College, this PowerPoint slide set combines graphics and text in a colorful format to help you convey sociological principles in a new and exciting way. Created in PowerPoint, an easy-to-use, widely available software program, this set contains over 300 slides keyed to each chapter in the text. For easy download, they are available on our instructor resource site at http://www.prenhall.com/sociology_central

Prentice Hall Color Transparencies: Sociology Series VII. Full-color illustrations, charts, and other visual materials from the text as well as outside sources have been selected to make up this useful in-class tool.

Instructor's Guide to Prentice Hall Color Transparencies: Sociology Series VII. This guide offers suggestions for effectively using each transparency in the classroom.

MEDIA SUPPLEMENTS

Interactive CD-ROM. Using video as a window to the world outside of the classroom, this innovative CD-ROM offers students videos and animations arranged according to theme (Global Perspective, Social Diversity, or Critical Thinking) within each chapter. Students can view relevant ABC News clips and author video tips, interact with the global and national maps, and review sociological concepts through video. The CD-ROM is available free with all new copies of *Sociology, Ninth Edition.*

Census 2000 Update CD-ROM. Capturing the rich picture of our nation drawn by Census 2000, this CD-ROM brings related Census data into your classroom in a multimedia format. It is free when packaged with *Sociology, Ninth Edition.*

Companion Website™. In tandem with the text, students and professors can now take full advantage of the Internet to enrich their study of sociology. The Macionis *Companion Website™* continues to lead the way in providing students with avenues for delving deeper into the topics covered in the text. Features of the Web site include chapter objectives, study questions, and faculty resources, as well as links to interesting material and information from other sites on the Web that will reinforce and enhance the content of each chapter. Use of the site is free to both students and faculty. Please visit the site at http://www. prenhall.com/macionis and click on the cover of *Sociology, Ninth Edition*.

ContentSelect. Developed by Prentice Hall and EBSCO, the world leader in online journal subscription management, ContentSelect is a customized research database for students of sociology. A collection of over 125 sources—peer-reviewed journals as well as popular magazines, but *all* with relevance to sociology—provide students with a reputable starting point for their research. If you would like to integrate this resource into your course, a free student access code can be packaged with *Sociology, Ninth Edition*. Please contact your Prentice Hall representative for more information or visit the ContentSelect Web site at www.prenhall.com/contentselect

Distance Learning Solutions. Prentice Hall is committed to providing our leading content to the growing number of courses being delivered over the Internet by developing relationships with the leading vendors—Blackboard™, Web CT™, and CourseCompass, Prentice Hall's own easy-to-use course management system powered by Blackboard™. Please visit our technology solutions site at http://www.prenhall.com/demo

Sociology on the Internet: A Critical Thinking Guide, 2001. This guide focuses on developing the critical thinking skills necessary to evaluate and use online sources. The guide also provides a brief introduction to navigating the Internet, along with complete references related specifically to the discipline of sociology. This supplementary book is free to students when packaged with *Sociology, Ninth Edition*. Please contact your Prentice Hall representative for more information.

FOR THE STUDENT

Study Guide. This complete guide helps students to review and reflect on the material presented in *Sociology, Ninth Edition*. Each of the twenty-four chapters in the Study Guide provides an overview of the corresponding chapter in the student text, summarizes its major topics and concepts, offers applied exercises, and features end-of-chapter tests with solutions.

Practice Tests. This collection of study questions offers students a learning opportunity that is free when packaged with *Sociology, Ninth Edition*.

The New York Times Supplement, Themes of the Times, for Introductory Sociology. *The New York Times* and Prentice Hall are sponsoring *Themes of the Times*, a program designed to enhance student access to current information relevant to the classroom. Through this program, the core subject matter provided in this text is supplemented by a collection of timely articles from one of the world's most distinguished newspapers, *The New York Times*. These articles demonstrate the vital, ongoing connection between what is learned in the classroom and what is happening in the world around us.

To enjoy the wealth of information of *The New York Times* daily, a reduced subscription rate is available. For information, call toll-free 1-800-631-1222.

Prentice Hall and *The New York Times* are proud to co-sponsor *Themes of the Times*. We hope it will make the reading of both textbooks and newspapers a more dynamic and involving process.

10 Ways to Fight Hate Brochure. Produced by the Southern Poverty Law Center, the leading hate-crime and crime-watch organization in the United States, it walks students through ten steps that they can take on their own campus or in their own neighborhood to fight hate everyday.

Critical Thinking Audiocassette Tape. In keeping with the text's critical thinking approach, a sixty-minute audio tape is available to help students think and read critically.

IN APPRECIATION

The conventional practice of designating a single author obscures the efforts of dozens of women and men that have resulted in *Sociology, Ninth Edition*. I would like to express my thanks to the Prentice Hall editorial team, including Yolanda de Rooy, division president, Laura Pearson, editorial director, Nancy Roberts, publisher, Chris DeJohn, senior acquisitions editor in sociology, and Christina Scalia, editorial assistant, for their steady enthusiasm and for pursuing both innovation and excellence. Day-to-day work on the book is shared by the author and the production team. Susanna Lesan, developmental editor-in-chief at Prentice Hall, has played a vital role in the development of all my texts for more than fifteen years, coordinating and supervising the editorial process. Barbara Reilly, production editor at Prentice Hall, is an essential member of the team. Barbara deserves much of the credit for the attractive page layout of the book; indeed, if anyone "sweats the details" more than the author, it is Barbara! Amy Marsh Macionis, the text's "in house" editor, checks virtually everything, untangling awkward phrases, and eliminating errors and inconsistencies in all the statistical data. Amy is a most talented editor who is relentless in her pursuit of quality; my debt to her is great, indeed.

I also have a large debt to the members of the Prentice Hall sales staff, the men and women who have given this text such remarkable support over the years. Thanks, especially, to Beth Mejia who directs our marketing campaign.

Thanks, too, to Laura Gardner for providing the interior design of the book, which was coordinated by art director Nancy Wells. Developmental and copy editing of the manuscript was provided by Harriett Prentiss, Carol Peschke, and Amy Marsh Macionis. Barbara Salz did the research for our photographs and fine art.

It goes without saying that every colleague knows more about some topics covered in this book than the author does. For that reason, I am grateful to the hundreds of faculty and students who have written to me to offer comments and suggestions. More formally, I am grateful to the following people who have reviewed some or all of this manuscript:

Sampson Lee Blair, Arizona State University
Lovberta Cross, Southwestern Tennessee Community College
Isaac W. Eberstein, Florida State University
Mike Hart, Broward County Community College
Steve Light, SUNY Plattsburgh
Dale Lund, University of Utah
Tim Tuinstra, Kalamazoo Valley Community College
Rich Yinger, Palm Beach Community College

I also wish to thank the following colleagues for sharing their wisdom in ways that have improved this book: Doug Adams (The Ohio State University), Richard Alford (East Central University), Sally Archer (The College of New Jersey), Kip Armstrong (Bloomsburg University), Rose Arnault (Fort Hays State University), Patricia S. Astry (SUNY College at Fredonia), Judith Barker (Ithaca College), Scott Beck (Eastern Tennessee State University), Paul J. Becker (Morehead State University), Lois Benjamin (Hampton University), Philip Berg (University of Wisconsin, La Crosse), Jane Bock (University of Wisconsin—Green Bay), Charlotte Brauchle (Southwest Texas Junior College), Bill Brindle (Monroe Community College), John R. Brouillette (Colorado State University), Cathryn Brubaker (Georgia Perimeter College), Brent Bruton (Iowa State University), Richard Bucher (Baltimore City Community College), Karen A. Callaghan (Barry University), Karen Campbell (Vanderbilt University), Harold Conway (Blinn College), Gerry Cox (Fort Hays State University), Robert Daniels (Mount Vernon Nazarene College), James A. Davis (Harvard University), Sumati Devadutt (Monroe Community College), Keith Doubt (Northeast Missouri State University), Denny Dubbs (Harrisburg Area Community College), Lois Easterom (Onondaga Community College), Travis Eaton (Northeast Louisiana State University), Helen Rose Fuchs Ebaugh (University of Houston), John Ehle (Northern Virginia Community College), Roger Eich (Hawkeye Community College), Heather Fitz Gibbon (The College of Wooster), Kevin Fitzpatrick (University of Alabama-Birmingham), Jerry Flattum (University of Minnesota), Dona C. Fletcher (Sinclair Community College), Abby Foster (University of Colorado at Colorado Springs), Charles Frazier (University of Florida), Karen Lynch Frederick (St. Anselm College), Mary Theresa Bonhage Freund (Alma College), Patricia Gagné (University of Kentucky, Louisville), Pam Gaiter (Collin County Community College), Timothy J. Gallagher (Kent State University), Jarvis Gamble (Owen's Technical College), Steven Goldberg (City College, City University of New York), Charlotte Gotwald (York College of Pennsylvania), Norma B. Gray (Bishop State Community College), Rhoda Greenstone (DeVry Institute), Jeffrey Hahn (Mount Union College), Harry Hale (Northeast Louisiana State University), Dean Haledjian (Northern Virginia Community College), Dick Haltin (Jefferson Community College), Roma Stouall Hanks (University of South Alabama), Marvin Hannah (Milwaukee Area Technical College), Charles Harper (Creighton University), Christine L. Himes (Syracuse University), Gary Hodge (Collin County Community College), Elizabeth A. Hoisington (Heartland Community College), Sara Horsfall (Stephen F. Austin State University), Peter Hruschka (Ohio Northern University), Glenna Huls (Camden County College), Jeanne Humble (Lexington Community College), Cynthia Imanaka (Seattle Central Community College), G. David Johnson (University of South Alabama), Patricia Johnson (Houston Community College), Ed Kain (Southwestern University), Paul Kamolnick (Eastern Tennessee State University), Irwin Kantor (Middlesex County College), Thomas Korllos (Kent State University), Rita Krasnow (Virginia Western Community College), Donald Kraybill (Elizabethtown College),

Michael Lacy (Colorado State University), Michael Levine (Kenyon College), George Lowe (Texas Tech University), Don Luidens (Hope College), Larry Lyon (Baylor University), Li-Chen Ma (Lamar University), N. Jane McCandless (State University of West Georgia), Karen E. B. McCue (University of New Mexico, Albuquerque), Meredith McGuire (Trinity College), Setma Maddox (Texas Wesleyan University), Errol Magidson (Richard J. Daley College), Marguerite Martin (Gonzaga University), Allan Mazur (Syracuse University), Jack Melhorn (Emporia State University), Ken Miller (Drake University), Michael Miller (University of Texas at San Antonio), Richard Miller (Navarro College), Daniel J. Monti (Boston University), Joe Morolla (Virginia Commonwealth University), Craig Nauman (Madison Area Technical College), David Naylor (Charleston Southern University), Toby Parcel (The Ohio State University), Anne Peterson (Columbus State Community College), Marvin Pippert (Roanoke College), Lauren Pivnik (Monroe Community College), Nevel Razak (Fort Hays State College), Jim Rebstock (Broward Community College); George Reim (Cheltenham High School), Virginia Reynolds (Indiana University of Pennsylvania), Laurel Richardson (The Ohio State University), Keith Roberts (Hanover College), Ellen Rosengarten (Sinclair Community College), Howard Schneiderman (Lafayette College), Ray Scupin (Lindenwood University), Steve Severin (Kellogg Community College), Robert Shelly (Ohio University), Harry Sherer (Irvine Valley College), Walt Shirley (Sinclair Community College), Anson Shupe (Indiana University-Purdue University at Fort Wayne), Ree Simpkins (Missouri Southern State University), Glen Sims (Glendale Community College), Blasco Sobrinho (University of Cincinnati), Nancy Sonleitner (University of Oklahoma), Dee Southard (Central Washington University), Steven Spitzer (Suffolk University), Leslie Stanley-Stevens (Tarleton University), Larry Stern (Collin County Community College), Randy Ston (Oakland Community College), Verta Taylor (The Ohio State University), Vickie H. Taylor (Danville Community College), Jan Thomas (Kenyon College), Mark J. Thomas (Madison Area Technical College), Len Tompos (Lorain County Community College), Christopher Vanderpool (Michigan State University), Phyllis Watts (Tiffin University); Murray Webster (University of North Carolina, Charlotte), Debbie White (Collin County Community College), Rhys H. Williams (Southern Illinois University—Carbondale), Marilyn Wilmeth (Iowa University), Stuart Wright (Lamar University), William Yoels (University of Alabama, Birmingham), Dan Yutze (Taylor University), Wayne Zapatek (Tarrant County Community College), and Frank Zulke (Harold Washington College).

Finally, I would like to dedicate this edition of the book to all the men and women who became heroes in the wake of events of September 11, 2001, in ways big and small, including those known to many and those known to just a few. In the face of terror, they rose up, reached out to others even at the cost of their own lives, and displayed the very best that lies within us.

ABOUT THE AUTHOR

John J. Macionis (pronounced ma-SHOW-nis) was born and raised in Philadelphia, Pennsylvania. He received his bachelor's degree from Cornell University and his doctorate in sociology from the University of Pennsylvania. His publications are wide-ranging, focusing on community life in the United States, interpersonal intimacy in families, effective teaching, humor, new information technology, and the importance of global education. He and Nijole V. Benokraitis have edited the companion volume to this text, *Seeing Ourselves: Classic, Contemporary, and Cross-Cultural Readings in Sociology*. Macionis has also authored *Society: The Basics*, the leading brief text in the field, and he collaborates on international editions of the texts: *Sociology: Canadian Edition* (with Linda M. Gerber, from Prentice Hall Canada), *Society: The Basics, Canadian Edition* (with Cecelia Benoit and Mikael Jansson, also from Prentice Hall Canada), and *Sociology: A Global Introduction* (with Ken Plummer, published by Prentice Hall Europe). *Sociology* is also available in various international and foreign language editions. In addition, Macionis and Vincent Parrillo have written the urban studies text, *Cities and Urban Life* (Prentice Hall). Macionis's most recent new text is *Social Problems* (Prentice Hall), which is the first text to take a social-constructionist approach to the study of social problems and public policy. The latest on all the Macionis textbooks, as well as news, information, and dozens of Internet links of interest to students and faculty in sociology, can be found at the author's personal Web site, http://www.macionis.com or http://www.TheSociologyPage.com Additional information, as well as online study guides for the texts, is available at the Prentice Hall site, http://www.prenhall.com/macionis

John Macionis is Professor and Prentice Hall Distinguished Scholar of Sociology at Kenyon College in Gambier, Ohio. During a career of almost twenty-five years at Kenyon, he has chaired the Anthropology-Sociology Department, directed the college's multidisciplinary program in humane studies, and presided over the campus senate and also the college's faculty.

In 1998, the North Central Sociological Association named Macionis recipient of the Award for Distinguished Contribution to Teaching, citing his work with textbooks and his pioneering use of new technology in sociology.

Professor Macionis has been active in academic programs in other countries, having traveled to some fifty nations. In the fall of 1994, he directed the global education course for the University of Pittsburgh's Semester at Sea program, teaching 400 students on a floating campus that visited twelve countries as it circled the globe.

Macionis writes, "I am an ambitious traveler, eager to learn and, through the texts, to share much of what I discover with students, many of whom know so little about the rest of the world. For me, traveling and writing are all dimensions of teaching. First and foremost, I am a teacher—a passion for teaching animates everything I do." At Kenyon, Macionis offers a wide range of upper-level courses, but his favorite course is Introduction to Sociology, which he schedules every semester. He enjoys extensive contact with students and each term invites his students to enjoy a home-cooked meal.

The Macionis family—John, Amy, and children McLean and Whitney—live on a farm in rural Ohio. Their home serves as a popular bed and breakfast where they enjoy visiting with old friends and making new ones. In his free time, John enjoys bicycling through the Ohio countryside, swimming, sailing, and playing oldies rock and roll on his guitar. He is currently learning to play the Scottish bagpipes.

Professor Macionis welcomes (and responds to) comments and suggestions about this book from faculty and students. Write to the Sociology Department, Palme House, Kenyon College, Gambier, Ohio 43022, or direct e-mail to MACIONIS@KENYON.EDU

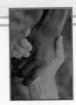

CHAPTER

1

John Sloan (1871–1951)
Traveling Carnival, Santa Fe, 1924

Oil on canvas, 76.5 × 91.6 cm.
Smithsonian American Art Museum, Washington, D.C./Art Resource, N.Y.

THE SOCIOLOGICAL PERSPECTIVE

Whitney Linnea is a happy, well-adjusted ten-year-old living in a small Midwestern town in the United States. Like most of her friends, she loves sports. It is a warm fall day, and Whitney is headed from school to soccer practice. She climbs into her mother's van and settles back with a snack for the five-mile trip to the playing fields. Her mother will drive back again in an hour to pick her up. On Saturday, there are soccer games: The away games can be a two-hour drive each way.

Soccer is not the only sport Whitney enjoys. As the weather turns colder, soccer fades and swimming takes

over, with the season lasting until the end of March. Daily practices are held at the pool of the nearby college—a twenty-minute drive each way—with meets around the state on Saturdays.

In spring, Whitney splits her afternoons between soccer and Little League baseball. On Saturdays in April and May, she is likely to hurry from a morning soccer game to a noon baseball game that may be thirty miles away. With all the driving to and from Whitney's practices and sporting events, Whitney's mother and father put more than 5,000 miles on their car (adapted from Ferguson, 1999).

Some 40 million young people in the United States—about three out of four—participate in one or more organized sports from soccer to swimming to squash. If you asked them why they do it, probably most would say they play sports just to have fun. But there is more to the story than children doing what they enjoy. Consider that the United States has a fascination with competitive sports that is far greater than what we find in much of the world. In other words, if we view Whitney's behavior in context, we see that the choices we make every day have much to do with the larger society around us. Here and elsewhere, how people decide to spend their time does not result from the process philosophers call "free will." More correctly—and this is the essential wisdom that we gain from a study of sociology—our social world guides our actions and life choices in much the same way that the seasons influence our selection of clothing and activities.

THE SOCIOLOGICAL PERSPECTIVE

Sociology is *the systematic study of human society*. At the heart of sociology is a distinctive point of view called "the sociological perspective."

SEEING THE GENERAL IN THE PARTICULAR

Peter Berger (1963) described the sociological perspective as *seeing the general in the particular*. By this he meant that sociologists identify general patterns in the behavior of particular people. Although every individual is unique, a society guides people to act in certain ways, such as enjoying competitive sports. In addition, within any one country society acts differently on various *categories* of people (say, women as opposed to men, the rich as opposed to the poor, and children as opposed to adults). We begin to think sociologically by realizing how the general categories into which we fall shape our particular life experiences.

1

Every page of the Annotated Instructor's Edition of *Sociology* contains information and data—revised for this edition—that will enhance the usefulness of the text. The annotations, as well as the separately bound *Data File*, offer substantial material directly related to the topic at hand. Annotations are of 14 types:

(1) **SUPPLEMENTS:** Cross-references to material in the *Data File*, video library, or other supplementary material.

(2) **CYBER:** Material concerning the social implications of new information technology.

(3) **APPLIED:** Applications of sociological thinking to the world of work and popular culture.

(4) **THEN AND NOW:** Data on the extent of change during recent decades.

We can easily grasp the power of society over the individual by imagining how different our lives would be had we been born in place of any of these children from, respectively, Bolivia, Sri Lanka, Ethiopia, Botswana, the People's Republic of China, and El Salvador.

This text explores the power of society to shape our thoughts, feelings, and actions. People with high incomes, for example, are likely to enjoy expensive sports (such as downhill skiing), whereas people with low incomes prefer less expensive sports (such as baseball and basketball). More generally, people who come from more privileged social backgrounds tend to be confident and optimistic about their lives. This is not surprising when we realize that they have had more opportunities and the training and skills to take advantage of them.

Seeing the world sociologically also makes us aware of the importance of gender. As Chapter 13 ("Gender Stratification") describes, every society attaches meaning to being female or male and gives women and men different kinds of work and family responsibilities. Here, again, society influences us throughout the course of our lives by suggesting that certain sports, college courses, and career goals correspond to our sex.

SEEING THE STRANGE IN THE FAMILIAR

At first, using the sociological perspective amounts to *seeing the strange in the familiar*. This does not mean that sociologists focus on the bizarre elements of society. Rather, looking sociologically means giving up the familiar idea that human behavior is simply a matter of what people *decide* to do in favor of the initially strange notion that society shapes our lives.

For individualistic North Americans, learning to see how society affects us may take a bit of practice. Say someone asked you why you "chose" to enroll at your particular college. In response, you might offer one of the following reasons:

"I wanted to stay close to home."

"I got a basketball scholarship."

"With a journalism degree from this university, I can get a good job."

(5) **GLOBAL:** Facts or observations comparing the U.S. to other countries or otherwise placing the topic at hand in a global context.

(6) **DIVERSITY:** Comparative data or analysis of the issue in terms of race, ethnicity, age, gender, or class.

(7) **THE MAP:** Comments about the Windows on the World global maps and the Seeing Ourselves national maps.

(8) **RESOURCE:** An article or book useful for further reading or for enhancing a class discussion.

(9) **Q:** A noteworthy quotation by a sociologist, historical figure, or contemporary newsmaker.

(10) **SOCIAL SURVEY:** Data from the National Opinion Research Center's *General Social Survey* or other survey data. GSS entries are taken from the *GSS Codebook*.

"My girlfriend goes to school here."

"I didn't get into the school I *really* wanted to attend."

Such responses may well be true. But do they tell the whole story?

Thinking sociologically about going to college, we might first realize that, around the world, about five people in one hundred gets a college degree. Even in the United States a century ago, going to college was not an option for most people. Today a look around the classroom shows that social forces still have much to do with college attendance. Typically, U.S. college students are young, generally between eighteen and twenty-four. Why? Because in our society, attending college is linked to this period of life. But more than age is involved because fewer than half of all young men and women actually end up on campus.

Another factor is cost. Because higher education is so expensive, students tend to come from families with above-average incomes. As Chapter 20 ("Education") explains, if you are lucky enough to belong to a family earning more than $75,000, you are three times as likely to go to college as someone whose family earns less than

 For a closer look at college attendance by family income, go to http://www.prenhall.com/weblinks

$20,000 each year. This is one reason that a greater share of white people (63 percent) than African Americans (59 percent) "choose" to go to college.

INDIVIDUALITY IN SOCIAL CONTEXT

To see the power of society to shape individual choices, consider the number of children women have. In the United States, as shown in Global Map 1–1 on page 4, the average woman has slightly fewer than two children during her lifetime. In India, however, the average is about three; in South Africa, about four; in Cambodia, about five; in Saudi Arabia, about six; and in Niger, about seven.

Why these striking differences? As later chapters explain, women in poor countries have less schooling and fewer economic opportunities, are more likely to remain in the home, and are less likely to use contraception. Clearly, society has much to do with the decisions women and men make about childbearing.

Another illustration of the power of society to shape even our most private choices comes from the study of suicide. What could be a more personal choice than taking one's own life? But Emile Durkheim (1858–1917), one of sociology's pioneers, showed that

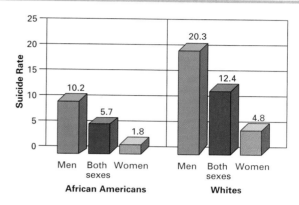

DIVERSITY SNAPSHOT

FIGURE 1–1 Rate of Death by Suicide, by Race and Sex, for the United States

Rates indicate the number of deaths by suicide for every 100,000 people in each category for 1998.

Source: U.S. National Center for Health Statistics (2000).

social forces are at work even in the apparently isolated act of self-destruction.

Examining official records in his native France, Durkheim found that some categories of people were more likely than others to take their own lives. He found that men, Protestants, wealthy people, and the unmarried had significantly higher suicide rates than did women, Catholics and Jews, the poor, and married people. Durkheim explained the differences in terms of *social integration:* Categories of people with strong social ties had low suicide rates, whereas more individualistic people had high suicide rates.

In the male-dominated society Durkheim studied, men certainly had more freedom than women. But despite its advantages, freedom also contributes to social isolation and thus a higher suicide rate. Likewise, more individualistic Protestants were more prone to suicide than more traditional Catholics and Jews, whose rituals foster stronger social ties. The wealthy have much more freedom than the poor, but, once again, at the cost of a higher suicide rate. Finally, can you see why single people are at greater risk than married people?

A century later, Durkheim's analysis still holds true (Thorlindsson & Bjarnason, 1998). Figure 1–1 shows suicide rates for four categories of the U.S. population. In 1998, there were 12.4 recorded suicides for every

(11) NOTE: A theoretical or methodological comment, information on the text's artwork or photography, or the etymology of an important term.
(12) DISCUSS: Topical information to provoke class discussion.
(13) EXERCISE: An instructional activity for students.
(14) CTQ: Suggestions for discussing the Critical-Thinking Questions at the end of each chapter.

SUPPLEMENTS: The *Data File* contains a chapter outline, discussion topics, and additional lecture material for this chapter. Interactive material for review, discussion, and further research is available at the Macionis Web site, http://www.prenhall.com/macionis
THEN AND NOW: U.S. suicide rate, *1950:* 11.4 per 100,000 people; *1960:* 10.6; *1970:* 11.6; *1980:* 11.9; *1990:* 12.4; *1999:* 10.7.
Q: "The farther one travels, the less one knows." George Harrison

WINDOW ON THE WORLD

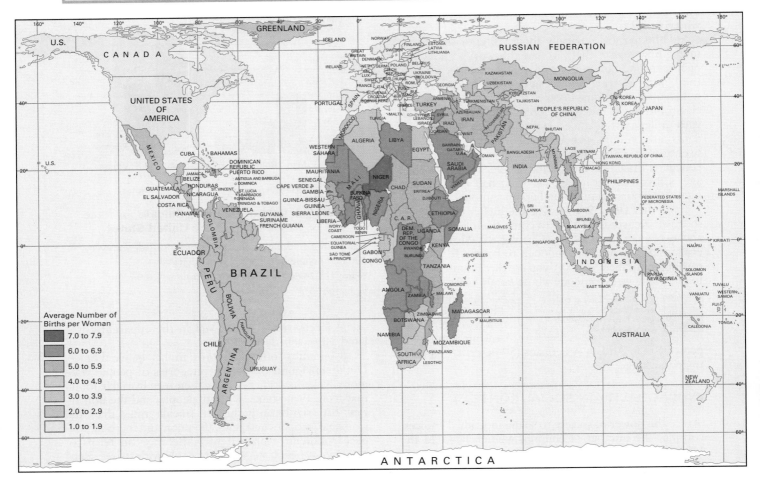

GLOBAL MAP 1–1 Women's Childbearing in Global Perspective

Is childbearing simply a matter of personal choice? A look around the world shows that it is not. In general, women living in poor countries have many more children than women in rich nations. Can you point to some of the reasons for this global disparity? In simple terms, such differences mean that if you had been born into another society (whether you are female or male), your life might have been quite different from what it is now.

Source: Data from Mackay (2000).

100,000 white people, more than twice the rate for African Americans (5.7). For both races, suicide was more common among men than among women; white men (20.3) were more than four times as likely as white women (4.8) to take their own lives. Among African Americans, the rate for men (10.2) was nearly six times higher than for women (1.8). Following Durkheim's logic, the higher suicide rate among white people and men reflects their greater wealth and freedom; the lower rate among women and people of color follows

NOTE: Recently, suicide among black youth has been on the rise (although it is still well below the rate for white teens). This rise may be due to upward mobility: a weakening of social ties among young people in families moving up into the middle class (Belluck, 1998).

GLOBAL: Support for Durkheim's thesis comes from rising suicide rates (especially among the young) in Hong Kong, Singapore, and other Asian countries experiencing rising affluence. Moreover, since the breakup of the former Soviet Union, Latvia, Lithuania, and Russia have the world's highest suicide rates (Jordan, 1998).

NOTE: Good travel is hard work: note the common root of "travel" and "travail"; "tour," by contrast, refers to simply "going in a circle." For cross-cultural experiences to involve learning rather than simply fun, in short, we need to work at it!

GLOBAL SOCIOLOGY

The Global Village: A Social Snapshot of Our World

The Earth is home to 6.2 billion people who live in the cities and villages of 192 nations. To grasp the social shape of the world, imagine for a moment that the planet's population is reduced to a single settlement of 1,000 people. In this "global village," more than half (610) of the inhabitants are Asian, including 210 citizens of the People's Republic of China. Next, in terms of numbers, we would find 130 Africans, 120 Europeans, 85 people from Latin America and the Caribbean, 5 from Australia and the South Pacific, and just 50 North Americans, including 45 people from the United States.

A study of the settlement's ways of life would reveal some startling facts:

The village is a rich place, with a seemingly endless array of goods and services for sale. Yet most of the inhabitants only dream about such treasures because 80 percent of the village's total income is earned by just 200 people.

For the majority, the greatest problem is getting enough food. Every year, village workers produce more than enough to feed everyone; even so, half the village's people, including most of the children, do not get enough to eat, and many fall asleep hungry. The worst-off 200 residents (who, together, have less money than the richest person in the village) lack both clean drinking water and safe shelter. Weak and unable to work, some of them fall victim to life-threatening diseases every day.

Villagers boast of their community's many schools, including a fine university. About 50 inhabitants have completed a college degree, but almost half of the village's people can neither read nor write.

We in the United States, on average, would be among the richest people in this global village. Although we tend to credit ourselves for living well, the sociological perspective reminds us that our achievements are largely products of the privileged position our nation holds in the worldwide social system.

Source: Calculations by the author based on data from United Nations and Population Reference Bureau publications.

from their limited social choices. Just as in Durkheim's day, then, we can see general patterns in the personal actions of particular individuals.

THE IMPORTANCE OF GLOBAL PERSPECTIVE

December 10, Fez, Morocco. This exotic medieval city—a web of narrow streets and alleyways—is alive with the laughter of playing children, the silence of veiled women, and the steady gaze of men leading donkeys laden with goods. Fez has changed little over the centuries. Here, in northwest Africa, we are just a few hundred miles from the more familiar rhythms of Europe. Yet this place seems a thousand years away. Never have we had such an adventure! Never have we thought so much about home!

As new information technology draws even the farthest reaches of the Earth closer to each other, many academic disciplines take a **global perspective,** *the study of the larger world and our society's place in it.* What is the importance of a global perspective for sociology?

First, global awareness is a logical extension of the sociological perspective. Sociology shows us that our place in society profoundly affects our life experiences. It stands to reason, then, that the position of our society in the larger world system affects everyone in the United States. The box describes a "global village" to show the social shape of the world and the place of the United States within it.

Global Map 1–2 provides a visual guide to the relative economic development of the world's countries. **High-income countries**[1] are *nations with very*

---

[1]The text favors this terminology over the traditional but outdated "First World," "Second World," and "Third World." See Chapter 12 ("Global Stratification") for a full discussion.

THE MAP: About 18% of the world's people live in high-income countries, 54% live in middle-income nations, and just over one-quarter live in low-income countries. Per capita GDP for the world as a whole stands at roughly $7,000.
THEN AND NOW: Percentage of Japanese households with cars: *1961,* 2.8%; *1994,* 79.7% (Japanese Economic Planning Agency).

NOTE: Some students may not know that the world is divided into 24 time zones. Whereas the U.S. has 4, the highly centralized People's Republic of China, although just as "wide," holds to 1 (everyone uses Beijing time).
THEN AND NOW: The number of telephone calls made from the United States to some other country: *1970,* 23 million; *1980,* 200 million; *1998,* 4.5 billion (a 195-fold increase) (FCC data).

WINDOW ON THE WORLD

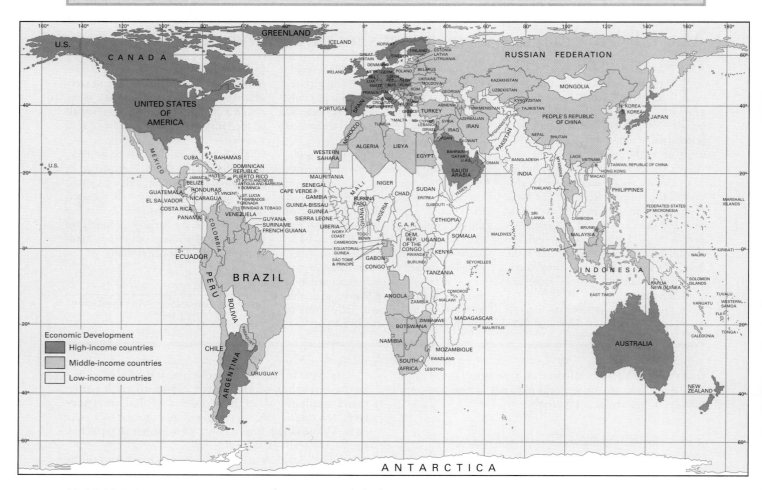

GLOBAL MAP 1–2 Economic Development in Global Perspective

In high-income countries—including the United States, Canada, Argentina, the nations of Western Europe, Israel, Saudi Arabia, Australia, and Japan—a highly productive economy provides people, on average, with material plenty. Middle-income countries—including most of Latin America and the nations of Eastern Europe—are less economically productive, with a standard of living about average for the world as a whole but far below that of the United States. These nations also have a significant share of poor people who barely scrape by with meager housing and diet. In the low-income countries of the world, poverty is severe and extensive. Although small numbers of elites live very well in the poorest nations, most people struggle to survive on a small fraction of the income common in the United States.

Note: Data for this map are provided by the United Nations. High-income countries have a per capita gross domestic product (GDP) of at least $10,000. Many are far richer than this, however; the figure for the United States exceeds $31,000. Middle-income countries have a per capita GDP ranging from $2,500 to $10,000. Low-income countries have a per capita GDP below $2,500. Figures used here reflect the new United Nations "purchasing power parities" system. Rather than directly converting income figures into U.S. dollars, this calculation estimates the local purchasing power of each domestic currency.

Sources: Prepared by the author using data from United Nations Development Programme (2001). Map projection from *Peters Atlas of the World* (1990).

productive economic systems in which most people have relatively high incomes. High-income countries include the United States and Canada, Argentina, the nations of Western Europe, Israel, Saudi Arabia, Japan, and Australia. Taken together, these forty nations produce most of the world's goods and services and control most of the wealth. On average, individuals in these countries live well, not because they are smarter than anyone else, but because they had the good fortune to be born in an affluent region of the world.

The world's **middle-income countries** are *nations with moderately productive economic systems in which people's incomes are about the global average.* Individuals living in any of these roughly ninety nations—most of the countries of Eastern Europe, some of southern Africa, and almost all of Latin America—are as likely to live in rural villages as in cities; to walk or ride tractors, scooters, bicycles, or animals as to drive automobiles; and, on average, to receive just a few years of schooling. Most middle-income countries also have marked social inequality, so that some people are extremely rich (members of the business elite in nations across North Africa, for example), but many more lack safe housing and adequate nutrition.

Finally, about half of the world's people live in the sixty **low-income countries**, *nations with less productive economic systems in which most people are poor.* As Global Map 1–2 shows, most of the poorest countries in the world are in Africa and Asia. Here, again, a few people are very rich, but the majority struggle to get by with poor housing, unsafe water, too little food, limited sanitation, and, perhaps most seriously of all, little chance to improve their lives.

Chapter 12 ("Global Stratification") details the causes and consequences of global wealth and poverty. But every chapter of this text highlights life in the world beyond our own borders for four reasons:

1. **Where we live makes a great difference in shaping our lives.** As we saw in Global Map 1–1, women's lives are strikingly different in rich and poor countries. To understand ourselves and appreciate the plight of others, we must grasp the social landscape of the world—one good reason to pay attention to the thirty global maps found throughout this text.

2. **Societies throughout the world are increasingly interconnected.** Historically, the United States has taken only passing note of the countries beyond its own borders. In recent decades, however, the United States and the rest of the world have become linked as never before. Electronic

One important reason to gain a global understanding is that, living in a high-income nation, we scarcely can appreciate the suffering that goes on in much of the world. This boy is growing up in the African nation of Ghana, where he carries water for cooking and drinking from a public faucet and sewerage flows freely over unpaved streets. In poor nations like this, children have only a fifty-fifty chance to grow to adulthood.

technology now transmits sounds, pictures, and written documents around the globe in seconds.

One consequence of new technology, as later chapters explain, is that people all over the world now share many tastes in music, clothing, and food. With their economic clout, high-income countries such as the United States influence other nations, whose people eagerly gobble up our hamburgers, dance to pop music, and, more and more, speak the English language.

We are spreading our way of life around the world, but the larger world also has an impact on us. Almost 1 million documented immigrants enter the United States each year, and we have been quick to adopt many of their fashions and foods, which greatly enhances the racial and cultural diversity of this country.

Commerce across national boundaries has also created a global economy. Large corporations make and market goods worldwide, and global financial markets linked by satellite communication operate around the clock. Stock traders in New York follow the financial markets in Tokyo and Hong Kong even as wheat farmers in Iowa watch the price of grain in the former Soviet republic of Georgia. With eight out of ten new U.S. jobs involving international trade, global understanding has never been more important.

3. **Many problems that we face in the United States are far more serious elsewhere.** Poverty is a serious problem in the United States, but as Chapter 12 ("Global Stratification") explains, poverty in Latin America, Africa, and Asia is both more common and more serious. Similarly, although women have lower social standing than men in the United States, gender inequality is much greater in poor countries of the world.

4. **Thinking globally is a good way to learn more about ourselves.** We cannot walk the streets of a distant city without becoming keenly aware of what it means to live in the United States. Making global comparisons also leads to unexpected lessons. For instance, in Chapter 12 we visit a squatter settlement in Madras, India. There, de-spite a lack of basic material goods, people thrive in the love and support of family members. Why, then, is poverty in the United States associated with isolation and anger? Are material comforts—so crucial to our definition of a "rich" life—the best way to gauge human well-being?

In sum, in an increasingly interconnected world, we can understand ourselves only to the extent that we comprehend others (Macionis, 1993).

APPLYING THE SOCIOLOGICAL PERSPECTIVE

It is easy to apply the sociological perspective when we encounter people who differ from us—whether around the world or in our own hometowns—because they remind us that society shapes individual lives. But two other kinds of situations also help us to see the world with a sociological perspective: being socially marginal and living through a social crisis.

SOCIOLOGY AND SOCIAL MARGINALITY

From time to time, everyone feels like an "outsider." For some categories of people, however, being an

outsider—not part of the dominant group—is an every-day experience. The greater people's social marginal-ity, the better able they are to use the sociological perspective.

For example, no African American grows up in the United States without understanding the impor-tance of race. But white people, as the dominant ma-jority, think less often about race and believe it affects only people of color, not themselves. Women, gay people, people with disabilities, and the very old are also, to some degree, "outsiders." People at the mar-gins of social life are aware of social patterns that oth-ers rarely think about. To become better at using the sociological perspective, therefore, we must step back from our familiar routines and look at our lives with new awareness and curiosity.

SOCIOLOGY AND SOCIAL CRISIS

Periods of change or crisis make everyone feel a little off balance and prompt us to use the sociological perspective. U.S. sociologist C. Wright Mills (1959) illustrated this idea with the Great Depression of the 1930s. As the unemployment rate soared to 25 per-cent, people out of work could not help but see gen-eral social forces at work in their particular lives. Rather than saying, "Something is wrong with me; I can't find a job," they took a sociological approach and realized, "The economy has collapsed; there are no jobs to be found!"

Just as social change fosters sociological thinking, sociological thinking can bring about social change. The more we learn how "the system" operates, the more we may want to change it in some way. Becom-ing aware of the power of gender, for example, many women and men have actively tried to reduce tradi-tional gender role differences.

In short, an introduction to sociology is an invita-tion to learn a new way of looking at familiar patterns of social life. But is this invitation worth accepting? What are the benefits of applying the sociological perspective?

BENEFITS OF THE SOCIOLOGICAL PERSPECTIVE

Applying the sociological perspective to our daily lives benefits us in four ways:

1. **The sociological perspective helps us assess the truth of "common sense."** We all take many things for granted, but that does not make

APPLYING SOCIOLOGY

The Sociological Imagination: Turning Personal Problems into Public Issues

The power of the sociological perspective lies not just in changing individual lives but in transforming society. As C. Wright Mills saw it, society, not people's personal failings, is the cause of poverty and other social problems. The sociological imagination brings people together to bring about change by transforming personal *problems* into public *issues*.

In the following excerpt* Mills explains the need for a sociological imagination:

When a society becomes industrialized, a peasant becomes a

worker; a feudal lord is liquidated or becomes a businessman. When classes rise or fall, a man is employed or unemployed; when the rate of investment goes up or down, a man takes new heart or goes broke. When wars happen, an insurance salesman becomes a rocket launcher; a store clerk, a radar man; a wife lives alone; a child grows up without a father. Neither the life of an individual nor the history of a society can be understood without understanding both.

Yet men do not usually define the troubles they endure in terms of historical change. . . . The well-being they enjoy, they do not usually impute to the big ups and downs of the society in which they live. Seldom aware of the intricate

connection between the patterns of their own lives and the course of world history, ordinary men do not usually know what this connection means for the kind of men they are becoming and for the kinds of history-making in which they might take part. They do not possess the quality of mind essential to grasp the interplay of men and society, of biography and history, of self and world. . . .

What they need . . . is a quality of mind that will help them to [see] . . . what is going on in the world and . . . what may be happening within themselves. It is this quality . . . that . . . may be called the sociological imagination.

*In this excerpt, Mills uses "man" and male pronouns to apply to all people. Note that even an outspoken critic of society such as Mills reflected the conventional writing practices of his time as far as gender was concerned.

Source: Mills (1959:3–5).

---

them true. One good example, noted earlier, is the notion that we are free individuals who are personally responsible for our own lives. If we think people decide their own fate, we may be quick to praise particularly successful people as superior and consider others with more modest achievements personally deficient. A sociological approach, by contrast, encourages us to ask whether commonly held beliefs are actually true and, to the extent that they are not, why they are so widely held.

2. **The sociological perspective helps us assess both opportunities and constraints in our lives.** Sociological thinking leads us to see that, in the game of life, we have a say in how to play our cards, but it is society that deals us the hand. The more we understand the game,

the better players we will be. Sociology helps us size up our world so we can pursue our goals more effectively.

3. **The sociological perspective empowers us to be active participants in our society.** The more we understand about how society works, the more active citizens we become. For some, this may mean supporting society as it is; others may attempt nothing less than changing the entire world in some way. Evaluating any aspect of social life—whatever your goal—requires identifying social forces and assessing their consequences.

In the box, C. Wright Mills describes the power of using the sociological perspective.

4. **The sociological perspective helps us live in a diverse world.** North Americans represent just

5 percent of the world's people, and, as the remaining chapters of this book explain, much of the other 95 percent live very differently than we do. Still, like people everywhere, we tend to define our own way of life as "right," "natural," and "better." The sociological perspective encourages us to think critically about the relative strengths and weaknesses of all ways of life, including our own.

SOCIOLOGY, POLICY, AND CAREERS

The benefits of sociology go well beyond personal growth. Sociologists have helped shape public policy and law in countless ways, involving school desegregation, school busing, pornography, and social welfare. For example, the work that Lenore Weitzman (1985) did on the financial hardships facing women after divorce "had a real impact on public policy and resulted in the passage of fourteen new laws in California" (1996:538).

A background in sociology is also good preparation for the working world. The American Sociological Association reports that sociologists are hired for hundreds of jobs in fields such as advertising, banking, criminal justice, education, government, health care, public relations, and research (Billson & Huber, 1993).

Most men and women who continue beyond a bachelor's degree to earn advanced training in sociology go on to careers in teaching and research. But an increasing number of professional sociologists work in

 In a short video, the author offers a personal response to the question, "why would someone want to be a sociologist?" See the Video Gallery at http://www.TheSociologyPage.com

all sorts of applied fields. For example, clinical sociologists work with troubled clients much as clinical psychologists do. A basic difference is that whereas psychologists focus on the individual, sociologists locate difficulties in a person's web of social relationships. Another type of applied sociology is evaluation research. In today's cost-conscious climate, administrators must evaluate the effectiveness of almost every kind of program and policy. Sociologists, especially those with advanced research skills, are in high demand for this kind of work (Deutscher, 1999).

THE ORIGINS OF SOCIOLOGY

Like the "choices" made by individuals, major historical events rarely just happen on their own. The birth of sociology resulted from powerful social forces.

SOCIAL CHANGE AND SOCIOLOGY

Striking transformations during the eighteenth and nineteenth centuries greatly changed European society. Three changes were especially important in the development of sociology: the rise of a factory-based industrial economy, the explosive growth of cities, and new ideas about democracy and political rights.

A New Industrial Economy

During the European Middle Ages, most people tilled fields near their homes or engaged in small-scale *manufacturing* (a word derived from Latin words meaning "to make by hand"). But by the end of the eighteenth century, inventors used new sources of energy—the power of moving water and then steam—to operate large machines in mills and factories. Instead of laboring at home or in tightly knit groups, workers became part of a large and anonymous labor force, toiling for strangers who owned the factories. This change in the system of production separated families and weakened the traditions that had governed community life for centuries.

The Growth of Cities

Across Europe, factories drew people in need of work. Along with this pull came the push of the *enclosure movement*. Landowners fenced off more and more ground, turning farms into grazing land for sheep, the source of wool for the thriving textile mills. Without land, countless tenant farmers left the countryside in search of work in the new factories.

As cities grew to unprecedented size, the new urban dwellers contended with mounting social problems, including pollution, crime, and homelessness. Living on streets crowded with strangers, they adapted to the new, impersonal social environment.

Political Change

During the Middle Ages, people viewed society as an expression of God's will: Royalty claimed to rule by "divine right," and each person up and down the social ladder played a part in the holy plan. This theological view of society is captured in lines from the old Anglican hymn "All Things Bright and Beautiful":

The rich man in his castle,
The poor man at his gate,
God made them high and lowly
And ordered their estate.

NOTE: The early Industrial Revolution saw the first U.S. courses in sociology. Williams College offered a course in social ethics in 1865; Johns Hopkins taught social science in its opening year, 1876, the same year William Graham Sumner taught his first sociology course at Yale; Cornell introduced a social science course in 1884; the University of Chicago founded the first formal sociology department in 1892.

NOTE: Lewis Coser (1977) notes that Comte first called his new discipline "social physics." Thinking the term stolen by Adolphe Quetelet, Comte renamed the fledgling field "sociology."

Q: "Savoir pour prévoir et prévoir pour pouvoir." Auguste Comte (Literally, "Know to foresee and foresee to be able to," or, translated more freely, "By knowing the laws of phenomena we can make predictions about them, and change the world to our advantage.")

The birth of sociology was prompted by rapid social change. The discipline developed in those regions of Europe where the Industrial Revolution most disrupted traditional ways of life, drawing people from isolated villages to rapidly growing industrial cities.

But economic development and the rapid growth of cities soon brought new political ideas. By about 1600, tradition was under spirited attack. In the writings of Thomas Hobbes (1588–1679), John Locke (1632–1704), and Adam Smith (1723–1790), we see a shift in focus from people's moral obligations to God and their rulers to the idea that people should pursue their own self-interest. In the new political climate, philosophers spoke of *individual liberty* and *individual rights*. Echoing Locke, our own Declaration of Independence asserts that every person has "certain unalienable rights," including "life, liberty, and the pursuit of happiness."

The French Revolution, which began in 1789, symbolized this dramatic break with political and social tradition. French social analyst Alexis de Tocqueville (1805–1859) declared that the changes in society brought about by the French Revolution amounted to "nothing short of the regeneration of the whole human race" (1955:13; orig. 1856).

A New Awareness of Society

Huge factories, exploding cities, a new spirit of individualism—these changes combined to make people aware of their surroundings. As the social ground trembled under people's feet, the new discipline of sociology was born in England, France, and Germany—precisely where the changes were greatest.

SCIENCE AND SOCIOLOGY

The nature of society fascinated the brilliant thinkers of the ancient world, including the Chinese philosopher K'ung Fu-tzu, or Confucius (551–479 B.C.E.), and the Greek philosophers Plato (c. 427–347 B.C.E.) and Aristotle (384–322 B.C.E.).[2] Later, the Roman emperor Marcus Aurelius (121–180), the medieval thinkers St. Thomas Aquinas (c. 1225–1274) and Christine de Pisan (c. 1363–1431), and the great English playwright William Shakespeare (1564–1616) took up the question.

Yet these thinkers were more interested in envisioning the ideal society than in analyzing society as it really was. In creating their new discipline, sociology's pioneers certainly cared how society could be improved, but their major goal was to understand how society actually operates. It was the French social thinker Auguste Comte (1798–1857) who coined the term *sociology* in 1838 to describe this new way of

[2]Throughout this text, the abbreviation B.C.E. designates "before the common era." We use this terminology in place of the traditional B.C. ("before Christ") in recognition of the religious plurality of our society. Similarly, in place of the traditional A.D. (*anno Domini*, or "in the year of our Lord"), we use the abbreviation C.E. ("common era").

NOTE: Comte considered sociology to be the "Queen of the Sciences," an assertion that inspired some of his followers to acts of arrogance. A century ago, for example, sociologists at Brown suggested that their entire university be reorganized under the sociology department.
GLOBAL: Brazil, a country that has long embraced ambitious social planning (consider the building of the new capital, Brasilia), was
guided by Comte's ideas. In fact, the Brazilians adopted for their national flag Comte's slogan, "Order and Progress."
Q: "The first and most intense passion that is produced by equality of condition is, I need hardly say, the love of that equality. . . . Among democratic nations, men easily attain a certain equality of condition, but they can never attain as much as they desire." Alexis de Tocqueville

Here we see Copernicus, the sixteenth-century astronomer, taking careful measurements of the world. Just as Copernicus challenged the common sense of his day, sociologists such as Auguste Comte later argued that society is neither fixed by God's will nor set by human nature. On the contrary, Comte claimed, society is a system we can study scientifically, and based on what we learn, we can act intentionally to improve our lives.

thinking. Therefore, sociology is among the youngest academic disciplines—far newer than history, physics, or economics, for example.

Comte (1975; orig. 1851–54) saw sociology as the product of a three-stage historical development. During the earliest, the *theological stage*, which spanned the time from the beginning of human history to the end of the European Middle Ages about 1350 C.E., people took a religious view of society, seeing it as an expression of God's will.

With the Renaissance, the theological approach gave way to what Comte called the *metaphysical stage*. During this period, people understood society as a natural rather than a supernatural phenomenon.

Thomas Hobbes (1588–1679), for example, thought that society reflected not the perfection of God so much as the failings of a selfish human nature.

What Comte called the *scientific stage* of history began with the work of early scientists such as the Polish astronomer Copernicus (1473–1543), the Italian astronomer and physicist Galileo (1564–1642), and the English physicist and mathematician Isaac Newton (1642–1727). Comte's contribution came in applying the scientific approach, which was first used to study the physical world, to the study of society.[3]

Comte thus favored **positivism**, defined as *a way of understanding based on science*. As a positivist, Comte believed that society conforms to invariable laws, much as the physical world operates according to gravity and other laws of nature.

At the beginning of the twentieth century, sociology emerged as an academic discipline in the United States, strongly influenced by Comte's ideas. Today, most sociologists still consider science a crucial part of sociology. But as Chapter 2 ("Sociological Investigation") explains, we now realize that human behavior is far more complex than the movement of planets or even the actions of other living things. Because humans are creatures of imagination and spontaneity, our behavior can never be fully explained by any rigid "laws of society." In addition, early sociologists such as Karl Marx (1818–1883), whose ideas are discussed in Chapter 4 ("Society"), were deeply troubled by the striking inequality of the new industrial society. They wanted the new discipline of sociology not just to understand society but to bring about change toward social justice.

 For a biographical sketch of Comte, go to the Gallery of Sociologists at http://www.TheSociologyPage.com

GENDER AND RACE: MARGINAL VOICES

Auguste Comte and Karl Marx stand among the giants of sociology. In recent years, though, we have come to see the important contributions that others—pushed to the margins of society because of gender or race—have made.

---

[3]Illustrating Comte's stages, the ancient Greeks and Romans viewed the planets as gods; Renaissance metaphysical thinkers saw them as astral influences (giving rise to astrology); by the time of Galileo, scientists understood planets as natural objects behaving in orderly ways.

NOTE: Harriet Martineau's lifelong activism was guided by a Comtean view of the world as comprehensible and changeable. Her achievements are all the more impressive in light of her almost total deafness from about the age of 12.

Q: "Liberals have devised whole disciplines like sociology and women's studies to prove that nothing is anybody's fault." P.J. O'Rourke

NOTE: The word "theory" is derived from the Greek *theoria*, meaning "a viewing." The Latin root of the word "structure" (*struct*) means "a piling up of."

Q: "My life had its significance and its only deep significance because it was part of a problem; but the problem was, I continue to think, the central problem of the greatest of the world's democracies and so the problem of the future world." W.E.B. Du Bois

We can use the sociological perspective to look at sociology itself. All of the most widely recognized pioneers of the discipline were men. This is because, in the nineteenth century, it was all but unheard of for women to be college professors, and few women took a central role in public life. But women, such as Harriet Martineau in England and Jane Addams in the United States, made contributions to sociology that we now recognize as important and lasting.

Harriet Martineau (1802–1876), born to a wealthy English family, first made her mark in 1853 by translating the writings of Auguste Comte from French into English. Subsequently, she became a noted scholar in her own right, revealing the evils of slavery and arguing for laws to protect factory workers and advance the standing of women.

In the United States, Jane Addams (1860–1935) was a sociological pioneer. Trained as a social worker, Addams spoke out on behalf of immigrants, who were entering the nation at the rate of 1 million per year. In 1889, Addams founded Hull House, a settlement house in Chicago that provided assistance to immigrant families. She also gathered sociologists and politicians to discuss the urban problems of the day. For her work on behalf of immigrants, Addams received the Nobel Peace Prize in 1931.

An important contribution to understanding race in the United States was made by yet another sociological pioneer, William Edward Burghardt Du Bois (1868–1963). Born to a poor Massachusetts family, Du Bois enrolled in Fisk University in Nashville, Tennessee, and then Harvard University, where he earned the first doctorate awarded by that university to a person of color. Like Martineau and Addams, Du Bois believed sociologists should try to solve social problems. He therefore studied the black community (1899), spoke out against racial inequality, and served as a founding member of the National Association for the Advancement of Colored People (NAACP).

Widespread belief in the inferiority of women and African Americans kept Martineau, Addams, and Du Bois at the margins of sociology. Looking back with a

sociological eye, we can see how the forces of society were at work shaping even the history of sociology itself.

SOCIOLOGICAL THEORY

Weaving observations into understanding brings us to another aspect of sociology: theory. A **theory** is *a statement of how and why specific facts are related*. More to the point, the job of sociological theory is to explain social behavior in the real world. Recall Emile Durkheim's theory that categories of people with low social integration (men, Protestants, the wealthy, and the unmarried) are especially prone to suicide. As Durkheim pondered the issue of suicide, he considered a number of possible theories. But which one was correct?

To evaluate a theory, as the next chapter explains, sociologists gather evidence using various methods of scientific research. Facts allow sociologists to confirm some theories while rejecting or modifying others. Thus, Durkheim collected data that revealed patterns showing that certain categories of people are more likely to commit suicide. These patterns allowed Durkheim to settle on a theory that best squared with all available evidence. National Map 1–1 displays the suicide rate for each of the fifty states and gives you a chance to do some theorizing of your own.

In building theory, sociologists face two basic questions: What issues should we study? How should we connect the facts? How they answer these questions depends on their theoretical "road map," or paradigm (Kuhn, 1970). A **theoretical paradigm** is *a*

THE MAP: The highest suicide rate for any state is Nevada (23.0 per 100,000 people), with Wyoming in second place (20.8). The District of Columbia is lowest (5.4).

NOTE: Durkheim influenced anthropology through the work of Arthur Radcliffe-Brown (1881–1955) and Bronislaw Malinowski (1884–1942), who first described this approach as "functionalist."

Q: "[Functional] theory aims at the explanation of anthropological facts at all levels of development by their function, by the part which they play within the integral system of culture, by the manner in which they are related to each other within the system." Bronislaw Malinowski

NOTE: Kingsley Davis (1959) pointed out that because any theoretical approach involves assessing part-whole relationships, every sociologist is a functionalist to some degree.

SEEING OURSELVES

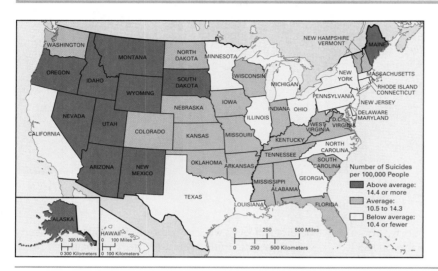

NATIONAL MAP 1–1
Suicide Rates across the United States

This map shows which states have high, average, and low suicide rates. Look for patterns. By and large, high suicide rates occur where people live far apart from one another. More densely populated states have low suicide rates. Do these data support or contradict Durkheim's theory of suicide? Why?

Source: U.S. National Center for Health Statistics (2000).

---

basic image of society that guides thinking and research. Sociology has three major approaches: the structural-functional paradigm, the social-conflict paradigm, and the symbolic-interaction paradigm.

THE STRUCTURAL-FUNCTIONAL PARADIGM

The **structural-functional paradigm** is *a framework for building theory that sees society as a complex system whose parts work together to promote solidarity and stability.* As its name suggests, this paradigm points to **social structure**, meaning *any relatively stable pattern of social behavior.* Social structure gives our lives shape, whether it be in families, the workplace, or the classroom. Second, this paradigm looks for a structure's **social functions**, or *consequences for the operation of society as a whole.* All social structure—from a simple handshake to complex religious rituals—functions to keep society going, at least in its present form.

The structural-functional paradigm owes much to Auguste Comte, who pointed to the importance of social integration during a time of rapid change. Emile Durkheim, who helped establish sociology in French universities, also based his work on this approach. A third structural-functional pioneer was the English sociologist Herbert Spencer (1820–1903). Spencer compared society to the human body. Just as the structural

parts of the human body—the skeleton, muscles, and various internal organs—function interdependently to help the entire organism survive, social structures work together to preserve society. The structural-functional paradigm, then, organizes sociological observations by identifying various structures of society and investigating their functions.

As sociology developed in the United States, many of the ideas of Comte, Spencer, and Durkheim were carried forward by Talcott Parsons (1902–1979), the major U.S. proponent of the structural-functional paradigm. Parsons treated society as a system, and sought to identify the basic tasks that any and all societies must perform to survive and the ways they accomplish these tasks.

 The Gallery of Sociologists includes a biography of Herbert Spencer. Go to http://www.TheSociologyPage.com

Contemporary U.S. sociologist Robert K. Merton critically expanded our understanding of the concept of social function. Merton (1968) explains, first, that people rarely perceive all the functions of social structure. He describes as **manifest functions** *the recognized and intended consequences of any social pattern.* By contrast, **latent functions** are *consequences that are largely unrecognized and unintended.* To illustrate, the obvious function of the U.S. system of higher

NOTE: Thanks to Larry Stern (Colin County College) for pointing out that Robert Merton's development of the functional paradigm was as an effort to bring conflict into the discussion. In other words, Merton saw himself more as a conflict thinker.

NOTE: Herbert Spencer wrote the first textbook on sociology, *Principles of Sociology*, in 1879 as part of a larger philosophical treatise.

NOTE: After Spencer's *Principles of Sociology* (1879), texts in sociology appeared only occasionally and included Lester Ward's *Dynamic Sociology* (1893), Robert Park and Ernest Burgess's *Introduction to the Science of Society* (1920), Ernest Ross's *Principles of Sociology* (1923), Robert MacIver's *Society* (1937), and William Ogburn and Meyer Nimkoff's *Introduction to Sociology* (1940).

The approach of the structural-functional paradigm is conveyed by the painting St. Regis Indian Reservation *by Amy Jones (1937). Here we see society composed of major rounds of life, each serving a particular purpose that contributes to the operation of the entire system.*

Amy Jones, *St. Regis Indian Reservation*, 1937. Photo courtesy Janet Marqusee Fine Arts Ltd.

education is to provide young people with the information and skills they need to perform jobs. Perhaps almost as important, although less often acknowledged, is college's function as a "marriage broker," bringing together people of similar social backgrounds. Another latent function of higher education is keeping millions of young people out of the labor market where, presumably, many of them would not find jobs.

Second, Merton explains, social patterns affect various members of a society differently (Stern, 1998). For example, conventional families may provide a good setting for rearing children, but they also confer privileges on men while limiting the opportunities of women.

Merton makes a third important point: Social structure is not always useful. **Social dysfunctions** are *the undesirable consequences of any social pattern for the operation of society.* People usually disagree about what is useful or harmful. What is functional for one category of people (say, factory owners or landlords) may well be dysfunctional for another category of people (factory workers or tenants).

Critical evaluation. The chief characteristic of the structural-functional paradigm is its vision of society as stable and orderly. The main goal of sociologists who use this approach, then, is to figure out "what makes society tick."

In the mid-1900s, most sociologists favored the structural-functional paradigm. In recent decades, however, its influence has declined. By focusing on social stability and unity, critics point out, structural-functionalism tends to ignore inequalities of social class, race, and gender, which can generate considerable tension and conflict. In general, focusing on stability at the expense of conflict makes this paradigm somewhat conservative. As a critical response to this approach, sociologists developed another theoretical orientation: the social-conflict paradigm.

THE SOCIAL-CONFLICT PARADIGM

The **social-conflict paradigm** is *a framework for building theory that sees society as an arena of inequality that generates conflict and change.* Unlike the structural-functional emphasis on solidarity, this approach highlights inequality. Sociologists guided by this paradigm investigate how factors such as social class, race, ethnicity, gender, and age are linked to the unequal distribution of money, power, education, and social prestige. A conflict analysis rejects the idea that social structure promotes the operation of society as a whole, pointing out instead how social patterns benefit some people while depriving others. The box highlights a key contribution regarding race made by W. E. B. Du Bois.

Sociologists using the social-conflict paradigm look at ongoing conflict between dominant and disadvantaged categories of people—the rich in relation to the poor, white people in relation to people of color, and men in relation to women. Typically, people on top strive to protect their privileges, while the disadvantaged try to gain more for themselves.

A conflict analysis of our educational system shows how schooling reproduces class inequality in every new generation. For example, secondary schools

DIVERSITY: RACE, CLASS, AND GENDER

An Early Pioneer: Du Bois on Race

One of sociology's pioneers in the United States, William Edward Burghardt Du Bois, did not consider sociology a dry, academic discipline. On the contrary, he wanted to apply sociology to solving the pressing problems of his time, especially racial inequality.

Du Bois spoke out against racial separation and served as a founding member of the National Association for the Advancement of Colored People (NAACP). He helped his colleagues in sociology—and people everywhere—to see the deep racial divisions in the United States. White people can simply be "Americans," Du Bois pointed out; African Americans, however, have a "double consciousness," reflecting their status as citizens who are never able to escape identification based on the color of their skin.

In his sociological classic *The Philadelphia Negro: A Social Study* (1899), Du Bois studied Philadelphia's African American community, identifying both the strengths and weaknesses of people wrestling with overwhelming social problems. He challenged the widespread belief in black

inferiority, attributing the problems of African Americans to white prejudice. His criticism extended also to successful people of color for being so eager to win white acceptance that they gave up all ties with the black community, which needed their help.

Du Bois described race as the major problem facing the United States in the twentieth century. Early in his career, he was optimistic about overcoming racial divisions. By the end of his life, however, he had grown bitter, believing that little had changed. At the age of ninety-three, Du Bois left the United States for Ghana, where he died two years later. Do you think, following Du Bois, that race is still a major problem in the twenty-first century?

Sources: Based, in part, on Baltzell (1967) and Du Bois (1967; orig. 1899).

assign students to either college preparatory or vocational training programs. From a structural-functional point of view, such "tracking" benefits everyone by providing schooling that fits students' abilities. But conflict analysis counters that tracking often has less to do with talent than with social background, so that well-to-do students are placed in higher tracks while poor children end up in the lower tracks.

In this way, young people from privileged families receive the best schooling and later pursue high-income careers. The children of poor families, on the other hand, are not prepared for college and, like their parents before them, typically enter low-paying jobs. In both cases, the social standing of one generation is passed on to another, with schools justifying the practice in terms of individual merit (Bowles & Gintis, 1976; Oakes, 1982, 1985).

Social conflict in the United States extends well beyond schools. Later chapters of this book explain how inequality based on class, gender, and race is rooted in the organization of society itself.

Many sociologists use the social-conflict paradigm not just to understand society but to bring about societal change that would reduce inequality. This was the goal of W. E. B. Du Bois and also Karl Marx, whose writing was especially important in the development of the social-conflict paradigm. Marx had little patience with those who sought only to analyze society. In a well-known declaration (inscribed on his monument in London's Highgate Cemetery), Marx asserted, "The philosophers have only interpreted the world, in various ways; the point, however, is to change it."

Critical evaluation. The social-conflict paradigm has gained a large following in recent decades. Yet, like other approaches, it has had its share of criticism. Because the paradigm focuses on inequality, it largely ignores how shared values and mutual interdependence

NOTE: Herbert Blumer first used the term "symbolic interactionism" in 1937.

NOTE: An interesting illustration of "the human process of attaching meaning to our surroundings": The first act of Adam and Eve in Genesis is to name the elements around them.

Q: "Situations that are defined as real are real in their consequences." W.I. Thomas

DISCUSS: The text asserts that "sociology advocates no one political orientation." Some students believe that the discipline has a left-leaning bias, however, and research shows sociologists, overall, do tend to favor liberal positions. Does a macro-structural orientation promote left-ish politics?

Q: "Theories should be as simple as possible, but not more so." Albert Einstein

unify members of a society. In addition, say critics, to the extent that this paradigm pursues political goals, it cannot claim scientific objectivity. As Chapter 2 ("Sociological Investigation") explains, however, conflict theorists counter that *all* theoretical approaches have political consequences, albeit different ones.

A final criticism of both the structural-functional and social-conflict paradigms is that they paint society in broad strokes in terms of "family," "social class," "race," and so on. A third theoretical paradigm depicts society less in terms of broad social structures and more as everyday experiences.

THE SYMBOLIC-INTERACTION PARADIGM

The structural-functional and social-conflict paradigms share a **macro-level orientation,** meaning *a concern with broad patterns that shape society as a whole.* Macro-level sociology takes in the big picture, rather like observing a city from high above in a helicopter and seeing how highways help people move from place to place or how housing differs from rich to poor neighborhoods. Sociology also has a **micro-level orientation,** *a close-up focus on social interaction in specific situations.* Exploring urban life in this way occurs at street level, perhaps observing how children interact on a school playground or how pedestrians respond to homeless people. The **symbolic-interaction paradigm,** then, is *a framework for building theory that sees society as the product of the everyday interactions of individuals.*

How does "society" result from the ongoing experiences of tens of millions of people? One answer, explained in Chapter 6 ("Social Interaction in Everyday Life"), is that society is nothing more than the shared reality that people construct as they interact with one another. That is, human beings are creatures who live in a world of symbols, attaching *meaning* to virtually everything. "Reality," therefore, is simply how we define our surroundings, our obligations toward others, even our own identities.

Of course, this process of definition is subjective and varies from person to person. For example, one person may define a homeless man as "just a bum looking for a handout" and ignore him, but another might see the man as a "fellow human being in need" and offer help. In the same way, one person may feel a sense of security passing by a police officer walking the beat, while another may be seized by nervous anxiety. Sociologists who take a symbolic-interaction approach, therefore, view society as a complex, ever-changing mosaic of subjective meanings.

The painting Furnishings, *by Paul Marcus, presents the essential wisdom of social-conflict theory: Society operates in a way that conveys wealth, power, and privilege to some at the expense of others. Looking at the painting, what are most of the people doing? What do you make of the head hanging on the wall? The classi cal scene between the drapes? What categories of people does the artist suggest are disadvantaged?*

© Paul Marcus, *Furnishings*, oil painting on canvas, 64 in. × 48 in. Studio SPM, Inc.

The symbolic-interaction paradigm has roots in the thinking of Max Weber (1864–1920), a German sociologist who emphasized the need to understand a setting from the point of view of the people in it. Weber's approach is discussed in Chapter 4 ("Society").

Since Weber's time, sociologists have taken micro-level sociology in a number of directions. Chapter 5 ("Socialization") discusses the ideas of George Herbert Mead (1863–1931), who explored how we build our personalities from social experience. Chapter 6 ("Social Interaction in Everyday Life") presents the work of Erving Goffman (1922–1982), whose *dramaturgical analysis* describes how we resemble actors on a stage as

attractiveness. Interactional analysis explores the gradual process by which most female (and male) prostitutes take on the role and identity of the streetwalker and the various negotiations that occur between sex workers and clients (and also pimps).

To understand how the social-interaction paradigm views society, consider Emil Bisttram's painting Domingo Chorus. *Society is never at rest; it is an ongoing process by which interacting individuals define and redefine reality.*

Emil Bisttram, American (1895–1976). *Domingo Chorus*, 1936, gouache and pencil on paper, 57.8 × 43.5 cm. Private Collection/Christie's Images/The Bridgeman Art Library.

"social class," the symbolic-interaction paradigm reminds us that society basically amounts to *people interacting.* That is, micro-level sociology tries to convey how individuals actually experience society. The other side of the coin is that, by focusing on day-to-day interactions, the symbolic-interaction paradigm ignores larger social structures, the effects of culture, and factors such as class, gender, and race.

Table 1–1 summarizes the main characteristics of the structural-functional paradigm, the social-conflict paradigm, and the symbolic-interaction paradigm. Each paradigm is helpful in answering particular kinds of questions. However, the fullest understanding of society comes from using the sociological perspective with all three, as we show with the following analysis of sports in the United States.

APPLYING THE PARADIGMS: THE SOCIOLOGY OF SPORT

In the opening to this chapter, we noted how people in the United States love sports. Not only do most young people engage in organized sports, but—for old and young alike—television is filled with sporting events, and a large share of daily news reports sports scores. In the United States, outstanding players such as Mark McGwire (baseball), Shaquille O'Neal (basketball), and Venus Williams (tennis) are among our most famous celebrities. Overall, sports in the United States are a multibillion-dollar industry. What sociological insights can the three theoretical paradigms give us about this familiar part of everyday life?

The Functions of Sports

A structural-functional approach directs attention to the ways in which sports help society operate. Their manifest functions include providing recreation, physical conditioning, and a relatively harmless way to "let off steam." Sports have important latent functions as well, from fostering social relationships to generating tens of thousands of jobs. Perhaps most important, sports encourage competition and the pursuit of success, both of which are central to our way of life.

Sports also have dysfunctional consequences. For example, colleges and universities intent on fielding winning teams sometimes recruit students for their athletic ability rather than their academic aptitude. Not only does this practice pull down the academic standards of a school, but it shortchanges athletes who devote little time to academic work (Upthegrove, Roscigno, & Charles, 1999).

we play out our various roles. Other contemporary sociologists, including George Homans and Peter Blau, have developed *social-exchange analysis.* In their view, social interaction is guided by what each person stands to gain and lose from others (Molm, 1997; Mulford et al., 1998). In the ritual of courtship, for example, people seek mates who offer at least as much—in terms of physical attractiveness, intelligence, and wealth—as they themselves have to offer.

Critical evaluation. The social-interaction paradigm corrects some of the bias found in macro-level approaches to society. Without denying the existence of macro-level social structures such as "the family" and

NOTE: Each orientation's key thinkers: *functional*, Comte, Durkheim, and Spencer; *conflict*, Marx and Weber; *interactional*, Weber, G.H. Mead, Blumer, and Garfinkel. Note that all sociological approaches challenge the utilitarian approach evident in the 18th-century thought of Thomas Hobbes and others (and which is now staging something of a comeback in the form of "rational-choice theory").

NOTE: The assertion that sports function to "build character" was widely expressed at the founding of the Young Men's Christian Association (YMCA) in 1844.

DIVERSITY: One sign of women moving into professional sports was the 1997 launch of the Women's National Basketball Association (WNBA). In 2000, 34% of players were white, 63% black, and 3% Latina.

TABLE 1–1 The Three Major Theoretical Paradigms: A Summary

Theoretical Paradigm	Orientation	Image of Society	Core Questions
Structural-functional	Macro-level	A system of interrelated parts that is relatively stable because of widespread agreement on what is morally desirable; each part has a particular function in society as a whole.	How is society integrated? What are the major parts of society? How are these parts interrelated? What are the consequences of each part for the overall operation of society?
Social-conflict	Macro-level	A system based on social inequality; each part of society benefits some categories of people more than others; social inequality leads to conflict, which, in turn, leads to social change.	How is society divided? What are the major patterns of social inequality? How do some categories of people try to protect their privileges? How do other categories of people challenge the status quo?
Symbolic-interaction	Micro-level	An ongoing process of social interaction in specific settings based on symbolic communication; individual perceptions of reality are variable and changing.	How is society experienced? How do human beings interact to create, maintain, and change social patterns? How do individuals try to shape the reality that others perceive? How does individual behavior change from one situation to another?

Sports and Conflict

A social-conflict analysis begins by pointing out that sports are closely linked to social inequality. Some sports—including tennis, swimming, golf, and skiing—are expensive, so participation is largely limited to the well-to-do. Football, baseball, and basketball, however, are accessible to people of all income levels. In short, the games people play are not simply a matter of choice but also reflect social standing.

Throughout history, sports have been oriented mainly toward males. For example, the first modern Olympic Games, held in 1896, barred women from competition; in the United States, even Little League teams in most parts of the country did not let girls play until recently. Such exclusion has been defended by incorrect notions that girls and women lack the strength and stamina to play sports or that they lose their femininity when they do. Thus, our society encourages men to be athletes while expecting women to be attentive observers and cheerleaders. Today, more women play professional sports than ever before, yet they continue to take a back seat to men, particularly in sports with the most earnings and social prestige.

Although our society long excluded people of color from big league sports, the opportunity to earn high incomes in professional sports has expanded in recent decades. Major League Baseball first admitted African American players when Jackie Robinson broke the color line and joined the Brooklyn Dodgers in 1947. More than fifty years later, in 2000, after professional baseball retired the legendary Robinson's number 42 on *all* teams, African Americans (12 percent of the U.S. population) accounted for 13 percent of Major League Baseball players, 67 percent of National Football League (NFL) players, and 78 percent of National Basketball Association (NBA) players (Center for the Study of Sport in Society, 2001).

One reason for the increasing proportion of people of African descent in professional sports is that athletic performance—in terms of batting average or number of points scored per game—can be precisely measured and is not influenced by racial prejudice. It is also true that some people of color make a particular effort to excel in athletics, where they perceive greater opportunity than in other careers (Steele, 1990; Hoberman, 1997, 1998; Edwards, 2000; Harrison, 2000). In recent years, in fact, African American athletes have earned higher salaries, on average, than white players.

But racial discrimination still taints professional sports in the United States. For one thing, race is linked to the *positions* athletes play on the field, in a pattern called "stacking." Figure 1–2 shows the result of the aggressive sports popular in North America. Anthropologists have also found that aggressive sports are favored by warlike peoples more than by those who are more peaceful (Sipes, 1973).

DIVERSITY: The National Collegiate Athletic Association (NCAA) reports that African American men—5% of all college students—make up 56% of men's collegiate basketball players and 46% of collegiate football players.

DIVERSITY SNAPSHOT

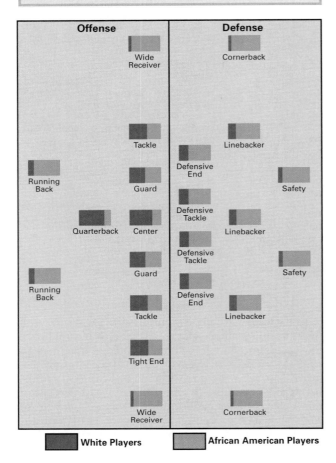

White Players   **African American Players**

FIGURE 1–2 Race and Sport: "Stacking" in Professional Football

Source: Center for the Study of Sport in Society (2001).

of a study of race in football. Notice that white players dominate in offense and also play the central positions on both sides of the line. More broadly, African Americans figure prominently in only five

For a look at racial "stacking" in professional baseball, go to http://www.prenhall.com/weblinks

sports: baseball, basketball, football, boxing, and track. Across all of professional sports, the vast majority of managers, head coaches, and owners of sports teams are white (Gnida, 1995; Smith & Leonard, 1997).

We might ask who benefits the most from professional sports. Although individual players get astronomical salaries, and millions of fans enjoy following their teams, sports are big business, generating property for a small number of people (predominantly white men). In sum, sports in the United States are bound up with inequalities based on gender, race, and economic power.

Sports as Interaction

At a micro-level, a sporting event is a complex drama of face-to-face interaction. In part, play is guided by the players' assigned positions and the rules of the game. But players are also spontaneous and unpredictable. Informed by the symbolic-interaction paradigm, then, we see sports less as a system than as an ongoing process.

From this point of view, too, we expect each player to understand the game a little differently. Some thrive in a setting of stiff competition, whereas, for others, love of the game may be greater than the need to win. (The ancient Romans coined the word *amateur*, literally, "lover," to designate someone who engages in some activity for the sheer love of it.)

Beyond different attitudes toward competition, team members also shape their particular realities according to the various prejudices, jealousies, and ambitions they bring to the game. Then, too, the behavior of any single player may change over time. A rookie in professional baseball, for example, may feel self-conscious during the first few games in the big leagues. In time, however, most players fit in comfortably with the team. Coming to feel at home on the field was slow and painful for Jackie Robinson (the first African American to play in the major leagues, beginning in 1947), who knew that many white players, and millions of white fans, resented his presence. In time, however, his outstanding ability and his confident and cooperative manner won him the respect of the entire nation.

The three theoretical paradigms—structural-functional, social-conflict, and symbolic-interaction—provide different insights, but none is more correct than the others. Applied to any issue, each paradigm generates its own interpretations; to appreciate fully the power of the sociological perspective, you should become familiar with all three. Together, they stimulate debates and controversies. In the final box, we review many of the ideas presented in this chapter by asking how sociological generalizations differ from common stereotypes.

DISCUSS: African Americans are overly represented in only 5 sports: basketball, football, baseball, boxing, and sprint events in track. If genetic factors are at work, why are blacks not also overly represented in tennis? Before baseball was desegregated in 1947, many considered blacks athletically *inferior* to whites. How would you explain this? And, why do we not ask whether Canadians excel in hockey because of a genetic difference (see Gnida, 1995)?

DIVERSITY: Latino representation in Major League Baseball has jumped from 13% in 1990 to 26% in 2000. Latinos make up less than 1% of all NFL players and 1% of NBA players.

THEN AND NOW: African Americans in the NBA: *1954*, 5%; *2000*, 78%; Major League Baseball: *1954*, 7%; *2000*, 13%; NFL: *1954*, 12%; *2000*, 67%.

CONTROVERSY & DEBATE

Is Sociology Nothing More Than Stereotypes?

"Protestants are the ones who kill themselves!"

"People in the United States? They're rich, they love to marry, and they love to divorce!"

"Everybody knows that you have to be black to play professional basketball!"

Everyone, including sociologists, loves to generalize. But beginning students of sociology may wonder how generalizations differ from stereotypes. For example, are the preceding statements sound generalizations or stereotypes?

These three statements are **stereotypes**, *exaggerated descriptions applied to every person in some category.* First, rather than describing averages, each statement paints every individual in a category with the same brush; second, each ignores facts and distorts reality (even though many stereotypes do contain an element of truth); third, a stereotype sounds more like a "put-down" than a fair-minded assertion.

Good sociology, by contrast, involves making generalizations, but with three important conditions. *First, sociologists do not indiscriminately apply any generalization to all individuals; second, sociologists are careful that a generalization squares with available facts; third, sociologists offer generalizations fair-mindedly, with an interest in getting at the truth.*

Earlier in this chapter, we noted that the suicide rate among Protestants is higher than among Catholics or Jews. However, the statement "Protestants are the ones who kill themselves" is not a reasonable generalization because most Protestants do no such thing. Moreover, it would be just as wrong-headed to assume that a particular friend, because he is a Protestant male, is on the verge of self-destruction. (Imagine refusing to lend money to a roommate who happens to be a Baptist, explaining, "Well, given your risk of suicide, I might never get paid back!")

Second, sociologists shape their generalizations to available facts. A more factual version of the second statement at the beginning of this box is that, on average and by world standards, the U.S. population has a very high standard of living. It is also true that our marriage rate is one of the highest in the world. And, although few people take pleasure in divorcing, so is our divorce rate.

Third, sociologists strive to be fair-minded; that is, they are motivated by a passion for truth. The third statement, about African Americans and basketball, is not good sociology for two reasons. First, it is simply not true, and, second, it seems motivated by bias rather than truth-seeking.

Good sociology stands apart from harmful stereotyping. But a sociology course is an excellent setting for talking over common stereotypes. The classroom encourages discussion and offers the factual information you need to decide whether a particular assertion is accurate or just a stereotype.

Continue the debate . . .

1. *Do people in the United States have stereotypes of sociologists? What are they? Are they valid?*

2. *Do you think taking a sociology course dispels people's stereotypes? Why or why not?*

3. *Can you cite a stereotype of your own that sociology challenges?*

SUMMARY

1. The sociological perspective shows "the general in the particular," or the power of society to shape our individual lives.

2. Because our culture emphasizes individual choice, seeing the power of society in our lives may seem, at first, like "seeing the strange in the familiar."

3. Differences in the number of children born to women around the world, as well as Emile Durkheim's research on suicide rates among some categories of people, show that society affects even our most personal choices and actions.

4. Global awareness is an important part of the sociological perspective because, first, people live very differently in various nations; second, societies around the world are becoming increasingly interconnected; third, many social problems are most

Q: "Serious differences among social scientists occur not between those who would observe without thinking and those who would think without observing; the differences have rather to do with what kinds of thinking, what kinds of observing, and what kinds of links, if any, there are between the two." C. Wright Mills

Q: "The world is a book and those who study just their own society read only a single page." Old saying

Q: "It might be supposed that, at least in their ability to run their own affairs, sociologists would have an edge over their fellow mortals, but any acquaintance with the American Sociological Association quickly dispels that notion." Pierre L. Van den Berghe (1978:4)

EXERCISE: To help students see the power of society, suggest that students speak to grandparents about their lives as children.

Q: "You gotta play the hand that's dealt you." James Brady

serious beyond the borders of the United States; and, fourth, global awareness helps us better understand ourselves.

5. Socially marginal people are more likely than others to see the power of society. For everyone, periods of social crisis foster sociological thinking.

6. The benefits of using the sociological perspective include, first, helping us assess common beliefs; second, helping us appreciate the opportunities and limits in our lives; third, encouraging more active participation in society; and, fourth, increasing our awareness of social diversity in the world around us.

7. Sociology arose in response to vast changes in Europe during the eighteenth and nineteenth centuries. Three changes—the rise of an industrial economy, the explosive growth of cities, and the emergence of new political ideas—focused people's attention on how society operates.

8. Auguste Comte gave sociology its name in 1838. Earlier social thinkers focused on what society ought to be, but Comte's new discipline used scientific methods to understand society as it is.

9. A theory weaves observations into insight and understanding. Sociologists use various theoretical paradigms to construct theories.

10. The structural-functional paradigm focuses on how patterns of behavior contribute to the operation of society. This approach highlights stability and integration while minimizing inequality and conflict.

11. While emphasizing inequality, conflict, and change, the social-conflict paradigm downplays a society's integration and stability.

12. In contrast to these broad, macro-level approaches, the symbolic-interaction paradigm is a micro-level framework that focuses on face-to-face interaction in specific settings.

13. Because each paradigm highlights different dimensions of any social issue, the richest sociological understanding is derived from applying all three.

14. Sociological thinking involves generalizations. But unlike a stereotype, a sociological statement (1) is not applied indiscriminately to everyone in some category, (2) is supported by facts, and (3) is put forward in the fair-minded pursuit of truth.

KEY CONCEPTS

sociology (p. 1) the systematic study of human society

global perspective (p. 5) the study of the larger world and our society's place in it

high-income countries (p. 5) nations with very productive economic systems in which most people have relatively high incomes

middle-income countries (p. 7) nations with moderately productive economic systems in which people's incomes are about the global average

low-income countries (p. 7) nations with less productive economic systems in which most people are poor

positivism (p. 12) a way of understanding based on science

theory (p. 13) a statement of how and why specific facts are related

theoretical paradigm (p. 13) a basic image of society that guides thinking and research

structural-functional paradigm (p. 14) a framework for building theory that sees society as a complex system whose parts work together to promote solidarity and stability

social structure (p. 14) any relatively stable pattern of social behavior

social functions (p. 14) the consequences of any social pattern for the operation of society as a whole

manifest functions (p. 14) the recognized and intended consequences of any social pattern

latent functions (p. 14) the unrecognized and unintended consequences of any social pattern

social dysfunctions (p. 15) the undesirable consequences of any social pattern for the operation of society

social-conflict paradigm (p. 15) a framework for building theory that sees society as an arena of inequality that generates conflict and change

macro-level orientation (p. 17) a concern with broad patterns that shape society as a whole

micro-level orientation (p. 17) a close-up focus on social interaction in specific situations

symbolic-interaction paradigm (p. 17) a framework for building theory that sees society as the product of the everyday interactions of individuals

stereotypes (p. 21) exaggerated descriptions applied to every person in some category

CRITICAL-THINKING QUESTIONS

1. How would you contrast psychology and sociology in terms of perspective?

2. In what ways does using the sociological perspective make us seem less in control of our lives? How does it give us greater power over our surroundings?

3. What factors help explain why sociology developed where and when it did?

4. Guided by the discipline's three major theoretical paradigms, what questions might you ask about (a) television, (b) war, and (c) colleges and universities?

APPLICATIONS AND EXERCISES

1. Packaged in the back of this new textbook is an interactive CD-ROM that offers a variety of study and review materials intended to help you better understand the material covered in this chapter. For this chapter, the CD-ROM contains an author's tip video, Real Life Sociology videos, interactive map animations, audio journal entries from the author, Web links, and much more. It also offers an interactive version of the timeline that is inside the front cover of this textbook.

2. Spend several hours exploring your local area until you can draw a sociological map of the community. The map might indicate the categories of people and types of buildings found in various places (for example, "big single-family homes," "run-down business area," "new office buildings," "student apartments," and so on). What patterns do you see?

3. Look ahead to Figure 18–3, which shows the U.S. divorce rate over the last century. Try to identify societal factors that pushed the divorce rate down after 1930, up again after 1940, down in the 1950s, and up again after 1960.

4. During a class, carefully observe the behavior of the instructor and other students. What patterns do you see in who speaks? What about how people use space? What categories of people are taking the class in the first place?

 ## SITES TO SEE

http://www.prenhall.com/macionis

The author and publisher of this book invite you to visit the interactive *Companion Website*™ that accompanies this text. Begin by clicking on the cover of your book. You will find a chapter-by-chapter study guide, practice tests, and a significant portion of the text for online review, as well as many suggested Web links.

http://www.macionis.com
(or http://www.TheSociologyPage.com)

You can find dozens of additional links to Internet sites, as well as information—including short videos—about the discipline of sociology, at the author's home page. Bookmark this page as your doorway to the discipline.

http://www.plasma.nationalgeographic.com/mapmachine
http://www.nationalatlas.gov

These two sites provide a number of maps showing patterns and trends of interest to sociologists.

http://quickfacts.census.gov/qfd
http://www.countrywatch.com

The first of these sites provides statistical data and other information about the United States, your own state, and your own county. The second offers a range of data about all 192 nations in the world.

 ## INVESTIGATE WITH CONTENTSELECT

Investigate issues discussed in this chapter using the ContentSelect database of scholarly journals and popular publications. To access ContentSelect through this book's *Companion Website*™, visit http://www.prenhall.com/macionis Click on the cover of your book. Select this or any chapter and click "Begin." Once in the chapter, click the ContentSelect icon at the bottom left of your screen. You will be prompted to enter your ContentSelect access code and then asked to create your personal User ID and Password. For all repeat visits, simply enter your personal User ID and Password. Enter keywords such as "sociology," "Auguste Comte," and "sports," and the search engine will help you become an effective researcher.

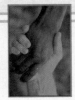

CHAPTER

2

Edvard Munch (1863–1944)
Rue Lafayette

National Gallery, Oslo, Norway, Scala/Art Resource, N.Y.
© Artists Rights Society (ARS), New York/ADAGP, Paris.

SOCIOLOGICAL INVESTIGATION

While on a visit to the city of Atlanta during the winter holiday season, sociologist Lois Benjamin (1991) called on the mother of an old friend from college. Benjamin was eager for news of her friend, Sheba, a woman who she knew had shared her own dream of earning a graduate degree, landing a teaching job, and writing books. Benjamin had fulfilled her lifelong dream, but as she soon found out, the news was not good for Sheba, who had fallen disastrously short of her goal.

There had been early signs of trouble, Benjamin recalled. After college, Sheba began graduate work at a university in Canada. But in her letters to Benjamin, Sheba became more and more critical of the world and seemed to be cutting herself off from others. The problem, as Sheba saw it, was racism. As an African American woman, she felt she was the target of racial hostility. Before long, she flunked out of school, blaming her white professors for her failure. Then she left North America, finally earning a PhD from an English university and settling in Nigeria. Since then, Benjamin had not heard a word from her long-time friend.

Benjamin was happy to learn that Sheba had returned to Atlanta. But her delight dissolved into shock when she saw Sheba and

realized that her friend, suffering a mental breakdown, was barely responsive to anyone.

For months after, Sheba's emotional collapse troubled Benjamin. She knew that many factors combine to cause such personal tragedy. But having experienced the sting of racism herself, Benjamin believed it had played a major role in Sheba's story. Partly as a tribute to her old friend, Benjamin set out to explore the effects of racial prejudice on the lives of bright and well-educated people of color in the United States.

Benjamin realized she was challenging the conventional wisdom that race poses less of a barrier today than in previous generations, especially to talented African Americans (Wilson, 1978). But her own experiences—and, she believed, Sheba's—seemed to contradict such thinking.

To test her ideas, Benjamin spent the next two years of her life asking 100 successful African Americans across the country how race affected their lives. In the words of these "Talented One Hundred"[1] men and women, she found evidence that, even among privileged African Americans, racism remains a heavy burden.

---

[1]Benjamin derived her concept from the term "Talented Tenth" used by W. E. B. Du Bois (1899) to describe African American leaders in his day.

25

SUPPLEMENTS: The *Data File* contains an annotated outline of Chapter 2, supplemental lecture material, and suggestions for class discussion.
NOTE: Science and religion do not conflict but complement one another. Scientific truths involve proximate causes of events; religious truths deal with ultimate causes.
Q: "The truth is rarely pure and never simple." Oscar Wilde

NOTE: Many traditional people (especially today) have a good sense of science. There is an old joke about a tribal shaman using his power to make rain, which always comes soon after. A visitor asks him, "I can't help but notice that you only do your rain ritual when dark clouds gather in the sky." "Of course," he responds, "I would be a fool to hope for rain when there are no clouds!"
Q: "Plato is dear to me, but dearer still is truth." Aristotle

Later in this chapter, we will take a closer look at Lois Benjamin's research. For the moment, notice how the sociological perspective helped her spot broad social patterns operating in the lives of individuals. Just as important, Benjamin's work demonstrates the *doing* of sociology, the process of *sociological investigation*.

Many people think that scientists work only in laboratories, carefully taking measurements using complex equipment. But as this chapter explains, whereas some sociologists conduct scientific research in laboratories, most work on neighborhood streets, in homes and workplaces, in schools and hospitals, in bars and prisons—in short, wherever people can be found.

This chapter examines the methods sociologists use to conduct research. Along the way, we shall see that research involves not just procedures for gathering information but controversies about values: Should researchers strive to be objective? Or should they point to the need for change? Certainly, Lois Benjamin did not undertake her study simply to show that racism exists; she wanted to bring racism out in the open as a way to challenge it. We shall tackle questions of values after addressing the basics of sociological investigation.

THE BASICS OF SOCIOLOGICAL INVESTIGATION

Sociological investigation starts with two simple requirements. The first was the focus of Chapter 1: *Use the sociological perspective*. This point of view reveals curious patterns of behavior all around us that call for further study. It was Lois Benjamin's sociological imagination that prompted her to wonder how race affects the lives of talented African Americans.

The first requirement of sociological investigation leads directly to the second: *Be curious and ask questions*. Benjamin sought to learn more about how race affects people with significant personal achievements. She asked questions: Who are the leaders of this nation's black community? What effect does being part of a racial minority have on their self-identity? On the way white people perceive them and their work?

Seeing the world sociologically and asking questions are fundamental to sociological investigation. Yet they are only the beginning. They spark our curiosity, but then we face the task of finding answers to our questions. To understand the kinds of insights sociology offers, we need to realize that there are various kinds of "truth."

SCIENCE AS ONE FORM OF TRUTH

When we say we "know" something, we can mean many things. Most members of U.S. society, for instance, claim to believe in the existence of God. Few would claim to have direct contact with God, but they say they believe all the same. We call this kind of knowing "belief" or "faith."

A second kind of truth rests on the pronouncement of some recognized expert. For example, parents with questions about raising their children may read books by an "expert" or consult a child psychologist.

A third type of truth is based on simple agreement among ordinary people. We come to "know" that, say, sexual intercourse among young children is wrong because just about everyone says it is.

People's "truths" differ the world over, and we often encounter "facts" at odds with our own. Imagine being a Peace Corps volunteer who has just arrived in a small, traditional village in Latin America. Your job is to help local people increase their crop yield. On your first day in the fields, you observe a curious practice: After planting the seeds, the farmers lay dead fish on top of the soil. In response to your question, they reply that the fish are a gift to the god of the harvest. A village elder adds sternly that the harvest was poor one year when no fish were offered.

From that society's point of view, using fish as gifts to the harvest god makes sense. The people believe in it, their experts endorse it, and everyone seems to agree that the system works. But with scientific training in agriculture, you shake your head and wonder. The scientific truth in this situation is something entirely different: The decomposing fish fertilize the ground, producing a better crop.

Science represents a fourth way of knowing. **Science** is *a logical system that bases knowledge on direct, systematic observation*. **Scientific sociology**, then, is *the study of society based on systematic observation of social behavior*. Standing apart from faith, the wisdom of experts, and general agreement, scientific knowledge rests on **empirical evidence,** that is, *information we can verify with our senses*.

Our Peace Corps example does not mean that people in traditional villages ignore what their senses tell them, or that members of technologically advanced societies reject nonscientific ways of knowing. A medical researcher using science to develop a new drug for treating cancer, for example, may still practice her religion as a matter of faith; she may turn to experts when making financial decisions; and she may derive political opinions from family and friends. In short, we all hold various kinds of truths at the same time.

NOTE: Two examples of misleading common sense: The birth rate of "welfare mothers" is actually below that of all women; remarriages are more prone to divorce than first marriages.

Q: "It's not the things we don't know that get us into trouble. It's the things we know that just ain't so." Artemus Ward

Q: "There are other avenues to knowledge besides the objective experience of our senses." Ralf Dahrendorf

NOTE: Facts, standing alone, do not constitute compelling truth. Myth (from the Greek *mythos*, meaning "story" or "word") is a means of conveying broad cultural truths without relying on factual details. The success of the film *E.T.* resulted partly from its mythic elements: a main character who was born elsewhere, came to Earth, underwent a great testing, and finally returned to his origins. The same four elements underlie the lives of Moses, Jesus, and Superman.

Myths as well as scientific facts are an important dimension of human existence. In his painting, The Creation of the Earth, *Mexican painter Diego Rivera (1886–1957) offers a mythic account of human origins. A myth (from the Greek, meaning "story" or "word") may or may not be factual in the literal sense. Yet, it conveys some basic truth about the meaning and purpose of life. Indeed, it is science, rather than art, that has no power to address such questions of meaning.*

Diego Rivera, Mexican (1886–1957). *The Creation of the Earth* page from *Popol Vuh*, watercolor on paper. Museo Casa Diego Rivera (INBA), Guanajuato, Mexico. Index/The Bridgeman Art Library. © 2003 Banco de Mexico Diego Rivera and Frida Kahlo Museums Trust.

COMMON SENSE VERSUS SCIENTIFIC EVIDENCE

Scientific evidence sometimes challenges our common sense. Here are six statements that many North Americans assume are true:

1. **Poor people are far more likely than rich people to break the law.** Watching a television show such as *Cops*, one might well conclude that police arrest only people from "bad" neighborhoods. Chapter 8 ("Deviance") explains that poor people do stand out in the official arrest statistics. But research also shows that police and prosecutors are more likely to respond leniently to wrongdoing by well-to-do people. Furthermore, some laws are written in a way that criminalizes poor people more and affluent people less.

2. **The United States is a middle-class society in which most people are roughly equal.** Data presented in Chapter 11 ("Social Class in the United States") show that the richest 5 percent of our people control more than half the nation's total wealth. If people are equal, then some are much "more equal" than others.

3. **Most poor people don't want to work.** Research described in Chapter 11 indicates that this statement is true of some but not most poor people. In fact, about half of poor people in the United States are children and elderly people whom no one would expect to work.

4. **Differences in the behavior of females and males reflect "human nature."** Much of what we call "human nature" is constructed by the society in which we are raised, as Chapter 3 ("Culture") explains. Furthermore, as Chapter 13 ("Gender Stratification") argues, some societies define "feminine" and "masculine" very differently from the way we do.

5. **People change as they grow old, losing many interests as they focus on their health.** Chapter 15 ("Aging and the Elderly") reports that aging changes our personalities very little. Problems of health increase in old age, but, by and large, elderly people keep their distinctive personalities.

6. **Most people marry because they are in love.** To members of U.S. society, few statements are so self-evident. Surprisingly, however, in many societies marriage has little to do with love. Chapter 18 ("Family") explains why.

These examples confirm the old saying that "It's not what we don't know that gets us into trouble as much as things we *do* know that just aren't so." We have

 For another example of sociology challenging common sense, go to http://www.prenhall.com/weblinks

all been brought up believing conventional truths, being bombarded

Common sense suggests that, in a world of possibilities, people fall in love with that "special someone." Sociological research reveals that the vast majority of people select partners who are very similar in social background to themselves.

by expert advice, and being pressured to accept the opinions of people around us. As adults, we need to evaluate critically what we see, read, and hear. Sociology can help us to do just that.

SCIENCE: BASIC ELEMENTS AND LIMITATIONS

In Chapter 1, we explained how early sociologists such as Auguste Comte and Emile Durkheim applied science to the study of society just as natural scientists investigate the physical world. The scientific approach to knowing, called *positivism*, assumes that an objective reality exists "out there." The job of the scientist is to discover this reality by gathering empirical evidence, facts we can verify with our senses.

In this chapter, we begin by introducing the major elements of scientific sociology. Then we shall discuss some limitations of scientific (or positivist) sociology and present alternative approaches.

CONCEPTS, VARIABLES, AND MEASUREMENT

A basic element of science is the **concept,** *a mental construct that represents some part of the world in a simplified form.* "Society" is a concept, as are the structural parts of societies, such as "the family" and "the economy." Sociologists also use concepts to describe individuals, as when we speak of someone's "race" or "social class."

A **variable** is *a concept whose value changes from case to case.* The familiar variable "price," for example, changes from item to item in a supermarket. Similarly, we use the concept "social class" to identify people as upper class, middle class, working class, or lower class.

The use of variables depends on **measurement,** *a procedure for determining the value of a variable in a specific case.* Some variables are easy to measure, as when the checkout clerk adds up the cost of our groceries. But measuring sociological variables can be far more difficult. For example, how would you measure a person's social class? You might look at clothing, listen to patterns of speech, or note a home address. Or, trying to be more precise, you might ask about income, occupation, and education.

Because almost any variable can be measured in more than one way, sociologists often have to make a judgment about which factors to consider. For example, having a very high income might qualify a person as "upper class." But what if the income comes from selling automobiles, an occupation most people think of as "middle class"? Would having only an eighth-grade education make the person "lower class"? In this case, sociologists sensibly (but arbitrarily) combine these three measures—income, occupation, and education—to assign social class, as described in Chapter 10 ("Social Stratification") and Chapter 11 ("Social Class in the United States").

Sociologists face another interesting problem in measuring variables: dealing with vast numbers of people. For instance, how do you describe income for millions of U.S. families? Reporting streams of numbers carries little meaning and tells us nothing about the people as a whole. Therefore, sociologists use *statistical measures* to describe people. The box explains how.

Defining Concepts

Measurement is always somewhat arbitrary because the value of any variable partly depends on how it is

NOTE: The mode is a nominal level of measurement, the median is ordinal, and the mean is an interval/ratio measure.

NOTE: U.S. household income (mean of $57,045, median of $42,148) provides another example of a mean pulled up by extreme scores.

Q: "It is the essence of the human mind to take apart what experience presents as a whole." Peter Berger

NOTE: Awards in medical malpractice cases illustrate wild variations in statistical measures. One study noted the modal settlement was zero (the most common award); median award was around $20,000 because most awards are small; yet the mean award was about $100,000 because the average is skewed upward by a few high awards.

Q: "Let us lay the facts aside, for they do not affect the question." Jean Jacques Rousseau

APPLYING SOCIOLOGY

Three Useful (and Simple) Statistical Measures

We all talk about "averages," whether it is the average price of a gallon of gasoline or the average salary for new college graduates. Sociologists, too, are interested in averages, and they use three different statistical measures to describe what is typical.

Assume that we want to describe the salaries paid to seven members of a sociology department at a local college:

$35,000 $41,700 $35,000 $35,000
$43,000 $42,000 $78,295

The simplest statistical measure is the *mode*, the value that occurs most often in a series of numbers. In this example, the mode is $35,000 because that value occurs three times and each of the others occurs only once. If all the values occurred only once, there would be no mode; if two values occurred three times (or twice), there would be two modes. Although it is easy to identify, sociologists rarely use the mode because it is a very crude measure of the "average."

A more common statistical measure, the *mean*, is the arithmetic average of a series of numbers, calculated by adding all the values together and dividing by the number of cases. The sum of the seven incomes is $309,995; dividing by seven yields a mean income of $44,285. But notice that the mean is higher than the income of six of the seven sociologists. Because the mean is pulled up or down by an especially high or low value (in this case, the $78,295 paid to one sociologist, who also serves as a dean), it has the drawback of giving a distorted picture of any distribution that contains extreme scores.

The *median* is the middle case: the value that occurs midway in a series of numbers arranged from lowest to highest. Here the median income for the seven people is $41,700 because three incomes are higher and three are lower. (With an even number of cases, the median is halfway between the two middle cases.) Because a median is unaffected by an extreme score, it gives a better picture of what is "average" than the mean does.

Calculate simple statistics on your own. An example is found at http://www.prenhall.com/weblinks

---

defined. In addition, deciding what abstract concepts such as "love," "family," or "intelligence" mean in real life can lead to lengthy debates before any attempt is made to measure them as variables.

Good research, therefore, includes **operationalizing a variable,** which means *specifying exactly what one is to measure before assigning a value to a variable.* Before measuring the concept of social class, for example, we would have to decide exactly what we were going to measure (say, income level, years of schooling, occupational prestige). Sometimes sociologists measure several of these things; in such cases, they need to specify exactly how they plan to combine these variables into one overall score. When reading about research, always notice the way researchers operationalize each variable. How they define terms can greatly affect the results.

When deciding how to operationalize variables, sociologists may take into account the opinions of the people they study. Since 1977, for example, researchers at the U.S. Census Bureau defined race and ethnicity as white, black, Hispanic, Asian or Pacific Islander, and American Indian or Alaskan Native. One problem with this list is that someone can be both Hispanic and white or black; similarly, people of Arab ancestry might not identify with any of these choices. Just as important, an increasing number of people in the United States are *multiracial* (Cose, 1997; O'Hare, 1998). As a result of such problems, the census in the year 2000 allowed people to describe their race and ethnicity by selecting more than one category.

Reliability and Validity

For a measurement to be useful, it must be reliable and valid. **Reliability** refers to *consistency in measurement.* In other words, the procedure must yield the same result if repeated time after time. But consistency is no guarantee of **validity,** which means *precision in measuring exactly what one intends to measure.* In other words, valid

NOTE: Precision and accuracy have an inverse relationship: The more precise our statement, the more likely it is to be wrong. Consider: When weather forecasters predict that the high temperature 5 days from now will be, say, 73, they are almost always wrong.

NOTE: An independent variable in one situation may be a dependent variable in another; the designation is arbitrary and determined by the specific experiment in question.

NOTE: Earl Babbie describes bad measurement as bullet holes scattered all around a target, reliable but not valid measurement as holes clustered together on a target but not in the bull's eye, reliable and valid measurement as holes clustered on the bull's-eye. Note that validity implies reliability, but not vice versa.

Q: "It is the pursuit of truth that gives us life, and it is to that pursuit that our loyalty is due." William Graham Sumner

Young people who live in the crowded inner city are more likely than those who live in the spacious suburbs to have trouble with the police. But does this mean that crowding causes delinquency? Researchers know that crowding and arrest rates do vary together, but they have demonstrated that the connection is spurious: Both factors rise in relation to a third factor—declining income.

measurement means more than hitting the same spot on a target again and again; it means hitting the bull's-eye.

Valid measurement is more difficult than it may at first seem. Say you want to study how religious people are. A reasonable strategy might be to ask how often respondents attend religious services. But is going to a church or temple really the same thing as being religious? It may be that religious people attend services more frequently, but people also join in religious rituals out of habit or because someone else wants them to. Moreover, some devout believers avoid organized religion altogether. Thus, even when a measurement

yields consistent results (making it reliable), it can still miss the real, intended target (and lack validity). Later on, in Chapter 19 ("Religion"), we suggest that measuring religiosity should take account of not only church attendance but also a person's beliefs and the degree to which a person lives by religious convictions. In sum, careful measurement is vital to sociological research and often a challenge.

Relationships between Variables

Once measurements are made, investigators can pursue the real payoff: seeing how variables are related. The scientific ideal is **cause and effect,** *a relationship in which change in one variable causes change in another.* Cause-and-effect relationships occur around us every day, as when studying for an exam results in a high grade. *The variable that causes the change* (in this case, studying) is called the **independent variable.** *The variable that changes* (the exam grade) is called the **dependent variable.** In other words, the value of one variable depends on the value of another. Why is linking variables in terms of cause and effect important? Because this kind of relationship allows us to *predict* how one pattern of behavior will produce another.

But just because two variables change together does not mean that they are linked by a cause-and-effect relationship. For instance, the marriage rate in the United States falls to its lowest point in January, exactly the same month that our national death rate peaks. This hardly means that people die because they fail to marry (or that they don't marry because they die). In fact, it is the dreary weather in much of the nation during January (and maybe also the post-holiday blahs) that causes both a low marriage rate and a high death rate. The converse holds as well: The warmer and sunnier summer months have the highest marriage rates and the lowest death rates. Thus researchers must look below the surface to untangle cause-and-effect relationships.

To take a second case, sociologists have long recognized that juvenile delinquency is more common among young people who live in crowded housing. Say we operationalize the variable "juvenile delinquency" as the number of times (if any) a person under age eighteen has been arrested, and we define "crowded housing" to mean a home's amount of square feet of living space per person. We would find the variables related; that is, delinquency rates are high in densely populated neighborhoods. But should we conclude that crowding in the home (in this case, the independent variable) is what causes delinquency (the dependent variable)?

Not necessarily. **Correlation** is *a relationship by which two (or more) variables change together*. We know that density and delinquency are correlated because they change together, as shown in part (a) of Figure 2–1. This relationship *may* mean that crowding causes misconduct, but it could also mean that some third factor is at work causing change in *both* of the variables under observation. To identify a third variable, think what kind of people live in crowded housing: people with little money and few choices—the poor. Poor children are also more likely to end up with police records. Therefore, crowded housing and juvenile delinquency are found together because *both* are caused by a third factor—poverty—as shown in part (b) of Figure 2–1. In short, the apparent connection between crowding and delinquency is "explained away" by a third variable—low income—that causes them both to change. So our original connection turns out to be a **spurious correlation,** *an apparent, although false, relationship between two (or more) variables caused by some other variable.*

Unmasking a correlation as spurious takes a bit of detective work, assisted by a technique called **control,** *holding constant all variables except one in order to see clearly the effect of that variable*. In this example, we suspect that income level may be causing a spurious link between housing density and delinquency. To check, we control for income (that is, we hold income constant by looking at only young people of one income level) and see whether a correlation between density and delinquency remains. If the correlation between density and delinquency is still there despite the control (that is, if young people living in more crowded housing show higher rates of delinquency than young people in less crowded housing, all with the same family income), we have more reason to think that crowding does, in fact, cause delinquency. But if the relationship disappears when we control for income, as shown in part (c) of the figure, we then know we have a spurious correlation. In fact, research shows that the correlation between crowding and delinquency just about disappears if income is controlled (Fischer, 1984). So we have now sorted out the relationships between the three variables, as illustrated in part (d) of the figure. Housing density and juvenile delinquency have a spurious correlation; evidence shows that both variables rise or fall according to people's income.

To sum up, correlation means only that two or more variables change together. Cause and effect rests on three conditions: (1) demonstrated correlation, (2) an independent (or causal) variable that precedes the dependent variable in time, and (3) no evidence that a

FIGURE 2–1 Correlation and Cause: An Example

(a)

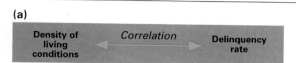

If two variables vary together, they are said to be correlated. In this example, density of living conditions and juvenile delinquency increase and decrease together.

(b)

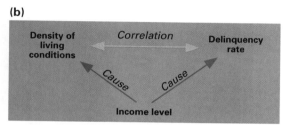

Here we consider the effect of a third variable: income level. Low income level may cause *both* high-density living conditions *and* a high delinquency rate. In other words, as income level decreases, both density of living conditions and the delinquency rate increase.

(c)

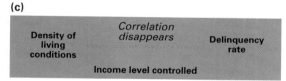

If we control income level—that is, examine only cases with the same income level—do those with higher-density living conditions still have a higher delinquency rate? The answer is *no*. There is no longer a correlation between these two variables.

(d)

This finding leads us to conclude that income level is a cause of both density of living conditions and delinquency rate. The original two variables (density of living conditions and delinquency rate) are thus correlated, but neither one causes the other. Their correlation is therefore *spurious*.

DISCUSS: As another example of spuriousness: A negative correlation links state-by-state tallies of the number of PhDs and the number of mules. Does a dying mule create a PhD? (Warren Street, Central Washington University)

RESOURCE: Max Weber's statement on value-free research is among the classics in the Macionis and Benokraitis reader, *Seeing Ourselves*, 5th ed.

Q: "Instructors who feel called upon to intervene in the struggles of world views and party opinions . . . may do so outside, in the marketplace, in the press, in meetings. . . . But after all it is somewhat too convenient to demonstrate one's courage in taking a stand where the audience and possible opponents are condemned to silence." Max Weber, "Science as a Vocation"

THE IDEAL OF OBJECTIVITY

Assume that ten people who work for a magazine in Fort Lauderdale, Florida, are collaborating on a story about that city's best restaurants. With the magazine picking up the tab, they head out on the town for a week of fine dining. Later, they get together to compare notes. Do you think one restaurant will be everyone's clear favorite? That hardly seems likely.

In scientific terms, each of the ten probably operationalizes the concept "best restaurant" differently. For one, it might be a place that serves delicious steaks at reasonable prices; for another, the choice might turn on a menu keyed to nutrition and health; for still another, stunning decor and attentive service might be the deciding factors. Like so many other things in life, the best restaurant turns out to be mostly a matter of individual taste.

Personal values are fine when it comes to restaurants, but they pose a challenge to scientific research. Remember, science assumes an objective reality. Scientists need to study this reality without changing it in any way. Therefore, science demands that researchers strive for **objectivity**, *a state of personal neutrality in conducting research*. Objectivity means that researchers carefully hold to scientific procedures while reining in their own attitudes and beliefs in order not to bias the results.

Scientific objectivity is an ideal rather than a reality, of course, because no one can be completely neutral about anything. Even the subject a researcher chooses to study reflects a personal interest of one sort or another, as Lois Benjamin's research on race attests. But the scientific ideal is to keep a professional sense of detachment from how the results turn out. Holding to this ideal, we do our best to see that conscious or unconscious biases do not distort research. As an extra precaution, many researchers inform their readers about their personal leanings so that their conclusions are taken in the proper context.

One principle of scientific research is that sociologists and other investigators should strive to be objective in their work, so that their personal values and beliefs do not distort their findings. But such an aloof attitude may discourage the relationship needed in order for people to open up and share information. Thus, as sociologists study human relationships, they have to be especially mindful of their own—when it comes to their subjects.

Max Weber: Value-Free Research

The influential German sociologist Max Weber expected that people would select their research topics according to their personal beliefs and interests. After all, why else would one person study world hunger, another investigate the effects of racism, and still another examine how children fare in one-parent families? Knowing that people select topics that are *value-relevant*, Weber cautioned researchers to be *value-free* in their investigations. Only by being dispassionate (as we expect any professional to be) can researchers study the world *as it*

third variable could be causing a spurious correlation between the two.

Natural scientists usually have an easier time than social scientists identifying cause-and-effect relationships because they can control many variables in a laboratory. Carrying out research in a workplace or on the streets, however, is a more difficult task, and sociologists often must be satisfied with demonstrating only correlation. Moreover, human behavior is highly complex, involving dozens of causal variables at any one time, so establishing all the cause-and-effect relationships in any situation is extremely difficult.

Q: "We may remind ourselves that disinterestedness is not disinterest. The passionate commitment to scholarly detachment and free inquiry . . . needs all the self-restraint we can muster to support it precisely because self-restraint goes against our natural preference for our own, including our own views." Pamela Jensen

NOTE: Only a small proportion of social science research is actually subjected to replication (far less than in the natural sciences).

Q: "We can no longer view the world as Descartes and Laplace would have us do, as 'rational onlookers,' from outside. Our place is within the same world that we are studying, and whatever scientific understanding we achieve must be a kind of understanding that is available to participants within the process of nature, i.e., from inside." Stephen Toulmin

A basic lesson of social research is that being observed affects how people behave. Researchers can never be certain precisely how this will occur; while some people resent public attention, others become highly animated when they think they have an audience.

is rather than tell how they think *it should be.* For Weber, this detachment is a crucial element of science that sets it apart from politics. In other words, politicians are committed to particular outcomes; scientists try to maintain an open-minded readiness to accept the results of their investigations, whatever they may be.

Weber's argument still carries much weight in sociology, although most sociologists concede that we can never be completely value-free or even aware of all our biases (Demerath, 1996). Moreover, sociologists are not "average" people: Most are white people who are highly educated and more politically liberal than the population as a whole (Wilson, 1979). Sociologists need to remember that they, too, are influenced by their own social backgrounds.

One way to limit distortion caused by personal values is **replication,** *repetition of research by other investigators.* If other researchers repeat a study using the same procedures and obtain the same results, we gain confidence that the results are accurate. The need for replication in scientific investigation probably explains why the search for knowledge is called *re*-search in the first place.

In any case, keep in mind that the logic of science does not guarantee objective, absolute truth. What science offers is an approach to knowledge that is *self-correcting* so that, in the long run, researchers stand the best chance of overcoming their biases. Thus, objectivity and truth lie not in any particular research but in the scientific process itself.

SOME LIMITATIONS OF SCIENTIFIC SOCIOLOGY

Science is one important way of knowing. Yet, applied to social life, science has several important limitations:

1. **Human behavior is too complex for sociologists to predict precisely any individual's actions.** Astronomers calculate the movement of objects in the heavens with remarkable precision, but comets and planets are unthinking objects. Humans, by contrast, have minds of their own, so no two people react to any event in exactly the same way. Sociologists, therefore, must be satisfied with showing that *categories* of people typically act in one way or another. This is not a failing of sociology. It simply reflects the reality of what we do: study creative, spontaneous people.

2. **Because humans respond to their surroundings, the mere presence of a researcher may affect the behavior being studied.** An astronomer's gaze has no effect whatever on a distant comet. But most people react to being observed. Some become anxious, angry, or defensive; others try to "help" by doing what they think the researcher expects of them.

3. **Social patterns change; what is true in one time or place may not hold true in another.** The laws of physics apply tomorrow as well as

today; they hold true all around the world. But human behavior is so variable that there are no unchanging sociological laws.

4. **Because sociologists are part of the social world they study, being value-free when conducting social research is difficult.** Barring a laboratory mishap, chemists are rarely personally affected by what goes on in test tubes. But sociologists live in their "test tube": the society they study. Therefore, social scientists face a greater challenge in controlling, or even recognizing, personal values that may distort their work.

A SECOND FRAMEWORK: INTERPRETIVE SOCIOLOGY

All sociologists agree that studying social behavior scientifically presents some real challenges. But some sociologists go further, suggesting that science as it is used to study the natural world misses a vital part of the social world: *meaning*.

Human beings do not simply act; we engage in *meaningful* action. Max Weber, who pioneered this framework, argued that the proper focus of sociology, therefore, is *interpretation*, or understanding the meanings involved in everyday life. **Interpretive sociology** is *the study of society that focuses on the meanings people attach to their social world.*

Interpretive sociology differs from scientific, or positivist, sociology in three ways. First, scientific sociology focuses on action, what people do; interpretive sociology, by contrast, focuses on the meaning people attach to behavior. Second, whereas scientific sociology sees an objective reality "out there," interpretive sociology sees reality constructed by people themselves in the course of their everyday lives. Third, whereas scientific sociology tends to favor *quantitative* data—that is, numerical measurements of social behavior—interpretive sociology favors *qualitative* data, researchers' perceptions of how people understand their surroundings.

In sum, the scientific approach is well suited to research in a laboratory, where investigators stand back and take careful measurements. The interpretive approach is better suited to research in a natural setting where investigators interact with people, learning how they make sense of their everyday lives.

Weber believed that the key to interpretive sociology lay in *Verstehen*, the German word for "understanding." It is the interpretive sociologist's job not just to observe *what* people do but to share in their world of meaning and come to appreciate *why* they act

as they do. Subjective thoughts and feelings—which science tends to dismiss as "bias"—now become the focus of the researcher's attention (Berger & Kellner, 1981; Neuman, 1997).

A THIRD FRAMEWORK: CRITICAL SOCIOLOGY

There is a third methodological approach in sociology. Like the interpretive approach, critical sociology developed in reaction to scientific research. This time, however, the issue was the scientific goal of objectivity.

Scientific sociology holds that reality is "out there," and the researcher's task is to study and document this reality. But Karl Marx, who founded the critical approach, rejected the idea that society exists as a natural system with a fixed order. To assume this, he claimed, amounts to saying that society cannot be changed. From this point of view, scientific sociology ends up supporting the status quo.

Critical sociology, by contrast, is *the study of society that focuses on the need for social change.* Rather than asking the scientific question "How does society work?" critical sociologists ask moral and political questions, especially "Should society exist in its present form?" Their answer, typically, is that it should not. The point, said Marx (1972:109; orig. 1845), is not merely to study the world as it is but to *change* it. In making value judgments about how society should be improved, critical sociology rejects Weber's goal that researchers be value-free.

Sociologists using the critical approach seek to change not only society but also the character of research itself. They consider their research subjects equals and encourage their participation in deciding what to study and how to do the work. Often, researchers and subjects use their findings to provide a voice for less powerful people and advance the political goal of a more equal society (Nielsen, 1990; Stanley, 1990; Reinharz, 1992; Wolf, 1996; Hess, 1999).

Scientific sociologists object to taking sides in this way, charging that critical sociology (whether feminist, Marxist, or some other critical approach), because of its political nature, lacks objectivity and is unable to correct for its own biases. Critical sociologists respond that *all* research is political or biased in that either it calls for change or it does not. Sociologists thus have no choice about their work being political, but they can choose *which* positions to support.

Critical sociology is an activist approach tying knowledge to action, seeking not just to understand the world but also to improve it. Generally speaking, scientific

NOTE: In principle, the issue can be cast as a choice between "scientific correctness" (based on empirical data) and "political correctness" (based on political priorities).
NOTE: Eichler's gender issues noted here are both threats to sound research and barriers to gender equality.
Q: "Advocacy research often justifies playing fast and loose with the facts in service to a noble cause." Neil Gilbert

Q: "The work [on AIDS and the gay community] done by gay male sociologists submitted to scholarly journals has been rejected as too angry or as theoretically un-novel, too critical or lacking in hard data." Stephen O. Murray
NOTE: Anthony Jones (1989) describes sociology as having "weak boundaries," a trait that allows political events and values to seep easily into research.

TABLE 2–1 Three Methodological Approaches in Sociology

	Scientific	Interpretive	Critical
What Is Reality?	Society is an orderly system; reality is "out there."	Society is ongoing interaction; reality is socially constructed meanings.	Society is patterns of inequality; reality is that some dominate others.
How Do We Conduct Research?	Gather empirical data, ideally, quantitative; researcher tries to be an objective observer.	Develop a qualitative account of the subjective sense people make of their world; researcher is a participant.	Research is a strategy to bring about desired change; researcher is an activist.
Corresponding Theoretical Paradigm	Structural-functional paradigm	Symbolic-interaction paradigm	Social-conflict paradigm

sociology tends to appeal to researchers with more conservative political views; critical sociology appeals to those whose politics range from liberal to radical-left.

What about the link between methodological approaches and theory? There is no precise connection; a sociologist who favors the critical approach, for example, may well use scientific methods to collect data. But each of the three methodological approaches does stand closer to one of the theoretical paradigms presented in Chapter 1 ("The Sociological Perspective"). The scientific approach corresponds to the structural-functional paradigm, the interpretive approach to the symbolic-interaction paradigm, and the critical approach to the social-conflict paradigm. Table 2–1 summarizes the differences between the three methodological approaches. Many sociologists favor one approach over another; however, it is important to become familiar with all three (Gamson, 1999).

GENDER AND RESEARCH

In recent years, sociologists have become aware that research is affected by **gender,** *the personal traits and social positions that members of a society attach to being female and male.* Margrit Eichler (1988) identifies five ways in which gender can shape research:

1. **Androcentricity.** *Androcentricity* (*andro* is the Greek word for "male"; *centricity* means "being centered on") refers to approaching an issue from a male perspective. Sometimes researchers act as if only men's activities are important, ignoring what women do. For years researchers studying occupations focused on the paid work of men and overlooked the housework and child care traditionally performed by women. Clearly, research

that seeks to understand human behavior cannot ignore half of humanity.

Gynocentricity—seeing the world from a female perspective—is equally limiting to sociological investigation. However, in our male-dominated society, this problem arises less often.

2. **Overgeneralizing.** This problem occurs when researchers use data drawn from people of only one sex to support conclusions about "humanity" or "society." Gathering information about a community from a handful of male public officials and then drawing conclusions about the entire community illustrates the problem of overgeneralizing. In another case, studying child-rearing practices by collecting data only from women would allow researchers to draw conclusions about "motherhood" but not about the more general issue of "parenthood."

3. **Gender blindness.** Failing to consider the variable of gender at all is called "gender blindness." As is evident throughout this book, the lives of men and women differ in countless ways. A study of growing old in the United States would be flawed by gender blindness if it overlooked the fact that most elderly men live with spouses whereas elderly women typically live alone.

4. **Double standards.** Researchers must be careful not to distort what they study by judging men and women differently. For example, a family researcher who labels a couple "man and wife" may define the man as the "head of household" and treat him accordingly while assuming that the woman simply engages in family "support work."

5. **Interference.** Gender distorts a study if a subject reacts to the sex of the researcher and

DISCUSS: In the past, investigators (especially psychologists) readily used deception in research; a well-known example is Asch's experiment (see Ch. 5). If the research depends on deception, is it ethical? When does deception move from benign to dangerous?

DISCUSS: Here are three examples of research operations funded by organizations with an interest in the results: Credit Research Center (Georgetown University), funded primarily by the consumer credit industry; Transportation Research Institute (University of Michigan), with almost half its funding from the auto industry; Center for VDT and Health Research (Johns Hopkins University), funded by the computer industry. Does such funding threaten research or make research possible?

Q: "People kill each other for prophetic certainties, hardly for falsifiable hypotheses." Peter Berger

thereby interferes with the research operation. While studying a small community in Sicily, for instance, Maureen Giovannini (1992) found many men responding to her as a woman rather than as a researcher. Gender dynamics prevented her from performing certain activities such as private conversations with men, which were considered inappropriate for a single woman. Local residents also denied Giovannini access to places they considered off-limits to women.

There is nothing wrong with focusing research on one sex or the other. But all sociologists, as well as people who read their work, should be mindful of the importance of gender in any investigation.

RESEARCH ETHICS

Like all other researchers, sociologists are aware that research can harm as well as help subjects or communities. For this reason, the American Sociological Association (ASA)—the major professional association of sociologists in North America—has established formal guidelines for conducting research (1997).

Sociologists must strive to be both technically competent and fair-minded in their work. Sociologists must disclose all research findings, without omitting significant data. They are ethically bound to make their results available to other sociologists, especially those who want to replicate a study.

Sociologists must also ensure the safety of subjects taking part in a research project. Should research develop in a manner that threatens the well-being of participants, investigators must stop their work immediately. Researchers must also protect the privacy of

 Read the American Sociological Association's code of ethics at http://www.asanet.org

anyone involved in a research project. This last promise can be difficult to keep because researchers sometimes come under pressure (even from the police or courts) to disclose information. Therefore, researchers must think carefully about their responsibility to protect subjects, and they should discuss this issue with participants. In fact, ethical research requires the *informed consent* of participants, which means that subjects understand the responsibilities and risks that the research involves and agree—before the work begins—to take part.

Another important guideline concerns funding. Sociologists must include in their published results the sources of all financial support. They must also avoid conflicts of interest that may compromise the integrity of their work. For example, researchers must never accept funding from an organization that seeks to influence the research results for its own purposes.

Finally, there are global dimensions to research ethics. Before beginning research in other countries, investigators must become familiar enough with that society to understand what people *there* are likely to perceive as a violation of privacy or a source of personal danger. In a multicultural society such as the United States, the same rule applies to studying people whose cultural background differs from one's own. The box offers some tips about how outsiders can effectively and sensitively study Hispanic communities.

THE METHODS OF SOCIOLOGICAL RESEARCH

A **research method** is *a systematic plan for conducting research*. The remainder of this chapter introduces four commonly used methods of sociological investigation. None is inherently better or worse than any other. Rather, in the same way that a carpenter selects a particular tool for a specific task, researchers choose a method according to who they want to study and what they want to learn.

TESTING A HYPOTHESIS: THE EXPERIMENT

The logic of science is most clearly expressed in the **experiment**, *a research method for investigating cause and effect under highly controlled conditions*. Experimental research is *explanatory*, meaning that it asks not just what happens but why. Typically, researchers devise an experiment to test a **hypothesis**, *an unverified statement of a relationship between variables*.

The ideal experiment consists of four steps. First, the experimenter specifies the variable that changes (the dependent variable, or "the effect") and the variable that one assumes is causing the change in the dependent variable (the independent variable, or "the cause"). Second, the investigator measures the dependent variable. Third, the investigator exposes the dependent variable to the independent variable (the "treatment"). Fourth, the researcher again measures the dependent variable to see whether the predicted change took place. If the expected change did occur, the experiment supports the hypothesis; if not, the hypothesis must be modified.

NOTE: The word "experiment" contains the Latin root *per*, "to try out." This is also the root of the word "peril," a link demonstrated by the Zimbardo research.

RESOURCE: Earl Babbie's article, "The Importance of Social Research," appears in the 5th edition of the Macionis and Benokraitis reader, *Seeing Ourselves*.

Q: "Prediction is very difficult. Especially of the future." Niels Bohr

Q: "All human errors are impatience, a premature breaking off of methodical procedure, an apparent fencing in of what is apparently at issue." Franz Kafka

Q: "We have an obligation to tell the truth no matter how good the news may be." Jeanne Kirkpatrick

Q: "Information is difference that makes a difference." Gregory Bateson

DIVERSITY: RACE, CLASS, AND GENDER

Studying the Lives of Hispanics

In a society as racially, ethnically, and religiously diverse as the United States, sociologists are always studying people who differ from themselves. Learning—in advance—some of the distinctive traits of any category of people can ease the research process and ensure that no hard feelings are left when the work is finished.

Gerardo Marín and Barbara VanOss Marín have identified five areas of concern in conducting research with Hispanics:

1. **Terminology.** The Maríns point out that the term "Hispanic" is a label of convenience used by the Census Bureau. Few people of Spanish descent think of themselves as "Hispanic" or "Latino"; most identify with a particular country (generally, with a Latin American nation such as Mexico or Argentina, or with Spain).

2. **Cultural values.** By and large, the United States is a nation of individualistic, competitive people. Many Hispanics, by contrast, have a more collective orientation. Therefore, an outsider may judge the behavior of a Hispanic subject as conformist or overly trusting when, in fact, the person is simply trying to be courteous. Researchers should also realize that Hispanic respondents might agree with a particular statement out of politeness rather than conviction.

3. **Family dynamics.** Generally speaking, Hispanic cultures have strong family loyalties. Asking subjects to reveal information about another family member may make them uncomfortable or even angry. The Maríns add that, in the home, a researcher's request to speak privately with a Hispanic woman may provoke suspicion or outright disapproval from her husband or father.

4. **Time and efficiency.** Spanish cultures, the Maríns explain, tend to be

more concerned with the quality of relationships than with simply getting a job done. A non-Hispanic researcher who tries to hurry an interview with a Hispanic family, perhaps wishing not to delay the family's dinner, may be considered rude for not proceeding at a more sociable and relaxed pace.

5. **Personal space.** Finally, as the Maríns point out, people of Spanish descent typically maintain closer physical contact than many non-Hispanics. Consequently, researchers who seat themselves across the room from their subjects may appear "standoffish." Conversely, researchers may inaccurately label Hispanics "pushy" when they move closer than the non-Hispanic researcher finds comfortable.

Of course, Hispanics differ among themselves, just like people in every other category, and these generalizations apply to some more than to others. But the challenge of being culturally aware is especially great in the United States, where hundreds of categories of people make up our multicultural society.

Source: Marín & Marín (1991).

But a change in the dependent variable could be due to something other than the supposed cause. To be certain that they identify the correct cause, researchers carefully control other factors that might intrude into the experiment and affect the outcome. Such control is most easily accomplished in a laboratory, a setting specially constructed for research purposes. Another strategy for neutralizing outside influences is dividing subjects into an *experimental group* and a *control group*. Early in the study, the researcher measures the dependent variable for subjects in both groups but later exposes only the experimental group to the independent variable or treatment. (The control group typically gets a *placebo*, a treatment that seems to be the same but really has no effect on the experiment.) Then the investigator measures the subjects in both groups again. Any factor occurring during the

SUPPLEMENTS: W.S. Slater's "The Proper Study," an amusing poem about sociological research, is found in the *Data File*.
NOTE: *Literary Digest* began political polling in 1916; in 1932, the publication correctly predicted Franklin Delano Roosevelt's victory over Herbert Hoover. Three months before the 1936 election, however, George Gallup disputed the *Digest* poll foretelling Alf Landon's victory. The *Digest* predicted the Landon margin at 57%, although he actually received only 37% of the vote. The *Digest* sent out 20 million postcards based on telephone listings and automobile registrations, of which only 3 million came back. Gallup's prophecy made him the national pollster, although he subsequently erred on occasion, as when he wrongly predicted the victory of Thomas Dewey over Harry Truman in the tight presidential race of 1948 (Reeves, 1983).

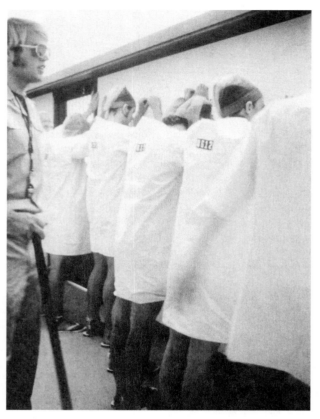

Philip Zimbardo's research helps to explain why violence is a common element in our society's prisons. At the same time, his work demonstrates the dangers that sociological investigation poses for subjects and the need for investigators to observe ethical standards that protect the welfare of people who participate in research.

course of the research that influences people in the experimental group (say, a news event) would do the same to those in the control group, thus "washing out" the factor. By comparing the before and after measurements of the two groups, a researcher can assess how much of the change is due to the independent variable.

The Hawthorne Effect

Another concern of experimenters is that subjects may change their behavior simply because they are getting special attention, as one classic experiment revealed. In the late 1930s, the Western Electric Company hired researchers to investigate worker productivity in its Hawthorne factory near Chicago (Roethlisberger & Dickson, 1939). One experiment tested the hypothesis that increasing the available lighting would raise worker output. First, researchers measured worker productivity (the dependent variable). Then they increased the lighting (the independent variable) and measured output a second time. Productivity increased, supporting the hypothesis. But when the research team later turned the lighting back down, productivity increased again. What was going on? In time, the researchers realized that the employees were working harder (even if they could not see as well) simply because people were paying attention to them. From this research, social scientists coined the term **Hawthorne effect** to refer to *a change in a subject's behavior caused simply by the awareness of being studied.*

An Illustration: The Stanford County Prison

Prisons can be violent settings, but is this simply a result of the "bad" people who end up there? Or, as Philip Zimbardo suspected, does the prison itself somehow generate violent behavior? This question led Zimbardo to devise a fascinating experiment, which he called the "Stanford County Prison" (Zimbardo, 1972; Haney, Banks, & Zimbardo, 1973).

Zimbardo contended that, once inside a prison, even emotionally healthy people are prone to violence. Thus, Zimbardo treated the *prison setting* as the independent variable capable of causing *violence*, the dependent variable.

To test this hypothesis, Zimbardo's research team first constructed a realistic-looking "prison" in the basement of the psychology building on the campus of Stanford University. Then they placed an ad in a Palo Alto newspaper, offering to pay young men to help with a two-week research project. To each of the seventy who responded they administered a series of physical and psychological tests and then selected the healthiest twenty-four.

The next step was to assign randomly half the men to be "prisoners" and half to be "guards." The plan called for the guards and prisoners to spend the next two weeks in the mock prison. The prisoners began their part of the experiment soon afterward when the Palo Alto police "arrested" them at their homes. After searching and handcuffing the men, the police drove them to the local police station, where they were fingerprinted. Then police transported their captives to the Stanford prison, where the guards locked them up. Zimbardo started his video camera rolling and watched to see what would happen next.

The experiment turned into more than anyone had bargained for. Both guards and prisoners soon became embittered and hostile toward one another. Guards humiliated the prisoners by assigning them tasks such as cleaning out toilets with their bare hands. The prisoners resisted and insulted the guards. Within four days, the researchers removed five prisoners who displayed "extreme emotional depression, crying, rage and acute anxiety" (Haney, Banks, & Zimbardo, 1973:81). Before the end of the first week, the situation had become so bad that the researchers canceled the experiment. Zimbardo explains,

> The ugliest, most base, pathological side of human nature surfaced. We were horrified because we saw some boys (guards) treat others as if they were despicable animals, taking pleasure in cruelty, while other boys (prisoners) became servile, dehumanized robots who thought only of escape, of their own individual survival and of their mounting hatred for the guards. (Zimbardo, 1972:4)

The events that unfolded at the "Stanford County Prison" supported Zimbardo's hypothesis that prison violence is rooted in the social character of jails themselves, not in the personalities of guards and prisoners. This finding raises questions about our society's prisons, suggesting the need for basic reform. But also note how this experiment reveals the potential of research to threaten the physical and mental well-being of subjects. Such dangers are not always as obvious as they were in this case. Therefore, researchers must consider carefully the potential harm to subjects at all stages of their work and end any study, as Zimbardo did, if subjects may suffer harm of any kind.

ASKING QUESTIONS: SURVEY RESEARCH

A **survey** is *a research method in which subjects respond to a series of statements or questions in a questionnaire or an interview*. The most widely used of all research methods, surveys are particularly well suited to studying attitudes—such as beliefs about politics, religion, or race—because there is no way to observe directly what people think. Sometimes surveys provide clues about cause and effect, but typically they yield *descriptive* findings, painting a picture of people's views on some issue.

Population and Sample

A survey targets a **population,** *the people who are the focus of research*. In her study of racism described at the

beginning of this chapter, Lois Benjamin's population was talented African Americans. At the broadest level, political pollsters predict election returns using surveys that treat every adult in the country as the population.

Obviously, contacting millions of people would overwhelm even the most well-funded and patient researcher. Fortunately, there is an easier way that yields accurate results: Researchers collect data from a **sample,** *a part of a population that represents the whole*. Everyone uses the logic of sampling all the time. If you look around the classroom and notice five or six heads nodding off, you might conclude that the class finds the day's lecture dull. In reaching this conclusion, you are making a judgment about *all* the people (the "population") from observing *some* of the people (the "sample"). But how can we know if a sample actually represents the entire population?

A good way to do this is *random sampling*, in which researchers draw a sample from the population by chance so that every element in the population has an equal opportunity to be selected. The mathematical laws of probability dictate that a random sample is quite likely to represent the population.

Beginning researchers sometimes make the mistake of assuming that "randomly" walking up to people on a street produces a sample that is representative of the entire city. Unfortunately, such a strategy does not give every person an equal chance to be included in the sample. For one

For a discussion of the use of polls in political campaigns, go to http://www.faculty.vassar.edu/lowry/polls.html

thing, any street, whether in a rich neighborhood or a college town, contains more of some kinds of people than others. For another, any researcher is apt to find some people more approachable than others, again introducing a bias.

Although good sampling is no simple task, it can save a great deal of time and money. We are spared the tedious work of contacting everyone in a population, yet we can obtain essentially the same results.

Using Questionnaires

Selecting subjects is only the first step in carrying out a survey. Also needed is a plan for asking questions and recording answers. Most surveys do this with a questionnaire.

A **questionnaire** is *a series of written questions a researcher presents to subjects*. One type of questionnaire provides not only the questions but a series of fixed responses (similar to a multiple-choice examination).

NOTE: Some questions elicit "expected" answers. For example, a recent Harris poll found that 64% of U.S. adults "expect to go to heaven," but just 2% say they "expect to go to hell."

NOTE: Survey organizations have found that enclosing a small amount of money with a questionnaire (say, a dollar bill) greatly improves the response rate. Even with follow-up mailings, however, response rates rarely exceed 75%.

NOTE: The Census Bureau reports that 67% of people returned the 2000 census forms.

NOTE: "Pop" research often is flawed because of poor surveys. For example, the last "Hite survey" of male-female relationships was based on a survey return rate of only 4.5%.

NOTE: Although widely used in survey research, "snowball sampling" is crude and unlikely to represent a population accurately.

CRITICAL THINKING

Survey Questions: A Word or Two Makes All the Difference

Do people approve of their president? Pollsters find that approval ratings rise or fall depending on a few small words. During the Clinton years, surveys showed that a majority of adults held a favorable opinion of Mr. Clinton as president. But when researchers asked people what they thought of Mr. Clinton *as a person*, his approval ratings typically tumbled 20 percent.

This difference shows that how researchers word questions affects people's responses. In 1998, *Newsweek* magazine hired a team of researchers to measure public attitudes toward abortion. The results of this national survey showed once again just how important a few words can be in shaping public response. One question put it this way: "Do you personally believe that abortion is wrong?" In this case, 57 percent of respondents said "yes," and 36 percent said "no" (the rest either were not sure or did not answer). Looking at these results, one might well conclude that a majority of people are antiabortion. Another question was worded this way: "Whatever your own personal view of abortion, do you favor or oppose a woman in this country having the choice to have an abortion with the advice of her doctor?" Now 69 percent favored available abortion, and just 24 percent opposed it—clear support for the abortion-rights side of the debate.

Are people of two minds on the abortion question? Probably most people listen carefully to the wording of the questions. Although a slight majority *personally* consider abortion wrong, a larger majority believe that women—with medical advice—should be able to have an abortion if they decide to.

One final example: Look at the wording in these questions. The first is "Do you think that the police force is doing a good job?" The second is "Do you agree that the police force is doing a good job?" Which one is more likely to show stronger support for the police? Why?

Source: Data from Witt (1999).

This *closed-ended format* makes it easy to analyze the results, but by narrowing the range of responses, it can also distort the findings. For example, Frederick Lorenz and Brent Bruton (1996) found that how many hours per week students say they study for a college course depends on the options offered to them. When the researchers presented students with options ranging from one hour or less to nine hours or more, 75 percent said that they studied four hours or less per week. But when a comparable group was given choices ranging from four hours or less to twelve hours or longer (a higher figure that suggests that students should study more) they suddenly became more studious, with only 34 percent reporting that they studied four hours or less each week.

A second type of questionnaire, using an *open-ended format*, allows subjects to respond freely, expressing various shades of opinion. The drawback of this approach is that the researcher has to make sense out of what can be a bewildering array of answers.

The researcher must also decide how to present questions to subjects. Most often, researchers use a *self-administered survey*, mailing or e-mailing questionnaires to respondents and asking them to complete the form and send it back. Because no researcher is present when subjects read the questionnaire, it must be both inviting and clearly written. *Pretesting* a self-administered questionnaire with a small number of people before sending it to the entire sample can avoid the costly problem of finding out—too late—that instructions or questions were confusing.

Using the mail or e-mail allows a researcher to contact a large number of people over a wide geographic area at minimal expense. But many people treat such questionnaires as junk mail, so that typically no more than half of the questionnaires are completed and returned (in 2000, the public returned just two-thirds of U.S. Census Bureau forms as requested). Researchers must send follow-up mailings (or, as the Census Bureau does, visit people's homes) to coax reluctant subjects to respond.

Finally, keep in mind that many people are not capable of completing a questionnaire on their own. Young children obviously cannot, nor can many hospital patients, and a surprising number of adults simply lack the necessary reading and writing skills.

NOTE: Conducting interviews, as Lois Benjamin did, is something like traveling abroad. We have some idea of our direction and destination, but the unexpected always arises along the way. Imaginative improvisation is needed to make the most of an interview opportunity and sometimes even to save a situation.

Q: "Unfettered thought is the essence of research methods." Stanislav Andreski

NOTE: The utilitarians embraced scientific truth to the exclusion of almost any other form of knowing; recall Charles Dickens's spoofing of their preoccupation with "Just the facts!" in his novel *Hard Times*.

Q: "One unerring mark of the love of truth is not entertaining any proposition with greater assurance than the proofs it is built on will warrant." John Locke (1690)

Conducting Interviews

An **interview** is *a series of questions a researcher administers in person to respondents*. In a closed-format design, researchers read a question or statement and then ask the subject to select a response from several alternatives. Generally, interviews are open-ended so that subjects can respond as they choose and researchers can probe with follow-up questions. However, the researcher must guard against influencing a subject, which is as easy as raising an eyebrow when a person begins to answer.

Although subjects are more likely to complete a survey if contacted personally by the researcher, interviews have some disadvantages: Tracking people down is costly and time-consuming, especially if subjects do not live in the same area. Telephone interviews allow far greater "reach," but the impersonality of cold calls by telephone (and reaching answering machines) can lower the response rate.

In both questionnaires and interviews, how a question is worded greatly affects how people answer. For example, when asked whether they object to homosexuals serving in the military, most adults in the United States say "yes." Yet, when asked whether the government should exempt homosexuals from military service, most say "no" (NORC, 1991). Emotionally loaded language can also sway subjects. For instance, using the term "welfare mothers" rather than "women who receive public assistance" adds an emotional element to a question that encourages people to answer negatively. The box takes a closer look at the importance of wording in conducting public opinion polls.

Finally, researchers may confuse respondents by asking a double question, such as "Do you think that the government should reduce the deficit by cutting spending and raising taxes?" The problem here is that a subject could agree with one part of the question but reject the other, so that forcing a subject to say "yes" or "no" distorts the opinion the researcher is trying to measure.

An Illustration:
Studying the African American Elite

We opened this chapter by recounting how Lois Benjamin came to investigate the effects of racism on talented African American men and women. Benjamin suspected that personal achievement did not prevent hostility based on color. She based this view on her own experiences as the only black professor in the history of the University of Tampa. But was she the exception or the rule? To answer this question, Benjamin

These African American women and men are members of the Congressional Black Caucus; they are movers and shakers on the national scene. But, according to Lois Benjamin, who conducted interviews with 100 highly successful African Americans, "making it" does not eliminate the sting of racial prejudice. On the contrary, she found, even the highest achievers still have to contend with barriers based on skin color.

set out to discover whether—and how—racism had plagued others like her.

Opting to conduct a survey, Benjamin chose to interview subjects rather than distribute a questionnaire because, first, she wanted to enter into a conversation with her subjects, to ask follow-up questions, and to pursue topics that she could not anticipate. A second reason Benjamin favored interviews over questionnaires is that racism is a sensitive topic. A supportive investigator can make it easier for subjects to respond to painful questions (Bergen, 1993).

Choosing to conduct interviews made it necessary to limit the number of people in the study. Benjamin settled for 100 men and women. Even this small number kept Benjamin busy for more than two years scheduling, traveling, and meeting with respondents.

NOTE: Lois Benjamin did not clearly operationalize "talented African Americans," so the population her sample represents remains only vaguely defined.

Q: "Don't dissect destiny with tools more precise than destiny itself." Marianne Moore

Q: "There is no position from which sociological research is not biased in one way or another." Howard S. Becker

NOTE: Among the first systematic participant observers of U.S. society was Alexis de Tocqueville, who, along with his companion, Gustave Beaumont, traveled some 7,000 miles across the U.S. and Canada between May 11, 1831, and February 20, 1832, before writing *Democracy in America*.

Q: "The world belongs to me because I understand it." Honoré de Balzac

TABLE 2–2 The Talented One Hundred: Lois Benjamin's African American Elite

Sex	Age	Childhood Racial Setting	Childhood Region	Highest Educational Degree	Occupational Sector	Income	Political Orientation
Male 63%	35 or younger 6%	Mostly black 71%	West 6%	Doctorate 32%	College or university 35%	More than $50,000 64%	Radical left 13%
Female 37%	36 to 54 68%	Mostly white 15%	North or Central 32%	Medical or law 17%	Private, profit 17%	$35,000 to $50,000 18%	Liberal 38%
	55 or older 26%	Racially mixed 14%	South 38%	Master's 27%	Private, nonprofit 9%	$20,000 to $34,999 12%	Moderate 28%
			Northeast 12%	Bachelor's 13%	Government 22%	Less than $20,000 6%	Conservative 5%
			Other 12%	Less 11%	Self-employed 14%		Depends on issue 14%
					Retired 3%		Unknown 2%
100%	100%	100%	100%	100%	100%	100%	100%

Source: Adapted from Lois Benjamin, *The Black Elite: Facing the Color Line in the Twilight of the Twentieth Century* (Chicago: Nelson-Hall, 1991), p. 276.

She spent two more years transcribing the tapes of her interviews, sorting out what the hours and hours of talk told her about racism, and writing up her results.

In selecting a sample, Benjamin first considered using all the people listed in *Who's Who in Black America*. But she rejected this idea in favor of starting out with people she knew and asking them to suggest others. This strategy is called *snowball sampling* because the number of subjects included grows rapidly over time.

Snowball sampling is appealing because it is an easy way to do research: We begin with familiar people who provide introductions to their friends and colleagues. The drawback is that snowball sampling rarely produces a sample that is representative of the larger population. Benjamin's sample probably contained many like-minded individuals, and it was certainly biased toward people willing to talk openly about race. She understood these problems and tried to make her sample as varied as she could in terms of sex, age, and region of the country. Table 2–2 presents a statistical profile of Benjamin's respondents; the box provides some tips on how to read tables.

Benjamin based all her interviews on a series of questions, with an open-ended format so that her subjects could say whatever they wanted. As usually happens, the interviews took place in a wide range of settings. She met subjects in offices (hers or theirs), in hotel rooms, and in cars. In each case, Benjamin tape-recorded the conversation, which lasted from two-and-one-half to three hours, so she would not be distracted by taking notes.

As research ethics demand, Benjamin offered full anonymity to participants. Even so, many—including notables such as Vernon E. Jordan, Jr. (former president of the National Urban League) and Yvonne Walker-Taylor (first woman president of Wilberforce University)—were accustomed to being in the public eye and permitted Benjamin to use their names.

What surprised Benjamin most about her research was how eagerly many informants responded to her request for an interview. These normally busy men and women appeared to go out of their way to contribute to her project. Furthermore, once the interviews were underway, many became very emotional. Benjamin reports that, at some point in the conversation, about forty of her subjects cried. For them, apparently, the research provided an opportunity to release feelings and share experiences never revealed before. How did Benjamin respond to such sentiments? She reports that she laughed and cried along with her respondents.

Benjamin's research is less scientific and more interpretive sociology (she wanted to find out what race

Q: "We cannot work without hoping that others will advance further than we have." Max Weber

Q: "At least in science, we show the greatest respect for an author by leaving him behind." Peter Berger

Q: "Sciences seek constantly to go beyond their founders, but ideologies do not." Robert Nisbet

NOTE: David Hume (1711–1776) argued that science can empirically determine correlation and temporal ordering of variables but not an actual causal connection, which defies observation. Perhaps with Hume's thought in mind, the National Cancer Institute acknowledged higher cancer rates among people living near nuclear power plants but argued that research "can neither confirm nor deny a link . . . because statistical studies, by their very nature, cannot prove cause and effect."

APPLYING SOCIOLOGY

Reading Tables: An Important Skill

A table provides a lot of information in a small amount of space, so learning to read tables can increase your reading efficiency. When you spot a table, look first at the title to see what information it contains. The title tells you that Table 2–2 presents a profile of the 100 subjects participating in Lois Benjamin's research. Across the top of the table, you will see eight variables that define these men and women. Reading down each column, note the categories within each variable; the percentages in each column add up to 100.

Starting at the top left, we see that Benjamin's sample was mostly men (63 percent men versus 37 percent women). In terms of age, most of the respondents (68 percent) were in the middle stage of life, and most grew up in a predominantly black community in the South, North, or Central regions of the United States.

These people are, indeed, a professional elite. Notice that half have earned either a doctorate (32 percent) or a medical or law degree (17 percent). Given their extensive education (and Benjamin's own position as a professor),

we should not be surprised that the largest share (35 percent) work in academic institutions. In terms of income, these are well-off individuals, with most (64 percent) earning more than $50,000 annually (a salary that only 25 percent of all U.S. workers made at the time).

Finally, we see that these 100 people are generally left-of-center in their political orientation. In part, this reflects their extensive schooling (which encourages progressive thinking) and the tendency of academics to fall on the liberal side of the political spectrum.

---

meant to her subjects) and critical sociology (she undertook the study partly to document that racial prejudice still exists). Indeed, many subjects reported fearing that race might someday undermine their success, and others spoke of a race-based "glass ceiling" preventing them from reaching the highest positions in our society. Summarizing her findings, Benjamin concluded that despite the improving social standing of African Americans, black people in the United States still feel the sting of racial hostility.

IN THE FIELD: PARTICIPANT OBSERVATION

Lois Benjamin's research demonstrates that sociological investigation takes place not only in laboratories but in the field, that is, where people carry on their everyday lives. The most widely used strategy for field study is **participant observation,** *a research method in which investigators systematically observe people while joining in their routine activities.*

Participant observation allows researchers an inside look at social life in settings ranging from nightclubs to religious seminaries. Cultural anthropologists commonly use participant observation (which they call *fieldwork*) to

study communities in other societies. They call their descriptions of unfamiliar cultures *ethnographies.* Sociologists prefer to call their accounts of people in particular settings *case studies.*

At the outset of a field study, most investigators do not have a specific hypothesis in mind. In fact, they may not yet realize what the important questions will turn out to be. Thus, most field research is *exploratory* and *descriptive.*

As its name suggests, participant observation has two sides. On one hand, getting an "insider's" look depends on becoming a participant in the setting: spending time with others, trying to act, think, and even feel the way they do. Compared with experiments and survey research, then, participant observation has fewer rules. But it is precisely this flexibility that allows investigators to explore the unfamiliar and adapt to the unexpected.

Unlike other research methods, participant observation requires that the researcher become immersed in the setting, not for a week or two but for months or even years. At the same time, however, the researcher must maintain some distance as an observer, mentally stepping back to record field notes and eventually to interpret them. Because the investigator must both "play the participant" to win acceptance and gain access to

NOTE: The interpretive approach claims that all reality is subjective. Sociological research into how people understand their world, then, amounts to interpretations of interpretations.

RESOURCE: John Brewer's article "Sensitivity in Field Research: A Study of Policing in Northern Ireland" is included in the Macionis and Benokraitis reader, *Seeing Ourselves*, 5th ed.

GLOBAL: Cultural differences may significantly impede research in unfamiliar settings. Language problems, for example, may slow interviewing and generate errors of understanding. A researcher abroad may also unintentionally "steer" subjects, perhaps even coercing agreement to participate in the study in the first place.

Q: "[Community studies are] the poor sociologist's substitute for the novel." Ruth Glass

Anthropologists and photographers Angela Fisher and Carol Beckwith have documented fascinating rituals around the world. As part of their fieldwork, they lived for months with the Himba in Namibia, in order to gain their acceptance and trust. During this time, a village man was killed by a lion. Later, his wives fell under the control of a lion spirit, apparently sent by the husband to bring these women to him in the afterlife. In the ritual shown above, photographed by Fisher and Beckwith, the women seek to rid themselves of the curse.

people's lives and "play the observer" to maintain the distance needed for thoughtful analysis, there is an inherent tension in this method. Carrying out the twin roles of insider participant and outsider observer often comes down to a series of careful compromises.

Most sociologists carry out participant observation alone, so they—and readers—must remember that the results depend on the work of a single individual. Participant observation usually falls within interpretive sociology, yielding mostly qualitative data—impressions and understandings—although researchers sometimes collect some quantitative (numerical) data. From a scientific point of view, participant observation is a "soft" method that relies heavily on personal judgment and lacks scientific rigor. Yet, its personal approach is also a strength: Whereas a highly visible team of sociologists attempting to administer, say, formal surveys would disrupt many social settings, a sensitive participant-observer can often gain considerable insight into people's natural behavior.

An Illustration: *Street Corner Society*

In the late 1930s, a young graduate student at Harvard University named William Foote Whyte (1914–2000)

was fascinated by the lively street life of a nearby, run-down section of Boston. His curiosity ultimately led him to carry out four years of participant observation in this neighborhood, which he called "Cornerville," in the process producing a sociological classic.

At the time, Cornerville was home to first- and second-generation Italian immigrants. Many were poor, and popular wisdom in Boston considered Cornerville a place to avoid: a poor, chaotic slum inhabited by racketeers. Unwilling to accept easy stereotypes, Whyte set out to discover for himself exactly what kind of life went on inside this community. His celebrated book, *Street Corner Society* (1981; orig. 1943), describes Cornerville as a highly organized community with a distinctive code of values, complex social patterns, and particular social conflicts.

In beginning his investigation, Whyte considered a range of research methods. He could have taken questionnaires to one of Cornerville's community centers and asked local people to fill them out. Or he could have invited members of the community to come to his Harvard office for interviews. But it is easy to see that such formal strategies would have prompted little cooperation from the local people and yielded few insights. Therefore, Whyte decided to

NOTE: Other well-known examples of participant-observation studies include Robert and Helen Lynd's *Middletown* and *Middletown in Transition* (Muncie, Ind.), W. Lloyd Warner's *Yankee City* series (Newburyport, Mass.), Herbert Gans's *The Levittowners* (Willingboro, N.J.), and Elliot Liebow's *Tally's Corner* (Washington, D.C.).
Q: "To know is nothing at all. To imagine is everything." Anatole France

Q: "The possibility of drawing inferences from what has been observed and described in London, as to what we might expect in New York or Chicago, rests on the assumption that the same forces create everywhere essentially the same conditions." Robert Park
RESOURCE: In the methodological appendix to *Street Corner Society* (1981; orig. 1943), William Foote Whyte candidly assesses how his own values influenced his work.

ease into Cornerville life and patiently build an understanding of this rather mysterious place.

Soon enough, Whyte discovered the challenges of getting started in field research. After all, an upper-middle-class graduate student from Harvard did not exactly fit into Cornerville life. He soon found out, for example, that even a friendly overture, made by an outsider, could seem pushy and rude. Early on, Whyte dropped in at a local bar, hoping to buy a woman a drink and encourage her to talk about Cornerville. But looking around the room, he could find no woman alone. Presently, he thought he might have an opportunity when a man sat down with two women. He gamely asked, "Pardon me. Would you mind if I joined you?" Instantly, he realized his mistake:

> There was a moment of silence while the man stared at me. Then he offered to throw me down the stairs. I assured him that this would not be necessary, and demonstrated as much by walking right out of there without any assistance. (1981:289)

As this incident suggests, gaining entry to a community is the crucial (and sometimes hazardous) first step in field research. "Breaking in" requires patience, ingenuity, and a little luck. Whyte's big break came in the form of a young man named "Doc," whom he met in a local social service agency. Listening to Whyte's account of his bungled efforts to make friends in Cornerville, Doc was sympathetic and decided to take Whyte under his wing and introduce him to others in the community. With Doc's help, Whyte soon became a neighborhood regular.

Whyte's friendship with Doc illustrates the importance of a *key informant* in field research. Such people not only introduce a researcher to a community but often remain a source of information and help. Using a key informant also has its risks. Because any person has a particular circle of friends, a key informant's guidance is certain to "spin" the study in one way or another. Moreover, in the eyes of others, the reputation of the key informant—for better or worse—usually rubs off on the investigator. In sum, a key informant is helpful at the outset, but a participant-observer soon must seek a broad range of contacts.

Having entered the Cornerville world, Whyte began his work in earnest. But he soon realized that a field researcher needs to know when to speak up and when simply to look, listen, and learn. One evening, he joined a group discussing neighborhood gambling. Wanting to get the facts straight, Whyte asked innocently, "I suppose the cops were all paid off?" In a heartbeat,

> The gambler's jaw dropped. He glared at me. Then he denied vehemently that any policeman had been paid off and immediately switched the conversation to another subject. For the rest of that evening I felt very uncomfortable.

The next day, Doc offered some sound advice:

> "Go easy on that 'who,' 'what,' 'why,' 'when,' 'where' stuff, Bill. You ask those questions and people will clam up on you. If people accept you, you can just hang around, and you'll learn the answers in the long run without even having to ask the questions." (1981:303)

In the months and years that followed, Whyte became familiar with life in Cornerville and even married a local woman, with whom he spent the rest of his life. In the process, he learned that this neighborhood was hardly the stereotypical slum. On the contrary, most immigrants worked hard, many were successful, and some even boasted of sending children to college. In short, Whyte's book is fascinating reading about the deeds, dreams, and disappointments of one ethnic community, and it contains a richness of detail that can come only from long-term participant observation.

Whyte's work shows that participant observation is a method rife with tensions and contrasts. Its flexibility allows a researcher to respond to the unexpected, but it also makes replication difficult. Participation means getting close to people, but observation depends on keeping some distance. Because no elaborate equipment or laboratory is needed, little expense is involved. But this method is costly in terms of time: Most studies take a year or more, which probably explains why participant observation is used less often than the other methods described in this chapter. Yet the depth of understanding gained through interpretive research of this kind greatly enriches our knowledge of many types of human communities.

USING AVAILABLE DATA: SECONDARY AND HISTORICAL ANALYSIS

Not all research requires investigators to collect their own data. Sometimes, sociologists conduct **secondary analysis,** *a research method in which a researcher uses data collected by others.*

The most widely used statistics in social science are gathered by government agencies (for easy access to many data links, visit http://www.TheSociologyPage.com).

RESOURCE: The *Statistical Abstract* is the single best source of statistical data about the population of the U.S. (order by telephone: 301-763-4100). For global data, see the World Bank's *World Development Report* (202-473-1155) and the United Nations's *Human Development Report* (212-963-8302). See this text's Web site for links to statistical data: http://www.prenhall.com/macionis
NOTE: Anecdotal ways to describe the difference between the two

The Census Bureau continuously updates information on the U.S. population. Comparable data on Canada are available from Statistics Canada, a branch of that nation's government. For international data, consult various publications of the United Nations and the World Bank. In short, a wide range of data about the whole world is as close as your library or the Internet.

Using available data—whether government statistics or the findings of individual researchers—saves time and money. Therefore, this approach has special appeal to sociologists with low budgets. Even more important, government data generally are better than what most researchers could obtain on their own.

Still, secondary analysis has inherent problems. For one thing, available data may not exist in precisely the form needed. Furthermore, there are always questions about the meaning and accuracy of work done by others. For example, in his classic study of suicide, Emile Durkheim acknowledged that there was no way to know whether a death classified as a suicide was really an accident or vice versa. In addition, various agencies use different procedures and categories in collecting data, making comparisons difficult. In the end, then, using secondhand data is a little like shopping for a used car: Bargains are plentiful, but you have to shop carefully to avoid ending up with a "lemon."

To illustrate, let's assume that reading about Lois Benjamin's account of African American elites sparks our interest in this country's well-off minorities. How many such people are there? Where do they live? National Map 2–1 graphically displays Census Bureau data that address these questions. These statistics are the best available and at no cost. Yet to use them means accepting the Census Bureau's racial and ethnic categories (until 2000, for example, people could check only one racial category). It also means accepting people's self-reported income on government questionnaires as accurate. Furthermore, if you were to use this map for your own purposes, you would also have to accept the given definitions of "well-off" and "above average" even though they may not exactly fit your purpose.

An Illustration: A Tale of Two Cities

To people trapped in the present, secondary analysis offers a key to unlocking secrets of the past. The award-winning study *Puritan Boston and Quaker Philadelphia*, by E. Digby Baltzell (1979b), exemplifies a researcher's power to analyze the past using historical sources.

cities: Puritan Boston named streets after great families, Quaker Philadelphia named streets after trees. A Boston accent often leads people to overestimate someone, a Philadelphia accent confers little prestige. Boston's leading university (Harvard) was founded within a decade of the city's settlement and is at the top of the Ivy League; Philadelphia's founders did not establish the University of Pennsylvania for 60 years, and it remains the least well-known Ivy.

A chance visit to Bowdoin College in Maine prompted Baltzell to begin his investigation. Entering the college library, he gazed at portraits of the celebrated author Nathaniel Hawthorne, the eminent poet Henry Wadsworth Longfellow, and Franklin Pierce, the fourteenth U.S. president. He was startled to learn that all three of these great men were members of a single class at Bowdoin, graduating in 1825. How could it be, Baltzell mused, that this small college had graduated more famous people in a single year than his own, much bigger University of Pennsylvania had graduated in its entire history? To answer this question, Baltzell was soon poring over historical documents to see whether New England had indeed produced more famous individuals than his native Pennsylvania.

For data, Baltzell turned to the *Dictionary of American Biography*, twenty volumes profiling more than 13,000 outstanding men and women in fields such as politics, law, and the arts. The *Dictionary* told Baltzell *who* was great; but he also wanted some way to measure *how* great people were. He decided to base his ranking on the *Dictionary's* statement that, the more impressive the person's achievements, the longer the biography. So counting the number of lines in a biography yielded a reasonable measure of "greatness."

By the time Baltzell had identified the seventy-five individuals with the longest biographies, he saw a striking pattern. Massachusetts had the most by far, with twenty-one of the seventy-five top achievers. The New England states combined claimed thirty-one of the entries. By contrast, Pennsylvania could boast of only two, and the entire Middle Atlantic region had just twelve. Looking more closely, Baltzell discovered that most of New England's great achievers had grown up in and around the city of Boston. Again, in stark contrast, almost no one of comparable standing came from his own Philadelphia, a city with many more people than Boston.

What could explain this remarkable pattern? Baltzell drew inspiration from the German sociologist Max Weber (1958; orig. 1904–5), who argued that a region's record of achievement was largely a result of its predominant religious beliefs (see Chapter 4, "Society"). In the religious differences that set Boston apart from Philadelphia, Baltzell found the answer to his puzzle. Boston was a Puritan settlement, founded by people who were determined in their pursuit of excellence and public achievement. Philadelphia, by contrast, was settled by Quakers, who were equally determined to shun public notice.

Both the Puritans and the Quakers were fleeing religious persecution in England, but the two religious

THE MAP: Generally speaking, African Americans, Asian Americans, and Latinos are concentrated in different regions of the country (look ahead to National Map 14–4). The largest urban regions (surrounding New York and Los Angeles) are home to well-off minorities of all kinds (although they often live in distinctive neighborhoods). In most cases, however, a single county contains a disproportionate share of well-off people of only one minority category. In general, at all income levels, people of various racial and ethnic categories live in different regions of the country and in different communities.

NOTE: In conducting historical research, sociologists can discern the contours and impacts of most significant social developments (such as industrialization or deindustrialization), which come to light only over long periods.

SEEING OURSELVES

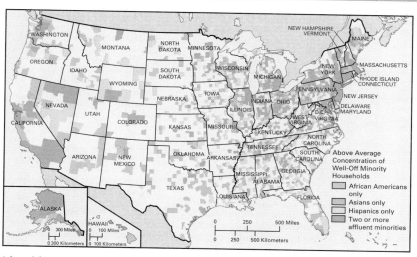

NATIONAL MAP 2–1
Well-Off Minorities across the United States

Based on 1990 census data, this map identifies the counties of the United States with an above-average share of well-off minority households—people earning at least $50,000 annually. (For the entire country in 2000, about one-third of African American and Hispanic families and more than half of Asian families fell into this category.) Where in the United States do well-off members of each minority category live? Do members of one category tend to live where members of another category predominate? Can you explain this pattern?

Adapted from *American Demographics* magazine, December 1992, pp. 34–35. Reprinted with permission. © 1992, *American Demographics* magazine, Ithaca, New York. Data from the 1990 decennial census.

beliefs produced very different cultural patterns. Convinced of humanity's innate sinfulness, Boston Puritans built a rigid society in which family, church, and school regulated people's behavior. They celebrated hard work as a means of glorifying God and viewed public success as a reassuring sign of God's blessing. In other words, Puritanism fostered a disciplined life in which people both sought and respected achievement.

Philadelphia's Quakers, on the other hand, built their way of life on the belief that all human beings are basically good. They saw little need for strong social institutions to "save" individuals from sinfulness. They believed in equality, so that even people who became rich considered themselves no better than anyone else. Thus, rich and poor alike lived modestly and discouraged one another from standing out by seeking fame or even public office.

In Baltzell's sociological imagination, Boston and Philadelphia took the form of two social "test tubes": Puritanism was poured into one, Quakerism into the other. Centuries later, we can see that different "chemical reactions" occurred in each case. The two belief systems apparently led to different attitudes toward personal achievement, which, in turn, shaped the history of each region. Moreover, we can see the results of these cultural differences even today. Boston's Kennedy family (despite being Catholic) still exemplifies the Puritan pursuit of recognition and leadership, but there has never been a family with such public stature in the entire history of Philadelphia.

Baltzell's study uses scientific logic, but it also illustrates the interpretive approach. His research reminds us that sociological investigation often involves various methodological approaches and a lively sociological imagination.

Table 2–3 on page 48 summarizes the four major methods of sociological investigation. We now turn to our final consideration: the link between research results and sociological theory.

THE INTERPLAY OF THEORY AND METHOD

No matter how they gather data, sociologists must turn facts into meaning by building theory. They do this in two ways: inductive logical thought and deductive logical thought.

Inductive logical thought is *reasoning that transforms specific observations into general theory*. In this mode, a researcher's thinking runs from the specific to

DISCUSS: Inductive logical thought amounts to saying, "If this is what happens, then what is true?" Deductive logical thought runs the other way: "If this is true, then what ought to happen?"

NOTE: Sherlock Holmes, celebrated for his great powers of deduction, actually engaged in *inductive reasoning*. While investigating a particular crime scene, for example, Holmes spoke with the woman of the house when he suddenly noticed the housekeeper searching for the cord to close the drapes. "Why did you dismiss your previous servant?" he asked. "How did you know!?" came her startled reply. "Elementary," he explained, "your present servant is obviously new to her duties."

Q: "Science is meaningless because it gives no answer to the question, the only question of importance for us: 'What shall we do and how shall we live?'" Leo Tolstoy

TABLE 2–3 Four Research Methods: A Summary

Method	Application	Advantages	Limitations
Experiment	For explanatory research that specifies relationships between variables; generates quantitative data	Provides the greatest opportunity to specify cause-and-effect relationships; replication of research is relatively easy	Laboratory settings have an artificial quality; unless the research environment is carefully controlled, results may be biased
Survey	For gathering information about issues that cannot be directly observed, such as attitudes and values; useful for descriptive and explanatory research; generates quantitative or qualitative data	Sampling, using questionnaires, allows surveys of large populations; interviews provide in-depth responses	Questionnaires must be carefully prepared and may yield a low return rate; interviews are expensive and time-consuming
Participant observation	For exploratory and descriptive study of people in a "natural" setting; generates qualitative data	Allows study of "natural" behavior; usually inexpensive	Time-consuming; replication of research is difficult; researcher must balance roles of participant and observer
Secondary analysis	For exploratory, descriptive, or explanatory research whenever suitable data are available	Saves time and expense of data collection; makes historical research possible	Researcher has no control over possible biases in data; data may only partially fit current research needs

the general and goes something like this: "I have some interesting data here; I wonder what they mean?" E. Digby Baltzell's research illustrates the inductive logical model. His data showed that one region of the country (the Boston area) had produced many more high achievers than another (the Philadelphia region). He worked upward, from ground-level observations to the more general theory that religious values were a key factor that shaped people's attitudes toward achievement.

A second type of logical thought moves downward: **Deductive logical thought** is *reasoning that transforms general theory into specific hypotheses suitable for testing*. The researcher's thinking runs from the general to the specific: "I have this hunch about human behavior; let's collect some data and put it to the test." Working deductively, the researcher first states the theory in the form of a hypothesis and then selects a method by which to test it. To the extent that the data support the hypothesis, we conclude that the theory is correct; data that refute the hypothesis tell us that the theory should be revised or perhaps rejected entirely.

Philip Zimbardo's Stanford County Prison experiment illustrates deductive logic. Zimbardo began with the general idea that prisons change human behavior. He then developed a specific, testable hypothesis:

Placed in a prison setting, even emotionally well-balanced young men will behave violently. The violence that erupted soon after his experiment began supported Zimbardo's hypothesis. Had his experiment produced friendly behavior between prisoners and guards, his original theory clearly would have needed reformulation.

Just as researchers often use several methods over the course of one study, they typically make use of *both* kinds of logical thought. Figure 2–2 illustrates both types of reasoning: inductively building theory from observations and deductively making observations to test a theory.

Finally, turning facts into meaning usually involves organizing and presenting statistical data. Precisely how sociologists arrange their numbers affects the conclusions they reach. In short, preparing one's results amounts to spinning reality in one way or another.

Often, we conclude that an argument must be true simply because there are statistics to back it up. However, we must look at statistics with a cautious eye. After all, researchers choose what data to present, they interpret their statistics, and they may use tables and graphs to steer readers toward particular conclusions. The final box, on pages 50–51, takes a closer look at this important issue.

NOTE: The ten steps are all important but need not necessarily follow the rigid order suggested here (cf. Lynch & Bogen, 1997).
Q: "The direction of our scientific exertions . . . is conditioned by the society in which we live, and most directly by the political climate. . . . Students turn to research on issues that have obtained political importance." Gunnar Myrdal

EXERCISE: Motivated students can learn a great deal from reading research reports. For example, Elliot Liebow's classic *Tally's Corner* (1967) or his last book *Tell Them Who I Am: The Lives of Homeless Women* (1993) both detail the research experience.
EXERCISE: Students come across research reports in the media all the time. Ask them to bring one to class and offer some critical comment about how well the research was carried out.

PUTTING IT ALL TOGETHER: TEN STEPS IN SOCIOLOGICAL INVESTIGATION

We can draw the material in this chapter together by outlining ten steps in the process of carrying out sociological investigation. Each step is represented by an important question:

1. **What is your topic?** Being curious and using the sociological perspective can generate ideas for social research any time and any place. The issue you choose for study is likely to have some personal significance.

2. **What have others already learned?** You are probably not the first person with an interest in some issue. Visit the library to see what theories and methods other researchers have applied to your topic. In reviewing the existing research, note problems that have come up.

3. **What, exactly, are your questions?** Are you seeking to explore an unfamiliar social setting? To describe some category of people? To investigate cause and effect between variables? If your study is exploratory or descriptive, identify *who* you want to study, *where* the research will take place, and *what* kinds of issues you want to explore. If it is explanatory, you also must formulate the hypothesis to be tested and operationalize each variable.

4. **What will you need to carry out research?** How much time and money are available to you? Are special equipment or skills necessary? Can you do the work yourself? You should answer all these questions as you plan the research project.

5. **Are there ethical concerns?** Not all research raises serious ethical questions, but you must be sensitive to the possibility. Can the research cause harm or threaten anyone's privacy? How might you design the study to minimize the chances for injury? Will you promise anonymity to the subjects? If so, how will you ensure that anonymity is maintained?

6. **What method will you use?** Consider all major research strategies, as well as combinations of approaches. Keep in mind that the appropriate method depends on the kinds of questions you are asking and the resources available to you.

7. **How will you record the data?** The research method you choose is the system for data collection. Record all information accurately and in a way that will make sense later (it may be some time before you write up the results of your work). Be alert for any bias that may creep into the research.

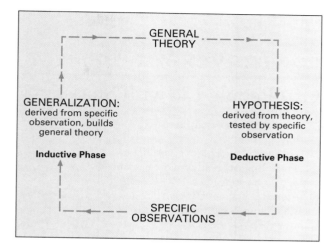

FIGURE 2–2 Deductive and Inductive Logical Thought

8. **What do the data tell you?** Study the data in terms of your initial questions and decide how to interpret the data you have collected. If your study involves a specific hypothesis, you must decide whether to confirm, reject, or modify the hypothesis. Keep in mind that there may be several ways to look at your data, depending on which theoretical paradigm you apply, and you should consider all interpretations.

9. **What are your conclusions?** Prepare a final report stating your conclusions. How does your work advance sociological theory? Improve research methods? Does your study have policy implications? What would the general public find interesting in your work? Finally, evaluate your own work, noting problems that arose and questions left unanswered.

10. **How can you share what you've learned?** Consider sending your research paper to a campus newspaper or magazine or making a presentation to a class, campus gathering, or perhaps a meeting of professional sociologists. The point is to share what you have learned with others and to let them respond to your work.

NOTE: Why is there not more fraud in research? Probably because the gains of dishonesty are significant only in situations in which the odds of detection are very high.

Q: "As soon as those who are considered promoters of science become persuaded of their infallibility, they naturally proclaim as indubitable things that are not only unnecessary but often absurd, and having proclaimed them they cannot repudiate them." Leo Tolstoy

DISCUSS: Consider Plato's idea that "truth" exists as an ideal "form" only approximated by worldly ideas.

Q: "From my earliest years, I have accepted many false opinions as true." René Descartes

Q: "Theories and concepts emerge in sociology like popcorn, puffed up by their own steam." Joseph Gusfield, explaining why no "social scientific Newton" is likely to emerge from sociology

CONTROVERSY & DEBATE

Can People Lie with Statistics?

Is research—especially research involving numbers—always as "factual" as we think? Not according to the great English politician Benjamin Disraeli, who remarked, "There are three kinds of lies: lies, damned lies, and statistics!" In a world that bombards us with numbers—often described as "scientific facts" or "official figures"—it is worth pausing to consider that statistical evidence is not necessarily the same as truth. For one thing, any researcher can make mistakes. For another, because data do not speak for themselves, someone has to interpret what they mean. Sometimes, people dress up their data the way politicians deliver campaign speeches: with an eye more to winning you over than getting at the truth.

The best way not to fall prey to statistical manipulation is to understand how people can mislead with statistics:

1. **People select their data.** Many times, the data presented are not wrong, but they are not the whole story. Let's say someone who thinks that television is ruining our way of life presents statistics indicating that

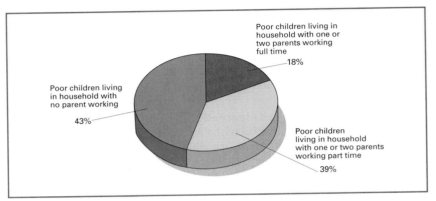

Poor children living in household with one or two parents working full time — 18%

Poor children living in household with no parent working — 43%

Poor children living in household with one or two parents working part time — 39%

we watch more TV today than a generation ago. Moreover, during the same period, SAT scores have fallen. Both sets of data may be correct, but the suggestion that television is lowering test scores remains unproven. Moreover, a person more favorable to television might counter with the additional "fact" that the U.S. population spends much more money buying books today than it did a generation ago, suggesting that television creates new intellectual interests. In sum,

people can find statistics that seem to support just about any argument.

2. **People interpret their data.** Another way people manipulate statistics is to package them with a ready-made interpretation, as if numbers can mean only one thing. One publication, for example, presented the results of a study of U.S. children living in poverty (National Center for Children in Poverty, cited in *Population Today*, 1995). As the figure shows, the researchers

SUMMARY

1. Two basic requirements for sociological investigation are (1) using the sociological perspective and (2) being curious and asking questions about the world around us.

2. Scientific sociology studies society by systematically observing social behavior. This methodological approach requires carefully operationalizing concepts and ensuring that measurement is both reliable (consistent) and valid (precise).

3. A goal of science is to discover how variables are related. Correlation means that two or more variables change

value together. A cause-and-effect relationship means that change in one variable causes the change in another variable. When a cause-and-effect relationship exists, a researcher who knows the value of an independent variable can predict the value of some dependent variable.

4. Although investigators select topics according to their personal interests, the scientific ideal of objectivity demands that they try to suspend personal values and biases as they conduct research.

5. Interpretive sociology is a methodological approach that focuses on the meaning that people attach to

NOTE: "Facts" rarely speak for themselves. Surveys show that among people over the age of 80, men are much more sexually active than women. Does this suggest a biological difference allowing older men to continue to be sexually active? Or is it the fact that, given the difference in longevity, most older men live with wives, whereas older women live alone?

EXERCISE: You can have your sociological imagination working even when watching television. For example, national surveys suggest that television sitcom watchers tend to be young, single, and politically liberal, whereas network news watchers tend to be older, married, and more conservative. Watch both kinds of television and, based on the commercial advertising, see whether your perceptions confirm this pattern. What exactly would you look for in each case? Sketch a research plan.

reported that 43 percent of these children lived in a household with no working parent, 39 percent lived in a household with one or two parents employed part time, and 18 percent lived in a household with one or two parents working full time. The researchers labeled this figure "Majority of Children in Poverty Live with Parents Who Work." Do you think this interpretation is accurate or misleading?

3. **People use graphs to spin the truth.** Especially in newspapers and other popular media, we find statistics in the form of charts and graphs. Graphs help explain data, showing, for example, an upward or downward trend. But they also give people the opportunity to "spin" data in various ways. What trend we think we see depends, in part, on the time frame used in a graph. Looking at just the last few years, for instance, we would see the U.S. crime rate going downward. But looking at the last few decades, we would see an opposite trend: The crime rate pushes sharply upward.

The scale used to draw a graph is also important because it lets a researcher "inflate" or "deflate" a trend. Both of the following graphs present identical data for College Board SAT scores between 1967 and 2000. But the left-hand graph stretches the scale to show a dip in the middle; the right-hand graph compresses the scale, making the dip disappear. So, understanding what statistics mean—or don't mean—depends on being a careful reader!

Continue the debate . . .

1. *Why do you think people are so quick to accept statistics as true?*

2. *From a scientific point of view, is spinning the truth acceptable? What about from a critical approach, trying to advance social change?*

3. *Can you find a news story on some social issue that you think presents biased data or conclusions? What are the biases?*

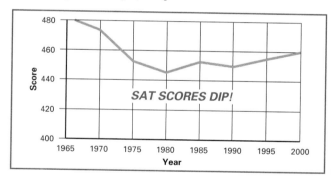

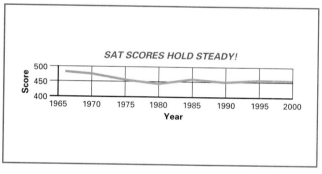

their behavior. Reality is not "out there" but is constructed by people in their everyday interactions.

6. Critical sociology is a methodological approach that uses research as a means of social change. Critical sociology rejects the scientific principle of objectivity, claiming that all research has a political character.

7. The logic of science is most clearly expressed in the experiment, which is performed under controlled conditions and tries to specify cause-and-effect relationships between two (or more) variables.

8. Surveys measure people's attitudes or behavior using questionnaires or interviews.

9. Participant observation is a method in which a researcher directly observes a social setting while participating in it for an extended period of time.

10. Secondary analysis is making use of existing data. This method is easier and often more efficient than collecting data firsthand and allows the study of historical issues.

11. Theory and research are linked in two ways. Deductive logical thought starts with general theories and generates specific hypotheses suitable for testing. Inductive logical thought starts with specific observations and builds general theories.

Q: "Philosophers know very little about what is very important; scientists know a great deal about what is far less worth knowing." E. Digby Baltzell

CTQ1: Science is one kind of truth, as are common sense, tradition, faith, and so on. Science has the advantage of being self-correcting, yet it cannot address questions of human values (the "ought" questions).

Q: "In science as in love, a concentration on technique is likely to lead to impotence." Peter Berger (1963)

CTQ2: Scientific (positivist) sociology lends itself to studying observable behavior, interpretive sociology is more concerned with meanings, and critical sociology has a normative and activist character. Crudely, Durkheim is the most positivist, Weber the most interpretive, and Marx the most critical.

KEY CONCEPTS

science (p. 26) a logical system that bases knowledge on direct, systematic observation

scientific sociology (p. 26) the study of society based on systematic observation of social behavior

empirical evidence (p. 26) information we can verify with our senses

concept (p. 28) a mental construct that represents some part of the world in a simplified form

variable (p. 28) a concept whose value changes from case to case

measurement (p. 28) a procedure for determining the value of a variable in a specific case

operationalizing a variable (p. 29) specifying exactly what one is to measure before assigning a value to a variable

reliability (p. 29) consistency in measurement

validity (p. 29) precision in measuring exactly what one intends to measure

cause and effect (p. 30) a relationship in which change in one variable (the independent variable) causes change in another (the dependent variable)

independent variable (p. 30) a variable that causes change in another (dependent) variable

dependent variable (p. 30) a variable that is changed by another (independent) variable

correlation (p. 31) a relationship by which two (or more) variables change together

spurious correlation (p. 31) an apparent, although false, relationship between two (or more) variables caused by some other variable

control (p. 31) holding constant all variables except one in order to see clearly the effect of that variable

objectivity (p. 32) a state of personal neutrality in conducting research

replication (p. 33) repetition of research by other investigators

interpretive sociology (p. 34) the study of society that focuses on the meanings people attach to their social world

critical sociology (p. 34) the study of society that focuses on the need for social change

gender (p. 35) the personal traits and social positions that members of a society attach to being female and male

research method (p. 36) a systematic plan for conducting research

experiment (p. 36) a research method for investigating cause and effect under highly controlled conditions

hypothesis (p. 36) an unverified statement of a relationship between variables

Hawthorne effect (p. 38) a change in a subject's behavior caused simply by the awareness of being studied

survey (p. 39) a research method in which subjects respond to a series of statements or questions in a questionnaire or an interview

population (p. 39) the people who are the focus of research

sample (p. 39) a part of a population that represents the whole

questionnaire (p. 39) a series of written questions a researcher presents to subjects

interview (p. 41) a series of questions a researcher administers in person to respondents

participant observation (p. 43) a research method in which investigators systematically observe people while joining in their routine activities

secondary analysis (p. 45) a research method in which a researcher uses data collected by others

inductive logical thought (p. 47) reasoning that transforms specific observations into general theory

deductive logical thought (p. 48) reasoning that transforms general theory into specific hypotheses suitable for testing

CRITICAL-THINKING QUESTIONS

1. What does it mean to say that there are various kinds of truth? What are the advantages and limitations of science as a way of knowing?

2. How does interpretive sociology differ from scientific sociology? What about critical sociology? Which approach best describes the work of each of these sociology founders: Emile Durkheim, Max Weber, and Karl Marx?

3. Why do some sociologists argue that objectivity is essential to sound research? Why do other sociologists disagree?

4. What are some differences between "hard" research (such as scientific experiments) and "soft" research (such as participant observation)?

Q: "The most incomprehensible thing about the world is the fact that it is comprehensible." Albert Einstein

CTQ3: The positivist tradition sees reality as "out there," and thus human subjectivity amounts to bias and error. The interpretive tradition see subjectivity as essentially human. The critical tradition sees "objectivity" as a strategy to neutralize efforts toward deliberate change.

Q: "Truth must have one face, the same and universal." Michel de Montaigne

CTQ4: Although many students tend to see "hard" science as superior to "soft" research, each approach is appropriate for different kinds of questions and settings. Scientific experiments, for example, require controlled settings; participant observation allows researchers to study behavior in a more natural environment.

APPLICATIONS AND EXERCISES

1. Imagine that you are observing your instructor in an effort to assess his or her skills as a teacher. Operationalize the concept "good teaching." What specific traits might you identify as relevant evidence? Do you think students are always good judges of strong teaching?

2. Drop by to see at least three sociology instructors (or other social science instructors) during their office hours. Ask each the extent to which sociology is an objective science. Do they agree about the character of their discipline? Why or why not?

3. Conduct a practice interview with a roommate or friend on the general topic of "How do I expect that completing a college education will affect the rest of my life?" Before the actual interview, prepare a list of specific questions or issues you think are relevant. Afterward, give some thought to why carrying out an effective interview is much harder than it initially may seem.

4. You can do sociological research while watching television. In recent years, some critics have claimed that African Americans are not very visible on prime-time television. Select a sample of prime-time shows and systematically keep track of the race of major characters. Notice that you will have to decide what "prime-time" means, what a "major" character is, how to gauge someone's "race," and other issues before you begin. Sketch out a research plan.

5. Packaged in the back of this new textbook is an interactive CD-ROM that offers a variety of study and review materials intended to help you better understand the material covered in this chapter. For this chapter, the CD-ROM contains an author's tip video, Real Life Sociology videos, other relevant audio and video, interactive map animations, audio journal entries from the author, Web links, and much more.

 ## SITES TO SEE

http://www.prenhall.com/macionis

Visit the interactive *Companion Website*™ that accompanies this text. Begin by clicking on the cover of your book. You will find a chapter-by-chapter study guide, practice tests, and a significant portion of the text for on-line review, as well as many suggested Web links.

http://www.macionis.com
(or http://www.TheSociologyPage.com)

You can find more than fifty Web links to sociological journals and other sources of data and information by visiting the Links Library at the author's personal Web site.

http://www.ropercenter.uconn.edu

To learn more about public opinion research, visit the Roper Center's Web site.

http://quickfacts.census.gov/qfd/

Data for any county in the United States are available from this Census Bureau Web site. Visit this site and prepare a profile of your local area.

http://ssda.anu.edu.au/

Learn more about Australia by visiting this Web site that provides social science data for that country.

 ## INVESTIGATE WITH CONTENTSELECT

Follow the instructions found on page 23 of this textbook to enter this chapter of the book's *Companion Website*™. Once in the chapter, click on the Content-Select icon at the bottom left of your screen and enter your personal User ID and Password. Enter keywords such as "science" and "objectivity," and the search engine will help you become an effective researcher.

WELCOME TO THE INFORMATION REVOLUTION!

Now that we have begun a new century (and a new millennium), we are witnessing astounding changes brought on by a new kind of technology. For the last two centuries, the Industrial Revolution has shaped our society, dictating the kind of work people do and how we think about the world. But now another transformation is underway—dubbed the Information Revolution—that is already redefining our world in novel ways.

At the end of each of the five parts of this text, we present a special section called "cyber.scope." These features highlight how computers and new information technology affect the issues raised in the preceding chapters. In this first cyber.scope, we extend our discussion of the sociological perspective (Chapter 1) and sociological research (Chapter 2) to explain what the Information Revolution is all about.

The Age of Machines: Industrial Society

The time line found inside the front cover of this book places the onset of the modern era about 250 years ago, the dawn of the Industrial Revolution. At that time—first in England and soon afterward in the United States—new sources of energy led imaginative people to create new products in new ways. First rivers and then steam generated by coal furnaces provided the power to operate large machines. Soon afterward, the Industrial Revolution was changing all aspects of social life, drawing people away from home to

work in the new factories and demanding that they learn the skills needed to operate machinery. As time went on, the increasing size and number of factories encouraged migration from the countryside to rapidly growing cities, where most people experienced a faster-paced, more impersonal way of life and, in time, came to enjoy a higher material standard of living. As we have noted, these changes sparked people's interest in studying society and played a key role in the birth of sociology.

The Age of Computers: Information Society

The final decades of the twentieth century witnessed the unfolding of another technological transformation—the Information Revolution—which promises to change our world once again. The technology that will define the twenty-first century is

Familiarity with computers is far more common among younger members of our society than older generations. Today's young people, who will live out their lives during the twenty-first century, will find computers a natural and indispensable part of day-to-day living.

based on *information:* the computer and related technology including the Internet, facsimile machines, modems and cellular telephones, as well as fiber optics and satellite communications. The fact that we already have shorthand names for such devices—the "Net," "fax," "cell phone," and "dish"—suggests how quickly they have become a part of our lives.

The age of the computer began in 1946 when U.S. engineers in a Philadelphia laboratory switched on a room-sized machine stuffed with wires and vacuum tubes. Despite its giant size, this "mother of all computers" could do no more than today's ten-dollar hand-held calculator. No wonder Thomas Watson, head of IBM, thought his company would end up selling "maybe five computers." Thirty years later, Ken Olson, founder of Digital Equipment Corporation, was just as skeptical, stating, "There is no reason anyone would want a computer in the home" (quoted in Lunsford, 1996).

For better or worse, these two men were quite wrong. In the final decades of the twentieth century, increasingly sophisticated computers quickly became a basic element of our lives. We now find microprocessors at work in the vast majority of U.S. households and businesses, and in cars and trucks as well. Surveys show that in

NOTE: The term "cyberspace" was coined by William Gibson in his 1984 novel *Neuromancer*. In the 1940s, mathematician Norbert Weiner adapted the Greek *kybernan* (meaning "to steer") to coin "cybernetics," the science of automated systems (Wallis, 1996).

Q: "But what . . . is it good for?" An engineer at the Advanced Computing System Division of IBM, commenting on the microchip (1968)

CYBER: In the industrial age we thought of value in terms of material objects; in the information age, value lies in symbols. Thus, a new version of, say, Windows may have as much value as a new line of automobiles, but it exists only as a stored configuration of electrons.

Q: "Computers make it easier to do a lot of things, but most of the things they make it easier to do don't need to be done." Andy Rooney

2001, almost 55 percent of U.S. households had at least one personal computer, and almost 45 percent of U.S. households

For the latest government reports on computer use and Internet availability, visit http://www. census.gov/ population/www/ socdemo/ computer.html

were connected to the Internet (U.S. Census Bureau, 2001). As computers become more numerous—as well as more powerful, smaller, and more portable—they will rewrite the rules of social life in the twenty-first century just as monstrous machines defined the industrial era now coming to a close.

What's different about new information technology? Most basically, the change involves the kind of work people do. Yesterday's industrial technology empowered people to create more and more *things*; information technology leads us to work with *ideas*, creating and manipulating symbols. The industrial age was represented by the factory's assembly line, with workers toiling to make steel or assemble cars. But the typical worker in the information age peers at a computer screen, entering data, writing, calculating, composing, drawing, or designing.

A second key change brought about by the Information Revolution is the declining importance of distance and physical space. Just as industrial technology demands that people work in centralized factories (where the machinery and energy sources are located), information

The earliest computers, including the 1946 ENIAC (Electronic Numerical Integrator and Computer) were monstrous contraptions that filled an entire room. (In fact, in 1949, Popular Mechanics *magazine confidently predicted that computers in the future would weigh no more than 1.5 tons!) It wasn't until the development of small, personal computers in the 1980s that the Information Revolution began to change the everyday lives of most people in the United States.*

technology allows people to work almost anywhere that they can carry a computer or flip on a cell phone. Note, too, that when we use this technology to communicate with others, we often have no idea where they are. The term "cyberspace" suggests that our emerging world is less and less bounded by physical dimensions. Of course, just as we gauged the output of industrial engines with a reference to the "horsepower" they made obsolete, so we now cling to older, physical images in describing new cyber-realities: We talk about the information superhighway,[1] read electronic bulletin boards, and enter online chat rooms. Yet these places are a "virtual reality," meaning that they are computer simulations that we see

and interact with, yet they have no physical existence. In fact, they exist only in the flow of electrons that illuminates our computer, electrons that can circle the world at the speed of light.

As later chapters of the text explain, this new technology is changing nearly every dimension of our lives: reshaping culture and how we learn about the world, connecting us to people in new ways, generating new kinds of crime as well as new ways of pursuing criminals, and even altering patterns of social inequality. There is little doubt that as we move through the new century we will see more changes that will spark people's sociological interest in the surrounding world.

New Information Technology: Thoughts on Theory

Chapter 1 ("The Sociological Perspective") discusses sociology's three major theoretical paradigms. What insights do these paradigms give us into new information technology?

A structural-functional analysis would point up the fact that because society is a system of countless interdependent elements, a new form of technology is likely to affect nearly all aspects of our lives. Since

---

[1]The rapidly increasing number of people logging on to the Internet has overwhelmed existing telephone lines and sometimes results in long delays in transmitting and receiving information. Until high-speed connections are more common, the information "superhighway" may remain more of a "dirt road."

THE MAP: Internet access is best in urban areas; regionally, this includes the Northeast corridor, the Florida coasts, and the West coast. The central part of the country, where access is limited, has fewer people who are, on average, older. Across the country, affluent counties have more Internet access than poor counties.

DIVERSITY: Computer ownership is linked to income and race.

About 1¹/₂ times as many white households as African American households report owning a computer. However, among all households earning more than $40,000, white and black people's Internet access is about equal. Among all households earning less than $40,000, white people are six times more likely to use the Internet than black people (*Science*, April 1998). For more on cyber-stratification, see the cyber.scope on pages 406–7.

SEEING OURSELVES

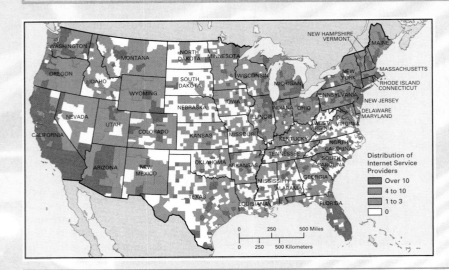

**NATIONAL MAP Cyber I-1
Available Internet Service
across the United States**

The counties that have the most Internet service providers are those with high population densities and thus large markets. These same counties also have a large number of affluent people who can afford to log on. Thus, although high technology is transforming the United States, the pace of change is faster in urban than rural areas.

Source: *Time*, March 22, 1999. Copyright © 1999, *Time*, Inc. Reprinted by permission.

Distribution of
Internet Service
Providers
- Over 10
- 4 to 10
- 1 to 3
- 0

---

the invention of television in 1939, more than 2 billion TV sets have been built (and, in high-income nations such as the United States, we add televisions faster than we add people). Television has altered what we know, how we learn, patterns of recreation, and even the ways family members interact. The computer will almost certainly change our lives even more. Its manifest (that is, intended and expected) effects will range from decentralizing the workplace to encouraging entire cities to spread outward because talking to or working with others no longer requires being physically with them. The latent (that is, unintended) effects are certainly harder to foresee, but they may well include new kinds of human communities as people pay less attention to their physical neighbors and spend more time communicating online with like-minded others.

A social-conflict analysis of the rise of new information technology offers contrasting insights, especially regarding social inequality. Here, we might note that the spread of new information technology has been rapid among affluent people but far less among the poor, a pattern illustrated in National Map Cyber I–1. There is already evidence that the information age will be marked by two distinct classes: educated people with sophisticated symbolic skills (who are likely to prosper) and people without symbolic skills (who are likely to remain in low-income jobs). Statistical comparisons show that, among workers in the same job, those able to use a computer earn 15 percent more than those who cannot (Ratan, 1995).

Finally, the symbolic-interaction paradigm asks questions at the micro-level of analysis. For example, how does communication via electronic mail differ from face-to-face interaction? Obviously, lacking facial expression or tone of voice,

electronic communication cannot convey emotion very well. For this reason, as shown in Figure Cyber I–1, people have creatively turned the characters found on their keyboards into symbols, generating a new cyber-language.

New Information Technology: What about Research?

How is new information technology changing sociological research, the focus of Chapter 2? A generation of sociologists has been trained to use computers to select random samples, to perform complex statistical analysis, and prepare written reports efficiently. Obviously, electronic mail enables researchers to "travel" almost anywhere almost instantly and with minimal cost. In the coming years, more and more surveys will take place online. Electronic surveys raise some interesting questions: Will this technology improve survey response rates or be discarded as electronic junk mail?

Will cyber-surveys end up protecting respondents' anonymity or threatening their privacy?

What seems sure is that new information technology will greatly enhance communication between researchers throughout the world. The Internet—highlighted in the next cyber.scope, on pages 244–45—now links some 400 million people in almost all of the world's 192 nations. It gives sociologists a powerful tool for building networks, sharing information, and joining together to conduct research. Just as important, faculty and students now have ready access to a rapidly increasing amount of statistical information. For example, the U.S. Census Bureau (see their Web site at http://www.census.gov) publishes reports of all kinds online and will respond to questions from individuals doing research of their own.

Visit Us Online!

Please visit the Web site that accompanies this text. Travel to the author's home page at http://www.TheSociologyPage.com (or http://www.macionis.com) to review our family of textbooks, read sociological news, view videos, enter the Gallery of Sociologists, and find a library of links to a wide range of interesting organizations. The author and publisher have also prepared an interactive Web site that serves as a study guide to help you throughout this course. Visit http://www.prenhall.com/macionis and click on the cover of this book. There, you will find a chapter-by-chapter study guide, self-scoring practice tests, and many links to other instructive Web sites. These sites, along with the CD-ROM that is included with your new textbook, are our invitation to you to join the Information Revolution. Welcome, and enjoy!

FIGURE Cyber I-1 Cyber-Symbols: An Emerging Language

It all started with the "smiley" figure that shows one is happy or telling a joke. Now a new language of gestures is emerging as creative people use computer keystrokes to create emoticons, symbols that convey thoughts and emotions. Here is a sampling of the new cyber-language. (Rotate this page 90° to the right to appreciate the emoticon faces.)

: -)	I'm smiling at you.
: `-)	I'm so happy (laughing so hard) that I'm starting to cry.
: - O	Wow!
: - x	My lips are sealed!
: -||	I'm angry with you!
: - P	I'm sticking my tongue out at you!
: - (	I feel sad.
: - |	Things look grim.
% -}	I think I've had too much to drink.
-:(	Somebody cut my hair into a mohawk!
+O:-)	I've just been elected Pope!
@}——->———	Here's a rose for you!

Computers are as popular in Japan as they are in the United States. The Japanese have their own emoticons:

(^_^)	I'm smiling at you.
(*^o^*)	This is exciting!
(^o^)	I am happy.
\(^o^)/	Banzai! This is wonderful!

How far will this new keyboard language go? If you're creative enough, anything is possible. Here's a routine that has been making the rounds on the Internet. It's called "Mr. Asciihead learns the Macarena"! To see Mr. Asciihead in action, go to the link at http://www.TheSociologyPage.com

```
o       o       o       o       o      <o      <o>     o>      o
.I.     \I.     \I/     //      X       \       I       <I     <I>
/\      >\      /<      >\      /<      >\      /<      >\      /<
```

Sources: Pollak (1996) and Krantz (1997). "Mr. Asciihead" is the creation of Leow Yee Ling.

CHAPTER

3

Diego Rivera (1866–1957)
La Piñata, 1953

CULTURE

Don Domingo is a priest and member of the Q'ero, a small society that lives 15,000 feet up in the peaks of the Andes, South America's highest mountain range. The Q'ero are among the most socially isolated people on Earth, rarely making contact with the world beyond their home. But in 2000, the world came to the Q'ero. A messenger from the United Nations arrived to invite Don Domingo and several other Q'ero people to attend the Millennium World Peace Summit in New York City. Don Domingo considered the invitation but made one request: He asked whether the UN officials would provide horses for the group to travel the three days needed to reach the nearest paved road. When the messenger agreed, Don Domingo smiled at the thought of visiting the United States.

A few weeks later, Don Domingo and five of his fellow priests were in Peru's capital city, Cuzco, boarding a DC-10 airliner. Because the Quechua language has no word for "airplane," they spoke of the plane using their word for "big bird." As the plane roared down the runway, the men anxiously gazed out the window. Then, shortly after take-off, they smiled and nodded as the flight attendant handed them cans of Coke, although they had no idea what to do with them.

Hours later, the plane touched down at Newark

Airport, a few miles west of New York. In their brightly colored clothing, the visitors followed their UN hosts to a waiting van. Only minutes later, the van was stuck in the late afternoon traffic that clogs the New Jersey Turnpike. "A horse moves faster than this," Don Domingo commented to the others. Alongside the highway was a small rocky hill, which prompted the question, "What is the name of this mountain?" The interpreter shook her head and responded that, as far as she knew, the hill had no name. This disturbed the Q'ero priests, who view all mountains as gods. As the traffic began to move, the van headed into the Lincoln Tunnel. The five priests became even more uneasy. "Uccu Pacha," Don Domingo said quietly to the others, "We are entering the underworld."

United Nations officials pronounced the conference a success, having brought together people from hundreds of societies—large and small—to discuss ways to promote peace and protect the Earth's natural environment. The Q'ero priests, too, were pleased with their travels. Back in the Andes, Don Domingo and the others have spent many hours trying to convey to the Q'ero people something of life in New York, including the mysterious trip to the underworld that people make in cars that barely move (based on Van Biema, 2000).

SUPPLEMENTS: Chapter 3 of the *Data File* includes a detailed chapter outline, supplementary lecture material, and discussion questions.

Q: What we have loved,
   Others will love,
   And we will teach them how.
   Wordsworth

DISCUSS: An interesting question, in light of rapid technological advance, is how different people from various parts of the world, as shown here, will appear a century from now.

Q: "Natives who beat drums to drive off evil spirits are objects of scorn to smart Americans who blow horns to break up traffic jams." Mary Ellen Kelly

Q: "Man has no nature; what he has is history." José Ortega y Gassett

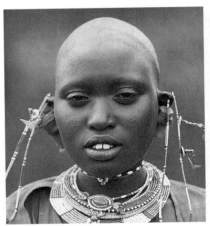

Human beings around the globe create diverse ways of life. Such differences begin with outward appearance: Contrast the women shown here from Brazil, Kenya, New Guinea, and Morocco, and the men from Taiwan (Republic of China), India, Peru, and New Guinea. Less obvious, but of even greater importance, are internal differences, since culture also shapes our goals in life, our sense of justice, and even our innermost personal feelings.

NOTE: The Latin root of "culture," *cultur(a)*, means "a tilling." Note that "cultivate" and "agriculture" have the same root. In this sense, culture is the means by which humans cultivate the world.

Q: "Culture . . . is that complex whole which includes knowledge, belief, art, morals, laws, customs, and any other capabilities and habits acquired by man as a member of society." Edward B. Tylor, who offered perhaps the first formal definition of culture

DISCUSS: Culture shock happens even in our own communities as we confront people of other colors, cultures, and class positions. Can students provide examples from their own lives?

NOTE: Note that sociologists use "culture" in an all-inclusive way, not with highbrow connotations ("cul-chah").

Q: "I was a student in the department of anthropology. They taught me that nobody was ridiculous or bad or disgusting." Kurt Vonnegut

The world is home to more than 6 billion human beings, who have developed thousands of different ways of life. As the Q'ero visitors discovered, the dif-

 For additional photos of the Q'ero, visit http://www.suu.edu/hss/psychology/Gordon/Images/photos/PhotoAlbum/Qero.html

ferences can delight, puzzle, and disturb us. Indeed, we might imagine the reaction of a small group of New Yorkers if they were parachuted into a tiny Q'ero village at the top of the Andes.

Some differences in how people live are not important. Whereas many New Yorkers wear conservative business suits, the Q'ero prefer clothing that is brightly colored. Other cultural differences, however, can be quite profound. A survey of the world's people would show that some people have many children, whereas others have few; some honor the elderly, while others push them aside; some are peaceful, and others are warlike; and people have thousands of different religious beliefs and ideas about what is polite or rude, beautiful or ugly, pleasant or repulsive. This amazing capacity for difference is a matter of human culture.

WHAT IS CULTURE?

Culture is *the values, beliefs, behavior, and material objects that, together, form a people's way of life.* Culture includes what we think, how we act, and what we own. Culture is both a bridge to our past and a guide to the future (Soyinka, 1991).

To understand all that culture entails, we must distinguish between thoughts and things. **Nonmaterial culture** is *the intangible world of ideas created by members of a society,* ideas that range from altruism to zen. **Material culture,** on the other hand, is *the tangible things created by members of a society,* everything from armaments to zippers.

Not only does culture shape what we do, it also helps form our personalities—what we commonly, but wrongly, describe as "human nature." The warlike Yąnomamö of the Brazilian rain forest think aggression is natural, whereas, halfway around the world, the Semai of Malaysia live in peace and cooperation. The cultures of the United States and Japan both stress achievement and hard work, but members of our society value individualism more than the Japanese, who are more traditional and group-oriented.

Given the extent of cultural differences in the world and people's tendency to view their own way of life as better or more "natural" than others, it is no wonder that travelers—such as the Q'eros described in

Behavior people in one society consider routine can be chilling to members of another culture. In the Russian city of St. Petersburg, this young mother and her six-week-old son brave the 17°F temperatures for a dip in a nearby lake. To Russians, this is something of a national pastime. To some members of our society, however, this practice may seem cruel or even dangerous.

the opening to this chapter—often feel uneasy when they enter a different culture. This uneasiness is known as **culture shock,** *personal disorientation when experiencing an unfamiliar way of life.* The box on page

 The author offers a short video discussing the challenges and benefits of travel at http://www.TheSociologyPage.com

62 presents another experience of culture shock: the story of a researcher making his first visit to the home of the Yąnomamö people living in the Amazon region of South America.

December 1, Istanbul, Turkey. Harbors everywhere, it seems, have two things in common: ships and cats. Istanbul, the tenth port on our voyage, is awash with felines, prowling about in search of an easy meal. People certainly change from place to place—but not cats.

DISCUSS: Napoleon Chagnon did not speak the Yąnomamö language, working instead through a translator. How might this practice have affected his understanding of these people? (Thanks to Doug Shocke, PhD, Northern Virginia Community College.)

NOTE: In 2000, Patrick Tierney's book *Darkness in El Dorado* attacked Napoleon Chagnon for fomenting violence among the Yąnomamö, allegedly in support of his theory that they are an aggressive people. Other social scientists have come to Chagnon's defense, claiming that Tierney has long opposed Chagnon's work as politically incorrect (Lasswell, 2000).

NOTE: The early human ancestor Lucy lived about 3 million years ago, stood about 3 ft. 6 in. tall, and weighed 65 lbs.; at that time, men might have reached 5 ft. and 100 lbs. Today's global averages are 5 ft. 6 in. tall and 150 lbs. for men, 5 ft. 2 in. and 125 lbs. for women.

GLOBAL SOCIOLOGY

Confronting the Yąnomamö: The Experience of Culture Shock

A small aluminum motorboat chugged steadily along the muddy Orinoco River, deep within South America's vast tropical rain forest. Anthropologist Napoleon Chagnon was nearing the end of a three-day journey to the home territory of the Yąnomamö, one of the most technologically simple societies on Earth.

Some 12,000 Yąnomamö live in villages scattered along the border of Venezuela and Brazil. Their way of life could hardly be more different from our own. The Yąnomamö wear little clothing and live without electricity, automobiles, or other familiar conveniences. Their traditional weapon, used for hunting and warfare, is the bow and arrow. Most Yąnomamö have had little contact with the outside world, so Chagnon would be as strange to them as they would be to him.

By 2:00 in the afternoon, Chagnon had almost reached his destination. The hot sun and humid air were almost unbearable. He was soaked with perspiration, and his face and hands swelled from the bites of gnats swarming around him. But he scarcely noticed, so excited was he that in just a few moments he would be face to face with people unlike any he had ever known.

Chagnon's heart pounded as the boat slid onto the riverbank. Chagnon and his guide climbed from the boat and headed toward the sounds of a nearby village, pushing through the dense undergrowth. Chagnon describes what happened next:

> I looked up and gasped when I saw a dozen burly, naked, sweaty, hideous men staring at us down the shafts of their drawn arrows! Immense wads of green tobacco were stuck between their lower teeth and lips making them look even more hideous, and strands of

dark green slime dripped or hung from their nostrils—strands so long that they clung to their [chests] or drizzled down their chins.

> My next discovery was that there were a dozen or so vicious, underfed dogs snapping at my legs, circling me as if I were to be their next meal. I just stood there holding my notebook, helpless and pathetic. Then the stench of the decaying vegetation and filth hit me and I almost got sick. I was horrified. What kind of welcome was this for the person who came here to live with you and learn your way of life, to become friends with you? (1992:11–12)

Fortunately for Chagnon, the Yąnomamö villagers recognized his guide and lowered their weapons. Though reassured that he would survive the afternoon, Chagnon was still shaken by his inability to make any sense of the people surrounding him. And this was to be his home for a year and a half! He wondered why he had forsaken physics to study human culture in the first place.

Source: Chagnon (1992).

No way of life is "natural" to humanity, even though most people around the world view their own behavior that way. What comes naturally to members of our species is creating culture. Every other form of life—from ants and crocodiles to robins and zebras—behaves in uniform, species-specific ways. To a traveler, the enormous diversity of human life stands out in contrast to the behavior of, say, cats, which is the same everywhere. This uniformity follows from the fact that most living creatures are guided by *instinct*, biological programming over which an animal has no control. A few animals—notably chimpanzees and related primates—have the capacity for limited culture, as researchers have noted by observing them use tools and teach simple skills to their offspring. But the creative power of humans far exceeds that of any other form of life. In short, *only humans rely on culture rather than instinct to ensure the survival of their kind* (Harris, 1987).

NOTE: Light from the nearest galaxy (Andromeda) takes 2 million years to reach the earth; thus, the light we see in the night sky left all the stars before humans existed on the earth.

Q: "There can obviously be no culture without a society [and] no cultureless human society is known; it would even be hard to imagine. But it does not hold on the subhuman level . . . ants and bees do have genuine societies without culture." A.L. Kroeber

GLOBAL: Societies show significant cultural variation in their favorite sports. Canada, ice hockey; Brazil, soccer; Jamaica, cricket; China, tai chi chuan; Thailand, kite flying (Davis, 1997).

RESOURCE: Leslie White's article "Symbol: The Basic Element of Culture" and Robert Merton's "Manifest and Latent Functions" are two classics on culture found in the Macionis and Benokraitis reader, *Seeing Ourselves.*

To understand how human culture came to be, we need to look back at the history of our species.

CULTURE AND HUMAN INTELLIGENCE

In a universe 15 billion years old, our planet is a much younger 4.5 billion (see the time lines inside the front cover of this text). Not for a billion years after the Earth was formed did life appear. Several billion more years went by before dinosaurs ruled the Earth, only to disappear. It was then, 65 million years ago, that our history took a crucial turn with the appearance of the creatures we call primates.

What sets primates apart is their intelligence: They have the largest brains relative to body size of all living creatures. About 12 million years ago, primates began to evolve along two different lines, setting humans apart from the great apes, our closest relatives. But our common lineage is evident in the traits that humans share with chimpanzees, gorillas, and orangutans: great sociability, affectionate and long-lasting bonds for child rearing and mutual protection, the ability to walk upright (normal in humans but less common among other primates), and hands that manipulate objects with great precision.

Some 3 million years ago, our distant human ancestors descended from the trees to the tall grasses of central Africa. There, walking upright, they learned the advantages of hunting in groups and made use of fire, tools, and weapons; they built simple shelters and fashioned basic clothing. These Stone Age achievements may seem modest, but they mark the point at which our ancestors set off on a distinct evolutionary course, making culture their primary survival strategy. By about 250,000 years ago, our own species—*Homo sapiens* (derived from the Latin term meaning "thinking person")—finally emerged. Humans continued to evolve so that about 40,000 years ago, people who looked almost like us roamed the Earth. With larger brains, these "modern" *Homo sapiens* rapidly developed culture, as the wide range of tools and cave art from this period suggests.

About 12,000 years ago, the founding of permanent settlements and growth of specialized occupations in the Middle East (in what is today Iraq and Egypt) marked the "birth of civilization." At this point, the biological forces we call instincts were long gone in favor of a more efficient survival scheme: *refashioning the environment for ourselves.* Ever since, humans have made and remade their worlds in countless ways, which explains today's fascinating cultural diversity.

CULTURE, NATION, AND SOCIETY

Three similar terms—"culture," "nation," and "society"—have slightly different meanings. *Culture* is a shared way of life. A *nation* is a political entity, that is, a territory with designated borders, such as the United States, Canada, Peru, or Zimbabwe. *Society*, the topic of the next chapter, is the organized interaction of people in a nation or within some other boundary.

The United States, then, is both a nation and a society. But many societies, including the United States, are *multicultural*, meaning that their people follow various ways of life that blend (and sometimes clash).

In the United States, how many cultures are there? The Census Bureau lists several hundreds of languages spoken by this country's people, many of which were brought by immigrants from around the world. Globally, experts have documented more than 5,000 languages, suggesting that at least this many cultures have existed at various times (Durning, 1993; Crispell, 1997a). Fewer cultures exist today, however, because of high-technology communication, increasing international migration, and an expanding global economy. Even so, as the story of the Q'ero suggests, some cultures remain isolated and largely unaffected by change in the rest of the world.

And what of world nations? The tally goes up or down as a result of political events. The dissolution of the former Soviet Union and the former Yugoslavia, for example, added nineteen nations to the count. In 2001, there were 192 politically independent nations in the world.

THE COMPONENTS OF CULTURE

Although cultures vary greatly, they all have five common components: symbols, language, values and beliefs, norms, and material culture, including technology. We begin with the one that underlies all the others: symbols.

SYMBOLS

Like all other creatures, humans sense the surrounding world, but unlike others, we also create a reality of *meaning.* Humans transform elements of the world into **symbols,** *anything that carries a particular meaning recognized by people who share culture.* A word, a whistle, a wall of graffiti, a flashing red light, a raised fist—all serve as symbols. We can see the human capacity to create and manipulate symbols reflected in the very

GLOBAL: Other examples of potential cultural conflict: Because Muslims consider the bottom of the foot to be unclean, they require people to remove shoes before entering a mosque. In other societies, including Japan, counting change is taken as an insult because it implies distrust. The Chinese find "looking someone straight in the eye" to be rudely direct.

GLOBAL: Helen Colton (1983) asked, if one disturbs a woman in the bath, what body parts does she cover? An Islamic woman covers her face; a prerevolutionary Chinese woman covered her feet; a Sumatran woman covers her knees; a Laotian woman covers her breasts; a Samoan woman covers her navel; a North American or European woman covers her breasts with one hand and her genital area with the other.

People throughout the world communicate not just with spoken words but also with bodily gestures, which vary from culture to culture. To most North Americans, there is nothing unusual about the young woman shown in the left-hand photo. But to people living in Muslim societies—who typically use the left hand for bathroom hygiene—eating this way is disturbing, to say the least! Similarly, the familiar "A-OK" gesture, by which we express approval and pleasure, is likely to insult a French person, who "reads" the message as "You're worth zero." Finally, even the commonplace "thumbs up" gesture we take to mean "Good job!" can get you into trouble in Australia, where people take it to mean "Up yours!"

different meanings associated with the simple act of winking the eye, which can convey interest, understanding, or insult.

We are so dependent on our culture's symbols that we take them for granted. Sometimes, however, we become keenly aware of a symbol when someone uses it in an unconventional way, as when a person burns a U.S. flag during a political demonstration. Entering an unfamiliar culture also reminds us of the power of symbols; culture shock is really the inability to "read" meaning in new surroundings. Not understanding the symbols of a culture leaves a person feeling lost and isolated, unsure of how to act, and sometimes frightened.

Culture shock is a two-way process. On one hand, travelers *experience* culture shock when encountering people whose way of life is different. For example, North Americans who consider dogs beloved household pets might be put off by the Masai of eastern Africa, who ignore and never feed them. The same travelers might be horrified to find that, in parts of Indonesia and the northern regions of the People's Republic of China, people roast dogs for dinner.

On the other hand, a traveler *inflicts* culture shock by acting in ways that offend others. A North American who asks for a cheeseburger in an Indian restaurant offends Hindus, who consider cows sacred and never to be eaten.

Global travel provides almost endless opportunities for misunderstanding. In unfamiliar settings, we need to remember that even behavior that seems innocent and normal to us can offend others, as the photos above suggest.

Symbolic meanings also vary within a single society. A fur coat may represent a prized symbol of success or the inhumane treatment of animals. Similarly, the Confederate flag symbolizes regional heritage and pride to some, but others see it as a symbol of racial oppression (cf. Reingold & Wike, 1998; Broughton, 2001).

LANGUAGE

In infancy, an illness left Helen Keller (1880–1968) blind and deaf. Without these two senses, she was cut off from the symbolic world, which greatly limited her social development. Only when her teacher, Anne Mansfield Sullivan, broke through Keller's isolation using sign language did Helen Keller begin to realize her human potential. This remarkable woman, who

 To learn more about the life of Helen Keller, go to http://helen-keller.freeservers.com/

later became a renowned educator herself, recalls the moment she grasped the concept of language.

> We walked down the path to the well-house, attracted by the smell of honeysuckle with which it was covered. Someone was drawing water, and my teacher placed my hand under the spout. As the cool stream gushed over one hand, she spelled into the other the word *water*, first slowly, then rapidly. I stood still, my whole attention fixed upon the motions of her fingers. Suddenly I felt a misty consciousness as of something forgotten—a thrill of returning thought; and somehow the mystery of language was revealed to me. I knew then that "w-a-t-e-r" meant the wonderful cool something that was flowing over my hand. That living word awakened my soul; gave it light, hope, joy, set it free! (1903:21–24)

Language, the key to the world of culture, is *a system of symbols that allows people to communicate with one another*. Humans have devised hundreds of alphabets. Even conventions for writing differ: Most people in Western societies write from left to right, but people in northern Africa and western Asia write right to left, and people in eastern Asia write from top to bottom. Global Map 3–1 on page 66 shows where one finds the three most widely spoken languages.

Language not only allows communication but also ensures the continuity of culture. Language is a cultural heritage and the key to **cultural transmission,** *the process by which one generation passes culture to the next.* Just as our bodies contain the genes of our ancestors, so our culture contains countless symbols of those who came before us. Language is the key that unlocks centuries of accumulated wisdom.

Every society transmits culture through speech, a process sociologists call the *oral cultural tradition.* Some 5,000 years ago, however, humans invented writing, although just a favored few ever learned to read and write. Not until the twentieth century did high-income nations boast of nearly universal literacy. Still, at least 10 percent of U.S. adults (some 20 million people) are functionally illiterate, unable to read and write in a society that increasingly demands symbolic skills. In low-income countries of the world, about one-third of men and almost two-thirds of women are illiterate (United Nations Development Programme, 2001).

Language not only links us with the past but also sets free the human imagination. Connecting symbols in new ways, we can conceive of an almost limitless range of future possibilities. Language sets humans apart as the only creatures who are self-conscious, aware of our limitations and ultimate mortality yet able to dream and hope for a future better than the present.

Language: Only for Humans?

Creatures great and small direct sounds, smells, and gestures toward one another. In most cases, these signals are instinctive. But some animals have at least some ability to use symbols to communicate with one another and with humans.

Consider the remarkable achievement of a twelve-year-old pygmy chimp named Kanzi. Chimpanzees lack the physical ability to mimic human speech. But researcher E. Sue Savage-Rumbaugh discovered that Kanzi could learn language by listening to and observing people. Under Savage-Rumbaugh's supervision, Kanzi has developed a vocabulary of several hundred words, and he has learned to "speak" by pointing to pictures on a special keyboard. He can respond to requests such as "Will you get a diaper for your sister?" or "Put the melon in the potty." Kanzi's abilities go beyond mere rote learning because he can respond to requests he has not heard before. In short, Kanzi has the language ability of a human child of two-and-one-half years (Linden, 1993).

Still, the language skills of chimps, dolphins, and a few other animals are limited. Even specially trained animals cannot pass on language skills to others of their kind. But the achievements of Kanzi and others caution us against assuming that humans alone can lay any claim to culture.

Does Language Shape Reality?

Do the Q'ero, who think using the Quechua language, experience the world differently from North Americans who think in, say, English or Spanish? The answer is "yes" because each language has its own distinctive symbols that serve as the building blocks of reality.

Edward Sapir and Benjamin Whorf proposed that languages are not just different sets of labels for the same reality (Sapir, 1929, 1949; Whorf, 1956). Rather, each symbolic system has at least some unique words or expressions. In addition, all languages fuse symbols with distinctive emotions. Thus, as multilingual people can attest, a single idea may "feel" different when spoken in Spanish rather than in English or Chinese (Falk, 1987). The **Sapir-Whorf thesis** states that *people perceive the world through the cultural lens of language.*

WINDOW ON THE WORLD

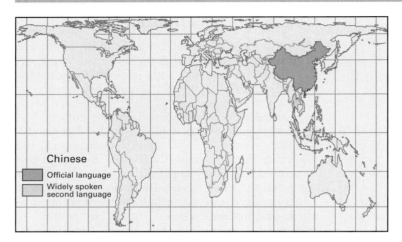

GLOBAL MAP 3–1
Language in Global Perspective

Chinese (including Mandarin, Cantonese, and dozens of other dialects) is the native tongue of one-fifth of the world's people, almost all of whom live in Asia. Although all Chinese people read and write with the same characters, they use several dozen dialects. The "official" dialect, taught in schools throughout the People's Republic of China and the Republic of Taiwan, is Mandarin (the dialect of Beijing, China's historic capital city). Cantonese, the language of Canton, is the second most common Chinese dialect; it differs in sound from Mandarin roughly the way French differs from Spanish.

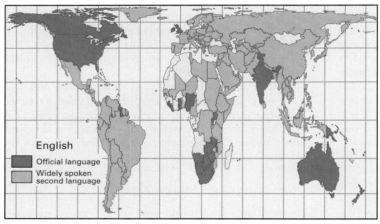

English is the native tongue or official language in several world regions (spoken by 10 percent of humanity) and has become the preferred second language in most of the world.

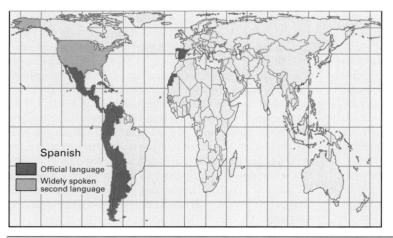

The largest concentration of Spanish speakers is in Latin America and, of course, Spain. Spanish is also the preferred second language of the United States.

Source: *Peters Atlas of the World* (1990); updated by the author.

GLOBAL: Regarding Williams's 10 points for traditional societies—*Pts. 1 and 2*: Traditional societies generally embrace fate as a key value; *Pt. 3*: Spiritual comfort and well-being; *Pt. 4*: Greater reflectiveness (especially Eastern cultures); *Pt. 5*: Implies a rational worldview; this value also suggests why we devalue academics as "eggheads "; *Pt. 6*: Members of most traditional societies are not optimistic (even the Japanese are less so); *Pt. 7*: Religion plays much more of a role than science; *Pt. 8*: Collective sentiment is higher, as is compliance to official authority; for example, Moroccans accept high-handed police direction with little evident complaint; *Pt. 9*: Most of the world is less individualistic than we are; *Pt. 10*: Most of the traditional world is much more group-oriented than we are.

Q: "What Western man needs to learn is how to be content in an empty room." Blaise Pascal

VALUES AND BELIEFS

What accounts for the popularity of films with characters such as James Bond, Dirty Harry, Rambo, and Erin Brockovich? Each is ruggedly individualistic, relying on personal skill and savvy to challenge "the system." In applauding such characters, we are endorsing certain **values,** *culturally defined standards by which people assess desirability, goodness, and beauty and that serve as broad guidelines for social living.* Values are statements, from the standpoint of a culture, of what ought to be.

Values are broad principles that underlie **beliefs,** *specific statements that people hold to be true.* In other words, values are abstract standards of goodness, and beliefs are particular matters that individuals consider true or false. For example, because most adults in the United States share the value of providing equal opportunities for all, they believe a qualified woman could serve as president of the nation (NORC, 2001).

Cultural values and beliefs not only affect how we perceive our surroundings, they also form the core of our personalities. We learn from families, friends, schools, and religious organizations to think and act according to particular principles, to believe worthy truths, and to pursue worthy goals. Even so, in a nation as large and diverse as the United States, few cultural values and beliefs are shared by everyone. Our long history of immigration has made the United States a cultural mosaic. In this regard, our country differs from many nations—such as China and Japan—that are more culturally homogeneous.

Australian feminist artist Sally Swain alters a famous artist's painting to make fun of our culture's tendency to ignore the everyday lives of women. This spoof is entitled Mrs. Picasso Dusts the Mantlepiece.

Key Values of U.S. Culture

Although U.S. culture is not uniform, Robin Williams (1970) has identified ten values that are widespread and viewed by many as central to our way of life:

1. **Equal opportunity.** People in the United States endorse not *equality of condition* but *equality of opportunity.* This means that society should provide everyone with the chance to get ahead according to individual talents and efforts.

2. **Achievement and success.** Our way of life encourages competition so that each person's rewards should reflect personal merit. Moreover, success confers worthiness on a person—the mantle of being a "winner."

3. **Material comfort.** Success in the United States generally means making money and enjoying what it will buy. Although people sometimes say that "money won't buy happiness," most pursue wealth all the same.

4. **Activity and work.** Popular U.S. heroes, from fictional archaeologist Indiana Jones to golf champion Tiger Woods, are "doers" who get the job done. Our culture values *action* over *reflection* and controlling events over passively accepting one's fate.

5. **Practicality and efficiency.** People in the United States value the practical over the theoretical, or "doing" over "dreaming." Activity has value to the extent that it earns money. "Major in something that will help you get a job!" parents say to their children.

6. **Progress.** We are an optimistic people who, despite waves of nostalgia, believe that the present

CRITICAL THINKING

Don't Blame Me! The New "Culture of Victimization"

A University of North Carolina law student walked down the street, took aim with an M-1 rifle, and killed two men he never met. Later, from a psychiatric hospital, he sued his therapist for not doing enough to prevent his actions. A jury awarded him $500,000. A New York man leaped in front of a subway train; lucky enough to survive, he sued the city, claiming that the train failed to stop in time to prevent his serious injuries. His award: $650,000. In Washington, D.C., after realizing that he had been videotaped smoking crack cocaine in a hotel room, the city's mayor blamed his woman companion for "setting him up" and suggested that the police were racially motivated in arresting him. After more than a dozen women accused an Oregon senator of sexual

harassment, he claimed his behavior was caused by his problem with alcohol. In the most celebrated case of its kind, a former city politician gunned down the mayor of San Francisco and a city council member, blaming his violence on

Since the 1980s, "tell all" television programs have reinforced the emerging "culture of victimization."

insanity caused by eating too much junk food (the so-called "Twinkie defense").

In each of these cases, someone denied personal responsibility for an action, claiming instead to be a victim. More and more, members of our society are pointing the finger elsewhere, which prompted Irving Horowitz (1993) to declare that our way of life is becoming a "culture of victimization" in which "everyone is a victim" and "no one accepts responsibility for anything."

One indication of this victimization trend is the proliferation of "addictions," a term once associated only with uncontrollable drug use. We now hear about gambling addicts, compulsive overeaters, sex addicts, and even people who excuse runaway credit card debt as a shopping addiction. Bookstores overflow with manuals to help people deal

is better than the past. We celebrate progress, equating the "very latest" with the "very best."

7. **Science**. We look to science and advanced technology to solve problems and improve our lives. We believe we are rational people, which probably explains our cultural tendency (especially among men) to devalue emotion and intuition as sources of knowledge.

8. **Democracy and free enterprise**. Members of our society recognize individual rights that should not be overridden by government. We believe that a just political system is based on free elections in which adults select their leaders and on an economy that responds to the choices of individual consumers.

9. **Freedom**. Our cultural value of freedom means that we place a higher value on individual

initiative than on collective conformity. Although we know that everyone has responsibilities to others, we believe that people should be free to pursue their own personal goals with minimal interference from government.

10. **Racism and group superiority**. Despite strong notions about individualism and freedom, most people in the United States still evaluate individuals according to gender, race, ethnicity, and social class. In general, U.S. culture values males above females, whites above people of color, people with northwest European backgrounds above those whose ancestors came from other lands, and rich above poor. Although we like to describe ourselves as a nation of equals, there is little doubt that some of us rank as "more equal than others."

NOTE: Of course, the notion of victims implies the existence of victimizers, which explains the link between the developing culture of victimization and rising political conflict.

Q: "Social sciences show that values do not fly on their own wings; they must be embodied in our rituals." Amitai Etzioni

NOTE: Illustrate the changing norms of language on TV: In 1952, Lucy and Desi couldn't say "pregnant" to describe her condition.

NOTE: "Norm" is derived from Latin *norm(a)*, meaning "a carpenter square, a rule, or a pattern." The root of "moral" is *mor* or *mos*, meaning "custom." The rarely used singular form of "mores" is "mos."

NOTE: Not all norms are neatly characterized as mores or folkways; these concepts are most effectively used as endpoints of a continuum.

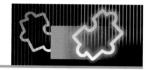

with numerous new medical or psychological conditions ranging from the "Cinderella complex" to the "Casanova complex" and even "soap opera syndrome." And U.S. courts are clogged by lawsuits blaming someone for misfortunes that we used to accept as part of life.

What's going on here? Is U.S. culture changing? Historically, our cultural ideal was rugged individualism, the idea that people are responsible for whatever triumph or tragedy befalls them. But this value has been eroded in a number of ways. First, everyone is more aware (partly through the work of sociologists) of how society shapes our lives. Therefore, categories of people other than those who have suffered real historical disadvantages (such as Native Americans, African Americans, and women) now say they are victims. The latest victims include white men who claim that "everybody gets special treatment but us."

Second, especially since they began advertising their services in 1977, many lawyers have encouraged a sense of injustice among clients they hope to represent in court. The number of million-dollar lawsuit awards has risen more than twenty-five-fold in the last twenty-five years.

Finally, a proliferation of "rights groups" promotes what Amitai Etzioni calls "rights inflation." Beyond the traditional constitutional liberties are many newly claimed rights: those of hunters (as well as animals), the rights of smokers (and nonsmokers), the right of women to control their bodies (and the rights of the unborn), and the right to own a gun (and the right to be safe from violence). Expanding claims for unmet rights create victims (and victimizers) on all sides.

Does this shift toward victimization signal a fundamental realignment in our individualistic culture? Perhaps, but the new popularity of being a victim also springs from some established cultural forces. For example, the claim to victimization depends on a longstanding belief that everyone has the right to life, liberty, and the pursuit of happiness. What is new, however, is that the explosion of "rights" now does more than alert us to clear cases of injustice: It lessens our responsibility for our own lives.

What do you think?

1. *Do you think our cultural emphasis on individualism is weaker today than in the past? Why?*

2. *Do you think the United States has experienced "rights inflation"? Why or why not?*

3. *Does using the sociological perspective encourage us to view people as victims? Why or why not?*

Sources: Based on Etzioni (1991), Taylor (1991), Hollander (1995), and Roche (1999).

Values: Sometimes in Conflict

Looking over Williams's list, we see that some values are inconsistent and even opposed to one another (Lynd, 1967; Bellah et al., 1985; Ray, 1997). For example, people in the United States believe in equality of opportunity, yet they may also discriminate against others because of their sex or race.

Conflict between values reflects the cultural diversity of U.S. society and also cultural change by which new trends develop alongside older traditions. Recently, for example, what some observers call a "culture of victimization" has arisen to challenge our society's longstanding belief in individual responsibility (Best, 1997; Furedi, 1998). The box takes a closer look.

Value conflict causes strain and often leads to awkward balancing acts in our beliefs. Sometimes we decide one value is more important than another by, for example, supporting equal opportunity while opposing the acceptance of homosexual people in the U.S. military. In such cases, we simply learn to live with the contradictions.

NORMS

Most people in the United States are eager to gossip about "who's hot" and "who's not." Members of Peru's Q'ero society, however, condemn such behavior as rude and divisive. Both patterns illustrate the operation of **norms**, *rules and expectations by which a society guides the behavior of its members.* Some norms are *proscriptive:* They state what we should *not* do, as, for example, when health officials warn us to avoid casual sex. *Prescriptive* norms, on the other hand, state what

Standards of beauty—including the color and design of everyday surroundings—vary significantly from one culture to another. These two Nankani women put the finishing touches on their lavishly decorated homes. Members of North American and European societies, by contrast, make far less use of bright colors and intricate detail so that their housing appears much more subdued.

we *should* do, as when U.S. schools teach "safe-sex" practices.

Most important norms in a culture apply everywhere and at all times. For example, parents expect obedience from young children regardless of the setting. Other norms depend on the situation. In the United States, we expect the audience to applaud after a musical performance, we may applaud (although it is not expected) at the end of a classroom lecture, but we do not applaud when a priest or rabbi finishes a sermon.

Mores and Folkways

William Graham Sumner (1959; orig. 1906), an early U.S. sociologist, recognized that some norms are more important to our lives than others. Sumner coined the term **mores** (pronounced "more-ays") to refer to *norms that are widely observed and have great moral significance.* Mores, or *taboos,* include our society's prohibition against adults engaging in sexual relations with children.

People pay less attention to **folkways,** *norms for routine, casual interaction.* Examples include ideas about appropriate greetings and proper dress. In short, mores distinguish between right and wrong, whereas folkways draw a line between right and rude. A man who does not wear a tie to a formal dinner party may raise eyebrows for violating folkways. However, if he were to arrive at the party wearing *only* a tie, he would violate cultural mores and invite more serious sanctions.

Social Control

Mores and folkways are the basic rules of everyday life. Although we sometimes bristle when others pressure us to conform, we all can see that norms make our dealings with others more orderly and predictable. Observing or breaking the rules of social life prompts a response from others, in the form of reward or punishment. *Sanctions*—whether an approving smile or a raised eyebrow—operate as a system of **social control,** *various means by which members of a society encourage conformity to norms.*

As we learn cultural norms, we acquire the capacity to evaluate our own behavior. Doing wrong (say, downloading a term paper from the Internet) can cause both *shame* (the painful sense that others disapprove of our actions) and *guilt* (a negative judgment we make of ourselves). Only cultural creatures can experience shame and guilt. This is probably what Mark Twain had in mind when he remarked that people "are the only animals that blush—or need to."

"IDEAL" AND "REAL" CULTURE

Values and norms do not describe actual behavior so much as they suggest how we *should* behave. We must remember that *ideal* culture always differs from *real* culture—what actually occurs in everyday life. To illustrate, most women and men agree on the importance of sexual fidelity in marriage. Even so, in one study, about 25 percent of married men and 10 percent of married women reported being sexually unfaithful to their spouses at some point in their marriage (Laumann et al., 1994). But a culture's moral prodding is important all the same, calling to mind the old saying "Do as I say, not as I do."

EXERCISE: Consider the cultural significance of a survey of 8- to 12-year-olds whose holiday wish list included a swimming pool, 97%; big-screen TV, 96%; hot tub, 91%; trip to Disney World, 90% (*American Demographics*, 1998).

NOTE: As Donald Kraybill and Marc Olshan (1994) point out, the tension between the Amish and the surrounding society has only increased with the escalation of modern technology.

NOTE: For a detailed discussion of how technology has historically shaped human society, see Chapter 4 ("Society").

NOTE: More complex technology empowers humanity to manipulate the natural world; members of industrial societies therefore risk losing sensitivity to the natural environment and the requirements of living in an ecological system. Look ahead to Chapter 22 ("Population, Urbanization, and Environment").

MATERIAL CULTURE AND TECHNOLOGY

In addition to intangible elements such as values and norms, every culture includes a wide range of tangible (from the Latin word meaning "touchable") human creations, which sociologists call *artifacts*. The Chinese eat with chopsticks rather than knives and forks, the Japanese put mats rather than rugs on the floor, many men and women in India prefer flowing robes to the close-fitting clothing common in the United States. The material culture of a people may seem as strange to outsiders as their language, values, and norms.

A society's artifacts partly reflect underlying cultural values. The warlike Yąnomamö carefully craft their weapons and prize the poison tips on their arrows. By contrast, our society's emphasis on individualism and independence goes a long way toward explaining our high regard for the automobile: We own some 208 million motor vehicles—one for every licensed driver—and, on average, U.S. cars are the biggest in the world. Figure 3–1 shows that, even compared with other high-income nations, the United States stands out as a car-loving nation.

In addition to reflecting values, material culture also reflects a society's **technology,** *knowledge that people use to make a way of life in their surroundings.* The more complex a society's technology, the more its members are able (for better or worse) to shape the world for themselves.

Because we attach great importance to science and praise sophisticated technology, people in our society tend to judge cultures with simpler technology as less advanced. Some facts support such an assessment. For example, life expectancy for children born in the United States now exceeds seventy-six years; the life span of the Yąnomamö is only about forty years.

However, we must be careful not to make self-serving judgments about other cultures. Although many Yąnomamö are eager to acquire modern technology (such as steel tools and shotguns), they are generally well fed by world standards, and most are very satisfied with their lives (Chagnon, 1992). Also, although our powerful and complex technology has produced work-reducing devices and seemingly miraculous medical treatments, it has also contributed to unhealthy levels of stress, degraded the natural environment, and created weapons capable of destroying in a blinding flash everything that humankind has achieved.

Finally, technology is not equally distributed within our population. Although many of us cannot imagine life without personal computers, televisions,

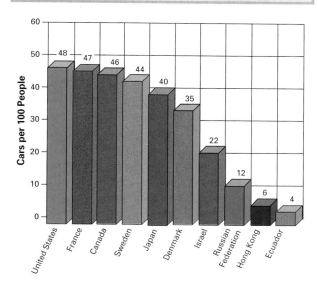

GLOBAL SNAPSHOT

FIGURE 3–1 Car Ownership in Global Perspective
Source: The World Bank (2001).

and CD players, many members of U.S. society cannot afford these luxuries. Others, including the Amish, reject them on principle. These "Plain People," who live in small farming communities across Pennsylvania, Ohio, and Indiana, shun most modern conveniences on religious grounds. With their traditional black garb and horse-drawn buggies, the Amish may seem like a curious relic of the past. Yet their communities flourish, grounded in strong families that give everyone a sense of identity and purpose. Some researchers have studied the Amish only to conclude that these communities are "islands of sanity in a culture gripped by commercialism and technology run wild" (Hostetler, 1980:4; Kraybill, 1994:28).

NEW INFORMATION TECHNOLOGY AND CULTURE

Many high-income nations, including the United States, have entered a postindustrial phase in which an increasing share of economic activity is based on computers and

DISCUSS: The concept of "collective memory" refers to significant events that become part of a people's cultural heritage. Paul Revere's ride, Washington's crossing the Delaware, M.L. King's "I have a dream" speech, and the 9/11 terrorist attacks are examples.

Q: "Cultures are dramatic conversations about things that matter to their participants." Robert Bellah

Q: "It is poor strategy, poor history and poor logic . . . to bemoan . . . 'Anglo' culture. . . . After all, does anyone expect that there is more tolerance for multiculturalism in Tokyo, Caracas, Istanbul, Copenhagen, Mexico City, or Beijing than there is in New York or Los Angeles?" Kenneth T. Jackson

Q: "Every immigrant who comes here should be required within five years to learn English or leave the country." Theodore Roosevelt

CRITICAL THINKING

Virtual Culture: Is It Good for Us?

January 16, Orlando, Florida. Disney World is a delight to the kids but a little disturbing to sociologists. It is ready-made culture: Streets, stores, and events re-create a nineteenth-century small town, populated with Disney characters. Here, life is carefully controlled to ensure a good time, with the ultimate purpose of relieving us of whatever cash we have left.

The Information Revolution is generating symbols—words, sounds, and images—faster than ever before and spreading these symbols across the nation and around the world. What does this new information technology mean for our way of life?

In centuries past, culture was a way of life transmitted from generation to generation. It was a heritage—a society's collective memory—that was authentically our own because it belonged to our ancestors (Schwartz, 1996). But in the emerging cyber-society, more and more cultural symbols are new, intentionally *created* by a small cultural elite of composers, writers, filmmakers, and others who work in the expanding information economy.

To illustrate, consider the changing character of cultural heroes, people who serve as role models and represent cultural ideals. A century ago, our heroes were real men and women who made a difference in the life of this nation: George Washington, Abigail Adams, Betsy Ross, Davy Crockett, Daniel Boone, Abraham Lincoln, and Harriet Tubman. Of course, when a society makes a hero of someone (almost always well after the person has died), they "clean up" the person's biography, highlighting the successes and overlooking the shortcomings. Even so, these people were authentic parts of our history.

Today's youngsters, by contrast, are fed a steady diet of *virtual culture*, images that spring from the minds of contemporary culture makers and reach them via a screen: on television, in the movies, or through computer networks. Today's "heroes" are Crocodile Dundee, Rug Rats, Pokémon, Batman, Barbie, Barney, a continuous flow of Disney characters, and the ever-smiling Ronald McDonald. Some of these cultural icons embody values that shape our way of life. But they have no historical reality, and almost all have been created for a single purpose: to make money.

What do you think?

1. *As the Information Revolution proceeds, do you think virtual culture will become increasingly important? Why or why not?*

2. *Does virtual culture erode or enhance our cultural traditions? Is that good or bad?*

3. *What image of this country do U.S. movies and television shows give to people abroad?*

Source: Thanks to Roland Johnson (1996) for the basic idea for this box.

new information technology. Whereas industrial production is centered on factories and machinery generating material goods, postindustrial production is based on computers and other electronic devices that create, process, store, and apply information.

In an information economy, workers need symbolic skills in place of the mechanical skills of the industrial age. Symbolic skills include the ability to speak, write, compute, design, and create images in art, advertising, and entertainment. New information technology also enables us to *generate culture* on an unprecedented scale. The box takes a closer look.

CULTURAL DIVERSITY: MANY WAYS OF LIFE IN ONE WORLD

In the United States, we are aware of our cultural diversity when we hear the distinctive accents of people from various geographic regions of the country, including New England, the Midwest, and the deep South. Ours is also a nation of religious pluralism, a land of class differences, and a home to individualists who try to be like no one else. Over the centuries, heavy immigration has made the United States the most *multicultural* of all high-income countries. By

NOTE: "Culture" shares a Latin root with the word "cultivate," explaining the view of "cultured" people as highbrows who cultivate their tastes.

NOTE: In *Highbrow, Lowbrow: The Emergence of Cultural Hierarchy in America*, Lawrence Levine claims that until the time of the Civil War, all classes were familiar with poetry and quoted Shakespeare. Then, as class hierarchy grew, so did cultural hierarchy.

Q: "The growth of democracy endowed mass culture with political legitimacy." Paul Jerome Croce

Q: "Highbrow: a person who can listen to the William Tell Overture without thinking of 'The Lone Ranger.'" Jack Perlis

Q: "If Hamlet is broadcast on network television, does it represent popular culture (since millions presumably see it) or elite culture, since it is a classic work of art?" Arthur Asa Berger

GLOBAL SNAPSHOT

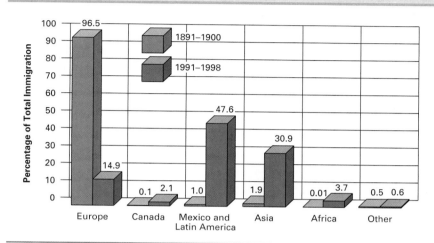

FIGURE 3–2
Recorded Immigration to the United States, by Region of Birth, 1891–1900 and 1991–1998

Sources: U.S. Department of Commerce (1930) and U.S. Immigration and Naturalization Service (1999).

contrast, historic isolation has made Japan the most *monocultural* of all high-income nations.

Between 1820 (when the U.S. government began keeping track of immigration) and 2000, more than 65 million people have come to these shores. Moreover, our cultural mix continues to increase as each year almost 1 million more people arrive. A century ago, as shown in Figure 3–2, almost all immigrants hailed from Europe; today, most newcomers are from Latin America and Asia. To understand the reality of life in the United States, we must move beyond broad cultural patterns and shared values to consider cultural diversity.

HIGH CULTURE AND POPULAR CULTURE

Cultural diversity can involve social class. In fact, in everyday talk, we usually use the word "culture" to mean art forms such as classical literature, music, dance, and painting. We describe people who regularly go to the opera or the theater as "cultured" because we think they appreciate the "finer things in life."

We speak less generously of ordinary people, assuming that everyday culture is somehow less worthy. We are tempted to judge the music of Beethoven as "more cultured" than the blues, couscous as better than cornbread, and polo as more polished than Ping-Pong.

Such judgments imply that many cultural patterns are readily accessible to only some members of a society (Hall & Neitz, 1993). Sociologists use the term **high culture**[1] to refer to *cultural patterns that distinguish a society's elite*; **popular culture** designates *cultural patterns that are widespread among a society's population*. At the same time, because common sense seems to suggest that high culture is superior to popular culture, sociologists prefer the term "culture" to refer to *all* elements of a society's way of life, including patterns of rich and poor alike.

Moreover, we should resist distinctions between high culture and popular culture for two reasons. First, neither elites nor ordinary people share all the same tastes and interests; people in both categories differ in numerous ways. Second, do we praise high culture because it is inherently better than popular culture or simply because its supporters have more money, power, and prestige? For example, there is no difference between a violin and a fiddle; however, we name the instrument one way when it is used to produce music typically enjoyed by a person of higher position and the other way when the musician plays works appreciated by people with lower social standing.

---

[1]The term "high culture" is derived from the term "highbrow." A century ago, people influenced by phrenology—the bogus nineteenth-century notion that personality was affected by the shape of the human skull—praised the tastes of those they called "highbrows" while dismissing the appetites of "lowbrows."

THE MAP: Consumers of wine are higher-income, more educated people who live in urban areas. Beer drinkers (especially those who drink low-cost domestic brands) predominate in rural, lower-income regions. The West is a curious mix of lowbrow locals and highbrow transplants.

DIVERSITY: In terms of sales, salsa has now surpassed catsup as the number-one condiment in the U.S.

DIVERSITY: See the national maps in Chapter 14, which highlight the increasing cultural diversity of the United States.

GLOBAL: Why do people of European background tend to think of people from the Southern Hemisphere as "having rhythm"? The reason is that Western European music emphasizes not rhythm but harmonics. Similarly, European (and U.S.) music has strong bass lines, a trait not found in most of the world's music.

SEEING OURSELVES

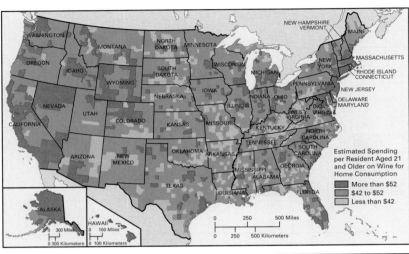

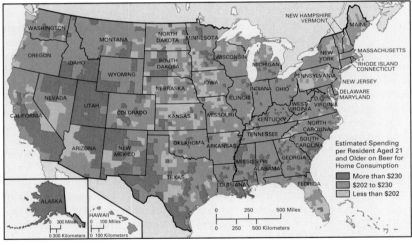

NATIONAL MAP 3–1
What'll Ya Have?
Popular Beverages across the United States

What people consume is one mark of their status as a "highbrow" or "lowbrow." Drinking wine at home is an indicator of highbrow standing. Well-to-do people not only enjoy a glass of wine with dinner but drink water from bottles rather than the tap, prefer Grey Poupon to Gulden's mustard, and favor Häagen-Daz over the local Tastee-Freeze. Drinking beer, on the other hand, marks a person as a "lowbrow." Such a person has a low to moderate income, consumes a good deal of snack foods, and frequents fast-food restaurants. Looking at the maps, where have the "highbrows" and the "lowbrows" created centers of "high culture" and "popular culture"?

Source: *American Demographics* magazine, March 1998, p. 19. Reprinted with permission. © 1998, *American Demographics* magazine, Ithaca, New York.

National Map 3–1 looks at preferred alcoholic beverages to show the distribution of high and popular culture across the United States.

SUBCULTURE

The term **subculture** refers to *cultural patterns that set apart some segment of a society's population.* Young people who enjoy rap music, Polish Americans, frequent-flyer executives, New England Yankees, Colorado cowboys, the southern California beach crowd, jazz musicians, computer "nerds," campus poets, and wilderness campers—all display subcultural patterns.

It is easy, but often inaccurate, to place people in some subcultural category because almost everyone participates in many subcultures without necessarily having much commitment to any of them. In some cases, however, ethnicity and religion set people apart from one another, sometimes with tragic results.

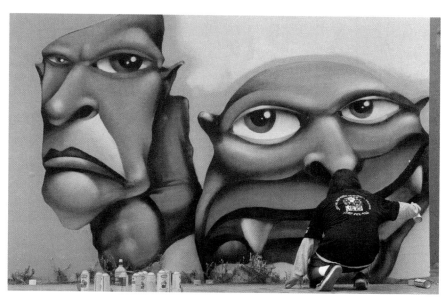

Whether visual expression in lines and color is revered as "art" or dismissed as "graffiti" or even condemned as "vandalism" depends on the social standing of the creator. How would you characterize images such as this one, common in cities across North America? Is this art? Why or why not?

Consider the former nation of Yugoslavia in southeastern Europe. The recent Balkan war is only the latest chapter in a long history of hatred based on cultural differences. Before its breakup, this *one* small country used *two* alphabets, professed *three* religions, spoke *four* languages, was home to *five* major nationalities, was divided into *six* political republics, and absorbed the cultural influences of *seven* surrounding countries. Clearly, subcultures are a source not only of pleasing variety but also of tension and outright violence (cf. Sekulic, Massey, & Hodson, 1994).

Historically, we have viewed the United States as a melting pot where many nationalities blend into a single "American" culture. But given our cultural diversity, how accurate is the "melting pot" image? For one thing, subcultures involve not just *difference* but *hierarchy*. Too often, what we view as "dominant" or "mainstream" culture is a set of patterns favored by powerful segments of the population, and we view the lives of disadvantaged people as "subculture." Some sociologists, therefore, prefer to level the playing field of society by emphasizing multiculturalism.

MULTICULTURALISM

Multiculturalism is *an educational program recognizing the cultural diversity of the United States and promoting the equality of all cultural traditions.* Multiculturalism is a sharp turn away from the past, when our society downplayed cultural diversity and defined itself primarily in terms of its European (and especially English) immigrants. Today, a spirited debate asks whether we should continue to stress these historical traditions or highlight our cultural diversity (Orwin, 1996; Rabkin, 1996).

E pluribus unum, the familiar Latin phrase that appears on all U.S. coins, means "out of many, one." This motto symbolizes not only our national political union but also the idea that immigrants from around the world have come together to form a new way of life.

From the outset, however, the many cultures did not melt together so much as harden into a hierarchy. At the top were the English, who formed a majority early in U.S. history and established English as the nation's dominant language. Further down, people of other backgrounds were advised to model themselves after "their betters." In practice, then, "melting" was really a process of Anglicization (adoption of English ways). As multiculturalists see it, early in our history, this society set up the English way of life as an ideal to which all should aspire and by which all should be judged.

Ever since, historians have reported events from the point of view of the English and other people of European ancestry, paying little attention to the perspectives and accomplishments of Native Americans

DIVERSITY: In the U.S., the need for multicultural skills is greatest among the young. Compare the age-based diversity (in 1999) among people ages 70 to 74 (8.5% African American, 5.6% Latino, 2.5% Asian and Pacific Islander) with the percentages among preschoolers (14.8% African American, 18.3% Latino, 4.8% Asian and Pacific Islander) (U.S. Census Bureau, 2000).

GLOBAL: Problems of multiculturalism arise in other societies as well. Consider Sri Lanka, where Sinhalese and Tamil (different languages using different alphabets) replaced English in an effort to end colonial influences. Within two decades, civil war broke out between the two populations. (But remember that in Germany, both the Jews and the Germans spoke German, and that didn't prevent the Holocaust.)

Any society is actually made up of countless different cultural patterns, some of which may seem strange, indeed, to most people. What cultural values are evident in the pierced noses and tattoos of these two men? Are these values completely at odds with our individualistic way of life?

and people of African and Asian descent. Multiculturalists call this view **Eurocentrism,** *the dominance of European (especially English) cultural patterns.* Molefi Kete Asante, an advocate of multiculturalism, argues that, like "the fifteenth-century Europeans who could not cease believing that the Earth was the center of the universe, many today find it difficult to cease viewing European culture as the center of the social universe" (1988:7).

One contested issue involves language. Some people believe English should be the official language of the United States. By 2001, legislatures in twenty-six states had enacted such laws. But some 45 million men and women—nearly one in six—speak a language

other than English at home. Spanish is the second most commonly spoken language, but several hundred other tongues are also heard across the country, including Italian, German, French, Filipino, Japanese, Korean, Vietnamese, and a host of Native American languages. National Map 3–2 shows where in the United States large numbers of people speak a language other than English at home.

Proponents also paint multiculturalism as a way of coming to terms with our country's increasing social diversity. With the Asian and Hispanic populations of this country increasing rapidly, some analysts predict that today's children will live to see people of African, Asian, and Hispanic ancestry become a *majority* of this country's population.

Proponents also claim that multiculturalism is a good way to strengthen the academic achievement of African American children. To offset Eurocentrism, some multicultural educators are calling for **Afrocentrism,** *the dominance of African cultural patterns,* which they see as a corrective for centuries of minimizing or ignoring the cultural achievements of African societies and African Americans.

Although multiculturalism has found favor in recent years, it has provoked criticism as well. Opponents say it encourages divisiveness rather than unity, urging people to identify with their own category rather than with the nation as a whole. Instead of recognizing any common standards of truth, say critics, multiculturalism maintains that we should evaluate ideas according to the race (and sex) of those who present them. Our common humanity thus dissolves into an "African experience," an "Asian experience," and so on.

The bottom line, say critics, is that multiculturalism does not help minorities, as its supporters claim. Some multicultural policies (from African American studies to all-black dorms) seem to endorse the same racial segregation that our nation has struggled so long to end. Furthermore, in the early grades an Afrocentric curriculum may deny children a wide range of important knowledge and skills by teaching only certain topics from a single point of view. The historian Arthur Schlesinger, Jr. (1991:21), puts the matter bluntly: "If a Kleagle of the Ku Klux Klan wanted to use the schools to handicap black Americans, he could hardly come up with anything more effective than the 'Afrocentric' curriculum."

Is there any common ground in this debate? Almost everyone agrees that we need greater appreciation of our cultural diversity. But precisely where the balance is to be struck—between the *pluribus* and the *unum*—is likely to remain an issue for some time to come.

SEEING OURSELVES

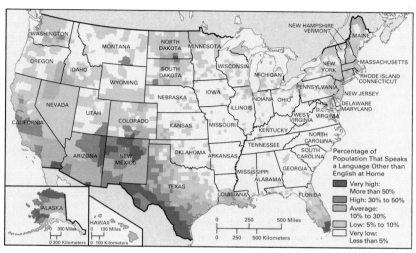

NATIONAL MAP 3–2
Language Diversity across the United States

Of nearly 255 million people over the age of five in the United States, the 2000 census reports that 45 million (18 percent) typically speak a language other than English at home. Of these people, 60 percent speak Spanish, 15 percent use an Asian language, and the remaining 25 percent communicate with some other tongue (the Census Bureau lists 25 languages, each of which is favored by more than 100,000 people in the United States). The map shows that non–English speakers are concentrated in certain regions of the country. Which ones? What do you think accounts for this pattern?

Source: *Time*, January 30, 1995. Copyright © 1995 *Time*, Inc. Reprinted by permission.

COUNTERCULTURE

Cultural diversity also includes outright rejection of conventional ideas or behavior. **Counterculture** consists of *cultural patterns that strongly oppose those widely accepted within a society.*

In many societies, counterculture is linked to youth (Spates, 1976, 1983; Spates & Perkins, 1982). The youth-oriented counterculture of the 1960s, for example, rejected mainstream culture as overly competitive, self-centered, and materialistic. Instead, hippies and other counterculturalists favored a cooperative lifestyle in which "being" took precedence over "doing," and the capacity for personal growth—or "expanded consciousness"—was prized over material possessions such as homes and cars. Such differences led some people to "drop out" of the larger society.

Countercultures are still flourishing. In the 1990s, militaristic bands of men and women, deeply suspicious of the federal government, advocated dropping out of the political system. Countercultural extremism of this kind led to the bombing of the Oklahoma City federal building in 1995, killing 168 people.

CULTURAL CHANGE

Perhaps the most basic human truth of this world is "All things shall pass." Even the dinosaurs, which thrived on this planet for 160 million years (see the time line), remain today only as fossils. Will humanity survive for millions of years to come? All we can say with certainty is that, given our reliance on culture, for as long as we survive, the human record will show continuous change.

Table 3–1 compares student attitudes in 1968 (the height of the 1960s counterculture) and 2000. Some attitudes have changed only slightly. Today, as they did a generation ago, most men and women look forward to raising a family. But today's students are much more interested in making money than in developing a philosophy of life.

Change in one dimension of a culture usually sparks changes in others. For example, women's increased participation in the labor force parallels changing family patterns, including first marriages at a later age and a rising divorce rate. Such connections illustrate the principle of **cultural integration,** *the close relationships among various elements of a cultural system.*

DIVERSITY: Table 3–1 shows that changes in attitudes are generally greater among women than among men. The difference can be traced to the women's movement, which intensified after 1968.

RESOURCE: Another jumping-off point for a discussion of ethnocentrism and cultural relativity is Horace Miner's "Body Ritual among the Nacirema" (*American Anthropologist* 58, 3 (1956):503–7), included in the Macionis and Benokraitis reader, *Seeing Ourselves*.

NOTE: Dietary differences offer illustrations of ethnocentrism. We find the drinking of goat's blood by the Masai of eastern Africa to be revolting; however, few Chinese drink cow's milk, which we consider a very healthful drink.

Q: "There is nothing so vile or repugnant to nature, but you may plead prescription for it in the customs of some nation or other." Tobias Smollett

TABLE 3–1 Attitudes among Students Entering U.S. Colleges, 1968 and 2000

Life Objectives ("Essential" or "Very Important")		1968*	2000	Change
Develop a philosophy of life	Men	79%	43%	−36%
	Women	87	42	−45
Keep up with political affairs	Men	52	32	−20
	Women	52	25	−27
Help others in difficulty	Men	50	53	+ 3
	Women	71	69	− 2
Raise a family	Men	64	73	+ 9
	Women	72	73	+ 1
Be successful in my own business	Men	55	45	−10
	Women	32	35	+ 3
Be very well off financially	Men	51	76	+25
	Women	27	71	+44

*To allow comparisons, data from the early 1970s rather than 1968 are used for some items.

Sources: Richard G. Braungart and Margaret M. Braungart, "From Yippies to Yuppies: Twenty Years of Freshmen Attitudes," *Public Opinion*, vol. 11, no. 3 (September–October 1988): 53–56; Linda J. Sax, Alexander W. Astin, William S. Korn, and Kathryn M. Mahoney, *The American Freshman: National Norms for Fall 2000* (Los Angeles: UCLA Higher Education Research Institute, 2000).

Cultural Lag

Some elements of culture change faster than others. William Ogburn (1964) observed that technology moves quickly, generating new elements of material culture (such as test-tube babies) faster than nonmaterial culture (such as ideas about parenthood) can keep up with them. Ogburn called this inconsistency **cultural lag,** *the fact that some cultural elements change more quickly than others, which may disrupt a cultural system.* How are we to apply traditional notions about motherhood and fatherhood when one woman can give birth to a child using another woman's egg, which has been fertilized in a laboratory with the sperm of a total stranger?

Causes of Cultural Change

Cultural changes are set in motion in three ways. The first is *invention*, the process of creating new cultural elements. Invention has given us the telephone (1876), the airplane (1903), and the computer (the late 1940s), each of which has had a tremendous impact on our

way of life. The process of invention goes on constantly, as indicated by the thousands of applications submitted annually to the U.S. Patent Office. The time line inside the front cover of this text shows other inventions that have changed our way of life.

Discovery, a second cause of cultural change, involves recognizing and better understanding something already in existence—from a distant star, to the foods of another culture, to women's athletic prowess. Many discoveries result from painstaking scientific research, but others are a stroke of luck, as in 1898, when Marie Curie left a rock on a piece of photographic paper, noticed that emissions from the rock exposed the paper, and thus discovered radium.

The third cause of cultural change is *diffusion*, the spread of cultural traits from one society to another. Because new information technology sends information around the globe in seconds, cultural diffusion has never been greater than it is today.

Certainly our own society has contributed many significant cultural elements to the world, ranging from jazz music to computers. Of course, diffusion works the other way, too, so that much of what we assume to be "American" actually comes from elsewhere. Clocks, newspapers, money, most clothing and furniture, and even the English language are derived from other cultures (Linton, 1937a).

ETHNOCENTRISM AND CULTURAL RELATIVISM

December 10, a small village in rural Morocco. Watching many of our shipmates browsing through a tiny ceramic factory, we feel confident in saying that North Americans are among the world's greatest shoppers. We delight in admiring hand-woven carpets in China or India, inspecting finely crafted metals in Turkey, or collecting the beautifully colored porcelain tiles we find here in Morocco. And, of course, all these items are wonderful bargains. But one major reason for the low prices is unsettling: Many products from the world's low- and middle-income countries are produced by children—some as young as five or six—who work long days for extremely low wages.

Q: "No man ever looks at the world with pristine eyes. He sees it edited by a definite set of customs and institutions and ways of thinking." Ruth Benedict
Q: "We have failed to understand the relativity of cultural habits, and we remain debarred from much profit and enjoyment in our human relations with people of different cultural standards, and untrustworthy in our dealings with them." Ruth Benedict

DISCUSS: In 1997, two Iraqi brothers, ages 34 and 28, were charged under Nebraska law with the statutory rape of their wives, ages 13 and 14, whom they married according to Muslim law and the customs of their native southern Iraq. Were the charges appropriate or ethnocentric?
DISCUSS: For a discussion of child labor, look ahead to Global Map 5–1 on page 130.

We think of childhood as a time of innocence and freedom from adult burdens such as regular work. In poor countries throughout the world, however, families depend on income earned by children. So what people in one society think of as right and natural, people elsewhere find puzzling and even immoral. Perhaps the Chinese philosopher Confucius had it right when he noted that "All people are the same; it's only their habits that are different."

Just about every imaginable idea or behavior is commonplace somewhere in the world, and this cultural variation causes travelers equal measures of excitement and distress. The Australians flip light switches down to turn them on, whereas North Americans flip them up; the Japanese name intersections rather than streets, a practice that regularly confuses North Americans, who do the opposite; Egyptians stand very close to others in conversation, which irritates North Americans, used to maintaining several feet of "personal space." In rural Morocco, most bathrooms lack toilet paper, causing considerable consternation among Westerners unaccustomed to using the left hand for bathroom hygiene.

Given that a particular culture is the basis for everyone's reality, it is no wonder that people everywhere exhibit **ethnocentrism,** *the practice of judging another culture by the standards of one's own culture.* Some ethnocentrism is necessary for people to be emotionally attached to their way of life. But ethnocentrism also generates misunderstanding and sometimes conflict.

Even our language is culturally biased. Centuries ago, people in Europe and North America called China the "Far East." But this term, unknown to the Chinese, is an ethnocentric expression for a region that is far east *of us.* The Chinese name for their country translates as "Central Kingdom," suggesting that they, like us, see their own society as the center of the world. The map on page 80 shows ethnocentrism at work in a "down under" view of the Western Hemisphere.

The logical alternative to ethnocentrism is **cultural relativism,** *the practice of evaluating a culture by its own standards.* Cultural relativism is a difficult attitude to adopt: It requires understanding unfamiliar values and norms and suspending cultural standards we have known all our lives. At the same time, as people of the world come into increasing contact with one another, the importance of understanding other cultures becomes ever greater.

Businesses in the United States are learning that success in the global economy depends on cultural awareness. For example, General Motors learned the hard way that its Nova wasn't selling well

Most people in the affluent United States take for granted that childhood should be a carefree time of life devoted to learning and play. In low-income societies of the world, however, poor families depend on the income earned by children, some of whom perform long days of heavy physical labor. We may not want to accept all cultural practices as "natural" just because they exist. But what universal standards can be used to judge social patterns as either right or wrong?

in Spanish-speaking nations because the name in Spanish means "No Go." Coors's phrase "Turn It Loose" startled customers by proclaiming that the beer would cause diarrhea. Braniff Airlines turned "Fly in Leather" into clumsy Spanish reading "Fly Naked." Eastern Airlines transformed its slogan "We Earn Our Wings Daily"

 In two brief videos, the author considers issues of cultural relativism: http://www.TheSociologyPage.com

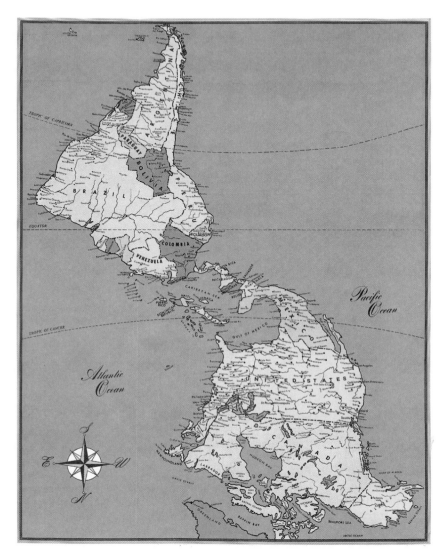

The View from "Down Under"

North America should be "up" and South America "down," or so we think. But, because we live on a globe, such notions are conventions rather than absolutes. The reason that this map of the Western Hemisphere looks wrong to us is not that it is geographically inaccurate; it simply violates our ethnocentric assumption that the United States should be "above" the rest of the Americas.

into "We Fly Every Day to Heaven." Frank Purdue fell victim to poor marketing when his pitch "It Takes a Tough Man to Make a Tender Chicken" ended up as "A Sexually Excited Man Will Make a Chicken Affectionate" in Spanish (Helin, 1992).

But cultural relativism introduces problems of its own. If almost any kind of behavior is normative *somewhere* in the world, does that mean everything is equally right? Does the fact that poor Moroccan families benefit from having their children work long hours justify child labor?

Because we all are members of a single species, surely there must be some universal standards of proper conduct. But what are they? And, in trying to develop them, how can we avoid imposing our own standards of fair play on others? There are no simple answers. But when confronting an unfamiliar cultural practice, resist making judgments before grasping what members of that culture think of the issue. Remember, also, to think about your own way of life as others might see it. After all, what we gain most from studying others is better insight into ourselves.

NOTE: Ralph Linton (1937) first used the term "cultural universals" to refer to cultural traits found throughout a *single* society. The term has come to be used to designate a surprising number of cultural traits common to *all* societies.
NOTE: Anthropology has traditionally focused attention on traits common to all cultures and those unique to one.

DISCUSS: An interesting way to launch a functional analysis of culture is to analyze cultural heroes. What makes an act heroic?
Q: "The function of any recurrent activity, such as the punishment of a crime, or a funeral ceremony, is the part it plays in the social life as a whole and therefore the contribution it makes to the maintenance of the structural continuity." A.R. Radcliffe-Brown, *American Anthropologist* 37 (1935):395–96.

A GLOBAL CULTURE?

Today, more than ever before, we can observe many of the same cultural practices the world over. Walking the streets of Seoul (South Korea), Kuala Lumpur (Malaysia), Madras (India), Cairo (Egypt), and Casablanca (Morocco), we find jeans, hear familiar pop music, and see advertising for many of the same products we use at home. Recall from Global Map 3–1 that English is rapidly emerging as the preferred second language of most of the world. Are we witnessing the birth of a single global culture?

It is true that societies around the world have more contact with one another than ever before, involving the flow of goods, information, and people:

1. **The global economy: the flow of goods.** There has never been more international trade. The global economy has spread many of the same consumer goods (from cars and TV shows to music and fashions) throughout the world.

2. **Global communication: the flow of information.** Satellite-based communication enables people to experience the sights and sounds of events taking place thousands of miles away, often as they happen.

3. **Global migration: the flow of people.** Knowing about the rest of the world motivates people to move where they imagine life will be better. Moreover, today's transportation technology, especially air travel, makes relocating easier than ever before. As a result, in most countries, significant numbers of people were born elsewhere (including some 30 million people who are now in the United States, 11 percent of the population).

These global links make the cultures of the world more similar. But there are three important limitations to the global culture thesis. First, the global flow of goods, information, and people is uneven. Generally speaking, urban areas (centers of commerce, communication, and people) have stronger ties to one another, and rural villages remain isolated. Furthermore, the greater economic and military power of North America and Western Europe means that these regions influence the rest of the world more than happens the other way around.

Second, the global culture thesis assumes that people everywhere are able to afford various new goods and services. As Chapter 12 ("Global Stratification") explains, desperate poverty in much of the world deprives people of even the basic necessities of a safe and secure life.

Third, although many cultural practices are found throughout the world, people everywhere do not attach the same meanings to them. Do teenagers in Tokyo understand hip hop the way their counterparts in New York or Los Angeles do? Similarly, we enjoy foods from around the world while knowing little about the lives of the people who created them. In short, people everywhere look at the world through their own cultural lenses (Featherstone, 1990; Hall & Neitz, 1993).

THEORETICAL ANALYSIS OF CULTURE

Culture helps us make sense of ourselves and the surrounding world. And sociologists have the special task of comprehending culture. They use several theoretical approaches.

STRUCTURAL-FUNCTIONAL ANALYSIS

The structural-functional paradigm depicts culture as a complex strategy for meeting human needs. Borrowing from the philosophical doctrine of *idealism*, this approach considers values as the core of a culture (Parsons, 1966; Williams, 1970). In other words, cultural values give meaning to life and bind people together. Countless other aspects of culture function in various ways to support a way of life.

Thinking functionally helps us understand an unfamiliar way of life. Take, for example, the Amish farmer plowing hundreds of acres of an Ohio farm with a team of horses. His farming methods may violate our cultural value of efficiency, but from the Amish point of view, hard work functions to develop the discipline necessary for a highly religious way of life. Long days of working together make the Amish self-sufficient while unifying families and communities.

Of course, Amish practices have dysfunctions as well. The hard work and strict religious discipline are too demanding for some, who end up leaving the community. Then, too, religious devotion sometimes prevents compromise, resulting in lasting divisions within the Amish world (Hostetler, 1980; Kraybill, 1989; Kraybill & Olshan, 1994).

If cultures are strategies for meeting human needs, we would expect to find many common patterns around the world. **Cultural universals** are *traits that are part of*

NOTE: More detailed analysis of the social conflict approach to society is found in the section of Chapter 4 ("Society") dealing with the work of Karl Marx.

RESOURCE: Dianne Herman's gender conflict article "The Rape Culture" is a selection in the Macionis and Benokraitis reader.

Q: "To most people a savage nation is one that wears comfortable clothes." Finley Peter Dunne

RESOURCE: David Barash's *The Whispering Within* (1981) clearly probes the politics of sociobiology (see Chapter 8).

EXERCISE: Consider ways in which humans, as cultural creatures, differ from other animals. List pairs of terms that fit the following sentence: "Although all forms of life have _____, only human beings have _____." Examples: consciousness, self-consciousness; violence, prejudice; self-preservation, awareness of mortality.

Following the structural-functional paradigm, what do you make of the Amish practice of "barn raising," by which everyone in a community joins together to raise a family's new barn in a day? Why is such a ritual almost unknown in rural areas outside of Amish communities?

every known culture. Comparing hundreds of cultures, George Murdock (1945) identified dozens of cultural universals. One common element is the family, which functions everywhere to control sexual reproduction and oversee the care of children. Funeral rites, too, are found everywhere, because all human communities cope with the reality of death. Jokes are another cultural universal, serving as a safe means of releasing social tensions.

Critical evaluation. The strength of the structural-functional paradigm is showing how culture operates to meet human needs. Yet, by emphasizing a society's dominant cultural patterns, this approach largely ignores cultural diversity. Moreover, because this approach emphasizes cultural stability, it downplays the importance of change. In short, cultural systems are not as stable or as free of conflict as structural functionalism leads us to believe.

SOCIAL-CONFLICT ANALYSIS

The social-conflict paradigm stresses the link between culture and inequality. From this point of view, any cultural trait benefits some members of society at the expense of others.

We might well begin a conflict analysis by asking why certain values dominate a society in the first place. Many conflict theorists, especially Marxists, argue that culture is shaped by a society's system of economic production. "It is not the consciousness of men that determines their being," Marx asserted, "it is their social being that determines their consciousness" (Marx & Engels, 1978:4; orig. 1859). Social-conflict theory, then, is rooted in the philosophical doctrine of *materialism*, which holds that a society's system of material production (such as our own industrial-capitalist economy) has a powerful effect on the rest of a culture. This materialist approach contrasts with the idealist leanings of structural functionalism.

Social-conflict analysis ties our competitive values to our society's capitalist economy, which serves the interests of our nation's wealthy elite. The culture of capitalism further teaches us to think that rich and powerful people have more energy and talent than others and therefore deserve their wealth and privileges. Viewing capitalism as somehow "natural" also discourages efforts to reduce economic disparity.

Eventually, however, the strains of inequality erupt into movements for social change. Two recent examples in the United States are the civil rights movement and the women's movement. Both seek greater equality, and both encounter opposition from defenders of the status quo.

Critical evaluation. The social-conflict paradigm proposes that cultural systems do not address human needs

Q: "Although the genes have given away most of their sovereignty, they maintain a certain amount of influence in at least the behavioral qualities that underlie the variations between cultures." Edward O. Wilson

NOTE: Scientists discovered 50 years ago that DNA (deoxyribonucleic acid) is analogous to a 3-billion-bit-long computer program, shaped like a double helix, that generates protein and transmits human heredity. Scientists expect to complete the mapping of human DNA early in the 21st century. As this work proceeds, we will learn much more about how genetics affects human culture.

NOTE: From the point of view of sociobiology, genes use bodies (and societies) to create more genes. Thus, the chicken and egg dilemma is solved in the following way: Eggs come first; eggs use chickens to create more eggs.

Using an evolutionary perspective, sociobiologists point to a double standard by which men treat women as sexual objects more than women treat men that way. While this may be so, many sociologists counter that behavior—such as that shown in Ruth Orkin's photograph, American Girl in Italy—*is more correctly understood as resulting from a culture of male domination.*

Copyright 1952, 1980 Ruth Orkin/Getty Images, Inc.

equally, allowing some people to dominate others. This inequity, in turn, generates pressure toward change.

Yet, by stressing the divisiveness of culture, this paradigm understates the ways in which cultural patterns integrate members of society. Therefore, we should consider both social-conflict and structural-functional insights for a fuller understanding of culture.

SOCIOBIOLOGY

We know culture is a human creation, but does human biology influence how culture unfolds? A third theoretical paradigm, standing with one leg in biology and one in sociology, is **sociobiology**, *a theoretical paradigm that explores ways in which human biology affects how we create culture.*

Sociobiology rests on the theory of evolution proposed by Charles Darwin (1859) in his book *On the Origin of Species.* Darwin asserted that living organisms change over long periods of time as a result of *natural selection*, a matter of four simple principles. First, all living things live to reproduce themselves. Second, the blueprint for reproduction is in the genes, the basic units of life that carry traits of one generation into the next. Third, random variation in genes allows a species to "try out" new life patterns in a particular environment. This variation allows some organisms to survive better than others and pass on their advantageous genes to their offspring. Finally, over thousands of generations, the genetic patterns that promote reproduction survive and become dominant. In this way, as biologists say, a species *adapts* to its environment, and dominant traits emerge as the "nature" of the organism.

Sociobiologists claim that the large number of cultural universals reflects the fact that all humans are members of a single biological species. It is our common biology that underlies, for example, the apparently universal "double standard" of sexual behavior. As sex researcher Alfred Kinsey put it, "Among all people everywhere in the world, the male is more likely than the female to desire sex with a variety of partners" (quoted in Barash, 1981:49). But why?

We all know that children result from joining a woman's egg with a man's sperm. But the biological importance of a single sperm and of a single egg are quite different. For healthy men, sperm are a renewable resource produced by the testes throughout most of the life course. A man releases hundreds of millions of sperm in a single ejaculation—technically, enough to fertilize every woman in North America (Barash, 1981:47). A newborn female's ovaries, however, contain her entire lifetime allotment of follicles, or immature eggs. A woman generally releases a single egg cell from her ovaries each month. So, whereas a man is biologically capable of fathering thousands of offspring, a woman is able to bear only a small number of children.

Q: Father, mother, and me,
  Sister and Auntie say
  All the people are like We,
  And everyone else is They.
  And They live over the sea
  While We live over the way,
  But—would you believe it?—they look upon We

As only a sort of They!?
Rudyard Kipling, "We and They"

NOTE: The final section of Chapter 5 ("Socialization") explores the "constraint versus freedom" controversy.

Q: "The child that is born into any society finds that most of the problems . . . confronted in the course of . . . life have already been met and solved by those who have lived before." Ralph Linton

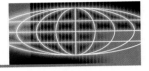

GLOBAL SOCIOLOGY

The United States and Canada: Are They Culturally Different?

To many people in the United States, this country *is* "America." But, to the north lies another large, high-income nation: Canada. How does the culture of Canada compare with U.S. culture?

One important point to make at the start is that both nations are *multicultural*. Just as immigration has brought people to the United States from all over the world, it has done the same in Canada. Also as in the United States, most early immigrants came from Europe, and most recent immigrants have come from Asia and Latin America. Vancouver, for example, on the western Canadian coast, has a large Chinese community on the same order as the Spanish community in Los Angeles.

Canada and the United States differ in one important respect. Historically, Canada has had *two* dominant cultures: French (about 25 percent of the population) and British (roughly 40 percent). People of French ancestry are a large majority of the province of Quebec (where French is the official language) and a large minority of New Brunswick (which is officially bilingual).

Otherwise, do Canada and the United States share the same dominant values? Seymour Martin Lipset (1985) finds that the two nations differ to some degree. The United States declared independence from Great Britain in 1776; Canada formally separated from Great Britain only in 1982. Thus, Lipset continues, the dominant culture of Canada lies somewhere between the cultures of the United States and Great Britain.

For example, the culture of the United States is more individualistic, whereas Canada's is more collective. In the United States, individualism is seen in the historical importance of the cowboy—a self-sufficient person—and even outlaws such as Jessie James and Billy the Kid are looked on as heroes because they bucked authority. In Canada, by contrast, it is the Mountie—Canada's well-known police officer—who is looked on with great respect.

Politically, people in the United States tend to think individuals ought to do things for themselves. In Canada, however, there is a strong sense that government should look after the interests of everyone, much as there is in Great Britain. This is one reason, for example, that Canada has a much broader social welfare system (including universal health care) than the United States (the only high-income nation without such a program). Likewise, about half of all U.S. households own one or more guns, and the idea that individuals are entitled to own a gun is strong—although controversial—in this country. In Canada, few households have a gun, and government greatly restricts gun ownership, as in Great Britain.

Sources: Lipset (1985) and Macionis & Gerber (2001).

Given this biological difference, men reproduce their genes most efficiently by being promiscuous, readily engaging in sex. However, this scheme opposes the reproductive interests of women. Each of a woman's pregnancies demands that she carry the child for nine months, give birth, and provide care for some time afterward. Therefore, efficient reproduction on the part of the woman depends on carefully selecting a mate whose qualities (beginning with the likelihood that he will simply stay around) will contribute to their child's survival and, later, successful reproduction (Remoff, 1984).

The "double standard" certainly involves more than biology and is tangled up with the historical domination of women by men (Barry, 1983). But sociobiology suggests that this cultural pattern, like many others, has an underlying bio-logic. Simply put, the double standard exists around the world because women and men everywhere tend toward distinctive reproductive strategies.

Critical evaluation. Sociobiology has generated intriguing theories about the biological roots of some cultural patterns. But the approach remains controversial for several reasons.

First, some critics fear that sociobiology may revive biological arguments from a century ago that touted the superiority of one race or sex. But defenders counter that sociobiology rejects the past pseudoscience of racial superiority. In fact, sociobiology unites all of humanity because all people share a single evolutionary history. Sociobiology does assert that

Q: "What is truth on one side of the Pyrenees is error on the other."
Blaise Pascal (17th-century philosopher and mathematician)
GLOBAL: "Travel" implies a commitment to learn; its root is the
same as "travail," or work. "Touring" implies a passive observation
of the unfamiliar; literally, this word means simply going in a circle.
Q: "Don't be so open minded that your brains fall out." Richard
Rorty

NOTE: Chemists tell us that only 92 elements occur naturally on
the earth, but sociologists know that the world is home to countless
variations of human culture.
Q: "The problem with other cultures is that other people don't behave the way we expect them to, that is, like us." Craig Storti
Q: "Absolute truth can belong to only one class of humans . . . the
class of absolute fools." Ashley Montagu

men and women differ biologically in some ways that culture cannot overcome. But, far from claiming that males are somehow more important than females, sociobiology emphasizes that both sexes are vital to human reproduction.

Second, say the critics, sociobiologists have little evidence to support their theories. Research to date suggests that biological forces do not determine human behavior in any rigid sense. Rather, humans *learn* behavior within a cultural system. The contribution of sociobiology, then, lies in explaining why some cultural patterns are learned more readily than others (Barash, 1981).

CULTURE AND HUMAN FREEDOM

Underlying the discussion in this chapter is an important question: To what extent are cultural creatures free? Does culture bind us to each other and to the past? Or does culture enhance our capacity for individual thought and independent choices?

CULTURE AS CONSTRAINT

Humans cannot live without culture. But the capacity for culture does have some drawbacks. We may be the only animals who name ourselves, but living in a symbolic world means that we are also the only creatures who experience alienation. Moreover, culture is largely a matter of habit, limiting our choices and driving us to repeat troubling patterns, such as racial prejudice, in each new generation. In addition, in this age of new information technology, we may wonder at the extent to which business-dominated media manipulate our culture in pursuit of profits.

Finally, our society's emphasis on competitive achievement urges us toward excellence, yet this pattern also isolates us from one another. Material things comfort us in some ways but divert us from the security and satisfaction that come from close relationships and spiritual strength.

CULTURE AS FREEDOM

For better or worse, human beings are cultural creatures, just as ants and bees are prisoners of their biology. But there is a crucial difference. Biological instincts create a ready-made world; culture, by contrast, forces us to choose as we make and remake a world for ourselves. No better evidence of this freedom exists than the cultural diversity of our own society and the even greater human diversity around the world.

Learning more about this cultural diversity is one goal shared by sociologists. The final box offers some contrasts between the cultures of the United States and Canada. But, wherever we may live, the better we understand the workings of the surrounding culture, the better prepared we are to use the freedom it offers us.

SUMMARY

1. Culture is a way of life shared by members of a society. Several species have limited capacity for culture, but only human beings rely on culture for survival.

2. As the human brain evolved, the first elements of culture appeared some 3 million years ago; culture replaced biological instincts as our species' primary strategy for survival.

3. Culture relies on symbols. Language is the symbolic system by which one generation transmits culture to the next.

4. Values are culturally defined standards of what ought to be; beliefs are statements that people who share a culture hold to be true.

5. Cultural norms, which guide human behavior, are of two kinds: Mores have great moral significance, whereas folkways are everyday matters of politeness.

6. High culture consists of patterns that distinguish a society's elite; popular culture consists of widespread social patterns.

7. The United States stands among the most culturally diverse societies in the world. Subculture consists of distinctive cultural patterns supported by some part of a population, and counterculture of patterns strongly at odds with a conventional way of life. Multiculturalism is an educational effort to enhance awareness and appreciation of cultural diversity.

8. Invention, discovery, and diffusion all generate cultural change. Cultural lag results as some parts of a cultural system change faster than others.

9. Ethnocentrism involves judging others by the standards of one's own culture. By contrast, cultural relativism means evaluating another culture according to its own standards.

10. Global cultural patterns result from the worldwide flow of goods, information, and people.

11. Structural-functional analysis views culture as a generally stable system built on core values. Cultural patterns function to maintain the overall system.

12. The social-conflict paradigm envisions culture as a dynamic arena of inequality and conflict. Cultural patterns benefit some categories of people more than others.

13. Sociobiology studies how evolution shapes the human creation of culture.

14. Culture can constrain social possibilities, yet as cultural creatures, we have the capacity to shape and reshape our world to meet our needs and pursue our dreams.

KEY CONCEPTS

culture (p. 61) the values, beliefs, behavior, and material objects that, together, form a people's way of life

nonmaterial culture (p. 61) the intangible world of ideas created by members of a society

material culture (p. 61) the tangible things created by members of a society

culture shock (p. 61) personal disorientation when experiencing an unfamiliar way of life

symbols (p. 63) anything that carries a particular meaning recognized by people who share culture

language (p. 65) a system of symbols that allows people to communicate with one another

cultural transmission (p. 65) the process by which one generation passes culture to the next

Sapir-Whorf thesis (p. 65) the thesis that people perceive the world through the cultural lens of language

values (p. 67) culturally defined standards by which people assess desirability, goodness, and beauty and that serve as broad guidelines for social living

beliefs (p. 67) specific statements that people hold to be true

norms (p. 69) rules and expectations by which a society guides the behavior of its members

mores (p. 70) norms that are widely observed and have great moral significance

folkways (p. 70) norms for routine, casual interaction

social control (p. 70) various means by which members of a society encourage conformity to norms

technology (p. 71) knowledge that people use to make a way of life in their surroundings

high culture (p. 73) cultural patterns that distinguish a society's elite

popular culture (p. 73) cultural patterns that are widespread among a society's population

subculture (p. 74) cultural patterns that set apart some segment of a society's population

multiculturalism (p. 75) an educational program recognizing the cultural diversity of the United States and promoting the equality of all cultural traditions

Eurocentrism (p. 76) the dominance of European (especially English) cultural patterns

Afrocentrism (p. 76) the dominance of African cultural patterns

counterculture (p. 77) cultural patterns that strongly oppose those widely accepted within a society

cultural integration (p. 77) the close relationships among various elements of a cultural system

cultural lag (p. 78) the fact that some cultural elements change more quickly than others, which may disrupt a cultural system

ethnocentrism (p. 79) the practice of judging another culture by the standards of one's own culture

cultural relativism (p. 79) the practice of evaluating a culture by its own standards

cultural universals (p. 81) traits that are part of every known culture

sociobiology (p. 83) a theoretical paradigm that explores ways in which human biology affects how we create culture

CRITICAL-THINKING QUESTIONS

1. In the United States, hot dogs, hamburgers, French fries, and ice cream have long been considered national favorites. What cultural patterns help explain the love for these kinds of foods?

Q: "Society is indeed a contract between those who are living, those who are dead, and those who are yet to be born." Edmund Burke

CTQ2: All these games express individual competition, with singular winners and many losers.

CTQ3: Certainly, some degree of global culture is emerging, evidenced by the spread of trade, information, and rising migration. Supporters see global culture as a "convergence" that encourages poor nations to develop economically. Critics see global "McCulture" as the spread of Western ideas and capitalist markets to the advantage of rich nations but not poor nations.

CTQ4: Almost everyone is a member of several subcultures, defined by region, interests, ethnicity, or accident. But most are memberships of limited liability that do not define people in the sense of a master status.

2. What cultural lessons do games such as King of the Mountain, Tag, or Keep-Away teach our children? What about a schoolroom spelling bee? What cultural values are expressed by children's stories such as *The Little Engine That Could* and board games such as "Chutes and Ladders," "Monopoly," and "Risk"?

3. To what extent, in your opinion, is a global culture emerging? Do you regard the prospect of a global culture as positive or negative? Why?

4. Have you ever identified with one or more subcultures? If so, which? How are they distinctive?

APPLICATIONS AND EXERCISES

1. Try to find someone on campus who has lived in another country. Ask for a chance to discuss how the culture of that society differs from the way of life here. Does the other person see U.S. culture differently from most of us?

2. Make a list of words with the prefix *self* (*self-service, self-image, self-esteem, self-destructive,* and so on); there are hundreds of them. What does this high number suggest about our way of life?

3. An easy way to study popular culture is to pick up a number of superhero comic books. Examine them to see why some people are defined as heroes and others as villains. Does gender figure in this process? (cf. Hall & Lucal, 1999)

4. Watch a Disney film such as *The Little Mermaid, Aladdin, Pocahontas,* or *Mulan.* All of these films share cultural themes, which explains their popularity. According to these films, how should young people behave toward their parents? What makes these films especially "American"?

5. Packaged in the back of this new textbook is an interactive CD-ROM that offers a variety of study and review materials intended to help you better understand the material covered in this chapter. For this chapter, the CD-ROM contains an author's video, Real Life Sociology videos, other relevant audio and video, interactive map animations, audio journal entries from the author, Web links, and much more.

SITES TO SEE

http://www.prenhall.com/macionis
Visit the interactive *Companion Website*™ that accompanies this text. Begin by clicking on the cover of your book. You will find a chapter-by-chapter study guide, practice tests, and a significant portion of the text for on-line review, as well as many suggested Web links.

http://www.macionis.com
(or http://www.TheSociologyPage.com)
Visit the author's Web page to view short videos on the lessons and challenges of traveling in an unfamiliar setting.

http://www.nationalgeographic.com
Visit the Web site for the National Geographic Society.

This site offers information on world cultures, including search engines and a library of maps.

http://www.gorilla.org
The Gorilla Foundation operates a Web site where you can follow the progress researchers are making in teaching a 450-pound gorilla named Koko to use sign language.

http://www.aaanet.org
Anthropologists study cultures all over the world. This is the Web site for the American Anthropological Association, where you can find out more about this discipline, which is closely related to sociology.

INVESTIGATE WITH CONTENTSELECT

Follow the instructions found on page 23 of this textbook to enter this chapter of the book's *Companion Website*™. Once in the chapter, click on the ContentSelect icon at the bottom left of your screen and enter your personal User ID and Password. Enter keywords such as "Amish," "multiculturalism," and "immigration," and the search engine will help you become an effective researcher.

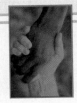

CHAPTER

4

Tosa (attributed to)
People along the River
Detail from screen representing the River Festival. 17th century. Painting on paper. Photo: Arnaudet. Musée des Arts
Asiatiques–Guimet, Paris, France. Réunion des Musées Nationaux/Art Resource, N.Y.

SOCIETY

Sididi Ag Inaka has never logged on to the Internet, sent a fax, or even spoken on a cell phone. In today's high-technology world, these facts may seem strange enough. But neither Inaka nor anyone else in his family has ever seen a television or read a newspaper.

Who are these people? They are Tuareg nomads who wander the vastness of the Sahara in western Africa, north of the city of Timbuktu in the nation we know as Mali. Known as the "blue men of the desert" for the flowing blue robes worn by both men and women, the Tuareg herd camels, goats, and sheep and live in camps where the sand blows and the daytime temperature often reaches 120 degrees. Life is hard, but most try to

hold onto traditional ways. With a look of determination, Inaka says, "My father was a nomad, his father was a nomad, I am a nomad, my children will be nomads."

The Tuaregs are among the poorest people of the world, living a simple and difficult existence. When the rains fail to come, they and their animals are at risk for their lives. Inaka and his people are a society set apart, isolated from the rest of humanity and nearly untouched by modern ideas and advanced technology. To many, no doubt, they seem a curious throwback to the past. But Inaka does not complain: "This is the life of my ancestors. This is the life that we know" (Buckley, 1996; Matloff, 1997; Lovgren, 1998).

Many kinds of human societies have existed in the past, and we still find remarkable diversity today, as the story of the Tuareg shows. But what is a society? How and why have societies changed over the course of human history?

Society is *people who interact in a defined territory and share culture.* In this chapter, we shall examine this deceptively simple term from four different angles. We begin with **Gerhard Lenski,** who described the changing character of human societies over the last 10,000 years. He explained the importance of *technology* and its revolutionary consequences for social life. Then we turn to three of sociology's founders. **Karl Marx,** like Lenski, understood human history as a long and complex process. For Marx, however, the story of society centered on *social conflict* that arises from how people produce material goods. **Max Weber** took another approach, showing that the power of *ideas* also shapes society. Weber contrasted the traditional thinking of simple societies with the rational thought that dominates our modern way of life. Finally, **Emile Durkheim** helped us see the different

ways in which traditional and modern societies hang together.

All four visions of society answer important questions: What makes people like the Tuareg of the Sahara so different from the society familiar to us? How and why do all societies change? What forces divide a society? What forces hold it together? Finally, after looking at the trends over time, we conclude this chapter by asking whether societies are getting better or worse.

GERHARD LENSKI: SOCIETY AND TECHNOLOGY

Members of our society, who take telephones and television as well as schools and hospitals for granted, must wonder at the nomads of the Sahara, who live the same simple life their ancestors did centuries ago. The work of Gerhard Lenski (Lenski, Nolan, & Lenski, 1995; Nolan & Lenski, 1999) helps us understand the great differences among societies that have flourished and declined throughout human history.

SUPPLEMENTS: The *Data File* provides an outline of Chapter 4 along with discussion questions and supplementary lecture material.

NOTE: Use this chapter in any number of ways. Assign all of it to give students a detailed introduction to important historical material and key theorists whose ideas inform later chapters. Or assign sections separately along with later chapters: Use the Weber section to preface the discussion of bureaucracy in Chapter 7, the Durkheim section before the structural-functional analysis of deviance in Chapter 8, and the Marx section before discussion of social inequality in Chapter 10. Instructors may also omit the chapter entirely without breaking the flow of the text.

NOTE: Gerhard Lenski is well known for his research on religion, social inequality, and history.

Drawing on Lenski's work, we will describe five types of societies according to their technology: hunting and gathering societies, horticultural and pastoral societies, agrarian societies, industrial societies, and postindustrial societies.

HUNTING AND GATHERING SOCIETIES

The simplest of all kinds of societies live by **hunting and gathering,** *the use of simple tools to hunt animals and gather vegetation.* From the emergence of our species 3 million years ago until just 12,000 years ago, *all* humans were hunters and gatherers. Even in 1800, there were many hunting and gathering societies in the world. Today, however, just a few remain, including the Aka and Pygmies of central Africa, the Bushmen of southwestern Africa, the Aborigines of Australia, the Kaska Indians of northwest Canada, and the Batek and Semai of Malaysia (Endicott, 1992; Hewlett, 1992).

With little control over their environment, hunters and gatherers spend most of their time searching for game and collecting edible plants. Only in lush areas where food is plentiful do hunters and gatherers have leisure time. Moreover, it takes a lot of land to support even a few people, so hunting and gathering societies are small bands with a few dozen members. They must also be nomadic, moving on as they deplete vegetation in an area or follow migratory animals. Although they return periodically to favored sites, they rarely form permanent settlements.

Hunting and gathering societies are built on kinship. The family obtains and distributes food, protects its members, and teaches the children. Everyone's life is much the same and is focused on getting the next meal. There is some specialization related to age and gender. The very young and the very old contribute what they can, and healthy adults secure most of the food. Women gather vegetation—the most reliable food source—and men take on the less certain task of hunting. Although men and women perform different tasks, most hunters and gatherers probably saw the sexes as having about the same social importance (Leacock, 1978).

Hunting and gathering societies have few formal leaders. Most recognize a *shaman,* or spiritual leader, who enjoys high prestige but receives no greater material rewards and must work to find food like everyone else. In short, hunting and gathering societies are egalitarian.

Hunters and gatherers use simple weapons—the spear, bow and arrow, and stone knife—but rarely to

In technologically simple societies, successful hunting wins men great praise. However, the gathering of vegetation by women is a more dependable and easily available source of nutrition.

Lenski uses the term **sociocultural evolution** to refer to *the changes that occur as a society acquires new technology.* Societies with simple technology, such as the Tuareg, have little control over nature, so they can support only a small number of people. Technologically complex societies, though not necessarily better, support large numbers of people who live highly specialized lives.

In addition, the more technological information a society has, the faster it changes. Technologically simple societies change very slowly; Sididi Ag Inaka says he "lives the life of his ancestors." Modern, high-technology societies, on the other hand, change so quickly that dramatic transformations can occur during a single lifetime. Imagine asking someone who lived just a few generations ago for his or her opinion of beepers, phone sex, artificial hearts, test-tube babies, genetic engineering, e-mail, smart bombs, space shuttles, the threat of nuclear holocaust, transsexualism, computer hackers, and "tell all" talk shows.

In short, new technology sends ripples of change through a society's entire way of life. When our ancestors first discovered how to harness the power of the wind using a sail, they set the stage for building sailing ships, which took them to new lands, stimulated trade, and increased their military might. As a more recent example, consider how our lives are being changed by the spread of computer technology.

Pastoralism historically has flourished in regions of the world where arid soil does not support crops. Pastoral people still thrive in northern Africa, living today much as they did a thousand years ago.

wage war. Their real enemy is the forces of nature: Storms and droughts can destroy their food supply, and there is little they can do in the event of accident or illness. Such vulnerability encourages cooperation and sharing, raising everyone's odds of survival. Nonetheless, many die in childhood, and no more than half reach age twenty (Lenski, Nolan, & Lenski, 1995:104).

During the twentieth century, technologically complex societies slowly closed in on the few remaining hunters and gatherers, reducing their food supply. Lenski claims that hunting and gathering societies are now disappearing from the Earth. Fortunately, study of this way of life has produced valuable information about human history and our fundamental ties to the natural world.

HORTICULTURAL AND PASTORAL SOCIETIES

Ten to twelve thousand years ago, a new technology began to change the lives of human beings (see the time line inside the front cover). People discovered **horticulture,** *the use of hand tools to raise crops.* Using a hoe to work the soil and a digging stick to punch holes in the ground to plant seeds may seem simple and obvious, but horticulture allowed people to give up gathering in favor of "growing their own." Humans first planted gardens in the fertile regions of the Middle East and then in Latin America and Asia. Within 5,000 years, cultural diffusion spread knowledge of horticulture throughout most of the world.

Not all societies abandoned hunting and gathering in favor of horticulture. Hunters and gatherers living amid plentiful vegetation and game probably took little note of the new technology (Fisher, 1979). Then, too, people inhabiting arid regions (such as the Sahara in western Africa or the Middle East) or mountainous areas found horticulture of little value. Such people (including the Tuareg) turned to **pastoralism,** *the domestication of animals.* Today, societies that mix horticulture and pastoralism thrive in South America, Africa, and Asia.

Domesticating plants and animals greatly increased food production, so societies could support not dozens but hundreds of people. Pastoralists remained nomadic, leading their herds to fresh grazing lands. Horticulturalists, by contrast, formed settlements, moving only when they depleted the soil. Joined by trade, these settlements formed societies with populations climbing into the thousands.

Once a society is capable of producing a *material surplus*—more resources than needed to support day-to-day living—not everyone has to secure food. Some make crafts, engage in trade, cut hair, apply tattoos, or

NOTE: *Hort* is a Latin root meaning "garden." Latin *horti cultura* thus means "cultivation of a garden"; *agri cultura* means "cultivation of a field." "Pastoral" is derived from the Latin meaning "shepherd" or, literally, "feeder."

NOTE: Horticulturalists practice *slash and burn* or *swidden* horticulture. This practice involves regular clearing of new land as land in use suffers depleted nutrients.

NOTE: Warfare is probably more common among horticulturalists and rare among hunting and gathering people because increasing population density limits available land and game.

Q: "You can lead a horticulture, but you can't make her think." Dorothy Parker

NOTE: Probably the "oldest profession" is not prostitution but shamanism.

Of Egypt's 130 pyramids, the Great Pyramids at Giza are the largest. Each of the three major structures stands more than forty stories high and is composed of 3 million massive stone blocks. Some 4,500 years ago, tens of thousands of people labored to construct these pyramids so that one man, the pharaoh, might have a godlike monument for his tomb. Clearly social inequality in this agrarian society was striking.

serve as priests. Compared with hunting and gathering societies, then, horticultural and pastoral societies are more specialized and complex.

Hunters and gatherers believe many spirits inhabit the world. Horticulturalists practice ancestor worship and conceive of God as Creator. Pastoral societies carry this belief further, seeing God directly involved in the well-being of the entire world. This view of God ("The Lord is my shepherd," Psalm 23) is widespread among members of our own society because Christianity, Islam, and Judaism all began as Middle Eastern pastoral religions.

Expanding productive technology creates social inequality. As some families produce more food than others, they assume positions of power and privilege. Forging alliances—including marriage—with other elite families allows social advantages to endure over generations. Along with social hierarchy, simple government, backed by military force, emerges to shore up the dominance of elites. However, without the ability to communicate or to travel over large distances, a ruler can control only a small number of people, so there is little empire building.

Domestication of plants and animals made simpler societies more productive. But advancing technology is never entirely beneficial. Lenski points out that, compared with hunters and gatherers, horticulturalists and pastoralists have more social inequality and, in many cases, engage in slavery, protracted warfare, and even cannibalism.

AGRARIAN SOCIETIES

About 5,000 years ago, another technological revolution was underway in the Middle East and eventually transformed most of the world. This was the discovery of **agriculture**, *large-scale cultivation using plows harnessed to animals or more powerful energy sources.* So great was the social significance of the animal-drawn plow and other technological innovations of the period—including irrigation, the wheel, writing, numbers, and various metals—that this era qualifies as "the dawn of civilization" (Lenski, Nolan, & Lenski, 1995:177).

Using animal-drawn plows, farmers could cultivate fields vastly larger than the garden-sized plots worked by horticulturalists. Plows have the additional advantage of turning and aerating the soil to increase fertility. As a result, farmers work the same land for generations, which, in turn, encourages permanent settlements. Large food surpluses, transported on animal-powered wagons, allow agrarian societies to expand their land area and population greatly. About 100 C.E., for example, the agrarian Roman Empire boasted a population of 70 million spread over 2 million square miles (Stavrianos, 1983; Nolan & Lenski, 1999).

As before, increasing production meant more specialization. Tasks once performed by everyone, such as clearing land and securing food, became distinct occupations. Specialization also made the early barter

DIVERSITY: RACE, CLASS, AND GENDER

Technology and the Changing Status of Women

In the earliest human societies, women produced more food than men did. Hunters and gatherers valued meat highly, but men's hunting was not a dependable source of nourishment. The vegetation gathered by women was the primary means of ensuring survival. Similarly, it was women who took charge of the tools and seeds used in horticulture. For their part, men engaged in trade and tended herds of animals. Only at harvest time did men and women work side by side.

Then, about 5,000 years ago, humans discovered how to mold metals. This technology spread by cultural diffusion, primarily along male-dominated trade networks. Therefore, it was men who developed the metal plow and, because they already managed animals, thought to hitch the implement to a cow.

The metal plow marked the beginning of agriculture, and for the first time men took over the dominant role in food production. Elise Boulding explains how this technological breakthrough undermined the social standing of women:

The shift of the status of the woman farmer may have happened quite rapidly, once there were two male specializations relating to

agriculture: plowing and the care of cattle. This situation left women with all the subsidiary tasks, including weeding and carrying water to the fields. The new fields were larger, so women had to work just as many hours as they did before, but now they worked at more secondary tasks. . . . This would contribute further to the erosion of the status of women.

Sources: Based on Boulding (1976) and Fisher (1979).

---

system obsolete, and money became the standard of exchange. Because money made trade easier, cities grew, and their populations soared into the millions.

Agrarian societies exhibit dramatic social inequality. In many cases, including the United States early in its history, peasants or slaves represent a significant share of the population. Freed from manual work, elites can then engage in the study of philosophy, art, and literature. This explains the historical link between "high culture" and social privilege noted in Chapter 3.

Among hunters and gatherers and also among horticulturists, women are the primary providers of food. Agriculture, however, propels men into a position of social dominance (Boulding, 1976; Fisher, 1979). The box looks more closely at the declining position of women at this point in the course of sociocultural evolution.

In many societies, religion reinforces the power of agricultural elites by defining work as a moral obligation. Many of the wonders of the ancient world, such as the Great Wall of China and the Great Pyramids of Egypt, were possible only because emperors and pharaohs wielded absolute power, commanding their people to a lifetime of labor without wages.

In agrarian societies, then, elites acquire unparalleled power. To maintain control of large empires, leaders need the services of a wide range of administrators. Therefore, along with the growing economy, the political system emerges as a distinct sphere of life.

 To see several wonders of the ancient world, all made primarily with muscle power, click on http://unmuseum. mus.pa.us/wonders.htm

Of the societies described so far, agrarian societies have the greatest specialization and the most social inequality. Agrarian technology also gives people a greater range of life choices, which is why agrarian societies differ more from one another than horticultural and pastoral societies do.

INDUSTRIAL SOCIETIES

Industrialism, as found in the United States, Canada, and other rich nations of the world, is *the production of goods using advanced sources of energy to drive large machinery.* Until the industrial era, the major source of energy was the muscles of humans and other animals. But

NOTE: Chapter 16 ("The Economy and Work") details the facets of the Industrial Revolution: (1) new forms of energy, (2) factories, (3) mass production, (4) productive specialization, and (5) wage labor.

NOTE: Lenski notes that the term "Industrial Revolution" only entered common usage in the final decades of the 19th century; at that point, it described events that began almost two centuries before.

GLOBAL: The long-run consequences of the Industrial Revolution may be the emergence of a global culture, as suggested by modernization theory (Chapter 12, "Global Stratification"); see also Chapter 24 ("Social Change").

NOTE: Marion Levy suggests that a good index of modernization is the ratio of inanimate to animate sources of energy (that is, fuel to muscle power).

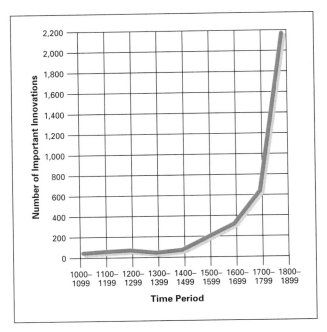

FIGURE 4–1 The Increasing Number of Technological Innovations

This figure illustrates the dramatic change in the number of technological innovations in Western Europe after the beginning of the Industrial Revolution in the mid-eighteenth century. Technological innovation occurs at an accelerating rate because each innovation combines with existing cultural elements to produce many additional innovations.

Source: Lenski, Nolan, & Lenski (1995).

in about 1750, mills and factories began to use water and then steam boilers to power ever-larger machinery.

With industrial technology, societies began to change faster, as shown in Figure 4–1. Industrial societies transformed themselves more in one century than they had during the past thousand years. As explained in Chapter 1 ("The Sociological Perspective"), this stunning change prompted the birth of sociology itself. During the nineteenth century, railroads and steamships revolutionized transportation, and steel-framed skyscrapers dwarfed the cathedrals that symbolized an earlier age.

In the twentieth century, automobiles further changed Western societies, and electricity powered modern conveniences such as lighting, refrigerators, elevators, and washing machines. Electronic communication, including the telephone, radio, and television, soon followed, making the world seem smaller and smaller. During the last generation, computers have dramatically increased our ability to process information.

Work also has changed. In agrarian societies, most men and women work in the home or in the nearby fields. Industrialization draws people away from home to factories situated near energy sources (such as coal fields) and filled with large machinery. Industrial workers are far more productive, of course, but lost in the process are close working relationships, strong kinship ties, and many of the traditional values, beliefs, and customs that guide agrarian life.

Occupational specialization has become more pronounced than ever. In fact, industrial people begin to size up one another in terms of their jobs rather than according to their kinship ties (as nonindustrial people do). Rapid change and movement from place to place also generate anonymity, cultural diversity, and numerous subcultures and countercultures, as described in Chapter 3.

Industrial technology recasts the family, too, lessening its traditional significance as the center of social life. No longer does the family serve as the primary setting for economic production, learning, and religious worship. And, as Chapter 18 ("Family") explains, technological change also underlies the trend away from traditional families to greater numbers of single people, divorced people, single-parent families, and stepfamilies.

Lenski explains that early in the industrialization process, only a small segment of the population enjoys the benefits of advancing technology. In time, however, wealth spreads and more people live longer and more comfortably. Although poverty remains a serious problem in industrial societies, compared with a century before the standard of living has risen fivefold and social inequality has declined. Some social leveling, described in Chapter 10 ("Social Stratification"), occurs because industrial societies need an educated and skilled labor force. Whereas most people in nonindustrial societies are illiterate, industrial societies provide state-funded schooling and confer numerous political rights on almost everyone. In fact, industrialization intensifies demands for a political voice, as seen most recently in South Korea, Taiwan, the People's Republic of China, the nations of Eastern Europe, and the former Soviet Union.

POSTINDUSTRIAL SOCIETIES

Many industrial societies, including the United States, have entered yet another phase of technological development, and we can extend Lenski's analysis to take

NOTE: Further discussion of postindustrial society is found in Chapter 16 ("The Economy and Work").

DISCUSS: Consider how modern communication and information technology mass produces culture and directs it *at* people, rather than the earlier pattern by which culture emerged organically from our own lives.

NOTE: In the industrial era, "setting the clocks" used to mean adjusting the bedroom clock and kitchen wall clock. Now it involves addressing dozens of electronic devices: TVs, computers, VCRs, faxes, cellular phones, and so on.

NOTE: One indicator of our society moving into the postindustrial era is that we now spend more money on computers than on televisions.

RESOURCE: John Macionis's article "Welcome to Cyber-Society!" is included in the 5th edition of the *Seeing Ourselves* reader.

Does advancing technology make society better? In some ways, perhaps. However, many films—including Frankenstein *(1931) and* Jurassic Park III *(2001)—have expressed the concern that new technology not only solves old problems but creates new ones. All the sociological theorists discussed in this chapter shared this ambivalent view of the modern world.*

account of recent trends. A generation ago, sociologist Daniel Bell (1973) coined the term **postindustrialism** to refer to *technology that supports an information-based economy.* Whereas production in industrial societies centers on factories and machinery generating material goods, postindustrial production is based on computers and other electronic devices that create, process, store, and apply information. Members of industrial societies learn and apply mechanical skills, and people in postindustrial societies develop information-based skills for working with computers and other forms of high-technology communication.

With this shift in key skills and the emergence of postindustrialism, a society's occupational structure changes dramatically. Chapter 16 ("The Economy and Work") explains that a postindustrial society uses less and less of its labor force for industrial production. At the same time, the ranks of clerical workers, managers, and other people who process information (in fields ranging from academia and advertising to marketing and public relations) swell.

The Information Revolution is most pronounced in rich nations, yet the new technology affects the entire world. As discussed in Chapter 3 ("Culture"), a new, worldwide flow of goods, people, and information ties societies together and creates a global culture. And, just as industrial technology joined local communities to create a national economy, postindustrial technology joins nations to build a global economy.

Table 4–1 summarizes how technology shapes societies at different stages of sociocultural evolution.

THE LIMITS OF TECHNOLOGY

Technology remedies many human problems by raising productivity, reducing infectious disease, and sometimes simply relieving boredom. But it provides no quick fix for social problems. Poverty, for example, remains the plight of millions of women and men in the United States (detailed in Chapter 11, "Social Class in the United States") and 1 billion people worldwide (see Chapter 12, "Global Stratification"). Moreover, technology creates new problems that our ancestors (and people like the chapter-opening story's Sididi Ag Inaka today) could not imagine. Industrial societies provide more personal freedom, but often at the cost of the sense of community that characterized

TABLE 4–1 Sociological Evolution: A Summary

Type of Society	Historical Period	Productive Technology	Population Size
Hunting and Gathering Societies	Only type of society until about 12,000 years ago; still common several centuries ago; the few examples remaining today are threatened with extinction	Primitive weapons	25–40 people
Horticultural and Pastoral Societies	From about 12,000 years ago, with decreasing numbers after about 3000 B.C.E.	Horticultural societies use hand tools for cultivating plants; pastoral societies are based on the domestication of animals	Settlements of several hundred people, connected through trading ties to form societies of several thousand people
Agrarian Societies	From about 5,000 years ago, with large but decreasing numbers today	Animal-drawn plow	Millions of people
Industrial Societies	From about 1750 to the present	Advanced sources of energy; mechanized production	Millions of people
Postindustrial Societies	Emerging in recent decades	Computers that support an information-based economy	Millions of people

preindustrial life. Furthermore, although the most powerful nations in the world today rarely engage in all-out warfare, they have stockpiles of nuclear weapons that could return us to a technologically primitive state—if we survived at all.

Advancing technology has also contributed to major social problems involving the environment. Each stage in sociocultural evolution has introduced more powerful sources of energy and increased our appetite for the earth's resources. An issue of vital concern, discussed in Chapter 22 ("Population, Urbanization, and Environment"), is whether humanity can continue to pursue material prosperity without permanently damaging our planet.

In some respects, then, technological advances have improved life and brought the world's people closer to a "global village." But establishing peace, ensuring justice, and protecting the environment are problems that technology alone cannot solve.

KARL MARX: SOCIETY AND CONFLICT

The first of our classic visions of society comes from Karl Marx (1818–1883), an early giant in the field of sociology. A keen observer of the industrial transformation of Europe, Marx spent most of his adult life in London, then the capital of the vast British Empire. He was awed by the productive power of the new factories. Great Britain and other industrial nations were producing more goods than ever before, with resources from around the world funneling into their factories at a dizzying rate.

 For biographical information on Karl Marx, go to http://www.TheSociologyPage.com and click on Marx in the Gallery of Sociologists.

What astounded and disturbed Marx was that industry's riches were concentrated in the hands of a few. A walk around London revealed striking contrasts of

Type of Society	Settlement Pattern	Social Organization	Examples
Hunting and Gathering Societies	Nomadic	Family centered; specialization limited to age and sex; little social inequality	Pygmies of central Africa Bushmen of southwestern Africa Aborigines of Australia Semai of Malaysia Kaska Indians of Canada
Horticultural and Pastoral Societies	Horticulturalists form small permanent settlements; pastoralists are nomadic	Family centered; religious system begins to develop; moderate specialization; increased social inequality	Middle Eastern societies about 5000 B.C.E. Various societies today in New Guinea and other Pacific islands Yạnomamö today in South America
Agrarian Societies	Cities become common, but they generally contain only a small proportion of the population	Family loses significance as distinct religious, political, and economic systems emerge; extensive specialization; increased social inequality	Egypt during construction of the Great Pyramids Medieval Europe Numerous predominantly agrarian societies of the world today
Industrial Societies	Cities contain most of the population	Distinct religious, political, economic, educational, and family systems; highly specialized; marked social inequality persists, diminishing somewhat over time	Most societies today in Europe and North America, Australia, and Japan generate most of the world's industrial production
Postindustrial Societies	Population remains concentrated in cities	Similar to industrial societies, with information processing and other service work gradually replacing industrial production	Industrial societies noted above are now entering postindustrial stage

splendid affluence and wretched squalor. A handful of aristocrats and industrialists lived in luxury in mansions staffed by dozens of servants. But most people labored long hours for low wages and lived in slums or even slept in the streets, where many eventually died from disease brought on by poor nutrition.

Marx wrestled with a basic contradiction: In a society so rich, how could so many be so poor? Just as important, Marx asked, how can this situation be changed? Many people think Karl Marx set out to tear societies apart. But he was motivated by compassion and sought to help a badly divided society forge a new and just social order.

The key to Marx's thinking is the idea of **social conflict**, *struggle between segments of society over valued resources.* Of course, social conflict can take many forms: Individuals may quarrel, some colleges have longstanding sports rivalries, and nations sometimes go to war. For Marx, however, the most significant form of social conflict was class conflict arising from the way a society produces material goods.

SOCIETY AND PRODUCTION

Living in the nineteenth century, Marx observed the early stage of industrial capitalism in Europe. He noted that this economic system turned a small part of the population into **capitalists**, *people who own and operate factories and other businesses in pursuit of profits.* A capitalist seeks profit by selling a product for more than it costs to produce. Capitalism transforms most of the population into industrial workers, whom Marx called the **proletarians**, *people who sell their productive labor for wages.* To Marx, conflict between capitalists and workers is inevitable in a system of capitalist production. To keep profits high, capitalists keep wages low. Workers, naturally, want higher wages. Because profits and wages come from the same pool of funds,

NOTE: "Capitalism" is derived from the Latin word *caput*, meaning "head." The term was first used in 12th-century Europe at a time of expanding commerce. "Conflict" is derived from the Latin meaning "a striking together."

Q: The economic structure of society always furnishes the real basis, starting from which we can alone work out the ultimate explanation of the whole superstructure of judicial and political institutions as well as of the religious, philosophical, and other ideas of a given historical period." Friedrich Engels

NOTE: Marx used the term "species being" to imply that humans are *social* beings. Thus, he maintained, humans are neither individualistic nor self-serving but derive satisfactions from social pursuits. In this view, Marx opposed the utilitarian thought of James Mill, John Stuart Mill, and Jeremy Bentham.

Norbert Goeneutte's painting Pauper's Meal on a Winter's Day in Paris *suggests the numbing poverty common to migrants drawn to cities as the Industrial Revolution was getting underway. Karl Marx saw in such suffering a fundamental contradiction of modern society: Industrial technology promises material plenty for all, but capitalism concentrates wealth in the hands of a few.*

conflict is the result. As Marx saw it, this conflict could end only with the end of capitalism itself.

All societies are composed of **social institutions,** defined as *the major spheres of social life, or societal subsystems, organized to meet human needs.* In his analysis of society, Marx argued that one institution—the economy—dominates all the others and defines the character of a society. Drawing on the philosophical doctrine of *materialism*, which says that how humans produce material goods shapes their experiences, Marx believed that the political system, family, religion, and education operate largely to support a society's economy. Just as Lenski argued that technology molds a society, Marx argued that the economy is a society's "real foundation" (1959:43; orig. 1859).

Marx viewed the economic system as society's *infrastructure* (*infra* is Latin for "below"). Other social institutions, including the family, the political system, and religion, are built on this foundation, forming society's *superstructure.* These institutions apply economic principles to other areas of life, as illustrated in Figure 4–2. In practical terms, social institutions maintain capitalists' dominant position by protecting their wealth and lawfully transmitting property from one generation to the next through the family.

Generally speaking, members of industrial-capitalist societies do not view their legal or family systems as hotbeds of social conflict. On the contrary, individuals come to see their right to private property as "natural." People in the United States find it easy to think that affluent people have earned their wealth and that those who are poor or out of work lack skills or motivation. Marx rejected this reasoning, arguing that grand wealth clashing with grinding poverty is merely one set of human possibilities—the one generated by capitalism (Cuff & Payne, 1979).

Therefore, Marx rejected capitalist beliefs as **false consciousness,** *explanations of social problems as the shortcomings of individuals rather than the flaws of society.* Marx was saying, in effect, that industrial capitalism itself is responsible for many social problems. False consciousness, he continued, harms people by hiding the real cause of their problems.

CONFLICT AND HISTORY

Marx believed that most societies evolve gradually over time. But sometimes they erupt in rapid, revolutionary change. Marx observed (as did Lenski) that change is caused partly by technological advance. But most change, he maintained, results from social conflict.

To put Lenski's analysis in Marxist terms, early hunters and gatherers formed primitive communist societies. *Communism* is a system by which people share roughly equally in the production of food and other material goods. Although resources were meager, they were shared by all rather than privately owned. In addition, everyone did much the same work, so there was little chance for social conflict.

Horticulture introduced social inequality, Marx noted. Among horticultural, pastoral, and early agrarian societies—which Marx lumped together as the "ancient world"—warfare was frequent, and the victors made their captives slaves. A small elite (the "masters") and their slaves were locked into an irreconcilable pattern of social conflict (Zeitlin, 1981).

RESOURCE: The *Manifesto of the Communist Party* is included in the Macionis and Benokraitis reader, *Seeing Ourselves.*
Q: "The bourgeoisie, wherever it has got the upper hand, has put an end to all feudal, patriarchal, idyllic relations. It has pitilessly torn asunder the motley fuedal ties that bound man to his 'natural superiors' and left no other nexus between man and man than naked self-interest, than callous 'cash payment'." Marx and Engels

SOCIAL SURVEY: "Inequality continues to exist because it benefits the rich and powerful." (GSS 2000, N=1,272; *Codebook*, 2001:943)
"Strongly agree" 12.3%   "Strongly disagree" 4.4%
"Agree" 32.5%   "Can't choose" 4.4%
"Neither agree nor disagree" 24.3%   DK/NR 6.1%
"Disagree" 16.0%

Agriculture brought still more wealth to members of the elite, fueling further social conflict. Agrarian serfs, occupying the lowest reaches of European feudalism from about the twelfth to the eighteenth century, were only slightly better off than slaves. In Marx's view, both the church and the state defended the feudal system as God's will. Thus, to Marx, feudalism amounted to little more than "exploitation, veiled by religious and political illusions" (Marx & Engels, 1972:337; orig. 1848).

Gradually, new productive forces eroded the feudal order. As trade increased steadily, the merchants and skilled craftsworkers in cities formed a class, the *bourgeoisie* (a French word meaning "of the town"). Expanding trade made the bourgeoisie richer and richer. After about 1800, the bourgeoisie also controlled factories, becoming true capitalists with power that soon rivaled that of the ancient, landed nobility. For their part, the nobility looked down their noses at this upstart "commercial" class, but, in time, it was the capitalists who gained control of European societies. To Marx's way of thinking, then, new technology was only part of the Industrial Revolution. It was also a class revolution by which capitalists overthrew the old, agrarian elite.

Industrialization also led to the growth of the proletariat. English landowners converted fields once tilled by serfs into grazing land for sheep to produce wool for the textile mills. Forced from the land, serfs migrated to cities to work in factories. Marx envisioned these workers one day joining together to form a unified class and thereby setting the stage for a historic confrontation. This time, he hoped, the class revolution would lift the exploited workers over the oppressing capitalists.

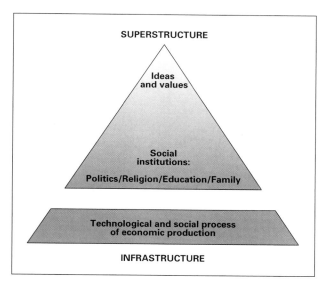

FIGURE 4–2 Karl Marx's Model of Society

This diagram illustrates Marx's materialist view that economic production underlies and shapes the entire society. Economic production involves both technology (industry, in the case of capitalism) and social relationships (for capitalism, the relationship between the capitalists, who control economic production, and the workers, who are a source of labor). On this infrastructure, or foundation, rests society's superstructure, which includes its major social institutions as well as core cultural values and ideas. Marx maintained that every part of a society supports the economic system.

CAPITALISM AND CLASS CONFLICT

"The history of all hitherto existing society is the history of class struggles." With these words, Marx and his collaborator, Friedrich Engels, began their best-known statement, the *Manifesto of the Communist Party* (1972:335; orig. 1848). Industrial capitalism, like earlier types of society, contains two major social classes—the ruling class and the oppressed—reflecting the two basic positions in the productive system. Like masters and slaves in the ancient world and nobles and serfs in feudal systems, capitalists and proletarians are engaged in class conflict now. Today, as in the past, one class controls the other as productive property. Marx used the term **class conflict** (and sometimes *class struggle*) to refer to *conflict between entire classes over the distribution of a society's wealth and power.*

Class conflict is nothing new. What distinguishes the conflict in capitalist society, Marx pointed out, is how out in the open it is. Agrarian nobles and serfs, for all their differences, were bound together by long-standing traditions and mutual obligations. Industrial capitalism dissolved those ties so that pride and honor were replaced by "naked self-interest." With no personal ties to their oppressors, Marx saw no reason for the proletarians to put up with their situation.

Although industrial capitalism brought class conflict out in the open, Marx realized that revolution would not quickly follow. First, workers must *become aware* of their oppression and see capitalism as its true cause. Second, they must *organize and act* to address their problems. This means workers must replace false consciousness with **class consciousness,** *workers' recognition of themselves as a class unified in opposition to*

NOTE: In opposing capitalism, Marx encouraged workers to cease to be merely a social class *in* themselves and become a social class acting *for* themselves.

NOTE: The following quotations suggest that the Roman Catholic church has taken differing positions on the morality of capitalism.

Q: "Every man has by nature the right to possess property as his own." Pope Leo XIII

Q: "It is impossible to reduce society to one level." Pope Leo XIII

Q: "The needs of the poor must take priority over the desires of the rich; and the rights of workers over the maximization of profits." Pope John Paul II

Q: "The bourgeoisie, during its rule of scarcely one hundred years, has created more massive and more colossal productive forces than have all preceding generations together." Marx and Engels

Karl Marx, shown here at work on the Manifesto of the Communist Party *with his friend, benefactor, and collaborator Friedrich Engels, was surely the pioneering sociologist who had the greatest influence on the world as a whole. Through the second half of the last century, 1 billion people—nearly one-fifth of humanity—lived in societies organized on Marxist principles.*

capitalists and, *ultimately, to capitalism itself.* Because the inhumanity of early capitalism was plain for him to see, Marx concluded that industrial workers would soon rise up to destroy capitalism.

And what of the capitalists? The capitalists' vast wealth made them strong. But Marx saw a weakness in the capitalist armor. Motivated by a desire for personal gain, capitalists fear competition with other capitalists. Therefore, Marx thought that capitalists would be slow to band together even though they, too, share common interests. Furthermore, he reasoned, because capitalists keep employees' wages low to maximize profits, the workers' resolve grows ever stronger. In the long run, Marx believed, capitalists contribute to their own undoing.

CAPITALISM AND ALIENATION

Marx also condemned capitalism for producing **alienation,** *the experience of isolation and misery resulting from powerlessness.* Dominated by capitalists, workers are nothing more than a commodity—a source of labor—hired and fired at will. Dehumanized by their jobs (especially monotonous, repetitive factory work), workers find little satisfaction and feel unable to improve their situation. Here we see another contradiction of capitalist society: As people develop technology to gain power over the world, the capitalist economy gains more control over people.

Marx cited four ways in which capitalism alienates workers:

1. **Alienation from the act of working.** Ideally, people work to meet immediate needs and to develop their personal potential. Capitalism, however, denies workers a say in what they make or how they produce it. Furthermore, much work is tedious, a constant repetition of routine tasks. The fact that we replace workers with machines whenever possible would not have surprised Marx. As far as he was concerned, capitalism had turned human beings into machines long ago.

2. **Alienation from the products of work.** The product of work belongs not to workers but to capitalists, who sell it for profit. Therefore, Marx reasoned, the more workers invest of themselves in their work, the more they lose.

3. **Alienation from other workers.** Through work, Marx claimed, people build bonds of community. However, industrial capitalism makes work competitive rather than cooperative. As the box illustrates, factory work provides little opportunity for human companionship.

4. **Alienation from human potential.** Industrial capitalism alienates workers from their human potential. Marx argued that a worker "does not fulfill himself in his work but denies himself, has a feeling of misery rather than well-being, does not freely develop his physical and mental energies, but is physically exhausted and mentally debased. The worker, therefore, feels himself to be at home only during his leisure time, whereas at work he feels homeless" (1964a:124–25; orig. 1844). In short, industrial capitalism distorts activity that should express the best qualities in human beings into a dull and dehumanizing experience.

Q: "Marxist social scientists typically ask questions about matters on which they already believe to have the answers, at least in broad outline. This is a useful methodology for prophets; it decisively flaws the work of social scientists." Peter Berger (1986:5)

RESOURCE: The *Seeing Ourselves* reader also includes Marx's selection "Alienated Labor."

SOCIAL SURVEY: "On the whole, how satisfied are you with the work you do—would you say you are very satisfied, moderately satisfied, a little dissatisfied, or very dissatisfied?" (GSS 2000, N=2,275; *Codebook*, 2001:213) In GSS survey items, workers do not express strong dissatisfaction with their work.

"Very satisfied"	43.1%	"Very dissatisfied"	3.4%
"Moderately satisfied"	40.4%	DK/NR	5.0%
"A little dissatisfied"	8.2%		

APPLYING SOCIOLOGY

Alienation and Industrial Capitalism

These excerpts from the book *Working* by Studs Terkel illustrate how dull, repetitive jobs can alienate a worker.

Phil Stallings is a twenty-seven-year-old auto worker in a Ford assembly plant in Chicago:

I start the automobile, the first welds. From there it goes to another line, where the floor's put on, the roof, the trunk, the hood, the doors. Then it's put on a frame. There is hundreds of lines. . . . I stand in one spot, about two- or three-feet area, all night. The only time a person stops is when the line stops. We do about thirty-two jobs per car, per unit. Forty-eight units an hour, eight hours a day. Thirty-two times forty-eight times eight. Figure it out. That's how many times I push that button.

The noise, oh it's tremendous. You open your mouth and you're liable to get a mouthful of sparks. [Shows his arms.] That's a burn, these are burns. You don't compete against the noise. You go to yell and at the same time you're straining to maneuver the gun to where you have to weld.

You got some guys that are uptight, and they're not sociable. It's too rough. You pretty much stay to yourself. You get involved with yourself. You dream, you think of things you've done. I drift back continuously to when I was a kid and what me and my brothers did. The things you love most are what you drift back into.

It don't stop. It just goes and goes and goes. I bet there's men who have lived and died out there, never seen the end of the line. And they never will—because it's endless. It's like a serpent. It's just all body, no tail. It can do things to you.

Twenty-four-year-old Sharon Atkins is a college graduate working as a telephone receptionist for a large midwestern business:

I don't have much contact with people. You can't see them. You don't know if they're laughing, if they're being satirical or being kind. So your conversations become very abrupt. I notice that in talking to people. My conversation would be very short and clipped, in short sentences, the way I talk to people all day on the telephone. . . .

You try to fill up your time with trying to think about other things: what you're going to do on the weekend or about your family. You have to use your imagination. If you don't have a very good one and you bore easily, you're in trouble. Just to fill in time, I write real bad poetry or letters to myself and to other people and never mail them. The letters are fantasies, sort of rambling, how I feel, how depressed I am. . . .

I never answer the phone at home.

Source: Terkel (1974).

Marx viewed alienation, in its various forms, as a barrier to social change. But he hoped that industrial workers would overcome their alienation by uniting into a true social class, aware of the cause of their problems and ready to transform society.

REVOLUTION

The only way out of the trap of capitalism, argued Marx, is to remake society. He envisioned a more humane productive system, one in which people would be equals. He called this system *socialism*. Although Marx understood the obstacles to a socialist revolution, he was nevertheless disappointed that he did not live to see workers in England rise up. Convinced of the immorality of capitalism, he was sure that, in time, the working majority would realize that they hold the key to a better future. This change would certainly be revolutionary, and perhaps even violent. In the end, Marx believed, a socialist society could meet the needs of all.

Chapter 10 ("Social Stratification") explains more about changes in industrial-capitalist societies since Marx's time and why the revolution he wanted never took place. In addition, as Chapter 17 ("Politics and Government") explains, Marx failed to see that the revolution he imagined would take the form of repressive

NOTE: Weber was born to a rich family. His father was a major politician (giving Weber his interest in politics), and his mother was a devout Calvinist (sparking Weber's interest in religion). Weber's wife, Marianne, was a leading feminist of her day. For much of his life, Weber suffered from mental problems, which limited his productivity.

NOTE: The German word *weltanschauung* (*welt* = world, *anschauung* = perception), designating the distinctive ideas with which people embrace the world, has no English equivalent. For Weber, early Protestantism was more than a religion, as capitalism was more than an economic system: Both represented a distinctive *weltanschauung*.

NOTE: In times of trouble, traditional people consult religious leaders (as the Irish people did during the 19th-century potato famines). Today, people consult physicians and lawyers.

For years, the conventional wisdom in the United States was that, once established, socialism stifled its opposition, rendering government immune to overthrow. But that notion collapsed along with the socialist regimes of Eastern Europe and the Soviet Union. The political transformation of this world region during the 1990s was symbolized, in city after city, by the removal of statues of Vladimir Lenin (1870–1924), architect of Soviet Marxism.

regimes—such as Stalin's government in the Soviet Union—that would take the lives of tens of millions of people (Hamilton, 2001). But, in his own time, Marx looked toward the future with hope (Marx & Engels, 1972:362; orig. 1848): "The proletarians have nothing to lose but their chains. They have a world to win."

MAX WEBER: THE RATIONALIZATION OF SOCIETY

With knowledge of law, economics, religion, and history, Max Weber (1864–1920) produced what many regard as the greatest individual contribution to sociology. This scholar, born to a prosperous family in Germany, generated ideas so wide ranging that, in this discussion, we can touch on only his vision

For biographical information about Max Weber, visit http://www.TheSociologyPage.com and click on his name in the Gallery of Sociologists.

of how modern society differs from earlier types of social organization.

In line with the philosophical approach called *idealism*, Weber emphasized how human ideas shape society. He understood the power of technology, and he shared many of Marx's ideas about social conflict. But he countered Marx's materialist analysis by arguing that societies differ mainly in terms of how their members think about the world. For Weber, then, ideas—especially beliefs and values—are the key to understanding society. Weber saw modern society as the product not just of new technology and capitalism but also of a new way of thinking. This emphasis on ideas, in contrast with Marx's focus on production has led scholars to describe Weber's work as "a debate with the ghost of Karl Marx" (Cuff & Payne, 1979:73–74).

Weber compared social patterns in different times and places. To make the comparisons, he relied on the **ideal type,** *an abstract statement of the essential characteristics of any social phenomenon.* He explored religion by contrasting the "ideal Protestant" with the "ideal Jew," "ideal Hindu," and "ideal Buddhist," knowing that these models precisely described no actual individuals. Note that Weber's use of the word *ideal* does not mean that something is "good" or "the best." We can analyze criminals as well as priests in ideal terms. We have already used ideal types in comparing hunting and gathering societies with industrial societies and capitalism with socialism.

TWO WORLDVIEWS: TRADITION AND RATIONALITY

Rather than categorizing societies by their technology or productive systems, Max Weber focused on ways people view the world. In simple terms, Weber said, members of preindustrial societies are *traditional*, whereas people in industrial-capitalist societies are *rational*.

By **tradition,** Weber meant *sentiments and beliefs passed from generation to generation.* In other words, traditional people are guided by the past. They consider particular actions right and proper solely because they have been accepted for so long.

But, argued Weber, people in modern societies favor **rationality,** *deliberate, matter-of-fact calculation of the most efficient means to accomplish a particular task.* Sentiment has no place in a rational worldview, which treats tradition simply as one kind of information. Typically, modern people choose to think and act on the basis of present and future consequences, evaluating jobs, schooling, and even relationships in terms of what

NOTE: The Protestant ethic and the spirit of capitalism are not synonymous. Weber explained that the former becomes the latter only as it is *disenchanted*. The disenchanted spirit of Calvinism is then evident in three impersonal modern "types," all of which are highly disciplined but devoid of piety: the *capitalist* (devotion to profits), the *scientist* (devotion to knowledge), and the *bureaucrat* (devotion to duty). Drawings in Chapter 24 illustrate these three types.

GLOBAL: The Portuguese founded the colony of Macau in 1557 and introduced a Catholic culture; the British founded Hong Kong almost three centuries later in 1840 with a Protestant culture. Economically speaking, the latter greatly surpassed the former. (Hong Kong reverted to PR China in 1997 and Macau in 1999.)

Q: Victor Hugo observed that nothing is as powerful as "an idea whose time has come."

they put into them and what they expect to receive in return.

Weber viewed both the Industrial Revolution and capitalism as evidence of a surge of rationality. He used the phrase **rationalization of society** to mean *the historical change from tradition to rationality as the dominant mode of human thought*. He went on to say that modern society has been "disenchanted" as scientific thinking and technology have swept away sentimental ties to the past.

The willingness to adopt the latest technology, then, is one strong indicator of how rationalized a society is. To illustrate the global pattern of rationalization, Global Map 4–1 on page 104 shows where in the world personal computers are found. In general, the high-income countries of North America and Europe use personal computers the most, whereas in low-income nations they are rare.

Using Weber's comparative perspective and the data found in the map, we can say that various societies value technological advance differently. What one society might consider a breakthrough another might deem unimportant and a third might strongly oppose as a threat to tradition. The Tuareg nomads, described at the beginning of this chapter, shrug off the notion of using telephones: Why would anyone want such a thing in the desert? In the United States, the Amish refuse to have telephones in their homes for religious reasons.

In Weber's view, then, the extent of technological innovation in a society depends on how people understand their world. Many people throughout history have had the opportunity to adopt new technology; however, only in the rational cultural climate of Western Europe did people exploit scientific discoveries to spark the Industrial Revolution (1958; orig. 1904–5).

IS CAPITALISM RATIONAL?

Is industrial capitalism a rational economic system? Here, again, Weber and Marx came down on opposite sides. Weber considered industrial capitalism the essence of rationality because capitalists pursue profit in whatever ways they can. Marx believed capitalism was irrational because it failed to meet the basic needs of most of the people (Gerth & Mills, 1946:49).

WEBER'S GREAT THESIS: PROTESTANTISM AND CAPITALISM

To look more closely at Weber's analysis we must consider how industrial capitalism emerged in the first place. Weber contended that industrial capitalism is

A key element of U.S. culture has long been a "work ethic," with its roots in the Calvinist thinking that fascinated Max Weber. This Currier and Ives lithograph from 1875 makes a statement that people should shun the stock market, race track, lotteries, and even labor strikes as ways to improve their lives in favor of climbing the "Ladder of Fortune" based on personal virtue and individual effort.

the legacy of Calvinism, a Christian religious movement that arose from the Protestant Reformation. Calvinists, Weber explained, approached life in a highly disciplined and rational way. Moreover, central to the religious doctrine of John Calvin (1509–1564) was *predestination*, the idea that an all-knowing and all-powerful God has predestined some people for salvation and others for damnation. With everyone's fate set before birth, Calvinists believed that people could do nothing to change their destiny. Worse, they did not even know what their destiny was. Therefore, Calvinists swung between hopeful visions of spiritual salvation and anxious fears of eternal damnation.

THE MAP: Another indicator of the uneven pace of rationalization in the world is that half the world's scientific output is generated by six nations: United States, United Kingdom, Japan, former Soviet Union, France, and Germany.

GLOBAL: Illustrating the link between cultural ethos and achievement, Peter Berger (1986:155) notes that certain ethnic groups everywhere stand out as more productive: the Chinese in Southeast Asia, Buddhists in Thailand and Sri Lanka, Sikh peasants in the Punjab of India, and the Ibos in Nigeria.

GLOBAL: The importance of worldview to achievement is suggested by the fact that in the Philippines, 9 of the 10 richest families are Chinese. Also recall Baltzell's comparative analysis of the Puritan ethic of Boston and Philadelphia's Quaker heritage (see Chapter 2).

WINDOW ON THE WORLD

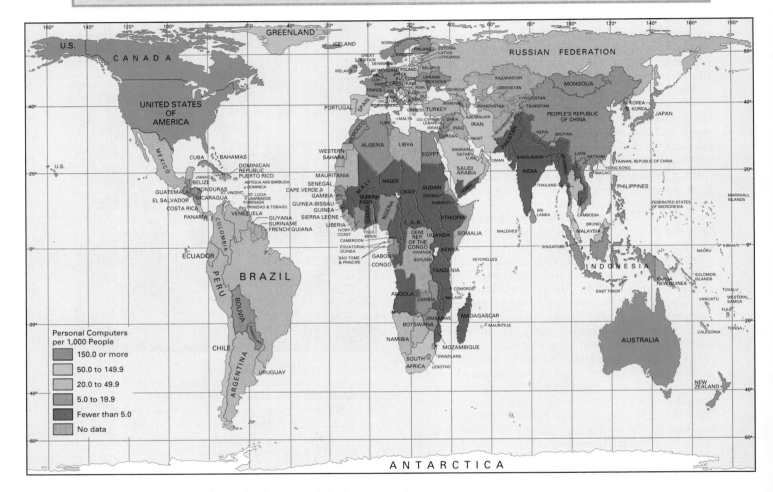

GLOBAL MAP 4–1 High Technology in Global Perspective

Countries with traditional cultures either cannot afford, ignore, or sometimes even resist technological innovation; nations with highly rationalized ways of life quickly embrace such changes. Personal computers, central to today's high technology, are numerous in high-income countries such as the United States. In low-income nations, by contrast, they are unknown to most people.

Source: *World Bank Atlas* by The World Bank. Copyright © 2001 by World Bank. Reproduced with permission of World Bank in textbook format via Copyright Clearance Center.

Not knowing one's fate was intolerable, and Calvinists gradually came to a resolution of sorts. Why shouldn't those chosen for glory in the next world, they reasoned, see signs of divine favor in *this* world? Such a conclusion prompted Calvinists to interpret worldly prosperity as a sign of God's grace. Eager to acquire this reassurance, Calvinists threw themselves into a quest for success, applying rationality, discipline, and hard work to their tasks. Their pursuit of wealth was not for its own sake because

104 CHAPTER 4 Society

NOTE: A full discussion of formal organization is found in Chapter 7 ("Groups and Organizations").
RESOURCE: Ferdinand Tönnies's "*Gemeinschaft* and *Gesellschaft*" is one classic included in the *Seeing Ourselves* reader. Also find four selections by Weber: "The Case for Value-Free Sociology," "The Characteristics of Bureaucracy," "The Protestant Ethic and the Spirit of Capitalism," and "The Disenchantment of Modern Life."

Q: "The decisive reason for the advance of bureaucratic organization has always been its purely technical superiority over any other form of organization. The fully developed bureaucratic apparatus compares with other organizations exactly as does the machine with the nonmechanical modes of production." Max Weber (1978:973; orig. 1921)

self-indulgent spending was clearly sinful. But neither were Calvinists moved to share their wealth with the poor because poverty was a sign of God's rejection. Their duty was to carry forward what they held to be a personal *calling* from God: reinvesting their profits for still greater success. Calvinists thus built the foundation of capitalism. With religious conviction, they used wealth to create more wealth, saved their money, and eagerly adopted new technology that helped their efforts.

The pursuit of wealth distinguished Calvinism from other world religions. For example, Catholicism, the traditional religion in most of Europe, gave rise to a passive, "otherworldly" view: Good deeds performed humbly on earth would bring rewards in heaven. For Catholics, material wealth had none of the spiritual significance that motivated Calvinists. And so it was, Weber concluded, that industrial capitalism developed primarily in areas of Europe where Calvinism was strong.

Weber's study of Calvinism provides striking evidence of the power of ideas to shape society (compared with Marx's contention that ideas merely reflect the process of economic production). But Weber was not one to accept simple explanations; he knew that industrial capitalism has many causes. In fact, one purpose of Weber's research was to counter Marx's narrow, strictly economic explanation of modern society.

Although later generations of Calvinists were less religious, their success-seeking and personal discipline remained, and a *religious* ethic became simply a *work* ethic. In other words, industrial capitalism can be seen as "disenchanted" religion, with wealth now valued for its own sake. It is revealing that the practice of "accounting," which to early Calvinists meant keeping a daily record of moral deeds, before long was simply a matter of keeping track of money.

RATIONAL SOCIAL ORGANIZATION

According to Weber, then, rationality gave rise to the Industrial Revolution and capitalism and thereby defined modern society. Weber went on to identify seven characteristics of rational social organization:

1. **Distinctive social institutions.** Among hunters and gatherers, the family is the center of all activity. Gradually, however, other social institutions, including religious, political, and economic systems, become separate from family life. In modern societies, new institutions—education and health care—also appear. The separation of social institutions is a rational way to meet human needs efficiently.

2. **Large-scale organizations.** Modern rationality is evident in the spread of large-scale organizations. As early as the horticultural era, political officials oversaw religious observances, public works, and warfare. In medieval Europe, the Catholic church grew into a huge organization with thousands of officials. In our modern, rational society, the federal government employs millions, and most people work for one large organization or another.

3. **Specialized tasks.** Unlike members of traditional societies, individuals in modern societies perform a wide range of specialized jobs. Flipping through the classified section of any city's telephone directory shows just how many different occupations there are today.

4. **Personal discipline.** Modern society puts a premium on self-discipline. For early Calvinists, discipline was rooted in religious belief. Although now distanced from its religious origins, discipline is still encouraged by cultural values such as achievement, success, and efficiency.

5. **Awareness of time.** In traditional societies, people measure time according to the rhythm of the sun and seasons. Modern people, by contrast, schedule events precisely by the hour and even the minute. Interestingly, clocks began appearing in European cities some 500 years ago, about the time commerce began to expand. Soon, people began to think (to borrow Benjamin Franklin's phrase) that "time is money."

6. **Technical competence.** Members of traditional societies size up one another on the basis of *who* they are—how they are joined to others in the web of kinship. Modern rationality prompts us to judge people according to *what* they are—that is, with an eye toward their skills and abilities.

7. **Impersonality.** Finally, in a rational society technical competence takes priority over close relationships, making the world impersonal. People interact as specialists concerned with particular tasks rather than as individuals broadly concerned with one another. Because feelings are difficult to control, modern people tend to devalue emotion.

Max Weber agreed with Karl Marx that modern society is alienating to the individual, but the two thinkers identified different causes of this estrangement. For Marx, economic inequality is the culprit; for Weber, the issue is pervasive and dehumanizing bureaucracy. George Tooker's painting Landscape with Figures *echoes Weber's sentiments.*

George Tooker, *Landscape with Figures*, 1963, egg tempera on gesso panel, 26 x 30 in. Private collection.

Rationality and Bureaucracy

The medieval church grew large, Weber explained, but it remained basically traditional and resisted change. Truly rational organizations that are both efficient and open to change appeared only in the last few centuries. The kind of organization Weber called *bureaucracy* arose along with capitalism as an expression of the rationality that shapes modern society. Indeed, Weber explained, bureaucracy and capitalism have much in common:

> Today, it is primarily the capitalist market economy which demands that the official business of public administration be discharged precisely, unambiguously, continuously, and with as much speed as possible. Normally, the very large capitalist enterprises are themselves unequaled models of strict bureaucratic organization. (1978:974; orig. 1921)

As Chapter 7 ("Groups and Organizations") explains, we find aspects of bureaucracy in today's businesses, government agencies, labor unions, and universities. Weber considered bureaucracy highly rational because its elements—offices, duties, and policies—help achieve specific goals as efficiently as possible. Therefore, Weber concluded, the defining elements of modern society—capitalism, bureaucracy, and science—are all expressions of the same underlying factor: rationality.

Rationality and Alienation

Max Weber joined with Karl Marx in recognizing the efficiency of industrial capitalism. Weber also agreed that modern society generates widespread alienation, although he offered different reasons. Whereas Marx thought alienation was caused by economic inequality, Weber blamed the stifling effect of bureaucracy's countless rules and regulations. Bureaucracies treat people as a series of cases rather than as unique individuals, Weber warned. In addition, working for large organizations entails highly specialized and often tedious routines. In the end, Weber envisioned modern society as a vast and growing system of rules seeking to regulate everything and threatening to crush the human spirit.

Like Marx, Weber found it ironic that modern society, meant to serve people, turns on its creators and enslaves them. Just as Marx described the human toll of industrial capitalism, Weber portrayed the modern individual as "only a small cog in a ceaselessly moving mechanism that prescribes to him an endlessly fixed routine" (1978:988; orig. 1921). Although Weber could see the advantages of modern society, he was

Durkheim's observation that people with weak social bonds are prone to self-destructive behavior stands as stark evidence of the power of society to shape individual lives. When rock-and-roll singers become famous, they are wrenched out of familiar life patterns and existing relationships, sometimes with deadly results. The history of rock and roll contains many tragic stories of this kind, including (from left) Janis Joplin's and Jimi Hendrix's deaths by drug overdose (both 1970) and Jim Morrison's (1971) and Kurt Cobain's (1994) suicides.

deeply pessimistic about the future. He feared that, in the end, the rationalization of society would reduce human beings to robots.

EMILE DURKHEIM: SOCIETY AND FUNCTION

"To love society is to love something beyond us and something in ourselves." These are the words of Emile Durkheim (1858–1917), another of sociology's founders. In this curious statement (1974:55; orig. 1924) we find one more influential vision of human society.

Durkheim is included in the Gallery of Sociologists at http://www.TheSociologyPage.com

STRUCTURE: SOCIETY BEYOND OURSELVES

Emile Durkheim's great insight was recognizing that society exists beyond ourselves. Society is more than the individuals who compose it; society has a life of its own that stretches beyond our personal experience. Society is here long before we are born, it shapes us while we live, and it will remain long after we are gone. Patterns of human behavior—cultural norms, values, and beliefs—exist as established structures and thus are *social facts* that have an objective reality beyond the lives of individuals.

Because society looms larger than any one of us, it has the *power* to guide our thoughts and actions. This is why studying individuals alone (as many psychologists

or biologists do) can never capture the essence of the human experience. Society is more than the sum of its parts; it exists as a complex organism rooted in our collective life. A classroom of third graders taking a math test, a family gathered around a table sharing a meal, people quietly waiting their turn in a doctor's office—all are examples of the countless situations that have a familiar organization apart from any particular individual who has ever participated in them.

Once created by people, then, society takes on a life of its own and demands a measure of obedience from its creators. We experience the reality of society in the order of our lives or as we face temptation and feel the tug of morality.

FUNCTION: SOCIETY AS SYSTEM

Having established that society has structure, Durkheim turned to the concept of *function*. The significance of any social fact, he explained, is more than what individuals see in our immediate lives; social facts help society as a whole to operate.

To illustrate, consider crime. Of course, individuals experience pain and loss as a result of crime. But, taking a broader view, Durkheim saw that crime is vital to the ongoing life of society itself. As Chapter 8 ("Deviance") explains, only by defining acts as criminal do people construct and defend morality, which gives purpose and meaning to our collective life. For this reason, Durkheim rejected the common view of crime as "pathological." On the contrary, he concluded, crime is

NOTE: By arguing that society has an objective existence, Durkheim (like Comte) may have been attempting to establish a natural social order as a moral authority to replace tradition.
Q: "For Durkheim, the sacredness of the person could become one of the few cultural ideals capable of providing a crucial point of unification for an increasingly differentiated, yet interdependent, world." Mike Featherstone (1990:4)

NOTE: Durkheim linked mechanical solidarity to the extent of repressive (criminal) law and organic solidarity to the extent of restitutive (civil) law.
GLOBAL: As Edward A. Tiryakian (1994) points out, neither Durkheim nor other social theorists predicted the reemergence of mechanical solidarity in the form of religious, ethnic, racial, and gender conflict around the world and on the U.S. campus.

Historically, members of human societies engaged in many of the same activities: searching out food and securing shelter. Modern societies, explained Durkheim, display a rapidly expanding division of labor. Increasing specialization is evident in the streets of countries in the process of industrialization: On a Bombay street, a man earns a small fee for cleaning ears.

"normal" for the most basic reason: A society could not exist without it (1964a, orig. 1893; 1964b, orig. 1895).

PERSONALITY: SOCIETY IN OURSELVES

Durkheim contended that society is not only "beyond ourselves" but also "in ourselves." In other words, each of us builds a personality by internalizing social facts. How we act, think, and feel—our essential humanity—is drawn from the society that nurtures us. Moreover, society regulates our behavior through moral discipline. Durkheim held that human beings are naturally insatiable and in constant danger of being overpowered by their own desires. That is, "the more one has, the more one wants, since satisfactions received only stimulate instead of filling needs" (1966:248; orig. 1897). Having given us life, then, society must also rein us in.

Nowhere is the need for societal regulation better illustrated than in Durkheim's study of suicide (1966; orig. 1897), described in Chapter 1 ("The Sociological Perspective"). Why is it that rock stars—from Janis Joplin to Jim Morrison and Jimi Hendrix to Kurt Cobain—seem so prone to self-destruction? Durkheim had the answer long before anyone made electric music: A century ago, just as today, the *least* regulated categories of people suffer the *highest* rates of suicide.

The enormous freedom of the young, rich, and famous exacts a high price in terms of the risk of suicide.

MODERNITY AND ANOMIE

Compared with traditional societies, modern societies impose fewer restrictions on everyone. Durkheim acknowledged the advantages of modern-day freedom, but he warned of increased **anomie,** *a condition in which society provides little moral guidance to individuals.* The pattern by which many celebrities are "destroyed by fame" well illustrates the destructive effects of anomie. Sudden fame tears people from their families and familiar routines, it disrupts established values and norms, and it breaks down society's support and regulation of an individual, sometimes with fatal results. Therefore, Durkheim explains, an individual's desires must be balanced by the claims and guidance of society—a balance that is sometimes difficult in the modern world.

EVOLVING SOCIETIES: THE DIVISION OF LABOR

Like Marx and Weber, Durkheim saw firsthand the rapid social transformation of Europe during the nineteenth century. But Durkheim made his own sense of this change.

In preindustrial societies, explained Durkheim, tradition operates as the social cement that binds people together. In fact, what he called the *collective conscience* is so strong that the community moves quickly to punish anyone who dares to challenge conventional ways of life. Durkheim used the term **mechanical solidarity** to refer to *social bonds based on common sentiments and shared moral value that are strong among members of preindustrial societies.* In practice, mechanical solidarity springs from *likeness.* Durkheim called these bonds "mechanical" because people feel an automatic sense of belonging together.

With industrialization, Durkheim continued, mechanical solidarity becomes weaker and weaker, and people cease to be bound by tradition. But this does not mean that society dissolves. Modern life generates a new type of solidarity. Durkheim called this new social integration **organic solidarity,** *social bonds based on specialization and interdependence that are strong among members of industrial societies.* Where solidarity was once rooted in likeness, it is now based on *differences* among people who find that their specialized work—as plumbers, consultants, midwives, or sociology instructors—make them rely on one another for many of their daily needs.

Q: The term "tyranny of the tribe" suggests the power of the collective conscience in traditional societies.

RESOURCE: An example of a small society that approximates Durkheim's concept of mechanical solidarity is the Amish, described in John Hostetler's article in the Macionis and Benokraitis reader, *Seeing Ourselves*, 5th ed. The Amish practice of shunning illustrates the operation of collective conscience in today's U.S. society.

Q: "The nail that stands up gets hit down." Japanese proverb that might describe social control in a traditional society

Q: "In a word, we must discover the rational substitutes for those religious notions that for a long time have served as the vehicle for the most essential moral ideas." Emile Durkheim, *Moral Education* (1961:9). (This is the idea behind the concept of "civil religion"; see Chapter 19, "Religion.")

APPLYING SOCIOLOGY

The Information Revolution:
What Would Durkheim (and Others) Have Thought?

New technology is rapidly reshaping our society. Were they alive today, the founding sociologists discussed in this chapter would be eager observers of the current scene. Let's imagine for a moment the questions Emile Durkheim, Max Weber, and Karl Marx might ask about the effects of computer technology on society.

Emile Durkheim, who emphasized the increasing division of labor in modern society, probably would wonder whether new information technology is pushing specialization even further. There is good reason to think that it is. Because electronic communication (say, a Web site) gives anyone a vast market (already, 400 million people access the Internet), people can specialize far more than if they were confined to a limited geographic area. For example, whereas most small-town lawyers have a general practice, an information-age attorney (living anywhere) could become a specialist in, say, prenuptial agreements or electronic copyright law. Indeed, as we move into the electronic age, the number of highly specialized

microbusinesses in all fields—some of which become very large—is increasing rapidly.

Durkheim might also point out that the Internet threatens to increase anomie. In part, this is because computer use tends to isolate people, weakening personal relationships. Also, as the Internet offers a flood of information, it provides little in the way of moral guidance about what is true or worth knowing.

Max Weber believed that modern societies are distinctive because their members share a rational worldview, and nothing illustrates this better than bureaucracy. But will bureaucracy continue to dominate the social scene in the new century? Here is one reason to think it may not: Although it may make sense for organizations to regulate workers performing the kinds of routine tasks that were common in the industrial era, much work in the postindustrial era involves imagination. Consider such "new age" work as designing homes, composing music, and writing software. The creativity involved cannot

be regulated in the same way as, say, building automobiles on an assembly line. Perhaps this is why many high-technology companies have done away with dress codes and time clocks.

Finally, what might Karl Marx make of the Information Revolution? Because Marx considered the earlier Industrial Revolution a *class* revolution that allowed the owners of industry to dominate society, he would probably wonder whether a new symbolic elite is gaining power over us. For example, some analysts point out that film and television writers, producers, and performers now enjoy vast wealth, international prestige, and enormous power (Lichter, Rothman, & Lichter, 1990). Similarly, just as people without industrial skills stayed at the bottom of the class system in past decades, so people without symbolic skills are likely to become the "underclass" in the new century.

Durkheim, Weber, and Marx gave us an understanding of industrial societies. As we continue into the postindustrial age, there is plenty of room for new generations of sociologists to carry on.

For Durkheim, then, the key to change in a society is an expanding **division of labor,** or *specialization of economic activity.* Max Weber said that modern societies specialize in order to become more efficient, and Durkheim filled out the picture by showing that members of modern societies count on tens of thousands of others—most of them strangers—for the goods and services needed every day. That is, as members of modern societies, we depend more and more on people we trust less and less. Why do we look to people we hardly know and whose

beliefs may well differ from our own? Durkheim's answer is, "Because we can't live without them."

So modernity rests far less on *moral consensus* and far more on *functional interdependence.* Herein lies what we might call "Durkheim's dilemma": The technological power and greater personal freedom of modern society come at the cost of declining morality and the rising risk of anomie.

Like Marx and Weber, Durkheim worried about the direction society was taking. But of the three,

NOTE: Various assessments of social change, corresponding to the ideas of Marx, Weber, and Durkheim, are found in Chapter 24 ("Social Change").
Q: "Man will never fly. Not in a thousand years." Wilbur Wright
Q: "The optimist proclaims that we live in the best of all possible worlds, and the pessimist fears that this is true." James Cabell

Q: "We have too many men of science, too few of God. We have grasped the mystery of the atom and rejected the Sermon on the Mount. . . . Ours is a world of nuclear giants and ethical infants. We know more about war than we do about peace, more about killing than about living." General Omar N. Bradley (1948)
Q: "Our lives are connected by a thousand different threads." Herman Melville

Durkheim was the most optimistic. He praised our greater freedom and privacy while hoping we could create laws to regulate our behavior.

Finally, can we apply Durkheim's views to the Information Revolution? The box on page 109 suggests that he and the other theorists we have considered in this chapter would have had much to say about new computer technology.

CRITICAL EVALUATION: FOUR VISIONS OF SOCIETY

This chapter opened with several important questions about society. We conclude by summarizing how each of the four visions of society answers these questions.

What Holds Societies Together?

How is something as complex as society possible? Lenski believes that members of a society are united by a shared culture, although cultural patterns vary according to a society's level of technological development. He also points out that as technology becomes more complex, inequality divides a society more and more, although industrialization reduces inequality somewhat.

Marx saw not unity but social division based on class position. From his point of view, elites may force an uneasy peace, but true social unity will come about only if production becomes a cooperative endeavor. To Weber, members of a society share a worldview. Just as tradition joined people together in the past, modern societies have created rational, large-scale organizations that connect people's lives. Finally, Durkheim made solidarity the focus of his work. He contrasted the mechanical solidarity of preindustrial societies, which is based on shared morality, with modern society's organic solidarity, which is based on specialization.

How Have Societies Changed?

According to the Lenski model of sociocultural evolution, societies differ primarily in terms of changing technology. Modern society stands out in this regard with its enormous productive power. Marx also stressed historical differences in productive systems yet pointed to the persistence of social conflict (except perhaps among hunters and gatherers). For Marx, modern society is distinctive only because it brings that conflict out in the open. Weber considered the question of change from the perspective of how people look at the world. Members of preindustrial societies have a traditional outlook, whereas modern people take a rational worldview. Finally, for Durkheim, traditional societies are characterized by mechanical solidarity based on moral likeness. In industrial societies, mechanical solidarity gives way to organic solidarity based on productive specialization.

Why Do Societies Change?

As Lenski sees it, social change is first and foremost a matter of technological innovation that, over time, transforms an entire society. Marx's materialist approach highlights the struggle between classes as the "engine of history," pushing societies toward revolution and reorganization. Weber pointed out how ideas contribute to social change. He demonstrated how a particular world view—Calvinism—advanced the Industrial Revolution, which, in turn, reshaped just about all of society. Finally, Durkheim pointed to an expanding division of labor as the key dimension of social change.

The fact that these four approaches are so different does not mean that any one of them is right or wrong in an absolute sense. Society is exceedingly complex, and we benefit from using all four visions, as shown in the final box.

SUMMARY

Gerhard Lenski

1. Sociocultural evolution explores the effects of technological advances on societies.

2. The earliest hunting and gathering societies were composed of a small number of family-centered nomads. Such societies have all but vanished from today's world.

3. Horticulture began some 12,000 years ago as people created hand tools for cultivation. Pastoral societies domesticate animals and trade extensively.

4. Agriculture, about 5,000 years old, is large-scale cultivation using animal-drawn plows. This technology allows societies to expand into vast empires, with greater productivity, more specialization, and increasing inequality.

SOCIAL SURVEY: "Do you think that most people would try to take advantage of you if they got a chance, or would they try to be fair?" (GSS 2000, N=1,896; *Codebook*, 2001:178). This item is one possible index of anomie.
"Would take advantage of you" 37.9%   "Depends" 9.1%
"Would try to be fair"   51.3%   DK/NR 1.7%
Q: "How is society possible?" Georg Simmel

DISCUSS: Ask how many students are confident that their lives will be better than those of their parents.
Q: "Had there been no technological innovations during the last 10,000 years, all societies would be small, nomadic populations of hunters and gatherers living much the way our Stone Age ancestors did." Gerhard and Jean Lenski

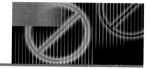

CONTROVERSY & DEBATE

Is Society Getting Better or Worse?

Optimism has been a defining trait of U.S. culture: As time goes on, we think, life gets better. But these days, our historic optimism may be on the decline. Consider that a recent national survey found 67 percent of U.S. adults agreeing that life for the average person is getting worse, not better (30 percent disagreed, and 3 percent offered no opinion; NORC, 2001:210).

What's going on here? To begin, there are reasons for our society's long-time belief in progress. Since the beginning of the twentieth century, for example, we have seen a tenfold increase in the share of college graduates among U.S. adults. Moreover, even taking inflation into account, the average U.S. income is up fourfold.

Back in 1900, it was the rare home that had a telephone and, outside of large cities, none had electricity. No one had even heard of television, and cars were still on the drawing board. Today, almost every home has at least one telephone, a host of electric appliances, television sets, and videocassette recorders; most are equipped with cable

TV and air conditioning, and about half have at least one home computer. Indeed, not only is life better, but there is also more of it: People born in 1900 lived an average of just forty-seven years; children born today can look forward to reaching age seventy-six.

But some trends, especially during the last twenty-five years, have been troubling. Members of our society have been losing confidence that hard work pays off. Despite an increasing share of two-income couples, average family earnings have risen only slightly. At the same time, the divorce rate has soared, and there is four times as much violent crime as in 1960. Our relative affluence, coupled with our capacity to move farther and faster than ever before, seems to have unleashed a wave of individualism that sometimes turns into pure selfishness. As a result, not only is pessimism on the rise, but a majority of U.S. adults report thinking that "they can't be too careful in dealing with people" (NORC, 2001:178).

So, which is it? Is society getting better or worse?

The theorists whose ideas we have examined in this chapter shed some light on this issue. It is easy to equate technology with progress. But, echoing Lenski, history shows us that although advancing technology offers real advantages, it is no guarantee of a better life. Marx, Weber, and Durkheim also noted the growing wealth of societies over time; yet all criticized modern society for a dangerous tendency toward individualism. For Marx, capitalism is the culprit, elevating money to a godlike status and fostering a culture of selfishness. In Weber's analysis, the modern spirit of rationality erodes traditional ties of kinship and neighborhood while expanding bureaucracy, which, he warned, manipulates and isolates people. For Durkheim, members of modern societies may need one another, but they have little moral framework by which to judge right and wrong.

In the end, what societies gain through technological advances may be offset, to some extent, by the loss of human community.

5. Industrialization began 250 years ago in Europe as people used new energy sources to operate large machinery.

6. In postindustrial societies, production shifts from heavy machinery making material things to computers and related technology processing information.

Karl Marx

7. Marx's materialist analysis points out conflict between social classes.

8. Conflict in "ancient" societies involved masters and slaves; in agrarian societies, nobles oppose serfs; in industrial-capitalist societies, capitalists oppose the proletariat.

9. Industrial capitalism alienates workers in four ways: from the act of working, from the products of work, from other workers, and from human potential.

10. Marx believed that once workers overcame their false consciousness, they would overthrow the industrial-capitalist system.

Max Weber

11. Weber's idealist approach argues that ideas have a powerful effect on society.

12. Weber contrasted the tradition of preindustrial societies with the rationality of modern, industrial societies.

13. Weber traced the origins of capitalism to Calvinist religious beliefs. In his analysis, capitalism is "disenchanted" religion.

14. Weber feared that rationality, especially in efficient bureaucratic organizations, would stifle human creativity.

Emile Durkheim

15. Durkheim explained that society has an objective existence apart from individuals.

16. Durkheim related social elements to the larger society through their functions.

17. Societies need solidarity. Traditional societies have mechanical solidarity, which is based on moral likeness; modern societies depend on organic solidarity, which is based on the division of labor.

KEY CONCEPTS

society (p. 89) people who interact in a defined territory and share culture

sociocultural evolution (p. 90) Lenski's term for the changes that occur as a society acquires new technology

hunting and gathering (p. 90) the use of simple tools to hunt animals and gather vegetation

horticulture (p. 91) the use of hand tools to raise crops

pastoralism (p. 91) the domestication of animals

agriculture (p. 92) large-scale cultivation using plows harnessed to animals or more powerful energy sources

industrialism (p. 93) the production of goods using advanced sources of energy to drive large machinery

postindustrialism (p. 95) technology that supports an information-based economy

social conflict (p. 97) struggle between segments of society over valued resources

capitalists (p. 97) people who own and operate factories and other businesses in pursuit of profits

proletarians (p. 97) people who sell their productive labor for wages

social institutions (p. 98) the major spheres of social life, or societal subsystems, organized to meet human needs

false consciousness (p. 98) Marx's term for explanations of social problems as the shortcomings of individuals rather than the flaws of society

class conflict (p. 99) conflict between entire classes over the distribution of a society's wealth and power

class consciousness (p. 99) Marx's term for workers' recognition of themselves as a class unified in opposition to capitalists and, ultimately, to capitalism itself

alienation (p. 100) the experience of isolation and misery resulting from powerlessness

ideal type (p. 102) an abstract statement of the essential characteristics of any social phenomenon

tradition (p. 102) sentiments and beliefs passed from generation to generation

rationality (p. 102) deliberate, matter-of-fact calculation of the most efficient means to accomplish a particular task

rationalization of society (p. 103) Weber's term for the historical change from tradition to rationality as the dominant mode of human thought

anomie (p. 108) Durkheim's term for a condition in which society provides little moral guidance to individuals

mechanical solidarity (p. 108) Durkheim's term for social bonds based on common sentiments and shared moral values that are strong among members of preindustrial societies

organic solidarity (p. 108) Durkheim's term for social bonds based on specialization and interdependence that are strong among members of industrial societies

division of labor (p. 109) specialization of economic activity

CRITICAL-THINKING QUESTIONS

1. Would you say that development of new technology is the same as progress? Why or why not?

2. Explain how Marx's materialist view of society differed from the idealist view held by Weber.

CTQ1: Lenski's view is that technological advance may or may not be accompanied by overall improvement in people's lives. Clearly, Marx and especially Weber were highly critical of modern societies.

CTQ2: Marx considered the economy to be the foundation of society. Weber held that culture could be just as influential (see his *Protestant Ethic*) and that the economy and culture influenced each other.

CTQ3: Marx's alienation is a product of hierarchy; Weber's alienation is the product of rationalization (especially bureaucracy); Durkheim's anomie is the product of increasing tolerance and cultural relativism.

CTQ4: None of the theories deals explicitly with gender, but students should be able to see that each helps explain the increasing gender equality characteristic of modern society.

3. Both Marx and Weber were concerned that modern society alienated people. How are their approaches different? How do their concepts of alienation compare with Durkheim's concept of anomie?

4. Apply the visions of society discussed in this chapter to the changing status of women. How might each theorist explain increasing gender equality? Can you criticize these theories from a feminist perspective?

APPLICATIONS AND EXERCISES

1. Hunting and gathering people mused over stars, and we still know the constellations in terms they used—mostly the names of animals and hunters. As a way of revealing what's important to *our* way of life, write a short paper imagining the meanings we would give clusters of stars if we were starting from scratch.

2. Spend an hour in your home trying to identify every device that has a computer chip in it. How many did you find? Were you surprised by the number?

3. Watch an old Tarzan movie or another film about technologically simpler people. How are they portrayed in the film?

4. Packaged in the back of this new textbook is an interactive CD-ROM that offers a variety of study and review materials intended to help you better understand the material covered in this chapter. For this chapter, the CD-ROM contains an author's tip video, Real Life Sociology videos, other relevant audio and video, interactive map animations, audio journal entries from the author, Web links, and much more.

 ## SITES TO SEE

http://www.prenhall.com/macionis

Visit the interactive *Companion Website*™ that accompanies this text. Begin by clicking on the cover of your book. You will find a chapter-by-chapter study guide, practice tests, and a significant portion of the text for on-line review, as well as many suggested Web links.

http://www.hewett.norfolk.sch.uk/curric/soc/durkheim/durk.htm
http://csf.colorado.edu:80/psn/marx/index.html

These two sites provide close-up looks at the work of two great sociologists.

http://www2.pfeiffer.edu/~lridener/DSS/INDEX.HTML

Visit the Dead Sociologists Society to learn more about Marx, Weber, Durkheim, and other sociologists.

http://www.macionis.com
(or http://www.TheSociologyPage.com)

Biographical sketches of Marx, Weber, Durkheim, and other social thinkers are found on the author's Web site.

http://www.gwu.edu/~ccps/

Visit the Web site for the Communitarian Network, an organization concerned with balancing modern individuality with traditional social responsibility.

 ## INVESTIGATE WITH CONTENTSELECT

Follow the instructions found on page 23 of this textbook to enter this chapter of the book's *Companion Website*™. Once in the chapter, click on the ContentSelect icon at the bottom left of your screen and enter your personal User ID and Password. Enter keywords such as "Karl Marx," "horticulture," and "Industrial Revolution," and the search engine will help you become an effective researcher.

CHAPTER

5

Andrew Macara
Footballers, Kos, 1993

Oil on canvas, 63.5 × 76.2 cm. Private Collection/
The Bridgeman Art Library.

SOCIALIZATION

On a cold winter day in 1938, a social worker walked quickly to the door of a rural Pennsylvania farmhouse. Investigating a case of possible child abuse, the social worker entered the home and discovered a five-year-old girl hidden in a second-floor storage room. The child, whose name was Anna, was wedged into an old chair with her arms tied above her head so that she couldn't move. She was wearing filthy clothes, and her arms and legs were as thin as matchsticks (Davis, 1940).

Anna's situation can only be described as tragic. She was born in 1932 to an unmarried and mentally impaired woman of twenty-six who lived with her strict father. Enraged by his daughter's "illegitimate" motherhood, the grandfather did not even want the child in his house.

For her first six months, therefore, Anna was shuttled between various welfare agencies. When her mother was no longer able to pay for her care, Anna returned to the hostile home of her grandfather.

To lessen the grandfather's anger, Anna's mother moved Anna to the storage room and gave her just enough milk to keep her alive. There she stayed— day after day, month after month, with almost no human contact—for five long years.

Learning of the discovery of Anna, sociologist Kingsley Davis (1940) immediately went to see her. He found her with local authorities at a county home. Davis was appalled by the sight of the emaciated child who was not able to laugh, speak, or even smile. Anna was completely unresponsive, as if alone in an empty world.

SOCIAL EXPERIENCE: THE KEY TO OUR HUMANITY

Here is a terrible case of a child deprived of social contact. Although physically alive, Anna hardly seemed human. Her plight reveals that without social experience a child is incapable of thought, emotion, or meaningful action—more an object than a person.

Sociologists use the term **socialization** to refer to *the lifelong social experience by which individuals develop their human potential and learn culture.* Unlike other living species whose behavior is biologically set, humans need social experience to learn their culture and survive. Social experience is also the foundation of **personality,** *a person's fairly consistent patterns of acting, thinking, and feeling.* We build a personality by internalizing—or taking in—our surroundings. But without social experience, as Anna's case shows, personality does not develop at all.

HUMAN DEVELOPMENT: NATURE AND NURTURE

Helpless at birth, the human infant depends on others to provide nourishment and care. Anna's case makes these facts clear. But a century ago, most people mistakenly believed that human behavior was the product of our biology.

Charles Darwin: The Role of Nature

Charles Darwin's groundbreaking study of evolution, described in Chapter 3 ("Culture"), explained that each species evolves over thousands of generations as

115

SUPPLEMENTS: An outline of Chapter 5, along with supplementary lecture material and discussion questions, is found in the *Data File*.

NOTE: The term *tabula rasa* (Latin, meaning "clean slate") was introduced by English philosopher John Locke (1632–1704). An empiricist, Locke believed that human personalities were "written on" by experience.

NOTE: "Nature" has the Latin root *nat(us)*, meaning "born"; "nurture" has the Latin root *nutrit(us)*, meaning "nourished."

NOTE: An interesting twist on the nature-nurture debate: Throughout history, naturalists believed an untaught child would speak but wondered what language. The naturalist Holy Roman Emperor Frederick II thought it would be Latin or Greek; James I of Scotland opined it would be Hebrew.

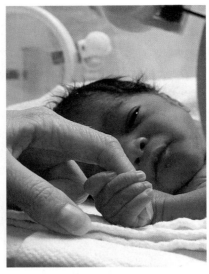
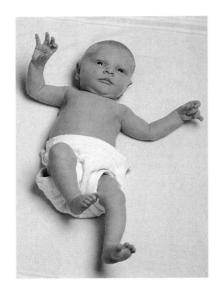

Human infants display various reflexes—biologically based behavior patterns that enhance survival. The sucking reflex, which actually begins before birth, enables the infant to obtain nourishment. The grasping reflex, triggered by placing a finger on the infant's palm causing the hand to close, helps the infant to maintain contact with a parent and, later on, to grasp objects. The Moro reflex, activated by startling the infant, has the infant swinging both arms outward and then bringing them together across the chest. This action, which disappears after several months of life, probably developed among our evolutionary ancestors so that a falling infant could grasp the body hair of a parent.

genetic variation improves its ability to survive and reproduce. Traits that enhance survival emerge as a species' "nature." For this reason people once assumed that humans, like other life forms, had an instinctive "human nature." Given our tendency to see our own way of life as natural, people argued that our economic system reflects "instinctive human competitiveness," that some people are "born criminals," or that women are "naturally" emotional while men are "innately" rational (Witkin-Lanoil, 1984).

People trying to understand cultural diversity also misunderstood Darwin's thinking. From centuries of world exploration, Western Europeans knew that people around the world behaved quite differently from each other. But Europeans linked these differences to biology rather than culture. It was an easy, but very damaging, next step to claim that members of technologically simple societies were biologically less evolved and thus less human. This ethnocentric view helped justify colonialism: Why not exploit others if they seem not to be human in the same sense in which you are?

The Social Sciences: The Role of Nurture

In the twentieth century, biological explanations of human behavior came under fire. Psychologist John B. Watson (1878–1958) developed a theory called *behaviorism*, which held that behavior is not instinctive but learned. Thus, people everywhere are equally human, differing only in their cultural patterns. In short, Watson rooted human behavior not in nature but in *nurture*.

Today, social scientists are cautious about describing *any* human behavior as instinctive. This does not mean that biology plays no part in human behavior. After all, human life depends on the functioning of the body. We also know that children often share biological traits (such as height and hair color) with their parents and that heredity plays a part in intelligence, musical and artistic aptitude, and personality (such as how one reacts to frustration). In fact, unless children use their brains early in life, the brain itself does not fully develop. At the same time, whether a person *realizes* any inherited potential depends on environmental factors, which create opportunities to develop it (Plomin & Foch, 1980; Goldsmith, 1983; Begley, 1995).

Without denying the importance of nature, then, nurture matters more in shaping human behavior. More precisely, *nurture is our nature.*

SOCIAL ISOLATION

Of course, researchers must never experiment on human beings by placing them in total isolation. But forty years ago, researchers did carry out a revealing study of the effects of social isolation using nonhuman primates.

Studies of Nonhuman Primates

Psychologists Harry Harlow and Margaret Harlow (1962) placed rhesus monkeys—whose behavior is in some ways surprisingly similar to human behavior—in various conditions of social isolation. They found that complete isolation (with adequate nutrition) for even six months seriously disturbed the monkeys' development. When returned to their group, these monkeys were passive, anxious, and fearful.

The Harlows then placed infant rhesus monkeys in cages with an artificial "mother" made of wire mesh with a wooden head and the nipple of a feeding tube where the breast would be. These monkeys, too, were later unable to interact with others.

But when the researchers covered the artificial mother with soft terry cloth, the infant monkeys would cling to it. The monkeys benefited from this closeness, the Harlows concluded, because they showed less developmental damage than earlier monkeys. The experiment confirmed how important it is that adults cradle infants affectionately.

Finally, the Harlows discovered that infant monkeys could recover from about three months of isolation. But by about six months, isolation caused irreversible emotional and behavioral damage.

Studies of Isolated Children

Tragic cases of children isolated by abusive family members show the damage caused by depriving human beings of social experience. We will review three such cases.

Anna: The rest of the story. The rest of Anna's story squares with the Harlows' findings. After her discovery, Anna received extensive attention and soon showed

Early in the twentieth century, most people in the United States thought biology shaped human behavior. The discipline of anthropology helped demonstrate the primary importance of environment to human development. The best known of all anthropologists is Margaret Mead, shown here with a mother and child during a 1953 research project on the Admiralty Islands near New Guinea in the South Pacific.

improvement. When Kingsley Davis visited her after ten days, he found her more alert and even smiling with obvious pleasure. Over the next year, Anna made steady progress, showing more interest in other people and gradually learning to walk. After a year and a half, she could feed herself and play with toys.

As the Harlows might have predicted, however, Anna's five years of social isolation had caused permanent damage. At age eight, her mental development was less than a two-year-old's. Not until she was almost ten did she begin to use words. Because Anna's mother was mentally retarded, perhaps Anna was similarly challenged. The riddle was never solved because Anna died at age ten from a blood disorder, possibly related to years of abuse (Davis, 1940, 1947).

Another case: Isabelle. A second case involves another girl, found at about the same time as Anna and under very similar circumstances. After more than six years of isolation, this child—known as Isabelle—displayed the same lack of responsiveness as Anna. Unlike Anna, though, Isabelle benefited from a special learning program directed by psychologists. Within a week, Isabelle was attempting to speak and, a year and a half later, she knew some 2,000 words. The psychologists concluded that intensive effort had propelled

NOTE: The violence in Genie's family stemmed from a father who wanted no children. The first child in the family died from exposure at 2½ months; the second child died at 2 years; the third child survived but only after the paternal grandmother took him into her own home; Genie was the family's fourth child. Genie's mother was almost blind; she isolated Genie to protect her. When Genie came to the attention of social workers, the father shot himself.

NOTE: Another way to present the theorists is to pose the question "How do we learn?" Freud emphasizes *internalization* of culture; Piaget underscores internal *cognitive development*; behaviorists Watson and Skinner highlight *environmental stimulation*; Mead advances a *social behaviorist* approach based on gaining the capacity for symbolic interaction.

Q: "Anatomy is destiny." Sigmund Freud

The personalities we develop depend largely on the environment in which we live. As William Kurelek shows in this painting, Prairie Childhood, *based on his childhood in the Alberta, Canada, prairies, a young person's life on a farm is often characterized by periods of social isolation and backbreaking work. How would such a boy's personality be likely to differ from that of his wealthy cousin raised in a large city, such as Montreal?*

Isabelle through six years of normal development in only two years. By the time she was fourteen, Isabelle was attending sixth-grade classes, damaged by her early ordeal but on her way to a somewhat normal life (Davis, 1947).

A third case: Genie. A more recent case of childhood isolation involves a California girl abused by her parents (Curtiss, 1977; Pines, 1981; Rymer, 1994). From

 Read a transcript of the PBS *Nova* television program about the life of Genie at http://www.pbs.org/wgbh/nova/transcripts/2112gchild.html

age two, Genie was tied to a potty chair in a dark garage. In 1970, when she was found at age thirteen, Genie weighed only fifty-nine pounds and had the mental development of a one-year-old. With intensive treatment, she became physically healthy, but her language ability remains that of a young child. Genie lives today in a home for developmentally disabled adults.

Conclusion. All the evidence points to the crucial role of social experience in forming personality. Human beings can sometimes recover from abuse and isolation. But there is a point—precisely when is unclear from the small number of cases studied—at which isolation in infancy causes permanent developmental damage.

UNDERSTANDING SOCIALIZATION

Socialization is a complex, lifelong process. The following sections highlight the work of six researchers who made lasting contributions to our understanding of human development.

SIGMUND FREUD: THE ELEMENTS OF PERSONALITY

Sigmund Freud (1856–1939) lived in Vienna at a time when most Europeans considered human behavior

 For a biographical sketch of Sigmund Freud, see the Gallery of Sociologists at http://www.TheSociologyPage.com

biologically fixed. Trained as a physician, Freud gradually turned to the study of personality and eventually developed the celebrated theory of psychoanalysis.

Basic Human Needs

Freud believed that biology plays a major part in human development, although not in terms of specific instincts, as in other species. He theorized that humans have two basic needs. First is a need for bonding, which Freud called the life instinct, or *eros* (from the

NOTE: Champions of psychoanalysis include Franz Boas, Margaret Mead, and Ruth Benedict, all of whom interpreted this approach as favoring nurture over nature.

RESOURCE: The most sociological of Freud's 24 books is *Civilization and Its Discontents*. The sociological implications of Freud's work are explored in Philip Rieff's *Freud: The Mind of the Moralist* (Doubleday, 1961).

NOTE: A revealing example of Freud's influence on popular culture: the characterization of anything unintended as "Freudian."

Q: "The principal task of civilization, its actual *raison d'être*, is to defend us against nature." Sigmund Freud

Q: "The mind, of course, is just what the brain does for a living." Sharon Begley

Q: "It was my fate to be a scholar for a while." Nietzsche

Greek god of love). Second, we also have an aggressive drive he called the death instinct, or *thanatos* (from the Greek word meaning "death"). These opposing forces operate at an unconscious level and generate deep inner tension.

Freud's Model of Personality

Freud joined basic needs with the influence of society to devise a model of personality with three parts: id, ego, and superego. The **id** (the Latin word for "it") represents *the human being's basic drives*, which are unconscious and demand immediate satisfaction. Rooted in biology, the id is present at birth, making a newborn a bundle of demands for attention, touching, and food. But society opposes the self-centered id, which is why one of the first words a child learns is "no."

To avoid frustration, a child must learn to approach the world realistically. This is done through the **ego** (Latin for "I"), which is *a person's conscious efforts to balance innate pleasure-seeking drives with the demands of society*. The ego develops as we become aware of ourselves but also realize that we cannot have everything we want.

Finally, the human personality develops the **superego** (Latin meaning "above" or "beyond" the ego), which is *the cultural values and norms internalized by an individual*. The superego operates as our conscience, telling us *why* we cannot have everything we want. The superego begins to form as a child becomes aware of parental control and matures as the child comes to understand that everyone's behavior must take into account cultural norms.

Personality Development

To the id-centered child, the world is a bewildering array of physical sensations that bring either pleasure or pain. As the superego develops, however, the child learns the moral concepts of right and wrong. In other words, initially children can feel good only in a physical way, but after three or four years, they feel good or bad according to how they judge their behavior against cultural norms.

The id and superego remain in conflict, but in a well-adjusted person, the ego manages these two opposing forces. When conflicts are not resolved during childhood, they may surface as personality disorders later on.

Culture, in the form of superego, *represses* selfish demands, forcing people to look beyond themselves. Often, the competing demands of self and society result in a compromise that Freud called *sublimation*. Sublimation redirects selfish drives into socially acceptable behavior. Sexual urges, for example, may lead to marriage, just as aggression gives rise to competitive sports.

Critical evaluation. Freud's work was controversial in his own time. More recently, critics charge that Freud's work presents humans in male terms and devalues women (Donovan & Littenberg, 1982). But Freud influenced everyone who later studied the human personality. Of special importance to sociology is his notion that we internalize social norms and that childhood experiences have a lasting impact on our personalities.

JEAN PIAGET: COGNITIVE DEVELOPMENT

Swiss psychologist Jean Piaget (1896–1980) studied human *cognition*—how people think. As Piaget watched his own three children, he wondered not just *what* they knew but *how* they made sense of the world. Piaget went on to identify four stages of cognitive development.

 For a closer look at Piaget and his work, go to http://www.piaget.org

The Sensorimotor Stage

Stage one is the **sensorimotor stage**, *the level of human development at which individuals experience the world only through their senses*. For about the first two years of life, the infant knows the world only through the five senses: touching, tasting, smelling, looking, and listening. "Knowing" to young children amounts to direct, sensory experience.

The Preoperational Stage

About age two, children enter the **preoperational stage**, *the level of human development at which individuals first use language and other symbols*. Now children begin to think about the world mentally and with imagination. But "pre-op" children between about two and six still attach meaning only to specific experiences and objects. They can identify a favorite toy but cannot explain what *kinds* of toys they like.

Lacking abstract concepts, a child also cannot judge size, weight, or volume. In one of his best-known experiments, Piaget placed two identical glasses containing equal amounts of water on a table. He asked

NOTE: Stress that Piaget's stages of development are *maturational*; in this, he stands apart from George Herbert Mead, for whom biology played almost no role in social development. (Piaget was trained as a biologist.)

NOTE: An example of preoperational thinking: Young children prefer nickels to dimes because nickels are bigger.

Q: "If we examine the intellectual development of the individual . . . we shall find that the human spirit goes through a certain number of stages, each different from the other." Jean Piaget

NOTE: Because of their egocentric worldview, young children may see themselves as responsible for family conflict and divorce.

In a well-known experiment, Jean Piaget demonstrated that children over the age of seven had entered the concrete operational stage of development because they could recognize that the quantity of liquid remained the same when poured from a wide beaker into a tall one.

several children ages five and six whether the amount in both glasses was the same. They nodded that it was. The children then watched Piaget take one of the glasses and pour its contents into a taller, narrower glass, raising the level of the water. He asked again whether the glasses held the same amount. The children insisted that the taller glass held more water. By about age seven, children are able to think abstractly and realize that the amount of water stays the same.

The Concrete Operational Stage

Next comes the **concrete operational stage,** *the level of human development at which individuals first perceive causal connections in their surroundings.* Between ages seven and eleven, children focus on how and why things happen. In addition, children in this stage attach more than one symbol to a particular event or object. For example, if you say to a child of five, "Today is Wednesday," she might respond, "No, it's my birthday!" indicating that she can use just one symbol at a time. But a ten-year-old at the concrete operational stage would be able to respond, "Yes, and this Wednesday is my birthday!"

The Formal Operational Stage

The last stage in Piaget's model is the **formal operational stage,** *the level of human development at which individuals think abstractly and critically.* At about age twelve, young people begin to reason abstractly rather than thinking only of concrete situations. For example, if you were to ask a child of seven, "What would you like to be when you grow up?" you might receive a concrete response such as "a teacher." But most teenagers can think more abstractly and might reply, "I would like a job that helps others." This capacity for abstract thought also lets young people understand metaphors. Hearing the expression "A penny for your thoughts" might lead a child to ask for a coin, but the adolescent will recognize a gentle invitation to intimacy.

Critical evaluation. Whereas Freud saw human beings torn by opposing forces of biology and culture, Piaget saw the mind as active and creative. He saw an ability to engage the world unfolding in stages as the result of both biological maturation and social experience.

But do people in all societies pass through all four of Piaget's stages? Living in a traditional society that changes slowly limits the capacity for abstract and critical thought. Even in our own society, perhaps 30 percent of people never reach the formal operational stage (Kohlberg & Gilligan, 1971).

LAWRENCE KOHLBERG: MORAL DEVELOPMENT

Lawrence Kohlberg (1981) built on Piaget's work in studying *moral reasoning,* the ways in which individuals judge situations as right or wrong. Here, again, development occurs in stages.

Young children who experience the world in terms of pain and pleasure (Piaget's sensorimotor stage) are at the *preconventional* level of moral development. At this early stage, "rightness" amounts to "what feels good to me."

The *conventional* level, Kohlberg's second stage, appears by the teen years (corresponding to Piaget's final, formal operational stage). At this point, young people lose some of their selfishness as they learn to define right and wrong in terms of what pleases parents and what is consistent with broader cultural norms. Individuals at this stage also try to assess intention in reaching moral judgments instead of simply observing what others do.

In Kohlberg's final stage of moral development, the *postconventional* level, individuals move beyond their society's norms to consider abstract ethical principles. Now they think about liberty, freedom, or justice, perhaps arguing that what is legal still may not be right.

GLOBAL: Kohlberg claims, in essence, that good and evil span a continuum from selflessness at one end to selfishness at the other. This is an almost universal theme of world religions.

SOCIAL SURVEY: One of Gilligan's interview items asked girls, "How often do you feel happy the way you are?" Sixty percent of elementary school girls, but only 29% of high school girls, answered "always." Corresponding figures for boys were 67% and 46%.

Q: "In Gilligan's studies females moved from an early 'selfish' stage to an overly altruistic stage. The developmental task for the women in Gilligan's study was to achieve a position where they could take their own interests into account. . . . A mature person, according to the ethic of care, recognizes her connection to others . . . and at the same time can articulate her own wants and needs." John R. Hall and Mary Jo Neitz (1993:37)

CRITICAL THINKING

The Importance of Gender in Research

Carol Gilligan, an educational psychologist at Harvard University, has shown how gender guides social behavior. Her early work exposed the gender bias in studies by Kohlberg and others who had used only male subjects. But as her research progressed, Gilligan (1990) made a major discovery: Boys and girls use different strategies in making moral decisions. Thus, by ignoring gender, we end up with an incomplete view of human behavior.

More recently, Gilligan has looked at the effect of gender on self-esteem. Her research team interviewed more than 2,000 girls, ages six to eighteen, over a five-year period. She found a clear pattern: Young girls start out eager and confident, but their self-esteem slips away as they pass through adolescence.

Why? Gilligan claims that the answer lies in the way our culture defines females. In our society, the ideal woman is calm, controlled, and eager to please. Also, as girls move from the elementary grades to secondary school, they encounter fewer women teachers and find that most authority figures are men. As a result, by their late teens, girls must struggle to regain the personal strength they had a decade before.

Ironically, when Gilligan and her colleagues returned to a private school—one site of their research—to present their findings, they found further evidence of their theory. Most younger girls who had been interviewed were eager to have their names appear in the forthcoming book, but the older girls were hesitant: Many were fearful that they would be talked about.

What do you think?

1. *How does Gilligan's research show the importance of gender in understanding society?*

2. *How does her work show that socialization may not be a direct and linear progression?*

3. *Do you think boys are subject to some of the same pressures and difficulties as girls? How?*

Sources: Gilligan (1990) and Winkler (1990).

Critical evaluation. Like the work of Piaget, Kohlberg's model presents moral development in distinct stages. But, here again, whether this model applies to people in all societies remains unclear. Many people in the United States apparently never reach the postconventional level of moral reasoning, although exactly why is still an open question.

Another problem with Kohlberg's research is that his subjects were all boys. Kohlberg commits the research error, described in Chapter 2 ("Sociological Investigation"), of generalizing the results of male subjects to all people. This problem led a colleague, Carol Gilligan, to investigate how gender affects moral reasoning.

CAROL GILLIGAN: THE GENDER FACTOR

Carol Gilligan, whose approach is highlighted in the box, compared the moral development of girls and boys and concluded that the two sexes use different standards of rightness.

Gilligan (1982, 1990) claims that males have a *justice perspective*, relying on formal rules to define right and wrong. Girls have a *care and responsibility perspective*, judging a situation with an eye toward personal relationships. For example, as boys see it, stealing is wrong because it breaks the law. Girls are more likely to wonder why someone would steal and to be sympathetic toward a person who steals to, say, feed a hungry child.

Kohlberg considers rule-based male reasoning superior to the person-based female approach. But Gilligan notes that impersonal rules dominate men's lives in the workplace, whereas personal relationships are more relevant to women's lives as mothers and caregivers. Why, then, Gilligan asks, should we set up male standards as the norms by which to judge everyone?

Critical evaluation. Gilligan's work sharpens our understanding of human development and gender issues in research. But what accounts for the differences she documents between females and males? Is it nature or nurture? In Gilligan's view, cultural conditioning is at work. Therefore, as more women organize their lives

RESOURCE: Mead's statement "The Self" is among the classics included in the *Seeing Ourselves* reader.

RESOURCE: Besides believing in the plasticity of human personality, George Herbert Mead also believed in people's ability to reform society. For a discussion of his views on social reform, see Dmitri N. Shalin, *American Journal of Sociology* 93, 4 (January 1988):913–51.

NOTE: Piaget argued that social behavior is shaped by maturational stages; by contrast, Mead implied that stages of life are defined and structured by society.

RESOURCE: Italian playwright Luigi Pirandello (1867–1936) made use of the sociological perspective in his work. Many of his plays reveal a striking similarity to the ideas of George Herbert Mead (and also Erving Goffman). See, especially, *The Pleasure of Honesty*.

George Herbert Mead wrote: "No hard-and-fast line can be drawn between our own selves and the selves of others." The painting Manyness *by Rimma Gerlovina and Valeriy Gerlovin conveys this important truth. Although we tend to think of ourselves as unique individuals, each person's characteristics develop in an ongoing process of interaction with others.*

Rimma Gerlovina & Valeriy Gerlovin, *Manyness*, 1990. © the artists, New City, N.Y.

around the workplace, the moral reasoning of women and men will become more similar.

GEORGE HERBERT MEAD: THE SOCIAL SELF

George Herbert Mead (1863–1931) developed a theory of *social behaviorism* to explain how social experience creates individual personality (1962; orig. 1934). His approach calls to mind the behaviorism of psychologist John B. Watson, described earlier. Both saw the power of environment to shape behavior. But whereas Watson focused on outward behavior, Mead studied inward *thinking*, humanity's defining trait.

A short biography of George Herbert Mead is included in the Gallery of Sociologists at http://www.TheSociologyPage.com

The Self

Mead's central concept is the **self**, *the part of an individual's personality composed of self-awareness and self-image.*

Mead's genius was in seeing the self as the product of social experience.

First, said Mead, *the self develops only with social experience.* The self is not part of the body, and it does not exist at birth. Mead rejected the position that personality is guided by biological drives (as Freud asserted) or biological maturation (as Piaget claimed). For Mead, self develops only as the individual interacts with others. In the absence of interaction, as we see from cases of isolated children, the body grows, but no self emerges.

Second, Mead explained, *social experience is the exchange of symbols.* Only people use words, a wave of the hand, or a smile to create meaning. We can train a dog by rewarding correct behavior, but the dog attaches no meaning to its actions. Human beings, by contrast, find meaning in action by imagining people's underlying intentions. In short, a dog responds to *what you do*; a human responds to *what you have in mind* as you do it. Thus, you can train a dog to go to the hallway and bring back an umbrella. But without understanding intention, if the dog cannot find the umbrella, it is incapable of the *human* response: to look for a raincoat instead.

Third, Mead continues, *understanding intention requires imagining the situation from the other's point of view.* Using symbols, we imagine ourselves "in another person's shoes" and see ourselves as that person does. We can therefore anticipate how others will respond to us even before we act. A simple toss of a ball requires stepping outside ourselves to imagine how another will catch our throw. Social interaction, then, involves seeing ourselves as others see us—a process Mead called *taking the role of the other.*

The Looking-Glass Self

In effect, others represent a mirror (which people used to call a "looking glass") in which we can see ourselves. What we think of ourselves, then, depends on what we think others think of us. For example, if we think others see us as clever, we will think of ourselves in the same way. But if we feel they think of us as clumsy, then that is how we will see ourselves. Charles Horton Cooley (1864–1929) used the phrase **looking-glass self** to mean *a self-image based on how we think others see us* (1964; orig. 1902).

The I and the Me

Mead's fourth point is that *by taking the role of the other, we become self-aware.* The self, then, has two parts. As subject, the self is active and spontaneous. Mead called

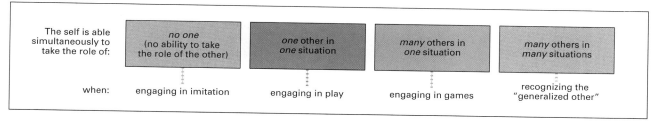

FIGURE 5–1 Building on Social Experience

George Herbert Mead described the development of the self as a process of gaining social experience. That is, the self develops as we expand our capacity to take the role of the other.

the active side of the self the *I* (the subjective form of the personal pronoun). But the self is also an object, as we imagine ourselves as others see us. Mead called the objective side of the self the *me* (the objective form of the personal pronoun). All social experience has both components: We initiate an action (the I-phase of self) and then we continue the action (or not) based on how others respond to us (the me-phase of self).

Development of the Self

The key to developing the self, then, is learning to take the role of the other. With limited social experience, infants can do this only through *imitation*. That is, they mimic behavior without understanding underlying intentions, and so they have no self.

As children learn to use language and other symbols, the self emerges through *play*, which involves taking the roles of *significant others*, especially parents. Playing "mommy and daddy" (often putting themselves literally "in the shoes" of a parent) helps young children imagine the world from a parent's point of view.

Gradually, children learn to take the roles of several others at once. They can move from simple play (say, playing catch) involving one other to complex *games* (such as baseball) involving many others. By about age seven, most children have the social experience needed to engage in team sports.

Figure 5–1 charts the progression from imitation to play to games. But a final stage in the development of self remains. A game involves taking the role of others in just one situation, but social life demands that we see ourselves in terms of cultural norms as *anyone* else might. Mead used the term **generalized other** to refer to *the widespread cultural norms and values we use as a reference in evaluating ourselves.*

As life goes on, the self continues to change along with our social experiences. But no matter how much

events and circumstances affect us, we always remain creative beings. Thus, Mead concluded, we play a key role in our own socialization.

Critical evaluation. Mead's work explores the character of social experience itself. In symbolic interaction, he found the root of both self and society.

Some critics say Mead's view is completely social, allowing no biological element at all. In this, Mead stands apart from Freud (who identified general drives within the organism) and Piaget (whose stages of development are tied to biological maturity).

Be careful not to confuse Mead's concepts of the I and the me with Freud's id and superego. For Freud, the id originates in our biology, whereas Mead rejected any biological element of self (although he never specified the origin of the I). Moreover, whereas the id and superego are locked in continual combat, the I and the me work together cooperatively (Meltzer, 1978).

ERIK H. ERIKSON: EIGHT STAGES OF DEVELOPMENT

All the thinkers discussed so far point to childhood as the crucial time when personality takes shape. Erik H. Erikson (1902–1994) took a broader view of socialization. He believed that we face challenges throughout the life course (1963; orig. 1950).

Stage 1—Infancy: the challenge of trust (versus mistrust). Between birth and about eighteen months, infants face the first of life's challenges: to establish a sense of trust that their world is a safe place. Family members play a key role in how the child meets this challenge.

Stage 2—Toddlerhood: the challenge of autonomy (versus doubt and shame). The

EXERCISE: For motivated students, assign a special report on George Herbert Mead's ideas about teaching. Sources include "The Psychology of Social Consciousness Implied in Instruction" (*Science* XXXI, 1910:688–93) and "The Teaching of Science in College" (*Science* XXIV, 1906:390–97).

Q: "The powerful play goes on and you may contribute a verse." Walt Whitman
DISCUSS: What does the class make of the fact that a substantial majority of people incarcerated for violent crimes had poor family lives as children?

Sociological research indicates that affluent parents tend to encourage creativity in their children while poor parents tend to foster conformity. While this general difference may be valid, parents at all class levels can and do provide loving support and guidance by simply involving themselves in their children's lives. Henry Ossawa Tanner's painting The Banjo Lesson *stands as a lasting testament to this process.*

Henry Ossawa Tanner, *The Banjo Lesson*, 1893. Oil on canvas. Hampton University Museum, Hampton, Virginia.

next challenge, up to age three, is to learn skills to cope with the world in a confident way. Failing to gain self-control leads children to doubt their abilities.

Stage 3—Preschool: the challenge of initiative (versus guilt). Four- and five-year-olds must learn to engage their surroundings—including people outside the family—or experience guilt at failing to meet the expectations of parents and others.

Stage 4—Preadolescence: the challenge of industriousness (versus inferiority). Between ages six and thirteen, children enter school, make friends, and strike out on their own more and more. They feel proud of their accomplishments, or fear that they do not measure up.

Stage 5—Adolescence: the challenge of gaining identity (versus confusion). During the teen years, young people struggle to establish their own identity. In part, teenagers identify with others, but they also want to be unique. Almost all teens experience some confusion as they struggle to establish an identity.

Stage 6—Young adulthood: the challenge of intimacy (versus isolation). The challenge for young adults is to form and maintain intimate relationships. Falling in love (as well as making close friends) involves balancing the need to bond with the need to have a separate identity.

Stage 7—Middle adulthood: the challenge of making a difference (versus self-absorption). The challenge of middle age is contributing to the lives of others in the family, at work, and in the larger world. Failing at this, people become stagnant, caught up in their own limited concerns (think of Scrooge in Dickens's classic *A Christmas Carol*).

Stage 8—Old age: the challenge of integrity (versus despair). Near the end of our lives, Erikson explains, people hope to look back on what they have accomplished with a sense of integrity and satisfaction. For those who have been self-absorbed, old age brings only a sense of despair over missed opportunities.

Critical evaluation. Erikson's theory views personality formation as a lifelong process. Furthermore, success at one stage (say, an infant gaining trust) prepares us for meeting the next challenge.

One problem with this model is that not everyone confronts these challenges in the exact order presented by Erikson. Nor is it clear that failure to meet the challenge of one stage of life means that a person is doomed to fail later on. A broader question, raised earlier in our discussion of Piaget's ideas, is whether people in other cultures and in other times in history would define a successful life in the same terms as Erikson.

In sum, Erikson's model helps us make sense of socialization and points out how the family, the school, and other settings shape us. We turn now to take a close look at these agents of socialization.

AGENTS OF SOCIALIZATION

Every social experience we have affects us in at least a small way. However, several familiar settings have special importance in the socialization process.

THE FAMILY

The family has the greatest impact on socialization. Infants are totally dependent on others, and the responsibility typically falls on parents and other family members. At least until children begin school, the family also has the job of teaching children skills, values, and beliefs. Even teenagers continue to place their greatest trust in their parents, according to a recent survey shown in Figure 5–2. Overall, research suggests, nothing is more likely to produce a happy, well-adjusted child than being in a loving family (Gibbs, 2001).

Not all family learning results from intentional teaching by parents. Children also learn from the kind of environment that adults create. Whether children learn to see themselves as strong or weak, smart or stupid, loved or simply tolerated, and, as Erik Erikson suggests, whether they see the world as trustworthy or dangerous, depends largely on their surroundings.

The family also gives children a social position in terms of race, religion, ethnicity, and class. In time, all these elements become part of a child's self-concept.

Research shows that the class position of parents affects how they raise their children (Ellison, Bartkowski, & Segal, 1996). Class position shapes not just how much money parents have to spend but also what they expect of their children. Surveys show that when asked to pick from a list of traits that are most desirable in a child, lower-class people in the United States favor obedience and conformity. Well-to-do people, by contrast, choose good judgment and creativity (NORC, 2001).

Why the difference? Melvin Kohn (1977) explains that people of lower social standing usually have limited education and perform routine jobs under close supervision. Expecting that their children will hold similar positions, they encourage obedience and may even use physical punishment such as spanking to get it. Well-off parents, with more schooling, usually have jobs that demand imagination and provide more personal freedom. Therefore, these parents try to inspire the same qualities in their children. In short, parents act in ways that encourage their children to follow in their footsteps.

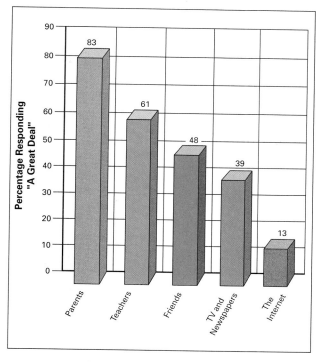

FIGURE 5–2 Whom Do You Trust?

Survey Question: "How much do you trust the information you get from . . . ?"

Sample of 409 U.S. teens, ages 13 to 17, 341 (83%) responding using the Internet. Survey taken April 1999 by Yankelovich Partners, Inc.

Source: Data from Okrent (1999).

THE SCHOOL

Schooling enlarges children's social worlds to include people with backgrounds different from their own. In the process, they learn the importance that society attaches to race and gender. Studies confirm that children tend to cluster in play groups made up of one race and gender (Lever, 1978; Finkelstein & Haskins, 1983).

Schools teach children a wide range of knowledge and skills. But schools informally convey other lessons, which might be called the *hidden curriculum*. Activities such as spelling bees and sports foster the value of competition and showcase success. Children also receive countless informal lessons that their society's way of life is morally good.

School is also most children's first experience with bureaucracy. The school day runs on impersonal rules and a strict time schedule. Not surprisingly, these are

NOTE: The word "peer" is derived from the Latin *par*, meaning "equal."

DIVERSITY: Mean daily TV viewing time for individuals is 4.3 hrs. Women watch more than men, people over 55 more than those under 25, and African Americans more than whites.

GLOBAL: In Brazil, about three-fourths of all homes have a television, yet only one-fourth have a refrigerator.

GLOBAL: Some 250,000 television sets are built each day, more than the number of people added to the earth's population. In global perspective, the mass media (especially television) are most widespread in industrial and postindustrial societies that change quickly; however, the media are a powerful force for change when introduced to traditional societies—see the box about Brazil's Kaiapo Indians in Chapter 24.

GLOBAL SNAPSHOT

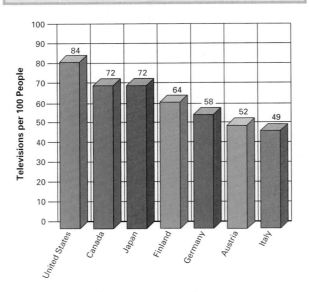

FIGURE 5–3 Television Ownership in Global Perspective

Source: The World Bank (2001).

the hallmarks of the many organizations that will employ them later in life.

Finally, schools socialize children into gender roles. Raphaela Best (1983) notes that at school, boys engage in more physical activities and spend more time outdoors, whereas girls often volunteer to help teachers with various housekeeping chores. Gender differences continue in college as women tend toward majoring in the arts or humanities and men lean toward economics, the physical sciences, and computing.

PEER GROUPS

By the time they enter school, children have discovered the **peer group,** *a social group whose members have interests, social position, and age in common.* Unlike the family and school, the peer group lets children escape the direct supervision of adults. Among their peers, children learn how to form relationships on their own. Peer groups also offer the chance to discuss interests that adults may not share (such as clothing and popular music) or tolerate (such as drugs and sex).

Not surprisingly, then, parents express concern about who their children's friends are. In a rapidly changing society, peer groups have great influence, and the attitudes of young and old may differ because of a "generation gap." The importance of peer groups typically peaks during adolescence, when young people begin to break away from their families and think of themselves as adults.

Even during adolescence, however, parental influence on children remains strong. Peers may affect short-term interests such as music or films, but parents retain greater sway over long-term goals such as going to college (Davies & Kandel, 1981).

Finally, any neighborhood or school is a social mosaic of many peer groups. As Chapter 7 ("Groups and Organizations") explains, individuals tend to view their own group in positive terms and discredit others. Moreover, people are influenced by peer groups they would like to join, a process sociologists call **anticipatory socialization,** *learning that helps a person achieve a desired position.* In school, for example, young people may mimic the styles and slang of the group they hope to join. Or a young lawyer who hopes to become a partner in her law firm may conform to the attitudes and behavior of the firm's partners in order to be accepted.

THE MASS MEDIA

`September 29, the Pacific Ocean, nearing Japan.` We have been out of sight of land for two weeks now, which makes this ship our entire social world. But more than land, many of the students miss television! A few students have brought videotapes of old "Beverly Hills 90210" shows, which are a hot item.

The **mass media** are *impersonal communications aimed at a vast audience.* The term "media" comes from the Latin word meaning "middle," suggesting that media connect people. *Mass* media arise as communication technology (first newspapers and then radio and television) spreads information on a mass scale.

In the United States today, the mass media have an enormous effect on our attitudes and behavior. Television, introduced in 1939, soon became the dominant medium: 98 percent of U.S. households have a TV (just 94 percent have telephones), and 88 percent have more than one. Two out of three households also have cable television. As Figure 5–3 shows, the United States has the highest rate of television ownership in

SEEING OURSELVES

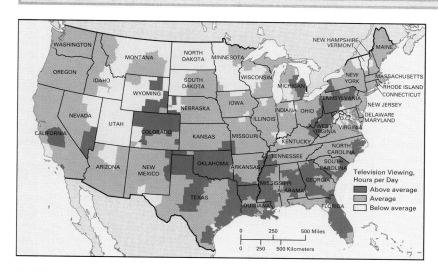

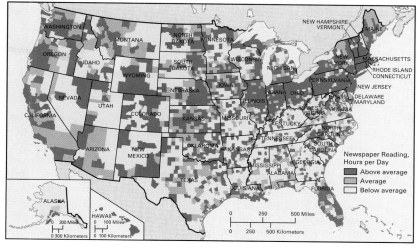

NATIONAL MAP 5–1
Television Viewing and Newspaper Reading across the United States

The map on the left identifies U.S. counties where television watching is above average, average, and below average. The map below provides comparable information for time devoted to reading newspapers. What do you think accounts for the high level of television viewing across much of the South and in rural West Virginia? Does your theory also account for patterns of newspaper reading?

Source: *American Demographics* magazine, August 1993, p. 64; *American Demographics* magazine, November 1998, p. 46. Reprinted with permission. © 1993, 1998 *American Demographics* magazine, Ithaca, New York.

the world. Some categories of people, including those with lower incomes, spend more time watching TV than others do. National Map 5–1 shows where in the United States people are more likely to be television watchers and where they are more likely to spend their leisure time reading newspapers.

Just how "glued to the tube" are we? Survey data show that the average household has at least one set turned on for seven hours each day, and people spend almost half their free time watching television

(Nielsen, 1997; Seplow & Storm, 1997; Cornell, 2000). A study by the Kaiser Family Foundation found that youngsters between age two and age eighteen average five-and-one-half hours per day "consuming media," including almost three hours a day watching television and the rest divided between watching videotapes and playing video games (McPherson, 1999).

Years before children learn to read, television watching is a regular routine. In fact, children grow up

DIVERSITY: RACE, CLASS, AND GENDER

How Should the Media Portray Minorities?

On an old *Saturday Night Live* sketch, director Ron Howard tells comedian Eddie Murphy about a new film, *Night Shift*, in which two mortuary workers decide to open their own sideline business: a prostitution ring. Murphy asks whether there are any black actors in the film; Howard shakes his head "no." Murphy then thunders, "A story about two pimps and there wasn't no brothers in it? I don't know whether to thank you or punch you in the mouth, man!"

Murphy's response points to twin criticisms of the U.S. mass media: Films and television either portray minorities in stereotypical fashion or ignore them altogether (Press, 1993:219). Back in the 1950s, minorities were all but absent from television and films. Even the wildly successful comedy *I Love Lucy* initially was turned down by major television studios because it featured Desi Arnaz—a Cuban—in a starring role. Since then, the media have steadily included more minorities. But despite top-rated programs such as *The Cosby Show* in the 1980s, *visibility* remains an issue: The 1990s came to an end with just a handful of African American stars on prime time television.

But what about *how* the media portray minorities? The few African Americans who managed to break into television in the 1950s played stereotypical low-status characters such as Amos and Andy and Jack Benny's butler, Rochester. Today, more television shows feature African American stars, but most are situation comedies that feature crude humor and bumbling characters.

Certainly, the image of minorities in the mass media is better than it used to be. But how minorities should be portrayed on television is still a matter of debate (MacDonald, 1992). Should television portray minorities *as they are*, which risks perpetuating stereotypes? Should shows present minorities *as they should be*, which risks being unrealistic about our nation's problems? Or should programs just present *individuals*, who may or may not match anyone's expectations?

spending as many hours in front of a television as they do in school or interacting with their parents. This is so despite research that suggests that television makes children more passive and less likely to use their imagination (Singer & Singer, 1983; APA, 1993; Fellman, 1995).

Comedian Fred Allen once quipped that we call television a "medium" because it is rarely well done. For a variety of reasons, television (as well as other mass media) provokes plenty of criticism. Some liberal critics argue that television shows mirror our society's patterns of inequality and rarely challenge the status quo. Most programs involve men in positions of power over women. Moreover, although racial and ethnic minorities watch about 40 percent more television than white people, they are largely absent from programming (Gans, 1980; Cantor & Pingree, 1983; Ang, 1985; Parenti, 1986; Brown, 1990). The box provides a closer look at how the U.S. entertainment industry characterizes minorities.

On the other side of the fence, conservative critics charge that the television and film industries are led by a liberal "cultural elite." In recent years, they claim, "politically correct" media have advanced liberal causes—including feminism and gay rights—while excluding a conservative perspective (Lichter, Rothman, & Rothman, 1986; Woodward, 1992b; Prindle, 1993; Prindle & Endersby, 1993; Rothman, Powers, & Rothman, 1993).

A final concern involves the mass media and violence. In 1996, the American Medical Association (AMA) declared that violence in the mass media, especially television and films, had reached levels that were hazardous to the well-being of this country's people. More recently, a study found a strong link between the amount of time elementary school children spend watching television and using video games and aggressive behavior (Robinson et al., 2001). The public as a whole seems to share concerns over the violent content of the mass media: Three-fourths of U.S. adults reported having walked out of a movie or turned off a television show because of high levels of violence. A more recent national study found that almost two-thirds of television programs contain violence and that

RESOURCE: D. Terri Heath's article about childhood socialization in global perspective is one of the cross-cultural selections in the *Seeing Ourselves* reader.
RESOURCE: See Ruth Benedict's (1938) classic article on the social construction of childhood.
DISCUSS: If children are becoming more like adults, are adults becoming more like children?

DISCUSS: This nation's 71 million children under age 18 are affected by political elections but cannot vote. Should they have this right? (Remember that about half of their parents do not vote.)
NOTE: The International Save the Children Alliance reports that some 300,000 children under 18 are active participants in 36 armed conflicts worldwide. Children are easy to recruit and often deemed expendable. Girls are sometimes recruited for sex.

In recent decades, some analysts suggest that U.S. society is shortening childhood by pushing children to grow up faster and faster. What role do you think the mass media have in this process? What about the rising number of children left to fend for themselves while their parents work? What other factors are affecting the experience of childhood today?

in most violent scenes, characters show no remorse and are not punished (Wilson, 1998).

In 1997, the television industry adopted a rating system for shows. But larger questions remain: Does watching sexual or violent programming harm people as much as critics say? More important, why do the mass media contain so much sex and violence in the first place?

In sum, television and the other mass media enrich our lives with entertaining and educational programming. The media also increase our exposure to diverse cultures and provoke discussion of current issues. At the same time, the power of the media, especially television, to shape how we think remains highly controversial.

Finally, other spheres of life beyond the family, school, peer groups, and the media also play a part in social learning. For most people in the United States, these include religious organizations, the workplace, the military, and social clubs. Considering the variety of sources, we end up with different messages. In the end, therefore, socialization proves to be not a simple matter of learning but a complex process of taking in and evaluating all sorts of conflicting information.

SOCIALIZATION AND THE LIFE COURSE

Although childhood has special importance in the socialization process, learning continues throughout our lives. An overview of the life course reveals that our

society organizes human experience according to age: childhood, adolescence, adulthood, and, finally, old age.

CHILDHOOD

A few years ago, the Nike corporation, maker of sportswear and athletic shoes, came under fire. Their shoes are made in Taiwan and Indonesia, in many cases by young children who work in factories rather than going to school. Some 250 million of the world's children work, at least 120 million of them full time, earning about fifty cents an hour (Human Rights Watch, 2001). Global Map 5–1 shows that child labor is most common in the nations of Africa and Asia.

Criticism of Nike sprang from the fact that most North Americans think of *childhood*—roughly the first twelve years of life—as a carefree time for learning

 A Web site that reports on the state of children serving as soldiers around the world is http://www.hrw.org/campaigns/crp/

and play. But a century ago, children in North America and Europe led much the same life as children in poor countries today: Many worked long hours, often under dangerous conditions, for little pay. In fact, explains historian Philippe Ariès (1965), the whole idea of childhood is fairly new. During the Middle Ages, children of four or five were treated like adults and expected to fend for themselves.

We defend our idea of childhood because youngsters are biologically immature. But a look back in time and around the world shows that the concept of childhood is grounded in culture. In rich countries, not

WINDOW ON THE WORLD

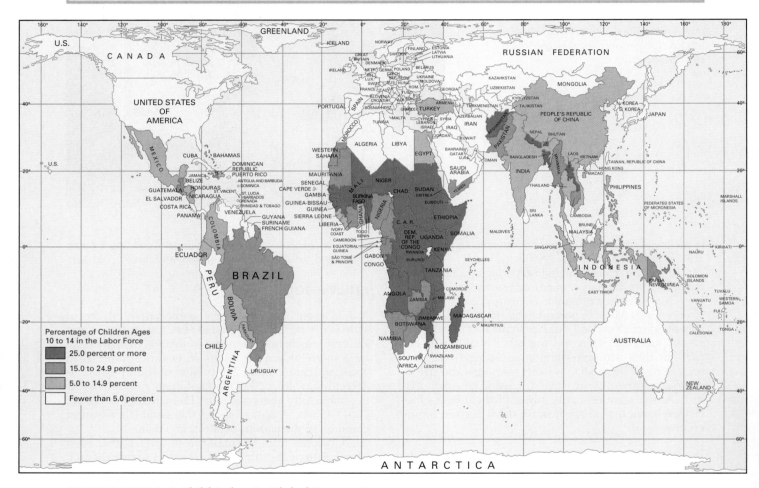

GLOBAL MAP 5–1 Child Labor in Global Perspective

Industrialization prolongs childhood and discourages children from work and other activities deemed suitable only for adults. Thus, child labor is uncommon in the United States and other high-income countries. In less economically developed nations of the world, however, children are a vital economic asset, and they typically begin working as soon as they are able.

Source: The World Bank (2001) and author estimates; map projection from *Peters Atlas of the World* (1990).

everyone has to work, so childhood can be extended to allow time for young people to learn the skills they will need in a high-technology workplace.

Given this extended childhood, many people worry about children growing up too fast. According to one executive of a children's television channel, today's

ten- to twelve-year-olds have many of the same interests and experiences typical of twelve- to fourteen-year-olds a generation ago (Hymowitz, 1998). In part, this "hurried child" syndrome results from changes in the family—including high divorce rates and both parents in the labor force—that leave children with less

Q: "From birth to age 18, a girl needs good parents; from 18 to 35, she needs good looks; from 35 to 55, she needs a good personality; from 55 on she needs cash." Sophie Tucker

NOTE: Income peaks between ages 45 and 54. Median income (2000): 25–34, $44,473; 35–44, $53,240; 45–54, $58,218; 55–64, $44,992; 65 and older, $23,048 (U.S. Census Bureau, 2001).

NOTE: "Adult" is derived from the Latin word *adultus*, meaning "grown."

Q: "Life is like a B-movie: You don't want to leave in the middle, but you also don't want to see it again." Ted Turner

RESOURCE: Robert N. Butler's "The Tragedy of Old Age in America" is among the classics included in the Macionis and Benokraitis reader.

supervision. Then, too, "adult" programming on television (not to mention films and the Internet) carries grown-up concerns such as sex, drugs, and violence into young people's lives. Perhaps it should be no surprise that, compared with kids fifty years ago, today's children have higher levels of stress and anxiety (Gorman, 2000).

ADOLESCENCE

Just as industrialization created childhood as a distinct stage of life, adolescence emerged as a buffer between childhood and adulthood. We generally link adolescence, or the teenage years, to emotional and social turmoil as parents spar with young people who are trying to develop their own identities. We are tempted to attribute teenage turbulence to the biological changes of puberty, but this turmoil more correctly reflects cultural inconsistency. For example, the mass media glorify sex, and schools hand out condoms, while, at the same time, parents urge restraint. An eighteen-year-old male may face the adult duty of going to war, but he lacks the adult right to drink alcohol. In short, adolescence is a time of social contradictions when people are no longer children but not yet adults.

As is true of all stages of life, adolescence varies according to social background. Most young people from working-class families move directly from high school into the adult world of work and parenting. Wealthier teens, however, have the resources to attend college and perhaps graduate school, thereby stretching adolescence into the late twenties and even the thirties.

ADULTHOOD

Adulthood, which begins between the late teens and early thirties, depending on social background, is a time of accomplishment. Having completed their schooling, people embark on careers and raise families of their own. Personalities are now largely formed, although a marked change in a person's environment—such as unemployment, divorce, or serious illness—may cause significant change in the self.

Early Adulthood

During early adulthood—until about age forty—young adults learn to manage day-to-day affairs for themselves, often juggling conflicting priorities: parents, partner, children, schooling, and work (Levinson et al., 1978). Women, especially, often try to "do it all," because our

culture gives them major responsibility for child rearing and housework even if they have demanding jobs outside the home (Hochschild & Machung, 1989).

Middle Adulthood

In middle adulthood—roughly ages forty to sixty—people sense that their life circumstances are pretty well set. They also become more aware of the fragility of health, which the young typically take for granted. Women who have spent many years raising a family find middle adulthood especially trying. Children grow up and need less attention, and husbands become absorbed in their careers, leaving some women with spaces in their lives that are difficult to fill. Many women who divorce also face serious financial problems (Weitzman, 1985, 1996). For all these reasons, an increasing number of women in middle adulthood return to school and seek new careers.

For everyone, growing older means facing physical decline, a prospect our culture makes more painful for women. Because good looks are defined as more important for women, wrinkles, added weight, and graying hair can be traumatic. Of course, men have their own difficulties. Some must admit that they are never going to reach their career goals. Others realize that the price of career success has been neglect of family or personal health (Farrell & Rosenberg, 1981; Wolf, 1990).

OLD AGE

Old age—the later years of adulthood and the final stage of life itself—begins about the mid-sixties. Again, societies attach different meanings to this stage of life. As explained in Chapter 15 ("Aging and the Elderly"), traditional societies often give older people control over most of the land and other wealth. Also, because traditional societies change slowly, older people amass great wisdom during their lifetime, which earns them much respect (Sheehan, 1976; Hareven, 1982).

In industrial societies, however, most younger people work apart from the family, becoming independent of their elders. Rapid change fosters a youth orientation that leads us to define what is old as unimportant or even obsolete. To younger people, the elderly appear unaware of new trends and fashions, and their knowledge and experience may seem of little value.

It is likely that U.S. society's anti-elderly bias will diminish as the share of older people steadily increases. The percentage of the U.S. population over age sixty-five has more than tripled since the beginning of the

DIVERSITY: RACE, CLASS, AND GENDER

The Development of Self among High School Students

Adolescence is a time when people are concerned about identity, asking questions such as "Who am I?" and "What should I strive to become?" Depending on their race and ethnicity, however, young people develop very different answers to these questions.

Grace Kao (2000) investigated the identity and aspirations of students enrolled in Johnstown High School, a large (3,000-student) school in a Chicago suburb. Johnstown High is considered a good school, with above-average test scores. It is also racially and ethnically diverse: 47 percent of the students are white, 43 percent are African American, 7 percent are Hispanic, and 3 percent are of Asian descent.

Kao interviewed sixty-three Johnstown students—female and male—both in small groups with others of their race and ethnicity and also individually. From these interviews, she documented the importance of racial and ethnic stereotypes in the students' developing sense of self. Moreover, Kao

found, not only is there wide agreement about these stereotypes, but students in various racial and ethnic categories apply these stereotypes to themselves.

What are these stereotypes? White students are seen as hard working and studious, motivated by a desire for high grades. African American students, by contrast, are viewed as less studious. As some see it, this is because they are less intelligent; as others see it, this is simply because they don't try as hard. Hispanics are seen as destined for manual occupations—as gardeners or laborers—so that doing well in school is less important to them. Finally, Asian American students are seen as hard working and high achievers. Again, some attribute this achievement to "being smart," whereas others see it as a focus on academics rather than, say, sports.

From her interviews, Kao concludes that most students take these stereotypes very personally. That is, they assume these beliefs are true and that they will perform in school the way the

stereotype predicts. One reason for this, Kao explains, is that white, black, Hispanic, and Asian students tend to socialize—both in and out of school—with others like themselves, which reinforces existing beliefs.

Another reason is that although students of all racial and ethnic categories say they *want* to do well in school, they measure success *only in relation to their own category*. In other words, to African American students "success" means doing as well as other black students and not flunking out. To Hispanics, "success" means avoiding manual labor and ending up with any job in an office. Whites and Asians, by contrast, define "success" as earning high grades and living up to the high achievement embodied in the stereotype. For all these young people, then, "self" develops through the lens of how U.S. society defines race and ethnicity.

Source: Kao (2000).

---

twentieth century, so that today there are more seniors than there are teenagers. Moreover, because life expectancy is still increasing, most men and women in their mid-sixties (the "young elderly") can look forward to decades more of life. In the twenty-first century, the Census Bureau (1999) predicts that the fastest-growing segment of our population may be those over eighty-five ("the oldest old"), whose numbers could soar nearly fivefold.

Old age differs in an important way from earlier stages in the life course. Growing up typically means entering new roles and assuming new responsibilities. Growing old, by contrast, is the opposite experience:

leaving roles that provided both satisfaction and social identity. Retirement can be a period of restful activity, or it can mean the loss of valued routines and sometimes outright boredom. Like any life transition, retirement demands learning new, different patterns while *un*learning familiar habits from the past. A nonworking wife or husband who must now accommodate a partner at home has an equally difficult transition to make.

DYING

Through most of human history, low living standards and simple medical technology meant that death,

GLOBAL: Death practices display remarkable cultural variety. Societies burn, bury, leave out in the weather, embalm, smoke, and even pickle their dead members. Similarly, funerals are times for laughter, tears, revelry, solemnity, fighting, or even sex—depending on the culture.
Q: "Always go to other people's funerals. Otherwise they won't come to yours." Yogi Berra

Q: Beware ye as ye pass by,
   As ye be now so once was I.
   As I be now, so must ye be.
   Prepare for death and follow me.
   18th-century New England epitaph
Q: "All my possessions for a moment of time." The last words of Queen Elizabeth I

caused by disease or accident, came at any stage of life. Today, however, more than 85 percent of people in the United States die after the age of fifty-five (U.S. National Center for Health Statistics, 2001).

After observing many dying people, Elisabeth Kübler-Ross (1969) described death as an orderly transition involving five distinct responses. A person's first reaction to the prospect of dying usually is *denial*, because our culture tends to ignore the reality of death. The second phase is *anger*, when a person facing death views it as a gross injustice. Third, anger gives way to *negotiation* as the person imagines avoiding death by striking a bargain with God. The fourth response, *resignation*, is often accompanied by psychological depression. Finally, adjustment to death is completed in the fifth stage, *acceptance*. Rather than being paralyzed by fear and anxiety, the person whose life is ending now sets out to make the most of whatever time remains.

As the share of women and men in old age increases, we can expect our culture to become more comfortable with the idea of death. In recent years, for example, people in the United States and elsewhere discuss death more openly, and the trend is to view dying as preferable to painful or prolonged suffering. Moreover, more married couples now prepare for death with legal and financial planning. This openness may ease somewhat the pain of the surviving spouse, a consideration for women who, more often than not, outlive their husbands.

THE LIFE COURSE: AN OVERVIEW

This survey of the life course leads us to two major conclusions. First, although each stage of life is linked to the biological process of aging, the life course is largely a social construction. For this reason, people in other societies may experience a stage of life very differently, or they may not recognize it at all. Second, in any society, the stages of the life course present characteristic problems and transitions that involve learning something new and, in many cases, unlearning familiar routines.

Societies organize the life course according to age, but other forces such as class, race, ethnicity, and gender also shape people's lives. Therefore, the general patterns we have described apply somewhat differently to various categories of people (cf. Duncan et al., 1998). The box provides an example, showing how race and ethnicity can shape the academic performance of high-school students.

The penal system's requirement that new inmates suffer the indignity of having their heads shaved is more than a matter of hair style; such a degrading ritual is also the first stage in the process by which a total institution attempts to break down an individual's established social identity.

Finally, people's life experiences also vary according to when, in the history of the society, they are born. A **cohort** is *a category of people with a common characteristic, usually their age.* Age cohorts are likely to be influenced by the same economic and cultural trends so that members have similar attitudes and values (Riley, Foner, & Waring, 1988). Women and men born in the 1940s and 1950s, for example, grew up during a time of economic expansion that gave them a sense of optimism. Today's college students, who have grown up in an age of economic uncertainty, are less confident of the future.

RESOCIALIZATION: TOTAL INSTITUTIONS

A final type of socialization, currently experienced by more than 2 million people in the United States, involves being confined—often against their will—in prisons or mental hospitals. This is the special world of the **total institution,** *a setting in which people are isolated from the rest of society and manipulated by an administrative staff.*

NOTE: The prison population of the U.S. is approaching 2 million and has doubled every 10 years. Mandatory sentences, especially for drug offenses, are driving the trend.
Q: "Are you going to let the system eat you up and relieve you of your humanity? Or are you going to use the system to human purposes?" Joseph Campbell
Q: "A basic social arrangement in modern society is that the individual tends to sleep, play, and work in different places, with different co-participants, under different authorities, and without an overall rational plan. The central feature of total institutions can be described as the breakdown of the barriers ordinarily separating these three spheres of life." Erving Goffman (1961:6)
Q: "Humanity has survived thanks only to inconsistency." Leszek Kolakowski

CONTROVERSY & DEBATE

Are We Free within Society?

Throughout this chapter, we have stressed one key theme: Society shapes how we think, feel, and act. If this is so, then in what sense are we free? To answer this question, consider the Muppets, puppet stars of television and film. Watching the antics of Kermit the Frog, Miss Piggy, and the rest of the troupe, we almost believe they are real rather than objects animated from backstage. Similarly, as the sociological perspective points out, human beings are like puppets in that we, too, respond to backstage forces. Society gives us a culture and shapes our lives according to class, race, and gender. In the face of such social forces, can we really claim to be free?

Sociologists speak with many voices when addressing this question. One response, with politically liberal overtones, is that individuals are *not* free of society; in fact, as social creatures, we never could be. But if we are constrained to life within society, it is important to make our home as just as possible. That is, we should work to lessen class differences and other barriers to opportunity for minorities, including women.

Another approach, this time with conservative overtones, is that we *are* free because society can never dictate our dreams. Our history as a nation, right from the revolutionary act that led to its founding, is one story after another of individuals pursuing personal goals despite great odds.

We find both attitudes in George Herbert Mead's analysis of socialization. Mead recognized that society makes demands on us and sometimes limits us. But he also saw that human beings are spontaneous and creative, capable of continually acting back—individually and collectively—on society. Thus Mead noted the power of society while still affirming the human capacity to evaluate, criticize, and, ultimately, to choose and change.

In the end, then, we may resemble puppets, but only on the surface. A crucial difference—one that gives us a large measure of freedom—is that we can stop, look up at the "strings" that animate much of our action, and even yank on them defiantly (Berger, 1963:176). If our pull is persistent enough, we can do more than we might think. As Margaret Mead once mused, "Do not make the mistake of thinking that concerned people cannot change the world; it's the only thing that ever has."

Continue the debate . . .

1. *Do you think our society affords more freedom to males than to females? Why or why not?*

2. *What about modern, high-income countries compared with traditional, low-income nations: Are some of the world's people more free than others?*

3. *Does an understanding of sociology increase your freedom? Why?*

According to Erving Goffman (1961), total institutions have three distinctive characteristics. First, staff members supervise all spheres of daily life, including where residents (often called "inmates") eat, sleep, and work. Second, the environment of a total institution is highly standardized, with institutional food, uniforms, and one set of activities for everyone. Third, formal rules and daily schedules dictate when, where, and how inmates perform their daily routines.

Total institutions impose such regimentation for one purpose: **resocialization,** *radically changing an inmate's personality by carefully controlling the environment.* Prisons and mental hospitals physically isolate inmates behind fences, barred windows, and locked doors and control their access to the telephone, mail, and visitors. The institution becomes the inmate's entire world, making it easier for the staff to produce long-term change—or at least short-term compliance—in the inmate.

Resocialization is a two-part process. First, the staff breaks down the new inmate's existing identity, using what Goffman describes as "abasements, degradations, humiliations, and profanations of self" (1961:14). For example, an inmate must give up personal possessions, including clothing and grooming articles used to maintain a distinctive appearance. Instead, the staff provides standard-issue clothes so everyone looks alike. The staff subjects new inmates

Q: For of all sad words, of tongue or pen; / The saddest are these: "It might have been!" / John Greenleaf Whittier

Q: "Let me be myself and then I am satisfied. I know that I am a woman with inward strength and plenty of courage." Anne Frank

Q: "After all is said and done, more is said than done." Anonymous

Q: "Humility is the final achievement." Anonymous

Q: "The beasts have the same senses as ourselves; and very nearly the same appetites." Tocqueville

Q: "He was a bold man that first ate an oyster." Jonathan Swift

Q: "Idealism is what precedes experience; cynicism is what follows." David Wolf

Q: "And, in the end, the love you take is equal to the love you make." The Beatles

to "mortifications of self," including searches, head-shaving, medical examinations, and fingerprinting, and then assigns each a serial number. Once inside the walls, individuals also give up their privacy, as guards routinely monitor their living quarters.

In the second part of the resocialization process, the staff tries to build a new self in the inmate through a system of rewards and punishments. Having a book to read, watching television, or making a telephone call may seem trivial to outsiders, but in the rigid environment of the total institution, these simple privileges can be powerful motivations to conform. In the end, the length of confinement typically depends on how well the inmate cooperates with the staff.

Resocialization can bring about profound change in an inmate, but total institutions affect different people in different ways. Whereas some inmates are considered "rehabilitated" or "recovered," others may change little, and still others may become hostile and bitter. Furthermore, over a long period of time, the rigidly controlled environment can leave some *institutionalized*, without the capacity for independent living.

But what about the rest of us? Does socialization crush our individuality or empower us? The final box takes a closer look at this important question.

SUMMARY

1. Socialization is the way individuals develop their humanity and particular identities.

2. A century ago, people thought most human behavior was guided by biological instinct. Today, we recognize that human behavior is mostly a result of nurture rather than nature.

3. The permanently damaging effects of social isolation reveal that social experience is essential to human development.

4. Sigmund Freud's model of the human personality has three parts: The id represents innate human drives (the life and death instincts), the superego is internalized cultural values and norms, and the ego resolves competition between the demands of the id and the restraints of the superego.

5. Jean Piaget believed that human development reflects both biological maturation and increasing social experience. He identified four stages of cognitive development: sensorimotor, preoperational, concrete operational, and formal operational.

6. Lawrence Kohlberg applied Piaget's approach to moral development. Individuals first judge rightness in preconventional terms, according to their individual needs. Next, conventional moral reasoning takes account of parental attitudes and cultural norms. Finally, postconventional reasoning allows people to criticize society itself.

7. In response to Kohlberg's use of only male subjects, Carol Gilligan discovered that whereas males rely on abstract standards of rightness, females look at the effect of decisions on relationships.

8. To George Herbert Mead, social experience generates the self, which he described as partly autonomous (the I) and partly guided by society (the me). Although infants engage in imitation, the self develops through play and games and eventually includes the "generalized other."

9. Charles Horton Cooley used the term "looking-glass self" to explain that we see ourselves as we imagine others see us.

10. Erik H. Erikson identified characteristic challenges that individuals face at each stage of life from infancy to old age.

11. Usually the first setting of socialization, the family has the greatest influence on a child's attitudes and behavior.

12. Schools expose children to greater social diversity and introduce them to impersonal performance evaluations.

13. Peer groups free children from adult supervision and take on great significance during adolescence.

14. The mass media, especially television, have a great impact on the socialization process. The average U.S. child spends as much time watching television as attending school or interacting with parents. Research has linked television and video games to aggressive behavior in young children.

15. Each stage of the life course—childhood, adolescence, adulthood, and old age—is socially constructed in ways that vary from society to society.

16. People in high-income countries typically fend off death until old age. Accepting death is part of socialization for the elderly.

17. Total institutions, such as prisons and mental hospitals, try to resocialize inmates—that is, to radically change their personalities.

18. Socialization shows the power of society to shape our thoughts, feelings, and actions. Yet, as humans, we have the ability to act back, shaping both ourselves and our social world.

KEY CONCEPTS

socialization (p. 115) the lifelong social experience by which individuals develop their human potential and learn culture

personality (p. 115) a person's fairly consistent patterns of acting, thinking, and feeling

id (p. 119) Freud's term for the human being's basic drives

ego (p. 119) Freud's term for a person's conscious efforts to balance innate pleasure-seeking drives with the demands of society

superego (p. 119) Freud's term for the cultural values and norms internalized by an individual

sensorimotor stage (p. 119) Piaget's term for the level of human development at which individuals experience the world only through their senses

preoperational stage (p. 119) Piaget's term for the level of human development at which individuals first use language and other symbols

concrete operational stage (p. 120) Piaget's term for the level of human development at which individuals first perceive causal connections in their surroundings

formal operational stage (p. 120) Piaget's term for the level of human development at which individuals think abstractly and critically

self (p. 122) George Herbert Mead's term for the part of an individual's personality composed of self-awareness and self-image

looking-glass self (p. 122) Cooley's term for self-image based on how we think others see us

generalized other (p. 123) George Herbert Mead's term for the widespread cultural norms and values we use as a reference in evaluating ourselves

peer group (p. 126) a social group whose members have interests, social position, and age in common

anticipatory socialization (p. 126) learning that helps a person achieve a desired position

mass media (p. 126) impersonal communications aimed at a vast audience

cohort (p. 133) a category of people with a common characteristic, usually their age

total institution (p. 133) a setting in which people are isolated from the rest of society and manipulated by an administrative staff

resocialization (p. 134) radically changing an inmate's personality by carefully controlling the environment

CRITICAL-THINKING QUESTIONS

1. What do cases of social isolation teach us about the importance of social experience to human beings?

2. State the two sides of the nature–nurture debate. In what sense are human nature and nurture not opposed to one another?

3. We have all seen young children place their hands in front of their faces and exclaim, "You can't see me!" They assume that if they cannot see you, then you cannot see them. What does this behavior suggest about a young child's ability to "take the role of the other"? Can a parent expect a young child to "see things from *my* point of view"?

4. What are the common themes in the ideas of Freud, Piaget, Kohlberg, Gilligan, Mead, and Erikson? In what ways do their theories differ?

APPLICATIONS AND EXERCISES

1. Work with several members of your sociology class to gather data on socialization. Each person should ask several friends and classmates to name traits that are elements of "human nature." Then compare notes and discuss the extent to which these traits are the product of nature or nurture.

2. Find a copy of the book (or video) *Lord of the Flies*, a tale by William Golding based on a Freudian model of personality. Jack (and his hunters) represent the power of the id, Piggy consistently opposes them as the superego, and Ralph stands between the two as the ego, the voice of reason. Golding wrote the book after taking part in the bloody D-Day landing in France during World War II. Do you agree with his belief that violence is part of human nature?

3. Make a list of personality traits that characterize you. If you have the courage, ask several others who know you well what they think. Can you explain where these traits came from?

4. Watch several hours of prime time programming on network or cable television. Keep track of every time any element of violence is shown. For fun, assign each program a "YIP rating," for the number of Years in Prison a person would serve for committing all the violent acts you witness (Fobes, 1996). On the basis of observing this small (and unrepresentative) sample of programs, what are your conclusions?

5. Packaged in the back of this new textbook is an interactive CD-ROM that offers a variety of study and review materials intended to help you better understand the material covered in this chapter. For this chapter, the CD-ROM contains an author's tip video, Real Life Sociology videos, and other relevant audio and video, interactive map animations, audio journal entries from the author, Web links, and much more.

 ## SITES TO SEE

http://www.prenhall.com/macionis

Visit the interactive *Companion Website*™ that accompanies this text. Begin by clicking on the cover of your book. You will find a chapter-by-chapter study guide, practice tests, and a significant portion of the text for on-line review, as well as many suggested Web links.

http://www.macionis.com
(or http://www.TheSociologyPage.com)

At the author's Web site, you can find brief biographies of George Herbert Mead, Charles Horton Cooley, and other sociologists discussed in this chapter.

http://freud.t0.or.at

Visit the Sigmund Freud Museum of Vienna, Austria, at this site.

http://www.piaget.org/

The Jean Piaget Society hosts this Web site, which presents the work of this celebrated social psychologist.

http://www.nd.edu/~rbarger/kohlberg.html

This Web site is dedicated to the ideas and research of Lawrence Kohlberg.

http://www.prenticehall.ca/macionis/massmedia.html

An online chapter on the mass media is available at the Web site for Macionis Canadian texts.

http://www.nncc.org/Maintitles/info.page.html

This site, operated by the National Network for Child Care, is a gateway to information about a wide range of children's issues, including child abuse, literacy, and the increasing racial and ethnic diversity of U.S. children.

 ## INVESTIGATE WITH CONTENTSELECT

Follow the instructions found on page 23 of this textbook to enter this chapter of the book's *Companion Website*™. Once in the chapter, click on the ContentSelect icon at the bottom left of your screen and enter your personal User ID and Password. Enter keywords such as "Sigmund Freud," "childhood," and "mass media," and the search engine will help you become an effective researcher.

CHAPTER

6

Georges Jean (20th c)
Dance Hall, 1972

Haitian art. Coll. Manu Sassoonian,
New York, N.Y./Art Resource, N.Y.

SOCIAL INTERACTION IN EVERYDAY LIFE

arold and Sybil are on their way to another couple's home in an unfamiliar area near Ticonderoga, New York. They are late because for the last twenty minutes they have traveled in circles looking for Graphite Mountain Road. Harold, gripping the wheel ever more tightly, is doing a slow burn. Sybil, sitting next to him, looks straight ahead, afraid to utter a word. Both realize the evening is off to a bad start (Tannen, 1990:62).

Harold and Sybil are lost in more ways than one: They are unable to grasp why they are growing more and more enraged at their situation and at each other. Consider their plight from Harold's point of view. Like most men, Harold hates getting lost. The longer he drives around, the more incompetent he feels. Sybil, on the other hand, cannot understand why Harold does not pull over and ask someone where Graphite Mountain Road is. If she were driving, she fumes to herself,

they already would have arrived and would now be comfortably settled with drink in hand.

Why don't men like to ask for directions? Because men value their independence, they are uncomfortable asking for help (and also reluctant to accept it). To men, asking for assistance is the same as saying "You know something I don't." If it takes Harold a few more minutes to find the address on his own—and keep his self-respect in the process—he thinks it's a good bargain.

If men value self-sufficiency and are sensitive to hierarchy, women are more attuned to others and strive for connectedness. From Sybil's point of view, asking for help is right because sharing information reinforces social bonds. Asking for directions seems as natural to her as searching on his own is to Harold. Obviously, getting lost is sure to generate conflict as long as neither one understands the other's point of view.

Everyday experiences such as Harold's and Sybil's are the focus of this chapter. We begin by presenting the building blocks of common experience and then explore the almost magical way in which face-to-face interaction between two or more people generates reality. The central concept that we will look at is **social interaction,** *the process by which people act and react in relation to others.* Through social interaction, we create the reality in which we live. Social structure, in turn, guides our interaction.

SOCIAL STRUCTURE: A GUIDE TO EVERYDAY LIVING

October 21, Ho Chi Minh City, Vietnam. This morning we leave the ship and make our way along the docks toward the center of Ho Chi Minh City, known to an earlier generation as Saigon. The government security officers wave us

139

SUPPLEMENTS: An outline of Chapter 6, as well as supplemental lecture material and topics for class discussion, appears in the *Data File*.

Q: "A status, as distinct from the individual who may occupy it, is simply a collection of rights and duties." Ralph Linton (1937:113)

DISCUSS: Ask members of the class to identify elements of their own status set.

NOTE: "Status" has two Latin roots: *Sta* is derived from *stare*, meaning "to stand"; *tus* means "the use of." Thus, status is literally "the use of standing." The term "role" appears to be derived from the French word *rôle*, meaning a roll (of paper) that contains an actor's part.

NOTE: In reality, ascribed status and achieved status operate as two endpoints on a continuum.

In any rigidly ranked setting, no interaction can proceed until people assess each other's social standing. Thus, military personnel wear clear insignia to designate their level of authority. Don't we size up one another in much the same way in routine interactions, noting a person's rough age, quality of clothing, and manner for clues about social position?

through the heavy metal gates. Pressed against the fence surrounding the port are dozens of men who operate cyclos (bicycles with a small carriage attached to the front), the Vietnamese

For a short video on the difficulties of traveling to strange places, see http://www.TheSociologyPage.com

equivalent of taxicabs. We wave them off but spend the next twenty minutes shaking our heads at several drivers who pedal alongside, pleading for our business. The pressure is uncomfortable. We decide to cross the street but realize suddenly that there are no stop signs or signal lights, and the street is an unbroken stream of bicycles, cyclos, motorbikes, and small trucks. What to do? The locals don't bat an eye; they

just walk at a steady pace across the street, parting waves of vehicles that close in again immediately behind them. Walk right into traffic? With our small children on our backs? Yup, we did it; that's the way it works in Vietnam.

Members of every society rely on social structure to make sense out of everyday situations. As one family's introduction to the streets of Vietnam suggests, the world can be disorienting—even frightening—when cultural norms are not what we expect. So what, then, are the building blocks of our daily lives?

STATUS

One building block of social structure is **status**, *a social position that an individual occupies*. Sociologists do not use the term "status" in its everyday meaning of "prestige," as when a college president has "more status" than a newly hired assistant professor. Rather, both "president" and "professor" are statuses within the collegiate organization.

Every status is part of our social identity and helps define our relationship to others. As Georg Simmel (1950:307), one of the founders of sociology, put it, "The first condition of having to deal with somebody . . . is knowing with *whom* one has to deal."

STATUS SET

Everyone occupies many statuses at once. A **status set** consists of *all the statuses a person holds at a given time*. A teenage girl is a *daughter* to her parents, a *sister* to her brother, a *friend* to members of her social circle, and a *goalie* to others on her soccer team. Just as status sets branch out in many directions, they also change over the life course. A child grows into a parent, a student becomes a lawyer, and people marry to become husbands and wives, sometimes becoming single again as a result of death or divorce. Joining an organization or finding a job enlarges our status set; withdrawing from activities makes it smaller. Over a lifetime, individuals gain and lose dozens of statuses.

ASCRIBED AND ACHIEVED STATUS

Sociologists classify statuses in terms of how people obtain them. An **ascribed status** is *a social position a*

Q: "It is crucial that responsibilities, resources, and rights be assigned to statuses, not to particular individuals. For only by doing so can societies establish general and uniform rules or norms that will apply to many and diverse individuals who are to occupy the statuses." Melvin Tumin (1985:21)

GLOBAL: Typically, members of rich societies have a larger status set than people in traditional countries for whom kinship represents the core of social organization.
NOTE: Statuses sometimes have differing consequences for social identity. Consider introducing the concept of *status consistency*—the degree of consistency in social ranking—discussed in Chapter 11 ("Social Class in the United States").

Role models teach us that any one person can truly make a difference for our world. In December, 1955, the driver of a city bus in Montgomery, Alabama, asked passenger Rosa Parks to give up her seat, as required by law, so a white man could sit down. She refused and was arrested, fingerprinted, and later fined $14 for the offense. This courageous act prompted Birmingham's African American population to boycott city buses, leading to the repeal of the bus-segregation law.

person receives at birth or assumes involuntarily later in life. Examples of ascribed statuses include being a daughter, a Cuban, a teenager, or a widower. Ascribed statuses are matters about which people have little or no choice.

By contrast, an **achieved status** is *a social position a person assumes voluntarily that reflects personal ability and effort.* Achieved statuses in the United States include honors student, Olympic athlete, spouse, computer programmer, and thief.

In practice, most statuses involve some combination of ascription and achievement. That is, people's ascribed statuses influence the statuses they achieve. People who achieve the status of lawyer, for example, are likely to share the ascribed benefit of being born into well-off families. By the same token, many less desirable statuses, such as criminal or unemployed person, are more easily achieved by people born into poverty.

MASTER STATUS

Some statuses matter more than others. A **master status** is *a status that has special importance for social identity, often shaping a person's entire life.* For most people, one's occupation is a master status because it conveys a great deal about social background, education, and income. In a few cases, being a "Bush" or a "Kennedy" is enough by itself to push a person into the limelight.

In a negative sense, serious illness also operates as a master status. Sometimes even lifelong friends avoid people with cancer or acquired immune deficiency syndrome (AIDS) simply because of their illness. Most societies of the world also limit the opportunities of women, whatever their abilities, making gender a master status (cf. Webster & Hysom, 1998).

Sometimes a physical disability serves as a master status to the point that we dehumanize people by perceiving them only in terms of their disability. In the box on page 142, two people with disabilities describe the problem.

ROLE

A second component of social interaction is **role**, *behavior expected of someone who holds a particular status.* People *hold* a status and *perform* a role (Linton, 1937b). Holding the status of student, for example, means one will attend classes, complete assignments, and, more broadly, devote a lot of time to personal enrichment through academic study.

Both statuses and roles vary by culture. In the United States, the status "uncle" refers to a sibling of either mother or father. In Vietnam, however, the word for "uncle" is different on the mother's and father's sides of the family, and the two men have different responsibilities. Of course, in every society, actual

NOTE: Barbara Laslett (1978) points out that role conflict and role strain probably were more pronounced in the Middle Ages than they are today because parents not only raised children but produced their food, schooled them, guided their worship, and saw to their health.

DISCUSS: Ask students to identify potential role sets linked to the statuses of college student, public school teacher, member of the military, and U.S. senator.

Q: "Status and role serve to reduce the ideal patterns for social life to individual terms." Ralph Linton (1937:114)

DIVERSITY: RACE, CLASS, AND GENDER

Physical Disability as Master Status

Physical disability operates in much the same ways as class, gender, or race in defining individuals in the eyes of others. In the following interviews, two women explain how a physical disability can become a master status—an all-important trait that overshadows everything else about them. The first voice is twenty-nine-year-old Donna Finch, who lives with her husband and son in Muskogee, Oklahoma, and holds a master's degree in social work. She is also blind.

Most people don't expect handicapped people to grow up, they are always supposed to be children. . . . You aren't supposed to date, you aren't supposed to have a job, somehow you're just supposed to disappear. I'm not saying this is true of anyone else, but in my own case I think I was more intellectually mature than

most children, and more emotionally immature. I'd say that not until the last four or five years have I felt really whole.

Rose Helman is an elderly woman who has retired and lives near New

York City. She has spinal meningitis and is also blind.

You ask me if people are really different today than in the '20s and '30s. Not too much. They are still fearful of the handicapped. I don't know if *fearful* is the right word, but uncomfortable at least. But I can understand it somewhat; it happened to me. I once asked a man to tell me which staircase to use to get from the subway out to the street. He started giving me directions that were confusing, and I said, "Do you mind taking me?" He said, "Not at all." He grabbed me on the side with my dog on it, so I asked him to take my other arm. And he said, "I'm sorry, I have no other arm." And I said, "That's all right, I'll hold onto the jacket." It felt funny hanging onto the sleeve without the arm in it.

Source: Orlansky and Heward (1981).

role performance varies according to an individual's personality, although some societies permit more individual expression of a role than others.

ROLE SET

Because we occupy many statuses at once—a status set—everyday life is a mix of multiple roles. Robert Merton (1968) introduced the term **role set** to identify *a number of roles attached to a single status*.

Figure 6–1 shows four statuses of one individual, each status linked to a different role set. First, as a

professor, the woman interacts with students (the teacher role) and with other academics (the colleague role). Second, in her work as a researcher, she gathers data (the laboratory role) that she uses in her publications (the author role). Third, the woman occupies the status of "wife," with a conjugal role (such as confidante and sexual partner) toward her husband, with whom she shares a domestic role toward the household. Fourth, she holds the status of "mother," with routine responsibilities for her children (the maternal role) and toward their school and other organizations (the civic role).

ROLE CONFLICT AND ROLE STRAIN

Most people in industrial societies juggle a host of responsibilities demanded by their various statuses and roles. As many mothers can testify, parenting as well as working outside the home can be both physically and emotionally draining. Sociologists thus recognize **role conflict** as *conflict between roles corresponding to two or more statuses.*

We experience role conflict when we find ourselves pulled in various directions while trying to respond to the many statuses we hold. Sometimes we decide that "something has to go." For example, a well-known person may decide not to run for political office because the demands of a campaign would interfere with family life. In other cases, some people delay having children so they can stay on the "fast track" for career success.

Even roles linked to a single status may make competing demands on us. **Role strain** is *tension between roles connected to a single status.* A plant supervisor may enjoy being friendly with other workers. At the same time, however, the supervisor has production goals and must maintain the personal distance needed to evaluate employees. In short, although not all cases of role strain present serious problems, performing the various roles attached to even one status can be a balancing act (Gigliotti & Huff, 1995).

One strategy for minimizing role conflict is to "compartmentalize" our lives so that we perform roles linked to one status at one time and place and carry out roles corresponding to another status in a completely different setting. A familiar example of this scheme is deciding to "leave the job at work" before heading home to one's family.

ROLE EXIT

After she left the life of a Catholic nun to become a university sociologist, Helen Rose Fuchs Ebaugh (1988) began to study *role exit*, the process by which people disengage from important social roles. Studying a range of "exes," including ex-nuns, ex-doctors, ex-husbands, and ex-alcoholics, Ebaugh identified elements common to the process of becoming an "ex."

According to Ebaugh, the process begins as people come to doubt their ability to continue in a certain role. As they imagine alternative roles, they ultimately reach a tipping point when they decide to pursue a new life. Even at this point, however, a past role can continue to influence our lives. "Exes" carry away a

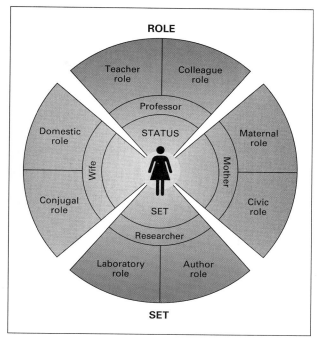

FIGURE 6–1 Status Set and Role Set

self-image shaped by an earlier role, which can interfere with building a new sense of self. An ex-nun, for example, may hesitate to wear stylish clothing and makeup.

"Exes" must also rebuild relationships with people who knew them in their earlier life. Learning new social skills is another challenge. For example, Ebaugh reports, nuns who begin dating after decades in the church often are startled to learn that sexual norms are very different from those they knew as teenagers.

THE SOCIAL CONSTRUCTION OF REALITY

More than sixty years ago, the Nobel Prize–winning Italian playwright Luigi Pirandello wrote the play *The Pleasure of Honesty*. The main character is Angelo Baldovino, a brilliant man with a checkered past. Baldovino enters the fashionable home of the Renni family and introduces himself in a peculiar way:

Inevitably we construct ourselves. Let me explain.
I enter this house and immediately I become

Flirting is an everyday experience in reality construction. Each person offers information to the other, and hints at romantic interest. Yet the interaction proceeds with a tentative and often humorous air so that either individual can withdraw at any time without further obligation.

what I have to become, what I can become: I construct myself. That is, I present myself to you in a form suitable to the relationship I wish to achieve with you. And, of course, you do the same with me. (1962:157–58)

Baldovino's introduction suggests that although behavior is guided by status and role, we also have the ability to shape what happens moment to moment. In other words, "reality" is not as fixed as we may think.

The phrase **social construction of reality** describes *the process by which people creatively shape reality through social interaction.* This idea is the familiar foundation of the symbolic-interaction paradigm, described in earlier chapters (Berger & Luckmann, 1966; Maines, 2000). As Angelo Baldovino's remark suggests, quite a bit of "reality" remains unclear in everyone's mind, especially in unfamiliar situations. So we present ourselves in terms that suit the setting and our purposes, and, as others do the same, reality emerges.

Social interaction, then, amounts to a complex negotiation. Most everyday situations involve at least some agreement about what's going on, in part because people recognize the various statuses of the people involved. Even so, people have to act in expected

To further investigate the social construction of reality, enter the phrase at the ContentSelect Web site: http://www.prenhall.com/contentselect

ways in order to make the status believable to others; that is, a professor who expects to be taken seriously must act in a professorial manner (Ridgeway & Erickson, 2000).

Of course, participants are likely to hold different perceptions of events to the extent that they have different interests and intentions. In other words, in any interaction each participant has at least slightly different ideas about what "reality" should be. Our very choice of words is one way we put a "spin" on events. The box applies this idea to the language used by the military to create (or conceal?) reality.

"STREET SMARTS"

What people commonly call "street smarts" really amounts to constructing reality. In his biography *Down These Mean Streets*, Piri Thomas recalls moving to an apartment in Spanish Harlem. Returning home one evening, young Piri found himself cut off by Waneko, the leader of the local street gang, who was flanked by a dozen others.

"Whatta ya say, Mr. Johnny Gringo," drawled Waneko.

Think man, I told myself, *think your way out of a stomping. Make it good.* "I hear you 104th Street coolies are supposed to have heart," I said. "I don't know this for sure. You know there's a lot of streets where a whole 'click' is made out of punks who can't fight one guy unless they all jump him for the stomp." I hoped this would push Waneko into giving me a fair one. His expression didn't change.

NOTE: Other terms that spin reality in different ways: "unemployed" vs. "between jobs"; "elderly" vs. "elders"; "ladies" vs. "women"; "handicapped children" vs. "exceptional children"; "remedial" vs. "refresher"; "primitive" vs. "nonliterate"; "broken families" vs. "one-parent households"; "sexually active" vs. "promiscuous"; "pre-driven" vs. "used."

NOTE: Nowhere is the fascination with use of language more

intense than on campus, where words are our stock in trade. Consider, for example, the ramifications of using two similar phrases "people of color" and "colored people."

NOTE: Ethnomethodology has roots not only in symbolic interaction but also in Alfred Schutz's phenomenology. Moreover, it shares with Berger and Luckmann's work an interest in the everyday round of life, not just a society's grand values or political ideologies.

APPLYING SOCIOLOGY

The "Spin" Game: Choosing Our Words Carefully

Military organizations choose their words carefully in order to "sanitize" the horror of war and make military action seem necessary and good. William Lutz, an English professor at Rutgers University, collected examples of language used by U.S. military officers in the Persian Gulf War. Compare the following military terminology and the straight-talk translations. Do these military terms convey a reality or do you think they try to alter it?

Military Language	Everyday Meaning
Incontinent ordnance	Bombs or shells that miss their targets and hit civilians
Area denial weapons	Cluster bombs that kill or destroy everything within a particular area
Coercive potential	The capacity of bombs and shells to kill or injure the enemy
Suppressing assets	Reducing the enemy's ability to fight by killing people and destroying equipment
Ballistically induced aperture	Bullet hole
Scenario dependent, post-crisis environment	Whether we win or lose

"Maybe we don't look at it that way."

Crazy, man, I cheer inwardly, *the* cabron *is falling into my setup.* . . . "I wasn't talking to you," I said. "Where I come from, the pres is president 'cause he got heart when it comes to dealing."

Waneko was starting to look uneasy. He had bit on my worm and felt like a sucker fish. His boys were now light on me. They were no longer so much interested in stomping me as seeing the outcome between Waneko and me. "Yeah," was his reply. . . .

I knew I'd won. Sure, I'd have to fight; but one guy, not ten or fifteen. If I lost, I might still get stomped, and if I won I might get stomped. I took care of this with my next sentence. "I don't know you or your boys," I said, "but they look cool to me. They don't feature as punks."

I had left him out purposely when I said "they." Now his boys were in a separate class. I had cut him off. He would have to fight me on his own, to prove his heart to himself, to his boys, and most important, to his turf. He got away from the stoop and asked, "Fair one, Gringo?" (1967:56–57)

This situation reveals the drama—sometimes subtle, sometimes savage—by which human beings

creatively build reality. But, of course, not everyone enters a situation with equal standing. Had a police officer come upon the scene while Piri and Waneko were facing off for a fight, both young men might have ended up in jail.

THE THOMAS THEOREM

By displaying his wits and fighting with Waneko until they both tired, Piri Thomas won acceptance and became one of the gang. What took place that evening in Spanish Harlem is an example of the **Thomas theorem,** named after W. I. Thomas (1966:301; orig. 1931): *Situations that are defined as real are real in their consequences.*

Applied to social interaction, the Thomas theorem means that although reality is initially "soft" as it is fashioned, it can become "hard" in its effects. In the case we have described, local gang members saw Piri Thomas act in a worthy way, so in their eyes he *became* worthy.

ETHNOMETHODOLOGY

Rather than assume that reality is something "out there," the symbolic-interaction paradigm states that people create reality in everyday encounters. But how exactly do we define reality for ourselves? Answering this question is the objective of *ethnomethodology*, a specialized approach within the symbolic-interaction paradigm.

The term itself has two parts: The Greek *ethno* refers to people and how they understand their surroundings; *methodology* designates a set of methods or principles. Combining the two makes **ethnomethodology,** *the study of the way people make sense of their everyday surroundings.*

Ethnomethodology is largely the creation of Harold Garfinkel (1967), who challenged the then-dominant view of society as a broad, abstract "system" (recall the structural-functional approach of Emile Durkheim, described in Chapter 4, "Society"). Garfinkel wanted to explore how we make sense of countless familiar situations. Our talk and behavior, explained Garfinkel, rest on deeper assumptions about the world that typically we take for granted.

Think for a moment about what we assume in asking someone the simple question, "How are you?" Do we mean physically? Mentally? Spiritually? Financially? Do we even want an answer, or are we just being polite?

Ethnomethodology, then, explores the process of making sense of social encounters. Garfinkel argues that the only way to discover how we make sense of events is to purposely *break the rules.* By deliberately ignoring conventional rules and observing how people respond, we "tease out" how people build a reality. Thus, Garfinkel directed his students to refuse to "play the game" in a wide range of situations. Some students living with their parents started acting as if they were boarders rather than children; others entered stores and insisted on bargaining for items; others recruited people into simple games (such as tic-tac-toe) only to intentionally flout the rules; still others started conversations while slowly moving closer and closer to the other person.

The students later reported on people's reactions. Typically, the "victims" became annoyed, suggesting how important our everyday reality is to us. Trying to identify exactly *why* people were disturbed led students to consider the unspoken agreements that underlie family and community life, shopping, fair play, and the like.

Some sociologists view ethnomethodology as less-than-serious research because it focuses on common experiences and uses unusual, even bizarre methods. Still, ethnomethodology heightens our awareness of the unnoticed patterns of everyday life.

REALITY BUILDING: CLASS AND CULTURE

People do not build everyday experience out of thin air. In part, how we act or what we see in our surroundings depends on our interests. Scanning the night sky, for example, lovers discover romance, whereas scientists view the same stars as hydrogen atoms fusing into helium. Social background also directs our perceptions, so that residents of, say, Spanish Harlem experience the world somewhat differently from those living on Manhattan's upscale East Side.

In truth, the reality construction that goes on across the United States is very diverse. Take golf, a popular sport among some segments of the U.S. population but not among others. National Map 6–1 shows where people are—and are not—likely to tee off.

Remember that all the maps in this text become interactive at the *Companion Website*™: http://www.prenhall.com/macionis

In global perspective, reality construction varies even more. Consider these everyday situations: People waiting for a bus in London typically "queue up" in a straight line; people in New York rarely are so orderly. The law forbids women in Saudi Arabia to drive cars, a ban unheard of in the United States. Fear of crime in our big cities is much greater than it is elsewhere, including London, Paris, Rome, Calcutta, and Hong Kong; this sense of public danger shapes the daily realities of tens of millions of our citizens.

The general conclusion is that people build reality from the surrounding culture. Chapter 3 ("Culture") explains how people the world over find different meanings in specific gestures, so that sometimes travelers find themselves building an unexpected reality. Similarly, in a study of popular culture, JoEllen Shively (1992) showed western films to men of European descent and to Native American men. Both categories claimed to enjoy the films but for different reasons. White men interpreted the films as praising rugged people striking out for the West to impose their will on nature. Native American men, by contrast, saw in the same films a celebration of land and nature apart from any human ambitions.

Finally, what about the range of human emotions? Are emotions much the same for people everywhere? Or do we draw our feelings from our culture? Cross-cultural research, described in the box on pages 148–49, indicates that emotions are rooted in both biology and culture.

SEEING OURSELVES

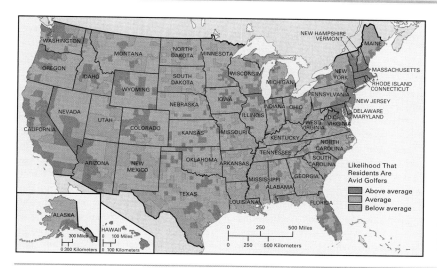

NATONAL MAP 6–1
Teeing Off across the United States

The map shows the popularity of the game of golf for all 3,141 counties in the United States in 2000. More than 25 million people across the country enjoy golf, but they are not typical in a number of respects. Looking at the map, what patterns can you see? As a hint, serious golfers tend to be white men who are somewhat older than the national average and who have much higher than average incomes.

Source: This map first appeared in the August 2000 edition of *American Demographics* magazine. It is reprinted with permission from Media Central, a Primedia Company.

DRAMATURGICAL ANALYSIS: "THE PRESENTATION OF SELF"

Erving Goffman (1922–1982) spent much of his life explaining how people in their everyday behavior are very much like actors performing on a stage. If we imagine ourselves as directors observing what goes on in some situational "theater," we can understand Goffman's **dramaturgical analysis:** *the study of social interaction in terms of theatrical performance.*

Dramaturgical analysis offers a fresh look at the concepts of status and role. A status is like a part in a play, and a role serves as a script, supplying dialogue and action for the characters. Goffman described each individual's "performance" as the **presentation of self,** *an individual's efforts to create specific impressions in the minds of others.* This process, sometimes called *impression management,* has several distinct elements (Goffman, 1959, 1967).

PERFORMANCES

As we present ourselves in everyday situations, we convey information—consciously and unconsciously—to others. A person's performance includes dress (costume), objects carried along (props), and tone of voice and particular gestures (manner). In addition, people craft their performance according to the setting (stage). We may joke loudly in a restaurant, for example, but lower our voices when entering a church. People design settings, such as homes or offices, to bring about desired reactions in others.

An Application: The Doctor's Office

Consider how a physician uses an office to convey particular information to the audience of patients. Physicians enjoy high prestige and power in the United States, a fact evident upon entering a doctor's office. First, the physician is nowhere to be seen. Instead, in what Goffman describes as the "front region" of the setting, the patient encounters a receptionist who serves as a gatekeeper, deciding whether and when the patient can meet the doctor. Who waits to see whom is a power game. And a simple survey of the doctor's waiting room, with patients (often impatiently) waiting to gain entry to the inner sanctum, leaves little doubt that the physician controls events.

The physician's private office and examination room are the "back region" of the setting. Here, the patient confronts a wide range of props, such as medical

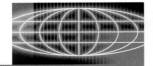

GLOBAL SOCIOLOGY

The Sociology of Emotions: Do People Everywhere Feel the Same?

On a busy New York City sidewalk, a woman reacts angrily to an in-line skater who zooms past her. Her facial expression, together with a few choice words, broadcasts a strong emotion that North Americans easily recognize. But would an observer from Nigeria, Nicaragua, or New Guinea interpret her emotion the same way? In other words, do all people share similar feelings, and do they express them in the same way?

Paul Ekman and his colleagues studied people's emotions in many countries, including a small society in New Guinea. From this research, they concluded that people the world over share six basic emotions: anger, fear, disgust, happiness, surprise, and sadness. Moreover, people everywhere display these feelings using the same distinctive facial expressions. To Ekman, this commonality is evidence that much of our emotional life is universal rather than

culturally variable and that the display of emotion is biologically programmed in our facial features, muscles, and central nervous system.

But Ekman notes three ways in which emotional life does differ according to culture. First, *what triggers an emotion differs from one society to another.* Whether people define a particular situation as an insult (causing anger), a loss (calling forth sadness), or a mystical event (provoking surprise and awe) depends on culture. In other words, people in various societies react differently to the same event.

Second, *people display emotions according to the norms of their culture.* Every society has rules about when, where, and to whom a person may exhibit certain emotions. Members of our society, for example, express emotions more freely at home among family members than in the workplace among colleagues. Similarly, we expect children to express emotions to parents, although

parents are taught to guard their emotions in front of children.

Third, *societies differ in terms of how people cope with emotions.* Some societies encourage the expression of feelings, whereas others belittle emotions and expect members to suppress their feelings. Societies also display significant gender differences in this regard. Our culture labels emotional expression as feminine, expected of women but a sign of weakness among men. In other societies, however, this gender pattern is less pronounced or even reversed.

In sum, people everywhere experience the same basic emotions. But what sparks a particular emotion, how and where a person expresses it, and how people define emotion in general all vary as matters of culture.

Sources: Ekman (1980a, 1980b), Lutz & White (1986), and Lutz (1988).

books and framed degrees, that reinforce the impression that the physician has the specialized knowledge necessary to call the shots. In the office, the physician usually remains seated behind a desk—the larger and grander the desk, the greater the statement of power—while the patient has only a chair.

The physician's appearance and manner convey still more information. The usual costume of white lab coat may have the practical function of keeping clothes from becoming soiled, but its social function is to let others know at a glance the physician's status. A stethoscope around the neck or a black medical bag in hand has the same purpose. A doctor's highly technical language is also a statement of power. Finally, patients

use the title "doctor," but they, in turn, often are addressed by their first names, which further underscores the physician's dominant position. The overall message of a doctor's performance is clear: "I will help you, but you must allow me to take charge."

NONVERBAL COMMUNICATION

Novelist William Sansom describes a fictional Mr. Preedy, an English vacationer on a beach in Spain:

> He took care to avoid catching anyone's eye. First, he had to make it clear to those potential companions of his holiday that they were of no concern to

Q: "We are, I fear, getting to know one another. Reticence, secrecy, concealment of self have been transformed into social problems; once they were aspects of civility." Philip Rieff

DISCUSS: What techniques do people in public places (airport waiting area, bus station, or in a cafe) use to claim a certain private space as their own?

RESOURCE: Roger Axtell's "The DOs and TABOOs of Body Language around the World" is a cross-cultural selection in the *Seeing Ourselves* reader.

Q: "Male nonverbal communication has certain elements and effects that distinguish it from its female counterpart." Henley, Hamilton, & Thorne (1992:10)

To most people in the United States, these expressions convey anger, fear, disgust, happiness, surprise, and sadness. But do people elsewhere in the world define them in the same way? Research suggests that all human beings experience the same basic emotions and display them to others in the same basic ways. But culture plays a part by specifying the situations that trigger one emotion or another.

him whatsoever. He stared through them, round them, over them—eyes lost in space. The beach might have been empty. If by chance a ball was thrown his way, he looked surprised; then let a smile of amusement light his face (Kindly Preedy), looked around dazed to see that there were people on the beach, tossed it back with a smile to himself and not a smile *at* the people. . . .

[He] then gathered together his beach-wrap and bag into a neat sand-resistant pile (Methodical and Sensible Preedy), rose slowly to stretch his huge frame (Big-Cat Preedy), and tossed aside his sandals (Carefree Preedy, after all). (1956; quoted in Goffman, 1959:4–5)

Without uttering a single word, Mr. Preedy offers a great deal of information about himself to anyone observing him. This illustrates the process of **nonverbal communication,** *communication using body movements, gestures,* and *facial expressions rather than speech.*

People use many parts of the body to generate *body language* through which they convey information to others. Facial expressions are the most significant form of body language. Smiling conveys pleasure, for instance, although we distinguish between the deliberate smile of Kindly Preedy on the beach, a spontaneous smile of joy at seeing a friend, a pained smile of embarrassment, and the full, unrestrained smile of

CHAPTER 6 Social Interaction in Everyday Life **149**

DISCUSS: Is hypocrisy really such a bad thing, or is some dishonesty necessary to civilized life? What would life be like if everyone agreed to tell the truth in all interactions?

Q: "If we never tried to seem a little better than we are, how could we improve or 'train ourselves from the outside inward'?" Charles Horton Cooley (1964:352; orig. 1902)

Q: "It is easier to ask forgiveness than to ask permission." Old saying

Q: "There is no crime more infamous than the violation of truth. It is apparent that men can be social beings no longer than they believe each other. When speech is employed only as the vehicle of falsehood, every man must disunite himself from others, inhabit his own cave and seek prey only for himself." Samuel Johnson

DISCUSS: Ask members of the class to identify other social situations that are gendered. Can they identify any that are *not* gendered?

Hand gestures vary widely from one culture to another. Yet people everywhere define a chuckle, grin, or smirk in response to someone's performance as an indication that one does not take another person seriously. Therefore, the world over, people who cannot restrain their mirth tactfully cover their faces.

self-satisfaction we often associate with the "cat who ate the canary."

Eye contact is another crucial element of nonverbal communication. Generally, we use eye contact to invite social interaction. Someone across the room "catches our eye," sparking a conversation. Avoiding another's eyes, by contrast, discourages communication. Hands, too, speak for us. Common hand gestures in our society can convey, among other things, an insult, a request for a ride, an invitation for someone to join us, or a demand that others stop in their tracks. Gestures also supplement spoken words. Pointing in a menacing way at someone gives greater emphasis to a word of warning, just as shrugging the shoulders adds an air of indifference to the phrase "I don't know," and rapidly waving the arms lends urgency to the single word "Hurry!"

Body Language and Deception

As any actor knows, it is very difficult to pull off a perfect performance. In everyday performances, unintended body language can contradict our planned meaning. A teenage boy offers an explanation for getting home late, for example, but his mother doubts his words because he avoids looking her in the eye. The movie star on a television talk show claims that her recent flop at the box office is "no big deal," but the nervous swing of her leg suggests otherwise. In practical terms, careful observation of nonverbal communication (most of which is not easily controlled) provides clues to deception, in much the same way that a lie detector records telltale changes in breathing, pulse rate, perspiration, and blood pressure.

Look at the two photographs in the box. Can you tell which smile is honest and which one is meant to deceive? Detecting phony performances is difficult because no bodily gesture directly indicates that one is lying. Even so, because any performance involves so many expressions, few people can lie without making a slip and raising the suspicions of a careful observer. Therefore, the key to detecting deceit is to scan the whole performance with an eye for inconsistencies. The box provides a closer look at everyday lie detection.

 For more information about facial expression and honesty, visit the following Web site: http://www.bbc.co.uk/science/ humanbody/humanface/ expertarticle_ekman.shtml

GENDER AND PERSONAL PERFORMANCES

Because women are socialized to be less assertive than men, they tend to be more sensitive to nonverbal communication. Moreover, gender plays an important part in personal performances. Based on the work of Nancy Henley, Mykol Hamilton, and Barrie Thorne (1992), we can extend our discussion of personal performances to spotlight the importance of gender.

APPLYING SOCIOLOGY

Hide Those Lyin' Eyes: Can You Do It?

Poker players and police officers have long realized that a good liar has a real advantage. Deception is a familiar element of everyday interaction, if only because common politeness sometimes demands that we not say what we really think.

Can you tell when another person is trying to deceive you? Paul Ekman suggests paying close attention to four elements of a performance: words, voice, body language, and facial expressions.

1. **Words.** Good liars mentally rehearse their lines, but they cannot always avoid a simple slip of the tongue—something the performer did not mean to say in quite that way. For example, a young man who is deceiving his parents by claiming that his roommate is a male friend rather than a female lover might mistakenly use the word "she" rather than "he" in conversation. The more complicated the deception, the more likely a performer is to make a revealing mistake.

2. **Voice.** Tone and patterns of speech contain clues to deception because they are hard to control. Especially when trying to hide a powerful emotion, a person cannot easily prevent the voice from trembling or breaking. Similarly, the person may speak more quickly (suggesting anger) or slowly (indicating sadness). Nervous laughter, inappropriate pauses between words, or nonwords, such as "ah" and "ummm," also hint at discomfort.

3. **Body language.** A "leak" from body language may tip off an observer to deception as well. Subtle body movements, for example, give the impression of nervousness, as does sudden swallowing or rapid breathing. These are especially good clues to deception because few people can control them. Sometimes, *not* using the body in the expected way—as when a person's body fails to confirm words that suggest excitement—also reveals deception.

4. **Facial expressions.** Because facial expressions, too, are hard to control, they give away many phony performances. Have you picked the lying face? It's the one on the left. Whereas a real smile usually has a relaxed expression and lots of "laugh lines" around the eyes, a phony smile seems forced and unnatural, with fewer wrinkles around the mouth and eyes.

Sources: Based on Ekman (1985) and Golden (1999b).

Demeanor

Demeanor—general conduct or deportment—is a clue to personal power. Simply put, powerful people enjoy more freedom in how they act; subordinates act more formally and self-consciously. Off-color remarks, swearing, or putting one's feet on the desk may be acceptable for the boss but not for a secretary. Similarly, powerful people can interrupt others whenever they want, whereas subordinates are expected to display deference through silence (Smith-Lovin & Brody, 1989; Henley, Hamilton, & Thorne, 1992; Johnson, 1994).

Because women generally occupy positions of lesser power, demeanor is a gender issue as well. As Chapter 13 ("Gender Stratification") explains, about half of all working women in the United States hold clerical or service jobs that place them under the control of supervisors, who are usually men. Women, then, craft their personal performances more carefully than men and defer to others more often in everyday interaction.

DISCUSS: In public settings, just as we expect a small amount of personal space, we also expect people to avoid private or personal discussion in the immediate presence of strangers. In recent years, the spread of cellular phones is changing this norm: In airports and on airplanes, for example, people seated right next to you often begin an audible personal conversation on the phone. How do students feel about such experiences?

GLOBAL: Use of space is another pattern subject to cultural interpretation (or misinterpretation). Across North Africa, from Cairo to Casablanca, people routinely move to within a foot or two when speaking in public. The U.S. traveler may easily consider such "in your face" behavior to be provocative, which it is not necessarily.
DISCUSS: Ask students how faculty idealize their performances.

Use of Space

How much space does a personal performance require? Power plays a key role because using more space is a sign of personal importance. Men typically command more space than women, whether pacing back and forth before an audience or casually lounging on a beach. Why? Our culture traditionally has measured femininity by how *little* space a woman occupies (the standard of "daintiness") and masculinity by how *much* territory a man controls (the standard of "turf").

For both sexes, the concept of **personal space** refers to *the surrounding area over which a person makes some claim to privacy*. In the United States, people typically position themselves several feet apart when speaking; throughout the Middle East, by contrast, people stand much closer. But just about everywhere, men routinely intrude into women's personal space. A woman's encroachment into a man's personal space, however, is often seen as a sexual overture. Here, again, women have less power in everyday interaction than men.

Staring, Smiling, and Touching

Eye contact encourages interaction. Women more than men work to sustain eye contact. But men have their own distinctive brand of eye contact: *staring*. As Henley, Hamilton, and Thorne see it, men staring at women are claiming dominance and defining women as sexual objects.

Although often conveying pleasure, *smiling* can also be a sign of appeasement or submission. In a male-dominated world, therefore, women smile more than men.

Finally, mutual *touching* conveys intimacy and caring. Apart from close relationships, however, touching generally is something men do to women (and rarely, in our culture, to other men). A male physician touches the shoulder of his female nurse as they examine a report, a young man touches the back of his woman friend as he guides her across the street, or a male skiing instructor touches young women as he teaches them to ski. In such examples, the touching may evoke little response, but it amounts to a subtle ritual by which men claim dominance over women.

IDEALIZATION

Complex motives underlie human behavior. Even so, Goffman suggests, we construct performances to *idealize* our intentions. That is, we try to convince others (and perhaps ourselves) that what we do reflects ideal cultural standards rather than selfish motives.

Idealization is easily illustrated in the world of physicians and patients. In a hospital, physicians engage in a performance commonly called "making rounds." Entering the room of a patient, the physician often stops at the foot of the bed and silently examines the patient's chart. Afterward, physician and patient converse briefly. In ideal terms, this routine involves a physician making a personal visit to inquire about a patient's condition.

In reality, the picture is not so perfect. A physician may see several dozen patients a day and remember little about many of them, so that reading the chart is a chance to recall the patient's name and medical problems. Revealing the impersonality of such medical care would undermine the cultural ideal of the physician as one who is deeply concerned about the welfare of others.

Physicians, college professors, and other professionals typically idealize their motives for entering their chosen careers. They describe their work as "making a contribution to science," "helping others," "serving the community," and even "answering a calling from God." Rarely do they concede the less honorable, but common, motives of seeking the income, power, prestige, and leisure these occupations provide.

More generally, idealization is part of civility. Smiling and speaking politely to people we do not like are little lies that ease our way through social interactions. Even when we suspect that others are putting on an act, we are unlikely to challenge their performances, for reasons we explain next.

EMBARRASSMENT AND TACT

The visiting speaker mispronounces the college's name; the senator rises from the table to speak, unaware of the napkin that still hangs from her neck; the president becomes ill at a state dinner. As carefully as people craft their performances, slip-ups of all kinds occur. The result is *embarrassment*, or discomfort resulting from a spoiled performance. Goffman describes embarrassment simply as "losing face."

Embarrassment is an ever-present danger because, first, all performances typically contain some deception. And second, most performances involve many elements that, in a thoughtless moment, can shatter the intended impression.

Q: "Tact is the ability to describe others the way they see themselves." Abraham Lincoln
GLOBAL: Few comparative data exist regarding tact. But, logically, one imagines that traditional societies engage in less of it because reality is more well established.

NOTE: "Androcentrism" is a masculine bias—in this case, of language. (*Andro* is Greek, meaning "male.")
GLOBAL: Worth noting is the fact that English does not follow the pattern of Romance languages of designating all nouns as either female or male.

A curious fact is that an audience usually overlooks flaws in a performance, allowing an actor to avoid embarrassment. If we do point out a misstep ("Excuse me, but did you know your fly is open?"), we do it quietly and only to help someone avoid even greater loss of face. In Hans Christian Andersen's classic fable "The Emperor's New Clothes," the child who blurts out that the emperor is parading about naked tells the truth but is scolded for being rude.

Often, members of an audience actually help the performer recover a flawed performance. *Tact* amounts to helping someone "save face." After hearing a supposed expert make an embarrassingly inaccurate remark, for example, people may tactfully ignore the comment as if it were never spoken. Or mild laughter may indicate that they choose to treat what was said as a joke. Or a listener may simply respond, "I'm sure you didn't mean that," noting the statement but not allowing it to destroy the actor's performance. With this in mind, we can understand Abraham Lincoln's comment that "Tact is the ability to describe others the way they see themselves."

Why is tact so common? Because embarrassment provokes discomfort not only for the actor but for everyone. Just as a theater audience feels uneasy when an actor forgets a line, people who observe awkward behavior are reminded of how fragile their own performances are. Socially constructed reality thus works like a dam holding back a sea of chaos. If one person's performance springs a leak, others tactfully help make repairs. After all, everyone lends a hand in building reality, and no one wants it suddenly swept away.

In sum, Goffman's research shows that although behavior is spontaneous in some respects, it is more patterned than we like to think. Almost 400 years ago, Shakespeare captured this idea in memorable lines that still ring true:

> All the world's a stage,
> And all the men and women merely players:
> They have their exits and their entrances;
> And one man in his time plays many parts.
> (*As You Like It*, II)

INTERACTION IN EVERYDAY LIFE: TWO APPLICATIONS

We have examined the major elements of social interaction. The final sections of this chapter apply these lessons to two important yet very different aspects of everyday life: language and humor.

Why do we associate ownership with men and characterize what is owned as feminine? How easily can you imagine renaming this boat with the gender reversed?

LANGUAGE: THE GENDER ISSUE

As Chapter 3 ("Culture") explains, language is the thread that joins members of a society in the symbolic web we call culture. Language conveys not only a surface meaning but also deeper levels of meaning. One such level involves gender. Language defines men and women differently in at least three ways, involving power, value, and attention.[1]

Language and Power

A young man astride his new motorcycle proudly rolls up his friend's driveway and eagerly asks, "Isn't she a beauty?" On the surface, the question has little to do

[1]The following sections draw primarily on Henley, Hamilton, & Thorne (1992). Additional material comes from Thorne, Kramarae, & Henley (1983) and Romaine (1999).

RESOURCE: Deborah Tannen's article on gender and communication is included among the contemporary selections in the companion reader *Seeing Ourselves*.

NOTE: Deborah Tannen describes her research as "interactional sociolinguistics."

DISCUSS: Why are boys—but not girls—designated as Jr., II, III, etc.?

DISCUSS: What is the symbolism of a married woman choosing to use her husband's last name or to keep her own last name?

DIVERSITY: "Widower" is the derivative term (from "widow"), suggesting that marital standing is a master status for women more than for men.

NOTE: The value function of language is also evident in terms such as "lady doctor," which suggests an exceptional case.

DIVERSITY: RACE, CLASS, AND GENDER

Gender and Language: "You Just Don't Understand!"

In the story that opened this chapter, a couple faces a situation that rings all too true to many people: When lost, men grumble to themselves, perhaps blame their partners, but avoid asking others for directions. For their part, women can't seem to understand such behavior.

Deborah Tannen, who has conducted extensive research on the linguistic differences that separate the sexes, explains. Men, she claims, see most daily encounters as competitive situations; getting lost is bad enough without asking for help and thereby letting someone else get "one up" on them. By contrast, because women in the United States hold a generally subordinate position, they are socialized to ask for help. Sometimes, Tannen points out, women ask for assistance even when they don't need it.

A similar gender-linked problem common to couples involves what men call "nagging." Consider the following exchange (Adler, 1990:74):

SYBIL: What's wrong, honey?

HAROLD: Nothing . . .

SYBIL: Something is bothering you; I can tell.

HAROLD: I told you nothing is bothering me. Leave me alone.

SYBIL: But I can see that something is wrong.

HAROLD: OK. Just why do you think something is bothering me?

SYBIL: Well, for one thing, you're bleeding all over your shirt.

HAROLD [NOW IRRITATED]: It doesn't bother me.

SYBIL [LOSING HER TEMPER]: "WELL, IT SURE IS BOTHERING ME!"

HAROLD: "I'll go change my shirt."

The problem couples face in communicating is that what one partner *intends* by a comment is not always what the other *hears* in the words. To Sybil, her opening question is an attempt at cooperative problem solving. She can

see that something is wrong with Harold (who has cut himself while doing yard work), and she wants to help him. But Harold interprets her pointing out his problem as belittling, and he tries to close off the discussion. Sybil, confident that Harold needs just to understand that she only wants to be helpful, repeats herself. This reaction sets in motion a vicious circle in which Harold, thinking his wife is nagging because she must believe he cannot take care of himself, responds by digging in his heels. His response, in turn, makes Sybil all the more sure that she needs to do something. And around and around it goes until somebody gets really angry.

In the end, Harold gives in only to the extent that he agrees to change his shirt. But notice that he still refuses to discuss the original problem—his injury. Misunderstanding his wife's motives, Harold just wants Sybil to leave him alone. Likewise, Sybil fails to understand her husband's view of the situation and walks away thinking that he is a stubborn grouch.

Sources: Adler (1990) and Tannen (1990).

with gender. Yet why does he use the pronoun "she" rather than "he" or "it" to refer to his prized possession? The answer is that men often use language to establish control over their surroundings. That is, a man attaches a female pronoun to a motorcycle (or car, boat, or other object) because it reflects the power of *ownership*.

Another power function of language relates to people's names. Traditionally in the United States and in many other parts of the world, a woman takes the family name of her husband when she marries. Although few people in this country consider this an explicit statement of a man's ownership of a woman,

NOTE: Humor's origin in incongruity is evident in Woody Allen's line, "More than any time in history, mankind faces a crossroads. One path leads to despair and utter hopelessness, the other to total extinction. Let us pray that we have the wisdom to choose correctly."
NOTE: Another incongruous thought: "My wife and I have no secrets from one another . . . at least none that she knows of."
NOTE: "Most weight lifters are biceptual." John Rostoni

NOTE: Humor can also be generated by leading an audience to expect two incongruent realities, one of which fails to materialize. Groucho Marx once quipped, "I worked myself up from nothing to a state of extreme poverty."
NOTE: The link between humor and contrasting realities is inherent in the Monty Python troupe's signature line, "Now for something completely different."

many think it reflects male dominance. For this reason, an increasing share of married women (almost 15 percent) have kept their own name or merged the two family names.

Language and Value

The English language usually treats as masculine whatever has greater value, force, or significance. For instance, the adjective "virtuous," meaning "morally worthy" or "excellent," is derived from the Latin word *vir*, meaning "man." By contrast, the disparaging adjective "hysterical" is derived from the Greek word *hyster*, meaning "uterus."

In many familiar ways, language also confers different value on the two sexes. Traditional masculine terms such as "king" and "lord" have retained their positive meaning, whereas comparable terms, such as "queen," "madam," and "dame" have acquired negative connotations in contemporary usage. Language thus both mirrors social attitudes and helps perpetuate them.

Similarly, use of the suffixes "ette" and "ess" to denote femininity usually devalues the words to which they are added. For example, a "major" has higher standing than a "majorette," as does a "host" in relation to a "hostess." And, certainly, men's groups with names such as the *Los Angeles Rams* carry more stature than women's groups with names such as the *Radio City Music Hall Rockettes*.

Language and Attention

Language also shapes reality by directing greater attention to masculine activity. In the English language, the plural pronoun "they" is gender-neutral. But the corresponding singular pronouns "he" and "she" specify gender. According to traditional grammatical practice, many people use "he," along with the possessive "his" and objective "him," to refer to *all* people. Thus, we assume that the bit of wisdom "He who hesitates is lost" refers to women as well as to men. But this practice also reflects the cultural pattern of neglecting the existence of women.

The English language has no gender-neutral, third-person singular personal pronoun. In recent years, however, the plural pronouns "they" and "them" have gained some currency as a singular pronoun ("A person should do as they please"). This usage violates grammatical rules, yet there is no doubt that English is changing to accept such gender-neutral constructions.

Grammar aside, the mix of gender and language is likely to remain a source of miscommunication between women and men. In the box, Harold and Sybil, whose misadventures in trying to find a friend's home opened this chapter, return to illustrate how the two sexes often seem to be speaking different languages.

HUMOR: PLAYING WITH REALITY

Humor is an important part of everyday life. But, although everyone laughs at jokes, few people think about what makes something funny or why humor is a part of every culture in the world. We can apply many of the ideas developed in this chapter to explore the character of humor.[2]

The Foundation of Humor

Humor is a product of reality construction; specifically, it stems from the contrast between two different realities. Generally, one reality is *conventional*, that is, what people expect in a specific situation. The other reality is *unconventional*, an unexpected violation of cultural patterns. Thus, humor arises from contradiction, ambiguity, and double meanings found in differing definitions of the same situation. Note how this principle works in the newspaper headlines in the box on page 156.

There are countless ways to mix realities and thereby generate humor. Contrasting realities emerge from statements that contradict themselves, such as "Nostalgia is not what it used to be." Switching words can create humor, as in Oscar Wilde's line: "Work is the curse of the drinking class." Even reordering syllables does the trick, as in the case of the (probably fictitious) country song, "I'd rather have a bottle in front of me than a frontal lobotomy."

Of course, a joke can be built the other way around, so that the comic leads the audience to *expect* an unconventional answer then delivers a very ordinary one. When a reporter asked the famous desperado Willy Sutton why he robbed banks, for example, he replied dryly, "Because that's where the money is." However a joke is constructed, the greater the opposition or incongruity between the two definitions of reality, the greater the humor.

---

[2]The ideas discussed here are those of the author (1987), except as otherwise noted. The general approach draws on work discussed in this chapter, especially on the ideas of Erving Goffman.

NOTE: Examples for eliciting the pleasure of getting jokes: What campus departments or offices would use these call letters for their radio station? WIXL (honors program), WSOS (security office), WURU (counseling service), WYMI (philosophy department), WYYY (religion department), WYRU (sociology department) (Barry Glassner and John Western).
Q: "He who laughs, lasts." Dr. Robert Anthony

NOTE: What do you get when you cross a mafiosi with a sociologist? You get an offer you can't understand.
NOTE: Example of the audience having to "finish a joke" is Woody Allen's line that, after some guy backed into his car, he told the fellow, "Be fruitful and multiply—but not in those words."
Q: "There are very few jokes about sociologists." Peter Berger (1963:1)

CRITICAL THINKING

Double Take: Real Headlines That Make People Laugh

Humor is generated by mixing two distinct and opposing realities. Here are several real headlines from newspapers. Read each one and identify the conventional meaning intended by the writer as well as the unconventional interpretation that generates humor.

"Include Your Children When Baking Cookies"

"Drunk Gets Nine Months in Violin Case"

"Survivor of Siamese Twins Joins Parents"

"Iraqi Head Seeks Arms"

"Stud Tires Out"

"Prostitutes Appeal to Pope"

"Panda Mating Fails: Veterinarian Takes Over"

"Soviet Virgin Lands Short of Goal Again"

"Typhoon Rips Through Cemetery: Hundreds Dead"

"Squad Helps Dog Bite Victim"

"Miners Refuse to Work after Death"

"Killer Sentenced to Die for Second Time in Ten Years"

"Something Went Wrong in Jet Crash"

"British Left Waffles on Falkland Islands"

"Stolen Painting Found by Tree"

What do you think?

1. *For each headline, do you see the expected and unexpected meanings?*

2. *Which headlines are funniest? Why?*

3. *Can you think of other everyday examples of humor?*

Source: Thanks to Kay Fletcher.

When telling jokes, the comedian can strengthen this opposition in various ways. One common technique is for the comic to present the first, or conventional, remark in conversation with another actor, then to turn toward the audience to deliver the second, unexpected line. In a Marx Brothers film, Groucho waxes philosophical when he says, "Outside of a dog, a book is a man's best friend." Then, dropping his voice and turning to the camera, he counters, "And *inside* of a dog, it's too dark to read!" Such "changing channels" underscores the incongruity of the two parts. Following the same logic, stand-up comics may "reset" the audience to conventional expectations by interjecting "But, seriously, folks . . ." after one joke and before the next one.

To construct the strongest contrast in meaning, comedians pay careful attention to their performances—the precise words they use and the timing of their delivery. A joke is "well told" if the comic creates the sharpest possible opposition between the realities, just as humor falls flat in a careless performance. Because the key to humor lies in the opposition of realities, we can see why the climax of a joke is called the "*punch*" line.

The Dynamics of Humor: "Getting It"

Someone who does not understand both the conventional and unconventional realities in a joke may complain, "I don't get it." To "get" humor, the audience must understand the two realities involved well enough to appreciate their difference. But comics may make getting the joke harder still by leaving out some important piece of information. Therefore, the audience must pay attention to the *stated* elements of the joke and then fill in the missing pieces on their own.

As a simple case, consider the reflection of movie producer Hal Roach upon reaching his one hundredth birthday: "If I had known I would live to be one hundred, I would have taken better care of myself!" Here, getting the joke depends on realizing that Roach must have taken pretty good care of himself because he lived to be one hundred in the first place. Or take one of W. C. Fields's lines: "Some weasel took the cork out of my lunch." "Some lunch!" we think to ourselves to "finish" the joke.

Here is an even more complex joke: What do you get if you cross an insomniac, a dyslexic, and an agnostic? Answer: A person who stays up all night wondering

NOTE: Two simple examples to illustrate the elements of humor:

#1: "What do you get when you cross the Atlantic with the *Titanic*?"

#2: "I dunno, what?"

#1: "About halfway."

An elderly Jewish woman in a Miami park sees a new face sitting on a bench. "I haven't seen you before," she offers. "I just finished forty years in jail," he replies. "What did you do?" "I killed my wife." "So," she concludes hopefully, "you're *single*."

NOTE: Laughter also accompanies tickling. This is a disruption of what is conventional in a physical sense. Tickling is also an ambiguous situation in which one does not know whether the other's motives are loving or aggressive.

whether there is a dog. To get this one, you must know, first, that insomnia is an inability to sleep; second, that dyslexia causes a person to reverse letters in words; and, third, that an agnostic doubts the existence of God.

Why would an audience be required to make this sort of effort in order to understand a joke? Simply because our enjoyment of a joke is heightened by the pleasure of having completed the puzzle. In addition, getting the joke confers a favored insider status. We can also understand the frustration of *not* getting a joke: fear of being judged stupid coupled with being excluded from a pleasure shared by others. Not surprisingly, outsiders in such a situation sometimes fake getting the joke, or someone may tactfully explain the joke so the other person doesn't feel left out.

But, as the old saying goes, if you have to explain a joke, it won't be very funny. Besides taking the edge off the language and timing on which the punch depends, an explanation removes the mental involvement and greatly reduces the listener's pleasure.

The Topics of Humor

People throughout the world smile and laugh, making humor a universal human trait. But the world's people differ in what they find funny, so humor rarely travels well.

October 1, Kobe, Japan. Can you share a joke with people who live halfway around the world? At dinner, I ask two Japanese college women to tell me a joke. "You know 'crayon'?" Asako asks. I nod. "How do you ask for a crayon in Japanese?" I respond that I have no idea. She laughs out loud as she says what sounds like "crayon crayon." Her companion, Mayumi, laughs, too. My wife and I sit awkwardly, straight-faced. Asako relieves some of our embarrassment by explaining that the Japanese word for "give me" is <u>kureyo</u>, which sounds like <u>crayon</u>. I force a smile.

What is humorous to the Japanese, then, may not seem funny in China, Iraq, or the United States. To some degree, too, the social diversity of our own country means that different types of people find humor in different situations. New Englanders, southerners, and

Because humor involves challenging established conventions, most U.S. comedians—including Margaret Cho—have been social "outsiders," members of racial and ethnic minorities.

westerners have their own brands of humor, as do Latinos and Anglos, fifteen- and forty-year-olds, Wall Street bankers and southwestern rodeo riders.

But, for everyone, humor deals with topics that lend themselves to double meanings or *controversy*. For example, the first jokes many of us learned as children were about culturally taboo bodily functions. The mere mention of "unmentionable acts" or even certain parts of the body can dissolve young faces in laughter.

Are there jokes that break through the culture barrier? Yes, but they must touch upon universal human experiences such as betraying a friend.

I think of a number of jokes, but none seems likely to work. Understanding jokes about the United States is difficult for people who have never been there. Is there something more universal? Inspiration: "Two fellows

NOTE: Here's an example of a one-line joke bordering on "sick": "Hey, do you know if, when you shoot a mime, you're supposed to use a silencer?"

NOTE: In other words, some topics are off limits because people expect them to be understood in only one way. The terrorist attack on the World Trade Center was such a case. Few "sick" jokes have circulated since the tragedy.

GLOBAL: Illustrating the use of humor to critique society, Soviets used to joke, "We pretend to work, and they pretend to pay us."

Q: "Imagination was given to man to compensate him for what he is not; a sense of humor was provided to console him for what he is." Robert Walpole

Q: "Clothes make the man. Naked people have little or no influence on society." Mark Twain

There are two sides to humor. On the one hand, people use humor as a safety valve to express potentially disruptive sentiments with little harm. On the other hand, people also make fun of others, elevating themselves at the expense of someone else.

lightly risk being defined as deviant or even mentally ill (a common stereotype depicts insane people as laughing uncontrollably, and we have long dubbed mental hospitals "funny farms").

Also, every social group considers certain topics too sensitive for humorous treatment. One can joke about such things, but doing so may bring criticism for telling a "sick" joke (and, therefore, *being* sick). People's religious beliefs, tragic accidents, or appalling crimes are the stuff of "sick" jokes.

The Functions of Humor

Humor is found everywhere because it works as a safety valve that vents potentially disruptive sentiments with little harm. That is, humor provides a way to express an opinion on a sensitive topic without being serious. Having said something controversial, a person can also use humor to diffuse the situation by simply stating, "I didn't mean anything by what I said; it was just a joke!"

Similarly, people use humor to relieve tension in uncomfortable situations. One study of medical examinations found most patients begin to joke with doctors to ease their own nervousness (Baker et al., 1997).

Humor and Conflict

If humor holds the potential to comfort those who laugh, it can also be used to harm others. Men who tell jokes about women, for example, typically are voicing some measure of hostility toward them (Powell & Paton, 1988; Benokraitis & Feagin, 1995). Similarly, jokes at the expense of homosexuals reveal the tensions surrounding sexual orientation in the United States. Humor often is a sign of real conflict in situations in which one or both parties choose not to bring the conflict out into the open (Primeggia & Varacalli, 1990).

"Put-down" jokes make one category of people feel good at the expense of another. After collecting and analyzing jokes from many societies, Christie Davies (1990) concluded that conflict between ethnic groups is one driving force behind humor almost everywhere. The typical ethnic joke makes fun of some disadvantaged category of people, thereby making the jokester and the audience superior. Given the Anglo-Saxon traditions of U.S. society, Poles and other ethnic and racial minorities have long been the butt of jokes, as have Newfoundlanders ("Newfies") in

are walking in the woods and come upon a huge bear. One guy leans over and tightens up the laces on his running shoes. 'Jake,' says the other, 'what are you doing? You can't outrun this bear!' 'I don't have to outrun the bear,' responds Jake, 'I just have to outrun you!' Smiles all around.

Humor and health have always been related. During the Middle Ages, people used the word *humors* (derived from the Latin word *humidus*, meaning "moist") to mean a balance of bodily fluids that regulate a person's well-being. Researchers today document the power of humor to reduce stress and improve health, confirming the old saying "Laughter is the best medicine" (Robinson, 1983; Haig, 1988). But, at the extreme, people who always take conventional reality eastern Canada, the Irish in Scotland, Sikhs in India, Turks in Germany, Hausas in Nigeria, Tasmanians in Australia, and Kurds in Iraq.

Disadvantaged people also make fun of the powerful, although usually with some care. Women in the United States joke about men, just as African Americans find humor in white people's ways, and poor people poke fun at the rich. Throughout the world, people target their leaders with humor, and officials in some countries take such jokes seriously enough to suppress them (cf. Speier, 1998).

In sum, the significance of humor is much greater than we may think. Humor is a means of mental escape from a conventional world that is never entirely to our liking (Flaherty, 1984, 1990; Yoels & Clair, 1995). Indeed, this fact explains why so many of our nation's comedians come from among the ranks of historically oppressed peoples, including Jews and African Americans. As long as we maintain a sense of humor, we assert our freedom and are not prisoners of reality. By putting a smile on our faces, we change ourselves and the world just a little.

SUMMARY

1. Social structure provides guidelines for behavior, which helps to make everyday life understandable and predictable.

2. A major component of social structure is status. Within an entire status set, a master status has special significance for a person's identity.

3. Ascribed statuses are involuntary, whereas achieved statuses are earned. In practice, most statuses are both ascribed and achieved.

4. Role is the dynamic expression of a status. Incompatible roles linked to two or more statuses generate role conflict; likewise, incompatible roles linked to a single status cause role strain.

5. "The social construction of reality" refers to the idea that we build the social world through our interactions with others.

6. The Thomas theorem states that situations defined as real become real in their consequences.

7. Ethnomethodology reveals the assumptions and understandings people have of their social world.

8. Dramaturgical analysis views everyday life as theatrical performance, noting that people try to create particular impressions in the minds of others.

9. Social power affects performances, which is one reason men's behavior typically differs from women's.

10. Everyday behavior carries the ever-present danger of embarrassment, or "loss of face." People use tact to prevent others' performances from breaking down.

11. Language is vital to the process of socially constructing reality. In various ways, language defines women and men differently, generally to the advantage of men.

12. Humor stems from the difference between conventional and unconventional definitions of a situation. Because humor is an element of culture, people throughout the world find different situations funny.

KEY CONCEPTS

social interaction (p. 139) the process by which people act and react in relation to others

status (p. 140) a social position that an individual occupies

status set (p. 140) all the statuses a person holds at a given time

ascribed status (p. 140) a social position a person receives at birth or assumes involuntarily later in life

achieved status (p. 141) a social position a person assumes voluntarily that reflects personal ability and effort

master status (p. 141) a status that has special importance for social identity, often shaping a person's entire life

role (p. 141) behavior expected of someone who holds a particular status

role set (p. 142) a number of roles attached to a single status

role conflict (p. 143) conflict between the roles corresponding to two or more statuses

role strain (p. 143) tension between roles connected to a single status

CTQ1: People may wrongly assume individuals with physical impairments have mental impairments or are not sexually active.

CTQ3: Nathan's quote suggests that reality is not objective but exists in the mind of the beholder. If I can't change *you*, he implies, I can change *the way I see you*. The element of humor lies in contrasting Nathan's line to our expectation that one drinks to make *oneself* more interesting.

CTQ2: Unless one enters into a conversation open-mindedly, change is unlikely; in such a case, one might say the talk does not proceed in good faith.

CTQ4: There are not many jokes about sociologists because most people aren't sure what we do. To get the joke, one would have to recognize sociology's tendency to highlight social structure rather than the actions of individuals.

social construction of reality (p. 144) the process by which people creatively shape reality through social interaction

Thomas theorem (p. 145) W. I. Thomas's assertion that situations that are defined as real are real in their consequences

ethnomethodology (p. 146) Harold Garfinkel's term for the study of the way people make sense of their everyday surroundings

dramaturgical analysis (p. 147) Goffman's term for the study of social interaction in terms of theatrical performance

presentation of self (p. 147) Goffman's term for an individual's efforts to create specific impressions in the minds of others

nonverbal communication (p. 149) communication using body movements, gestures, and facial expressions rather than speech

personal space (p. 152) the surrounding area over which a person makes some claim to privacy

CRITICAL-THINKING QUESTIONS

1. Consider ways in which a physical disability can serve as a master status. What assumptions do people commonly make about the mental ability of someone with a physical disability such as cerebral palsy? What assumptions are made about the person's sexuality?

2. The word "conversation" has the same root as the religious term "convert," suggesting that we engage one another with the expectation of change on the part of everyone involved. In what sense, then, does good-faith conversation necessitate open-mindedness on everyone's part?

3. George Jean Nathan once quipped, "I only drink to make other people interesting." What does this mean in terms of reality construction? Can you identify the elements of humor in this statement?

4. Here is a joke about sociologists: "Question—How many sociologists does it take to change a light bulb? Answer—None, because there is nothing wrong with the light bulb; it's *the system* that needs to be changed!" What makes this joke funny? What sort of people are likely to get it? What kind of people probably won't? Why?

APPLICATIONS AND EXERCISES

1. Write down as many of your own statuses as you can. Do you consider any of your statuses a master status? To what extent is each of your statuses ascribed and achieved?

2. During the next twenty-four hours, every time somebody asks, "How are you?" stop and actually give a truthful answer. What happens when you respond to a "polite" question in an unexpected way? (Listen to what people say and also note their body language.) What does this experiment suggest about everyday interactions?

3. This chapter illustrated Erving Goffman's ideas with a description of a physician's office. Investigate the offices of several professors in the same way. What furniture is there, and how is it arranged? What "props"

do professors use? How are the offices of physicians and professors different? Which are tidier? Why?

4. Spend an hour or two walking around the businesses of your town (or shops at a local mall). Observe the presence of women and men at each location. Based on your observations, would you conclude that physical space is "gendered"?

5. Packaged in the back of this new textbook is an interactive CD-ROM that offers a variety of study and review materials intended to help you better understand the material covered in this chapter. For this chapter, the CD-ROM contains an author's tip video, Real Life Sociology videos, other relevant audio and video, interactive map animations, audio journal entries from the author, Web links, and much more.

SITES TO SEE

http://www.prenhall.com/macionis

Visit the interactive *Companion Website*™ that accompanies this text. Begin by clicking on the cover of your book. You will find a chapter-by-chapter study guide, practice tests, and a significant portion of the text for on-line review, as well as many suggested Web links.

http://www.census.gov/genealogy/www/

Many interesting patterns of everyday life involve names. This Census Bureau Web site has a search engine for names. Study the frequency of different last names (or investigate first names) in the U.S. population. What patterns can you find? How many others share your own name?

http://www.ai.mit.edu/projects/humanoid-robotics-group/kismet.html

Is it possible to build a machine capable of human interaction? That is the goal of robotics engineers at the Massachusetts Institute of Technology. Their Web site provides

details and photographs. Look over their work and think about issues raised in this chapter. In what ways are machines able—and unable—to mimic human behavior?

http://www.georgetown.edu/faculty/tannend/

Here is the personal home page for Deborah Tannen, whose research is noted in the chapter.

http://www.achievement.org/autodoc/page/par0pro-1

Read more about the life and activism of Rosa Parks, who helped launch the civil rights movement in 1955.

http://www.paulekman.com

Discover more about Paul Ekman's research on human emotions.

http://www.people.brandeis.edu/~teuber/goffmanbio.html

Read more about the life and work of Erving Goffman at this site.

INVESTIGATE WITH CONTENTSELECT

Follow the instructions found on page 23 of this textbook to enter this chapter of the book's *Companion Website*™. Once in the chapter, click on the ContentSelect icon at the bottom left of your screen and enter your personal User ID and Password. Enter keywords such as "ethnomethodology," "Goffman," and "emotions," and the search engine will help you become an effective researcher.

Colin William Moss (b. 1914, English)
Hunger Marchers, 1936

Oil on canvas, 64 × 76.5 cm.
The Bridgeman Art Library.

GROUPS AND ORGANIZATIONS

Back in 1948, people in Pasadena, California, paid little attention to the opening of a new restaurant. Yet one small business—owned by brothers Maurice and Richard McDonald—would not only transform the restaurant industry but also introduce a new organizational model copied by countless businesses of all kinds.

The McDonald brothers' basic concept, which we now call "fast food," was to serve meals quickly and cheaply to large numbers of people. The brothers trained employees to perform highly specialized jobs, so that one person grilled hamburgers while others "dressed" them, made French fries, whipped up milkshakes, and presented the food to the customers in assembly-line fashion.

As the years went by, the McDonald brothers prospered, and they decided to move their single restaurant from Pasadena to San Bernardino. It was there, in 1954, that Ray Kroc, a traveling blender and mixer merchant, paid them a visit.

Kroc was fascinated by the efficiency of the brothers' system and saw the potential for a whole chain of fast-food restaurants. The three launched the plan as partners. Soon, however, Kroc bought out the McDonalds, and he went on to become one of the greatest success stories of all time. Today, about 28,000 McDonald's restaurants have served more than 150 billion hamburgers to people throughout the United States and in 120 other nations around the world.

The success of McDonald's is evidence of more than just the popularity of hamburgers. The larger importance of McDonald's lies in the extent to which the principles that guide this company are coming to dominate social life in the United States and elsewhere (Ritzer, 1993, 1998, 2000).

We begin with an examination of *social groups*, the clusters of people with whom we interact in much of our daily lives. As we shall see, the scope of group life expanded greatly during the course of the twentieth century. Having evolved from a close-knit world of families, local neighborhoods, and small businesses, our society now turns on the operation of huge businesses and other bureaucracies that sociologists describe as *formal organizations*. Understanding how this expanding scale of life came to be—and what it means for us as individuals—are this chapter's main objectives.

SOCIAL GROUPS

Almost everyone seeks a sense of belonging, which is the experience of group life. A **social group** is made up of *two or more people who identify and interact with one another*. Human beings come together in couples, families, circles of friends, churches, clubs, businesses, neighborhoods, and large organizations. Whatever its form, a group is made up of people with shared experiences, loyalties, and interests. In short, while keeping their individuality, members of social groups also think of themselves as a special "we."

Not every collection of individuals can be called a group. People with a status in common, such as women, homeowners, gay men, soldiers, millionaires, and Roman Catholics, are not a group but a *category*. Although they know others who hold the same status, most are strangers to one another.

163

SUPPLEMENTS: An outline and supplementary lecture material for Chapter 7 are included in the *Data File*.
RESOURCE: An excerpt of Cooley's analysis of primary groups appears in the Macionis and Benokraitis companion reader, *Seeing Ourselves*.
NOTE: "Primary" is derived from the Latin word *prime*, meaning "first"; "secondary" is from the Latin *secund(us)*, meaning "following."

NOTE: Cooley used only the term "primary group"; others introduced the term "secondary group" into sociological terminology, inferring the concept from Cooley's writings. Cooley did his first research for the U.S. Census, collecting statistics on street railways.
GLOBAL: The importance of traditional solidarities—of race, ethnicity, religion, or clan—typically surprises the U.S. traveler in less economically developed countries.

As human beings, we live our lives as members of groups. Such groups may be large or small, temporary or long-lasting. The United States is regarded as a country where people are especially likely to form groups based on kinship, heritage, or some shared interest.

What about students sitting together in a lecture hall or bathers enjoying a hot day at the beach? Some people in such settings may interact, but only with a few others. These temporary, loosely formed collections of people are better termed a *crowd*. In general, crowds are too anonymous and transitory to qualify as groups.

The right circumstances, however, can turn a crowd into a group. People riding in an elevator that stalls between floors generally recognize their common plight and turn to each other for help. Sometimes out of accidents and disasters, people form lasting relationships.

PRIMARY AND SECONDARY GROUPS

Acquaintances commonly greet one another with a smile and a "Hi! How are you?" The response is usually, "Just fine, thanks. How about you?" This answer is often more scripted than truthful. In most cases, providing a detailed account of how you are *really* doing would make most people feel so awkward they would beat a hasty retreat.

Sociologists designate two types of social groups, depending on the degree of genuine personal concern that members show for one another. According to Charles Horton Cooley (1864–1929), a **primary group** is *a small social group whose members share personal and enduring relationships*. Bound by *primary relationships*, people typically spend a great deal of time together, engage in a wide range of activities, and feel that they know one another well. Although not without conflict from time to time, members of primary groups display real concern for each other's welfare. The family is every society's most important primary group.

> For a biographical sketch of Charles Horton Cooley, see the Gallery of Sociologists at http://www.TheSociologyPage.com

Cooley called these personal and tightly integrated groups *primary* because they are among the first groups we experience in life. In addition, the family and early play groups hold primary importance in the socialization process, shaping attitudes, behavior, and social identity.

Primary relationships give people a comforting sense of security. In the familiar social circle of family or friends, people feel they can "be themselves" without worrying about the impression they are making.

Members of primary groups help one another in many ways, but they generally think of their ties as ends in themselves rather than as means to some other end. In other words, we prefer to think that kinship and friendship link people who belong together. Moreover, members of a primary group tend to view each other as unique and irreplaceable. Especially in the family, we are bound to others by emotion and loyalty. Brothers and sisters may not always get along, but they always remain siblings.

In contrast to the primary group, the **secondary group** is *a large and impersonal social group whose members pursue a specific goal or activity*. In most respects, secondary groups have precisely the opposite characteristics of primary groups. *Secondary relationships* involve weak emotional ties and little personal knowledge of one another. Most secondary groups are short term, beginning and ending without particular significance. Students in a college sociology course, for instance, who probably will not see many of the others again after the semester ends, exemplify the secondary group.

Secondary groups include many more people than primary groups. For example, dozens or even hundreds of people may work together in the same office, yet most of them pay only passing attention to one another. In some cases, time may transform a group from

NOTE: Primary groups involve bonds of affection but not necessarily of intimacy. Parents generally strive to treat children in an evenhanded and equal, if therefore impersonal, fashion. The adjectival form of "family"—*familiar*—also implies something less than intimacy. See the marriage box in Chapter 18 ("Family").

NOTE: Some categories of groups—peer groups, for example—cut across the primary-secondary continuum.

DISCUSS: Under what circumstances does somebody feel "used" by a friend? What does this feeling tell us about the character of ideal friendship?

NOTE: Emphasizing the expressive component while discounting the instrumental element of primary relationships is an example of Goffman's concept of idealization.

Q: "Blood is thicker than water." Old saying

secondary to primary, as with co-workers who share an office for many years. But, generally, members of a secondary group do not think of themselves as "we."

Whereas members of primary groups display a *personal orientation*, people in secondary groups have a *goal orientation*. Secondary ties need not be hostile or cold, of course. Interaction between students, co-workers, and business associates often is pleasant even if it is impersonal. But whereas primary group members define themselves according to *who* they are in terms of kinship or personal qualities, people in secondary groups look to one another for *what* they are or what they can do for each other. Put simply, people in secondary groups tend to "keep score," mindful of what they give others and what they receive in return. This goal orientation means that secondary group members usually remain formal and polite. In a secondary relationship, therefore, we ask the question "How are you?" without expecting a truthful answer.

Table 7–1 summarizes the characteristics that distinguish primary and secondary groups. Keep in mind that these traits define two types of groups in ideal terms; many real groups contain elements of both. But putting these concepts at opposite ends of a continuum helps us describe and analyze group life.

Many people think that small towns and rural areas have mostly primary relationships and that large cities are characterized by more secondary ties. This generalization holds much truth, but some urban neighborhoods—especially those populated by people of a single ethnic or religious category—are very tightly knit.

GROUP LEADERSHIP

How do groups operate? One important element of group dynamics is leadership. Many small friendship groups have no leader at all, but most large secondary groups have a formal chain of command.

Two Leadership Roles

Groups typically benefit from two kinds of leadership. **Instrumental leadership** is *group leadership that emphasizes the completion of tasks.* Members look to instrumental leaders to get things done. **Expressive leadership,** on the other hand, is *group leadership that focuses on collective well-being.* Expressive leaders take less of an interest in achieving goals than in raising group morale and minimizing tension and conflict between members.

Because they concentrate on performance, instrumental leaders usually have formal, secondary relationships with other group members. Instrumental

TABLE 7–1 Primary Groups and Secondary Groups: A Summary		
	Primary Group ←→	**Secondary Group**
Quality of Relationships	Personal orientation	Goal orientation
Duration of Relationships	Usually long term	Variable; often short term
Breadth of Relationships	Broad; usually involving many activities	Narrow; usually involving few activities
Subjective Perception of Relationships	As ends in themselves	As means to an end
Typical Examples	Families; circles of friends	Co-workers; political organizations

leaders give orders and reward or punish members according to their contribution to the group's efforts. Expressive leaders build more personal, primary ties. They offer sympathy to a member going through a tough time, keep the group united, and lighten a tense moment with humor. Whereas successful instrumental leaders enjoy more *respect* from members, expressive leaders generally receive more personal *affection*.

In the traditional North American family, the two types of leadership are linked to gender. Historically, cultural norms bestowed instrumental leadership on men, who, as fathers and husbands, assumed primary responsibility for earning income and making major family decisions. Expressive leadership traditionally belonged to women: Mothers and wives encouraged supportive and peaceful relationships between family members. One result of this division of labor was that many children had greater respect for their fathers but closer personal ties with their mothers (Parsons & Bales, 1955; Macionis, 1978a).

Greater equality between men and women has blurred this gender-based distinction between instrumental and expressive leadership. In most group settings, women and men now assume both leadership roles.

Three Leadership Styles

Sociologists also characterize leadership in terms of decision-making style. *Authoritarian leadership* focuses

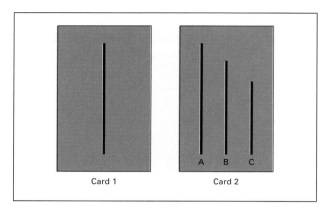

FIGURE 7–1 Cards Used in Asch's Experiment in Group Conformity

Source: Asch (1952).

on instrumental concerns, takes personal charge of decision making, and demands strict compliance from subordinates. Although this leadership style may win little affection from the group, a fast-acting authoritarian leader is appreciated in a crisis.

Democratic leadership is more expressive and makes a point of including everyone in the decision-making process. Although less successful when crises leave little time for discussion, democratic leaders generally draw on the ideas of all members to develop creative solutions to problems.

Laissez-faire leadership (a French phrase roughly meaning "to leave alone") allows the group to function largely on its own. This style typically is the least effective in promoting group goals (White & Lippitt, 1953; Ridgeway, 1983).

GROUP CONFORMITY

Groups influence the behavior of members and promote conformity. "Fitting in" provides a secure feeling of belonging, but, at the extreme, group pressure can be unpleasant and, at times, dangerous. Moreover, even strangers can foster conformity, as experiments by Solomon Asch and Stanley Milgram showed.

Asch's Research

Solomon Asch (1952) conducted a classic experiment that showed the power of groups to generate conformity. Asch recruited students allegedly for a study of visual perception. Before the experiment began, he explained to all but one member in a small group that

their real purpose was to put pressure on the remaining person. Arranging six to eight students around a table, Asch showed them a "standard" line, as drawn on Card 1 in Figure 7–1, and asked them to match it to one of three lines on Card 2.

Anyone with normal vision could easily see that the line marked "A" on Card 2 is the correct choice. Initially, as planned, everyone made the matches correctly. But then Asch's secret accomplices began answering incorrectly, leaving the naive subject (seated at the table in order to answer next to last) bewildered and uncomfortable.

What happened? Asch found that one-third of all subjects conformed to the others by answering incorrectly. Apparently, many of us are willing to compromise our own judgment to avoid being different, even from people we do not know.

Milgram's Research

Stanley Milgram, a former student of Solomon Asch, conducted conformity experiments of his own. In Milgram's controversial study (1963, 1965; Miller, 1986), a researcher explained to male recruits that they would be taking part in a study of how punishment affects learning. One by one, he assigned subjects to the role of "teacher" and placed another individual—actually an accomplice of Milgram—in a connecting room to pose as a "learner."

The teacher watched as the learner was seated in a contraption that looked like an electric chair. The researcher applied electrode paste to one of the learner's wrists, explaining that this would "prevent blisters and burns." The researcher then attached an electrode to the wrist and secured the leather straps, explaining that these would "prevent excessive movement while the learner is being shocked." Although the shocks would be painful, the researcher assured the teacher that they would cause "no permanent tissue damage."

The researcher then led the teacher back to the next room, explaining that the "electric chair" was connected to a "shock generator," a phony but realistic-looking piece of equipment with a label that read "Shock Generator, Type ZLB, Dyson Instrument Company, Waltham, Mass." On the front was a dial that supposedly regulated electric current from 15 volts (labeled "Slight Shock") to 300 volts (marked "Intense Shock") to 450 volts (marked "Danger: Severe Shock").

Seated in front of the "shock generator," the teacher was told to read aloud pairs of words. Then the teacher was to repeat the first word of each pair

NOTE: Keep in mind that pressure to conform comes from many sources other than groups, including media presentations, pronouncements of experts, and opinions of significant others.

Q: "I was only following orders." Adolf Eichmann, Nazi death camp officer

Q: "It is our nature to conform; it is a force not many can successfully resist." Mark Twain

Q: "With higher levels of aspiration than the less educated, the better educated man had more to lose in his own eyes and in the eyes of his friends by failure to achieve some sort of status in the army. Hence, frustration was greater for him than for others if a goal he sought was not attained." Samuel A. Stouffer (1949:153)

Q: "Whatever crushes individuality is despotism, by whatever name it may be called." John Stuart Mill

and wait for the learner to recall the second word. Whenever the learner failed to answer correctly, the teacher was told to apply an electric shock.

The researcher directed the teacher to begin at the lowest level (15 volts) and to increase the shock by 15 volts every time the learner made a mistake. And so the teacher did. At 75, 90, and 105 volts, the teacher heard moans from the learner; at 120 volts, shouts of pain; at 270 volts, screams; at 315 volts, pounding on the wall; after that, deadly silence. None of forty subjects assigned to the role of teacher during the initial research even questioned the procedure before reaching 300 volts, and twenty-six of the subjects—almost two-thirds—went all the way to 450 volts. Even Milgram was surprised at how readily people obeyed authority figures.

Milgram (1964) then modified his research to see whether Solomon Asch had documented such a high degree of group conformity only because the task he used to measure group conformity was trivial. Could groups of ordinary people—not authority figures—also pressure people to administer electrical shocks?

This time, Milgram formed a group of three teachers, two of whom were his accomplices. Each of the three teachers was to suggest a shock level when the learner made an error; the group would then administer the *lowest* of the three suggestions. This arrangement gave the naive subject the power to deliver a lesser shock regardless of what the others proposed.

The accomplices suggested increasing the shock level with each error, putting pressure on the third member to do the same. And, in fact, they succeeded. The subjects applied voltages three to four times higher than subjects who acted alone under control conditions. Thus Milgram's research suggests that people are likely to follow directions from not only "legitimate authority figures" but also from groups of ordinary individuals, even when it means inflicting harm on another person.

Janis's Research

Experts also cave in to group pressure, says Irving L. Janis (1972, 1989). Janis contends that a number of U.S. foreign policy errors, including the failure to foresee the Japanese attack on Pearl Harbor during World War II and the ill-fated Vietnam War, resulted from group conformity among our highest-ranking political leaders.

Common sense tells us that group discussion improves decision making. Janis counters that group members often seek consensus that closes off other points of view. Janis called this process **groupthink,** *the tendency of group members to conform, resulting in a narrow view of some issue.*

A classic example of groupthink led to the disastrous 1961 invasion of the Bay of Pigs in Cuba. Looking back, Arthur Schlesinger, Jr., an advisor to President Kennedy, confessed to feeling guilty for "having kept so quiet during those crucial discussions in the Cabinet Room," adding that the group discouraged anyone from challenging what, in hindsight, Schlesinger considered "nonsense" (quoted in Janis, 1972:30, 40).

REFERENCE GROUPS

How do we assess our own attitudes and behavior? Often we use a **reference group,** *a social group that serves as a point of reference in making evaluations and decisions.*

A young man who imagines his family's response to a woman he is dating is using his family as a reference group. Similarly, a supervisor who tries to gauge her employees' reactions to a new vacation policy is using them as a standard of reference. As these examples suggest, reference groups can be primary or secondary. In either case, our need to conform means that others' attitudes greatly affect us.

We also use groups that we do *not* belong to for reference. Being well prepared for a job interview means showing up dressed the way people in that company dress for work. Conforming to groups we do not belong to as a strategy to win acceptance illustrates the process of *anticipatory socialization*, described in Chapter 5 ("Socialization").

Stouffer's Research

Samuel A. Stouffer (1949) conducted a classic study of reference group dynamics during World War II. Researchers asked soldiers to rate their own or any competent soldier's chances of promotion in their army unit. One might guess that soldiers serving in outfits with a high promotion rate would be optimistic about their own advancement. Yet Stouffer's research pointed to the opposite conclusion: Soldiers in army units with low promotion rates actually were more positive about their chances to move ahead.

The key to understanding Stouffer's results lies in the groups against which soldiers measured themselves. Those having assignments with lower promotion rates looked around them and saw people making no more headway than they were. That is, although

RESOURCE: Georg Simmel's "The Dyad and the Triad" is one of the classics included in the companion reader, *Seeing Ourselves*.
GLOBAL: Marriage in our society is dyadic; ideally, powerful emotional ties unite husbands and wives. However, marriage in other societies may involve more than two people. In that case, the household usually is more stable, although many of the marital relationships are weaker.

Q: "A dyad . . . depends on each of its two elements alone—in its death, though not in its life: For its life, it needs both, but for its death, only one." Georg Simmel (1950:124)
NOTE: Ethnocentrism is one expression of valuing one's own ingroup while undervaluing those who differ as an outgroup.
NOTE: In the dyad, there can be no "social loafing."

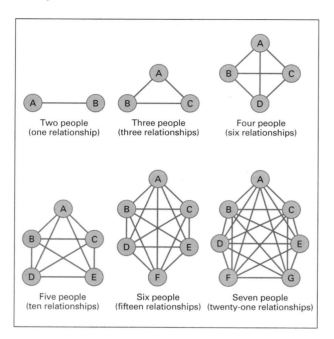

Two people (one relationship)
Three people (three relationships)
Four people (six relationships)
Five people (ten relationships)
Six people (fifteen relationships)
Seven people (twenty-one relationships)

FIGURE 7–2 Group Size and Relationships

they had not been promoted, neither had many others, so they did not feel deprived. On the other hand, soldiers in units with a higher promotion rate could easily think of people who had been promoted sooner or more often than they had. With such people in mind, even soldiers who had been promoted were likely to feel shortchanged.

The lesson is that we do not make judgments about ourselves in isolation, nor do we compare ourselves with just anyone. Regardless of our situation in *absolute* terms, we form a subjective sense of our well-being by looking at ourselves in relation to specific reference groups (Merton, 1968; Mirowsky, 1987).

INGROUPS AND OUTGROUPS

Everyone favors some groups over others, whether because of political outlook, social prestige, or just manner of dress. On the college campus, for example, left-leaning student activists may look down on fraternity members, whom they consider conservative; the Greeks, in turn, may snub the computer "nerds" and "grinds," who work too hard. Nearly every social landscape has a comparable mix of positive and negative evaluations.

Such judgments illustrate another element of group dynamics: the opposition of ingroups and outgroups. An **ingroup** is *a social group commanding a member's esteem and loyalty.* An ingroup exists in relation to an **outgroup**, *a social group toward which one feels competition or opposition.* Ingroups and outgroups are based on the idea that "we" have valued traits that "they" lack.

Tensions among groups sharpen their boundaries and give people a clearer social identity. At the same time, these group dynamics foster stereotypes and distort reality. Specifically, members of ingroups generally hold overly positive views of themselves and unfairly negative views of various outgroups.

Power also plays a part in intergroup relations. A powerful ingroup can define others as a lower-status outgroup. Historically, for example, white people have viewed people of color as an outgroup and subordinated them socially, politically, and economically. Internalizing these attitudes, minorities must struggle to overcome negative self-images. In short, ingroups and outgroups foster loyalty but also generate conflict (Tajfel, 1982; Bobo & Hutchings, 1996).

GROUP SIZE

If you are the first person to arrive at a party, you are in a position to watch some fascinating group dynamics. Until about six people enter the room, everyone usually shares a single conversation. But as more people arrive, the group soon divides into two or more clusters. Size plays an important role in how group members interact.

To understand the effects of group size, consider the mathematical number of relationships between two to seven people. As Figure 7–2 shows, two people form a single relationship, adding a third person results in three relationships, and adding a fourth person yields six. Increasing the number of people one at a time expands the number of relationships much more rapidly because every new person can interact with everyone already there. Thus, by the time seven people join one conversation, twenty-one "channels" connect them. With so many open channels at this point, the group usually divides.

The Dyad

German sociologist Georg Simmel (1858–1918) studied the social dynamics in the smallest groups. Simmel (1950; orig. 1902) used the term **dyad** to designate *a social group with two members.*

Simmel explained that social interaction in a dyad typically is more intense than in larger groups because neither member shares the other's attention with anyone else. In the United States, love affairs, marriages, and the closest friendships are dyadic.

For more about Georg Simmel, see his biography in the Gallery of Sociologists at http://www.TheSociologyPage.com

But like a stool with only two legs, dyads are unstable. Both members of a dyad must work to keep the relationship going; if either withdraws, the group collapses. Because the stability of marriages is important to society, the marital dyad is supported with legal, economic, and often religious ties.

The Triad

Simmel also studied the **triad,** *a social group with three members.* A triad contains three relationships, each joining two of the three people. A triad is more stable than a dyad because one member can act as a mediator should the relationship between the other two become strained. Such group dynamics help explain why members of a dyad (say, a married couple) often seek out a third person (a counselor) to air tension between them.

On the other hand, two of the three can pair up to press their views on the third, or two may intensify their relationship, leaving the other feeling left out. For example, when two of the three develop a romantic interest in each other, they will understand the old saying, "Two's company, three's a crowd."

As groups grow beyond three people, they become more stable and capable of withstanding the loss of even several members. At the same time, increases in group size reduce the intense personal interaction possible only in the smallest groups. Larger groups therefore are based less on personal attachment and more on formal rules and regulations. Such formality helps a group persist over time, although the group is not immune to change. After all, their numerous members give large groups more contact with the outside world, opening the door to new attitudes and behavior (Carley, 1991).

SOCIAL DIVERSITY: RACE, CLASS, AND GENDER

Race, ethnicity, class, and gender also affect group dynamics. Peter Blau (1977; Blau, Blum, & Schwartz, 1982; South & Messner, 1986) points out four ways in which social diversity influences intergroup contact:

The triad, illustrated by Jonathan Green's painting Friends, *includes three people. A triad is more stable than a dyad because conflict between any two persons can be mediated by the third member. Even so, should the relationship between any two become more intense in a positive sense, those two are likely to exclude the third.*

Jonathan Green, *Friends,* 1992. Oil on masonite, 14 in. × 11 in. © Jonathan Green, Naples, Florida. Collection of Patric McCoy.

1. **Large groups turn inward.** Blau explains that the larger a group, the more likely its members are to have relationships just between themselves. Say a college is trying to enhance social diversity by increasing the number of international students. These students may add a dimension of difference, but as their numbers rise, they become more likely to form their own social group. Thus, efforts to promote social diversity may have the unintended effect of promoting separatism.

2. **Heterogeneous groups turn outward.** The more internally diverse a group is, the more

Today's college campuses value social diversity. One of the challenges of this movement is ensuring that all categories of students are fully integrated into campus life. This is not always easy. Following Blau's theory of group dynamics, as the number of minority students increases, these men and women are able to form a group unto themselves, perhaps interacting less with others.

likely its members are to interact with outsiders. Campus groups that recruit people of both sexes and various social backgrounds typically have broader social contact than those with members of one social type.

3. **Social equality promotes contact.** To the extent that all groups have the same social standing, members of all the groups will interact. Thus, whether groups keep to themselves depends on how much the groups form a social hierarchy.

4. **Physical boundaries create social boundaries.** To the extent that a social group is physically segregated from others (by having its own dorm or dining area, for example), its members are less likely to associate with other people.

NETWORKS

A **network** is *a web of weak social ties*. Think of a network as a "fuzzy" group containing people who come into occasional contact but who lack a sense of boundaries and belonging. If we think of a group as a "circle of friends," then we might describe a network as a "social web" expanding outward, often reaching great distances and including large numbers of people.

Some networks are close to being groups, as is the case with college friends who stay in touch after graduation by e-mail and telephone. More commonly, however, a network includes people we *know of*—or who *know of us*—but with whom we interact rarely, if at all. As one woman with a widespread reputation as a community organizer explains, "I get calls at home, someone says, 'Are you Roseann Navarro? Somebody told me to call you. I have this problem'" (quoted in Kaminer, 1984:94).

Network ties often give us the sense that we live in a small world. In another classic experiment, Stanley Milgram (1967; Watts, 1999) gave letters to subjects in Kansas and Nebraska intended for a few specific people in Boston who were unknown to the original subjects. No addresses were supplied, and the subjects in the study were instructed to send the letters to others they knew personally who might know the target people. Milgram found that letters reached the target people with, on average, six subjects helping out. This result led Milgram to conclude that just about everyone is connected to everyone else with "six degrees of separation."

Network ties may be weak, but they can be a powerful resource. For immigrants seeking to become established in a new community, businesspeople seeking to expand their operations, or anyone looking for a job, *whom you know* is often just as important as *what you know* (cf. Luo, 1997; Hagan, 1998; Petersen, Sapotra, & Seidel, 2000).

Networks are based on people's colleges, clubs, neighborhoods, political parties, and personal interests. Obviously, some networks contain people with much more wealth, power, and prestige than others, which is what the expression "well connected" means. The networks of more privileged categories of people—including whites in comparison to African Americans and Hispanics—are a more valuable form of "social capital," which is more likely to land people in those categories higher-paying jobs, for example (Kasinitz & Rosenberg, 1996; Green, Tigges, & Diaz, 1999).

Some people also have denser networks than others; that is, they are connected to more people. Typically, the most extensive social networks include people who are young, well educated, and living in large cities (Markovsky et al., 1993; Kadushin, 1995;

CYBER: In 1998, some 3.4 trillion e-mail messages passed through the U.S. Internet system. In 2000, the number probably was closer to 6.6 trillion. In 2000, more than 50% of households had a personal computer, most connected to an Internet account, and almost half of the work force uses the Internet on the job.

Q: "In our own life the intimacy of the neighborhood has been broken up by the growth of an intricate mesh of wider contacts which leaves us strangers to people who live in the same house." Charles Horton Cooley (1962:26; orig. 1909)

NOTE: One indicator of the character of social organization is the share of unlisted telephone numbers. In Albany, N.Y., and Minneapolis, about 12% are unlisted; in Los Angeles, 60% are unlisted.

GLOBAL SOCIOLOGY

The Internet: A Global Network

Its origins are reminiscent of the film popular during the cold war in the 1960s, *Dr. Strangelove*. Three decades ago, government officials and scientists trying to figure out how to run the country after an atomic attack, which, they assumed, would knock out telephones and television. The brilliant solution was to devise a communication system with no central headquarters, no one in charge, and no main power switch—in short, an electronic web that would link the country in one vast network.

By 1985, a web of high-speed data lines was in place, and the Internet was about to be born. Today, the Internet connects thousands of colleges and universities and tens of thousands of government offices, all of which share in the cost of its operation. Tens of millions of businesses and individuals at home also connect to this "information superhighway" using modems and subscriptions to commercial Internet service providers.

How many people use the Internet? A rough estimate is that, in 2002, more than 400 million people in 180 (of 192) countries around the world are connected by the largest network in history.

What does the network offer to individuals? Popular search engines such as YAHOO! (type in http://www.yahoo.com) provide site listings for just about any topic you can imagine. Through electronic mail you can start a cyber-romance with a pen pal, write to your textbook author (macionis@kenyon.edu), or even send a message to the president of the United States (president@whitehouse.gov). You can also use the Internet to join discussion groups, take "virtual tours" of museums, locate data from government agencies (a good starting point is http://www.census.gov), explore Web pages of sociological interest (try the author's Web site, at http://www.TheSociologyPage.com), or review for exams in this course (http://www.prenhall.com/macionis). With no formal rules for its use, the Internet's potential is limited only by our imagination.

Ironically, perhaps, it is precisely this freedom that disturbs some people. Critics claim that "electronic democracy" threatens our political system, parents fear that their children will access sexually explicit sites, and purists bristle as the Internet becomes flooded with advertising.

In its "anything-goes" character, the Internet is like the real world. Not surprisingly, therefore, more and more people now use passwords, fees, and other "gates" to create restricted sub-networks limited to people like themselves. From one vast network, then, is emerging a host of social groups.

Sources: Based on Elmer-DeWitt (1993, 1994b), Hafner (1994), and O'Connor (1997).

O'Brien, Hassinger, & Dershem, 1996; Fernandez & Weinberg, 1997; Podolny & Baron, 1997).

Gender also shapes networks. Although the networks of men and women typically are the same size, women include more relatives (and other women) in their networks, whereas men include more co-workers (and other men). Research suggests that women's ties do not carry quite the same clout as typical "old boy" networks. Even so, as gender equality increases in the United States, the networks of women and men are becoming more alike (Moore, 1991, 1992; Wright, 1995; Mencken & Winfield, 1999; Reskin & McBrier, 2000).

Finally, new information technology has generated a global network of unprecedented size in the form of the Internet. The box takes a closer look at this twenty-first century form of communication, and Global Map 7–1 on page 172 shows access to the Internet around the world.

FORMAL ORGANIZATIONS

A century ago, most people in the United States lived in small groups of family, friends, and neighbors. Today, our lives revolve increasingly around **formal organizations,** *large secondary groups that are organized to achieve their goals efficiently.*

Formal organizations, such as business corporations and government agencies, differ from families and neighborhoods in an important way: Their greater size makes social relations less personal and fosters a formal, planned atmosphere. In other words, formal organizations operate in a deliberate way, not

NOTE: The Cellular Communications Industry Association calculates that as of June 1999, there were more than 76 million cellular telephone subscribers in the U.S.

CYBER: In the electronic age, what is a file? Do bureaucrats have to save all electronic correspondence (emerging government regulations tend to say "yes")? Are people aware that their messages leave trails and may end up as files?

GLOBAL: Two global maps from other chapters may be of interest here. One, in Chapter 4 ("Society"), shows the availability of personal computers, a good measure of the relative rationalization of society. Another, in Chapter 13 ("Gender Stratification"), illustrates women's paid employment around the world. In many poor nations, women's lives remain bounded by the home despite the increase in formal organization.

WINDOW ON THE WORLD

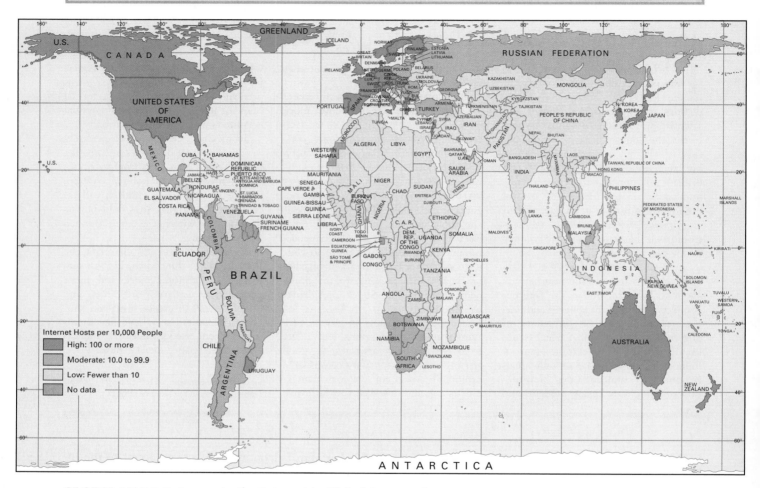

GLOBAL MAP 7–1 Access to the Internet in Global Perspective

This map shows access to the Internet around the world in terms of the number of Internet hosts for every 10,000 people. Most high-income countries and many middle-income nations are rated as having high Internet access. By contrast, about half the world's nations (mostly those with low average incomes) offer little access. What effect does this have on people's access to information? What are the likely consequences of this disparity for the future in terms of global inequality?

Source: The World Bank (2001).

NOTE: Even from one individual's viewpoint, there are combinations of Etzioni's organizational types: Being drafted into an army is partly coercive (restricting freedoms), partly utilitarian (offering pay), and partly normative (doing one's duty).

GLOBAL: Alvin and Heidi Toffler report that three-fourths of the world's 600 million telephones are in 9 countries.

NOTE: In formal organizations, Arne L. Kalleberg and Mark E. Van Buren (1996) found that "bigger is better" when it comes to employee rewards such as salaries and fringe benefits. Yet "small is beautiful" when it comes to giving employees autonomy.

RESOURCE: An excerpt from Max Weber's analysis of bureaucracy is among the classic selections found in the companion reader, *Seeing Ourselves*.

to meet personal needs but to accomplish complex jobs.

When you think about it, organizing some 285 million members of society is an incredible accomplishment, involving countless jobs, from collecting taxes to delivering the mail. To carry out most of these tasks, we rely on large formal organizations. The U.S. government, the nation's largest formal organization, employs more than 5 million people in hundreds of agencies and the armed forces. Large formal organizations develop lives and cultures of their own so that, as members come and go, their operation can stay the same over many years.

TYPES OF FORMAL ORGANIZATIONS

Amitai Etzioni (1975) identified three types of formal organizations, distinguished by the reasons people participate: utilitarian organizations, normative organizations, and coercive organizations.

Utilitarian Organizations

Just about everyone who works for income belongs to a *utilitarian organization*, one that pays people for their efforts. For example, large businesses generate profits for their owners and income for their employees. Joining utilitarian organizations usually is a matter of individual choice, although, obviously, most people must join one or another utilitarian organization to make a living.

Normative Organizations

People join *normative organizations* not for income but to pursue some goal they think is morally worthwhile. Sometimes called *voluntary associations*, these include community service groups (such as the Lions Club, the League of Women Voters, and the Red Cross), as well as political parties and religious organizations. In global perspective, people in the United States tend to join voluntary associations (Curtis, Grabb, & Baer, 1992). Figure 7–3 provides a comparative glance at membership in arts-related organizations for selected countries.

Coercive Organizations

Coercive organizations have an involuntary membership. That is, people are forced to join these organizations as a form of punishment (prisons) or treatment (psychiatric hospitals). Coercive organizations have special physical features, such as locked doors and

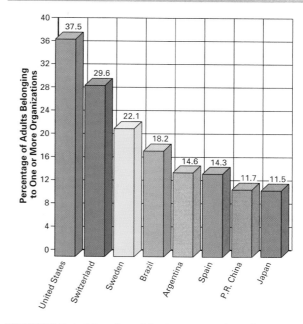

GLOBAL SNAPSHOT

FIGURE 7–3 Membership in Arts-Related Organizations

Source: Inglehart et al. (2000).

barred windows, and are supervised by security personnel. They isolate people as "inmates" or "patients" for a period of time, seeking to change attitudes and behavior radically. Recall from Chapter 5 ("Socialization") the power of *total institutions* to transform a human being's sense of self.

From differing vantage points, any particular organization may fall into all of these categories. A psychiatric hospital, for example, serves as a coercive organization for a patient, a utilitarian organization for a psychiatrist, and a normative organization for a part-time hospital volunteer.

ORIGINS OF BUREAUCRACY

Formal organizations date back thousands of years. Elites who controlled early empires relied on officials to collect taxes, undertake military campaigns, and construct monumental structures, from the Great Wall of China to the pyramids of Egypt.

NOTE: A section in Chapter 4, "Max Weber: The Rationalization of Society," provides general background for this discussion of bureaucracy. Chapter 4 introduces Weber's thesis of increasing rationalization; this section focuses more narrowly on bureaucracy as a major manifestation of that process.

NOTE: Modern bureaucracy arose at the same time as large, efficient armies; Weber's bureaucratic traits are very militaristic.

Q: "In small groups, members typically have a chance to interact directly with one another; once the group exceeds a relatively limited size, such interaction must be mediated through formal arrangements. . . . Thus, no large group can function without the creation of offices, the differentiation of status positions, and the delegation of tasks and responsibilities." Lewis A. Coser (1971:188)

Q: "Punctuality is the virtue of the bored." Evelyn Waugh

CHARACTERISTICS OF BUREAUCRACY

Bureaucracy is *an organizational model rationally designed to perform tasks efficiently.* Bureaucratic officials deliberately enact and revise policy in order to increase efficiency. To appreciate the power and scope of bureaucratic organization in the twenty-first century, consider this: Any one of nearly 300 million phones in the United States can connect you, within seconds, to any other phone—in homes, businesses, automobiles, or even a hiker's backpack on a remote mountain trail in the Adirondacks. Such instant communication was beyond the imagination of people who lived in the ancient world.

Of course, the telephone system depends on technology such as electricity, fiberoptics, and computers. But the system could not exist without the organizational ability to keep track of every telephone call—noting which phone called which other phone, when, and for how long—and then present this information in the form of more than 100 million monthly telephone bills.

What are the specific traits that promote organizational efficiency? Max Weber (1978; orig. 1921) identified six key elements of the ideal bureaucratic organization:

Although formal organization is vital to modern, high-income nations, it is far from new. Twenty-five centuries ago, the Chinese philosopher and teacher K'ung Fu-Tzu (known to Westerners as Confucius) endorsed the idea that government offices should be filled by the most talented young men. This led to what was probably the world's first system of civil service examinations. Here, would-be bureaucrats compose essays to demonstrate their knowledge of Confucian texts.

1. **Specialization.** Our ancestors spent most of their time looking for food and shelter. Bureaucracy, by contrast, assigns individuals highly specialized duties.

2. **Hierarchy of offices.** Bureaucracies arrange personnel in a vertical ranking of offices. Each person is supervised by "higher-ups" in the organization while supervising others in lower positions. Usually, with few people at the top and many at the bottom, bureaucratic organizations take the form of a pyramid.

3. **Rules and regulations.** Cultural tradition counts for little in a bureaucracy. Instead, rationally enacted rules and regulations guide a bureaucracy's operation. Ideally, a bureaucracy seeks to operate in a completely predictable way.

4. **Technical competence.** Bureaucratic officials and staff have the technical competence to carry out their duties. Bureaucracies typically recruit new members according to set criteria and regularly monitor their performance. Such impersonal evaluation contrasts sharply with the ancient custom of favoring relatives, whatever their talents, over strangers.

These early organizations had two limitations, however. First, they lacked the technology to communicate quickly, to travel over large distances, and to collect and store information. Second, tradition is strong in preindustrial societies, so organizational goals were to preserve cultural systems, not to change them. But during the last few centuries, what Max Weber called a "rational worldview" emerged in parts of the world, a process described in Chapter 4 ("Society"). In Europe and North America, the Industrial Revolution ushered in a new organizational structure concerned with efficiency, which Weber called *bureaucracy.*

CYBER: Will electronic communication, which gives almost anyone access to anyone else, let employees skip over levels to make bureaucratic pyramids flatter? Probably, although electronic screens may soon reinforce hierarchy online.

NOTE: Photocopier machines, now essential to bureaucratic organizations, first appeared in the 1950s. Many people were skeptical that they would catch on.

Q: "[Through bureaucracy,] the performance of each individual worker is mathematically measured, each man becomes a little cog in the machine and, aware of this, his one preoccupation is whether he can become a bigger cog." Max Weber (quoted in Coser, 1971:231)

NOTE: The "files" direct the future operation of an organization just as personality guides the future behavior of an individual.

5. **Impersonality.** Bureaucracy puts rules ahead of personal whim so that clients as well as workers are treated uniformly. From this detached approach stems the notion of the "faceless bureaucrat."

6. **Formal, written communication.** According to an old saying, the heart of bureaucracy is not people but paperwork. Rather than casual, face-to-face talk, bureaucracy relies on formal, written memos and reports, which accumulate in vast files and guide the operation of the organization.

Bureaucratic organization promotes efficiency by carefully recruiting personnel and limiting the unpredictable effects of personal taste and opinion. Table 7–2 summarizes the differences between small social groups and large formal organizations.

ORGANIZATIONAL ENVIRONMENT

No organization operates in a vacuum. How any organization performs depends not only on its own goals and policies but also on the **organizational environment,** *factors outside the organization that affect its operation.* These factors include technology, economic and political trends, the available work force, and other organizations.

Modern organizations are shaped by the *technology* of computers, telephone systems, and copiers. Computers give employees access to more information and people than ever before. At the same time, computer technology allows managers to monitor closely the activities of workers (Markoff, 1991).

Economic and political trends affect organizations. All organizations are helped or hindered by periodic economic growth or recession. Most industries also face competition from abroad as well as changes in law—such as new environmental standards—at home.

Population patterns, such as the size and composition of the surrounding populace, also affect organizations. The average age, typical education, and social diversity of a local community determine the available work force and, sometimes, the market for an organization's products or services.

Other organizations also contribute to the organizational environment. To be competitive, a hospital must be responsive to the insurance industry and organizations representing doctors, nurses, and other workers. It must also keep abreast of the equipment and procedures available at nearby facilities, as well as their prices.

TABLE 7–2 Small Groups and Formal Organizations: A Comparison		
	Small Groups	**Formal Organizations**
Activities	Members typically engage in many of the same activities	Members typically engage in distinct, highly specialized activities
Hierarchy	Often informal or nonexistent	Clearly defined, corresponding to offices
Norms	Informal application of general norms	Clearly defined rules and regulations
Membership Criteria	Variable, often based on personal affection or kinship	Technical competence to carry out assigned tasks
Relationships	Variable; typically primary	Typically secondary, with selective primary ties
Communications	Typically casual and face to face	Typically formal and in writing
Focus	Person-oriented	Task-oriented

THE INFORMAL SIDE OF BUREAUCRACY

Weber's ideal bureaucracy deliberately regulates every activity. In actual organizations, however, human beings are creative (and stubborn) enough to resist bureaucratic blueprints. Informality may amount to simply cutting corners in one's job, but it can also provide needed flexibility (Scott, 1981).

Informality comes partly from the personalities of organizational leaders. Studies of U.S. corporations document that the qualities and quirks of individuals—including personal charisma and interpersonal skills—can have a great effect on organizational outcomes (Halberstam, 1986; Baron, Hannan, & Burton, 1999).

Authoritarian, democratic, and laissez-faire types of leadership (described earlier in this chapter) reflect individual personality as much as they do any organizational plan. Also, in the real world of organizations, leaders and their cronies sometimes seek to benefit personally by abusing organizational power. Perhaps even more commonly, leaders take credit for the efforts of their subordinates. For example, many executive assistants have far more authority

George Tooker's painting Government Bureau *is a powerful statement about the human costs of bureaucracy. The artist depicts members of the public in monotonous similitude—reduced from human beings to mere "cases" to be disposed of as quickly as possible. Set apart from others by their positions, officials are "faceless bureaucrats" concerned more with numbers than with providing genuine assistance (notice that the artist places the fingers of the officials on calculators).*

George Tooker, *Government Bureau*, 1956. Egg tempera on gesso panel, 19⅝ x 29⅝ inches. The Metropolitan Museum of Art, George A. Hearn Fund, 1956 (56.78). Photograph © 1984 The Metropolitan Museum of Art.

and responsibility than their official job titles and salaries suggest.

Communication offers another example of informality within large organizations. Memos and other written communications are the formal way to spread information through the organization. Typically, however, individuals create informal networks, or "grapevines," that spread information quickly, if not always accurately. Grapevines, using both word-of-mouth and e-mail, are particularly important to subordinates because higher-ups may try to keep important information from them.

The spread of e-mail has "flattened" organizational hierarchies somewhat, because it allows even the lowest-ranking employee to bypass immediate superiors and communicate directly with the organization's leader or even with all fellow employees at once. Some organizations object to "open-channel" communication and limit employees' use of e-mail. Microsoft Corporation (whose founder, Bill Gates, has an unlisted address yet still receives hundreds of e-mail messages a day) has developed "screens" that allow messages only from approved people to reach a particular computer terminal (Gwynne & Dickerson, 1997).

Using new information technology and age-old human ingenuity, members of organizations try to personalize their procedures and surroundings. Such efforts suggest that we should now take a closer look at some of the problems of bureaucracy.

PROBLEMS OF BUREAUCRACY

We rely on bureaucracy to manage countless dimensions of everyday life, but many people are uneasy about large organizations. Bureaucracy can dehumanize and manipulate us, and some say it poses a threat to political democracy.

Bureaucratic Alienation

Max Weber touted bureaucracy as a model of productivity. Nonetheless, Weber was keenly aware of bureaucracy's ability to *dehumanize* the people it is supposed to serve. The same impersonality that fosters efficiency also keeps officials and clients from responding to each other's unique, personal needs. On the contrary, officials must treat each client impersonally, as a standard "case."

According to Weber, formal organizations create *alienation* by reducing the human being to "a small cog in a ceaselessly moving mechanism" (1978:988; orig. 1921). Although formal organizations are intended to benefit humanity, Weber feared that people could end up serving formal organizations.

Bureaucratic Inefficiency and Ritualism

Inefficiency, the failure of an organization to carry out the work that it exists to perform, is a familiar problem. According to one report, the General Services Administration, the government agency that buys

NOTE: Following Weber's analysis, the most effective way to destroy a bureaucratic organization would be to eliminate not its officers but its files.

NOTE: The U.S. Census Bureau was formed in 1902, more than a century after the first census was taken (1790).

Q: "Bureaucracy, the rule of no one, has become the modern form of despotism." Mary McCarthy

NOTE: "Oligarchy" is derived from the Greek root *oligo*, meaning "few."

Q: "It is organization which gives birth to the dominion of the elected over the electors, of the mandataries over the mandators, of the delegates over the delegators. Who says organization says oligarchy." Robert Michels

Q: "Hell hath no fury like a bureaucrat scorned." Milton Friedman

equipment for federal workers, takes up to three years to process a request for a new computer. This delay ensures that by the time the computer arrives, it is already out of date (Gwynne & Dickerson, 1997).

The problem of inefficiency is captured in the concept of *red tape* (reminiscent of the red tape used by eighteenth-century English administrators to wrap official records; Shipley, 1985). *Red tape* refers to a tedious preoccupation with organizational routine and procedures. Robert Merton (1968) points out that red tape amounts to a new twist to the familiar concept of group conformity. He coined the term **bureaucratic ritualism** to designate *a preoccupation with rules and regulations to the point of thwarting an organization's goals*.

Ritualism stifles individual creativity and impedes organizational performance. In part, ritualism arises from the fact that organizations, which pay modest, fixed salaries, give officials little financial stake in performing efficiently. Bureaucratic ritualism also stands as another form of alienation that Weber feared would arise from bureaucratic rigidity (Whyte, 1957; Merton, 1968; Coleman, 1990; Kiser & Schneider, 1994).

Bureaucratic Inertia

Although bureaucrats sometimes have little motivation to be efficient, they have every reason to protect their jobs. Officials may even strive to keep an organization going when its purpose has been realized. As Weber put it, "once fully established, bureaucracy is among the social structures which are hardest to destroy" (1978:987; orig. 1921).

Bureaucratic inertia is *the tendency of bureaucratic organizations to perpetuate themselves*. Formal organizations tend to take on a life of their own beyond their formal objectives. For example, the U.S. Department of Agriculture has offices in almost all U.S. counties, even though only one county in seven has working farms (Littman, 1992).

Usually, an organization stays in business by redefining its goals. For example, the Agriculture Department now performs a number of tasks not directly related to farming, including nutritional and environmental research.

OLIGARCHY

Early in the twentieth century, Robert Michels (1876–1936) pointed out the link between bureaucracy and political **oligarchy**, *the rule of the many by the few* (1949; orig. 1911). According to what Michels

According to Max Weber, bureaucracy is an organizational strategy that promotes efficiency. Impersonality, however, also fosters alienation among employees, who may become indifferent to the formal goals of the organization. The behavior of this municipal employee in Bombay, India, is understandable to members of formal organizations almost anywhere in the world.

called "the iron law of oligarchy," the pyramid shape of bureaucracy places a few leaders in charge of organizational resources.

Max Weber credited a strict hierarchy of responsibility with high organizational efficiency. But Michels countered that this hierarchical structure also concentrates power and thus endangers democracy because officials can—and often do—use their access to information, resources, and the media to promote their personal interests.

Furthermore, bureaucracy also insulates officials from the public, as in the case of the corporate president or public official who is "unavailable for comment" to the local press, or the U.S. president who withholds documents from Congress claiming "executive privilege." Thus, oligarchy thrives in the hierarchical structure of bureaucracy and reduces the accountability of leaders to the people (Tolson, 1995).

DIVERSITY SNAPSHOT

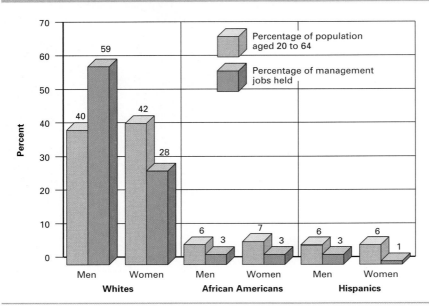

FIGURE 7–4
U.S. Managers in Private Industry by Race, Sex, and Ethnicity, 1999
Sources: U.S. Census Bureau (2001) and U.S. Equal Employment Opportunity Commission (2001).

Political competition, term limits, and a system of checks and balances prevent the U.S. government from becoming an out-and-out oligarchy. Even so, incumbents enjoy a significant advantage in U.S. politics. In the 2000 congressional elections, only 15 of 437 congressional officeholders running for reelection were defeated by their challengers (Giroux, 2000; Pierce, 2000).

THE EVOLUTION OF FORMAL ORGANIZATIONS

The problems of bureaucracy—especially the alienation it produces and its tendency toward oligarchy—stem from two organizational traits: hierarchy and rigidity. To Weber, bureaucracy was a top-down system: Rules and regulations made at the top guide every facet of people's lives down the chain of command. A century ago in the United States, Weber's ideas took hold in an organizational model called "scientific management." We begin with a look at this model and then describe three challenges over the course of the twentieth century that gradually led to a new model: the "flexible organization."

SCIENTIFIC MANAGEMENT

Frederick Winslow Taylor (1911) had a simple message: Most businesses in the United States were sadly inefficient. Managers had little idea of how to increase their businesses' output, and workers relied on the same tired skills of earlier generations.

To increase efficiency, Taylor explained, business should apply the principles of science. **Scientific management** is *the application of scientific principles to the operation of a business or other large organization.*

Scientific management involves three steps. First, managers carefully observe the task performed by each worker, identifying all the operations involved and measuring the time needed for each. Second, they analyze the data, trying to discover ways for workers to perform each task more efficiently. For example, managers might decide to provide workers with different tools or reposition work operations within the factory. Third, management provides guidance and incentives for workers to do their jobs more efficiently. A factory worker who moves twenty tons of pig iron in one day, for example, would be shown how to move forty tons a day and then given higher wages for higher productivity. Applying scientific principles in this way, Taylor

NOTE: Earlier editions of the text included (C. Northcote) Parkinson's Law ("Work expands to fill the time available for its completion") and the (Laurence J.) Peter Principle ("Bureaucrats are promoted to their level of incompetence"). Although they are amusing, most empirical evidence fails to support these principles.

DIVERSITY: A growing number of women are trying to resolve role conflicts by leaving organizational jobs ("cashing out") and starting their own small businesses; by 1999, 9.1 million women owned their own businesses.
DIVERSITY: An interesting question is whether women need to learn about organizations or organizations need to learn about women.

During the last fifty years in the United States, women have moved into management positions throughout the corporate world. While some men initially opposed women's presence in the executive office, it is now clear that women bring particular strengths to the job, including leadership flexibility and communication skills. Thus, some analysts speak of women offering a "female advantage."

concluded, companies become more profitable, workers earn higher wages, and, in the end, consumers end up paying lower prices. As auto pioneer Henry Ford put it, "Save ten steps a day for each of 12,000 employees, and you will have saved fifty miles of wasted motion and misspent energy" (Allen & Hyman, 1999:209).

In the early 1900s, the Ford Motor Company and many businesses followed Taylor's lead and improved their efficiency. As time went on, however, formal organizations faced three new challenges involving race and gender, rising competition from abroad, and changes in work itself. We look briefly at each in turn.

THE FIRST CHALLENGE: RACE AND GENDER

During the 1960s, critics pointed out that big businesses and other organizations were inefficient—and also unfair—in their hiring practices. Rather than hiring on the basis of competence, as Weber had proposed, they excluded women and other minorities. As a result, the vast majority of managers were white men.

Patterns of Exclusion

Even by the end of the twentieth century, as shown in Figure 7–4, white men in the United States—40 percent of the working-age population—still held 59 percent of management jobs. White women made up 42 percent of the population, but they held just 28 percent of managerial positions (U.S. Equal Employment Opportunity Commission, 2001). The members of other minorities lagged further behind.

According to Rosabeth Moss Kanter (1977; Kanter & Stein, 1979), excluding women and minorities from the workplace ignores the talents of more than half the population. Furthermore, underrepresented people in an organization often feel like socially isolated outgroups—uncomfortably visible, taken less seriously, and given fewer chances for promotion.

Opening up an organization to women and minorities, Kanter claims, improves everyone's on-the-job performance by motivating employees to work harder and be more committed to the company. By contrast, an organization with many dead-end jobs makes workers less productive. An open organization also encourages leaders to seek out the input of everyone, which benefits the organization. It is officials in rigid organizations—those who have little reason themselves to be creative—who jealously guard their privileges and ride herd over their employees.

The "Female Advantage"

Some organizational researchers argue that women have management skills that strengthen an organization. For example, Deborah Tannen (1994) claims that women have a greater "information focus" and more readily ask questions in order to understand an issue. Men, on the other hand, have an "image focus" that makes them wonder how asking questions in a particular situation will affect their reputation.

In another study of women executives, Sally Helgesen (1990) found three other gender-linked patterns. First, women place greater value on communication

During the 1980s, U.S. corporations turned their eyes to Japan, where competition from Japanese corporations was becoming intense. Japanese organizations are characterized by a collective orientation. Here, employees at the Texas Instruments plant in Kyushu participate in sports day, a company strategy to build work-team morale.

skills and share information more than men do. Second, women are more flexible leaders who typically give their employees greater autonomy. Third, compared with men, women tend to emphasize the interconnectedness of all organizational operations. Thus, women bring a "female advantage" to companies striving to be more flexible and democratic.

In sum, one challenge to conventional bureaucracy is to become more open and flexible to take advantage of everyone's experience, ideas, and creativity. The result goes right to the bottom line: greater profits.

THE SECOND CHALLENGE: THE JAPANESE ORGANIZATION

In 1980, U.S. corporations were shaken to discover that the most popular automobile model sold in this country was not a Chevrolet, Ford, or Plymouth but the Honda Accord, made in Japan. To people old enough to remember the 1950s, the words "made in Japan" generally meant a cheap, poorly made product. But times had changed. The success of the Japanese auto industry (and, soon after, companies making electronics, cameras, and other products) had analysts buzzing about the "Japanese organization." How else could so small a country challenge the world's economic powerhouse?

Japanese organizations reflect that nation's strong collective spirit. That is, whereas most members of our society prize rugged individualism, the Japanese

value cooperation. In effect, formal organizations in Japan are like very large primary groups. William Ouchi (1981) highlights five differences between formal organizations in Japan and in the United States:

1. **Hiring and advancement.** U.S. organizations hold out promotions and raises in salary as prizes to be won through individual competition. In Japanese organizations, however, companies hire new school graduates together, and all employees in the group receive the same salary and responsibilities. Only after several years is anyone likely to be singled out for special advancement.

2. **Lifetime security.** Employees in the United States expect to move from one company to another to advance their careers. U.S. companies are also quick to lay off employees during an economic setback. By contrast, most Japanese firms hire workers for life, fostering strong, mutual loyalties. If jobs become obsolete, Japanese companies avoid layoffs by retraining workers for new positions.

3. **Holistic involvement.** Whereas we tend to see the home and the workplace as distinct spheres, Japanese companies play a much larger role in workers' lives. They provide home mortgages, sponsor recreational activities, and schedule social events. Such interaction beyond the workplace strengthens collective identity and offers the respectful Japanese employees a chance to voice suggestions and criticisms informally.

NOTE: At Honda's plant at Marysville, Ohio—America's most productive—assembly line workers (called "associates") have considerable opportunity to shape the production process. All employees, from the president to the maintenance staff, wear similar uniforms in the plant to encourage exchange of ideas.

NOTE: Self-managed work teams are an outgrowth of so-called quality circles in which employees provide critical analyses of operations.

NOTE: Another contrast: Japan trains 10 engineers for each lawyer; the U.S. trains 10 lawyers for each engineer.

RESOURCE: Boye de Mente's excerpt, "Japanese Etiquette and Ethics in Business," is one of the cross-cultural selections included in the reader *Seeing Ourselves.*

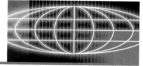

GLOBAL SOCIOLOGY

The Japanese Model: Will It Work in the United States?

What the company wants is for us to work like the Japanese. Everybody go out and do jumping jacks in the morning and kiss each other when they go home at night. You work as a team, rat on each other, and lose control of your destiny. That's not going to work in this country.

John Brodie
President, United Paperworkers
Local 448
Chester, Pennsylvania

Competition from Asia and, increasingly, from Europe is forcing U.S. companies to rethink how corporate organizations should operate in a global marketplace. Business leaders are looking at the Japanese manufacturing plants built here in the United States. These "transplant organizations," operated in the United States by Honda, Nissan, and Toyota, have adapted well to a new environment, achieving the same level of efficiency and quality that won these companies praise in Japan. They have

also provided more than 250,000 jobs for U.S. workers.

Yet some voices in this country—from the ranks of workers, union leaders, and managers—speak as bitterly about importing Japanese organizational techniques as they do about importing Japanese cars. Our corporate culture still favors hierarchy, praises individualism, and remembers its long history of labor-management conflict. As a result, workers and managers are wary of traditional Japanese practices, such as worker participation.

Some employees in the United States think worker participation ends up increasing their workload. While still responsible for building cars, for instance, workers also have to worry about quality control, unit costs, and overall efficiency—concerns usually shouldered by management. Moreover, some employees see the broad training favored by the Japanese as endlessly moving from job to job, always having to learn new skills. Many union leaders fear that any alliance of workers and managers undermines union strength.

Some managers, too, look warily on worker participation programs. Sharing the power to set production goals or schedule vacations does not come easily in light of past practices. Finally, U.S. corporations have a short-term outlook on profits, which discourages investing time and money in organizational restructuring.

But the pressure of rising global competition is slowly changing U.S. organizations. The government reports that 70 percent of large businesses have begun at least some reforms of this kind. Productivity and profits usually are higher when workers have a say in decision making. Moreover, most employees in worker participation programs—even those who may not want to sign up for morning jumping jacks—seem happier about their jobs. Workers who have long used only their bodies are now enjoying the opportunity to use their minds as well.

Sources: Hoerr (1989) and Florida & Kenney (1991).

---

4. **Broad-based training.** U.S. workers are highly specialized, and many spend an entire career doing one thing. But a Japanese organization trains workers in all phases of its operation, again with the idea that employees will remain with the company for life.

5. **Collective decision making.** In the United States, key executives make the important decisions. Although Japanese leaders also take responsibility for their organization's performance, they involve workers in "quality circles" to discuss decisions that affect them. A closer working relationship is also encouraged by Japan's lower

salary difference between executives and workers: about 10 percent of the difference that is typical in the United States.

These characteristics give the Japanese a strong sense of organizational loyalty. Because their personal interests are tied to company interests, workers realize their ambitions through the organization. In recent years, Japanese companies have become more like their U.S. counterparts by, for example, laying off some workers. Even so, the Japanese emphasis on *groupism* is the cultural equivalent of our society's emphasis on *individual* achievement.

The recent trend is toward breaking down the rigid structure of conventional bureaucracy. One example of more flexible organizational form is the self-managed work team, whose members have the skills to carry out their tasks creatively and with minimal supervision.

Many U.S. companies have been influenced by Japanese organizations. But transplanting an organizational system from one culture to another is not easy, as the box on page 181 explains.

THE THIRD CHALLENGE: THE CHANGING NATURE OF WORK

Beyond rising global competition, pressure to modify conventional organizations is also coming from changes in the nature of work itself. Chapter 4 ("Society") described the shift from industrial to postindustrial production. Rather than working in factories using heavy machinery to make *things*, more and more people are using computers and other electronic technology to create or process *information*. The postindustrial society, then, is characterized by information-based organizations.

Frederick Taylor developed his concept of scientific management at a time when jobs involved tasks that, though often backbreaking, were routine. Workers shoveled coal, poured liquid iron into molds, welded body panels to automobiles on an assembly line, or shot hot rivets into steel girders to build skyscrapers. In addition, a large proportion of U.S. workers in Taylor's day were immigrants, most of whom had little schooling and many of whom knew little English. The routine nature of industrial jobs coupled with the limited skills of the labor force led Taylor to treat work as a series of fixed tasks set down by management and followed by employees.

Many of today's information age jobs are very different: The work of designers, artists, writers, composers, programmers, business owners, and others now demands creativity and imagination. What does this mean for formal organizations? Here are several ways in which today's organizations differ from those of a century ago:

1. **Creative autonomy.** Organizations know that employees with information age skills are a vital resource. Executives can set production goals but cannot dictate how to accomplish tasks involving imagination and discovery. Thus, highly skilled workers have *creative autonomy*, which means they have little day-to-day supervision as long as they generate good ideas in the long run.

2. **Competitive work teams.** Many organizations give several groups of employees the freedom to work on a problem, offering the greatest rewards to those who come up with the best solution. Competitive work teams, a strategy first used by Japanese organizations, draw out the creative contributions of everyone and, at the same time, reduce the alienation often found in conventional organizations (Yeatts, 1991, 1994; Maddox, 1994).

3. **A flatter organization.** By spreading responsibility for creative problem solving throughout the work force, organizations take on a flatter shape. That is, the pyramid shape of conventional bureaucracy is replaced by an organizational form with fewer levels in the chain of command, as shown in Figure 7–5.

4. **Greater flexibility.** The typical industrial age organization was a rigid structure guided from the

RESOURCE: A selection by George Ritzer titled "McJobs: Mc-Donaldization and the Workplace" is among the contemporary selections found in the Macionis and Benokraitis reader, *Seeing Ourselves.*

NOTE: The U.S. averages one fast-food restaurant per 10,000 people. Which county has the most? It's Socorro County, N.M., with six fast-food places for 15,400 people.

NOTE: Kroc paid the McDonalds $1.6 million—a large amount, especially back then, but an amazing bargain in retrospect. In addition to the 20,000 McDonald's restaurants, there are also 5,000 Wendy's worldwide.

NOTE: Joan Beverly Kroc, widow of Ray Kroc, lives in Rancho Sante Fe, California, and is on the *Forbes* list of the wealthiest 400 families in the U.S., with assets of about $2.5 billion.

FIGURE 7–5 Two Organizational Models

The conventional model of bureaucratic organizations has a pyramid shape, with a clear chain of command. Directives flow from the top down, and reports of performance flow from the bottom up. Such organizations have extensive rules and regulations, and their workers have highly specialized jobs. More open and flexible organizations have a flatter shape, more like a football. With fewer levels in the hierarchy, responsibility for generating ideas and making decisions is shared throughout the organization. Many workers do their jobs in teams and have a broad knowledge of the entire organization's operation.

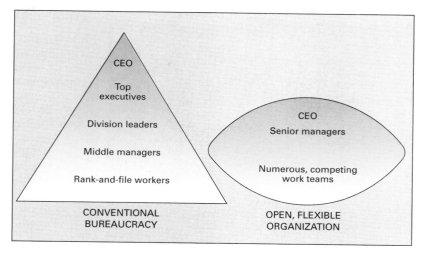

Source: Created by the author.

top. Such organizations may accomplish a good deal of work, but they are not especially creative or able to respond quickly to changes in their larger environment. The ideal model in the information age is a *flexible* organization, one that both generates new ideas and, in a rapidly changing global marketplace, adapts quickly.

As important as these changes are, many of today's jobs do not involve creative work at all. On the contrary, the postindustrial economy has created two very different types of work: highly skilled creative work and low-skill service work. For example, work in the fast-food industry is routine and highly supervised and thus has much more in common with factory work of a century ago than with the work of teams in information organizations. Whereas some organizations have taken on a flexible, flatter form, others continue to use the rigid chain of command, as we now explain.

THE "McDONALDIZATION" OF SOCIETY[1]

As noted in the opening to this chapter, McDonald's has enjoyed enormous success, now operating 28,000 restaurants in the United States and around the world. Japan has more than 2,400 Golden Arches, and the

[1]Much of the material in this section is based on Ritzer (1993, 1998, 2000).

world's largest McDonald's is found in China's capital city of Beijing.

```
October 9, Macau. Here we are, halfway
around the world, in the Portuguese
colony of Macau—a little nub jutting
from the coast of China. Few people here
speak English, and life on the streets
seems a world apart from the urban
rhythms of New York, Chicago, or Los
Angeles. Then I turn the corner and
stand face to face with (who else?)
Ronald McDonald! After eating who-
knows-what for so long, forgive me for
giving in to the lure of the Big Mac.
But the most amazing thing is that the
food—the burger, the fries, and the
drink—looks, smells, and tastes ex-
actly the same as it does back home
10,000 miles away!
```

McDonald's may be found almost everywhere these days but, in the United States, it is more than a restaurant: It is a symbol of our way of life. Not only do people around the world associate McDonald's with the United States, but, here at home, one poll found that 98 percent of schoolchildren could identify Ronald McDonald, making him as well known as Santa Claus.

NOTE: Ritzer (1998) reports that fast food represents 40% of the more than 6 million U.S. restaurant jobs; 70% of employees are age 20 or younger (for many it is their first job); about 15% of U.S. workers had their first job at McDonald's; one of eight U.S. adults has worked at McDonald's at some time; the average workweek is 30 hours.

NOTE: There are weak countertrends to McDonaldization. For example, the 20s generation is the most likely ever to drink micro-brewed beers—perhaps because the beers have distinctive tastes and are produced by local companies rather than the national giants.
NOTE: McDonald's even varies slightly by region in the U.S.: In Maine it sells lobster rolls.

Is McDonaldization becoming a global trend? Yes and no. The spread of McDonald's and other fast-food corporations around the world has been dramatic, and the company now earns most of its revenue from outside the United States. But in some nations, McDonald's has altered its formula to take account of local cultural norms. For example, these women in a shopping mall in Dhahran, Saudi Arabia, are ordering food from a "ladies only" counter, which reflects the traditional gender norms of that nation.

Even more important, the organizational principles that underlie McDonald's are coming to dominate our entire society. Our culture is becoming "McDonaldized," an awkward way of saying that we model many aspects of life on this restaurant chain: Parents buy toys at worldwide chain stores such as Toys 'Я' Us; we drive to Jiffy Lube for a ten-minute oil change; face-to-face communication is sliding more and more toward voice mail, e-mail, and junk mail; more vacations take the form of resort and tour packages; television presents news in the form of ten-second sound bites; college admissions officers size up students they have never met by their GPA and SAT scores; and professors assign ghost-written textbooks[2] and evaluate students with tests mass-produced by publishing companies. The list goes on and on.

McDonaldization: Four Principles

What do all such developments have in common? According to George Ritzer (1993), the McDonaldization of society involves four basic organizational principles:

1. **Efficiency.** Ray Kroc, the marketing genius behind the expansion of McDonald's, set out to serve a hamburger, French fries, and milkshake to a customer in fifty seconds. Today, one of the company's most popular items is the Egg McMuffin, an entire breakfast in a single sandwich. In the restaurant, customers bus their own trays, or they drive away from the pickup window taking the packaging and whatever mess they make with them.

   Efficiency is now central to our way of life. We tend to think that anything done quickly is, for that reason alone, good.

2. **Calculability.** The first McDonald's operating manual set the weight of a regular raw hamburger at 1.6 ounces, its size at 3.875 inches across, and its fat content at 19 percent. A slice of cheese weighs exactly half an ounce. Fries are cut precisely 9/32 of an inch thick.

   Think about how many objects around your home, the workplace, and campus are designed and mass-produced according to a uniform plan. Not just our environment but our life experiences—from traveling the nation's interstates to sitting at home viewing television—are more standardized than ever before.

3. **Uniformity and predictability.** A person can walk into a McDonald's restaurant almost anywhere and receive the same sandwiches, drinks, and desserts prepared in precisely the same way.[3] Predictability is the result of a highly rational system that specifies every course of action and leaves nothing to chance.

4. **Control through automation.** The most unreliable element in the McDonald's system is human beings. People, after all, have good and bad days, sometimes let their minds wander, or simply

---

[2]Several popular sociology texts were not authored by the person or persons whose names appear on the cover. This book is not one of them.

EXERCISE: Suggest that students who work try to personalize themselves more. Marketing researcher Michael Linn (1996) reports that waiters/waitresses who named themselves boosted their tips by 53%; a casual touch on the shoulder or hand by servers boosted tips 42%.

DISCUSS: With regard to social change: Durkheim characterized modernity as a gradual loss of moral bonds (collective conscience) with a concomitant rise of individualism and economic cooperation. But he recognized that modern culture generates limited social cohesion and argued that group memberships could enhance social solidarity. But do modern groups exert much moral pull on us?

decide to try something a different way. To minimize the unpredictable human element, McDonald's has automated its equipment to cook food at fixed temperatures for set lengths of time. Even the cash register at a McDonald's is little more than pictures of the items, so that the task of ringing up a customer's order is made as simple as possible.

Similarly, automatic teller machines are replacing banks, highly automated bakeries now produce bread with scarcely any human intervention, and chickens and eggs (or is it eggs and chickens?) emerge from automated hatcheries. In supermarkets, laser scanners are phasing out checking groceries by hand. We do most of our shopping in malls, where everything—from temperature and humidity to the kinds of stores and products—is carefully controlled and supervised (Ide & Cordell, 1994).

Can Rationality Be Irrational?

There can be no argument about the popularity or efficiency of McDonald's. But there is another side to the story.

Max Weber observed the expansion of formal organizations with alarm, fearing that they would cage the imagination and crush the human spirit. As Weber

 To learn more about Max Weber, go to http://www. TheSociologyPage.com

saw it, rational systems were efficient but dehumanizing, and McDonaldization bears him out. Each of the four principles just discussed limits human creativity, choice, and freedom. Echoing Weber, Ritzer states that "the ultimate irrationality of McDonaldization is that people could lose control over the system and it would come to control us" (1993:145).

---

[3]As McDonald's has "gone global," a few products have been added or modified according to local tastes. For example, in Uruguay, customers enjoy the McHuevo (hamburger with poached egg on top); Norwegians can buy McLaks (grilled salmon sandwiches); the Dutch favor Groenteburger (vegetable burger); in Thailand, McDonald's serves Samurai pork burgers (pork burgers with teriyaki sauce); the Japanese can purchase Chicken Tatsuta Sandwich (chicken seasoned with soy and ginger); Filipinos eat McSpaghetti (spaghetti with tomato sauce and bits of hot dogs); and in India, where Hindus eat no beef, McDonald's sells a vegetarian Maharaja Mac (Sullivan, 1995).

THE FUTURE OF ORGANIZATIONS: OPPOSING TRENDS

Early in the twentieth century, ever-larger organizations arose in the United States, most taking on the bureaucratic form described by Max Weber. In many respects, these organizations resembled armies led by powerful generals who issued orders to their captains and lieutenants. Foot soldiers, working in the factories, did what they were told.

With the emergence of a postindustrial economy after mid-century and with rising competition from abroad, many organizations have evolved toward a flatter, more flexible model that prizes communication and creativity. Such "intelligent organizations" (Pinchot & Pinchot, 1993) have become more productive than ever. Just as important, for highly skilled people whose information age work demands creative autonomy, these organizations create less of the alienation that so worried Max Weber.

But this is only half the story. Although the postindustrial economy has created many highly skilled jobs, it has created even more routine service jobs, as exemplified by McDonald's, where one in eight adults in the United States has worked at some time (Ritzer, 1998). Work of this kind, which Ritzer calls "McJobs," offers few of the benefits that today's highly skilled workers enjoy. On the contrary, the automated routines that define work in the fast-food industry, telemarketing, and similar fields are very much the same as Frederick Taylor described a century ago.

Moreover, the organizational flexibility that gives better-off workers more autonomy carries, for rank-and-file employees, the ever-present threat of "downsizing" (Sennett, 1998). That is, organizations facing global competition are eager to have creative employees, but they are just as eager to cut costs by eliminating as many routine jobs as possible. The net result is that some people are better off than ever while others worry about holding their jobs and struggle to make ends meet—a trend that Chapter 11 ("Social Class in the United States") explores in detail.

In sum, many analysts conclude that U.S. organizations remain the envy of the world for their productive efficiency. Indeed, there are few places on earth where the mail arrives as quickly and dependably as it does in the United States (J. Wilson, 1991). But we should remember that the future is far brighter for some than for others. In addition, as the final box on pages 186–87 explains, organizations pose an increasing threat to our privacy—something to keep in mind as we envision our organizational future.

SOCIAL SURVEY: "How concerned are you about threats to your personal privacy in America today?" (GSS 1982, N = 1,506; *Codebook*, 2001:290)

"Very concerned"   44.6%   "Not concerned at all" 10.9%
"Somewhat concerned"   28.6%   DK/NR   1.5%
"Only a little concerned" 14.4%

DISCUSS: What about implanting computer chips on individuals to provide their identity, medical history, insurance information, and credit card numbers? This might help Alzheimer's patients, but is it a boon or threat to everyone else?

Q: "Mind your own business." Phrase appearing on the first coin minted in the U.S. in 1778

CONTROVERSY & DEBATE

Computer Technology, Large Organizations, and the Assault on Privacy

Joe finishes dressing and calls a 1-800 number to check the pollen count. As he listens to a recorded message, a Caller ID computer identifies Joe, records the call, and pulls up Joe's profile from a public records database. The computer adds to the profile the fact that Joe suffers from allergies. Several weeks later, tens of thousands of profiles are sold to a drug company, which sends Joe and others a free sample of its new allergy medication.

At a local department store, Nina uses her American Express card to buy an expensive new watch and some sleepwear. The store's computer adds Nina's name to its database of "buyers of expensive jewelry" and "buyers of sexy lingerie." The store trades its database with other companies, and within a month Nina receives four jewelry catalogues and an adult video brochure (Bernstein, 1997).

Are these organizations providing consumers with interesting products, or are they violating people's privacy? The answer is both: The same systems that help organizations operate efficiently also let them invade our lives and manipulate us. So as large organizations have expanded in the United States, privacy has diminished.

Small-town life in the past gave people little privacy, but at least if people knew something about you, you were just as likely to know something about them. Today, unknown people can access information about any of us at any time.

In part, the loss of privacy is a result of more and more complex computer technology. Are you aware that every e-mail you send and every chat room message you post is recorded in one or more computers and can be retrieved by people you don't know? Even visiting a Web site leaves an electronic "footprint" that can be traced by anyone interested in your tastes and shopping habits.

Another part of today's loss of privacy reflects the number and size of formal organizations. As we have explained in this chapter, large organizations tend to treat people impersonally, and they have a huge appetite for information. Mix large organizations with ever-more complex computer technology, and it is no wonder that most people in the United States are concerned about who knows what about them and what people are doing with this information.

For decades, the level of personal privacy in the United States has been declining. Early in the twentieth century, when state agencies began issuing driver's licenses, for example, they generated files for every licensed driver. Today, officials can send this information at the touch of a button to other organizations, including police. Similarly, the Internal Revenue Service, the Social Security Administration, and government agencies that benefit veterans, students, the unemployed, and the poor all collect extensive information.

Business organizations now do much the same thing, although, as these examples show, people may not be aware that their choices and activities end up in a company's database. Most people find credit cards a great convenience—the U.S. population now holds more than 1 billion of them, averaging more than five per adult—but few people stop to think that credit card purchases automatically generate records that can end up almost anywhere.

Then there are the small cameras found in stores, public buildings, parking garages, and college campuses. The number of surveillance cameras that

SUMMARY

1. Social groups are building blocks of society that connect individuals with each other and perform various tasks.

2. Primary groups tend to be small and person-oriented; secondary groups are large and goal-oriented.

3. Instrumental leadership is concerned with realizing a group's goals; expressive leadership focuses on members' morale and well-being.

4. Because group members often seek consensus, groups may pressure members toward conformity.

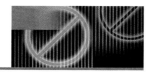

THE MAP: The more isolated the community, the larger the share of people who fear that big government and big companies are encroaching on our lives. Fears about privacy are greatest among people with moderate incomes, who are much more likely to spend a weekend hunting or fishing on their own than taking in a ballgame with friends.

Q: No man is an island, entire of itself;

every man is a piece of the continent,
a part of the main. . . .
any man's death diminishes me,
because I am involved in mankind.
And therefore never send to know
for whom the bell tolls; it tolls for thee.
John Donne

monitor our movements is rapidly increasing with each passing year. Such cameras may improve public safety in some ways—say, by discouraging muggers—but only at the cost of some of the privacy we have left.

Concern about the erosion of privacy in the United States is also on the rise. Across the United States, who is most concerned about the growing assault on

privacy? National Map 7–1 provides some insights.

There is some legal protection. All the states have enacted laws giving citizens rights to examine some records about themselves kept by employers, banks, and credit bureaus. The U.S. Privacy Act of 1974 also limits the exchange of personal information between government agencies and permits

citizens to examine and correct most government files. But so many private and public organizations now have information about us—experts estimate that 90 percent of U.S. households are profiled in databases somewhere—that current laws simply do not address the extent of the privacy problem. In the last ten years, the Internet revolution has made the problem of personal privacy more serious than ever, yet there are no national standards that protect public privacy.

Continue the debate . . .

1. *Look over National Map 7–1. Where are people most concerned about losing their privacy? Can you explain this pattern?*

2. *Internet search engines such as Yahoo! (http://www.yahoo.com) have "people search" programs that let you locate almost anyone. Do you think such programs pose a threat to privacy?*

3. *How have concerns about privacy changed in the wake of the September 11th terrorist attacks on the United States?*

SEEING OURSELVES

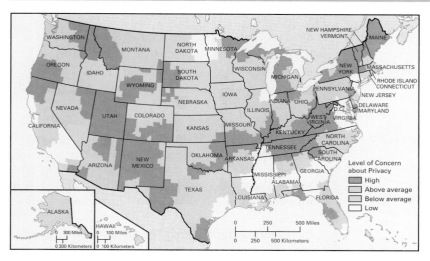

NATIONAL MAP 7–1 Concerns about Privacy across the United States

Source: *Business Geographics* © 1994 GIS World, Inc., 2101 S. Arlington Heights Boulevard, Arlington Heights, Ill., 60005-4185.

Sources: Bernstein (1997), Wright (1998), *Business Week* (2000), and Rosen (2000).

5. Individuals make use of reference groups—both ingroups and outgroups—to form attitudes and make evaluations.

6. Georg Simmel characterized the dyad—a social group with two members—as intense but unstable; a triad, he added, can easily dissolve into a dyad by excluding one member.

7. Peter Blau explored how group size, homogeneity, and social standing and physical segregation of groups all affect members' behavior.

8. Social networks are relational webs that link people with little common identity and limited interaction. The Internet is a vast electronic network linking millions of people worldwide.

9. Formal organizations are large secondary groups that seek to perform complex tasks efficiently. They are classified as utilitarian, normative, or coercive, based on their members' reasons for joining.

10. Bureaucratic organization expands in modern societies to perform tasks efficiently. Bureaucracy is based on specialization, hierarchy, rules and regulations, technical competence, impersonal interaction, and formal, written communications.

11. Technology, political and economic trends, population patterns, and other organizations all combine to form the environment in which a particular business or agency must operate.

12. Ideally, bureaucracy promotes efficiency, but it can also lead to alienation and oligarchy and contribute to the erosion of privacy.

13. Frederick Taylor's principles of scientific management shaped U.S. organizations a century ago. Since then, organizations have evolved toward a more open and flexible form as they have included a larger share of women and other minorities, responded to global competition, especially from Japan, and shifted their focus from industrial production to postindustrial information processing.

14. Reflecting the collective spirit of Japanese culture, formal organizations in Japan are based more on personal ties than their counterparts in the United States.

15. The "McDonaldization" of society involves increasing automation and impersonality.

16. The future of organizations probably will involve opposing trends: toward more creative autonomy for highly skilled information workers and toward supervision and discipline for less skilled service workers.

KEY CONCEPTS

social group (p. 163) two or more people who identify and interact with one another

primary group (p. 164) a small social group whose members share personal and enduring relationships

secondary group (p. 164) a large and impersonal social group whose members pursue a specific goal or activity

instrumental leadership (p. 165) group leadership that emphasizes the completion of tasks

expressive leadership (p. 165) group leadership that focuses on collective well-being

groupthink (p. 167) the tendency of group members to conform, resulting in a narrow view of some issue

reference group (p. 167) a social group that serves as a point of reference in making evaluations and decisions

ingroup (p. 168) a social group commanding a member's esteem and loyalty

outgroup (p. 168) a social group toward which one feels competition or opposition

dyad (p. 168) a social group with two members

triad (p. 169) a social group with three members

network (p. 170) a web of weak social ties

formal organization (p. 171) a large secondary group organized to achieve its goals efficiently

bureaucracy (p. 174) an organizational model rationally designed to perform tasks efficiently

organizational environment (p. 175) factors outside an organization that affect its operation

bureaucratic ritualism (p. 177) a preoccupation with rules and regulations to the point of thwarting an organization's goals

bureaucratic inertia (p. 177) the tendency of bureaucratic organizations to perpetuate themselves

oligarchy (p. 177) the rule of the many by the few

scientific management (p. 178) Frederick Taylor's term for the application of scientific principles to the operation of a business or other large organization

CRITICAL-THINKING QUESTIONS

1. How do primary groups differ from secondary groups? Identify examples of each in your own life.

2. According to Max Weber, what are the six characteristic traits of bureaucracy? In what ways do new, more flexible organizations differ?

3. George Ritzer (1996:1), a critic of "McDonaldization," suggests that fast-food restaurants carry the following label: "Sociologists warn us that habitual use of McDonald's systems are destructive to our physical and psychological well-being as well as to society as a whole." Do you agree? Why or why not?

4. The twentieth century was the first one with the widespread use of initials, such as IRS, IRA, IMF, IBM, CIA, WPA, PLO, NATO, CNN, WB, WWF, and CDC. What does this change suggest about so-cial trends?

APPLICATIONS AND EXERCISES

1. Spend several hours observing customers at a fast-food restaurant. Think about ways in which both employees and customers are trained to behave in certain ways. For example, customer norms include lining up to order and finding their own table. What other norms are at work?

2. Visit a large public building with an elevator. Ob-serve groups of people as they approach the elevator, and enter the elevator with them. Watch their be-havior: What happens to conversations as the eleva-tor doors close? Where do people fix their eyes? Can you account for these patterns?

3. Make a list of ingroups and outgroups on your cam-pus. What traits account for groups falling into each category? Ask several people to comment on your list to see whether they agree with your classifications.

4. Using available publications (and some assistance from an instructor), try to draw an organizational pyramid for your college or university showing the key offices and how they supervise and report to each other.

5. Packaged in the back of this new textbook is an inter-active CD-ROM that offers a variety of study and review materials intended to help you better under-stand the material covered in this chapter. For this chapter, the CD-ROM contains an author's tip video, Real Life Sociology videos, other relevant audio and video, interactive map animations, audio journal en-tries from the author, Web links, and much more.

 ## SITES TO SEE

http://www.prenhall.com/macionis

Visit the interactive *Companion Website*™ that accompa-nies this text. Begin by clicking on the cover of your book. You will find a chapter-by-chapter study guide, practice tests, and a significant portion of the text for on-line review, as well as many suggested Web links.

http://www.saturnbp.com

Visit the Saturn car company Web site to read about Sat-urn's flatter organizational structure.

http://www.mte.com/riot_site/webcam.html

This Web site uses a camera placed at New York City's Fifth Avenue at Forty-fifth Street. Do you think Internet technology of this kind threatens people's privacy? Why or why not?

http://groups.yahoo.com/local/news.html

A number of Web sites, including this one, let people build their own social groups for chat or posting photos and other information. Take a look and see what you think about "virtual groups."

 ## INVESTIGATE WITH CONTENTSELECT

Follow the instructions found on page 23 of this textbook to enter this chapter of the book's *Companion Website*™. Once in the chapter, click on the ContentSelect icon at the bottom left of your screen and enter your personal User ID and Password. Enter keywords such as "Max Weber," "bureaucracy," "social network," and "McDonald's," and the search engine will help you become an effective researcher.

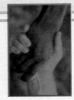

CHAPTER

8

Emil Kazaz
Saratoga, 1998

Oil on linen, 60 in. × 72 in.
Collection of Rafael and Marina Akopian. Courtesy of Noah's Ark Fine Art.

DEVIANCE

Ricky McGinn sat in his prison cell in Huntsville, Texas, wiping his mouth and looking at the floor. He had just finished the cheeseburger, French fries, and Dr. Pepper that he thought would be his last meal. Forty-three-year-old McGinn had been convicted of the brutal murder of his twelve-year-old stepdaughter and sentenced to death for his crime. In just several hours, the execution would be carried out.

Then, eighteen minutes before McGinn was to die, Texas governor George W. Bush halted the execution. Defense lawyers claimed that a DNA test would prove McGinn's innocence. The governor agreed to a postponement (Alter, 2000).

In recent years, public opinion about capital punishment has been

changing. The greatest fear is that people convicted of serious crimes and sentenced to death may be innocent. In 2000, Illinois Governor George Ryan ordered a halt to executions in that state in the wake of evidence that thirteen men on death row in Illinois prisons were actually innocent. Since 1973, nationwide, eighty-seven people sentenced to die have been set free based on new evidence.

In the case of Ricky McGinn, however, the reprieve was brief. Officials carried out the DNA tests McGinn's lawyers requested, and the evidence confirmed his guilt. With no further options to appeal, on September 27, 2000, McGinn again ordered a last meal and was put to death by lethal injection.

This chapter explores the problem of violent crime and other criminal offenses, profiles offenders, and looks at the criminal justice system. First, however, we tackle the broader issue of why societies develop standards of right and wrong in the first place. As we shall see, law is simply one part of a complex system of social control: Society teaches us all to conform, at least most of the time, to countless rules. We begin our investigation by defining several basic concepts.

WHAT IS DEVIANCE?

Deviance is *the recognized violation of cultural norms.* Because norms guide almost all human activities, the concept of deviance is quite broad. One category of deviance is **crime**, *the violation of a society's formally enacted criminal law.* Even criminal deviance spans a wide range of behavior, from minor traffic violations to sexual assault to murder.

Most examples of nonconformity that come readily to mind are negative instances of rule breaking, such as stealing from a convenience store, abusing a child, or driving while intoxicated. But we also define especially righteous people—students who speak up too much in class or people who are overly enthusiastic about new computer technology—as deviant, even if we accord them a measure of respect (Huls, 1987). What deviant actions or attitudes—whether negative or positive—have in common is some element of *difference* that causes us to regard another person as an "outsider" (Becker, 1966).

Not all deviance involves action or even choice. The very *existence* of some categories of people can be troublesome to others. To the young, elderly people may seem hopelessly "out of it," and to some whites, the mere presence of people of color may cause discomfort. Able-bodied people often view people with disabilities as an outgroup, just as affluent people may shun the poor for falling short of their standards.

191

SOCIAL CONTROL

All of us are subject to **social control,** *attempts by society to regulate people's thought and behavior*. Often, this process is informal, as when parents praise or scold their children or friends make fun of someone's musical taste. Serious deviance may involve the **criminal justice system,** *a formal response by police, courts, and prison officials to alleged violations of the law*.

In sum, deviance is much more than a matter of individual choice or personal failing. *How* a society defines deviance, *who* is branded as deviant, and *what* people decide to do about deviance all have to do with the way society is organized. Only gradually have people recognized this fact, as we shall now explain.

 Visit the Juvenile Justice and Delinquency Prevention Web site to see their available research reports: http://ojjdp. ncjrs.org/pubs/alpha.html

THE BIOLOGICAL CONTEXT

Chapter 5 ("Socialization") explained that people a century ago understood—or, more correctly, misunderstood—human behavior as an expression of biological instincts. Early interest in criminality thus emphasized biological causes. In 1876, Caesare Lombroso (1835–1909), an Italian physician who worked in prisons, proposed that criminals could be identified by physical traits: low foreheads, prominent jaws and cheekbones, big ears, lots of body hair, and unusually long arms. All in all, Lombroso claimed that criminals resembled our apelike ancestors.

But the physical features that Lombroso pointed to can be found throughout the entire population. We now know that no physical attributes of the kind described by Lombroso set off criminals from noncriminals (Goring, 1972; orig. 1913).

At mid-century, William Sheldon (Sheldon, Hartl, & McDermott, 1949) took a different tack, suggesting that body shape predicted criminality. He cross-checked hundreds of young men for body type and criminal history and concluded that criminality was most common among boys with muscular, athletic builds. Sheldon Glueck and Eleanor Glueck (1950) confirmed Sheldon's conclusion but cautioned that a powerful build does not necessarily cause criminality. Parents, they suggested, tend to be somewhat distant from powerfully built sons, who, in turn, grow up to show less sensitivity toward others. Moreover, in a self-fulfilling prophesy, people who expect muscular boys to act like bullies may provoke such aggressive behavior.

Today, genetics research seeks possible links between biology and crime. Although no conclusive evidence connects criminality to any specific genetic trait, people's overall genetic makeup, in combination with social influences, probably accounts for some tendency toward criminality. In other words, biological factors may have a real but modest effect on whether an individual becomes a criminal (Rowe, 1983; Rowe & Osgood, 1984; Wilson & Herrnstein, 1985; Jencks, 1987; Pallone & Hennessy, 1998).

Critical evaluation. At best, biological theories offer a limited explanation of crime. Researchers point out that violent crime is overwhelmingly male and that parents are more likely to abuse foster children than natural children. But we know too little about the links between genes and human behavior to draw firm conclusions (Daly & Wilson, 1988).

Furthermore, because a biological approach looks at the individual, it offers no insight as to how some kinds of behaviors come to be defined as deviant in the first place. Therefore, although there is much to be learned about how human biology may affect behavior, research currently puts far greater emphasis on social influences (Gibbons & Krohn, 1986; Liska, 1991).

PERSONALITY FACTORS

Like biological theories, psychological explanations of deviance focus on individual abnormality. Some personality traits are hereditary, but most psychologists think that personality is shaped primarily by social experience. Deviance, then, is viewed as the product of "unsuccessful" socialization.

Research by Walter Reckless and Simon Dinitz (1967) illustrates the psychological approach. Reckless and Dinitz began by asking a number of teachers to categorize twelve-year-old male students as either likely or unlikely to get into trouble with the law. They then interviewed both the boys and their mothers to assess each boy's self-concept and how he related to others. Analyzing their results, Reckless and Dinitz found that the "good boys" displayed a stronger conscience (what Freud called superego), could handle frustration, and identified with cultural norms and values. The "bad boys," by contrast, had a weaker conscience, displayed little tolerance for frustration, and felt out of step with conventional culture.

As we might expect, the "good boys" had fewer run-ins with the police than the "bad boys." Because all the boys lived in an area where delinquency was

NOTE: Psychology's more individualistic orientation is evident in that approach's tendency to speak of *personal disorders* rather than *social deviance.*

DISCUSS: To illustrate changing conceptions of deviance, ask students about the declining rate of traditionally moral offenses concerned with decorum and honesty and the rising rate of offenses concerned with sexual or racial harassment or other "insensitivity."

DISCUSS: To Polynesians, tattoos are symbols of high social standing. How are tattoos regarded in our society?

DISCUSS: Critics objected to rock-and-roll in the 1950s (Elvis Presley and the Everly Brothers), claiming that it undermined morality. Today, rock-and-roll is mainstream music. Given the increasingly outrageous character of rockers, ask the class whether they find any deviance in it.

widespread, the investigators attributed staying out of trouble to a personality that reined in deviant impulses. Based on this idea, Reckless and Dinitz called their analysis *containment theory.*

Critical evaluation. Psychologists have shown that personality patterns have some connection to deviance. However, the fact is that most serious crimes are committed by people whose psychological profiles are normal.

Overall, both biological and psychological research view deviance as an individual trait, without exploring how conceptions of right and wrong initially arise, why people define some rule breakers but not others as deviant, or what role power plays in shaping a society's system of social control. To explore these issues, we now turn to a sociological analysis of deviance.

THE SOCIAL FOUNDATIONS OF DEVIANCE

Although we tend to view deviance in terms of the free choice or personal failings of individuals, all behavior—deviance as well as conformity—is shaped by society. Three social foundations of deviance are identified here and explained in later sections of the chapter:

1. **Deviance varies according to cultural norms.**
   No thought or action is inherently deviant; it becomes deviant only in relation to particular norms. Norms vary from place to place, so deviance also varies. Parts of Nevada permit prostitution, a practice outlawed in all other states. Casinos in Atlantic City and Las Vegas and on Mississippi riverboats and numerous Native American reservations beckon high rollers, but everywhere else in the United States gambling is illegal. Furthermore, most cities and towns have at least one unique statute. For example, South Padre Island, Texas, bans wearing ties; Mount Prospect, Illinois, has a law against keeping pigeons or bees; Los Angeles bans gas-powered leaf blowers; Hoover, South Dakota, outlaws fishing with a kerosene lantern; and Beverly Hills regulates the number of tennis balls allowed on the court at one time (Sanders & Horn, 1998; Steele, 2000).
   Around the world, what is considered deviant is even more diverse. Albania outlaws any public display of religious faith, such as "crossing" oneself; Cuba and Vietnam can prosecute their citizens for "consorting with foreigners"; Singapore bans the sale of chewing gum; police in

The kind of deviance people create reflects the moral values they embrace. The Berkeley campus of the University of California has long celebrated its open-minded tolerance of sexual diversity. Thus, in 1992, when Andrew Martinez decided to attend classes wearing virtually nothing, people were reluctant to accuse "The Naked Guy" of immoral conduct. However, in Berkeley's politically correct atmosphere, it was not long before school officials banned Martinez from campus—charging that his nudity constituted a form of sexual harassment.

Iran can arrest a woman for wearing makeup; U.S. citizens risk arrest by traveling to Libya or Iraq.

2. **People become deviant as others define them that way.** Everyone violates cultural norms, sometimes to the extent of breaking the law. For example, most of us sometimes walk around talking to ourselves or "borrow" pens from the workplace. Whether such behavior defines us as mentally ill or criminal depends on how others perceive, define, and respond to our behavior.

3. **Both rule-making and rule-breaking involve social power.** The law, claimed Karl Marx, is the

RESOURCE: A classic selection from Durkheim on crime is included in the 5th edition of the Macionis and Benokraitis reader, *Seeing Ourselves.*

DISCUSS: Andres Serrano, who created "Piss Christ," a photograph of a crucifix submerged in Serrano's own urine, maintains that art reaches its greatest power when it is most provocative. Is such work art or obscenity?

DIVERSITY: Look ahead to Chapter 23 to the five photos showing changing hairstyles in the U.S. over recent decades; fashion is a matter of changing conceptions of conformity and deviance. Students can attach great significance to small fashion details: Recall how baseball caps became popular one year, then were worn backwards the next.

Q: "Innocence is being ashamed of nothing." Jean Jacques Rousseau

Artists have an important function in any society: to explore alternatives to conventional notions about how to live. For this reason, while we celebrate artists' creativity, we also accord them a mildly deviant identity. In today's more conservative political climate, some government officials have objected to art that seems to challenge traditional morality. For their part, some artists have found expressive ways to show their displeasure with such thinking.

means by which powerful people protect their interests. A homeless person who stands on a street corner denouncing the government risks arrest for disturbing the peace; a mayoral candidate during an election campaign does exactly the same thing and receives police protection. In short, norms and how we apply them reflect social inequality.

THE FUNCTIONS OF DEVIANCE: STRUCTURAL-FUNCTIONAL ANALYSIS

The key insight of the structural-functional paradigm is that deviance is a necessary part of social organization. This point was made a century ago by Emile Durkheim.

EMILE DURKHEIM: THE FUNCTIONS OF DEVIANCE

In his pioneering study of deviance, Emile Durkheim (1964a, orig. 1893; 1964b, orig. 1895) made the surprising statement that there is nothing abnormal about deviance. In fact, it performs four essential functions:

1. **Deviance affirms cultural values and norms.** As moral creatures, people must prefer some

attitudes and behaviors to others. But any conception of virtue rests on an opposing notion of vice: There can be no good without evil and no justice without crime. Deviance, then, is needed to define and sustain morality.

2. **Responding to deviance clarifies moral boundaries.** By defining some people as deviant, society draws a boundary between right and wrong. For example, a college marks the line between academic honesty and cheating by punishing students who plagiarize.

3. **Responding to deviance promotes social unity.** People typically react to serious deviance with collective outrage. In this way, Durkheim explained, they reaffirm the moral ties that bind them. For example, after the terrorist attacks on the World Trade Center and the Pentagon in 2001, feelings of anguish and outrage brought together not just those communities but the entire nation.

4. **Deviance encourages social change.** Deviant people push a society's moral boundaries, suggesting alternatives to the status quo and encouraging change. Today's deviance, declared Durkheim, can become tomorrow's morality (1964b:71). For example, rock and roll—condemned as morally degenerate in the 1950s—became a multibillion-dollar industry just a few years later.

NOTE: A new functional issue is the pattern of "defining deviance upward," the pattern of refocusing a prosecution from a "lesser" issue to a more important one. The O.J. Simpson case was about murder, but it was "defined up" to the issue of whether the criminal justice system is free of bias.

Q: "Puritanism is the lurking fear that someone, somewhere, may be happy." H.L. Mencken

DISCUSS: Erikson found that 3–4% of the Puritans were defined as deviant at any time. What would Durkheim say about the fact that, in the U.S. today, about 3% of adults are in prison, on parole, or on probation?

NOTE: Thomas Szasz (1995) suggests that, economically speaking, people fall into one of three categories: producers (Merton's conformists), predators (innovators), or parasites (retreatists).

An Illustration: The Puritans of Massachusetts Bay

Kai Erikson's (1966) study of the Puritans of Massachusetts Bay brings Durkheim's theory to life. Erikson shows that even the Puritans, a disciplined and highly religious group, created deviance to clarify their moral boundaries. In fact, Durkheim might well have had the Puritans in mind when he wrote,

> Imagine a society of saints, a perfect cloister of exemplary individuals. Crimes, properly so called, will there be unknown; but faults which appear [insignificant] to the layman will create there the same scandal that the ordinary offense does in ordinary consciousness. . . . For the same reason, the perfect and upright man judges his smallest failings with a severity that the majority reserve for acts more truly in the nature of an offense. (1964b:68–69)

In short, deviance is not a matter of a few "bad apples"; it is a necessary condition of "good" social living.

Deviance may be universal, but the *kind* of deviance people generate depends on the moral issues they seek to clarify. For example, the Puritans experienced a number of "crime waves," including the well-known outbreak of witchcraft in Salem in 1692. With each response, the Puritans sharpened their views on crucial moral issues. They answered questions about the range of proper beliefs by celebrating some of their members and condemning others as deviant.

Perhaps most fascinating of all, Erikson discovered that even though the offenses changed, the proportion of people the Puritans defined as deviant remained steady over time. This stability, concludes Erikson, confirms Durkheim's contention that deviants serve to mark a society's changing moral boundaries. In other words, by constantly defining a small number of people as deviant, the Puritans gave a moral shape to their society.

MERTON'S STRAIN THEORY

Some deviance may be necessary for a society to function, but Robert Merton (1938, 1968) argued that excessive deviance results from particular social arrangements. Specifically, the extent and kind of deviance depend on whether a society provides the *means* (such as schooling and job opportunities) to achieve cultural *goals* (such as financial success).

Conformity, says Merton, lies in pursuing conventional goals through approved means. Thus, our success stories celebrate people who acquire wealth

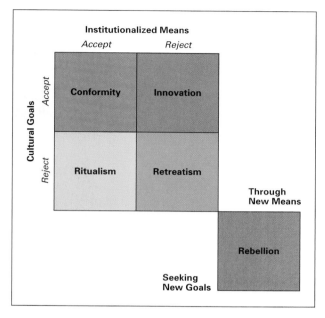

FIGURE 8–1 Merton's Strain Theory of Deviance
Source: Merton (1968).

and prestige through talent and hard work. But not everyone who seeks conventional success has the opportunity to attain it. People raised in poverty may see little chance of becoming successful if they play by the rules. As a result, they may try to make money through crime—say, by dealing cocaine. Merton called this type of deviance *innovation*: using unconventional means (drug sales) to achieve a culturally approved goal (becoming rich). Figure 8–1 shows that innovation involves accepting a cultural goal while rejecting the conventional means of getting there.

According to Merton, the strain between our culture's emphasis on wealth and the limited opportunity to get rich gives rise to theft and the sale of drugs or other street crime, especially among the poor. In some respects, notorious gangster Al Capone was quite conventional: He pursued the fame and fortune at the heart of the "American dream." But, like many minorities who find the doors to "legitimate" success hard to open, Capone blazed his own trail to the top. As one analyst put it,

> The typical criminal of the Capone era was a boy who had . . . seen what was rated as success in the society he had been thrust into—the Cadillac, the big bankroll, the elegant apartment. How could

In Kosovo, as in the United States, young people (especially males) cut off from legitimate opportunity may form deviant subcultures as a strategy to gain the prestige denied them by the larger society.

he acquire that kind of recognizable status? He was almost always a boy of outstanding initiative, imagination, and ability; he was the kind of boy who, under different conditions, would have been a captain of industry or a key political figure of his time. But he hadn't the opportunity of going to Yale and becoming a banker or broker; there was no passage for him to a law degree from Harvard. There was, however, a relatively easy way of acquiring these goods that he was incessantly told were available to him as an American citizen, and without which he had begun to feel he could not properly count himself as an American citizen. He could become a gangster. (Allsop, 1961:236)

Perhaps we should not be surprised that Capone, with little chance of attending Yale or Harvard, landed his first job with a gangster who called himself Mr. Frankie Yale and owned a nightclub named the "Harvard Inn."

The inability to become successful by normative means may also lead to another type of deviance that Merton calls *ritualism* (see Figure 8–1). Low-level bureaucrats, knowing they will achieve only limited financial success, stick closely to the rules in order to feel and appear respectable.

A third response to the inability to succeed is *retreatism*, the rejection of both cultural goals and means. In effect, one "drops out" of mainstream culture. Some alcoholics, drug addicts, and street people are retreatists. The deviance of retreatists lies in their unconventional lifestyle and, perhaps more seriously, in their choosing to live this way.

The fourth response to failure is *rebellion*. Like retreatists, rebels reject both the cultural definition of success and the normative means of achieving it. Rebels—such as radical "survivalists"—go one step further by forming a counterculture and advocating alternatives to the existing social order.

DEVIANT SUBCULTURES

Richard Cloward and Lloyd Ohlin (1966) extended Merton's theory, proposing that crime results not just from limited legitimate (legal) opportunity but also from readily accessible illegitimate (illegal) opportunity. In short, deviance or conformity arises from the *relative opportunity structure* that frames a person's life.

The life of Al Capone shows how an ambitious person denied legitimate opportunity could take advantage of an illegal opportunity: supplying alcohol during Prohibition (1920–1933). In other words, illegal opportunities foster the development of *criminal subcultures* that provide people with the knowledge, skills, and other resources to succeed in unconventional ways. Capone, for example, built a criminal empire. Indeed, gangs may specialize in one or another form of criminality according to available opportunities and resources (Sheley et al., 1995).

But what happens when people cannot identify *any* kind of opportunity, legal or illegal? Then, deviance often surfaces in the form of *conflict subcultures* (armed street gangs), where violence is ignited by frustration and a desire for respect. Alternatively, those who fail to succeed, even using criminal means, may fall into *retreatist subcultures*, dropping out through alcohol or other drug abuse.

Albert Cohen (1971; orig. 1955) suggests that delinquency is most pronounced among lower-class youths because they have the least opportunity to achieve conventional success. Neglected by society, they seek self-respect by creating a delinquent subculture that "defines as meritorious the characteristics they *do* possess, the kinds of conduct of which they *are* capable" (1971:66). Being feared on the street may win few points with society as a whole, but it may satisfy a youth's desire to "be somebody" in the local neighborhood.

Walter Miller (1970; orig. 1958) adds that delinquent subcultures are characterized by (1) *trouble*, arising from frequent conflict with teachers and police; (2) *toughness*, the value placed on physical size and strength, especially among males; (3) *smartness*, the ability to succeed on the streets, to outsmart or "con" others, and to avoid being similarly taken advantage of; (4) *a need for excitement*, the search for thrills, risk, or danger; (5) *a belief in fate*, a sense that people lack control over their own lives; and (6) *a desire for freedom*, often expressed as hostility toward figures of authority.

Finally, Elijah Anderson (1994) explains that most people in poor, urban neighborhoods conform to conventional ("decent") values. Some young men, however, faced with neighborhood crime and violence, hostility from police, and sometimes even neglect from their own parents, adopt a "street code." To show that he can take care of himself and thus survive on the street, a young man displays "nerve," a willingness to stand up to any threat. According to this code, explains Anderson, even a violent death is better than being "dissed" (disrespected) by others. Some manage to escape the dangers, but the risk of ending up in jail—or worse—is very high for these young men pushed to the margins of our society.

Critical evaluation. Durkheim made an important contribution by pointing out the functions of deviance. However, evidence shows that a community does not always come together in reaction to crime; sometimes fear of crime drives people to withdraw from public life (Liska & Warner, 1991; Warr & Ellison, 2000).

Merton's strain theory has been criticized for explaining some kinds of deviance (theft, for example) far better than others (such as crimes of passion or mental illness). Moreover, not everyone seeks success in conventional terms of wealth, as strain theory implies.

The general argument of Cloward and Ohlin, Cohen, Miller, and Anderson—that deviance reflects the opportunity structure of society—has been confirmed by subsequent research (cf. Allan & Steffensmeier, 1989; Uggen, 1999). However, these theories fall short in assuming that everyone shares the same cultural standards for judging right and wrong. Moreover, we must be careful not to define deviance in ways that unfairly target poor people. If we define crime to include stock fraud as well as street theft, then more affluent people will be counted among criminals. Finally, all structural-functional theories imply that everyone who breaks the rules is labeled deviant. However, becoming deviant is actually a highly complex process, as the next section explains.

Association's view on homosexuality. The *Diagnostic and Statistical Manual of Mental Disorders* (DSM) listed homosexuality as a "personality disorder" when it first appeared in 1952; later, it was called a "sexual orientation disorder"; next, gays unhappy with their sexuality were diagnosed with "ego dystonic homosexuality"; finally, in 1987, homosexuality was dropped entirely from the DSM (Livingston, 1999).

LABELING DEVIANCE: SYMBOLIC-INTERACTION ANALYSIS

The symbolic-interaction paradigm explains how people define deviance in everyday situations. From this point of view, definitions of deviance and conformity are surprisingly flexible.

LABELING THEORY

The central contribution of symbolic-interaction analysis is **labeling theory,** *the assertion that deviance and conformity result not so much from what people do as from how others respond to those actions.* Labeling theory stresses the relativity of deviance, meaning that people may define the same behavior in any number of ways. Thus, deviance is nothing more than behavior that people define as deviant (Becker, 1966).

Consider these situations: A woman takes an article of clothing from a roommate; a married man at a convention has sex with a prostitute; a mayor gives a big city contract to a major campaign contributor. In each case, "reality" depends on the response of others. Is the first situation a matter of borrowing or theft? The consequences of the second case depend largely on whether the man's behavior becomes known back home. In the third situation, is the official choosing a good contractor or paying off a political debt? The social construction of reality, then, is a highly variable process of detection, definition, and response.

More broadly, because "reality" depends on time and place, it is no surprise that one society's conformity may be another's deviance. The box describes cockfighting. Is this sport an important cultural ritual or a vicious abuse of animals?

Primary and Secondary Deviance

Edwin Lemert (1951, 1972) observed that some episodes of norm violation—say, skipping school or underage drinking—provoke slight reaction from others and have little effect on a person's self-concept. Lemert calls such episodes *primary deviance.*

But what happens if other people notice someone's deviance and make something of it? For example, if people begin to describe a young man as a "boozer" and evict him from their social circle, he may become embittered, drink even more, and seek the company of others who approve of his behavior. In this way, the response to initial deviance sets in motion *secondary deviance*, by which a person repeatedly violates a norm and begins to take on a deviant identity. The development of secondary deviance

DISCUSS: The psychosexual dimensions of the cockfighting rituals described below are fairly obvious.

RESOURCE: Initial insights into the importance of audience reaction to an episode of deviance in fostering a deviant career were made by Frank Tannenbaum in *Crime and the Community* (Columbia University Press, 1938).

NOTE: The term "stigma" is derived from a Greek root meaning "tattoo."

Q: "The Greeks, who were apparently strong on visual aids, originated the term *stigma* to refer to bodily signs designed to expose something unusual and bad about the moral status of the signifier." Erving Goffman, *Stigma* (1963)

GLOBAL SOCIOLOGY

Cockfighting: Cultural Ritual or Abuse of Animals?

You won't see it on television, but one of the world's most popular sports—from North America to Europe to Asia—is cockfighting. It is legal in parts of Louisiana, Texas, New Mexico, and Arizona, big business in Mexico, and something of a national pastime in the Philippines. There, the local cock pit is as important as the town square in the U.S. Midwest: Every village has one, and it draws a crowd on weekends and fiesta days.

On the surface, cockfights are about gambling. An afternoon or evening event might include ten fights. A fight begins with the cock owners displaying their birds to one another, calling out for bets as to the stronger bird. Members of the audience weigh in with cash. Keeping track of the bets is the *cristo*,

someone who stands, arms extended, taking money.

With the odds set and the money on the table, actual combat begins. Each rooster is outfitted with a small, sharp blade strapped to the rear of the left leg. The cocks need little encouragement to fight, but the owners do a bit of strutting themselves, swinging their birds in front of each other before dropping them on lines drawn in the pit sand. Upon hitting the ground, the birds fly at one another, merging in a blur of legs and feathers.

Within a few minutes, one bird may collapse from exhaustion; the owner steps in to revive his cock and the process is repeated. Before long, however, a blade finds its mark. The victor, the bird that will live to fight another day, perches on the vanquished, which will not.

In many parts of the world, cockfighting is an important male ritual. Men raise their roosters for about two years, often at great expense, and care for them like sons. In the ritual of the cockfight itself, men test their claims to manhood, establish their standing in the community's pecking order, and pass on to their sons lessons about honor, competition, and masculinity.

Many outside observers are repulsed by the spectacle. But cockfighting is obviously important to insiders. Should one condemn it as brutality or respect it as ceremony?

Sources: Based on *The Economist* (1994), Harris (1994), and the author's research in the Philippines.

---

is one application of the Thomas theorem (discussed in Chapter 6, "Social Interaction in Everyday Life"), which states that "situations defined as real become real in their consequences."

Stigma

Secondary deviance marks the start of what Erving Goffman (1963) calls a *deviant career*. As people develop a stronger commitment to deviant behavior, they typically acquire a **stigma,** *a powerfully negative label that greatly changes a person's self-concept and social identity.*

Stigma operates as a master status (see Chapter 6), overpowering other aspects of social identity so that a person is discredited in the minds of others, becoming socially isolated. Sometimes an entire community formally stigmatizes a person through what Harold Garfinkel (1956) calls a *degradation ceremony*. A criminal prosecution is one example, operating much like a high school graduation in reverse: A person stands

before the community to be labeled in a negative rather than a positive way.

Retrospective and Projective Labeling

Once people stigmatize a person, they may engage in *retrospective labeling*, interpreting someone's past in light of some present deviance (Scheff, 1984). For example, after discovering that a priest has sexually molested a child, others rethink his past, perhaps musing, "He always did want to be around young children." Retrospective labeling distorts a person's biography by being highly selective and helps deepen a deviant identity.

Similarly, people may engage in *projective labeling* of a stigmatized person. That is, they use a deviant identity to predict future action. People might say of the priest, for example, "He's just going to keep at it until he gets caught." Such expectations may increase the likelihood that they will come true.

NOTE: In the late 1950s, Thomas Szasz prepared a short article on the myth of mental illness and submitted it to every major U.S. psychiatric journal; every one rejected it. The article finally appeared in *The American Psychologist* (1960).
NOTE: The medicalization of deviance is one dimension of the cultural trend of victimization described in Chapter 3, "Culture."

SOCIAL SURVEY: "Morality is a personal matter and society should not force everyone to follow one standard." (GSS 1988, *N* = 1,481; *Codebook*, 2001:377)

"Agree strongly"	31.7%	"Disagree strongly"	7.6%
"Agree somewhat"	38.8%	DK/NR	4.4%
"Disagree somewhat"	17.5%		

Labeling and Mental Illness

Is a woman who believes that Jesus rides the bus to work with her every day mentally ill or just expressing her strong religious faith? Is a homeless man who refuses to allow police to take him to a city shelter on a cold night mentally ill or simply trying to live independently?

The psychiatrist Thomas Szasz (1961, 1970, 1994, 1995) charges that people apply the label "insanity" to what is only "difference." Therefore, he concludes, we should abandon the concept of mental illness entirely. Illness is physical, he continues, and afflicts only the body; "mental" illness is a myth. The world is full of people whose "differences" in thought or action may irritate us, but such differences are no grounds for defining someone as mentally ill. Such labeling, Szasz claims, simply enforces conformity to the standards of people powerful enough to impose their will on others.

Most health care professionals reject the notion that mental illness is a fiction. But some hail Szasz's work for pointing out the danger of using medicine to promote conformity. After all, most of us experience periods of extreme stress or other mental instability from time to time. Such episodes, although upsetting, usually are of passing importance. However, if others respond with negative labeling, the long-term result may be further deviance as a self-fulfilling prophecy (Scheff, 1984; Rosenfeld, 1997).

THE MEDICALIZATION OF DEVIANCE

Labeling theory, particularly the ideas of Szasz and Goffman, helps explain an important shift in the way our society understands deviance. Over the last fifty years, the growing influence of psychiatry and medicine in the United States has encouraged the **medicalization of deviance**, *the transformation of moral and legal deviance into a medical condition.*

Medicalization amounts to swapping one set of labels for another. In moral terms, we evaluate people or their behavior as "bad" or "good." However, the scientific objectivity of modern medicine passes no moral judgment, instead using clinical diagnoses such as "sick" or "well."

To illustrate, until the middle of this century, people generally viewed alcoholics as morally weak and easily tempted by the pleasure of drink. Gradually, however, medical specialists redefined alcoholism so that most people now consider alcoholism a disease, making people "sick" rather than "bad." Similarly, overeating, drug addiction, child abuse, sexual promiscuity, and other behaviors that used to be moral matters

The world is full of people who are unusual in one way or another. This Indian man grew the fingernails on one hand for more than thirty years just to do something that no one else had ever done. Should we define such behavior as harmless eccentricity or as evidence of mental illness?

are widely defined today as illnesses for which people need help rather than punishment.

The Difference Labels Make

Whether we define deviance as a moral or medical issue has three consequences. First, it affects *who responds* to deviance. An offense against common morality usually brings about a reaction from members of the community or the police. A medical label, however, places the situation under the control of clinical specialists, including counselors, psychiatrists, and physicians.

A second difference is *how people respond* to deviance. A moral approach defines the deviant as an "offender" subject to punishment. Medically, however, "patients" need treatment (for their own good, of course). Therefore, whereas punishment is designed to fit the crime, treatment programs are tailored to the patient and may

When people step out of line, should we consider their behavior "bad" or "sick"? In 2000, Atlanta Braves pitcher John Rocker made comments about minorities that many considered offensive. Rocker was reprimanded and was also required to undergo psychological testing, suggesting that he has an illness. Do you think these kinds of cases warrant "treatment," or is "punishment" more appropriate? Why?

involve almost any therapy that a specialist thinks will prevent future illness (von Hirsh, 1986). As a result, whereas punishment is closely monitored by the law, treatment provides less assurance of "due process."

Third, and most important, the two labels differ on *the personal competence of the deviant person.* Morally speaking, whether we are right or wrong, at least we take responsibility for our own behavior. Once defined as sick, however, we are seen as lacking the capacity to control (or, if "mentally ill," even understand) our actions. People who are incompetent are, in turn, subject to treatment against their will. For this reason alone, attempts to define deviance in medical terms should be made only with extreme caution.

SUTHERLAND'S DIFFERENTIAL ASSOCIATION THEORY

Learning any behavioral pattern—whether conventional or deviant—is a social process that takes place in groups. Therefore, according to Edwin Sutherland (1940), a person's tendency toward conformity or deviance depends

on the amount of contact with others who encourage or reject conventional behavior. This is Sutherland's theory of *differential association.*

We can illustrate Sutherland's theory with a study of drug and alcohol use among young adults in the United States (Akers et al., 1979). Questionnaires completed by juniors and seniors in high school showed a close connection between the extent of alcohol and drug use and the degree to which peer groups encouraged such activity. The researchers concluded that young people accept delinquent patterns to the extent that they receive praise and other rewards for defining deviance—rather than conformity—in positive terms.

HIRSCHI'S CONTROL THEORY

The sociologist Travis Hirschi (1969; Gottfredson & Hirschi, 1995) developed *control theory,* which states that social control depends on imagining the consequences of one's behavior. Hirschi assumes that everyone finds at least some deviance tempting. But imagining the reaction of family and friends deters most people; almost everyone else would stop at the prospect of a ruined career. On the other hand, people who feel they have little to lose from deviance are likely to become rule-breakers.

Specifically, Hirschi continues, there are four types of social control:

1. **Attachment.** Strong social attachments encourage conformity; weak relationships in the family, peer group, and school leave people freer to engage in deviance.

2. **Commitment.** The greater a person's commitment to legitimate opportunity, the greater the advantages of conformity. By contrast, someone with little confidence in future success is more likely to drift toward deviance.

3. **Involvement.** Extensive involvement in legitimate activities—such as holding a job, going to school, and playing sports—inhibits deviance. People who simply "hang out," waiting for something to happen, have time and energy for deviant activity.

4. **Belief.** Strong belief in conventional morality and respect for authority figures control tendencies toward deviance. People with a weak conscience who are left unsupervised are more vulnerable to temptation (Osgood et al., 1996).

Hirschi's analysis draws together a number of earlier ideas about the causes of deviant behavior. Note

Gang violence is a common occurrence in many large cities of the United States. Young people pushed to the margins of U.S. society may turn to gangs and violence as a means to gain a sense of belonging and importance. But the price is often high, indeed. This graffiti memorial to a fallen gang member is found in Bridgeport, Connecticut.

that a person's relative social privilege and strength of moral character give him or her a stake in conforming to conventional norms (Wiatrowski, Griswold, & Roberts, 1981; Sampson & Laub, 1990; Free, 1992).

Critical evaluation. The various symbolic-interaction theories see deviance as process. Labeling theory links deviance not to *action* but to the *reaction* of others. Thus, some people come to be defined as deviant while others who think or behave in the same way are not. The concepts of secondary deviance, deviant careers, and stigma demonstrate how being labeled deviant can become a lasting self-concept.

Yet labeling theory has several limitations. First, this theory's highly relative view of deviance ignores the fact that some kinds of behavior, such as murder, are condemned just about everywhere (Wellford, 1980). Labeling theory thus works best in the case of less serious deviance, such as illegal drug use or mental illness. Second, research on the consequences of deviant labeling is inconclusive (Smith & Gartin, 1989; Sherman & Smith, 1992). Does deviant labeling produce further deviance or discourage it? Third, not everyone resists being labeled as deviant; some people actually seek it out (Vold & Bernard, 1986). For example, people take part in civil disobedience and willingly subject themselves to arrest in order to call attention to social injustice.

Both Sutherland's differential association theory and Hirschi's control theory have had considerable influence in sociology. But they provide little insight into why a society's norms and laws define certain kinds of activities as deviant in the first place. This important question is addressed by social-conflict analysis, the focus of the next section.

DEVIANCE AND INEQUALITY: SOCIAL-CONFLICT ANALYSIS

The social-conflict paradigm demonstrates how deviance reflects social inequality. This approach holds that who or what is labeled "deviant" depends on which categories of people hold power in a society.

DEVIANCE AND POWER

Alexander Liazos (1972) points out that the people we commonly consider deviants—"nuts, sluts, and 'preverts'"—are people who share the trait of powerlessness. That is, bag ladies (not corporate polluters) and unemployed men on street corners (not arms dealers) carry the stigma of deviance.

Social-conflict theory explains this pattern in three ways. First, the norms—and especially laws—of any society generally reflect the interests of the rich and powerful. People who threaten the wealthy, either by taking their property or by advocating a more egalitarian society, are defined as "common thieves" or "political radicals." As noted in Chapter 4 ("Society"), Karl Marx argued that the law—and all social institutions—support the interests of the rich. Or, as Richard Quinney puts it, "Capitalist justice is by the capitalist class, for the capitalist class, and against the working class" (1977:3).

Q: "Public opinion in regard to picking pockets would not be well organized if most of the information regarding this crime came to the public directly from the pickpockets themselves." Edwin H. Sutherland

NOTE: Much of the underground economy involves criminal activity in that it evades taxes. The federal government estimates that $80 billion due in income taxes is not paid, which equals the combined budgets of Congress and the federal judicial system, the Departments of Commerce, Education, and Energy, the EPA, and NASA.

NOTE: With regard to corporations protecting individuals from criminal prosecutions, imagine holding a street gang, but not its individual members, responsible for violence.

Q: "In this century, America's only permanent growth industry has been organized crime." Selwyn Raab

Second, even if their behavior is called into question, the powerful have the resources to resist deviant labels. Corporate executives who order the dumping of hazardous wastes are rarely held personally accountable. Moreover, as the O. J. Simpson trial made clear, even when charged with violent crimes, the rich have the resources to resist being labeled criminal.

Third, the widespread belief that norms and laws are natural and good masks their political character. For this reason, we may condemn the unequal application of the law but give little thought to whether the laws themselves are inherently fair (Quinney, 1977).

DEVIANCE AND CAPITALISM

In the Marxist tradition, Steven Spitzer (1980) argues that deviant labels are applied to people who interfere with the operation of capitalism. First, because capitalism is based on private control of wealth, people who threaten the property of others—especially the poor who steal from the rich—are prime candidates for being labeled deviant. Conversely, the rich who exploit the poor are unlikely to be defined as deviant. For example, landlords who charge poor tenants high rents and evict anyone who cannot pay are not considered a threat to society; they are simply "doing business."

Second, because capitalism depends on productive labor, people who cannot or will not work risk being labeled deviant. Many members of our society think people who are out of work, even through no fault of their own, are somehow deviant.

Third, capitalism depends on respect for authority figures, so people who resist authority are labeled deviant. Examples are children who skip school or talk back to parents and teachers and adults who do not cooperate with employers or police.

Fourth, anyone who directly challenges the capitalist status quo is likely to be defined as deviant. In this category are antiwar activists, radical environmentalists, and labor organizers.

On the other side of the coin, society positively labels whatever promotes the capitalist system. Winning athletes, for example, enjoy celebrity status because they express the values of individual achievement and competition that are vital to capitalism. Moreover, Spitzer notes, we condemn using drugs of escape (marijuana, psychedelics, heroin, and crack) as deviant but endorse drugs that promote adjustment to the status quo (alcohol, tobacco, and caffeine).

The capitalist system also strives to control people who don't fit into the system. The elderly, people with mental or physical disabilities, and Robert Merton's retreatists (people addicted to alcohol or other drugs) are considered a "costly yet relatively harmless burden" on society. Such people, claims Spitzer, are subject to control by social welfare agencies. But people who openly challenge the capitalist system, including the inner-city underclass and revolutionaries—Merton's innovators and rebels—are controlled by the criminal justice system and, in times of crisis, by military forces such as the National Guard.

Notice that both the social welfare and criminal justice systems blame individuals, not the system, for social problems. Welfare recipients are deemed unworthy freeloaders; poor people who vent their rage are labeled rioters; anyone who challenges the government is branded a radical or a Communist; and those who attempt to acquire illegally what they cannot obtain otherwise are rounded up as common criminals.

WHITE-COLLAR CRIME

In 1987, a Wall Street stockbroker named Michael Milken made headlines for becoming the highest-paid U.S. worker in half a century. His yearly salary and bonuses totaled $550 million, *about $1.5 million a day.* Such a sum placed Milken right behind Al Capone, whose earnings in 1927 reportedly reached $600 million in current dollars (Swartz, 1989). Milken had something else in common with Capone: He was jailed—in his case, for business fraud.

Milken committed a **white-collar crime,** defined by Edwin Sutherland (1940) as *crime committed by people of high social position in the course of their occupations* (Sutherland & Cressey, 1978). As the Milken case indicates, white-collar crimes do not involve violence and rarely bring police with guns drawn to the scene. Rather, white-collar criminals use their powerful occupational positions to enrich themselves and others, often causing significant public harm in the process (Hagan & Parker, 1985; Vold & Bernard, 1986). For this reason, sociologists sometimes call white-collar offenses that occur in government offices and corporate board rooms *crime in the suites* as opposed to *crime in the streets.*

The most common white-collar crimes are bank embezzlement, business fraud, bribery, and antitrust violations. Certainly, some white-collar crime causes little public harm. But many cases—such as the savings and loan scandal of the 1980s—attract a great deal of attention and cause great loss to the public (Weisburd et al., 1991). The government program to bail out the savings and loan industry ended up costing

Q: "The laws are best explained, interpreted, and applied by those whose interest and abilities lie in perverting, confounding, and eluding them. . . . Reward and punishment [are] the two hinges upon which all government turns." Jonathan Swift, *Gulliver's Travels*

GLOBAL: Socialist societies also have organized crime; hundreds of criminal organizations now operate in Russia, and the number is rising as a market system develops and political freedom expands.

GLOBAL: A new form of crime, both high-tech and global in character, is pirating copyrighted software. The Internet now allows anyone with a computer and modem to send or receive materials globally. Software piracy is especially pronounced in lower-income countries such as Mexico, Brazil, Pakistan, and Malaysia, where perhaps 85% of all software is procured illegally.

Q: "Good laws derive from evil habits." Macrobius

U.S. taxpayers $600 billion, which amounts to $2,500 per person.

Sutherland (1940) explains that white-collar offenses typically end up in a civil hearing rather than a criminal courtroom. *Civil law* regulates business dealings between private parties, whereas *criminal law* defines the individual's moral responsibilities to society. In practice, then, someone who loses a civil case pays for damage or injury but is not labeled a criminal. Furthermore, corporate officials are protected by the fact that most charges of white-collar crime target the organization rather than individuals.

In the rare cases in which white-collar criminals are charged and convicted, the odds are almost fifty-fifty that they will not go to jail. One accounting shows that just 54 percent of the embezzlers convicted in the U.S. federal courts served prison sentences; the rest were put on probation or paid a fine (U.S. Bureau of Justice Statistics, 2000).

CORPORATE CRIME

Sometimes whole companies, rather than individuals, break the law. **Corporate crime** is *the illegal actions of a corporation or people acting on its behalf.*

Corporate crime ranges from knowingly selling faulty or dangerous products to deliberately polluting the environment (Benson & Cullen, 1998). If wrongdoing on the part of corporate officers or their agents can be proven, these people are subject to criminal prosecution. However, as is the case with white-collar crime, most cases go unpunished, and many never become a part of the public record.

Even so, the cost of corporate crime is high, going beyond dollars to human lives. For example, for decades coal mining companies put miners at risk from inhaling coal dust, so that hundreds of people die annually from "black lung" disease. The death toll from all job-related hazards that are *known to companies* probably exceeds 100,000 annually (Reiman, 1998; Carroll, 1999; Jones, 1999b). More recently, some charge, the Bridgestone Firestone company marketed unsafe tires and concealed their knowledge of the hazard before recalling 6.5 million tires. Tread separation on Bridgestone Firestone tires is alleged to have caused 271 deaths in the United States, and numerous lawsuits are pending (Eisenberg, 2000; Morris & Lavelle, 2000).

ORGANIZED CRIME

Organized crime is *a business supplying illegal goods or services.* Sometimes crime organizations force people to

Laws regulate the operation of businesses just as they direct the actions of individuals. But, as social-conflict analysis points out, powerful corporate leaders who head up corporations charged with law-breaking are rarely thought of as criminals, and rarely are they subject to the punishment accorded to ordinary people.

do business with them, as when a gang extorts money from shopkeepers for "protection." In most cases, however, organized crime involves selling illegal goods and services—including sex, drugs, and gambling—to a willing public.

For more than a century, organized crime has flourished in the United States. Its operations expanded as waves of immigrants found that this society was not willing to share its opportunities with them. Thus, some ambitious minorities (such as Al Capone, described earlier) made their own success, especially when Prohibition banned the production and sale of alcoholic beverages coast to coast from 1920 to 1933.

The Italian Mafia is a well-known example of organized crime. But other criminal organizations involve African Americans, Chinese, Colombians, Cubans, Haitians, Russians, and almost every other racial and ethnic category. Moreover, today's organized crime involves a wide range of activities, from selling illegal drugs to prostitution to credit-card fraud to marketing false identification papers to illegal immigrants (Valdez, 1997).

TABLE 8–1 Sociological Explanations of Deviance: A Summary	
Theoretical Paradigm	**Major Contributions**
Structural-functional analysis	What is deviant may vary, but deviance is found in all societies; deviance and the social response it provokes sustain the moral foundation of society; deviance may also guide social change.
Symbolic-interaction analysis	Nothing is inherently deviant but may become defined as such through the response of others; the reactions of others are highly variable; labeling someone deviant may lead to the development of secondary deviance and deviant careers.
Social-conflict analysis	Laws and other norms reflect the interests of powerful members of society; those who threaten the status quo generally are defined as deviant; social injury caused by powerful people is less likely to be considered criminal than is social injury caused by people who have little social power.

Critical evaluation. According to social-conflict theory, inequality in wealth and power guides the creation and application of laws and other norms. The criminal justice and social welfare systems thus act as political agents, controlling categories of people who threaten the capitalist system.

As with other approaches to deviance, however, social-conflict theory has its critics. First, this approach implies that laws and other cultural norms are created directly by the rich and powerful. At the very least, this is an oversimplification because laws also protect workers, consumers, and the environment, sometimes opposing the interests of the rich.

Second, social-conflict analysis implies that criminality springs up only to the extent that a society treats its members unequally. However, as Durkheim noted, deviance exists in all societies, whatever the economic system.

The sociological explanations for crime and other types of deviance that we have discussed are summarized in Table 8–1.

DEVIANCE AND SOCIAL DIVERSITY

What is defined as deviant has much to do with the relative power and privilege of different categories of people. The following sections offer two examples: how racial and ethnic hostility motivate hate crimes and how gender is linked to deviance.

HATE CRIMES

A **hate crime** is *a criminal act against a person or person's property by an offender motivated by racial or other bias.* A hate crime may express hostility toward someone's race, religion, ancestry, sexual orientation, or physical disability.

Most people were stunned by the brutal killing in 1998 of Matthew Shepard, a gay student at the University of Wyoming, by two men filled with hate toward homosexuals. The National Gay and Lesbian Task Force reports that one in five lesbians and gay men is physically assaulted and more than 90 percent verbally abused because of sexual orientation (cited in Berrill, 1992:19–20). Victims of hate-motivated violence are especially likely to be people who contend with multiple stigmas, such as gay men of color. The federal government records more than 8,000 hate crimes each year.

By 2001, forty-three states and the federal government had enacted legislation that increased penalties for crimes motivated by hatred. Supporters are gratified, but opponents say such laws punish thoughts, not actions. The box takes a closer look at the issue of hate-crime laws.

DEVIANCE AND GENDER

Virtually every society in the world applies more stringent normative controls to women than to men. Historically, our society has centered the lives of women in the home. Even today, in the United States, women's opportunities in the workplace, politics, athletics, and the military are limited. Elsewhere in the world, women face even greater barriers. In Saudi Arabia, women cannot vote or legally operate motor vehicles; in Iran, women who dare to expose their hair or wear makeup in public can be whipped.

Gender also figures in the theories of deviance noted earlier. Robert Merton's strain theory, for example, seems masculine in that it defines cultural goals in terms of financial success. Traditionally at least, accumulating wealth has more to do with the lives of men, whereas women are socialized to define success in terms of relationships, particularly marriage and motherhood (Leonard, 1982). A more woman-focused theory might recognize the strain that results from the cultural ideal of equality clashing with the reality of gender-based inequality.

CRITICAL THINKING

Hate-Crime Laws: Do They Punish Actions or Attitudes?

On a cool October evening, Todd Mitchell, an African American teenager, was standing with some friends in front of their apartment complex in Kenosha, Wisconsin. They had just seen the film *Mississippi Burning* and were fuming over a scene that showed a white man beating a young black boy who is kneeling in prayer.

"Do you feel hyped up to move on some white people?" asked Mitchell. Minutes later, they saw a young white boy walking toward them on the other side of the street. Mitchell commanded: "There goes a white boy; go get him!" The group swarmed around the youngster, beating him bloody and leaving him on the ground in a coma. The attackers took the boy's tennis shoes as a trophy.

Police soon arrested the boys and charged them with the beating. A jury found Mitchell guilty of aggravated battery *motivated by racial hatred*. Instead of the usual two-year prison sentence, he went to jail for four years.

As this case illustrates, hate-crime laws punish a crime more severely if the offender is motivated by bias against some category of people. Supporters make three arguments in favor of hate-crime

legislation. First, the offender's intentions are always important in weighing criminal responsibility, so considering hatred an intention is nothing new. Second, crimes motivated by racial or other bias inflame the public mood more than crimes carried out, say, for monetary gain. Third, victims of hate crimes typically suffer greater injury than victims of crimes with other motives.

Critics counter that although some hate-crime cases involve hard-core racism, most are impulsive acts by young people. Even more important, critics maintain, hate-crime laws are a threat to First Amendment guarantees

The murder of gay student Matthew Shephard in 1998 prompted candlelight vigils and other demonstrations across the country. Why do you think hate crimes so inflame the public?

of free speech. Hate-crime laws allow courts to sentence offenders not just for actions but for their attitudes. As Harvard law professor Alan Dershowitz cautions, "As much as I hate bigotry, I fear much more the Court attempting to control the minds of its citizens." In short, according to critics, hate-crime statutes open the door to punishing beliefs rather than behavior.

In 1993, the U.S. Supreme Court upheld Mitchell's sentence. In a unanimous decision, the justices stated that the government should not punish an individual's beliefs. But, they reasoned, a belief is no longer protected when it becomes the motive for a crime.

What do you think?

1. Do you think crimes motivated by hate are more harmful than those motivated by, say, greed? Why or why not?

2. On balance, do you favor or oppose hate-crime laws? Why?

3. Do you think minorities such as African Americans should be subject to hate-crime laws just as white people are? Why or why not?

Sources: Greenhouse (1993), Jacobs (1993), and Terry (1993).

In labeling theory, gender influences how we define deviance because people commonly use different standards to judge the behavior of women and men. Furthermore, because society puts men in positions of power over women, men often escape direct responsibility for actions that victimize women. In the past, at least, men who sexually harassed or assaulted women were labeled only mildly deviant, if they were punished at all.

On the other hand, women who are victimized may have to convince an unsympathetic audience that they did not bring sexual harassment on themselves. Research confirms an important truth: Whether people define a situation as deviance—and, if so, whose deviance it is—depends on the sex of both the audience and the actors (King & Clayson, 1988).

Finally, despite its focus on social inequality, social-conflict analysis neglects the importance of gender. If

THE MAP: Arrest rates are higher for poor, young minority men, who make up a higher share of the population of the "above average" counties.

NOTE: The *corpus delecti* ("body of a crime") is composed of (a) *actus reus* ("guilty act"), which is the physical act (or omission) in violation of criminal law; (b) *mens rea* ("guilty mind"), or mental resolve to commit the crime; (c) causal order, by which the criminal intent precedes and is related to the criminal act; and (d) all legal elements, the factors attached to the specific crime in a particular jurisdiction according to the wording of the criminal statute.

NOTE: A significant percentage of violent and property crimes are committed by young people. Under 21: 29.8% of arrests for violent crime; 48.3% of arrests for property crime. Under 18: 15.9% of arrests for violent crime; 32.0% for property crime (U.S. Federal Bureau of Investigation, 2001).

SEEING OURSELVES

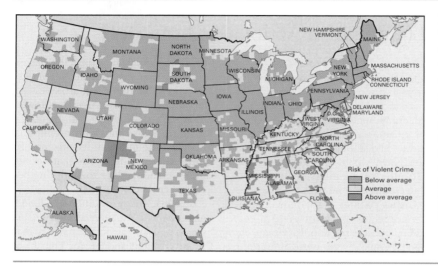

NATIONAL MAP 8–1
The Risk of Violent Crime across the United States

This map shows the risk of becoming a victim of violent crime. In general, the risk is highest in low-income, rural counties that have a large population of men between the ages of fifteen and twenty-four. After reading through this section of the text, see whether you can explain this pattern.

Source: This map first appeared in the December 2000 edition of *American Demographics* magazine. It is reprinted with permission from Media Central, a Primedia Company.

Risk of Violent Crime
- Below average
- Average
- Above average

---

economic disadvantage is a primary cause of crime, as social-conflict theory suggests, why do women (whose economic position is much worse than men's) commit far fewer crimes than men do?

CRIME

Crime is the violation of criminal laws enacted by a locality, state, or the federal government. Technically, all crimes are composed of two elements: the *act* itself (or, in some cases, the failure to do what the law requires) and *criminal intent* (in legal terminology, *mens rea*, or "guilty mind"). Intent is a matter of degree, ranging from a planned action to negligence. Someone who is negligent does not deliberately set out to hurt anyone but acts (or fails to act) in a way that might reasonably cause harm to another. Prosecutors weigh the degree of intent in deciding whether, for example, to charge someone with first-degree murder, second-degree murder, or negligent manslaughter. Alternatively, there may be no prosecution if officials consider a killing justifiable, as in self-defense.

TYPES OF CRIME

In the United States, the Federal Bureau of Investigation gathers information on criminal offenses and regularly reports the results in a publication called *Crime in the United States.* Two major types of crime make up the FBI "crime index."

Crimes against the person are *crimes that direct violence or the threat of violence against others.* Such violent crimes include murder and manslaughter (legally defined as "the willful killing of one human being by another"), aggra-

Read a report by the Department of Housing and Urban Development on gun violence in public housing projects: http://www.huduser.org/periodicals/rrr/rrr_3_2000/0300_1.html

vated assault ("an unlawful attack by one person upon another for the purpose of inflicting severe or aggravated bodily injury"), forcible rape ("the carnal knowledge of a female forcibly and against her will"), and robbery ("taking or attempting to take anything of value from the care, custody, or control of a person or persons by force or threat of force or violence and/or putting the victim in fear"). National Map 8–1 shows the risk of violent crime for all the counties across the United States.

Crimes against property are *crimes that involve theft of property belonging to others.* Property crimes include burglary ("the unlawful entry of a structure to commit a [serious crime] or a theft"), larceny-theft ("the unlawful taking, carrying, leading, or riding away of property from the possession of another"), auto theft ("the theft or attempted theft of a motor

NOTE: The Los Angeles–Long Beach, Calif., metropolitan area reports the highest number of murders in the U.S.; during 2000, 1,006 were recorded.

NOTE: Changes in our view of violence are suggested by how common violence between officials was two centuries ago. For example, Vice President Aaron Burr shot and killed Alexander Hamilton (first U.S. Secretary of the Treasury) in a duel in 1804.

DIVERSITY: Juveniles figure disproportionately not only among offenders but among victims, representing one-fourth of victims of violent crime.

NOTE: There were 645 workplace homicides in 1999; such violence is the third leading cause of workplace death for women. By occupation, truck drivers lead the risk list.

Q: "I am as pure as the driven slush." Tallulah Bankhead

vehicle"), and arson ("any willful or malicious burning or attempt to burn the personal property of another").

A third category of offenses, not included in major crime indexes, is **victimless crimes,** *violations of law in which there are no readily apparent victims.* Also called "crimes without complaint," they include illegal drug use, prostitution, and gambling. The term "victimless crime" is misleading, however. How victimless is a crime when people have to steal to support a drug habit? What about a pregnant woman who smokes crack and permanently harms her baby? Perhaps it is more correct to say that people who commit such crimes are both offenders and victims.

Because public views of victimless crimes vary so much, laws differ from place to place. In the United States, gambling is legal only in a few locations within twenty-three states; prostitution is lawful only in one (rural counties of Nevada). Yet both activities are common across the country. Homosexual (and some heterosexual) behavior among consenting adults is legally restricted in about half the states. Where such laws exist, enforcement is light and selective.

CRIMINAL STATISTICS

Statistics gathered by the Federal Bureau of Investigation show crime rising between 1960 and 1990 but declining thereafter. Even so, police tally nearly 12 million serious crimes each year. Figure 8–2 on page 208 shows the trends for various serious crimes.

Read crime statistics with caution, however; they include only crimes known to the police. Almost all homicides are reported, but assaults—especially among people who know each other—often are not. Police records include an even smaller share of property crimes, especially when the losses are small.

Researchers check official crime statistics using *victimization surveys,* which ask a representative sample of people about their experience with crime. According to these surveys, the crime rate is two to four times higher than what official reports indicate (Russell, 1995b).

THE STREET CRIMINAL: A PROFILE

Government crime reports paint a broad-brush picture of people arrested for violent and property crimes. We now break down these arrest statistics by age, gender, social class, race, and ethnicity.

Criminal statistics can be used to construct a portrait of offenders in the United States. But these data have some limitations. For one thing, they are based not on convictions in a court of law but on arrests made and reported to the FBI by police. Two patterns are clear: Those arrested for serious crimes are likely to be young and they are likely to be male.

Age

Official crime rates rise sharply during adolescence and peak in the late teens, falling thereafter. People between the ages of fifteen and twenty-four represent just 14 percent of the U.S. population, but they represent 39.1 percent of all arrests for violent crimes and 46.8 percent for property crimes in 2000.

A disturbing trend is that young people are responsible for a larger share of serious crimes. During the 1990s, juveniles accounted for a rising share of arrests for rape, robbery, and arson (U.S. Federal Bureau of Investigation, 2001).

Gender

Although each sex constitutes roughly half the population, police collared males in 70.1 percent of all property crime arrests in 2000. In other words, men are arrested more than twice as often as women for property crimes. In the case of violent crimes, the

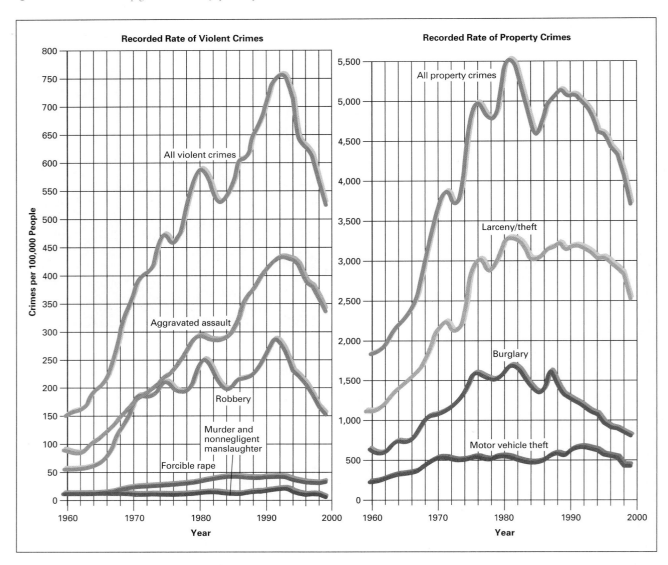

FIGURE 8–2 Crime Rates in the United States, 1960–2000

The graphs represent crime rates for various violent crimes and property crimes during recent decades.

Source: U.S. Federal Bureau of Investigation (2001).

disparity is even greater: 82.6 percent of arrests were males, and just 17.4 percent were females (a five-to-one ratio).

One reason for the difference is that law enforcement officers are reluctant to define women as criminals. Even so, the difference in arrest rates for women and men is narrowing, which probably reflects increasing sexual equality in our society. Between 1991 and 2000, a 17.6 percent *increase* in arrests of women contrasted with a *drop* of 3.8 percent in arrests of men (U.S. Federal Bureau of Investigation, 2001). A similar pattern holds globally, with the greatest gender difference in crime rates in societies that most severely limit the opportunities of women.

Social Class

The FBI does not assess the social class of arrested persons, so no statistical data are available. But research confirms that street crime is more widespread among people of lower social position (Wolfgang, Figlio, & Sellin, 1972; Clinard & Abbott, 1973; Braithwaite, 1981; Thornberry & Farnsworth, 1982; Wolfgang, Thornberry, & Figlio, 1987). Yet the link between class and crime is more complicated than it appears on the surface. For one thing, many people look on the poor as less worthy than the rich, whose wealth and power confer "respectability" (Tittle & Villemez, 1977; Tittle, Villemez, & Smith, 1978; Elias, 1986). Moreover, although crime—especially violent crime—is a serious problem in the poorest inner-city neighborhoods, most of these crimes are committed by a few hard-core offenders; the majority of the people who live in poor communities have no criminal records at all (Wolfgang, Figlio, & Sellin, 1972; Elliott & Ageton, 1980; Harries, 1990).

Moreover, the connection between social standing and criminality depends on what kind of crime one is talking about (Braithwaite, 1981). If we expand our definition of crime beyond street offenses to include white-collar crime and corporate crime, the "common criminal" suddenly looks much more affluent.

Race and Ethnicity

Both race and ethnicity are strongly correlated to crime rates, although the reasons are many and complex. Official statistics show that 69.7 percent of arrests for index crimes in 2000 involved white people. However, arrests of African Americans were higher than for whites in proportion to their numbers. African Americans represent 12.3 percent of the population but 31.0 percent of arrests for property crimes (versus 66.2 percent for whites) and 37.8 percent of arrests for violent crimes (59.9 percent for whites) (U.S. Federal Bureau of Investigation, 2001).

What accounts for the higher arrest rate among African Americans? First, to the degree that prejudice related to color or class encourages white police to arrest black people or citizens to report African Americans to police as potential offenders, people of color are overly criminalized (Liska & Tausig, 1979; Unnever, Frazier, & Henretta, 1980; Smith & Visher, 1981; Holmes et al., 1993; Covington, 1995).

Second, race in the United States closely relates to social standing, which, as we have already explained, affects the likelihood of engaging in street crimes.

In the United States, African Americans contend with higher rates of poverty, which goes a long way to explaining their proportionately higher involvement in crime—as victims as well as offenders. Especially in inner cities, where there is little available work, young people can be consumed by despair and anger, perhaps turning to crime or drugs. Paul Marcus captures one man's self-defeating efforts to escape his situation in the painting Cracked-up.

© Paul Marcus, *Cracked-up*, oil on panel, 24 in. × 30 in. Studio SPM Inc.

Many poor people living in the midst of affluence come to perceive society as unjust and therefore are more likely to turn to crime (Blau & Blau, 1982; Anderson, 1994; Martinez, 1996).

Third, black and white family patterns differ: Two-thirds of non-Hispanic black children (compared to one-fifth of non-Hispanic white children) are born to single mothers. In general, single-parenting means children grow up with less supervision and are more likely to be poor than children raised by both parents. With one-third of African American children growing up in poverty (compared to one in eight white children), no one should be surprised at higher crime rates for African

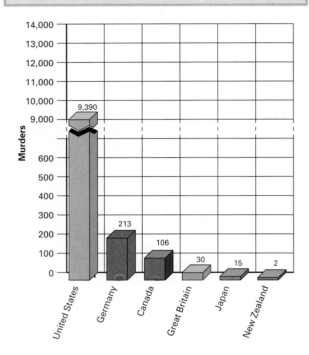

FIGURE 8–3 Number of Murders by Handguns, 1996

Source: Handgun Control, Inc. (2001).

Asian Americans enjoy higher than average educational achievement and income. Moreover, Asian American culture emphasizes family solidarity and discipline, both of which keep criminality down.

CRIME IN GLOBAL PERSPECTIVE

Although recent crime trends in the United States are downward, by world standards, the U.S. crime rate is high. There were 15,517 murders in the United States in 2000, about one every half-hour around the clock. In large cities such as New York, rarely does a day pass with no murder; in fact, more New Yorkers are hit with stray bullets than people deliberately gunned down in most large cities elsewhere in the world.

Overall, the U.S. violent crime rate is about five times greater than Europe's; the U.S. property crime rate is twice as high. The contrast is even greater between our society and the nations of Asia, including India and Japan, where rates of violent and property crime are among the lowest in the world.

Elliott Currie (1985) suggests that crime stems from our culture's emphasis on individual economic success, often at the expense of strong families and neighborhoods. The United States also has extraordinary cultural diversity, resulting from centuries of immigration, which can weaken community ties. Moreover, economic inequality can have the same effect, and it is higher in this country than in most other high-income nations. Thus, our society's relatively weak social fabric, combined with frustration among the have-nots, generates a large amount of criminal behavior.

Another contributing factor to violence in the United States is extensive private ownership of guns. About two-thirds of murder victims in the United States die from shootings. Since the early 1990s, in Texas and several other southern states shooting deaths have exceeded automobile-related fatalities. As Figure 8–3 shows, the United States is the runaway leader in handgun deaths among high-income nations.

Surveys suggest that almost half of U.S. households own at least one gun (J. Wright, 1995; NORC, 2001). Put differently, there are as many guns as there are adults in this country, and one-third of these weapons are handguns that figure in violent crime. In large part, gun ownership reflects people's fear of crime, yet easy availability of guns in this country also makes crime more deadly.

But as critics of gun control point out, waiting periods and background checks at retail gun stores (mandated by the 1993 "Brady bill") do not keep guns out of the hands of criminals, who almost always obtain guns

Americans (Sampson, 1987; Courtwright, 1996; Jacobs & Helms, 1996; U.S. Census Bureau, 2001).

Fourth, remember that the official crime index excludes arrests for offenses ranging from drunk driving to white-collar violations. This omission contributes to the view of the typical criminal as a person of color. If we broaden our definition of crime to include driving while intoxicated, business fraud, embezzlement, and cheating on income tax returns, the proportion of white criminals rises dramatically.

Finally, some categories of the population have unusually low rates of arrest. People of Asian descent, who account for about 4 percent of the population, figure in only 1.2 percent of all arrests. As Chapter 14 ("Race and Ethnicity") documents,

Here is a government report on racial differences in violent crime victimization: http://www.ojp.usdoj.gov/bjs/abstract/vvr98.htm

SOCIAL SURVEY: "Do you think the use of marijuana should be made legal or not?" (GSS 2000, N = 1,896; Codebook, 2001:124) "Should" 31.5%   "Should not" 62.4%   DK/NR 6.1%

DIVERSITY: The U.S. average is 25 police officers per 10,000 people. By state, the top 3 are Washington, D.C., 68; New York, 40; and Louisiana, 39. The lowest are South Dakota, 16; and Washington and Oregon, both at 17. Washington, D.C., with the highest

police ratio, also has the highest homicide rate, suggesting that police cannot effectively control crime by themselves.

DIVERSITY: Although varying by jurisdiction, women make up about 17% of U.S. police officers and detectives; African Americans (men and women) represent about 19%, and Latinos about 8% (U.S. Department of Labor, 2001).

illegally (J. Wright, 1995). Moreover, we should be cautious about seeing gun control as the magic bullet in the war on crime. Elliott Currie (1985) notes that the number of Californians killed each year by knives alone exceeds the number of Canadians killed by weapons of all kinds. However, most experts think that gun control would lower the level of deadly violence.

Crime rates are soaring in some of the largest cities of the world, including Manila in the Philippines and São Paulo, Brazil, where rapid population growth has produced millions of desperately poor people. Outside such cities, however, the traditional character of low-income societies and their strong family structure allow local communities to control crime informally (Clinard & Abbott, 1973; Der Spiegel, 1989).

Some kinds of crime have always been multinational, such as terrorism, espionage, and arms dealing (Martin & Romano, 1992). But, today, the "globalization" we are experiencing on many fronts also extends to crime. A recent case in point is the illegal drug trade. In part, the problem of illegal drugs in the United States is a "demand" issue. That is, there is a high demand for cocaine and other drugs in this country, and legions of young people risk arrest or even violent death to take part in the lucrative drug trade. But the "supply" side of the issue is just as important. In the South American nation of Colombia, at least 20 percent of the people depend on cocaine production for their livelihood. Furthermore, not only is cocaine Colombia's most profitable export, but it outsells all other exports—including coffee—combined. Clearly, then, understanding global crime such as drug dealing means understanding social and economic conditions both in this country and elsewhere.

Countries have different strategies for dealing with crime. The use of the death penalty is an example. Global Map 8–1 on page 212 identifies countries that use capital punishment in response to crime and those that do not. The global trend is toward abolition of the death penalty: Amnesty International (2001) reports that since 1976 more than fifty nations have ended this practice entirely.

THE CRIMINAL JUSTICE SYSTEM

December 10, Casablanca, Morocco. Casablanca! An exciting mix of African, European, and Middle Eastern cultures. Returning from a stroll through the medina, the medieval section of this coastal north African city, we confront lines of police along a boulevard, standing between us and our ship in the harbor. The police are providing security for many important leaders attending an Islamic conference in a nearby hotel. Are the streets closed? No one asks; people seem to observe an invisible line some fifty feet from the police officers. I play the brash urbanite and start across the street to inquire (in broken French) whether we can pass by, but I stop cold as several officers draw a bead on me with their eyes. Their fingers nervously tap at the grips on their automatic weapons. This is no time to strike up a conversation.

The criminal justice system is a society's formal system of social control. In some of the world's countries, military police keep a tight rein on people's behavior; in others, including the United States, police have more limited powers and only respond to specific violations of criminal law. We shall briefly introduce the major components of the criminal justice system: police, the courts, and the punishment of convicted offenders.

POLICE

The police are the primary point of contact between the population and the criminal justice system. In the United States, unlike many other countries, police are responsive and accountable to citizens (Bayley, 1998). Of course, there is only so much the 654,601 full-time police officers in the United States (in 2000) can do to monitor the activities of 281 million people. As a result, the police must exercise a high degree of discretion about which situations warrant their attention and how to handle them.

How do police carry out their duties? In a study of police behavior in five cities, Douglas Smith and Christy Visher (1981; Smith, 1987) concluded that because they must respond swiftly, police quickly size up a situation in terms of six factors. First, *how serious is the alleged crime?* The more serious police consider the situation, the more likely they are to make an arrest. Second, *what is the victim's preference?* Generally, if a victim demands that police make an arrest, they are likely to do so. Third, *is the suspect cooperative or not?* Resisting the police increases a suspect's chances of arrest. Fourth, *have they arrested the suspect before?* Police are more likely to take into custody

GLOBAL: China executes more people than the rest of the world combined; the death penalty can be applied for minor offenses such as tax evasion. The current practice is to execute offenders minutes after their convictions and then to harvest their organs before cremating the body (Smith, 2001).

GLOBAL: In France, the guillotine was used from 1791 until 1977; in 1981, France abolished the death penalty.

GLOBAL: Fewer than half the world's nations have a death penalty. According to Amnesty International, the largest number of executions of criminals occurs in these nations: P.R. China, Saudi Arabia, Nigeria, and Kazakhstan. The U.S. and Japan are the only high-income nations that retain the death penalty.

NOTE: The last public execution in England took place in 1868.

WINDOW ON THE WORLD

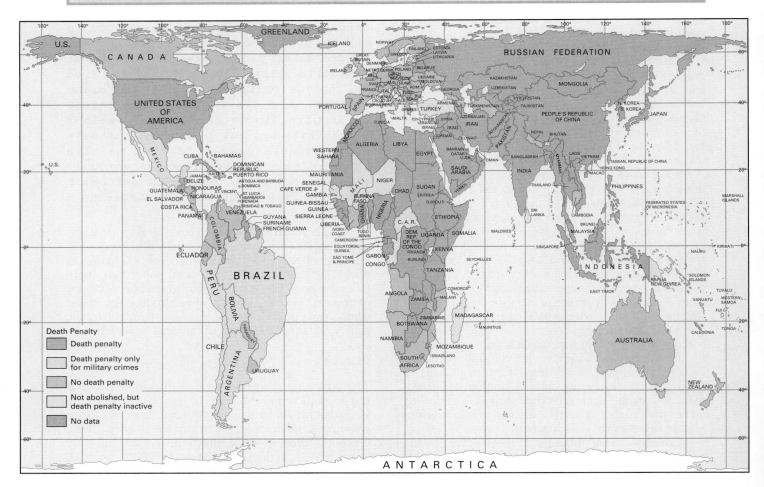

GLOBAL MAP 8–1 Capital Punishment in Global Perspective

The map identifies eighty-six countries and territories in which the law provides for the death penalty for ordinary crimes; in fourteen more, the death penalty is reserved for exceptional crimes under military law or during times of war. The death penalty does not exist in seventy-five countries and territories; in twenty more, although the death penalty remains in law, no execution has taken place in more than a decade. Compare rich and poor nations: What general pattern do you see? In what way do the United States and Japan stand out?

Source: Amnesty International Website against the Death Penalty, http://www.web.amnesty.org/ Accessed September 20, 2001.

NOTE: Of 6.3 million U.S. adults in the criminal justice system, 60% are on probation, 20% are in prison, 11% are on parole, and 9% are in local jails (U.S. Bureau of Justice Statistics, 2000).
DISCUSS: Consider the divergent reactions to the O.J. Simpson acquittal: Most whites were stunned, most blacks were elated. How and why does race shape our views of the criminal justice system?
GLOBAL: The U.S. incarceration rate is the world's highest.

THEN AND NOW: Retribution is evident in virtually all ancient codes of law. The Latin concept *lex talionis* refers to the "law of retaliation" by which an offender's punishment fits the crime.
NOTE: In 1999, California had more people incarcerated than all of Europe.
Q: "To be good is noble. To tell people how to be good is even nobler, and much less trouble." Mark Twain

someone they have arrested before, presumably because previous arrest suggests guilt. Fifth, *are bystanders present?* Smith and Visher claim that the presence of observers prompts police to take stronger control of a situation, if only to move the encounter from the street (the suspect's turf) to the police department (where law officers have the edge). Sixth, *what is the suspect's race?* All else being equal, Smith and Visher contend, police are more likely to arrest people of color than whites, perceiving suspects of African or Hispanic descent as either more dangerous or more likely to be guilty.

COURTS

After arrest, a court determines a suspect's guilt or innocence. In principle, our courts rely on an adversarial process involving attorneys—one representing the defendant and another the state—in the presence of a judge, who monitors legal procedures.

In practice, however, about 90 percent of criminal cases are resolved prior to court appearance through **plea bargaining,** *a legal negotiation in which a prosecutor reduces a charge in exchange for a defendant's guilty plea.* For example, the state may offer a defendant charged with burglary a lesser charge of possessing burglary tools in exchange for a guilty plea.

Plea bargaining is widespread because it spares the state the time and expense of court trials. A trial is unnecessary if there is little disagreement as to the facts of the case. Moreover, because the annual number of cases entering the system has doubled over the last decade, prosecutors could not possibly bring every case to trial. By quickly resolving most of their work, the courts channel their resources into the most important cases.

But plea bargaining pressures defendants (who are presumed innocent) to plead guilty. A person can exercise the right to a trial, but only at the risk of receiving a more severe sentence if found guilty. Furthermore, low-income defendants enter the process with the guidance of a public defender: an attorney, often underpaid, who may devote little time to even a serious case (Novak, 1999). Overall, plea bargaining may be efficient, but it compromises the adversarial process as well as the rights of some defendants.

PUNISHMENT

When a young girl is murdered—as in the case described in the opening to this chapter—some people may wonder why, but almost everyone believes that someone should have to pay for the crime. Indeed,

During the 1990s, the United States built prisons at an unprecedented rate. There are now almost twice as many people in jail—2 million—than there were in 1990. The public's "get tough with criminals" attitude has also led to the spread of "road gangs"—a return of the "chain gangs" common in the early decades of the twentieth century. As some see it, putting criminals to work along busy highways reminds the public of the consequences of law-breaking.

sometimes the desire to punish an offender is so great that justice is lost.

Such cases force us to ask why a society should punish its wrongdoers. Over many years, scholars have pointed to four basic reasons to punish: retribution, deterrence, rehabilitation, and societal protection.

Retribution

The oldest justification for punishment is the public's craving for revenge. Knowing the power of this passion, U.S. Supreme Court justice Oliver Wendell Holmes stated that "the law has no choice but to satisfy [that] craving" (quoted in Carlson, 1976).

The first reason to punish, then, is to satisfy a society's need for **retribution,** *an act of moral vengeance by which society inflicts suffering on an offender comparable to that caused by the offense.* Retribution rests on a view of society as a moral balance. When criminality upsets this balance, punishment exacted in comparable measure

DIVERSITY: The proportion of men ages 20 to 39 behind bars, according to the U.S. Bureau of Justice Statistics (2000), is: white, 1 in 65; Hispanic, 1 in 25; African American, 1 in 9.
SOCIAL SURVEY: "Do you favor or oppose the death penalty for persons convicted of murder?" (GSS 2000, N = 2,817; *Codebook*, 2001:119)
"Favor" 62.6%   "Oppose" 28.4%   DK/NR 8.9%

NOTE: Gun control advocates suggest that the presence of guns encourages deadly behavior, a view critics describe as the "trigger pulls the finger" hypothesis.
RESOURCE: Elijah Anderson's "The Code of the Streets" is included in the Macionis and Benokraitis reader, *Seeing Ourselves*.
Q: "I'm the one who has to die when it's time for me to die; so let me live my life the way I want to." Jimi Hendrix

GLOBAL SNAPSHOT

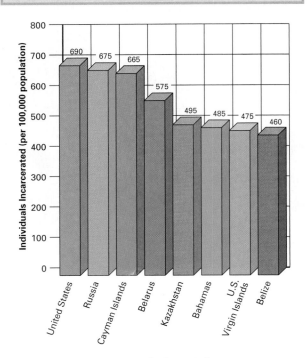

FIGURE 8–4 Nations with the Highest Incarceration Rates, 2000

Source: Walmsley (2000).

restores the moral order, as suggested in the biblical dictum "An eye for an eye."

During the Middle Ages, most people viewed crime as a sin—an offense against God as well as society—that warranted a harsh response. Today, although critics point out that retribution does little to reform the offender, many people consider vengeance reason enough for punishment.

Deterrence

A second justification for punishment is **deterrence,** *the use of punishment to discourage criminality.* Deterrence is based on the eighteenth-century Enlightenment idea that humans are calculating and rational creatures who will not break the law if they think that the pain of punishment will outweigh the pleasure of crime.

Deterrence emerged as reform in response to the harsh punishments based on retribution. Why put someone to death for stealing, reformists reasoned, if theft can be discouraged with a prison sentence? As the concept of deterrence gained widespread acceptance, execution and physical mutilation of criminals in most industrial societies were replaced by milder forms of punishment such as imprisonment.

Punishment can deter in two ways. *Specific deterrence* convinces an individual offender that crime does not pay. Through *general deterrence*, the punishment of one person serves as an example to others.

Rehabilitation

The third justification for punishment is **rehabilitation,** *a program for reforming the offender to prevent subsequent offenses.* Rehabilitation arose along with the social sciences in the nineteenth century. Sociologists of that time (and also since) saw crime and other deviance springing from a social environment marked by poverty or a lack of parental supervision. Logically, then, if offenders learn to be deviant, they can also learn to obey the rules; the key is controlling the environment. *Reformatories* or *houses of correction* provided controlled settings where people could learn proper behavior (recall the description of total institutions in Chapter 5, "Socialization").

Like deterrence, rehabilitation motivates the offender to conform. But rehabilitation emphasizes constructive improvement, whereas deterrence and retribution make the offender suffer. In addition, where retribution demands that the punishment fit the crime, rehabilitation tailors treatment to each offender. Thus, identical crimes would prompt similar acts of retribution but might call for different rehabilitation programs.

Societal Protection

A final justification for punishment is **societal protection,** *a means by which society renders an offender incapable of further offenses temporarily through incarceration or permanently by execution.* Like deterrence, societal protection is a rational approach to punishment intended to protect society from crime.

Currently, 2 million people are incarcerated in the United States, and another 4.5 million are on parole or probation. In response to tougher public attitudes and an increasing number of arrests for drug offenses, the U.S. prison population has tripled since 1980. The size of inmate populations is going up in most high-income countries, yet as Figure 8–4 shows, the

United States incarcerates a larger share of its population than all other countries in the world (Sutton, 2000; Walmsley, 2000).

Critical evaluation. Table 8–2 summarizes the four justifications for punishment. Assessing the actual consequences of punishment, however, is no simple task.

The value of retribution lies in Durkheim's contention that punishing the deviant person increases people's moral awareness. Appropriately, then, punishment traditionally was carried out in public. Although the last public execution in the United States took place in Kentucky in 1937, today's mass media ensure that the population is aware of executions carried out within prison walls (Kittrie, 1971).

Certainly, punishment deters some crime. Yet our society also has a high rate of **criminal recidivism,** *subsequent offenses by people convicted of crimes.* About three-fourths of state prisoners have been jailed before and, once released, about half will be back in prison within a few years (McNulty, 1994; Petersilia, 1997). In light of such patterns, we may well wonder about the extent to which punishment really deters crime. Furthermore, only about one-third of all crimes are known to police, and only about one in five of these crimes results in an arrest. The adage "Crime doesn't pay" rings hollow when we consider that only a small share of offenses are ever punished.

General deterrence is even harder to investigate scientifically because we have no way of knowing how people might act if they were unaware of punishments given to others. In the debate over capital punishment, opponents point to research suggesting that the death penalty has limited value as a general deterrent. Moreover, the United States is the only Western, high-income society that routinely executes offenders. Even more troubling is the fact that some death sentences turn out to be flawed as noted at the beginning of this chapter, and since 1973, eighty-seven people have been released from death row, which amounts to putting the death penalty itself on trial (Sellin, 1980; van den Haag & Conrad, 1983; Archer & Gartner, 1987; Lester, 1987; Bailey & Peterson, 1989; Bailey, 1990; Bohm, 1991; Tanber, 1998; Alter, 2000). National Map 8–2 on page 216 identifies the thirty-eight states that have the death penalty and shows that half the prisoners on death row are in just five of these states.

Prisons provide short-term societal protection by keeping offenders off the streets, but they do little to reshape attitudes or behavior in the long term (Carlson, 1976; Wright, 1994). Perhaps rehabilitation is an unrealistic expectation because, according

TABLE 8–2	Four Justifications for Punishment: A Summary
Retribution	The oldest justification for punishment. Punishment is atonement for a moral wrong; in principle, punishment should be comparable in severity to the deviance itself.
Deterrence	An early modern approach. Deviance is considered social disruption, which society acts to control. People are viewed as rational and self-interested; deterrence works because the pains of punishment outweigh the pleasures of deviance.
Rehabilitation	A modern strategy linked to the development of social sciences. Deviance is viewed as the product of social problems (such as poverty) or personal problems (such as mental illness). Social conditions are improved; treatment is tailored to the offender's condition.
Societal Protection	A modern approach easier to implement than rehabilitation. If society is unable or unwilling to rehabilitate offenders or reform social conditions, people are protected by incarcerating or executing the offender.

to Sutherland's theory of differential association, locking up criminals together for years probably

 Rape in prison is an old problem that is gaining more attention. To read a report on prison rape by the activist organization Human Rights Watch, go to http://www.hrw.org/reports/2001/prison/

strengthens criminal attitudes and skills. Incarceration also severs whatever social ties inmates may have to the outside world, which, following Hirschi's control theory, leaves them likely to commit more crimes upon their release.

Finally, the stigma of being an ex-convict can be a powerful barrier to building a new life. One study of young offenders in Philadelphia found that boys who were sentenced to long prison terms—and thus were likely to acquire a criminal stigma—went on to commit both more crimes and more serious ones when released (Wolfgang, Figlio, & Sellin, 1972).

Ultimately, we should never assume that the criminal justice system can eliminate crime. As the box on page 217 explains, police, courts, and prisons have played a part in the recent downturn in crime rates. But more is involved. As this chapter has described, crime and other deviance result not just from the acts of "bad people" but from the operation of society itself.

THE MAP: In general, the "execution belt" of the U.S. extends across the southern half of the country; this region is characterized by more conservative political opinions.

DISCUSS: Between 1977 and 2000, 6,588 people were sentenced to death; 683 were executed. Does this make the death penalty an "arbitrary lottery," as opponents claim, or a filter reserving death for only the worst offenders, as supporters claim?

NOTE: The minimum age at which an offender can be put to death is now effectively 16, based on the Supreme Court's decision in *Thompson v. Oklahoma* (June 1988). The essential issue is how old a person has to be to be consciously evil and act accordingly.

NOTE: Fifteen states have laws banning the execution of people considered to be mentally retarded; in 2001, Texas governor Rick Perry vetoed such a bill.

SEEING OURSELVES

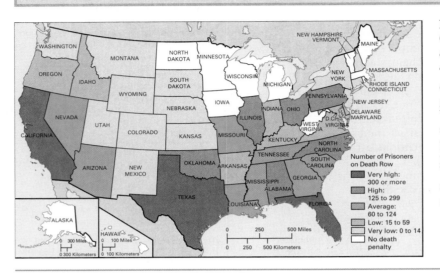

NATIONAL MAP 8–2
Capital Punishment across the United States

The United States and Japan are the only high-income nations in which the government imposes the death penalty. Yet within the United States, the fifty states have broadly divergent capital punishment laws: Half of the 3,527 prisoners on death row are in five states. What regional pattern do you see in the map? Can you account for this pattern?

Source: U.S. Bureau of Justice Statistics (2000).

SUMMARY

1. *Deviance* refers to norm violations ranging from mild breaches of etiquette to serious violence.

2. Biological research, from Caesare Lombroso's nineteenth-century observations of convicts to recent research in human genetics, has not offered much insight into the causes of deviance.

3. Psychological study links deviance to abnormal personality resulting from either biological or environmental causes. Psychological theories help explain some kinds of deviance.

4. Deviance has societal rather than individual roots because it (a) varies according to cultural norms, (b) is socially defined, and (c) reflects patterns of social power.

5. Using the structural-functional paradigm, Durkheim explained that deviance affirms norms and values, clarifies moral boundaries, promotes social unity, and encourages social change.

6. The symbolic-interaction paradigm is the basis of labeling theory, which holds that deviance lies in people's reaction to a person's behavior, not in the behavior itself. Acquiring a stigma of deviance can lead to secondary deviance and a deviant career.

7. Based on Karl Marx's ideas, social-conflict theory holds that laws and other norms reflect the interests of powerful members of society. Although white-collar and corporate crime cause extensive social harm, offenders rarely are branded as criminals.

8. Official statistics indicate that arrest rates peak in late adolescence, then drop steadily with advancing age. Seventy percent of those arrested for property crimes and 83 percent of those arrested for violent crimes are male.

9. People of lower social position commit more street crime than people with greater social privilege. When white-collar and corporate crimes are included among criminal offenses, however, the disparity in overall criminal activity goes down.

10. More whites than African Americans are arrested for street crimes. However, African Americans are arrested more often than whites in proportion to their respective populations. Asian Americans have lower-than-average rates of arrest.

11. Police exercise a great deal of discretion in their work. Arrest is more likely if the offense is serious, bystanders are present, or the accused is African American or Hispanic.

NOTE: The 683 executions between 1977 and 2000, by method: Lethal injection, 518; electrocution, 149; gas chamber, 11; hanging, 3; firing squad, 2.
DISCUSS: Does the increasing use of lethal injection illustrate the "medicalization of death"? Some oppose this practice because it involves less evident suffering; others approve of it as humane; still others object to any form of capital punishment.

DISCUSS: The moratorium on executions in the U.S. from 1967 to 1977 was based partly on evidence that black offenders were more likely to be put to death than white offenders. In recent years, evidence suggests that a racial bias may now work against white offenders (cf. Langbein, 1999).
Q: "The fundamental sociological problem is not crime but the law." Peter Berger (1963:37)

APPLYING SOCIOLOGY

Violent Crime Is Down—But Why?

During the 1980s, crime rates shot upward. Just about everyone lived in fear of violent crime, and in many larger cities, the numbers killed and wounded turned whole neighborhoods into war zones. There seemed to be no solution to the problem.

Then, in the 1990s, something good and unexpected happened: Serious crime rates began to fall until, by 2000, they were at levels not seen in more than a generation. Why? Applying the perspectives and theories presented in this chapter, we can identify several reasons:

1. **A reduction in the youth population.** We have already noted that young people (particularly males) are responsible for much violent crime. Between 1990 and 2000, the share of the population aged fifteen to twenty-four dropped by about 5 percent (in part because abortion was legalized in 1973), presumably making a modest contribution to the decline in serious crime.

2. **Changes in policing.** Much of the drop in crime (and the earlier rise in crime) has taken place in large cities. New York City, where the number of murders fell from 2,245 in 1990 to just 673 in 2000, has adopted a policy of *community policing*, which means that police are concerned not just with making arrests but with preventing crime before it happens. Officers get to know the areas they patrol and stop young men for jaywalking or other minor infractions to check them for concealed weapons (the word has gotten around that you risk arrest for carrying a gun). Moreover, there are *more* police at work in large cities. For example, Los Angeles added more than 2,000 police during the 1990s, and it, too, has seen its violent crime rate fall.

3. **More prisons.** From 1985 until 2000, the number of inmates in U.S. jails and prisons soared from 750,000 to 2 million. The main reason for this increase is tough laws that demand prison time for many crimes, especially drug offenses. As one analyst put it, "When you lock up an extra million people, it's got to have some effect on the crime rate" (Zimring, cited in Witkin, 1998:31).

4. **A better economy.** The U.S. economy has boomed during the last ten years. With unemployment down, more people are working, which reduces the likelihood that some will turn to crime out of economic desperation. The logic here is simple: More jobs, fewer crimes. However, as the economy weakened after 2000, reductions in crime have also slowed.

5. **The declining drug trade.** Many analysts agree that the most important factor in reducing violent crime rates is the decline of crack cocaine. Crack came on the scene about 1985, and violence spread as young people—especially in the inner cities and increasingly armed with guns—became part of a booming drug trade. With legitimate job opportunities low and rising opportunity to make money illegally, a generation of young people became part of a wave of violence. Widespread crack cocaine use also explains the trend, noted earlier, of the younger age of violent criminals.

By the early 1990s, however, the popularity of crack began to fall as people saw the damage it was causing to entire communities. This realization, coupled with steady improvement in the economy and stiffer sentences for drug offenses, brought the turnaround in violent crime.

Keep in mind that the current picture looks better compared with what it was a decade ago. The crime problem, says one researcher, "looks better, but only because the early 1990s were so bad. So let's not fool ourselves into thinking everything is resolved. It's not."

Sources: Based on Boggess & Bound (1997), Blumstein & Rosenfeld (1998), Fagan, Zimring, & Kim (1998), Witkin (1998), Winship & Berrien (1999), and Donahue & Leavitt (2000).

12. In the United States, most prosecutions of criminal cases never go to trial but are resolved through the process of plea bargaining. Though efficient, it is widely believed that this method puts less powerful people at a disadvantage.

13. Justifications of punishment include retribution, deterrence, rehabilitation, and societal protection. Because its consequences are difficult to evaluate scientifically, punishment—like deviance itself—sparks controversy among sociologists and the public as a whole.

CTQ1: The general theme of this chapter is that deviance is the creation of society, not the result of individual choices.
CTQ2: Durkheim suggested that no society could be free from deviance because deviance is a necessary element of social organization that generates social cohesion.
CTQ3: From a labeling perspective, situations defined as real may well become real in their consequences.

CTQ4: A number of factors are involved, including higher rates of poverty and racial discrimination (emphasized by liberals) and higher rates of single parenting (highlighted by conservatives).
EXERCISE: Students might investigate the rise in cheating on campus, which seems to be linked to use of materials from the Internet. Computer technology is also making it easier to catch cheaters.

KEY CONCEPTS

deviance (p. 191) the recognized violation of cultural norms

crime (p. 191) the violation of a society's formally enacted criminal law

social control (p. 192) attempts by society to regulate people's thought and behavior

criminal justice system (p. 192) a formal response by police, courts, and prison officials to alleged violations of the law

labeling theory (p. 197) the assertion that deviance and conformity result not so much from what people do as from how others respond to those actions

stigma (p. 198) a powerfully negative label that greatly changes a person's self-concept and social identity

medicalization of deviance (p. 199) the transformation of moral and legal deviance into a medical condition

white-collar crime (p. 202) crime committed by people of high social position in the course of their occupations

corporate crime (p. 203) the illegal actions of a corporation or people acting on its behalf

organized crime (p. 203) a business supplying illegal goods or services

hate crime (p. 204) a criminal act against a person or person's property by an offender motivated by racial or other bias

crimes against the person (p. 206) (violent crimes) crimes that direct violence or the threat of violence against others

crimes against property (p. 206) (property crimes) crimes that involve theft of property belonging to others

victimless crimes (p. 207) violations of law in which there are no readily apparent victims

plea bargaining (p. 213) a legal negotiation in which a prosecutor reduces a charge in exchange for a defendant's guilty plea

retribution (p. 213) an act of moral vengeance by which society inflicts suffering on an offender comparable to that caused by the offense

deterrence (p. 214) the use of punishment to discourage criminality

rehabilitation (p. 214) a program for reforming the offender to prevent subsequent offenses

societal protection (p. 214) a means by which society renders an offender incapable of further offenses temporarily through incarceration or permanently by execution

criminal recidivism (p. 215) subsequent offenses by people convicted of crimes

CRITICAL-THINKING QUESTIONS

1. How does a sociological view of deviance differ from the common-sense notion that bad people do bad things?

2. List Durkheim's functions of deviance. From his point of view, can society ever be free from deviance? Why or why not?

3. You probably have heard the old saying, "Sticks and stones can break my bones, but names can never hurt me." Explain how labeling theory challenges this statement.

4. A recent study found that one in three black men between the ages of twenty and twenty-nine is in jail, on probation, or on parole (The Sentencing Project, 2000). What factors noted in this chapter help explain this pattern?

APPLICATIONS AND EXERCISES

1. Research computer crime. What new kinds of crime are emerging in the information age? Is computer technology also generating new ways to track lawbreakers?

2. Rent a wheelchair (check with a local pharmacy or medical supply store) and use it as much as possible for a day or two. Not only will you gain a firsthand understanding of the physical barriers to getting

EXERCISE: Study the rapid increase in maximum security prisons: There were 36 in 31 states by the beginning of 1999. These expensive facilities hold the most violent offenders, typically isolating them for 23 hours a day. Critics (and some wardens) claim these prisons cause marked psychological stress.

Q: "The inescapable conclusion is that society secretly wants crime and needs crime." Karl Menninger, *The Crime of Punishment*

RESOURCE: David Rosenhan writes "On Being Sane in Insane Places" in the Macionis and Benokraitis reader, *Seeing Ourselves.*

RESOURCE: Good illustrations of how crime functions to reaffirm norms and increase social unity are found in Truman Capote's *In Cold Blood* (Signet, 1965); see especially pp. 279–80.

Q: "There is so much good in the worst of us, and so much bad in the best of us." Anonymous

around, but you will also discover that people respond to you in many different ways.

3. Watch an episode of the real-action police show *COPS*. Based on this program, how would you profile the people who commit crimes?

4. Packaged in the back of this new textbook is an interactive CD-ROM that offers a variety of study and review materials intended to help you better understand the material covered in this chapter. For this chapter, the CD-ROM contains an author's tip video, Real Life Sociology videos, other relevant audio and video, interactive map animations, audio journal entries from the author, Web links, and much more.

SITES TO SEE

http://www.prenhall.com/macionis

Visit the interactive *Companion Website*™ that accompanies this text. Begin by clicking on the cover of your book. You will find a chapter-by-chapter study guide, practice tests, and a significant portion of the text for on-line review, as well as many suggested Web links.

http://www.telalink.net/~police/risk/

Visit this site, run by the Nashville Police Department, that rates your chances of becoming a victim of a serious crime.

http://www.civilrights.org/

The Leadership Conference on Civil Rights maintains this site on hate crimes and other civil rights issues.

http://www.igc.apc.org/spr/

The organization Stop Prisoner Rape hosts this site dealing with the problem of rape in U.S. prisons.

http://www.ncadp.org
http://www.uaa.alaska.edu/just/death/intl.html

These sites provide information on the death penalty. The first presents the views of the National Coalition to Abolish the Death Penalty. The second provides data on the death penalty in global perspective.

http://www.cybercrime.gov

This site, operated by the U.S. Department of Justice, provides a great deal of information on computer crime and intellectual property issues.

http://www.crime.com/info/jailcam_redirect.html

This site provides live video coverage inside the Maricopa County, Arizona, jail.

INVESTIGATE WITH CONTENTSELECT

Follow the instructions found on page 23 of this textbook to enter this chapter of the book's *Companion Website*™. Once in the chapter, click on the ContentSelect icon at the bottom left of your screen and enter your personal User ID and Password. Enter keywords such as "crime," "murder," "prisons," and "cyber-crime," and the search engine will help you become an effective researcher.

CHAPTER

9

Andy Warhol
Marilyn, 1967
© 2001 Andy Warhol Foundation for the Visual Arts/Artists Rights Society (ARS), New York. Tate Gallery, London/Art Resource, N.Y.

SEXUALITY

It was a typical autumn day in Sacramento, California, and students were buzzing as they returned to Center High School for the beginning of classes. Large groups of young people moved together down the hallways as young men and women exchanged stories about summer vacation and caught up with friends. But one story dominated the discussion: the return of teacher David Warfield, who, over the summer, changed his sex from being a man to being a woman and adopted the new name Dana Rivers.

Warfield, who had taught at Center High for almost ten years, was a popular, award-winning journalism teacher who also served as announcer for the school's football games. The previous year, he had informed school officials of his "gender dysphoria," a medical condition

whereby he was physically a man but felt himself to be a woman. This condition went back to his childhood, he explained. As much as he had tried to "be a man," he just couldn't do it. Warfield had already begun hormone treatments and planned to undergo a sex-change operation to become a woman within the following year.

School board officials were uneasy about Warfield's plan. They insisted that upon returning to classes in the fall she not share any details about her operation or transformation. However, Rivers discussed her change with a number of students, leading several parents to file complaints. The incident divided the school community between those who supported and those who opposed keeping Rivers as a teacher. Soon after, the school board fired Rivers (Hornblower, 1999).

One thing that is clear about the Dana Rivers case is that in U.S. society, sexuality is an important—and controversial—issue. It is also clear that many young people, and a number of their parents, understand too little about sexuality. This chapter presents some of what researchers have learned about human sexuality. From a sociological point of view, our main concern is how society defines sexuality and how people sexually express themselves.

UNDERSTANDING SEXUALITY

How much of the day goes by without your giving any thought at all to sexuality? If you are like most people, the answer is "not very much." That is because sexuality is not just about "having sex." Sexuality is a theme found throughout society and apparent on campus, in

the workplace, and especially in the mass media. In addition, the sex industry—including pornography and prostitution—is a multibillion-dollar business in its own right. As Dana Rivers's story shows us, sexuality is an important part of how we think about ourselves and how others evaluate us. In truth, there are few areas of life in which sexuality does *not* play some part.

But despite its importance, few people understand sexuality. Through much of our history, sex has been a cultural taboo so that, at least in polite conversation, people do not talk about it. As a result, although sex can produce much pleasure, it also causes confusion and sometimes outright fear. Even scientists long considered sex off limits as a research topic. It was not until the mid-twentieth century that researchers turned their attention to this vital dimension of social life. Since then, as this chapter reports, we have learned a great deal about human sexuality.

SUPPLEMENTS: An outline of this chapter, supplementary lecture material, and suggested discussion topics are found in the *Data File*.
Q: "Human beings are the only living creatures who blush—or need to." Mark Twain

NOTE: The ratio of male to female fetuses is actually higher than 105/100 because male embryos are more likely to abort spontaneously than female embryos are. This further complicates the issue of which is the "weaker" sex.

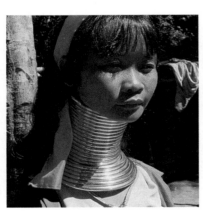

We claim that beauty is in the eye of the beholder, which suggests the importance of culture in setting standards of attractiveness. All of the people pictured here—from Morocco, South Africa, Nigeria, Myanmar (Burma), Japan, and Ecuador—are beautiful to members of their own society. At the same time, sociobiologists point out that, in every society on Earth, people are attracted to youthfulness. The reason is that, as sociobiologists see it, attractiveness underlies our choices about reproduction, which is most readily accomplished in early adulthood.

SEX: A BIOLOGICAL ISSUE

Sex is *the biological distinction between females and males.* From a biological point of view, sex is the means by which humans reproduce. A female ovum and a male sperm, each containing twenty-three chromosomes (biological codes that guide physical development), combine to form a fertilized embryo. One of these pairs of chromosomes determines the child's sex. To this pair the mother contributes an X chromosome and the father contributes either an X or a Y. An X chromosome from the father combines with the mother's X to produce a female (XX) embryo; a Y from the father produces a male (XY) embryo. Thus, a child's sex is determined biologically at the moment of conception.

Within weeks, the sex of an embryo starts to guide its development. If the embryo is male, testicular tissue starts to produce testosterone, a hormone that triggers the development of male genitals. If no testosterone is present, the embryo develops female genitals. In the United States, about 105 boys are born for every 100 girls, but a higher death rate among males reverses this trend and makes females a slight majority by the time people reach their mid-thirties (U.S. National Center for Health Statistics, 2001).

SEX AND THE BODY

What sets females and males apart are differences in the body. Right from birth, the two sexes have different **primary sex characteristics,** namely, *the genitals, organs used for reproduction.* At puberty, as people reach sexual maturity, additional sex differentiation takes place. At this point, people develop **secondary sex characteristics,** *bodily development apart from the genitals, that distinguishes biologically mature females and males.* To allow for pregnancy, childbirth, and breast feeding, mature females have wider hips, breasts, and soft fatty tissue that provides a reserve supply of nutrition. Mature males typically develop more muscle in the upper body, more extensive body hair, and deeper voices. Of course, these are general differences: Some males are smaller and have less body hair and higher voices than some females.

Hermaphrodites

Sex is not always as clear-cut as we have just described. In rare cases, a hormone imbalance before birth produces a **hermaphrodite** (a word derived from Hermaphroditus, the offspring of the mythological Greek gods Hermes and Aphrodite, who embodied both sexes), *a human being with some combination of female and male genitalia.*

Because our culture is uneasy about sexual ambiguity, some people respond to hermaphrodites with confusion or even disgust. But other cultures lead people to respond quite differently. For example, the Pokot of eastern Africa pay little attention to what they consider a simple biological error, and the Navajo look on hermaphrodites with awe, seeing in them the full potential of both the female and the male (Geertz, 1975).

Transsexuals

Some hermaphrodites undergo genital surgery to appear (and occasionally function as) a sexually normal female or male. Other people deliberately change their sex: **Transsexuals** are *people who feel they are one sex even though biologically they are the other.* This was the case with Dana Rivers. In fact, tens of thousands of people in the United States feel trapped in a body of the wrong sex. Most become *transgendered,* meaning that they begin to disregard conventional ideas about how females and males should look and behave. Many go one step further and become transsexuals by surgically altering their genitals (Tewksbury & Gagné, 1996; Gagné, Tewksbury, & McGaughey, 1997).

Like so many elements of our lives, notions about kissing vary from place to place. The Maori people of New Zealand rub noses to show affection.

SEX: A CULTURAL ISSUE

Sexuality has a biological foundation. But like all dimensions of human behavior, sexuality is also very much a cultural issue. Biology is sufficient to explain the fascinating mating rituals of the animal world, but humans have no similar biological program. That is, humans have a biological "sex drive" in the sense that they find sex pleasurable and want to engage in sexual activity, but our biology does not dictate any specific way of being sexual any more than our desire to eat dictates any particular foods or table manners.

Cultural Variation

Almost any sexual practice shows wide variation from one society to another. In his pioneering study of sexuality in the United States, Alfred Kinsey (1948) found that most couples in the United States reported having intercourse in a single position: face to face, with the woman on the bottom and the man on top. Halfway around the world, in the South Seas, most couples *never* have sex in this way. In fact, when the people of the South Seas learned of this practice from Western missionaries, they poked fun at it as the strange "missionary position."

Even the simple practice of showing affection has extensive cultural variation. Whereas most people in the United States readily kiss in public, the Chinese kiss only in private. The French kiss publicly, often twice (once on each cheek), and Belgians kiss three times (starting on either cheek). The Maoris of New Zealand rub noses, and most people in Nigeria don't kiss at all.

Modesty also is a culturally variable matter. If a woman entering a bath is disturbed, what body parts does she cover? Helen Colton (1983) reports that an Islamic woman covers her face, a Laotian woman covers her breasts, a Samoan woman her navel, a Sumatran woman her knees, and a European woman covers her breasts with one hand and her genital area with the other.

Around the world, some societies tend to restrict sexuality, and others are more permissive. In China, for example, norms closely regulate sexuality so that few people have sexual intercourse before they marry. In the United States, at least in recent decades intercourse before marriage has become the norm, and people may choose to have sex even when there is no strong commitment between them.

THE INCEST TABOO

Are any cultural views of sex the same everywhere? The answer is yes. One cultural universal—an element found in every society the world over—is the **incest taboo,** *a norm forbidding sexual relations or marriage between certain relatives.* In the United States, the law and cultural mores prohibit close relatives (including brothers and sisters, parents and children) from having sex or marrying. But exactly which family members are included in a society's incest taboo varies from one place to another. Some societies (such as the North American Navajo) apply incest taboos to the mother and others on her side of the family. There are also societies (including ancient Peru and Egypt) on record that have approved brother-sister marriages among the nobility (Murdock, 1965; orig. 1949).

Why does the incest taboo exist everywhere? Biology is part of the reason: Reproduction between close relatives of any species risks offspring with mental or physical problems. But this fact does not explain why, of all living species, only humans observe an incest taboo. In other words, controlling sexuality among close relatives seems a necessary element of social organization. First, the incest taboo limits sexual competition in families by restricting sex to spouses (ruling out, for example, sex between parent and child). Second, because family ties define people's

rights and obligations toward each other, reproduction between close relatives would hopelessly confuse kinship; if a mother and son had a daughter, for example, what would the child's relationship be to the other two? Third, by requiring people to marry outside their immediate families, the incest taboo integrates the larger society as people look widely for partners to form new families.

The incest taboo has been an enduring sexual norm in the United States and elsewhere. But in this country, many sexual norms have changed over time. During the twentieth century, as we now explain, our society experienced both a sexual revolution and, later, a sexual counterrevolution.

SEXUAL ATTITUDES IN THE UNITED STATES

What do people in the United States think about sex? Our cultural orientation toward sexuality has always been inconsistent. On one hand, most European immigrants arrived with rigid notions about "correct" sexuality, which ideally meant that sex was only for the purpose of reproduction within marriage. As explained in Chapter 8 ("Deviance"), the Puritan settlers of New England demanded conformity in all attitudes and behavior, and they imposed severe penalties for any misconduct, even if the sexual "misconduct" took place in the privacy of one's home. Efforts to regulate sexuality continued long after: As late as the 1960s, for example, some states legally banned the sale of condoms in stores. Even today, a number of states have laws on the books banning homosexuality and various "unnatural" acts.

But this is just one side of the story of sexuality in the United States. As Chapter 3 ("Culture") explains, our culture is also individualistic, and many believe in giving people freedom to do pretty much as they wish, as long as they cause no direct harm to others. Such thinking—that what people do in the privacy of their own home is *their* business—makes sex a matter of individual freedom and personal choice.

So which is it? Is the United States a restrictive or a permissive society when it comes to sexuality? The answer is that we are both. On one hand, many people in the United States still view sexual conduct as an important indicator of personal morality. On the other, sex is exploited and glorified everywhere in our culture and strongly promoted by the mass media.

Within this general framework, we turn now to changes in sexual attitudes and behavior over the

DISCUSS: The U.S. ambivalence about sex was evident in public response to the Clinton sex scandals. Liberals defended Clinton against what they saw as our tradition of oppressive Puritanism; conservatives condemned Clinton as embodying 1960s permissiveness. What do students think?

DISCUSS: Why was the legalization of abortion in 1973 another important dimension of the sexual revolution?

RESOURCE: The companion reader, *Seeing Ourselves*, 5th ed., features a contemporary excerpt on "Sex in America: How Many Partners Do We Have?" by Robert T. Michael et al.

NOTE: Another documented dimension of the sexual revolution is a wider range of sexual practices. Laumann et al. (1994) report that in recent decades, a larger share of adults engaged in oral and anal sex.

course of the twentieth century. As we shall see, sexual attitudes have changed considerably over time.

THE SEXUAL REVOLUTION

During the twentieth century, people witnessed profound changes in sexual attitudes and practices. The first indications of this change occurred in the 1920s as millions of women and men migrated from farms and small towns to rapidly growing cities. There, living apart from their families and meeting in the workplace, young people enjoyed greater sexual freedom. Indeed, this is one reason the decade became known as the "Roaring Twenties."

In the 1930s and 1940s, the Great Depression and World War II slowed the rate of change. But in the postwar period, after 1945, Alfred Kinsey set the stage for what later came to be known as the *sexual revolution*. Kinsey and his colleagues published their first study of sexuality in the United States in 1948, and it raised eyebrows everywhere. It was not so much what Kinsey said about sexual behavior—although he did present some surprising results—as simply the fact that scientists were studying sex that set off a national conversation. At that time, after all, many people were uneasy talking about sex even privately at home.

Kinsey's two books (1948, 1953) became bestsellers partly because they revealed that people in the United States, on average, were far less conventional in sexual matters than most had thought. Thus, these books fostered a new openness toward sexuality, which helped advance the sexual revolution.

In the late 1960s, the sexual revolution truly came of age. Youth culture dominated public life, and expressions such as "if it feels good, do it" and "sex, drugs, and rock and roll" summed up a new freedom about sexuality. Some people were turned off by the idea of "turning on," of course, but the baby boom generation, born between 1945 and 1960, became the first cohort in U.S. history to grow up with the idea that sex was part of everyone's life, married or not.

Technology also played a part in the sexual revolution. "The pill," introduced in 1960, not only prevented pregnancy but made sex more convenient. Unlike a condom or diaphragm, which has to be used at the time of intercourse, the pill could be taken any time during the day. Now women as well as men could engage in sex without any special preparation.

The sexual revolution had special significance for women because historically women were subject to greater sexual regulation than men. According to the

The sexual revolution was well underway by the late 1960s, when the youth counterculture embraced the idea of "free love." This term is something of an exaggeration, but many people did enter into more casual sexual relationships.

double standard, society allows (and even encourages) men to be sexually active while expecting women to remain chaste before marriage and faithful to their husbands afterward. The survey data shown in Figure 9–1 on page 226 support this conclusion. Among people born in the United States between 1933 and 1942 (that is, people in their sixties today), 56 percent of men but just 16 percent of women report having had two or more sexual partners by the time they were age twenty. Compare this wide gap with the pattern among the baby boomers born between 1953 and 1962 (people now in their forties), who came of age after the sexual revolution. In this category, 62 percent of men and 48 percent of women say they had two or more sexual partners by age twenty (Laumann et al., 1994:198). Thus, the sexual revolution increased

NOTE: Alfred Kinsey found that of women born before 1900, only 8% had sexual intercourse before age 20; for women born between 1910 and 1929, the share rose to 22% (Davis, 1971:333).

SOCIAL SURVEY: The Laumann data for a younger cohort born between 1963 and 1972, after the sexual revolution was well along, indicate that the gap is smaller still: 62% of men and 51% of women report having five or more sexual partners by age 20 (Laumann et al., 1994:198).

NOTE: 1999 recorded the lowest syphilis rate since 1941: 2.5 new cases per 100,000 people. There were 6,657 cases reported in 1999, half of them in just 22 counties, mostly in the South; 79% of U.S. counties reported no new cases at all.

DIVERSITY SNAPSHOT

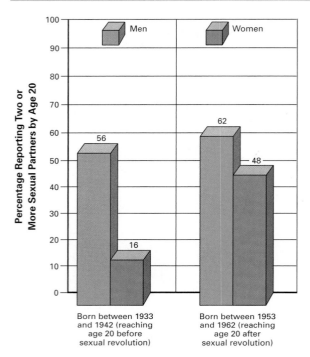

FIGURE 9–1 The Sexual Revolution: Closing the Double Standard

Source: Laumann et al. (1994:198).

sexual activity overall, but it changed behavior among women more than among men.

A general trend, then, is greater openness about sexuality as societies develop economically and as the opportunities for women increase. With these facts in mind, we can understand the global pattern of birth control use shown in Global Map 9–1.

THE SEXUAL COUNTERREVOLUTION

The sexual revolution made sex a topic of everyday discussion and sexual activity more a matter of individual choice. But given that U.S. society has always had two minds about sex, the sexual revolution was also controversial. By 1980, the climate of sexual freedom that had marked the late 1960s and 1970s was criticized by some as evidence of our country's moral decline. Thus, the *sexual counterrevolution* began.

Politically speaking, the sexual counterrevolution was a conservative call for a return to "family values," replacing sexual freedom with sexual responsibility. In practice, this turnaround meant moving sex back within marriage. Critics objected not just to the idea of "free love" but to trends such as cohabitation (living together) and having children out of wedlock.

Looking back, we can see that the sexual counterrevolution did not greatly change the idea that individuals should decide for themselves when and with whom to have a sexual relationship. What did happen, however, is that more people began choosing to limit their number of sexual partners or to abstain from sex entirely. In many cases, such decisions are made on moral grounds. For others, however, the decision to limit sexual activity reflects a fear of sexually transmitted diseases (STDs). As Chapter 21 ("Health and Medicine") explains, although rates of most infectious diseases fell after 1960, rates of STDs rose sharply. Moreover, the fact that some STDs (such as genital herpes) are incurable and others (AIDS) are deadly has given people good reason to consider carefully their sexual choices.

PREMARITAL SEX

In light of the sexual revolution and the sexual counterrevolution, how much has sexual behavior in the United States really changed? One interesting trend involves premarital sex, that is, the likelihood that young people will have sexual intercourse before marriage.

Consider first what U.S. adults *say* about premarital intercourse. Table 9–1 on page 228 shows that about 35 percent characterize sexual relations before marriage as "always wrong" or "almost always wrong." Another 20 percent consider premarital sex "wrong only sometimes," and about 40 percent say premarital sex is "not wrong at all." Public opinion is more accepting of premarital sex today than a generation ago, but even so, our society remains divided on this issue.

Now first consider what young people *do* regarding premarital intercourse. For women, there has been marked change over time. The Kinsey studies (1948, 1953; see also Laumann et al., 1994) reported that for people born in the early 1900s, about 50 percent of men but just 6 percent of women had premarital sexual intercourse before age nineteen. Studies of baby boomers born after World War II show a slight increase in premarital intercourse among men but a large increase—to about one-third—among women.

NOTE: Laumann's study was based on a national survey involving 3,432 adults aged 18 to 59. Subjects responded to the first two items using a self-administered, anonymous questionnaire that they sealed in an envelope before giving it to the interviewer; subjects responded verbally to the third item in an interview.

DIVERSITY: In Laumann's study, 54% of men but only 19% of women claimed to "think about sex daily" (cited in Elmer-DeWitt, 1994c:64).

DISCUSS: How many words can students think of to characterize a sexually loose female? How many comparable words apply to men? Why the difference?

WINDOW ON THE WORLD

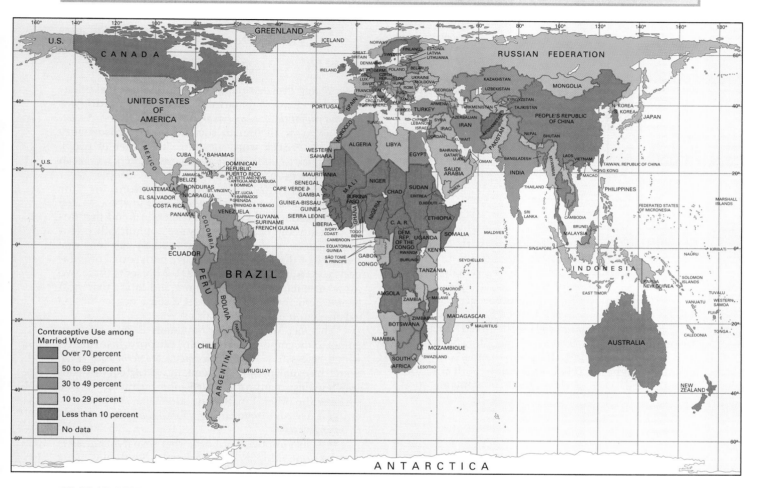

GLOBAL MAP 9–1 Contraceptive Use in Global Perspective

The map shows the percentage of married women using modern contraception methods (such as barrier methods, contraceptive pill, implants, injectables, intra-uterine contraceptive devices [IUD], or sterilization). In general, how do high-income nations differ from low-income nations? Can you explain this difference?

Source: Data from Mackay (2000).

The most recent studies, targeting men and women born in the 1970s, show that 76 percent of men and 66 percent of women had premarital sexual intercourse by their senior year in high school (Laumann et al., 1994:323–24). Thus, although general public attitudes remain divided on premarital sex, the behavior is broadly accepted among young people.

SEX BETWEEN ADULTS

To hear the mass media tell it, people in the United States are very active sexually. But do popular images exaggerate reality? The Laumann study (1994) found that frequency of sexual activity varied widely in the U.S. population. The patterns break down like this:

"Not at all?"   21.2%   "About once a week"   16.3%
"Once or twice"   8.4%   "2 or 3 times a week"   18.6%
"About once a month"   8.5%   "More than 3 times a week" 6.3%
"2 or 3 times a month" 15.0%   DK/NR   5.7%

GLOBAL: Although many people think of the French as more

SOCIAL SURVEY: "About how often did you have sex during the last 12 months?"

sexual and the British as less so, survey results indicate that the share of adults reporting having five or more sexual partners is about the same. More U.S. adults make this claim than French or British adults (cited in Elmer-DeWitt, 1994c:64).

SOCIAL SURVEY: Asked whether their last sexual encounter included oral sex, 27% of men and 19% of women said yes (Laumann et al., 1994).

TABLE 9–1 How We View Premarital and Extramarital Sex

Survey Question: "There's been a lot of discussion about the way morals and attitudes about sex are changing in this country. If a man and a woman have sexual relations before marriage, do you think it is always wrong, almost always wrong, wrong only sometimes, or not wrong at all? What about a married person having sexual relations with someone other than the marriage partner?"

	Premarital Sex	Extramarital Sex
"Always wrong"	26.7%	77.8%
"Almost always wrong"	8.4	10.6
"Wrong only sometimes"	20.5	7.0
"Not wrong at all"	39.9	2.5
"Don't know"/No answer	4.5	2.1

Source: *General Social Surveys, 1972–2000: Cumulative Codebook* (Chicago: National Opinion Research Center, 2001), pp. 17–18.

One-third of adults report having sex with a partner a few times a year or not at all; another one-third have sex once or several times a month; the remaining one-third have sex with a partner two or more times a week. In short, no single stereotype accurately describes sexual activity in the United States.

Moreover, despite the widespread image of "swinging singles," it is married people who have sex with partners the most. In addition, married people report the highest level of satisfaction, both emotional and physical, with their partners (Laumann et al., 1994).

EXTRAMARITAL SEX

What about married people having sex with someone other than their marriage partner? What people commonly call "adultery" (sociologists prefer a more neutral term such as "extramarital sex") is widely condemned. Table 9–1 shows that nearly 90 percent of U.S. adults consider a married person having sex with someone other than the marital partner "always wrong" or "almost always wrong." The norm of sexual fidelity within marriage has been and remains a strong element of U.S. culture.

But in terms of behavior, the cultural ideal often differs from real life. It probably comes as no surprise that extramarital sexual activity is more common than people say it should be. At the same time, extramarital sex is not as frequent as many believe. The Laumann study reports that about 25 percent of married men and 10 percent of married women have had at least

one extramarital sexual experience. Or, the other way around, 75 percent of men and 90 percent of women remain sexually faithful to their partners throughout their married lives (Laumann et al., 1994:214; NORC, 2001:1135).

SEXUAL ORIENTATION

Over recent decades, public opinion about sexual orientation has changed remarkably. **Sexual orientation** is *a person's romantic and emotional attraction to another person.* The norm in all human societies is **heterosexuality** (*hetero* is a Greek word meaning "the other of two"), meaning *sexual attraction to someone of the other sex.* Yet in every society a significant share of people favor **homosexuality** (*homo* is the Greek word for "the same"), *sexual attraction to someone of the same sex.* When thinking about these categories, keep in mind that homosexuality and heterosexuality are not mutually exclusive. That is, people do not necessarily fall into one category or the other but may have both sexual orientations to varying degrees. Figure 9–2 presents these two sexual orientations as a continuum, indicating that most people actually experience at least some degree of sexual attraction to people of both sexes.

The fact that sexual orientation is not clear-cut points to the importance of a third category: **bisexuality,** which refers to *sexual attraction to people of both sexes.* Some bisexual people are equally attracted to males and females; many others are more attracted to one sex over the other. Finally, one additional sexual orientation is **asexuality,** meaning *no sexual attraction to people of either sex.*

It is also important to note that sexual *attraction* is not the same thing as sexual *behavior.* No doubt, many people have experienced attraction to someone of the same sex, but fewer ever experience same sex behavior. This is in large part because of cultural constraints on our actions.

Cultural systems do not accept all sexual orientations equally. In the United States and around the world, heterosexuality is the norm because, biologically speaking, heterosexual relations permit human reproduction. Even so, most societies tolerate homosexuality. In fact, among the ancient Greeks, upper-class men considered homosexuality the highest form of relationship, partly because they looked down on

For a summary of recent research on sexual orientation, go to http://www.davidmyers.org/sexorient/

DIVERSITY: Part of the sexual folklore of the U.S. is the idea that minorities are more sexual than whites. Why is this? Data from the Laumann et al. (1994) study show that although African Americans have first intercourse about a year earlier, there are no significant differences among adults in this regard.

RESOURCE: An excerpt on "Understanding Sexual Orientation" by Alfred Kinsey, Wardell Pomeroy, and Clyde Martin is among the classics in the Macionis and Benokraitis reader, *Seeing Ourselves*.
NOTE: In 1975, the American Psychological Association followed in the footsteps of the American Psychiatric Association, removing homosexuality from its list of mental disorders.

women as intellectually inferior. As men saw it, heterosexuality was necessary only so they could have children, and "real" men preferred homosexual relations (Kluckhohn, 1948; Ford & Beach, 1951; Greenberg, 1988).

WHAT GIVES US A SEXUAL ORIENTATION?

The question of *how* people come to have a sexual orientation in the first place is vigorously debated. But the arguments cluster into two general positions: first, that sexual orientation is a product of society, and second, that sexual orientation is a product of biology.

Sexual Orientation: A Product of Society

This view argues that people in any society construct a set of meanings that lets them make sense of sexuality. Therefore, understandings of sexuality differ from place to place and over time. For example, Michel Foucault (1990; orig. 1978) points out that there was no distinct category of people called "homosexuals" until a century ago, when scientists and, eventually, the public as a whole began labeling people that way. Through most of history, in other words, some people no doubt had what we would call homosexual experiences. But neither they nor others saw in this behavior the basis for any special identity.

Anthropologists provide further evidence that sexual orientation is socially constructed. Studies show that various kinds of homosexuality exist in different societies. In Siberia, for example, the Chukchee Eskimo have a ritual practice in which one man dresses like a woman and does a woman's work. The Sambia, who dwell in the eastern highlands of New Guinea, have a ritual in which young boys perform oral sex on older men in the belief that ingesting semen will enhance their masculinity. The existence of such diverse patterns around the world points to the fact that sexual orientation and sexual expression have much to do with society itself (Herdt, 1993; Murray & Roscoe, 1998).

Sexual Orientation: A Product of Biology

A growing body of evidence suggests that sexual orientation is innate, that it is rooted in human biology, in much the same way that people are born right-handed or left-handed. Arguing this position, Simon LeVay (1993) links sexual orientation to the structure of the human brain. LeVay studied the brains of both homosexual and heterosexual men and found a small

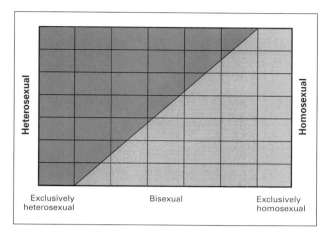

FIGURE 9–2 The Sexual Orientation Continuum
Source: Adapted from Kinsey et al. (1948).

but important difference in the size of the hypothalamus, a part of the brain that regulates hormones. Such an anatomical difference, some claim, plays a part in shaping sexual orientation.

Genetics also may influence sexual orientation. One study of forty-four pairs of brothers, all homosexual, found that thirty-three pairs had a distinctive genetic pattern involving the X chromosome. Moreover, the gay brothers had an unusually high number of gay male relatives, but only on their mother's side, the source of the X chromosome. Such evidence leads some researchers to think there may be a "gay gene" (Hamer & Copeland, 1994).

Critical evaluation. Mounting evidence supports the conclusion that sexual orientation is rooted in biology, although the best guess at present is that it is derived from *both* society and biology (Gladue, Green, & Hellman, 1984; Weinrich, 1987; Troiden, 1988; Isay, 1989; Puterbaugh, 1990; Angier, 1992; Gelman, 1992). Furthermore, we must

 The American Psychological Association posts answers to commonly asked questions regarding sexual orientation at http://www.apa.org/pubinfo/answers.html

bear in mind that sexual orientation is not a matter of neat categories. That is, most people who think of themselves as homosexual have had some heterosexual experiences, just as many people who think of themselves as heterosexual have had some homosexual experiences. Thus, the task of explaining sexual orientation is extremely complex.

FIGURE 9–3 Sexual Orientation in the United States: Survey Data

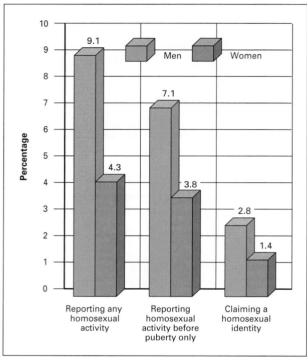

(a) How Many Gay People?

Source: Adapted from Laumann et al. (1994).

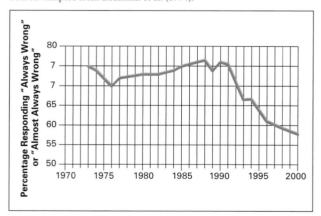

(b) Attitudes toward Homosexual Relations, 1973–2000

Survey Question: "What about sexual relations between two adults of the same sex—do you think it is always wrong, almost always wrong, wrong only sometimes, or not wrong at all?"
Source: NORC (2001).

There is also a political issue here with great importance for gay men and lesbians. To the extent that sexual orientation is based in biology, homosexuality is not a matter of choice any more than, say, skin color. If this is so, shouldn't gay men and lesbians expect the same legal protection from discrimination as African Americans? (Herek, 1991)

HOW MANY GAY PEOPLE?

What share of the U.S. population is gay? This is a difficult question to answer because, as we have explained, sexual orientation not a matter of neat categories. Moreover, people are not always willing to reveal their sexuality to strangers or even to family members. Pioneering sex researcher Alfred Kinsey (1948, 1953) estimated that about 4 percent of males and 2 percent of females have an exclusively same-sex orientation, although he thought that at least one-third of men and one-eighth of women have at least one homosexual experience leading to orgasm.

In light of the Kinsey studies, many social scientists put the gay share of the population at 10 percent. But a more recent national survey of sexuality in the United States indicates that how one operationalizes "homosexuality" makes a big difference in the results (Laumann et al., 1994). As part (a) of Figure 9–3 shows, about 9 percent of U.S. men and about 4 percent of U.S. women between ages eighteen and fifty-nine reported homosexual activity *at some time* in their lives. The second set of numbers shows that a significant share of men (less so women) have a homosexual experience during childhood but not after puberty. And 2.8 percent of men and 1.4 percent of women define themselves as partly or entirely homosexual.

Finally, Kinsey treated sexual orientation as an "either/or" trait: To be more homosexual was, by definition, to be less heterosexual. But same-sex and other-sex attractions can operate independently. At one extreme, then, bisexual people feel strong attraction to people of both sexes; at the other, asexual people experience little sexual attraction to people of either sex.

In the national survey mentioned earlier, less than 1 percent of adults described themselves as bisexual. But bisexual experiences appear to be fairly common (at least for a time) among younger people, especially on college campuses (Laumann et al., 1994; Leland, 1995). Many bisexuals, then, do not think of themselves as either gay or straight, and their behavior reflects elements of both gay and straight living.

RESOURCE: J. M. Carrier looks at "Homosexual Behavior in Cross-Cultural Perspective" in the Macionis and Benokraitis reader, *Seeing Ourselves.*
Q: "A narcissist is somebody who is better looking than you are." Gore Vidal

NOTE: Although the rate of pregnancy among teenage girls between ages 15 and 20 has gone down, the pregnancy rate for *younger* girls has gone up. The reason is girls and boys becoming sexually active at a younger age.

THE GAY RIGHTS MOVEMENT

In recent decades, the public attitude toward homosexuality has been moving toward greater acceptance. In 1973, as shown in part (b) of Figure 9–3, about three-fourths of U.S. adults claimed homosexual relations were "always wrong" or "almost always wrong." That percentage changed little during the 1970s and 1980s, but by 2000 it dropped to less than 60 percent (NORC, 2001:243).

In large measure, this change came about through the gay rights movement that arose in the middle of the twentieth century (Chauncey, 1994). At that time, most people did not discuss homosexuality, and it was common for companies (including the federal government and the armed forces) to fire anyone who was thought to be gay. Mental health professionals also took a hard line, describing homosexuals as "sick," and sometimes sending them to mental hospitals where, presumably, they might be cured.

In this climate of intolerance, most lesbians and gay men remained "in the closet," closely guarding the secret of their sexual orientation. But the gay rights movement gained strength during the 1960s. One early milestone occurred in 1973, when the American Psychiatric Association declared that homosexuality was not an illness but simply "a form of sexual behavior."

Gay rights advocates also began using the term **homophobia** to describe *the dread of close personal interaction with people thought to be gay, lesbian, or bisexual* (Weinberg, 1973). The concept of homophobia (literally, "fear of sameness") turns the tables on society: Instead of asking "What's wrong with gay people?" the question becomes "What's wrong with people who can't accept a different sexual orientation?"

SEXUAL CONTROVERSIES

Sexuality lies at the heart of a number of controversies in the United States. Here we take a look at four issues: teen pregnancy, pornography, prostitution, and sexual violence.

TEEN PREGNANCY

Being sexually active—especially having intercourse—demands a high level of responsibility because pregnancy can result. Teenagers may be biologically mature, but many are not socially mature and may not appreciate all the consequences of their actions. Indeed, although the rate of teen pregnancy has been

This gathering took place on June 27, 1999, at New York's Stonewall Inn to celebrate the thirtieth anniversary of the so-called "Stonewall Riot" in 1969, when gay people first fought back against harassment by the police, sparking the gay rights movement.

dropping, surveys indicate that 1 million U.S. teens become pregnant each year, and most did not intend to.

Pregnancy means not only that many young women (and sometimes young fathers-to-be) cannot finish school, but they are at high risk of poverty. As Figure 9–4 on page 232 shows, this country's rate of births among teens is higher than that of other high-income countries.

Did the sexual revolution lead to an increase in teenage pregnancy? Surprisingly, perhaps, the answer is no. The rate in 1950 was actually higher than the rate today, but this is because people

 Find out about a global report from the Alan Guttmacher Institute on teenage sex and pregnancy: http://www.agi-usa.org/pubs/new_world_engl.html

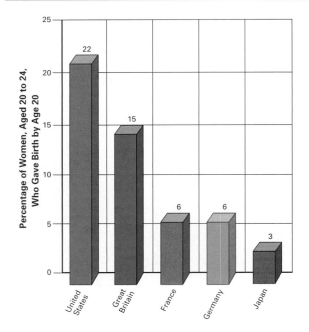

GLOBAL SNAPSHOT

FIGURE 9–4 Births to Teenage Women

Source: The Alan Guttmacher Institute (2000).

married younger at the time. Also, many pregnancies led to quick marriages. As a result, there were many pregnant teenagers, but most were married women. Today, by contrast, most teenagers who become pregnant are not married. In about half of all cases, these women have abortions; in the other half, they keep their babies (Voydanoff & Donnelly, 1990; Holmes, 1996a). National Map 9–1 shows the distribution of births to females between ages fifteen and nineteen in the United States.

Concern about the high rate of teenage pregnancy has led to sex education programs in schools. But such programs are controversial, as the box explains.

PORNOGRAPHY

In general terms, **pornography** is *sexually explicit material that causes sexual arousal*. But what exactly is or is not pornographic has long been a matter of debate. Recognizing that people view the portrayal of sexuality

differently, the U.S. Supreme Court gives local communities the power to decide for themselves what violates "community standards" of decency and lacks any redeeming social value.

Definitions aside, pornography is surely popular in the United States: X-rated videos, commercial telephone numbers for sexual conversations, and a host of sexually explicit movies and magazines together constitute roughly a $10-billion-a-year industry. The figure is rising as people find more pornography at more and more sites—now estimated to be in the hundreds of thousands—on the Internet.

Traditionally, people have criticized pornography on *moral* grounds. As national surveys confirm, 60 percent of U.S. adults are concerned that "sexual materials lead to a breakdown of morals" (NORC, 2001:244). Today, however, pornography is also seen as a *power* issue because it depicts women as the sexual playthings of men.

Some critics also see pornography as a cause of violence against women. Although it is difficult to document a scientific cause-and-effect relationship between what people view and how they act, research does support the idea that pornography makes men think of women as objects rather than as people. The public shares a concern about pornography and violence, with almost half of adults holding the opinion that pornography encourages people to commit rape (NORC, 2001:245).

People everywhere object to material they find offensive, but many also value freedom of speech and artistic expression. Nevertheless, opposition to pornography is building from an unlikely coalition of conservatives (who condemn pornography on moral grounds) and progressives (who oppose it for political reasons).

PROSTITUTION

Prostitution is *the selling of sexual services*. Often called "the world's oldest profession," prostitution has always been widespread, and about one in five adult men in the United States reports having paid for sex at some time (NORC, 2001:1135). Even so, to the extent that people think of sex as an expression of interpersonal intimacy, they find the idea of sex for money disturbing. As a result, prostitution is against the law everywhere in the United States, except for parts of Nevada.

Around the world, prostitution is greatest in lower-income countries where patriarchy is strong and traditional cultural norms limit women's ability to earn a living. Global Map 9–2 on page 234 shows where in the world prostitution is most widespread.

SOCIAL SURVEY: "There is nothing inherently wrong with prostitution, so long as the health risks can be minimized. If consenting adults agree to exchange money for sex, that is their business." (GSS 1996, *N* = 1,444; *Codebook*, 2001:624)

"Agree strongly"	15.4%	"Disagree strongly"	43.1%
"Agree somewhat"	23.7%	DK/NR	2.7%
"Disagree somewhat"	15.2%		

CRITICAL THINKING

Sex Education: Solution or Problem?

Most schools today have sex education programs that teach the basics of sexuality. Instructors explain to young people how their bodies grow and change, how reproduction occurs, and how to avoid pregnancy by using birth control or abstaining from sex.

Because half of teenage boys in the United States report having sex by the time they reach sixteen, and half of girls report doing so by seventeen, "sex ed" programs seem to make sense. But critics point out that as the number of sex education programs has expanded, the level of teenage sexual activity has gone *up*. This trend seems to suggest that sex education may not be discouraging sex among youngsters and, maybe, that learning more about sex encourages young people to become sexually active sooner. Critics also say that it is parents who should be instructing their children about sex because, unlike teachers, parents can also teach their beliefs about what is right and wrong.

But supporters of sex education counter that research does not support the conclusion that sex education results in young people being more sexually active. More generally, they argue that it is the larger culture—one that celebrates sexuality—that encourages children to become sexually active. If this is the case, the sensible strategy is to ensure that they understand what they are doing and that they take reasonable precautions to protect themselves from unwanted pregnancy and sexually transmitted diseases.

What do you think?

1. *Schools can teach the facts about sexuality. But do you think they can address the emotional issues that often accompany sex? What about the moral issues involved? Why or why not?*

2. *What about parents? Are they doing their job in instructing children about sex? Ask members of your class how many received instruction in sexual matters from their parents.*

3. *Overall, do you think young people know too little about sexuality? Do you think they know too much? What specific changes would you suggest to address the problem of unwanted pregnancy among teens?*

SEEING OURSELVES

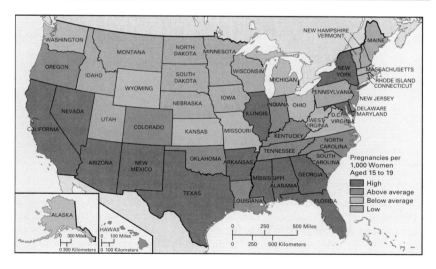

NATIONAL MAP 9–1 Teenage Pregnancy Rates across the United States

The map shows pregnancy rates in the mid-1990s for women aged fifteen to nineteen. In what regions of the country are rates high? Where are they low? What explanation can you offer for these patterns?

Source: The Alan Guttmacher Institute (1999).

Sources: Gibbs (1993), Stodghill (1998), and Voss & Kogan (2001).

GLOBAL: A clear case of ethnocentrism is that the Japanese child pornography industry—the biggest in the world—almost never uses Japanese girls; it "imports" other Asian girls.

GLOBAL: Around the world, perhaps 100 million children live on the streets selling sex to survive. Some are orphaned by AIDS or war, and almost all of them are poor.

NOTE: The ancient Greeks had much the same prostitution hierarchy as we do now. Low-cost brothel workers occupied the lowest position; street walkers were only slightly more rewarded. At the top, the elite call girls of the time—the *hetirae*—were educated in the arts and philosophy and provided intellectual as well as sexual stimulation (cf. Davis, 1971).

WINDOW ON THE WORLD

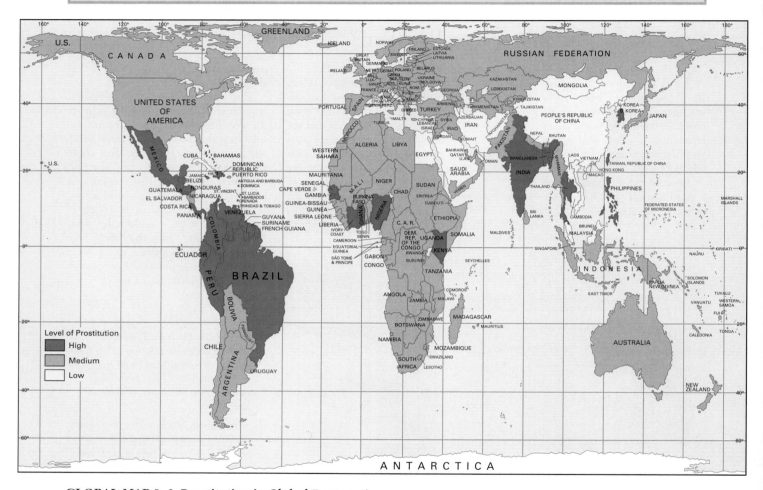

GLOBAL MAP 9–2 Prostitution in Global Perspective

Generally speaking, prostitution is widespread in societies where women have low standing. Officially, at least, the People's Republic of China boasts of gender equality, including the elimination of "vice," such as prostitution, which oppresses women. By contrast, in much of Latin America, where patriarchy is strong, prostitution is common. In many Islamic societies patriarchy is also strong, but religion is a counterbalance, so prostitution is limited. Western, high-income nations have a moderate amount of prostitution.

Sources: *Peters Atlas of the World* (1990) and Mackay (2000).

Types of Prostitution

Most prostitutes (many prefer the morally neutral term "sex workers") are women, but they fall into different categories. *Call girls* are elite prostitutes, typically women who are young, attractive, and well educated and arrange their own appointments with clients by telephone. The classified pages of any large city newspaper contain numerous ads for "escort services," through which women (and a much smaller number of men) offer both companionship and sex for a fee.

Sex workers in a middle category are employed in "massage parlors" or brothels under the control of managers. These people have less choice about their clients, receive less money for their services, and get to keep no more than half of what they make.

At the bottom of the sex-worker hierarchy are *street walkers*, women and men who work the streets of large cities. Female street walkers often are under the control of male pimps who take most of their earnings. Street walkers are at the highest risk of violence from pimps and clients (Gordon & Snyder, 1989; Davidson, 1998).

Most prostitutes offer heterosexual services. Gay prostitutes also trade sex for money. Researchers report that many gay prostitutes have suffered rejection by family and friends because of their sexual orientation (Weisberg, 1985; Boyer, 1989; Kruks, 1991).

A Victimless Crime?

Prostitution is against the law almost everywhere in the United States, but many people consider it a victimless crime (see Chapter 8, "Deviance"). Therefore, instead of enforcing prostitution laws all the time, police stage occasional crackdowns. Our society seems to want to control prostitution while assuming that nothing will eliminate it.

Is selling sex a victimless crime that hurts no one? Certainly, many people who take a "live and let live" attitude about prostitution would say it is. But this view overlooks the fact that prostitution subjects many women to abuse and violence and plays a part in spreading sexually transmitted diseases, including AIDS. In addition, many poor women become trapped in a life of selling sex, generally to the benefit of others, while they put their own lives at risk.

SEXUAL VIOLENCE AND ABUSE

Although sexual activity often occurs within a loving relationship, sex can be twisted by hate and violence. Sexual violence, which ranges from verbal abuse to rape and assault, is widespread in the United States.

Rape

Although some people think rape is a form of sex, it is actually an expression of power, a violent act that uses sex to hurt, humiliate, or control another person. The U.S. Federal Bureau of Investigation reports that about 90,000 women are raped each year. This number reflects only the reported cases, and the actual number of rapes is several times higher (McCormick, 1994; U.S. Federal Bureau of Investigation, 2001).

The official definition of rape, according to the federal government, is "the carnal knowledge of a female forcibly and against her will." Thus, official rape statistics include only victims who are women. But men, too, are raped—in perhaps 10 percent of all cases. Most men who rape men are not homosexual: They are heterosexuals who are motivated by a desire not for sex but to dominate another person (Groth & Birnbaum, 1979; Gibbs, 1991a).

Date Rape

A common myth is that rape involves strangers. In reality, however, most rapes involve people who know one another, and they usually take place in familiar surroundings, especially the home. For this reason, the terms "date rape" and "acquaintance rape" refer to forcible sexual violence against women by men they know.

Many victims of date rape do not report the crime. A new government report on the sexual victimization of college women is available at http://www.ojp.usdoj.gov/bjs/abstract/svcw.htm Some believe that because they know the offender, an attack could not have been rape. But the tide is turning, with more and more women speaking out. The box on page 236 takes a closer look.

THEORETICAL ANALYSIS OF SEXUALITY

We can better understand human sexuality by using sociology's various theoretical paradigms. In the following sections, we apply the three major paradigms in turn.

STRUCTURAL-FUNCTIONAL ANALYSIS

The structural-functional approach highlights the contributions of any social pattern to the overall operation of society. Because sexuality is an important dimension of social life, society regulates sexual behavior.

The Need to Regulate Sexuality

From a biological point of view, sex allows our species to reproduce. But culture and social institutions regulate *with whom* and *when* people reproduce. For example, most societies condemn married people for having sex with someone other than their spouse. To do otherwise—to give the forces of sexual passion free

NOTE: Public support for rape victims has prompted more women to come forward, a trend reflected in a steady rise in the number and percentage of forcible rapes reported to police during the 1980s and 1990s.
NOTE: Men also rape men, of course, and there are rare cases of women raping men. Although the federal definition of "forcible rape" focuses on a man raping a woman, other patterns are noted separately by the FBI.
GLOBAL: Interpol data indicate that the worst nation in the world with regard to rape is South Africa, with about 1.6 million rapes per year (a rate of 104 per 100,000 people versus 34 in the U.S.). Only about 3 in 100 rapes are reported to police (Hawthorne, 1999).

CRITICAL THINKING

Date Rape: Exposing Dangerous Myths

April Sanders was beside herself with excitement: She had a date with Bob McMahon, a senior she had admired all semester. On Saturday night, she met Bob at 10 o'clock at the south end of the Arts Quad, and they talked easily as they walked across campus to a party. The more Bob talked, the more April liked him.

The music was live and loud as they joined the crowd at a favorite campus hangout, and the beer was flowing freely. They had a few beers and danced. Then they joined some of Bob's friends at a table where everyone was downing shots of hard liquor. Bob handed April a glass. She paused, but then smiled and drank it down. He kept refilling her glass, and soon April's head was spinning. She knew she had drunk too much and just wanted to go home and lie down. Embarrassed, she said she wanted to go back to her dorm room. "No problem," Bob responded, insisting on walking her home.

When they reached her room, April let Bob come in while she looked for some aspirin. They were sitting on her couch talking, when Bob tried to kiss her. At that point, he seemed to change, forcefully pushing April into having sex. "Bob, no!" April pleaded, overcome with fear. But Bob was determined and strong, and she simply could not stop him.

Ten minutes later, the attack was over, and Bob got up and left. April's first reaction was to take a shower. "I felt so filthy," she recalled later. "I washed myself over and over." For hours, she sat crying, trying to make sense of a night that had gone terribly wrong. "Was I raped?" she asked herself, "I told him 'no,' I tried to stop him." But she also worried, "Who will believe me? We were out drinking together. I let him into my room."

In the morning, April Sanders went to the dean's office to report the attack. Later that day, she spoke with two city police officers. The police conducted an investigation, but they were reluctant to act because Bob claimed the sex was consensual, and there was no other evidence such as bruises, a medical ex- amination, or torn clothes to back up April's story.

The case of April Sanders is all too typical. In fact, at least half of all victims of sexual attack make no report to police. One reason is that many women and men do not understand what rape is. In fact, three wrong ideas about rape are so common in the United States that they might be called "rape myths."

Myth #1: Rape involves strangers. A sexual attack brings to mind a strange man lurking in the shadows who suddenly springs on an unsuspecting victim. In four out of five rapes, however, the victim knows the offender. For this reason, it is more realistic to speak of *acquaintance rape* or *date rape*.

Myth #2: Women provoke their attackers. Many people think a woman who has been raped must have done something to make the man think she wanted to have sex. In April Sanders's case, didn't she agree to go drinking? Didn't she let Bob into her room late at night? Such self-doubt often paralyzes

rein—would threaten family life and, especially, the raising of children.

Another example, discussed earlier in this chapter, is the incest taboo. The fact that this norm exists everywhere clearly shows that no society permits completely free choice in sexual partners. Reproduction by family members other than married partners would break down the system of kinship and muddle relationships between people.

Historically, the social control of sexuality was strong, mostly because sex commonly led to childbirth. Moreover, offspring, as well as parents, were subject to these controls. We see this in the traditional distinction between "legitimate" reproduction (within marriage) and "illegitimate" reproduction (outside of marriage). But once a society can effectively control births, its norms become more permissive. This occurred in the United States where, over the course of the twentieth century, sex moved beyond its basic reproductive function and became accepted as a form of intimacy and even recreation (Giddens, 1992).

Latent Functions: The Case of Prostitution

It is easy to see that prostitution is harmful because it spreads disease and exploits women. But are there latent functions that help explain why prostitution is widespread despite society's attempts to limit it? Definitely,

NOTE: Kingsley Davis argued that prostitution was functional to the extent that it provided sexual access for people without committed partners and a sexual outlet that might even keep some marriages together. Generally, however, functionalism views sexually transmitted diseases, teen pregnancy, pornography, prostitution, and sexual violence as dysfunctional patterns that result from the failure of social institutions—notably the family and the church—to operate as they should. Ideally, at least, a society in which children grow up in two-parent families learning to respect conventional moral standards should have little problem with pornography, sexual violence, teenage pregnancy, and sexually transmitted diseases.

victims. But going out with a man—or even inviting him into her room—is not consent to have sex with him any more than it would be consent to have him beat her with a club.

Myth #3: Rape is simply sex. If there is no knife held to a woman's throat or if she is not bound and gagged, what's the crime? The answer is that, under the law, forcing a woman to have sex without her consent is a *violent crime*. "Having sex" implies intimacy, caring, and, most important of all, consent, none of which is present in rape. Beyond the brutality of being physically violated, rape by an acquaintance also undermines a victim's sense of trust. Psychological scars are especially serious among the half of rape victims who are under eighteen; one-third of these young victims are attacked by their own fathers or stepfathers (Greenfield, 1996).

The more people believe rape myths, the more women will fall victim to sexual violence. The ancient Babylonians stoned married women who were raped, convinced that they had committed adultery. Ideas about rape have

Is a person who drinks alcohol to excess capable of making a responsible decision about having sex? What role does alcohol play in date rape on the campus?

changed little over thousands of years, which helps explain why, even today, only about one in twenty rapes results in an offender being sent to jail.

Nowhere has the issue of date rape been more widely discussed than on campuses. The collegiate environment promotes easy friendships and encourages trust. At the same time, many young students have much to learn about relationships and about themselves. So although college life encourages communication, it also invites sexual violence.

To counter the problem, many schools now actively address myths about rape and the place of alcohol in campus life. College men and women alike need to understand two simple truths: Sex without a woman's consent is rape, and when a woman says "no," she means just that.

What do you think?

1. *In your opinion, why are myths about rape so widespread?*

2. *What programs or policies exist on your campus to address sexual assault?*

3. *What else needs to be done?*

Sources: Gibbs (1991a, 1991b) and Gilbert (1992).

explains Kingsley Davis (1971): Prostitution performs several useful functions. Prostitution is one way to meet the sexual needs of a large number of people who do not have ready access to sex, including soldiers, travelers, and people who are not physically attractive or who have trouble establishing relationships. Moreover, adds Davis, the availability of sex without commitment may even help stabilize some loveless marriages that might otherwise collapse.

Critical evaluation. The structural-functional paradigm helps us appreciate how sexuality plays an important part in the way society is organized. The incest taboo and other cultural norms also suggest that

society has always paid attention to who has sex with whom and, especially, who reproduces with whom.

At the same time, this approach pays little attention to the great diversity of sexual ideas and practices found within every society. Moreover, sexual patterns change over time, just as they differ in remarkable ways around the world. To appreciate the varied and changeable character of sexuality, we turn to the symbolic-interaction paradigm.

SYMBOLIC-INTERACTION ANALYSIS

The symbolic-interaction paradigm highlights how, as people interact, they construct everyday reality. As

NOTE: Another interactional example involves the meaning attached to AIDS. Various precautions (dentists using gloves and masks, carefully disposing of needles, and so on) began after the AIDS crisis, even though other diseases such as hepatitis are more contagious and have been around far longer. Why? Probably because AIDS was defined as a gay disease.

DISCUSS: Actress Brooke Shields filmed her famous "Nothing comes between me and my Calvins" ad when she was 15. Describe the ad to the class and ask them whether they think sexual advertising of this kind is helpful or harmful to young people.

Chapter 6 ("Social Interaction in Everyday Life") explains, the process of constructing reality is highly variable, so that one group's or society's views of sexuality may well differ from another's. In the same way, how people understand sexuality can and does change over time.

The Social Construction of Sexuality

Almost all social patterns involving sexuality changed greatly over the course of the twentieth century. One good illustration is the changing importance of virginity. A century ago, our society's norm—for women, at least—was virginity before marriage. This norm was strong because, without effective birth control, virginity was the only assurance a man had that his bride-to-be was not carrying another man's child. Today, however, we have gone a long way toward separating sex from reproduction, and, as a result, the virginity norm has weakened. In the United States, among those born between 1963 and 1974, just 16.3 percent of men and 20.1 percent of women report being virgins at first marriage (Laumann et al., 1994:503).

Another example of our society's construction of sexuality involves young people. A century ago, childhood was a time of innocence in sexual matters. In recent decades, however, our thinking has changed. Although we expect that children will not be sexually active, most people believe children should be educated about sex by the time they are teenagers so that they can make intelligent choices about their sexual behavior.

Global Comparisons

The broader our view, the more variation we see in the meanings people attach to sexuality. One classic study showed that some cultures are far more accepting of childhood sexuality than others. Anthropologist Ruth Benedict (1938), who spent years learning the ways of life of the Melanesian people of southeast New Guinea, reported that adults paid little attention when young children engaged in sexual experimentation with one another. Parents in Melanesia shrugged off such activity because, before puberty, sex cannot lead to reproduction. Is it likely that most parents in the United States would respond the same way?

Sexual practices, too, vary as a part of culture. Male circumcision of infant boys (the practice of removing all or part of the foreskin of the penis) is common in the United States but rare in most other parts of the world. Similarly, female circumcision (the practice of removing the clitoris) is rare in the United States but common in parts of Africa and the Middle East (Crosette, 1995, Huffman, 2000). (For more about female circumcision, see the box in Chapter 13 ["Gender Stratification"] on page 342.)

Critical evaluation. The strength of the symbolic-interaction paradigm lies in revealing the constructed character of familiar social patterns. Understanding that people "construct" sexuality, we can better appreciate the variety of sexual practices found over the course of history and around the world.

One limitation of this approach is that not everything is so variable. Throughout our own history—and around the world—men are more likely to see women in sexual terms than the other way around. If this pattern is widespread, some broader social structure must be at work, as we shall see in the next section.

SOCIAL-CONFLICT ANALYSIS

The social-conflict paradigm highlights dimensions of inequality. Therefore, this approach shows how sexuality both reflects patterns of social inequality and helps create them.

Sexuality: Reflecting Social Inequality

Recall our discussion of prostitution, a practice outlawed almost everywhere in the United States. Even so, enforcement is uneven at best, especially when it comes to who is and is not likely to be arrested. Although two parties are involved, the record shows that police are far more likely to arrest (less powerful) female prostitutes than (more powerful) male clients. Similarly, of all women engaged in prostitution, it is street walkers—women with the least income and those most likely to be minorities—who face the highest risk of arrest (COYOTE, 2000). Also, we might wonder whether so many women would be involved in prostitution at all if they had equal economic opportunities with men.

Sexuality: Creating Social Inequality

Social-conflict theorists, especially feminists, point to sexuality as the root of inequality between women and men. How can this be? Defining women in sexual terms amounts to devaluing them from full human beings into objects of men's interest and attention. Is it

DISCUSS: In 1920, one analyst offered the following explanation for the pattern of arresting prostitutes more than "johns": "The professional prostitute being a social outcast may be periodically punished without disturbing the usual course of society....The man is something more than partner in an immoral act: He discharges important social and business relations, is a father or brother responsible for the maintenance of others....He cannot be imprisoned

without [disrupting] society" (Abraham Flexner, *Prostitution in Europe* [New York, Century, 1920:108]). How do students react to this analysis?

DISCUSS: Various "isms" can build on one another. Some queer theorists point out that the disadvantage of homosexuality is more severe for gay men who are black than for those who are white (Seidman, 1996).

any wonder that the word "pornography" comes from the Greek word *porne*, meaning "a man's sexual slave"?

If men define women in sexual terms, it is easy to see why many people consider pornography—almost all of which is consumed by males—a power issue. Because pornography typically depicts women seeking to please men, it supports the idea that men have power over women.

Some more radical critics doubt that this element of power can ever be removed from heterosexual relations (Dworkin, 1987). Whereas most social-conflict theorists do not reject heterosexuality entirely, they do agree that sexuality can and does degrade women. Critics point out that our culture often depicts sexuality in terms of sport (men "scoring" with women) and violence ("slamming," "banging," and "hitting on," for example, are verbs used for both fighting and sex).

Queer Theory

Finally, social-conflict theory has taken aim not only at men dominating women but also at heterosexuals dominating homosexuals. In recent years, just as many lesbians and gay men have come out in search of public acceptance, some sociologists have tried to add a gay voice to their discipline. **Queer theory** is *a growing body of research findings that challenges the heterosexual bias in U. S. society.*

Queer theory begins with the assertion that our society is characterized by **heterosexism,** *a view stigmatizing anyone who is not heterosexual as "queer."* Our heterosexual culture victimizes a wide range of people, including gay men, lesbians, bisexuals, transsexuals, and even asexual people. Furthermore, although most people agree that bias against women (sexism) and people of color (racism) is wrong, heterosexism is widely tolerated and sometimes well within the law. This country's military forces, for example, cannot legally discharge a female soldier for "acting like a woman," because that would be a clear case of gender discrimination. But the military forces can discharge her for homosexuality if she is a sexually active lesbian.

Heterosexism also exists at a more subtle level in our everyday understanding of the world. When we describe something as "sexy," for example, don't we really mean attractive to *heterosexuals?*

Critical evaluation. Applying the social-conflict paradigm shows how sexuality is both a cause and effect of inequality. In particular, this paradigm helps us understand men's power over women and heterosexual people's domination of homosexual people.

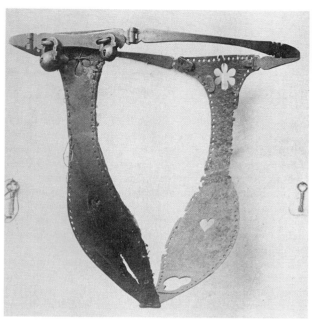

The control of women's sexuality is a common theme in human history. During the Middle Ages, Europeans devised the "chastity belt"—a metal device locked about a woman's groin that prevented sexual intercourse (and probably interfered with other bodily functions as well). While such devices are all but unknown today, the social control of sexuality continues. Can you point to examples?

At the same time, this approach overlooks the fact that sexuality is not a power issue for everyone: Many couples enjoy a vital sexual relationship that deepens their commitment to one another. In addition, the social-conflict paradigm pays little attention to strides our society has made toward eliminating injustice. Men, in public at least, are less likely to describe women as sex objects than they were a few decades ago; moreover, our rising public concern about sexual harassment (see Chapter 13, "Gender Stratification") has had some effect in reducing the role of sexuality in the workplace. Likewise, there is ample evidence that the gay rights movement has secured greater opportunities and social acceptance for homosexuals.

We close this chapter with a look at what is perhaps the most divisive sexuality issue of all: **abortion,** *the deliberate termination of a pregnancy.* Many people on both sides of this issue feel strongly about abortion because, as we shall see in the box on pages 240–41, it cuts to the heart of almost everyone's sense of justice.

NOTE: In the decades since 1973, new laws and court decisions have restricted—but not eliminated—women's access to abortion. In 1977, Congress (the Hyde Amendment) declared that Medicaid funds could not be used to pay for abortions except to save a mother's life. In 1980, the Supreme Court (*Harris v. McRae*) ruled that state and federal governments may decide not to use welfare funds to pay for abortions for poor women. In 1989, the Supreme Court supported a state's law forbidding state doctors and hospitals from performing abortions except to save a mother's life. Most states have also enacted laws requiring girls under legal age to obtain parental consent before receiving an abortion.

Q: "If conception occurs in excess . . . have abortion induced before sense and life have begun in the embryo." Aristotle, revealing that the ancient Greeks had developed some ability to control birth.

CONTROVERSY & DEBATE

The Abortion Controversy

A black van pulls up in front of the storefront in a busy section of the city. Two women get out of the front seat and cautiously scan the sidewalk. After a moment, one nods to the other and they open the rear door to let a third woman out of the van. Standing to the right and left of their charge, the two quickly whisk her into the building.

Is this a description of two federal marshals escorting a convict to a police station? It might be. But it is actually an account of two clinic workers escorting a woman who has decided to have an abortion. Why are they so cautious? Anyone who has read the papers in recent years knows about the heated confrontations at abortion clinics across North America. In fact, some opponents have even targeted and killed several doctors who perform abortions. Overall, the 1.3 million abortions performed each year make this probably the most hotly contested issue in the United States today.

Abortion has not always been so controversial. During the colonial era, midwives and other healers performed abortions with little community opposition and with full approval of the law. But controversy arose about 1850, when early medical doctors sought to eliminate the competition they faced from midwives and other traditional health providers, whose income was derived largely from terminating pregnancies. By 1900, medical doctors succeeded in getting every state to pass a law banning abortion.

Such laws did not end abortion, but they greatly reduced the numbers. In addition, these laws drove abortion underground, so that many women—especially those who were poor—had little choice but to seek help from unlicensed "back alley" abortionists, sometimes with tragic results.

By the 1960s, opposition to abortion laws was rising. In 1973, the U.S. Supreme Court rendered a landmark decision (in the cases of *Roe* v. *Wade* and *Doe* v. *Bolton*), striking down all state laws banning abortion. In effect, this action established a woman's legal access to abortion.

In the wake of the Court's decision, the abortion controversy has grown. On one side of the issue are people who describe themselves as "pro-choice," supporting a woman's right to choose abortion. On the other side are those who call themselves "pro-life," opposing abortion as morally wrong; these people would like to see the Supreme Court reverse its 1973 decision.

How strong is the support for each side of the abortion controversy? A recent national survey asked a sample of adults this question: "Should it be possible for a pregnant woman to obtain a legal abortion if the woman wants it for any reason?" In response, 37.9 percent said "yes" (placing them in the pro-choice camp) and 57.1 percent said "no" (the pro-life position); the remaining 5.0 percent offered no opinion (NORC, 2001:234).

However, a closer look shows that particular circumstances make a big difference in how people see this issue. The figure shows that a large majority of U.S. adults favor legal abortion if a pregnancy seriously threatens a woman's health, if she became pregnant as a result of rape, or if a fetus is very likely to have a serious defect. The bottom line,

SUMMARY

1. U.S. culture had long defined sex as a taboo topic, until the Kinsey studies (1948, 1953). They were among the first publications by social scientists on human sexuality.

2. Sex is the biological distinction between females and males, which is determined at conception when a male sperm joins a female ovum.

3. Males and females are distinguished not only by their genitals (primary sex characteristics) but also by bodily development as they mature (secondary sex characteristics). Hermaphrodites have some combination of both male and female genitalia. Transsexuals are people who feel that they are one sex, although, biologically, they are the other.

4. For most species, sex is rigidly directed by biology, but for human beings sex is a matter of cultural definition as well as personal choice. Patterns of kissing, modesty, and beauty vary around the world, revealing the cultural foundation of sexual practices.

NOTE: The Supreme Court has also ruled that states may require doctors to evaluate whether a fetus can survive outside the mother's body before performing an abortion (*Webster* v. *Reproductive Health Services*). Congress has twice passed a law banning "partial birth" abortion, a controversial type of abortion procedure during the third trimester. These laws were vetoed by President Clinton.

NOTE: The ancients used a wide range of plants, including Queen Anne's lace and myrrh, to make contraceptive potions (Riddle, Estes, & Russell, 1994).

DISCUSS: Where will the marketing of the "morning after" pill or the controversial RU-486 abortion pill take the current abortion debate?

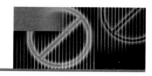

then, looks like this: About 38 percent support access to abortion under *any* circumstances, but about 80 percent support access to abortion under *some* circumstances.

Many pro-life people feel strongly that abortion is nothing more than killing unborn children. To them, people never have the right to end innocent life in this way. But pro-choice people are no less committed to their position. As they see it, the abortion debate is really about the standing of women in society.

Why? For the simple reason that women must have control over their own sexuality. If pregnancy dictates the course of women's lives, women will never be able to compete with men on equal terms, whether it is on campus or in the workplace. Thus, the pro-choice position concludes, women must have access to legal, safe abortion as a necessary condition to full participation in society.

Continue the debate . . .

1. *The more conservative pro-life people see abortion as a moral issue, whereas more liberal pro-choice people see abortion as a power issue. Can you see a parallel to how conservatives and liberals view the issue of pornography?*

2. *Surveys show that men and women have almost the same opinions about abortion. Does this surprise you? Why?*

3. *Why do you think the abortion controversy is often so bitter? Why has our nation been unable to find a middle ground on which all can agree?*

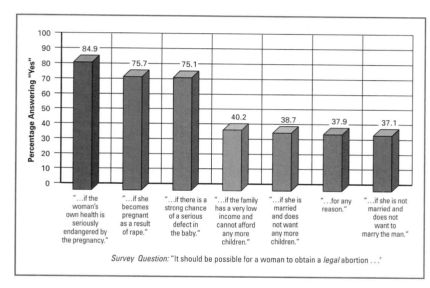

Survey Question: "It should be possible for a woman to obtain a *legal* abortion . . ."

When Should the Law Allow a Woman to Choose Abortion?
Source: NORC (2001).

Sources: Based in part on Luker (1984), Tannahill (1992), and various news reports.

5. Historically, our society has held rigid attitudes toward sexuality, although these attitudes have become more permissive over time. Thus, we see that sex is a social, as well as a biological, issue.

6. The sexual revolution, which has roots back to the 1920s but came of age in the 1960s and 1970s, increased openness in matters of sexuality. Research shows that changes in sexuality were greater for women than for men. By 1980, a sexual counterrevolution was taking form, condemning permissiveness and urging a return to more conservative "family values."

7. The share of people in the United States who have premarital sexual intercourse increased during the twentieth century. Research shows that about three-fourths of young men and two-thirds of young women have intercourse by their senior year in high school.

8. The level of sexual activity varies within the population of U.S. adults: One-third report having sex with a partner a few times a year or not at all; another one-third have sex once or several times a month; the remaining one-third have sex with a partner two or more times a week.

EXERCISE: Visit a local supermarket and examine the covers of the magazines displayed at the checkout line. To what extent is sexuality used to sell products? More specifically, are men or women more commonly portrayed in sexual terms?

CTQ1: Increased geographic mobility, greater individualism, more opportunities for women, and birth control technology all played a part in the sexual revolution, which increased the rate of premarital sex and, more generally, separated sex from reproduction.

9. Although extramarital sex is widely condemned, about 25 percent of married men and 10 percent of married women report being sexually unfaithful to their spouses at some time.

10. Sexual orientation refers to a person's romantic and emotional attraction to another person. Four major orientations are heterosexuality, homosexuality, bisexuality, and asexuality. Sexual orientation is caused by some combination of biological factors, cultural factors, and human choice.

11. The share of the population that is homosexual depends on how researchers define "homosexuality." About 9 percent of adult men and 4 percent of adult women report having some homosexual experience, compared with 2.8 percent of men and 1.4 percent of women who say they have a homosexual identity.

12. The gay rights movement has worked to gain greater acceptance for homosexuals. Largely because of this movement, the share of the U.S. population condemning homosexuality as morally wrong has steadily decreased and stands now at about half.

13. Some 1 million teenagers become pregnant each year in the United States. The rate of teenage pregnancy has dropped since 1950, when many teens married and had children. Today, however, most pregnant teens are not married and, especially when they drop out of school, are at high risk of poverty.

14. With no universal definition of pornography, the law allows local communities to set standards of decency. Many conservatives condemn pornography as immoral; by contrast, many liberals condemn it as demeaning to women.

15. Prostitution, the selling of sexual services, is illegal almost everywhere in the United States. Although many people think of prostitution as a victimless crime, it victimizes women and spreads sexually transmitted diseases.

16. Some 90,000 rapes are reported each year, but the actual number is several times greater. Although many people think of rape as a sexual act, rape is really a violent expression of power. Most rapes involve people who know one another.

17. Structural-functional theory highlights society's need to regulate sexual activity. A universal norm in this regard is the incest taboo, which keeps kin relationships clear.

18. The symbolic-interaction paradigm emphasizes how people attach various meanings to sexuality. Thus, societies differ from one another in terms of sexual attitudes and practices; similarly, sexual patterns change within any one society over time.

19. Social-conflict theory links sexuality to inequality. From this point of view, men dominate women in part by devaluing them as sexual objects.

KEY CONCEPTS

sex (p. 222) the biological distinction between females and males

primary sex characteristics (p. 223) the genitals, organs used for reproduction

secondary sex characteristics (p. 223) bodily development, apart from the genitals, that distinguishes biologically mature females and males

hermaphrodite (p. 223) a human being with some combination of female and male genitalia

transsexuals (p. 223) people who feel they are one sex even though biologically they are the other

incest taboo (p. 224) a norm forbidding sexual relations or marriage between certain relatives

sexual orientation (p. 228) a person's romantic and emotional attraction to another person

heterosexuality (p. 228) a sexual orientation in which a person is sexually attracted to someone of the other sex

homosexuality (p. 228) a sexual orientation in which a person is sexually attracted to someone of the same sex

bisexuality (p. 228) a sexual orientation in which a person is sexually attracted to people of both sexes

asexuality (p. 228) a sexual orientation in which a person is not sexually attracted to people of either sex

homophobia (p. 231) the dread of close personal interaction with people thought to be gay, lesbian, or bisexual

pornography (p. 232) sexually explicit material that causes sexual arousal

prostitution (p. 232) the selling of sexual services

queer theory (p. 239) a growing body of research findings that challenges the heterosexual bias in U. S. society

heterosexism (p. 239) a view stigmatizing anyone who is not heterosexual as "queer"

abortion (p. 239) the deliberate termination of a pregnancy

CTQ2: Sexual orientation is a person's romantic and emotional attraction to another person. This concept is hard to measure because many people do not fit into clear-cut categories; in addition, people are not always honest in their responses about sex.

CTQ3: Generally, conservatives oppose sexually explicit material as harmful to community moral standards. By contrast, liberals support free artistic expression. Even so, some liberals oppose some forms of sexual expression as demeaning to women.

CTQ4: Examples of society's regulation of sexuality range from formal norms such as the incest taboo, rape and statutory rape laws, sodomy laws, and sexual harassment regulations and statutes to informal norms involving sexual orientation and standards of beauty.

CRITICAL-THINKING QUESTIONS

1. What do sociologists mean by the term "sexual revolution"? What did the sexual revolution change? Can you suggest some reasons that these changes occurred?

2. What is sexual orientation? Why is this characteristic difficult for researchers to measure?

3. Do you think laws should regulate the portrayal of sex in books, films, or on the Internet? Why or why not?

4. In what ways do societies regulate sexuality? In what ways does sexuality play a part in social inequality?

APPLICATIONS AND EXERCISES

1. The most complete study of sexual patterns in the United States to date is *The Social Organization of Sexuality: Sexual Practices in the United States* by Edward Laumann and others. You can find this book in your campus or community library. Get a copy and browse through some of the chapters most interesting to you. Afterwards, think about the value of doing sociological research on sexuality.

2. Contact your school's student services office and ask for information about the extent of sexual violence on your campus. Do people report such crimes? What policies and procedures does your school have to respond to sexual violence?

3. Do some research on transgendered people such as Dana Rivers, profiled in the opening to this chapter. When you first read her story, would you have supported or opposed firing Rivers? After reading this chapter, do you hold the same opinion? Why?

4. Packaged in the back of this new textbook is an interactive CD-ROM that offers a variety of study and review materials intended to help you better understand the material covered in this chapter. For this chapter, the CD-ROM contains an author's tip video, Real Life Sociology videos, other relevant audio and video, interactive map animations, audio journal entries from the author, Web links, and much more.

 ## SITES TO SEE

http://www.prenhall.com/macionis

Visit the interactive *Companion Website*™ that accompanies this text. Begin by clicking on the cover of your book. You will find a chapter-by-chapter study guide, practice tests, and a significant portion of the text for on-line review, as well as many suggested Web links.

http://www.teenpregnancy.org

Visit the Web site of the National Campaign to Prevent Teen Pregnancy, an organization formed to guide teens toward responsible sexual behavior. You can find data for your state at this site. What are the key parts of this organization's program? How effective would you imagine it is? Why?

http://www.qrd.org

This Web site, the Queer Resources Directory, looks at a wide range of issues—including family, religion, education, and health—from a queer theory perspective. Visit this site to see in what ways various social institutions can be considered heterosexist. Do you agree? Why?

http://www.gay.com

This is a search engine for all sorts of information on issues involving homosexuality.

 ## INVESTIGATE WITH CONTENTSELECT

Follow the instructions found on page 23 of this textbook to enter this chapter of the book's *Companion Website*™. Once in the chapter, click on the ContentSelect icon at the bottom left of your screen and enter your personal User ID and Password. Enter keywords such as "sexuality," "incest taboo," "transgender," and "abortion," and the search engine will help you become an effective researcher.

cyber.scope

HOW NEW TECHNOLOGY IS CHANGING OUR WAY OF LIFE

Marshall McLuhan (1969) summed up his pioneering research in the study of communications this way: "Any new technology tends to create a new human environment." In other words, technology not only affects how we work but also shapes and colors our entire way of life. In this second cyber.scope, we pause to reflect on some of the ways the Information Revolution is changing our culture and society.

The Information Revolution and Cultural Values

Chapter 3 ("Culture") noted the importance members of our society attach to material comfort. Throughout our history, many people have defined "success" to mean earning a good income and enjoying the things money will buy, including a home, a car, and fashionable clothing.

But there are signs that as we move through this new century, our values may shift from a single-minded focus on the accumulation of things (the products of industrial

"Travel" to an Adirondack mountaintop and enjoy the view by visiting http://adirondack.net/adnet/bluemt/bluemt1.html or tour the Tower of London at http://www.toweroflondontour.com

technology) to an appreciation of ideas (the product of information technology). Such new-age ideas include both travel and countless experiences with virtual reality, to concern with well-being, including the self-actualization that has become popular in recent decades (Newman, 1991).

Socialization in the Computer Age

Half a century ago, television rewrote the rules for socialization in the United States, and as Chapter 5 ("Socialization") explained, young people now spend more time watching TV than talking to their parents. Today, screens are not just for television; they are our windows into a cyber-world in which we look to computers to link, entertain, and educate us. But this trend toward cyber-socialization raises several important questions.

First, will the spread of computer-based information erode the regional diversity that has marked this country's history, setting off New England from the Deep South and the Midwest from the West Coast? We know that new information technology is

linking our nation and the world, so we might well expect to see a more national culture emerge and, with time, a more global culture as well.

Second, how will this cyber-culture affect our children? Is having computers at the center of their lives good for them? For most children, at least, computer-based images and information play a significant role in teaching them about themselves and the world. Is this trend reducing the importance of parents in children's lives, as television did? Cyber-socialization can certainly entertain and instruct, but can it meet the emotional needs of children? Will it contribute to their moral development? After all, there is nothing more important to a child—and more "low-tech"—than a warm hug.

Almost unlimited access to information can be a mixed blessing, as parents can well understand. How can we prevent children from gaining access to pornography or other objectionable material on the Internet? Or, should we?

Third, who will control cyber-socialization? Just as parents have long expressed concerns about what their children watch on television, they now worry about what kids encounter as they surf the 'Net. To date, the federal courts have taken the position that the Internet should operate with minimal government interference. Do we, as citizens and as parents, have expectations for the content of virtual culture? Should the information industry operate for profit? Should there be standards to ensure some measure of educational content? Who should decide?

The Cyber-Self

A person using the name "VegDiet" enters one of thousands of chat rooms found on the Internet, the vast global network described in Chapter 7 ("Groups and Organizations"). Within a few seconds, VegDiet is actively debating the state of the world with three other people: "MrMaine," "Ferret," and "RedWine."

The growing popularity of computer chat gives us a chance to highlight ways in which online interaction differs from more conventional modes of interaction. After studying online interaction, Dennis Waskul (1997) described the self we transmit via a computer as "disembodied." Using Erving Goffman's dramaturgical approach (see Chapter 6), Waskul notes that computer technology screens out a host of "cues" about people's identities—where they are, what they look like, how they dress, and their age and sex—and conveys only the identities they choose to present.

Cyberspace thus affords us great freedom to try on identities, with few or no lasting consequences. As one chat room participant explained, "Online is a game. . . . Only here, I play with who I am" (Waskul, 1997:21).

But Wait a Minute: The Neo-Luddites

In the eighteenth century, groups of English weavers who opposed the Industrial Revolution traveled about demolishing new machinery whenever they could gain access to a factory. The Luddites (named after Ned Ludd, their leader) were convinced that the new technology of their day would end up eliminating jobs and generally make life worse (Zachary, 1997).

"On the Internet, nobody knows you're a dog."

Although the Luddites lost their battle to stem the tide of change, their spirit lives on today in people opposed to the Information Revolution. These neo-Luddites, as they are called, speak with many voices. But they agree that we should not race headlong into a cyber-future without thinking critically about how new technology is likely to make our lives better and worse.

The neo-Luddites remind us, first, that technology is never socially neutral. That is, technology does not simply exist in the world: It *changes* the world, pushing human lives in one direction while closing off other alternatives. By venerating technology as good in and of itself, Theodore Roszak (1986) points out, we give up the power to decide for ourselves how we should live. Is putting computers in the classroom a substitute for good teaching? We might well remember that no computer ever created a painting, penned a poem, or composed a symphony. Perhaps most important, computers have no ability to address ethical questions about right and wrong.

Living in a forward-looking culture, we easily imagine the benefits of new technology. But we need to remember that just as technology can serve us, it also can diminish us and even destroy us. After all, the Luddites were not anti-technology; they simply wanted to be sure that technology responded to human needs—and not the other way around.

CHAPTER

10

Paul Marcus
Upstairs–Downstairs

© Paul Marcus, *Upstairs–Downstairs*,
Studio SPM, Inc.

SOCIAL STRATIFICATION

On April 10, 1912, the ocean liner *Titanic* slipped away from the docks of Southampton, England, on its maiden voyage across the North Atlantic to New York. A proud symbol of the new industrial age, the towering ship carried 2,300 men, women, and children, some enjoying more luxury than most travelers today could imagine. Poor people crowded the lower decks, journeying to what they hoped would be a better life in the United States.

Two days out, the crew received radio warnings of icebergs in the area but paid little notice. Then, near midnight, as the ship steamed swiftly westward, a lookout was stunned to see a massive

shape rising out of the calm ocean directly ahead. Moments later, the *Titanic* collided with a huge iceberg, as tall as the ship itself, which split open its side as if the grand vessel were just a giant tin can.

Seawater flooded the lower levels, pulling the ship down by the bow. Within twenty-five minutes of impact, people were rushing for the lifeboats. By 2:00 A.M., the bow was completely submerged, and the stern high above the water. Within minutes, all lights went out. Clinging to the deck, in silence and darkness, hundreds of helpless passengers and crew passed their final minutes before the ship disappeared into the frigid Atlantic (Lord, 1976).

The tragic loss of more than 1,600 lives made news around the world. Looking back dispassionately at this terrible accident with a sociological eye, however, we note that some categories of passengers had much better odds of survival than others. In an age of conventional gallantry, women and children boarded the lifeboats first, so that 80 percent of the casualties were men. Class also was at work. More than 60 percent of people holding first-class tickets were saved because they were on the upper decks, where warnings were sounded first and lifeboats were accessible. Only 36 percent of the second-class passengers survived, and of the third-class passengers on the lower decks, only 24 percent escaped drowning. On board the *Titanic*, class turned out to mean much more than the quality of one's cabin. Class was a matter of life or death.

The fate of those aboard the *Titanic* dramatically illustrates how social inequality affects the way people live—and sometimes whether they live at all. This chapter explores the important concept of social stratification. Chapter 11 continues the story by examining social inequality in the United States, and Chapter 12 examines how our country fits into a global system of wealth and poverty.

WHAT IS SOCIAL STRATIFICATION?

For tens of thousands of years, humans the world over lived in small hunting and gathering societies. Although members of these bands might single out one person as swifter, stronger, or particularly skillful in collecting food, everyone had roughly the same social standing. As societies became more complex—a process detailed in Chapter 4 ("Society")—a major change came about. Societies began to elevate some categories of people above others, giving segments of the population more money, power, and prestige than others.

Social stratification is *a system by which a society ranks categories of people in a hierarchy*. Social stratification is a matter of four basic principles:

247

SUPPLEMENTS: The *Data File* contains a detailed outline of Chapter 10, along with supplementary lecture material and additional discussion topics.

DISCUSS: Conforming to the traditional norm, "Women and children first," 80% of the *Titanic* casualties were men. Perhaps times have changed: In a 1992 *Pittsburgh Post–Gazette* survey, 65% of men said they would not give up their lifeboat seat for a woman or child.

Q: "All the animals are equal, but some are more equal than others." George Orwell, *Animal Farm*

DIVERSITY: Regarding point 4 below, Joan Huber Rytina, William H. Form, and John Pease found that people of higher social position saw the U.S. as a more "open" society. Moreover, they found that whites perceived more opportunity than blacks did. [See *American Journal of Sociology* 75, 4 (January 1970):703–16.]

The personal experience of poverty is captured in Sebastiao Salgado's haunting photograph, which stands as a universal portrait of human suffering. The essential sociological insight is that, however strongly individuals feel its effects, our social standing is largely a consequence of the way in which a society (or a world of societies) structures opportunity and reward. To the core of our being, then, we are all the products of social stratification.

1. **Social stratification is a trait of society, not simply a reflection of individual differences.** Many of us think of social standing in terms of personal talent and effort and, as a result, we often exaggerate the extent to which we control our own fate. Did a higher percentage of the first-class passengers on the *Titanic* survive because they were smarter or better swimmers than second- and third-class passengers? Hardly. They fared better because of the system of privilege at work on the ship. Similarly, children born into wealthy families are more likely than children born into poverty to enjoy good health, achieve academically, succeed in their life's work, and live a long life. Neither the rich nor the poor people are responsible for creating social stratification, yet this system shapes the lives of us all.

2. **Social stratification persists over generations.** To see that stratification is a trait of societies rather than individuals, we need only look at how inequality persists across generations. In all societies, parents pass their social position on to their children.

    Some individuals, especially in high-income societies, experience **social mobility,** *change in one's position in the social hierarchy.* Social mobility may be upward or downward. We celebrate the achievements of Britney Spears or Michael Jordan, both of whom rose from modest beginnings to fame and fortune. But people also move downward because of business setbacks, unemployment, or illness. More often, people move *horizontally,* that is, they switch one job for another at about the same social level. For most people, social standing remains much the same over a lifetime.

3. **Social stratification is universal but variable.** Social stratification is found everywhere. Yet *what* is unequal and *how* unequal it is varies from one society to another. In some societies, inequality is mostly a matter of prestige; in others, wealth or power is the key dimension of difference. Moreover, some societies display more inequality and others less.

4. **Social stratification involves not just inequality but beliefs.** Any system of inequality not only gives some people more than others but also defines these arrangements as fair. Just as *what* is unequal differs from society to society, so does the explanation of *why* people should be unequal.

CASTE AND CLASS SYSTEMS

Sociologists distinguish between "closed" systems, which allow for little change in social position, and "open" systems, which permit considerable social mobility (Tumin, 1985).

THE CASTE SYSTEM

A **caste system** is *social stratification based on ascription, or birth.* A pure caste system is closed because birth alone determines one's destiny, with little or no opportunity for social mobility based on individual effort. Caste systems rank people in rigid categories, where they live out their lives.

Two Illustrations: India and South Africa

Many of the world's societies, most of them agrarian, approximate caste systems. One example is India, or at least India's traditional villages, where most of the people still live. The Indian system of castes (or *varna,* a Sanskrit word that means "color") is composed of four categories: Brahmin, Kshatriya, Vaishya, and

NOTE: The Latin root of "caste," *cast(us)*, means "chaste" or "pure"; its later use (for example, the Portuguese word *casta*) means "race" or "blood."
GLOBAL: Hope for India's economic development rests on three key elements that should attract foreign investment: (a) widespread use of the English language, (b) a democratic political system, and (c) a legal system suitable for modern business.

DISCUSS: Our contemporary class system still subjects women to castelike expectations: They should perform traditional tasks as a moral duty, while men are financially rewarded for their efforts. Consider the ideological element in the fact that most chefs are men who work for income while most household cooks are women performing a household duty.

In India, the traditional caste system still guides people's choice of work, especially in rural areas. Below the four basic castes are the Harijans, people defined as "outcasts" or "untouchables." These people perform jobs, such as turning leather into shoes, defined as unclean for others of higher social position.

Shudra. On the local level, however, each of these is composed of hundreds of subcaste (or *jati*) groups.

Caste has also played an important role in the history of South Africa. Until recently, this nation's policy of *apartheid* gave the 5 million South Africans of European ancestry a commanding share of wealth and power, dominating some 35 million black South Africans. In a middle position were another 3 million mixed-race people, known as "coloreds," and about 1 million Asians. The box on pages 250–51 describes the current state of South Africa's racial caste system.

In a caste system, birth shapes people's lives in four ways. First, traditional caste groups have specific occupations, so generations of a family perform the same type of work. In rural India, although some occupations (such as farming) are open to all, castes are identified with the work their members do (as priests, barbers, leather workers, sweepers, and so on). In South Africa, whites still hold most of the desirable jobs, and most blacks perform manual labor and other low-level service work.

Second, maintaining a rigid social hierarchy depends on people marrying within their own categories; "mixed" marriages would blur the ranking of children. Therefore, caste systems demand that people marry others like themselves. Sociologists call this pattern *endogamous* marriage (*endo* comes from the Greek word meaning "within"). Traditionally, Indian parents select their children's marriage partners, often before the children reach their teens. Before 1985,

South Africa outlawed marriage (and even sex) between the races; today, interracial couples are legal, but because most blacks and whites still live in separate areas, they are rare.

Third, caste norms guide people to stay in the company of "their own kind." Hindus in India support this segregation, believing that a ritually "pure" person of a higher caste will be "polluted" by contact with someone of lower standing. Apartheid in South Africa operated in much the same way.

Finally, caste systems rest on powerful cultural beliefs. Indian culture is built on Hindu moral belief in accepting one's life work, whatever it is. In South Africa, although apartheid is no longer law, most people still distinguish "white jobs" from "black jobs."

Caste and Agrarian Life

Caste systems exist in agrarian societies because the lifelong routines of agriculture depend on a rigid sense of duty and discipline. Therefore, caste persists in rural India more than sixty years after being formally outlawed and even as its grip has relaxed in big cities, where people exercise greater choice in their work and marriage partners. Similarly, the rapid industrialization of South Africa made personal choice and individual rights more important, so the abolition of apartheid was only a matter of time. In mature industrial nations such as the United States, some caste elements survive, but treating people categorically on the

RESOURCE: Daphne Topouzis's article, "Women's Poverty in Africa," is included in the 5th edition of the Macionis and Benokraitis reader, *Seeing Ourselves.*

Q: "I have used one cake of soap for three months and it is not nearly finished yet." Mahatma Gandhi

Q: "Nobody chooses his parents, but anyone, in principle, can accumulate capital." Peter Berger

Q: "In this world, a man must be either an anvil or a hammer." Henry Wadsworth Longfellow

GLOBAL SOCIOLOGY

Race as Caste: A Report from South Africa

At the southern tip of the African continent lies South Africa, a country about the size of Alaska with a population of about 44 million in 2001. Long inhabited by black people, the region attracted white Dutch traders and farmers in the mid-seventeenth century. Early in the nineteenth century, a second wave of colonization saw British immigrants push the Dutch inland. By the early 1900s, the British had taken over the country, proclaiming it the Union of South Africa. In 1961, the United Kingdom gave up control and recognized the independence of the Republic of South Africa.

But freedom was a reality only for the white minority. Years before, to ensure their political control over the black majority, whites had instituted a policy of *apartheid*, or racial separation. Apartheid was made law in 1948, denying blacks national citizenship, ownership of land, and any formal voice in the government. In effect, black South Africans became a lower caste, receiving little schooling and performing menial, low-paying jobs. Under this system, even "middle class" white households had at least one black household servant.

The prosperous white minority defended apartheid, claiming that blacks threatened their cultural traditions or, more simply, were inferior beings. But resistance to apartheid rose steadily, prompting whites to resort to brutal military repression to maintain their power.

Steady resistance—especially from younger blacks, impatient for a political voice and economic opportunity—gradually forced change. Adding to the pressure was criticism from many other nations, including the United States. By the mid-1980s, the tide began to turn as the South African government granted limited political rights to people of mixed race and Asian ancestry. Then came the right for all people to form labor unions, to enter occupations once restricted to whites, and to own property. Officials also began to dismantle the system of laws that separated the races in public places.

basis of race or sex now invites charges of racism and sexism.

Note that the erosion of caste does not signal an end to social stratification. On the contrary, it simply marks a change in its character, as the next sections explain.

THE CLASS SYSTEM

Farming demands the lifelong discipline created by caste systems. But industrial production depends on developing people's talents, giving rise to a **class system,** *social stratification based on both birth and individual achievement.*

A class system is more open, so those who acquire schooling and skills may be socially mobile in relation to their parents and siblings. Such mobility blurs class distinctions, so that even blood relatives may have different social standings. Social boundaries also break down as people immigrate from abroad or move from the countryside to the city, lured by greater opportunity for education and work (Lipset & Bendix, 1967; Cutright, 1968; Treiman, 1970). Typically, newcomers

take low-paying jobs, thereby pushing others up the social ladder (Tyree, Semyonov, & Hodge, 1979).

Categorizing people according to their color, sex, or social background comes to be seen as wrong in industrial and postindustrial societies, and all people gain political rights and roughly equal standing before the law. Moreover, in such high-income societies, work is not fixed at birth but involves some personal choice. Greater individualism also translates into more freedom in selecting a marriage partner.

Meritocracy

Compared with agrarian societies, where caste is the rule, industrial societies move toward **meritocracy,** *social stratification based on personal merit.* Because industrial societies need to develop a broad range of capabilities (beyond farming), stratification is based not only on birth but also on "merit," by which we mean the job one does and how well one does it. To advance meritocracy, industrial societies expand equality of opportunity, although people expect inequality of outcomes.

Q: "Chiefly, the mold of a man's future is in his own hands." Francis Bacon

NOTE: The term "meritocracy" is associated with Michael Young and his 1957 book *The Rise of the Meritocracy*. He is also Lord Young of Dartington, member of Parliament. He wrote, "If the soil creates castes, the machine manufactures classes." See an article by Young in *Society* 31, 6 (September/October 1994):84–89.

Q: "You can do business with anyone, but only sail with a gentleman." J.P. Morgan

SOCIAL SURVEY: "How important for getting ahead in life is ambition?" (GSS 1987, *N* = 1,285; *Codebook*, 2001:940)

"Essential"	41.6%	"Not very important"	0.7%
"Very important"	44.9%	"Not important at all"	0.2%
"Fairly important"	10.4%	DK/NR	8.2%

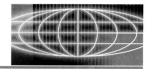

The rate of change increased in 1990, with Nelson Mandela's release from prison. In 1994, the first national election open to all people of all races elected Mandela president, ending centuries of white minority rule.

Despite this dramatic political change, social stratification in South Africa is still based on race. Even with the right to own property, one-third of black South Africans have no jobs, and the majority remain dirt poor. The worst off are some 7 million *ukuhleleleka*, which means "marginal people" in the Xhosa language. Soweto-by-the-Sea may sound like a summer getaway, but it is home to thousands of ukuhleleleka who live crammed into shacks made of packing cases, corrugated metal, cardboard, and other discarded materials. There is no

electricity for lights or refrigeration. Without plumbing, people use buckets to haul sewerage; women line up to take a turn at a single water tap that serves more than 1,000 people. Any job is hard to come by, and those who do find work are lucky to earn $200 a month.

South Africa's current president, Thabo Mbeki, elected in 1999, leads a nation still twisted by centuries of racial caste. Tourism is up and holds out promise of an economic boom in years to come. But the country can shed its past only by providing all its people with real opportunity.

Sources: Fredrickson (1981), Wren (1991), Hawthorne (1999), and Mabry & Masland (1999).

In a pure meritocracy, social position would depend entirely on a person's ability and effort. Such a system would have ongoing social mobility, blurring social categories as individuals continuously move up or down in the system, depending on their latest performance. In caste societies, "merit" (from the Latin word meaning "worthy of praise") means persisting in low-skill jobs such as farming. Caste systems honor those who do their work dutifully and remain "in their place."

Caste systems waste human potential, of course, but they are very orderly. And herein lies the answer to an important question: Why do industrial and postindustrial societies keep castelike qualities (such as letting wealth pass from generation to generation) rather than becoming complete meritocracies? Simply because a pure meritocracy diminishes the importance of families and other social groupings. Economic performance is not everything, after all. Would we want to evaluate our family members solely on their jobs? Probably not. Therefore, class systems in high-income nations move toward meritocracy to promote productivity and efficiency but retain caste elements to maintain order and social cohesion.

Status Consistency

Status consistency is the *degree of consistency in a person's social standing across various dimensions of social inequality*. A caste system has limited social mobility and high status consistency, so that the typical person has the same relative ranking with regard to wealth, power, and prestige. The greater mobility of class systems, however, produces less status consistency. In the United States, then, a college professor with an advanced degree might enjoy high social prestige but earn only a modest income. Low status consistency means that *classes* are less well defined than *castes*.

ASCRIPTION AND ACHIEVEMENT: THE UNITED KINGDOM

The mix of caste and meritocracy in class systems is well illustrated by the United Kingdom (composed of England, Wales, Scotland, and Northern Ireland), an industrial nation with a long agrarian history.

NOTE: In one sense, the English clergy cannot be considered a caste in that, until the Reformation, at least, they could not legally marry. Thus the "caste" depended on the steady flow of younger sons without inheritance.

NOTE: In the estate system, "gentleman" and "lady" designated people of noble birth. In more democratic North America, the words have come to refer indiscriminately to men and women.

The Estate System

In the Middle Ages, England had a castelike system of three *estates*. The *first estate* was a hereditary nobility composed of barely 5 percent of the population; they controlled most of the land, the chief form of wealth (Laslett, 1984). Most nobles had no occupation because they deemed engaging in trade or any other work for income beneath them. Well tended by servants, nobles used their leisure time to develop skills in riding and the martial arts and to cultivate a refined taste in art, music, and literature.

To prevent vast landholdings from being divided by heirs, the law of *primogeniture* (from the Latin words meaning "first born") demanded that all landholdings pass to the oldest son or other male relation. Younger sons had to find other means of support. Some entered the clergy—often called the *second estate*—where their spiritual power was upheld by the church's extensive landholdings. Other young men of high birth became military officers or lawyers or took up other professions considered honorable for gentlemen. In an age when no woman could inherit her father's property and few women had the opportunity to earn a living, a noble daughter depended for her security on marrying well.

Below the nobility and the clergy, most men and women formed the *third estate*, or commoners. Most commoners were serfs working land owned by nobles. With little education, most were illiterate.

As the Industrial Revolution expanded England's economy, some commoners living in cities made enough money to challenge the nobility. Greater emphasis on meritocracy, the growing importance of money, and expanded schooling and legal rights eventually blurred social rankings and gave rise to a class system.

Perhaps it is a sign of the times that these days traditional titles are put up for sale by nobles who simply need the money. In 1996, for example, the title "Lord of Wimbledon" was put on the block by the Earl Spencer—Princess Diana's brother—to raise the $300,000 he needed to redo the plumbing in one of his large homes (McKee, 1996).

The United Kingdom Today

Today, the United Kingdom has a class system, though it retains the mark of a long, feudal past. A small cluster of British families own inherited estates, attend expensive schools, and exercise great political influence. A traditional monarch, Queen Elizabeth II, stands as the United Kingdom's head of state, and Parliament's

NOTE: In 1999, the British labor party introduced a bill to abolish inherited peerages, who tend to be conservative. Blair would replace them with more life peers, who are called "Tony's cronies."

THEN AND NOW: Share of Britons who think the country would be worse off without the monarchy: *1984*, 77%; *2001*, 43% (McAllister, 2001).

House of Lords is composed of peers, about half of noble birth. However, control of the government has passed to the House of Commons, where the prime minister and other commoners typically attain positions by achievement—winning an election—rather than by birth.

Further down, roughly one-fourth of the British people form the "middle class." Many earn comfortable incomes from professions and business and are likely to have investments in the form of stocks and bonds.

Below the middle class, about half of all Britons think of themselves as "working class," earning modest incomes through manual work. In recent decades, the decline of British industries such as coal mining and steel production has led to high unemployment among working-class families. Some have slipped into poverty, joining the remaining one-fourth of Britons who are socially and economically deprived. Lower-class people—or, more simply, the poor—are heavily concentrated in northern and western regions of the United Kingdom, which are plagued by economic decay.

Today's British class system mixes caste elements and meritocracy, producing a highly stratified society in which people are quite unequal, although some move upward or downward. One legacy of the historical estate system is that social mobility is less

 London's *Sunday Times* recently presented a list of the richest people in Great Britain and various other nations. Find "The Rich List" at http://www.sunday-times.co.uk/richlist/

common in the United Kingdom than in the United States (Kerckhoff, Campbell, & Winfield-Laird, 1985). This more rigid system of inequality in the United Kingdom is reflected in the importance attached to accent. Distinctive patterns of speech develop in any society when people are separated from one another over many generations. Whereas people in the United States treat accent as a clue to where one lives (there is little mistaking a Midwestern "twang" or a southern "drawl"), Britons use accent as a mark of social class, distinguishing elites who speak the "King's English" from all others. So different are these two accents that the British seem to be a single people divided by a common language, as the saying goes.

ANOTHER EXAMPLE: JAPAN

Social stratification in Japan also mixes caste and meritocracy. Japan is at once the world's oldest, continuously operating monarchy and a modern society where wealth follows individual achievement.

GLOBAL: The average income in Japan is below that in the U.S. (see Table 12–1); to the observer, however, Japan appears as a more "middle-class society." There is little of the striking urban poverty found in the U.S.; even so, the recent emergence of homelessness has challenged the positive view many Japanese have of their society.
GLOBAL: The status/honor element of Japanese society is still evident in young people aspiring to join *ichi-ryu* (meaning "first-class")

corporations even if their income would be greater elsewhere (DeMente, 1987).
GLOBAL: After World War II, General Douglas MacArthur represented the U.S. as the ruler of occupied Japan. MacArthur modeled the new Japanese government after that of the U.S. and advanced the rights and opportunities of women; he allowed the emperor to remain as a means of stabilizing the otherwise decimated society.

The traditional caste system, with its concern for people's different social rankings, is still evident in Japan today. Here the women who work at a Japanese inn bow as a sign of respect to a male guest as he departs (in a vintage U.S. automobile that looks to be a 1957 Plymouth).

Feudal Japan

By the fifth century C.E., Japan was an agrarian society with a rigid caste system composed of nobles and commoners and ruled by an imperial family. The emperor ruled by divine right, and his military leader (or *shogun*) oversaw a number of regional warlords.

Below the nobility were the *samurai*, a warrior caste whose name means "to serve." This second rank of Japanese society was made up of soldiers who learned martial skills and who lived by a code of honor based on absolute loyalty to their leaders.

As in Great Britain, most people in Japan at this time in history were commoners who labored to scrape out a bare subsistence. Unlike their European counterparts, however, Japanese commoners were not lowest in rank. At the bottom were the *burakumin*, or "outcasts," shunned by lord and commoner alike. Much like the lowest caste groups in India, these outcasts lived apart from others, performed the most distasteful work, and, like everyone else, could not change their standing.

Japan Today

By the 1860s (the time of the Civil War in the United States), the nobles realized that Japan could not enter the modern, industrial era with its traditional caste system. Besides, as in Britain, some nobles were happy to have their children marry wealthy commoners who

had more money than they did. As Japan opened up to the larger world, the traditional caste system weakened. In 1871, the Japanese legally banned the social category of "outcast," although even today people look down on descendants of this rank. After Japan's defeat in World War II, the nobility lost legal standing, and the emperor remains only as a symbol of Japan's traditions, with little real power.

Social stratification in Japan is a far cry from the rigid caste system of centuries ago. Today, Japanese society consists of "upper," "upper-middle," "lower-middle," and "lower" classes. But no firm boundaries exist, and many people move between classes over time. But because Japanese people revere tradition, family background is never far from the surface in sizing up someone's social standing. Officially, everyone has equal standing before the law, although in practice many people still look at one another through the centuries-old lens of caste (Hiroshi, 1974; Norbeck, 1983).

Finally, traditional ideas about gender continue to shape Japanese society. Legally, the two sexes are equal, but men dominate women in many ways. Japanese par-

 For information on Japanese society, visit this University of Pittsburgh site: http://www. pitt.edu/libraries/jic/jic.html

ents are more likely to send sons rather than daughters to college, so a significant gender gap exists in education (Brinton, 1988). Consequently, most women who work have lower-level support positions in the corporate world, only rarely assuming leadership roles. Thus, individual

After the collapse of the Soviet Union in 1991, that nation began a transition toward a market economy. Since then, some people have become quite rich, but others have lost their jobs as old, inefficient factories closed. As a result, the problem of poverty has become widespread, affecting perhaps one-third of the Russian people. Scenes like this one—a Moscow woman begging for money—have become all too common.

achievement in Japan's modern class system operates in the shadow of centuries of traditional male privilege.

THE FORMER SOVIET UNION

The former Union of Soviet Socialist Republics (U.S.S.R.), which rivaled the United States as a military superpower during much of the twentieth century, was born out of revolution in 1917. The Russian Revolution ended the feudal estate system ruled by a hereditary nobility and transferred farms, factories, and other productive property from private ownership to state control.

A Classless Society?

The Russian Revolution was guided by the ideas of Karl Marx, who wrote that private ownership of productive property is the basis of social classes (see Chapter 4, "Society"). When the state took control of the economy, Soviet officials boasted that they had engineered the first classless society.

Outside the Soviet Union, however, analysts were skeptical of this claim (Lane, 1984). They pointed out that the jobs people held actually fell into four unequal categories. At the top were high government officials, or *apparatchiks*. Next came the Soviet intelligentsia, including lower government officials, college professors, scientists, physicians, and engineers. Below them were manual workers and, at the lowest level, the rural peasantry.

These categories enjoyed very different living standards, so the former Soviet Union was not really classless at all. But putting factories, farms, colleges, and hospitals under state control did limit economic inequality (although doing so probably increased differences of power) compared with that of capitalist societies such as the United States.

The Second Russian Revolution

After decades of organizing Soviet society according to the ideas of Karl Marx (and revolutionary leader Vladimir Lenin), the Soviet Union shook with change after Mikhail Gorbachev became president in 1985. Gorbachev introduced a program popularly known as *perestroika*, meaning "restructuring." He saw that although the Soviet system had reduced economic inequality, nearly everyone was poor, and living standards lagged far behind those of higher-income nations in the West. Gorbachev sought to generate economic expansion by reducing inefficient centralized control of the economy.

Gorbachev's economic reforms turned into one of the most dramatic social movements in history. Throughout Eastern Europe, socialist governments toppled, and in 1991 the Soviet Union itself collapsed. People blamed their poverty and their lack of basic freedoms on a repressive ruling class of Communist party officials. In the Soviet Union, for

GLOBAL: The Soviet empire in Eastern Europe included the Baltic nations of Estonia, Latvia, and Lithuania, Poland, East Germany, Czechoslovakia, Romania, Hungary, and Bulgaria. Between 1989 and 1991, all established their political independence from what is now the Russian Federation.
NOTE: Estimates placed the fortune of the Soviet Communist party, dissolved in August 1991, at roughly $175 billion.

NOTE: Figure 10–1 is consistent with Figure 10–2, the Kuznets curve. Lower-income countries typically have greater economic inequality than higher-income nations do. Note, however, that income inequality also reflects intentional policies and ranges from an income ratio of 3:1 or 4:1 in socialist nations and Japan to around 11:1 in the U.S.

example, just 6 percent of the population formed the Communist party, which ran the whole country.

The Soviet story shows that social inequality involves more than economic resources. Soviet society may not have had the extremes of wealth and poverty found in Great Britain, Japan, and the United States. But an elite class existed all the same, one based on power rather than wealth. Thus, despite the fact that both Mikhail Gorbachev and his successor, Boris Yeltsin, earned far less than a U.S. president, they wielded awesome power.

What about social mobility in the Soviet Union? During the twentieth century there was as much upward social mobility in the Soviet Union as in Great Britain, Japan, and even the United States. Rapidly expanding industry and government drew many poor rural peasants into factories and offices (Dobson, 1977; Lane, 1984; Shipler, 1984). This trend illustrates what sociologists call **structural social mobility**, *a shift in the social position of large numbers of people due more to changes in society itself than to individual efforts.*

November 24, Odessa, Ukraine. The first snow of our voyage flies over the decks as our ship puts in at Odessa, the former Soviet Union's southernmost port on the Black Sea. A short distance from the dock, we gaze up the Potemkin Steps—the steep stairway leading to the city proper where the first shots of the Russian Revolution rang out. It has been six years since our last visit, and much has changed; indeed, the Soviet Union itself has collapsed. Has life improved? For some people, certainly: There are now chic boutiques where well-dressed shoppers buy fine wines, designer clothes, and imported perfumes. Outside, shiny new Volvos, Mercedes, and even a few Cadillacs stand next to the small Ladas from the "old days." But for most, life seems much worse. Flea markets line the curbs as families sell home furnishings. Many are desperate in a town where meat sells for $4 a pound and the average person earns about $30 a month. Even the city has to save money by shutting off street lights at eight o'clock. The spirits of most people seem as dim as Odessa's streets.

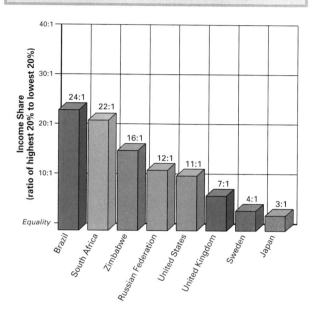

GLOBAL SNAPSHOT

FIGURE 10–1 Economic Inequality in Selected Countries, 1990–2000

These data are the most recent available, representing income share for various years between 1990 and 2000.

Sources: U.S. Census Bureau (2001) and The World Bank (2001).

During the 1990s structural social mobility in the Russian Federation took a downturn. In fact, between 1990 and 1998, the average life span for Russian men dropped by eight years and for women, two years. Many factors are involved in this decline, including Russia's poor health care system, but the Russian people clearly are suffering from a turbulent period of economic change (Róna-Tas, 1994; Specter, 1997b; Bohlen, 1998; Gerber & Hout, 1998).

In the long run, closing inefficient state industries may improve the nation's economic performance. In the short run, however, most citizens face hard times as living standards fall. Moreover, as state-run businesses become privately owned, the gulf between rich and poor grows, a trend reflected in Figure 10–1. Thus, while some praise the recent changes, others do little more than hang on, hoping for a higher living standard.

Medieval Europeans accepted rigid social hierarchy as part of a divine plan for the world. This fifteenth-century painting by the Limbourg brothers shows nobles and high church officials well served by soldiers and servants.

Limbourg Brothers, *Les Tres Riches Heures–January–Purged*, 1400–D. 1416, Flemish. By courtesy of The Board of Trustees of The Victoria & Albert Museum, London/Bridgeman Art Library, London/SuperStock.

IDEOLOGY: THE POWER BEHIND STRATIFICATION

Noting the extent of social inequality around the world, we might wonder how societies persist without sharing resources more equally. Castelike systems in Great Britain and Japan lasted for centuries, placing land and power in the hands of several hundred families. For 2,000 years, people in India have accepted the idea that they should be privileged or poor because of the accident of birth.

A major reason social hierarchies endure, then, is **ideology,** *cultural beliefs that justify social stratification.* A belief—for example, the idea that the rich are smart and the poor are lazy—is ideological to the extent that it defines the wealthy as worthy and suggests that poor people deserve their plight.

Plato and Marx on Ideology

The ancient Greek philosopher Plato (427–347 B.C.E.) defined *justice* as agreement about who should have what. Every culture considers some type of inequality "fair," Plato explained. Karl Marx, too, understood this fact, although he was far more critical of inequality than Plato. Marx took capitalist societies to task for channeling wealth and power to a few and defending the process as "a law of the marketplace." Capitalist law defines the right to own property, Marx continued, and inheritance ensures that money stays within the same families from one generation to the next. In short, Marx concluded, culture and institutions combine to shore up a society's elite, which is why established hierarchies last a long time.

Historical Patterns of Ideology

Ideology changes as a society's economy and technology change. Because agrarian societies depend on the routine labor of their people, they develop caste systems that view performing the duties of one's "station" as a moral responsibility within a natural order. With the rise of industrial capitalism, personal initiative acquires value, and an ideology of meritocracy develops. Wealth and power become prizes won by those who perform the best. Under industrial capitalism, the poor, the object of charity under feudalism, are scorned as personally undeserving. This harsh view is expressed in the work of Herbert Spencer, as explained in the box.

History shows how difficult it is to change social stratification. However, challenges to the status quo always arise. Traditional notions of a "woman's place," for example, are giving way to economic opportunity for women. The continuing progress toward racial equality in South Africa also exemplifies widespread rejection of the ideology of apartheid.

THE FUNCTIONS OF SOCIAL STRATIFICATION

Why are societies stratified at all? One answer, consistent with the structural-functional paradigm, is that social inequality plays a vital part in the operation of

Q: "The ruling ideas of each age have ever been the ideas of its ruling class." Karl Marx, *Manifesto of the Communist Party*

NOTE: Andrew G. Walder (1995) argues that communist organizations allocate rewards to members to promote conformity to the party line, a case of stratification enhancing political correctness rather than market productivity.

DISCUSS: Davis and Moore's thesis suggests that agrarian societies, with little productive specialization, do not have to provide differential rewards to the mass of "commoners." However, such societies demand persistence; thus, faithfully performing one's duty carries the reward of honor.

RESOURCE: Davis and Moore's analysis is one of the classics in the companion reader, *Seeing Ourselves.*

CRITICAL THINKING

Is Getting Rich "The Survival of the Fittest"?

"The survival of the fittest"—we have all heard these words used to describe society as a competitive jungle. The phrase was coined by one of sociology's pioneers, Herbert Spencer (1820–1903), whose ideas about social inequality are still widespread today.

Spencer, who lived in England, eagerly followed the work of the natural scientist Charles Darwin (1809–1882). Darwin's theory of biological evolution holds that a species changes physically over many generations as it adapts to the natural environment. Spencer, thinking to apply Darwin's theory to the operation of society, proposed that society is a "jungle," with the "fittest" people rising to the top and the weak gradually sinking into miserable poverty.

In the United States, Spencer's distortion of Darwin's theory was popular among the powerful industrialists of that time. John D. Rockefeller (1839–1937), who made a vast fortune building the oil industry, recited Spencer's "social gospel" to young children in Sunday school. As Rockefeller saw it, the growth of giant corporations—and the astounding wealth of their owners—was merely a basic fact of nature. Neither Spencer nor Rockefeller had much sympathy for the poor, seeing poverty as evidence of not measuring up in a competitive world. Spencer opposed social welfare programs for penalizing society's "best" members (through taxes) and rewarding society's "worst" members (through welfare benefits).

Today's sociologists are quick to point out that social standing is not a simple matter of personal effort, as Spencer contended. Nor is it the case that companies or people who generate more money necessarily benefit society. Yet Spencer's view that people get what they deserve in life remains part of our individualistic culture.

What do you think?

1. *What did Herbert Spencer mean when he said society encourages "the survival of the fittest"?*

2. *Why do you think Spencer's ideas are still popular in the United States?*

3. *In what sense do highly paid people benefit society? In what ways do they not?*

society. This argument was set forth more than fifty years ago by Kingsley Davis and Wilbert Moore (1945).

THE DAVIS-MOORE THESIS

The **Davis-Moore thesis** states that *social stratification has beneficial consequences for the operation of a society.* How else, ask Davis and Moore, can we explain the fact that some form of social stratification has been found in every known society?

Davis and Moore note that modern societies have hundreds of occupational positions of varying importance. Certain jobs—say, washing windows or answering telephones—are fairly easy and can be performed by almost anyone. Other jobs—such as designing computers or transplanting human organs—are difficult and demand the scarce talents of people with extensive (and expensive) training.

Therefore, Davis and Moore explain, the greater the functional importance of a position, the more

rewards a society attaches to it. This strategy promotes productivity and efficiency because rewarding important work with income, prestige, power, and leisure encourages people to do these jobs and to work better, longer, and harder. Unequal rewards benefit some individuals, then, and a system of unequal rewards (which is what social stratification is) benefits society as a whole.

Davis and Moore concede that any society can be egalitarian, but only to the extent that people are willing to let *anyone* perform *any* job. Equality also demands that someone who carries out a job poorly be rewarded the same as someone who performs well. Such a system clearly offers little incentive for people to try their best and thereby reduces a society's productive efficiency.

The Davis-Moore thesis suggests why some form of stratification exists everywhere; it does not state precisely what rewards a society should give to any occupational position or just how unequal the rewards

CRITICAL THINKING

Big Bucks: Are the Rich Worth What They Earn?

For an hour of work, a Los Angeles priest earns about $5, a hotel maid in New Orleans about $7, a bus driver in San Francisco about $15, a Phoenix bartender about $20, and a Detroit auto worker roughly $25. By comparison, Barry Bonds earns $40,000 per hour playing baseball for the San Francisco Giants. And what about the $100,000 actor Jim Carrey makes for every hour he spends making a movie? Or the $200,000 Oprah Winfrey collects for each hour she chats with guests before the television cameras? Or the $1 million Tim Allen recently earned for filming each half-hour episode of the sitcom *Home Improvement*?

The Davis-Moore thesis suggests that rewards reflect an occupation's value to society. But are the talents of Michael Jordan, who earned $33 million in just one year playing basketball (more than all the other Chicago Bulls combined) worth more than the efforts of all 100 U.S. senators or 1,000 police officers? In short, do earnings really reflect people's social importance?

In industrial-capitalist societies such as the United States, salaries reflect the market forces of supply and demand. In simple terms, the more you create value in a market system, the more rewards you command. According to this view, movie and television stars, top athletes, writers of popular songs, doctors and other professionals, and many business executives have rare talents that are much in demand; thus, they earn many times more than the typical worker in the United States. Even Elvis Presley's estate—more than twenty-five years after the popular singer's death—still pulls in about $35 million in royalties each year.

But critics of the Davis-Moore thesis question whether the market is really a good evaluator of occupational importance. First, they say, the U.S. economy is dominated by a small proportion

Julia Roberts is among the highest-paid women in the film industry, making millions for starring in each picture. Why does she earn so much more than many lower-paid actors?

of people who manipulate the system for their own benefit. Corporate executives pay themselves multimillion-dollar salaries and bonuses whether their companies do well or not. Lawrence Ellison, CEO of Oracle computer corporation, earned more than $350 million in 2000, even as the price of his company's stock fell dramatically. Moreover, say the critics, many people who make very real contributions to society get little reward in return. The average teacher would have to work more than 10,000 years to earn Ellison's 2000 income.

Equating income with social worth, then, is risky business. Those who defend the market as a measure of occupational worth ask what would be better. But as critics see it, our economic system amounts to a closed game in which only a handful of people have the money to play.

What do you think?

1. *Do you think that highly paid entertainers such as Julia Roberts deserve a thousand times more than an average worker? Why or why not?*

2. *We would all agree that parents perform a vital task as they raise children. Why is parenting unpaid work?*

3. *What about the argument that higher pay would improve the quality and performance of teachers? Do you agree? Why or why not?*

should be. Davis and Moore merely point out that positions a society considers very important must carry enough reward to draw talent away from less important work.

Critical evaluation. Although the Davis-Moore thesis is an important contribution to sociological analysis, it has provoked criticism. Melvin Tumin (1953) wondered, first, how we assess how important any occupation is.

DISCUSS: In 1996, Tiger Woods earned nearly $1 million winning his first two tournaments right after turning pro at age 20. By the time he won the Masters in 1997, he was signing endorsement contracts for some $40 million. Why does he rate such amounts? (The secretary-general of the UN makes $205,809 annually plus a house, car and chauffeur, and entertainment allowance.)

Q: "The small tradespeople, shopkeepers, and retired tradespeople generally, the handicraftsmen and peasants—all these sink gradually into the proletariat." Karl Marx and Friedrich Engels

Q: "That all men are born to equal rights is true . . . but to teach that all men are born with equal powers and faculties, to equal influence in society, to equal property and advantages through life is . . . gross fraud." John Adams

Obviously, we cannot say that important jobs are simply those with high rewards because that amounts to circular reasoning (that is, we assume important jobs have high rewards, but then we define a job's importance by its level of reward so that our thesis is correct by definition). Perhaps the high rewards our society gives to, say, physicians, results partly from deliberate efforts by the medical profession to limit the supply of physicians and thereby increase the demand for their services.

Moreover, do rewards really reflect the contribution someone makes to society? With an income approaching $100 million per year, television personality

 Do corporate CEOs deserve their high salaries? The AFL-CIO offers a critical view at their site where they track CEO salaries: http://www.aflcio.org/paywatch/index.htm

Oprah Winfrey earns more in two days than George W. Bush makes all year as president. Would anyone argue that hosting a talk show is more important than leading the country? The box takes a critical look at the link between pay and societal importance.

Second, Tumin claims that the Davis-Moore thesis ignores ways in which social stratification can *prevent* the development of individual talent. Born to privilege, rich children may develop their abilities, something many gifted poor children may never do.

Third, by suggesting that social stratification benefits all of society, the Davis-Moore thesis ignores how social inequality promotes conflict and even outright revolution. This criticism leads us to the social-conflict paradigm, which provides a very different explanation for social hierarchy.

STRATIFICATION AND CONFLICT

Social-conflict analysis argues that rather than benefiting society as a whole, social stratification provides some people with advantages over others. This analysis draws heavily on the ideas of Karl Marx, with contributions from Max Weber.

KARL MARX: CLASS AND CONFLICT

Karl Marx, whose ideas are discussed fully in Chapter 4 ("Society"), explained that most people have one of two basic relationships to the means of production: They can either own productive property or work for others. This productive role is the basis of social class. In medieval Europe, the nobility and church officials owned the productive land; peasants toiled as farmers. Similarly, in industrial class systems, the

capitalists (or the bourgeoisie) control factories, which use the labor of workers (the proletariat).

Marx saw great inequality in wealth and power arising from capitalism, which, he argued, made class conflict inevitable. In time, he believed, oppression and misery would drive the working majority to organize and ultimately overthrow capitalism.

Marx lived at a time when a small number of industrialists were amassing huge fortunes. Andrew Carnegie, J. P. Morgan, John D. Rockefeller, and John Jacob Astor (one of the few very rich passengers to perish on the *Titanic*) lived in fabulous mansions adorned with priceless art and staffed by dozens of servants. Their wealth was staggering: Andrew Carnegie, founder of U.S. Steel, reportedly earned some $20 million a year at the beginning of the twentieth century (more than $100 million in today's dollars), at a time when the average worker earned roughly $500 a year (Baltzell, 1964; Pessen, 1990).

But according to Marx, the capitalist elite draws strength not just from the operation of the economy. Through the family, opportunity and wealth are passed down from generation to generation. Moreover, the legal system defends private property and inheritance. Finally, elite children mix at exclusive schools, forging social ties that will benefit them throughout their lives. In short, from Marx's point of view, capitalist society *reproduces the class structure in each new generation.*

Critical evaluation. Marx's analysis of how capitalism creates conflict between classes has greatly influenced sociological thinking. But because it is revolutionary, calling for the overthrow of capitalist society, Marxism is also highly controversial.

One of the strongest criticisms of Marxism is that it denies a central tenet of the Davis-Moore thesis: that motivating people to perform various social roles requires some system of unequal rewards. Marx separated reward from performance, endorsing a roughly equal system based on the principle of "from each according to his ability; to each according to his needs" (1972:388; orig.1848). Critics argue that severing rewards from performance is exactly what caused low productivity in the former Soviet Union and other socialist economies around the world.

Defenders of Marx counter that there is much evidence supporting Marx's view of humanity as inherently social rather than selfish (Clark, 1991; Fiske, 1991). Therefore, we should not assume that individual rewards (much less, money alone) are the only way to motivate people to perform their social roles.

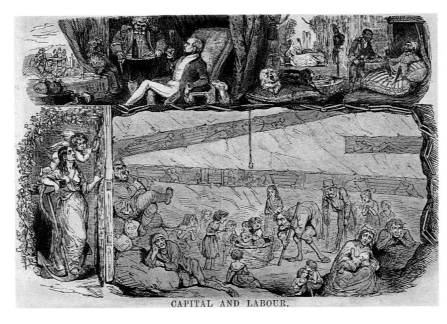

CAPITAL AND LABOUR.

This cartoon, titled "Capital and Labour," appeared in the English press in 1843, when the ideas of Karl Marx were first gaining attention. It links the plight of that country's coal miners to the privileges enjoyed by those who owned coal-fired factories.

A second problem is that the revolutionary developments Marx considered inevitable within capitalist societies have, by and large, failed to happen. The next section explores why the socialist revolution Marx predicted has not occurred, at least not in advanced capitalist societies.

WHY NO MARXIST REVOLUTION?

Despite Marx's prediction, capitalism is still thriving. Why have workers in the United States and other industrial societies not overthrown capitalism? Ralf Dahrendorf (1959) suggests four reasons:

1. **The fragmentation of the capitalist class.** Today, millions of stockholders, rather than single families, own most large companies. Moreover, day-to-day operation of large corporations is now in the hands of a managerial class, whose members may or may not be major stockholders. With stock widely held—by the late 1990s, about 40 percent of U.S. adults were in the market— more and more people have a direct stake in preserving the capitalist system.

2. **A higher standard of living.** As Chapter 16 ("The Economy and Work") explains, a century ago most workers were in factories or on farms performing **blue-collar occupations,** *lower-prestige work that involves mostly manual labor.* Today, most workers hold **white-collar occupations,** *higher-prestige work that involves mostly mental activity.* These jobs are in sales, management, and other service fields. Most of today's white-collar workers do not think of themselves as an "industrial proletariat." Just as important, the average U.S. worker's income rose almost tenfold over the course of the twentieth century, even allowing for inflation, and the workweek decreased. As a result, most workers consider themselves better off than their parents and grandparents, a case of structural mobility encouraging people to accept the present system (Edwards, 1979; Gagliani, 1981; Wright & Martin, 1987).

3. **More worker organizations.** Workers today have organizational clout that they lacked a century ago. With the right to organize into labor unions, workers make demands of management backed up by threats of work slowdowns and strikes. In other words, worker-management disputes are settled without threatening the capitalist system.

4. **More extensive legal protections.** During the twentieth century, the government passed laws to make the workplace safer and developed programs such as unemployment insurance,

TABLE 10–1 Two Explanations of Social Stratification: A Summary

Structural-Functional Paradigm	Social-Conflict Paradigm
Social stratification keeps society operating. Linking greater rewards to more important social possessions benefits society as a whole.	Social stratification is the result of social conflict. Differences in social resources serve the interests of some and harm others.
Social stratification matches talents and abilities to appropriate occupational positions.	Social stratification ensures that much talent and ability in society will not be developed at all.
Social stratification is both useful and inevitable.	Social stratification is useful only to some people; it is not inevitable
The values and beliefs that legitimize social inequality are widely shared throughout society.	Values and beliefs tend to be ideological; they reflect the interests of the more powerful members of society.
Because systems of social stratification are useful to society as a whole and are supported by cultural values and beliefs, they are usually stable over time.	Because systems of social stratification reflect the interests of only part of society, they are unlikely to remain stable over time.

Source: Adapted in part from Arthur L. Stinchcombe, "Some Empirical Consequences of the Davis-Moore Theory of Stratification," *American Sociological Review*, Vol. 28, No. 5 (October 1963):808.

disability protection, and Social Security to provide workers with greater financial security.

A Counterpoint

These developments suggest that society has smoothed many of capitalism's rough edges. Yet many claim that Marx's analysis of capitalism is still largely valid (Miliband, 1969; Edwards, 1979; Giddens, 1982; Domhoff, 1983; Stephens, 1986; Boswell & Dixon, 1993; Hout, Brooks, & Manza, 1993). First, wealth remains highly concentrated, with 40 percent of all privately owned property in the hands of just 1 percent of our population (Keister, 2000). Second, many of today's white-collar jobs offer no more income, security, or satisfaction than factory work did a century ago. Third, many benefits enjoyed by today's workers came about through the class conflict Marx described, and workers still struggle to hold on to what they have. Fourth, although workers have gained legal protections, the law still protects the private property of the rich. Therefore, social-conflict theorists conclude, the absence of a socialist revolution in the United States does not negate Marx's analysis of capitalism.

Table 10–1 summarizes the contributions of the two contrasting sociological approaches to understanding social stratification.

MAX WEBER: CLASS, STATUS, AND POWER

Max Weber, whose approach to social analysis is described in Chapter 4 ("Society"), agreed with Karl Marx that social stratification causes social conflict, but he considered Marx's two-class model simplistic. Instead, he thought social stratification involves three distinct dimensions of inequality.

The first dimension is economic inequality—the issue so vital to Marx—which Weber called *class* position. Weber did not think of "classes" as crude categories but as a continuum ranging from high to low. Weber's second dimension of social stratification is *status*, or social prestige, and the third is *power*.

The Socioeconomic Status Hierarchy

Marx viewed social prestige and power as simple reflections of economic position and did not treat them as distinct dimensions of inequality. But Weber noted that status consistency in modern societies often is quite low: A local government official, for instance, might wield great power yet have little wealth or social prestige.

Weber's contribution, then, is portraying social stratification in industrial societies as a multidimensional ranking rather than a hierarchy of clearly defined classes. In line with Weber's thinking, sociologists use the term **socioeconomic status (SES)** to refer to *a composite ranking based on various dimensions of social inequality.*

Because people vary on the three dimensions of class, status, and power, Weber saw society not in terms of distinct classes, as Marx did, but as a broad range of self-interested social categories. For Weber, social conflict is therefore both variable and complex.

The extent of social inequality in agrarian systems is greater than that found in industrial societies. One indication of the unchallenged power of rulers is the monumental structures built over years with the unpaid labor of common people. Although the Taj Mahal in India is among the world's most beautiful buildings, it is merely a tomb for a single individual.

Inequality in History

Weber noted that each of his three dimensions of social inequality stands out at different points in the evolution of human societies. Agrarian societies emphasize status or social prestige, typically in the form of honor. Members of these societies gain status by conforming to cultural norms that correspond to their rank.

Industrialization and the development of capitalism level traditional rankings based on birth but generate striking financial inequality. Thus, Weber argued, the crucial difference between people in industrial societies is the economic dimension of class.

Over time, industrial and, especially, postindustrial societies witness the growth of a bureaucratic state. Bigger government and the spread of all kinds of other organizations make power more important in the stratification system. Especially in socialist societies, because government regulates many aspects of life, high-ranking officials become the new elite.

Historical analysis points to a final difference between Weber and Marx. Marx thought societies could eliminate social stratification by abolishing private ownership of productive property. Weber doubted that overthrowing capitalism would significantly diminish social stratification. It might lessen economic disparity, he reasoned, but socialism would simultaneously increase inequality by expanding government and concentrating power in the hands of a political elite. Popular uprisings against entrenched bureaucracies in Eastern Europe and the former Soviet Union support Weber's position.

Critical evaluation. Weber's multidimensional view of social stratification has strongly influenced sociologists. But critics (particularly those who favor Marx's ideas) argue that although social class boundaries may have blurred, industrial and postindustrial nations still show striking patterns of social inequality.

Moreover, as we shall see in Chapter 11 ("Social Class in the United States"), income inequality has increased in recent years. In light of this trend, whereas some people favor Weber's multidimensional hierarchy, others think Marx's view of the rich versus the poor is closer to the mark.

STRATIFICATION AND TECHNOLOGY: A GLOBAL PERSPECTIVE

We can weave together a number of observations made in this chapter by considering the relationship between a society's technology and its type of social stratification. This analysis draws on Gerhard Lenski's model of sociocultural evolution, detailed in Chapter 4 ("Society").

HUNTING AND GATHERING SOCIETIES

With simple technology, hunters and gatherers produce only what is necessary for day-to-day living. Some people may produce more than others, but the

NOTE: Lenski's analysis of historical changes in human societies, including the types noted here, is found in the first section of Chapter 4, "Society."
Q: "Whether we like to admit it or not, a society which encourages the full flowering of individual liberty is, and can only be, a stratified society." Andrew Hacker

Q: "Men may not get all they pay for in this world; but they must certainly pay for all they get." Frederick Douglass
NOTE: The shrinking stature of the U.S. rich is suggested by this comparison: When William Henry Vanderbilt died in 1885, his obituary covered the entire front page of *The New York Times*. When Sam Walton died in 1992, his death was reported on 1/20th of a page.

group's survival depends on all sharing what they have. Thus, no categories of people emerge as better off than others.

HORTICULTURAL, PASTORAL, AND AGRARIAN SOCIETIES

As technological advances create a surplus, social inequality increases. In horticultural and pastoral societies, a small elite controls most of the surplus. Large-scale agriculture is more productive still, and marked inequality—as great as any time in human history—means that various categories of people lead strikingly different lives. Agrarian nobility typically exercises godlike power over the masses.

INDUSTRIAL SOCIETIES

Industrialization turns the tide, lessening inequality. Prompted by the need to develop individual talents, meritocracy takes hold and erodes the power of traditional elites. Industrial productivity also raises the standard of living of the historically poor majority. Furthermore, the specialized work performed in industrial societies demands schooling for all, sharply reducing illiteracy. A literate population, in turn, presses for a greater voice in political decision making, further diminishing social inequality and lessening men's domination of women.

Over time, even wealth becomes somewhat less concentrated (countering the trend predicted by Marx). In the 1920s, the richest 1 percent of the U.S. population owned about 36 percent of all wealth, a figure that fell to 30 percent by the 1980s (Williamson & Lindert, 1980; Beeghley, 1989; *1991 Green Book*). Such trends help explain why Marxist revolutions occurred in *agrarian* societies—such as the former Soviet Union (1917), Cuba (1959), and Nicaragua (1979)—where social inequality is most pronounced, rather than in industrial societies, as Marx predicted. However, wealth inequality turned up again after 1990 (Keister, 2000).

THE KUZNETS CURVE

In human history, technological progress first increases but then moderates the extent of social stratification. Greater inequality is functional for agrarian societies, but industrial societies benefit from a more egalitarian climate. This historical trend, recognized by the Nobel

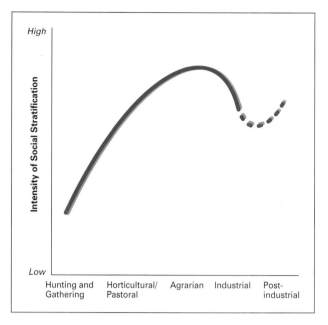

FIGURE 10–2 Social Stratification and Technological Development: The Kuznets Curve

The Kuznets curve shows that greater technological sophistication generally is accompanied by more pronounced social stratification. The trend reverses itself as industrial societies relax rigid castelike distinctions in favor of greater opportunity and equality under the law. Political rights are more widely extended, and there is even some leveling of economic differences. The Kuznets curve may also be usefully applied to the relative social standing of the two sexes. However, the emergence of postindustrial society has brought an upturn in economic inequality, as indicated by the broken line added by the author.

Source: Created by the author, based on Kuznets (1955) and Lenski (1966).

Prize–winning economist Simon Kuznets (1955, 1966), is illustrated by the Kuznets curve, shown in Figure 10–2.

Patterns of social inequality around the world today generally square with the Kuznets curve. Global Map 10–1 on page 264 shows that high-income nations that have passed through the industrial era (including the United States, Canada, and nations of Western Europe) have somewhat less income inequality than nations in which agriculture remains a major part of the economy (as is common in Latin America

DIVERSITY: In every society, income inequality ratios are greater for men than for women, who are underrepresented at the highest income levels (cf. Hout, Brooks, & Manza, 1993).

GLOBAL: Data for share of income (%) received by top and bottom 20%, by country: Lesotho, 60.1/2.8; Dominican Republic, 53.3/5.1; Australia, 41.3/5.9; Spain, 40.3/7.5; Canada, 39.3/7.5; India, 46.1/8.1; Sweden, 34.5/9.6 (World Bank, 2001).

GLOBAL: Figure 12–1 shows the distribution of the world's income by fifths of humanity:
Richest 20%: 80% of income
Second 20%: 10% of income
Middle 20%: 6% of income
Fourth 20%: 3% of income
Poorest 20%: 1% of income

WINDOW ON THE WORLD

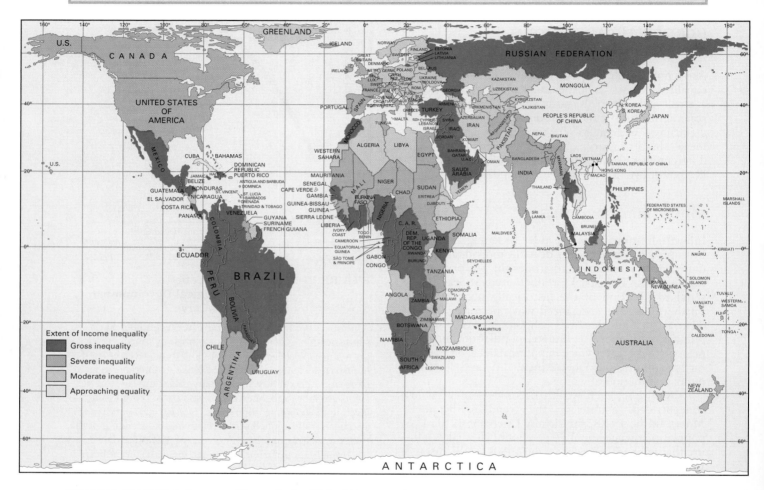

GLOBAL MAP 10–1 Income Disparity in Global Perspective

Societies throughout the world differ in the rigidity and extent of social stratification and in overall standard of living. This map highlights income inequality. Generally speaking, countries that have centralized, socialist economies (including the People's Republic of China and Cuba) display the least income inequality, although their standard of living is low. Postindustrial societies with predominantly capitalist economies, including the United States and most of Western Europe, have higher overall living standards accompanied by severe income disparity. The less economically developed countries of Latin America and Africa (including Mexico, Brazil, and the Democratic Republic of the Congo), as well as the Russian Federation and much of the Arab world, exhibit the most pronounced inequality of income.

Sources: *Peters Atlas of the World* (1990); updates by the author from United Nations Development Programme (1999).

264 CHAPTER 10 Social Stratification

The early industrial era, according to Simon Kuznets, is marked by extreme social inequality that affords aristocratic people a life of leisure while others toil at manual labor for pennies a day. U.S. artist Ford Madox Brown (1821–1893) captures such class distinctions in his painting, Work. *Today, more than a century after Brown lived, do you think class differences in the United States have become smaller or greater? Why?*

and Africa). Of course, income disparity reflects not just technological development but also political and economic priorities. Of all high–income nations, the United States has the most income inequality.

And what of the future? A glance back at Figure 10–2 shows that we have extended the trend described by Kuznets to the postindustrial era (the broken line) to show increased social inequality. That is, as the Information Revolution moves ahead, we are experiencing some economic polarization (discussed in the next chapter), suggesting that the long-term trend may differ from what Kuznets observed half a century ago (Nielsen & Alderson, 1997).

SOCIAL STRATIFICATION: FACTS AND VALUES

> The year was 2081 and everybody was finally equal. They weren't only equal before God and the law. They were equal every which way. Nobody was smarter than anybody else. Nobody was better looking than anybody else. Nobody was stronger or quicker than anybody else. All this equality was due to the 211th, 212th, and 213th Amendments to the Constitution and the

unceasing vigilance of agents of the Handicapper General.

With these words, novelist Kurt Vonnegut, Jr. (1961) begins the story of *Harrison Bergeron,* an imaginary account of a future United States in which all social inequality has been abolished. Vonnegut warns that although perhaps appealing in principle, equality can be a dangerous concept in practice. His story describes a nightmare of social engineering whereby every individual talent that makes one person different from another is systematically neutralized by the government.

To eradicate differences that make one person "better" than another, Vonnegut's state requires that physically attractive people wear masks that make them average looking, that intelligent people wear earphones that generate distracting noise, and that the best athletes and dancers be fitted with weights to make them as clumsy as everyone else. In short, although we may imagine that social equality would liberate people to make the most of their talents, Vonnegut concludes that an egalitarian society could exist only by reducing everyone to the lowest common denominator.

Like Vonnegut's story, all of this chapter's explanations of social stratification involve value judgments.

GLOBAL: Intriguing in light of the "bell curve" debate, the People's Republic of China adopted a policy to ban marriages between people deemed likely to produce physically or mentally defective children that would undermine the "quality of the population."
Q: "Our thesis is that . . . the twenty-first [century] will open on a world in which cognitive ability is the decisive dividing force." Richard Herrnstein and Charles Murray

Q: "The more complex a society becomes, the more valuable are the people who are especially good at dealing with complexity." Richard Herrnstein and Charles Murray
Q: "The very same people who scream freedom of expression for Snoop Doggy Dogg or Robert Mapplethorpe . . . would be only too happy to silence—or academically lynch—Charles Murray or his late partner, Richard Herrnstein." Leon R. Kass

CONTROVERSY & DEBATE

The Bell Curve Debate: Are Rich People Really Smarter?

It is rare when a social science book captures the attention of people across the country. But *The Bell Curve: Intelligence and Class Structure in American Life*, by Richard J. Herrnstein and Charles Murray, did that and more. The book ignited a firestorm of controversy over why social stratification divides our society and, just as important, what should be done about it.

The Bell Curve is a long (800-page) book that addresses many complex issues, but at bottom it puts forth eight propositions:

1. There exists something we can describe as "general intelligence"; people with more of it tend to be more successful in their careers than those with less.

2. At least half the variation in human intelligence is transmitted genetically from one generation to another; the remaining variability results from environmental factors.

3. Over the course of the twentieth century—and especially since the Information Revolution began several decades ago—intelligence has become more necessary in our society's most important jobs.

4. At the same time, the best U.S. colleges and universities have shifted their admission policies away from favoring children of inherited wealth to admitting young people with high grades and the highest scores on standardized tests, such as the Scholastic Assessment Test (SAT), American College Testing Program (ACT), and Graduate Record Examination (GRE).

5. As a result of these changes in the workplace and higher education, our society is coming to be dominated by a "cognitive elite," who are, on average, not only better trained than most people but actually more intelligent.

6. Intelligent people tend to interact with others like themselves—both on the campus and in the workplace—which raises the odds that they will pair up, marry, and have intelligent children, thus extending the "cognitive elite" into another generation.

7. The same process is at work at the other end of the social ladder: Poor people, who have lower intelligence on average, are also socially segregated, tend to marry others with similar social background, and thus pass along their more modest abilities to their children.

Thus, Herrnstein and Murray conclude,

8. Because membership in the affluent elite or the impoverished underclass is at least partly rooted in intelligence received mostly by genetic inheritance, we should not be

---

The Davis-Moore thesis states not only that social stratification is universal but that it is actually necessary to efficient social organization. Class differences in U.S. society, then, reflect both variation in human abilities and the relative importance of different jobs. From this point of view, equality is undesirable because it could be achieved only through oppressive measures to impose uniformity on the population.

Social-conflict analysis, advocated by Karl Marx, reflects egalitarian values. Marx considered inequality dysfunctional to societies, causing both suffering and conflict. As he saw it, social stratification springs from injustice and greed. Therefore, he advocated sharing resources equally. Marx believed that equality would not diminish but enhance human well-being.

The box addresses the connection between intelligence and social class. This issue—also a mix of fact and value—is among the most troublesome in social science. The difficulty lies partly in defining and measuring "intelligence" and partly in the very idea that elites are somehow "better" than others, which challenges our democratic culture.

Chapter 11 ("Social Class in the United States") examines inequality in our own nation, highlighting recent economic polarization. Then, in Chapter 12 ("Global Stratification"), we survey the entire world, asking why some nations have so much more wealth than others. At all levels, as we shall see, the study of social stratification involves a mix of facts and values about the shape of a just society.

Q: "I hate the impudence of a claim that in fifty minutes you can judge a human being's predestined fitness in life. . . . I hate the sense of superiority it creates and the sense of inferiority it imposes." Walter Lippmann, on IQ tests (1922)

NOTE: Two comprehensive critiques of the "bell curve thesis" are the *New Yorker* article "Curveball" by Stephen Jay Gould (November 28, 1994:139–49) and Melvin Kohn's (1996) essay.

Q: "Suppose a man, having plowed and cultivated his farm, should take in his hand a bag of mixed seeds . . . and walk straight across his land, sowing as he went. All pieces on his path would be sown alike: the rocks, the sandy ground, the good upland soil . . . but there would be great variety in the result when harvest time came around. . . . Something like this, I think, is the case with a stock of men passing through history." Charles Horton Cooley (1897)

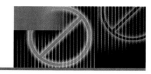

surprised that the poor contend with high levels of social problems, such as crime and drug abuse. Furthermore, we should expect that programs to help the poor (including Head Start and Affirmative Action) will have few practical results.

Evaluating the claims made in *The Bell Curve* must begin with a hard look at the concept of intelligence. Critics of the book argue that most of what we call "intelligence" is the result not of genetic inheritance but of socialization. In other words, intelligence tests do not measure cognitive *ability* as much as they measure cognitive *performance*. If this is so, we might well expect rich children to perform better on such tests because they have had the best schooling. In short, whatever innate abilities children have can develop only in a supportive environment.

Most researchers who study intelligence agree that genetics plays a part in children's intelligence, but the consensus is that no more than 25 to 40 percent is inherited—less than what Herrnstein and Murray claim. Therefore, *The Bell Curve* misleads readers into thinking that social stratification is both natural and inevitable. In fact, say critics, this book amounts to a new version of the social Darwinism popular a century ago, which justified the great wealth of industrial tycoons as "the survival of the fittest."

Perhaps the more today's competitive society seems like a jungle, the more people think of stratification as a matter of blood rather than upbringing. But despite any flaws, *The Bell Curve* raises issues we cannot easily ignore. If some people are, indeed, smarter than others, shouldn't we expect that most will end up in higher social positions? Is that fair or not? Wouldn't we want the top people in various fields to be at least a little smarter than the rest of us? Are there also dangers in having a smart elite? Is it true that our society's elites live apart from the problems—including crime, homelessness, and poor schools—that plague most of the population? Finally, what can our society do to ensure that all people have the opportunity to develop their abilities as fully as possible?

Continue the debate . . .

1. *Do you think there is such a thing as "general intelligence"? Why or why not?*

2. *Do you think that well-off people, on average, are more intelligent than people of low social position? If so, how do we know which factor is causing the other?*

3. *Do you think social scientists should study controversial issues such as differences in human intelligence? Why or why not?*

Sources: Herrnstein & Murray (1994), Jacoby & Glauberman (1995), and Kohn (1996).

SUMMARY

1. Social stratification is the ranking of people in a hierarchy. Stratification (a) is a trait of society, not just a result of individual differences, (b) endures over many generations; (c) is universal yet variable in form; and (d) is supported by cultural beliefs.

2. Caste systems, common in agrarian societies, are based on ascription (birth), permit little social mobility, and shape a person's entire life, including occupation and marriage.

3. Class systems, with an element of meritocracy, are found in industrial and postindustrial societies and allow social mobility based on individual achievement.

4. With public ownership of productive property, socialist societies claim to be classless. Although such societies usually exhibit less economic inequality than their capitalist counterparts, there is much greater inequality in power.

5. Social stratification is difficult to change because it is supported by various social institutions and because cultural values and beliefs—ideology—define certain kinds of inequality as both natural and just.

6. The Davis-Moore thesis states that social stratification is universal because it promotes economic productivity in a society. In class systems, unequal

Q: "The chief vice of every egalitarian society is envy. . . . Such constant comparing is really the quintessence of vulgarity." Hannah Arendt

CTQ1: To some extent, social position does reflect individual merit, but mostly it reflects people's family background. Moreover, stratification itself is a trait of a society, and individuals have positions within it.

CTQ2: Both are statements of fairness about who gets what. But one is based on birth and the other is based on one's relation to production, which has a significant achieved element. Industrialization, more than agriculture, demands the development of human potential, thus explaining the shift toward a greater (but limited) element of meritocracy.

rewards attract the most able people to the most important jobs.

7. Critics of the Davis-Moore thesis note that (a) it is difficult to assess objectively the functional importance of any job; (b) stratification prevents many people from developing their abilities; and (c) social stratification benefits some at the expense of others, causing social conflict.

8. For Karl Marx, the main architect of social-conflict analysis, conflict in industrial societies places the capitalists (bourgeoisie), who own the means of production and seek to maximize profits, in opposition to the proletariat, who provide labor in exchange for wages.

9. The socialist revolution Marx predicted has not occurred in high-income nations such as the United States. Some sociologists consider this evidence that Marx's analysis was flawed; others point out that our society is marked by pronounced social inequality and class conflict.

10. Max Weber identified three dimensions of social inequality: economic class, social status or prestige, and power. Because people's standing on the three dimensions may differ, stratification takes the form of a multidimensional hierarchy rather than distinct classes.

11. Historically, says Gerhard Lenski, technological advances have made societies more unequal. Some reversal of this trend occurs in industrial societies, as shown by the Kuznets curve. However, the new postindustrial economy in the United States shows some increase in economic inequality.

12. The study of social inequality deals not only with facts but also with politics and values concerning how a society should be organized.

KEY CONCEPTS

social stratification (p. 247) a system by which a society ranks categories of people in a hierarchy

social mobility (p. 248) change in one's position in the social hierarchy

caste system (p. 248) social stratification based on ascription, or birth

class system (p. 250) social stratification based on both birth and individual achievement

meritocracy (p. 250) social stratification based on personal merit

status consistency (p. 251) the degree of consistency in a person's social standing across various dimensions of social inequality

structural social mobility (p. 255) a shift in the social position of large numbers of people due more to changes in society itself than to individual efforts

ideology (p. 256) cultural beliefs that justify social stratification

Davis-Moore thesis (p. 257) the assertion that social stratification is a universal pattern because it benefits the operation of a society

blue-collar occupations (p. 260) lower-prestige work that involves mostly manual labor

white-collar occupations (p. 260) higher-prestige work that involves mostly mental activity

socioeconomic status (SES) (p. 261) a composite ranking based on various dimensions of social inequality

CRITICAL-THINKING QUESTIONS

1. How is social stratification a creation of society rather than simply a reflection of individual differences?

2. How do caste and class systems differ? What do they have in common? In what ways does industrialization introduce a measure of meritocracy to social stratification?

3. According to the Davis-Moore thesis, why should a college president earn more than a professor or a secretary? What would happen if all employees were paid the same?

4. In what respects have Karl Marx's predictions about capitalism failed? In what respects are they correct?

CTQ3: According to the thesis, a president should receive more rewards (some combination of prestige, pay, power, etc.) than a secretary only if the presidency has greater functional importance for the organization than the secretary's position. How do we know if one job is more functionally important than another? In principle, switching jobs might give some indication: Would the president perform the secretary's job better than the secretary would perform the president's job?

CTQ4: Marx's predicted revolution did not take place in advanced capitalist societies but in agrarian societies. Yet Marx's vision of production generating conflict and conflict driving social change seems valid.

Q: "All wealth and power are like clouds passing by." Chinese Poet Li Bi (Bye)

APPLICATIONS AND EXERCISES

1. Is social stratification evident on your college campus? What categories of people are unequal? In what ways are they unequal?

2. Sit down with parents, grandparents, or other relatives and assess how your family's lifestyle has changed over the last three generations. Has social mobility taken place? If so, describe the change. Was it caused by the efforts of individuals or changes in society itself?

3. What are the "seven deadly sins," the human failings recognized by the Catholic church during the Middle Ages? Why are these traits dangerous to an agrarian caste system? Are they a threat to a modern, capitalist class system? Why?

4. Packaged in the back of this new textbook is an interactive CD-ROM that offers a variety of study and review materials intended to help you better understand the material covered in this chapter. For this chapter, the CD-ROM contains an author's tip video, Real Life Sociology videos, other relevant audio and video, interactive map animations, audio journal entries from the author, Web links, and much more.

 ## SITES TO SEE

http://www.prenhall.com/macionis

Visit the interactive *Companion Website*™ that accompanies this text. Begin by clicking on the cover of your book. You will find a chapter-by-chapter study guide, practice tests, and a significant portion of the text for online review, as well as many suggested Web links.

http://www.macionis.com
(or **http://www.TheSociologyPage.com**)

You can find additional links pertaining to social stratification at the author's home page.

http://www.bea.doc.gov

This Web site is run by the U.S. government's Bureau of Economic Analysis. Here you will find income data by county and many other statistics about social inequality. See what you can learn about stratification in your part of the country.

http://www.cbpp.org

This site, developed by the Center on Budget and Policy Priorities, provides data and analysis of issues involving social inequality.

 ## INVESTIGATE WITH CONTENTSELECT

Follow the instructions found on page 23 of this textbook to enter this chapter of the book's *Companion Website*™. Once in the chapter, click on the ContentSelect icon at the bottom left of your screen and enter your personal User ID and Password. Enter keywords such as "social class," "meritocracy," "Karl Marx," and "apartheid," and the search engine will help you become an effective researcher.

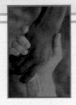

Beauford Delaney (1901–1979)
Can Fire in the Park, 1946

Oil on canvas, 24 × 30 in. (61.0 × 76.2 cm).
Smithsonian American Art Museum, Washington, D.C./Art Resource, N.Y.

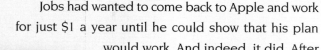

SOCIAL CLASS
IN THE UNITED STATES

The board of directors of Apple Computer had a problem on their hands: How were the directors to thank CEO Steve Jobs for leading the company through a striking economic recovery? In the mid-1990s, Apple Computer—the company Jobs had founded—was struggling for its very existence. In 1997, Jobs returned to lead the company, and by early 2000, Apple's sales were higher than ever and its stock price sky high. "This guy has saved the company," beamed one board member.

Jobs had wanted to come back to Apple and work for just $1 a year until he could show that his plan would work. And indeed, it did. After much discussion, the board came up with what they thought was an appropriate compensation: Jobs would receive 10 million stock options (the right to buy company stock at a low price that was worth roughly $200 million) and $90 million to buy a Gulfstream V jet aircraft for his personal use. "How do you motivate somebody who already has everything?" commented one observer (Jackson, 2000).

Many people joked that the fortune given to Jobs (including the jet airplane) took CEO pay to new "heights." But this story also reveals an important fact about U.S. society: The benefits of this economy—the largest, most productive in the world—are far greater for some people than for others. Indeed, we may all live in one country, but we also live in different worlds, depending on our social standing. This chapter explores social stratification in the United States. We shall see what separates us, how different we are, and why the differences are getting greater.

DIMENSIONS OF SOCIAL INEQUALITY

Many people think of the United States as a more or less equal society. Unlike countries in Europe, this nation never had a nobility. With the significant exception of our racial history, we have never known a caste system that rigidly ranks categories of people.

Even so, U.S. society is highly stratified. Not only do the rich have most of the money, but they also receive more schooling, enjoy better health, and consume the lion's share of goods and services. Such privileges contrast sharply with the poverty of millions of women and men in this same country who worry about paying next month's rent or a doctor's bill when a child becomes ill.

So why do many people think of the United States as a middle-class society? We underestimate the extent of social inequality for many reasons. For one thing, our legal system declares that everyone stands equal before the law. Second, our culture celebrates individual effort and downplays the importance of birth. Third, most of us do not know people who are "super rich" or very poor; we interact mostly with people like ourselves (Kelley & Evans, 1995). Finally, because the United States is such a rich country, it seems that everyone is at least pretty well off.

When people do face up to social inequality, they often speak of a "ladder of social class," as if inequality were a matter of a single factor such as money. But social class in the United States has several dimensions. Socioeconomic status (SES), as discussed in Chapter 10 ("Social Stratification"), reflects not just money (income and wealth and the power they provide) but also occupational prestige and schooling.

271

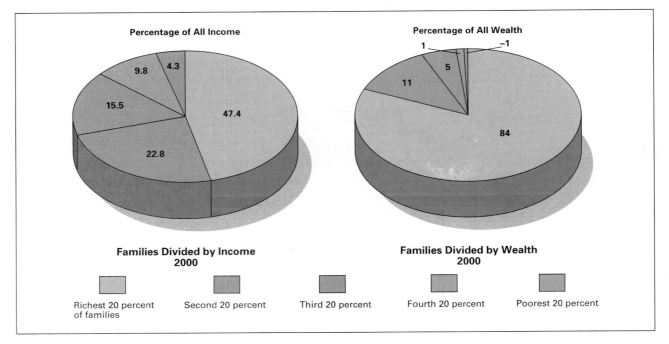

FIGURE 11–1 Distribution of Income and Wealth in the United States

Sources: Income data from U.S. Census Bureau (2001); wealth data are author estimates based on Keister (2000) and Russell & Mogelonsky (2000).

INCOME

One important dimension of inequality is **income,** *wages or salary from work and earnings from investments.* The Census Bureau reports that the median U.S. family income in 2000 was $50,891. The first part of Figure 11–1 illustrates the distribution of income among all U.S. families.[1] The richest 20 percent of families (earning at least $91,701 annually, with a mean of $155,531) received 47.4 percent of all income, while the bottom 20 percent (earning less than $24,000, with a mean of $14,228) received only 4.3 percent.

Table 11–1 provides a closer look at income distribution. In 2000, the highest-paid 5 percent of U.S. families earned at least $160,250 (averaging $272,354), or 20.8 percent of all income, more than the total earnings of the lowest-paid 40 percent. At the very top of the income pyramid, the richest half of 1 percent earned at least $1.5 million. In short, while a small number of people earn very high incomes, the majority make do with far less.

Chapter 10 ("Social Stratification") explained that social inequality declines as a society industrializes (illustrated by the Kuznets curve, Figure 10–2). Thus, the United States has less income inequality than, say, Venezuela (in South America), Nigeria (Africa), or Malaysia (Asia). However, as Figure 11–2 indicates, the United States has more income inequality than most other high-income nations.

Compare economic inequality in the United States and Canada by visiting http://www.ccsd.ca/facts.html

WEALTH

Income is only one part of a person or family's **wealth,** *the total value of money and other assets, minus outstanding*

---

[1]The Census Bureau reports both mean and median income for families ("two or more persons related by blood, marriage or adoption") and households ("two or more persons sharing a living unit"). In 2000, mean family income was $65,574, higher than the median because high-income families pull up the mean but not the median. For households, the figures are somewhat lower—a mean of $57,045 and a median of $42,148—mostly because families average 3.2 persons, whereas households average 2.6.

NOTE: Below, we mean "privately held wealth" because public property (lands, forests, roads, transportation systems, and the military) are excluded from such considerations. According to the World Bank, if all public and private wealth in the U.S. were divided equally, each person would have about $425,000.

NOTE: Another indicator of high income is employing a household maid: About 9% of U.S. households do.

debts. Wealth—including stocks, bonds, and real estate—is distributed even less equally than income.

The second part of Figure 11–1 shows the distribution of privately owned wealth in the United States. The richest 20 percent of families own roughly 80 percent of the country's entire wealth. High up in this privileged category are the wealthiest 5 percent of families: the

 A government report on the distribution of wealth in the United States is found at http://www.census.gov/hhes/www/wealth/1995/wealth95.html

"very rich," who own 60 percent of all private property. Richer still—with wealth into the tens of millions—are the 1 percent of families that qualify as "super rich" and own about 40 percent of this nation's privately held resources (Keister, 2000; Keister & Moller, 2000). Capping the wealth pyramid, the one dozen richest families have a combined net worth exceeding $262 billion (*Forbes*, 2001). This equals the total property of 3.7 million average families, including enough people to fill the cities of Chula Vista, California; Chicago, Illinois; Cleveland, Ohio; Chattanooga, Tennessee; and Clearwater, Florida.

The wealth of the average U.S. household rose through the 1990s to about $71,600 in 1999, although this figure probably fell during the economic downturn beginning in 2000. Household wealth reflects the value of homes, cars, investments, insurance policies, retirement pensions, furniture, clothing, and all other personal property, minus home mortgages and other debts. The wealth of average people not only is less than that of the rich, but is also different in kind. Whereas most people's wealth centers on a home and a car—that is, property that generates no income—the

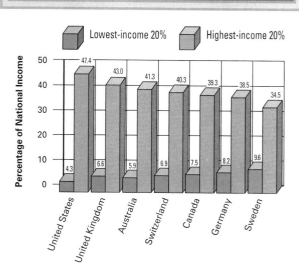

FIGURE 11–2 Income Disparities for Selected High-Income Countries

Sources: U.S. Census Bureau (2001) and The World Bank (2001).

wealth of the rich is mostly in the form of stocks and other income-producing investments.

When financial assets are balanced against debits, the lowest-ranking 40 percent of families in the United States have virtually no wealth at all. The negative percentage shown in Figure 11–1 for the poorest 20 percent of the population means that these families are in debt.

POWER

In the United States, wealth is an important source of power. Therefore, the small share of families that controls most of the nation's wealth also shapes the agenda of an entire society. Thomas Jefferson (1953; orig. 1785), the third U.S. president and a wealthy man himself, cautioned that a true democracy could not exist if property remained in the hands of a small number of families.

Chapter 17 ("Politics and Government") presents the debate surrounding wealth and power. Some analysts argue that although the rich have certain advantages, they do not dominate the political process.

TABLE 11–1 U.S. Family Income, 2000

Highest paid . . .	Annually earns at least . . .
0.5%	$1,500,000
1	330,000
5	160,000
10	110,000
20	92,000
30	73,000
40	61,000
50	52,000
60	41,000
70	31,000
80	24,000
90	10,000

Sources: Kennickell, Starr-McCluer, & Surette (2000), U.S. Census Bureau (2001), and author calculations.

NOTE: How much money do people need "to get by"? The average person says $25,000; people in the top 1% (those with income over $250,000 or assets over $2.5 million) say $80,000. "To live in reasonable comfort"? Average: $41,000; rich: $150,000. "To fulfill all dreams"? Average: $102,000; rich: $500,000 (*American Demographics*, 1998).

CYBER: As we move into a postindustrial society, will prestige be less a matter of owning things and more a matter of developing personal creative potential?

NOTE: If wealth were in the form of bricks, the richest individuals in the U.S. would have a pile as high as the Eiffel Tower (1,056 feet), whereas most people would have a stack only a few feet from the ground. The bottom few percent would be "in the hole."

TABLE 11–2 The Relative Social Prestige of Selected Occupations in the United States

White-Collar Occupations	Prestige Score	Blue-Collar Occupations	White-Collar Occupations	Prestige Score	Blue-Collar Occupations
Physician	86		Funeral director	49	
Lawyer	75		Realtor	49	
College/university professor	74		Bookkeeper	47	
Architect	73			47	Machinist
Chemist	73			47	Mail carrier
Physicist/astronomer	73		Musician/computer	47	
Aerospace engineer	72			46	Secretary
Dentist	72		Photographer	45	
Member of the clergy	69		Bank teller	43	
Psychologist	69			42	Tailor
Pharmacist	68			42	Welder
Optometrist	67			40	Farmer
Registered nurse	66			40	Telephone operator
Secondary-school teacher	66			39	Carpenter
Accountant	65			36	Brick/stone mason
Athlete	65			36	Child-care worker
Electrical engineer	64		File clerk	36	
Elementary-school teacher	64			36	Hairdresser
Economist	63			35	Baker
Veterinarian	62			34	Bulldozer operator
Airplane pilot	61			31	Auto body repairperson
Computer programmer	61		Retail apparel salesperson	30	
Sociologist	61			30	Truck driver
Editor/reporter	60		Cashier	29	
	60	Police officer		28	Elevator operator
Actor	58			28	Garbage collector
Radio/TV announcer	55			28	Taxi driver
Librarian	54			28	Waiter/waitress
	53	Aircraft mechanic		27	Bellhop
	53	Firefighter		25	Bartender
Dental hygienist	52			23	Farm laborer
Painter/sculptor	52			23	Household laborer
Social worker	52			22	Door-to-door salesperson
	51	Electrician		22	Janitor
Computer operator	50			09	Shoe shiner

Source: Adapted from *General Social Surveys 1972–2000: Cumulative Codebook* (Chicago: National Opinion Research Center, 2001), pp. 1391–1409.

Others counter that the political system serves mostly the interests of the "super rich."

OCCUPATIONAL PRESTIGE

In addition to being a source of income, work also provides social prestige. We commonly evaluate each other according to the kind of work we do, respecting some and looking down on others.

Sociologists monitor the relative prestige of various occupations (Counts, 1925; Hodge, Treiman, & Rossi, 1966; NORC, 2001). Table 11–2 shows that people accord high prestige to occupations (such as medicine, law, and engineering) that require extensive training

and generate high income. On the other hand, less prestigious work (waiting tables, for example) not only pays less but usually requires less ability and schooling.

Occupational prestige rankings are much the same in all industrial societies (Ma, 1987; Lin & Xie, 1988). Almost everywhere, white-collar work that involves mental activity with little supervision carries greater prestige than blue-collar work that involves supervised, manual labor.

In any society, high-prestige occupations go to privileged categories of people. In Table 11–2, for example, the highest-ranking occupations are dominated by men. More than a dozen jobs down the list we find "registered nurse," where most workers are women.

NOTE: The government has long curtailed inheritance using taxation. The first such tax existed from 1797 to 1802, another was enacted from 1862 to 1870, and a third from 1898 to 1902; all were intended to generate revenue. The current tax, exacted in 1916 to pay for World War I, was not later repealed (Bartlett, 2000). The tax reforms of 2001 will phase out estate taxes by 2011, although estate taxes will return in 2012 unless Congress enacts further legislation.

DIVERSITY: The social dominance of white Anglo Saxon Protestants (the acronym WASP was first used by E. Digby Baltzell, 1964) is evident in the widespread perception that racial, ethnic, or religious identity applies to everyone but them.
Q: Noting the favor accorded to the rich, C. Wright Mills commented that "prestige is the shadow of money and power" (1956:83).

Similarly, many of the lowest-prestige jobs are commonly performed by people of color.

SCHOOLING

Industrial societies make schooling widely available to prepare workers for specialized tasks. Table 11–3 shows schooling in 1999 for U.S. women and men aged twenty-five and older. Whereas 84 percent completed high school, only about 26 percent were college graduates.

Nevertheless, dimensions of inequality are once again linked. Schooling affects both occupation and income; a college degree or other advanced study is needed for most (but not all) of the better-paying white-collar jobs shown in Table 11–2. Most blue-collar jobs, which bring lower income and social prestige, require less schooling.

SOCIAL STRATIFICATION AND BIRTH

As we discussed in Chapter 10, the class system in the United States is to some extent a meritocracy—that is, social position reflects individual talent and effort. But birth also plays a big part in shaping what we become later in life.

ANCESTRY

Nothing affects social standing in the United States as much as being born into a particular family. Family is our point of entry into the social system and has a strong bearing on schooling, occupation, and income. Research suggests that at least half our country's richest individuals—those worth hundreds of millions of dollars or more—derived their fortunes mostly from inheritance (Thurow, 1987; Queenan, 1989). By the same token, "inherited" poverty just as surely shapes the future of others.

GENDER

Of course, both men and women are found in families at every class level. Yet, on average, women have less income, wealth, and occupational prestige than men. Therefore, in the United States there are about six times more poor families headed by women (3.1 million) than there are poor families headed by men (489,000). From another angle, families headed by women are more than twice as likely to be poor (24.7 percent) as families headed by men (11.5 percent)

TABLE 11–3 Schooling of U.S. Adults, 1999 (aged 25 and over)

	Women	Men
Not a high school graduate	**16.0%**	**15.8%**
8 years of less	6.8	7.1
9–11 years	9.2	8.7
High school graduate	**84.0**	**84.2**
High school only	34.3	31.9
1–3 years college	26.1	24.5
College graduate or more	23.6	27.8

Source: U.S. Census Bureau (2000).

(U.S. Census Bureau, 2001). Chapter 13 ("Gender Stratification") examines the connection between gender and social stratification.

RACE AND ETHNICITY

Race is closely linked to social position in the United States. White people receive more schooling and have higher overall occupational standing than African Americans. Thus, the median African American family's income was $34,204 in 2000, just 64 percent of the $53,256 earned by white families. As you can imagine, this disparity makes a huge difference in people's lives. For example, white families are more likely to own their homes (70 percent do) than black families (46 percent) (U.S. Census Bureau, 2000).

Much of the disparity in income is related to the larger share of single-parent families among African Americans. Comparing only families headed by married couples, African Americans earned 85 percent as much as whites.

Over time, as Figure 11–3 on page 276 shows, the income differential creates a large wealth gap (Altonji et al., 2000). A recent survey of U.S. households by the Federal Reserve found that median wealth for minority families, including African American, Hispanics, and Asians (about $16,400), is just 17 percent of the median ($94,900) for white families. Race is significant even among affluent families, as the box on page 277 explains.

Social ranking involves ethnicity as well. Historically, people of English ancestry have enjoyed the most wealth and wielded the greatest power in the United States. The rapidly growing Latino population, by contrast, has long been disadvantaged. In 2000, median income among Hispanic families was $35,050, which is 66 percent of the comparable figure

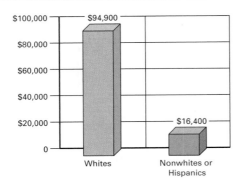

DIVERSITY SNAPSHOT

**FIGURE 11–3 Average Wealth for Whites
and Nonwhite or Hispanic
Minorities, 1998**

Source: Kennickell, Starr-McCluer, & Surette (2000).

for all white families. A detailed examination of how
race and ethnicity affect social standing is presented in
Chapter 14 ("Race and Ethnicity").

RELIGION

Religion, too, has a bearing on social standing in the
United States. Among Protestant denominations, with
which almost two-thirds of individuals are affiliated,
Episcopalians and Presbyterians have significantly
higher social standing, on average, than Lutherans and
Baptists. Jews also have high social standing, and
Roman Catholics hold a more modest position (Roof,
1979; Davidson, Pyle, & Reyes, 1995).

Even John Fitzgerald Kennedy, a member of one
of this country's wealthiest and most powerful families, had to overcome religious opposition to become
our first Catholic president in 1960. Throughout our
history, upward mobility has sometimes meant converting to a higher-ranking religion (Baltzell, 1979b).

SOCIAL CLASSES
IN THE UNITED STATES

As Chapter 10 ("Social Stratification") explained,
rankings in a caste system are rigid and obvious to all.

Defining social categories in a more fluid class system
is not so easy, however.

Consider the joke about a couple who orders a
pizza, asking that it be cut into six slices because they
aren't hungry enough to eat eight. All sociologists
agree that social inequality exists in the United States;
they just can't agree on how to divide up the population. Some, following Karl Marx, see two major
classes: capitalists and proletariat. Others find as many
as six classes (Warner & Lunt, 1941) or even seven
(Coleman & Rainwater, 1978). Still others side with
Max Weber, favoring not clear-cut classes but a multidimensional status hierarchy.

Defining classes in U.S. society is difficult because
of our relatively low level of status consistency. Especially near the middle of the hierarchy, standing on
one dimension often contradicts standing on another.
For example, a government official may have the
power to administer a multimillion-dollar budget yet
earn a modest personal income. Similarly, members of
the clergy enjoy great prestige but moderate power
and low pay. Or consider a lucky day trader on the
stock market who wins no special respect but makes a
lot of money.

Finally, the social mobility typical of class systems—again, most pronounced at the middle—
means that social position may change during a person's lifetime, further blurring class lines. With these
reservations in mind, we can describe four general social classes in the United States: the upper class, the
middle class, the working class, and the lower class.

THE UPPER CLASS

Families in the upper class—5 percent of the U.S. population—earn at least $160,000 annually and may earn
ten times that much. As a general rule, the more a family's income comes from inherited wealth in the form
of stocks and bonds, real estate, and other investments,
the stronger a family's claim to being upper class.

In 2001, *Forbes* magazine profiled the richest 400
people in the United States and noted that they had
a *minimum* net worth of $600 million and included
266 billionaires. The combined wealth of the *Forbes*
mega-rich was $951 billion (more than $2.3 billion per
person). This economic upper class is Karl Marx's
"capitalists"—those who own most of the nation's private wealth. Many members of the upper class work as
top corporate executives or senior government officials. Historically, though far less so today, the upper
class was composed of white Anglo-Saxon Protestants
(WASPs) (Baltzell, 1964, 1976, 1988).

DIVERSITY: RACE, CLASS, AND GENDER

The Color of Money: Being Rich in Black and White

African American families earn 64 cents for every dollar a white family earns, which helps explain why black families are three times as likely to be poor. But there is another side to black America—an affluent side—that has expanded dramatically in recent decades.

The number of affluent families—those with annual incomes over $80,000—is increasing faster among African Americans than among whites. In 2000, 1.2 million African American families (13 percent) were financially privileged, 50 percent more than the number in 1990 and ten times the number in 1970, taking account of inflation. About 12 percent of Latino families also rank as well-off, along with 30 percent of non-Hispanic white families.

The color of money is the same for everyone, but black and white affluence differs in several ways. First, well-off people of African descent are not *as rich* as their white counterparts. Sixty-five percent of affluent non-Hispanic white families (20 percent of all non-Hispanic white families) earn more than $100,000 a year, compared to 60 percent

of affluent African American families (8 percent of all black families).

Second, African Americans are more likely than white people to achieve affluence through multiple incomes. From another angle, 10.5 percent of non-Hispanic white men and 2.5 percent of non-Hispanic white women earn more

Rich people come in all colors. But are they all the same?

than $80,000, compared to just 2.9 percent of black men and 1.0 percent of black women. Rich black families, then, are more likely to contain two, and perhaps more, working people.

Third, affluent African Americans are more likely to derive their income from salaries rather than from investments. Among wealthy white families, more than 80 percent of families have investment income, compared to two-thirds of affluent African American families.

Beyond differences in income, affluent people of color contend with social barriers that do not limit whites. Even African Americans with the money to purchase a home, for example, may find that they are unwelcome as neighbors. This is one reason that a smaller share of well-off African American families (40 percent) live in the suburbs (the richest areas of the country) than affluent white families (61 percent).

Affluent Americans come in all colors. Yet race has a powerful effect on the lives of rich people, just as it does on the lives of us all.

Sources: O'Hare (1989), Weicher (1995), Lach (1999), and U.S. Census Bureau (2001).

Upper-Uppers

The *upper-upper class*, sometimes called "blue bloods" or simply "society," includes less than 1 percent of the U.S. population (Warner & Lunt, 1941; Coleman & Neugarten, 1971; Baltzell, 1995). Membership almost always comes at birth, as suggested by the quip that the easiest way to become an upper-upper is to be born one. Most of these families possess enormous wealth, primarily inherited. For this reason, members of the upper-upper class are said to have *old money*.

Set apart by their wealth, upper-uppers live in old, exclusive neighborhoods, such as Beacon Hill in Boston, Rittenhouse Square or the Main Line in Philadelphia, the Gold Coast of Chicago, and Nob Hill in San Francisco. Their children typically attend private schools with others of similar background and high-prestige colleges and universities. In the tradition of European aristocrats, they study liberal arts rather than vocational skills.

Women of the upper-upper class often maintain a full schedule of volunteer work for charitable

NOTE: The special "Forbes Four Hundred" issue appears in October of each year and contains interesting facts and patterns about U.S. wealth. For example, in 1982, 13 people in the U.S. were billionaires. In 2001, two-thirds of those on the list were worth billions. The new-rich corporate and technology elite, whose wealth is mostly in the form of stocks (rather than, say, art) make up a large portion of the list.

NOTE: If we consider only financial wealth—that is, investments—the top 1% owns almost half of the pie (Keister, 2000).
Q: "If you can actually count your money, then you are not a rich man." J. Paul Getty
NOTE: By the late 1990s, the number of millionaire families in the U.S. had increased to 4 million from less than 1 million in 1990.

People often distinguish between the "new rich" and those with "old money." Men and women who suddenly begin to earn high incomes tend to spend their money on "status symbols" because they enjoy the new thrill of high-roller living and they want others to know of their success. Those who grow up surrounded by wealth, on the other hand, are used to a privileged way of life and are more quiet about it. Thus, the "conspicuous consumption" of the lower-upper class (left) can differ dramatically from the more private pursuits and understatement of the upper-upper class (right).

organizations. While helping the larger community, such charitable activities also build networks that broaden this elite's power (Ostrander, 1980, 1984).

Lower-Uppers

Most upper-class people actually fall into the *lower-upper class*. To most of us, these people seem every bit as privileged as the upper-upper class. The major difference, however, is that lower-uppers (including Steve Jobs, profiled in the opening to this chapter) are the "working rich"; their primary source of income is earnings rather than inherited wealth. Although "new rich" families generally live in exclusive communities, most do not gain entry to the clubs and associations of "old money" families.

Historically, the American Dream has been to earn enough to join the ranks of the lower-upper class. The athlete who signs a million-dollar contract, the actor who lands a starring role in a Hollywood film, the computer whiz who becomes an Internet entrepreneur—these are the talented and lucky achievers who reach the lower-upper class. The box sharpens the distinction between "society" and the high achievers of the lower-upper class, people very much like the rest of us—except that they make a lot of money.

THE MIDDLE CLASS

Including 40 to 45 percent of the U.S. population, the large middle class has a tremendous influence on our culture. Television programs and movies usually depict middle-class people, and most commercial advertising is directed toward these "average" consumers. The middle class contains far more racial and ethnic diversity than the upper class.

Upper-Middles

The top half of this category is called the *upper-middle class*, based on above-average income in the range of $80,000 to $160,000 a year. Such income allows upper-middle-class families to accumulate valuable property: a comfortable house in a fairly expensive area, several automobiles, and investments. Two-thirds of upper-middle-class children receive college educations, and postgraduate degrees are common. Many go on to high-prestige careers as physicians, engineers, lawyers, accountants, and business executives. Lacking the power of the richest people to influence national or international events, upper-middles often play an important role in local political affairs.

NOTE: Regional editions of the *Social Register* were published for Newport, R.I. (1887; discontinued), New York (beginning in 1888), Philadelphia and Boston (1890), Baltimore (1892), Chicago (1893), Washington, D.C. (1906), and Cleveland-Cincinnati-Dayton (1910). In 1976, these listings were merged into a single, national edition (Baltzell, 1995).

NOTE: The *Social Register* is owned by the Forbes family.

NOTE: The 945-page winter edition of the 1996 *Social Register* contains 26,402 names, or about 1/10 of 1 percent of the U.S. population. There is also a summer edition for vacation homes and boats.

NOTE: Max Weber called old rich "rentiers" versus new rich "entrepreneurs."

NOTE: Thorstein Veblen (1857–1929) coined the term "conspicuous consumption" in his book *Theory of the Leisure Class.*

CRITICAL THINKING

Caste and Class: The *Social Register* and *Who's Who*

Small and exclusive, the upper-upper class comes closest to being a true social group. There is even a list of these privileged families: the *Social Register*, first published in 1887 as fortunes grew along with the industrial economy. Today, some 40,000 families are included in this inventory of our society's "blue bloods."

Because membership typically is based on birth, the upper-upper class operates much like a caste: You are either "in" or "out." Traditional upper-upper parents urge their children to seek partners of their own kind, sustaining the class into another generation. Family is thus crucial to the upper-upper class, as it is to all caste groups. This is why the *Social Register* lists *families*, not *individuals*.

The listing for David Rockefeller, a member of one of the most socially prominent U.S. families, indicates his family's address and home telephone number, Mrs. Rockefeller's maiden name, the names of the Rockefeller children and the boarding schools and colleges they are attending, and exclusive social clubs to which the family belongs. Because achievement is not the issue, the *Social Register* never mentions anyone's occupation or place of business.

The lower-upper class, by contrast, is an achievement elite. This larger category of "new rich" individuals has no clear boundaries, and its members do not engage in formal rituals (such as debutante parties) as many "old money" families do.

There is also a list—roughly speaking—of people at this class level: the national edition of *Who's Who in America*. Here, instead of established families, we find distinguished individuals: outstanding athletes, highly successful businesspeople, college presidents, Nobel prize winners, and famous entertainers.

Who's Who contains a few people, including David Rockefeller, who are also listed in the *Social Register*, but the information provided is quite different. David Rockefeller's entry in *Who's Who* includes a brief biography (date of birth, schooling, honorary degrees), a list of accomplishments (military decorations, government service, books authored), and—most important—his position as board chair of Chase Manhattan Bank. The address provided in *Who's Who* is his place of business.

These two publications show that there are two kinds of elites in the United States. The castelike *Social Register* lists high-prestige families according to *who they are*. The more classlike *Who's Who* lists individuals on the basis of *what they have done*. But as the dual listings for David Rockefeller suggest, social privilege and personal achievement sometimes go together.

What do you think?

1. *In what sense are the rich* not *all the same?*
2. *Why are "old money" families more a caste and "new money" families more a class?*
3. *With time, of course, "new money" becomes "old money." How did the ancestors of some of today's "old money" families (including the Rockefellers or the Kennedys) get their start?*

Average-Middles

The rest of the middle class falls near the center of the U.S. class structure. *Average-middles* typically work in less prestigious white-collar occupations (middle managers, high school teachers, and salesclerks) or in highly skilled blue-collar jobs (say, as building contractors). Household income is between $40,000 and $80,000 a year, which is roughly the national average.

Middle-class people accumulate a small amount of wealth over the course of their working lives (half of all U.S. households now own at least some stock and other investments). Yet most wealth for middle-class people is likely to be in the form of a house. Middle-class men and women are likely to be high school graduates, but the odds are just fifty-fifty that they will complete a college degree, generally at a less expensive, state-supported school.

THE WORKING CLASS

About one-third of the population is working class (sometimes called the *lower-middle class*). In Marxist terms, the working class forms the core of the industrial proletariat. Their blue-collar jobs usually yield a family income between $25,000 and $40,000 a year,

NOTE: The importance of a college education to middle-class standing is suggested by the practice, common in the U.S., of placing college decals on the windows of automobiles.

DIVERSITY: Attention to the term "underclass" has been considerable, although this category includes only about 5% of the poor. The term is used to designate those who are (1) chronically poor, (2) in inner-city areas, and (3) dependent on welfare.

Q: "[U]nderclass has become the code word for lower-income blacks and Puerto Ricans." Leslie Dunbar (1988:16)

Q: "A great many people are in the working class and don't know it." Marshal Berman

NOTE: Joan Rodgers (1995) estimates that the children of poor parents in the U.S. have a 16 to 28% chance (with 95% confidence) of becoming poor as adults.

For decades, farm families who worked hard could expect to fall within the U.S. middle class. But the trend toward large-scale agribusiness has put the future of the small family farm in doubt. While many young people in rural areas are turning away from farming toward other careers, some carry on, incorporating high technology into their farm management in their determined efforts to succeed.

somewhat below the national average, and they have little or no wealth. Working-class families thus are vulnerable to financial problems caused by unemployment or illness.

Many working-class jobs provide little personal satisfaction—requiring discipline but rarely imagination—and subject workers to constant supervision. These jobs also offer fewer benefits, such as medical insurance and pension plans. About half of working-class families own their own homes, usually in lower-cost neighborhoods. College is a goal that only about one-third of working-class children realize.

THE LOWER CLASS

The remaining 20 percent of our population constitutes the lower class. Low income makes their lives unstable and insecure. In 2000, the federal government classified 31.1 million people (11.3 percent of the population) as poor. Millions more, called the "working poor," are just barely better off, holding low-prestige jobs that provide not only little satisfaction but close to minimum wage. Barely half manage to complete high school, and only one in four reaches college.

Society segregates the lower class, especially when the poor are racial or ethnic minorities. About 40 percent of lower-class families own their own homes, typically in the least desirable neighborhoods. Although poor neighborhoods usually are found in the inner cities, lower-class families also live in rural communities, especially across the South.

THE DIFFERENCE CLASS MAKES

September 2, Mount Vernon, Ohio. My bike leans right, leaving the trail for the rest station that offers a stretch and a drink of water. Here I encounter Linda, a thirty-something woman having trouble with her roller blades. Eye contact and a perplexed look are a call for help, so I walk over to see what I might do. Several of her boot buckles need adjustment. Close up, she doesn't look well. "Are you OK?" I ask gently. "Very tired," Linda responds, and goes on to explain why. Now divorced, she cannot pay off her debts with one low-income job. So she works an 11 A.M. to 7 P.M. shift as a computer clerk at a bank in town, catches four hours of sleep, and then drives an hour to Columbus, where she sits at another computer, processing catalog orders from 2 A.M. until 10 A.M. That leaves just enough time to drive back to Mount Vernon to start all over again at the bank.

Social stratification affects nearly every dimension of our lives. We will briefly examine some of the ways social standing is linked to our health, values, politics, and family life.

HEALTH

Health is closely related to social standing. Children born into poor families are three times more likely to die from disease, neglect, accidents, or violence during their first years of life than children born to rich families. Among adults, people with above-average incomes are twice as likely as low-income people to describe their health as excellent. Moreover, richer people live, on average, seven years longer because they eat more

DISCUSS: What do students think of the Bush tax cuts? Conservatives support tax cuts to spur investment and to allow people to keep more of what they earn. Liberals oppose tax cuts because taxes pay for social programs. Across-the-board cuts always favor the rich, who pay most income tax in the first place: The richest half of U.S. households pays more than 95% of all income taxes.

SOCIAL SURVEY: "On the whole, do you think it should or should not be the government's responsibility to reduce the differences between the rich and the poor?" (GSS 1998, N = 1,284; *Codebook*, 2001:899)
"Definitely should be" 16.8% "Definitely should not be" 25.0%
"Probably should be" 25.9% DK/NR 9.0%
"Probably should not be" 23.3%

nutritious food, live in safer and less stressful environments, and receive better medical care (U.S. National Center for Health Statistics, 1999).

VALUES

Cultural values also vary from class to class. The "old rich" have an unusually strong sense of family history because their social position is based on wealth passed down from generation to generation (Baltzell, 1979b). With their birthright privileges, upper-uppers also favor understated manners and tastes, whereas many "new rich" practice *conspicuous consumption*, buying things they know others will notice. They use clothes, homes, cars, and even airplanes to make a statement about their social position.

Affluent people with more education and financial security also are more tolerant of controversial behavior such as homosexuality. Working-class people, who grow up in an atmosphere of greater supervision and discipline and are less likely to attend college, tend to be less tolerant (Kohn, 1977; NORC, 2001).

POLITICS

Political affiliations flow along class lines. By and large, more privileged people support the Republican party, and people with fewer advantages favor the Democrats.

But issue by issue, the pattern is more complex. A desire to protect their wealth prompts well-off people to be more conservative on *economic* issues, favoring, for example, lower taxes. But on *social* issues, such as abortion and other feminist concerns, highly educated, affluent people are more liberal. People of lower social standing, on the other hand, tend to be economic liberals, favoring expanded government social programs, but support a more conservative social agenda (Erikson, Luttbeg, & Tedin, 1980; NORC, 2001).

Another clear pattern emerges when it comes to political involvement. Higher-income people, who are better served by the system, are more likely to vote and to join political organizations than people in the lower class.

FAMILY AND GENDER

Social class also shapes family life. Most lower-class families are somewhat larger than middle-class families because of earlier marriage and less use of birth control. In addition, working-class parents encourage children to conform to conventional norms and respect authority figures. Parents of higher social standing

Compared to high-income people, low-income people are half as likely to report good health and, on average, live about seven fewer years. The toll of low income—played out in inadequate nutrition, little medical care, and high stress— is easy to see on the faces of the poor, who look old before their time.

transmit a different "cultural capital" to their children, teaching them to express their individuality and imagination. In both cases, parents are looking to the future: The odds are that less privileged children will take jobs that require them to closely follow rules, whereas more advantaged children will enter fields that require more creativity (Kohn, 1977; McLeod, 1995).

Of course, the more money a family has, the better parents can develop their children's talents and abilities. For example, an affluent family earning $95,800 a year will spend $241,770 raising a child born in 2000 to the age of eighteen. Middle-class people, with an income of $50,600 a year, will spend $165,630, and a lower-income family earning less than $38,000 will spend about $121,230 (Lino, 2001). Privilege, then, tends to beget privilege as family life reproduces the class structure in each generation.

RESOURCE: Lillian Rubin's *Worlds of Pain* (Basic, 1976) shows the influence of class on family life. While middle-class women seek personal qualities such as sensitivity and sharing in a spouse, working-class women have greater concern for basic traits such as holding a steady job and refraining from excessive drinking and domestic violence. In short, until economic standing is secure, women and men have little ability to consider other relational issues.

NOTE: To help students keep the terms straight, note that *intra* is Latin for "within" and *inter* means "between."

GLOBAL: An example of structural downward mobility was China's Cultural Revolution, which forced 17 million urban youths to live in rural areas (Zhou & Hou, 1999).

Industrial class systems provide the opportunity for social mobility—both upward and downward. Typically, social mobility is modest and gradual. Sociologists track this change by comparing the social standing of people in different generations of the same family—for example, in the achievement of a son that makes his father proud.

Class also shapes our world of relationships. Elizabeth Bott (1971) found that most working-class couples divide their responsibilities according to gender; middle-class couples, by contrast, are more egalitarian, sharing more activities and expressing greater intimacy. More recently, Karen Walker (1995) discovered that working-class friendships typically provide material assistance; middle-class friendships, however, are likely to involve shared interests and leisure pursuits.

SOCIAL MOBILITY

Ours is a dynamic society marked by significant social movement. Earning a college degree, landing a higher-paying job, or marrying someone who earns a high income contributes to *upward social mobility;* dropping out of school, losing a job, or divorce (especially for women) may signal *downward social mobility.*

Over the long term, though, social mobility is not so much a matter of individual changes as changes in society itself. During the first half of the twentieth century, for example, industrialization expanded the U.S. economy, pushing up living standards. Even without being very good swimmers, so to speak, people rode a rising tide of prosperity. More recently, *structural social mobility* in a downward direction has dealt many people economic setbacks.

Sociologists distinguish between shorter- and longer-term changes in social position. **Intragenerational social mobility** is *a change in social position occurring during a person's lifetime.* **Intergenerational social mobility,** *upward or downward social mobility of children in relation to their parents,* is important because it usually reveals long-term changes in society that affect almost everyone.

MYTH VERSUS REALITY

In few societies do people think about "getting ahead" as much as in the United States. After all, moving up is the American Dream. But is there as much social mobility as we like to think?

Studies of intergenerational mobility (almost all of which, unfortunately, have focused exclusively on men) show that almost 40 percent of the sons of blue-collar workers attain white-collar jobs and almost 30 percent of sons born into white-collar families end up doing blue-collar work. *Horizontal mobility*—a change of occupation at one class level—is even more common, so that about 80 percent of sons show at least some type of social mobility in relation to their fathers (Blau & Duncan, 1967; Featherman & Hauser, 1978; Hout, 1998).

Research points to four general conclusions about social mobility in the United States:

1. **Social mobility, at least among men, has been fairly high.** The widespread belief that social mobility in the United States is high is true. Mobility is what we would expect in an industrial class system.

2. **The long-term trend in social mobility has been upward.** Industrialization, which greatly expanded the U.S. economy, and the growth of white-collar work over the course of the twentieth century have boosted living standards.

3. **Within a single generation, social mobility usually is small.** Most young families increase their income over time (Duncan et al., 1998). Yet only a very few people move "from rags to riches." Although sharp rises or falls in individual fortunes may attract the media, social mobility usually involves limited movement *within* one class level rather than striking moves *between* classes.

4. **Social mobility since the 1970s has been uneven.** Real income (that is, adjusted for inflation) rose steadily during the twentieth century until the 1970s, when it hit a plateau. During the 1980s, real income changed little for many people, rising slowly by the end of the 1990s.

MOBILITY BY INCOME LEVEL

General trends often mask the experiences of different categories of people. Figure 11–4 shows how U.S. families at different income levels fared between 1980 and 2000. Well-to-do families (the highest 20 percent, but not all the same families over the entire period) saw their incomes jump 59 percent, from an average $97,991 in 1980 to $155,531 in 2000. People in the middle of the population saw more modest gains of about 20 percent during this time, while the lowest-income 20 percent saw a smaller gain of only 11.5 percent.

For families at the top of the income scale (the highest 1 percent), the last fifteen years have been a windfall. These families, with an average income of $132,451 in 1980, were earning $500,000 in 2000, almost four times as much (Edmondson, 1995; Nielsen & Alderson, 1997; U.S. Census Bureau, 2001).

MOBILITY: RACE, ETHNICITY, AND GENDER

White people, in a more privileged position to begin with, have been more upwardly mobile in recent decades than people of African or Hispanic ancestry. Through the economic expansion of the 1980s and 1990s, many more African Americans entered the ranks of the wealthy. But the real income of African Americans overall has changed little in two decades. African Americans earned only a slightly greater share of average white family income in 2000 (64 percent) as in 1970 (61 percent). Compared with non-Hispanic

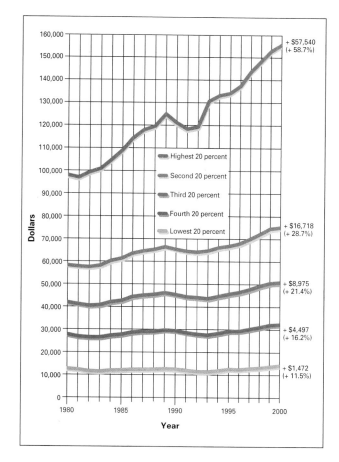

FIGURE 11–4 Mean Income, U.S. Families, 1980–2000 (in 2000 dollars, adjusted for inflation)
Source: U.S. Census Bureau (2001).

white families, Latinos lost ground between 1975 (when their average income was 67 percent of white family income) and 2000 (when it had fallen to 66 percent) (Featherman & Hauser, 1978; Pomer, 1986; U.S. Bureau of the Census, 2001).

Historically, women have had less opportunity for upward mobility than men because most working women hold clerical jobs (such as secretary) and service positions (say, serving food in a restaurant) that offer few promotions. In addition, when marriages end in divorce (as almost half do), women commonly experience downward social mobility; they lose not only income but a host of benefits, including health care and insurance coverage (Weitzman, 1996).

THE MAP: Generally speaking, lower-income counties are those in which pessimism about the future is widespread. One interesting exception is counties containing large college campuses where many people, although fairly affluent, are doomsayers.

Q: "What is important for democracy is not that great fortunes should not exist, but that great fortunes should not remain in the same hands." Alexis de Tocqueville

Q: "When some learn that all the American Dream does not fit all that is true about the realities of our life, they denounce the Dream and deny the truth of any of it. Fortunately, most of us are wiser and better adjusted to social reality; we recognize that, though it is called a Dream and some of it is false, by virtue of our firm belief in it we have made some of it true." W. Lloyd Warner, *Social Class in America*

SEEING OURSELVES

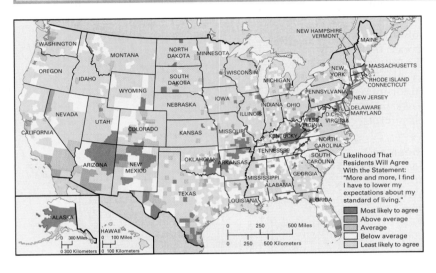

NATIONAL MAP 11–1
"Fear of Falling"
across the United States

This map shows, by county, how likely people are to agree with the statement "More and more, I find I have to lower my expectations about my standard of living." What characterizes regions (including Appalachia in Kentucky and West Virginia) where pessimism is high? But pessimism is pronounced not only in poor rural areas. In rich cities, including New York, Chicago, and Los Angeles, people are also afraid of losing their jobs.

Source: *American Demographics* magazine, February 1994, p. 60, Reprinted with permission. © 1994, *American Demographics* magazine, Ithaca, New York. Data from Yankelovich *Monitor* and Clarita's *Prizm* system.

Over time, however, the earnings gap between women and men has been narrowing. Women working full time in 1980 earned 60 percent as much as men working full time; by 2000, women earned 74 percent as much. Unfortunately, some of the change was due to a *drop* in men's earnings through the 1980s while women's income stayed about the same (U.S. Census Bureau, 2001).

THE AMERICAN DREAM: STILL A REALITY?

The expectation of upward social mobility is deeply rooted in our culture. Through most of our history, economic expansion fulfilled this promise by raising living standards. But about 1970 this upward trend leveled off, starting a period of income stagnation for many families that has shaken our national confidence. Note these recent trends:

1. **For many workers, earnings have stalled.** The annual income of a fifty-year-old man working full time climbed more than 50 percent between 1958 and 1974 (from $22,849 to $37,747 in constant 2000 dollars). Between 1974 and 2000, however, this worker's income rose only slightly, even as the number of hours worked increased and the cost of necessities such as housing, education, and medical care went up (Russell, 1995a; U.S. Census Bureau, 2001).

2. **Multiple job-holding is up.** According to the Bureau of Labor Statistics, 4.7 percent of the U.S. labor force worked at two or more jobs in 1975; by 2000, the share had risen to 5.6 percent.

3. **More jobs offer little income.** In 1979, the Census Bureau classified 12 percent of full-time workers as "low-income earners" because they made less than $6,905; by 1998, this segment increased to 15.4 percent, earning less than the comparable figure of $15,208.

4. **Young people are remaining at home.** Fully 53 percent of young people aged eighteen to twenty-four are living with their parents. Since 1975, the average age at marriage has moved upward three years (to 25.0 years for women and 26.7 years for men).

In sum, over the last generation, the rich have become richer. Moreover, the number of rich people has also increased, to at least 5 million millionaires in the United States, four times the number a decade ago (D'Souza, 1999). So, for some at least, the American Dream is alive and well. But most are less optimistic about the future, and a significant share worry that the

NOTE: Mark Western and Erik Olin Wright (1994) argue that *authority boundaries* (separating managers from nonmanagers) are more permeable than *expertise boundaries* (separating experts from nonexperts); least permeable are *property boundaries* (dividing capitalists from wage laborers).

NOTE: Our society's belief in opportunity—and even the personal obligation to be upwardly mobile—is suggested by admonitions such as "pull yourself up by your own bootstraps," which, curiously, is a physical impossibility.

NOTE: To some extent, getting ahead economically today depends on limiting or entirely avoiding the expenses of child rearing. "Yuppies" (young, upwardly mobile professionals) often are "Dinks" (double-income-no-kids).

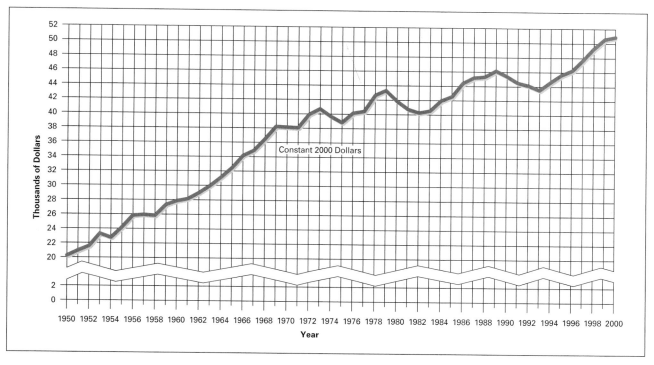

FIGURE 11–5 Median Income, U.S. Families, 1950–2000
Source: U.S. Census Bureau (2001).

chance for a middle-class life is slipping away (Kerckhoff, Campbell, & Winfield-Laird, 1985; Newman, 1993). National Map 11–1 shows where in the United States pessimism about the future is most widespread.

Dubbed the *middle-class slide*, this downward structural mobility came along with a rising share of low-pay jobs. As Figure 11–5 shows, although median family income doubled between 1950 and 1973, it has grown by only 25 percent since then (U.S. Census Bureau, 2001).

THE GLOBAL ECONOMY AND U.S. CLASS STRUCTURE

Underlying the recent shifts in U.S. class structure is global economic change. Much of the industrial production that gave U.S. workers high-paying jobs a generation ago has moved overseas. With less industry at home, the United States now serves as a vast market for industrial goods such as cars and popular items such as stereos, cameras, and computers made in Japan, Korea, and elsewhere.

High-paying jobs in manufacturing, held by 26 percent of the U.S. labor force in 1960, support only 15 percent of workers today. In their place, the economy now offers service work, which often pays far less. A traditionally high-paying corporation such as USX (formerly United States Steel) now employs fewer people than McDonald's. Meanwhile, McDonald's continues to expand, and fast-food clerks make only a fraction of what steel workers earn.

The global reorganization of work is not bad news for everyone. On the contrary, the global economy creates upward social mobility for educated people who specialize in areas such as law, finance, marketing, and computer technology. Moreover, global economic expansion has helped push up the stock market (even with the recent declines) almost tenfold between 1980 and 2000, reaping profits for families with money to invest.

But the same trend has hurt many "average" workers who have seen their factory jobs disappear. Moreover, many companies have "downsized"—cut the ranks of their work force, blue-collar and white-collar alike—

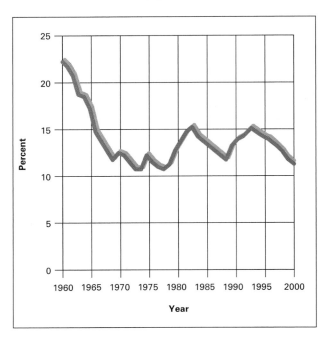

**FIGURE 11–6 The Poverty Rate
in the United States, 1960–2000**

Source: U.S. Census Bureau (2001).

to become competitive in world markets. As a result, although half of all households contain two or more workers—twice the share in 1950—many people are working harder simply to hold on to what they have (Reich, 1989, 1991; Nelson, 1998; Schlesinger, 1998; Sennett, 1998).

POVERTY IN THE UNITED STATES

Social stratification creates both "haves" and "have-nots." All systems of social inequality create poverty, or at least **relative poverty,** *the deprivation of some people in relation to those who have more.* A more serious but preventable problem is **absolute poverty,** *a deprivation of resources that is life threatening.*

As Chapter 12 ("Global Stratification") explains, upwards of 1 billion human beings—one in six—are at risk of absolute poverty. Even in the affluent United States, families go hungry, live in inadequate housing, and suffer poor health because of wrenching poverty.

THE EXTENT OF U.S. POVERTY

In 1964, the federal government established an official *poverty line* and began counting the poor and offering certain benefits. The idea was to identify people living close to absolute poverty. Mollie Orshansky, the architect of the poverty line, described it as the income needed "to purchase a nutritionally adequate diet on the assumption that no more than a third of the family income is used for food" (1969:38). In other words, the poverty threshold is three times what the government estimates people must spend to eat. The government sets the exact dollar amount according to family size, with annual adjustments to reflect the changing cost of living.

Figure 11–6 shows the official poverty rate as calculated annually since 1960. During the 1960s, poverty fell sharply, but there has been little overall change in the rate since. In 2000, the government tallied 31.1 million men, women, and children—11.3 percent of the U.S. population—as poor. Another 12.3 million people—the *near poor*—lived on income no greater than 125 percent of the poverty threshold.

For a family of four, the 2000 poverty line was set at $17,603. But the income of the average poor family was much lower—just $10,783. This means that the typical poor family must get by on about 60 percent of poverty-line income (U.S. Census Bureau, 2001).

Poor people know very well the consequences of living on the edge: not being able to afford the jackets or expensive sneakers their children want so badly and, worse, worrying about what will happen if one of the family becomes injured or ill. In short, poverty means a life of daily stress, insecurity, and—for several million adults and children in the United States—hunger.

WHO ARE THE POOR?

Although the poor fit no single stereotype, certain categories of our population are at high risk of poverty. Where these categories overlap, the problem is especially serious.

Age

A generation ago, it was the elderly who were at greatest risk for poverty, but no longer. From 30 percent in 1967, the poverty rate for seniors over the age of sixty-five fell to 10.2 percent in 2000, or 3.4 million elderly poor. The elderly now have a poverty rate below the national average because of better

DISCUSS: What is the significance of ATMs? The ubiquitous automatic teller machines (165,000 in the U.S. in 1997; about 130 million people have cards to use them) symbolize the declining demand for lower-skill workers in the service sector.
NOTE: All welfare payments account for only about one-fourth of the income of all poor people.

NOTE: Some estimates suggest that half of homeless women are fleeing abusive partners.
Q: "The difference of natural talents in different men is, in reality, much less than we are aware of. . . . The difference between . . . a philosopher and a street porter, for example, arises not so much from nature, as from habit, custom, and education." Adam Smith, *The Wealth of Nations*, Bk. 1, sec. 2, 15

In the 1952 painting Laundress, *U.S. artist George Tooker captures the humanity and humility of impoverished people. This message—that the poor are human beings, most doing the best they can to get by—is important to remember in a society that tends to define poor people as morally unworthy and deserving of their bitter plight.*

George Tooker (b. 1920), *Laundress*, 1952. Oil on gesso panel, 23 1/2 × 24 in. (59.7 × 61 cm). Christie's Images, N.Y. © George Tooker.

retirement programs from private employers and better government benefits. Even so, with the number of older people increasing, about 11 percent of the poor are elderly people.

Today, the burden of poverty falls most heavily on children. In 2000, 16.2 percent of people under age eighteen (11.6 million children) were poor. Tallied another way, nearly four in ten of the U.S. poor are children under the age of eighteen. The poverty problem contributes to the high *infant mortality rate*, a measure of how likely children are to survive their first year of life. Despite being the richest country in the world, the United States has one of the highest infant mortality rates among high-income nations. The box on page 288 takes a closer look at child poverty in the United States.

Race and Ethnicity

Two-thirds of all poor people are white; 25 percent are African Americans. But in relation to their overall numbers, African Americans are about three times as likely as non-Hispanic whites to be poor. In 2000, 22.1 percent of African Americans (7.7 million people) lived in poverty, compared to 21.2 percent of Hispanics (7.5 million), 10.8 percent of Asians and Pacific Islanders (1.1 million), and 7.5 percent of non-Hispanic white people (13.2 million). The poverty gap between whites and minorities has changed little since 1975 (U.S. Census Bureau, 2001).

Gender and Family Patterns

Of all poor people over age eighteen, 61 percent are women and 39 percent are men. This disparity reflects the fact that women who head households bear the brunt of poverty. Of all poor families, 50 percent are headed by women with no husband present, while just 8 percent of poor families are headed by single men.

The term **feminization of poverty** describes *the trend by which women represent an increasing proportion of the poor.* In 1960, 25 percent of all poor families were headed by women; the majority of poor families had

THE MAP: High child poverty rates are found across the South, which is also the region of high African American concentration.

THEN AND NOW: The child poverty rate stood at about 25% in 1960; it fell to 14% by 1969 and is now 16.2%.

NOTE: Because women and children tend to suffer together from poverty, the feminization of poverty might also be termed the "juvenilization of poverty." Children are now the poorest of the U.S. poor.

DIVERSITY: Although the U.S. infant mortality rate is 6.8, in poor cities such as Camden, N.J., the figure is 20, the same as in much poorer countries such as Venezuela, Colombia, and Uzbekistan.

DIVERSITY: RACE, CLASS, AND GENDER

U.S. Children: Bearing the Burden of Poverty

We cringe at the sight of starving children in Somalia, the war-torn African nation where the average person struggles to live on less than $200 per year. But child poverty in the United States may be an even greater tragedy because ours is such a rich nation, with more than 100 times the per capita income of Somalia. Applying the sociological perspective, what can we learn about child poverty in the United States?

To begin, one in six (16.2 percent) U.S. children under age eighteen is poor—almost 12 million boys and girls. This is the same number as almost forty years ago, when the government began its "war on poverty." National Map 11–2 shows that the problem of child poverty is greatest across the South.

Like that of poverty in general, the risk of child poverty varies within our population. Whereas 9 percent of non-Hispanic white children are poor, 28 percent of Latino children and 31 percent of African American youngsters are poor.

From another angle, 63 percent of poor children are white, 30 percent are African American, and 4 percent are Asian; 29 percent of poor children are culturally Hispanic. But although poor children are a diverse lot, they share one trait: They all live in households with low income.

To explain the problem of child poverty, researchers point to the rising share of single-parent households. Today, about eight in ten poor children live in a household with a single mother. In the same share of cases, this household has no full-time worker.

The reasons for poverty are complex and controversial. But everyone agrees that children are not to blame. Tragically, however, this is precisely where the burden of poverty falls. Practically speaking, reducing child poverty is certainly cheaper than dealing with its later effects, including lower achievement in school and higher risk of drug use and crime. Whether we look at this issue from a moral or a practical standpoint, can we permit our society's most vulnerable members to suffer this way?

What do you think?

1. *National Map 11–2 shows that the problem of child poverty is greatest across the southern and southwestern United States. Why do you think this is the case?*

2. *More than twice as many poor children are white as are black. Does this surprise you? Why or why not?*

3. *Why, in your opinion, does the United States have such a high level of child poverty? What do you think U.S. society could do to address this problem?*

SEEING OURSELVES

NATIONAL MAP 11–2 Child Poverty across the United States

Source: U.S. Census Bureau (2001).

Sources: Children's Defense Fund (1995), Duncan et al. (1998), and U.S. Census Bureau (2001).

THE MAP: The 50 richest counties are found around large metropolitan areas, including New York (10), San Francisco (5), and Washington, D.C. (5). Although some rural counties are also rich, these tend to be areas popular as affluent getaways, including Pitkin County, Colo. (Aspen) and Nantucket, Mass. Low-income counties are likely to be rural, and many also have a high immigrant population. Worth noting is that the patterns are very much the same as in our earlier maps with data from 1990.

NOTE: Since 1959, poverty rates have declined; then, 18% of whites and 55% of African Americans were poor.

Q: "I can see the end of public assistance in America." President Franklin Delano Roosevelt (1935)

SEEING OURSELVES

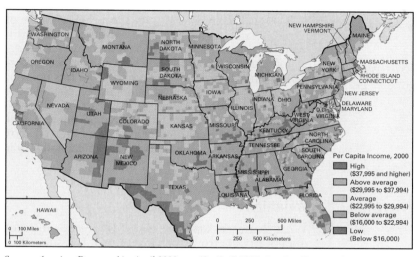

NATIONAL MAP 11–3
Per Capita Income across the United States, 2000

This map shows the median per-person income (that is, how much money, on average, a person has to spend) for the more than 3,000 counties that make up the United States for the year 2000. The richest counties, shown in dark green, are not spread randomly across the country. Nor are the poorest U.S. counties, which are shown in dark red. Looking at the map, what patterns do you see in the distribution of wealth and poverty across the United States? Do these patterns support our assertion linking affluence to urban living and poverty to rural places?

Per Capita Income, 2000
- High ($37,995 and higher)
- Above average ($29,995 to $37,994)
- Average ($22,995 to $29,994)
- Below average ($16,000 to $22,994)
- Low (Below $16,000)

both wives and husbands in the home. By 2000, however, the share of poor families headed by a single woman had doubled to 50 percent.

The feminization of poverty is thus part of a larger change: the rapidly increasing number of households at all class levels headed by single women. This trend, coupled with the fact that households headed by women are at high risk of poverty, is why women (and their children) make up an increasing share of the U.S. poor.

Urban and Rural Poverty

The greatest concentration of poverty is found in central cities, where the 2000 poverty rate stood at 16.1 percent. Suburbs also have destitute people, but their poverty rate is just 7.8 percent. Thus, the poverty rate for urban areas as a whole is 10.8 percent—a bit lower than the 13.4 percent found in rural areas. National Map 11–3 presents income levels across the United States and shows where poverty is most pronounced.

EXPLAINING POVERTY

For the richest nation on earth to have tens of millions of poor people raises serious questions. It is true, as some analysts remind us, that many of the people counted among the officially poor in the United States are far better off than the poor in other countries: 41 percent of U.S. poor families own their home (with an average of three bedrooms and a garage), 60 percent have a clothes washer, 70 percent own a car, and 97 percent have a color television. Moreover, only a few percent report often going without food (Rector, 1998; Gallagher, 1999). Nevertheless, millions of people in the United States have too little income to lead healthy lives.

A report on food scarcity in the United States is found at this Internet address: http://www.econ.ag.gov/epubs/pdf/fanrr2/fanrr2.pdf

Figure 11–7 on page 290 shows that the U.S. public is divided over what to do about poverty. One-fourth of respondents to this national survey look to the government to help poor people; slightly more than that think people must take responsibility for themselves. Almost 42 percent straddle the fence, thinking both government and individuals share this responsibility.

We now focus on two different explanations for poverty. Together, they lead to a lively and important political debate.

NOTE: About 1.6 million U.S. workers earn the minimum wage (and 2.8 million earn less than the minimum wage). The minimum wage was first set in 1938 at $.25 per hour.
Q: "Poverty is in the eye of the beholder." Mollie Orshansky, creator of the poverty line
Q: "To drive men from independence to live on alms is itself a great cruelty." Edmund Burke

Q: "Anyone who can walk to the welfare office can walk to work." Al Capp
NOTE: Edward Banfield (1974) is another proponent of the social Darwinist view that the poor are largely responsible for their own poverty. More recently, Richard Herrnstein and Charles Murray (1994) echoed this logic, asserting that today's poor are largely people handicapped by low intelligence.

Counterpoint: Blame Society

Another position, argued by William Julius Wilson (1996a, 1996b; Mouw, 2000), holds that *society is primarily responsible for poverty*. Wilson points to the loss of jobs in the inner cities as the primary cause of poverty, claiming that there is simply not enough work to support families. Thus, Wilson sees any lack of trying on the part of poor people as a *result of little opportunity* rather than a *cause of poverty*. From this point of view, Oscar Lewis's analysis amounts to blaming the victims for their own suffering (Ryan, 1976). The view that looks to government to overcome poverty is at the left side of the continuum in Figure 11–7. The box provides a closer look at Wilson's argument and how it would shape public policy.

Survey Question: "Some people think that the government in Washington should do everything possible to improve the living standards of all poor Americans [they are at point 1 below]. Other people think it is not the government's responsibility, and that each person should take care of himself [they are at point 5 below]. Where would you place yourself on this scale, or haven't you made up your mind on this?"

1	2	3	4	5	Don't know/ no answer
13.9%	12.5%	41.5%	16.3%	12.0%	3.9%

"I strongly agree the government should improve living standards"

"I agree with both answers"

"I strongly agree that people should take care of themselves"

FIGURE 11–7 Government or Individuals: Who Is Responsible for Poverty?
Source: NORC (2001:311).

One View: Blame the Poor

One approach holds that *the poor are mostly responsible for their own poverty*. Throughout our history, people in the United States have valued self-reliance and believed that social standing is mostly a matter of individual talent and effort. This view sees society offering plenty of opportunity to anyone able and willing to take advantage of it. Thus, anyone who is poor either cannot or will not work. These are people with few skills, little schooling, and little motivation. This argument represents the right side of the continuum in Figure 11–7.

In a study of Latin American cities, the anthropologist Oscar Lewis (1961) concluded that the poor become trapped in a *culture of poverty*, a lower-class subculture that can destroy people's ambition. Socialized in poor families, children become resigned to their plight, producing a self-perpetuating cycle of poverty.

In 1996, hoping to break the cycle of poverty in the United States, Congress changed the welfare system that had provided federal funds to assist poor people since 1935. Now the federal government sends money to the states to give to needy people, but benefits carry strict time limits: in most cases, no more than two years at a stretch and a total of five years if a person moves in and out of the welfare system. The objective is to move people from depending on the government to supporting themselves.

Weighing the Evidence

What evidence supports one side or the other of the poverty controversy? Government statistics show that 48 percent of the heads of poor households did not work at all during 2000, and an additional 32 percent worked only part time (U.S. Census Bureau, 2001). Such facts seem to support the "blame the poor" side because one major cause of poverty is *not holding a job*.

But the *reasons* that people do not work seem more consistent with the "blame society" position. Middle-class women may be able to combine working and child rearing, but this is much harder for poor women who cannot afford child care, and few employers provide child-care programs for their employees. Moreover, as William Julius Wilson explains, many people are idle not because they are avoiding work but because there are not enough jobs. In short, most poor people in the United States find few options (Popkin, 1990; Schiller, 1994; Edin & Lein, 1996; Wilson, 1996a; Pease & Martin, 1997; Duncan, 1999).

The Working Poor

But not all poor people are jobless, and the *working poor* command the sympathy and support of people on both sides of the poverty debate (Schwartz & Volgy, 1992). In 2000, 20 percent of poor heads of households (1.3 million women and men) worked at least fifty weeks of the year and yet could not escape poverty. Another 32 percent of these heads of families (2.1 million people) remained poor despite part-time employment. Put differently, about 3 percent of

SOCIAL SURVEY: A U.S. Census Bureau survey of poor adults yielded these explanations for not working among those who did not work at all: Ill/ disabled, 18%; retired, 3%; home or family reasons, 44%; school/other, 23%; could not find work, 13%.

Q: "[I]t is a vicious cycle: You cannot get a job because you do not have an address, you do not have an address because you do not have any money, and you do not have any money because you do not have a job." Danny Cahill, *Forgotten Voices, Unforgettable Dreams*

NOTE: One critic of Wilson notes that the population of the Chicago neighborhoods in Wilson's research declined from 250,000 in 1950 to 86,000 in 1990. This drop, suggests Marvin Kosters (1996), seems to indicate that most people succeeded over time in moving on and up.

CRITICAL THINKING

When Work Disappears: The Result Is Poverty

The U.S. economy has created tens of millions of new jobs in recent decades. Yet African Americans who live in inner cities have faced a catastrophic loss of work. William Julius Wilson points out that while people continue to talk about welfare reform, neither major political party (Democrats or Republicans) has said anything about the lack of work in central cities.

With the loss of inner-city jobs, Wilson continues, for the first time in U.S. history a large majority of the adults in our inner cities are not working. Studying the Washington Park area of Chicago, Wilson found a troubling trend. Back in 1950, most adults in the African American community had jobs, but by the mid-1990s, two-thirds did not. As one elderly woman who moved to the neighborhood in 1953 explains,

> When I moved in, the neighborhood was intact. It was intact with homes, beautiful homes, mini-mansions, with stores, laundromats, with Chinese cleaners. We had drugstores. We had hotels. We had doctors over on 39th Street. We had doctor's offices in the neighborhood. We had the middle class and the upper-middle class. It has gone from affluent to where it is today. (1996b:28)

But *why* has this neighborhood declined? Wilson's eight years of research point to one answer: There are barely any jobs. It is the loss of work that has pushed people into desperate poverty, weakened families, and made people turn to welfare. In nearby Woodlawn, Wilson identified more than 800 businesses that operated in 1950; today, just 100 remain. Moreover, a number of major employers a generation ago—including Western Electric and International Harvester—closed their plant doors in the late 1960s. The inner cities have fallen victim to economic change, including downsizing and jobs being moved overseas.

Wilson paints a grim picture. But he also believes there is an answer: Create jobs. Wilson proposes attacking the problem in stages. First, the government could hire people to do all kinds of work, including clearing slums and putting up new housing. Such a program, modeled on the Works Progress Administration (WPA) enacted in 1935 during the Great Depression, would move people from welfare to work and create much-needed hope. In addition, federal and state governments must improve schools by imposing performance standards and providing more funding. Of special importance is teaching children language skills and computer skills to prepare them for the jobs being created by the Information Revolution. Improved regional public transportation would connect cities (where people need jobs) and suburbs (where most jobs are). In addition, more child-care programs would help single mothers and fathers balance the responsibilities of parenting and work.

Wilson claims that his proposals are well grounded in research. But he knows politics revolves around other considerations as well. For one thing, to the extent that the public *thinks* there are plenty of jobs, they will conclude that the poor are simply avoiding work, making any change unlikely. Moreover, he concedes that his proposals, at least in the short term, are more expensive than continuing to funnel welfare assistance to jobless communities.

But for the long term, he asks, what are the costs of allowing our cities to decay while suburbs prosper? Of allowing a new generation of preschoolers to join the ranks of the restless and often angry people for whom there is no work? What would be the benefits of affording everyone the hope and satisfaction that are supposed to define our way of life?

What do you think?

1. *According to Wilson, why are many of this country's inner-city neighborhoods so poor?*

2. *What does he think we can do to address this problem?*

3. *Do you agree with his analysis of poverty? Why or why not?*

Source: Based on Wilson (1996b).

heads of families, people of color, people isolated from the larger society in inner-city areas—who face special barriers and limited opportunities.

HOMELESSNESS

There is no precise count of homeless people. Fanning out across the cities of the United States on the night of March 27, 2000, in a one-day tabulation of homeless people Census Bureau officials tallied 170,706 people at emergency and homeless shelters. But experts agree that a full count of the homeless might reach 500,000 *on any given night*, with as many as three times that number—1.5 million people—homeless *at some time during the course of a year* (Kozol, 1988; Wright, 1989; U.S. Census Bureau, 2000; Wickham, 2000).

The familiar stereotypes of homeless people—men sleeping in doorways and women carrying everything they own in a shopping bag—have been replaced by the "new homeless": people thrown out of work because of plant closings, those forced out of apartments by rent increases or condominium conversions, and others unable to meet mortgage or rent payments because of low wages or no work at all. Today, no stereotype paints a complete picture of the homeless.

Most homeless people report that they do not work, but 44 percent say they work at least part-time (HUD, 1999). But working or not, virtually all homeless people have one thing in common: *poverty*. For that reason, the explanations of poverty already offered also apply to homelessness. Some blame the *personal traits* of the homeless themselves. One-third of homeless people are substance abusers, and one-fourth are mentally ill. More broadly, it should not be surprising that a fraction of 1 percent of our population, for one reason or another, is unable to cope with our complex and highly competitive society (Bassuk, 1984; Whitman, 1989).

 Find the HUD report on homelessness at http://www.huduser.org/publications/homeless/homelessness/contents.html

Others see homelessness resulting from *societal factors*, including low wages and a lack of low-income housing (Kozol, 1988; Schutt, 1989; Bohannan, 1991). Supporters of this position point out that one-third of all homeless people are entire families, and children are the fastest-growing category of the homeless. A minister in a Pennsylvania town that has lost hundreds of industrial jobs because of plant closings describes the real-life effects of economic recession:

About 2.4 million people in the United States work full time yet do not earn enough to escape poverty. These laundry workers in San Francisco's Chinatown earn $7 per hour, about $14,500 per year, in one of the most expensive cities in the country.

full-time workers earn so little that they remain poor (U.S. Census Bureau, 2001). In short, the working poor suffer from low income because they work too few hours and earn low wages. Keep in mind that a full-time worker making $6 (above the minimum wage of $5.15 per hour) cannot lift an urban family of four above the poverty line.

To sum up, individual ability and personal initiative do play a part in shaping everyone's social position. However, the weight of sociological evidence points to society—not individual character traits—as the primary cause of poverty. Society must be at fault because the poor are *categories* of people—female

NOTE: The $50-billion home mortgage interest tax deduction (85% of which goes to households in the top 20% of income) amounts to more than six times the $8 billion the government spends annually on low-income housing.

RESOURCE: The key conservative criticisms of public assistance are found in Charles Murray's *Breaking Ground* (1984); his thesis is that the outlay for welfare must continue to grow because the system fails to alleviate the problems it has set out to fix, actually making matters worse.

Q: "Homeless people are poor people. Forced to choose between feeding their families and paying the rent, many of these families are soon driven to the streets." Jonathan Kozol

Homelessness is found throughout the United States as well as other high-income nations. Here, homeless people gather under a bridge in Hamburg, Germany. Why do you think that the public tends not to view homelessness (and, more generally, poverty) as a serious social problem?

Yes, there are new jobs. There's a new McDonald's and a Burger King. You can take home [enough to] barely pay the rent. What do you do if someone gets sick? What do you do for food and clothes? These may be good jobs for a teenager. Can you ask a thirty-year-old man who's worked for GM since he was eighteen to keep his wife and kids alive on jobs like that? There are jobs cleaning rooms in the hotel. . . . Can you expect a single mother with three kids to hold her life together with that kind of work? (Kozol, 1988:6)

No one disputes that a large proportion of homeless people are personally impaired to some degree, but how much is cause and how much is effect is difficult to untangle. Structural changes in the U.S. economy, coupled with reduced aid to low-income people and a real estate market that puts housing out of reach of low-income people, all contribute to homelessness (Ratnesar, 1999).

Most homeless people live in urban areas. A Housing and Urban Development (HUD) study of more than 4,000 poor people across the United States, most of them homeless at the time they were interviewed, reports that 92 percent are urban: 71 percent reside in central cities and 21 percent live in suburbs.

Just 8 percent live in rural areas (HUD, 1999). Rural homelessness is not only less common but also less visible. As one volunteer in a rural Ohio county explains, "Here, you don't see people sleeping in a park or under a bridge" (Splain, 2000:1a). Yet social services agencies in this small county (of 15,000 people) serve about 400 people a year. Some are transients, moving from place to place; some are living with friends or relatives; and some are sleeping in a car. This varied pattern explains why people who live in rural areas may not be aware that they, too, have homeless in their communities.

 A report by the U.S. Conference of Mayors on homelessness in this country is found at http://www.usmayors.org/uscm/news/press_releases/documents/hunger_121101.asp

We close this chapter with a look at welfare, a topic that focuses our thinking about how to respond to issues such as poverty and homelessness.

Finally, social stratification extends far beyond the borders of the United States. In fact, the most striking social inequality is found not within any one nation but in the different living standards among nations of the world. In Chapter 12, we broaden our investigation of social stratification by looking at global inequality.

CONTROVERSY & DEBATE

The Welfare Dilemma

In 1996, Congress ended the federal public assistance that guaranteed some income to all poor people. Now state-run programs require that people receiving aid enroll in a job training program or find work—or have their benefits cut off.

Almost no one likes public assistance, or welfare. Liberals criticize welfare for doing too little to help the poor, conservatives charge that it hurts the people it is supposed to help, and the poor themselves find welfare a complex and often degrading program.

So what exactly *is* welfare? The term "welfare" refers to a host of policies and programs designed to improve the well-being of the U.S. population. Until the welfare reform of 1996, most people used the term to refer to one part of the overall system: Aid for Dependent Children (AFDC), a program of monthly financial support to parents (mostly single women) to care for themselves and their children. In 1996, some 5 million households received AFDC for some part of the year.

Did AFDC help or hurt the poor? There are two sides to the debate. Conservative critics argue that rather than reducing child poverty, AFDC actually made the problem worse for two reasons. First, this form of welfare weakened families by subsidizing living single as an alternative to marriage. For years, poor mothers received benefits *only if no husband lived in the home*. As conservatives saw it, therefore, AFDC was an economic incentive to women to have children outside marriage

and one reason for the increase in out-of-wedlock births among poor people. Conservatives see a clear connection between being poor and not being married: Fewer than one in ten married-couple families were poor; more than nine in ten families receiving AFDC were headed by an unmarried woman.

Second, conservatives also believe that welfare made poor people dependent on government handouts rather than working to support themselves. This, they say, is the main reason that eight of ten poor heads of households did not have steady, full-time jobs. Furthermore, more than half of nonpoor, single mothers worked full-time, compared to only 5 percent of single mothers receiving AFDC. Conservatives sum up by concluding that welfare strayed from its original purpose of giving temporary help to women with children (typically, after divorce or death of a husband) until they could find work. Instead, welfare became a way of life. Once trapped in dependency, poor

Do welfare programs such as food stamps do too much, or too little, to help the poor?

women are likely to raise children who will be poor as adults.

Liberals charge that their opponents use a double standard in evaluating government programs. Why, they ask, do people object to government money going to poor mothers and children when most "welfare" actually goes to relatively rich people? The AFDC budget was $25 billion annually—no small sum, to be sure, but just half of the $50 billion in home mortgage interest deductions that homeowners pocket each year. And it pales in comparison to the $300 billion in annual Social Security benefits Uncle Sam provides to senior citizens, most of whom are quite well-off. And what about "corporate welfare" to big companies? Their tax write-offs and other benefits amount to hundreds of billions of dollars a year. As liberals see it, "wealthfare" is far greater than "welfare."

Second, liberals claim that conservatives have a distorted picture of public assistance. The popular image of do-nothing "welfare queens" masks the fact that most poor families who turn to public assistance are truly needy. Moreover, the typical household receiving AFDC received barely $400 per month, hardly enough to attract people to a "life of welfare dependency." And, in constant dollars, AFDC payments actually declined over recent decades. In fact, liberals fault public assistance as a "Band-Aid approach" to the serious social problems of too few jobs and too much income inequality in the United States.

NOTE: According to the Cato Institute, the hourly value of welfare benefits in 1995 ranged from $5.53 in Mississippi to $17.50 in Hawaii (Tanner & Moore, 1995).

Q: "Nobody likes welfare. Conservatives worry that it erodes the work ethic, retards productivity, and rewards the lazy. Liberals view the American welfare system as incomplete, inadequate, and punitive. Poor people, who rely on it, find it degrading, demoralizing, and mean." Michael B. Katz (1986:ix)

DISCUSS: Why do only about half of all poor people eligible for public assistance programs enroll?

Q: "A long time ago I concluded that the current welfare system undermines the basic values of work, responsibility, and family, trapping generation after generation in dependency. . . . Welfare . . . was meant to be a second chance, not a way of life." President Bill Clinton

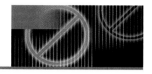

As for the charge that public assistance weakens families, liberals concede that the proportion of single-parent families has risen, but they doubt AFDC was to blame. Rather, single parenting is a broad cultural trend found at all class levels in many countries.

Thus, liberals conclude, AFDC was attacked not because it failed but because it benefitted a part of the population that many consider undeserving. Our cultural tradition of equating wealth with virtue and poverty with vice allows rich people to display privilege as a badge of ability, whereas poverty is a sign of personal failure. According to Richard Sennett and Jonathan Cobb (1973), the negative stigma of poverty is the "hidden injury of class."

Figure 11–8 shows that people in the United States, more than people in other industrial societies, see poverty as a mark of laziness and personal failure. This fact goes a long way to explaining why the U.S. public offers limited support for social programs to assist the poor. It should not be surprising, then, that Congress replaced the federal AFDC program with state-run programs called Temporary Assistance for Needy Families (TANF). The federal government provides funding, and states set their own qualifications and benefits, but they must limit assistance to two consecutive years (with a lifetime limit of five years). By 2002, TANF expects to move half of single parents on welfare into jobs or job training. By 2000, four years after the welfare reform bill took effect, the welfare rolls had shrunk by 56 percent (the number of people receiving benefits dropped from 14.1 million to 6.3 million). Half of those people have found jobs; others are in school or job-training programs. Supporters declare the reform successful. However, opponents note that many of those with jobs receive very low pay and fear that many families will end up worse off than before.

Continue the debate . . .

1. *How does our cultural emphasis on self-reliance help explain the controversy surrounding public assistance? Why, then, do people not criticize benefits (such as home mortgage interest deductions) for more well-off people?*

2. *Do you think public assistance has become a way of life and eroded the family? Why or why not?*

3. *Do you approve of the benefit time limits built into the new TANF program? Why or why not?*

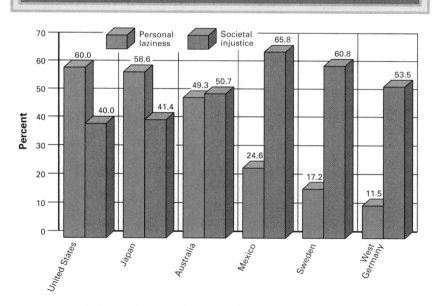

GLOBAL SNAPSHOT

FIGURE 11–8 Assessing the Causes of Poverty

Survey Question: "Why are there people in this country who live in need?" Percentages reflect respondents' identification of either "personal laziness" or "societal injustice" as the primary cause of poverty.

*Percentages for each country may not add up to 100 because less frequently identified causes of poverty were omitted from this figure.

Source: Inglehart et al. (2000).

Sources: Church (1996), Murray (1996), Broder (1997), Dervarics (1998), Jones (1999a), Corcoran et al. (2000), U.S. Department of Health and Human Services (2000), and Rogers-Dillon (2001).

CTQ1: Because social class is multidimensional, no single question provides a valid measurement. But asking about occupation probably is a good choice because one's work also suggests level of education and level of income.
CTQ2: At best he becomes a member of the lower-upper class. A financial windfall does nothing, at least in the short run, to change the cultural patterns of this man's life.

CTQ3: Support for class-based affirmative action assumes that our birth plays a significant role in our opportunities and achievement through most of life. Opposition to such a policy assumes it does not.
Q: "The most dangerous illusion of them all is the illusion that all is well." William Nicholson
Q: "Stay humble. Always answer your own phone, no matter who else is in the car." Jack Lemmon

SUMMARY

1. Social stratification in the United States involves inequality of many kinds, including income, wealth, and power.

2. White-collar jobs generally offer greater income and prestige than blue-collar work. Many jobs typically held by women offer little social prestige or income.

3. Schooling is also a resource that is distributed unequally. More than 80 percent of people over age twenty-five complete high school, but only one-fifth are college graduates.

4. Family ancestry, race and ethnicity, gender, and religion all affect a person's social position.

5. The upper class (5 percent of the population) includes the richest and most powerful families. Most members of the upper-upper class, or the "old rich," inherit their wealth; the lower-upper class, or the "new rich," amass wealth from high incomes.

6. The middle class (40 to 45 percent) enjoys financial security, but only some of these people (the upper-middle class) have substantial wealth.

7. With below-average incomes, most members of the working class or lower-middle class (33 percent) have blue-collar jobs, and only one-third of their children reach college.

8. About one-fifth of the U.S. population belongs to the lower class; about half of these people live below the government's poverty line. People of African and Hispanic descent, as well as women, are disproportionately represented in the lower class.

9. Social class shapes our lives, affecting our health, attitudes, and patterns of family living.

10. Social mobility is common in the United States and other high-income countries; typically, though, only small changes occur from one generation to the next.

11. The growing global economy has increased the wealth of rich families in the United States but stalled or even lowered the standard of living of low-income families.

12. The government classifies 31.1 million people as poor. Nearly 40 percent of the poor are children under age eighteen. Two-thirds of the poor are white, but African Americans and Hispanics are disproportionately represented among people with low income. The *feminization of poverty* means that more poor families are headed by women.

13. The *culture of poverty* thesis suggests that poverty is caused by shortcomings in the poor themselves. Others believe that poverty is caused by society's unequal distribution of jobs and wealth.

14. Our cultural emphasis on individual responsibility helps explain why public assistance for the poor has long been controversial.

KEY CONCEPTS

income (p. 272) wages or salary from work and earnings from investments

wealth (p. 272) the total value of money and other assets, minus outstanding debts

intragenerational social mobility (p. 282) a change in social position occurring during a person's lifetime

intergenerational social mobility (p. 282) upward or downward social mobility of children in relation to their parents

relative poverty (p. 286) the deprivation of some people in relation to those who have more

absolute poverty (p. 286) a deprivation of resources that is life threatening

feminization of poverty (p. 287) the trend by which women represent an increasing proportion of the poor

CRITICAL-THINKING QUESTIONS

1. If you were trying to assess a person's social class and could ask the person only one question, what would it be? Why?

2. In June, 2001, a 66-year-old retired grocer in California claimed a $141-million lottery prize, which will provide a lump sum payment of $42.3 million after taxes. Does this windfall make the man a member of the upper class? Explain your answer.

3. Would you be in favor of class-based affirmative action? That is, should our society give people born to

lower-class families an edge in college admission and company hiring? Why or why not?

4. Our society is always ready to assist the "worthy" poor, including elderly people, whom we do not expect to fend for themselves. At the same time, we are less generous toward the "unworthy poor," able-bodied people who, we think, could take care of themselves but do not. If this is so, why do you think we have not done more to reduce poverty among children, who surely fall into the "worthy" category?

APPLICATIONS AND EXERCISES

1. Develop several simple questions that, taken together, would let you measure someone's social class position. The trick is to decide exactly what you think social class really means. Then try your questions on several adults, refining the questions as you proceed.

2. During an evening of television viewing, assess the social class level of the characters you see in various shows. In each case, explain why you assign someone a particular social position. What patterns do you find?

3. Visit the social services office that oversees financial assistance to people with low incomes in your community. See what you can learn about the effect of the 1996 welfare reforms.

4. Packaged in the back of this new textbook is an interactive CD-ROM that offers a variety of study and review materials intended to help you better understand the material covered in this chapter. For this chapter, the CD-ROM contains an author's tip video, Real Life Sociology videos, other relevant audio and video, interactive map animations, audio journal entries from the author, Web links, and much more.

 ## SITES TO SEE

http://www.prenhall.com/macionis

Visit the interactive *Companion Website*™ that accompanies this text. Begin by clicking on the cover of your book. You will find a chapter-by-chapter study guide, practice tests, and a significant portion of the text for on-line review, as well as many suggested Web links.

http://quickfacts.census.gov/qfd/index.html
http://www.bea.doc.gov

These two sites, the first run by the Census Bureau and the second by the government's Bureau of Economic Analysis, provide state-by-state and county-by-county income data. Visit these sites and see what you can learn about social standing in your part of the country.

http://www.iwpr.org

The Institute for Women's Policy Research investigates the interplay of gender and poverty.

http://www.ssc.wisc.edu/irp
http://www.jcpr.org
http://www.nber.org

Here are three Web sites that are worth a visit to learn more about poverty in the United States. The first is operated by the Institute for Research on Poverty, the second by the Joint Center for Poverty Research, and the third by the National Bureau of Economic Research.

http://www.researchforum.org
http://www.childrensdefense.org

In the United States, children are at high risk of poverty. These two sites introduce you to the Research Forum on Children, Families, and the New Federalism and the Children's Defense Fund, both of which are concerned with child poverty.

 **Journal Research Collections from** *ContentSelect*

INVESTIGATE WITH CONTENTSELECT

Follow the instructions found on page 23 of this textbook to enter this chapter of the book's *Companion Website*™. Once in the chapter, click on the ContentSelect icon at the bottom left of your screen and enter your personal User ID and Password. Enter keywords such as "social class," "wealth," and "poverty," and the search engine will help you become an effective researcher.

CHAPTER

12

José Belon (d. 1927, French)
Famine in India

Illustration from *Le Petit Journal*, c. 1899 (colored engraving).
Private Collection. The Bridgeman Art Library.

GLOBAL STRATIFICATION

For months, the monsoon rains had soaked the Philippines. Finally, to everyone's relief, the rain ended. At the foot of Manila's enormous garbage dump, families gathered in front of their shacks to enjoy the warm sunshine. Soon enough, these poorest of the poor would begin picking through the final resting place for Manila's garbage in search of anything of value that they might sell.

Suddenly, the morning turned to tragedy as one of the high mountains of garbage rumbled and swept down, covering homes and people. In minutes the landslide was over, leaving only an eerie silence.

Within several hours, rescuers began digging with backhoes and shovels in hopes of finding survivors. Workers and volunteers held rags across their faces to protect them from the stench of the decomposing garbage. By mid-afternoon, about 60 people had been saved. But it was apparent that at least 300 more were buried, and only a few more would be found alive.

As the day drew to a close, families and friends sat helplessly, weeping. They gazed at what was left of their community, which—ironically—had been known as "Promised Land" (based on Associated Press, 2000).

It may surprise you to learn that thousands of people live in Manila's garbage dump. The same is true of dumps in Cairo, Mexico City, and many other large cities in lower-income nations of the world. These people are only a small share of roughly 1 billion of the world's people who work hard every day and yet are miserably poor. As this chapter explains, although poverty is a reality in the United States, we can understand the full dimensions of poverty only by taking a global perspective.

GLOBAL STRATIFICATION: AN OVERVIEW

Chapter 11 ("Social Class in the United States") described social inequality in the United States. In global perspective, however, social stratification is far more pronounced. Figure 12–1 on page 300 divides the world's total income by fifths of the population. Recall that the richest 20 percent of the U.S. population earns about 47 percent of the national income (see Figure 11–1). However, the richest 20 percent of global population receives about 80 percent of world income. At the other extreme, the poorest 20 percent of the U.S. population earns 4 percent of our national income, but the poorest fifth of the world's people struggles to survive on just 1 percent of global income.

Because global income is so concentrated, even people in the United States with income below the government's poverty line live far better than the majority of the earth's people. The average person living in a rich nation such as the United States is quite well-off by world standards. At the very top of the pyramid, the wealth of the world's three richest *individuals* roughly equals the annual economic output of the world's forty-eight poorest *countries* (Annan, 1998).

A WORD ABOUT TERMINOLOGY

A familiar model for describing global stratification, developed after World War II, labeled rich, industrial countries the "First World"; less industrialized, socialist

SUPPLEMENTS: The *Data File* contains a detailed outline of Chapter 12, along with discussion topics and supplementary lecture material.
GLOBAL: When discussing Figure 12–1, note that the richest 20% of the world's people consume 45% of all meat and fish, 58% of all energy, and 84% of all paper and own 87% of all motor vehicles (Annan, 1998).

Q: "Half the world does not know how the other half lives." Rabelais
Q: "We now live in a global village." Marshall McLuhan (1969)
GLOBAL: The world's richest person is probably Bill Gates, with wealth of about $58 billion.
Q: "One billion more people are being fed today than in the early 1970s, but the number of hungry people continues to increase." John W. Helmuth

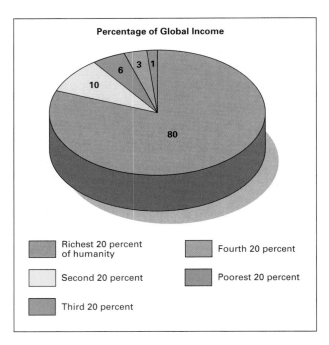

FIGURE 12–1 Distribution of World Income

Sources: Calculated by the author based on United Nations Development Programme (2000) and The World Bank (2001).

countries the "Second World"; and nonindustrialized, poor countries the "Third World." But the "Three Worlds" model is now less useful. For one thing, it was a product of cold war politics by which the capitalist West (the First World) faced off against the socialist East (the Second World), while other nations (the Third World) remained more or less on the sidelines. But the sweeping changes in Eastern Europe and the collapse of the former Soviet Union mean that a distinctive Second World no longer exists.

A second problem is that the "Three Worlds" model lumped together more than 100 countries as the Third World. In reality, some relatively better-off nations of the Third World (such as Chile in South America) have fifteen times the per-person productivity of the poorest countries of the world (including Ethiopia in east Africa).

These facts call for a modestly revised system of classification. Here, we define *high-income countries* as the richest forty nations with the highest overall standard of living. Next, the world's ninety *middle-income countries* are somewhat poorer, with economic development more or less typical of the world as a whole.

Finally, the remaining sixty *low-income countries* have the lowest productivity and the most severe and extensive poverty.

This new model has two advantages over the older "Three Worlds" system. First, it focuses on economic development rather than whether societies are capitalist or socialist. Second, it gives a better picture of the relative economic development of various countries because it does not lump together all lower-income nations into a single "Third World."

Still, classifying the 192 nations on Earth into any three categories ignores many striking differences. These nations have rich and varied histories, speak different languages, and take pride in their distinctive cultures.

Keep in mind, too, that every country is also internally stratified. Thus, the extent of global inequality is actually greater than national comparisons suggest because the most well-off people in rich countries (such as the United States) live worlds apart from the poorest people in low-income countries (such as Haiti, Sudan, and India).

HIGH-INCOME COUNTRIES

In nations where the Industrial Revolution first took place more than two centuries ago, productivity increased more than one-hundredfold. To understand the power of industrial technology—and even newer technology that is part of the Information Revolution—consider that the small European nation of Holland is more productive than the vast continent of Africa south of the Sahara Desert; likewise, tiny Belgium outproduces all of India.

A look back at Global Map 1–2 on page 6 identifies the forty high-income countries of the world. They include the United States and Canada, Argentina, the nations of Western Europe, Israel, Saudi Arabia, Singapore, Hong Kong (now part of the People's Republic of China), Japan, South Korea, Australia, and New Zealand.

Taken together, countries with the most developed economies cover roughly 25 percent of the earth's land area—including parts of five continents—and lie mostly in the Northern Hemisphere. In 2002, the population of these nations was about 1 billion, or about 18 percent of the Earth's people. About three-fourths of the people in high-income countries live in or near cities.

Significant cultural differences exist among high-income countries. For example, the nations of Europe

GLOBAL: The world total GDP is about $30 trillion; total world wealth is about $600 trillion (United Nations Development Programme, 2001).

GLOBAL: The 1999 UN *Human Development Report* states that the assets of the world's 200 richest people exceeded $1 trillion in 1998. The assets of the 3 richest people were greater than the combined GNP of the 48 least developed countries.

NOTE: By and large, poor countries have more internal stratification than the U.S. Thus, the chasm separating the rich of the U.S. and the world's poorest people is truly immense. One manifestation of this is the pattern of wealthy U.S. households employing immigrant service workers.

NOTE: A useful illustration here is to refer back to the "global village" box on page 5 in Chapter 1 ("The Sociological Perspective").

When natural disasters strike high-income countries, such as Hurricane Andrew that devasted much of southern Florida in 1992, property loss is great but the loss of life is low. In low-income countries, by contrast, the converse is true; the death toll from Hurricane Mitch's rampage through Honduras in 1998 reached 5,000.

recognize more than thirty official languages. But these societies share an industrial capacity that generates, on average, a rich material life for their people. Per capita income ranges from about $10,000 annually (in Slovakia and Saudi Arabia) to more than $25,000 annually (in the United States and Norway).[1] In fact, people in high-income countries enjoy more than half the world's total income.

Production in rich nations is capital-intensive; that is, it is based on factories, big machinery, and advanced technology. High-income countries also stand at the forefront of the Information Revolution; not only do these countries have the most computer users, but they are headquarters for most of the largest corporations that design and market computers. In addition, high-income countries control the world's financial markets, so that daily events on the financial exchanges of New York, London, and Tokyo affect people throughout the world.

MIDDLE-INCOME COUNTRIES

Middle-income countries have per capita income ranging between $2,500 and $10,000, roughly the median for the world's *nations* (but above that for the world's *people* because most people live in the poorest countries). Two-thirds of the people live in cities, and industrial jobs are common. The remaining one-third of the people live in rural areas, where most are poor and lack access to schools, medical care, adequate housing, and even safe drinking water.

Looking back at Global Map 1–2 (page 6), we see that about ninety of the world's nations fall in the middle-income category. At the high end are Chile (Latin America), South Africa (Africa), and Malaysia (Asia), where annual income is about $8,500. At the low end are Ecuador (Latin America), Albania (Europe), Egypt (Africa), and Indonesia (Asia) with roughly $3,000 annually in per capita income.

One cluster of middle-income countries includes the former Soviet Union and the nations of Eastern Europe (in the past, known as the Second World). These countries had mostly socialist economies until popular revolts between 1989 and 1991 swept aside their governments. Since then, these nations have begun to introduce market systems, but so far the results have been uneven. Some (including Estonia) have improving economies, whereas living standards in others (including Russia) have fallen.

---

[1]High-income countries have per capita annual income of at least $10,000. For middle- and low-income countries, the comparable figures are $2,500 to $10,000 and $2,500 and less. All data reflect the United Nations' concept of "purchasing power parities," which avoids distortion caused by exchange rates when converting currencies to U.S. dollars. Instead, the data represent the local purchasing power of each nation's currency.

GLOBAL: A country's level of economic development reflects the distribution of the labor force by sectors of the economy. The relative percentages in agriculture, industry, and services (men/women): low-income countries, 61/75–15/10–25/14; middle-income countries, 50/56–23/17–26/27; high-income countries, 5/4–34/17–53/73 (World Bank, 1999).

NOTE: Perhaps 5% of the U.S. population (14 million) are poor enough to experience the life of most residents of low-income nations. (That's roughly the population of Cambodia or Kazakhstan.)

GLOBAL: One indicator of economic development is the rate of passenger car ownership (per 1,000 people, 1999): U.S., 478; Sweden, 437; Kuwait, 317; Panama, 83; Paraguay, 14; Syria, 9; Pakistan, 5 (World Bank, 2001).

Japan represents the world's high-income countries, in which industrial technology and economic expansion have produced material prosperity. The presence of market forces is evident in this view of downtown Tokyo (above, left). The Russian Federation represents the middle-income countries of the world. Industrial development and economic performance were sluggish under socialism; as a result, Moscow residents had to wait in long lines for their daily needs (above, right). The hope is that the introduction of a market system will raise living standards, although in the short run, Russian citizens must adjust to increasing economic disparity. Bangladesh (left) represents the world's low-income countries. As the photograph suggests, these nations have limited economic development and rapidly increasing populations. The result is widespread poverty.

A second, and larger, category of middle-income nations includes Chile and Brazil in South America, and Algeria and Botswana in Africa. Although South Africa's white minority lives as well as people in the United States, the country is considered less developed because its majority black population has far less income.

Taken together, middle-income countries span roughly 47 percent of the earth's land area and include about 3.3 billion people, or more than one-half of humanity. Some countries (such as Russia) are far less crowded than others (such as El Salvador), but compared with high-income countries, these societies are densely populated.

LOW-INCOME COUNTRIES

Low-income countries, where most people are very poor, are largely agrarian societies with some industry. Most of these sixty nations, identified in Global

Map 1–2, are found in Africa and in southern Asia. Low-income countries cover 28 percent of the planet's land area and are home to 28 percent of its people. Population density is generally high, although it is greater in Asian countries (such as Bangladesh and India) than in central African nations (such as Chad and the Democratic Republic of the Congo).

In poor countries, 31 percent of the people live in cities; most inhabit villages and farms, living much as their families have for centuries. In fact, half the world's people are peasants who, by and large, follow cultural traditions. With limited industrial technology, peasants are not very productive, one reason that many endure severe poverty. Hunger, disease, and unsafe housing frame the lives of the world's poorest people.

People living in affluent nations such as the United States find it hard to grasp the scope of human want in much of the world. From time to time, televised pictures of famine in very poor countries such as Ethiopia and Bangladesh give us a shocking glimpse of

GLOBAL: A society's mode of transportation is a shorthand index of development that is evident to a traveler. The poorest societies of the world depend on the muscle power of humans and their animals, illustrated by the waves of pedestrians and bicyclists in the streets of Beijing. Developing nations (such as Taiwan) make extensive use of mopeds, motorcycles, and other lightweight, gasoline-powered vehicles. Rich societies use high numbers of automobiles; in the U.S., the number of motor vehicles exceeds the number of adults. (And on college campuses, there is a curious return to low-tech walking and bicycling.)

GLOBAL: Daily caloric consumption for some of the world's poorest countries (1997): Tanzania, 1,995; Niger, 1,992; Benin, 1,958; Haiti, 1,869; Ethiopia, 1,858; Mozambique, 1,832; Burundi, 1,685; Eritrea, 1,622 (United Nations Development Programme, 2000).

the poverty that makes every day a life-and-death struggle. Behind these images lie cultural, historical, and economic forces that we explore in the remainder of this chapter.

GLOBAL WEALTH AND POVERTY

October 14, Manila, the Philippines. What caught my eye was how clean she was—a girl no more than seven or eight years old. She was wearing a freshly laundered dress, and her hair was carefully combed. She followed us with her eyes: Camera-toting Americans stand out in this neighborhood, one of the poorest in the entire world.

Fed by methane from decomposing garbage, the fires never go out on Smokey Mountain, the vast garbage dump on the north side of Manila (referred to in the chapter opener). Smoke envelopes the hills of refuse like a thick fog. But Smokey Mountain is more than a dump; it is a neighborhood that is home to thousands of people. The residents of Smokey Mountain are the poorest of the poor. It is hard to imagine a setting more hostile to human life. Amid the smoke and the squalor, men and women do what they can to survive. They pick plastic bags from the garbage and wash them in the river and collect cardboard boxes or anything else they can sell. And all over Smokey Mountain are children who must already sense the enormous odds against them. What chance do they have, living in families that earn scarcely a few hundred dollars a year? With barely any opportunity for schooling? Year after year, breathing this air?

Against this backdrop of human tragedy, one lovely little girl has put on a fresh dress and gone out to play.

Now our taxi driver threads his way through heavy traffic as we head for the other side of Manila. The change is amazing: The smoke and smell of the dump give way to neighborhoods that could be in Miami or Los Angeles. On the bay in the distance floats a cluster of yachts. No more rutted streets; now we glide quietly along wide boulevards lined with trees and filled with expensive Japanese cars. We pass shopping plazas, upscale hotels, and high-rise office buildings. Every block or so we see the gated entrance to an exclusive residential enclave with security guards standing watch. Here, in large, air-conditioned homes, the rich of Manila live and many of the poor work.

A visit to the Philippines, which is a middle-income nation, or (even more so) India, which is a low-income country, reveals the striking extent of poverty. Indeed, in much of the world, most of the population gets by on incomes of barely several hundred dollars a year. Clearly, this means that the burden of poverty is far greater than among the poor of the United States. This is not to suggest that poverty at home is a minor problem. In so rich a country, too little food, substandard housing, and no medical care for tens of millions of people—almost half of them children—amount to a national tragedy. Yet poverty in poor countries is both *more severe* and *more extensive* than in the United States.

THE SEVERITY OF POVERTY

Poverty in poor countries is more severe than it is in rich countries. The data in Table 12–1 on page 304 show why. The first column of figures gives gross domestic product (GDP) for representative high-, middle-, and low-income countries.[2] The United States, a large

---

[2]Gross domestic product (GDP) includes all the goods and services on record as produced by a country's economy in a given year, excluding income earned outside the country by individuals or corporations. Gross national product (GNP) adds in the foreign earnings. For countries that invest heavily abroad (Kuwait, for example), GDP is much smaller than GNP; for countries in which other nations invest heavily (Hong Kong), GDP is much greater than GNP. For countries that both invest heavily abroad and have high foreign investment at home (including the United States), the two measures are about the same.

GLOBAL: The world's labor force numbers about 2.9 billion people; about 30% (some 900 million people) are unemployed or underemployed, almost all living in poor nations.

GLOBAL: The UN quality of life aggregate figures are: high-income countries, .926; middle-income countries, .740; and low-income countries, .549.

GLOBAL: Life expectancy at birth (1999) is a major indicator of quality of life: Japan, 81; Hong Kong, 79; Canada, 79; Germany, 78; U.K., 77; U.S., 77; Poland, 73; P.R. China, 70; Romania, 69; Russian Federation, 66; Nigeria, 52; Angola, 45; Ethiopia, 44; Uganda, 43 (World Bank, 2001).

NOTE: Global production statistics also exclude the value of housework.

TABLE 12–1 Wealth and Well-Being in Global Perspective, 1999

Country	Gross Domestic Product ($ billion)	GDP per Capita (PPP$)*	Quality of Life Index
High Income			
Norway	153	28,433	.939
Australia	404	24,574	.936
Canada	635	26,251	.936
Sweden	239	22,636	.936
United States	9,152	31,872	.934
Japan	4,347	24,898	.928
France	1,432	22,897	.924
United Kindgom	1,442	22,093	.923
South Korea	407	15,712	.875
Middle Income			
Eastern Europe			
Poland	155	8,450	.828
Lithuania	11	6,656	.803
Russian Federation	401	7,473	.775
Ukraine	39	3,458	.742
Latin America			
Mexico	484	8,297	.790
Venezuela	102	5,495	.765
Brazil	752	7,037	.750
Asia			
Malaysia	79	8,209	.774
Thailand	124	6,132	.757
China, P.R.	990	3,617	.718
Middle East			
Iran	111	5,531	.714
Syria	19	4,454	.700
Africa			
Algeria	48	5,063	.693
Botswana	6	6,872	.577
Low Income			
Latin America			
Honduras	5	2,340	.634
Haiti	4	1,464	.467
Asia			
India	447	2,248	.571
Bangladesh	46	1,483	.470
Africa			
Democratic Republic of the Congo	6	801	.429
Guinea	4	1,934	.397
Ethiopia	6	628	.321
Sierra Leone	1	448	.258

*These data are the United Nations' purchasing power parity calculations, which avoid currency rate distortion by showing the local purchasing power of each domestic currency.

Source: United Nations Development Programme, *Human Development Report, 2001* (New York: Oxford University Press, 2001).

industrial nation, had a 1999 GDP of more than $9 trillion; Japan's GDP was more than $4 trillion. Comparing GDP figures shows that the world's richest nations are thousands of times more productive than the poorest countries.

The second column of figures in Table 12–1 indicates per capita GDP in terms of what the United Nations (1995) calls "purchasing power parities"—what people can buy using their income in the local economy. The per capita GDP for rich countries such as the United States, France, and Canada is very high—more than $20,000. For middle-income countries, such as Botswana and Lithuania, the figures are much lower—about $6,500. In the world's low-income countries, per capita annual income is just a few hundred dollars. In the Democratic Republic of the Congo or in Ethiopia, for example, a typical person labors all year to make what the average worker in the United States earns in several days.

The last column of Table 12–1 measures quality of life in these nations. This index, calculated by the United Nations, is based on income, education (extent of adult literacy and average years of schooling), and longevity (how long people typically live). Index values are decimals that fall between hypothetical extremes of 1 (highest) and zero (lowest). By this calculation, Norwegians enjoy the highest quality of life (.939), with residents of the United States close behind (.934). At the other extreme, people in the African nation of Sierra Leone have the lowest quality of life (.258).

One reason that quality of life differs so much around the world is that economic productivity is lowest in precisely the regions of the globe where population growth is highest. Figure 12–2 shows the division of global population and global income for countries at each level of economic development. High-income countries are by far the most advantaged, with 79 percent of global income supporting just 18 percent of humanity. In middle-income nations, 54 percent of the world's people earn 18 percent of global income. This leaves 28 percent of the planet's population with just 3 percent of global income. In short, for every dollar received by individuals in a low-income country, someone in a high-income nation takes home $41.

Relative versus Absolute Poverty

The distinction between relative and absolute poverty, made in Chapter 11, has an important application to global inequality. People living in rich countries generally focus on *relative poverty*, meaning that some

NOTE: Illiteracy rates are high in poor societies (about half of all Africans and one-fourth of all Latin Americans can neither read nor write). Throughout the world, illiteracy is much more common among women than men. Examples (percentage illiterate, 1999): Algeria, 23% of men, 44% of women; Bangladesh, 48%, 71%; Brazil, 15%, 15%; P.R. China, 9%, 25%; Saudi Arabia, 17%, 34%; Tunisia, 20%, 41% (United Nations Development Programme, 2001).

GLOBAL: Another way to describe the relationship in Figure 12–2 is that half the world's people account for about 18% of global GDP; the richest 18% account for three-quarters of global GDP.

GLOBAL: Asia has the largest absolute number of poor (some 750 million people; between 20% and 25%); Africa has the highest proportion of poor people (35%).

people lack resources that others take for granted. Relative poverty, by definition, cuts across every society, rich or poor.

More important in global perspective, however, is *absolute poverty*, a lack of resources that is life threatening. Human beings in absolute poverty lack the nutrition necessary for health and long-term survival. To be sure, some absolute poverty exists in the United States. But such immediately life-threatening poverty strikes only a small proportion of the U.S. population; in low-income countries, by contrast, one-third or more of the people are in desperate need.

Because absolute poverty is deadly, one global indicator of this problem is median age at death. Global Map 12–1 on page 306 identifies the age by which half of all people born in a nation die. In rich societies, most people die after age seventy-five; in poor countries, half of all deaths occur among children under age ten.

THE EXTENT OF POVERTY

Poverty in poor countries is more extensive than it is in rich nations such as the United States. Chapter 11 ("Social Class in the United States") indicated that the U.S. government officially classifies about 11 percent of the population as poor. In low-income countries, however, most people live no better than the poor in the United States, and many are far worse off. As Global Map 12–1 shows, the high death rates among children in

Read a report on world hunger by the Food and Agriculture Organization of the United Nations: http://www. fao.org/NEWS/1999/img/ SOFI99-E.PDF

Africa indicate that absolute poverty is greatest there, where half the population is malnourished. In the world as a whole, at any given time, 15 percent of the people (about 1 billion) suffer from chronic hunger, which leaves them less able to work and puts them at high risk of disease (Kates, 1996; United Nations Development Programme, 2001).

The typical adult in a rich nation, such as the United States, consumes about 3,500 calories a day, an excess that contributes to obesity and related health problems. The typical adult in a low-income country not only does more physical labor but consumes just 2,000 calories a day. The result is undernourishment: too little food or not enough of the right kinds of food.

In the ten minutes it takes to read this section of the chapter, about 300 people in the world who are sick and weakened from hunger will die. This amounts to about 40,000 people a day, or 15 million people

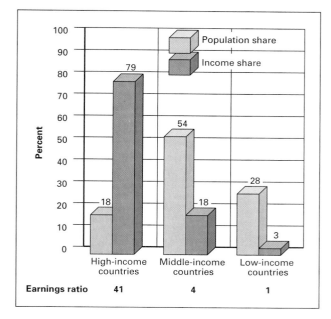

FIGURE 12–2 The Relative Share of Income and Population by Level of Economic Development

Sources: Calculated by the author based on United Nations Development Programme (2000) and The World Bank (2001).

each year. Clearly, easing world hunger is one of the most serious responsibilities facing humanity in the twenty-first century.

POVERTY AND CHILDREN

Death comes early in poor societies, where families lack adequate food, safe water, secure housing, and access to medical care. Organizations combating child poverty estimate that at least 100 million city children in poor countries beg, steal, sell sex, or work for drug gangs to provide income for their families. Such a life almost always means dropping out of school and puts children at high risk of disease and violence. Many girls, with little or no access to medical assistance, become pregnant: a case of children who cannot support themselves being forced to have still more children.

About 100 million of the world's children leave their families altogether, sleeping and living on the streets as best they can. Roughly half of all street children are found in Latin America (United Nations

THEN AND NOW: Life expectancy in sub-Saharan Africa has risen from about 37 in 1960 to 51 today; but that's still about 25 years off the U.S. level.

THE MAP: The high mortality in low-income societies is all the more striking in light of the fact that infant mortality has actually dropped by half since 1965, from about 125 (per 1,000 live births) to about 62 today.

GLOBAL: One indicator of patterns of child poverty is the UN's calculation of seriously underweight children below the age of 5. In high-income countries, the figure is about 3%. The ten worst rates are these low-income countries: Bangladesh, 56%; Cambodia, 52%; Niger, 50%; Ethiopia, 47%; Nepal, 47%; Yemen, 46%; Maldives, 43%; Lao PDR, 40%; Mali, 40% (United Nations Development Programme, 2001).

WINDOW ON THE WORLD

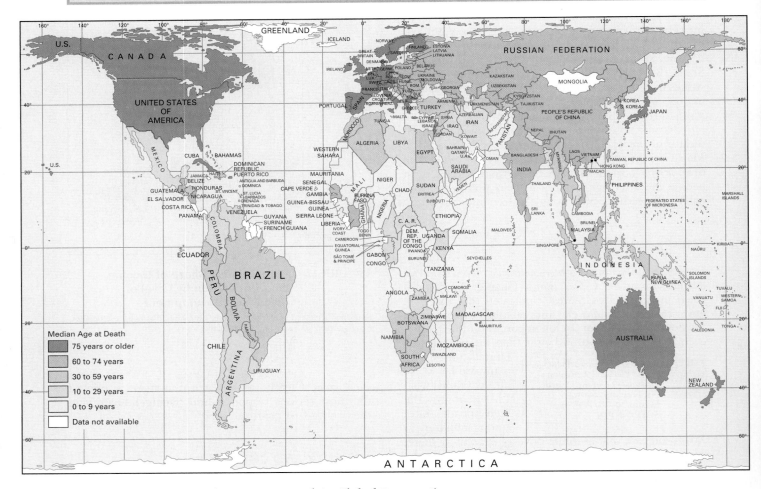

GLOBAL MAP 12–1 Median Age at Death in Global Perspective

This map identifies the age below which half of all deaths occur in any year. In the high-income countries of the world, including the United States, it is mostly the elderly who face death—that is, people age seventy-five or older. In middle-income countries, including most of Latin America, most people die years or even decades earlier. In low-income countries, especially in Africa and parts of Asia, it is children who die, half of them never reaching their tenth birthday.

Sources: The World Bank (1993); map projection from *Peters Atlas of the World* (1990).

Development Programme, 2000). Some 10,000 homeless children roam throughout Mexico City alone (Ross, 1996). In Brazil,

This site profiles the plight of street children in poor nations of the world: http://www.hrw.org/children/street.htm

millions of street children live in makeshift huts, under bridges, or in alleyways. In Rio de Janeiro, known to many in the United States as Brazil's seaside resort, police try to keep the numbers of street children in check; at times, death squads may sweep

Tens of millions of children fend for themselves on the streets of Latin America, where many fall victim to disease, drug abuse, and outright violence. What do you think must be done to put an end to scenes like this one in San Salvador, the capital city of El Salvador?

through a neighborhood in a bloody ritual of "urban cleansing." Reports indicate that several hundred street children are murdered in that city each year (Larmer, 1992; U.S. House of Representatives, 1992).

POVERTY AND WOMEN

In rich societies, the work women do typically is unrecognized, undervalued, and underpaid. In poor societies, this is even more the case. Workers in sweatshops—factories that make much of the clothing and other products consumed in rich countries, including the United States—are mostly women.

At this site, read about a woman who spent six years working in a sweatshop in Saipan producing clothing for sale by the Gap in the United States: http://www.globalexchange.org/education/speakers/CarmencitaChieAbad.html

Families in poor societies depend on women's income. At the same time, tradition bars many women from attending school and gives them primary responsibility for raising children and maintaining the household. The United Nations estimates that in poor countries, men own 90 percent of the land, a far greater gender disparity in wealth than that in high-income nations. Thus, about 70 percent of the world's 1 billion people living near absolute poverty are women (Hymowitz, 1995).

Women in poor countries have limited access to birth control (which, in turn, raises the birth rate), and they typically give birth without the assistance of trained health personnel. Figure 12–3 on page 308 draws a stark contrast between low- and high-income countries in this regard.

SLAVERY

Poor societies are vulnerable to many problems: hunger, illiteracy, warfare, and slavery. The British Empire banned slavery in 1833; the United States followed suit in 1865. But according to Anti-Slavery International (ASI), as many as 400 million men, women, and children (almost 7 percent of humanity) live today in conditions that amount to slavery (Janus, 1996).

ASI distinguishes four types of slavery. In *chattel slavery*, one person owns another. The number of chattel slaves is difficult to estimate because this practice is against the law almost everywhere. Nevertheless, the buying and selling of slaves still takes place in many countries in Asia, the Middle East, and especially

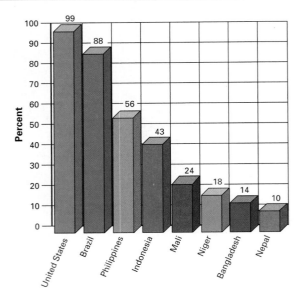

GLOBAL SNAPSHOT

FIGURE 12–3 Percentage of Births Attended by Trained Health Personnel

Source: The World Bank (2001).

Africa. The box describes the reality of one slave's life in the African nation of Mauritania.

A second, more common form of bondage is *child slavery*. Desperately poor families make their children take to the streets to fend for themselves. Perhaps 100 million children—many in poor countries of Latin America—fall into this category.

Third, *debt bondage* is the practice by which employers hold workers by paying them too little to cover their debts. In this case, workers receive wages but not enough to cover the food and housing the employer provides. Thus, for practical purposes, they are enslaved. Many workers in sweatshops in poor countries fall into this category (McCarthy, 1998).

Fourth, *servile forms of marriage* may also amount to slavery. In India, Thailand, and some African nations, families marry off women against their will. Many end up as slaves working for their husband's family; some are forced into prostitution.

 Read the United Nations' Universal Declaration of Human Rights at http://www.un.org/rights/50/decla.htm

In 1948, the United Nations issued its Universal Declaration of Human Rights, which states; "No one shall be held in slavery or servitude; slavery and the slave trade shall be prohibited in all their forms." Unfortunately, more than fifty years later, this social evil persists.

CORRELATES OF GLOBAL POVERTY

What accounts for the severe and extensive poverty throughout much of the world? The rest of this chapter weaves together explanations from the following facts about poor societies:

1. **Technology.** About one-quarter of people in low-income countries farm the land using human muscle or beasts of burden. Because these energy sources fall far short of the force of steam, oil, or nuclear power, only limited use of complex machinery is possible.

2. **Population growth.** As Chapter 22 ("Population, Urbanization, and Environment") explains, the poorest countries have the world's highest birth rates. Despite the death toll from poverty, the populations of poor countries in Africa, for example, double every twenty-five years. In these countries, half the people are teenagers or younger. With such numbers entering their childbearing years, a wave of population growth will roll into the future. In recent years, for example, the population of Chad swelled by 3.3 percent annually, so that even with economic development living standards have fallen.

3. **Cultural patterns.** Poor societies usually are traditional. Adhering to long-established ways of life, people resist innovation, even if it promises a richer material life. The box on page 310 explains why traditional people in India respond to their poverty differently than poor people in the United States.

4. **Social stratification.** Low-income societies distribute their wealth very unequally. Chapter 10 ("Social Stratification") explained that social inequality is more pronounced in agrarian societies than in industrial societies. In Brazil, for example, half of all farmland is owned by just 1 percent of the people (Bergamo & Camarotti, 1996).

5. **Gender inequality.** Extreme gender inequality in poor societies deprives women of opportunities,

NOTE: With a current rate of population growth of 1.7%, India's population passed the 1 billion mark in 2000 and will double again by 2042.

GLOBAL: Marlise Simons explains how economic development has undermined the cultural traditions of the Kaiapo in Brazil's Amazon region. See her article in the Macionis and Benokraitis reader or the box in Chapter 24.

GLOBAL: Refugees are on the rise, predominantly in the poorest regions of the world. Some 20 million people are displaced across international borders, with another 25 million displaced within their own countries. As the numbers rise, rich countries are becoming more restrictive about admitting refugees.

GLOBAL: Compared to an average of about 13 years of schooling in the U.S., China averages 5 years, Indonesia 4, and Pakistan 2.

GLOBAL SOCIOLOGY

"God Made Me to Be a Slave"

Fatma Mint Mamadou is a young woman living in North Africa's Islamic Republic of Mauritania. Asked her age, she pauses and smiles. She has no idea when she was born. Nor can she read or write. What she knows is tending camels, herding sheep, hauling bags of water, washing clothes, sweeping, and serving tea to her owners. This young woman is one of perhaps 90,000 slaves in Mauritania.

In the central region of this nation, having dark brown skin almost always means being a slave to an Arab owner. Fatma accepts her situation; she has known nothing else. She explains in a matter-of-fact voice that she is a slave as was her mother before her. And her grandmother before that. "Just as God created a camel to be a camel," she shrugs, "he created me to be a slave."

Fatma, her mother, and her brothers and sisters live in a squatter settlement on the edge of Nauakchott, Mauritania's capital city. Their home is a nine- by twelve-foot hut that they built from wood scraps and other materials taken from construction sites. The roof is nothing more than a piece of cloth; there is no plumbing or furniture. The nearest water comes from a well a mile down the road.

Human slavery continues to exist in the twenty-first century.

In this region, slavery began 500 years ago, about the time Columbus sailed west toward the New World. Then, as Arab and Berber tribes moved across the region spreading Islam, they raided local villages and made slaves of the people. So it has been for dozens of generations ever since. In 1905, the French colonial rulers of Mauritania banned slavery. After the nation gained independence in 1961, the new government banned slavery once again. But such proclamations have done little to change strong traditions. Indeed, people like Fatma have no idea what freedom to choose means.

The next question is more personal: "Are you and other girls ever raped?" Again, Fatma hesitates. With no hint of emotion, she responds, "Of course, in the night the men come to breed us. Is that what you mean by rape?"

Source: Based on Burkett (1997).

which typically means they have many children. An expanding population, in turn, slows economic development. Thus, many analysts conclude, raising living standards in much of the world depends on improving the social standing of women.

6. **Global power relationships.** A final cause of global poverty lies in the relationships between the nations of the world. Historically, wealth flowed from poor societies to rich nations through **colonialism,** *the process by which some nations enrich themselves through political and economic control of other nations.* The countries of Western Europe colonized much of Latin America and Africa beginning roughly 500 years ago.

Such global exploitation allowed some nations to develop economically at the expense of other nations.

Although 130 former colonies gained their independence during the twentieth century, exploitation continues through **neocolonialism** (*neo* is the Greek word for "new"), *a new form of global power relationships that involves not direct political control but economic exploitation by multinational corporations.* **Multinational corporations**—*huge businesses that operate in many countries*—wield tremendous economic power. Corporate decision makers often impose their will on countries where they do business, just as colonizers did in the past.

GLOBAL: Starvation has been caused by social policies more than by natural forces such as droughts. Examples: 1846–50, Irish potato famine as food is diverted to England; 1932–34, some 5 million Soviet people die during Stalin's farm collectivization; 1958–61, perhaps 25 million starve during China's failed "Great Leap Forward."
GLOBAL: Types of foods change with rising income. People in low-income countries eat basic cereals; middle-income nations consume basic packaged foods; the availability of frozen foods marks high-income countries. In the highest-income countries, prepared foods are popular, with fresh foods and health foods enjoyed by the richest of the world's people.
NOTE: The loss of life due to poor nutrition every 5 years surpasses the death toll from war, revolution, and murder during the last 150 years.

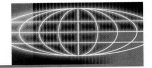

GLOBAL SOCIOLOGY

A Different Kind of Poverty: A Report from India

Most North Americans know that India is one of the poorest nations on Earth. A vast country with per capita gross domestic product (GDP) of only $2,248 a year (see Table 12–1), India is home to one-third of all the world's hungry people.

But most North Americans do not readily understand the reality of poverty in India. Most of the country's 1 billion people live in conditions far worse than those our society labels "poor." A traveler's first experience of Indian life can be shocking. Madras, one of India's largest cities with 7 million inhabitants, seems chaotic to an outsider: streets choked with motorbikes, trucks, carts pulled by oxen, and waves of people. Along the roadway, vendors sit on burlap cloth and hawk fruit, vegetables, and cooked food while people nearby work, talk, bathe, and sleep.

Madras is dotted with thousands of shanty settlements, home to half a million people from rural villages who have come in search of a better life. Shantytowns are clusters of huts built with branches, leaves, and pieces of discarded cardboard and tin. These dwellings offer little privacy and lack refrigeration, running water, and bathrooms. A visitor from the United States may feel uneasy in such an area, knowing that the poorest sections of our own inner cities seethe with frustration and sometimes explode with violence.

But India's people understand poverty differently than we do. No restless young men hang out on corners, no drug dealers work the streets, and there is little danger of violence. In the United States, poverty often means anger and isolation; in India, even

shantytowns are organized around strong families—children, parents, and often grandparents—who offer a smile and a welcome to a stranger.

For traditional people in India, life is shaped by *dharma*, the Hindu concept of duty and destiny that teaches people to accept their fate, whatever it may be. Mother Teresa, who worked among the poorest of India's people, went to the heart of the cultural differences: "Americans have angry poverty," she explained. "In India, there is worse poverty, but it is a happy poverty."

Perhaps we should not describe anyone who clings to the edge of survival as happy. But poverty in India is eased by the strength and support of families and communities, a sense that existence has a purpose, and a worldview that encourages each person to accept whatever life offers. As a result, a visitor may well come away from a first encounter with Indian poverty in confusion: "How can people be so poor and yet apparently content, active, and *joyful*?"

Source: Based on the author's research in Madras, India, November 1988.

GLOBAL STRATIFICATION: THEORETICAL ANALYSIS

There are two major explanations for the unequal distribution of the world's wealth and power: *modernization theory* and *dependency theory*. Each theory suggests a different path toward relieving the suffering of hungry people in much of the world.

MODERNIZATION THEORY

Modernization theory is *a model of economic and social development that explains global inequality in terms of technological and cultural differences between societies.* Modernization theory emerged in the 1950s, a time when U.S. society was fascinated with new technology and many people in poor countries were hostile toward the United States. With the socialist Soviet

In rich nations such as the United States, most parents expect their children to enjoy years of childhood, largely free from the responsibilities of adult life. This is not the case in poor nations across Latin America, Africa, and Asia. Poor families depend on whatever income their children can earn, and many children as young as six or seven work full days weaving or performing other kinds of manual labor. Child labor lies behind the low prices of many products imported for sale in this country.

Union gaining influence abroad, U.S. policy makers drafted a foreign policy that was promarket and has been with us ever since.[3]

Historical Perspective

Modernization theorists point out that as recently as several centuries ago, the entire world was poor. Because poverty is the norm throughout human history, it is *affluence* that demands an explanation.

Affluence came within reach of a growing share of people in Western Europe during the late Middle Ages as world exploration and trade expanded. Soon, the Industrial Revolution was underway, transforming first Western Europe and then North America. Industrial technology coupled with the spirit of capitalism created new wealth on an unprecedented scale. At the outset, this new wealth benefitted only a few. But industrial technology was so productive that gradually the living standard of even the poorest people began to improve. The specter of absolute poverty, which had cast a menacing shadow over humanity, was finally being routed.

During the twentieth century, the standard of living in high-income countries, where the Industrial Revolution began, jumped at least fourfold. Many middle-income nations in Asia and Latin America are now industrializing, and they, too, are becoming richer. But without industrial technology, low-income countries have changed little.

The Importance of Culture

Why didn't the Industrial Revolution sweep away poverty the world over? Modernization theory points out that not every society has been eager to seek out new technology. A society's cultural environment must emphasize the benefits of materialism and innovation.

Modernization theory thus identifies *tradition* as the greatest barrier to economic development. In societies with strong family systems and a reverence for the past, "cultural inertia" discourages people from adopting new technologies that would raise their living standards. Even today, many people—from the North American Amish to Islamic people of Iran to the Semai of Malaysia—oppose technological advances as a threat to their family relationships, customs, and religious beliefs.

As Max Weber (1958; orig. 1904–5) explained, at the end of the Middle Ages, the cultural environment of Western Europe favored change. As discussed in Chapter 4 ("Society"), the Protestant Reformation

---

[3]The following discussion of modernization theory draws primarily on Rostow (1960, 1978), Bauer (1981), and Berger (1986); see also Firebaugh (1996) and Firebaugh & Sandu (1998).

Q: "Economic achievement and progress depend largely on human aptitudes and attitudes, on social and political institutions and arrangements which derive from these." P.T. Bauer

RESOURCE: The cultural value placed on achievement is regarded by some sociologists as the crucial factor in advancing or inhibiting development. Cf. Daniel Lerner, *The Passing of Traditional Society: Modernizing the Middle East* (Free Press, 1958).

NOTE: The subtitle of Walt Whitman Rostow's (1960) work, "A Non-Communist Manifesto," suggests its opposition to Marx's thinking.

GLOBAL: Hong Kong (about the size of Los Angeles) has twice the economic productivity of Colombia and four times that of Bangladesh.

had reshaped traditional Catholicism to generate a progress-oriented way of life. Wealth, regarded with suspicion by the Catholic church, became a sign of personal virtue, and the growing importance of individualism steadily replaced the traditional emphasis on kinship and community. Taken together, these new cultural patterns nurtured the Industrial Revolution, which propelled a large segment of the population from poverty to prosperity.

Rostow's Stages of Modernization

Modernization theory holds that the door to affluence is open to all. Indeed, as technological advances spread around the world, all societies should gradually industrialize. According to W. W. Rostow (1960, 1978), modernization occurs in four stages:

1. **Traditional stage.** Socialized to venerate the past, people in traditional societies cannot easily imagine how life could be different. Therefore, they build their lives around families and local communities and follow well-worn paths that allow little individual freedom or change. Life often is spiritually rich but lacking in material goods.

   A century ago, much of the world was in this initial stage of economic development. Nations such as Bangladesh, Niger, and Somalia are still at the traditional stage and remain impoverished.

2. **Take-off stage.** As a society shakes off the grip of tradition, people start to use their talents and imagination, sparking economic growth. A market emerges as people produce goods not just for their own consumption but to trade with others for profit. Greater individualism, a willingness to take risks, and a desire for material goods also take hold, often at the expense of family ties and time-honored norms and values.

   Great Britain reached take-off by about 1800, the United States by 1820. Thailand, a middle-income country in eastern Asia, is now at this stage. Such development typically is speeded by progressive influences from rich nations, including foreign aid, advanced technology and investment capital, and opportunities for schooling abroad.

3. **Drive to technological maturity.** During this stage, "growth" is a widely accepted concept that fuels a society's pursuit of higher living standards. A diversified economy drives a population eager to enjoy the benefits of industrial technology. At the same time, however, people begin to realize

(and sometimes lament) that industrialization is eroding traditional family and local community life. Great Britain reached this point by about 1840, the United States by 1860. Today, Mexico, the U.S. territory of Puerto Rico, and South Korea are among the nations driving to technological maturity.

   Societies in stage three have greatly reduced absolute poverty. Cities swell with people who leave rural villages in search of economic opportunity, occupational specialization makes relationships less personal, and heightened individualism generates social movements demanding greater political rights. Societies approaching technological maturity also provide basic schooling for all their people and advanced training for some. The newly educated consider tradition "backward," opening the door to further change. The social position of women steadily becomes more equal to that of men. Even so, in the short term, the process of development may subject women to unexpected problems, as the box explains.

4. **High mass consumption.** Economic development steadily raises living standards as mass production stimulates industrial consumption. Simply put, people soon learn to "need" the expanding array of goods their society produces.

   The United States, Japan, and other rich nations moved into this stage by 1900. Now entering this level of economic development are two former British colonies that are prosperous small societies of eastern Asia: Hong Kong (part of the People's Republic of China) and Singapore (independent since 1965).

The Role of Rich Nations

Modernization theory claims that high-income countries play four important roles in global economic development:

1. **Helping control population.** Because population growth is greatest in the poorest societies, it can overtake economic advances. Rich nations can help limit population growth by exporting birth control technology and promoting its use. Once economic development is underway, birth rates should decline, as they have in industrialized nations, because children are no longer an economic asset.

2. **Increasing food production.** Rich nations can export high-tech farming methods to poor

NOTE: Modernization theory is loosely linked to structural-functional theory; dependency theory is more obviously connected to social-conflict theory.

GLOBAL: During the 1990s, the population of poor countries increased by about 2% annually versus 0.5% for rich nations; economic growth in poor countries was negative, against positive growth for rich societies.

Q: "The plight of women [in modernizing Bangladesh] is all too obvious in the streams of unattached mothers and children who pour into towns to beg, in the growth of prostitution, in the desperation with which rural women have left the seclusion of their homes to seek work." Sultana Alam

Q: "Women-headed households are of fairly recent origin in the Third World." Sultana Alam

DIVERSITY: RACE, CLASS, AND GENDER

Modernization: New Challenges for Women

In global perspective, gender inequality is greatest where people are poorest. Economic development, then, depends on giving women opportunities for schooling and work outside the home. In the process, birth rates decline and traditional male domination weakens.

But modernization also poses dangers for women. Investigating the lives of women in a poor, rural district of Bangladesh, Sultana Alam (1985) reports several hazards.

First, as economic opportunity draws men from rural areas to cities in search of work, women and children must fend for themselves. Some men sell their land and simply abandon their wives, who are left with nothing but their children.

Second, the diminishing strength of the family and neighborhood leaves women who are deserted with little assistance. The same holds true for women who become single through divorce or the death of a spouse. In the past, Alam reports, kin or neighbors readily took in a Bangladeshi woman who found herself alone. But, today, as Bangladesh struggles to advance economically, the number of households headed by single women is increasing, and most are poor. Thus, rather than enhancing women's autonomy, Alam argues, a new spirit of individualism has lowered the social standing of women.

In Rajshahi, Bangladesh, women meet to address their common problems.

Third, economic development—as well as the growing influence of Western movies and mass media—undermine women's traditional roles as wives, sisters, and mothers, defining them instead as objects of sexual attention. A new cultural emphasis on sexuality encourages men in poor countries to abandon aging spouses for younger, more physically attractive partners. The same emphasis contributes to the world's rising level of prostitution.

Modernization, then, does not affect men and women in the same ways. In the long run, the evidence suggests, modernization gives the sexes more equal standing. In the short run, however, many women suffer economic setbacks as they face problems virtually unknown in traditional societies.

Sources: Based on Alam (1985) and Mink (1989).

---

nations and thus raise agricultural yields. Such techniques, collectively called the Green Revolution, involve new hybrid seeds, modern irrigation methods, chemical fertilizers, and pesticides.

3. **Introducing industrial technology.** Rich nations can accelerate economic growth in poor societies by introducing machinery and information technology, which raise productivity. Industrialization also shifts the labor force from farming to skilled industrial and service jobs.

4. **Providing foreign aid.** Investment capital from rich nations can boost the prospects of poor societies striving to reach Rostow's take-off stage. Foreign aid can purchase fertilizer and fund irrigation projects, which increase agricultural productivity. Financial and technical assistance can also build power plants and factories to increase industrial output.

Critical evaluation. Modernization theory has many influential supporters among social scientists (Parsons, 1966; W. Moore, 1977, 1979; Bauer, 1981; Berger, 1986; Firebaugh & Beck, 1994; Firebaugh, 1996, 1999; Firebaugh & Sandu, 1998). Moreover,

Was the arrival of Europeans in the Western Hemisphere a tale of brave explorers or greedy conquerors? The painting Colonial Domination, *a mural by Mexican artist Diego Rivera, clearly presents the artist's point of view.*

Diego Rivera, *Colonial Domination.* The Granger Collection. © Banco de Mexico Diego Rivera Museums Trust.

for decades it has shaped the foreign policy of the United States and other rich nations. Proponents point to rapid economic development in Asia—including South Korea, Taiwan, Singapore, and Hong Kong—as proof that the affluence that accompanied industrialization in Western Europe and North America is within reach of all countries.

But modernization theory comes under fire from socialist countries (and left-leaning analysts in the West) as a thinly veiled defense of capitalism. Its most serious flaw, according to critics, is that modernization simply has not occurred in many poor countries. The United Nations recently reported that living standards in a number of nations, including Haiti and Nicaragua in Latin America and Sudan, Ghana, and Rwanda in Africa, are actually lower than in 1960 (United Nations Development Programme, 1996).

A second criticism of modernization theory is that it fails to recognize how rich nations, which benefit from the status quo, often block paths to development for poor countries. Centuries ago, critics charge, rich countries industrialized from a position of global *strength.* Can we expect poor countries today to do so from a position of global *weakness?*

Third, critics continue, modernization theory treats rich and poor societies as separate worlds, ignoring how international relations affect all nations. To begin with, it was colonization that boosted the fortunes of Europe. This economic windfall has left countries in Latin America and Asia reeling to this day.

Fourth, critics contend that modernization theory holds up the world's most developed countries as the standard for judging the rest of humanity, thus revealing an ethnocentric bias. We should remember that our Western conception of "progress" led us to degrade the physical environment throughout the world and to rush headlong into a competitive, materialistic way of life.

Fifth, and finally, modernization theory draws criticism for suggesting that the causes of global poverty lie almost entirely in the poor societies themselves. Critics see this analysis as little more than blaming the victims for their own plight. Instead, they argue, an analysis of global inequality should focus as much on the behavior of rich nations as of poor nations (Wiarda, 1987).

Such concerns reflect a second major approach to understanding global inequality. This is dependency theory.

DEPENDENCY THEORY

Dependency theory is *a model of economic and social development that explains global inequality in terms of the historical exploitation of poor societies by rich ones.* This analysis puts primary responsibility for global poverty on rich nations. It holds that rich countries have systematically impoverished low-income countries, making poor nations dependent on rich ones. This destructive process extends back for centuries and persists today.

Historical Perspective

Everyone agrees that before the Industrial Revolution there was little affluence in the world. Dependency theory asserts, however, that people living in poor countries were actually better off economically in the past than their descendants are now. André Gunder Frank (1975), a noted proponent of this theory, argues that the colonial process that helped develop rich nations also *underdeveloped* poor societies.

Dependency theory is based on the idea that the economic positions of rich and poor nations of the world are linked and cannot be understood in isolation from one another. Poor nations are not simply lagging behind rich ones on the "path of progress"; rather, the prosperity of the most developed countries came largely at the expense of less developed nations. In short, then, some nations became rich only because other nations became poor. Both are products of the global commerce beginning five centuries ago.

The Importance of Colonialism

Late in the fifteenth century, Europeans began surveying the Americas to the west, Africa to the south, and Asia to the east in order to establish colonies. They were so successful that a century ago Great Britain controlled about one-fourth of the world's land, boasting that "the sun never sets on the British Empire." The United States, itself originally thirteen small British colonies on the eastern seaboard, soon pushed across the North American continent, purchased Alaska, and gained control of Haiti, Puerto Rico, Guam, the Philippines, the Hawaiian Islands, and part of Cuba.

Meanwhile, Europeans and Africans engaged in a brutal form of human exploitation—the slave trade—from about 1500 until 1850. But even as the world was rejecting slavery, Europeans took control of Africa itself. As Figure 12–4 shows, European powers domi-

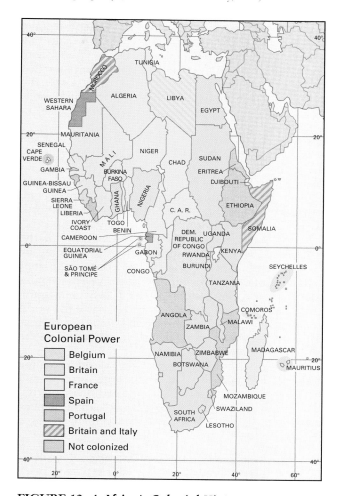

FIGURE 12–4 Africa's Colonial History

nated most of the African continent until the early 1960s.

Formal colonialism has almost disappeared from the world. However, according to dependency theory, political liberation has not translated into economic autonomy. Far from it: The economic relationship between poor and rich nations perpetuates the colonial pattern of domination. This neocolonialism is the essence of the capitalist world economy.

Wallerstein's Capitalist World Economy

Immanuel Wallerstein (1974, 1979, 1983, 1984) explains global stratification using a model of the capitalist world

NOTE: Some analysts distinguish between multinational and global corporations. MNCs consume only raw material and labor from a poor nation. Global corporations also locate research and development in the local country, which stimulates economic development. One global corporation is Hewlett Packard, which has a major research and development center in Guadalajara, Mexico.

GLOBAL: Some poor countries (such as Nicaragua, Mozambique, and Tanzania) have external debt that runs several times higher than annual GNP. Nicaragua's long-term debt of $5.9 billion amounts to more than $1,000 per person. With a per capita GNP of $430, people owe many years' income.

DISCUSS: Operating in 119 countries, McDonald's has nearly 30,000 restaurants; KFC has 9,400. Does this expansion constitute desirable development? Why or why not?

economy.[4] The term "world economy" suggests that the prosperity or poverty of any country is the product of a global economic system. According to Wallerstein, today's global economy is rooted in the colonization that began 500 years ago when Europeans first saw the wealth of the rest of the world. Because the world economy is based in high-income countries, it is capitalist in character.

Wallerstein calls the rich nations the *core* of the world economy. Colonialism enriched this core by funneling raw materials from around the world to Western Europe, where they fueled the Industrial Revolution. Today, multinational corporations operate profitably worldwide, channeling wealth to North America, Western Europe, Australia, and Japan.

Low-income countries are the *periphery* of the world economy. Drawn into the world economy by colonial exploitation, poor nations continue to support rich ones by providing inexpensive labor and a vast market for industrial products. The remaining countries are considered the *semiperiphery* of the world economy. They include prospering countries such as Mexico and South Africa that have closer ties to the global economic core.

According to Wallerstein, the world economy benefits rich societies (by generating profits) and harms the rest of the world (by perpetuating poverty). The world economy thus makes poor nations dependent on rich ones. This dependency involves three factors:

1. **Narrow, export-oriented economies.** Poor nations produce only a few crops for export to rich countries. Examples include coffee and fruit from Latin American nations, oil from Nigeria, hardwoods from the Philippines, and palm oil from Malaysia.

   Today's multinational corporations purchase raw materials cheaply in poor societies and transport them to core nations, where factories process them for profitable sale. This practice discourages poor nations from developing industries of their own and from trading with one another.

2. **Lack of industrial capacity.** Without an industrial base, poor societies face a double bind:

They count on selling inexpensive raw materials to rich nations, and then they buy whatever expensive manufactured goods they can afford. In a classic example of this dependency, British colonialists encouraged the people of India to raise cotton but prohibited them from weaving their own cloth. Instead, the British shipped Indian cotton to English textile mills in Birmingham and Manchester, manufactured the cloth, and shipped finished goods back to India for profitable sale.

Dependency theorists claim that the Green Revolution, widely praised by modernization theorists, works the same way. Poor countries sell cheap raw materials to rich nations and then try to buy expensive fertilizers, pesticides, and machinery in return. Rich countries profit from this exchange much more than poor nations.

3. **Foreign debt.** Unequal trade patterns have plunged poor countries into debt to the core nations. Collectively, the poor nations of the world owe rich countries more than $2.5 trillion, including hundreds of billions of dollars to the United States. Such staggering debt paralyzes a country with high unemployment and rampant inflation (Walton & Ragin, 1990; World Bank, 2001).

The Role of Rich Nations

Nowhere is the difference between modernization theory and dependency theory drawn more sharply than in the role each assigns to rich nations. Modernization theory maintains that rich societies *produce wealth* through capital investment and technological innovation. Accordingly, as poor nations adopt progrowth policies and more productive technology, they, too, will prosper. By contrast, dependency theory views global inequality in terms of how countries *distribute wealth*, arguing that rich nations have *over*developed themselves as they have *under*developed the rest of the world.

Dependency theorists dismiss the idea that programs developed by rich countries to control population and boost agricultural and industrial output raise living standards in poor countries. Instead, they contend, such programs benefit rich nations and the ruling elites, not the poor majority, in low-income countries (Lappé, Collins, & Kinley, 1981).

Hunger activists Frances Moore Lappé and Joseph Collins (1986) maintain that the capitalist

---

[4]Though based on Wallerstein's ideas, this section also reflects the work of Frank (1980, 1981), Delacroix & Ragin (1981), Bergesen (1983), Dixon & Boswell (1996), and Kentor (1998).

Q: "We are not without cunning. We will not make Britain's mistake. Too wise to govern the world, we shall simply own it." Ludwell Denny (cited in Vaughan, 1978:20)

GLOBAL: Inflation is a stunning problem in many poor societies, making the problem of simply maintaining one's standard of living difficult. In Argentina, for example, annual inflation has at times soared to 80,000%.

NOTE: Lenin attributed the failure of Marxist revolutions to occur in rich societies to the development of international capitalism that raised living standards at home based on exploitation of colonies abroad.

GLOBAL: Latin America represents a mixed case of economic development. Whereas the standing of some countries (Colombia and Chile) has improved, that of others (Peru, for example) has declined.

In the United States, most affluent people manage to distance themselves from the struggles of the poor. This is far more difficult to do in low-income countries, if only because there are so many more poor people. In the cities in India, for example, people routinely approach foreigners traveling by car in the hopes of receiving money in return.

culture of the United States encourages people to think of poverty as somehow inevitable. Following this line of reasoning, poverty results from "natural" processes, including having too many children, and natural disasters such as droughts. But global poverty is far from inevitable; it results from deliberate policies. Lappé and Collins point out that the world already produces enough food to allow every person on the planet to become fat. Moreover, India and most of Africa actually *export* food, even though many of their own people go hungry.

According to Lappé and Collins, the contradiction of poverty amid plenty stems from the rich nation policy of producing food for profit, not for people. That is, corporations in rich nations cooperate with elites in poor countries to grow and export profitable crops such as coffee, which means using land that could otherwise produce staples such as beans and corn for local families. Governments of poor countries support the practice of "growing for export" because they need food profits to repay foreign debt. At the core of this vicious cycle, according to Lappé and Collins, is the capitalist corporate structure of the global economy.

Critical evaluation. The main idea of dependency theory is that no country develops (or fails to develop) in isolation because the global economy shapes the destiny of all nations. Citing Latin America and other poor regions of the world, dependency

theorists claim that development simply cannot proceed under the constraints imposed by rich countries. Rather, they call for radical reform of the entire world economy so that it operates in the interests of the majority of people.

Critics charge that dependency theory wrongly treats wealth as a zero-sum commodity, as if no one gets richer without someone else getting poorer. Not so, critics continue, because corporations, small business owners, and farmers can and do create new wealth through their drive and imaginative use of new technology. After all, they point out, the entire world's wealth has swelled sixfold since 1950.

Second, critics continue, dependency theory is wrong in blaming rich nations for global poverty because many of the world's poorest countries (such as Ethiopia) have had little contact with rich nations. On the contrary, a long history of trade with rich countries has dramatically improved the economies of nations, including Sri Lanka, Singapore, and Hong Kong (all former British colonies), as well as South Korea and Japan. In short, say the critics, most evidence shows that foreign investment by rich nations fosters economic growth, as modernization theory claims, not economic decline, as dependency theorists assert (Vogel, 1991; Firebaugh, 1992).

Third, critics contend that dependency theory is simplistic for pointing the finger at a single factor—world capitalism—as the cause of global inequality (Worsley, 1990). Dependency theory thereby casts

DISCUSS: National policies in poor countries can have major effects on public well-being. Costa Rica, with average income at one-fourth the U.S. level, has the same life expectancy due largely to disbanding its army in 1949 and spending more on health and education. Brazil, with about the same average income as Costa Rica but different policies, has a life expectancy 10 years lower (Sachs, 1998).

Q: "In China, we waste nothing but time; in America, you waste everything but time." Comment made to the author by a student in the People's Republic of China

DISCUSS: The mass media are a powerful force making the world smaller. For example, Cable News Network (CNN) currently broadcasts to more than 60 nations. How do the media portray poor countries to us? How do they portray us to people abroad?

TABLE 12–2 Modernization Theory and Dependency Theory: A Summary

	Modernization Theory	Dependency Theory
Historical Pattern	The entire world was poor several centuries ago; the Industrial Revolution brought affluence to high-income countries; as industrialization gradually transforms poor societies, all nations are likely to become more equal and alike.	Global parity was disrupted by colonialism, which made some countries rich while making others poor; barring radical change in the world capitalist system, rich nations will grow richer and poor nations will become poorer.
Primary Causes of Global Poverty	Characteristics of poor societies cause their poverty, including lack of industrial technology, traditional cultural patterns that discourage innovation, and rapid population growth.	Global economic relations—historical colonialism and now multinational corporations—have enriched high-income countries while making low-income nations economically dependent.
Role of Rich Nations	Rich countries can and do assist poor nations through population control programs, technology transfers that increase food production and stimulate industrial development, and capital investment in the	Rich countries have concentrated global resources, conferring advantages on themselves while generating massive foreign debt in low-income countries; rich nations impede the economic development of poor nations.

poor societies as passive victims and ignores factors inside these countries that contribute to their economic plight. Sociologists have long recognized the vital role of culture in shaping people's willingness to embrace or resist change. Iran's brand of fundamentalist Islam, for example, has deliberately discouraged economic ties with other countries. Therefore, capitalist societies need hardly accept the blame for Iran's economic stagnation.

Nor should rich societies be saddled with responsibility for the reckless behavior of foreign leaders whose corruption and militaristic campaigns impoverish their countries (examples include the regimes of Ferdinand Marcos and, more recently, Joseph Estrada in the Philippines, François Duvalier in Haiti, Manuel Noriega in Panama, Mobutu Sese Seko in Zaire, and Saddam Hussein in Iraq). Governments may even use food supplies as a weapon in internal political struggles, a strategy that left the masses starving in the African nations of Ethiopia, Sudan, and Somalia. Other regimes throughout the world (the Taliban regime in Afghanistan stands out) have done little to improve the status of women or control population growth.

Fourth, critics chide dependency theorists for downplaying the economic dependency fostered by the former Soviet Union. The Soviet army seized control of most of Eastern Europe during World War II and then politically and economically dominated those countries. Many see the uprisings between 1989 and 1991 as a wholesale rejection of the Soviet Union's socialist colonial system.

Fifth, critics claim that this approach is more protest than policy because it offers only vague solutions to global poverty. Most dependency theorists urge poor nations to end all contact with rich countries, and some call for nationalizing foreign-owned industries. In other words, dependency theory amounts to a thinly disguised call for some sort of world socialism. In light of the difficulties socialist societies have had in meeting the needs of their own people, critics ask, should we really expect such a system to rescue the entire world from poverty?

Table 12–2 summarizes the main arguments of modernization theory and dependency theory.

GLOBAL STRATIFICATION: LOOKING AHEAD

Among the most important trends in recent decades is the development of a global economy. In the United States, rising production and sales abroad have brought record profits to many corporations and their stockholders, especially those who already have substantial wealth. At the same time, the global economy has cut factory jobs in this country, hurting many average workers. The net result: economic polarization in the United States. As this chapter has noted, however, social inequality is far more striking in global context. The concentration of wealth among high-income countries, coupled with the grinding poverty of low-income nations, may well be the

GLOBAL: The share of the world's GNP by fifths of the global population resembles the distribution of wealth in the United States (compare Figures 11–1 and 12–1).

NOTE: Many products from rich countries—electricity, technology, communication equipment—are getting cheaper, which helps raise living standards abroad. In other words, the manufactured goods–raw goods exchange rate has improved over time.

NOTE: Although the *economic* gap between rich and poor countries has remained stable, the divide is narrowing between the two categories of nations on many *social* indicators. This is because rising income produces greater improvement in living standards for lower-income countries.

WINDOW ON THE WORLD

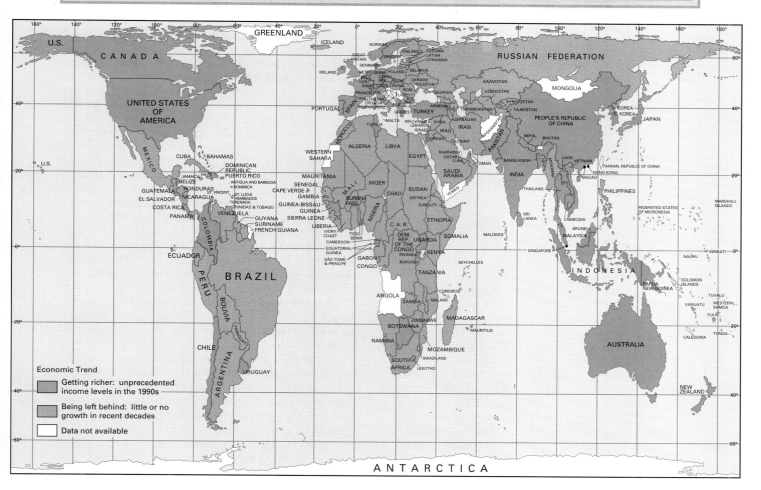

Economic Trend

- Getting richer: unprecedented income levels in the 1990s
- Being left behind: little or no growth in recent decades
- Data not available

GLOBAL MAP 12–2 Prosperity and Stagnation in Global Perspective

In about sixty nations of the world, people are enjoying a higher standard of living than ever before. These prospering countries include some rich nations (such as the United States and the countries of Western Europe) and some poor nations (especially in Asia). For most countries, however, living standards have remained steady or even slipped in recent decades. Especially in Eastern Europe and the Middle East, some nations have experienced economic setbacks since the 1980s. And in sub-Saharan Africa, some nations are no better off than they were in 1960. The overall pattern is economic polarization, with an increasing gap between rich and poor nations.

Source: United Nations Development Programme (1996); updates by the author.

DISCUSS: "Divided" countries shed light on the merits of each theory. South Korea (well within the capitalist world economy) has per capita GDP of $13,590 compared to isolated North Korea's figure of $4,058. For West Germany (1988), $14,730; East Germany, $8,000.

Q: "For hunger is a curious thing: At first it is with you all the time, waking and sleeping and in your dreams, and your belly cries out

incessantly, and there is a gnawing and a pain. . . . Then the pain is no longer sharp but dull, and this too is with you always so that you think of food many times a day. . . . Then that too is gone, all pain, all desire, only a great emptiness is left, like the sky, like a well in drought, and it is now that the strength drains from your limbs." K. Markandaya, *Nectar in a Sieve*

DISCUSS: Do you think there should be a universal "right to food"?

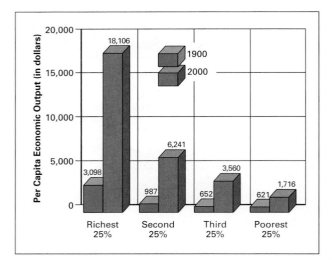

FIGURE 12–5 The World's Increasing Economic Inequality

Source: International Monetary Fund (2000).

biggest problem facing humanity in the twenty-first century.

Therefore, finding answers to questions about global poverty takes on some urgency. Which theory is right: modernization theory or dependency theory? Both have their merits and their limitations.

In searching for truth, we must consider empirical evidence. Over the course of the twentieth century, living standards rose around the world. Even so, as shown in Figure 12–5, the extent of income inequality increased dramatically. While the economic output of the poorest quarter of the world's people almost tripled over the course of the twentieth century, the economic output of the richest quarter of the world's people increased almost six-fold. By this measure, then, there was twice as much economic inequality in the world in 2000 as there was in 1900.

What are the trends in recent decades? There is evidence that income inequality between nations is stabilizing (Schultz, 1998; Firebaugh, 1999, 2000). The United Nations (1996) reports that people in about one-third of the world's countries are living better than they were in 1980. These nations, identified in Global Map 12–2 on page 319, include most of the high-income countries, but they also include dozens of poorer countries, especially in Asia. These prospering nations are evidence that the market forces endorsed by modernization theory can raise living standards.

In another one-third of the world's countries, however, living standards were lower in 1996 than they were in 1980. A rising wave of poverty, especially in the nations of sub-Saharan Africa, supports the dependency theory assertion that current economic arrangements are leaving hundreds of millions of people behind.

This evidence calls into question both modernization and dependency theories, and both camps are revising their views of proper paths to development. On one hand, few societies seeking economic growth favor a market economy completely free of government control, which challenges orthodox modernization theory and its free-market approach to development. On the other hand, the upheavals in the former Soviet Union and Eastern Europe demonstrate that a global reevaluation of socialism is underway. Because these uprisings follow decades of poor economic performance and political repression, many poor societies are reluctant to consider a wholly government-controlled path to development. Because dependency theory has historically supported socialist economic systems, changes in world socialism will generate new thinking here as well.

Perhaps the basic problem caused by poverty is hunger. As the final box explains, many analysts wonder whether we have the determination to provide for everyone on the planet.

Although the world's future is uncertain, we have learned a great deal about global stratification. One insight, offered by modernization theory, is that poverty is partly a *problem of technology*. A higher standard of living for a surging world population depends on raising agricultural and industrial productivity. A second insight, derived from dependency theory, is that global inequality is also a *political issue*. Even with higher productivity, the human community must address crucial questions concerning how resources are distributed, both within societies and around the globe.

Note, too, that while economic development increases living standards, it also places greater strains on the natural environment. Imagine, for example, if the 1 billion people in India suddenly became middle class, with automobiles guzzling gasoline and spewing hydrocarbons into the atmosphere.

Finally, the vast and increasing gulf that separates the world's richest and poorest people puts everyone at greater risk of war, as the most impoverished people challenge the social arrangements that threaten their lives. In the long run, we can achieve peace on this planet only by ensuring that all people enjoy a significant measure of dignity and security.

NOTE: Modernization theory is sometimes called "convergence theory" (especially by economists); dependency theory is also called "polarization theory."
Q: "I am convinced that the global economy makes it more difficult to devise and enact redistributive policies." Robert A. Dahl
DISCUSS: H. W. Longfellow said, "Out of the shadows of night, the world rolls into light. It is daybreak everywhere." Is he right or not?

NOTE: Crudely speaking, the "optimists" in the world hunger debate lean toward modernization theory; the "pessimists" typically favor dependency theory.
EXERCISE: Ask students to look over past issues of *National Geographic*. How does this popular magazine portray life in poor nations? In light of facts noted in this chapter, is the portrayal realistic or not?

CONTROVERSY & DEBATE

Will the World Starve?

The animals' feet leave their prints
  on the desert's face.
Hunger is so real, so very real,
that it can make you walk
  around a barren tree looking
  for nourishment.
Not once,
Not twice,
Not thrice . . .

These lines, by Indian poet Amit Jayaram, describe the appalling hunger found in Rajasthan, in northwest India. As this chapter has explained, however, hunger casts its menacing shadow not only over Asia but also over much of Africa and parts of Latin America, Asia, and even North America. Throughout the world, hundreds of millions of adults do not eat enough food to enable them to work. Most tragically, about 10 million children die each year as a result of hunger. As we begin the twenty-first century, what are the prospects for ending the wretched misery of daily hunger?

Pessimists point out that the populations of poor countries are increasing by 74 million people annually—equivalent to adding another Egypt to the world every year. Poor countries can scarcely feed the people they have now; how will they ever feed *twice* as many people a generation in the future?

In addition, hunger forces poor people to exploit the earth's resources by using short-term strategies for food production that lead to long-term disaster.

For example, farmers are cutting rain forests to increase their farmland. But without the protective canopy of trees, it is only a matter of time before much of this land turns to desert. Taken together, rising populations and short-sighted policies raise the specter of unprecedented hunger, human misery, and political calamity.

But there are also some grounds for optimism. Thanks to the Green Revolution, food production the world over has increased sharply over the last fifty years, well outpacing the growth in population. The world's economic productivity has risen steadily, so that the average person on the planet now has more income to purchase food and other necessities than ever before. This growth has also increased daily calorie intake, life expectancy, access to safe water, and adult literacy. Around the world, infant mortality is half of what it was in 1960.

So what are the prospects for eradicating world hunger? Overall, we see less hunger in both rich and poor countries, and a smaller *share* of the world's people are hungry now than in 1960. But as global population increases, with 96 percent of children born in middle- and low-income countries, the *number* of lives at risk is as great today as ever before. Thus, many low-income countries have made solid gains, but many more are stagnating or even losing ground.

The "best case" region of the world is eastern Asia, where incomes controlled for inflation have tripled over

the last generation. It is to Asia that optimists in the global hunger debate point for evidence that poor countries can and do raise living standards and reduce hunger. The "worst case" region of the world is sub-Saharan Africa, where living standards have fallen over the last decade. It is here that high technology is least evident and birth rates are highest. Pessimists typically look to Africa when they argue that poor countries are losing ground in the struggle to feed their people.

Television brings home the tragedy of hunger when news cameras focus on starving people in places such as Ethiopia and Somalia. But hunger—and early death from illness—are the plight of millions year-round. The world has the technical means to feed everyone; the question is, do we have the moral determination?

Continue the debate . . .

1. *In your opinion, what are the primary causes of global hunger?*
2. *Do you place more responsibility for eradicating world hunger on poor countries or rich ones? Why?*
3. *Do you consider yourself an optimist or a pessimist about the problem of global hunger? Why?*

Sources: United Nations Development Programme (1996, 1997, 1998, 1999, 2000, 2001).

SUMMARY

1. Around the world, social stratification is more pronounced than in the United States. About 18 percent of the world's people live in industrialized, high-income countries such as the United States and receive 79 percent of all income. Another 54 percent of humanity lives in middle-income countries with limited industrialization and receives about 18 percent of all income. Twenty-eight percent of the world's population lives in low-income countries with limited industrialization and earns only 3 percent of global income.

2. Although relative poverty is found everywhere, poor societies grapple with widespread absolute poverty. Worldwide, the lives of about 1 billion people are at risk because of poor nutrition. About 15 million people, most of them children, die annually from various causes because they lack adequate nourishment.

3. Women are more likely than men to be poor nearly everywhere in the world. Gender bias against women is greatest in poor, agrarian societies.

4. The poverty found in much of the world is a complex problem reflecting limited industrial technology, rapid population growth, traditional cultural patterns, internal social stratification, male domination, and global power relationships.

5. Modernization theory maintains that successful development hinges on breaking out of traditional cultural patterns to acquire advanced technology.

6. Modernization theorist W. W. Rostow identifies four stages of development: traditional, take-off, drive to technological maturity, and high mass consumption.

7. Arguing that rich societies hold the keys to creating wealth, modernization theory claims that rich nations can help poor nations by providing population control programs, agricultural technology such as hybrid seeds and fertilizers to increase food production, industrial technology including machinery and information technology, and foreign aid to help pay for power plants and factories.

8. Critics of modernization theory say that this approach has produced limited economic development in the world. Furthermore, they claim, poor nations cannot follow the same path to development taken by rich nations centuries ago.

9. Dependency theory claims that global wealth and poverty are the historical products of the capitalist world economy, first because of colonialism and, more recently, because of multinational corporations.

10. Immanuel Wallerstein views high-income countries as the advantaged "core" of the capitalist world economy, middle-income nations as the "semiperiphery," and poor societies as the global "periphery."

11. Three key factors—export-oriented economies, a lack of industrial capacity, and foreign debt—perpetuate poor countries' dependency on rich nations.

12. Critics of dependency theory argue that it overlooks the sixfold increase in the world's wealth since 1950. Furthermore, the world's poorest societies are not those with the strongest ties to rich countries.

13. Both modernization and dependency theories offer useful insights into global inequality. Some evidence supports each view. But as global inequality continues to increase, there is an urgent need to address the various problems caused by worldwide poverty.

KEY CONCEPTS

colonialism (p. 309) the process by which some nations enrich themselves through political and economic control of other nations

neocolonialism (p. 309) a new form of global power relationships that involves not direct political control but economic exploitation by multinational corporations

multinational corporation (p. 309) a large business that operates in many countries

modernization theory (p. 310) a model of economic and social development that explains global inequality in terms of technological and cultural differences between societies

dependency theory (p. 315) a model of economic and social development that explains global inequality in terms of the historical exploitation of poor societies by rich ones

CRITICAL-THINKING QUESTIONS

1. Based on what you have read here and elsewhere, what is your prediction about the extent of global hunger fifty years from now? Will the problem be more or less serious? Why?

CTQ2: In general, relative poverty is the greater concern in the U.S. and absolute poverty the greater concern for the world as a whole.
CTQ3: Women with schooling and jobs not only are economically more productive, but they also have fewer children.
CTQ4: Review the discussion of each approach, especially Table 12–2.

2. What is the difference between relative and absolute poverty? Use these two concepts to describe social stratification in the United States and around the world.

3. Why do many analysts argue that economic development in low-income countries depends on raising the social standing of women?

4. State the basic tenets of modernization theory and dependency theory. Spell out several criticisms of each approach.

APPLICATIONS AND EXERCISES

1. Keep a log book of mass media advertising mentioning low-income countries (selling, say, coffee from Colombia or exotic vacations to India). What image of life in low-income countries does the advertising present? In light of this chapter, do you think this image is accurate?

2. Millions of students from abroad study on U.S. campuses. See whether you can identify a woman and a man on your campus who were raised in a poor country. Approach them, explain that you have been studying global stratification, and ask whether they are willing to share what life is like back home. You may be able to learn quite a bit from them.

3. Use the Global Maps in this text (or the animated maps on the CD-ROM) to identify social traits associated with the world's richest and poorest nations. Try to use both modernization theory and dependency theory to build theoretical explanations of the patterns you find.

4. Packaged in the back of this new textbook is an interactive CD-ROM that offers a variety of study and review materials intended to help you better understand the material covered in this chapter. For this chapter, the CD-ROM contains an author's tip video, Real Life Sociology videos, other relevant audio and video, interactive map animations, audio journal entries from the author, Web links, and much more.

 ## SITES TO SEE

http://www.prenhall.com/macionis

Visit the interactive *Companion Website*™ that accompanies this text. Begin by clicking on the cover of your book. You will find a chapter-by-chapter study guide, practice tests, and a significant portion of the text for on-line review, as well as many suggested Web links.

http://members.aol.com/casmasalc

This is the Web site for the Coalition against Slavery in Mauritania and Sudan. This site provides information about the problem of slavery and links to similar organizations.

http://www.worldbank.org/data/

The site, operated by the World Bank, provides data and analysis of global poverty.

http://www.fh.org
http://www.worldconcern.org
http://www.worldvision.org
http://www.care.org

Here are a number of additional Web sites that address global inequality. The first is operated by Food for the Hungry International, the second takes you to the home page for World Concern, the third organization is World Vision, and the fourth is CARE. Visit them all and look for differences in their focus and strategies.

http://www.census.gov/ipc/www/idbnew.html
http://www.prb.org/

These two sites—operated by the U.S. Bureau of the Census and the Population Reference Bureau—present a statistical profile of world nations.

 INVESTIGATE WITH CONTENTSELECT

Follow the instructions found on page 23 of this textbook to enter this chapter of the book's *Companion Website*™. Once in the chapter, click on the ContentSelect icon at the bottom left of your screen and enter your personal User ID and Password. Enter keywords such as "global poverty," "world hunger," and "slavery," and the search engine will help you become an effective researcher.

CHAPTER

13

GENDER STRATIFICATION

At first we traveled quite alone. . . but before we had gone many miles, we came on other wagon-loads of women, bound in the same direction. As we reached different cross-roads, we saw wagons coming from every part of the country and, long before we reached Seneca Falls, we were a procession.

So wrote Charlotte Woodward in her journal as she made her way along the rutted dirt roads to Seneca Falls, a small town in upstate New York. The year was 1848, a time when slavery was legal in much of the United States and the social standing of all women—regardless of color—was subordinate in every way to that of men. Back then, in much of the United States, women could not own property or keep their wages if they were married; women could not

draft a will; women were barred from filing lawsuits in court, including suits seeking custody of their children; women could not attend college; and husbands could legally beat their wives as long as the stick they used was no thicker than a thumb (the origin of today's phrase "rule of thumb").

Some 300 women gathered at Wesleyan Chapel in Seneca Falls to challenge their second-class citizenship. They listened as their leader, Elizabeth Cady Stanton, called for expanding women's rights and opportunities, including the right to vote. To many, such a proposal seemed absurd and outrageous; even many attending the conference were shocked by the idea. Stanton's husband, Henry, rode out of town in protest.[1]

_____

[1]This material is drawn from Gurnett (1998).

Much has changed in the century and a half since the Seneca Falls convention, and many of Stanton's proposals are now accepted as a matter of basic fairness. But, as this chapter explains, women and men still lead different lives in the United States and elsewhere around the world; in most respects, men still dominate. This chapter explores the importance of gender and explains how gender, like class position, is a major dimension of social stratification.

GENDER AND INEQUALITY

Chapter 9 ("Sexuality") discussed the biological differences that divide the human population into categories of female and male. **Gender** refers to *the personal traits and social positions that members of a society attach to being female and male.* Gender, then, is a dimension of social organization, shaping how we interact with others and how we think about ourselves. Just as important, gender involves *hierarchy*, ranking men and women differently in terms of power, wealth, and other resources. Sociologists therefore speak of **gender stratification,** *the unequal distribution of wealth, power, and privilege between men and women.* In short, gender affects the opportunities and constraints each of us faces throughout our lives (Ferree & Hall, 1996; Riley, 1997).

MALE-FEMALE DIFFERENCES

Many people think there is something "natural" about gender distinctions because there are biological differences between the sexes. But we must be careful not to think of social differences in biological terms. In 1848, for example, women were denied the vote because many people assumed that they "naturally" lacked sufficient

SUPPLEMENTS: An outline of this chapter, along with supplementary lecture material, is included in the *Data File*.

Q: "The male is by nature fitter for command than the female, just as the elder and full-grown is fitter than the younger and immature. . . . The courage of a man is shown in commanding, of a woman in obeying." Aristotle, *Politics*

Q: "Most human beings live in single-sex worlds, women in a female world and men in a male world, and . . . the two are different from one another in a myriad of ways, both subjectively and objectively." Jessie Bernard (1981:3)

Q: "Gender is what gender means. It has no basis in anything other than the social reality its hegemony constructs." Catharine MacKinnon

Sex is a biological distinction that develops prior to birth. Gender is the meaning that a society attaches to being female or male. Gender differences are a matter of power, as what is masculine typically has social priority over what is feminine. The importance of gender is not evident among infants, of course, but the ways in which we think of boys and girls set in motion patterns that will continue for a lifetime.

intelligence and political interest. But such attitudes had nothing to do with biology. Rather, they reflected the *cultural conventions* of that time and place.

Figure 13–1 presents another example of women's "natural" inferiority: athletics. In 1925, most people would have doubted that the best women runners could ever finish a marathon in anywhere near the time that men could. Yet today, as the figure shows, the best women routinely post better times than the fastest men of decades past, and the performance gap between the sexes has greatly narrowed. Here, again, most of the differences between men and women turn out to be socially created.

There are some physical differences between the sexes. On average, males are 10 percent taller, 20 percent heavier, and 30 percent stronger, especially in their upper bodies (Ehrenreich, 1999). On the other hand, women outperform men in the ultimate game of life itself: Whereas life expectancy for men is 74.1 years, women can expect to live 79.5 years (U.S. National Center for Health Statistics, 2001).

In adolescence, males show greater mathematical ability and females excel in verbal skills, a difference that reflects both biology and socialization (Maccoby & Jacklin, 1974; Baker et al., 1980; Lengermann & Wallace, 1985; Hoffman, 2001). However, research points to no overall differences in intelligence between males and females.

Biologically, then, men and women differ in limited ways, with neither one naturally superior. But culture can define the two sexes very differently, as the global study of gender shows.

GENDER IN GLOBAL PERSPECTIVE

The best way to see the cultural foundation of gender is by making global comparisons. Here, we review three studies that highlight how different the ideas of "masculine" and "feminine" can be.

The Israeli Kibbutzim

In Israel, collective Jewish settlements are called *kibbutzim*. The *kibbutz* (singular form) is especially important for gender research because gender equality is one of its goals, with men and women sharing in both work and decision making.

Members of kibbutzim consider sex irrelevant to most of everyday life. Both men and women take care of children, cook and clean, and repair buildings. Girls and boys are raised in the same way, and, from the first weeks of life, children live together in dormitories. Women and men in kibbutzim have achieved remarkable (although not complete) social equality. Thus, kibbutzim are evidence of the wide latitude cultures have in defining what is feminine and what is masculine.

Margaret Mead's Research

Anthropologist Margaret Mead carried out groundbreaking research on gender. To the extent that gender reflects biological facts of sex, she reasoned, people everywhere should define "feminine" and "masculine" in the same way; if gender is cultural, the two concepts should vary.

Q: "The [comparison of the three societies] suggests that . . . many, if not all, of the personality traits which we have called masculine or feminine are as lightly linked to sex as are the clothing, the manners, and the form of head-dress that a society at a given period assigns to either sex. . . . We are forced to conclude that human behavior is almost unbelievably malleable, responding accurately and contrastingly to contrasting cultural conditions." Margaret Mead

RESOURCE: An excerpt from Margaret Mead's *Sex and Temperament in Three Primitive Societies* is one of the classic selections in the Macionis and Benokraitis reader.
Q: "At the bottom of it all, man's job is to protect woman, and woman's job is to protect her infant; all else is luxury." Steven Goldberg
Q: "Suffer women once to arrive at equality with you, and they will from that moment on become your superiors." Cato the Elder

Mead studied three societies in New Guinea (1963; orig. 1935). In the mountainous home of the Arapesh, Mead observed men and women with remarkably similar attitudes and behavior. Both sexes were cooperative and sensitive to others—in short, what our culture would label "feminine."

Moving south, Mead then studied the Mundugumor, head-hunters and cannibals who stood in striking contrast to the gentle Arapesh. In this culture, both sexes typically were selfish and aggressive, traits we define as more "masculine."

Finally, traveling west to the Tchambuli, Mead discovered a culture that, like our own, defined females and males differently. But, Mead reported, the Tchambuli reversed many of our notions of gender: Females were dominant and rational, and males were submissive, emotional, and nurturing toward children. Based on her observations, Mead concluded that culture is the key to gender: What one culture defines as masculine, another may consider feminine.

Some critics view Mead's findings as "too neat," as if she saw in these three societies just the patterns she was looking for. Deborah Gewertz (1981) challenged Mead's "reversal hypothesis," claiming that Tchambuli males are really more aggressive and Tchambuli females more submissive. Gewertz explains that Mead visited the Tchambuli (who actually call themselves the Chambri) during the 1930s, after they had lost much of their property in tribal wars. Men working in the home, she claims, was a temporary role for Chambri men.

George Murdock's Research

In a broader study of more than 200 preindustrial societies, George Murdock (1937) found some global agreement on which tasks are feminine and which masculine. Hunting and warfare generally fall to men, and home-centered tasks such as cooking and child care tend to be women's work. With their simple technology, preindustrial societies apparently assign roles reflecting men's and women's physical attributes. With greater size and strength, men hunt game and protect the group; because women bear children, they assume domestic duties.

But beyond this general pattern, Murdock found significant variation. Consider agriculture: Women did the farming in about the same number of societies as men, but in most the two sexes divided this work. When it came to many other tasks—from building shelters to tattooing the body—Murdock found societies of the world were as likely to turn to one sex as the other.

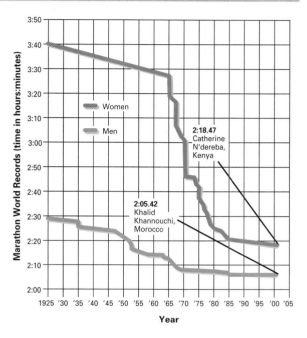

DIVERSITY SNAPSHOT

FIGURE 13–1 Men's and Women's Athletic Performance

Do men naturally outperform women in athletic competition? The answer is not obvious. Early in the twentieth century, men outdistanced women by many miles in marathon races. But as opportunities for women in athletics increased, women have been closing the performance gap. Thirteen minutes separate the current world marathon records for women (set in 2001) and for men (set in 1999).

Sources: *The Christian Science Monitor* (1995) and www.marathonguide.com (2001). Adapted with permission of *The Christian Science Monitor.* © 1995 The Christian Science Publishing Society. All rights reserved.

In Sum: Gender and Culture

Global comparisons show us that societies do not consistently define most tasks as either feminine or masculine. With industrialization, moreover, the importance of muscle power declines, giving people even more options and further reducing gender differences (Nolan & Lenski, 1999). Thus, gender is simply too variable across cultures to be considered a simple expression of

NOTE: Although scholars continue to debate the connection between biology and gender, the larger point is that any innate differences that do exist certainly are inadequate as an explanation of gender.
NOTE: Patriarchy implies that paternity is the central social relationship. Note the Old Testament emphasis on "begats," one man begetting a son (Rothman, 1995).

Q: "There is in fact no true 'matriarchal,' as distinct from 'matrilineal,' society in existence or known from literature, and the chances are there never has been." Kathleen Gough
NOTE: Sandra Bem (1993) uses the term "androcentrism" to refer to the belief in male superiority.
Q: "Why isn't 'man's best friend' woman?" Carol Tavris and Carole Offir

In every society, people assume certain jobs, patterns of behavior, and ways of dressing are "naturally" feminine while others are just as obviously masculine. But in global perspective, we see remarkable variety in such social definitions. These men, Wodaabe pastoral nomads who live in the African nation of Niger, are proud to engage in a display of beauty most people in our society would consider feminine.

biology. Instead, as with many other elements of culture, what it means to be female and male is mostly a creation of society.

PATRIARCHY AND SEXISM

Although conceptions of gender vary, everywhere in the world we find some degree of **patriarchy** (literally, "the rule of fathers"), *a form of social organization in which males dominate females.* Despite mythical tales of societies dominated by female "Amazons," **matriarchy,** *a form of social organization in which females dominate males,* has never been documented in human history (Gough, 1971; Harris, 1977; Lengermann & Wallace, 1985).

Although some degree of patriarchy may be universal, Global Map 13–1 shows significant variation in the relative power and privilege of females and males around the world. According to the United Nations, three Nordic countries—Norway, Sweden, and Finland—afford women the highest social standing. By contrast, women in the central African nations of Niger and Chad, the East African nation of Djibouti, and the Asian nation of Afghanistan have the lowest social standing compared with men. Of the world's nations, the United States ranked eighth in terms of gender equality (United Nations, 1995).

Sexism, *the belief that one sex is innately superior to the other,* is the ideological basis of patriarchy. Sexism is not just a matter of individual attitudes; it is built into the institutions of our society. *Institutional*

sexism is part of the economy, for example, so that women are highly concentrated in low-paying jobs. Similarly, the legal system has long excused violence against women, especially on the part of boyfriends, husbands, and fathers (Landers, 1990).

The Costs of Sexism

Sexism stunts the talents and limits the ambitions of women, who make up half the population. Although men benefit in some respects from sexism, their privilege comes at a high price. Masculinity in our culture calls for men to engage in many high-risk behaviors, including greater use of tobacco and alcohol, participation in physically dangerous sports, and reckless driving, so that motor vehicle accidents are the leading cause of death among young males. Moreover, as Marilyn French (1985) argues, patriarchy compels men to seek control, not only of women but of themselves and their world. Thus, masculinity is closely linked not only to accidents but suicide, violence, and stress-related diseases. The Type A personality—characterized by chronic impatience, driving ambition, competitiveness, and free-floating hostility—is a recipe for heart disease and almost perfectly matches the behavior that our culture considers masculine (Ehrenreich, 1983).

Finally, insofar as men seek control over others, they lose opportunities for intimacy and trust. As one analyst put it, competition is supposed to separate "the men from the boys." In practice, however, it separates men from men and everyone else (Raphael, 1988).

Q: "Fifty-three percent of the world's population are women, they perform two-thirds of the world's work, receive one-tenth of its income, and own one-hundredth of its property." Patricia Schroeder, former representative from Colorado

RESOURCE: Naomi Neft and Ann Levine take a cross-cultural look at "Women in Today's World" in the Macionis and Benokraitis reader, *Seeing Ourselves*.

NOTE: Several "firsts" for U.S. women: first woman physician, Elizabeth Blackwell, 1847; ordained minister, Antoinette Blackwell, 1853; surgeon, Mary Thompson, 1863; dentist (DDS), Lucy Hobbs, 1866; lawyer, Arabella Mansfield, 1869; college president, Frances Willard, 1871.

DIVERSITY: In 1999, there were 78 women's colleges in the U.S., down sharply from about 300 in 1960.

WINDOW ON THE WORLD

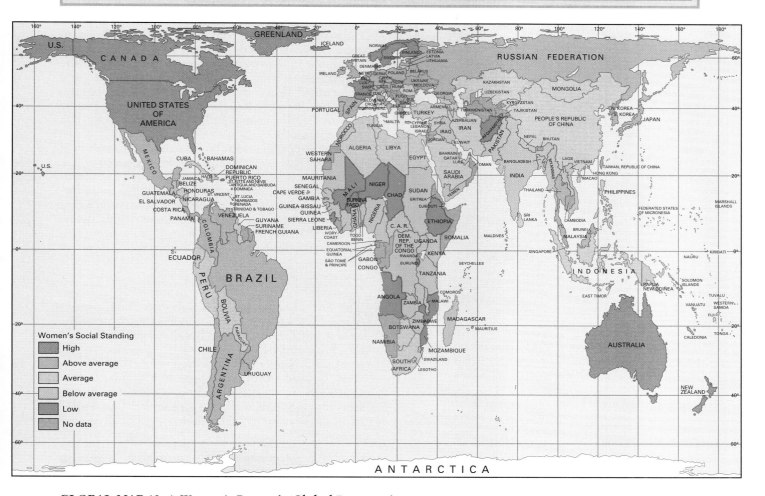

GLOBAL MAP 13–1 Women's Power in Global Perspective

Women's social standing, in relation to men's, varies around the world. In general, women fare better in rich countries than in poor countries. Even so, some nations stand out: In the Nordic nations of Norway, Sweden, and Finland, women come closest to social equality with men.

Source: Data from Seager (1997).

Is Patriarchy Inevitable?

In preindustrial societies, women have little say over pregnancy and childbirth, which limits the scope of their lives. At the same time, men's greater height and physical strength are highly valued resources. But industrialization—and especially the development of birth control technology—gives people choices about how to live. In today's postindustrial societies, such as our own, biological differences offer little justification for patriarchy.

But males are dominant in the United States and elsewhere. Does this mean that patriarchy is

Q: "Differences between the male and female endocrine/central nervous system are such that—statistically speaking—males have a greater tendency to exhibit whatever behavior is necessary in any environment to attain dominance in hierarchies." Steven Goldberg
RESOURCE: By and large, sociologists accept the view that biology plays no significant role in gender formation. Goldberg's quote (above) therefore is likely to elicit strong disapproval. Goldberg presents his

evidence in "Reaffirming the Obvious" and "Utopian Yearning versus Scientific Curiosity," *Society*, Vol. 23, No. 6 (September/October 1986):4–7, 29–39.
DISCUSS: Androgyny is the fusing of conventional traits of femininity and masculinity in a single personality. To what extent are most people androgynous? To what extent could we be? Is androgyny the fulfillment of "total humanity"? Why or why not?

GENDER AND SOCIALIZATION

From birth until death, gender shapes human feelings, thoughts, and actions. Children quickly learn that their society considers females and males different kinds of people; by about age three, they begin to apply gender standards to themselves.

Table 13–1 presents the traits that people in the United States traditionally link to "feminine" and "masculine" behavior. Note the pattern of opposites, even though research suggests that most young people do not develop consistently feminine or masculine personalities (Bernard, 1980; Bem, 1993).

Just as gender affects how we think of ourselves, it teaches us how to act. **Gender roles** (or sex roles) are *attitudes and activities that a society links to each sex.* Insofar as our culture defines males as ambitious and competitive, we expect them to play team sports and aspire to positions of leadership. To the extent that we define females as deferential and emotional, we expect them to be supportive helpers and quick to cry.

GENDER AND THE FAMILY

The first question people usually ask about a newborn—"Is it a boy or a girl?"—looms large because the answer involves not just sex but the likely direction of the child's entire life.

In fact, gender is at work even before the birth of a child, because most parents hope to have a boy rather than a girl. Soon after birth, family members usher infants into the "pink world" of girls or the "blue world" of boys (Bernard, 1981). Parents even send gender

Among the most striking consequences of patriarchy in China is the practice of foot-binding, by which the feet of young girls (especially those of high social position) are tightly wrapped as they grow, with predictable results. Conventional thinking suggests that this practice produces women of "dainty" proportions, but it also greatly limits women's physical mobility. Although rare today, cases of foot binding are still reported and documented with photographs.

inevitable? Some sociologists claim that biological factors set limits on the behavior of the two sexes so that, on average, females and males have different motivations and behaviors, with more aggressiveness in males. To the extent to which this is so, patriarchy may be difficult to eliminate (Goldberg, 1974, 1987; Rossi, 1985; Popenoe, 1993b; Udry, 2000). However, most sociologists believe that gender is a social construct that can be changed. Just because no society has yet eliminated patriarchy does not mean that we must be prisoners of the past.

To understand the persistence of patriarchy, we now examine how gender is rooted and reproduced in society, a process that begins in childhood and continues throughout our lives.

TABLE 13–1 Traditional Notions of Gender Identity	
Feminine Traits	**Masculine Traits**
Submissive	Dominant
Dependent	Independent
Unintelligent and incapable	Intelligent and competent
Emotional	Rational
Receptive	Assertive
Intuitive	Analytical
Weak	Strong
Timid	Brave
Content	Ambitious
Passive	Active
Cooperative	Competitive
Sensitive	Insensitive
Sex object	Sexually aggressive
Attractive because of physical appearance	Attractive because of achievement

DIVERSITY: Without knowing the sex of the person involved, wouldn't people tend to evaluate the traits traditionally linked to females (Table 13–1) as negative?

NOTE: Research suggests that undergraduate women and men have somewhat different expectations of advisers. One-fourth of women and two-thirds of men had the primary concern that advisers "make concrete and directive suggestions." Three-fourths of women and one-third of men asked advisers to "take the time to know me personally" (The Harvard Assessment Seminars: Explorations with Students and Faculty about Teaching, Learning, and Student Life).

Q: "[Men] think themselves superior to women, but they mingle that with the notion of equality between men and women. It's very odd." Jean-Paul Sartre

APPLYING SOCIOLOGY

Masculinity as Contest

By the time I was ten, the central fact in my life was the demand that I become a man. By then, the most important relationships by which I was taught to define myself were those I had with other boys. I already knew that I must see every encounter with another boy as a contest in which I must win or at least hold my own. . . . The same lesson continued [in school], after school, even in Sunday school. My parents, relatives, teachers, the books I read, movies I saw, all taught me that my self-worth depended on my manliness, my willingness to stand up to the other boys. This usually didn't mean a physical fight, though the willingness to stand up and "fight like a man" always remained a final test. But the relationships between us usually had the character of an armed truce. Girls weren't part of this social world at all yet, just because they weren't part of this contest. They didn't have to be bluffed, no credit was gained by cowing them, so they were more or less ignored. Sometimes when there were no grownups around we would let each other know that we liked each other, but most of the time we did as we were taught.

Source: Silverstein (1977).

messages in the way they handle daughters and sons. One researcher at an English university presented an infant dressed as either a boy or a girl to a number of women; her subjects handled the "female" child tenderly, with frequent hugs and caresses, and the "male" child more aggressively, often lifting him up high in the air or bouncing him on the knee (Bonner, 1984). The lesson is clear: The female world revolves around passivity and emotion, whereas the male world puts a premium on independence and action.

GENDER AND THE PEER GROUP

About the time they enter school, children move outside the family and make friends with others of the same age. Peer groups teach additional lessons about gender. The box explains how play groups shaped one young boy's sense of himself as masculine.

After spending a year watching children at play, Janet Lever (1978) concluded that boys favor team sports with complex rules and clear objectives such as scoring a run or making a touchdown. Such games nearly always have winners and losers, which reinforces masculine traits of aggression and control.

Girls, too, play team sports. But girls also play hopscotch, jump rope, or simply talk, sing, or dance. These activities have few rules, and rarely is "victory" the ultimate goal. Instead of teaching girls to be competitive, Lever explains, female peer groups promote interpersonal skills of communication and cooperation, presumably the basis for girls' future roles as wives and mothers.

Lever's observations recall Carol Gilligan's (1982) gender-based theory of moral reasoning, discussed in Chapter 5 ("Socialization"). Boys reason according to abstract principles, Gilligan contends. For them, "rightness" amounts to "playing by the rules." Girls, on the other hand, consider morality a matter of social responsibility to others. Thus, the games we play have serious implications for our later lives.

GENDER AND SCHOOLING

In high school, more girls than boys learn secretarial skills and take vocational classes such as cosmetology and food service. Classes in woodworking and auto maintenance, conversely, attract mostly young men.

In college, men are disproportionately represented in mathematics and the sciences, including physics, chemistry, and biology. Women cluster in the humanities (such as English), the fine arts (painting, music, dance, and drama), and the social sciences (including anthropology and sociology). New areas of study are also likely to be gender-typed. Computer science enrolls mostly men, for example, whereas courses in gender studies enroll more women.

DIVERSITY: RACE, CLASS, AND GENDER

Pretty Is As Pretty Does: The Beauty Myth

The Duchess of Windsor once quipped, "A woman cannot be too rich or too thin." The first half of her observation might apply to men as well, but certainly not the second. It is no surprise that most ads placed by the $20-billion-a-year cosmetics industry and the $40-billion diet industry target women.

According to Naomi Wolf (1990), our culture promotes a "beauty myth" that is damaging to women. The beauty myth arises, first, because society teaches women to measure themselves in terms of physical appearance (Backman & Adams, 1991). Yet the standards of beauty (such as the *Playboy* centerfold or the 100-pound New York fashion model) are unattainable for most women.

The beauty myth also teaches women to prize relationships with men and to use beauty to attract men. Striving for beauty drives women to be superficial and forces them to be highly attuned and responsive to men. Beauty-minded women try to please men and avoid challenging male power.

The beauty myth affects males as well: Men should want to possess beautiful women. Thus, our ideas about beauty

reduce women to objects and motivate men to possess women as if they were dolls rather than human beings.

In sum, there can be little doubt that the idea of beauty is important in everyday life. The question, according to Wolf, is whether beauty is about how we look or how we act.

What do you think?

1. *We might be tempted to say that physical attraction is simply a biological issue about "looks." How does Wolf's argument make beauty a social issue?*

2. *Do you think the beauty myth is still strong today? What messages about beauty and women does today's advertising send?*

3. *Are men harmed by the beauty myth? If so, how?*

Source: Based on Wolf (1990).

GENDER AND THE MASS MEDIA

Since television first captured the public imagination in the 1950s, white males have held center stage. Racial and ethnic minorities were all but absent from prominent television roles until the early 1970s. Even when both sexes appear on camera, men generally play the brilliant detectives, fearless explorers, and skilled surgeons. Women, by contrast, play the less capable characters, unnecessary except for the sexual interest they add to the story.

Historically, advertisements have presented women in the home, happily using cleaning products, serving food, trying out appliances, and modeling clothes. Men, on the other hand, predominate in ads for cars, travel, banking services, industrial companies, and alcoholic beverages. The authoritative voiceover—the faceless voice that describes a product on television and radio—is almost always male (Courtney & Whipple, 1983; Davis, 1993).

In studying magazine and newspaper ads, Erving Goffman (1979) documented the pattern by which men usually appear taller than women, implying male superiority. Women, he found, were more frequently presented lying down (on sofas and beds) or, like children, seated on the floor. Men's facial expressions exuded competence and authority, whereas women often appeared childlike. While men focused on the

DIVERSITY: Although sex segregation in the labor force remains high, it is declining over time: rapidly during the 1980s and more slowly since 1990 (see Wells, 1999).

SOCIAL SURVEY: "Do you approve or disapprove of a married woman earning money in business or industry if she has a husband capable of supporting her?" (GSS 1998, N = 1,871; Codebook, 2001:229) "Approve" 80.7% "Disapprove" 17.5% DK/NR 1.8%

DIVERSITY: In 1998, 86% of Fortune 500 companies (429) had at least 1 woman director; overall, women held 11.1% (women of color, 1%) of seats on boards of directors (Catalyst, 2000).

THEN AND NOW: Women now represent 40% of business fliers on major airlines, up from 2% in 1970.

NOTE: A study of married women found that 68% preferred the title "Mrs."; 6% "Ms."; 26% were unsure (Des Moines Register).

DIVERSITY SNAPSHOT

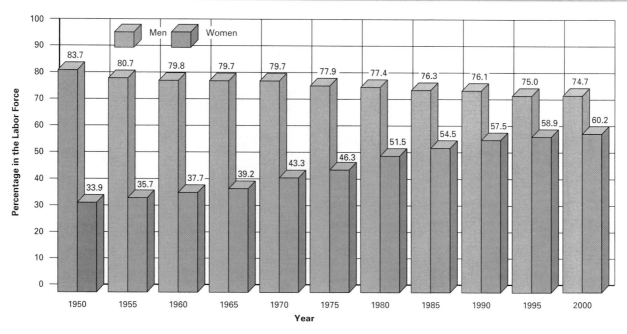

FIGURE 13–2 Men and Women in the U.S. Labor Force

Source: U.S. Department of Labor (2001).

products being advertised, women focused on the men, playing a supportive and submissive role.

In recent years, advertising has portrayed women and men in more equal terms. Still, advertising does not give women a fair shake, actively perpetuating what Naomi Wolf calls the "beauty myth." The box takes a closer look.

GENDER AND SOCIAL STRATIFICATION

Gender implies more than how people think and act. It is also about social hierarchy. The reality of gender stratification can be seen, first, in the world of work.

WORKING WOMEN AND MEN

Back in 1900, just one-fifth of U.S. women were in the labor force. In 2000, as shown in Figure 13–2, 60 percent of women aged sixteen and over worked for income, and three-fourths of working women worked full time. The traditional view that earning an income is exclusively a man's role no longer holds true.

Factors that have changed the U.S. labor force include the decline of farming as an occupation, the growth of cities, a shrinking family size, and a rising divorce rate. Thus, the United States, along with most other nations of the world, considers women working for income the rule rather than the exception. In fact, 62 percent of U.S. married couples depend on two incomes. As Global Map 13–2 on page 334 shows, women represent almost half of the U.S. work force; however, this is not the case in many of the poorer nations of the world.

In the past, many women in the U.S. labor force were childless. But today, 62 percent of married women with children under age six work for income, as do 77 percent of married women with children between six and seventeen years of age. For divorced

THEN AND NOW: Percentage of the labor force women represent, 1970 and 1999: United Arab Emirates, 4% and 15%; Ireland, 26% and 34%; U.K., 36% and 44%; Norway, 29% and 46%; Japan, 39% and 41%; U.S., 37% and 46%; Sweden, 36% and 48% (World Bank, 2001).

GLOBAL: The nation closest to earnings parity is Sweden, 90%. Other countries: France, 77%; Germany, 70%; Japan, 67%.

THEN AND NOW: In 1950, the U.S. gender earnings ratio was 57%; it is 73% today.

NOTE: Extending the current trend, gender parity in top management positions will take another 75 years; however, congressional parity would take 500 years.

Q: "Women who seek to be equal with me lack ambition." Timothy O'Leary

WINDOW ON THE WORLD

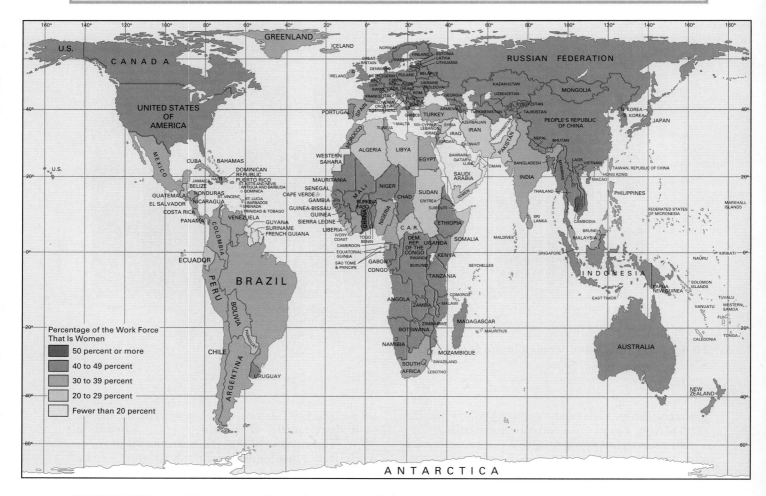

GLOBAL MAP 13–2 Women's Paid Employment in Global Perspective

This map shows the percentage of the labor force made up of women. A country's level of technological development plays an important part here. In 2000, women were 47 percent of the labor force in the United States—up almost 10 percent over the last generation. In high-income nations, overall, nearly one-half of the labor force is made up of women. In poor societies, however, women work even harder than in this country, but they are less likely to be paid for their efforts. In Latin America, for example, women represent about one-third of the paid labor force; in Islamic societies of northern Africa and the Middle East, the figure is significantly lower. One exception to this rule is central and southern Africa, where, traditionally, women make up a large share of farmers.

Sources: *Peters Atlas of the World* (1990); updated by the author from The World Bank (2001).

women with children, the comparable figures are 77 percent of women with younger children and 82 percent of women with older children (U.S. Census Bureau, 2000).

Gender and Occupations

Although the shares of men and women in the labor force have been converging, the work they do remains different. The U.S. Department of Labor (2001) reports that nearly half of working women hold one of two types of jobs. Administrative support work draws 23 percent of working women. These office jobs sometimes are called "pink-collar" jobs because 79 percent are filled by women. Another 16 percent of employed women do service work. Most of these jobs are in food services, child care, and health care.

Table 13–2 shows the ten occupations with the highest concentrations of women. Overall, although more women now work for pay, they remain segregated in the labor force in jobs at the low end of the pay scale, with limited opportunities for advancement, and usually supervised by men (Charles, 1992; Bianchi & Spain, 1996; U.S. Department of Labor, 2001).

Men dominate most other job categories, including the building trades, where 99 percent of brick and stone masons, structural metalworkers, and heavy equipment

Read more about the small number of women in top corporate jobs at http://www.catalystwomen.org/press/factsheets/factscote00.html top

mechanics are men. Likewise, 90 percent of engineers, 83 percent of police officers, 72 percent of physicians, 70 percent of judges and lawyers, and 55 percent of corporate managers are men. According to a recent survey, the top earners in Fortune 500 corporations include 2,162 men and 93 women, or about 4 percent women. Just nine of the 1,000 largest corporations in the United States have a woman as their chief executive officer (Catalyst, 2001; U.S. Department of Labor, 2001).

Gender stratification in the workplace is easy to see: Female nurses assist male physicians, female administrative assistants serve male executives, and female flight attendants are under the command of male airplane pilots. Moreover, in any field, the greater the income and prestige associated with a job, the more likely it is to be held by a man. For example, 98 percent of kindergarten teachers, 83 percent of elementary school teachers, 58 percent of secondary school teachers, 42 percent of college and university professors, and 16 percent of college and university presidents are women (U.S. Department of Labor, 2001).

TABLE 13–2 Jobs with the Highest Concentrations of Women, 2000

Occupation	Number of Women Employed	Percentage in Occupation Who Are Women
1. Secretary	2,594,000	98.9%
2. Dental hygienist	110,000	98.5
3. Prekindergarten and kindergarten teacher	617,000	98.5
4. Family child-care provider	446,000	97.7
5. Private household child-care worker	268,000	97.5
6. Receptionist	983,000	96.7
7. Dental assistant	210,000	96.4
8. Early childhood teacher's assistant	457,000	95.2
9. Private household cleaner or servant	474,000	94.8
10. Stenographer	146,000	94.7

Source: U.S. Department of Labor, Bureau of Labor Statistics, *Employment and Earnings*, vol. 48, no. 1, January 2001, pp. 178–83.

How are women kept out of certain jobs? By defining some kinds of work as "masculine," companies define women as unsuitable workers. In a study of coal mining in West Virginia, Suzanne E. Tallichet (2000) found that most men considered it "unnatural" for women to work in the mines. Women who did work in the mines were themselves defined as "unnatural" and subject to labeling as "sexually loose" or lesbian. Such labeling made these women outcasts, presented a challenge to holding the job, and made advancement all but impossible.

But one challenge to male domination in the workplace comes from women who are entrepreneurs. Women now own more than 9 million small businesses in the United States, twice the number just a decade ago and more than one-third of the total. Although the majority of women-owned businesses are one-person operations, these businesses employ one-fourth of the entire labor force. By starting their own businesses, women have shown that they can make opportunities for themselves outside larger, male-dominated companies (Ando, 1990; O'Hare & Larson, 1991; Mergenhagen, 1996c; NFWBO, 1996; Winters, 1999; U.S. Department of Labor, 2001).

HOUSEWORK

In the United States, housework has always been a cultural contradiction: We claim that it is essential for

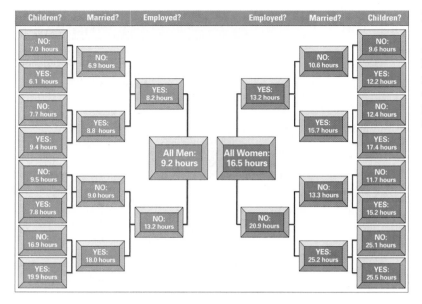

FIGURE 13–3 Housework: Who Does How Much?

Overall, women average 16.5 hours of housework per week, compared to 9.2 hours for men. This pattern holds whether people are employed or not, married or not, and parenting or not.

Source: Adapted from Stapinski (1998).

family life but give housework little prestige or other reward (Bernard, 1981). With women's entry into the labor force, the amount of housework performed by women has declined, but the *share* women do has stayed about the same. Figure 13–3 shows that, overall, women average 16.5 hours a week of housework, compared to 9.2 hours for men. Among all categories of people, the figure shows, women do significantly more housework than men (Stapinski, 1998).

In sum, men support the idea of women entering the labor force, and most count on the money women earn. But most men also resist taking on a more equal share of household duties. Holding primary responsibility for housework is likely to continue to reduce women's available time for paid work or schooling (Cowan, 1992; Robinson & Spitze, 1992; Lennon & Rosenfeld, 1994; Heath & Bourne, 1995; Harpster & Monk-Turner, 1998; Stratton, 2001).

GENDER, INCOME, AND WEALTH

In 2000, the median earnings for women working full time were $27,355, whereas men working full time earned $37,339. This means that, for every dollar earned by men, women earned about 73 cents.

Among full-time workers, 42 percent of women earned less than $25,000 in 2000, compared to 26 percent of comparable men. At the upper end of the income scale, men were three-and-one-half times more likely than women (14.8 percent versus 4.1 percent) to earn more than $75,000 (U.S. Census Bureau, 2001).

The main reason women earn less is the *kind* of work they do: largely clerical and service jobs. In effect, jobs and gender interact. People still perceive jobs with less clout as "women's work," just as people devalue certain jobs simply because they are performed by women (Parcel, Mueller, & Cuvelier, 1986; Blum, 1991; England, 1992; Bellas, 1994; Huffman, Velasco, & Bielby, 1996; England, Hermsen, & Cotter, 2000).

During the 1980s, proponents of gender equality proposed a policy of comparable worth. That is, people should be paid not according to the historical double standard but according to the worth of what they actually do. Several nations, including Great Britain and Australia, have adopted comparable worth policies, but not the United States. As a result, women in this country lose as much as $1 billion annually.

A second cause of gender-based income disparity has to do with the family. Both men and women have children, of course, but our culture defines parenting as more a woman's duty than a man's. Pregnancy and raising small children keep many younger women out of the labor force at a time when their male peers are making significant career advancements. As a result, women workers have less job seniority than their male counterparts (Fuchs, 1986; Stier, 1996; Waldfogel, 1997).

NOTE: A recent study found the highest-paid female corporate executives earn 68 percent as much as the highest-paid male executives (not controlling for organization size). Median earnings were $518,596 vs. $765,000 (Catalyst study, cited in *USA Today*, November 10, 1998:10).
NOTE: In 1998, there were 6.9 million men and 8.6 million women enrolled in U.S. colleges.

DIVERSITY: Among African Americans, the gender gap in education is greater than among whites: Of all African American college graduates, 58% are women.
DIVERSITY: Although among whites men receive 54% of doctorates, among African Americans women earn 55% of doctorates; among Native Americans, 49%; Hispanics, 48%; Asians, 36%.

Moreover, women who choose to have children may be reluctant or unable to maintain fast-paced jobs that tie up their evenings and weekends. To avoid role strain, they may take jobs that offer a shorter commuting distance, more flexible hours, or employer child-care services. Women pursuing both a career and a family are often torn between their dual responsibilities in ways that men are not. Consider what one researcher found: At age forty, 90 percent of men but only 35 percent of women in executive positions have at least one child (F. Schwartz, 1989).

These two factors—type of work and family responsibilities—account for about two-thirds of the earnings disparity between women and men. A third factor—discrimination against women—accounts for most of the remainder (Pear, 1987; Fuller & Schoenberger, 1991). Because discrimination is illegal, it is practiced in subtle ways. Corporate women often encounter a *glass ceiling*, a barrier that is invisible because it is denied by company officials even though it effectively prevents women from rising above middle management (Benokraitis & Feagin, 1995; Yamagata et al., 1997).

For all these reasons, then, women earn less than men in all major occupational categories. As shown in Table 13–3, this disparity varies from job to job, but in only five of the major job classifications do women earn more than 75 percent as much as men.

Finally, perhaps because women typically outlive men, many people think that women own most of this country's wealth. Government statistics tell a different story: Sixty-one percent of individuals with $1 million or more in assets are men, although widows are highly represented in this millionaires' club (U.S. Internal Revenue Service, 2000). Just 12 percent of the people identified in *Forbes* magazine as the richest people in the United States are women.

 A report by the Department of Labor traces women's earnings over the second half of the twentieth century: http://www.dol.gov/dol/wb/public/wb_pubs/wagegap2000.htm

GENDER AND EDUCATION

In the past, women received little schooling because their lives revolved around the home. But times have changed. By 1980, women earned a majority of all associate and bachelor degrees; in 1998, that proportion stood at 56 percent (U.S. National Center for Education Statistics, 2001).

College doors have opened to women, and differences in men's and women's majors are becoming smaller. In 1970, for example, women earned just

TABLE 13–3 Earnings of Full-Time U.S. Workers,* by Sex, 2000			
Selected Occupational Categories	Median Income		Women's Income as a Percentage of Men's
	Men	Women	
Executives, administrators, and managers	$57,162	$36,953	65%
Professional specialties	58,364	39,319	67
Technologists and technicians	46,717	35,818	77
Sales	41,266	25,619	62
Clerical and other administrative support workers	32,622	25,197	77
Precision production, craft, and repair workers	35,197	26,101	74
Machine operators and tenders	28,918	19,196	66
Material moving equipment operators	29,461	25,613	87
Handlers, equipment cleaners, helpers, and laborers	22,157	17,384	78
Service workers	25,052	16,873	67
Farming, forestry, and fishing workers	19,586	17,618	90
All occupations listed above	37,339	27,355	73

*Workers aged 15 and over.
Source: U.S. Census Bureau (2001).

17 percent of bachelor degrees in the natural sciences, computer science, and engineering; by 1998, that proportion had increased to 31 percent.

In 1993, for the first time, women also earned a majority of postgraduate degrees, often a springboard to high-prestige jobs. For all areas of study in 1995, women earned 57 percent of master's degrees and 42 percent of doctorates (including 56 percent of all Ph.D.s in sociology). Women have also broken into many graduate fields that used to be almost all male. For example, in 1970 only a few hundred women received a master's of business administration degree, compared to more than 39,000 in 1998 (39 percent of all such degrees) (U.S. National Center for Education Statistics, 2001).

Men continue to dominate some professional fields, however. In 1998, men received 56 percent of

SOCIAL SURVEY: Top 10 nations in terms of share of women in national legislatures (2001): 1) Sweden, 42.7%; 2) Finland, 36.5%; 3) Netherlands, 36.0%; 4) Norway, 35.8%; 5) Iceland, 34.9%; 6) Germany, 31.1%; 7) New Zealand, 30.8%; 8) Mozambique, 30.0%; 9) South Africa, 29.8%; 10) Spain, 28.3%; 48) U.S., 14.0% (Inter-Parliamentary Union, 2001).

DIVERSITY: The gender gap in politics is real: 11.1% more women

TABLE 13–4 Significant "Firsts" for Women in U.S. Politics

Year	Event
1869	Law allows women to vote in Wyoming territory; Utah follows suit in 1870.
1872	First woman to run for the presidency (Victoria Woodhull) represents the Equal Rights party.
1917	First woman elected to the House of Representatives (Jeannette Rankin of Montana).
1924	First women elected state governors (Nellie Taylor Ross of Wyoming and Miriam ["Ma"] Ferguson of Texas); both followed their husbands into office. First woman to have her name placed in nomination for vice-presidency at the convention of a major political party (Lena Jones Springs).
1931	First woman to serve in the Senate (Hattie Caraway of Arkansas); completed the term of her husband upon his death and won reelection in 1932.
1932	First woman appointed to the presidential cabinet (Frances Perkins, secretary of labor in the cabinet of President Franklin D. Roosevelt).
1964	First woman to have her name placed in nomination for the presidency at the convention of a major political party (Margaret Chase Smith, a Republican).
1972	First African American woman to have her name placed in nomination for the presidency at the convention of a major political party (Shirley Chisholm, a Democrat).
1981	First woman appointed to the U.S. Supreme Court (Sandra Day O'Connor).
1984	First woman to be successfully nominated for the vice-presidency (Geraldine Ferraro, a Democrat).
1988	First woman chief executive to be elected to a consecutive third term (Madeleine Kunin, governor of Vermont).
1992	Political "Year of the Woman" yields record number of women in the Senate (six) and the House (forty-eight), as well as (1) first African American woman to win election to U.S. Senate (Carol Moseley-Braun of Illinois), (2) first state (California) to be served by two women senators (Barbara Boxer and Dianne Feinstein), and (3) first woman of Puerto Rican descent elected to the House (Nydia Valasquez of New York).
1996	First woman appointed secretary of state (Madeleine Albright).
2000	Record number of women in the Senate (thirteen) and the House (fifty-nine).
2000	First "First Lady" to win elected political office (Hillary Rodham Clinton, senator from New York).

Sources: Based on data compiled from Sandra Salmans, "Women Ran for Office before They Could Vote," *New York Times*, July 13, 1984, p. A11; and news reports.

law degrees, 58 percent of medical degrees, and 62 percent of dental degrees (U.S. National Center for Education Statistics, 2001). Our society still defines high-paying professions (and the drive and competitiveness needed to succeed in them) as masculine; this

fact helps explain why an equal number of women and men begin most professional graduate programs, but women are less likely to complete their degrees (Fiorentine, 1987; Fiorentine & Cole, 1992). Nonetheless, the proportion of women in all these professions is rising steadily: For example, the American Bar Association reports that the law school class of 2004 across the United States is about evenly split between women and men (Gest, 2001).

 A report from the National Center for Educational Statistics on gender and education can be found at http://nces.ed.gov/pubs2000/2000030.pdf

GENDER AND POLITICS

A century ago, almost no women held elected office in the United States. In fact, women were legally barred from voting in national elections until passage of the Nineteenth Amendment to the Constitution in 1920. However, a few women were candidates for political office even before they could vote. The Equal Rights party supported Victoria Woodhull for the U.S. presidency in 1872; perhaps it was a sign of the times that she spent election day in a New York City jail. Table 13–4 identifies later milestones in women's gradual movement into political life.

Today, thousands of women serve as mayors of cities and towns across the United States, and tens of thousands hold responsible administrative posts in the federal government. At the state level, 22 percent of legislators in 2001 were women (up from just 6 percent in 1970). National Map 13–1 shows where in the United States women have made the greatest political gains.

Less change has occurred at the highest levels of politics, although a majority of U.S. adults claim they would support a qualified woman for any office, including the presidency. After the 2000 national elections, 5 of the 50 state governors were women (10 percent), and women held 59 of 435 seats in the House of Representatives (14 percent) and 13 of 100 seats (13 percent) in the Senate.

In global perspective, although women are half the Earth's population, they hold just 13.9 percent of seats in the world's 179 parliaments. Although this represents a rise from 3 percent fifty years ago, only in the Nordic nations of Norway, Sweden, Finland, and Denmark (38.7 percent) and Iceland (34.9 percent) and the Netherlands (32.9 percent) does the share of parliamentary seats held by women even approach

THE MAP: Roughly speaking, women hold the most power in state government in the western states (the region in which women first became state governors). By contrast, the South remains the region in which women are least likely to be in the labor force and where the political clout of women is lowest.

DIVERSITY: In 1992, the U.S. Senate chamber added a women's bathroom.

SOCIAL SURVEY: "If your party nominated a woman for president, would you vote for her if she were qualified for the job?" (GSS 1998, N = 1,871; *Codebook*, 2001:229) [In a 1937 Gallup poll, 37% endorsed a qualified woman for president.]
"Yes"   90.2%   "No"   6.2%   DK/NR   3.6%

RESOURCE: Nijole Benokraitis describes "How Subtle Discrimination Works" in the 5th edition of the *Seeing Ourselves* reader.

SEEING OURSELVES

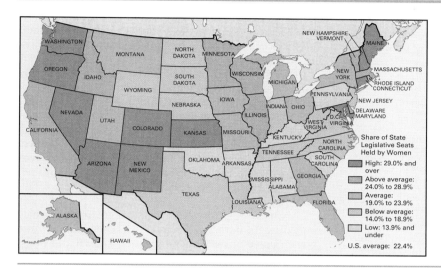

NATIONAL MAP 13–1
Women in State Government across the United States

Although women represent half of U.S. adults, just 22 percent of seats in state legislatures are held by women. Look at the state-by-state variation in the map. In which regions of the country have women gained the greatest political power? What factors do you think account for this pattern?

Source: Center for American Women and Politics, Eagleton Institute of Politics, Rutgers University, "Women in State Legislatures 2001." [Online] Available http://www.rci.rutgers.edu/~cawp/pdf/stleg.pdf, October 23, 2001.

their share of the population (Inter-Parliamentary Union, 2001).

GENDER AND THE MILITARY

Since colonial times, women have served in the armed forces. Yet in 1940, at the outset of World War II, just 2 percent of armed forces personnel were women. By the 1991 Persian Gulf War, 35,000 women made up 6.5 percent of a total deployment of 540,000 U.S. troops. Five of the 148 Gulf War casualties were women.

In 2001, 15 percent of all armed forces personnel were women. Only the Coast Guard makes all assignments available to women; at the other extreme, the Marine Corps denies women access to two-thirds of its jobs. Those who defend limited roles for women in the military claim that, on average, women lack the physical strength of men. Critics counter that military women are better educated and score higher on intelligence tests than their male counterparts. But the heart of the issue is our society's deeply held view of women as *nurturers*—people who give life and help others—which clashes intolerably with the image of women trained to kill.

Although incorporating women into military culture has been difficult, women in all branches of the

U.S. armed forces are taking on more and more military assignments. One reason is that reliance on high technology blurs the distinction between combat and noncombat personnel. A combat pilot can fire missiles at a radar-screen target miles away, while nonfighting medical evacuation teams go to the battle site (McNeil, 1991; May, Segal, & Hansen, 1992; Wilcox, 1992; Kaminer, 1997).

ARE WOMEN A MINORITY?

Sociologists define a **minority**[2] as *any category of people, distinguished by physical or cultural difference, that a society sets apart and subordinates*. Given the clear economic disadvantage our society imposes on women, it seems reasonable to say that U.S. women are a minority even though they outnumber men.

Subjectively speaking, however, most white women do not think of themselves this way (Hacker, 1951; Lengermann & Wallace, 1985). This is partly because, unlike racial minorities (including African

---

[2]We use the term "minority" instead of "minority group" because, as explained in Chapter 7 ("Groups and Organizations"), a minority is a category, not a group.

Americans) and ethnic minorities (say, Hispanics), white women are well represented at all levels of the class structure, including the very top.

Bear in mind, however, that at every class level, women typically have less income, wealth, education, and power than men. In fact, patriarchy makes women dependent for much of their social standing on men—first their fathers and later their husbands (Bernard, 1981).

MINORITY WOMEN

If women are defined as a minority, what about minority women? Are they doubly handicapped? Generally speaking, they are, as we can show with some income comparisons. Looking first at race and ethnicity, the median income in 2000 for African American women working full time was $25,117, which is 85 percent as much as the $29,604 earned by non-Hispanic white women; Hispanic women earned $20,527—just 69 percent as much as their white, non-Hispanic counterparts. Looking at gender, African American women earned 83 percent as much as African American men, and Hispanic women earned 83 percent as much as Hispanic men.

Combining these disadvantages, African American women earned 61 percent as much as non-Hispanic white men, and Hispanic women earned 50 percent as much (U.S. Census Bureau, 2001). These disparities reflect minority women's lower positions in the occupational and educational hierarchies compared with white women (Bonilla-Santiago, 1990). These data confirm that, although gender has a powerful effect on our lives, it never operates alone. Class position, race and ethnicity, and gender intersect to form a multilayered system of disadvantage for some and privilege for others (Ginsburg & Tsing, 1990; St. Jean & Feagin, 1998).

VIOLENCE AGAINST WOMEN

As noted in the opening to this chapter, the phrase "rule of thumb" entered our language about 150 years ago when common decency prevented a man from beating his wife with a stick thicker than his thumb. Even today, a great deal of "manly" violence is directed at women. A U.S. government report estimates 383,000 sexual assaults against women annually, including 201,000 rapes or attempted rapes. To this number can be added perhaps 2 million physical assaults (Goetting, 1999; U.S. Bureau of Justice Statistics, 2001).

Gender violence is also an issue on college and university campuses. A new report from the Department of Justice (2001) states that in 2000, 1.7 percent of female college students were victims of rape, and another 1.1 percent were victims of attempted rape. In 90 percent of all cases, the victims knew the offenders, and most of the assaults took place in the woman's living quarters.

Off the campus as well, most gender-linked violence occurs where men and women interact most: in the home. Richard Gelles (cited in Roesch, 1984) argues that with the exception of the police and the military the family is the most violent organization in the United States. Both sexes suffer from family violence, although women sustain more serious injuries than men (Straus & Gelles, 1986; Schwartz, 1987; Shupe, Stacey, & Hazlewood, 1987; Gelles & Cornell, 1990; Smolowe, 1994).

Violence against women also occurs in casual relationships. As noted in Chapter 8 ("Deviance"), most rapes involve not strangers but men known and often trusted by the victim. Dianne Herman (2001) believes

 Here is a United Nations report on violence against women and girls around the world: http://www.unicef-icdc.org/publications/pdf/digest6e.pdf

that abuse of women is built into our way of life. All forms of violence against women—from the wolf whistles that intimidate women on city streets to a pinch in a crowded subway to physical assaults that occur at home—express what she calls a "rape culture" of men trying to dominate women. Sexual violence, she explains, is fundamentally about *power*, not sex, and therefore should be understood as a dimension of gender stratification.

In global perspective, violence against women is built into culture in other ways. One case in point is the practice of female genital mutilation, found in some

 This German site provides information on female genital mutilation in twenty-eight African nations and related links: http://www.gtz.de/fgm

three dozen countries and known to occur in the United States, as shown in Global Map 13–3. The box on page 342 presents a case of genital mutilation that took place in California.

Sexual Harassment

Sexual harassment consists of *comments, gestures, or physical contact of a sexual nature that are deliberate, repeated, and unwelcome.* During the 1990s, sexual harassment became an issue of national importance that rewrote the rules for workplace interaction.

NOTE: E. Digby Baltzell points out that control of women's sexuality is not designed simply to ensure the domination of women; it is society's means of promoting endogamy, thus defending racial and class hegemony.

Q: "We all live in single-sex worlds, and most of what we know—from history, the humanities, the social and behavioral sciences—deals with the male world." Jessie Bernard

Q: "Consider, I address you as a legislator, whether, when men contend for their freedom, and to be allowed to judge for themselves their own happiness, it be not inconsistent and unjust to subjugate women, even though you firmly believe that you are acting in the manner best calculated to promote their happiness? Who made man the exclusive judge, if woman partake with him the gift of reason?" Mary Wollstonecraft, *A Vindication of the Rights of Woman* (1792)

WINDOW ON THE WORLD

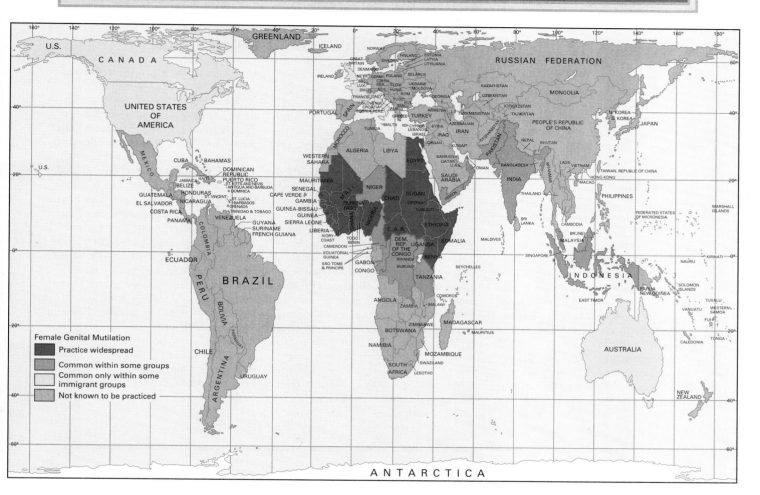

GLOBAL MAP 13–3 Female Genital Mutilation in Global Perspective

Female genital mutilation, also called female circumcision, is known to be performed in more than forty countries around the world. Across Africa, the practice is common and affects a majority of girls in the eastern African nations of Sudan, Ethiopia, and Somalia. In several Asian nations, including India, the practice is limited to a few ethnic minorities. In the United States, Canada, several European nations, and Australia, there are reports of the practice among some immigrants.

Source: Data from Seager (1997).

Most victims of sexual harassment are women. This is because, first, our culture encourages men to be sexually assertive and to perceive women in sexual terms. As a result, social interaction in the workplace, on campus, and elsewhere can readily take on sexual overtones. Second, most people in positions of power—including business executives, physicians, assembly line supervisors, professors, and military officers—are men

DISCUSS: Ask how the class distinguishes between "erotic" and "pornographic" material. Debate a proper balance among conservative moral concerns, liberal support for freedom of expression, and feminist opposition to the patriarchal dimensions of pornography.
Q: "To be born a woman means to inhabit, from early infancy to the last day of life, a psychological world which differs from the world of man." Mirra Komarovsky

DISCUSS: There are some 3,000 gentlemen's clubs in the U.S., employing some 250,000 dancers. Does this multibillion-dollar industry exploit women? Exploit men? Is it just sleazy for everybody? Or is it a matter of personal choice?
Q: "Sexual objectification is the primary process of the subjugation of women." Catharine MacKinnon

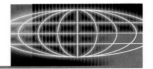

GLOBAL SOCIOLOGY

Female Genital Mutilation: Violence in the Name of Morality

Meserak Ramsey, a woman born in Ethiopia and now working as a nurse in California, paid a visit to a friend's home. Soon after arriving, she noticed her friend's eighteen-month-old daughter huddled in the corner of a room in obvious distress. "What's wrong?" she asked.

Ramsey was shocked when the woman said her daughter recently had a clitoridectomy, or female circumcision, whereby the clitoris is surgically removed. This procedure—performed by a midwife, a tribal practitioner, or a doctor and typically without anesthesia—is common in two dozen African nations, including Nigeria, Togo, Somalia, and Egypt, and is known to exist among certain cultural groups in other nations around the world.

Among members of highly patriarchal societies, husbands demand that their wives be virgins at marriage and remain sexually faithful thereafter. The point of genital mutilation is to eliminate sexual sensation, which, people as-

sume, makes the girl less likely to violate sexual norms and thus be more desirable to men. In about one-fifth of all cases, an even more severe procedure, called infibulation, is performed, in which the entire external genital area is removed and the surfaces are stitched together, leaving only a small hole for urination. Before marriage, a husband retains the right to open the wound and assure himself of his bride's virginity.

How many women have undergone genital mutilation? Worldwide, estimates place the number at more than 100 million. In the United States, hundreds and probably thousands of such procedures are performed every year. In most cases, immigrant mothers and grandmothers who have themselves been mutilated insist that young girls in their family follow their example. Indeed, many immigrant women demand the procedure *because* their daughters now live in the United States, where sexual mores are more lax. "I don't have to worry about her now," one

California parent explained to Meserak Ramsey; "She'll be a good girl."

Medically, the consequences of genital mutilation include more than loss of sexual pleasure. Pain is intense and can persist for years. There is also danger of infection, infertility, and even death. Meserak Ramsey underwent genital mutilation as a young girl. She is one of the lucky ones who has had few medical problems since. But the extent of her suffering is suggested by this story: She had invited a young U.S. couple to stay at her home. Late at night, she heard the woman's cries and burst into their room to investigate, only to learn that the couple was making love and the woman had just had an orgasm. "I didn't understand," Ramsey recalls; "I thought that there must be something wrong with American girls. But now I know that there is something wrong with me." Or with a system that inflicts such injury in the name of traditional morality.

Source: Based on Crossette (1995).

who oversee the work of women. In surveys carried out in widely different work settings, half of women respondents report receiving unwanted sexual attention (Paul, 1991; NORC, 2001).

Sexual harassment is sometimes blatant and direct: A supervisor solicits sexual favors from a subordinate by threatening reprisal if the advances are refused. Courts have declared such *quid pro quo* sexual harassment (the Latin phrase means "one thing in return for another") a violation of civil rights.

More often, however, sexual harassment involves subtle behavior—sexual teasing, off-color jokes, or pinups displayed in the workplace—that may not even be intended to harass anyone. But under the *effect* standard favored by many feminists, such actions create a

hostile environment (Cohen, 1991; Paul, 1991). Incidents of this kind are far more complex because they involve different perceptions of the same behavior. For example, a man may think that complimenting a co-worker on her appearance is simply a friendly gesture; she, on the other hand, may feel his behavior hinders her job performance.

Pornography

Chapter 9 ("Sexuality") defined *pornography* as sexually explicit material that causes sexual arousal. However, people have different views of what is and what is not pornographic. Likewise, the law gives local municipalities the power to draw the lines that define what sexually

DISCUSS: To draw out the link between aggression and masculinity, ask the class what makes a man a "wimp"? A "real man"?
NOTE: The phrase "the opposite sex" clearly conveys the idea that gender is a matter of opposition.
RESOURCE: An excerpt from Deborah Tannen's *You Just Don't Understand* is included in the Macionis and Benokraitis reader, *Seeing Ourselves.*

Q: "The Lord said to Moses, 'Say to the people of Israel, When a man makes a special vow of persons to the Lord at your valuation, then your valuation of a male from 20 years old to 60 years old shall be 50 shekels of silver, according to the shekel of the sanctuary. If the person be a female, your valuation shall be 30 shekels.'" (Leviticus 27:1–4)

Many private companies and public organizations have adopted policies to discourage forms of behavior that might create a "hostile or intimidating environment." In practice, such policies seek to remove sexuality from the workplace so that employees can do their jobs while steering clear of traditional notions about female and male relationships. The hope is that sexual harassment policies will develop a comfortable informal atmosphere in which people can interact freely and easily.

explicit materials violate "community standards" of decency and lack redeeming social value.

People may disagree about what pornography is, but there is little doubt that in the United States pornography is big business. Taken together, sexually explicit videos, movies, magazines, telephone chat lines, and Internet sites represent more than $10 billion in sales each year.

Traditionally, U.S. society has viewed pornography as a *moral* issue. National survey data show that 57 percent of U.S. adults express concern that "sexual materials lead to a breakdown of morals" (NORC, 2001:244). But pornography also plays a part in gender stratification. From this point of view, pornography is a *power* issue because most pornography dehumanizes women as the playthings of men. It is worth noting that the term *pornography* comes from the Greek word *porne*, meaning a prostitute who acts as a man's sexual slave.

In addition, there is widespread concern that pornography promotes violence against women. Depicting women as merely the sexual playthings of men amounts to defining women as weak and undeserving of respect. Men may show contempt for women defined this way by striking out against them. Surveys show that about half of U.S. adults think that pornography encourages men to commit rape (NORC, 2001:245).

Like sexual harassment, pornography raises complex and conflicting issues. Most people object to offensive material, but many also think we must protect free speech and artistic expression. Nevertheless, public support to restrict pornography has increased, both from more conservative people who oppose pornography on moral grounds and from more liberal people who oppose it as demeaning and threatening to women.

THEORETICAL ANALYSIS OF GENDER

Each of sociology's major theoretical paradigms addresses the significance of gender in social organization.

STRUCTURAL-FUNCTIONAL ANALYSIS

The structural-functional paradigm views society as a complex system of many separate but integrated parts. From this point of view, gender functions to organize social life.

As Chapter 4 ("Society") explained, members of hunting and gathering societies had little power over the forces of biology. Lacking birth control, women often were pregnant, and the responsibilities of child care kept them close to home. At the same time, men's greater strength made them more suited for warfare and hunting. Over the centuries, this sexual division of labor became institutionalized and largely taken for granted (Lengermann & Wallace, 1985).

Industrial technology opens up vastly greater cultural possibilities. Because human muscles are no

Q: "Presumably there is continuity from sub-human origins in one critical respect, namely the centering of the earliest child-care responsibilities on the mother. This fact, plus the disabilities of pregnancy and the fact that only recently has other than breast-feeding become widely feasible, lie at the basis of the differentiation of sex roles." Talcott Parsons (1951:155)
DISCUSS: The term "transgendered" has emerged to refer to

people, including transsexuals and cross-dressers, who violate gender norms. Why, according to Talcott Parsons, would such people encounter strong disapproval from others? Why, following a conflict approach, could such behavior be viewed as an act of resistance? (cf. Gagne & Tewksbury, 1998)
Q: "Pregnancy and warfare test the limits of equality." Wendy Kaminer

In the 1950s, Talcott Parsons proposed that sociologists interpret gender as a matter of *differences. As he saw it, masculine men and feminine women formed strong families and made for an orderly society. In recent decades, however, social-conflict theory has reinterpreted gender as a matter of* inequality. *From this point of view, U.S. society places men in a position of dominance over women.*

Parsons further argued that socialization teaches the two sexes appropriate gender identity and skills needed for adult life. Thus, society teaches boys—presumably destined for the labor force—to be rational, competitive, and self-assured. This complex of traits Parsons called *instrumental.* To prepare girls for child rearing, their socialization stresses what Parsons called *expressive* qualities, such as emotional responsiveness and sensitivity to others.

Society promotes gender conformity, Parsons explained, by instilling in men and women a fear that straying too far from accepted standards courts rejection by the opposite sex. In simple terms, women learn to view nonmasculine men as sexually unattractive, and men learn to shun unfeminine women.

Critical evaluation. Structural functionalism puts forward a theory of complementarity by which gender integrates society both structurally (in terms of what people do) and morally (in terms of what they believe). Influential at midcentury, this approach has lost much of its standing today.

For one thing, functionalism assumes a singular vision of society that is not shared by everyone. For example, many women have always worked outside the home because of economic necessity, a fact not reflected in Parsons's conventional, middle-class view of family life. Second, Parsons's analysis ignores the personal strains and social costs of rigid, traditional gender roles (Giele, 1988). Third, for those who seek sexual equality, what Parsons describes as gender "complementarity" amounts to little more than women submitting to male domination.

SOCIAL-CONFLICT ANALYSIS

From a social-conflict point of view, gender involves differences not just in behavior but in power. Consider the striking parallel between the way ideas about gender have benefited men and the way oppression of racial and ethnic minorities has benefited whites (Hacker, 1951, 1974; Collins, 1971; Lengermann & Wallace, 1985). That is, conventional ideas about gender promote not cohesion but division and tension, with men seeking to protect their privileges as women challenge the status quo.

As earlier chapters explain, the social-conflict paradigm draws heavily on the ideas of Karl Marx. Yet Marx was a product of his time insofar as his writings focused almost exclusively on men. However, his friend and collaborator Friedrich Engels did develop a theory of gender stratification (1902; orig. 1884).

longer the main energy source, the physical strength of men becomes less significant. In addition, the ability to control reproduction gives women greater choice in shaping their lives. Modern societies have come to see that traditional gender roles waste an enormous amount of human talent, yet change comes slowly because gender is deeply embedded in culture.

Talcott Parsons: Gender and Complementarity

As Talcott Parsons (1942, 1951, 1954) observed, gender helps to integrate society, at least in its traditional form. Gender forms a *complementary* set of roles that links men and women into family units for carrying out various important tasks. Women take primary responsibility for managing the household and raising children. Men connect the family to the larger world as they participate in the labor force.

Q: "Differences of age and sex no longer have distinctive social validity for the working class. All are instruments of labor, more or less expensive to use, according to their age and sex." Karl Marx and Friedrich Engels

Q: "Anyone who knows anything about history knows that great social changes are impossible without the feminine ferment." Karl Marx

Q: "Conventionality is not morality." Charlotte Brontë

Friedrich Engels: Gender and Class

Looking back through history, Engels noted that in hunting and gathering societies, the activities of women and men, though different, had the same importance. A successful hunt brought men great prestige, but the vegetation gathered by women provided most of a group's food supply. As technological advances led to a productive surplus, however, social equality and communal sharing gave way to private property and, ultimately, a class hierarchy. At this time, men gained pronounced power over women. With surplus wealth to pass on to heirs, upper-class men wanted to be sure of paternity, which led them to control the sexuality of women. In other words, the desire to control property led to the creation of monogamous marriage and the family. Women were then taught to remain virgins until marriage, to stay faithful to their husbands thereafter, and to build their lives around bearing and raising one man's children.

Furthermore, said Engels, capitalism intensifies this male domination. First, capitalism creates more wealth, which confers greater power on men as owners of property and primary wage earners. Second, an expanding capitalist economy depends on turning people—especially women—into consumers who seek personal fulfillment by buying and using products. Third, to free men to work in factories, society assigns women the task of maintaining the home. The double exploitation of capitalism, as Engels saw it, lies in paying low wages for male labor and no wages for female work (Eisenstein, 1979; Barry, 1983; Jagger, 1983; Vogel, 1983).

Critical evaluation. Social-conflict analysis highlights how society places the two sexes in unequal positions of wealth, power, and privilege. It is decidedly critical of conventional ideas about gender, claiming that society would be better off if we minimized or even eliminated this dimension of social structure.

But social-conflict analysis has its critics. One problem is that this approach sees conventional families—defended by traditionalists as morally positive—as a social evil. Second, from a more practical point of view, social-conflict analysis minimizes the extent to which women and men live together cooperatively, and often happily, in families. A third problem lies in the assertion that capitalism is the basis of gender stratification. In fact, agrarian countries typically are more patriarchal than industrial-capitalist societies, and socialist nations—including the People's Republic of China and Cuba—are more patriarchal than the United States (Moore, 1992; Rosendahl, 1997).

Q: "The early socialists often argued that problems associated with gender stratification would simply disappear under socialism. The leadership in socialist countries still gives lip service to the ideal of gender equality and includes it among its long-term goals." Charlotte G. O'Kelly and Larry S. Carney

Q: "Law may prescribe that the male nipple may be equal to the female one, but they will still not give milk." Allan Bloom

FEMINISM

Feminism is *the advocacy of social equality for men and women, in opposition to patriarchy and sexism.* The first wave of the feminist movement in the United States began in the 1840s as women opposed to slavery, including Elizabeth Cady Stanton and Lucretia Mott, drew parallels between the oppression of African Americans and the oppression of women. The Seneca Falls convention, described in the chapter opening, began the social movement by which women finally won the right to vote in 1920. But other disadvantages persisted, and a second wave of feminism arose in the 1960s and continues today.

BASIC FEMINIST IDEAS

Feminism views the personal experiences of women and men through the lens of gender. How we think of ourselves (gender identity), how we act (gender roles), and our sex's social standing (gender stratification) are all rooted in the operation of our society.

Although people who consider themselves feminists disagree on many issues, most support five general principles:

1. **The importance of change.** Feminist thinking is decidedly political, linking ideas to action. Feminism is critical of the status quo and advocates change toward social equality for women and men.

2. **Expanding human choice.** Feminists maintain that cultural conceptions of gender divide the full range of human qualities into two opposing and limited spheres: the female world of emotions and cooperation and the male world of rationality and competition. As an alternative, feminists propose a "reintegration of humanity" by which each person develops *all* human traits (French, 1985).

3. **Eliminating gender stratification.** Feminism opposes laws and cultural norms that limit the education, income, and job opportunities of women. For this reason, feminists advocate passage of the Equal Rights Amendment (ERA) to the U.S. Constitution, which states, "Equality of rights under the law shall not be denied or abridged by the United States or any State on account of sex." The ERA, first proposed in Congress in 1923, has the support of two-thirds of U.S. adults (NORC, 2001:267). Even so, it has yet to become law, which probably reflects the

These three women made enormous contributions to the women's movement during the twentieth century. Margaret Higgins Sanger (1883–1966) was a pioneer activist in the crusade for women's reproductive rights. Margaret Mead (1901–1978), probably the best known anthropologist of all time, showed how definitions of femininity and masculinity are rooted in culture rather than biology. In 1949, Simone De Beauvoir (1908–1986) published The Second Sex, *one of the first books to explore systematically the importance of gender to social life.*

fact that most of the men who dominate state legislatures oppose the amendment.

4. **Ending sexual violence.** Today's women's movement seeks to eliminate sexual violence. Feminists argue that patriarchy distorts the relationships between women and men, encouraging violence against women in the form of rape, domestic abuse, sexual harassment, and pornography (Millet, 1970; Bernard, 1982, orig. 1973; Dworkin, 1987).

5. **Promoting sexual freedom.** Finally, feminism supports women's control over their sexuality and reproduction. Feminists support the free availability of birth control information. As Figure 13–4 shows, contraceptives are much less available in most of the world than they are in the United States. Most feminists also support a woman's right to choose whether to bear a child or terminate a pregnancy, rather than allowing men—as husbands, physicians, and legislators—to control their reproduction. Finally, many feminists also support homosexuals' efforts to overcome the many barriers they face in a predominantly heterosexual culture (Deckard, 1979; Barry, 1983; Jagger, 1983).

TYPES OF FEMINISM

Although feminists agree on the importance of gender equality, they disagree on how to achieve it: through liberal feminism, socialist feminism, or radical feminism (Barry, 1983; Jagger, 1983; Stacey, 1983; Vogel, 1983).

Liberal Feminism

Liberal feminism is based on classic liberal thinking that individuals should be free to develop their own talents and pursue their own interests. Liberal feminists accept the basic organization of our society but seek to expand the rights and opportunities of women, in part by passing the Equal Rights Amendment.

Liberal feminists also endorse reproductive freedom for all women. They respect the family as a social institution but seek changes, including more widely available maternity leave and child care for mothers who want to work.

Given their belief in the rights of individuals, liberal feminists do not think that all women need to work together collectively. Both women and men, through their individual achievement, are capable of improving their lives as long as society removes legal and cultural barriers.

NOTE: Socialist feminists also oppose the family because living in isolated units discourages the solidarity that leads to collective action by women and men.

NOTE: Radical feminism dovetails with the "children's rights" movement that aspires to free children from dependence on adults.

Q: "To consider such traits as aggressiveness or passivity to be sex-linked is not possible in light of the facts." Margaret Mead

SOCIAL SURVEY: "How important is the women's rights issue to you?" (GSS 1996, N = 1,460; Codebook, 2001:230)
"One of the most important" 11.2%   "Not important at all" 9.9%
"Important"   52.1%   DK/NR   1.8%
"Not very important"   25.1%
NOTE: In general, support for feminism is stronger on both coasts than in the Midwest and the South.

Socialist Feminism

Socialist feminism evolved from the ideas of Karl Marx and Friedrich Engels, in part as a critical response to Marx's inattention to gender (Philipson & Hansen, 1992). From this point of view, capitalism increases patriarchy by concentrating wealth and power in the hands of a small number of men.

Socialist feminists do not think the reforms sought by liberal feminism go far enough. They argue that the bourgeois family fostered by capitalism amounts to domestic slavery and should be replaced by some collective means of carrying out housework and child care. Moreover, replacing the traditional family can come about only through a socialist revolution that creates a state-centered economy to meet the needs of all. Such a basic transformation of society requires that women and men pursue their personal liberation not individually, as liberal feminists propose, but collectively.

Radical Feminism

Radical feminism, too, finds liberal feminism inadequate. Moreover, radical feminists claim that even a socialist revolution would not end patriarchy. Instead, to attain equality, society must eliminate gender itself.

One way to achieve this goal is to use new reproductive technology (see Chapter 18, "Family") to separate women's bodies from the process of childbearing. With an end to motherhood, radical feminists reason, society could leave behind the entire family system, liberating women, men, and children from the tyranny of family, gender, and sex itself (Dworkin, 1987). Thus, radical feminism envisions an egalitarian and gender-free society, a revolution more radical than that sought by Marx.

OPPOSITION TO FEMINISM

Feminism provokes criticism and resistance from both men and women who hold conventional ideas about gender. Some men oppose sexual equality for the same reasons that many white people have historically opposed social equality for people of color: They want to preserve their own privileges. Other men and women, including those who are neither rich nor powerful, distrust a social movement (especially its more radical expressions) that attacks the traditional family and rejects centuries-old patterns of male-female relationships.

For some men, feminism threatens the basis of their status and self-respect: their masculinity. Men who have been socialized to value strength and dominance feel uneasy about feminist ideas of men as gentle

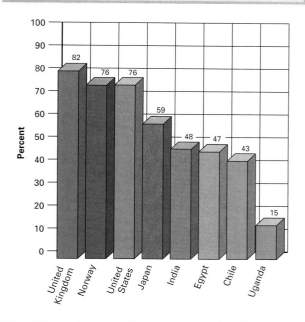

GLOBAL SNAPSHOT

FIGURE 13–4 Use of Contraception by Women of Childbearing Age

Source: United Nations Development Programme (2001).

and warm (Doyle, 1983). Similarly, many women whose lives center on their husbands and children think feminism disparages the social roles that give meaning to their lives (Marshall, 1985).

Race and ethnicity play some part in shaping people's attitudes toward feminism. In general, African Americans (especially African American women) express the greatest support of feminist goals, followed by whites, with Hispanic Americans holding somewhat more traditional attitudes when it comes to gender (Kane, 2000).

Most sociologists support feminism, but some charge that feminism willfully ignores a growing body of evidence that men and women think and act in somewhat different ways, which would make gender equality impossible. Furthermore, say critics, with its drive to enhance women's presence in the workplace, feminism belittles the crucial and unique contribution women make to the development of children, especially in the first years of life (Baydar & Brooks-Gunn, 1991; Popenoe, 1993b; Gibbs, 2001).

Q: "A woman's brain evolves emotion rather than intellect; and whilst this feature fits her admirably as a creature burdened with the preservation and happiness of the human species, it painfully disqualifies her for the sterner duties to be performed by the intellectual facilities. The best wife and mother and sister would make the worst legislator, judge, and police officer." 19th-century politician opposed to women's suffrage

DISCUSS: Is the "rational-emotional" distinction inherently hierarchical? We might tell someone to "control your emotions!" but never "control your intellect!" Rationality tends to be allied with males and dominance.
NOTE: In 1992, Congress passed the Family Leave Act, by which the U.S. joined more than 100 nations in guaranteeing maternity leave (but not pay) for all working women.

As a general rule, patriarchy is strongest in nations with traditional cultures and less economic development. Here we see a husband dragging his wife through the streets of Dhaka, Bangladesh, reportedly because she did not do the cooking on time. But while violence against women in the United States may not be so public, it remains a serious problem linked to women's subordination here as well.

Finally, there is the question of *how* women should go about improving their social standing. A large majority of U.S. adults believe women should have equal rights, but 70 percent also say that women should advance individually, according to their abilities; only 10 percent favor women's rights groups or collective action (NORC, 2001:364).

In sum, opposition to feminism is directed primarily at its socialist and radical forms, whereas support for liberal feminism is widespread. Moreover, we are seeing an unmistakable trend toward greater gender equality. In 1977, 65 percent of all adults endorsed the statement "It is much better for everyone involved if the man is the achiever outside the home and the woman takes care of the home and family." By 2001, however, support for this statement had dropped sharply, to 39 percent (NORC, 2001:266).

LOOKING AHEAD: GENDER IN THE TWENTY-FIRST CENTURY

At best, predictions about the future are informed speculation. So just as economists disagree about what the inflation rate will be a year from now, sociologists can offer only general observations about the likely future state of gender and society.

To begin, change so far has been remarkable. A century and a half ago, women occupied a position of striking subordination. Husbands controlled property in marriage, and laws barred women from most jobs, from holding office, and from voting. Although women today remain socially disadvantaged, the movement toward equality has surged ahead. Two-thirds of people entering the work force during the 1990s were women, and the economy of the new century depends on the earnings of women.

Many factors have contributed to this transformation. Perhaps most important, industrialization has both broadened the range of human activity and shifted the nature of work from physically demanding tasks that favored male strength to jobs that require thought and imagination. In this respect, women and men are on an even footing. Additionally, because we have greater control over reproduction, women's lives are less constrained by unwanted pregnancies.

Many women and men have also deliberately pursued social equality. For example, sexual harassment complaints now are taken much more seriously in the workplace. Furthermore, as more women assume positions of power in the corporate and political worlds, social changes in the new century may be as great as those we have already witnessed.

Gender is an important part of personal identity and family life, and it is deeply woven into the moral fabric of our society. Therefore, efforts to change social patterns involving gender will continue to provoke opposition, as the final box illustrates. On balance, although changes may be incremental, we are seeing movement toward a society in which women and men enjoy equal rights and opportunities.

NOTE: Of all people arrested for drunk driving, 84% are men.
NOTE: Another dimension of male disadvantage is education. Boys are more likely to drop out, be kicked out, or flunk out of school than girls; they are less likely to enter college, receive lower grades, and are several times more likely to be diagnosed with a learning disability (cf. Kleinfeld, 1999).

Q: "For a guy to walk into a bar and have every woman there be ready to jump into bed with him, he would have to be the world's richest, best looking, and bravest guy. For a woman to get the same response from men, she only has to do her hair." Bill Maher, *Politically Incorrect*
Q: "We can no longer go to war without women." U.S. Secretary of State Colin Powell

CONTROVERSY & DEBATE

Counterpoint: Are Males Really So Privileged?

Anti-male discrimination has become far greater in scope, in degree, and in damage than any which may exist against women.
Men's rights advocate Richard F. Doyle

It is men, this chapter argues, who dominate society. Men enjoy higher earnings, control more wealth, exercise more power, do less housework, and get more respect than women. But Doyle's assertion is an important counterpoint advanced by the "men's rights movement"—that the male world is not nearly as privileged as some people think.

If men are so privileged in our society, why do they turn to crime more often than women? Moreover, the criminal justice system does not give men any special privileges. Few people are surprised to learn that many police are reluctant to arrest a woman, especially if she has children. This fact helps explain why 78 percent of arrests for serious crime put the handcuffs on a man. Nor do men get a break from the courts: They make up 93 percent of the U.S. prison population. And even though women can and do kill, all but 2 of the roughly 400 offenders executed during the last several decades have been men.

Culture is not always generous to men, either. "Real men" work and play hard; they typically drink and smoke and speed on the highways. Given this view of maleness, is it any wonder that men are twice

as likely as women to suffer serious assault, three times more likely to fall victim to homicide, and four times more likely to commit suicide? In light of such statistics, how do we explain our national preoccupation with violence against women? Perhaps, critics suggest, we are in the grip of a cultural double standard: We accept harm that comes to males while showing sympathy in the far fewer cases in which violence victimizes women. It is this same double standard, the argument continues, that moves women and children out of harm's way and expects men to "go down with the ship" or die defending their country on the battlefield.

In school, it is boys more than girls who flunk out, drop out, or are kicked out. Boys are also several times more likely than girls to be diagnosed with a learning disability. Boys are less likely than girls to go to college, and those who do earn lower grades.

Child custody is another sore point from the perspective of many men. Despite decades of consciousness-raising for gender fairness and clear evidence that men earn more than women, courts across the United States routinely award primary care of children to mothers. And, to make matters worse, men separated from their children by the courts often are stigmatized as "runaway fathers" or "deadbeat dads," even though government studies show that women are more likely to refuse to pay

court-ordered child support (45 percent of cases) than men (31 percent of cases).

Finally, male advocates point out that affirmative action laws now cover three-fourths of the population but notably exclude white males. Therefore, in today's affirmative action climate, women have the inside track to college (where they now outnumber men) and the work force (where businesses know they will be called to account for hiring practices).

Even nature seems to plot against men, as, on average, women live five years longer. The controversial question is this: When society plays favorites, who is favored?

Continue the debate . . .

1. *Do you think the criminal justice system favors women over men? Or do men simply get what they deserve? Why, in your opinion, are so many more men than women in prison?*

2. *On your campus, do men's organizations (such as fraternities and athletic teams) enjoy special privileges? What about women's organizations and teams?*

3. *On balance, do you agree or disagree with the "men's rights" perspective? Which specific points do you find convincing or wrong-headed? Why?*

Sources: Based on Doyle (1980), Scanlon (1992), Rosenfeld (1998), and Kleinfeld (1999).

SUMMARY

1. Gender refers to the meaning a culture attaches to being female or male. Because society gives men more power and other resources than women, gender is an important dimension of social stratification.

2. Although some degree of patriarchy exists everywhere, gender varies historically and across cultures.

3. Through the socialization process, people incorporate gender into their personalities (gender identity)

EXERCISE: An enlightening independent research project might focus on the U.S. "dream home." Surveys show that women are more likely than men to desire a "state-of-the-art kitchen" and "walk-in closets," both sexes agree on "in-ground pool," men ask for "game/billiard room," "workshop," and "high-tech entertainment center" (see Mogelonsky, 1997).

CTQ1: Sex is a biological issue; gender is a societal issue. Most sociologists treat the two dimensions as unrelated so that gender (and even how we express our sexuality) is a cultural issue.

CTQ2: Much advertising idealizes women in terms of beauty and men in terms of power and control; in other words, society puts forward proper kinds of consumption as the path to pursue cultural ideals for femininity and masculinity as well as attractiveness to members of the other sex.

and their actions (gender roles). The major agents of socialization—family, peer groups, schools, and the mass media—reinforce cultural definitions of what is feminine and masculine.

4. Gender stratification shapes the workplace. Although a majority of women are now in the paid labor force, most hold clerical or service jobs. Unpaid housework remains a task performed mostly by women, whether or not they hold jobs outside the home.

5. On average, women earn 73 percent as much as men. This disparity stems from differences in jobs and family responsibilities and from discrimination.

6. Women now earn a slight majority of all bachelor's and master's degrees. Men still receive a majority of all doctorates and professional degrees.

7. The number of women in politics has increased sharply in recent decades. Still, most elected officials, especially at the national level, are men. Moreover, women make up only 15 percent of U.S. military personnel.

8. Because women have a distinctive social identity and are disadvantaged, they are a minority, although most white women do not think of themselves that way. Minority women encounter greater social disadvantages than white women. Overall, minority women earn only about 55 percent as much as white men.

9. Violence against women is a widespread problem in the United States. Our society is also grappling with the issues of sexual harassment and pornography.

10. Structural-functional analysis suggests that in preindustrial societies distinctive roles for males and females reflect biological differences between the sexes. In industrial societies, marked gender inequality becomes dysfunctional and gradually decreases. Talcott Parsons claimed that complementary gender roles promote the social integration of families and society as a whole.

11. Social-conflict analysis views gender as a dimension of social inequality and conflict. Friedrich Engels tied gender stratification to the development of private property.

12. Feminism endorses the social equality of the sexes and opposes patriarchy and sexism. Feminism also seeks to eliminate violence against women and give women control over their reproduction.

13. There are three variants of feminist thinking: Liberal feminism seeks equal opportunity for both sexes within current social arrangements, socialist feminism advocates abolishing private property as the means to social equality, and radical feminism seeks to create a gender-free society.

14. Although two-thirds of adults in the United States support the Equal Rights Amendment, this legislation, first proposed in Congress in 1923, has yet to become part of the U.S. Constitution.

KEY CONCEPTS

gender (p. 325) the personal traits and social positions that members of a society attach to being female and male

gender stratification (p. 325) the unequal distribution of wealth, power, and privilege between men and women

patriarchy (p. 328) a form of social organization in which males dominate females

matriarchy (p. 328) a form of social organization in which females dominate males

sexism (p. 328) the belief that one sex is innately superior to the other

gender roles (sex roles) (p. 330) attitudes and activities that a society links to each sex

minority (p. 339) any category of people, distinguished by physical or cultural difference, that a society sets apart and subordinates

sexual harassment (p. 340) comments, gestures, or physical contact of a sexual nature that are deliberate, repeated, and unwelcome

feminism (p. 345) the advocacy of social equality for men and women, in opposition to patriarchy and sexism

CRITICAL-THINKING QUESTIONS

1. In what ways are sex and gender related? In what respects are they distinct?

2. What techniques do the mass media use to sell conventional ideas about gender to women and men?

CTQ3: Gender involves not just difference but hierarchy. Sociology's recent emphasis on the "intersections" of class, gender, race, and ethnicity shows these to be cumulative dimensions of privilege or disadvantage.

CTQ4: See the review of types of feminism at the end of the chapter. These three are rough categorizations; new feminist thinking is always mixing and extending these positions in novel ways.

CTQ5: Generally, the U.S. public has been critical of "quotas" because of our cultural ideal that people should earn their positions through talent and effort. At the same time, our ideas about gender also equate masculinity with power and competence, which helps explain why men continue to dominate national politics. Note, however, that women's role in national politics is increasing.

3. Why is gender a dimension of social stratification? How does gender intersect other dimensions of inequality based on class, race, and ethnicity?

4. What are the key assertions of feminism? How do liberal, socialist, and radical feminism differ from one another?

5. A number of European nations, including Great Britain, Norway, Denmark, and Finland, require that at least 25 percent of candidates for national offices be women. Because just 14 percent of people in the U.S. Congress are women, should the United States do likewise?

APPLICATIONS AND EXERCISES

1. Take a walk through a business area of your local community. Which businesses are frequented almost entirely by women? By men? By both men and women? Try to explain the patterns you find.

2. Watch several hours of children's television programming on a Saturday morning. Notice the advertising, which mostly sells toys and breakfast cereal. Keep track of what share of toys are "gendered," that is, aimed at one sex or the other. What traits are associated with toys intended for boys and those intended for girls?

3. Do some research on the history of women's issues in your state. When was the first woman sent to Congress? What laws once existed that restricted the work women could do? Are there any such laws today? Did your state support the passage of the Equal Rights Amendment? What percentage of political officials today is women?

4. Packaged in the back of this new textbook is an interactive CD-ROM that offers a variety of study and review materials intended to help you better understand the material covered in this chapter. For this chapter, the CD-ROM contains an author's tip video, Real Life Sociology videos, other relevant audio and video, interactive map animations, audio journal entries from the author, Web links, and much more.

 SITES TO SEE

http://www.prenhall.com/macionis

Visit the interactive *Companion Website*™ that accompanies this text. Begin by clicking on the cover of your book. You will find a chapter-by-chapter study guide, practice tests, and a significant portion of the text for on-line review, as well as many suggested Web links.

http://www.now.org

Visit the Web site for the National Organization of Women to discover the goals and strategies of this organization.

http://www.iwpr.org

Another informative site is run by the Institute for Women's Policy Research. Identify the issues this organization finds most important. Would you characterize this site as feminist? Why or why not?

http://www.wwwomen.com/

This site provides a search engine to locate all sorts of information concerning women.

http://www.educationindex.com/women/

This site provides numerous and widely varied links to sites concerned with women's issues.

http://www.feminist.org

The Feminist Majority Foundation Online offers information about feminist issues and the feminist movement.

http://www.ncjrs.org/pdffiles1/nij/182369.pdf

A report from the U.S. Department of Justice about sexual violence on the college campus can be found at this Web site.

 INVESTIGATE WITH CONTENTSELECT

Follow the instructions found on page 23 of this textbook to enter this chapter of the book's *Companion Website*™. Once in the chapter, click on the ContentSelect icon at the bottom left of your screen and enter your personal User ID and Password. Enter keywords such "gender," "feminism," and "sexual harassment," and the search engine will help you become an effective researcher.

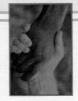

CHAPTER

14

Paul Marcus
Dreaming of Fred and Ginger

© Paul Marcus. Oil painting on wood, 24 × 28 in.
Studio SPM, Inc.

RACE
AND ETHNICITY

On a bright fall day almost fifty years ago, in the city of Topeka, Kansas, a minister and his nine-year-old daughter walked hand in hand to the public elementary school four blocks from their home. But school officials refused to enroll Linda Brown. Instead, they said that she must attend another school two miles away, which meant a daily six-block walk to a bus stop where she sometimes waited half an hour for the bus. In bad weather, the child could be soaking wet by the time the bus came; one day she was so cold at the bus stop that she walked back home. Why, she asked her parents, could she not attend the school that was so close to home?

The answer, difficult for loving parents to give their daughter, was Linda Brown's introduction to a harsh fact: Skin color made her a second-class citizen in the United States. The injustice of separate schools for black and white children led the Browns and others to file a lawsuit on behalf of Linda Brown and other children, and, in 1954, Linda's question was put to the Supreme Court of the United States. In *Brown v. the Board of Education of Topeka*, the Supreme Court ruled unanimously that racially segregated

schools provide African Americans with inferior schooling, thus striking down the practice, dating back to 1896, of "separate but equal" education for the two races.

Many people greeted the Supreme Court's decision as a major turning point in U.S. education. Yet as the twenty-first century begins, most children in the United States still attend racially imbalanced schools. Although our society is officially committed to the principle that all people are created equal, it is a fact that race and ethnicity continue to guide the lives of men, women, and children in all sorts of ways.

The pattern of inequality and conflict based on color and culture is even more pronounced in other parts of the world. Since the fall of the former Soviet Union in the early 1990s, Ukrainians, Moldavians, Azerbaijanis, and a host of other ethnic peoples in Eastern Europe have been struggling to recover their cultural identity. In the Middle East, Arabs and Jews are trying to overcome deep-rooted tensions, as are Protestants and Catholics in Northern Ireland. In dozens of the world's nations, color and culture often flare in violent confrontation.

The range of biological variation in human beings is far greater than any system of racial classification allows. This fact is made obvious by trying to place all of the people pictured here into simple racial categories.

An irony of the human condition is that color and culture—sources of great pride—also cause people to degrade themselves with hatred and violence. This chapter examines the meaning of race and ethnicity, explains how these social constructs have shaped our history, and suggests why they continue to play such a central part, for better or worse, in the world today.

THE SOCIAL MEANING OF RACE AND ETHNICITY

People often confuse race and ethnicity. For this reason, we begin by defining these terms.

RACE

A **race** is *a socially constructed category composed of people who share biologically transmitted traits that members of a society consider important.* People may classify each other racially based on physical characteristics such as skin color, facial features, hair texture, and body shape.

Physical diversity appeared among our human ancestors as the result of living in different geographic regions of the world. In regions of intense heat, for example, humans developed darker skin (from the natural pigment melanin) as protection from the sun; in regions with moderate climates, people have lighter skin. Such differences are literally only skin deep because all human beings the world over are members of a single biological species.

The variety of physical traits found today is also the product of migration, in that genetic characteristics once common to a single place are now found in many lands. Especially distinctive is the racial mix found in the Middle East (that is, western Asia), historically a crossroads of human migration. Greater racial uniformity, by contrast, characterizes more isolated people, such as the island-dwelling Japanese. But every population has some genetic mixture, and increasing contact among the world's people ensures even more racial blending in the future.

Although racial categories point to some biological elements, race is a socially constructed concept.

GLOBAL: People the world over differ not only in skin color but in height. The Masai of eastern Africa are tall and thin (which helps to dissipate heat in that equatorial climate); the Eskimos and Aleuts of North America, by contrast, are short and stout, which serves to protect them in a far colder habitat.

Q: "Race is not biologically definable; we are far too similar." Kenneth Kidd (Yale University geneticist)

DIVERSITY: Worth stressing is that race and ethnicity are categories that interact with class and gender.

DISCUSS: Does "American" represent an ethnic identity?

DIVERSITY: Underlying the trend favoring interracial marriages is the rising affluence of African Americans: 1 of 3 black families earns more than $50,000 annually, compared to 1 in 17 who earned a comparable amount in 1970.

This means that racial categories come into being only because a society considers some physical traits important. Around the world, societies show wide variation in this regard: Typically, people in the United States attach more meaning to skin color than, say, people in Brazil. In addition, definitions and meanings concerning race change over time. For example, about 1900, many people in the United States viewed people of Irish and Italian ancestry as racially different, but this practice was far less common by about 1950 (Loveman, 1999). Today, the Census Bureau allows people to describe themselves using more than one racial category (a total of sixty-three racial options), thus recognizing a wide range of multiracial people (Porter, 2001).

Racial Types

Race came into being as a social category when nineteenth-century biologists tried to organize the world's physical diversity by constructing three racial types. They defined people with light skin and fine hair *Caucasoid*, they called people with darker skin and coarse hair *Negroid*, and they labeled people with yellow or brown skin and distinctive folds on the eyelids *Mongoloid*.

Sociologists consider such terms misleading at best and harmful at worst. For one thing, no society contains biologically "pure" people. The skin color of people we might call "Caucasoid" (or "Indo-European," "Caucasian," or, more commonly, "white" people) ranges from very light (typical in Scandinavia) to very dark (in southern India). The same variation exists among so-called "Negroids" (Africans, or, more commonly, "black" people) and "Mongoloids" (that is, "Asians"). In fact, many "white" people (say, in southern India) have darker skin than many "black" people (such as the Negroid Aborigines of Australia). From another angle, on average, the three racial categories differ in about 6 percent of their genes—less than the genetic variation *within* each category (Gloash, 2000).

The population of the United States also is quite mixed. Over many generations and throughout the Americas, the genetic traits of Negroid Africans, Caucasoid Europeans, and Mongoloid Native Americans (whose ancestors came from Asia) have intermingled. Many "black" people therefore have a significant Caucasoid ancestry, and many "white" people have some Negroid genes. In short, whatever people may think, race is no black-and-white issue.

Why do people construct these racial categories in the first place? The reason is that such categories allow societies to rank people in a hierarchy, claiming that some are inherently "better" than others, although no sound scientific research supports such beliefs. But because so much is at stake, societies may construct racial categories in extreme ways. Throughout much of the twentieth century, for example, many southern states labeled as "colored" anyone with as little as one thirty-second African ancestry (that is, one African American great-great-great-grandparent). Today, the law allows parents to declare the race of a child as they wish. Even so, most members of our society are still very sensitive to people's racial background.

A Trend toward Mixture

The number of officially recorded interracial births has tripled in the last three decades to 159,000 annually, or about 5 percent of all births. Moreover, when completing their 2000 census forms, almost 7 million people described themselves by checking two or more racial categories. Although members of our society attach great social importance to race, biologically speaking, race has less and less meaning in the United States.

ETHNICITY

Ethnicity is *a shared cultural heritage*. People define themselves—or others—as members of an *ethnic category* based on having common ancestors, language, or religion that confers a distinctive social identity. The United States is a multiethnic society: Although most people speak the English language, some 45 million people speak Spanish, Italian, German, French, or some other tongue in their homes and local communities. Similarly, the United States is a predominantly Protestant nation, but most people of Spanish, Italian, and Polish descent are Roman Catholic, and many of Greek, Ukrainian, and Russian descent belong to the Eastern Orthodox church. More than 6 million Jewish Americans with ancestral ties to various nations share a religious history. Similarly, more than 7 million men and women are Muslim, which means that there are now more Muslims than Episcopalians in the United States (Blank, 1998).

Like the reality of race, the reality of ethnicity is socially constructed. On an individual level, people play up or play down cultural traits so that they fit in or stand apart from the surrounding society. More broadly, societies define some ethnic differences as important and others as not. For example, a century ago Catholics and Jews were considered "different" in the predominantly Protestant United States. This is

Q: "We may define a minority as a group of people who, because of their physical or cultural characteristics, are singled out from the others in the society in which they live for differential and unequal treatment and who therefore regard themselves as objects of collective discrimination." Louis Wirth

DISCUSS: Should homosexuals be counted as a minority? Why or why not?

DISCUSS: Do you think a sociologist has to be a member of a minority category to study that category? That is, do, say, Hispanics have a special claim to study Hispanics, women to study women, and so on? Explain your position.

APPLIED: Check the advertising in any popular magazine and note the share of ads that show people of two or more racial categories interacting. Do you think your results reflect social reality?

TABLE 14–1 Racial and Ethnic Categories in the United States, 2000

Racial or Ethnic Classification*	Approximate U.S. Population	Percentage of Total Population
Hispanic descent	**35,305,818**	**12.5%**
Mexican	20,640,711	7.3
Puerto Rican	3,406,178	1.2
Cuban	1,241,685	0.4
Other Hispanic	10,017,244	3.6
African descent	**34,658,190**	**12.3**
Native American descent	**2,475,956**	**0.9**
American Indian		
Eskimo		
Aleut		
Asian or Pacific Island descent	**10,641,833**	**3.7**
Chinese	2,432,585	0.9
Filipino	1,850,314	0.7
Asian Indian	1,678,765	0.6
Vietnamese	1,122,528	0.4
Korean	1,076,872	0.4
Japanese	796,700	0.3
Hawaiian	140,652	<
Samoan	91,029	<
Guamanian	58,240	<
Other Asian or Pacific Islander	1,394,148	0.5
Non-Hispanic European descent	**194,552,774**	**70.9**
German		
Irish		
English		
Italian		
French		
Polish		
Scottish		
Scots-Irish		
Dutch		
Norwegian		
Swedish		
Russian		
French Canadian		
West Indian		
Welsh		
Two or more races	**6,826,228**	**2.4**

*People of Hispanic descent may be of any race. Many people also identify with more than one ethnic category. Thus, figures total more than 100 percent.

< Indicates less than 1/10 of 1 percent.

Source: U.S. Census Bureau (2001).

not the case today. Similarly, U.S. society defines people of Spanish descent as "Latin," but not people of Italian descent, even though Italy probably has a more "Latin" culture than Spain. Instead, Italians generally are defined simply as "European" and thus less different (Camara, 2000; Brodkin, 2001).

Race and ethnicity, then, both come to be important because a society defines them as such. Even so, keep in mind that race involves highlighting biological traits, whereas ethnicity involves highlighting cultural traits. Of course, the two may go hand in hand. For example, Japanese Americans have distinctive physical traits and—for those who maintain a traditional way of life—a distinctive culture as well. Table 14–1 presents the broad sweep of racial and ethnic diversity in the United States, as recorded by the 2000 census.

People can modify their ethnicity fairly easily: Immigrants may discard their cultural traditions over time or, like many people of Native American descent in recent years, try to revive their heritage (Nagel, 1994; Spencer, 1994). However, if people mate with others like themselves, racial distinctiveness persists over generations.

Finally, ethnicity involves even more variability and mixture than race because most people identify with more than one ethnic background. For example, golf star Tiger Woods describes himself as one-eighth white, one-eighth American Indian, one-fourth black, one-fourth Thai, and one-fourth Chinese (White, 1997).

MINORITIES

As Chapter 13 ("Gender Stratification") described, a **minority** is *any category of people, distinguished by physical or cultural difference, that a society sets apart and subordinates*.

Both race and ethnicity are the basis for minority standing. As shown in Table 14–1, white people of non-Hispanic background (70 percent of the total) continue to predominate numerically. But the absolute numbers and share of population for virtually every minority are growing rapidly, so that minorities are a majority in three states and half of this country's 100 largest cities. Within a century, minorities, taken together, probably will form a majority of the entire U.S. population. National Map 14–1 shows where a minority-majority already exists.

Minorities have two major characteristics. First, they share a *distinctive identity*. Because societies attach importance to race, and these physical traits are almost impossible for a person to change, most minority men and women are keenly aware of their physical appearance. The significance of ethnicity (which people *can* change) is more variable. Throughout U.S. history, some people (such as Reform Jews) have downplayed their historic ethnicity, whereas others (including many Orthodox Jews) have maintained distinctive cultural traditions and even formed their own neighborhoods.

THE MAP: Minority-majority counties predominate in the South (where the proportion of African Americans historically has been high) and the Southwest (with immigration from Latin America and Asia). Between 1990 and 2000 in the U.S., the white, non-Hispanic population increased 3%; Asians and Pacific Islanders were up 41%; Hispanics, 58%; Native Americans, Eskimos, and Aleuts, 19%; African Americans, 16%. Over half the growth was in California, Florida, and Texas.

DIVERSITY: Among people over 35 years of age, one-fifth are racial or Hispanic minorities; among those under 35, one-third are. Thus, young people will reach a minority-majority first (before 2050), and older people will remain mostly white. Similarly, during the 21st century, central cities will become minority-majority settings while suburbs will remain mostly white.

SEEING OURSELVES

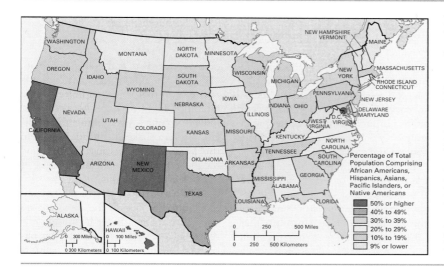

NATIONAL MAP 14–1
Where the Minority-Majority Already Exists

By 2000, minorities had become a majority in three states—Hawaii, California, and New Mexico—as well as the District of Columbia. With a 45 percent minority population, Texas is approaching a minority-majority. At the other extreme, Vermont and Maine have the lowest share of racial and ethnic minorities (about 2 percent). Why are states with high minority populations in the South and Southwest?

Source: "America 2000: A Map of the Mix," *Newsweek*, September 18, 2000, p. 48. Copyright ©2000 Newsweek, Inc. All rights reserved. Reprinted by permission.

Percentage of Total Population Comprising African Americans, Hispanics, Asians, Pacific Islanders, or Native Americans

- 50% or higher
- 40% to 49%
- 30% to 39%
- 20% to 29%
- 10% to 19%
- 9% or lower

March 3, Dallas, Texas. Sitting in the lobby of just about any major hotel presents a lesson in contrasts: The majority of the guests checking in and out are white; the majority of the employees who carry luggage, serve the food, and clean the rooms are people of color.

A second characteristic of minorities is *subordination*. As the remainder of this chapter shows, minorities typically have lower income, lower occupational prestige, and limited schooling. These facts mean that class, race, and ethnicity, as well as gender, are intersecting and reinforcing dimensions of social stratification. The box on page 358 profiles the struggles of Latin Americans who are recent immigrants to the United States.

Of course, not all members of any minority category are disadvantaged. For example, some Latinos are very wealthy, certain Chinese Americans are celebrated business leaders, and African Americans are included among our nation's leading scholars. But even the greatest success rarely allows individuals to escape their minority standing (Benjamin, 1991). That is, race or ethnicity often serves as a *master status* (described in Chapter 6, "Social Interaction in Everyday Life") that overshadows personal accomplishments.

The term "minority" suggests that these categories of people constitute a small proportion of a society's population. But not always. For example, black South Africans are disadvantaged even though they are a numerical majority in their country. In the United States, women are slightly more than half the population but are still struggling for the opportunities and privileges enjoyed by men.

PREJUDICE

November 19, Jerusalem, Israel. We are driving along the outskirts of this historic city—a holy place to Jews, Christians, and Muslims—when Razi, our taxi driver, spots a small group of fellasha—Ethiopian Jews—on a streetcorner. "Those people," he begins, "may be Jews like me, but they are different. They don't drive cars. They don't want to improve themselves. Even when our country offers them schooling, they don't take it." He shakes his head and pronounces the Ethiopians "socially incorrigible."

Prejudice is *a rigid and irrational generalization about an entire category of people.* Prejudice is irrational insofar as people hold inflexible attitudes supported by little or no direct evidence. Furthermore, prejudice

DIVERSITY: Asian Americans are increasing in number primarily due to immigration, Latinos because of both immigration and natural increase, and African Americans mainly due to natural increase.
SOCIAL SURVEY: "What if a person refuses to work with people of different racial or ethnic background: Is this person a bad citizen, or not?" Of U.S. born, 72% say "bad citizen"; of foreign born, 77% say the same (Public Agenda, 1998).

NOTE: A century ago, people believed that race (and biology, in general) directly affected human behavior; early anthropology and sociology were central in dispelling this view.
DISCUSS: Consider how stereotypes figure in the following expressions: "Dutch treat," "French kiss," "Russian roulette," or "gypping" someone (derived from "Gypsy"). What traits make up stereotypes concerning the Irish? the Italians? the English?

DIVERSITY: RACE, CLASS, AND GENDER

Hard Work: The Immigrant Life in the United States

Early in the morning, it is already hot in Houston as a line of pickup trucks snakes slowly into a dusty yard where 200 laborers have been gathering since dawn, hoping for a day's work. The driver of the first truck opens his window and tells the foreman that he is looking for a crew to spread boiling tar on a roof. The foreman turns to the crowd and, after a few minutes, three workers step forward and climb into the back of the truck. The next driver is looking for two experienced house painters. The scene is repeated over and over, as men and a few women leave to dig ditches, spread cement, hang drywall, open clogged septic tanks, or crawl under houses to poison rats.

To each driver who enters, Abdonel Cespedes, the foreman, asks "How much?" Most of the people in the trucks offer five dollars an hour. Cespedes automatically responds, "Six-fifty; the going rate is $6.50 for an hour's hard work." Sometimes he convinces people to pay that much, but usually not. The workers, who come from Mexico, El Salvador, and Guatemala, know that dozens of them will end up with no work at all this day. Most jump at the offer of five dollars an hour because they know that when the long day is over, they will have fifty dollars.

Labor markets such as this one are common in large cities, especially across the southwestern United States. The surge in immigration in recent years has brought millions of people in search of work, and most have little schooling and speak little English.

Manuel Barrera has taken a day's work moving the contents of a store that has closed to a storage site. He arrives at the boarded-up store and gazes at the mountains of heavy furniture that he must carry out to a moving van,

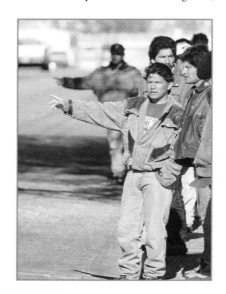

drive across town, and then carry again. He sighs when he realizes how hot it is outside and that it is even hotter in the building. He will have no break for lunch. No one says anything about toilets. Barrera shakes his head, "I will do this kind of work because it puts food on the table. But I did not foresee it would turn out like this."

The hard truth is that immigrants to the United States do the jobs that no one else wants. Indeed, immigrants represent the bottom level of the national economy, working in restaurants and hotels, on construction crews, and in private homes cooking, cleaning, and caring for children. Many well-off families take the labor of immigrants as much for granted as their sport utility vehicles and cell phones. Few immigrants make much more than minimum wage ($5.15 per hour), and rarely do immigrant workers receive health or pension benefits. Across the United States, about half of all housekeepers, household cooks, tailors, and restaurant waiters are men or women born abroad. In sum, much low-paying service work is performed by immigrants who are, literally, "at your service."

Source: Based on Booth (1998).

leads people to characterize all members of an entire category, most of whom they have never even met. Prejudice may target people of a particular social class, sex, sexual orientation, age, political affiliation, physical disability, race, or ethnicity.

Prejudices are *prejudgments*, and they may be positive or negative. Our positive prejudices tend to exaggerate the virtues of people like us, and our negative

prejudices condemn those who differ from us. Because attitudes are rooted in culture, everyone has at least some measure of prejudice.

STEREOTYPES

Prejudice often takes the form of a **stereotype** (*stereo* is derived from Greek meaning "hard" or "solid"), *an*

DIVERSITY: Illustrating the power of race, Charles Dryden, one of the Tuskegee airmen—the U.S. Army Air Corps' first unit of African American combat pilots—recalled being forced to give up his seat and moved to Negro cars on trains so that white, German POWs could sit down, and being barred from military cafeterias where Italian POWs ate (Farley, 1995).

DIVERSITY: Through most of human history, people identified and responded to one another in terms of social categories. However, the individualistic culture of industrial societies has transformed such categorical responses into social problems. From a modern point of view, various "isms" (racism, ageism, sexism, etc.) all are problematic because they deny people their individuality and value as distinct persons.

exaggerated description applied to every person in some category. Many white people hold stereotypical views of minorities. But minorities, too, use stereotypes, sometimes of whites and sometimes of other minorities, including themselves. Some Koreans, for example, portray African Americans as dishonest. Some African Americans express the same attitude toward Jewish people (Smith, 1996; Cummings & Lambert, 1997).

RACISM

A powerful and destructive form of prejudice, **racism** is *the belief that one racial category is innately superior or inferior to another.* Racism pervades world history. The ancient Greeks, the peoples of India, and the Chinese—despite their many notable achievements—were all quick to consider people unlike themselves inferior.

Racism has also been widespread in the United States, where notions about racial inferiority supported slavery. Today, overt racism in this country has subsided because our more egalitarian culture urges us to evaluate people, in Dr. Martin Luther King's words, "not by the color of their skin but by the content of their character."

 Racism can give rise to hate crimes; for information on such crimes, go to http://www. civilrights.org/issues/hate

Even so, racism remains a serious problem everywhere, and people still contend that some racial and ethnic categories are "better" than others. As the box on pages 360–61 explains, however, racial differences in mental abilities result from environment rather than biology.

Racial and ethnic stereotypes are deeply embedded in our culture and language. Many people speak of someone "gypping" another without realizing that this word insults European Gypsies, a category of people long pushed to the margins of European societies. What about terms such as "Dutch treat," "French kiss," or "Indian giver"?

THEORIES OF PREJUDICE

What are the origins of prejudice? Social scientists have suggested various answers to this vexing question, focusing on frustration, personality, culture, and social conflict.

Scapegoat Theory

Scapegoat theory holds that prejudice springs from frustration among people who are themselves disadvantaged (Dollard, 1939). Take the case of a white woman frustrated by the low wages she earns working in a textile factory. Directing hostility at the powerful people who operate the factory carries obvious

risk; therefore, she may attribute her low pay to the presence of minority co-workers. Her prejudice does not improve her situation, but it serves as a safe way to vent anger, and it may give her the comforting feeling that at least she is superior to someone.

A **scapegoat**, then, is *a person or category of people, typically with little power, whom people unfairly blame for their own troubles.* Because they are usually "safe targets," minorities often are used as scapegoats.

Authoritarian Personality Theory

According to T. W. Adorno et al. (1950), extreme prejudice is a personality trait in certain individuals. This

CRITICAL THINKING

Does Race Affect Intelligence?

Are Asian Americans smarter than white people? Is the typical white person more intelligent than the average African American? Throughout the history of the United States, many people have painted one category of people as more intellectually gifted than another. Moreover, people have used such thinking to justify the privileges of an allegedly superior category or to bar supposedly inferior people from entering this country.

Scientists know that the distribution of human intelligence forms a bell-shaped curve, as shown in the figure. By convention, average intelligence is defined as an *intelligence quotient* (IQ) score of 100 (technically, an IQ score is mental age, as measured by a test, divided by age in years, with the result multiplied by 100; thus, an eight-year-old who performs like a ten-year-old has an IQ of 10/8 = 1.25 × 100 = 125).

In a controversial study of intelligence and social inequality, Richard Herrnstein and Charles Murray (1994) report that much research shows a link between race and intelligence. Specifically, they explain, the average IQ of people with European ancestry is 100, that of people with East Asian ancestry is 103, and for people of African descent the average is 90.

Of course, assertions of this kind are explosive because they fly in the face of our democratic and egalitarian conviction that no racial type is inherently "better" than another. Some critics of Herrnstein and Murray charge that intelligence tests are flawed, and others question whether what we call "intelligence" has much real meaning at all.

Most social scientists acknowledge that IQ tests do measure something important that we think of as "intelligence," and they agree that *individuals* vary in intellectual aptitude. But they reject the idea that any *category* of people, on average, is "smarter" than any other. That is, categories of people may show small differences on intelligence tests, but the crucial question is *why*.

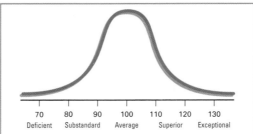

70 80 90 100 110 120 130
Deficient Substandard Average Superior Exceptional

IQ: The Distribution of Intelligence

conclusion is supported by research showing that people who display strong prejudice toward one minority usually are intolerant of all minorities. These *authoritarian personalities* rigidly conform to conventional cultural values and see moral issues as clear-cut matters of right and wrong. People with authoritarian personalities also look upon society as naturally competitive and hierarchical, with "better" people (like them) inevitably dominating those who are weaker. Adorno also found that people tolerant toward one minority are likely to be accepting of all; they tend to be more flexible in their moral judgments and treat all people as equals.

Adorno thought that people with little education who are raised by cold and demanding parents tend to develop authoritarian personalities. Filled with anger and anxiety as children, they grow into hostile, aggressive adults, seeking scapegoats, whom they consider inferior.

Culture Theory

A third theory contends that extreme prejudice may be characteristic of certain people, but some prejudice is found in everyone because it is embedded in culture. Emory Bogardus (1968) studied the effects of culturally rooted prejudices for more than forty years. He developed the concept of *social distance* to gauge how close or how distant people feel toward various racial and ethnic categories. Bogardus found that most people in the United States feel closest to people of English, Canadian, and Scottish background, even welcoming marriage with them. Attitudes are less favorable toward the French, Germans, Swedes, and Dutch, and the most negative prejudices target people of African and Asian descent.

According to Bogardus, prejudice is so widespread that we cannot explain intolerance as a trait of authoritarian personalities, as Adorno suggests. Rather,

DISCUSS: In 2000, Douglas Massey had student teams telephone realtors about available apartments. Among those using standard white English, 76% of men and 60% of women were told the flat was available; among those using a black accent, the comparable figures were 63% and 57%; among those using black English, the figures were 44% and 38% (Massey, 2000).

Q: "Despite the emotionally charged philosophical and political issues involved, [the connection between race and intelligence] is ultimately an empirical question" Thomas Sowell

Q: "The ordinary English worker hates the Irish worker as a competitor who lowers his standard of life. . . . This antagonism is the secret of the impotence of the English working class. . . . It is the secret by which the capitalist class maintains its power." Karl Marx

Thomas Sowell explains that most of the documented racial differences in intelligence result not from biology but from environment. In some skillful sociological detective work, Sowell traced IQ scores for various racial and ethnic categories from the early twentieth century. He found that, on average, immigrants from European nations such as Poland, Lithuania, Italy, and Greece and from Asian countries including China and Japan scored ten to fifteen points below the U.S. average. But people in these same categories today have IQ scores that are average or above average. Among Italian Americans, for example, average IQ jumped almost ten points in fifty years; among Polish and Chinese Americans, the increase was almost twenty points.

Because genetic changes occur over thousands of years and most of these people intermarried among themselves, biological factors cannot explain the higher IQ scores. The only plausible explanation is changing cultural patterns. The descendants of early immigrants improved their intellectual performance as their living conditions improved and their opportunity for schooling increased.

Sowell found that a similar pattern applies to African Americans. Historically, the average IQ test score of African Americans living in the North is about ten points higher than the average score of those living in the South. And among descendants of African Americans who migrated from the South to the North after 1940, IQ scores went up, just as they did with descendants of earlier immigrants. Thus, if environmental factors are the same for various categories of people, racial IQ differences largely disappear.

What IQ test score disparities do tell us, according to Sowell, is that *cultural patterns* matter. If Asians, on average, score high on tests, it is because they have been raised to value learning and pursue excellence, not because all Asians are smart. For their part, African Americans are no less intelligent than anyone else, but they carry a legacy of disadvantage that can undermine self-confidence and discourage achievement.

What do you think?

1. *If IQ scores and other measures of intelligence always reflect people's environment, to what extent are they valid measures? In what ways are they harmful?*

2. *Why, according to Thomas Sowell, do some racial and ethnic categories show dramatic, short-term changes in average IQ scores?*

3. *What could schools do to raise the IQ scores of children, especially those from disadvantaged backgrounds?*

Sources: Herrnstein & Murray (1994) and Sowell (1994, 1995).

Bogardus believed, everyone in U.S. society expresses some bigotry because we live in a "culture of prejudice" that has taught us to view certain categories of people as "better" or "worse" than others.

Conflict Theory

A fourth explanation proposes that powerful people use prejudice to justify oppressing others. To the extent that Anglos look down on illegal Latino immigrants in the Southwest, for example, the well-off among them can pay the immigrants low wages for hard work. Similarly, all elites benefit when prejudice divides workers along racial and ethnic lines and discourages them from working together to advance their common interests (Geschwender, 1978; Olzak, 1989).

Another conflict-based argument, advanced by Shelby Steele (1990), is that minorities themselves cultivate a climate of *race consciousness* in order to win greater power and privileges. To promote race consciousness, Steele explains, minorities claim that they are victims and therefore are entitled to special consideration based on their race. Although this strategy may yield short-term gains, Steele points out that such thinking can spark a backlash from white people or others who oppose "special treatment" for anyone on the basis of race or ethnicity.

DISCRIMINATION

Closely related to prejudice is **discrimination**, *treating various categories of people unequally.* Whereas prejudice consists of attitudes, discrimination is a matter of action. Like prejudice, discrimination can be either positive (providing special advantages) or negative (subjecting

DISCUSS: Discrimination always involves *making distinctions*; the question is which kinds of distinctions are deemed fair and just and which are viewed as unfair and wrong. Is a college wrong to admit students with better grades over those with lower grades?

Q: "Racism is both overt and covert. It takes two, closely related forms: individual whites acting against individual blacks, and acts by the white community against the black community. We call these

individual racism and *institutional racism.*" Stokely Carmichael and Charles V. Hamilton, *Black Power* (Vintage, 1967:4)

DISCUSS: According to the U.S. Bureau of Labor Statistics, African Americans make up 11% of the labor force but only 6.3% of all computer and data-processing employees. Does this fact support the conclusion that the high-tech industry is guilty of racial discrimination? Why or why not?

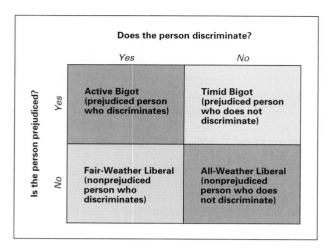

FIGURE 14–1 Patterns of Prejudice and Discrimination

Source: Merton (1976).

people to obstacles). Discrimination also ranges from subtle to blatant.

Prejudice and discrimination often occur together: For example, a prejudiced personnel manager may refuse to hire minorities. Robert Merton (1976) describes such a person as an *active bigot* (Figure 14–1). But prejudice and discrimination do not always occur together, as in the case of the prejudiced personnel manager who, out of fear of lawsuits, *does* hire minorities. Merton calls this person a *timid bigot.* People who are tolerant of minorities yet discriminate when it is to their advantage are *fair-weather liberals.* Finally, Merton's *all-weather liberal* is free of prejudice and discrimination.

INSTITUTIONAL PREJUDICE AND DISCRIMINATION

We typically think of prejudice and discrimination as the hateful ideas or actions of specific people. But thirty years ago, Stokely Carmichael and Charles Hamilton (1967) pointed out that far greater harm results from **institutional prejudice and discrimination,** *bias inherent in the operation of society's institutions,* including schools, banks, law enforcement, and the workplace. For example, researchers have shown that banks reject home mortgage applications from minorities at a higher rate than applications from white

people, even when income and quality of neighborhood are held constant (Gotham, 1998).

According to Carmichael and Hamilton, the white majority is slow to condemn or even to recognize institutional prejudice and discrimination because they often involve respected public officials and long-established traditions. A case in point is the Supreme Court's *Brown* decision in 1954, described in the opening to this chapter. The principle of "separate but equal" had been the law of the land, upholding institutional racism in the form of an educational caste system. Today, half a century later, the law may have changed, but most U.S. students still attend schools that are overwhelmingly one race or the other. Indeed, in 1991 the courts declared that neighborhood schools will never provide equal education as long as our population is divided into racially segregated neighborhoods, with most African Americans living in central cities and most white people (and Asian Americans) living beyond the city limits in suburbs.

PREJUDICE AND DISCRIMINATION: THE VICIOUS CYCLE

Prejudice and discrimination reinforce each other. The Thomas theorem, discussed in Chapter 6 ("Social Interaction in Everyday Life"), offers a simple explanation of this fact: *Situations defined as real become real in their consequences* (Thomas, 1966:301; orig. 1931).

As W. I. Thomas recognized, stereotypes become real to those who believe them and sometimes even to those who are victimized by them. Power also plays a role here because some categories of people can enforce their prejudices to the detriment of others. Prejudice on the part of whites toward people of color, for example, does not produce *innate* inferiority but can produce *social* inferiority, pushing minorities into low-paying jobs, inferior schools, and racially segregated housing. Then, if white people interpret social disadvantage as evidence that minorities do not measure up to their standards, they unleash a new round of prejudice and discrimination, giving rise to a *vicious cycle* (see Figure 14–2).

MAJORITY AND MINORITY: PATTERNS OF INTERACTION

Social scientists describe patterns of interaction between racial and ethnic categories in terms of four models: pluralism, assimilation, segregation, and genocide.

PLURALISM

Pluralism is *a state in which racial and ethnic minorities are distinct but have social parity.* In other words, everyone accepts the idea that society is multicultural and, even though categories of people are distinctive, they all have roughly the same average social standing.

The United States is pluralistic to the extent that our society promises equal standing under the law. Moreover, large cities contain countless "ethnic villages," where people proudly practice their ethnic traditions. In New York these include Spanish Harlem, Little Italy, and Chinatown; in Philadelphia, Italian South Philly; in Miami, Little Havana; in Chicago, Little Saigon; and Latino East Los Angeles.

But the United States is not really pluralistic for three reasons. First, although many people value their cultural heritage, only a small proportion want to live apart from others and exclusively with their "own kind" (NORC, 2001). Second, our tolerance for social diversity is limited. One reaction to the rising proportion of minorities in the United States is a social movement to establish English as this nation's official language. Third, as we shall see later in this chapter, it is simply a fact that people of various colors and cultures have unequal social standing.

ASSIMILATION

Assimilation is *the process by which minorities gradually adopt patterns of the dominant category.* Assimilation involves changing modes of dress, values, religion, language, and friends.

Many people think of the United States as a "melting pot" where different nationalities blend together. This concept was well expressed in a play that was popular in early 1900s:

> America is God's Crucible, the great melting-pot where all races of Europe are melting and reforming. Here you stand, good folks, think I, when I see them at Ellis Island [historical entry point for many immigrants in New York], here you stand with your fifty groups, with your fifty languages and histories, and your fifty blood-hatreds and rivalries. But you won't be long like that, brothers, for these are the fires of God. . . . Germans and Frenchmen, Irishmen and Englishmen, Jews and Russians, into the Crucible with you all! God is making an American! (Zangwill, 1921:33; orig. 1909)

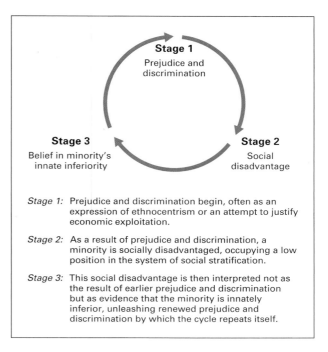

FIGURE 14–2 Prejudice and Discrimination: The Vicious Cycle

Prejudice and discrimination can form a vicious cycle, perpetuating themselves.

Stage 1: Prejudice and discrimination begin, often as an expression of ethnocentrism or an attempt to justify economic exploitation.

Stage 2: As a result of prejudice and discrimination, a minority is socially disadvantaged, occupying a low position in the system of social stratification.

Stage 3: This social disadvantage is then interpreted not as the result of earlier prejudice and discrimination but as evidence that the minority is innately inferior, unleashing renewed prejudice and discrimination by which the cycle repeats itself.

In truth, however, rather than everyone "melting" into some new cultural pattern, most minorities adopt the dominant culture established by the earliest settlers. Why? Assimilation is both a path to upward social mobility and a way to escape the prejudice and discrimination directed at more visible foreigners (Newman, 1973).

The degree of assimilation varies by category. For example, Germans and Irish have "melted" more than Italians, and the Japanese more than the Chinese or Koreans. Multiculturalists, however, oppose assimilation because it suggests that minorities are "the problem" and defines them (rather than majority people) as the ones who need to do all the changing.

Note that assimilation involves changes in ethnicity but not in race. For example, many descendants of Japanese immigrants discard their traditions but retain their racial identity. Racial traits can diminish over time only through **miscegenation,** *biological reproduction by partners of different racial categories.* Although the rate of interracial marriage is rising, it is still low; just 5 percent of all U.S. births are to parents of different races.

Q: First they came for the Jews,
   but I did not speak out
   because I was not a Jew.
   Then they came for the Communists,
   and I did not speak out
   because I was not a Communist.
   Then they came for the trade unionists,

and I did not speak out
because I was not trade unionist.
Then they came for me,
and no one was left
to speak out for me.
Pastor Martin Niemoeller, victim of the Nazis

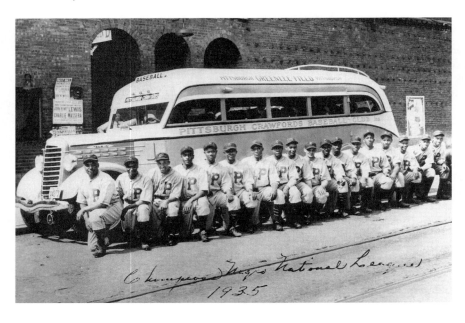

In the years following the founding of the National League in 1876, a handful of talented African American players joined a number of professional baseball teams. By the 1890s, however, a "color line" had been drawn, racially segregating professional baseball and giving rise to the "Negro leagues," which reached their greatest popularity in the 1930s and 1940s. After professional baseball was once again integrated in 1947 (first by Jackie Robinson of the Brooklyn Dodgers and, months later, by Larry Dobie of the Cleveland Indians), the "Negro leagues" faded away in the 1950s.

SEGREGATION

Segregation is *the physical and social separation of categories of people.* Some minorities, especially religious orders such as the Amish, voluntarily segregate themselves. Usually, however, majorities segregate minorities by excluding them. Residential neighborhoods, schools, occupations, hospitals, and even cemeteries can be segregated. Whereas pluralism fosters distinctiveness without disadvantage, segregation enforces separation to the detriment of a minority.

Racial segregation has a long history in the United States, beginning with slavery and evolving into racially separate housing, schools, buses, and trains. Decisions such as the 1954 *Brown* case have reduced *de jure* (Latin, meaning "by law") discrimination in this country. However, *de facto* ("in fact") segregation continues to this day in the form of countless neighborhoods that are home predominantly to people of a single race.

Racial segregation in the United States has declined somewhat during recent decades (Farley, 1997). Yet Douglas Massey and Nancy Denton (1989) have documented the *hypersegregation* of poor African Americans in some inner cities. These people have little contact of any kind with other people beyond their own communities. Hypersegregation disadvantages about one-fifth of all African Americans but only a few percent of comparably poor whites (Jagarowsky & Bane, 1990; Krivo et al., 1998).

Segregated minorities understandably resent their second-class citizenship, and sometimes the action of even a single person can bring about change. On December 1, 1955, Rosa Parks boarded a bus in Montgomery, Alabama, and sat in the section designated by law for African Americans. When a crowd of white passengers boarded, the driver asked four black people to give up their seats to white people. Three did so, but Rosa Parks refused. The driver left the bus and returned with police, who arrested her for violating the racial segregation laws. A court later convicted Parks and fined her $14. Her standing up (or sitting) for justice led the African American community of Montgomery to boycott city buses and ultimately end this form of segregation (King, 1969).

GENOCIDE

Genocide is *the systematic killing of one category of people by another.* Although this deadly form of racism and ethnocentrism violates every moral standard, it has erupted time and again in human history.

Genocide figured prominently in the European conquest of the Americas. From the sixteenth century on, the Spanish, Portuguese, English, French, and Dutch forcibly colonized vast empires. Some native people fell victim to calculated killing, but most succumbed to European diseases for which they had no natural immunity (Matthiessen, 1984; Sale, 1990).

THE MAP: Indian reservation land is spread out across the West, the region to which native peoples retreated in the face of population pressure and military campaigns against them. Today, they occupy land that has little value, one reason for the high poverty rate among them.

Q: "Illegal aliens have always been a problem in the United States; ask any Indian." Robert Orben

Q: "They made us many promises, more than I can remember, but they never kept but one; they promised to take our land, and they took it." Anonymous Native American (cited in Dee Brown, *Bury My Heart at Wounded Knee*)

NOTE: Thousands of Cherokees died on a forced march—the Trail of Tears—from their homes in the southeastern U.S. to reservations in Indian Territory, later Oklahoma, during 1838–39.

SEEING OURSELVES

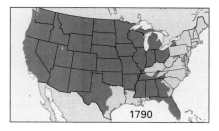
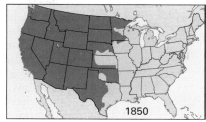
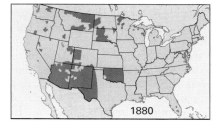

NATIONAL MAP 14–2
Land Controlled by Native Americans, 1790–1998

Two hundred years ago, Native Americans controlled three-fourths of the land that would eventually become today's United States. Today, Native Americans control 314 reservations—scattered across the United States—that, together, account for just 2 percent of the country's land area. How would you characterize these locations?

Source: Copyright © 1998 by The New York Times Co. Reprinted by permission. All rights reserved.

Genocide also occurred in the twentieth century. Unimaginable horror befell European Jews during the Holocaust of the 1930s and 1940s, when Hitler's Nazis exterminated more than 6 million Jewish men, women, and children. Soviet dictator Josef Stalin murdered on an even greater scale, killing perhaps 30 million real and imagined enemies. Between 1975 and 1980, Pol Pot's communist regime in Cambodia butchered all "capitalists," including anyone able to speak a Western language and even people who wore eyeglasses, viewed as an elitist symbol. In all, some 2 million people (one-fourth of the population) perished in the Cambodian "killing fields" (Shawcross, 1979).

Tragically, genocide continues. Recent examples include Hutus killing Tutsis in Rwanda and Serbs killing Bosnians in the Balkans of Eastern Europe.

The four minority-majority patterns just described have all been played out in the United States. Although many people proudly point to patterns of pluralism and assimilation, it is also important to recognize the degree to which our society has been built on segregation (of African Americans) and genocide (of Native Americans). The remainder of this chapter examines how these four patterns have shaped the history and present social standing of major racial and ethnic categories in the United States.

RACE AND ETHNICITY IN THE UNITED STATES

> Give me your tired, your poor,
> Your huddled masses yearning to breathe free,
> The wretched refuse of your teeming shore,
> Send these, the homeless, tempest-tossed to me:
> I lift my lamp beside the golden door.

These words by Emma Lazarus, inscribed on the Statue of Liberty, express cultural ideals of human dignity, personal freedom, and opportunity. Indeed, the United States has provided more of the "good life" to more immigrants than any other nation. But as the history of this nation's racial and ethnic minorities reveals, our country's golden door has opened more widely for some than for others.

NATIVE AMERICANS

The term "Native Americans" refers to the societies—including Aleuts, Eskimos, Cherokee, Zuni, Sioux, Mohawk, Aztec, and Inca—who first settled the Western Hemisphere. Some 30,000 years before Christopher Columbus (1446–1506) stumbled on the Americas, migrating peoples crossed a land bridge from Asia to North America where the Bering Strait

NOTE: Native Americans had casinos in 28 states (in 1998), earning more than $6 billion annually. Such financial clout commands growing attention from government leaders; unemployment stands at about zero in reservations with casinos.
RESOURCE: C. Matthew Snipp considers the increasing numbers of people claiming a Native American heritage in "A Comeback for American Indians" in the Macionis and Benokraitis reader.

NOTE: As non-WASP immigration increased, elite WASPs closed themselves off as an exclusive group, publishing the *Social Register* (1887), a list of members of "society," and establishing various genealogical organizations such as the Daughters of the American Revolution (1890) and the Society of Mayflower Descendants (1894). Such organizations further insulated wealthy WASPs from newly arrived immigrants (Baltzell, 1964).

TABLE 14–2 The Social Standing of Native Americans, 2000

	Native Americans	Entire United States
Median family income	$31,064	$50,891
Percentage in poverty	27.1%	11.3%
Completion of four or more years of college (age 25 and over)	9.3%*	25.6%

*Author estimate based on latest available data.

Source: U.S. Census Bureau (2001).

(off the coast of Alaska) lies today. Gradually, they made their way throughout North and South America.

When the first Europeans arrived late in the fifteenth century, Native Americans numbered in the millions. But by 1900, after relentless subjugation and acts of genocide, the "vanishing Americans" numbered a mere 250,000 (Dobyns, 1966; Tyler, 1973); the lands they controlled had also shrunk dramatically, as shown in National Map 14–2 on page 365.

It was Christopher Columbus who first called Native Americans "Indians" because he wrongly thought he had reached India. Actually, Columbus had landed in the Bahama Islands in the Caribbean. Columbus found the island people passive and peaceful, a stark contrast to materialistic and competitive Europeans (Matthiessen, 1984; Sale, 1990). Yet early Europeans justified seizing the land by calling their victims thieves and murderers (Unruh, 1979; Josephy, 1982).

After the Revolutionary War, the new U.S. government took a pluralist approach to Native American societies and sought to gain more land through treaties. Payment for land was far from fair, however, and when Native Americans resisted surrendering their homeland, the U.S. government simply used superior military power to evict them. By the early 1800s, few Native Americans remained east of the Mississippi River.

 For more information on Native Americans, visit this site, operated by Syracuse University: http://www.nativeweb.org

In 1871, the United States declared Native Americans wards of the government and adopted a strategy of forced assimilation. Native Americans continued to lose their land and were well on their way to losing their culture. Reservation life fostered dependency, replacing ancestral languages with English and traditional religion with Christianity. Officials of the Bureau of Indian

Affairs took children from their parents and put them in boarding schools, where they were resocialized as "Americans." Authorities gave local control of reservation life to the few Native Americans who supported government policies, and they distributed reservation land—traditionally held collectively—as private property to individual families (Tyler, 1973).

Not until 1924 were Native Americans entitled to U.S. citizenship. After that, many migrated from reservations, adopting more mainstream cultural patterns and marrying non–Native Americans. Many large cities have sizable Native American populations. Overall, however, Native Americans control just a small share of land in this country; the median family income of Native Americans is far below the U.S. average, and relatively few Native Americans earn a college degree (see Table 14–2).[1]

From in-depth interviews with Native Americans in a western city, Joan Albon (1971) concluded that lower Native American social standing reflects a range of cultural factors, including a noncompetitive view of life and a reluctance to pursue higher education. In addition, she noted, many Native Americans have dark skin, which makes them victims of prejudice and discrimination.

Like other racial and ethnic minorities in the United States, Native Americans have recently reasserted pride in their cultural heritage. Native American organizations report a surge in membership, and many children can speak native languages better than their parents (Fost, 1991; Johnson, 1991; Nagel, 1996). Moreover, the legal autonomy of reservations has turned out to be an ace-up-the-sleeve for many tribes, who have built lucrative casinos and now control 20 percent of all U.S. gambling. But such financial windfalls affect relatively few Native peoples; most endure their disadvantages with a profound sense of the injustice they have suffered at the hands of white people.

WHITE ANGLO-SAXON PROTESTANTS

White Anglo-Saxon Protestants (WASPs) were not the first people to inhabit the United States, but they

---

[1]In making comparisons of education and, especially, income, keep in mind that various categories of the U.S. population have different median ages. The 2000 median age for all U.S. people was 35.3 years. Non-Hispanic white people have a median age of 38.6 years; for Native Americans, the figure is 28.0 years. Because people's schooling and income increase over time, such an age difference accounts for some of the disparities shown in Table 14–2.

THE MAP: South Texas is a heavily Hispanic region; the upper Plains states are home to the descendants of Scandinavian immigrants. Note that WASPs are a substantial part of the U.S. population almost everywhere.

NOTE: E. Digby Baltzell, who coined the term "WASP," notes that to many people in the U.S., a true WASP is a person whose first name is a last name.

NOTE: Research documents that African Americans have a lower subjective sense of well-being than whites (see Hughes & Thomas, 1998).

THEN AND NOW: In the 1960s, whites tended to blame both whites and blacks for the disadvantages suffered by blacks; today, surveys show, most whites blames blacks for an alleged lack of motivation (Schuman & Krysan, 1999).

SEEING OURSELVES

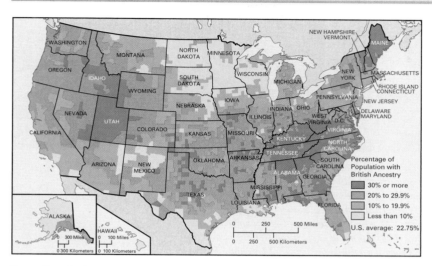

NATIONAL MAP 14–3
The Concentration of People of WASP Ancestry across the United States

Many people associate white Anglo-Saxon Protestants with elite communities along the eastern and western seaboards of the United States. But the highest concentrations of WASPs are in Utah (because of migrations of Mormons with English ancestry), Appalachia, and northern New England (because of historic immigration). Overall, however, WASPs form a large share of the U.S. population almost everywhere except Alaska, South Texas, and the upper Great Plains. Do you know why?

Source: From Rodger Doyle, *Atlas of Contemporary America*. Copyright © 1994 by Facts on File, Inc. Reprinted with permission of Facts on File, Inc.

came to dominate this nation once European colonization began. Most WASPs are of English ancestry, but the category also includes Scots and Welsh. More than 50 million people in our society, or one in five, claims some WASP background. National Map 14–3 shows where in the United States the highest concentrations of WASPs are found.

Historically, WASP immigrants were highly skilled and motivated to achieve by what we now call the Protestant work ethic. Because of their numbers and power, WASPs were not subject to the prejudice and discrimination experienced by other categories of immigrants. In fact, their historical dominance has led others to want to become like them.

WASPs were never one single social group; especially in colonial times, hostility separated English Anglicans and Scots-Irish Presbyterians (Parrillo, 1994). But during the nineteenth century, most WASPs joined together to bemoan the arrival of "undesirable foreigners": Germans in the 1840s and Italians in the 1880s. Political movements managed to pass laws that limited the flow of immigrants. Those who could afford to sheltered themselves in exclusive neighborhoods and restrictive clubs. Thus, the 1880s—the decade that saw the Statue of Liberty first welcome immigrants to the

United States—also saw the founding of the first country club with only WASP members (Baltzell, 1964).

By about 1950, WASP command of wealth and privileges had peaked, as indicated by the 1960 election of John Fitzgerald Kennedy as the first Irish-Catholic president. But the majority of people in the upper-upper class (but not the "new rich" lower-upper class) are still WASPs (Baltzell, 1964, 1976, 1979b, 1988). The WASP cultural legacy also remains. English is this country's dominant language, and Protestantism is the majority religion. Our legal system also reflects its English origins. But the historical dominance of WASPs is most evident in the widespread use of the terms "race" and "ethnicity" to describe everyone but them.

AFRICAN AMERICANS

Although African Americans accompanied European explorers to the New World in the fifteenth century, most accounts mark the beginning of black history in the United States as 1619, when a Dutch trading ship brought twenty Africans to Jamestown, Virginia. Whether these people arrived as slaves or indentured servants who paid their passage by laboring for a

SOCIAL SURVEY: "On the average, (Negroes/Blacks/African Americans) have worse jobs, income, and housing than white people. Do you think these differences are . . . " (GSS 2000, N = 1,877; *Codebook*, 2001:274–75)

	"Yes"	"No"	DK/NR
" . . . mainly due to discrimination?"	36.5%	56.6%	6.9%
" . . . because most blacks have less in-born ability to learn?"	12.1%	83.8%	4.1%
" . . . because most blacks don't have the chance for education?"	45.0%	50.5%	4.5%
" . . . because most blacks just don't have the motivation or will power?"	45.0%	47.1%	7.9%

Q: "There is no Negro problem in the United States; there is only a white problem." Richard Wright

The efforts of these four women greatly advanced the social standing of African Americans in the United States. Pictured above, from left to right: Sojourner Truth (1797–1883), born a slave, became an influential preacher and outspoken abolitionist who was honored by President Lincoln at the White House. Harriet Tubman (1820–1913), after escaping from slavery herself, masterminded the flight from bondage of hundreds of African American men and women via the "Underground Railroad." Ida Wells-Barnett (1862–1931), born to slave parents, became a partner in a Memphis newspaper and served as a tireless crusader against the terror of lynching. Marian Anderson (1902–1993), an exceptional singer whose early career was restrained by racial prejudice, broke symbolic "color lines" by singing in the White House (1936) and on the steps of the Lincoln Memorial to a crowd of almost 100,000 people (1939).

specified period, being of African descent on these shores soon became virtually synonymous with being a slave. In 1661, Virginia enacted the first law recognizing slavery (Sowell, 1981).

Slavery was the foundation of the southern colonies' plantation system. White people ran plantations with slave labor, and, until 1808, some were also slave traders. Traders—including Europeans, Africans, and North Americans—forcibly transported some 10 million Africans to various countries in the Americas, including 400,000 to the United States. On small sailing ships, hundreds of slaves were chained together for the several weeks it took to cross the Atlantic Ocean. Filth and disease killed many and drove others to suicide. Overall, perhaps half died en route (Tannenbaum, 1946; Franklin, 1967; Sowell, 1981).

Surviving the journey was a mixed blessing because it brought only a life of servitude. Although some slaves worked in cities at various trades, most labored in the fields, often from daybreak until sunset and even longer during the harvest. The law allowed owners to impose whatever disciplinary measures they deemed necessary to ensure that slaves were obedient and productive. Even killing a slave rarely prompted legal action. Owners often divided slave families at public auctions where human beings were bought and sold as pieces of property. Unschooled and dependent on their owners for all their basic needs, slaves had little control over their destinies (Franklin, 1967; Sowell, 1981).

Some free people of color lived in both the North and the South, laboring as small scale farmers, skilled workers, and small business owners. But the lives of most African Americans stood in glaring contradiction to the principles of equality and freedom on which the United States was founded. The Declaration of Independence states,

> We hold these Truths to be self-evident, that all Men are created equal, that they are endowed by their Creator with certain unalienable Rights, that among these are Life, Liberty, and the Pursuit of Happiness.

However, most white people did not apply these ideals to black people. In the *Dred Scott* case of 1857, the U.S. Supreme Court addressed the question, "Are blacks citizens?" by writing, "We think they are not, and that they are not included, and were not intended to be included, under the word 'citizens' in the

Constitution, and can therefore claim none of the rights and privileges which that instrument provides for and

Read the first-person accounts of slavery in the United States at this Library of Congress site: http://lcweb2.loc.gov/ammem/snhtml/

secures for citizens of the United States" (quoted in Blaustein & Zangrando, 1968:160). Thus arose what Swedish sociologist Gunnar Myrdal (1944) called the *American dilemma*: a democratic society's denial of basic rights and freedoms to an entire category of people. To resolve this dilemma, many white people simply defined black people as innately inferior.

In 1865, the Thirteenth Amendment to the Constitution outlawed slavery. Three years later, the Fourteenth Amendment reversed the *Dred Scott* ruling, conferring citizenship on all people born in the United States. The Fifteenth Amendment, ratified in 1870, stated that neither race nor previous condition of servitude could deprive anyone of the right to vote. However, so-called Jim Crow laws—classic cases of institutional discrimination—still segregated U.S. society into two racial castes. Especially in the South, white people beat and lynched black people (and some white people) who challenged the racial hierarchy.

The twentieth century brought dramatic changes for African Americans. After World War I, tens of thousands of men, women, and children joined the Great Migration, leaving the rural South for the North to take jobs in factories. Although most found greater economic opportunity, few escaped the racial prejudice and discrimination that ranked them lower in the class hierarchy than white immigrants arriving from Europe.

In the 1950s and 1960s, a national civil rights movement grew out of the landmark judicial decisions that outlawed segregated schools and overt discrimination in employment and public accommodations. In addition, the "black power" movement gave African Americans a renewed sense of pride and purpose.

Gains notwithstanding, people of African descent continue to occupy a subordinate position in the United States, as shown in Table 14–3. The median income of African American families in 2000 ($34,204) was only 64 percent of white family income ($53,256),[2]

TABLE 14–3 The Social Standing of African Americans, 2000		
	African Americans	Entire United States
Median family income	$34,204	$50,891
Percentage in poverty	22.1%	11.3%
Completion of four or more years of college (age 25 and over)	16.6%	25.6%

Source: U.S. Census Bureau (2001).

a ratio that has changed little in thirty years. Black families remain three times as likely as white families to be poor.

The number of African American families securely in the middle class rose by more than half between 1980 and 2000; 49 percent earn more than $35,000 a year, and 32 percent earn $50,000 or more annually. But most African Americans are still working class or poor; indeed, for many African Americans, earnings have

Policies by which banks provide mortgages to African Americans in inner cities have been controversial. Read a Housing and Urban Development (HUD) report at http://www.hud.gov/library/bookshelf18/pressrel/subprime.html

slipped during the last fifteen years as factory jobs, vital to residents of inner cities, have been lost to other countries where labor costs are lower. Thus, black unemployment is almost twice as high as white unemployment; among African American teenagers in many cities, the figure exceeds 40 percent (Horton et al., 2000; DeJong & Madamba, 2001; U.S. Department of Labor, 2001).

In the last generation, African Americans have made remarkable educational progress. The share of adults completing high school rose from half to more than three-fourths, nearly closing the gap between whites and blacks. Between 1980 and 2000, the share of African American adults with at least a college degree rose from 8 percent to more than 16 percent. But as Table 14–3 shows, African Americans are still at just over half the national standard when it comes to completing four years of college.

The political clout of African Americans has also increased. As a result of black migration to the cities and white movement to the suburbs, half of this country's ten largest cities have elected African American mayors. At the national level, however, only 2 percent of elected leaders are African Americans. After the 2000 congressional elections, 36 (of 435) members of

---

[2]Here again, a median age difference (non-Hispanic white people, 38.6; black people, 30.2) accounts for some of the income and educational disparities. Disparities also reflect a higher proportion of one-parent families among blacks than whites. Comparing only married-couple families, African Americans (median income $50,741 in 2000) earned 85 percent as much as whites ($59,953).

NOTE: Before the Industrial Revolution, few people moved from one country to another. The word "immigrant" entered the English language only around 1790.

NOTE: The current wave of immigration began in 1965 with liberalization of the old quota system dating from 1924. In essence, "country of origin" ceased to be a key criterion for admission to the U.S. in favor of special skills and family ties. This sparked a shift from Europe to Latin America and Asia as the source of immigrants and also allowed many families to join earlier immigrants.

NOTE: In 1943, the U.S. government extended the right of citizenship to Chinese Americans born abroad partly in response to China's status as a military ally in the war against Japan (Japanese Americans born abroad could not become U.S. citizens until 1952).

TABLE 14–4 The Social Standing of Asian Americans, 2000

	All Asian Americans	Chinese Americans	Japanese Americans	Korean Americans	Filipino Americans	Entire United States
Median family income	$60,825*	$59,494*	$74,231*	$48,828*	$67,244*	$50,891
Percentage in poverty	10.8%	10.8%*	5.4%*	10.5%*	4.9%*	11.3%
Completion of four or more years of college (age 25 and over)	43.9%	47.4%*	40.2%*	40.2%*	45.6%*	25.6%

*Author estimates based on latest available data.

Source: U.S. Census Bureau (2001).

the House of Representatives were black, and not one senator (of 100) was black.

In sum, for more than 350 years, people of African ancestry have struggled for social equality. As a nation, we have come far in this pursuit. Overt discrimination is now illegal, and research documents a long-term decline in prejudice against African Americans (Firebaugh & Davis, 1988; Wilson, 1992; NORC, 2001).

In 1913, fifty years after the abolition of slavery, W. E. B. Du Bois pointed to the extent of black achievement. But Du Bois also cautioned that racial caste remained strong in the United States, and in the twenty-first century, the racial hierarchy persists.

ASIAN AMERICANS

Although Asian Americans share some racial traits, enormous cultural diversity characterizes this category of people with ancestors from dozens of nations. In 2000, the total number of Asian Americans exceeded 10 million, approaching 4 percent of the U.S. population. The largest category of Asian Americans is people of Chinese ancestry (2.4 million), followed by those of Filipino (1.8 million), Asian Indian (1.6 million), Vietnamese (1.1 million), Korean (1 million), and Japanese (796,000) descent. More than one-third of Asian Americans live in California.

Young Asian Americans command respect as high achievers and are disproportionately represented at our country's best colleges and universities. Many of their elders also have made economic and social gains; most Asian Americans now live in middle-class suburbs (O'Hare, Frey, & Fost, 1994). Yet despite (and sometimes because of) their exceptional record of achievement, Asian Americans often find that others are aloof or hostile to them (Chua-Eoan, 2000).

At the same time, the "model minority" image of Asian Americans obscures the poverty found within their ranks. We now focus on the history and current standing of Chinese Americans and Japanese Americans—the longest-established Asian American minorities—and conclude with a brief look at the most recent arrivals.

Chinese Americans

Chinese immigration to the United States began in 1849 with the economic boom of California's gold rush. New towns and businesses sprang up overnight, and the demand for cheap labor attracted some 100,000 Chinese immigrants. Most Chinese workers were young men willing to take tough, low-status jobs shunned by whites. But the economy soured in the 1870s, and desperate whites began to compete with the Chinese for whatever work could be found. Suddenly the hardworking Chinese posed a threat. In short, economic hard times led to prejudice and discrimination (Ling, 1971; Boswell, 1986).

Soon, courts withdrew legal protection, barring Chinese workers from many occupations, and the public mood turned vicious against "the Yellow Peril." As everyone seemed to line up against the Chinese, a popular phrase described someone up against great odds as not having "a Chinaman's chance" (Sung, 1967; Sowell, 1981).

In 1882, the U.S. government passed the first of several laws curbing Chinese immigration. Because Chinese men outnumbered women by almost twenty to one, the sex imbalance limited marriages and sent the Chinese population plummeting

For a number of links offering information on Chinese Americans, visit http://www.chinatown-online.co.uk/pages/new_year/red_packets.html

DIVERSITY: Percentage of Asian Americans who speak a language other than English at home: All Asians, 65%; Hmong, 97%; Chinese, 83%; Koreans, 81%; Filipinos, 66%; Japanese, 43%; Indians, 15% (U.S. Census Bureau).

DIVERSITY: The sense that the Chinese would never assimilate is suggested by historic records such as this population count: "1,200 souls and two Chinamen" (Winnick, 1990).

NOTE: The suburban area with the largest Asian population is Los Angeles (528,608 in 1990); the only suburban area with an absolute majority of Asian Americans is Honolulu (57%; 270,000).

Q: "You cannot become thorough Americans if you think of yourselves in groups. America does not consist of groups. A man who thinks of himself as belonging to a particular national group has not yet become an American." Woodrow Wilson

to about 60,000 by 1920 (Hsu, 1971; Lai, 1980). Chinese women already in the United States were in high demand, and they soon shed their traditional submissiveness to men (Sowell, 1981).

Responding to racial hostility, some Chinese moved eastward; many more sought the safety of urban Chinatowns. There, Chinese traditions flourished, and kinship networks, called clans, provided financial help to individuals and represented the interests of all. At the same time, however, Chinatowns discouraged residents from learning the English language, which limited their job opportunities (Wong, 1971).

A renewed need for labor during World War II prompted President Franklin Roosevelt to end the ban on Chinese immigration in 1943 and to extend the rights of citizenship to Chinese Americans born abroad. Many responded by moving out of Chinatowns and pursuing cultural assimilation. In 1900, for example, 70 percent of Honolulu's Chinese people lived in that city's Chinatown; today, the figure is below 20 percent.

Since 1950, Chinese Americans have made great strides. Today, people of Chinese ancestry are no longer limited to self-employment in laundries and restaurants; they work in various high-prestige occupations, especially in the fields of science and new information technology.

As shown in Table 14–4, the median family income of Chinese Americans in 2000 ($59,494) stood above the national average ($50,891). The higher income of all Asian Americans reflects, on average, a larger number of family members in the labor force.[3] Chinese Americans also have an enviable record of educational achievement, with nearly twice the national average of college graduates.

Despite their success, many Chinese Americans still grapple with subtle (and sometimes overt) prejudice and discrimination. Such hostility is one reason poverty among Chinese Americans stands above the national average. Poverty is higher yet among those who remain in the restrictive circle of Chinatowns, working in restaurants or other low-paying jobs. In fact, sociologists debate whether racial and ethnic

Of all ethnic minorities, people of Asian Indian descent are the most well off, with a large share working in medicine or holding other professional positions. How do you explain the pattern by which some ethnic categories, on average, have higher or lower social standing than others?

enclaves help their residents or exploit them (Portes & Jensen, 1989; Zhou & Logan, 1989; Kinkead, 1992; Gilbertson & Gurak, 1993).

Japanese Americans

Japanese immigration to the United States started slowly in the 1860s, reaching only 3,000 by 1890. Most of these immigrants came to the Hawaiian Islands (annexed by the United States in 1898 and made a state in 1959) as a source of cheap labor. After 1900, however, as the number of Japanese immigrants to

---

[3]Median age for all Asian Americans in 2000 was 32.7, somewhat below the national median of 35.3 and the non-Hispanic white median of 38.6. But specific categories vary widely in median age: Japanese, 36.1; Chinese, 32.1; Filipino, 31.1; Korean, 29.1; Asian Indian, 28.9; Cambodian, 19.4; Hmong, 12.5 (U.S. Census Bureau, 2000, 2001).

DIVERSITY: Family size varies among Asian Americans, from 3.1 persons among Japanese Americans to 6.6 among the Hmong. Typically, income and family size are negatively correlated.

DIVERSITY: Educational gender gaps: Only among Filipinos are a larger share of women college graduates (42%) than men (36%). Among Koreans, 47% of men but only 26% of women hold a college degree.

DIVERSITY: About 18% of the U.S. population aged five and older speak a language other than English at home, a total of 45 million people in 2000. In 1980, the share was 11% and 23.5 million people. Most of these (60%) are Spanish speakers (in 1980: 48%); 15% (6.9 million) speak an Asian language (up from 2.2 million in 1980). More than half of all non–English speakers live in California, New York, and Florida (U.S. Census Bureau, 2001).

Between 1942 and 1944, more than 100,000 men, women, and children of Japanese ancestry were forcibly removed from their homes and businesses and taken to detention camps. Here, a mother fights back tears as the army prepares to move her and her three small children (note the identification tags) from Bainbridge Island (off the coast of Washington state) to the mainland.

California rose and they demanded better pay, white people responded by seeking limits to immigration (Daniels, 1971). In 1907, the United States signed an agreement with Japan curbing the entry of men—the chief economic threat—while allowing women to enter this country to ease the sex ratio imbalance. In the 1920s, state laws in California and elsewhere mandated segregation and banned interracial marriage, largely ending further Japanese immigration. Not until 1952 did the United States extend citizenship to foreign-born Japanese.

Japanese and Chinese immigrants differed in three ways. First, there were fewer Japanese immigrants, so they escaped some of the hostility directed at the more numerous Chinese. Second, the Japanese knew more about the United States than the Chinese did, which helped them assimilate (Sowell, 1981). Third, Japanese immigrants preferred rural farming to clustering in cities. But many white people objected to Japanese ownership of farmland, so in 1913, California barred further purchases. Many foreign-born Japanese (called *Issei*) responded by placing farmland in the names of their U.S.-born children (*Nisei*), who were constitutionally entitled to citizenship.

Japanese Americans faced their greatest challenge after December 7, 1941, when Japan bombed the U.S. naval fleet at Hawaii's Pearl Harbor. Rage toward Japan was directed at the Japanese living in the United States, and some feared that Japanese Americans would spy for Japan or otherwise sabotage the U.S. war effort. Within a year, President Franklin Roosevelt signed Executive Order 9066, an unprecedented action that detained people of Japanese descent in military camps. Authorities soon relocated 110,000 people (90 percent of all U.S. Japanese and more than 2,000 Japanese people living in thirteen Latin American nations) to remote inland reservations (Sun, 1998).

Concern about national security always rises in times of war, but Japanese internment was sharply criticized. First, it targeted an entire category of people, not one of whom was known to have committed any disloyal act. Second, roughly two-thirds of those imprisoned were *Nisei*, U.S. citizens by birth. Third, although the United States was also at war with Germany and Italy, no sweeping action of this kind was taken against people of German or Italian ancestry.

Relocation meant selling homes, furnishings, and businesses on short notice for pennies on the dollar. As a result, almost the entire Japanese American population was economically devastated. In military prisons, surrounded by barbed wire and guarded by armed soldiers, families crowded into single rooms, often in buildings that had previously sheltered livestock (Fujimoto, 1971; Bloom, 1980). The internment ended in 1944, when the Supreme Court declared it unconstitutional. In 1988, Congress awarded $20,000 as token compensation to each victim.

After World War II, Japanese Americans staged a dramatic recovery. Having lost their traditional businesses, they pursued a wide range of new occupations, and because their culture highly values education and hard work, Japanese Americans have enjoyed remarkable success. In 2000, the median income of Japanese American households was almost 50 percent above the national average. The rate of poverty among Japanese Americans was less than half the national figure.

Upward social mobility has encouraged cultural assimilation and interracial marriage. The third and fourth generations of Japanese Americans (the *Sansei* and *Yonsei*) rarely live in residential enclaves, as many Chinese Americans still do, and a majority marry non-Japanese. In the process, some have abandoned their traditions, including the Japanese language. However, a large proportion of Japanese Americans belong to associations as a way of maintaining their ethnic identity (Fugita & O'Brien, 1985). Unfortunately, some appear to be caught between two worlds, no longer culturally Japanese but not completely accepted in the larger society because of racial differences.

Recent Asian Immigrants

More recent immigrants from Asia include Filipinos, Indians, Koreans, Vietnamese, Samoans, and Guamanians. When added to the existing population of Chinese and Japanese descent, Asian Americans are this country's fastest-growing minority, accounting for one-third of all immigration to the United States (U.S. Immigration and Naturalization Service, 1999). A brief look at Koreans and Filipinos, both from countries that have had special ties to the United States, reveals the social diversity of newly arriving people from Asia.

Koreans. Korean immigration to the United States followed the U.S. involvement in the Korean War (1950–53). U.S. troops in South Korea experienced Korean culture firsthand, and some soldiers found Korean spouses. For South Koreans, contact with the troops raised interest in the United States.

The entrepreneurial spirit is strong among Asian immigrants. Asians are slightly more likely than whites, three times more likely than Latinos, and four times more likely than African Americans to own and operate small businesses (U.S. Census Bureau, 1995). Among all Asian Americans, Koreans are the most likely to be small business owners. For example, residents of New York City know that the majority of grocery stores there are Korean-owned; similarly, Los Angeles residents know that Koreans operate a large share of liquor stores.

Many Koreans work long hours; nonetheless, Korean American family income is slightly below the national average, as shown in Table 14–4. Moreover, Korean Americans face limited social acceptance, even among other Asian American people.

Filipinos. The large number of immigrants from the Philippines is explained partly by the fact that the United States controlled the Philippine Islands between 1898 (when Spain ceded it as partial settlement of the Spanish-American War) and 1946 (when the Philippines became an independent republic).

The data in Table 14–4 suggest that Filipinos generally have fared well. But a closer look reveals a mixed pattern, with some Filipinos highly successful in the professions (especially in medicine) and others struggling to get by in low-skill jobs (Parrillo, 1994).

For many Filipino families, the key to high income is working women. Almost three-fourths of Filipino American women are in the labor force, compared to just half of Korean American women. Moreover, many of these women are professionals, reflecting the fact that 42 percent of Filipino American women have a four-year college degree, compared to just 26 percent of Korean American women.

In sum, a survey of Asian Americans presents a complex picture. The Japanese come closest to having achieved social acceptance, but especially for Koreans and the Chinese, economic success has not toppled historical prejudice and discrimination. Although many Asian Americans have prospered, others remain poor. One clear trend is an exceptionally high immigration rate, which means that people of Asian ancestry will play a central role in our society in the twenty-first century (Lee, 1994).

HISPANIC AMERICANS

In 2000, Hispanics numbered more than 35 million, 12.5 percent of the U.S. population. According to the 2000 census, Hispanics are the most numerous minority category, surpassing African Americans (12.3 percent of the population). Few people who fall into this category actually describe themselves as "Hispanic" or "Latino," however. Like Asian Americans, Hispanics are really a cluster of distinct populations, each of which identifies with a particular ancestral nation (Marín & Marín, 1991). About two out of three Hispanics (20 million) are Mexican Americans, sometimes called Chicanos. Puerto Ricans are next in population size (3 million), followed by Cuban Americans (1.2 million). Many other nations of Latin America are represented by smaller numbers.

For the results of a national Latino ethnic attitude survey, visit http://falcon.cc.ukans.edu/~droy/

Much of the U.S. Hispanic population lives in the Southwest. One out of four Californians is a Latino (in greater Los Angeles, almost half the people are Latino). National Map 14–4 on page 374 locates the Hispanic, African American, and Asian American populations across the United States.

THE MAP: Hispanics, African Americans, and Asian Americans cluster in different regions of the U.S. Hispanics settle near the "Latin American" side of the country; similarly, most Asian immigrants come to California. Despite a marked northward migration after World War I, the highest concentrations of African Americans remain in the South.

DIVERSITY: The seven leading states in attracting immigrants from abroad (1998) were California, New York, Florida, Texas, New Jersey, Illinois, and Washington.

THEN AND NOW: In 1890, 15% of the U.S. population was foreign born; today, the figure is about 10%.

Q: "Remember, remember always that all of us . . . are descended from immigrants and revolutionists." Franklin Delano Roosevelt (1938)

SEEING OURSELVES

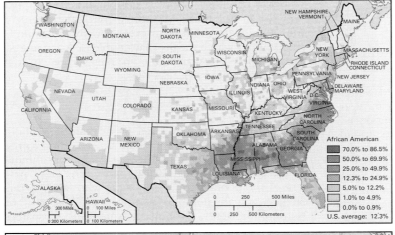

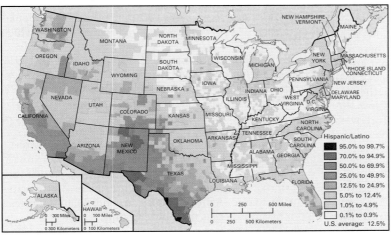

NATIONAL MAP 14–4
The Concentration of Asian Americans, African Americans, and Hispanics or Latinos, by County, 2000

In 2000, Asian Americans represented 3.6 percent of the U.S. population, compared with 12.3 percent African Americans and 12.5 percent people of Hispanic or Latino descent. These three maps show the geographic distribution of these categories of people in 2000. Comparing them, we see that the southern half of the United States is home to far more minorities than the northern half. But do the three concentrate in the same areas? What patterns do the maps reveal?

Source: U.S. Census Bureau (2001).

TABLE 14–5 The Social Standing of Hispanic Americans, 2000

	All Hispanics	Mexican Americans	Puerto Ricans	Cuban Americans	Entire United States
Median family income	$35,050	$31,123*	$30,129*	$38,312*	$50,891
Percentage in poverty	21.2%	24.1%*	25.8%*	17.3%*	11.3%
Completion of four or more years of college (age 25 and over)	10.6%	6.9%	13.0%	23.0%	25.6%

*Data for 1999.

Source: U.S. Census Bureau (2001).

Median family income for all Hispanics—$35,050 in 2000—stands well below the national average.[4] As the following sections discuss, some categories of Hispanics have fared better than others.

Mexican Americans

Some Chicanos are descendants of people who lived in a part of Mexico annexed by the United States after the Mexican American War (1846–48). However, most Mexican Americans are more recent immigrants. In fact, in recent decades, more immigrants have come to the United States from Mexico than from any other country.

Like many other immigrants, many Mexican Americans have worked as low-wage laborers on farms or elsewhere. Table 14–5 shows that the 1999 median family income for Mexican Americans was $31,123, about two-thirds of the national standard. One-fourth of Chicano families are poor, more than twice the national average. And despite gains since 1980, Mexican Americans still acquire less schooling than U.S. adults as a whole and have a high dropout rate.

Puerto Ricans

Puerto Rico (like the Philippines) came under U.S. control with the end of the Spanish-American War in 1898. In 1917, Puerto Ricans (but not Filipinos) became U.S. citizens.

New York City is the center of Puerto Rican life in the continental United States and is home to about 1 million Puerto Ricans. However, about 40 percent of this community is counted among that city's poor, and only 13 percent aged twenty-five and older have

earned a college degree. Adjusting to cultural patterns on the mainland—including, for many, learning English—is one challenge. Also, Puerto Ricans with dark skin encounter especially strong prejudice and discrimination. As a result, more people return to Puerto Rico each year than arrive, so New York lost about 100,000 Puerto Ricans during the 1990s (Navarro, 2000).

This "revolving door" pattern hampers assimilation. Three-fourths of Puerto Rican families in the United States speak Spanish at home, compared to about half of Mexican American families (Sowell, 1981; Stevens & Swicegood, 1987). Speaking only Spanish maintains a strong ethnic identity, but it limits economic opportunity. Puerto Ricans also have a higher incidence of women-headed households than other Hispanics, a pattern that puts families at greater risk of poverty.

Table 14–5 shows that the 1999 median family income for Puerto Ricans was $30,129, 60 percent of the national average. Although long-term mainland residents have made economic gains, more recent immigrants from Puerto Rico struggle to find work. Averaging out the differences, Puerto Ricans remain the most socially disadvantaged Hispanic minority (Rivera-Batiz & Santiago, 1994; Holmes, 1996b).

Cuban Americans

Within a decade after the 1959 Marxist revolution led by Fidel Castro, 400,000 Cubans had immigrated to the United States. Those who fled were highly educated business and professional people who wasted little time becoming as successful in the United States as in their homeland (Fallows, 1983; Krafft, 1993).

Table 14–5 shows that the median household income for Cuban Americans in 1999 was $38,312, well above that of other Hispanics yet still below the national average. The 1 million Cuban Americans living in the United States have managed a delicate balancing act, achieving success in the larger society

---

[4]The 2000 median age of the U.S. Hispanic population was 25.8 years, well below the national median of 35.3 years. This differential accounts for some of the disparity in income and education.

DISCUSS: Is it true that, generally speaking, involuntary immigrants (such as African Americans) have been more disadvantaged than voluntary immigrants (such as white ethnics and many Asians)?
DISCUSS: How likely, in your opinion, is the election of a U.S. president who is African American? Jewish? Asian American? Hispanic American? Give reasons for your opinion.

NOTE: In recent decades, African Americans have become more evident in the mass media, and especially television, where they appear in more favorable roles. In part this is due to advertisers' recognition of the growing African American audience: Blacks watch about 40% more television, on average, than whites do.
Q: "The issue of race could benefit from a period of benign neglect." Daniel Moynihan

The strength of family bonds and neighborhood ties is evident in this painting of street life in old San Juan, La Vida en Broma, *by Puerto Rican artist Nick Quijano.*

© Nick Quijano 1997. *La Vida en Broma, 1988: Streetlife in Old San Juan.*

while retaining much of their traditional culture. Of all Hispanics, Cubans are the most likely to speak Spanish in their homes: Eight out of ten families do. However, their cultural distinctiveness and highly visible communities, such as Miami's Little Havana, provoke hostility from some people.

WHITE ETHNIC AMERICANS

The term "white ethnics" recognizes the ethnic heritage and social disadvantages of many white people. White ethnics are non-WASPs whose ancestors lived in Ireland, Poland, Germany, Italy, or other European countries. More than half the U.S. population falls into a white ethnic category (U.S. Census Bureau, 2001).

Unprecedented emigration from Europe during the nineteenth century first brought Germans and Irish and then Italians and Jews to our shores. Despite cultural differences, all shared the hope that the United States would offer greater political freedom and economic opportunity than their homelands. Most did live better in this country, but the belief that "the streets of America were paved with gold" turned out to be a far cry from reality. Many immigrants found only hard labor for low wages.

White ethnics also endured their share of prejudice and discrimination. Nativist organizations opposed the entry of non-WASP Europeans to the United States, and many newspaper ads seeking workers warned new arrivals, "None need apply but Americans" (Handlin, 1941:67).

In 1921, the nativists declared victory when the federal government passed legislation that imposed a quota on immigration. Not until 1968 were restrictions lifted. The most severely targeted were southern and eastern Europeans—people likely to have darker skin and different cultural backgrounds from the dominant WASPs (Fallows, 1983).

In response to widespread bigotry, many white ethnics—like other immigrants—formed supportive residential enclaves. Some also established footholds in certain businesses and trades: Italian Americans entered the construction industry, the Irish worked in construction and civil service jobs, Jews predominated in the garment industry, and many Greeks (like the Chinese) worked in the retail food business (Newman, 1973).

Many working-class people still live in traditional neighborhoods, although those who prospered gradually assimilated. Most descendants of immigrants who labored in sweatshops and lived in overcrowded tenements now lead comfortable lives. As a result, their ethnic heritage is a source of pride.

RACE AND ETHNICITY: LOOKING AHEAD

The United States has been and will long remain a land of immigrants. Immigration has brought striking cultural diversity and tales of success, hope, and struggle told in hundreds of tongues.

DISCUSS: Ask students to comment on California's Proposition 187, passed in November 1994, prohibiting illegal immigrants from using state public services, but not yet put into practice. Also, Californians passed Proposition 209 in 1996, mandating that governments treat people in a racially and ethnically blind manner.

Q: "Once America was a microcosm of European nationalities; today, America is a microcosm of the world." Molefi Asante

Q: "Once I thought to write a history of the immigrants in America. Then I discovered that the immigrants were American history." Oscar Handlin, Pulitzer Prize–winning historian

DIVERSITY: As Chapter 19 ("Religion") details, 56% of U.S. adults identify themselves as Protestants, 25% as Catholics, 2% as Jews, and 15% claim no affiliation or preference (GSS 2000, N = 2,707; Codebook, 2001:129).

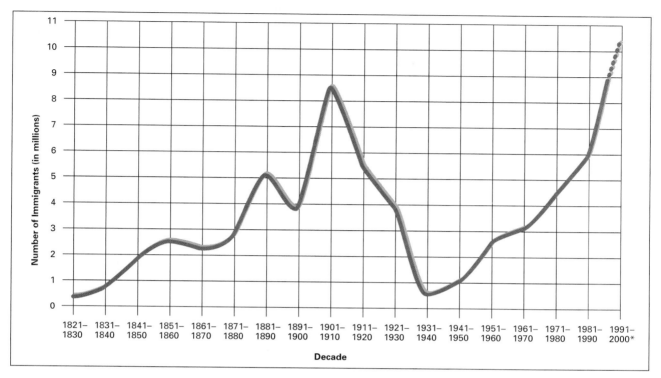

FIGURE 14–3 Immigration to the United States, by Decade

*Projection based on 1991–1998 data.

Source: U.S. Immigration and Naturalization Service (1999).

Most immigrants arrived in a great wave that peaked about 1910. The next two generations saw gradual economic gains and some assimilation. The government also extended citizenship to Native Americans (1924), foreign-born Filipinos (1942), Chinese Americans (1943), and Japanese Americans (1952).

As Figure 14–3 indicates, another wave of immigration began after World War II and swelled as the government relaxed immigration laws in the 1960s. During the 1990s, about 1 million people came to the United States each year, more than twice the number that arrived during the Great Immigration a century ago (although newcomers now enter a country that has five times as many people). However, today's immigrants come not from Europe but from Latin America and Asia, with Mexicans, Filipinos, and South Koreans arriving in the largest numbers.

New arrivals face the same kind of prejudice and discrimination experienced by those who came before them. Indeed, recent years have witnessed rising hostility toward foreigners (sometimes called *xenophobia*, with Greek roots meaning "fear of what is strange"). In 1994, California voters passed Proposition 187, which cut off social services (including schooling) to illegal immigrants. More recently, voters there mandated that all children learn English in school. In 2000, some landowners along the southwest border of the United States took up arms to discourage the large number of immigrants crossing the border from Mexico, and some political candidates have called for drastic action to cut off further immigration. Furthermore, as the final box explains, the debate over affirmative action rages as hotly as ever.

Like their predecessors, many immigrants try to blend into U.S. society without completely giving up their traditional culture. Some have formed racial and ethnic enclaves, so that the Little Havanas and Koreatowns of today stand alongside the Little Italys and Germantowns of the past. Like those who came before them, new arrivals also share the hope that their racial and ethnic identity can be a source of strength and not a badge of inferiority.

CONTROVERSY & DEBATE

Affirmative Action: Solution or Problem?

Adarand Constructors, a white-owned Colorado highway construction company, submitted the low bid for a federal project erecting guard rails. But Adarand did not get the job. Despite having to pay a higher price, the government selected Gonzales Construction, a minority-owned firm. Adarand sued, and a bitter company manager, Randy Perch, explained, "What is prejudice? It's when government makes a decision based on something that doesn't matter, like race or gender."

Should race or ethnicity or gender matter in how we treat people? This question lies at the heart of the affirmative action debate. To begin, what exactly is this controversial policy, and how did it start?

After World War II, the U.S. government funded higher education for veterans of all races. The G.I. Bill held special promise for African Americans, most of whom needed financial assistance to enroll in college. The program was so successful that by 1960, some 350,000 black men and women

were on college campuses with government funding.

But a problem remained: These people were not finding the kinds of jobs for which they were qualified. In short, *educational* opportunity was not producing *economic* opportunity.

Thus, in the early 1960s, the Kennedy administration introduced a program called "affirmative action" to provide a broader "net of opportunity" for qualified minorities in the job market.

Supporters argue that affirmative action in college admissions is needed to ensure a socially diverse campus.

Employers were instructed to monitor hiring, promotion, and admissions policies to eliminate discrimination—even if unintended—against minorities.

Defenders of affirmative action see it, first, as a sensible response to our nation's racial and ethnic history, especially for African Americans, who suffered through two centuries of slavery and a century of segregation under Jim Crow laws. Throughout our history, they claim, being white gave people a big advantage. Thus, minority preference today is a step toward just compensation for unfair majority preference in the past.

Second, given our racial history, the promise of a colorblind society strikes many analysts as hollow. Because prejudice and discrimination are deep in the fabric of U.S. society, simply endorsing the principle of colorblindness does not mean everyone will compete fairly.

Third, proponents maintain that affirmative action has worked. Where would minorities be if the government had not enacted this policy three decades ago? Major

SUMMARY

1. Races are socially constructed categories that set people apart according to various physical traits. Although a century ago scientists identified three broad categories—Caucasoids, Mongoloids, and Negroids—there are no pure races.

2. Ethnicity is based not on biology but on shared cultural heritage. Individuals may choose to emphasize or minimize their cultural distinctiveness. Likewise, societies may or may not set people apart because of cultural heritage.

3. Minorities—including people of various racial and ethnic categories—are people society sets apart as both socially distinct and socially disadvantaged.

4. Prejudice is a rigid and biased generalization about a category of people. Racism, a destructive type of prejudice, asserts that one race is innately superior or inferior to another.

5. Discrimination is a pattern of action by which a person treats various categories of people unequally.

employers, such as fire and police departments in large cities, began hiring minorities and women for the first time only because of affirmative action. This program has played an important part in expanding the African American middle class. Furthermore, affirmative action has increased interracial interaction on campus and advanced the careers of a generation of black students (Bowen & Bok, 1999).

But affirmative action has always drawn criticism, and by the mid-1990s, courts began cutbacks in such policies. Critics argue, first, that affirmative action started out as a temporary remedy to ensure fair competition but became a system of "group preferences" and quotas. In other words, the policy did not remain true to the goal of promoting colorblindness, as set out in the 1964 Civil Rights Act. Within a decade, it had become "reverse discrimination," favoring people not because of their performance but because of their race, ethnicity, or sex.

Second, critics contend that affirmative action polarizes society. If racial preferences were wrong in the past, they are wrong now. Moreover, why should whites or men today—many of whom are far from privileged—be penalized for past discrimination that was in no way their fault? Our society has undone most of the institutionalized prejudice and discrimination of earlier times, opponents continue, so that minorities can and do enjoy success when they have the talent and make the effort. Giving entire categories of people special treatment inevitably compromises standards of excellence, calls into question the real accomplishments of minorities, and provokes a hostile response from white people.

A third argument against affirmative action is that it benefits those who need it least. Favoring minority-owned corporations or allocating places in law school helps already-privileged people. Affirmative action has done little for the African American underclass, which most needs a leg up.

In sum, there are good reasons to argue for and against affirmative action. Indeed, people who believe in a society where no racial or ethnic category dominates fall on both sides of the debate. The disagreement, then, is not whether people of all colors should have equal opportunity, but whether a particular policy—affirmative action— is part of the solution or part of the problem.

Continue the debate . . .

1. *Because, historically, society has favored males over females and whites over people of color, would you agree that white males have received more "affirmative action" than anyone? Why or why not?*

2. *Should affirmative action include only disadvantaged categories of minorities (say, African Americans and Native Americans) and exclude more affluent categories (such as Japanese Americans)? Why or why not?*

3. *Some people claim that the U.S. government should offer African Americans reparation—that is, money—for historical injustice at the hands of white people. Do you think this is a good idea? Why or why not?*

Sources: Carr (1995), Cohen (1995), Curry (1996), Bowen & Bok (1999), and NORC (2001).

6. Pluralism means that racial and ethnic categories, although distinct, have equal social standing. Assimilation is a process by which minorities gradually adopt the patterns of the dominant category. Segregation is a physical and social separation of categories of people. Genocide is the extermination of a category of people.

7. Native Americans, the earliest human inhabitants of the Americas, have endured genocide, segregation, and forced assimilation. Today, the social standing of Native Americans is well below the national average.

8. WASPs predominated among the original European settlers of the United States, and many continue to enjoy high social position today.

9. African Americans experienced two centuries of slavery. Emancipation in 1865 gave way to segregation by law. Today, despite legal equality, African Americans are still disadvantaged.

10. Chinese and Japanese Americans have suffered both racial and ethnic hostility. Although some prejudice and discrimination continue, both categories now have above-average income and schooling. Recent

CTQ2: Prejudice and discrimination can form a vicious cycle by creating disadvantages that people view as evidence of innate inferiority, leading to renewed prejudice and discrimination.

CTQ3: Among young people, there is considerable crossover in musical tastes, suggesting a more multiethnic national culture. Note, too, that rap and hip hop have outsold rock and roll in recent years.

immigration, especially of Koreans and Filipinos, has made Asian Americans the fastest-growing racial category of the U.S. population.

11. Hispanics include many ethnicities sharing a Spanish heritage. Mexican Americans, the largest Hispanic minority, are concentrated in the Southwest. Puerto Ricans, one-third of whom live in New York, are the poorest Hispanics; Cubans, concentrated in Miami, are the most affluent.

12. White ethnics are non-WASPs of European ancestry. While making gains during the twentieth century, many white ethnics still struggle for economic security.

13. Immigration has increased in recent years. No longer primarily from Europe, most immigrants now arrive from Latin America and Asia.

KEY CONCEPTS

race (p. 354) a socially constructed category composed of people who share biologically transmitted traits that members of a society consider important

ethnicity (p. 355) a shared cultural heritage

minority (p. 356) any category of people, distinguished by physical or cultural difference, that a society sets apart and subordinates

prejudice (p. 357) a rigid and irrational generalization about an entire category of people

stereotype (p. 358) an exaggerated description applied to every person in some category

racism (p. 359) the belief that one racial category is innately superior or inferior to another

scapegoat (p. 359) a person or category of people, typically with little power, whom people unfairly blame for their own troubles

discrimination (p. 361) any action that involves treating various categories of people unequally

institutional prejudice and discrimination (p. 362) bias inherent in the operation of society's institutions

pluralism (p. 363) a state in which racial and ethnic minorities are distinct but have social parity

assimilation (p. 363) the process by which minorities gradually adopt patterns of the dominant category

miscegenation (p. 363) biological reproduction by partners of different racial categories

segregation (p. 364) the physical and social separation of categories of people

genocide (p. 364) the systematic killing of one category of people by another

CRITICAL-THINKING QUESTIONS

1. Differentiate between race and ethnicity. What does it mean to say that race and ethnicity are socially constructed?

2. In what ways do prejudice and discrimination reinforce each other?

3. What does the growing significance of Latin music by performers such as Gloria and Emilio Estefan and Ricky Martin suggest about ethnicity in the United States?

4. Do you think U.S. society is becoming more or less colorblind? Is colorblindness a goal worth striving for? Why or why not?

CTQ4: Survey results suggest that many kinds of racial prejudices are eroding. Yet some critics suggest that calling for colorblindness may amount to supporting "business as usual" rather than, say, affirmative action policies.

NOTE: Shelby Steele claims that race consciousness is especially effective on the college campus, where the claim of black victimization is matched by widespread feelings of guilt among white people.

Q: "Morality cannot be legislated, but behavior can be regulated. Judicial decrees may not change the heart, but they can restrain the heartless." Martin Luther King, Jr.

Q: "A free man carries himself with dignity. He feels respect for others, and for himself. In a free society all are equals, and in a society of free men there exist no prejudices." Olof Palme

APPLICATIONS AND EXERCISES

1. Does your college or university take account of race and ethnicity in its admissions policies? Ask to speak with an admissions officer to see what you can learn about your school's policies and the reasons for them. Ask whether there is a "legacy" policy that favors applicants with a parent who attended the school.

2. Give several of your friends or family members a quick quiz, asking them what share of the U.S. population is white, Hispanic, African American, and Asian (see Table 14–1). If they are like most people, they will exaggerate the share of all minorities and understate the white proportion (Labovitz, 1996). What do you make of the results?

3. There are probably immigrants on your campus or in your local community. Have you ever thought about asking them to tell you about their homeland and their experiences in the United States? Most immigrants are pleased to be asked, and you can learn a great deal.

4. Packaged in the back of this new textbook is an interactive CD-ROM that offers a variety of study and review materials intended to help you better understand the material covered in this chapter. For this chapter, the CD-ROM contains an author's tip video, Real Life Sociology videos, other relevant audio and video, interactive map animations, audio journal entries from the author, Web links, and much more.

 ## SITES TO SEE

http://www.prenhall.com/macionis

Visit the interactive *Companion Website*™ that accompanies this text. Begin by clicking on the cover of your book. You will find a chapter-by-chapter study guide, practice tests, and a significant portion of the text for on-line review, as well as many suggested Web links.

http://www.naacp.org
http://www.jdl.org

These two organizations—the National Association for the Advancement of Colored People and the Jewish Defense League—are concerned with combating prejudice and discrimination and advancing the social standing of

minorities in the United States. Determine each organization's strategies and goals.

http://w3.access.gpo.gov/eop/ca/index.html

This worthwhile data site, operated by the Council of Economic Advisors, provides an assessment of social and economic well-being of various racial and ethnic categories of this country's population.

http://www.collegeboard.org/research/html/991017r.html

Read the report of the College Board's National Task Force on Minority High Achievement, which analyzes racial and ethnic differences in higher education.

 ## INVESTIGATE WITH CONTENTSELECT

Follow the instructions found on page 23 of this textbook to enter this chapter of the book's *Companion Website*™. Once in the chapter, click on the ContentSelect icon at the bottom left of your screen and enter your personal

User ID and Password. Enter keywords such as "race," "ethnicity," and "discrimination," and the search engine will help you become an effective researcher.

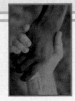

CHAPTER

15

Boris Kustodiev (1878–1927)
Easter Morning, 1911

Regional Gallery Art, Astrakhan, Russia.
Scala/Art Resource, N.Y.

AGING AND THE ELDERLY

Eldora Mitchell has just about seen it all: Born in 1903, she remembers when most homes had no electricity and there were more horses than cars on the streets. Looking back on her long life, what is most significant to her? "I have tried to live my life serving others and giving love," she explains. Growing up in a poor, African American family, she was scrubbing floors by the time she was twelve. She cleaned hospital rooms while she raised her own children, and later she spent years caring for her aging mother and her dying husband.

Now, at ninety-five, Mitchell smiles and says, "It's my turn." Four years ago, she moved across town to

live with her son, Charles, who is fifty-five and divorced. Charles Mitchell works the night shift as a police dispatcher in Durham, North Carolina, so he can spend days caring for his mother. In his home, Eldora Mitchell has a bedroom of her own. Bright green curtains hang around the windows, and a Bible with large print lies on the nightstand.

Eldora Mitchell does not have much money. She receives $45 per month as a pension from the hospital where she worked; her monthly Social Security check adds $568. Her life's savings is little more than $8,000. But as long as she has the love and care of her son, in her mind she is rich indeed (based on Rimer, 1998).

Across the United States, there are millions of families like the Mitchells, caring for aging parents. The United States is witnessing a revolution in aging, with people living longer and many—especially those with low incomes—turning to family members for assistance. In this chapter, we explore the graying of U.S. society, the various meanings different societies attach to their oldest members, and the transitions people face as they grow old.

THE GRAYING OF THE UNITED STATES

A quiet but powerful revolution is reshaping the United States. In 1900, the United States was a young nation, with half the population under age twenty-three; just 4 percent had reached sixty-five. But the number of elderly people—that is, women and men aged sixty-five or older—has increased more than tenfold in the past century. By 2000, the number of seniors reached 35 million. Seniors already outnumber

teenagers, and, as shown in Figure 15–1 on page 384, they accounted for 12.4 percent of the entire population in 2000.

By 2030, the number of seniors will double to 70 million, representing about 20 percent of the population. Then, almost half this country's people will be over age forty (U.S. Census Bureau, 2001).

Global Map 15–1 on page 385 shows that it is in the rich nations, such as the United States, that the share of elderly people is increasing most rapidly. Typically, two factors combine to drive up the elderly population: low birth rates (meaning that there are fewer children) and increasing longevity (meaning that people typically live longer).

In the United States, a third factor is also at work and will soon swell the ranks of the elderly: the aging of

Find information on aging and older people at the National Institute on Aging Web site: http://www.nia.nih.gov/

the baby boomers, the 75 million people born soon after the end of World War II. A generation later, after 1965, the birth rate took a sharp turn downward (the so-called baby bust

SUPPLEMENTS: An outline of this chapter, along with supplementary lecture material and discussion topics, is found in the *Data File*.

DIVERSITY: The odds of living to age 65 for people born in the U.S. in 1997 are 83% but vary for different categories. Whites: females, 87.1%; males, 78.8%. African Americans: females, 77.0%; males, 61.8% (U.S. National Center for Health Statistics, 1999).

NOTE: If today's longevity were the same as it was in 1900, half of the U.S. population would not be here at all: Half would have already died, and half would never have been born (White & Preston, cited in Crispell, 1997b).

NOTE: Between 1960 and 1999, the overall U.S. population grew 51%; the over-65 population increased 110%, and the 85 and older population soared 357%.

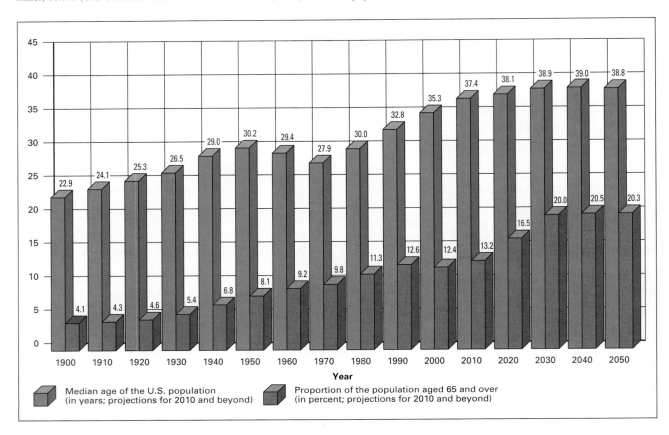

FIGURE 15–1 The Graying of U.S. Society

Source: U.S. Census Bureau (2000, 2001).

era), making the U.S. population more and more top-heavy in the twenty-first century.

THE BIRTH RATE: GOING DOWN

The first factor contributing to the graying of our society is a declining birth rate. The birth rate in the United States has been falling for more than a century. One reason is that as societies industrialize, children are more likely to survive to adulthood, so couples can have fewer. Another reason is that although children are an economic asset to farming families, they are an economic liability to families in industrial societies. Put otherwise, children no longer contribute to a family's financial well-being but are a major expense.

Also, as more and more women work outside the home for income, they want to have fewer children.

Advances in birth control technology during the twentieth century have provided the means to avoid unwanted births.

LIFE EXPECTANCY: GOING UP

The second factor contributing to the graying of U.S. society is an increase in life expectancy. It surprises many people to learn that in 1900, a typical female born in the United States lived just forty-eight years and a male lived just forty-six years. By contrast, females born in 2000 can look forward to living 79.5 years, and males can expect to live 74.1 years (U.S. National Center for Health Statistics, 2001).

A longer life span is one consequence of the Industrial Revolution. Greater material wealth and advances in medicine raise living standards; people benefit from better housing and nutrition and live

THE MAP: By 2020, almost all high-income nations will have high proportions of elderly people. Poor countries are those with high birth rates and limited longevity.

GLOBAL: Share of the population aged 65 and older, 2001: Italy, 18%; Japan, 17%; France, 16%; Germany, 16%; Canada, 13%; Argentina, 10%; Ethiopia, 3% (Population Reference Bureau, 2001).

GLOBAL: For all ages, women represent 50% of world population. For those aged 60+, 54%; for 80+, 62% (U.S. Census Bureau; see Dervarics, 1999).

GLOBAL: In terms of the size of the elderly population, P.R. China leads the world because of its population size, with about 88 million elderly people (about 7% of its total population).

WINDOW ON THE WORLD

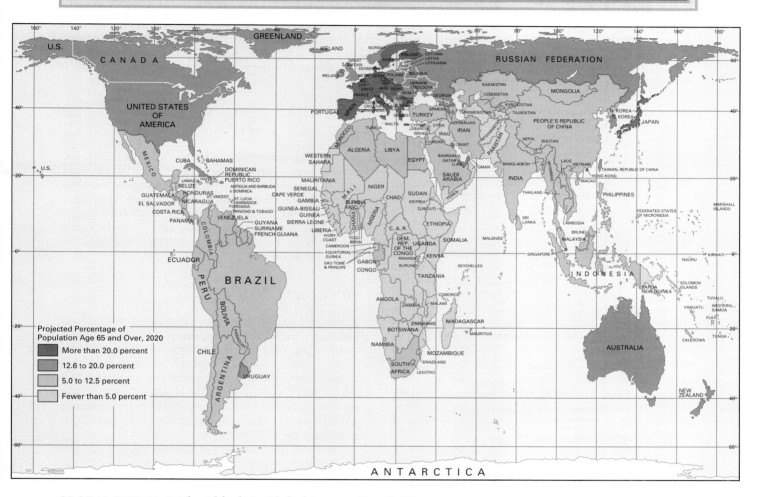

GLOBAL MAP 15–1 The Elderly in Global Perspective, 2020

Here we see projections for the share of population aged sixty-five and older in the year 2020, one generation from now. What relationship do you see between a country's income level and the size of its elderly population?

Source: U.S. Census Bureau (2000).

longer. At the same time, medical advances have almost eliminated infectious diseases such as smallpox, diphtheria, and measles that killed many infants and children a century ago. More recent medical strides help us fend off cancer and heart disease, which claim most of the U.S. population, but now later in life.

As life becomes longer, the fastest-growing segment of the U.S. population is people over eighty-five, who are already thirty-five times more numerous than they were in 1900. These men and women now number 4.2 million (about 1.5 percent of the total population). Projections put their number at 19 million

NOTE: Centenarians (people aged 100+): 35,000 in 1988, 62,000 in 1999, 1.1 million projected by 2050. The 78 million baby boomers will fuel the ranks of the elderly in the 21st century.

NOTE: Evidence of the graying of our society includes the rising proportion of college students over age 24: 39% in 1998 vs. 33% in 1974. The rise is due to larger older cohorts more than a change in the rate of college attendance (U.S. Census Bureau, 2000).

Q: "Life is one long process of getting tired." Robert Butler
NOTE: The graying of the U.S. would be even faster were it not for high immigration, which adds younger people to the population.

NOTE: As the ranks of the elderly swell, our society's share of people under 18 will drop dramatically. From 36% in 1960 and 26% in 1990, young people will account for just over 20% of the U.S. population by 2030.

(about 5 percent of the total) by the year 2050 (U.S. Census Office, 1902; Kaufman, 1990; Harbert & Ginsberg, 1991; U.S. Census Bureau, 2001).

We can only begin to imagine the changes that will accompany this major increase in the elderly population. As the number of older people retiring from the labor force goes up, the proportion of nonworking adults—already about ten times greater than in 1900—will demand more health care and other resources. Thus, the ratio of elderly people to working-age adults, called the *old-age dependency ratio*, will rise by 2050 from twenty to twenty-eight elderly people per 100 people aged eighteen to sixty-four. Government spending to support people over sixty-five is already increasing sharply. With tomorrow's swelling elderly population looking for support from a smaller share of younger workers, what security can today's young people expect in their old age? (Treas, 1995; Edmondson, 1996; Riche, 2000)

AN AGING SOCIETY: CULTURAL CHANGE

As the number of people and the share of the population over sixty-five push upward, cultural patterns are changing. For one thing, elderly people are becoming more and more visible in everyday life. Through much of the twentieth century, the young rarely mingled with the old, so that most people know little about old age. But as this country's elderly population steadily increases, age segregation will decline. Younger people will see more seniors at shopping malls, in movie theaters, at sporting events, and on the highways. Moreover, the design of buildings—from homes to stores to colleges—is likely to change to ease access for older people.

Of course, how frequently younger people interact with the elderly depends a great deal on where they live. This is because the elderly represent a far greater share of the population in some regions of the country than in others. National Map 15–1 looks at residential patterns of people aged sixty-five and older.

A larger share of old people certainly will change our way of life. Keep in mind, however, that seniors are socially diverse. Being "elderly" is a category open to everyone, if we are lucky to live long enough. Elders in the United States represent not just men and women but all cultures, classes, races, and ethnic backgrounds.

THE "YOUNG OLD" AND THE "OLD OLD"

Analysts sometimes distinguish two cohorts of the elderly. The younger elderly are between sixty-five and seventy-five and typically live independently, with good health and financial security; they are likely to be living as couples. The older elderly are past age seventy-five and more likely to have health and money problems and to be dependent on others. Because of their greater longevity, women outnumber men in the elderly population, an imbalance that grows greater with advancing age. Among the "oldest old," those over age eighty-five, about 60 percent are women.

GROWING OLD: BIOLOGY AND CULTURE

Studying the graying of the United States is the focus of **gerontology** (derived from the Greek word *geron*, meaning "an old person"), *the study of aging and the elderly*. Gerontologists—who work within many disciplines, including medicine, psychology, and sociology—investigate not only how people change as they grow old but also the different ways societies around the world define old age.

BIOLOGICAL CHANGES

Aging consists of gradual, ongoing changes in the body. But how individuals experience life's transitions—whether we welcome our maturity or complain about physical decline—depends largely on how a cultural system defines the various stages of life. In general, U.S. culture takes a positive view of biological changes that occur early in life. Through childhood and adolescence, people look forward to expanding opportunities and responsibilities.

But our youth-oriented culture takes a dimmer view of biological changes that develop later in life. Few people receive congratulations for getting old, at least not until they reach eighty-five or ninety. Rather, we commiserate with friends as they turn forty, fifty, and sixty and make jokes to avoid facing the fact that advancing age puts people, sooner or later, on a slippery slope of physical and mental decline. In short, we assume that by age fifty or sixty, people stop growing *up* and begin growing *down*.

Growing old brings on predictable changes: gray hair, wrinkles, loss of height and weight, and an overall decline in strength and vitality. After age fifty, bones become more brittle, so that injuries take longer to heal, and the odds of contracting chronic illnesses (such as arthritis and diabetes) and life-threatening conditions (such as heart disease and cancer) rise steadily. The sensory abilities—taste, sight, touch,

THE MAP: Young people migrate to regions of the country where jobs are plentiful; thus, counties with high proportions of elderly people are those that are economically contracting (especially rural counties in the middle of the country).

NOTE: The social clout of the baby-boomer generation is evident in the fact that they defined the 1960s, brought an end to the Vietnam War, got the vote by the time many of them were 18, initiated the second wave of feminism, celebrated the first Earth Day, and then raised the drinking age before their own children turned 18 (Longino, 1994).

THEN AND NOW: U.S. population 65 and older: *1974*, 10.3% (22 million); *2000*, 12.4% (35 million).

THEN AND NOW: Share of non-Hispanic whites in overall U.S. elderly population: *1980*, 88%; *1998*, 84%.

SEEING OURSELVES

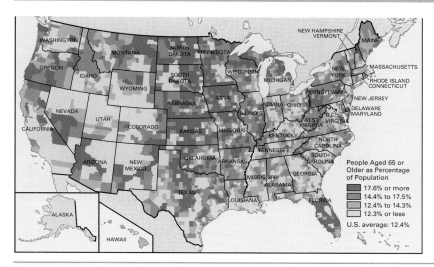

NATIONAL MAP 15–1
The Elderly Population of the United States

Common sense suggests that elderly people live in the Sunbelt, savoring the warmer climate of the South and Southwest. Although it is true that Florida has a disproportionate share of people over age sixty-five, it turns out that most counties with high percentages of older people are in the Midwest. What do you think accounts for this pattern? Hint: Which regions of the United States do *younger* people leave in search of jobs?

Source: U.S. Census Bureau (2001).

People Aged 65 or Older as Percentage of Population
- 17.6% or more
- 14.4% to 17.5%
- 12.4% to 14.3%
- 12.3% or less

U.S. average: 12.4%

---

smell, and especially hearing—become less keen with age (Colloway & Dollevoet, 1977; Treas, 1995).

Although health becomes more fragile with advancing age, most older people are not disabled by their physical condition. Only about one in ten seniors reports trouble walking, and fewer than one in twenty needs intensive care in a hospital or nursing home. No more than 1 percent of the elderly are bedridden. Overall, 27 percent of people over age sixty-five characterize their health as "fair" or "poor," and 73 percent consider their overall condition "good," "very good," or "excellent." In fact, the share of seniors reporting good or excellent health is going up (*Population Today*, 1997; U.S. National Center for Health Statistics, 1999).

However, patterns of well-being vary greatly within the elderly population. More health problems beset those over age seventy-five. Moreover, because women typically live longer than men, women spend more of their lives with chronic disabilities such as arthritis. In addition, well-to-do people live and work in healthful and safe environments and can afford better medical care. About 84 percent of elderly people with incomes exceeding $35,000 assess their own health as "excellent," "very good," or "good"; that figure drops below 60 percent among people with incomes under $10,000. Lower income and stress linked to prejudice and discrimination also explain why 60 percent of older African Americans assess their health in positive terms, compared to three-fourths of elderly white people (Feagin, 1997; U.S. National Center for Health Statistics, 1999).

PSYCHOLOGICAL CHANGES

Just as we tend to overstate the physical problems of old age, it is easy to exaggerate the psychological changes that accompany growing old. The conventional belief about intelligence over the life course can be summed up as "What goes up, must come down" (Baltes & Schaie, 1974).

If we operationalize intelligence to refer to skills such as sensorimotor coordination—the ability to arrange objects to match a drawing—we do find a steady decline after midlife. The ability to learn new material and think quickly also declines, although not until around age seventy. But the ability to apply familiar ideas holds steady with advancing age, and some studies show improvement in verbal and mathematical skills (Baltes & Schaie, 1974; Schaie, 1980).

We all wonder whether we will think or feel differently as we get older. Gerontologists report that, for better or worse, the answer is usually no. The only common personality change with advancing age is greater introspection. That is, people become less materialistic

NOTE: Six thoughts about getting older: (1) When people tell you how young you look, they're also telling you how old you are; (2) Anyone can get old; all you have to do is live long enough; (3) To worry about your age is silly. Every time you're a year older, so is everyone else; (4) Look at the bright side: No matter how old you are, you're younger than you will ever be again; (5) Wrinkles should merely indicate where smiles have been; (6) The one thing that comes without any effort is old age.

NOTE: We often assume that great figures of history were men and women of at least what we would call "middle age," but this is often not so. Joan of Arc, for example, was only 19 at the time of her martyrdom in 1431.

The reality of growing old is as much a matter of culture as it is of biology. In the United States, being elderly often means being inactive; yet, in rural regions of Iraq and other more traditional societies, old people commonly continue many familiar and productive routines.

and more engaged with their own thoughts and emotions. Generally, therefore, two elderly people who were childhood friends would recognize in each other the same personality traits that brought them together as youngsters (Neugarten, 1971, 1972, 1977; Wolfe, 1994).

AGING AND CULTURE

```
November 1, approaching Kandy, Sri
Lanka. Our little van struggles up the
steep mountain incline. Breaks in the
lush vegetation offer spectacular
views that interrupt our conversation
about growing old. "Then there are no
old age homes in your country?" I ask.
"In Colombo and other cities, I am
sure," our driver responds, "but not
many. We are not like you Americans."
"And how is that?" I counter, stiffen-
ing a bit. His eyes remain fixed on the
road: "We would not leave our fathers
and mothers to live alone."
```

When do people grow old? How do younger people regard society's oldest members? How do elderly people view themselves? The answers to these questions vary from place to place, showing that aging is not only a biological process but a matter of socially constructed meaning. In short, although aging is universal, the significance of growing old varies according to culture.

At one level, how well—and, more basically, how long—people live is closely linked to a society's technology and overall standard of living. Through most of human history, as English philosopher Thomas Hobbes (1588–1679) put it, people's lives have been "nasty, brutish, and short" (although Hobbes himself made it to the ripe old age of ninety-one). In his day, most people married and had children while in their teens, became middle-aged in their twenties, and succumbed to various illnesses in their thirties and forties. Thus, many greats of the past never reached what we would call old age at all: English poets Keats and Byron both died at age twenty-six; Mozart, the Austrian composer, died at thirty-five. Among famous writers, none of the three Brontë sisters lived to age forty, Edgar Allan Poe died at forty, Henry David Thoreau at forty-five, Oscar Wilde at forty-six, and Shakespeare at fifty-two.

About a century ago, rising living standards and advancing medical technology in the United States and Western Europe pushed longevity to about age fifty. As Global Map 15–2 shows, this life expectancy is still the case in many lower-income nations. During the twentieth century, increasing affluence in rich countries added almost thirty more years to the average life span.

THE MAP: Life expectancy closely parallels level of economic development; compare this map to Global Map 1–2 on page 6.

THEN AND NOW: Most of the increase in life expectancy occurred during the first half of the 20th century: *1900*, 47.3 years; *1950*, 68.2; *1960*, 69.7; *1970*, 70.8; *1980*, 73.7; *1990*, 75.4; *2000*, 76.9 (U.S. National Center for Health Statistics, 2001).

GLOBAL: Japan has the world's greatest life expectancy. In 1947, figures were: men, 50.1 years, women, 54.0 years; by 1997, comparable data were 76.8 and 82.9 years.

NOTE: Life expectancy is affected by changes in infant mortality and tends to exaggerate the change in life span for those who reach old age. In 1900, Americans reaching age 65 typically lived to age 77; by 1997, they could expect to reach 83.

WINDOW ON THE WORLD

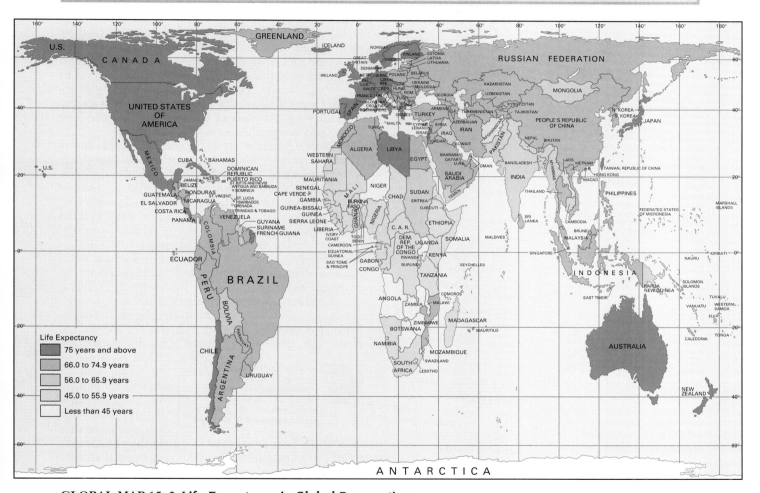

GLOBAL MAP 15–2 Life Expectancy in Global Perspective

Life expectancy has shot upward over the course of the twentieth century in high-income countries, including Canada, the United States, Western Europe, Japan, and Australia. A newborn in the United States can expect to live about seventy-seven years, and our life expectancy would be greater still were it not for the high risk of death among infants born into poverty. Because poverty is the rule in much of the world, lives are correspondingly shorter, especially in parts of Africa, where life expectancy may be less than forty years.

Source: Population Reference Bureau (2001).

Just as important as life expectancy is the value societies attach to their senior members. As Chapter 10 ("Social Stratification") explains, all societies distribute basic resources unequally. We now turn to the importance of age in this process.

AGE STRATIFICATION: A GLOBAL ASSESSMENT

Like race, ethnicity, and gender, age is a basis for social ranking. **Age stratification** is *the unequal distribution of wealth, power, and privilege among people at*

CHAPTER 15 Aging and the Elderly **389**

For data and graphics on aging in global perspective, visit this UN site: http://www.un.org/esa/population/publications/aging99/fa99.htm

different stages of the life course. As is true of other dimensions of social hierarchy, age stratification varies according to a society's level of technological development.

Hunting and Gathering Societies

As Chapter 4 ("Society") explains, without the technology to produce a surplus of food, hunters and gatherers must be nomadic. Therefore, survival depends on physical strength and stamina. As members of these societies grow old (in this case, about age thirty) they become less active and are considered an economic burden (Sheehan, 1976).

Pastoral, Horticultural, and Agrarian Societies

Once societies control food supplies by raising crops and animals, they can produce a surplus. Consequently, individuals can accumulate wealth over a lifetime. The most privileged members of these societies typically are the elderly, which gives rise to **gerontocracy,** *a form of social organization in which the elderly have the most wealth, power, and prestige.* Old people, particularly men, are honored (and sometimes feared) by their families, and, as the box reports in the case of the Abkhasians, they are leaders of society until they die. This veneration of the elderly also explains the widespread practice of ancestor worship in agrarian societies.

Industrial and Postindustrial Societies

We have noted that industrialization pushes living standards upward and advances medical technology, which increases human life expectancy. But although industrialization adds to the *quantity* of life, it does not necessarily improve the *quality* of life for old people. On the contrary, industrial societies give little power and prestige to the elderly. Why? Because the prime source of wealth shifts from land (typically controlled by the oldest members of society) to businesses and other goods (often owned and managed by younger people). Consider that in low-income countries the share of people over age sixty-five in the labor force is 76 percent of men and 44 percent of women. In high-income countries these percentages drop dramatically to 23 percent of men and 16 percent of women. These figures help explain why the peak earning years among

U.S. workers, on average, occur around age fifty; after that, earnings decline (UN Population Division, 1999; U.S. Census Bureau, 2000).

Modern living also physically separates the generations as younger people move away to pursue their careers, depending less on their parents and more on their own earning power. Furthermore, because industrial, urban societies change rapidly, the skills, traditions, and life experiences that served the old are not relevant to the young. Finally, the tremendous productivity of industrial nations means that not all members of a society need to work, so most of the very old and the very young play nonproductive roles (Cohn, 1982).

The long-term effect of all these factors transforms *elders* (a term with positive connotations) into *the elderly* (commanding far less prestige). In postindustrial societies such as the United States and Canada, economic and political leaders usually are middle-aged people who combine seasoned experience and up-to-date skills. In rapidly changing sectors of the economy, especially high-tech fields, many key executives are young, sometimes barely out of college. Industrial societies often consign older people to marginal participation in the economy because they lack the knowledge and training demanded in a fast-changing marketplace.

Some occupations are dominated by older people. Farming is one case in point: Whereas the average age of the U.S. labor force is thirty-eight, the average age

A U.S. Department of Agriculture report on the effects of aging in rural communities is found at http://www.ers.usda.gov/publications/rdrr90/rdrr90.pdf

of a U.S. farmer is fifty-seven, with 35 percent of farmers over age sixty-five. Certainly some older men and women remain at the helm of corporations and other businesses; more commonly, however, older people predominate only in traditional occupations (working as farmers, barbers, tailors, and shop clerks) and in jobs that involve minimal activity (night security guards, for instance) (Kaufman & Spilerman, 1982; Yudelman & Kealy, 2000).

Japan: An Exceptional Case

Japan stands out as an exception to the rule. Japan has about the same share of seniors as the United States, but its traditional culture reveres older people. Most aged people in Japan live with an adult daughter or son, and they play a significant role in family life. Elderly men in Japan are also more likely than their U.S. counterparts to stay in the labor force, and in many Japanese corporations, the oldest employees enjoy the

Q: "The older I grow, the more I distrust the familiar doctrine that age brings wisdom." H.L. Mencken
DISCUSS: Was John Glenn's 1999 flight into space at age 77 an important statement about the abilities of older people?
GLOBAL: People aged 65 and older were 6.8% of world population in 1998; by 2050, they will represent 15% (28% in Europe), according to the United Nations.

NOTE: Academics are aging far faster than the population as a whole. According to the U.S. National Center for Education Statistics, by the year 2000, a majority of full-time college faculty members will be aged 60 or older. In every discipline except mathematics, at least one-third of faculty members will be 65 or older by 2002. With increasing college enrollments and many coming retirements, our colleagues should be in rising demand.

GLOBAL SOCIOLOGY

Growing (Very) Old: A Report from Abkhasia

Anthropologist Sula Benet was sharing wine and conversation with a man in Tamish, a small village in the Republic of Abkhasia, once part of the Soviet Union. Based on the standards of her own society, she judged the man to be about seventy. She raised her glass and offered a toast to his long life. "May you live as long as Moses," she exclaimed. Her gesture of goodwill fell flat: Moses lived to 120, but Benet's companion was already 119.

In the Caucasus region of the world, a surprising number of people have lived past age 100. The *Guinness Book of World Records* lists the world's oldest person as Shirali Muslimov, who died twenty-five years ago at the reputed age of 168. Such reports give outsiders good reason to be skeptical. But government statistics confirm that even if many Abkhasians exaggerate their age, most handily outlive the average North American.

What accounts for the Abkhasians' remarkable longevity? The answer certainly is not advanced medical technology, so important to people in the United States; many Abkhasians have never seen a physician or entered a hospital.

The probable explanation for living so long is cultural, including diet and physical activity. Abkhasians eat little saturated fat (which is linked to heart disease), use no sugar, and drink no coffee or tea. Few smoke or chew tobacco. They consume large amounts of healthful fruits and vegetables and drink lots of buttermilk and low-alcohol wine. Abkhasians of all ages also lead active lives based on regular physical work.

Perhaps most important, Abkhasian culture gives everyone a strong feeling of belonging and clear sense of purpose. The elderly are valued members of the community, in marked contrast to our own practice of pushing old people to the margins of social life. As Benet explains,

"The old [in the United States], when they do not simply vegetate, out of view and out of mind, keep themselves 'busy' with bingo and shuffleboard." The Abkhasians do not even have a word for old people and have no concept of retirement. Furthermore, younger people accord senior members of society great prestige and respect because advanced age confers great wisdom. Elders, the indispensable guardians of culture, preside at important ceremonial occasions where they transmit their knowledge to the young. In short, people look to the old, rather than the young, for decisions and guidance in everyday life.

Given their positive approach to growing old, Abkhasians expect a long and useful life. They feel needed because—in their own minds and everyone else's—they are. Far from being a burden, elders stand at the center of society.

Sources: Based on Benet (1971) and Specter (1998).

Q: "Our society is getting older, but the old are getting younger. The 70-year-old of today is more like a person of 50 twenty years ago." Robert B. Maxwell, AARP

NOTE: In 1900, there were more men over 65 in the U.S. than there were women. The ratio has changed from 100:98 in 1900 to 100:141 in 1999. Higher past death rates for women (especially in childbirth) explain the pattern.

NOTE: Research suggests that, among subjects aged 25 to 74, subjective happiness rises with advancing age (Mroczek & Kolarz, 1998).

RESOURCE: The *Seeing Ourselves* reader includes an examination of "How the Grandparent Role Is Changing" by Roseann Giarrusso, Merril Silverstein, and Vern Bengston.

DIVERSITY: By age 75, 53% of women but only 22% of men live alone. At no age do most men live alone.

TABLE 15–1 Living Arrangements of the Elderly, 1999*

	Men	Women
Living alone	16.4%	40.1%
Living with spouse	73.6	41.8
Living with other relatives or nonrelatives	10.0	18.1

*In 2000, the percentage of elderly people living in a nursing home was 4.5 percent. These elders represent men and women who fall within each of the above categories.

Source: U.S. Census Bureau (2000).

greatest respect. But even Japan is steadily becoming more like other industrial societies, where growing old means giving up some measure of social importance (Harlan, 1968; Cowgill & Holmes, 1972; Treas, 1979; Palmore, 1982; Yates, 1986).

TRANSITIONS AND CHALLENGES OF AGING

We confront change at each stage of life. People learn to cope with new circumstances just as they must unlearn self-concepts and social patterns that no longer apply to their lives. Old age has its rewards, but of all stages of the life course, it presents the greatest challenges.

Physical decline in old age is less serious than most younger people think. But even so, older people endure more pain, become resigned to limiting their activities, adjust to greater dependence on others, lose dear friends and relatives, and face their own mortality. Moreover, because our culture places such high value on youthfulness, aging in the United States often means added fear and self-doubt (Hamel, 1990). As one retired psychologist commented about old age, "Don't let the current hype about the joys of retirement fool you. They are not the best of times. It's just that the alternative is even worse" (Rubenstein, 1991:13).

FINDING MEANING

Recall from Chapter 5 ("Socialization") Erik Erikson's (1963, 1980) theory that elderly people must resolve a tension of integrity versus despair. No matter how much they still may be learning and achieving, older people recognize that their lives are nearing an end. Thus the elderly spend much time reflecting on their past, including disappointments and accomplish-

ments. To Erikson, integrity means assessing one's life in a realistic way. Without such honesty, this stage of life may turn into a time of despair—a dead end with little positive meaning.

In a classic study of people in their seventies, Bernice Neugarten (1971) found that some people cope with growing older better than others. Worst off are those who fail to come to terms with aging; they develop *disintegrated and disorganized personalities* marked by despair. Many of these people end up as passive residents of hospitals or nursing homes.

A second segment of Neugarten's subjects, with *passive-dependent personalities*, are only slightly better off. They have little confidence in their abilities to cope with daily events, sometimes seeking help even if they do not need it. They are always in danger of social withdrawal, and their level of life satisfaction is low.

A third category, those with *defended personalities*, live independently but fear aging. They try to shield themselves from the reality of old age by fighting to stay youthful and physically fit. Their efforts to stay healthy certainly are positive, but setting unrealistic standards breeds stress and disappointment.

Most of Neugarten's subjects display what she calls *integrated personalities:* They cope well with the challenges of growing old. As Neugarten sees it, the key to successful aging lies in maintaining one's dignity and self-confidence and accepting the inevitability of advancing age.

SOCIAL ISOLATION

Being alone can cause anxiety at any age, but isolation is most common among elderly people. Retirement closes off one source of social interaction, physical problems may limit mobility, and negative stereotypes of the elderly as "over the hill" may discourage younger people from close social contact with them.

However, the greatest cause of social isolation is the inevitable death of significant others. Few human experiences affect people as profoundly as the death of a spouse. One study found that almost three-fourths of widows and widowers cited loneliness as their most serious problem (Lund, 1989). In such cases, people must rebuild their lives in the glaring absence of others with whom, in many cases, they spent most of their adult lives.

The problem of social isolation falls more heavily on women because they typically outlive their husbands. Table 15–1 shows that three-fourths of men aged sixty-five and over live with spouses, compared to only four in ten elderly women. Moreover, 40 percent of older women (especially the "older elderly") live

DIVERSITY: Percentage of U.S. population not in the paid labor force by age: under age 60, 14% of men and 27% of women; 60–64, 45% and 61%; 65–69, 72% and 82%; 70 and older, 88% and 95% (U.S. Department of Labor, 2000).

NOTE: In 1999, 4 million seniors (12% of seniors not in institutional care) were working or looking for work. Half of elderly workers do so full time.

NOTE: Research suggests factors encouraging retirement include (1) dissatisfaction with one's work, (2) being married, (3) marital satisfaction, and (4) having a nonworking spouse (see Reitzes, Mutran, & Fernandez, 1998).

NOTE: Despite the common image (in the middle class) of retirees heading south to Florida or west to Arizona, only 4% of elderly relocated during the past year (compared to 18% of people aged 20 to 64).

alone, compared to 16 percent of older men. Greater isolation among elderly women in the United States may account for the research finding that their mental health is not as sound as that of elderly men (Chappell & Havens, 1980). Also, living alone—which many older people value as a sign of independence—presumes the financial means to do so (Mutchler, 1992).

For most older people, including Eldora Mitchell, profiled in the opening to this chapter, family members are the major source of social support. The majority of older people have at least one adult child living no more than ten miles way. About half of these nearby children visit their parents at least once a week, although much research confirms that daughters are more likely than sons to visit regularly (Stone, Cafferata, & Sangl, 1987; Lin & Rogerson, 1994).

RETIREMENT

Work not only provides us with earnings but is also an important part of our personal identity. Thus, retirement means not only a reduction in income but also reduced social prestige and some loss of purpose in life.

Some organizations help ease this transition. Colleges and universities confer the title "professor emeritus" (from the Latin term meaning "fully earned") on retired faculty members, many of whom are permitted to maintain their library privileges, parking spaces, and e-mail accounts. Indeed, these highly experienced faculty can be a valuable resource to students and younger professors (Parini, 2001).

For many older people, new activities and interests minimize the personal disruption and loss of prestige brought on by retirement. Volunteer work can be very rewarding, allowing people to apply their career skills in new settings. AARP, the leading organization of U.S. seniors, has more than 15 million members over age fifty who engage in a wide range of volunteer activities. Surveys of the oldest baby boomers—those now in their mid-fifties—suggest that most expect to work at least part-time after they retire (Mergenhagen, 1996b; Gardyn, 2000).

Although we take retirement for granted, the concept emerged only within the last century in high-income countries. Industrial technology is so productive that not everyone needs to work; in addition, it places a premium on up-to-date skills. Therefore, retirement emerges as a strategy to permit younger workers—presumably those with the most current knowledge and training—to predominate in the labor force. Also, the introduction of private and public pension programs made it financially possible for older

Women and men experience stages of the life course in different ways. Most men, for example, pass through old age with the support of a partner. Women, who typically outlive men, endure much of their old age alone.

people to retire. In poor societies, most people work until they can work no more.

Given how varied the elderly population is, we might wonder exactly when (or even whether) we should expect people to retire. In our own history, Congress began phasing out mandatory retirement policies in the 1970s until, by 1987, almost none existed. Even so, the median age at retirement has fallen from sixty-eight in 1950 to sixty-three today. By age sixty-five, 83 percent of men and 91 percent of women can afford to leave the paid labor force. Indeed, in recent decades early retirement has been gaining popularity in the United States. Even so, given the fact that a sixty-five-year-old can look forward to ten to twenty more years of life, more people are remaining active:

DIVERSITY: Poverty rates for the elderly by race and ethnicity, 2000: Ages 65–74: all, 8.9%; non-Hispanic white, 6.8%; African American, 19.4%; Hispanic, 18.9%; ages 75 and over: all, 11.7%; non-Hispanic white, 10.0%; African American, 26.4%; Hispanic, 18.5% (U.S. Census Bureau, 2001).

NOTE: Looking at a cross-section of the U.S. population, income is highest at about age 50 and wealth is greatest at about age 67 (median wealth of $84,000, up from about $57,000 at age 40).

NOTE: Despite the present trend toward greater affluence for the elderly, several factors may undermine their future financial security: (1) the shift toward lower-income jobs noted in Chapter 11; (2) more people reaching 65 will have living parents who need support; and (3) an increasingly minority work force that historically has been underpaid will support the retirement system.

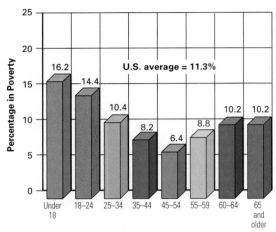

DIVERSITY SNAPSHOT

FIGURE 15–2 U.S. Poverty Rates, by Age, 2000
Source: U.S. Census Bureau (2001).

doing volunteer work, going back to school, or starting second careers. For their part, more companies recognize that many people reaching their sixties do not want to withdraw from work and are offering phased retirement by which people can retire in stages (Mergenhagen, 1994; U.S. Department of Labor, 2000; Gardyn, 2001; Walsh, 2001).

AGING AND POVERTY

By the time they reach sixty-five, most people have paid off their home mortgages and children's college expenses. But now medical care, household help, and home utility bills typically go up. At the same time, retirement often means a significant decline in income. Today's seniors are more affluent than ever before, yet many lack enough savings or pension benefits to be self-supporting. Social Security is the major source of income for most people over sixty-five. Not surprisingly, then, the risk of poverty rises after midlife, as shown in Figure 15–2.

The rate of poverty among the elderly has fallen sharply, from about 35 percent in 1960 to 10.2 percent in 2000, below the rate (11.3 percent) for the population as a whole. Moreover, since about 1980, seniors have posted a 25 percent increase in average income (in constant dollars), whereas income of people under thirty-five has held steady (U.S. Census Bureau, 2001).

Several factors have brought about this financial windfall: Better health now allows people who want to work to stay in the labor force, employer pension programs are more generous, and more couples enjoy double incomes. Government policy also has played a part, with programs benefiting the elderly (including Social Security) amounting to almost half of all government spending, even as spending on children has remained flat.

But disadvantages associated with race and ethnicity persist in old age. In fact, income inequality among the elderly is greater than among younger adults. In 2000, the poverty rate among elderly Hispanics (18.8 percent) and African Americans (22.3 percent) was two to three times higher than the rate for elderly non-Hispanic whites (8.3 percent) (U.S. Census Bureau, 2001).

Gender also continues to shape the lives of people as they age. Among full-time workers, women over sixty-five had median earnings of $34,159 in 2000, compared to $47,985 for men over sixty-five. A quick calculation shows that these older full-time working women earn just 71 percent as much as comparable men; thus, the income gap linked to gender is greater among older than younger people (recall that *all* working women earn 73 percent as much as *all* working men). This is because older women typically have much less schooling than men their age, so they hold lower-paying jobs.

But, of course, the majority of elderly people have retired from the labor force. Thus, a more realistic financial assessment must take account of the entire elderly population, nonworking as well as working. From this point of view, median individual income is far lower: $10,899 for women, which is 57 percent of the $19,168 earned by men (U.S. Census Bureau, 2001).

In the United States, then, although the elderly are faring better than ever, growing old (especially for women and other minorities) still raises the risk of poverty. One recent study found that poor elderly households typically spend three-fourths of their income on basic necessities, which means that these people are just getting by (Koelln, Rubin, & Picard, 1995).

Poverty among the elderly often is hidden from view. Because of personal pride and a desire to stay independent, many elderly people conceal financial problems even from their own families. People who have supported their children for years find it difficult to admit that they can no longer provide for themselves.

Q: "How can anyone deny that parents who have toiled for their children in their youth, have lost many a good night's sleep when they were ill, have washed their diapers long before they could talk and have spent about a quarter of a century bringing them up and fitting them for life, have the right to be fed by them and respected when they are old?" Chinese philosopher Lin Yutang

GLOBAL: In a 1994 effort to strengthen "family values," Singapore passed legislation allowing elderly people to sue their children for support.
DISCUSS: How will increasing responsibility to care for aging parents affect today's younger people? What are the financial and emotional concerns? Will this speed or delay their own retirement?

Typically, income drops by the time people pass the age of sixty. Therefore, the risk of poverty rises among the elderly. Research shows that poor elderly people need most of their income just to pay for necessities. For those who fall behind, homelessness can result. It is easy to imagine the struggle of homeless living for those whose desire for independence is offset by waning vitality.

CAREGIVING[1]

In an aging society, the need for caregiving is bound to increase. **Caregiving** consists of *informal and unpaid care provided to a dependent person by family members, other relatives, or friends.* Although parents provide caregiving to children, the term is more often applied to the needs of elderly men and women. Indeed, today's middle-aged adults are called the "sandwich generation" because many will spend as much time caring for their aging parents as for their own children.

Who Are the Caregivers?

Surveys show that 80 percent of caregiving to elders is provided by family members. Most caregivers live nearby, typically only minutes away from the older person. In addition, 75 percent of all caregiving is provided by women, most often daughters and, next, wives. The gender norm is so strong that daughters-in-law are more likely than sons to care for an aging parent.

About two-thirds of all caregivers are married, and one-third are also responsible for young children. When we add the fact that half of all caregivers also have

a part- or full-time job, it is clear that caregiving is a responsibility beyond what most people already consider a full day's work. Half of all primary caregivers spend more than twenty hours per week providing elder care.

Elder Abuse

Abuse of older people takes many forms, from passive neglect to active torment; it includes verbal, emotional, financial, and physical harm. Research suggests that 1 million elderly people (3 percent) suffer serious maltreatment each year, and three times as many (about one in ten) suffer abuse at some point. Like other forms of family violence, abuse of the elderly often goes unreported because victims are reluctant to talk about their plight (Bruno, 1985; Clark, 1986; Pillemer, 1988; Holmstrom, 1994; Thompson, 1997, 1998).

Certain factors increase the possibility of elder abuse. Risk is greater if the caregiver works full time, is also caring for young children, is poor, feels little affection for the older person, finds the elderly person very difficult, and gets no support or help from others.

Many caregivers contend with fatigue, emotional distress, and guilt over not being able to do more. But there is also a positive side to caregiving: Helping another person is a selfless act of human kindness that affirms the best in us and provides a source of personal enrichment and satisfaction (Lund, 1993).

---

[1]This section is based on Lund (1993) and helpful personal communication.

SOCIAL SURVEY: The National Aging Center on Elder Abuse reports that in about one-third of cases seniors are abused by adult children at home; spouses come next, with self-abuse through neglect third.
Q: "Aging is the neglected stepchild of the human life cycle." Robert Butler

DIVERSITY: A crucial difference between ageism and racism or sexism is that being old is an *open* category that intersects all others.
NOTE: Robert Butler coined the term "ageism" in 1969.
RESOURCE: Robert Butler's statement "The Tragedy of Old Age in America," which challenges various myths about old age, is included among the classics in the Macionis and Benokraitis reader, *Seeing Ourselves.*

AGEISM

In earlier chapters, we explained how ideology—including racism and sexism—serves to justify the social disadvantages of minorities. Sociologists use the parallel term **ageism** for *prejudice and discrimination against the elderly.*

Like racism and sexism, ageism can be blatant (as when a college decides not to hire a sixty-year-old professor because of her age) or subtle (as when a nurse speaks to elderly patients in a condescending tone, as if they were children). Also like racism and sexism, ageism builds physical traits into stereotypes; in the case of the elderly, people consider gray hair, wrinkled skin, and stooped posture signs of personal incompetence. Negative stereotypes portray the aged as helpless, confused, resistant to change, and generally unhappy (Butler, 1975). Even sentimental views of sweet little old ladies and eccentric old gentlemen are stereotypes that gloss over individuality and ignore years of experience and accomplishment.

Sometimes, ageism contains a kernel of truth. Statistically speaking, old people are more likely than young people to be mentally and physically impaired. But we slip into ageism when we make unwarranted generalizations about an entire category of people, most of whom do not conform to the stereotypes.

Betty Friedan (1993), a pioneer of today's feminist movement, believes ageism is deeply rooted in our culture. Friedan points out that few elderly people appear in the mass media; for example, only a small percentage of television shows include main characters over sixty. More generally, when most of us think about older people, it is often in negative terms: This older man *lacks* a job, that older woman has *lost* her vitality, and seniors *look back* to their youth. In short, says Friedan, we often treat being old as if it were a disease—marked by decline and deterioration—for which there is no cure.

Nevertheless, Friedan believes that older women and men in the United States are discovering that they have more to contribute than others give them credit for. Advising small business owners, designing housing for the poor, teaching children to read—there are countless ways in which older people can enhance their own lives and help others.

THE ELDERLY: A MINORITY?

No one doubts that as a category of people in this country, the elderly face social disadvantages. But sociologists disagree as to whether the aged form a minority in the same way as, say, African Americans or women.

Leonard Breen (1960) set out one side of the argument, concluding that the elderly are a minority because they have a clear social identity based on their age and they are subject to prejudice and discrimination. But Gordon Streib (1968) countered that minority status usually is both permanent and exclusive. That is, a person is an African American or woman *for life* and cannot become part of the dominant category of whites or men. Being elderly, says Streib, is an *open* status because people are elderly for only part of their lives, and everyone who has the good fortune to live long enough grows old.

Streib further pointed out that social disadvantages faced by the elderly are less substantial than those experienced by true minorities. For example, old people have never been deprived of the right to own property, vote, or hold office, as African Americans and women have. Some elderly people do suffer economic disadvantages, but not primarily because of old age. Rather, most of the aged poor fall into categories of people likely to be poor at any age. To Streib, it is not so much that the old grow poor as that the poor grow old.

In light of Streib's arguments—and the rising economic power of the elderly in recent decades—it seems reasonable to conclude that old people are not a minority in the same sense as other categories are. Instead, perhaps we should describe the elderly as a distinctive segment of our population with characteristic pleasures and challenges.

In sum, growing old involves problems and transitions. Some are brought on by physical decline. But others—including social isolation, adjustment to retirement, and risk of poverty, abuse, and ageism—are products of society. In the next section, we turn to theoretical perspectives on how society shapes the lives of the elderly.

THEORETICAL ANALYSIS OF AGING

Each of sociology's major theoretical paradigms sheds light on the process of aging in the United States. We examine each in turn.

STRUCTURAL-FUNCTIONAL ANALYSIS: AGING AND DISENGAGEMENT

Drawing on the ideas of Talcott Parsons, an architect of the structural-functional paradigm, Elaine Cumming and William Henry (1961) set the groundwork for this approach, explaining that aging threatens to disrupt

CYBER: Surveys show about 25% of seniors own a computer; 40% say they use one regularly.
DIVERSITY: The Age Discrimination in Employment Act (1967) prohibits age discrimination against workers or job applicants aged 40 to 65. As amended in 1975, it outlaws discrimination in federally funded job programs; in 1986, an additional change banned mandatory retirement in almost all types of jobs.

NOTE: The cultural value of individualism encourages elderly people to fend for themselves in order to be self-reliant. This kind of social disengagement is vividly evident in the single-room occupancy (SRO) hotels inhabited by many poor, elderly men (Cowgill, 1986:49).
NOTE: Another limitation of activity theory is putting too much emphasis on physical activity (Dale Lund).

There may be reasons to disengage elderly people from some critical work roles. But research shows that, for most people, satisfaction in old age (or, for that matter, at any age) depends on maintaining a high level of meaningful activity. A rising number of seniors are finding that they have much to contribute to others.

society as physical decline and death take their toll. In response, society disengages the elderly, gradually transferring statuses and roles from the old to the young so that tasks are performed with minimal interruption.

Disengagement is thus a strategy to ensure the orderly operation of society by removing aging people from productive roles while they are still able to perform them. Disengagement has an added benefit in a rapidly changing society because young workers typically bring the most up-to-date skills and training to their work. Formally, then, **disengagement theory** is *the idea that society enhances its orderly operation by disengaging people from positions of responsibility as they reach old age.*

Disengagement provides benefits to elderly people as well. Although most people in the United States who reach their sixties are quite able to continue working, the majority begin to think about retirement, or at least cutting back on their jobs. Exactly when people do this depends on a number of factors, including health, job satisfaction, and financial assets. Retirement does not necessarily mean inactivity; some people begin a different kind of job, and others develop or expand hobbies. In general, people in their sixties begin to think less about what they *have* been doing and begin to think more about what they *want* to do with the rest of their lives (Palmore, 1979b; Carstensen, 1995; Schultz & Heckhausen, 1996; Voltz, 2000).

Critical evaluation. Disengagement theory explains why rapidly changing high-income societies typically

define their oldest members as socially marginal. But there are several limitations to this approach.

First, many workers cannot disengage from paid work because they do not have the financial resources to fall back on. Second, many elderly people, regardless of their financial circumstances, do not want to disengage from their earlier productive roles. After all, disengagement comes at a high personal price, including loss of friends and social prestige. Third, it is far from clear that the societal benefits of disengagement outweigh its social costs, which include the loss of human resources and the need to care for people who might otherwise be able to care for themselves. Indeed, as the numbers of elderly people swell, finding ways to help seniors remain independent is a high priority. Fourth, a rigid system of disengagement does not take account of the widely differing abilities among the elderly.

SYMBOLIC-INTERACTION ANALYSIS: AGING AND ACTIVITY

Another approach draws heavily on the symbolic-interaction paradigm. **Activity theory** is *the idea that a high level of activity enhances personal satisfaction in old age.* Because various activities help build social identity, disengagement is bound to reduce satisfaction and meaning in elderly people's lives. What seniors need is not to be pushed out of roles but to find a wider range of productive or recreational activities. The importance of such options increases when we realize that

NOTE: In 1998, 62,000 people (.2%) aged 65 or older were enrolled in U.S. colleges and universities.
SOCIAL SURVEY: "As you know, many older people share a
home with their grown children. Do you think this is generally a
good idea or a bad idea?" (GSS 2000, N = 1,896; Codebook, 2001:206)
"A good idea"   50.7%   "Depends"   16.5%
"A bad idea"   31.2%   DK/NR   1.5%

Q: "The nation's rapidly aging white middle class will draw its retirement income from an increasingly black and Hispanic work
force." Franklin A. Thomas
DIVERSITY: The elderly are politically active: 67% of seniors
claim to have voted in the 1996 national elections, compared to
49% of people 25 to 44 years of age.

on average, seniors now have ten hours more leisure time a week than twenty years ago (Robinson, Werner, & Godbey, 1997).

Activity theory does not reject the notion of job disengagement; it simply says that people need to find new roles to replace those they leave behind. Research confirms that elderly people who maintain a high activity level derive the most satisfaction from their lives.

Activity theory also recognizes that the elderly are diverse, with highly variable interests, needs, and physical abilities. Therefore, the activities people pursue and the pace at which they pursue them is always an individual matter (Havighurst, Neugarten, & Tobin, 1968; Neugarten, 1977; Palmore, 1979b; Moen, Dempster-McClain, & Williams, 1992).

Critical evaluation. Activity theory shifts the focus of analysis from the needs of society (as stated in disengagement theory) to the needs of the elderly themselves. It emphasizes the social diversity among elderly people, an important consideration in formulating any government policy.

A limitation of this approach, from a structural-functionalist point of view, is the tendency to exaggerate the well-being and competence of the elderly. Do we really want to depend on elderly people to perform crucial roles? From another perspective, activity theory falls short by ignoring the fact that many problems older people face have more to do with society than with themselves. We turn now to that point of view: social-conflict theory.

SOCIAL-CONFLICT ANALYSIS: AGING AND INEQUALITY

A social-conflict analysis is based on the idea that different age categories have different opportunities and different access to social resources, creating a system of age stratification. Middle-aged people in the United States enjoy the greatest power and the most opportunities and privileges, and the elderly (and children) have less power and prestige and a higher risk of poverty. Employers often replace elderly workers with younger men and women to keep down wages. As a result, older people become second-class citizens (Atchley, 1982; Phillipson, 1982).

To conflict theorists, age-based hierarchy is inherent in an industrial-capitalist society. In line with Marxist thought, Steven Spitzer (1980) points out that a profit-oriented society devalues any category of people that is economically unproductive. To the extent that older people are less productive, then, our society labels them mildly deviant.

Social-conflict analysis also draws attention to social diversity in the elderly population. Differences of class, race, ethnicity, and gender divide older people, as they do everyone else. Some seniors have far greater economic security, access to better medical care, and more options for personal satisfaction in old age than others. Likewise, elderly WASPs typically enjoy many advantages denied to older minorities. And women—an increasing majority as people age—suffer the social and economic disadvantages of both sexism and ageism.

Critical evaluation. Social-conflict theory adds to our understanding of the aging process by underscoring age-based inequality and explaining how capitalism devalues elderly people who are less productive. But it is not capitalism that creates the lower social standing, according to critics; the real culprit is *industrialization*. Thus, the elderly are not better off under a socialist system, as a Marxist analysis claims. Furthermore, the notion that either industrialization or capitalism dooms the elderly to economic distress is challenged by a steady rise in income and well-being among the U.S. elderly in recent decades.

DEATH AND DYING

> To every thing there is a season,
> And a time for every matter under heaven:
> A time to be born and a time to die.

These well-known lines from the Bible's Book of Ecclesiastes state two basic truths about human existence: the fact of birth and the inevitability of death. Just as life varies throughout history and around the world, death, too, has many faces. We conclude this chapter with a brief look at the changing character of death, the final stage in the process of growing old.

HISTORICAL PATTERNS OF DEATH

In the past, confronting death was commonplace. No one assumed that a newborn child would live for long, a fact that led many parents to delay naming children until they were one or two years old. For those fortunate enough to survive infancy, illness, accident, and natural catastrophe made life uncertain at best.

Sometimes, in fact, food shortages forced societies to protect the majority by sacrificing the least productive members. *Infanticide* is the killing of newborn infants, and *geronticide* is the killing of the elderly.

Q: "Death itself is clearly among the biologically normal phenomena, and the changes which are inseparably connected with the passage of time are equally so. . . . [Even so,] it has sometimes been said that we Americans do our best to deny the reality of death. . . . The most important point seems to be that we (as Americans) cannot glorify death simply because we value achievement in this life, and death necessarily puts an end to that achievement." Talcott Parsons

NOTE: A grim demographic fact is that after age 30, a person's chance of death doubles every eight years (Waldrop, 1992).
NOTE: The modern avoidance of death is evident in the loss of the traditional custom of writing one's own epitaph. Today, even writing a will is considered to be a matter for late in life and is avoided entirely by two-thirds of U.S. people, who die without one.

If death was routine, it was also readily accepted. For example, medieval Christianity assured believers that death fit into the divine plan for human existence. Here is how the historian Philippe Ariès describes Sir Lancelot, one of King Arthur's Knights of the Round Table, preparing for death when he thinks he is mortally wounded:

> His gestures were fixed by old customs, ritual gestures which must be carried out when one is about to die. He removed his weapons and lay quietly upon the ground. . . . He spread his arms out, his body forming a cross . . . in such a way that his head faced east toward Jerusalem. (1974:7–8)

As societies gradually learned more about health and medicine, death became less of an everyday experience. Fewer children died at birth, and accidents and disease took a smaller toll among adults. People today view dying as extraordinary, except when it occurs among the very old or is associated with war or catastrophe. Consider that in 1900, about one-third of all deaths in the United States occurred before age five and fully two-thirds before age fifty-five. Today, by contrast, 85 percent of our population dies *after* age fifty-five. Death and old age are closely linked in our culture.

THE MODERN SEPARATION OF LIFE AND DEATH

Now removed from everyday experience, death somehow seems unnatural. If social conditions prepared our ancestors to accept their deaths, modern society, with its youth culture and aggressive medical technology, fosters a desire for eternal youth and immortality. Death has become separated from life.

Death is also *physically* removed from everyday activities. The clearest evidence of this is that many of us have never seen a person die. Our ancestors typically died at home in the presence of family and friends, but most deaths today occur in impersonal settings such as hospitals and nursing homes. Even in hospitals, dying patients occupy a special part of the building, and hospital morgues are located well out of sight of patients and visitors (Sudnow, 1967; Ariès, 1974).

ETHICAL ISSUES: CONFRONTING DEATH

Moral questions are more pressing than ever now that technological advances give humans the power to prolong life and thereby draw a line separating life from

In many traditional societies, people express great respect not only for elders but also for their ancestors. Dani villagers in New Guinea mummified the body of this elder in a sitting position so that they could continue to honor him and feel his presence in their daily lives.

death. We now grapple with how to use these new powers—or whether to use them at all.

When Does Death Occur?

Perhaps the most basic question is the most difficult: Exactly how do we define death? Common sense suggests that life ceases when breathing and heartbeat stop. But the ability of medical personnel to resuscitate someone after a heart attack and artificially sustain breathing makes such definitions of death obsolete. Medical and legal experts in the United States now define death as an *irreversible* state involving no response to stimulation, no movement or breathing, no reflexes, and no indication of brain activity (Ladd, 1979; Wall, 1980).

The Right-to-Die Debate

Today, many aging people are less afraid of death than the prospect of being kept alive at all costs. In other

NOTE: Philosophically, the right-to-die debate breaks down this way: Those who categorically view life—even with suffering—as preferable to death reject euthanasia. Those who recognize circumstances under which death is preferable to life endorse euthanasia, but they face the practical problem of determining just when life should be ended.

Q: "Death is a subject that is evaded, ignored, and denied by our youth-worshiping, progress-oriented society. It is almost as if we have taken on death as just another disease to be conquered." Joseph L. Braga and Laurie D. Braga (quoted in Kubler-Ross, 1975:x)

NOTE: In Oregon, according to a 1996 study, 21% of physicians reported being asked to assist in a suicide, and 7% said they had done so.

GLOBAL SOCIOLOGY

Death on Demand: A Report from the Netherlands

Marcus Erich picked up the telephone and dialed his brother Arjen's number. In a quiet voice, thirty-two-year-old Marcus announced, "It's Friday at 5 o'clock." When the time came, Arjen was there, having driven to his brother's farmhouse an hour south of Amsterdam. They said their final goodbyes. Soon afterward, Marcus's physician arrived. Marcus and the doctor spoke for a few moments, and then the doctor prepared a "cocktail" of barbiturates and other drugs. As Marcus drank the mixture, he made a face, joking, "Can't you make this sweeter?"

As the minutes passed, Marcus lay back and his eyes closed. But after half an hour, he was still breathing. At that point, according to their earlier agreement, the doctor administered a lethal injection. In a few minutes, Marcus's life came to an end.

Events like this take us to the heart of the belief that people have a right to die. Marcus Erich was dying of AIDS. For five years, his body had been wasting away, and he suffered greatly with no hope of recovery. He wanted his doctor to end his life.

The Netherlands, a small nation in northwestern Europe, has gone further than any other in the world in allowing mercy killing or euthanasia. A 1981 Dutch law allows a physician to assist in a suicide if the following five conditions are met:

1. The patient must make a voluntary, well-considered, and repeated request to the doctor for help in dying.

2. The patient's suffering must be unbearable and without prospect of improvement.

3. The doctor and the patient must discuss alternatives.

4. The doctor must consult with at least one colleague who has access to the patient and the patient's medical records.

5. The assisted suicide must be performed in accordance with sound medical practice.

Official records indicate that doctors end 3,000 to 4,000 lives per year in the Netherlands. But because many cases are never reported, the actual number may well be twice that many.

Sources: Based on della Cava (1997) and Mauro (1997).

words, medical technology now threatens personal autonomy by letting doctors rather than the dying person decide when life is to end. In response, many people now seek control over their deaths just as they seek control over their lives.

After deliberation, patients, families, and doctors may decide to forgo heroic measures to keep a person alive. *Living wills*—documents stating which medical procedures a person wants and does not want under specific conditions—are now widespread.

A more difficult issue involves mercy killing, or **euthanasia,** *assisting in the death of a person suffering from an incurable disease.* Euthanasia (from the Greek term meaning "a good death") poses an ethical dilemma because it involves not just refusing life-extending treatment but actively taking steps to end life. In euthanasia, some see an act of kindness, and others see a form of killing.

Is there a right to die? People with incurable diseases can forgo treatment that might prolong their lives. But whether a doctor should be allowed to help bring about death is a matter of debate. In 1994, three states—Washington, California, and Oregon—voted on propositions that would allow physicians to help people who wanted to die. Only in Oregon did voters pass the initiative, and opposition tied up enactment of the law in Oregon's state courts until 1997, when voters again endorsed it. Since then, Oregon doctors have legally assisted in the death of terminally ill patients. In 1997, however, the U.S. Supreme Court declared that the U.S. Constitution recognizes no right to die. In 2001, the attorney general took action to prevent physician-assisted suicide in Oregon and any other states. However, no change has been made to the law pending resolution by Oregon courts.

In the Netherlands, we find the most permissive euthanasia law in the world. How does the Dutch system operate? The box takes a closer look.

Should the United States hold the line on euthanasia or follow the lead of the Dutch? Right to-die

NOTE: In 1963, Jessica Mitford's *The American Way of Death* pointed out this culture's extravagant funereal rituals. Today, we spend half as much on funerals, largely because of the increasing popularity of cremation, up to about 20% of deaths from about 3% in 1960 (Gill, 1996).

Q: "Let us endeavor to live so that when we come to die even the undertaker will be sorry." Mark Twain

NOTE: People with one year or less to live consume 30% of all Medicare funds; the average person in the U.S. receives more than one-third of all medical care in the last six months of life.

CYBER: The first cyber-funeral service has begun operation: For about $6,500, Cybermourn will set up a camera at the funeral and post the live video to a Web site for anyone invited to "participate."

Our society has long been concerned with the "good life"; more recently, attention has turned to the idea of a good death. The hospice movement is an important part of this trend. In some cases, terminally ill patients move to a hospice facility, where a professional staff provides medical support and emotional comfort. In other cases, hospice workers provide care in the familiar surroundings of a person's home.

advocates maintain that a person facing unbearable suffering should be able to choose whether to live or die. And if death is the choice, medical assistance can help people toward a "good death." Surveys show that a majority of U.S. adults support the option to die with a doctor's help (Rosenbaum, 1997; NORC, 2001).

On the other side of the debate, opponents fear that laws allowing physician-assisted suicide invite abuse. Pointing to the Netherlands, critics cite surveys indicating that in most cases the five conditions for physician-assisted suicide are not met. In particular, most physicians do not consult with another doctor or even report the euthanasia to authorities. Of greater concern, however, is the fact that in about one-fifth of all doctor-assisted suicides, the patient never explicitly asks to die. This is so even though half of these patients are conscious and capable of making decisions for themselves (Gillon, 1999). Therefore, opponents fear that legalizing doctor-assisted suicide puts a nation on a slippery slope toward more and more euthanasia. Can anyone deny, they ask, that ill people may be pushed into accepting death by doctors who consider suicide the right choice for the terminally ill or by family members who are weary of caring for them or want to avoid the expenses of medical care?

However the right-to-die debate turns out in the future, our society has entered a new era when it comes

 For links to organizations worldwide advocating a right to die, see http://www.euthanasia.org/wfmap.html

to dying. Individuals, family members, and medical personnel must face death not as a medical fact but as a negotiated outcome (Flynn, 1991; Humphrey, 1991; Markson, 1992; Wolfson, 1998).

BEREAVEMENT

Elisabeth Kübler-Ross (1969) found that most people usually confront their own death in stages (see Chapter 5, "Socialization"). Initially, individuals react with *denial*, followed by *anger*; then they try to *negotiate* a divine intervention. Gradually, they fall into *resignation* and, finally, reach *acceptance*.

According to some researchers, bereavement follows the same pattern of stages. Those close to a dying person may initially deny the reality of impending death but with time gradually reach a point of acceptance. Other investigators question any linear "stage theory," arguing that bereavement is an unpredictable process (Lund, Caserta, & Dimond, 1986; Lund, 1989). However, experts do agree that how family and friends view an impending death affects the person who is dying. By accepting an approaching death, others help the dying person do the same; denying death isolates the dying person, who is unable to share feelings and experiences with others.

Many dying people find support in the *hospice movement*. Unlike a hospital, which is designed to cure disease, a hospice helps people have a good death. These care centers for dying people try to minimize

Looking ahead in the twenty-first century, the elderly will represent an increasing share of the U.S. population. How do you think this trend will affect the experiences and attitudes of the young?

pain and suffering—either there or at home—and encourage family members to stay close by.

Even under the most favorable circumstances, bereavement may involve profound grief and social disorientation that persist for some time. Research documents that bereavement is less intense for someone who accepts the death of a loved one and feels that the relationship with the dying person has reached a satisfactory resolution. Taking the opportunity to put appropriate closure on the relationship with a dying person allows family and friends to better comfort one another after death occurs (Atchley, 1983).

LOOKING AHEAD: AGING IN THE TWENTY-FIRST CENTURY

This chapter has explored the graying of the United States and other high-income nations. We can predict with confidence that the ranks of the elderly will swell dramatically in the twenty-first century: By 2050, the elderly population will exceed the population of the entire country in 1900. Moreover, one in four of these seniors will be over eighty-five. Within the next fifty years, then, society's oldest

 Government statistics and analysis of the well-being of the U.S. elderly population are available at http://www. agingstats.gov

members will gain a far greater voice in everyday life. *Gerontology*—the study of the elderly—is also sure to gain in importance.

The reshaping of our society's age structure raises many serious concerns. With more people in their old age (and living longer once they enter old age), will we have the support services to sustain them? Remember that as the elderly make demands, proportionately fewer younger people will be there to respond. What about the spiraling medical care costs of an aging society? As the baby boomers enter old age, some analysts paint a doomsday picture of the United States as a "twenty-first century Calcutta," with desperate and dying elderly people everywhere (Longino, 1994:13).

But not all the signs are ominous. For one thing, the health of tomorrow's elderly people (that is, today's young and middle-aged adults) is better than ever: Smoking is way down, and people are eating more healthfully. Such trends probably mean that the elderly of the twenty-first century will be more vigorous and independent than their counterparts today. Moreover, tomorrow's seniors will enjoy the benefits of steadily advancing medical technology, although, as the final box explains, the claim of the old on our nation's resources is already hotly debated.

Another positive sign is the financial strength of the elderly. Although the cost of living is sure to rise, tomorrow's elderly will draw on greater affluence than ever before. Also the baby boomers will be the first generation of U.S. seniors with women who have been in the labor force most of their lives, a fact reflected in their substantial savings and pensions.

One concern, as we look ahead, is that younger adults will face a mounting responsibility to care for aging parents. Indeed, a falling birth rate coupled with a growing elderly population means that caregiving in our society increasingly will include both the very young and the very old.

More and more people in the United States are learning to care for aging parents. Caregiving includes more than meeting physical needs. Many of us have much to learn about communicating, expressing love, and facing eventual death. In caring for parents, of course, we will also teach important lessons to our children, including the skills they will need, one day, to care for us.

Finally, an aging population will almost certainly change the way we view death. In all likelihood, death will become less of a social taboo and reestablish itself as a natural part of the life course. As this comes to pass, both young and old will benefit.

Q: Daniel Callahan advocates "an understanding of the process of aging and death that looks to our obligations to the young and to the future, that sees old age as a source of knowledge and insight of value to other age groups, that recognizes the necessity of limits and the acceptance of decline and death, and that values the old for their age and not their continuing youthful vitality." (1987:223)

Q: "It is possible that medicine's triumphant reconstruction of old age has also unwittingly created a demographic, economic, and medical avalanche, one that could ultimately (and perhaps already has) do great harm." Daniel Callahan
NOTE: Daniel Callahan's analysis raises important questions: Is getting older *good* for everyone? Is it even *possible* for everyone?

CONTROVERSY & DEBATE

Setting Limits: Must We "Pull the Plug" on Old Age?

Because death struck at any time, often without warning, our ancestors would have found the question, "Can people live too long?" absurd. In recent decades, however, as the elderly population soars in the United States, as new technology gives us more power to prolong life, and as life-extending care gets increasingly expensive, many now wonder just how much old age we can afford.

Currently, about half of the average person's lifetime spending for medical care occurs during the final years of life, and the share is rising. Against the spiraling costs of prolonging life, then, we well may ask whether what is technically possible is socially desirable. In this new century, warns gerontologist Daniel Callahan, an elderly population ready and eager to extend their lives will force us either to "pull the plug" on old age or shortchange everyone else.

To even raise this issue, Callahan concedes, seems cold and heartless. But consider that the bill for the elderly's health topped $200 billion in 2000—more than twice what it cost in 1980. This dramatic increase reflects our current policy of directing more and more medical resources to studying and treating the diseases and disabilities of old age.

So Callahan makes the case for limits. He reasons, first, that to spend more on behalf of the elderly we must spend less on others. But with poverty a growing problem among children, how can we spend more and more on the oldest members of our society?

Second, Callahan reminds us, a *longer* life is not necessarily a *better* life. Cost aside, does heart surgery that prolongs the life of an eighty-four-year-old woman a year or two truly improve the quality of her life? Cost considered, would those resources yield more quality of life if used to give a ten-year-old child a kidney transplant?

Third, Callahan urges us to reconsider our view of death as an enemy to be conquered at all costs. Rather, he suggests, a more realistic stance for an aging society is to treat death as a natural end to the life course. If we cannot make peace with death for our own well-being, given limited financial resources, we must do it for the benefit of others.

But not everyone agrees. Shouldn't people who have worked all their lives and made our society what it is enjoy our generosity in their final years? Moreover, given our cultural values of independence and responsibility, can we deny medical care to aging people able and willing to pay for it?

What is clear is that, in the twenty-first century, we will face questions that few would have imagined even fifty years ago: Is peak longevity good for everyone? Is it even *possible* for everyone?

Continue the debate . . .

1. *Should doctors and hospitals use a double standard, offering more complete care to the youngest people and more limited care to society's oldest members? Why or why not?*

2. *Do you think that a goal of the medical establishment should be to extend life at all costs?*

3. *Is the idea of rationing medical care really new? Hasn't our society always done this because some people have more wealth than others?*

Source: Callahan (1987).

SUMMARY

1. The proportion of elderly people in the U.S. population has risen from 4 percent in 1900 to 12 percent today; by 2030, 20 percent of our people will be elderly.

2. Gerontology, the study of aging and the elderly, focuses on how people change in old age and how various cultures define aging.

3. Most younger people exaggerate the extent of disability among the elderly. Growing old is accompanied by a rising rate of disease and disability, but most seniors are healthy.

4. Psychological research confirms that growing old does not result in overall loss of intelligence or radical changes in personality.

5. The age at which people are defined as old varies historically: Until several centuries ago, old age began as early as thirty. In poor societies today,

CTQ1: An aging population results from greater life expectancy coupled to a low birth rate, both of which are traits of postindustrial societies. Consequences include rising visibility for older people, more need for elder caregiving, and new products (Viagra) and designs (single-level homes) aimed at the increasing elder market.
CTQ2: Do students think younger professors are more "cool"? Is there a cultural gap between younger students and an older teacher?

Or do students admire a mature teacher with a lifetime of learning and experience?
CTQ3: Possible issues to consider are the average age of pop culture entertainers (films, television, music) and cultural attitudes about the young and the old. Students might supply adjectives that apply to the young and the old.

where life expectancy is much lower than in North America, people become old at fifty or even forty.

6. In global perspective, industrialization fosters a decline in the social standing of elderly people.

7. As people age, they face social isolation brought on by retirement, physical disability, and the death of friends or spouse. Even so, most elderly people enjoy the support of family members.

8. Since 1960, poverty among the elderly has dropped sharply. The aged poor include categories of people—such as single women and people of color—who are at high risk of poverty at any age.

9. An increasing elderly population raises the demand for caregiving, most of which is performed by family members, typically women, who are likely to be caring for children as well.

10. Ageism—prejudice and discrimination against old people—is used to justify age stratification.

11. Although many seniors are socially disadvantaged, the elderly include men and women of all races, ethnicities, and social classes. Therefore, older people do not qualify as a minority.

12. Disengagement theory, based on structural-functional analysis, suggests that society helps the elderly disengage from positions of social responsibility before the onset of disability or death. This process allows the orderly transfer of statuses and roles from the older to the younger generation.

13. Activity theory, based on symbolic-interaction analysis, claims that a high level of activity affords people personal satisfaction in old age.

14. Age stratification is one focus of social-conflict analysis. Capitalist society's emphasis on economic efficiency leads us to devalue those who are less productive, including the elderly.

15. Modern society has set death apart from everyday life, prompting a cultural denial of human mortality. In part, this attitude is related to the fact that most people now die after reaching old age. Recent trends suggest that people are confronting death more directly and seeking control over the process of dying.

KEY CONCEPTS

gerontology (p. 386) the study of aging and the elderly

age stratification (p. 389) the unequal distribution of wealth, power, and privilege among people at different stages of the life course

gerontocracy (p. 390) a form of social organization in which the elderly have the most wealth, power, and prestige

caregiving (p. 395) informal and unpaid care provided to a dependent person by family members, other relatives, or friends

ageism (p. 396) prejudice and discrimination against the elderly

disengagement theory (p. 397) the idea that society enhances its orderly operation by disengaging people from positions of responsibility as they reach old age

activity theory (p. 397) the idea that a high level of activity enhances personal satisfaction in old age

euthanasia (mercy killing) (p. 400) assisting in the death of a person suffering from an incurable disease

CRITICAL-THINKING QUESTIONS

1. What factors are causing the populations of high-income nations to become, on average, older? What are some of the likely consequences of "the graying of the United States"?

2. In general, are the most popular faculty on the campus young instructors or old instructors? How does age play into the way students evaluate a professor?

3. In what ways does the United States have a "youth culture"? Provide specific examples.

4. Political analyst Irving Kristol (1996) praised the elderly as "our most exemplary citizens" because, compared with younger people, they do not kill, steal, use illegal drugs, or fall deeply into debt. Moreover, they are twice as likely as young people to vote. Overall, do you think the elderly in this country receive the respect and social support they deserve? Why or why not?

Q: "Out of life comes death; and out of death, life; Out of the young, the old; and out of the old, the young; Out of waking, sleep; out of sleep, waking; the stream of creation and dissolution never stops." Heraclitus

CTQ4: In recent years, the elderly have received more attention from politicians. Would any political candidate dare to threaten Social Security?

Q: "We must wait until the evening to see how splendid the day has been." Sophocles

Q: "Do not go gentle into that good night; Rage, rage against the dying of the light." Dylan Thomas

EXERCISE: Ask students to prepare a list of social changes they might expect were life expectancy to increase another 20 years during the 21st century, much as it did during the 20th.

APPLICATIONS AND EXERCISES

1. What practices and policies does your college or university have for helping older faculty make the transition to retirement? Ask several faculty nearing retirement and several already retired for their views. In what ways does retiring from an academic career seem harder or easier than retiring from other kinds of work?

2. Look through an issue of any popular magazine— say, *Time, Newsweek,* or *People*—and notice the images of men and women featured in stories and pictured in advertising. Are elderly people fairly represented in such publications?

3. Obtain a copy of a living will and try to respond to all the questions it asks. Does filling out such a form help clarify your own thinking about confronting death?

4. The *Journal of Medical Ethics* (Vol. 25, No. 1, February 1999) has several research articles investigating alleged abuse of euthanasia laws in the Netherlands. Read the articles and decide whether you think, on balance, doctor-assisted suicide is a sound or unsound policy.

5. Packaged in the back of this new textbook is an interactive CD-ROM that offers a variety of study and review materials intended to help you better understand the material covered in this chapter. For this chapter, the CD-ROM contains an author's tip video, Real Life Sociology videos, other relevant audio and video, interactive map animations, audio journal entries from the author, Web links, and much more.

 ## SITES TO SEE

http://www.prenhall.com/macionis

Visit the interactive *Companion Website*™ that accompanies this text. Begin by clicking on the cover of your book. You will find a chapter-by-chapter study guide, practice tests, and a significant portion of the text for on-line review, as well as many suggested Web links.

http://www.nhpco.org

Learn about hospices by visiting the Web site for the National Hospice and Palliative Care Organization. Then check your local telephone book to contact people who operate a hospice in your community.

http://www.seniornet.org/php/

This is the site for SeniorNet, a nonprofit organization that is bringing seniors into the age of the Internet. Run by volunteers, SeniorNet offers low-cost computer and Internet instruction to the elderly at several hundred training sites across the United States.

http://www.aoa.gov

This site, operated by the Department of Health and Human Services, provides a look at likely trends involving the elderly over the course of the twenty-first century.

 ## INVESTIGATE WITH CONTENTSELECT

Follow the instructions found on page 23 of this textbook to enter this chapter of the book's *Companion Website*™. Once in the chapter, click on the ContentSelect icon at the bottom left of your screen and enter your personal

User ID and Password. Enter keywords such as "aging," "retirement," and "euthanasia," and the search engine will help you become an effective researcher.

cyber.scope

PART III

NEW INFORMATION TECHNOLOGY AND SOCIAL STRATIFICATION

Change in technology transforms the nature of work. Just as important, such shifts alter the reward structure, reshaping patterns of social inequality. This third cyber.scope considers several ways in which the spread of computer technology is linked to social stratification.

The Information Revolution and U.S. Stratification

Most analysts agree that recent decades have witnessed economic polarization in the United States, with economic growth primarily enriching families that already had high incomes (Persell, 1997; Keister, 2000). At the outset, at least, technological revolution typically concentrates income and wealth as a small number of people make key discoveries and, with the resulting products and services, establish and expand new markets. Just as John D. Rockefeller and Andrew Carnegie amassed great fortunes a century ago as captains of the Industrial Revolution, the Information Revolution has created a new elite today. For several years, the richest person in the country has been Bill Gates, a founder of Microsoft Corporation that produces not oil or steel but the operating systems found on most of today's personal computers. More broadly, it is those with money to invest (many of whom make up what Karl Marx called the capitalist class) who reap most of the profits from successful

new industries. During the 1990s, as the Information Revolution rolled ahead, key stock market indicators leaped fivefold, with new technology companies such as Microsoft (software), Intel (computer chips), Compaq (personal computers), and Cisco Systems (computer networking) making even more spectacular gains. A sharp downturn in the stock market during 2000 and 2001—especially affecting technology companies—trimmed these gains. Even so, high technology represents a larger and larger share of the U.S. economy.

But the wave of technological change does not benefit everyone. As companies adopt new technology in their efforts to become more efficient and profitable, some people lose out. In recent decades, for example, tens of millions of industrial jobs in the United States have simply disappeared. For each job lost, a worker—and usually an entire family—suffers.

Another key link between new information technology and social inequality concerns the unequal spread of computing skills. In 2000, more than half the U.S. population over age fifteen were Internet users. Yet these users are not average people; they represent an information elite, privileged in more ways than one. About 95 percent are white (compared to 85 percent of the population), 60 percent are men (compared to half the population), and 40 percent are professionals or managers (compared to 18 percent of the population). In short, computer users are people with above-average incomes. College students stand out among computer users, but even among them, differences emerge. Figure Cyber III–1 shows that students attending private (and more expensive) colleges and universities are more likely to be frequent e-mail users than those attending public institutions. Similarly, students at two-year and at historically black colleges also make less use of computers.

The trend has been that, over time, computer users are coming to mirror more closely the population as a whole. But there can be little doubt that, at least for now, new information technology is contributing to higher levels of economic inequality as it creates a cyber-elite and generates a new underclass made up of those without crucial symbolic skills (Wynter, 1995; Edmondson, 1997b; Sax et al., 1999).

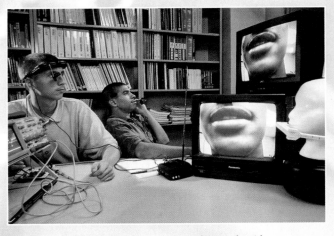

Computers provide expanded opportunities for people with disabilities. This computer system, for example, is helping to teach lip reading to a young man who is deaf.

The Information Revolution: Gender, Race, and Age

The Industrial Revolution ushered in a trend by which women and men are becoming more socially equal. Machinery eroded the link between work and physical strength, and more women entered the labor force as birth control technology helped lower the birth rate by making motherhood a matter of individual choice. The Information Revolution promises to continue this trend. Work in the computer age involves not making or moving *things* but manipulating *ideas*—activity that favors neither men nor women.

Also, communication via computers obscures a person's sex—obvious in face-to-face interaction—placing men and women on a more equal footing. The same holds for race and ethnicity, so that the coming cyber-society may well be marked by greater contact between people of all races and cultural backgrounds.

But an important counterpoint involves access to computer technology. To date, cultural biases within the new cyber-society have favored males: Most games that introduce children to computers are designed for boys, just as computer science courses in colleges enroll mostly men. Similarly, to the extent that racial and ethnic minorities are economically disadvantaged and attend less well-funded schools, this segment of our population will have less opportunity to own and operate computers—the key to success in the labor force in this new century.

Finally, the effects of computing on age stratification are likely to be mixed. On one hand, the fact that computing demands mental more than physical vitality—and allows work to be performed almost anywhere—should expand opportunities for people to continue to work

well past the standard retirement age that emerged during the industrial era. On the other hand, new technology is almost always age biased in that it is readily adopted by the young but regarded more cautiously by the old, whose life experiences have been shaped by earlier ways. Unless our society expands programs of adult education, then, younger people are likely to predominate in, and benefit from, work and other activities that rely heavily on new information technology.

The Information Revolution and Global Stratification

Worldwide, the elite pattern we have described holds even more: The Information Revolution directly involves only a tiny share of the planet's people. A look back at Global Map 4–1, on page 104, and Global Map 7–1, on page 172, shows that it is the rich regions of the world where computers and Internet access

are readily available, at least to those who can afford them. In most of Africa, by contrast, people are far less likely to have a computer, and in some countries there are few computers and almost no Internet access. Moreover, the large number of African languages and alphabets will slow the spread of computing there.

Although Internet access is found in most of Asia, at present, a cultural and technical problem limits the spread of computing in this world region: Almost all computer keyboards use the Latin alphabet. In China and other Asian nations, although members of the technical elite are likely to speak and write English, most people use complex character sets that have yet to be incorporated into computer technology. Overall, then, the Information Revolution has come to the part of the world already benefiting from industrial technology—yet another case of the rich getting richer.

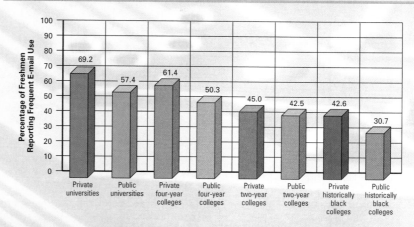

DIVERSITY SNAPSHOT

FIGURE Cyber III–1 Percentage of University and College Freshmen Reporting Frequent E-mail Use during the Past Year, 1999

Source: Sax et al. (1999).

CHAPTER

16

Christopher M. Chinn
Location and Dislocation

Courtesy of Latina/Latino Studies Program,
University of Illinois at Urbana–Champaign.

THE ECONOMY AND WORK

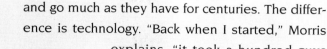

For more than thirty years, Alex Morris was a dockhand working the London waterfront. Today, at fifty-five, he considers himself retired. "I'm getting too old for the kind of work I used to do," he explains, "but the truth is there is no work for blokes like me anymore." These days, Morris spends most of his time in the company of other former dockworkers, sitting around the docks or in one of the local pubs.

It's not that the port of London is no longer operating; ships still come

and go much as they have for centuries. The difference is technology. "Back when I started," Morris explains, "it took a hundred guys five days to unload a ship. Then in the 1970s, they changed to container ships. Now it takes just eight people to unload a ship and they do it in just one day." Indeed, in ports around the world, enormous cranes lift the cargo containers, placing them directly on truck beds or railroad cars. Ships often are back to sea within twenty-four hours (based on Peters, 2000).

This chapter examines the economy, widely considered the most influential of all social institutions. (The other major social institutions are examined in Chapter 17, "Politics and Government"; Chapter 18, "Family"; Chapter 19, "Religion"; Chapter 20, "Education"; and Chapter 21, "Health and Medicine.") As Alex Morris's story demonstrates, the economy has been changing, and the changes have not been to the benefit of everyone. Indeed, as we shall see, sociologists debate how the economy ought to work, whose interests it ought to serve, and what companies and workers owe each other.

THE ECONOMY: HISTORICAL OVERVIEW

The **economy** is *the social institution that organizes a society's production, distribution, and consumption of goods and services.* As an institution, the economy operates in a generally predictable manner. *Goods* are commodities ranging from necessities (food, clothing, shelter) to luxury items (cars, swimming pools, yachts). *Services* are activities that benefit others (for example, the work of priests, physicians, teachers, and software specialists).

We value goods and services because they ensure survival or because they make life easier or more interesting. Also, what people produce (as workers) and buy (as consumers) are important parts of social identity. How goods and services are distributed shapes the lives of everyone in a number of important ways.

The economies of modern high-income nations are the result of centuries of social change. We turn now to three technological revolutions that reorganized production and, in the process, transformed social life.

THE AGRICULTURAL REVOLUTION

Members of the earliest human societies were hunters and gatherers living off the land. In these technologically simple societies, there was no distinct economy. Rather, producing and consuming were all part of family life.

As Chapter 4 ("Society") explained, when people harnessed animals to plows some 5,000 years ago, the new agricultural economy was fifty times as productive as hunting and gathering. The resulting surplus meant that not everyone had to produce food, so many took on specialized work: making tools, raising animals, or building dwellings. Soon towns sprang up, linked by networks of traders dealing in food, animals, and other goods (Jacobs, 1970). These four factors—agricultural technology, job specialization, permanent

SUPPLEMENTS: An outline of this chapter, supplementary mini-lectures, and suggested topics for discussion are found in the *Data File*.

DISCUSS: The Industrial Revolution went far beyond mere technological upheaval. What was it for Marx? A capitalist revolution. For Weber? The triumph of rationality. For Durkheim? A process of expanding specialization.

Q: "[The preindustrial economy] was limited to what could be organized within a family, and within the lifetime of its head." Peter Laslett (1984)

Q: "A fundamental characteristic of the world we have lost was the scene of labor, which was universally supposed to be the home." Peter Laslett (1984)

As societies industrialize, a smaller and smaller share of the labor force works in agriculture. In the United States, much of what agricultural work remains is performed by immigrants from lower-income nations. These people—new arrivals from Mexico—are harvesting aloe plants in south Texas.

settlements, and trade—made the economy a distinct social institution.

THE INDUSTRIAL REVOLUTION

By the mid-eighteenth century, a second technological revolution was underway, first in England and then in North America. The development of industry was to bring even greater changes than agriculture had. Industrialization changed the economy in five fundamental ways:

1. **New sources of energy.** Throughout history, "energy" meant the muscle power of people or animals. But in 1765, the English inventor James Watt introduced the steam engine. One hundred times more powerful than muscle power, early steam engines soon drove heavy machinery.

2. **Centralization of work in factories.** Steam-powered machines soon moved work out of homes and into factories, centralized and impersonal workplaces housing the machines.

3. **Manufacturing and mass production.** Before the Industrial Revolution, most people grew or gathered raw materials (such as grain, wood, or wool). In an industrial economy, the focus shifted so that most people's work day was spent turning raw materials into a wide range of finished products (such as furniture and clothing).

4. **Specialization.** Historically, artisans working at home made products from start to finish. In the factory, a laborer repeated a single task over and over, making only a small contribution to the finished product. Such specialization raised productivity but lowered the skill level of the average worker.

5. **Wage labor.** Instead of working for themselves in a household (called cottage industry), factory workers became wage laborers who sold their labor to strangers, who often cared less for them than for the machines they operated.

The Industrial Revolution gradually raised the standard of living as countless new products and services filled an expanding marketplace. Yet the benefits of industrial technology were not shared very equally, especially at the beginning. Some factory owners made vast fortunes, but the majority of industrial workers lived close to poverty. Children worked in factories or coal mines for pennies a day. Women factory workers, among the lowest paid, endured special problems, as the box explains.

THE INFORMATION REVOLUTION AND THE POSTINDUSTRIAL SOCIETY

By about 1950, the nature of production was changing once again. The United States was creating a

DIVERSITY: RACE, CLASS, AND GENDER

Women in the Mills of Lowell, Massachusetts

Few people paid much attention as Francis Cabot Lowell, ancestor of two prominent Boston families, the Cabots and the Lowells, stepped off a ship returning him from England in 1810. But Lowell carried with him documents that would change the course of the U.S. economy: plans, based on machinery operating in England, for this country's first power loom textile factory.

Lowell built his factory beside a waterfall on the Merrimack River in Massachusetts so he could use water power to turn large looms to weave cloth. Before long, Lowell's factory transformed a small farming village into a thriving industrial town that would be renamed at his death in his honor.

From the outset, 90 percent of the mill workers were women. Factory owners preferred women because they could be paid $2 to $3 a week, half the wages men received. Many immigrant men were willing to work for low wages, but prejudice disqualified "foreigners" from any job at all.

Recruiters, driving wagons through the small towns of New England, urged parents to send their daughters to the mills, where, they promised, the young women would be properly supervised as they learned skills and discipline. The offer appealed to many parents who could barely provide for their children, and the prospect of getting out on their own surely excited many young women. Back then, after all, there were few occupations open to women, and

those that were—including teaching and household service—paid even less than factory work.

At the Lowell factory, young women lived in dormitories, paying one-third of their wages for room and board. They were subject to a curfew and, as a condition of employment, regularly attended church. Any morally questionable conduct (such as bringing men to their rooms) brought firm disciplinary action.

Besides fulfilling their promise to parents, factory owners had another motive for their strict rules: They knew that closely supervised women could not organize among themselves. Working twelve or thirteen hours a day, six days a week, the Lowell employees had good reason to seek improvements in their working conditions. Yet any public criticism of the factory, or even possessing "radical" literature, could cost a worker her job.

Sources: Based on Eisler (1977) and Wertheimer (1982).

postindustrial economy, *a productive system based on service work and high technology.* Automated machinery (and, more recently, robotics) reduced the role of human labor in production so that fewer people work in industrial jobs and most now work in service positions, including sales, public relations, health care, advertising, and banking. Thus, the postindustrial era is distinguished by a shift from industrial work to service work.

Driving this change is a third technological breakthrough: the computer. Just as the Industrial Revolution introduced machines two centuries ago, the Information Revolution has introduced new kinds of products and new forms of communication that have

NOTE: The effects of technological advancement are summarized in Chapter 4's opening section, "Society and Technology." Marvin Harris estimates the rising productive capacity linked to societies at various stages of technological development in terms of the ratio of calories expended to calories produced: hunting and gathering, 1:3; horticultural and pastoral,.1:5; agrarian, 1:50; industrial, 1:5,000.

NOTE: The shift from an industrial to a service economy can be seen in the falling number of U.S. homes with a workshop and the rising number with a home office equipped with a computer.
DISCUSS: Is there a link between the rise of a service economy and the increasing number of overly committed two-career couples who use services ranging from housecleaning to take-out food?

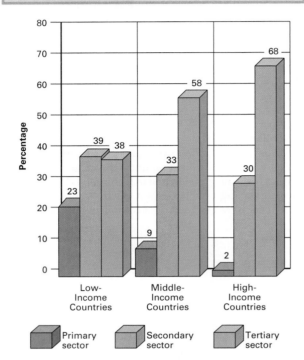

GLOBAL SNAPSHOT

FIGURE 16–1 The Size of Economic Sectors by Income Level of Country

Source: Author estimates based on United Nations Development Programme (2000) and The World Bank (2000).

altered the fundamental character of work. In general, we see three changes:

1. **From tangible products to ideas.** As we discussed in earlier chapters, the industrial era was defined by the production of goods; in the postindustrial era, work involves manipulating symbols. Computer programmers, writers, financial analysts, advertising executives, architects, editors, and all sorts of consultants make up the labor force of the information age.

2. **From mechanical skills to literacy skills.** The Industrial Revolution required mechanical skills, but the Information Revolution requires literacy skills: speaking and writing well and, of course, using computers. People able to communicate effectively enjoy new opportunities; people with limited literacy skills face declining prospects.

3. **From factories to almost anywhere.** Industrial technology drew workers into factories located near power sources, but computer technology allows workers to be almost anywhere. Laptop computers, cell phones, and portable fax machines now turn the home, car, or even an airplane into a "virtual office." New information technology blurs the line between work and home life.

SECTORS OF THE ECONOMY

The three revolutions we have just described reflect a shifting balance between the three sectors of a society's economy. The **primary sector** is *the part of the economy that draws raw materials from the natural environment.* The primary sector—agriculture, raising animals, fishing, forestry, and mining—is largest in low-income, preindustrial nations. Figure 16–1 shows that 23 percent of the economic output of low-income countries is in the primary sector, compared to 9 percent of economic activity in middle-income nations and just 2 percent in high-income countries such as the United States.

The **secondary sector** is *the part of the economy that transforms raw materials into manufactured goods.* This sector grows quickly as societies industrialize. It includes operations such as refining petroleum into gasoline and turning metals into tools and automobiles. The globalization of industry means that just about all the world's countries derive a significant share of their economic output from the secondary sector. Indeed, as Figure 16–1 shows, the secondary sector accounts for a greater share of economic output in low-income countries than it does in high-income nations.

The **tertiary sector** is *the part of the economy that involves services rather than goods.* Accounting for 38 percent of the economic output in low-income countries, the tertiary sector grows with industrialization and dominates the economies of middle-income countries (58 percent of economic output) and high-income, postindustrial nations (68 percent). Today, about 72 percent of the U.S. labor force is in service work, including clerical work and positions in food service, sales, law, health care, law enforcement, advertising, and teaching.

THE GLOBAL ECONOMY

New information technology is drawing people around the world closer together and creating a **global economy,** *expanding economic activity with little regard for national borders.*

THE MAP: The two maps show that the economies of low-income nations such as India are dominated by the primary sector. Middle-income countries, such as Russia and Mexico, have a secondary economic sector that is roughly the same size as their primary sector. The second global map is almost a reverse image of the first.

Q: "I believe that the most important, the most fundamental human right is how to ensure that the 1.2 billion Chinese people have adequate food and clothing." Jiang Zemin, president of PRC, when asked about human rights (1997)

GLOBAL: About half of all consumer items purchased in the U.S. are made outside the country.

WINDOW ON THE WORLD

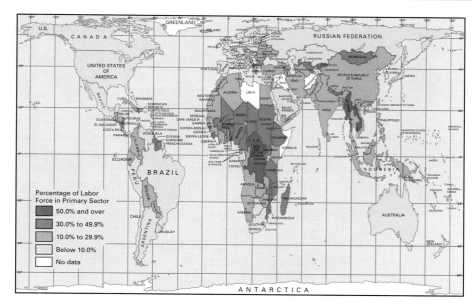

GLOBAL MAP 16–1
Agricultural Employment in Global Perspective

The primary sector of the economy is largest in societies that are least developed. Thus, in the poor countries of Africa and Asia, up to half of all workers are farmers. This picture is altogether different in the world's most economically developed countries—including the United States, Canada, Great Britain, and Australia—which have 2 percent of their work force in agriculture.

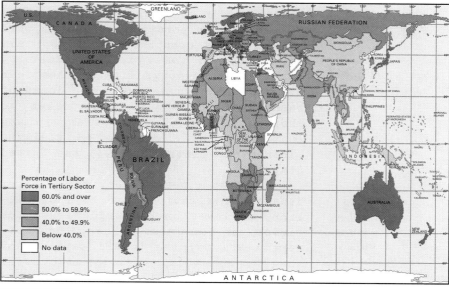

GLOBAL MAP 16–2
Service-Sector Employment in Global Perspective

The tertiary sector of the economy becomes ever larger as a nation's income level rises. In the United States, Canada, the countries of Western Europe, Australia, and Japan, about two-thirds of the labor force performs service work.

Sources: By the author, using data from United Nations Development Programme (2000) and The World Bank (2000, 2001); map projection from *Peters Atlas of the World* (1990).

The development of a global economy has four major consequences. First, we see a global division of labor so that different regions of the world specialize in one sector of economic activity. As Global Map 16–1 shows, agriculture represents more than half of the total economic output in the world's poorest countries. Global Map 16–2 indicates that most of the economic output in high-income countries is in the

DISCUSS: How many of your students work? The University of Michigan's Institute for Social Research estimates that three-fourths of high school seniors worked for income; 40% of all seniors work more than 20 hours a week.
EXERCISE: To help them become familiar with economic data, direct students to the *Statistical Abstract* (U.S. Census Bureau),

Human Development Report (United Nations), and *World Development Report* (World Bank). These three annual publications provide extensive data about the economies of the U.S. and other world nations.
Q: "The inherent vice of capitalism is the unequal sharing of blessing; the inherent virtue of socialism is the equal sharing of misery." Winston Churchill

The rise of a global economy means that more and more products originally produced in one country are now made and consumed around the world. What do you see as some of the good consequences of globalization? What about harmful consequences?

service sector. Thus, the poorest nations specialize in producing raw materials, and the richest nations, including the United States, specialize in the production of various services.

Second, an increasing number of products pass through more than one nation. Look no farther than your morning coffee, which may well have been grown in Colombia and transported to New Orleans on a freighter registered in Liberia, made in Japan using steel from Korea, and fueled by oil from Venezuela.

A third consequence of the global economy is that national governments no longer control the economic activity that takes place within their borders. In fact, governments cannot even regulate the value of their national currencies as dollars, pounds sterling, yen, and other currencies are traded around the clock in the financial centers of Tokyo, London, and New York. Global markets are the result of satellite communications that link the world's cities.

A fourth consequence of the global economy is that a small number of businesses, operating internationally, now control a vast share of the world's economic

activity. According to one estimate, the 600 largest multinational companies account for half the world's entire economic output (Kidron & Segal, 1991).

The world is still divided into 192 politically distinct nations. But increasing international economic activity makes nationhood less significant than it was even a decade ago.

ECONOMIC SYSTEMS: PATHS TO JUSTICE

October 20, Saigon, Vietnam. Sailing up the narrow Saigon River is an unsettling experience for anyone who came of age during the 1960s. We need to remember that Vietnam is a country, not a war, and more than twenty years have passed since the last U.S. helicopter lifted off the rooftop of the U.S. embassy, ending our country's presence there.

Saigon is on the brink of becoming a boomtown. Neon signs bathe the city's waterfront in color; hotels, bankrolled by Western corporations, push skyward from a dozen construction sites; taxi meters record fares in U.S. dollars, not Vietnamese dong; Visa and American Express stickers decorate the doors of fashionable boutiques that cater to shoppers from Japan, France, and (since the U.S. embargo on visiting Vietnam was lifted in 1994) the United States.

There is a heavy irony here: After decades of fighting, the loss of millions of lives on both sides, and the victory of Communist forces, the Vietnamese are turning toward capitalism. What we see today is what might well have happened had the U.S. forces won the war.

Every society's economic system makes a statement about justice because the economy broadly determines who gets what. Two general economic models are capitalism and socialism. No society has an economy that is completely one or the other; capitalism and

NOTE: The *Oxford English Dictionary* explains that the word "capitalism" entered the English language in the late 18th century. Peter Berger claims that Adam Smith never used the term. The etymology of the word reveals a Latin root, *caput*, meaning "of the head."

Q: "The engine that drives enterprise . . . is profit." John Maynard Keynes

DISCUSS: How does morality figure in the market system? Some say there is no morality in a market economy, only profit; the political left describes the market as implicitly immoral because it ignores social good; the political right says that self-seeking is inherently moral because it represents people freely serving their own chosen ends. Also, a market system offers people freedoms as producers and consumers and bridges national, religious, racial, ethnic, and other historic divides.

Although the United States has a mostly capitalist economy, the role of government increased over the course of the twentieth century and is now a familiar part of everyday life. By contrast, back in the 1800s in small towns across the country, the only evidence of government was a single building—a post office. Shown here is the original post office for Duluth, Minnesota.

socialism are two ends of a spectrum along which all actual economies can be located. We will look at each type in turn.

CAPITALISM

Capitalism is *an economic system in which natural resources and the means of producing goods and services are privately owned.* Ideally, a capitalist economy has three distinctive features:

1. **Private ownership of property.** In a capitalist economy, individuals can own almost anything. The more capitalist an economy is, the more private ownership there is of wealth-producing property such as factories, real estate, and natural resources.

2. **Pursuit of personal profit.** A capitalist society encourages the accumulation of private property and considers the profit motive natural, simply a matter of "doing business." Furthermore, claimed Scottish philosopher Adam Smith (1723–1790), the individual pursuit of self-interest helps the entire society prosper (1937:508; orig. 1776).

3. **Competition and consumer sovereignty.** A purely capitalist economy is a free-market system with no government interference (sometimes called a *laissez-faire* economy, from the French words meaning "to leave alone"). Adam Smith stated that a freely competitive economy regulates itself by the "invisible hand" of the laws of supply and demand.

Consumers regulate a free-market economy by selecting goods and services that offer the greatest value, Smith explained. Producers compete for customers' business by offering the highest-quality goods and services at the lowest price possible while still making a profit. As Smith put it, from narrow self-interest comes the "greatest good for the greatest number of people." Government control of the economy, on the other hand, distorts market forces by reducing producer motivation, diminishing quantity and quality of goods, and shortchanging consumers.

In a capitalist context, "justice" amounts to freedom of the marketplace, where one can produce, invest, and buy according to individual self-interest and the means to do so. The worth of products or workers is determined by the dynamic process of supply and demand. Replacing much of the work force with automatic machinery, as described in the opening to this chapter, is just if it is profitable to a company and its stockholders.

The United States is a capitalist nation in that the vast majority of businesses are privately owned. Even so, government plays an extensive role in economic affairs. The government itself owns and operates a number of businesses, including almost all of this country's

Capitalism still thrives in Hong Kong (left), evident in streets choked with advertising and shoppers. Socialism is more the rule in China's capital of Beijing (right), a city dominated by government buildings rather than a downtown business district.

schools, roads, parks and museums, the U.S. Postal Service, the Amtrak railroad system, and the entire U.S. military. The federal government also had a major part in building the Internet. In addition, governments use taxation and other forms of regulation to influence what companies produce, control the quality and cost of merchandise, influence what businesses import and export, and motivate consumers to conserve natural resources.

Furthermore, government sets minimum wage levels, enforces workplace safety standards, regulates corporate mergers, provides farm price supports, and supplements income in the form of Social Security, public assistance, student loans, and veterans' benefits for a majority of the people in the United States. In fact, local, state, and federal governments together are the country's biggest employer, with 14 percent of the labor force on their payrolls (U.S. Census Bureau, 2000).

SOCIALISM

Socialism is *an economic system in which natural resources and the means of producing goods and services are collectively owned.* In its ideal form, a socialist economy is the exact opposite of capitalism; its three distinctive features are:

1. **Collective ownership of property.** A socialist economy limits rights to private property, especially property used to generate income. Government controls such property and makes housing and other goods available to all, not just to people with the most money.

2. **Pursuit of collective goals.** The individualistic pursuit of profit is also at odds with the collective orientation of socialism. What capitalism celebrates as the entrepreneurial spirit, socialism condemns as greed. For this reason, socialist nations outlaw private transactions as "black market" activity.

3. **Government control of the economy.** Socialism rejects capitalism's laissez-faire approach in favor of a *centrally controlled* or *command economy* operated by the government. Socialism also rejects the idea that it is consumers who guide capitalist production, on the grounds that consumers lack the information necessary to evaluate products and are manipulated by advertising to buy what is profitable for factory owners rather than what

they genuinely need. Commercial advertising thus plays little role in socialist economies.

In a socialist context, "justice" is not freedom to compete and accumulate wealth but rather meeting everyone's basic needs in a roughly equal manner. From a socialist point of view, limiting workers' wages and benefits to boost company earnings is putting profits before people and is thus an injustice.

The People's Republic of China and some two dozen other societies in Asia, Africa, and Latin America model their economies on socialism, placing almost all wealth-generating property under state control (McColm et al., 1991; Freedom House, 2001). The extent of world socialism has declined in recent years as countries in Eastern Europe and the former Soviet Union have restructured their economies toward more of a market system.

Socialism and Communism

Many people think of *socialism* and *communism* as much the same. More precisely, **communism** is *a hypothetical economic and political system in which all members of a society are socially equal.* Karl Marx viewed socialism as a transitory stage on the path toward the ideal of a communist society that abolished all class divisions. In many socialist societies today, the dominant political party describes itself as communist, but nowhere has the communist goal been achieved.

Why? For one thing, social stratification involves differences of power as well as wealth. In general, socialist societies have reduced disparities in wealth by expanding government bureaucracies and extensively regulating daily life. In the process, government did not "wither away" as Karl Marx imagined. On the contrary, socialist political elites have enormous power and privilege.

Marx probably would have agreed that a communist society is a *utopia* (from the Greek words meaning "not a place"). Yet Marx considered communism a worthy goal and might well have disparaged reputedly Marxist societies such as the former Soviet Union, North Korea, the People's Republic of China, and Cuba for not fulfilling what he saw as the promise of communism.

WELFARE CAPITALISM AND STATE CAPITALISM

Some nations of Western Europe, including Sweden and Italy, have combined a market-based economy with broad social welfare programs. Analysts call this

Global comparisons indicate that socialist economies generate the greatest economic equality although living standards remain relatively low. Capitalist economies, by contrast, engender more income disparity although living standards are typically higher. As the former Soviet Union has moved towards a market system, however, the majority of people have suffered a decline in living standards, while some people have become quite rich.

"third way" **welfare capitalism**, *an economic and political system that combines a mostly market-based economy with extensive social welfare programs.*

Under welfare capitalism, the government owns some of the largest industries and services, such as transportation, the mass media, and health care. In Sweden and Italy, about 12 percent of economic production is "nationalized," or state controlled. That leaves most industry in private hands but subject to extensive government regulation. High taxation (aimed especially at the rich) funds a wide range of social welfare programs, including universal health care and child care (Olsen, 1996).

NOTE: Welfare capitalism is also called democratic socialism; state capitalism might also be called market socialism.

Q: "The function of socialism is to raise suffering to a higher level." Norman Mailer

RESOURCE: Karl Marx's analysis of "alienated labor" is one of the classic selections included in the Macionis and Benokraitis reader, *Seeing Ourselves.*

GLOBAL: The South Korean system of state capitalism has concentrated more than half of all GNP in just four major corporations, including Hyundai.

DISCUSS: Does socialism's lower productivity result from Marx's separation of reward from effort (implied in his famous call: "From each according to ability; to each according to need")?

TABLE 16-1 Participation in the Labor Force by Sex, Race, and Ethnicity, 2000

Category of the Population	In the Labor Force	
	Number (in millions)	Percentage
Men (aged 16 and over)	**75.2**	**74.7%**
White	63.8	75.4
African American	7.8	69.0
Hispanic	8.9	80.6
Women (aged 16 and over)	**65.6**	**60.2**
White	53.7	59.8
African American	8.7	63.2
Hispanic	6.4	56.9

Source: U.S. Department of Labor, *Employment and Earnings,* vol. 48, no. 1 (January 2001), pp. 168–71.

Yet another blend of capitalism and socialism is **state capitalism,** *an economic and political system in which companies are privately owned but cooperate closely with the government.* State capitalism is the rule in rapidly developing Asian countries along the Pacific Rim. Japan, South Korea, and Singapore, for example, are all capitalist countries, but their governments work in partnership with large companies, supplying financial assistance and controlling foreign imports to help their businesses compete in world markets (Gerlach, 1992).

RELATIVE ADVANTAGES OF CAPITALISM AND SOCIALISM

In practice, which economic system works best? Comparing economic models is difficult because all countries mix capitalism and socialism to varying degrees. Moreover, nations differ in cultural attitudes toward work, available natural resources, levels of technological development, and patterns of trade (Gregory & Stuart, 1985). Despite these complicating factors, some crude comparisons are revealing.

Economic Productivity

One key dimension of economic performance is productivity. A commonly used measure of economic output is gross domestic product (GDP), the total value of all goods and services produced annually. "Per capita," or per person, GDP allows us to compare the economic performance of nations of different population sizes.

The output of mostly capitalist countries at the end of the 1980s varied somewhat, but averaging the figures for the United States, Canada, and the nations of Western Europe yields a per capita GDP of about $13,500. The comparable figure for the former Soviet Union and nations of Eastern Europe is about $5,000. In other words, capitalist countries outproduced socialist nations by a ratio of 2.7 to 1 (United Nations Development Programme, 1990).

Economic Equality

How resources are distributed within a society is another important measure of how well an economic system works. A comparative study completed in the mid-1970s looked at income ratios based on the earnings of the richest and poorest 5 percent of the population (Wiles, 1977). The result was that societies with predominantly capitalist economies had an income ratio of about 10 to 1; the figure for socialist countries was 5 to 1. In other words, *capitalist economies support a higher overall standard of living but show greater income disparity.* Or, put another way, *socialist economies create more equality but with a lower overall living standard.*

Personal Freedom

One additional consideration in evaluating capitalism and socialism is the personal freedom of its people. Capitalism emphasizes *freedom to* pursue one's self-interest. After all, capitalism depends on the freedom of producers and consumers to interact, with little interference from the state. On the other hand, socialism emphasizes *freedom from* basic want. Equality is the goal, which requires state intervention in the economy, which in turn limits personal choices for citizens.

No system has yet been able to offer both political freedom and economic equality. In the capitalist United States, the political system guarantees many personal freedoms, but are these freedoms worth as much to a poor person as to a rich one? On the other side of the coin, China and Cuba have more economic equality but restrict the rights of their people to freely express themselves and move freely within and across their borders.

CHANGES IN SOCIALIST COUNTRIES

In 1989 and 1990, the nations of Eastern Europe that were seized by the Soviet Union at the end of World War II shook off their socialist regimes. These nations—including the German Democratic Republic, Czechoslovakia, Hungary, Romania, and Bulgaria—have introduced capitalist elements into

SEEING OURSELVES

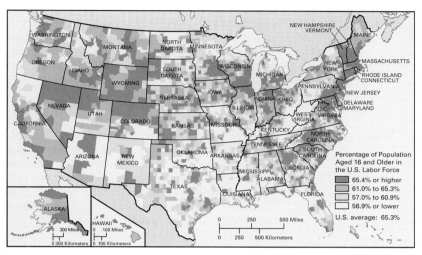

NATIONAL MAP 16–1
Labor Force Participation across the United States

Counties with high levels of labor force participation have steady sources of employment, including military bases, recreation areas, and large cities. By contrast, counties with low employment rates generally include a high proportion of elderly people (as well as students). Gender is another important consideration: What do you think is the typical level of employment in regions of the country (stretching from the South up into coal-mining districts of Kentucky and West Virginia) where traditional cultural norms encourage women to remain at home?

Percentage of Population Aged 16 and Older in the U.S. Labor Force

- 65.4% or higher
- 61.0% to 65.3%
- 57.0% to 60.9%
- 56.9% or lower

U.S. average: 65.3%

Sources: *American Demographics Desk Reference Series # 4.* Reprinted with permission. © 1992 *American Demographics* magazine, Ithaca, New York. Data from the 1990 decennial census.

what were centrally controlled economies. In 1992, the Soviet Union itself formally dissolved and has since introduced some free-market principles.

The reasons for these sweeping changes were complex. But two factors stand out: First, the mostly socialist economies grossly underproduced their capitalist counterparts. Although they achieved remarkable economic equality, living standards were low by Western European standards. Second, Soviet socialism was heavy-handed, rigidly controlling the media and restricting individual freedoms. In short, socialism did away with *economic* elites, as Karl Marx predicted. But as Max Weber foresaw, socialism increased the clout of *political* elites.

So far, the market reforms in Eastern Europe are proceeding unevenly. Some nations (Czech Republic, Slovakia, Poland, and the Baltic states of Latvia, Estonia, and Lithuania) are faring well, but others (Romania, Bulgaria, and the former Soviet republics) have been buffeted by price increases and falling living standards. Officials hope that expanding production eventually will bring a turnaround. However, there is already evidence that any improvement in living standards will be accompanied by increasing economic disparity (Pohl, 1996; Buraway, 1997; Specter, 1997a).

WORK IN THE POSTINDUSTRIAL ECONOMY

Economic change is not limited to the socialist world. In the United States in 2000, the government reported 141 million people in the U.S. labor force, representing two-thirds of the population age sixteen and over. As shown in Table 16–1, a larger proportion of men (74.7 percent) than women (60.2 percent) hold income-producing jobs, although this gap is closing. Among men, 69.0 percent of African Americans are in the labor force, compared to 75.4 percent of white people and 80.6 percent of Hispanics. Among women, 63.2 percent of African Americans are employed, compared to 59.8 percent of white people and 56.9 percent of Hispanics.

 Find a government report on youth in the U.S. labor force at this Web site: http://www.bls.gov/opub/rylf/rylfhome.htm

National Map 16–1 shows labor force participation across the United States. Because working is the major source of income for most people, regions of the country with greater labor force participation are more affluent.

THEN AND NOW: The decline of farming can be seen in the falling number of farms owned by African Americans: 926,000 in 1920 compared to 16,560 in 1997.
GLOBAL: Fueling the deindustrialization of the U.S. are the relatively low wage rates typical of poor societies: from $5.11 an hour in Taiwan to $1.89 an hour in Mexico (see Figure 16–4).

GLOBAL: A decline of agricultural employment characterizes all mature industrial societies, as Figure 16–1 suggests.
RESOURCE: Work in the secondary labor market is the focus of Mary Romero's article "Maid in the U.S.A." in the *Seeing Ourselves* reader.
THEN AND NOW: U.S. union membership in 2000 was 16.3 million, up 266,000 over the year before.

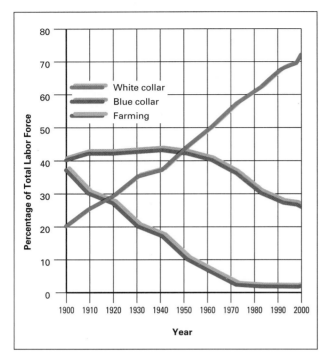

FIGURE 16–2 The Changing Pattern of Work in the United States, 1900–2000

Sources: Author estimates based on United Nations Development Programme (2000) and The World Bank (2000).

THE DECLINE OF AGRICULTURAL WORK

In 1900, almost 40 percent of the U.S. labor force engaged in farming. In 2000, just 2 percent were in agriculture. Figure 16–2 shows this rapid decline, which in turn reflects the shrinking role of the primary sector in the U.S. economy.

Although farming involves far fewer people today, it is more productive than ever. A century ago, a typical farmer grew food for five people; today, one farmer feeds seventy-five. This dramatic rise in productivity reflects new varieties of crops, pesticides that raise yields, and more efficient farm machinery and farming techniques. The average U.S. farm has also doubled in size since 1950, to about 500 acres.

The family farms of yesterday have been replaced by *corporate agribusinesses.* Agriculture may be more productive, but the transformation has required painful adjustments in farming communities across the country as a way of life is lost.

FROM FACTORY WORK TO SERVICE WORK

In the early 1900s, industrialization swelled the ranks of blue-collar workers. As shown in Figure 16–2, until about 1960, at least 40 percent of working people had industrial jobs—far more than were in agriculture. By 1950, however, a white-collar revolution had moved a majority of workers into service occupations. By 2000, 90 percent of new jobs were in the service sector, and 72 percent of the entire labor force performed service work.

As Chapter 11 ("Social Class in the United States") explained, the expansion of service work is one reason many people call the United States a middle-class society. But much service work—including sales and clerical positions and jobs in hospitals and restaurants—carries little of the income and prestige of white-collar professions and often fewer rewards than factory work. In sum, many jobs in this postindustrial era provide only a modest standard of living.

THE DUAL LABOR MARKET

Sociologists see the jobs in today's economy falling into two categories. The **primary labor market** includes *jobs that provide extensive benefits to workers.* This segment of the labor market includes the traditional white-collar professions such as medicine and law as well as upper-management positions. These are jobs that people think of as *careers,* interesting work that provides high income and job security. Such occupations require a broad education rather than specialized training and offer solid opportunity for advancement.

Few of these advantages apply to work in the **secondary labor market,** *jobs that provide minimal benefits to workers.* This segment of the labor force is employed in low-skilled, blue-collar assembly-line operations and low-level service-sector jobs, including clerical positions. Workers in the secondary labor market receive lower income, have less job security, and often feel dissatisfied with their jobs. One recent study found that about 15 percent of jobs in the United States lacked good pay, health benefits, or pension benefits. Women and other minorities are overrepresented in the secondary labor market work force (Hunnicutt, 1990; Greenwald, 1994; Nelson, 1994; Kalleberg, Reskin, & Hudson, 2000).

LABOR UNIONS

The changing U.S. economy has seen the role of labor unions diminish. **Labor unions** are *organizations of*

SOCIAL SURVEY: "How much confidence do you have in people running organized labor?" (GSS 2000, *N* = 1,896; *Codebook*, 2001:182)

| "A great deal" | 12.6% | "Hardly any" | 26.4% |
| "Only some" | 50.7% | DK/NR | 10.3% |

Q: "A profession is a conspiracy against the layman." George Bernard Shaw

Q: "Economics is the study of money and why it is good." Woody Allen

NOTE: In the U.S. there are about 17,000 sociologists, compared to 132,000 architects, 650,000 lawyers, and 1,250,000 accountants; annually about 500 doctorates in sociology are awarded, compared to 16,000 medical doctorates and 38,000 law doctorates (Neuman, 2000:8).

workers that seek to improve wages and working conditions through various strategies, including negotiations and strikes. During the Great Depression of the 1930s, union membership increased rapidly until, by 1950, more than one-third of nonfarm workers belonged to a union. By 1970, the number of union members peaked at almost 25 million. Since then, union rolls have declined to about 14 percent of nonfarm workers, or 16.3 million men and women. Looking more closely, 37 percent of government workers are members of unions, compared to just 9 percent of private sector (nongovernment) workers (Clawson & Clawson, 1999; Goldfield, 2000).

The pattern of union decline holds in other high-income countries as well. Yet unions claim a far smaller share of workers in the United States than elsewhere. In Canada and Japan, about 33 percent of workers belong to unions; across Europe, the share is about 40 percent; in the Scandinavian countries, the share is 80 percent (Western, 1993, 1995).

The global decline in union membership follows the shrinking industrial sector of the economy. In addition, the newer service jobs are less likely to be unionized. But as some analysts see it, decreased job security may make unions popular again in years to come. Indeed, in 1999 unions gained more than 250,000 members. However, unions will have to adapt to the new global economy. Union members in the United States, used to seeing foreign workers as "the enemy," will have to build new international alliances (Mabry, 1992; Church, 1994).

PROFESSIONS

All kinds of jobs today are called *professional*; we hear of professional tennis players, professional babysitters, and even professional exterminators. As distinct from *amateur* (from the Latin for "lover," meaning someone who acts out of love for the activity itself), a professional pursues some task for a living.

A **profession** is *a prestigious, white-collar occupation that requires extensive formal education.* The term "profession" suggests a public declaration to abide by certain principles. Traditional professions include the ministry, medicine, law, academia, and, more recently, architecture, accounting, and social work. Occupations are professions to the extent that they demonstrate the following four characteristics (Goode, 1960; Ritzer & Walczak, 1990):

1. **Theoretical knowledge.** Professionals have a theoretical understanding of their field

An increasing share of jobs in the postindustrial economy of the United States involves working with computers. These jobs lack the hard manual labor and health hazards common to much factory work in the past; at the same time, they provide only modest pay and limited opportunities for advancement.

rather than mere technical training. Anyone can master first-aid skills, for example, but physicians have a theoretical understanding of human health and illness.

2. **Self-regulating practice.** The typical professional is self-employed, "in practice" rather than working for a company. Professionals oversee their own work and observe a code of ethics.

3. **Authority over clients.** Based on extensive training, professionals advise clients and expect them to follow their direction.

4. **Community orientation rather than self-interest.** The traditional professing of duty is a vow to serve the community rather than merely seek personal income.

Many new occupations in the postindustrial economy seek to *professionalize* their services. Claiming professional standing often begins by renaming the work to imply special, theoretical knowledge, which also distances the field from its previously less distinguished reputation. For example, stockroom workers call their work "inventory supply," and exterminators are reborn as "insect control specialists."

Interested parties may also form a professional association to formally attest to their specialized skills.

THEN AND NOW: Between 1987 and 1999, the number of U.S. firms owned by women has doubled (+103%), while the number of employees has jumped 320% and sales have risen 436% (Rutherford, 1999).
DISCUSS: Is the home-based "virtual office" a good thing? Pluses include more freedom, no commute, more flexibility; cons include isolation, harder to get help, and blurring between home and work life.

DISCUSS: Measures of economic output do not include unpaid work (volunteer work and housework), which are historically the responsibilities of women. Should they? How does one measure the value of unpaid work?
GLOBAL: Unemployment rates (1998): Netherlands, 4.0%; Japan, 4.1%; U.S., 4.5%; U.K., 6.3%; Sweden, 8.3%; Canada, 8.4%; Germany, 9.4%; France, 11.7% (U.S. Census Bureau, 1999).

Jose Clemente Orozco's painting The Unemployed *is a powerful statement of the personal collapse and private despair that afflict men and women who are out of work. How does a sociological perspective help us to understand being out of work as more than a personal problem?*

Jose Clemente Orozco, *The Unemployed.* Oil. © Orozco Valladares Family. Reproduction authorized by the Instituto Nacional de Bellas Artes.

This organization then licenses people who perform the work and writes a code of ethics that emphasizes the occupation's role in the community. In its effort to win public acceptance, a professional association may also establish schools or other training facilities and perhaps start a professional journal (Abbott, 1988). Not all occupations try to claim professional status. Some *paraprofessionals*, including paralegals and medical technicians, possess specialized skills but lack the extensive theoretical education required of full professionals.

SELF-EMPLOYMENT

Self-employment—earning a living without working for an organization—was once common in the United States. About 80 percent of the labor force was self-employed in 1800, compared to 6.5 percent of workers today (8.2 percent of men and 5.7 percent of women) (U.S. Department of Labor, 2001).

Lawyers, physicians, and other professionals are well represented among the ranks of the self-employed. In addition, the number of people using the Internet to run small businesses is growing. But most self-employed workers are small business owners, plumbers, carpenters, freelance writers, editors, artists, and long-distance truck drivers. Overall, the self-employed are more likely to have blue-collar than white-collar jobs.

 Visit the Web site of the Small Business Administration: http://www.sba.gov

Finally, a notable trend in the U.S. economy is that women now own nearly 40 percent of this country's small businesses, and the share is rising. Moreover, the 9.1 million firms owned by U.S. women now employ almost 30 million people and generate close to $4 trillion in annual sales (Small Business Administration, 2001).

UNEMPLOYMENT AND UNDEREMPLOYMENT

Every society has some unemployment. Few young people entering the labor force find a job right away, workers may temporarily leave their jobs to seek new work or have children, some may be on strike, others suffer from long-term illnesses, and still others are illiterate or lack the skills to perform useful work.

But unemployment is also caused by the economy itself. Jobs disappear as occupations become obsolete, businesses close in the face of foreign competition or economic recession, and companies downsize to become more profitable. Since 1980, the 500 largest U.S. businesses have eliminated some 5 million jobs, one-fourth of the total.

In 2000, 5.7 million people over the age of sixteen were unemployed, about 4.0 percent of the civilian labor force. As a glance back at National Map 16–1 on page 419 shows, some regions of the country, including parts of West Virginia and New Mexico, have high unemployment, in some cases twice the national average. Indeed, research shows that rural residents in the United States are especially likely to experience unemployment or underemployment (Stofferahn, 2000).

Figure 16–3 shows that unemployment among African Americans (7.6 percent) is more than twice the rate among white people (3.5 percent). Overall, men and women of each race have about the same rates of unemployment.

SOCIAL SURVEY: "The government should provide a decent standard of living for the unemployed." (GSS 1985, N = 1,285; *Codebook*, 2001:954)

"Strongly agree"   6.2%   "Disagree"   29.2%
"Agree"   29.0%   "Strongly disagree"   5.7%
"Neither agree nor disagree" 25.8%   DK/NR 4.2%

THEN AND NOW: African American unemployment: 1930, about 4%; in 1999, 8%. Richard Vedder and Lowell Gallaway (1993) link this rise to black people's movement out of low-unemployment farming and into urban manufacturing jobs (where layoffs are common) but also to expanding entitlement programs, which have undermined employment.

DIVERSITY SNAPSHOT

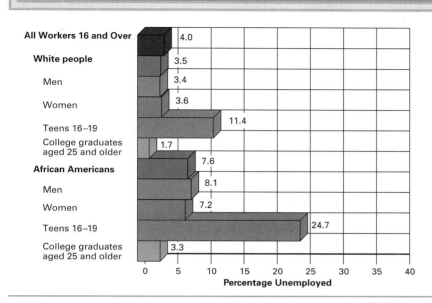

FIGURE 16–3
Official U.S. Unemployment Rates for Various Categories of Adults, 2000

Sources: U.S. Census Bureau (2000) and U.S. Department of Labor (2001).

Chart data:
All Workers 16 and Over: 4.0
White people: 3.5
Men: 3.4
Women: 3.6
Teens 16–19: 11.4
College graduates aged 25 and older: 1.7
African Americans: 7.6
Men: 8.1
Women: 7.2
Teens 16–19: 24.7
College graduates aged 25 and older: 3.3

(X-axis: Percentage Unemployed, 0 to 40)

Underemployment is a problem for millions of workers. The government reports that more than 30 million people work part time, meaning no more than thirty-four hours weekly. Of these, 80 percent are satisfied with the arrangement, but 20 percent (6 million workers) say they want more work but cannot find it (U.S. Department of Labor, 2001).

THE UNDERGROUND ECONOMY

The U.S. government requires individuals and businesses to report their economic activity, especially earnings. Unreported income makes a transaction part of the **underground economy**, *economic activity involving income unreported to the government as required by law.*

On a small scale, most people participate in the underground economy from time to time: A family makes extra money by holding a garage sale, or teenagers babysit for neighbors without reporting the income. Of course, far more of the underground economy is attributable to criminal activity, such as the sale of illegal drugs, prostitution, bribery, theft, illegal gambling, and loan-sharking.

But the single largest segment of contributors to the underground economy is people who fail to re-port some or all of their legally obtained income. Self-employed people such as carpenters, physicians, and owners of small businesses may understate their incomes on tax forms; food servers, taxicab drivers, and other service workers may not report their earnings from tips. Individually, the omissions and misrepresentations may be small, but millions of individuals hedging on income tax returns adds up to perhaps $170 billion annually in lost revenues (Speer, 1995).

DIVERSITY IN THE WORKPLACE: RACE AND GENDER

Traditionally, white men have been the mainstay of the U.S. labor force. As discussed in Chapter 14 ("Race and Ethnicity"), however, our nation's proportion of minorities is rising rapidly. Between 1990 and 2000, the African American population increased by 16 percent, more than five times the 3 percent rate for non-Hispanic white people. The jump in the Hispanic population was even greater, at 58 percent, and among Asian Americans, 41 percent. The box on page 424 takes a closer look at how the increasing social diversity of our society will affect the workplace.

NOTE: In 1995 (for the first time in 40 years) *Fortune* added service industries to its Fortune 400, including life insurance companies and banks. Showing the growing significance of information technology, Microsoft now rivals General Motors in value.
NOTE: National Maps 14–1 and 14–4, on pages 357 and 374, illustrate the areas of the country in which the character of the work force is most affected by racial and ethnic diversity.

NOTE: For young people, at least one of the jobs they will hold has yet to be invented.
RESOURCE: A selection from William Julius Wilson's research, "When Work Disappears," is included in the *Seeing Ourselves* reader.
THEN AND NOW: In 1980, half of 60-year-old male workers had been with the same company for more than 17 years; by 1998, the figure had fallen to 10 years.

DIVERSITY: RACE, CLASS, AND GENDER

Twenty-First Century Diversity: Changes in the Workplace

An upward trend in the U.S. minority population is changing the workplace. As the figure shows, the number of white men in the U.S. labor force will rise by a modest 7 percent between 1998 and 2008. The rate of increase among African American working men will be greater, at 18 percent, and that among Hispanic men will be greater still, at 29 percent. Among white women the projected increase is 13 percent, and among African American women it is 21 percent. Hispanic women will show the greatest gains, estimated at 49 percent.

The overall result is that within a decade, non-Hispanic white men will represent 38 percent of all workers, and that figure will continue to drop. Therefore, companies that welcome social diversity will tap the largest talent pool and enjoy a competitive advantage.

Welcoming social diversity means, first, recruiting talented workers of both sexes and all colors and cultural backgrounds. But developing the potential of all employees requires meeting the needs of women and other minorities,

which may not be the same as those of white men. For example, corporations are being pressed to provide child care at the workplace.

Second, businesses must develop effective ways to defuse tensions that arise from social differences. They will have to work harder at treating workers

equally and respectfully. Furthermore, no corporate culture can tolerate racial or sexual harassment.

Third, companies will have to rethink current promotion practices. At present, only 4 percent of Fortune 500 top executives are women, and just 1 percent are other minorities. In a broad survey of U.S. companies, the U.S. Equal Employment Opportunity Commission confirmed that white men (42 percent of adults aged twenty to sixty-four) hold 59 percent of management jobs; the comparable figures for white women are 42 and 28 percent; for African Americans, 12 and 6 percent; and for Hispanics, 13 and 4 percent.

In sum, "glass ceilings" that prevent skilled workers from advancing not only discourage effort but deprive companies of their largest source of talent: women and other minorities.

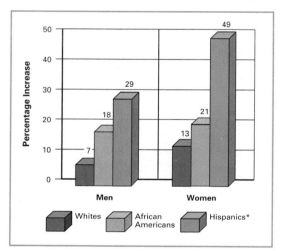

Projected Increase in the Numbers of People in the U.S. Labor Force, 1998–2008

*Hispanics can be of any race.
Source: U.S. Department of Labor (1999).

Sources: U.S. Department of Labor (1999), Catalyst (2001), and U.S. Equal Employment Opportunity Commission (2001).

NEW INFORMATION TECHNOLOGY AND WORK

July 2, Ticonderoga, New York. The manager of the local hardware store scans the barcodes on bags of lawn seed and fertilizer as I transfer them from

my shopping cart to the counter. "The computer not only totals the costs," she explains, "it also keeps track of inventory, places orders from the warehouse, and decides which products to continue to sell and which to discontinue." "Sounds like what you used

Although the Information Revolution is centered in high-income countries such as the United States, the effects of high technology are becoming evident even in low-income nations. Do you think the expansion of information technology will change the lives of rural people such as these peasants in Vietnam? If so, how?

to do, Maureen," I respond with a smile. "Yep," she nods, with no smile at all.

Another workplace issue is the increasing role of computers and other new information technology. The Information Revolution is changing the kind of work people do and where they do it. Computers are also changing the character of work in more subtle ways (Zuboff, 1982; Rule & Brantley, 1992; Vallas & Beck, 1996):

1. **Computers are deskilling labor.** Just as industrial machinery replaced the master craftsworkers of an earlier era, computers now threaten the skills of managers. More and more business decisions are based not on executive training and experience but on computer modeling. In other words, as in the hardware store just described, a machine makes decisions that people used to make, determining when to resupply inventory or even whether or not to approve a loan application.

2. **Computers are making work more abstract.** Most industrial workers have a hands-on relationship with their product. Postindustrial workers manipulate symbols in pursuit of abstract goals such as making a Web site more attractive, a company more profitable, or software more user-friendly.

3. **Computers limit workplace interaction.** As workers spend more time at computer terminals, they become isolated from one another.

4. **Computers enhance employers' control of workers.** Computers allow supervisors to monitor employees' output precisely and continuously, whether they work at computer terminals or on assembly lines.

Such changes remind us that technology is not socially neutral. Rather, it shapes the way we work and alters the balance of power between employers and employees. Understandably, then, people welcome some aspects of the Information Revolution and oppose others.

CORPORATIONS

At the core of today's capitalist economy lies the **corporation,** *an organization with a legal existence, including rights and liabilities, apart from that of its members.* Incorporating makes an organization a legal entity unto itself, able to enter into contracts and own property. Of more than 24 million businesses in the United States, 5 million are incorporated (U.S. Census Bureau, 2000). Incorporating also protects the wealth of owners from lawsuits arising from business debts or as a result of harm to consumers; often, it also means a lower tax rate on profits.

Q: "Growth for the sake of growth is the ideology of the cancer cell." John Nichols
SOCIAL SURVEY: "How much confidence do you have in the people running major companies?" (GSS 2000, N = 1,896; Codebook, 2001:181)
"A great deal"   27.8%   "Hardly any"   10.9%
"Only some"   56.8%   DK/NR   4.4%

NOTE: A significant portion of corporate stock is held by institutional investors (corporations investing in each other). In terms of individuals, about 50% of U.S. residents have such investments (the share increased dramatically during the 1990s). Extensive stock holdings characterize a much smaller proportion of the population, as noted in Chapter 11. Perhaps 20% of Britons are stockholders (exclusive of pension funds).

APPLYING SOCIOLOGY

Them That's Got, Gets: The Case of Corporate Welfare

What would you say if the government offered to slash your income taxes and abolish sales tax on your purchases? What if it offered you the money to buy a new house at a below-market interest rate? Would you like the government to hook up all your utilities for free and pay your water and electric bills?

For an ordinary individual, such deals sound too good to be true. But our tax money is doing exactly this—not for individuals but for big corporations. All a large company has to do is declare a willingness to relocate and then wait for the offers from state and local governments to come pouring in.

Supporters call government aid to corporations "public-private partnerships." They point to the jobs companies create, sometimes in areas hard hit by earlier business closings. For a city or county with a high unemployment rate, the promise of a new factory opening is simply too good to pass up. If some incentives in the form of tax relief or free utilities lure the company away from another possible site, it is considered money well spent.

However, critics call these arrangements corporate welfare. They concede that companies do create new jobs, but they also point out that the corporations get much more than they give. In 1991, for example, the state of Indiana offered $451 million in incentives to lure United Airlines to build an aircraft maintenance facility there. United Airlines built the facility and hired 6,300 people. But some simple math shows that the cost to Indiana came out to be a whopping $72,000 *per job*. Much the same happened in 1993, when Alabama offered $253 million in incentives to Mercedes-Benz to build an automobile assembly plant in Tuscaloosa. The plant opened and 1,500 people were hired—at an average cost to Alabama of $169,000 per worker. In 1997, Pennsylvania gave $307 million in incentives to a Norwegian company to reopen part of Philadelphia's naval shipyard. Once the deal was signed, 950 people were hired, at a cost of $323,000 per job. Across the country, the

pattern is much the same. During the 1990s, in fact, government support to corporations exceeded $15 billion each year—more than the welfare given to poor people.

Corporations willing to relocate their facilities attract very generous offers from politicians eager to "create jobs." But nationwide, although new plants do create some jobs, more often jobs are simply moved from one place to another. Nor do all the jobs pay well. And there is no guarantee that, once settled, a corporation will stay because businesses are free to make a better deal to move again to another location. In 1993, state and local governments in Kentucky granted General Electric $19 million in tax breaks to build a washing machine factory near Louisville. In 1999, GE pulled up stakes, announcing the loss of 1,500 local jobs because the company was moving to new factories in Georgia and Mexico, where wages were lower.

Source: Adapted from Bartlett & Steele (1998).

ECONOMIC CONCENTRATION

About half of U.S. corporations are small, with assets under $100,000. However, the largest corporations dominate our country's economy. In 1997, 549 corporations had assets exceeding $1 billion, representing three-fourths of all corporate assets and profits (U.S. Census Bureau, 2000).

The largest U.S. corporation in terms of sales is automaker General Motors, with $303 billion in total assets. GM employs more people than the state governments of California, Oregon, Washington, Alaska, and Hawaii combined. Its sales ($185 billion in 2000) equal the total tax revenues of half the states.

CONGLOMERATES AND CORPORATE LINKAGES

The largest businesses are **conglomerates,** *giant corporations composed of many smaller corporations.* Conglomerates form as corporations enter new markets, spin off new companies, or merge with other companies. For example, RJR-Nabisco is a conglomerate that sells not only cigarettes but also dozens of familiar household products.

Even conglomerates are linked because they own each other's stock, resulting in worldwide corporate alliances of staggering size. For example, General Motors owns Opel (Germany), Vauxhall (Great Britain), and

NOTE: Monopolies were outlawed in 1890 by the Sherman Antitrust Act.

NOTE: Oligopoly does not preclude successful economic challenges, either in well-established industries such as automaking (consider the success of the Japanese entering the U.S. auto market) or in new industries such as software (note Microsoft's outdistancing of IBM and other rivals to set a world standard).

Q: "If you have absolutely unrestrained competition in the marketplace, pretty soon you'll wind up with no competition at all." Lee Iacocca

DISCUSS: In 1996, the federal government probed Frito Lay for its domination (55% of sales dollars) of the snack food industry. Is this against the public interest or simply evidence that some companies perform better than others?

half of Saab (Sweden) and has partnerships with Suzuki, Isuzu, and Toyota (Japan). Similarly, Ford owns Jaguar and Aston Martin (Great Britain) and a share of Mazda (Japan), Kia (Korea), and Volvo (Sweden).

Corporations are also linked throughly *interlocking directorates*, networks of people who serve as directors of many corporations (Herman, 1981; Scott & Griff, 1985; Weidenbaum, 1995; Kono et al., 1998). These boardroom connections provide access to valuable information about each other's products and marketing strategies. Beth Mintz and Michael Schwartz (1981) found General Motors linked, through its board members, to 700 other companies. Such linkages do not in themselves run counter to the public interest, but they may encourage illegal activity, such as price-fixing, and they certainly concentrate wealth and power.

CORPORATIONS: ARE THEY COMPETITIVE?

According to the capitalist model, businesses operate independently in a competitive market. But large corporations have extensive linkages, which means they do not operate independently. Moreover, a small number of corporations dominate many large markets. Many large corporations therefore have little real competition.

Law forbids a large company from establishing a **monopoly**, *domination of a market by a single producer*, because a monopoly could simply dictate prices. But **oligopoly**, *domination of a market by a few producers*, is a legal and common practice. Oligopoly arises because the vast investment needed to enter a major market, such as the auto industry, is beyond the reach of all but the biggest companies. Moreover, true competition means risk, which big business tries to avoid.

Corporate power is now so great—and competition between corporations so limited—that government regulation may be the only way to protect the public interest. Yet the government is the corporate world's single biggest customer. The federal government also steps in to support struggling corporations, sometimes with billion-dollar bail-out programs. In addition, as the box explains, state government aid to corporations has drawn fire as "corporate welfare."

CORPORATIONS AND THE GLOBAL ECONOMY

Corporations have grown so big and powerful that they account for most of the world's economic output. The biggest corporations are based in the United

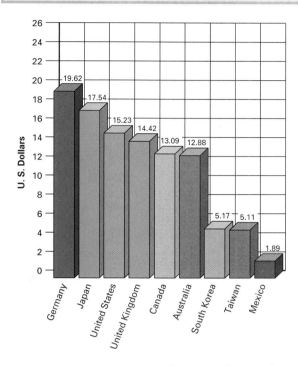

GLOBAL SNAPSHOT

FIGURE 16–4 Average Hourly Wages for Workers in Manufacturing, 1999

Source: Calculations by the author based on U.S. Department of Labor (2000).

States, Japan, and Western Europe, but they consider the entire world one huge marketplace. In fact, many large U.S. companies such as McDonald's generate most of their sales outside the United States.

Poor nations attract the attention of global corporations because most of the world's people and resources are found there. In addition, as shown in Figure 16–4, labor costs are far lower: A factory worker in Mexico works for two weeks to earn what a German worker earns in a single day.

The impact of multinationals on poor societies is controversial, as Chapter 12 ("Global Stratification") explains. On one side of the argument, modernization theorists claim that multinationals unleash the great productive power of capitalism to raise living standards in poor nations. Specifically, corporations offer poor

CONTROVERSY & DEBATE

The Market: Does the "Invisible Hand" Look Out for Us or Pick Our Pockets?

"The market" or "government planning"? Each is a means of economic decision making to determine what products and services companies will produce and what people will consume. So important is this process that the degree to which the market or government directs the economy largely determines how nations define themselves, choose their allies, and identify their enemies.

Historically, U.S. society has relied on the market's "invisible hand" for economic decisions. Market dynamics move prices up or down according to the supply of products and buyer demand. The market thus coordinates the efforts of countless people, each of whom—to return to Adam Smith's insight—is motivated only by self-interest.

Defenders of the market system praise it for discouraging social bad habits, such as racial prejudice. Industrialist J. P. Morgan, who once commented that he would sail only with a gentleman, would do business with *anyone*, making the point that market transactions focus on value, not the social traits of traders. Perhaps most

important of all, as economists Milton Friedman and Rose Friedman remind us, a freely operating market system is

J. Pierpont Morgan, railroad tycoon and founder of U.S. Steel (the first billion-dollar corporation), symbolized the operation of the market system at a time of little government regulation.

the key to U.S. society's unprecedented economic standard of living.

But others point to the contributions government makes to the U.S. economy. First, government must step in to carry out tasks that no private company could do as well. For example, Adam Smith looked to government to defend the country against external enemies. Government (in partnership with private companies) also plays a key role in constructing and maintaining public projects such as roads, utilities, schools, libraries, and museums.

But the Friedmans, as well as other believers in the free-market system, counter that whatever task government undertakes usually ends up being performed inefficiently. The least satisfying goods and services available today—including public schools, postal service, and passenger railroad service—are government-operated. The products we most enjoy—computers and other new electronics, household appliances, and the myriad offerings of supermarkets and shopping centers—are products of the market. Thus, while some government presence in the economy

Statistics and analysis for any number of economic issues can be found at the Web site of the U.S. Department of Labor: http://www.dol.gov

societies capital investment, tax revenues, new jobs, and advanced technology that accelerate economic growth (Rostow, 1978; Madsen, 1980; Berger, 1986; Firebaugh & Beck, 1994; Firebaugh & Sandu, 1998).

On the other hand, dependency theorists respond that multinationals intensify global inequality. Multinationals, they contend, actually create few jobs because they block the development of local industries and push poor countries to make goods for export rather than food and other products for local consumption. From this standpoint, multinationals make poor societies poorer and increasingly dependent on rich nations

NOTE: Beatrice Foods is a corporate "umbrella" containing more than 50 smaller corporations that manufacture well-known products, including Reddi-Whip, Wesson cooking oils, Peter Pan peanut butter, Hunt's foods, Tropicana fruit juices, La Choy foods, Orville Redenbacher popcorn, Max Factor cosmetics, Playtex clothing, and Samsonite luggage.

Q: "I have long dreamed of buying an island owned by no nation and of establishing the world headquarters of Dow Chemical Company on the truly neutral ground of such an island, beholden to no nation or society. . . . We could then really operate in the United States as U.S. citizens, in Japan as Japanese citizens, and in Brazil as Brazilians rather than being governed by the laws of the United States." Carl A. Gerstacker, chairman of Dow Chemical Company

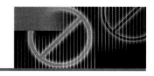

is necessary, the Friedmans and other supporters of free markets believe that minimal state regulation best serves the public interest.

But supporters of government intervention in the economy have additional arguments in their arsenal. For one thing, they claim, the market has little incentive to produce anything that is not profitable. This is why few private companies set out to meet the needs of poor people because, by definition, poor people have little money to spend.

Second, the market has certain self-destructive tendencies that only the government can curb. In 1890, for example, the government passed the Sherman Antitrust Act to break up monopolies that controlled the nation's oil and steel production. Since then—and especially since President Franklin Roosevelt's New Deal of the 1930s—government has taken a strong regulatory role to control inflation (by setting interest rates), enhance the well-being of workers (by imposing workplace safety standards), and ensure consumer satisfaction (by setting standards for product quality). Despite such interventions, advocates for a stronger government role point out that corporations in U.S. society are so powerful that the

government still cannot effectively challenge the capitalist elite.

Third, because the market magnifies social inequality, the government must step in on the side of social justice. Because capitalist economies concentrate income and wealth in the hands of a few, a government system of taxation that applies higher rates to the rich counters this tendency.

Does the market's "invisible hand" look out for us or pick our pockets?

Upon his election to the presidency, Franklin Delano Roosevelt announced a "New Deal" that greatly increased the role of government in the economic life of the United States. Here, Roosevelt signs historic Social Security legislation.

Although most people in the United States favor a free market, they also support government intervention that benefits the public. Indeed, government assists not only citizens but also business itself by providing investment capital, constructing roads and other infrastructures, and shielding companies from foreign competition. Yet in the United States and around the world, people continue to debate the optimal balance of market forces and government decision making.

Continue the debate . . .

1. *Why do free-market defenders assert that "a government is best that governs least"? What do you think?*

2. *What difference does it make in people's everyday lives if a society's economy is more a market system or more government-centered?*

3. *What is your impression of the successes and failures of socialist economic systems? What about welfare capitalism, as found in Sweden?*

Sources: Friedman & Friedman (1980) and Erber (1990).

(Vaughan, 1978; Wallerstein, 1979; Delacroix & Ragin, 1981; Bergesen, 1983; Walton & Ragin, 1990).

Whereas modernization theory hails the market as the key to progress and affluence for all the world's people, dependency theory calls for replacing market systems with government-based economic policies. The final box takes a closer look at the issue of market versus government economies.

LOOKING AHEAD: THE ECONOMY OF THE TWENTY-FIRST CENTURY

Social institutions are a society's way of meeting people's needs. But as we have seen, the U.S. economy only partly succeeds in this respect. Although highly

SEEING OURSELVES

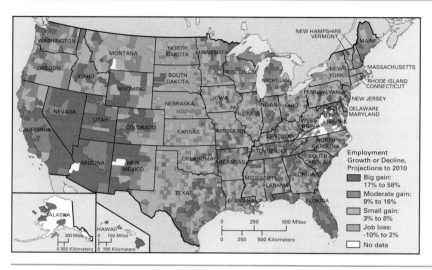

NATIONAL MAP 16–2
Where the Jobs Will Be: Projections to 2010

The economic prospects of counties across the United States are not the same. Much of the midsection of the country is projected to lose jobs. By contrast, the coastal regions and most of the West are rapidly gaining jobs. What factors might account for this pattern?

Source: Used with permission of Woods & Poole Economics, Washington, D.C.

productive, our economy provides for some much better than it does for others. Moreover, as we begin the twenty-first century, the Information Revolution continues to change our economy. In the postindustrial era, the share of the U.S. labor force engaged in manufacturing is half what it was in 1960; service work, especially computer-related jobs, makes up the difference. Therefore, our society must face the challenge of providing millions of men and women with the language and computer skills they need to succeed in the new information-based economy. We must also take into account that some regions of the country are experiencing an economic boom, as shown in National Map 16–2, whereas others—especially rural areas in the middle of the country—are projected to lose jobs. Can we afford to consign workers and their families to the margins of society because they happen to live in one region of the country rather than another?

In the new century the economy will also become increasingly global. Two centuries ago, the ups and downs of a local economy reflected events and trends in a single town. One century ago, communities were economically linked so that one town's prosperity depended on producing goods demanded by people elsewhere in the country. Today, it makes little sense to speak of a national economy because what people in

a Kansas farm town produce and consume may be affected more by what happens in the wheat-growing region of Russia than by events in their own state capital. In short, U.S. workers and business owners are generating products and services in response to factors and forces that are distant and unseen.

Finally, analysts around the world are rethinking conventional economic models. The global economy shows that socialism is less productive than capitalism, one important reason for the collapse of socialist regimes in Eastern Europe and the former Soviet Union. But capitalism also is changing. It now operates with significant government regulation, partly to address the economic inequality generated by market systems.

What are the long-term effects of these changes? Two conclusions seem inescapable. First, the economic future of the United States and other nations will be played out in a global arena. After all, the emergence of the postindustrial economy in the United States is inseparable from the increasing industrial production of other nations. Second, we must address the related issues of global inequality and population increase (Firebaugh, 1999, 2000). Whether the world economy ultimately reduces or deepens the disparity between rich and poor societies may well be what steers our planet toward peace or war.

SOCIAL SURVEY: "Should the government in Washington reduce income differences between the rich and the poor?" (1–7 Likert scale; GSS 2000, N = 1,896; *Codebook*, 2001:113)

(1) "Gov't should" 15.9% (5) 13.6%
(2) 11.4%   (6) 8.4%
(3) 15.5%   (7) "Gov't should not" 12.9%
(4) 19.7%   DK/NR 2.5%

Q: "The business of the United States is business." President Warren G. Harding

GLOBAL: The tax burden in the U.S. is considerably lower than that of most European nations. U.S. federal tax revenues represent 20% of GDP. Selected data for other nations: Norway, 33%; Sweden, 37%; France, 39%; Italy, 42% (United Nations Development Programme, 1999).

SUMMARY

1. The economy is the major social institution by which a society produces, distributes, and consumes goods and services.

2. In technologically simple societies, the economy is simply part of family life. Agrarian societies show some productive specialization. Industrialization rapidly expands the economy through greater specialization and new energy sources that power machines in large factories.

3. The postindustrial economy is characterized by a shift from producing goods to services. Just as the Industrial Revolution propelled the industrial economy of the past, the Information Revolution is now advancing the postindustrial economy.

4. The primary sector of the economy, which generates raw materials, dominates in preindustrial societies. The secondary, manufacturing sector prevails in industrial societies. The tertiary, service sector dominates in postindustrial societies.

5. The expanding global economy now produces and consumes products and services with little regard for national boundaries. Today, the 600 largest corporations, operating internationally, account for half of the world's economic output.

6. Capitalism is based on private ownership of productive property and the pursuit of profit in a competitive marketplace. Socialism is grounded in collective ownership of productive property through government control of the economy.

7. Although the economy of the United States is predominantly capitalist, government is broadly involved in economic life. Government plays a greater role in the welfare capitalist economies of some Western European nations, such as Sweden, and the state capitalism of many Asian nations, including Japan.

8. Capitalism is very productive, providing a high average standard of living. A capitalist system allows freedom to act according to one's self-interest. Socialism is less productive but generates greater economic equality. A socialist system offers freedom from basic want.

9. In the United States, agricultural work has declined to just 2 percent of the labor force. Blue-collar jobs have also dwindled, accounting for one-fourth of the labor force. The share of white-collar service occupations has risen to more than 70 percent of the labor force.

10. Although work in the primary labor market may provide greater rewards, many new jobs in the United States are service positions in the secondary labor market.

11. A profession is a special category of white-collar work based on theoretical knowledge, occupational autonomy, authority over clients, and a claim to serving the community.

12. Today, 6.5 percent of U.S. workers are self-employed. Although many professionals fall into this category, most self-employed workers have blue-collar occupations.

13. Unemployment has many causes, including the operation of the economy itself; in 2000, 4.0 percent of the U.S. labor force was without work.

14. The underground economy, which includes criminal as well as legal activity, generates income unreported to the government.

15. Corporations form the core of the U.S. economy. The largest corporations, which are conglomerates, account for most corporate assets and profits. Many large corporations operate as multinationals, producing and distributing products in nations around the world.

KEY CONCEPTS

economy (p. 409) the social institution that organizes a society's production, distribution, and consumption of goods and services

postindustrial economy (p. 411) a productive system based on service work and high technology

primary sector (p. 412) the part of the economy that draws raw materials from the natural environment

secondary sector (p. 412) the part of the economy that transforms raw materials into manufactured goods

tertiary sector (p. 412) the part of the economy that involves services rather than goods

global economy (p. 412) expanding economic activity with little regard for national borders

capitalism (p. 415) an economic system in which natural resources and the means of producing goods and services are privately owned

socialism (p. 416) an economic system in which natural resources and the means of producing goods and services are collectively owned

communism (p. 417) a hypothetical economic and political system in which all members of a society are socially equal

welfare capitalism (p. 417) an economic and political system that combines a mostly market-based economy with extensive social welfare programs

state capitalism (p. 418) an economic and political system in which companies are privately owned but cooperate closely with the government

primary labor market (p. 420) jobs that provide extensive benefits to workers

secondary labor market (p. 420) jobs that provide minimal benefits to workers

labor unions (p. 420) organizations of workers that seek to improve wages and working conditions through various strategies, including negotiations and strikes

profession (p. 421) a prestigious, white-collar occupation that requires extensive formal education

underground economy (p. 423) economic activity involving income unreported to the government as required by law

corporation (p. 425) an organization with a legal existence, including rights and liabilities, apart from that of its members

conglomerate (p. 426) a giant corporation composed of many smaller corporations

monopoly (p. 427) domination of a market by a single producer

oligopoly (p. 427) domination of a market by a few producers

CRITICAL-THINKING QUESTIONS

1. As a social institution, what is the economy supposed to do? How well do you think our economy does its job?

2. How did the Industrial Revolution alter the economy of the United States? How is the Information Revolution changing the economy once again?

3. What key characteristics distinguish capitalism from socialism? Compare these two systems in terms of productivity, economic inequality, and personal freedoms.

4. What does it mean to say that we now have a global economy? How does the operation of the global economy affect your life?

APPLICATIONS AND EXERCISES

1. Overall, a profile of the U.S. economy looks like this: 72 percent of output is in the service sector, 26 percent in the industrial sector, and 2 percent in the primary sector. But in any specific area, the percentages vary widely. Visit the library and locate data that profile your own city, county, or state.

2. Visit a discount store such as Wal-Mart or K-Mart and select a product area that interests you. Do a little fieldwork, inspecting the merchandise to see where it is made. Does your research support the existence of a global economy?

3. What share of the faculty on your campus has temporary teaching contracts? Talk with several tenured faculty, as well as several visiting professors: What differences can you discover in their working conditions and their attitude toward their jobs?

4. Packaged in the back of this new textbook is an interactive CD-ROM that offers a variety of study and review materials intended to help you better understand the material covered in this chapter. For this chapter, the CD-ROM contains an author's tip video, Real Life Sociology videos, other relevant audio and video, interactive map animations, audio journal entries from the author, Web links, and much more.

CTQ3: Capitalism is based on private ownership of productive property used to pursue profit in a competitive marketplace. Socialism is based on collective ownership of productive property through government control of the economy with the goal of social equality. Capitalism depends on the freedom to act in pursuit of self interest; socialism strives to secure freedom from basic want for all people.

CTQ4: An economy becomes global as more products and services (including information) move across national boundaries. An increasing number of familiar household products are made abroad; many involve components from and assembly in more than one nation.

Q: "The rare company that is able to retain its share of the market year after year and decade after decade does so by the means of productive efficiency—and deserves praise, not blame." Alan Greenspan

SITES TO SEE

http://www.prenhall.com/macionis

Visit the interactive *Companion Website*™ that accompanies this text. Begin by clicking on the cover of your book. You will find a chapter-by-chapter study guide, practice tests, and a significant portion of the text for on-line review, as well as many suggested Web links.

http://www.bls.gov

Visit this Web site, operated by the Bureau of Labor Statistics, where you will find a wide range of interesting data and reports.

http://www.nber.org

Another worthwhile site, run by the National Bureau of Economic Research, explains the operation of the economy.

http://www2.kenyon.edu/projects/famfarm/

Students at Kenyon College, in central Ohio, prepared this Web site to study family farms in the local, rural county.

http://www.fao.org

The Food and Agriculture Organization is a part of the United Nations concerned with how well the global economy meets the needs of the world's people. From their main page, look for their annual report, titled "State of Food Insecurity in the World."

 INVESTIGATE WITH CONTENTSELECT

Follow the instructions found on page 23 of this textbook to enter this chapter of the book's *Companion Website*™. Once in the chapter, click on the ContentSelect icon at the bottom left of your screen and enter your personal User ID and Password. Enter keywords such as "professions," "monopoly," and "underground economy," and the search engine will help you become an effective researcher.

CHAPTER
17

George Grosz (1893–1959)
Sonnenfinsternis (Eclipse of the Sun)

Oil on canvas, 207.3 × 182.6 cm. Huntington (N.Y.), Heckscher Museum.
Photo: AKG London. © Estate of George Grosz/Licensed by VAGA, New York, N.Y.

POLITICS
AND GOVERNMENT

Charlotte Williams sat straight up in the metal folding chair behind the ballot box, her eyes fixed on the open door in front of her. It was election day, and she was four hours into her day-long shift overseeing the voting in Washington, D.C., Precinct Number 15. To her left, a man of about sixty leaned over a table, completing his ballot. But except for the man and Williams herself, the large room was empty.

As the man walked over to deposit his ballot, he smiled and shrugged his shoulders. "Today we are picking a president," he began, "yet nobody bothers to come out to vote." "Tell me about it," Charlotte Williams responded, glad for the opportunity for conversation. "People ought to care, but—you know what—they don't. The welfare system is changing. You know what's

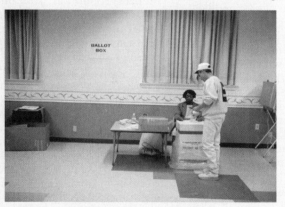

happening in our schools. There's way too much crime. I'm sorry, but I can't see it. I just can't see people not caring."

In the 2000 presidential election—a contest that turned on a few hundred votes—only about half the voting-age population of the United States bothered to go to the polls. And no category of the population is less likely to vote than the poor. In fact, more than three-fourths of high-income people vote in presidential elections compared to about 40 percent of low-income people.

What does this apathy mean? Is our political system failing to meet the needs of the people, especially the poor? Indeed, is it realistic to describe our nation as a democracy when most people don't participate in politics, even as once-a-year voters?

This chapter investigates *politics,* the dynamics of power within societies and between nations. Formally, **politics,** or "the polity," is *the social institution that distributes power, sets a society's agenda, and makes decisions.* But as the low turnout in many voting precincts suggests, politics may address the concerns of some far better than others.

POWER AND AUTHORITY

Every society rests on **power,** which sociologist Max Weber (1978; orig. 1921) defined as *the ability to achieve desired ends despite resistance from others.* To a

large degree, the exercise of power is the business of **government,** *a formal organization that directs the political life of a society.* Yet as Weber explained, few governments obtain compliance by openly threatening their people. Most of the time, people respect (or at least accept) their political system.

Practically speaking, it would be difficult for any large, complex society to persist if power derived *only* from sheer force, and life in such a society would be a nightmare of terror. Social organization depends on some degree of consensus among members of a society about proper goals (often in the form of cultural values) and suitable means of pursuing them (cultural norms).

SUPPLEMENTS: Consult the *Data File* for an outline of this chapter, supplementary lecture material, and discussion topics.
NOTE: As Hannah Arendt explained, the concept of authority is Roman in origin with roots in the Latin verb *augere*, meaning "to augment." Thus authority involves steadily augmenting some past foundation.

NOTE: Ferdinand Tönnies, too, described the social roots of authority. He linked authority to (1) advanced age, (2) force, and (3) wisdom or spirit.
GLOBAL: The British have melded traditional and bureaucratic authority in their recent practice of elevating individuals to noble rank based on distinguished accomplishment but mandating that the rank not pass to any descendants.

Every society, then, seeks to establish its power as legitimate. Weber therefore focused on the concept of **authority,** *power that people perceive as legitimate rather than coercive.* How is sheer power transformed into stable authority? Weber pointed to three ways, which vary according to a society's level of economic development.

TRADITIONAL AUTHORITY

Preindustrial societies, Weber explained, rely on **traditional authority,** *power legitimized through respect for long-established cultural patterns.* In ideal terms, traditional authority is power woven into a society's collective memory, so that people consider social arrangements almost sacred. Chinese emperors in antiquity were legitimized by tradition, as were nobles in medieval Europe. In both cases, the power of tradition was strong enough that—for better or worse—people typically viewed members of a hereditary ruling family as almost godlike.

But traditional authority declines as societies industrialize. Hannah Arendt (1963) pointed out that traditional authority is compelling only as long as everyone shares the same heritage and worldview. This form of authority is undermined by the specialization demanded by industrial production, by modern scientific thinking, and by the social change and cultural diversity that accompany immigration. Thus, it is quite unlikely that today's President George W. Bush would ever make the claim of ruling by grace of God. Even so, some well-established upper-class families with names such as Bush, Kennedy, Roosevelt, and Rockefeller have occupied a privileged position for several generations, so that when one of their number enters the political arena, it is with some measure of traditional authority (Baltzell, 1964).

If traditional authority plays only a small part in U.S. national politics, it persists in other aspects of everyday life. *Patriarchy,* the domination of women by men, is a traditional form of power that remains widespread, even though it is increasingly challenged. Less controversial is the traditional authority parents exert over their children. The fact that traditional authority is linked to a person's status as parent is obvious every time a parent answers a doubting child's "Why?" with "Because I said so!" There is no debating the parent's decision because that would defeat the parent's traditional authority over the child by putting the two on equal footing.

RATIONAL-LEGAL AUTHORITY

Weber defined **rational-legal authority** (sometimes called *bureaucratic authority*) as *power legitimized by legally enacted rules and regulations.* Rational-legal authority is power legitimized in the operation of lawful government.

As Chapter 7 ("Groups and Organizations") explained, Weber viewed bureaucracy as the organizational backbone of rational-thinking, modern societies. Moreover, just as a rational worldview promotes bureaucracy, it erodes traditional customs and practices. Instead of venerating the past, members of today's high-income societies look to formally enacted rules—especially law—for principles of justice.

Rationally enacted rules also underlie many power relationships in everyday life. For example, the authority of deans and classroom teachers rests on the offices they hold in bureaucratic colleges and universities. The police also are officers within the bureaucracy of local government. In contrast to traditional authority, rational-legal authority flows not from family background but from one's position in the formal organization of government. Thus, whereas a traditional monarch rules for life, a modern president accepts and gives up power according to law because presidential authority lies in the office, not the person.

CHARISMATIC AUTHORITY

Finally, Weber claimed power could be transformed into authority through charisma. **Charismatic authority** is *power legitimized through extraordinary personal abilities that inspire devotion and obedience.* Unlike tradition and rational law, then, charisma has less to do with social organization and is more a mark of an exceptionally forceful and magnetic personality.

Throughout history, some members of societies have been regarded as charismatic. Charisma enhances the stature of an established leader or strengthens the appeal of a challenger. Charismatics have the personal skills to turn an audience into followers and, in the process, they

Learn more about Dr. King and the civil rights movement at this Web site: http://www.umich.edu/politics/mlk/

may make their own rules and challenge the status quo. In 1917, for example, Vladimir Lenin guided the overthrow of Russia's feudal monarchy; after World War II, Mahatma Gandhi inspired the struggle to free India from British colonialism; soon after, Martin Luther King, Jr., galvanized the civil rights movement in the United States; and, over a lifetime of work ministering to the poor in Calcutta, India, Mother Teresa asked the world to confront its stunning poverty.

Because charismatic authority emanates from a single individual, any charismatic movement faces a

In 2000, just 28 of the world's 192 nations were political monarchies where single families pass power from generation to generation. The African nation of Swaziland recently celebrated the coronation of a young king.

crisis of survival upon the death of its leader. Thus, Weber explained, the persistence of a charismatic organization depends on the **routinization of charisma,** *the transformation of charismatic authority into some combination of traditional and bureaucratic authority.* For example, Christianity began as a cult driven by the personal charisma of Jesus of Nazareth. After the death of Jesus, followers institutionalized his teachings in a church eventually centered in Rome and built on both tradition and bureaucracy. Routinized in this way, the Roman Catholic church has flourished for 2,000 years.

POLITICS IN GLOBAL PERSPECTIVE

Political systems have taken many forms throughout history. The technologically simple hunting and gathering societies that once were found all over the planet operated like one large family. Leadership generally fell to a man with unusual strength, hunting skill, or personal charisma. But these leaders exercised little power because they lacked the resources to control their own people, much less extend their rule. In the simplest societies, then, leaders were barely discernible from everyone else, and government did not exist as a distinct sphere of life (Nolan & Lenski, 1999).

Larger and more complex agrarian societies are characterized by specialized activity and a material surplus. These societies become hierarchical, with a small elite gaining control of most wealth and power; politics moves outside the family to become a social institution in its own right. Leaders who manage to pass along their power over several generations may acquire traditional authority, perhaps even claiming divine right to govern. Such leaders also may benefit from Weber's rational-legal authority because they are served by a bureaucratic political administration and system of law.

As societies expand, politics eventually takes the form of a national government or *political state*. But the emergence of a political state depends on technology. Just a few centuries ago, armies moved slowly, and communication over even short distances was uncertain. For this reason, the early political empires—such as Mesopotamia in the Middle East about 5,000 years ago—took the form of many small *city-states*.

More complex technology helped the modern world develop the larger-scale system of *nation-states*. Currently, the world has 192 independent nation-states, each with a distinctive political system. Generally speaking, however, the world's political systems can be analyzed in terms of four categories: monarchy, democracy, authoritarianism, and totalitarianism.

MONARCHY

Monarchy (with Latin and Greek roots meaning "one ruler") is *a type of political system in which a single family rules from generation to generation.* Monarchy is typical in ancient agrarian societies; for example, the Bible tells of great kings such as David and Solomon. Today's British monarchy, the Windsor family, traces its lineage back roughly 1,000 years. In Weber's terms, then, monarchy is legitimized by tradition.

During the medieval era, *absolute monarchy*, in which hereditary rulers claimed a monopoly of power based on divine right, flourished from England to China and in parts of the Americas. Monarchs in some nations, including Saudi Arabia, still exercise nearly absolute control over their people.

During the twentieth century, however, a more egalitarian climate gradually weakened monarchs in favor of elected officials. Monarchs remain in several European nations—Great Britain, Spain, Norway, Sweden, Belgium, Denmark, and the Netherlands—but they now preside over *constitutional monarchies*. In other words, they are merely symbolic heads of state, and elected politicians, led by a prime minister, govern according to political principles embodied in a constitution. In these nations, then, the nobility may formally reign, but elected officials actually rule.

DEMOCRACY

The historical trend in the modern world is toward **democracy,** *a type of political system which gives power to the people as a whole.* But members of democratic societies rarely participate directly in decision making; numbers alone make this an impossibility. Instead, a system of *representative democracy* places authority in the hands of elected leaders, who are accountable to the people.

Most rich countries of the world claim to be democratic. Economic development and democratic government go together because both depend on a literate populace. Moreover, the traditional legitimization of power in an agrarian monarchy gives way, with industrialization, to rational-legal authority. A rational election process puts leaders in offices regulated by law. Thus democracy and rational-legal authority are linked just as monarchy and traditional authority are.

But countries such as the United States are not truly democratic for two reasons: First, there is the problem of bureaucracy. All democratic political systems rely on large numbers of bureaucratic officials. The federal government of the United States, for example, has more than 2 million regular, full-time employees, 6 million contract workers, 1.5 million uniformed military personnel, and 2.4 million workers paid for by various grants and special funding—about 12 million workers in all. In addition, another 15 million people work in 80,000 local governments across the country. Most people who operate the government are never elected by anyone and are not directly accountable to the people (Scaff, 1981; Edwards, 1985; Etzioni-Halevy, 1985; Light, 1999).

The second problem involves economic inequality. In a highly stratified society, the rich have far more political clout than the poor. One reason George W. Bush got off to such a fast start in the 2000 presidential race was that, as a rich man with many rich friends, he was able to raise more than $50 million in a short time. Magazine magnate Steve Forbes financed his own run for the White House, spending more than $50 million of his own fortune in 1996 and 2000 (although he did not get very far in the primaries). In short, in the game of politics, few doubt that "money talks." Given the even greater resources of billion-dollar corporations and labor unions, how can we think our "democratic" system responds to—or even hears—the voices of "average people"? (Burns, Francia, & Herrnson, 2000)

Democracy and Freedom: Capitalist and Socialist Approaches

Despite the problems we have just described, rich capitalist nations such as the United States claim to operate as democracies. Of course, socialist countries such as Cuba and the People's Republic of China make the same claim. This curious fact suggests that we need to look more closely at *political economy:* the interplay of politics and economics.

The political life of the United States, Canada, and the nations of Europe is shaped largely by the economic principles of capitalism. The pursuit of profit within a market system requires that "freedom" be defined in terms of people's right to act in their own self-interest. Thus, the capitalist approach to political freedom translates into personal liberty, the freedom to act in whatever ways maximize personal profit or other advantage. From this point of view, moreover, "democracy" means that individuals have the right to select their leaders from among those running for office.

However, as we noted earlier, capitalist societies are marked by a striking inequality of income and wealth. In other words, if everyone acts according to self-interest, the inevitable result is that some people have much more power to get their way than others. It is this elite that dominates the economic and political life of the society.

By contrast, socialist systems claim they are democratic because their economies meet everyone's basic needs for housing, schooling, work, and medical care. Despite being a much poorer country than the United States, for example, Cuba provides basic medical care to all without regard for people's ability to pay.

But critics of socialism counter that the extensive government regulation of social life in these countries

WINDOW ON THE WORLD

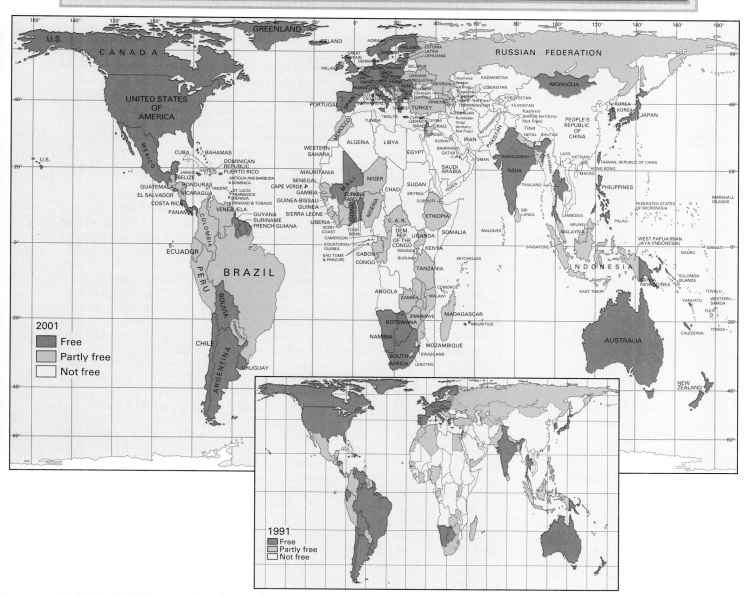

GLOBAL MAP 17–1 Political Freedom in Global Perspective

In 2001, 86 of the world's nations, containing 41 percent of all people, were politically "free"—that is, they offered their citizens extensive political rights and civil liberties. Another 58 countries, which included 24 percent of the world's people, were "partly free," with more limited rights and liberties. The remaining 48 nations, home to 35 percent of humanity, fall into the category of "not free." In these countries, government sharply restricts individual initiative. Between 1980 and 2000, democracy made significant gains, largely in Latin America and Eastern Europe. In Asia, India (containing 1 billion people) returned to the "free" category in 1999. In 2000, Mexico joined the ranks of nations considered "free" for the first time.

Source: Freedom House (2001).

NOTE: *Authoritarian* regimes are concerned mostly with overt compliance; *totalitarian* regimes seek to win "the hearts and minds" of their people.
NOTE: Totalitarianism opposes all pluralism. As an example, anti-Semitism in the former Soviet Union probably was less about religion and more an attempt to quash all loyalties except those to the state.

GLOBAL: The People's Republic of China installed wired radio soon after the communist revolution there. Although broadcast radio would have allowed more than one channel, the government provided only one message, hence the wiring strategy.
CYBER: Will new information technology enhance democracy by expanding available information or promote totalitarianism by increasing the technical capacity for social control?

is oppressive. For example, the socialist governments of China and Cuba do not allow their people to move freely within or across their borders, and they tolerate no organized political opposition.

These contrasting approaches to democracy and freedom raise an important question: Can economic equality and political liberty go together? To foster economic equality, socialism limits the choices of individuals. Capitalism, on the other hand, provides broad political liberties, which, in practice, mean little to the poor. A look back at Global Map 10–1, on page 264, shows the extent of income inequality in the world's nations. Global Map 17–1 on page 439 shows one organization's assessment of the extent of political freedoms around the world.

According to Freedom House, a New York–based organization that tracks global political trends, by 2001, eighty-six of the world's 192 nations (with 41 percent of global population) were "free," with great respect for basic civil liberties. This represents a strong gain for democracy: Just sixty-one nations were free a decade earlier (Freedom House, 2001).

AUTHORITARIANISM

As a matter of policy, some nations give their people little voice in politics. **Authoritarianism** is *a political system that denies popular participation in government.* An authoritarian government is indifferent to people's needs, lacks legal mechanisms to remove leaders from office, and gives people little or no way to voice their opinions. The Polish sociologist Wlodzimierz Wesolowski sums up authoritarianism this way: "The authoritarian philosophy argues for the supremacy of the state [over all other] organized social activity" (1990:435).

The absolute monarchies in Saudi Arabia and Kuwait are highly authoritarian, as are the military juntas in Congo and Ethiopia, where political dissatisfaction is widespread. But heavy-handed government does not always breed popular opposition. The box looks at the "soft authoritarianism" that thrives in the small Asian nation of Singapore.

TOTALITARIANISM

October 22, near Saigon, Vietnam. Six U.S. students on our study-abroad program have been arrested, charged with talking to Vietnamese students and taking pictures at the university. The Vietnamese Minister of Education has canceled the reception tonight, claiming that our students meeting their students threatens Vietnam's security.

The most controlling political form is **totalitarianism,** *a highly centralized political system that extensively regulates people's lives.* Totalitarian governments emerged only during the twentieth century, with the development of technological means for rigidly regulating a populace. The Vietnamese government closely monitors the activities of its citizens and visitors to the country. Similarly, the government of North Korea uses surveillance equipment and sophisticated computers to gather and store vast amounts of information about its people and thereby control them.

Although some totalitarian governments claim to represent the will of the people, most seek to bend people to the will of the government. As the term itself implies, such governments are *total* concentrations of power, allowing no organized opposition. Denying the populace the right to assemble for political purposes and controlling access to information, these governments thrive in an environment of social atomization and fear. For example, the government of the former Soviet Union did not permit ordinary citizens to own telephone directories, copying equipment, fax machines, or even accurate city maps.

Socialization in totalitarian societies is intensely political, seeking not just compliance but also personal commitment to the system. In North Korea, one of the world's most totalitarian states, pictures of leaders and political messages broadcast over loudspeakers constantly remind citizens that they owe total allegiance to the state. Government-controlled schools and mass media present only official versions of events.

Government indoctrination is especially intense whenever political opposition surfaces in a totalitarian society. After the 1989 prodemocracy movement in the People's Republic of China, for example, officials demanded that citizens report all "unpatriotic" people—even members of their own families—and subjected all students at Beijing's universities to political "refresher" courses (Arendt, 1958; Kornhauser, 1959; Friedrich & Brzezinski, 1965; Nisbet, 1966; Goldfarb, 1989).

Totalitarian governments span the political spectrum from fascist (including Nazi Germany) to communist (including North Korea). In some totalitarian states, businesses are privately owned (as was the case in Nazi Germany and, more recently, in Chile); in others, businesses are government owned (as in North

GLOBAL SOCIOLOGY

"Soft Authoritarianism" or Planned Prosperity?
A Report from Singapore

To many, Singapore, a tiny nation on the tip of the Malay Peninsula with a population of 4 million, seems an Asian paradise. Surrounded by poor societies grappling with rapidly rising populations, squalid, sprawling cities, and rising crime rates, Singapore, with its affluence, cleanliness, and safety, makes North American visitors think more of a theme park than of a country.

In fact, since it gained independence from Malaysia in 1965, Singapore has startled the world with its economic development; it is among the most prosperous of high-income nations. But compared to the United States, for example, Singapore has scarcely any social problems such as crime, slums, unemployment, or children living in poverty. In fact, people in Singapore don't even contend with traffic jams, graffiti on subway cars, or litter in the streets.

The key to Singapore's orderly environment is the ever-present hand of government, which actively promotes traditional morality and regulates just about everything. The state owns and manages most of the country's housing and has a hand in many businesses. It provides tax incentives for family planning and additional years of schooling. To keep traffic under control, the government slaps hefty surcharges on cars, pushing the price of a basic sedan up to around $40,000.

Singapore has tough anti-crime laws that mandate death by hanging for drug dealing and permit police to detain a person suspected of a crime without charge or trial. The government has outlawed some religious groups (including Jehovah's Witnesses) and banned pornography. To keep the city clean, the state forbids smoking in public and eating on a subway, imposes stiff fines for littering, and has even outlawed the sale of chewing gum.

In economic terms, Singapore defies familiar categories. Government control of scores of businesses, including television stations, telephone service, airlines, and taxis, seems socialist. Yet unlike most socialist enterprises, these businesses are operated efficiently and very profitably. Moreover, Singapore's capitalist culture applauds economic growth (although the government cautions people against the evils of excessive materialism), and hundreds of

multinational corporations are based here.

Singapore's political climate is as unusual as its economy. Freedom House characterizes Singapore as "partly free." The law provides for elections of political leaders, but one party—the People's Action party—dominates the political process and currently controls eighty-one of the eighty-three seats in the country's Parliament. In fact, the People's Action party has ruled Singapore without opposition since it gained independence more than thirty-five years ago. Just as important, members of this society feel the presence of government far more than their counterparts in the United States.

Clearly, Singapore is not a democratic country in the conventional sense. But most people in this prospering nation wholeheartedly endorse their way of life. What Singapore's political system offers is a simple bargain: Government demands unflinching loyalty from the populace; in return, it provides security and prosperity. Critics charge that this system amounts to a "soft authoritarianism" that stifles dissent and controls people's lives. However, most of the people of Singapore know the struggles of living elsewhere and, for now at least, consider the tradeoff a good one.

Sources: Adapted from Branegan (1993) and Freedom House (1999).

NOTE: Where does government money come from? The IRS took in $952 billion in individual income taxes in 2000, 48% of government revenue; corporate taxes, 10%; Social Security, retirement, and insurance premiums, 34%; excise, customs, gift, and estate taxes, 4%. Where it goes: Social Security, Medicare, and other retirement programs, 39%; national defense and veterans benefits, 19%; social programs, 13%; interest on debt, 20%; physical, human, and community development, 5%; law enforcement, 1% (U.S. Census Bureau, 2001).

THEN AND NOW: How long during an 8-hour workday one labors to pay taxes: *1929*, 0:52; *1940*, 1:29; *1950*, 2:02; *1960*, 2:20; *1970*, 2:32; *1980*, 2:40; *1999*, 2:51. Tax Freedom Day in 1929 was February 9; in 2001, it was May 11 (Tax Foundation, 2001).

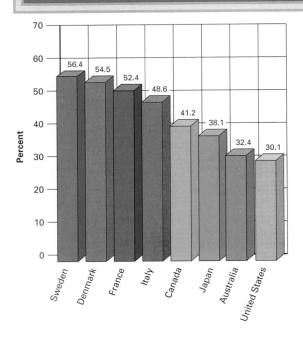

GLOBAL SNAPSHOT

FIGURE 17–1 The Size of Government: Government Expenditures as a Percentage of Gross Domestic Product, 1999

Source: U.S. Census Bureau (2000).

Korea, Cuba, and the former Soviet Union). In all cases, however, one party claims total control of the society and permits no opposition.

A GLOBAL POLITICAL SYSTEM?

Chapter 16 ("The Economy and Work") described the emergence of a global economy, by which more and more companies operate with little regard for national boundaries. Is there a parallel development of a global political system?

On one level, the answer is no. Although most of the world's economic activity now involves more than one nation, the planet remains divided into nation-states, just as it has been for centuries. The United Nations (founded in 1945) might seem a step toward global government, but to date its political role has been limited.

On another level, however, politics has become a global process. In the minds of some analysts, multinational corporations represent a new political order because they have enormous power to shape social life throughout the world. In other words, politics is dissolving into business as corporations grow larger than governments.

The Information Revolution has put even national politics onto the world stage. Electronic mail, the Internet, cellular phones, satellite transmission systems, and fax machines mean that countries can no longer conduct their political affairs in complete privacy.

Finally, several thousand nongovernmental organizations (NGOs) are now in operation, most with global membership and focus. Typically, these organizations seek to advance universal principles such as human rights (Amnesty International) or an ecologically sustainable world (Greenpeace). In the twenty-first century, NGOs will almost certainly play a key part in forming a global political culture (Boli & Thomas, 1997).

In sum, just as individual nations are losing control of their own economies, governments cannot fully manage the political events that occur within their borders.

POLITICS IN THE UNITED STATES

After winning a war against Great Britain to gain political independence, the United States replaced the British monarchy with a democratic political system. Since then, our nation's political development has reflected its distinctive history, capitalist economy, and cultural heritage.

U.S. CULTURE AND THE RISE OF THE WELFARE STATE

The political culture of the United States can be summed up in a word: individualism. This emphasis derives from the Bill of Rights, which guarantees freedom from undue government interference. It was this individualism that the nineteenth-century essayist Ralph Waldo Emerson had in mind when he said, "The government that governs best is the government that governs least."

But Emerson's assertion would find little support today among most of this nation's people, who recognize that government is necessary to maintain national defense, highway systems, schools, and law and order. Moreover, the government has grown into a vast and

Q: "When Justice Holmes uttered his now-famous remark that taxes were the price we pay for a civilized society, the year was 1904. Federal, state, and local taxes combined were $20 per person (in 1904 dollars) and only $340 per person in inflation-adjusted 1999 dollars. Now . . . the price of civilized society is $10,298 for every man, woman, and child in the United States." Tax Foundation (2000)
SOCIAL SURVEY: "Do you consider the amount of federal income tax which you have to pay as too high, about right, or too low?" (GSS 2000, N = 1,861; Codebook, 2001:115)

"Too high"   63.3%   "Too low"   0.9%
"About right" 31.0%   DK/NR   4.8%

Q: "The government's view of the economy could be summed up in a few short phrases: If it moves, tax it. If it keeps moving, regulate it. And if it stops, subsidize it." Ronald Reagan

TABLE 17-1 The Political Spectrum: A National Survey, 2000

Survey Question: "We hear a lot of talk these days about liberals and conservatives. I'm going to show you a seven-point scale on which the political views people might hold are arranged from extremely liberal—point 1—to extremely conservative—point 7. Where would you place yourself on this scale?"

1	2	3	4	5	6	7
Extremely liberal	Liberal	Slightly liberal	Middle of the road	Slightly conservative	Conservative	Extremely conservative
3.8%	10.9%	10.1%	37.4%	13.8%	14.6%	3.2%

[Don't know/no answer 6.1%]

Source: General Social Surveys, 1972–2000: Cumulative Codebook (Chicago: National Opinion Research Center, 2001), p. 96.

complex **welfare state,** *a range of government agencies and programs that provides benefits to the population.* Government benefits begin even before birth (through prenatal nutrition programs) and continue into old age (through Social Security and Medicare). Some programs are especially important to the poor, who are not well served by our capitalist economic system, but students, farmers, homeowners, small business operators, veterans, performing artists, and even executives of giant corporations also get subsidies and supports. In fact, a majority of U.S. adults now look to government for at least part of their income (Caplow et al., 1982; Devine, 1985; Bartlett & Steele, 1998).

Today's welfare state is the result of a gradual increase in the size and scope of government. In 1789, when the presence of the federal government amounted to little more than a flag in most communities, the entire federal budget was a mere $4.5 million ($1.50 for every person in the nation). Since then, it has steadily risen, reaching $1.8 trillion in 2000 (a per capita figure of $6,500).

Similarly, when our nation was founded, one government employee served every 1,800 citizens. Today, there is one official for every eleven citizens, a total of 25 million government employees, more than are employed in manufacturing (U.S. Census Bureau, 2000).

As much as government has grown in this country, the U.S. welfare state is still smaller than that in many other high-income nations. Figure 17–1 shows that government is larger in most of Europe and especially in Scandinavian countries such as Denmark and Sweden.

THE POLITICAL SPECTRUM

Who supports the welfare state? Who would like to see it grow larger? Who wants to cut back on the size of government? Such questions tap attitudes that form the *political spectrum.* Table 17–1 shows how adults in the United States describe their political orientation. One-fourth of the respondents fall on the liberal, or "left," side, and about one-third describe themselves as conservative to some degree, placing them on the political "right." The remaining 37 percent claim to be moderates in the political "middle" (NORC, 2001:96).

One reason so many people identify themselves as "moderates" is that most of us are conservative on some issues and liberal on others (Barone & Ujifusa, 1981; McBroom & Reed, 1990). In making sense of people's political attitudes, analysts distinguish two kinds of issues. *Economic issues* focus on economic inequality and the opportunities available for all categories of people. *Social issues* are moral concerns about how people ought to live.

Economic Issues

In the second half of the nineteenth century, industrialization generated enormous wealth in the United States, but much of it ended up in the pockets of a small elite. By the time of the Great Depression in 1929, mounting evidence suggested that a market system with little government regulation provided little financial security for much of the population. In response, President Franklin Delano Roosevelt initiated the New Deal programs, greatly expanding government efforts to promote well-being and building the foundation of our current welfare state.

To learn more about the New Deal, go to http://www.roosevelt.edu/newdeal/

Today, both the Democratic and Republican parties—the two major political organizations in the United States—support the basic outlines of the welfare

Lower-income people have more pressing financial needs and so they tend to focus on economic issues, such as the level of the minimum wage. Higher-income people, by contrast, provide support for many social issues, such as animal rights.

state, although they disagree about what the government should and should not do. Generally, the Democratic party supports the role of government in U.S. society, including government regulation of the economy. The Republican party, however, has sought to trim the size and scope of government in recent years, especially in the marketplace.

Thus, economic liberals (mostly on the Democratic side of the fence) expect the government to maintain a healthy economy and an adequate supply of jobs. Economic conservatives (likely to be Republicans) counter that government intervention inhibits economic productivity.

Social Issues

Social issues are moral matters, ranging from abortion to the death penalty to gay rights and treatment of minorities. Social liberals are broadly tolerant of social diversity. They endorse equal rights and opportunities for all categories of people, view abortion as a matter of individual choice, and oppose the death penalty because, in their view, it does little to discourage crime and has been unfairly applied to minorities.

On the other side of the political spectrum are social conservatives who advance a "family values" agenda.

They support traditional gender roles and oppose public acceptance of gay families, affirmative action, and other "special programs" for minorities that, as they see it, recognize group membership rather than reward individual initiative. Social conservatives also condemn abortion and support the death penalty as a just response to heinous crime.

Overall, the Republican party is more conservative on both economic and social issues, whereas the Democratic party takes a more liberal stand. In practice, then, Republicans endorse traditional values and individual initiative, and Democrats think the government should take an active role in enhancing social well-being and reducing inequality. Yet each party has its conservative and liberal wings, so there may be little difference between a liberal Republican and a conservative Democrat. Furthermore, both Republicans and Democrats favor big government—as long as it advances their particular aims. Conservative Republicans (such as Presidents Ronald Reagan and George W. Bush) have sought to increase U.S. military strength, for example, while more liberal Democrats (like President Bill Clinton) have tried to expand the government's "social safety net" that, for instance, extends government-regulated medical care coverage to all citizens.

Q: "One cannot fully grasp the political world unless one understands it as a confidence game." Peter Berger

NOTE: The policies of the major U.S. parties shift over time. Republicans were the party of civil rights for decades; now Democrats claim that mantle. Democrats supported large deficits; so did Reagan. Democrats endorsed intervention in foreign wars until 1950; now Republicans tend to (Dennis Dedrick).

NOTE: Top PAC donations by group: finance, insurance, and real estate, $154.4 million; lawyers and lobbyists, $69.8 m; labor, $60.8 m; health, $58.8 m; communication/electronics, $54.6 m; agribusiness, $43.4 m; ideological/single issue, $42.4 m; energy and natural resources, $41.4 m; transportation, $35.5 m; construction, $32.9 m; defense, $11.4 m; miscellaneous business, $90.6 m (Center for Responsive Politics, 2000).

Mixed Positions

Pegging the political views of individuals is difficult because most people do not hold the same positions on economic and social issues. Well-to-do men and women tend to be conservative on economic issues (because they have wealth to protect) but liberal on social issues (largely because of higher levels of education). Working-class people display the opposite pattern, combining economic liberalism with social conservatism (Nunn, Crockett, & Williams, 1978; Erikson, Luttbeg, & Tedin, 1980; McBroom & Reed, 1990). African Americans, both rich and poor, tend to be liberal (especially on economic issues) and, for half a century, have voted Democratic (more than 90 percent supported Democrat Al Gore in 2000). Historically, Latinos, Asian Americans, and Jews have also supported the Democratic party.

Party Identification

Because so many people hold mixed political attitudes—espousing liberal views on some issues and taking conservative stands on others—party identification in the United States is weak. In this way, our nation differs from European countries, where most people adhere strongly to one political party. Table 17–2 shows the results of a recent national survey of party identification among U.S. adults (NORC, 2001). Some 44 percent identified themselves to some degree as Democrats and about 34 percent as Republicans. Twenty percent claimed to be independents, voicing no preference for either party. Even though a large majority declare a party preference, their allegiance is weak. Republicans scored a landslide victory in the 1994 congressional elections, for example, while the Democrats held the White House in 1996 and gained ground in Congress in 1996, 1998, and 2000.

There is also an urban-rural divide in U.S. politics, by which people in urban areas typically vote Democratic and those in rural areas vote Republican.

 To learn more about how researchers conduct political polls, go to http://faculty. vassar.edu/lowry/polls.html The box on page 446 takes a closer look at the national political scene, and National Map 17–1 on page 447 shows the county-by-county results for the 2000 election.

SPECIAL-INTEREST GROUPS

Just about everyone is aware of the recent shootings in a number of public schools across the United States; in

TABLE 17–2 Political Party Identification in the United States, 2000

Party Identification	Percentage of Respondents
Democrat	**44.2%**
Strong Democrat	14.7
Not very strong Democrat	18.0
Independent, close to Democrat	11.5
Republican	**33.6**
Strong Republican	9.3
Not very strong Republican	14.2
Independent, close to Republican	10.1
Independent	**20.1**
Other party, no response	**2.1**

Source: *General Social Surveys, 1972–2000: Cumulative Codebook* (Chicago: National Opinion Research Center, 2001), p. 88.

the wake of these events, public support for gun control has been rising. The National Rifle Association, representing several million people who are active hunters and millions of social conservatives, has steadily worked in opposition to this goal.

The "gun lobby," which has been successful so far in fending off change, is an example of a **special-interest group:** *a political alliance of people interested in some economic or social issue.* Special-interest groups, which include associations of elderly people, tour bus operators, women's organizations, farmers, fireworks producers, environmentalists, and countless others, flourish in nations such as the United States where political parties tend to be weak. Special-interest groups employ *lobbyists* (Washington, D.C., is home to more than 75,000 of them) as their professional advocates in political circles.

One example of a special-interest group concerned with economic issues is the American Federation of Labor–Congress of Industrial Organizations (AFL-CIO), this nation's largest labor union. Special-interest groups lobbying on social issues include not only the conservative National Rifle Association but also the liberal American Civil Liberties Union.

Political action committees (PACs) are *organizations formed by special-interest groups, independent of political parties, to pursue political aims by raising and spending money.* Political action committees channel most of their funds directly to candidates likely to support their interests. Although legal reforms have limited direct contributions to candidates, since the 1970s the number of PACs has grown rapidly to 4,400 (U.S. Federal Election Commission, 2000).

NOTE: Voting among young people is most common in states where (1) education levels are high (the Midwest has the highest level of high school graduation in the country), (2) young people are likely to discuss political issues with parents (often by sharing meals), and (3) parents are likely to vote (the Midwest has high turnout among older voters).

THEN AND NOW: Recent high point of voter turnout was

62.8% in 1960 (Kennedy beat Nixon); all-time peak was 82.4% in 1876 (Rutherford Hayes beat Samuel Tilden and only men voted) (Johnston, 1996).

NOTE: Speaking of apathy, in a recent American Sociological Association election, just 23.4% of 11,179 voting members returned ballots. This represents a steady decline from more than 60% in the 1950s.

DIVERSITY: RACE, CLASS, AND GENDER

The Rural-Urban Divide: Election 2000

An important and often over-looked dimension of diversity in the United States involves where people live: in rural versus urban places. Sociologists have long debated how the two settings differ (see Chapter 22, "Population, Urbanization, and Environment"). But one thing is certain: Rural and urban politics are quite different.

Take a look at National Map 17–1, which shows the county-by-county results from the 2000 presidential election. The first thing that is striking about the map is that Republican George W. Bush won in almost 80 percent of U.S. counties: 2,477 out of a total of 3,153 (which appear in various shades of red). By contrast, Democrat Al Gore won in just 676 counties (which appear in a shade of blue). At the same time, Gore actually won the popular vote across the country (Bush was victorious in the election by winning the majority of votes in the electoral college).

The reason for this apparent contradiction is that the many counties won by Bush were mostly rural, with low populations. By contrast, Gore won the fewer counties containing large cities. In Nevada, for example, the map shows just the Las Vegas area in "Gore blue," but the remainder of the state is painted "Bush red." In Oregon, Gore won enough votes in Portland to carry the entire state, even though almost all the remaining counties went for Bush.

As political analyst Stuart Rothenberg (cited in Simon, 2000) concluded, "There is a cultural gap between liberal, urban, Democratic America and rural, small-town Republican America." In Washington, D.C., a politically divided Congress is trying to work together for the good of the country. Yet as the results of the 2000 election show, the country itself is divided in a way that is not likely to be overcome anytime soon.

Source: Based on Bai (2001).

Because of the rising costs of campaigns, most candidates eagerly accept support from political action committees. In the 1998 congressional elections, 40 percent of all funding came from PACs, and two-thirds of all senators seeking reelection received more than $1 million each in PAC contributions. Supporters maintain that PACs represent interests of a vast array of businesses, unions, and church groups, thereby increasing political participation. Critics counter that organizations supplying cash to politicians expect to be treated favorably in return so that, in effect, PACs try to buy political influence (Allen & Broyles, 1991; Cook, 1993; Center for Responsive Politics, 1998).

In 2000, the campaigns of presidential candidates cost a total of $3 billion, and another $3 billion was spent by congressional candidates and people running in state and local elections. Does having the most money matter? The evidence suggests that it is crucial because 90 percent of the candidates with the most money won their race. Concern about the power of money has prompted much discussion of campaign finance reform, but to date there has been little real change.

VOTER APATHY

As noted at the beginning of this chapter, a disturbing fact of U.S. political life is that many people seem indifferent to their right to vote. The long-term trend has been for greater *eligibility* to vote: The Fifteenth Amendment, ratified in 1870, enfranchised African American men; the Nineteenth Amendment extended

 For more information on voter apathy, visit this Harvard University site: http://www.vanishingvoter.org

voting rights to women in 1920; and in 1971 the Twenty-Sixth Amendment lowered the voting age to eighteen years. However, a countertrend shows that over the last century, a smaller and smaller share of eligible citizens *actually do vote*. In the 2000 presidential election, less than half the registered voters took the time to cast a ballot, below the comparable share in almost all other high-income nations. This was so despite the fact that

THE MAP: Urban areas tend to be Democratic; rural counties tend to be Republican. Immigrants, who tend to be young and vote Democratic, settle in urban areas; rural counties have, on average, older and more conservative populations.

Q: "Politics makes strange bedfellows." Charles Dudley Warner

Q: "Liberals can understand everything but the people who don't understand them." Lenny Bruce

DIVERSITY: Voting rates among 18- to 24-year-olds vary by gender and race: whites, 33%; blacks, 32%; Hispanics, 15%; black women, 38%; white women, 35%; Hispanic women, 19%; white men, 31%; black men, 26%; Hispanic men, 12% (Fetto, 1999).

Q: "What is conservatism? Is it not adherence to the old and tried against the new and untried?" Abraham Lincoln

SEEING OURSELVES

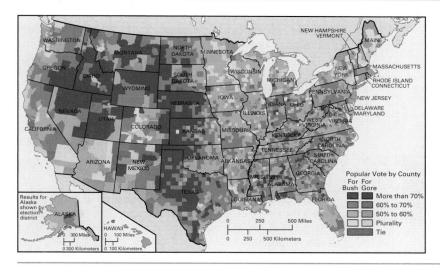

NATIONAL MAP 17–1
The Presidential Election, 2000: Popular Vote by County

The 2000 presidential election was the closest in more than a century. Almost 80 percent of the nation's counties went for George W. Bush, but densely populated areas—especially along both coasts—provided strong support for Al Gore. What social differences do you think distinguish the areas that voted Republican and Democratic? Why are rural areas mostly Republican whereas cities tend to be Democratic?

Source: "Red Zone vs. Blue Zone," *Newsweek*, January 22, 2001. Copyright © 2001 Newsweek, Inc. All rights reserved. Reprinted by permission.

the 2000 presidential race was decided in Florida (which gave George W. Bush enough electoral votes to win) by 537 votes (plus or minus a hanging chad or two) out of 2.5 million cast.

Who is and is not likely to vote? Women and men are equally likely to cast a ballot. White people are more likely to vote (64 percent voted in 2000) than African Americans (58 percent), with Hispanics (30 percent) the least likely of all to vote. Generally speaking, people with a bigger stake in society—homeowners, parents with children at home, people with good jobs and extensive schooling—are most likely to vote. Income matters, too: People earning more than $75,000 are twice as likely to vote (76 percent voted) as people earning between $5,000 and $10,000 (38 percent voted) (Lewis, McCracken, & Hunt, 1994; DeLuca, 1998; Fetto, 1999; U.S. Census Bureau, 2000).

Age is perhaps the most significant factor of all: People over sixty-five are three times as likely to vote as young adults aged eighteen to twenty-four. In fact, barely half of these young people even even bothered to register in 2000.

Of course, we should expect some nonvoting, because at any given time millions of people are sick, disabled, or away from home. Many more people move to a new neighborhood and forget to reregister. Registering and voting also depend on the ability to read and write, which discourages the tens of millions of U.S. adults who have limited literacy skills. Finally, people with physical disabilities that limit mobility have a lower turnout than the general population (Schur & Kruse, 2000).

Even so, the problem of political apathy is widespread in the population as a whole. Conservatives suggest that this apathy is not a serious problem because it reflects *indifference* to politics. That is, most people who do not vote are reasonably content with their lives. But liberals (and especially political radicals) counter that apathy is a symptom of a serious problem: Most nonvoters are *alienated* from politics. Although dissatisfied with the way society operates, they doubt that elections will make any real difference. Figure 17–2 on page 448 provides data that confirm the link between income and voting: In simple terms, most high-income people *do* and most low-income people *don't*. The fact that it is disadvantaged people who are least likely to vote suggests that the liberal explanation for low voter turnout probably is closer to the truth.

Are there small reforms that might make a difference in voting rates? Currently, many states require people to complete their voting registration well before election day. Research suggests that allowing people to register as late as election day would raise the turnout by about 7 percent (Brians & Grofman, 2001).

RESOURCE: An excerpt from C. Wright Mills's *The Power Elite* is among the classics included in the Macionis and Benokraitis reader, *Seeing Ourselves*.

NOTE: A more traditionally Marxist view of politics argues that elites need not circulate through the three sectors as Mills claims; the power of the capitalists is sufficient to ensure that politicians serve their interests.

Q: "The power elite is composed of men whose positions enable them to transcend the ordinary environments of ordinary men and women; they are in positions to make decisions having major consequences." C. Wright Mills (1956:3–4)

Q: "The less people know about how sausages and laws are made the better they'll sleep at night." Otto von Bismarck

Q: "If you can't convince 'em, confuse 'em." Harry S. Truman

DIVERSITY SNAPSHOT

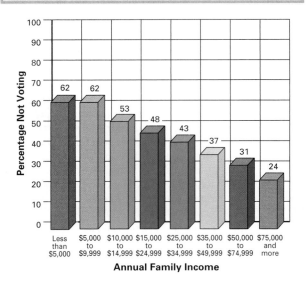

FIGURE 17–2 Political Apathy by Income Level

Percentage of adults who reported not voting in the 1996 presidential election, presented according to their annual family income.

Source: U.S. Census Bureau (1998).

THEORETICAL ANALYSIS OF POWER IN SOCIETY

Sociologists have long debated how power is distributed in the United States. Power is one of the most difficult topics to study scientifically because decision making is complex and takes place behind closed doors. Moreover, it is difficult to separate a theory of power from the theorist's political attitudes and personal values. Nevertheless, three competing models of power in the United States have emerged.

THE PLURALIST MODEL: THE PEOPLE RULE

The **pluralist model** is *an analysis of politics that sees power as dispersed among many competing interest groups.* This approach is closely tied to structural-functional theory.

Pluralists claim, first, that politics is an arena of negotiation. With limited resources, no organization can expect to realize all its goals. Organizations therefore operate as *veto groups*, realizing some success but mostly keeping opponents from achieving all their goals. The political process relies heavily on negotiating alliances and compromises between numerous interest groups so that policies gain wide support. In short, pluralists see power as widely dispersed throughout society, with all people having at least some voice in the political system (Dahl, 1961, 1982; Rothman & Black, 1998).

THE POWER-ELITE MODEL: A FEW PEOPLE RULE

The **power-elite model** is *an analysis of politics that sees power as concentrated among the rich.* This second approach is closely allied with the social-conflict paradigm.

The term *power elite* was coined by sociologist and social critic C. Wright Mills (1956), who argued that a small number of people in the United States control this nation's political system. Mills claimed that the power elite stands atop each of three major sectors of U.S. society: the economy, the government, and the military. Thus, the power elite is made up of the "super rich" (namely, the executives and large stockholders of major corporations), top officials in government (the most powerful figures in Washington, D.C., and state capitals around the country), and the highest-ranking officers in the U.S. military (senior Pentagon officials).

Furthermore, Mills explained, these elites move from one sector to another, consolidating their power as they go. For example, Alexander Haig has served as a top corporate executive, a member of Ronald Reagan's cabinet (and 1988 presidential candidate), and a general of the army. Haig is far from the exception: A majority of national political leaders enter government from powerful and highly paid positions—when President George W. Bush took office and assembled his cabinet in 2001, all but one person were already millionaires—and most return to the corporate world later on.

Power-elite theorists challenge the claim that the United States is a political democracy. They maintain that the concentration of wealth and power is simply too great for the average person's voice to be heard. They reject the pluralist idea that various centers of power serve as checks and balances on one another.

SOCIAL SURVEY: "How much confidence do you have in Congress?" (GSS 2000, *N* = 1,896; *Codebook*, 2001:183)
"A great deal"   12.0%   "Hardly any"   28.1%
"Only some"   55.1%   DK/NR   4.9%

Q: "The executive of the modern state is but a committee for managing the common affairs of the whole bourgeoisie." Marx and Engels

Q: "If voting changed anything, they'd make it illegal." Cousin Woodman

NOTE: The word "radical" is derived from the Latin, meaning "of the root" (a radish is also a root). Thus, radical politics seeks not reform but a change in the system itself.

Q: "Since all political systems were created by [people], it follows that [people] can also change them." Peter Berger (1963:128)

TABLE 17–3 Three Models of U.S. Politics: A Summary

	Pluralist Model	Power-Elite Model	Marxist Model
How is power distributed in U.S. society?	Highly dispersed	Concentrated	Concentrated
Is the United States basically democratic?	Yes, because voting offers everyone a voice, and no one group or organization dominates society	No, because a small share of the people dominates the economy, government, and military	No, because the bias of the capitalist system is to concentrate wealth and power
How should we understand voter apathy?	Apathy is indifference; after all, even poor people can organize for a greater voice if they want	Apathy is understandable, given how difficult it is for ordinary people to oppose the rich and powerful	Apathy is alienation generated by a system that will always leave most people powerless

Instead, the power-elite model holds that people at the top encounter no real opposition (Bartlett & Steele, 2000).

THE MARXIST MODEL: BIAS IN THE SYSTEM ITSELF

A third approach to understanding U.S. politics is the **Marxist political-economy model,** *an analysis that explains politics in terms of the operation of a society's economic system.* Like the power-elite model, the Marxist model rejects the idea that the United States operates as a political democracy. But whereas the power-elite model focuses on the disproportionate wealth of certain individuals and the control they have over our political system, the Marxist model highlights bias rooted in this nation's institutions, especially its economy. As noted in Chapter 4 ("Society"), Karl Marx claimed that a society's economic system (capitalist or socialist) goes a long way toward shaping how the political system operates. Therefore, the power elites do not simply appear on the scene; they are creations of capitalism itself.

From this point of view, any attempts to reform the political system—say, by limiting the amount of money rich people can contribute to political candidates—are unlikely to bring about true democracy. The problem does not lie in the *people* who exercise great power or the *people* who don't vote; the problem is rooted in the *system* itself, what Marxists call the political economy of capitalism. In other words, as long as the United States remains a predominantly capitalist economy, just as the majority of people are exploited in the workplace, they will be shut out of politics.

Critical evaluation. Table 17–3 summarizes the three models of the U.S. political system. Which of the models is correct? Over the years, research shows that a case can be made for all three. In the end, how one views this country's political system and how one thinks it ought to operate turn out to be a matter of political values as much as scientific fact.

Research by Nelson Polsby (1959) supports the pluralist model. Polsby studied the political scene in New Haven, Connecticut, and concluded that key decisions on various issues—including renewing urban areas, nominating political candidates, and operating the schools—were made by different groups. He found, too, that few of the upper-class families listed in New Haven's *Social Register* were also economic leaders. Thus, Polsby concluded, no one segment of society rules all the others.

Robert Dahl also investigated New Haven's history, finding that over time power had become more and more dispersed. Thus, Dahl's research also supports the pluralist model. As he put it, "No one, and certainly no group of more than a few individuals, is entirely lacking in [power]" (1961:228).

Supporting the power-elite position is research by Robert Lynd and Helen Lynd (1937) in Muncie, Indiana (which they called "Middletown," to suggest that it was a typical city). They documented the fortune amassed by a single family, the Balls, from their business manufacturing glass canning jars, and showed how the Ball family dominated the city's life. If anyone doubted the Balls' prominence, the Lynds explained, there was no need to look further than the local bank, a university, a hospital, and a department store, which all bear the family name. In Muncie, according to the Lynds, the power elite more or less boiled down to a single family.

In a study of Atlanta, Georgia, Floyd Hunter (1963; orig. 1953) found further support for the power-elite model. No one family dominated Atlanta, as was the case in Muncie. Yet Hunter found that about forty people held all the top positions in the city's businesses and controlled the city's politics.

From the Marxist perspective, the point is not to look at which individuals make political decisions at the local or even the national level. Rather, as Alexander Liazos (1982:13) explains, "The basic tenets of capitalist society shape everyone's life: the inequalities of social classes and the importance of profits over people." As long as the basic institutions of society are organized to meet the needs of the few rather than the many, Liazos concludes, a democratic society will elude us.

In the end, what are we to make of the U.S. political system? At one level, it affords almost everyone the right to participate in the political process through elections. This is an important opportunity, one that is not enjoyed by a majority of the world's people. At the same time, however, the power-elite and Marxist models point out that, at the very least, the U.S. political system is far less democratic than most people think. Most citizens may have the right to vote, but the major political parties and their candidates typically support only the positions acceptable to the most powerful segments of society and consistent with the operation of our capitalist economy (Bachrach & Baratz, 1970).

Whatever the reasons, many people in the United States do not report having very much confidence in their leaders. More than 80 percent of U.S. adults report having, at best, only "some confidence" that members of Congress and other government officials will do what is best for the country (NORC, 2001:904, 1037).

POWER BEYOND THE RULES

Politics always involves disagreement over a society's goals and the means to achieve them. Therefore, political systems try to resolve controversy within a system of rules. But political activity sometimes exceeds—or tries to do away with—established practices.

REVOLUTION

Political revolution is *the overthrow of one political system in order to establish another.* In contrast to reform, which involves change *within* a system, revolution involves change *of the system itself.* Thus, even one leader deposing another—called a *coup d'état* (in French, literally, "stroke concerning the state")—falls short of revolution because it involves only a change at the top. Whereas reform rarely escalates into violence, revolution often does. The revolutions in Eastern Europe beginning in 1989 were surprisingly peaceful, with the exception of Romania, where violence claimed thousands of lives.

No type of political system is immune to revolution, nor does revolution invariably produce any one kind of government. Our country's Revolutionary War transformed colonial rule by the British monarchy into democratic government. French revolutionaries in 1789 also overthrew a monarch, only to set the stage for the return of monarchy in the person of Napoleon. In 1917, the Russian Revolution replaced monarchy with a socialist government built on the ideas of Karl Marx. Then in 1992, the Soviet Union was reborn as the Russian Federation, moving toward a market system and a greater political voice for its people.

Despite their striking variety, revolutions share a number of traits (Tocqueville, 1955, orig. 1856; also Davies, 1962; Brinton, 1965; Skocpol, 1979; Lewis, 1984; Tilly, 1986):

1. **Rising expectations**. Although common sense suggests that revolution would be more likely when people are grossly deprived, history shows that most revolutions occur when people's lives are improving. Rising expectations, rather than bitter resignation, fuel revolutionary fervor.

2. **Unresponsive government**. Revolutionary zeal gains strength when a government is unwilling or unable to reform, especially when such demands are made by powerful segments of society.

3. **Radical leadership by intellectuals**. The English philosopher Thomas Hobbes (1588–1679) observed that intellectuals often provide the justification for revolution, and universities often are the center of sweeping political change. During the 1960s in the United States, students were at the forefront of much of the political unrest. Students also played a critical role in China's prodemocracy movement and the uprisings in Eastern Europe.

4. **Establishing a new legitimacy**. Overthrowing a political system is not easy, but more difficult still is ensuring a revolution's long-term success. Some revolutionary movements are unified

DISCUSS: What have been some of the longer-term consequences of the 9–11 terrorist attacks?

NOTE: The word "assassin" has the same root in Arabic as the word "hashish." This is because would-be assailants sometimes coaxed one of their numbers to violent action by visions stimulated by the drug.

Q: "When we discuss national security, we tend too often to give it a military label. It is, in fact, much broader than military power and much more complex. There can be no security without social betterment." Hubert H. Humphrey

Q: "In the Third World, where one child in ten dies before the age of five, there are six times as many soldiers as there are physicians." Ruth Leger Sivard (1993:6)

According to many analysts, our way of life changed with the events of September 11, 2001. Why? The power of terror lies in creating fear—fear that the unimaginable can actually happen. Unless we can take basic safety for granted, in short, it is difficult to get on with our lives. How has your life been different since that fateful day?

mostly by hatred of the past regime and fall apart once new leaders are installed. Revolutionaries must also guard against counterrevolutionary drives led by the deposed leaders. This explains the speed and ruthlessness with which victorious revolutionaries dispose of previous rulers.

Scientific analysis cannot declare that a revolution is good or bad. The full consequences of such an upheaval depend on one's values and become evident only after many years. In the wake of recent revolution, for example, the future of the former Soviet Union remains unsettled.

TERRORISM

On September 11, 2001, terrorists hijacked four commercial airliners, and although one airliner crashed in a wooded area, the other three were flown into public buildings full of people. The attack, which killed some 3,500 innocent people and injured many thousands more, completely destroyed the World Trade Center in New York City and seriously damaged the Pentagon in Washington, D.C. Not since the attack on Pearl Harbor at the outbreak of World War II had the United States suffered such a blow. Indeed, this event was the most serious terrorist act ever recorded, resulting in greater loss of life than all previous acts of terrorism combined.

Terrorism consists of *acts of violence or the threat of such violence used by an individual or group as a political strategy.* Like revolution, terrorism is a political act beyond the rules of established political systems. According to Paul Johnson (1981), terrorism has four distinguishing characteristics.

First, terrorists try to paint violence as a legitimate political tactic, despite the fact that such acts are condemned by nearly every nation. Terrorists also bypass (or are excluded from) established channels of political negotiation. Therefore, terror is a weak organization's strategy to harm a stronger foe. Indeed, terrorism has become almost common in international politics. In 2000, according to the U.S. State Department, there were 423 acts of terrorism worldwide, which claimed 405 lives and injured 791 people. Of these 423 terrorist acts, 200 (47 percent) were directed against the United States (U.S. State Department, 2001). Of course, in light of the September 11th attack on the United States, the 2001 casualties will be much higher.

Second, terrorism is used not just by groups but also by governments against their own people. *State terrorism* is the use of violence, generally without support of law, by government officials. State terrorism is lawful in some authoritarian and totalitarian states, which survive by inciting fear and intimidation. For example, Saddam Hussein shores up his power in Iraq through state terrorism.

Not all terrorism is the work of individuals or groups. Since 1950, China has sought to maintain control of Tibet by force. This Tibetan refugee displays instruments of torture used against him by officials of the Chinese government.

Third, democratic societies reject terrorism in principle, but they are especially vulnerable to terrorists because they afford extensive civil liberties to their people and have less extensive police networks. In contrast, totalitarian regimes make widespread use of state terrorism although, at the same time, their extensive police power minimizes opportunities for individual acts of terror.

Hostage-taking and outright killing provoke popular anger, but responding to such acts is difficult. Before taking action, a government must identify those responsible. However, because most terrorist groups are shadowy organizations with no formal connection to any established state, a reprisal may be all but impossible. Yet as terrorism expert Brian Jenkins warns, the failure to respond "encourages other terrorist groups, who begin to realize that this can be a pretty cheap way to wage war" (quoted in Whitaker, 1985:29). At the same time, a forcible military reaction to terrorism may risk confrontation with other governments.

Fourth, terrorism is always a matter of definition. Governments claim the right to maintain order, even

Read the U.S. State Department's latest annual report on global terrorism at http://www.usis.usemb.se/terror/rpt2000/index.html

by force, but brand opposition groups who use violence as "terrorists." Similarly, political differences may explain why one person's "terrorist" is another's "freedom fighter." Ironically, in Afghanistan, some of the "terrorists" that the United States and other nations targeted in the wake of the September 11th attacks were the same people who were widely praised as "freedom fighters" in the 1980s when they fought the invading Soviet army.

WAR AND PEACE

Perhaps the most critical political issue is **war,** *organized, armed conflict between the people of various societies, directed by their governments.* War is as old as humanity, of course, but understanding it now takes on greater urgency. Because we have the technological capacity to destroy ourselves, war poses unprecedented danger to the entire planet. Most scholarly investigation of war aims to promote peace, meaning the absence of war (but not necessarily the end of all political conflict).

Many people think of war as an extraordinary occurrence, yet for almost all of the twentieth century, nations somewhere on Earth were in violent conflict. In our nation's short history, we have participated in eleven large-scale wars, resulting in the deaths of more than 1.3 million U.S. men and women and injury to many times that number, as shown in Figure 17–3. Thousands more died in "undeclared wars" and "limited military actions" in the Dominican Republic, Lebanon, Grenada, Panama, and elsewhere.

THE CAUSES OF WAR

The frequency of war in human affairs might imply that there is something natural about armed confrontation. But whereas many animals are naturally aggressive, research provides no basis for concluding that human beings inevitably wage war under any particular circumstances. Indeed, as Ashley Montagu (1976) observes, governments around the world have to use considerable coercion to mobilize their people for war.

Like all other forms of social behavior, warfare is a product of society that varies in purpose and intensity from place to place. The Semai of Malaysia, among the most peace-loving of the world's people, rarely resort to violence. In contrast, the Yąnomamö, described in Chapter 3 ("Culture"), are far more likely to wage war.

If society holds the key to war or peace, under what circumstances do humans go to battle? Quincy Wright (1987) identifies five factors that promote war:

1. **Perceived threats.** Societies mobilize in response to a perceived threat to their people, territory, or culture. For example, the prospect of armed conflict between the United Sates and the former Soviet Union diminished as the two nations have become less fearful of each other; Russia even voiced support for the 2001 anti-terrorist attacks by the United States.

2. **Social problems.** When internal problems generate widespread frustration at home, a society's leaders may divert public attention by attacking an external "enemy" as a form of scapegoating. Some analysts see the lack of economic development in the People's Republic of China as underlying that nation's hostility toward Vietnam, Tibet, and the former Soviet Union.

3. **Political objectives.** Leaders sometimes use war as a political strategy. Poor societies, such as Algeria and Vietnam, have fought wars to end foreign domination. For powerful societies such as the United States, a periodic show of force (recall the recent deployments of troops in Somalia, Haiti, and Bosnia) enhances their global political stature.

4. **Moral objectives.** Rarely do nations claim to fight merely to increase their wealth and power. Leaders infuse military campaigns with moral urgency, rallying their people around visions of "freedom" or the "fatherland." U.S. leaders characterized the recent attack on the Taliban and the al Qaeda network in Afghanistan as a clear case of good against evil.

5. **The absence of alternatives.** A fifth factor promoting war is the absence of alternatives. Although it is the United Nations' job to maintain international peace, the UN has had limited success in resolving tensions between self-interested societies.

In short, war is rooted in social dynamics on both national and international levels. Moreover, even combat has rules, and breaking them can lead to charges of *war crimes*. The box on page 454 takes a closer look.

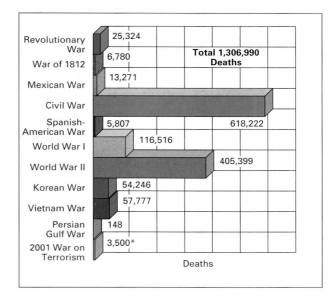

FIGURE 17–3 Deaths of Americans in Eleven U.S. Wars

*Preliminary, as of December 1, 2001.

Sources: Compiled from various sources by Maris A. Vinovskis (1989) and the author.

TERRORISM: A NEW KIND OF WAR?

In the wake of the terrorist attacks on September 11, 2001, U.S. government officials spoke of terrorism as a new kind of war. As we have explained, war is usually played out according to at least some rules, the warring parties are known to each other, and they clearly state their objectives, which generally involve control of territory.

Terrorism, however, breaks from these patterns. In cases of terrorism, the identity of terrorist individuals and organizations may not be known, those involved may deny their responsibility, and their goals may be unclear. Indeed, the recent terrorist attacks against the United States were not attempts to defeat the nation militarily, nor to secure territory. They were carried out by people representing not a country but a cause—one not well understood in the United States. In short, they were expressions of anger and hate, an effort to destabilize the country and shatter public morale by inciting widespread anger and fear.

Conventional warfare is "symmetrical," with two nations sending their armies into battle. By contrast,

GLOBAL SOCIOLOGY

Violence beyond the Rules: A Report from the Former Yugoslavia

War is violent, but it also has rules. Many of our current rules of warfare were written at the end of World War II, when the victorious Allies, including the United States, charged German and Japanese military officials with war crimes. The United Nations spells out the rules of war in a document called the Geneva Conventions.

One of the most important principles is that whatever violence soldiers inflict on each other, they should not imprison, torture, rape, or murder civilians. Nor should they deliberately destroy civilian property or wantonly bomb or shell cities. Even so, for years—and especially during the Balkan conflict in the 1990s—Serbs, Croats, and Muslims committed all these war crimes in the former Yugoslavia. Tens of thousands of civilians were killed, raped, and seriously injured; the loss of property was enormous. As early as 1993, a UN tribunal convened in the Netherlands to consider possible responses.

After World War II, the Allies successfully prosecuted (and, in several cases, executed) German officers for their crimes against humanity based on evidence obtained from extensive Nazi records. This time around, however,

the task of punishing offenders has turned out to be far more difficult. For one thing, there are few written records of the Balkan conflict; for another, UN officials fear that arrests may upset delicate diplomatic efforts to bring peace to the region.

Even so, since beginning its investigations, the United Nations has indicted dozens of military officers on all sides of the conflict and begun to hand down prison sentences. In 2001, Serbian president Slobodan Milosevic was taken to the Netherlands to stand trial for war crimes. Overall, however, only a handful of the many charged with such crimes have been taken into custody, so that it is doubtful that more than a few people responsible for a staggering number of civilian deaths will ever pay for their crimes.

Sources: Adapted from Nelan (1993), Sebastian (1996), Watson (1999), Hundley (2001), and various news reports.

terrorism is a new form of war, an "asymmetrical conflict" in which the small number of attackers use terror and their own willingness to die as a means to "level the playing field" against a much more powerful enemy. Furthermore, while the terrorists may be ruthless, the nation under attack must exercise restraint in its response to terror because little may be known about the identity and location of those responsible. It is for this reason that U.S. officials maintain that the reaction to the 2001 attacks is likely to unfold over a period of years.

THE COSTS AND CAUSES OF MILITARISM

The cost of armed conflict extends far beyond battlefield casualties. Together, the world's nations spend more than $1 trillion annually (roughly $160 for every person on the planet) for military purposes. Such expenditures divert resources from alleviating the desperate struggle for survival of millions of people. If the world's nations could muster the will and the political wisdom to redirect their military spending, they could greatly reduce global poverty.

Q: "The problem with defense spending is to figure out how far you should go without destroying from within what you are trying to defend from without." Dwight D. Eisenhower

Q: "The electron is the ultimate precision-guided weapon." CIA Director John M. Deutch

NOTE: The "doomsday clock," created in 1947 at the outset of the cold war, was initially set to 7 minutes to midnight. Its current setting, set in 1998, is 9 minutes to midnight (but was 17 minutes to midnight in 1991) (*Bulletin of the Atomic Scientists*, 2000).

GLOBAL: Among the most damaging elements of war are land mines. Experts estimate that more than 100 million mines remain in the ground in 65 countries, killing or maiming some 30,000 people annually, mostly civilians (Fedarko, 1996).

In recent years, defense has been the U.S. government's largest single expenditure, accounting for 16 percent of all federal spending, or $291 billion in 2000. This huge sum is the legacy of the *arms race*, a mutually reinforcing escalation of military power between the United States and the former Soviet Union that began after World War II.

Today, years after the collapse of the Soviet Union, military expenditures remain high. Thus, analysts who support power-elite theory say that the United States is dominated by a **military-industrial complex**, *the close association of the federal government, the military, and defense industries.* The roots of militarism, then, lie not just in external threats to our security but also within the institutional structures of our own society (Marullo, 1987).

Another reason for persistent militarism in the post–cold war world is regional conflict. During the 1990s, for example, localized wars broke out in Bosnia, Chechneya, and Zambia, and tensions remain high in a host of other areas, including the Middle East, Indonesia, and a divided Korea. Even wars of limited scope have the potential to escalate and involve other countries. In 1998, for example, India and Pakistan exploded atomic bombs, raising fears of nuclear confrontation in that region. As more and more nations acquire nuclear weapons, the risk that regional conflicts will erupt into deadly wars goes up.

NUCLEAR WEAPONS

Despite the easing of superpower tensions, nations still hold almost 25,000 nuclear warheads, a destructive force equivalent to five tons of TNT for every person on the planet. Should even a small fraction of this stockpile be used in war, life as we know it might well cease on much of the Earth. Albert Einstein, whose genius contributed to the development of nuclear weapons, reflected, "The unleashed power of the atom has changed everything *save our modes of thinking*, and we thus drift toward unparalleled catastrophe." In short, nuclear weapons make unrestrained war unthinkable in a world not yet capable of peace.

Great Britain, France, and the People's Republic of China all have substantial nuclear capability, but most nuclear weapons are based in the United States and the Russian Federation. The two superpowers have agreed to reduce their stockpiles of nuclear warheads by 75 percent by the year 2003. But even as the superpower rivalry winds down, the danger of catastrophic war increases with **nuclear proliferation**, *the acquisition of nuclear-weapon technology by more and more*

In recent years, the world has become aware of the death and mutilation caused by millions of land mines placed in the ground during wartime and left there afterward. Civilians— many of them children—maimed by land mines receive treatment in this Kabul, Afghanistan, clinic.

nations. Israel, India, and Pakistan also possess some nuclear weapons, and other nations (including Iran, Iraq, North Korea, and Libya) are developing them. Although some nations have taken steps to limit the development of nuclear weapons—Argentina and Brazil stopped their work in 1990 and South Africa dismantled its arsenal in 1991—by 2010, as many as fifty nations could be capable of fighting a nuclear war. Such a trend makes any regional conflict much more dangerous (McGeary, 1998; Thomas, Barry, & Liu, 1998).

PURSUING PEACE

How can the world reduce the danger of war? Here are the most recent approaches to peace:

1. **Deterrence.** The logic of the arms race linked security to a "balance of terror" between the superpowers. Based on the principle of *mutual assured destruction (MAD)*—meaning that the side

CRITICAL THINKING

Information Warfare: Let Your Fingers Do the Fighting

For decades, scientists and military officials have studied how to use computers to defend against missiles and planes. More recently, however, the military has recognized that new information technology can fundamentally transform warfare itself, replacing rumbling tanks and screaming aircraft with electronic "smart bombs" that would silently penetrate an enemy country's computer system and render it unable to transmit information.

In such "virtual wars," soldiers seated at workstation monitors would dispatch computer viruses to shut down the enemy's communication links, causing telephones to fall silent, air traffic control and railroad switching systems to fail, computer systems to feed phony orders to field officers, and televisions to broadcast false news bulletins urging people to turn against their leaders.

Like the venom of a poisonous snake, the weapons of information warfare might quickly paralyze an enemy before a conventional attack. Another, more hopeful possibility is that the use of new information technology weaponry might not just set the stage for conventional fighting but might prevent it entirely. If the victims of computer warfare could be limited to a nation's communication links rather than its citizens and cities, wouldn't we all be more secure?

Yet "info-war" also poses new dangers because a few highly skilled operators with sophisticated electronic equipment could also wreak havoc on the United States. This country may be militarily without equal in the world, but given our increasing reliance on high technology, we are also more vulnerable to cyber-attack than any other nation. As a result, in 1996 the Central Intelligence Agency began work on a defensive "cyber-war center" to prevent what one official called an "electronic Pearl Harbor." Congress has already appropriated more than $2 billion to ensure the security of the U.S. computer infrastructure, including several hundred scholarships to train computer specialists who agree to work for the government after they graduate.

What do you think?

1. *Do you think it is realistic to expect that virtual warfare could replace conventional battlefield fighting? Why or why not?*

2. *Can you see ways in which new information technology might be used to resolve disputes peacefully?*

3. *Do you think computer technology might increase the dangers of war? If so, how?*

Sources: Waller (1995), Weiner (1996), and Page (2000).

---

launching a first-strike nuclear attack against the other would be attacked in turn—deterrence has kept the peace for more than fifty years. But this strategy has three flaws. First, it has fueled an exorbitantly expensive arms race. Second, as missiles become capable of delivering their warheads more and more quickly, computers are left with less and less time to react to an apparent attack, thereby increasing the risks of unintended war. Third, deterrence cannot control nuclear proliferation, which poses a growing threat to peace.

2. **High-technology defense.** If technology created the weapons, some maintain, it can also deliver us from the threat of war. This is the idea behind the *strategic defense initiative (SDI)* proposed by the Reagan administration in 1981 and supported today by President Bush. Under SDI, satellites and ground installations provide a protective shield or umbrella against enemy missiles. In principle, the system would detect enemy missiles soon after launch and destroy them with lasers and particle beams before they could reenter the atmosphere. If perfected, advocates argue, such a "star wars" defense would render nuclear weapons obsolete (Thompson & Waller, 2001).

But critics charge that even years of research costing trillions of dollars would yield at best a leaky umbrella. The collapse of the Soviet Union also calls into question the need for such an extensive and costly defense scheme.

Worth noting, too, is that sophisticated technology raises not only new possibilities for defense but also new strategies for waging war.

The box takes a closer look at the possibilities for "information warfare."

3. **Diplomacy and disarmament.** Still other analysts point out that the best path to peace is diplomacy rather than technology (Dedrick & Yinger, 1990). Diplomacy can enhance security by reducing rather than building weapon stockpiles.

    But disarmament has limitations. No nation wants to become vulnerable by reducing its defenses. Successful diplomacy depends not on "soft" concessions or "hard" demands but on everyone involved sharing responsibility for a common problem (Fisher & Ury, 1988). Although the United States and the former Soviet Union have managed to negotiate arms reduction agreements, Libya, North Korea, Iraq, and other nations desire to build nuclear arsenals.

4. **Resolving underlying conflict.** As the United States attacked terrorist targets in Afghanistan, many people were aware that at least one nation bordering this poor country has nuclear weapons. Given the threat that any local conflict may erupt into a regional—and potentially nuclear—confrontation, it may be that the best way to reduce the danger of nuclear war is to resolve underlying conflicts. Some people in the Islamic world, for example, argue that the United States deserves to be attacked because it has stationed military personnel in a number of Islamic nations, enacted sanctions against Iraq, and supported what they see as Israel's oppression of Palestinians. While the vast majority of people in the United States and elsewhere in the world reject such "justifications" for terrorism, it remains true that establishing lasting peace depends on resolving the conflicts that have long divided the Middle East. And, if so, should the world's nations continue to spend thousands of times as much money on militarism as they do on peacekeeping? (Sivard, 1988; Kaplan & Schaffer, 2001)

LOOKING AHEAD: POLITICS IN THE TWENTY-FIRST CENTURY

Just as economic systems, the focus of Chapter 16, are changing, so are political systems. Over the course of the twenty-first century, several problems and trends will command widespread attention.

One vexing problem in the United States is the inconsistency between our democratic ideals and low public participation in politics. Perhaps, as the pluralists contend, many people do not bother to vote because they are basically satisfied with their lives. But on the other hand, perhaps the power-elite theorists are right: People withdraw from a system that concentrates wealth and power in the hands of a few. Or, as Marxist critics contend, perhaps people find that our political system gives little real choice, limiting options and policies to what is consistent with our capitalist economic system. In any case, it seems that the only way to reduce widespread apathy and low confidence in government is to move toward significant political reform.

A second trend discussed in this chapter is the expansion of a global political process. The Information Revolution is changing politics, just as it is reformulating the economy (although political change seems to be somewhat slower). Communication technology now allows news and political analysis to flow instantly from one point in the world to another. But will this global avalanche of information expand democracy by empowering individuals? Or will new information technology provide governments with new tools to manipulate their citizens? More basically, perhaps, some critics wonder whether we really want to give the average person—who is, after all, no expert—the power to decide important issues. The box on page 458 takes a look at the debate over computer-based "online democracy."

A third issue is the global rethinking of political models. The cold war between the United States and the Soviet Union cast political debate in the form of two rigid political alternatives based on capitalism and socialism. Today, in the post–cold war era, analysts envision a broader range of political systems, linking government to economic production in various ways. "Welfare capitalism," found in Sweden, and "state capitalism," found in Japan and South Korea, are just two possibilities.

Fourth, and finally, we still face the danger of war in many parts of the world. Even as tensions between the United States and the former Soviet Union have eased, vast stockpiles of weapons remain, and nuclear technology continues to proliferate around the world. New superpowers may arise (the People's Republic of China is a likely candidate), just as regional conflicts will surely continue to fester. One can only hope that, in the century now begun, a sense of political justice enables us to devise nonviolent solutions to the age-old problems that provoke war.

CONTROVERSY & DEBATE

"Online Democracy": Can Computers Increase Political Participation?

How about this as a way to get more people actively involved in politics: Give every home a personal computer and an Internet connection; allow anyone to propose new legislation, and, on the first Saturday of every month, every adult could use a password to vote and make law. What could be easier? Or more truly democratic?

Is it possible, as some predict, that new information technology is about to reverse the trend toward apathy and lead our nation into a new age of democracy? High technology promises to make citizens better informed about the workings of government than ever before by broadcasting government debates live to every home and providing telephone, e-mail, and fax links to all government officials.

Moreover, using computer technology, citizens everywhere could participate in electronic town meetings, pushing a button on a computer keyboard to help balance the budget, ban handguns, or, perhaps, close our borders to further immigration. In short, as some see it, we are entering the age of a "wired Congress" and "online democracy."

The push for high-tech politics finds most support from Republicans, who recognize that the majority of people in rural regions across the country hold more conservative political views (look back at National Map 17–1). As they see it, giving a greater voice to these small-town citizens can counter the generally liberal voice of the big-city media and urban politicians. In short, Republicans speak for people across the country who are fed up with the liberal, big-government politics favored "inside the Beltway" (a reference to the interstate that circles our nation's capital). Moreover, the Republicans point out, over the years Congress has managed to pass a number of unpopular programs only by shutting out the voices of "ordinary people." If the public had been polled on all the issues, they ask, would we have today's high levels of immigration, rigid affirmative action, or vast federal bureaucracy?

But Democrats and others disagree, and not everyone is rushing out to "wire" Congress to public opinion. One argument against computer-based "hyperdemocracy" is that the U.S. system of government was set up not as a *direct* democracy but as a *representative* democracy. That is, citizens elect officials to lead rather than follow the whims of the voters. The British philosopher Edmund Burke, himself a conservative, believed that government officials should do more than work hard for their constituents; leaders owe the people their judgment, he said. In these days of media frenzy and passion politics, when would-be leaders often seek to inflame public opinion, "online democracy" could result in questionable laws. In the early 1960s, for example, many people across the United States were too racially prejudiced to support the civil rights legislation enacted by Congress in 1964. But looking back, would we have wanted our representatives to do otherwise?

Like it or not, everyone agrees, new information technology will operate in two directions: It will give people a greater voice in government and also allow elected leaders to present and defend their own thinking to the public. But the question remains: Will this prescription for more direct democracy motivate a larger share of citizens to become politically active? More to the point, is a more direct democracy necessarily a *better* democracy?

Continue the debate . . .

1. Do you think new information technology will give the public a greater voice in government? Why or why not? Could political leaders use new information technology to manipulate the public? How?

2. Does technology that would give the public a greater voice necessarily mean that government would make better decisions? Why or why not? Should our leaders consult the people before making decisions, or should they rely mostly on their own judgment?

3. Some critics suggest that if we want more democracy, innovations in technology are no substitute for real change in the economic and power structures of this country. Do you agree? Why or why not?

Sources: Toffler & Toffler (1993), McConnell (1995), Roberts (1995), and R. Wright (1995).

SUMMARY

1. Politics is the major social institution by which a society distributes power and organizes decision-making. Max Weber explained that three social contexts transform coercive power into legitimate authority: tradition, rationally enacted rules and regulations, and the personal charisma of a leader.

2. Traditional authority is common to preindustrial societies; industrial societies legitimize power mostly through bureaucratic organizations and law. Charismatic authority, which arises in every society, sustains itself through routinization into traditional or rational-legal authority.

3. Monarchy is based on traditional authority and is common in preindustrial societies. Although constitutional monarchies persist in some industrial nations, industrialization favors democracy based on rational-legal authority and extensive bureaucracy.

4. Authoritarian political regimes deny popular participation in government. Totalitarian political systems go even further, tightly regulating people's everyday lives.

5. The world is divided into 192 politically independent nation-states. However, one global political trend is the growing wealth and power of multinational corporations. Additionally, new technology associated with the Information Revolution means that national governments can no longer control the flow of information across national boundaries.

6. Government has grown in the United States during the past two centuries and now acts in a wide range of ways to serve the public and regulate the economy. However, the welfare state in this country is less extensive than in most other high-income nations.

7. Liberals and conservatives take different positions on economic and social issues. Liberals call for government regulation of the economy and action to ensure economic equality; conservatives believe the government should not interfere in these areas. However, conservatives do support government regulation of moral issues such as abortion, whereas liberals argue that government should not interfere in matters of conscience.

8. Special-interest groups advance the political aims of specific segments of the population. These groups employ lobbyists and political action committees (PACs) to influence the political process.

9. Many people in the United States do not readily describe themselves in political terms, nor do they strongly identify with either the Democratic or the Republican party. Furthermore, less than half of those eligible to vote actually voted in the 2000 presidential election.

10. The pluralist model holds that political power is widely dispersed in the United States; the power-elite model takes an opposing view, arguing that power is concentrated in a small, wealthy segment of the population. The Marxist political-economy view claims that our political agenda is controlled by a capitalist economy.

11. Revolution radically transforms a political system. Terrorism, another unconventional political tactic, uses violence in the pursuit of political goals. States as well as individuals engage in terrorism. Terrorism is emerging as a new form of "asymmetrical" warfare.

12. War is armed conflict directed by governments. The development and proliferation of nuclear weapons have increased the threat of global catastrophe. World peace ultimately depends on resolving the tensions and conflicts that fuel militarism.

KEY CONCEPTS

politics (p. 435) the social institution that distributes power, sets a society's agenda, and makes decisions

power (p. 435) the ability to achieve desired ends despite resistance from others

government (p. 435) a formal organization that directs the political life of a society

authority (p. 436) power that people perceive as legitimate rather than coercive

traditional authority (p. 436) power legitimized through respect for long-established cultural patterns

rational-legal authority (also **bureaucratic authority**) (p. 436) power legitimized by legally enacted rules and regulations

charismatic authority (p. 436) power legitimized through extraordinary personal abilities that inspire devotion and obedience

routinization of charisma (p. 437) the transformation of charismatic authority into some combination of traditional and bureaucratic authority

monarchy (p. 437) a type of political system in which a single family rules from generation to generation

democracy (p. 438) a type of political system which gives power to the people as a whole

authoritarianism (p. 440) a political system that denies popular participation in government

totalitarianism (p. 440) a highly centralized political system that extensively regulates people's lives

welfare state (p. 443) a range of government agencies and programs that provides benefits to the population

special-interest group (p. 445) a political alliance of people interested in some economic or social issue

political action committee (PAC) (p. 445) an organization formed by a political-interest group, independent of political parties, to pursue political aims by raising and spending money

pluralist model (p. 448) an analysis of politics that sees power as dispersed among many competing interest groups

power-elite model (p. 448) an analysis of politics that sees power as concentrated among the rich

Marxist political-economy model (p. 449) an analysis that explains politics in terms of the operation of a society's economic system

political revolution (p. 450) the overthrow of one political system in order to establish another

terrorism (p. 451) acts of violence or the threat of such violence used by an individual or group as a political strategy

war (p. 452) organized, armed conflict between the people of various societies, directed by their governments

military-industrial complex (p. 455) the close association of the federal government, the military, and defense industries

nuclear proliferation (p. 455) the acquisition of nuclear-weapon technology by more and more nations

CRITICAL-THINKING QUESTIONS

1. What is the difference between authority and power? What forms of authority characterize preindustrial and industrial societies? Why does democracy gradually replace monarchy as societies industrialize?

2. Using the political spectrum, explain the range of attitudes of the U.S. population. How is class position linked to political opinions?

3. Contrast the pluralist, power-elite, and Marxist models of societal power. Which do you find most convincing? Why?

4. Do you think the danger of war today is greater or less than in past generations? Why?

APPLICATIONS AND EXERCISES

1. Immediately after every national election (held the first Tuesday in November), newspapers publish an analysis of who voted and for whom. Visit the library to obtain a "scorecard" for a recent national election (for example, check *The New York Times* for Wednesday, November 8, 2000; Wednesday, November 7, 2001; and Wednesday, November 6, 2002). To what extent do men and women vote for different presidential candidates? What about people of various racial categories? Ages? Religions? Income levels? Which variables affect political attitudes the most?

2. With several other people, make a list of leaders who have demonstrated personal charisma. Discuss why someone is on the list. Do you think personal

charisma today is something more than "being good on television"? If so, precisely what?

3. Do a little research to trace the increase in the size of the federal government over the last fifty years. Try to discover how organizations at different points along the political spectrum (from socialist organizations on the left through the Democratic and Republican parties to right-wing militia groups) view the size of the current welfare state.

4. Members of the all-volunteer army are drawn heavily from the working class in the United States. To share the burden and danger of defending this country, should the United States reintroduce a lottery system? Why or why not?

Q: "There is nothing wrong with the United States that a dose of smaller and less intrusive government will not cure." Milton and Rose Friedman

Q: "Just be glad you're not getting all the government you're paying for." Will Rogers

Q: "Don't think people can't change the world; they're the only ones who ever have." Margaret Mead

EXERCISE: Students can find many interesting facts and discussions at the following two Web sites. For information and statistics on all national and state political candidates and races, check out http://www.politics1.com; for information on voter apathy, visit http://www.vanishingvoter.org, a site run by Harvard's Center on Press, Politics, and Public Policy.

5. Freedom House, the organization that studies civil rights and political liberty around the world, publishes an annual report, *Freedom in the World*. Find a copy in the library (or write to the organization at 1319 Eighteenth Street, NW, Washington, D.C. 20036) and examine the trends or political profiles of countries that interest you.

6. Packaged in the back of this new textbook is an interactive CD-ROM that offers a variety of study and review materials intended to help you better understand the material covered in this chapter. For this chapter, the CD-ROM contains an author's tip video, Real Life Sociology videos, other relevant audio and video, interactive map animations, audio journal entries from the author, Web links, and much more.

SITES TO SEE

http://www.prenhall.com/macionis

Visit the interactive *Companion Website*™ that accompanies this text. Begin by clicking on the cover of your book. You will find a chapter-by-chapter study guide, practice tests, and a significant portion of the text for online review, as well as many suggested Web links.

http://www.uswc.org

The Internet provides enormous organizational potential, linking people who share an interest in some political issue. The goal of this Web site is to connect U.S. women to the global women's movement.

http://www.amnesty.org

Amnesty International operates a Web site that offers information about human rights around the world.

http://www.usis.usemb.se/terror/index.html

This Web site provides information on global terrorism.

http://www.coara.or.jp/~ryoji/abomb/e-index.html

Few of us have firsthand experience of the horrors of war. This Web site provides a personal account of the dropping of the first atomic bomb on the Japanese city of Hiroshima.

http://thomas.loc.gov

Review legislation currently before Congress by visiting this Web site.

INVESTIGATE WITH CONTENTSELECT

Follow the instructions found on page 23 of this textbook to enter this chapter of the book's *Companion Website*™. Once in the chapter, click on the ContentSelect icon at the bottom left of your screen and enter your personal User ID and Password. Enter keywords such as "charisma," "campaign finance reform," and "terrorism," and the search engine will help you become an effective researcher.

CHAPTER

18

Romare Bearden (1914–1988)
The Family, 1988

Collage on wood. Smithsonian American Art Museum, Washington, D.C./Art Resource, N.Y.
© Romare Bearden Foundation/Licensed by VAGA, New York, N.Y.

FAMILY

Tom Green is a family man—in a big way. The fifty-two-year-old resident of Snake Valley, Utah, lives with five wives, who range in age from twenty-four to thirty-one. Although Green married all five, he subsequently divorced four to avoid violating state law against bigamy (being married to more than one woman or man at one time). Green and the five women are parents to thirty children.

In 2001, Tom Green also became the focus of controversy when he appeared on several national television shows defending the practice of plural marriage. Apparently Green did not realize that he could still be prosecuted for his multiple marriages. State officials took action, charging him with bigamy. At his trial,

Green defended his way of life as morally right; his wives also defended Green and their family. Even so, after deliberating four days, a jury found him guilty, and he was sentenced to five years in prison. Green also faces statutory rape charges because his first wife was only thirteen when they wed (the others were between fourteen and sixteen).

Tom Green's ideas about plural marriage can be traced to the early years of the Mormon church in Utah. However, the Mormons banned plural marriage more than a century ago, and in 1980 the church excommunicated Tom Green for his plural marriage. But Tom Green is not alone: Estimates suggest that perhaps 25,000 plural marriage families exist in rural areas of Utah today.

No doubt, the vast majority of people in the United States do not support the kind of family life that led Tom Green to break the law. But that does not mean that people in this country agree on what families should be. On the contrary, recent decades have brought a spirited debate over the family. Consider these statistics: Among women under thirty, half of all pregnancies occur out of wedlock. The U.S. divorce rate has doubled over the past forty years so that, if the trend holds, almost half of today's marriages will end in divorce. The fact that one in three children is born to an unmarried woman, coupled with the high divorce rate, means that half of U.S. children will live with a single parent at some time before reaching age eighteen.

To hear some people tell it, the family is fast becoming an endangered species. Others counter that families are not disappearing so much as changing. Indeed, for better or worse, the family is probably changing faster than any other social institution (Bianchi & Spain, 1996). Not that long ago, the cultural ideal of the family consisted of a working husband, a homemaker wife, and their children. Today, fewer people have such a singular vision of the family and at any given time only about 30 percent of U.S. households fit that description.

This chapter explores changes in family life, asking why some people call the family the bedrock of social life and others predict—and some even encourage—the decline of the family. We begin with some basic concepts.

THE FAMILY: BASIC CONCEPTS

The **family** is *a social institution found in all societies that unites people in cooperative groups to oversee the bearing and raising of children.* Family ties are also called **kinship,**

SUPPLEMENTS: An outline of this chapter, suggested discussion topics, and supplementary lecture material highlighting cross-cultural family patterns are found in the *Data File*.

Q: "Some kind of family exists in all known human societies, although it is not found in every segment or class of all stratified, state societies. Greek and American slaves, for example, were prevented from forming families." Kathleen Gough (1989:239)

Q: "The happiest moments of my life have been the few which I have passed at home in the bosom of my family." Thomas Jefferson
NOTE: Of the 71.8 million U.S. families (2000), 40% were married couples without children, 37% were married couples with children, 15% were single parents with children, 8% were other families without children (U.S. Census Bureau, 2001).

Despite global variations in family form, people everywhere celebrate the ritual of marriage that extends kinship into a new generation. The great attention given to marriage is captured in this painting by Carmen Lomas Garza, titled The Blessing on Wedding Day/La bendición en el dia de la boda.

Carmen Lomas Garza, *The Blessing on Wedding Day/La bendición en el dia de la boda*. Alkyds on canvas, 24 × 32 inches. © 1993 Carmen Lomas Garza (reg. 1994). Photo credit: M. Lee Fatherree. Collection of Smith College Museum, Northampton, Mass.

a social bond based on blood, marriage, or adoption. Although all societies have families, just whom people call their kin has varied through history and varies today from one culture to another. In the United States, most people regard a **family unit** as *a social group of two or more people, related by blood, marriage, or adoption, who usually live together.* Initially, individuals are born into a family composed of parents and siblings; this is sometimes called the *family of orientation* because it is central to socialization. In adulthood, people form a *family of procreation* in order to have or adopt children of their own.

Throughout the world, families form around **marriage,** *a legally sanctioned relationship, usually involving economic cooperation as well as sexual activity and childbearing, that people expect to be enduring.* Our cultural belief that marriage is the right setting for procreation explains the historical use of the term *illegitimate* for children born out of wedlock. Moreover, *matrimony*, in Latin, means "the condition of motherhood." The link between childbearing and marriage has weakened, however, as the share of children born to single women (one in three) has increased.

Today, some people object to defining only married couples and children as families because it endorses a single standard of moral conduct. Many business and government programs use this conventional definition, so that unmarried but committed partners—whether heterosexual or homosexual—are

excluded from health care and other benefits. More and more, however, organizations are coming to recognize *families of affinity*, that is, people with or without legal or blood ties who feel that they belong together and want to define themselves as a family.

The U.S. Census Bureau, too, uses the conventional definition of family. Thus, sociologists who use Census Bureau data describing "families" must accept this definition.[1] But the national trend is toward a more inclusive definition of family.

THE FAMILY: GLOBAL VARIATIONS

In preindustrial societies, people take a broad view of family ties, recognizing the **extended family** as *a family unit that includes parents and children as well as other kin.* This group is also called the *consanguine family,* meaning that it includes everyone with "shared blood." With industrialization, however, increasing social mobility and geographic migration give rise to the **nuclear family,** *a family unit composed of one or two parents and their children.* The nuclear family is also

---

[1]According to the U.S. Census Bureau, there were 105.5 million U.S. households in 2000, of which 71.8 million (68 percent) were "family" households. The remaining living units contained single people or unrelated individuals living together. In 1960, 85 percent of all households were families.

called the *conjugal family,* meaning "based on marriage." Although many members of our society live in extended families, the nuclear family is most common in the United States.

Family change has been greatest in nations that have the most expansive welfare state (see Chapter 17, "Politics and Government"). In the box on pages 466–67, sociologist David Popenoe takes a look at Sweden, which, he claims, has the weakest families in the world.

MARRIAGE PATTERNS

Cultural norms, and often laws, identify people as suitable or unsuitable marriage partners. Some marital norms promote **endogamy,** *marriage between people of the same social category.* Endogamy limits marriage prospects to others of the same age, race, religion, or social class. By contrast, **exogamy** mandates *marriage between people of different social categories.* In rural areas of Pakistan and India, for example, people are expected to marry someone of the same caste (endogamy) but from a different village (exogamy). The logic of endogamy is that people of similar position pass along their standing to offspring, thereby maintaining traditional social patterns. Exogamy, on the other hand, builds alliances and encourages cultural diffusion.

In industrial societies, laws prescribe **monogamy** (from the Greek term meaning "one union"), *marriage that unites two partners.* However, our high level of divorce and remarriage suggests that *serial monogamy* might be a more accurate description of this nation's marital practice. Global Map 18–1 on page 468 shows that whereas monogamy is the rule throughout the Americas and in Europe, many lower-income societies—especially in Africa and southern Asia—permit **polygamy** (from the Greek term meaning "many unions"), *marriage that unites three or more people.* Polygamy takes two forms. By far the more common is **polygyny** (from the Greek term meaning "many women"), *marriage that unites one male and two or more females.* This is the family form favored by Tom Green, profiled in the opening to this chapter. Although it is illegal in the United States, many nations in Asia and most countries in Africa permit polygyny. This practice is linked to Islam, a world religion that allows men up to four wives. Even so, most Islamic families are monogamous because few men can afford to support several wives and even more children.

Polyandry (from the Greek term meaning "many men" or "many husbands") is *marriage that unites one* *female and two or more males.* One case of this rare pattern is in Tibet, a mountainous land where agriculture is difficult. There, polyandry discourages the division of land into parcels too small to support a family and divides the work of farming among many men. Polyandry has also been linked to female infanticide—aborting female fetuses or killing female infants—because a decline in the female population forces men to share women.

Most world societies, at some time, have permitted more than one marital pattern. Even so, researchers have long noted that most actual marriages have been monogamous (Murdock, 1965; orig. 1949). This cultural preference for monogamy reflects two facts of life: Supporting multiple spouses is a heavy financial burden, and the number of men and women in most societies is roughly the same.

RESIDENTIAL PATTERNS

Just as societies regulate mate selection, they designate where a couple resides. In preindustrial societies, most newlyweds live with one set of parents, who offer them protection and economic assistance. Most common is the norm of **patrilocality** (Greek for "place of the father"), *a residential pattern in which a married couple lives with or near the husband's family.* But some societies (such as the North American Iroquois) favor **matrilocality** (meaning "place of the mother"), *a residential pattern in which a married couple lives with or near the wife's family.* Societies that engage in frequent, local warfare tend toward patrilocality, so sons are close to home to offer protection. Societies that engage in distant warfare may be patrilocal or matrilocal, depending on whether sons or daughters have greater economic value (Ember & Ember, 1971, 1991).

Industrial societies show yet another pattern. Finances permitting, they favor **neolocality** (Greek meaning "new place"), *a residential pattern in which a married couple lives apart from both sets of parents.*

PATTERNS OF DESCENT

Descent is *the system by which members of a society trace kinship over generations.* Most preindustrial societies trace kinship through just the father's or mother's side of the family. The more common **patrilineal descent** is *a system tracing kinship through men.* Children are related to others only through their fathers, so that fathers typically pass property on to their sons. Patrilineal descent characterizes most pastoral and agrarian societies, in

GLOBAL SOCIOLOGY

The Weakest Families on Earth? A Report from Sweden

The Swedes have managed to avoid many of the social problems that plague us in the United States. Swedish cities have little of the violent crime, drug abuse, and savage poverty that blight whole communities, from New York to Los Angeles. Instead, this Scandinavian nation seems to fulfill the promise of the modern welfare state, with an extensive and professional government bureaucracy that sees to virtually all human needs.

But one drawback of an expanding welfare state, according to David Popenoe, is that Sweden has the weakest families on Earth. Because people look to the government, not spouses, for economic assistance, Swedes are less likely to marry than members of any other high-income society. For the same reason, Sweden also has a high share of adults living alone (more than 20 percent, about the same as in the United States). Moreover, a large proportion of

In Sweden, unmarried women bear half of all children, 50 percent higher than the percentage of births by single women in the United States.

couples live together without being married (25 percent versus 10 percent in the United States), and half of all Swedish children (compared to one in three in the United States) are born to unmarried parents. Average household size in Sweden is also the smallest in the world (2.2 people versus 2.6 in the United States). Finally, Swedish couples (whether married or not) are more likely to break up than partners in any other country. According to Popenoe, the family "has probably become weaker in Sweden than anywhere else—certainly among advanced Western nations. Individual family members are the most autonomous and least bound by the group" (1991:69).

Popenoe contends that a growing culture of individualism and self-fulfillment, along with the

---

which men produce the most valued resources. Less common is **matrilineal descent,** *a system tracing kinship through women.* Matrilineal descent, through which mothers pass property to their daughters, is found more frequently in horticultural societies, where women are the primary food producers.

Industrial societies with greater gender equality recognize **bilateral descent** ("two-sided descent"), *a system tracing kinship through both men and women.* In this pattern, children recognize people on both the father's side and the mother's side as relatives.

PATTERNS OF AUTHORITY

The predominance of polygyny, patrilocality, and patrilineal descent in the world reflects the universal presence of patriarchy. Wives and mothers exercise considerable power in every society, but as Chapter 13 ("Gender Stratification") explains, no truly matriarchal society has ever existed.

In industrial societies such as the United States, more egalitarian family patterns are evolving, especially as increasing numbers of women enter the labor force. However, even here, men are typically heads of households. Parents in the United States also still prefer boys to girls, and most give children their father's last name.

THEORETICAL ANALYSIS OF THE FAMILY

As in earlier chapters, several theoretical approaches offer a range of insights about the family.

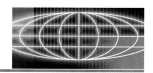

declining influence of religion, began eroding Swedish families in the 1960s. The movement of women into the labor force also played a part. Today, Sweden has the lowest proportion of women who are homemakers (10 percent versus about 22 percent in the United States) and the highest percentage of women in the labor force (77 percent versus 60 percent in the United States).

But most important, according to Popenoe, is the expansion of the welfare state. The Swedish government offers its citizens a lifetime of services. Swedes can count on the government to deliver and school their children, provide comprehensive health care, support them when they are out of work, and, when the time comes, pay for their funeral.

Many Swedes supported the growth of welfare, thinking it would *strengthen* families. But with the benefit of hindsight, Popenoe explains, we can see that with expanding benefits, government actually has been *replacing* families. Take the case of child care: The Swedish government operates public child-care centers, staffed by professionals and available regardless of parents' income. At the same time, however, the government offers no subsidy for parents who want to care for children in their own home. In effect, then, government benefits operate as incentives for people to let the state do what family members used to do for themselves.

But if Sweden's system has solved so many social problems, why should anyone care about the erosion of family life? For two reasons, says Popenoe. First, it is very expensive for government to provide many "family" services; this is the main reason that Sweden has one of the highest rates of taxation in the world. Second, can government employees in large child-care centers give children the amount of love and emotional security available from two parents living as a family? This is unlikely, says Popenoe, noting that small, intimate groups can accomplish some human tasks much better than large organizations.

Popenoe concludes that the Swedes have gone too far in delegating family responsibilities to government. But, he wonders, have we in the United States gone far enough? With the birth of a child, a Swedish parent may apply for up to eighteen months' leave at 90 percent of regular salary. In the United States, the 1993 Family and Medical Leave Act guarantees workers only ninety days—without pay—to care for newborns or sick family members. Should our society follow Sweden's lead? If we look to government to help working parents care for children, will it strengthen or weaken families?

Sources: Popenoe (1991, 1994); also Herrstrom (1990).

FUNCTIONS OF THE FAMILY: STRUCTURAL-FUNCTIONAL ANALYSIS

According to the structural-functional paradigm, the family performs several vital tasks. In fact, the family operates as the backbone of society.

1. **Socialization.** As explained in Chapter 5 ("Socialization"), the family is the first and most influential setting for socialization. Ideally, parents help children become well-integrated, contributing members of society (Parsons & Bales, 1955). Of course, family socialization continues throughout the life cycle. Adults change within marriage and, as any parent knows, mothers and fathers learn as much from their children as their children learn from them.

2. **Regulation of sexual activity.** Every culture regulates sexual activity in the interest of maintaining kinship organization and property rights. One universal regulation is the **incest taboo,** *a norm forbidding sexual relations or marriage between certain relatives.* Precisely which relatives fall within the incest taboo varies from one culture to another. The matrilineal Navajo, for example, forbid marrying any relative of one's mother. Our bilateral society applies the incest taboo to both sides of the family but limits it to close relatives, including parents, grandparents, siblings, aunts, and uncles. But even brother-sister marriages found approval among the ancient Egyptian, Incan, and Hawaiian nobility (Murdock, 1965; orig. 1949).

Reproduction between close relatives of any species can mentally and physically harm

NOTE: Teen pregnancy is increasing in poor societies, perhaps one indication of the breakdown of tradition. In Botswana, a southern African nation with a high population increase, one-fifth of female teens become pregnant, most unintentionally because of little knowledge about birth control.

DIVERSITY: Statistically speaking, the typical U.S. family is a married couple, both of whom are high school graduates and in the labor force, with one child (mean) or no children (mode), living in a (mortgaged) home that they own. At any given point in time, about 25% of all households have a wife, husband, and 1 or more children at home, although more than half take this form during the life course; at any given time, about 1 in 10 households include a working man, homemaker woman, and 1 or more children although, again, about 25% take this form at some point.

WINDOW ON THE WORLD

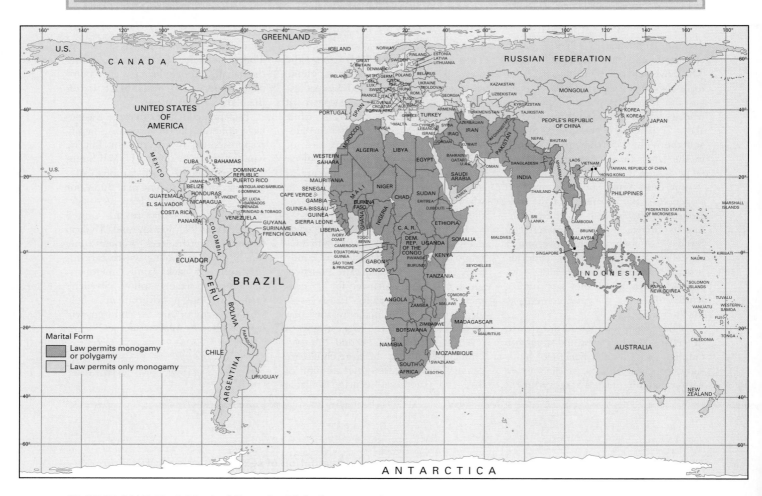

GLOBAL MAP 18–1 Marital Form in Global Perspective

Monogamy is the legally prescribed form of marriage throughout the Western Hemisphere and in much of the rest of the world. In most African nations and in southern Asia, however, polygamy is permitted by law. In many cases, this practice reflects the historic influence of Islam, a religion that allows a man to have up to four wives. Even so, most marriages in these traditional societies are monogamous, primarily for financial reasons.

Source: *Peters Atlas of the World* (1990).

offspring. Yet only human beings observe an incest taboo, suggesting that the main reason to control incest is social. Why? First, the incest taboo limits sexual competition in families by limiting sexuality to spouses. Second, forcing people to marry outside their immediate families integrates the larger society. Third, because kinship defines people's rights and obligations

The family is a basic building block of society because it performs important functions, such as conferring social position and regulating sexual activity. To most family members, however, the family (at least in ideal terms) is a "haven in a heartless world" in which individuals enjoy the feeling of belonging and find emotional support. Marc Chagall conveyed the promise of marriage in his painting, To My Wife. *Looking at the painting, how does the artist characterize marriage?*

Marc Chagall (1887–1985), *To My Wife*, 1933–44. Georges Pompidou Centre, Paris. The Bridgeman Art Library, London. © 2000 Artists Rights Society (ARS), New York/ADAGP, Paris.

toward each other, reproduction between close relatives would hopelessly confuse kinship ties and threaten social order.

3. **Social placement.** Families are hardly necessary for people to reproduce, but they help maintain social organization. Parents confer their own social identity—in terms of race, ethnicity, religion, and social class—on children at birth.

4. **Material and emotional security.** Many people view the family as a "haven in a heartless world," looking to kin for physical protection, emotional support, and financial assistance. Thus, people living in families tend to be healthier than people living alone.

Critical evaluation. Structural-functional analysis explains why society, at least as we know it, depends on families. But this approach glosses over the great diversity of U.S. family life and ignores how other social institutions (say, government) could meet some of the same human needs. Finally, structural-functionalism overlooks negative aspects of family life, including patriarchy and family violence.

INEQUALITY AND THE FAMILY: SOCIAL-CONFLICT ANALYSIS

The social-conflict paradigm also considers the family central to our way of life. But rather than focusing on ways that kinship benefits society, conflict theorists point out how the family perpetuates social inequality:

1. **Property and inheritance.** Friedrich Engels (1902; orig. 1884) traced the origin of the family to men's need (especially in the upper classes) to identify heirs so they could transmit property to their sons. Families thus support the concentration of wealth and reproduce the class structure in each succeeding generation (Mare, 1991).

2. **Patriarchy.** To know their heirs, men must control the sexuality of women. Families thus transform women into the sexual and economic property of men. A century ago in the United States, most wives' earnings belonged to their husbands. Today, despite striking economic gains, women still bear most of the responsibility for child rearing and housework (Hochschild & Machung, 1989; Presser, 1993; Keith & Schafer, 1994; Benokraitis & Feagin, 1995; Stapinski, 1998).

3. **Racial and ethnic inequality.** Racial and ethnic categories persist over generations only to the degree that people marry others like themselves. Thus endogamous marriage shores up racial and ethnic hierarchies.

Critical evaluation. Social-conflict analysis shows another side of family life: its role in social stratification. Engels criticized the family as part and parcel of capitalism. Yet noncapitalist societies also have families (and

NOTE: The Latin root of "intimacy" is *timere*, meaning "to fear" (an etymology shared with the word "intimidate"). Intimacy, then, is a relationship of "sharing fears."

NOTE: Social-exchange analysis is one kind of rational-choice theory.

NOTE: Social-exchange analysis also explains why people who perceive more potential new partners in their surroundings have higher divorce rates (cf. South & Lloyd, 1995).

RESOURCE: Among the classics included in the Macionis and Benokraitis reader, *Seeing Ourselves*, is Jessie Bernard's "'His' and 'Her' Marriage."

DIVERSITY: As people age, there are proportionately fewer males than females eligible for marriage. Regionally, this pattern is most pronounced in the Sunbelt; in San Diego, for example, there are three men aged 20–59 for every four women.

Here is another well-known painting by Carmen Lomas Garza, titled Una tarde *(An Afternoon). Garza is illustrating a distinctive quality of Hispanic cultures— the strong involvement of whole families in courtship, especially of a daughter. Young people get to know one another, in short, but only under the watchful eyes of the older generation.*

Carmen Lomas Garza, *Una tarde* (*An Afternoon*). Gouache painting, 18 × 25 inches. © 1990 Carmen Lomas Garza. Photo credit: Judy Reed. Collection of Sophie and Daniel Share, Birmingham, Michigan.

family problems). The family may be linked to social inequality, as Engels argued, but the family carries out societal functions not easily accomplished by other means.

CONSTRUCTING FAMILY LIFE: MICRO-LEVEL ANALYSIS

Both structural-functional and social-conflict analyses view the family as a structural system. By contrast, micro-level approaches explore how individuals shape and experience family life.

Symbolic-Interaction Analysis

Ideally, family living offers an opportunity for intimacy, a word with Latin roots meaning "sharing fear." That is, as family members share activities, they build emotional bonds. Of course, the fact that parents act as authority figures often limits their closeness with children. Only as people reach adulthood do kinship ties between generations open up to include confiding in and turning to one another for help with daily tasks and responsibilities (Macionis, 1978a).

Social-Exchange Analysis

Social-exchange analysis, another micro-level approach, depicts courtship and marriage as forms of

negotiation (Blau, 1964). Dating allows each person to assess the advantages and disadvantages of taking the other as a spouse, always keeping in mind the value of what one has to offer in return. In essence, say exchange analysts, individuals seek to make the best "deal" they can in a partner.

Physical attractiveness is an important dimension of exchange. In patriarchal societies, men bring wealth and power to the marriage marketplace, and women are expected to bring beauty. The importance of beauty explains women's traditional concern with their appearance and their sensitivity about revealing their age. But as women have joined the labor force, they are less dependent on men to support them, which means the terms of exchange are converging for men and women.

Critical evaluation. Micro-level analysis balances structural-functional and social-conflict visions of the family as an institutional system. Both the interaction and exchange viewpoints show how individuals shape the experience of family life for themselves. However, this approach misses the bigger picture, namely, that family life is similar for people in the same social and economic categories. U.S. families vary in predictable ways, according to social class and ethnicity, and as the next section explains, they typically evolve through distinct stages linked to the life course.

RESOURCE: Check Bron B. Ingoldsby's article, "Mate Selection and Marriage around the World," in the new edition of the Macionis and Benokraitis reader, *Seeing Ourselves.*

Q: "What's love got to do with it?" Tina Turner

Q: Caniel Cere (2001:53) defines courtship as "customs and rituals that help individuals negotiate the complex transition from sexual attraction, through love, to lasting marriage."

Q: "What does a woman do for herself and for her children by being fussy about her sexual partners? . . . If she focuses on male traits that are heritable, she sees to it that her kids start with a genetic edge. We aren't all created equal. . . . [She also] makes it possible to pick males who will stick around and help raise the kids. A woman is not simply competing for quality sperm; she's competing for the man who goes with it." Heather Trexler Remoff (1984)

GLOBAL SOCIOLOGY

Early to Wed: A Report from Rural India

Sumitra Jogi cries as her wedding is about to begin. Are they tears of joy? Not exactly. This "bride" is an eleven-month-old squirming in the arms of her mother. The groom? A boy of six.

In a remote, rural village in India's western state of Rajasthan, two families gather at midnight to celebrate a traditional wedding ritual. It is May 2, an especially good day to marry in Hindu tradition. Sumitra's father smiles as the ceremony begins; her mother cradles the infant, who has fallen asleep. The groom, dressed in a special costume with a red and gold turban on his head, gently reaches up and grasps the baby's hand. Then, as the ceremony reaches

its conclusion, the young boy leads the child and mother around the wedding fire three-and-one-half times, as the audience beams at the couple's first steps together as husband and wife.

Child weddings are illegal in India, but in the rural regions traditions are strong and marriage laws are hard to enforce. Thus, experts estimate, thousands of children marry each year. "In rural Rajasthan," explains one social welfare worker, "all the girls are married by age fourteen. These are poor, illiterate families, and they don't want to keep girls past their first menstrual cycle."

For the immediate future, Sumitra Jogi will remain with her parents. But in eight or ten years, a second ceremony

will send her to live with her husband's family, and her married life will begin.

If the responsibilities of marriage lie years in the future, why do families push their children to marry at such an early age? Parents of girls know that the younger the bride, the smaller the dowry offered to the groom's family. Also, when girls marry this young, there is no question about their virginity, which raises their value on the marriage market. Arranged marriages are an alliance between families. No one thinks about love or the fact that the children are too young to understand what is taking place.

Source: Based on Anderson (1995).

STAGES OF FAMILY LIFE

The family is a dynamic institution, with marked changes across the life course. New families begin with courtship and evolve as partners settle into the realities of married life. Next, for most couples at least, are the years spent raising children and, finally, the later years after children have left home to form families of their own. We will look briefly at each of these four stages.

COURTSHIP

November 2, Kandy, Sri Lanka. Winding through the rain forest of this beautiful island, our van driver, Harry, recounts how he met his wife. Actually, it was more of an arrangement: The two families were both Buddhist and of the same caste. "We got along well, right from the start," recalls

Harry. "We had the same background. I suppose she or I could have said 'no.' But love marriages happen in the city, not in the village where I grew up."

In rural Sri Lanka and in rural areas of low-and middle-income societies throughout the world, most people consider courtship too important to be left to the young (Stone, 1977). Arranged marriages represent an alliance between two extended families of similar social standing and usually involve not just an exchange of children but also wealth and favors. Romantic love has little to do with it, and parents may make such arrangements when their children are very young. A century ago in Sri Lanka and India, for example, half of all girls married before reaching age fifteen (Mayo, 1927; Mace & Mace, 1960). As the box explains, in some parts of the world, child marriage persists today.

Because traditional societies are culturally homogeneous, almost any member of the opposite sex has been suitably socialized to be a good spouse. Therefore,

Q: "Our forefathers had conceived a strange opinion on the subject of marriage; as they had noticed that the small number of love-matches in their time almost always turned out badly, they resolutely inferred that it was dangerous to listen to the dictates of the heart on the subject. Accident appeared to them a better guide than choice." Alexis de Tocqueville

THEN AND NOW: Age at first marriage: *1955*, 20.1 yrs. for women, 22.5 yrs. for men; *2000*, 25.1 yrs. for women, 26.8 yrs. for men.
DISCUSS: Distinguish *homogamy* (marriage between partners of similar background) from *endogamy* (marriage within some specific category).

People in every society recognize the reality of physical attraction. But the power of romantic love, captured in Christian Pierre's painting, I Do, *holds surprisingly little importance in traditional societies. In much of the world, it would be less correct to say that individuals marry individuals and more true to say that families marry families. In other words, parents arrange marriages for their children with an eye to the social position of the kin-groups involved.*

parents can arrange marriages with little thought to whether the two individuals involved are *personally* compatible; they can be confident that the partners will be *culturally* compatible.

Industrialization erodes the importance of extended families as it weakens tradition. Young people choose their own mates and delay marriage until they have financial security and the experience needed to select a suitable partner. Dating sharpens courtship skills and allows sexual experimentation.

Romantic Love

Our culture celebrates *romantic love*—affection and sexual passion for another person—as the basis for marriage. We find it hard to imagine marriage without love, and popular culture—from fairy tales such as "Cinderella" to today's romance novels—portrays love as the key to a successful marriage. However, as Figure 18–1 shows, in Pakistan, India, and many other countries where traditions remain strong, romantic love plays a much smaller role in marriage.

 Take a look at "virtual courtship" using the Internet to find a partner: http://www.loveme.com

Our society's emphasis on romance motivates young people to "leave the nest" to form new families of their own, and physical passion can help a new couple through difficult adjustments of living together (Goode, 1959). On the other hand, because feelings wax and wane, romantic love is a less stable foundation for marriage than social and economic considerations—one reason that the divorce rate is much higher in the United States than in nations where culture limits choices in partners.

But even here, sociologists point out, society aims Cupid's arrow more than we like to think. Most people fall in love with others of the same race, comparable age, and similar social class. Our society "arranges" marriages by encouraging **homogamy** (literally, "like marrying like"), *marriage between people with the same social characteristics.*

SETTLING IN: IDEAL AND REAL MARRIAGE

Our culture gives the young an idealized, "happily ever after" picture of marriage. Such optimism can lead to disappointment, especially for women, who are taught that marriage is the key to happiness. Then, too, romantic love involves a good deal of fantasy. We fall in love with others not necessarily as they are but as we want them to be (Berscheid & Hatfield, 1983). Only after marriage do many spouses face up to day-to-day responsibilities and routines.

Sexuality, too, can be a source of disappointment. In the romantic haze of falling in love, people may unrealistically expect marriage to be an endless sexual honeymoon, only to face the sobering realization that sex becomes a less than all-consuming passion. About two in three married people report that they are satisfied with the sexual dimension of their relationship, although marital sex does decline over time.

Many experts agree that couples with the most fulfilling sexual relationships experience the greatest satisfaction in their marriages. This correlation does not mean that sex is the key to marital bliss, but more often than not, good sex and good relationships go together (Hunt, 1974; Tavris & Sadd, 1977; Blumstein & Schwartz, 1983; Laumann et al., 1994).

Infidelity—*sexual activity outside marriage*—is another area where the reality of marriage does not coincide with our cultural ideal. In a recent survey, nearly 90 percent of U.S. adults said sex outside of marriage is "always wrong" or "almost always wrong." Even so, 21 percent of men and 13 percent of women indicated on a private, written questionnaire that they had been sexually unfaithful to their partners at least once (NORC, 2001:243, 1135).

CHILD REARING

Despite the demands children make on us, adults in the United States overwhelmingly identify raising children as one of life's greatest joys (NORC, 2001:979). However, today few people want more than three children, as Table 18–1 on page 474 documents. This is a change from two centuries ago, when *eight* children was the U.S. average.

Big families pay off in preindustrial societies because children supply needed labor. Thus, people regard having children as a wife's duty, and without effective birth control, childbearing is a regular event. Of course, a high death rate in preindustrial societies prevents many children from reaching adulthood; as late as 1900, one-third of children born in the United States died by age ten (Wall, 1980).

Economically speaking, industrialization transforms children from an asset to a liability. It now costs more than $200,000 to raise one child, including college tuition (Lino, 2001). No wonder the size of the U.S. family steadily dropped during the twentieth century to one child per family.[2]

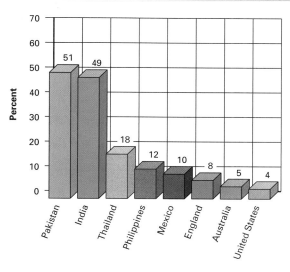

GLOBAL SNAPSHOT

FIGURE 18–1 Percentage of College Students Who Express a Willingness to Marry without Romantic Love

Source: Levine (1993).

The trend toward smaller families is most pronounced in higher-income nations. But the picture differs in lower-income countries in Latin America, Asia, and especially Africa, where many women have few alternatives to bearing children. In such societies, four to six children is still the norm.

Parenting is not only expensive, it is a lifetime commitment. As our society has given people greater choice about family life, more U.S. adults have opted to delay childbirth or to remain childless. In 1960, almost 90 percent of women between twenty-five and twenty-nine who had ever married had at least one child; by 1998, this proportion tumbled to 70 percent (U.S. Census Bureau, 2000).

About two-thirds of parents in the United States say they would like to devote more of their time to child rearing (Snell, 1990). But unless we are willing to accept a lower standard of living, economic realities demand that most parents pursue careers outside the home, even if that means giving less attention to their families.

[2]According to the U.S. Census Bureau, the mean number of children per family was 0.90 in 2000 and holding steady. Among married couples with children, the means were .89 for whites, 1.15 for African Americans, and 1.53 for Hispanics.

GLOBAL: Ideal family size is higher in poor societies. One recent survey in Honduras placed the ideal figure as 3.2 children. In rural areas (containing 60% of the people) the actual average family size is 6.9 children.

NOTE: According to the U.S. National Center for Health Statistics, 10% of births are unwanted; another 25% are "ill timed," meaning wanted but at a later date.

SOCIAL SURVEY: "How much satisfaction do you get from your family life?" (GSS 1994, N = 511; Codebook, 2001:180)

"A very great deal"	39.5%	"Some"	3.3%
"A great deal"	35.0%	"A little"	2.5%
"Quite a bit"	10.4%	"None"	2.0%
"A fair amount"	6.8%	DK/NR	0.4%

TABLE 18–1 The Ideal Number of Children for U.S. Adults, 2000

Number of Children	Proportion of Respondents
0	1.3%
1	3.4
2	50.4
3	23.4
4	8.2
5	0.7
6 or more	0.5
As many as you want	7.1
No response	5.0

Source: *General Social Surveys, 1972–2000: Cumulative Codebook* (Chicago: National Opinion Research Center, 2001), p. 238.

Children of working parents spend most of the day at school. But after school, more than 2 million children between five and fourteen (roughly 13 percent of the total) are *latchkey kids* who fend for themselves (Capizano, Tout, & Adams, 2001). Traditionalists in the "family values" debate charge that many mothers work at the expense of children, who receive too little parenting. Progressives counter that such criticism targets women for wanting the same opportunities that men have long enjoyed.

Here is a report about the quality of care children receive from relatives: http://newfederalism.urban.org/html/series_b/b28/b28.html

Congress took a step toward easing the conflict between family and job responsibilities by passing the Family and Medical Leave Act in 1993. This law allows up to ninety days of unpaid leave from work because of a new child or a serious family emergency. Still, most adults in this country have to juggle parental and occupational responsibilities. When mothers work, who cares for the kids? The box provides the answer.

THE FAMILY IN LATER LIFE

Increasing life expectancy in the United States means that, barring divorce, couples are likely to remain married for a long time. By about age fifty, most have completed the task of raising children. The remaining years of marriage bring a return to living with only one's spouse.

Like the birth of children, their absence—the "empty nest"—necessitates adjustments, although a marriage often becomes closer and more satisfying in midlife. Years of living together may diminish a couple's sexual passion for each other, but mutual understanding and companionship often increase.

Personal contact with children usually continues because most older adults live a short distance from at least one of their children. Moreover, one-third of all U.S. adults (60 million) are grandparents, many of whom help with child care and other responsibilities. Among African Americans (who have a high rate of single parenting), grandmothers hold a central position in family life (Crispell, 1993; Jarrett, 1994; Rutherford, 1999; Clemetson, 2000).

The other side of the coin is that more adults in midlife now care for their aging parents. The "empty nest" may not be filled by a parent actually moving in, but the responsibility for elderly parents can be more taxing than raising young children. The oldest of the baby boomers—now in their fifties—are called the "sandwich generation" because they (especially women) will spend as many years caring for their aging parents as they did caring for their children (Lund, 1993).

The final, and surely the most difficult, transition in married life comes with the death of a spouse. Wives typically outlive their husbands because of women's longer life expectancy and the fact that women usually marry men several years older. Wives can thus expect to spend some years as widows. The challenge of living alone after the death of a spouse is especially great for men, who usually have fewer friends than widows and may lack housekeeping skills.

U.S. FAMILIES: CLASS, RACE, AND GENDER

Dimensions of inequality—social class, ethnicity and race, and gender—are powerful forces that shape marriage and family life. This discussion addresses each factor in turn, but bear in mind that they overlap in our lives.

SOCIAL CLASS

Social class frames a family's financial security and range of opportunities. In a classic study of working-class women, Lillian Rubin (1976) found that wives thought a good husband was one who held a steady job, did not drink too much, and was not violent. By contrast, Rubin's middle-class informants never

APPLYING SOCIOLOGY

Who's Minding the Kids?

Traditionally, the task of providing daily care for young children fell to mothers. But with a majority of mothers and fathers now in the labor force, finding high-quality, affordable child care is a high priority for parents.

The figure shows how U.S. children under age five receive care while their mothers work. Nearly half of children receive care from a parent (24 percent) or a relative (23 percent); of those children receiving relative care, 9 percent are cared for in their own home and 14 percent are cared for in the relative's home. However, the majority of children are cared for by a nonrelative: 32 percent attend day care or preschool, 16 percent are cared for in a nonrelative's home, and only 6 percent of children are cared for in their own home by a nanny or babysitter. The proportion of children in day-care centers has doubled over the last decade because many parents cannot find affordable in-home care for their children.

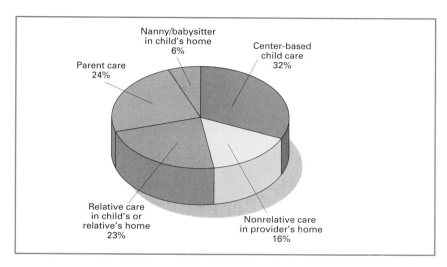

Some day-care centers are so big that they amount to "tot lots" where parents "park" their children for the day. The impersonality of such settings and the rapid turnover in staff prevent the warm and consistent nurturing that young children need to develop a sense of trust. Other child-care centers offer a secure and healthful environment. In short, *good* care centers are good for children; *bad* facilities are not.

Sources: U.S. Census Bureau (1997) and Capizzano, Adams, & Sonenstein (2001).

mentioned such things; these women simply *assumed* that a husband would provide a safe and secure home. Their ideal husband was someone they could talk to easily, sharing feelings and experiences.

This difference reflects the fact that people with higher social standing have more schooling and hold jobs that emphasize verbal skills. In addition, middle-class couples share a wide range of activities, whereas working-class life is more divided along gender lines. As Rubin explains, many working-class men have traditional ideas about masculinity and self-control, and they stifle emotional expressiveness. Women, then, turn to each other as confidants.

Clearly, what women (and men) think they can hope for in marriage—and what they end up with—is linked to their social class. Much the same holds for children; boys and girls lucky enough to be born into more affluent families enjoy better mental and physical health, develop more self-confidence, and go on to greater achievement than children born to poor parents (Komarovsky, 1967; Bott, 1971, orig. 1957; Rubin, 1976; Fitzpatrick, 1988; McLeod & Shanahan, 1993; Duncan et al., 1998).

ETHNICITY AND RACE

As described in Chapter 14 ("Race and Ethnicity"), ethnicity and race are powerful social forces, and the effects of both ripple through family life. Keep in mind, however, that like white families, Hispanic, African

NOTE: The Census Bureau reports that, in 2000, 53% of the 11.4 million African American children under 18 lived with only one parent (up 97% since 1970). Families with a woman heading the household (almost all of them) had a median income of $20,405, 40% of the comparable figure for black married-couple families ($50,741).
DIVERSITY: One-parent African American families represent about half the total but receive only one-third of all black family income.

THEN AND NOW: African American households with female heads: *1940*, 18%; *2000*, 45%; two-parent households: *1940*, 77%; *2000*, 46%. Percentage of African American children residing with both parents: *1960*, 75%; *2000*, 38% (U.S. Census Bureau, 2001).
DIVERSITY: About 70% of African American women ever marry, compared to 90% of white women.

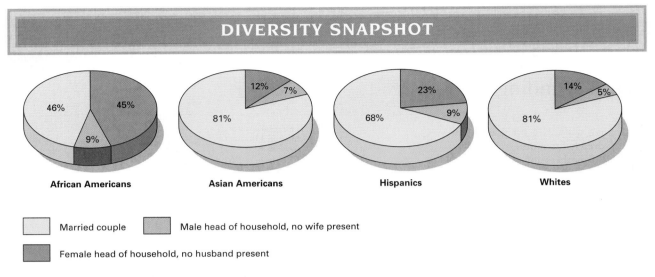

DIVERSITY SNAPSHOT

African Americans — 46%, 45%, 9%
Asian Americans — 81%, 12%, 7%
Hispanics — 68%, 23%, 9%
Whites — 81%, 14%, 5%

☐ Married couple   ☐ Male head of household, no wife present

☐ Female head of household, no husband present

FIGURE 18–2 Family Form in the United States, 2000
Source: U.S. Census Bureau (2001).

American, and other categories of families are diverse and conform to no single stereotype (Allen, 1995).

Hispanic Families

Many Latinos enjoy the loyalty and support of extended families. Traditionally, Hispanic parents exercise greater control over children's courtship, considering marriage an alliance of families, not just a union based on romantic love. Some Hispanic families also adhere to conventional gender roles, encouraging machismo—strength, daring, and sexual prowess—among men, whereas women are both honored and closely supervised.

However, assimilation into the larger society is changing these traditional patterns. For example, many Puerto Ricans who migrate to New York do not maintain the strong extended families they knew in Puerto Rico. Traditional male authority over women has also diminished, especially among affluent Hispanic families, whose number has tripled in the last twenty years (Moore & Pachon, 1985; Nielsen, 1990; O'Hare, 1990; Lach, 1999).

Although some Hispanics have prospered, the overall social standing of this segment of the U.S. population remains below average. The U.S. Census Bureau (2001) reports that the typical Hispanic family had an income of $35,050 in 2000, or 69 percent of the national average. As a result, many Hispanic families suffer the stress of unemployment and other poverty-related problems.

African American Families

African American families face economic disadvantages: As explained in earlier chapters, the typical African American family earned $34,204 in 2000, or 67 percent of the national average. People of African ancestry are also three times as likely as non-Hispanic whites to be poor, and poverty means families experience unemployment, underemployment, and in some cases a physical environment of crime and drug abuse.

Under these circumstances, maintaining stable family ties is difficult. For example, 25 percent of African American women in their forties have never married, compared to about 10 percent of white women of the same age (Bennett, Bloom, & Craig, 1989). This means that African American women—often with children—are more likely to be single heads of households. As Figure 18–2 shows, women headed 45 percent of all African American families in 2000, compared to 23 percent of Hispanic families, 12 percent of Asian or Pacific Islander families, and 14 percent of white families (U.S. Census Bureau, 2001).

Regardless of race, single-mother families are always at high risk of poverty. Seventeen percent of

THE MAP: Racially mixed marriages are most common in urban areas. In addition, the West Coast (especially California) has the greatest number of racially mixed marriages, reflecting both high minority populations and a relatively tolerant culture.

DIVERSITY: In 1998, there were 1,348,000 "mixed" marriages (some mix of African American/Asian/Native American/white), up from 651,000 in 1980. About 5% of U.S. births are racially mixed.

DISCUSS: What about interracial adoption? States vary sharply, from banning interracial adoption to promoting it. The National Association of Black Social Workers encourages the placement of children first with biological parents, then in "community of origin," then with others (of another race). About 40% of adopted children are African Americans.

SEEING OURSELVES

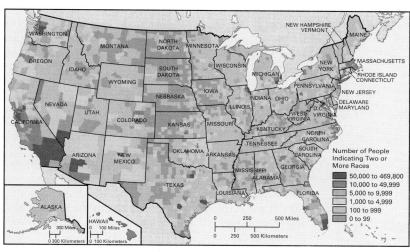

NATIONAL MAP 18–1
Racially Mixed People across the United States

Where are racially mixed marriages most common? No precise data of this kind are currently available, but the Census Bureau does publish the distribution of racially mixed people—those, presumably, who have parents of two different racial categories. This map shows the distribution of people who described themselves as racially mixed in the 2000 census. What can you say about where such people reside and, thus, where racially mixed marriages are most common?

Source: U.S. Census Bureau (2001).

families headed by non-Hispanic white women are poor, 34 percent of families headed by women of Hispanic ancestry are in poverty, and the proportion is 35 percent among African American women—good evidence of how class, race, and gender overlap to put women at a disadvantage. African American families with both wife and husband in the home, which represent half the total, are much stronger economically, earning 85 percent as much as comparable white families. But 72 percent of African American children are born to single women, and 31 percent of African American boys and girls are growing up poor, meaning that such families carry much of the burden of child poverty in the United States (Hogan & Kitagawa, 1985; U.S. Census Bureau, 2001; U.S. National Center for Health Statistics, 2001).

Racially Mixed Marriages

Many spouses have similar social backgrounds with regard to class, race, and ethnicity. But over the course of the twentieth century, ethnicity has mattered less and less. Thus, a woman of German and French ancestry might readily marry a man of Irish and English background without inviting disapproval from their families or from society in general.

Race remains a more formidable consideration, however. Before a 1967 Supreme Court decision (*Loving* v. *Virginia*), interracial marriage was illegal in sixteen states. Today, African, Asian, and Native Americans represent 17 percent of the U.S. population, so we would expect about the same share of marriages to be "mixed" if people ignored race in choosing spouses. The actual proportion of mixed marriages is 2.9 percent, showing that race still matters in social relations. But the number of racially mixed marriages is rising steadily, and most U.S. teens now claim they have dated someone of another race.

Black-white marriages are most numerous, as the large African American population (12 percent of the U.S. total) would lead us to expect. Proportionately, though, whites involved in racially mixed marriages are most likely to have partners of Asian ancestry (U.S. Census Bureau, 2001). National Map 18–1 shows where people who described themselves in Census 2000 as being multiracial live, which is one good indicator of the prevalence of racially mixed marriages.

GENDER

Regardless of race, Jessie Bernard (1982) says that every marriage is actually *two* different relationships:

NOTE: Whereas first marriages have a median duration of about eight years, second marriages typically last six years.

SOCIAL SURVEY: "Should divorce in this country be easier or more difficult to obtain than it is now?" (GSS 2000, N = 1,877; *Codebook*, 2001:241)
"Easier"   23.5%   "More difficult"   48.6%
"Same"   21.8%   DK/NR   6.0%

Q: "It is easier in these United States to walk away from a marriage than from a commitment to purchase a used car. Most contracts cannot be unilaterally abrogated; marriages in contemporary America can be terminated by practically anyone at any time, and without cause." Thomas Morgan
NOTE: The divorce rate among remarriages is held down by the fact of advancing age, which discourages marital dissolution.

During her long career conducting sociological research, Jessie Bernard provided evidence that marriage is something of a surprise for women. Taught to see marriage as a solution to life's problems, Bernard explained that many women who enter traditional marriages soon face problems they did not expect. Susan Pyzow's painting, Bridal Bouquet, *illustrates the idea.*

© Susan Pyzow, *Bridal Bouquet*, watercolor on paper, 10 × 13.5 in. Studio SPM Inc.

a woman's marriage and a man's marriage. Today, few marriages are composed of two equal partners. Patriarchy has weakened, but we still expect men to be older and taller than their wives and to have more prominent careers (McRae, 1986).

Why, then, do many people think that marriage benefits women more than men? (Bernard, 1982) The positive stereotype of the carefree bachelor contrasts sharply with the negative image of the lonely spinster, suggesting that women are fulfilled only by being wives and mothers.

But, Bernard claims, married women have poorer mental health, less happiness, and more passive attitudes toward life than single women. Married men, however, live longer than single men, are mentally better off, and report being happier. These differences suggest why, after divorce, men are more eager than women to find a new partner.

Bernard concludes that there is no better guarantor of long life, health, and happiness for a man than a woman well socialized to devote her life to taking care of him and providing the security of a well-ordered home. She is quick to add that marriage *could* be healthful for women if husbands did not dominate wives and expect them to perform virtually all the housework. Indeed, research confirms that husbands and wives with the best mental health share responsibilities for earning income, raising children, and keeping the home (Ross, Mirowsky, & Huber, 1983; Mirowsky & Ross, 1984).

TRANSITIONS AND PROBLEMS IN FAMILY LIFE

Ann Landers (1984), a well-known observer of the U.S. scene, once said that one marriage in twenty is wonderful, five in twenty are good, ten in twenty are tolerable, and the remaining four are "pure hell." Families can be a source of joy, but for some the reality falls far short of the ideal.

DIVORCE

U.S. society strongly supports marriage, and about nine out of ten people at some point "tie the knot." But many of today's marriages unravel. Figure 18–3 shows the tenfold increase in the U.S. divorce rate over the twentieth century. By 2000, more than four in ten marriages were ending in divorce (for African Americans, the rate was about six in ten). Ours is the highest divorce rate in the world: twice as high as the Canadian rate, four times as high as the Japanese, and ten times higher than in Italy (U.S. Census Bureau, 2000).

The high U.S. divorce rate has many causes (Thornton, 1985; Waite, Haggstrom, & Kanouse, 1985; Weitzman, 1985; Gerstel, 1987; Furstenberg & Cherlin, 1991; Etzioni, 1993; Popenoe, 1999):

1. **Individualism is on the rise.** Today's family members spend less time together. We have become more individualistic and more concerned

NOTE: Figure 18–3 illustrates the power of social forces in the individual decision to end a marriage: Besides climbing over the course of the century, divorce rates dropped during the Depression and rose rapidly at the end of World War II. Note, too, that the recent dip has a demographic component because the baby boomers are now passing 40, when divorce becomes less likely.

NOTE: California passed the first no-fault divorce law in 1969.
NOTE: The divorce rate may well ease downward in the future as the large baby-boomer cohort enters middle age, when divorce is less likely.
GLOBAL: Divorce rates for selected countries (1995; per 1,000 married women): U.S., 20; Sweden, 14; U.K., 13; Denmark, 12; Canada, 11; Germany, 9; Italy, 2 (U.S. Census Bureau, 1998).

with personal happiness than with the well-being of families and children.

2. **Romantic love often subsides.** Because our culture bases marriage on romantic love, relationships may fail when sexual passion fades. Many people end a marriage in favor of a new relationship that renews excitement and romance.

3. **Women are less dependent on men.** Marriage used to be an economic bond that provided support to partners, especially women. Increasing participation in the labor force has reduced wives' financial dependency on husbands. As a practical matter, then, women find it easier to leave unhappy marriages.

4. **Many of today's marriages are stressful.** With both partners working outside the home in most marriages, jobs leave less time and energy for family life. This makes raising children harder than ever. Children stabilize some marriages, but divorce is most common during the early years of marriage, when many couples have young children.

5. **Divorce is socially acceptable.** In past decades, marriage was upheld by cultural—and especially, religious—values. This is less true today. Divorce no longer carries the powerful stigma it did a century ago, and family and friends are now less likely to discourage couples in conflict from divorcing.

6. **Legally, a divorce is easier to get.** In the past, courts required divorcing couples to show that one or both were guilty of behavior such as adultery or physical abuse. Today, all states allow divorce if a couple simply thinks their marriage has failed. Surveys show that half of U.S. adults now think that a divorce should be harder to get (NORC, 2001:241).

Concern about easy divorce has led some states to consider rewriting their marriage laws. The box on page 480 explains.

Who Divorces?

At greatest risk of divorce are young spouses—especially those who marry after a brief courtship—with little money, who have yet to mature emotionally. The chance of divorce also rises if the couple marries after an unexpected pregnancy or if one or both partners have substance abuse problems. People whose parents

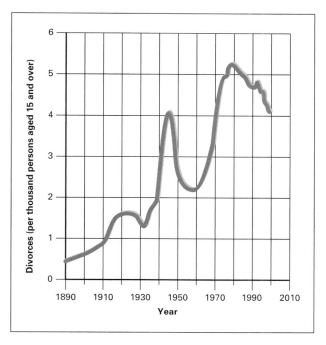

FIGURE 18–3 The Divorce Rate for the United States, 1890–2000
Sources: U.S. Census Bureau (2000) and U.S. National Center for Health Statistics (2001).

divorced also have a higher divorce rate themselves. Researchers suggest that a role-modeling effect is at work: Children who see parents go through divorce are more likely to consider divorce than those who have not had this experience (Amato, 2001). Finally, people who are not religious divorce more readily than those who are.

Divorce also is more common when both partners have successful careers, perhaps because of the strains of a two-career marriage but also because financially secure people do not feel compelled to stay in an unhappy home. Finally, men and women who divorce once are more likely to divorce again, presumably because problems follow them from one marriage to another (Booth & White, 1980; Yoder & Nichols, 1980; Glenn & Shelton, 1985).

Because mothers usually secure custody of children but fathers typically earn more income, the well-being of children often depends on fathers making court-ordered child-support payments. As Figure 18–4 on page 481 indicates, courts award child support in 56 percent of all divorces involving children. Yet in any

THEN AND NOW: Divorces per 1,000 marriages: *1970*, 328; *1998*, 488. Share of 30- to 34-year-old women not married: *1970*, 6.2; *1998*, 21.6%. Share of 30- to 34-year-old women who have not had a child: *1970*, 8.3%; *1998*, 27.4%.
Q: "For most [children of divorce], divorce was the most important cause of enduring pain and anomie in their lives." Judith S. Wallerstein and Sandra Blakeslee (1989)

DISCUSS: About $4 billion in court-ordered child support is unpaid in the U.S. each year. Is this problem caused by courts favoring mothers in custody disputes?
DIVERSITY: African American mothers are more likely than their white counterparts to receive child support, even holding fathers' income constant (Graham & Beller, 1996).

CRITICAL THINKING

Which Will It Be: Real Marriage or Marriage "Lite"?

"'Til death us do part," we say in the marriage vows. In reality, however, divorce is as likely as death to end today's marriages. Part of the reason is the no-fault divorce laws that were passed by all the states after the 1960s. Public opinion has turned, with half of people wanting to make divorces harder to get. Even so, no state has dropped the no-fault standard. But in 1997, Louisiana began offering not a new kind of divorce but a new kind of marriage (Walker, 1998).

The law in Louisiana, as well as Arizona (twenty other states are considering it), allows couples to choose a regular marriage or a *covenant* marriage. A covenant marriage requires both parties to agree that before they ever seek a divorce, they will turn to marital counseling. They also agree that they will not divorce unless one partner commits adultery, abandons the other for at least a year, becomes a drug or alcohol abuser, assaults the partner or a child, or is sent to prison for a serious crime. What spouses who select a covenant marriage cannot do is walk away from each other simply because they no longer want to stay married (Nock, Wright, & Sanchez, 1999).

Some people defend the covenant marriage law in the belief that it will bring down the high U.S. divorce rate. Some believe the law will make for better marriages: After all, if one partner balks at a covenant marriage, the other may well wonder why and reconsider the marriage.

However, critics claim that the new law will simply trap women and children in bad and perhaps abusive marriages. Then, too, the courts may end up filled with couples who are trying to escape their covenant bond. They point to early statistics showing that just a few percent of Louisiana's newlyweds are choosing covenant marriage as evidence that most people—even in marriage—want to keep their options open (Whelan, 1998).

What do you think?

1. *Do you think it is too easy for married couples to divorce? Why or why not?*

2. *Would you opt for a covenant marriage? Why or why not?*

3. *Should society try to keep people married who do not want to be? Why or why not?*

given year, more than half the children legally entitled to support receive only partial payments or no payments at all. Because some 2.5 million "deadbeat dads" fail to support their youngsters, federal legislation now mandates that employers withhold money from the earnings of parents who fail to pay up, and in 1998, refusing to make child-support payments or moving to another state to avoid making them became a felony (Weitzman, 1985; Waldman, 1992; Graham & Beller, 1996).

Divorce may be hardest on children. Divorce can tear young people from familiar surroundings, entangle them in bitter feuding, and distance them from a parent they love. Most seriously of all, many children blame themselves for their parents' breakup. For many children, divorce changes the course of their entire lives, causing emotional and behavioral problems and raising the risk of dropping out of school and getting into trouble with the law. Many experts counter that divorce is better for children than staying in a family torn by tension and violence. In any case, parents should remember that when couples think about divorce, more than their own well-being is at stake (Wallerstein & Blakeslee, 1989; Adelson, 1996; Popenoe, 1996; Cherlin, Chase-Lansdale, & McRae, 1998).

REMARRIAGE

Four out of five people who divorce remarry, most within five years. Nationwide, almost half of all marriages are now remarriages for at least one partner. Men, who derive greater benefits from wedlock, are more likely than women to remarry.

Remarriage often creates *blended families*, composed of children and some combination of biological parents and stepparents. Members of blended families thus have to define just who is part of the child's nuclear family. Adjustments are necessary: For example, an only child may suddenly find she has two older brothers. Nevertheless, blended families offer both young and old the opportunity to relax rigid family roles.

NOTE: Alan Booth and James Dabbs (1992) investigated records of 4,500 male veterans held by the Centers for Disease Control and found those with relatively high levels of testosterone were 50% less likely to marry than men in the low category. The high-testosterone men who married were 43% more likely to divorce, 38% more likely to have extramarital sex, and 12% more likely to abuse their wives. Conclude the researchers, "Testosterone has a consistent

negative relationship with getting and staying married and with multiple indicators of marital success."

Q: "It's ironic that in a world of commerce we have elaborate laws and contracts for insuring some protection and fairness in our financial dealings with one another, but to those we love most, we offer no such guarantees." Marcia Millman

FAMILY VIOLENCE

The ideal family is a source of pleasure and support. However, the disturbing reality of many homes is **family violence,** *emotional, physical, or sexual abuse of one family member by another.* Sociologist Richard J. Gelles calls the family "the most violent group in society with the exception of the police and the military" (quoted in Roesch, 1984:75).

Violence against Women

Family brutality often goes unreported to police. Even so, in 1999 the U.S. Bureau of Justice Statistics recorded more than 791,000 cases of violence between intimate partners. Of this total, 85 percent involved violence against women; the remaining 15 percent involved violence against men (U.S. Bureau of Justice Statistics, 2001). Thirty-two percent of women (but just 4 percent of men) who are victims of homicide are killed by spouses or, more often, ex-spouses. Nationwide, the death toll from family violence was 1,218 women in 1999. Overall, women are more likely to be injured by a family member than to be mugged or raped by a stranger or hurt in an automobile accident (Straus & Gelles, 1986; Schwartz, 1987; Shupe, Stacey, & Hazlewood, 1987; Blankenhorn, 1995).

Historically, the law defined wives as the property of their husbands, so that no man could be charged with raping his wife. Today, however, all states have enacted *marital rape laws.*

In the past, too, the law considered domestic violence a private, family matter, so victims had few options. Now, even without separation or divorce, a person can obtain court protection from an abusive spouse. Half the states have enacted stalking laws that prohibit an ex-partner from following or otherwise threatening someone. Finally, communities across the United States have established shelters to provide counseling and temporary housing for women and children driven from their homes by domestic violence.

Violence against Children

Family violence also victimizes children. In 1998, roughly 3 million cases of child abuse and neglect were reported; of these, about 1 million involved serious

The National Network for Child Care provides links to information on children's issues including abuse, literacy, and poverty: http://www.nncc.org/Maintitles/info.page.html

harm to children, including 1,100 deaths. Child abuse entails more than physical injury;

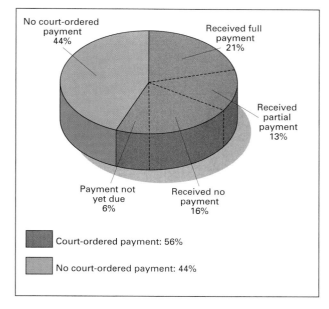

FIGURE 18–4 Payment of Child Support after Divorce

Source: U.S. Census Bureau (2000).

abusive adults misuse power and trust to damage a child's emotional well-being. Child abuse and neglect are most common among the youngest and most vulnerable children (Straus & Gelles, 1986; Van Biema, 1994; Besharov & Laumann, 1996; U.S. National Clearinghouse on Child Abuse and Neglect, 2000).

Child abusers are as likely to be women as men, and they conform to no simple stereotype. But most abusers do share one trait: having been abused themselves as children. Research shows that violent behavior in close relationships is learned; in families, then, violence begets violence (Widom, 1996; Browning & Laumann, 1997; Levine, 2001).

ALTERNATIVE FAMILY FORMS

Most families in the United States are still composed of a married couple who, at some point, raise children. But in recent decades, our society has displayed greater diversity in family life.

ONE-PARENT FAMILIES

Twenty-eight percent of U.S. families with children under eighteen have only one parent in the household,

THEN AND NOW: Number of teenage mothers: *1970*, 650,000; *1998*, 494,000. Although the numbers are down (fertility generally has decreased), the share of these who are unmarried has risen steadily and rapidly: In *1970*, 200,000 of 650,000 were unmarried; in *1998*, 391,000 of 494,000 were unmarried.

THEN AND NOW: In 1960, 17% of children under 18 lived without their biological fathers; today, the figure is 27% and rising.

NOTE: A Census Bureau study of the U.S. poor in 2000 found that 24.7% of people in female-headed households were poor vs. 4.7% of people in married-couple households. Of the chronic poor—people poor all year long—only 1.4% lived in married-couple households. Thus, one of the clearest predictors of whether a child will live in poverty is the marital status of the child's parents.

Not all marriages thrive "'til death us do part." The United States has the highest divorce rate in the world, with more than four in ten marriages ending because one or both partners want them to. The breakdown of communication that lies at the heart of failing relationships is clearly shown by Edward Hopper in his 1932 painting Room in New York.

Edward Hopper (1882–1967), *Room in New York*, 1932. Oil on canvas. 29 × 36 in. Sheldon Memorial Art Gallery, University of Nebraska–Lincoln. F. M. Hall Collection. 1932. H–166.

a proportion that more than doubled during the last generation. Put another way, 27 percent of U.S. children now live with only one parent, and about half will do so before reaching eighteen. One-parent families—78 percent of which are headed by a single mother—result from divorce, death, or an unmarried woman's decision to have a child. Figure 18–5 compares the share of U.S. births out of wedlock with those of other high-income nations.

Single parenthood increases a woman's risk of poverty because it limits her ability to work and to further her education. The converse is also true: Poverty raises the odds that a young woman will become a single mother (Trent, 1994). But single parenthood goes well beyond the poor because at least one-third of women in the United States become pregnant as unmarried teenagers, and many decide to raise their children themselves, whether they marry or not. Looking back to Figure 18–2, note that 54 percent of African American families are headed by a single parent. Single parenting is less common among Hispanics (32 percent), non-Hispanic whites (19 percent), and Asian Americans (19 percent). In many single-parent families, mothers turn to their own mothers for support. In the United States, then, the rise in single parenting is tied to a declining role for fathers and the growing importance of grandparenting.

Research shows that growing up in a one-parent family usually disadvantages children. Some studies claim that because a father and mother each make distinctive contributions to a child's social development, it is unrealistic to expect one parent alone to do as good a job. But the most serious problem for one-parent families, especially if that parent is a woman, is poverty. On average, children growing up in a single-parent family start out poorer, get less schooling, and end up with lower incomes as adults. Such children are also more likely to be single parents themselves (Wallerstein & Blakeslee, 1989; Astone & McLanahan, 1991; Li & Wojtkiewicz, 1992; Biblarz & Raftery, 1993; Popenoe, 1993a; Blankenhorn, 1995; Shapiro & Schrof, 1995; Webster, Orbuch, & House, 1995; Wu, 1996; Duncan et al., 1998; Kantrowitz & Wingert, 2001).

COHABITATION

Cohabitation is *the sharing of a household by an unmarried couple.* The number of cohabiting couples in the United States increased from about 500,000 in 1970 to about 5.5 million today (4.9 million heterosexual

NOTE: In 1992, *The Star Tribune* in Minneapolis became the first newspaper to list gay "domestic partnerships" on the wedding page.
NOTE: In the first year after Vermont's gay union law, 80% of the licenses went to nonresidents of the state.
NOTE: In 2000, about 60% of gay families and 45% of lesbian families lived in the largest 20 U.S. cities, which contained 26% of the overall U.S. population (Bianchi & Casper, 2000).

GLOBAL: Denmark legalized homosexual activity in 1930. Half the U.S. states still have laws restricting homosexual behavior (just as many outlaw adultery). The Danes, Norwegians, and Swedes allow gay and nongay couples equal rights with regard to marriage, inheritance, taxation, and property ownership but not with regard to adoption of children.

couples and 0.6 million homosexual couples), or about 10 percent of all couples (Miller, 1997b; U.S. Census Bureau, 2001).

In global perspective, cohabitation as a long-term form of family life, with or without children, is common in Sweden and other Scandinavian nations. But it is rare in more traditional (and Roman Catholic) nations such as Italy. Cohabitation is gaining in popularity in the United States, with almost half of people between ages twenty-five and forty-four having cohabited at some point. In addition, a rising share of cohabiting couples—already more than one-third—includes at least one child under eighteen (Blumstein & Schwartz, 1983; Macklin, 1983; Gwartney-Gibbs, 1986; Popenoe, 1988, 1991, 1992; Bumpass & Sweet, 1995; Raley, 1996).

Cohabiting tends to appeal to more independent-minded individuals and those who favor gender equality (Brines & Joyner, 1999). Most couples cohabit for no more than a few years, with about half then deciding to marry and half ending the relationship. Mounting evidence suggests that living together may actually discourage marriage because partners become used to low-commitment relationships. Furthermore, when cohabiting couples with children separate, the involvement of both parents—including financial support—is far from certain (Popenoe & Whitehead, 1999; Smock, 2000).

 For research reports on cohabitation and other intimate relationships, visit the Web site of The Marriage Project at Rutgers University: http://marriage.rutgers.edu

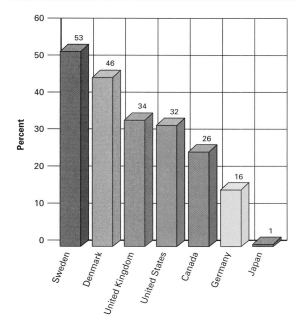

FIGURE 18–5 Percentage of Births to Unmarried Women, 1995

Source: U.S. Census Bureau (1998).

GAY AND LESBIAN COUPLES

In 1989, Denmark became the first country to lift its legal ban on same-sex marriages. This change extended social legitimacy to gay and lesbian couples and equalized advantages in inheritance, taxation, and joint property ownership. Norway (in 1993), Sweden (1995), and the Netherlands (2001) have followed suit. In 1996, however, the U.S. Congress passed a law banning gay marriage. Homosexual marriage is also illegal in all fifty states, although Vermont and Hawaii, as well as a number of major cities (including San Francisco, New York, and also Ontario, Canada), confer limited marital benefits on gay and lesbian couples.

Most of the U.S. gay couples with children are raising the offspring of previous, heterosexual unions; some couples have adopted children. But many gay parents are quiet about their sexual orientation, not wanting to draw unwelcome attention to their children. Moreover, in several widely publicized cases, courts have removed children from homosexual couples, citing the best interests of the children.

Gay parenting challenges many traditional ideas. But it also confirms that many gay people want to form families just as heterosexuals do (Bell, Weinberg, & Kiefer-Hammersmith, 1981; Gross, 1991; Pressley & Andrews, 1992; Henry, 1993).

SINGLEHOOD

Because nine out of ten people in the United States marry, we tend to see singlehood as a transitory stage of life. In recent decades, however, more people have deliberately chosen to live alone. In 1950, only one household in ten consisted of a single person. By 2000, this

SOCIAL SURVEY: "Methods of birth control should be available to teenagers between the ages of 14 and 16 if their parents do not approve." (GSS 2000, *N* = 1,877; *Codebook*, 2001:240)

"Strongly agree"	28.0%	"Strongly disagree"	20.2%
"Agree"	29.8%	DK/NR	2.7%
"Disagree"	19.3%		

For better or worse, the family is certainly changing. But the fact that young people still find marriage so attractive— even amid the most severe adversity—suggests that families will continue to play a central role in society for centuries to come.

proportion had risen to one in four, a total of 27 million single adults (U.S. Census Bureau, 2001).

Most striking is the rising number of single young women. In 1960, 28 percent of U.S. women aged twenty to twenty-four were single; by 2000, the proportion had soared to 75 percent. Underlying this trend is women's greater participation in the labor force. Women who are economically secure consider a husband a matter of choice rather than a financial necessity. In other words, a growing number of working women are not willing to "settle" just to get married (Edwards, 2000).

By midlife, however, many unmarried women sense a lack of available men. Because we expect a woman to "marry up," the older a woman is, the more education she has, and the better her job, the more difficulty she has finding a suitable husband (Leslie & Korman, 1989).

NEW REPRODUCTIVE TECHNOLOGY AND THE FAMILY

Recent medical advances involving *new reproductive technology* are changing families, too. A generation ago, England's Louise Brown became the world's first "test-tube baby"; since then, tens of thousands of children have been conceived this way. Within a decade, 2 or 3 percent of births in high-income nations may be the result of new reproductive technologies.

Test-tube babies are the products of *in vitro fertilization*, whereby doctors unite a woman's egg and a man's sperm "in glass" rather than in a woman's body. When successful, the doctor implants the resulting embryo in the womb of the woman who is to bear the child or freezes it for use at a later time.

At present, new reproductive technologies help some couples who cannot conceive normally to have children. These techniques eventually may help reduce the incidence of birth defects as genetic screening of sperm and eggs allows medical specialists to increase the odds of having a healthy baby. But new reproductive technology also raises fascinating and troubling questions: When one woman carries an embryo made from the egg of another, who is the mother? When a couple divorces, which spouse is entitled to use the frozen embryos? Can one partner later have a child against the will of the other? Such questions remind us that technology changes faster than our capacity to understand its uses and consequences (Thompson, 1994; Cohen, 1998; Nock, Wright, & Sanchez, 1999).

LOOKING AHEAD: THE FAMILY IN THE TWENTY-FIRST CENTURY

Family life in the United States will continue to change—and change causes controversy. In the case of the family, advocates of "traditional family values" line up against those who support greater personal choice; the final box on pages 486–87 sketches some of the issues. Sociologists cannot predict the outcome of this debate, but we can suggest five likely future trends.

First, divorce rates are likely to remain high, even in the face of evidence that marital breakups harm children. At the same time, bear in mind that today's marriages are no less durable than they were a century ago, when many were cut short by death (Kain, 1990). The difference is that more couples now *choose* to end marriages that fail to live up to their expectations. Thus, although the divorce rate has recently stabilized, it is unlikely to return to the low rates that marked the early decades of the twentieth century.

Second, family life in the twenty-first century will be highly variable. Cohabiting couples, one-parent families, gay and lesbian families, and blended families are all on the increase. Most families are still based on marriage, and most married couples still have children. But, taken together, the variety of family forms reveals a trend toward more personal choice.

Third, men will continue to play a limited role in child rearing. In the 1950s, a decade many people see as the "golden age" of families, men began to withdraw from active parenting (Snell, 1990; Stacey, 1990). In recent years, a small countertrend, the "stay-at-home dad," is evident, with some older, highly educated fathers of young children staying at home yet remaining active in their careers by using computer technology. But

Here is a resource Web site for stay-at-home fathers: http://www.slowlane.com

they represent no more than 15 percent of fathers with preschool children (Gardner, 1996). The bigger picture is that with the high U.S. divorce rate and the surge in single motherhood, more children are growing up with weak ties to fathers. At the same time, the evidence is building that the absence of fathers is harmful to children, at the very least because such families are at high risk of being poor.

Fourth, we will continue to feel the effects of economic changes in our families (Hochschild & Machung, 1989). In most homes, both household partners work, rendering marriage the interaction of weary men and women who try to squeeze in a little "quality time" for themselves and their children (Dizard & Gadlin, 1990). Two-career couples may advance the goal of gender equality, but the long-term effects on families as we have known them are likely to be mixed.

Fifth and finally, the importance of new reproductive technology will increase. Ethical concerns about whether what *can* be done *should* be done will surely slow these developments, but new forms of reproduction will continue to alter the traditional experience of parenthood.

Despite the changes and controversies that have buffeted the family in the United States, most people still report being happy as partners and parents. Marriage and family life will remain a foundation of our society for some time to come.

SUMMARY

1. All societies are built on kinship, although family forms vary across cultures and over time.

2. In industrial societies such as the United States, marriage is monogamous. Many preindustrial societies permit polygamy, of which there are two types: polygyny and polyandry.

3. In global perspective, patrilocality is most common, whereas industrial societies favor neolocality and a few societies have matrilocal residence. Industrial societies use bilateral descent, whereas preindustrial societies are either patrilineal or matrilineal.

4. Structural-functional analysis identifies major family functions: socialization of the young, regulation of sexual activity, social placement, and material and emotional support.

5. Social-conflict theories explore how the family perpetuates social inequality by transmitting divisions based on class, ethnicity, race, and gender from one generation to the next.

6. Micro-level analysis highlights the variety of family life as experienced by various family members.

7. Courtship leads to the formation of families. Romantic love is central to mate selection in the United States but not in much of the world. Even in this country, moreover, romantic love usually joins people with similar social backgrounds.

8. The vast majority of married couples have children, although family size has decreased over time. The main reason for this decline is industrialization, which transforms children into economic liabilities, encourages women to acquire an education and join the labor force, and reduces infant mortality.

9. Married life changes as children leave home to form families of their own. However, many middle-aged

CONTROVERSY & DEBATE

Should We Save the Traditional Family?

What are "traditional families"? Are they vital to our way of life or a barrier to progress? To begin, people use the term "traditional family" to mean a married couple who, at some point in their lives, raise children. Statistically speaking, traditional families are less common than they used to be. In 1950, as the figure shows, 90 percent of U.S. households were families: two or more people related by blood, marriage, or adoption. By 2000, just 68 percent of households were families because of rising levels of divorce, cohabitation, and singlehood.

Of course, "traditional family" is more than just a term; it is also a moral statement. That is, belief in the traditional family implies putting a high value on becoming and remaining married, placing children ahead of careers, and favoring two-parent families over various "alternative lifestyles."

On one side of the debate, David Popenoe warns that there has been a serious erosion of the traditional family since 1960. Then, married couples with young children accounted for almost half of all households; today, the figure is 24 percent. Singlehood is up, from 10 to 26 percent of present households.

The divorce rate has doubled since 1960, so that almost half of today's marriages will end in permanent separation. Moreover, because of both divorce and out-of-wedlock births, the share of youngsters who will live with a single parent before age eighteen has quadrupled since 1960, to 50 percent. In other words, just one in four of

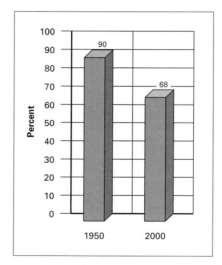

Share of U.S. Households That the Census Bureau Classifies as Families, 1950 and 2000

today's children will grow up with two parents and go on to maintain a stable marriage as an adult.

In light of such data, Popenoe concludes, it may not be an exaggeration to say that the family is falling apart. He sees a fundamental shift from a "culture of marriage" to a "culture of divorce." Traditional vows of marital commitment—" 'til death us do part"—now amount to little more than "as long as I am happy." Daniel Yankelovich (1994:20) sums it up this way:

> The quest for greater individual choice clashed directly with the obligations and social norms that held families and communities together in earlier years. People came to feel that questions of how to live and with whom to live were a matter of individual choice not to be governed by restrictive norms. As a nation, we came to experience the bonds of marriage, family, children, job, community, and country as constraints that were no longer necessary. Commitments have loosened.

The negative consequences of the cultural trend toward weaker families, Popenoe continues, are obvious and

couples care for aging parents, and many older couples are active grandparents. The final transition in marriage begins with the death of one's spouse, usually the husband.

10. Families differ according to class position, race, and ethnicity. For example, Hispanic families are more likely than others to maintain extended kinship ties. African American families are more likely than others to be headed by single women. Among all

categories of people, well-to-do families enjoy the most options and greatest financial security.

11. Gender affects family dynamics because husbands dominate in most marriages. Research suggests that marriage has more benefits for men than for women.

12. The divorce rate today is ten times what it was a century ago; at least four in ten current marriages will end in divorce. Most people who divorce—especially

Q: "An ideological concept that imposes mythical homogeneity on the diverse means by which people organize their intimate relationships, 'the family' distorts and devalues the rich variety of kinship stories. And, along with the class, racial, and heterosexual prejudices it promulgates, this sentimental fictional plot authorizes gender hierarchy." Judith Stacey (1990:269–70)

Q: "Marriage is a long, dull meal with the dessert at the beginning." Henri de Toulouse-Lautrec

NOTE: Hollywood, never keen on presenting traditional families, continues this trend in 2000's shows: *The Geena Davis Show* (cohabiting couple with kids), *Titus* (dysfunctional father and son), *Normal, Ohio* (gay father, estranged son), and *Gilmore Girls* (32-year-old mom living with 16-year-old daughter) (Poniewozik, 2000).

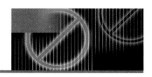

can be found everywhere: As we pay less and less attention to children, the juvenile crime rate goes up along with a host of other troublesome behaviors such as underage smoking and drinking and premarital sex.

As Popenoe sees it, then, we must act quickly and work hard to reverse current trends. Government cannot be the solution and may even be part of the problem: Since 1960, as government spending on social programs has soared fivefold, families have become weaker and weaker. Instead, says Popenoe, we need a cultural turnaround. We must replace our "me-first" attitudes in favor of commitment to our spouse and children. Such a switch is entirely possible, he continues; just look at how attitudes toward smoking have changed in recent decades. We can save the traditional family in two steps: first, by publicly affirming the value of staying married and, second, by endorsing the two-parent family as best for the well-being of children.

But Judith Stacey is unconvinced. She says "good riddance" to the traditional family and provides a counterpoint. To her, the traditional family is more problem than solution. Striking to the heart of the matter, Stacey writes (1990:269),

The family is not here to stay. Nor should we wish it were. On the contrary, I believe that all democratic people, whatever their kinship preferences, should work to hasten its demise.

The main reason for rejecting the traditional family is that it perpetuates social inequality, Stacey explains. Families play a key role in maintaining the class hierarchy, transferring wealth and "cultural capital" from one generation to another. Moreover, feminists criticize the traditional family's patriarchal form, which subjects women to their husbands' authority and saddles them with most of the responsibility for housework and child care. From a gay rights perspective, she adds, a society that values traditional families inevitably denies homosexual men and women equal participation in social life.

Stacey thus applauds the breakdown of the family as social progress. She does not consider the family a necessary social institution but rather a political construct that elevates one category of people—affluent white males—at the expense of others, including women, homosexuals, and poor people.

Stacey also claims that the concept of "traditional family" is increasingly irrelevant in a diverse society where both men and women work for income. What our society needs, Stacey concludes, is not a return to some "golden age" of the family but political and economic change, including income parity for women, universal health care and child care, programs to reduce unemployment, and expanded sex education in the schools. Only with such programs can we support our children and ensure that people in diverse family forms receive the respect everyone deserves.

Continue the debate . . .

1. *To strengthen families, David Popenoe suggests that parents put children ahead of their own careers by limiting their joint work week to sixty hours. Do you agree? Why or why not?*

2. *Judith Stacey thinks that marriage is weaker today because women are rejecting patriarchal relationships. What do you think about this argument?*

3. *Do we need to change family patterns for the well-being of our children? As you see it, what specific changes are called for?*

Sources: Popenoe (1993a), Stacey (1990, 1993), and Council on Families in America (1995).

men—remarry, often forming blended families that include children from previous marriages.

13. Most family violence victimizes women and children and is far more common than official records indicate. Most adults who abuse family members were themselves abused as children.

14. Our society's family life is becoming more varied. One-parent families, cohabitation, gay and lesbian couples, and singlehood have proliferated in recent years. Although the law does not recognize homosexual marriages, many gay men and lesbians form long-lasting relationships and increasingly are becoming parents.

15. Although ethically controversial, new reproductive technology is changing conventional ideas of parenthood.

KEY CONCEPTS

family (p. 463) a social institution found in all societies that unites people in cooperative groups to oversee the bearing and raising of children

kinship (p. 463) a social bond based on blood, marriage, or adoption

family unit (p. 464) a social group of two or more people, related by blood, marriage, or adoption, who usually live together

marriage (p. 464) a legally sanctioned relationship, usually involving economic cooperation as well as sexual activity and childbearing, that people expect to be enduring

extended family (consanguine family) (p. 464) a family unit that includes parents and children as well as other kin

nuclear family (conjugal family) (p. 464) a family unit composed of one or two parents and their children

endogamy (p. 465) marriage between people of the same social category

exogamy (p. 465) marriage between people of different social categories

monogamy (p. 465) marriage that unites two partners

polygamy (p. 465) marriage that unites three or more people

polygyny (p. 465) marriage that unites one male and two or more females

polyandry (p. 465) marriage that unites one female and two or more males

patrilocality (p. 465) a residential pattern in which a married couple lives with or near the husband's family

matrilocality (p. 465) a residential pattern in which a married couple lives with or near the wife's family

neolocality (p. 465) a residential pattern in which a married couple lives apart from both sets of parents

descent (p. 465) the system by which members of a society trace kinship over generations

patrilineal descent (p. 465) a system tracing kinship through men

matrilineal descent (p. 466) a system tracing kinship through women

bilateral descent (p. 466) a system tracing kinship through both men and women

incest taboo (p. 467) a norm forbidding sexual relations or marriage between certain relatives

homogamy (p. 472) marriage between people with the same social characteristics

infidelity (p. 473) sexual activity outside marriage

family violence (p. 481) emotional, physical, or sexual abuse of one family member by another

cohabitation (p. 482) the sharing of a household by an unmarried couple

CRITICAL-THINKING QUESTIONS

1. Identify several changes in the family since 1960. What factors are responsible for these changes?

2. A rising number of companies are extending marital benefits (such as health insurance) to unmarried gay partners. Do you approve of this trend? Why or why not? Should companies also extend benefits to cohabiting heterosexual partners?

3. Do you think that single-parent households do as good a job as two-parent households in raising children? Why or why not?

4. On balance, are families in the United States becoming weaker or simply different? What evidence can you cite?

APPLICATIONS AND EXERCISES

1. Parents and grandparents can be a wonderful source of information about changes in marriage and the family. Spend an hour or two with married people of two different generations and ask about when they married, what their married lives have been like, and what changes in family life today stand out for them.

2. Relationships with various family members differ. With which family member—mother, father, brother, sister—do you most readily and least readily share secrets? Why? Which family member would you turn to first in a crisis? Why?

3. Organize a debate for one class period with one team arguing each side of the "family values controversy." Present arguments for and against the statement: "Resolved: The traditional family is necessary for the survival of our country's way of life."

4. Packaged in the back of this new textbook is an interactive CD-ROM that offers a variety of study and review materials intended to help you better understand the material covered in this chapter. For this chapter, the CD-ROM contains an author's tip video, Real Life Sociology videos, other relevant audio and video, interactive map animations, audio journal entries from the author, Web links, and much more.

 SITES TO SEE

http://www.prenhall.com/macionis

Visit the interactive *Companian Website*™ that accompanies this text. Begin by clicking on the cover of your book. You will find a chapter-by-chapter study guide, practice tests, and a significant portion of the text for on-line review as well as many suggested Web links.

http://www.frc.org

This is the Web address for the Family Research Council, a conservative organization supporting what it calls "traditional family values." What does the council consider a "traditional family"? What values does it defend? Why? Are there family problems that it ignores?

http://www.redthreadmag.com

This site provides information about cross-cultural adoptions—specifically, the experiences of people in the United States adopting young girls from China.

http://childstats.gov

This is the site for the Federal Interagency Forum on Child and Family Statistics, which compiles information from eighteen government agencies.

http://www.polyamorysociety.org

Survey the increasing diversity of family life at the Web site for the Polyamory Society. What do you make of the society's views of family life?

 INVESTIGATE WITH CONTENTSELECT

Follow the instructions found on page 23 of this textbook to enter this chapter of the book's *Companion Website*™. Once in the chapter, click on the ContentSelect icon at the bottom left of your screen and enter your personal User ID and Password. Enter keywords such as "family values," "cohabitation," and "new reproductive technology," and the search engine will help you become an effective researcher.

CHAPTER

19

William Penhallow Henderson (1877–1943)
Feast Day: San Juan Pueblo (New Mexico), ca. 1924

Smithsonian American Art Museum,
Washington, D.C./Art Resource, N.Y.

RELIGION

A warm July wind blows through the open windows of the white-steepled New England church as it has this time of year for three centuries, since the Puritans settled the town of Chelmsford, Massachusetts. Many in the congregation slowly fan themselves with the worship program as they wait for the service to begin. Like Puritans of times past, these are conservative people, men and women who believe in prayer and follow a strict code of conduct, even abstaining from alcohol. Then their voices rise together, declaring, "God is great!" But these New Englanders are speaking Arabic: "Allah-u

Akhbar!" Muslims make up an increasing share of this Yankee town, as they do in communities all across the United States.

According to the most recent count, there are now between 7 and 10 million Muslims in the United States—more, in fact, than there are Episcopalians, Presbyterians, or Jews. In fact, Muslims in this nation now outnumber Mormons, Quakers, Unitarians, Seventh-Day Adventists, Christian Scientists, and Jehovah's Witnesses combined. As some see it, after Christianity, Islam is this country's second religion (adapted from Blank, 1998).

The names, languages, and rituals may change, but religion has always held a central part in U.S. society. This chapter explains what religion is, explores the changing face of religious belief throughout history and around the world, and examines the vital yet sometimes controversial place of religion in today's modern, scientific culture.

 Here is a new report on Muslims in the United States from the Council on American-Islamic Relations: http://www.cair-net.org/mosquereport/

RELIGION: BASIC CONCEPTS

The French sociologist Emile Durkheim stated that religion involves "things that surpass the limits of our knowledge" (1965:62; orig. 1915). As human beings, we define most objects, events, and experiences as **profane** (from Latin, meaning "outside the temple"), *that which people define as an ordinary element of everyday life.* But we define some things as **sacred,** *that which people set apart as extraordinary, inspiring a sense of awe and reverence.* Distinguishing the sacred from the profane is the essence of all religious belief. **Religion,** then, is *a social institution involving beliefs and practices based on a conception of the sacred.*

A global perspective reveals great variety in matters of faith, with nothing sacred to everyone on Earth. Although people regard most books as profane, Jews believe the Torah (the first five books of the Hebrew Bible or Old Testament) is sacred, in the same way that Christians revere the Old and New Testaments of the Bible and Muslims exalt the Qur'an (Koran).

But no matter how a community of believers draws religious lines, Durkheim (1965:62) explained, people understand profane things in terms of their everyday usefulness: We log onto the Web with our computer or turn a key to start our car. What is sacred we reverently set apart from everyday life and denote as "forbidden." Marking the boundary between the sacred and the profane, for example, Muslims remove their shoes before entering a mosque to avoid defiling a sacred place with soles that touch the profane ground outside.

The sacred is embodied in **ritual,** *formal, ceremonial behavior.* Holy communion is the central ritual of Christianity; to the Christian faithful, the wafer and wine consumed during communion are not treated in a profane way as food but as the sacred symbols of the body and blood of Jesus Christ.

491

SUPPLEMENTS: An outline for this chapter, supplemental lecture material, and suggested discussion topics are provided in the *Data File*.

Q: "Sociologists have a hard time coming to terms with the intensely religious character of the contemporary world. Whether politically on the left or not, they suffer from ideological blinders when it comes to religion, and the tendency is to explain away what cannot be explained. But, ideology apart, parochialism is an important factor here too. Sociologists live in truly secularized milieus—academia and the other institutions of the professional knowledge industry—and it appears that they are no more immune than the sociologically untrained to the common misconception that one can generalize about the world from one's own little corner." Peter Berger (1992:15–16)

Religion is founded on the concept of the sacred: that which is set apart as extraordinary and which demands our submission. Bowing, kneeling, or prostrating oneself are all ways of symbolically surrendering to a higher power. This monk is performing an act of prostration circumambulation, a complicated way of saying that he falls flat on the ground every few steps as he moves around a holy shrine. In this way, he expresses his complete surrender to his faith.

RELIGION AND SOCIOLOGY

Because religion deals with ideas and truth that transcend everyday experience, neither sociology nor any other scientific discipline can verify or disprove religious doctrine. Religion is a matter of **faith,** *belief anchored in conviction rather than scientific evidence.* The New Testament of the Bible, for instance, describes faith as "the assurance of things hoped for, the conviction of things not seen" (Heb. 11:1) and exhorts Christians to "walk by faith, not by sight" (2 Cor. 5:7).

Some people with strong faith may be disturbed by the thought of sociologists turning a scientific eye to what they hold sacred. However, a sociological study of religion poses no threat to anyone's faith. Sociologists study religion just as they study the family: to understand religious experiences around the world and how religion is tied to other social institutions. They make no judgments that a specific religion is right or wrong. Rather, scientific sociology takes a more worldly approach by delving into why religions take particular forms in one society or another and how religious activity affects society as a whole.

THEORETICAL ANALYSIS OF RELIGION

Sociologists have applied various theoretical paradigms to the study of religion. Each provides distinctive insights into the way religion shapes social life.

FUNCTIONS OF RELIGION: STRUCTURAL-FUNCTIONAL ANALYSIS

According to Durkheim (1965; orig. 1915), society has an existence and power of its own beyond the life of any individual. In other words, society itself is "godlike," surviving the death of its members, whose lives it shapes. Thus, people engage in religious life to celebrate the awesome power of their society.

No wonder, then, that people around the world transform certain everyday objects into sacred symbols of their collective life. Members of technologically simple societies do this with the **totem,** *an object in the natural world collectively defined as sacred.* The totem—perhaps an animal or an elaborate work of art—becomes the centerpiece of ritual, symbolizing the power of collective life over any individual. In our society, the flag is a quasi-sacred totem. It is not to be used in a profane manner (say, as clothing) or allowed to touch the ground.

Similarly, putting the inscription "In God We Trust" on all currency (a practice begun in the 1860s, at the time of the Civil War) implies that our society is bound by common beliefs. Local communities across the United States also create a sense of unity through totemic symbolism attached to sports teams, from the New England Patriots, to the Ohio State University Buckeyes, to the San Francisco 49ers.

Why is the religious dimension of social life so important? Durkheim pointed out three major functions of religion for the operation of society:

DISCUSS: Is the naming of sports teams an element of totemic symbolism in the U.S.? Honoring ancestors: Washington Redskins, Cleveland Indians, Atlanta Braves, Kansas City Chiefs, Pittsburgh Pirates, Dallas Cowboys, Philadelphia 76ers; honoring animals: Denver Broncos, Miami Dolphins, Detroit Tigers, Chicago Cubs, Baltimore Orioles.

NOTE: The Latin root of "religion" is *religare*, "to be tied back," suggesting the link between religion and tradition.
Q: "In everyday life it is just as important that some things can be silently taken for granted as that some things are reaffirmed in so many words. Indeed, the most fundamental assumptions about the world . . . are so 'obvious' that there is no need to put them into words." Peter Berger

1. **Social cohesion.** Religion unites people through shared symbolism, values, and norms. Religious thought and ritual establish rules of fair play that make organized social life possible.

2. **Social control.** Every society uses religious ideas to promote conformity. Societies give many cultural norms—especially mores that deal with marriage and reproduction—religious justification. Religion even legitimizes the political system. Although few of today's politicians claim to rule by divine right (as they did centuries ago), many publicly ask for God's blessing, implying to audiences that their efforts are right and just.

3. **Providing meaning and purpose.** Religious belief offers the comforting sense that our brief lives serve some greater purpose. Strengthened by their faith, people are less likely to despair when one of life's calamities strikes. For this reason, we mark major life course transitions—including birth, marriage, and death—with religious observances.

Critical evaluation. In Durkheim's structural-functional analysis, religion represents the collective life of society. The major weakness of this approach, however, is that it downplays religion's dysfunctions, especially the fact that strongly held beliefs can generate social conflict. During the early Middle Ages, for example, religious faith was the driving force behind the Crusades—the battles between European Christians and Muslims over the Holy Land, which both religions considered sacred. Conflict between Muslims, Jews, and Christians is still a source of political instability in the Middle East today. Similarly, tensions continue to divide Protestants and Catholics in Northern Ireland, and religious conflict persists in Algeria, India, Sri Lanka, and elsewhere. In short, many nations have marched to war under the banner of their God; in fact, few doubt that religious beliefs have provoked more violence in human history than differences in social class.

CONSTRUCTING THE SACRED: SYMBOLIC-INTERACTION ANALYSIS

From a symbolic-interaction point of view, religion (like all of society) is socially constructed (although perhaps with divine inspiration). Through various rituals—from daily prayers to annual religious observances such as Easter and Passover—individuals sharpen the distinction between the sacred and profane. Furthermore, as Peter Berger (1967:35–36)

explains, placing our fallible, brief lives within some "cosmic frame of reference" gives us "the semblance of ultimate security and permanence."

Marriage is a good example. If two people look on marriage as merely a contract, they can walk away whenever they want. But defined as holy matrimony, their bond makes far stronger claims on each of them. Indeed, the more religious people are, the less likely they are to divorce. More generally, whenever humans confront uncertainty or life-threatening situations—such as illness, war, and natural disaster—we turn to our sacred symbols.

Critical evaluation. Following the symbolic-interaction approach, religion puts everyday life under a "sacred canopy" of meaning (Berger, 1967). Of course, Berger adds, the sacred's ability to give meaning and stabilize society requires that people ignore its constructed character. After all, how much strength could we derive from beliefs we saw as mere strategies for coping with tragedy? Also, this micro-level analysis ignores religion's link to social inequality, to which we now turn.

INEQUALITY AND RELIGION: SOCIAL-CONFLICT ANALYSIS

The social-conflict paradigm highlights religion's support of social hierarchy. Religion serves ruling elites by legitimizing the status quo and diverting people's attention from social inequities, Karl Marx proclaimed.

Even today, for example, the British monarch is the formal head of the Church of England, showing the close alliance between religious and political elites. In practical terms, working for political change may mean opposing the church and, by implication, God. Religion also encourages people to look hopefully to a "better world to come," minimizing the social problems of this world. In a well-known statement, Marx dismissed religion as "the sigh of the oppressed creature, the sentiment of a heartless world, and the soul of soulless conditions. It is the opium of the people" (1964b:27; orig. 1848).

Religion and social inequality are also linked through gender. Virtually all the world's major religions are patriarchal, as the box on pages 494–95 explains.

For centuries, the powerful Christian nations of Western Europe justified the conquest of Africa, the Americas, and Asia by claiming that they were "converting heathens." In the United States, churches in

DIVERSITY: RACE, CLASS, AND GENDER

Religion and Patriarchy: Does God Favor Males?

Why do two-thirds of U.S. adults envision God as father rather than mother (NORC, 2001:144)? Probably because we link "godly" attributes such as wisdom and power to men. Thus, it is hardly surprising that organized religions tend to favor males, a fact evident in passages from the sacred writings of major world religions.

The Qur'an (Koran), the sacred text of Islam, stipulates that men dominate women:

> Men are in charge of women. . . . Hence good women are obedient. . . . As for those whose rebelliousness you fear, admonish them, banish them from your bed, and scourge them. (quoted in Kaufman, 1976:163)

Christianity, the major religion of the Western world, also supports patriarchy. Although many Christians revere Mary, the mother of Jesus, the New Testament also includes the following passages:

> A man . . . is the image and glory of God; but woman is the glory of man. For man was not made from woman, but woman from man.

Neither was man created for woman, but woman for man. (1 Cor. 11:7–9)

> As in all the churches of the saints, the women should keep silence in the churches. For they are not permitted to speak, but should be subordinate, as even the law says. If there is anything they desire to know, let them ask their husbands at home. For it is shameful for a woman to speak in church. (1 Cor. 14:33–35)

> Wives, be subject to your husbands, as to the Lord. For the husband is the head of the wife as Christ is the head of the church. . . . As the church is subject to Christ, so let wives also be subject in everything to their husbands. (Eph. 5:22–24)

the South believed enslaving African Americans was consistent with God's will. To this day, churches across the country remain segregated. In the words of African American author Maya Angelou, "Sunday at 11:30 A.M., America is more segregated than at any other time of the week."

Critical evaluation. Social-conflict analysis reveals the power of religion to legitimize social inequality. Yet religion also promotes change toward equality. For example, nineteenth-century religious groups in the United States were at the forefront of the movement to abolish slavery. During the 1950s and 1960s, religious organizations led by the Reverend Martin Luther King, Jr. and others formed the core of the civil rights movement. During the 1960s and 1970s, many clergy actively opposed the Vietnam War, and, as will be explained, some support revolutionary change in Latin America and elsewhere.

RELIGION AND SOCIAL CHANGE

Religion is not just the conservative force portrayed by Karl Marx. At some points in history, as Max Weber (1958; orig. 1904–5) noted, religion has promoted dramatic social transformation.

MAX WEBER: PROTESTANTISM AND CAPITALISM

Max Weber contended that new ideas often are engines of change. It was the religious doctrine of Calvinism, for example, that sparked the Industrial Revolution in Western Europe.

As Chapter 4 ("Society") explains in detail, John Calvin (1509–1564), a leader in the Protestant Reformation, preached the doctrine of predestination. According to Calvin, an all-powerful and all-knowing God predestined some people for salvation but condemned most

SOCIAL SURVEY: "Where would you place your image of God on the scale [between (1) Mother and (7) Father]?" (GSS 1998, *N* = 1,445; *Codebook*, 2001:144)

(1) 2.9%   (4) 24.5%   (7) 47.1%
(2) 1.1%   (5) 8.2%   DK/NR 4.4%
(3) 2.1%   (6) 9.6%

Q: "[Rationalization] means that principally there are no mysterious,

incalculable forces that come into play, but rather that one can, in principle, master all things by calculation." Max Weber

NOTE: The movement of women into the clergy has lagged behind their entry into law and medicine (Chaves, 1996).

DIVERSITY: The proportion of women serving as clergy in Protestant denominations ranges from 14% for Presbyterians to 35% for Unitarians.

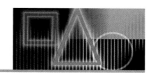

Let a woman learn in silence with all submissiveness. I permit no woman to teach or to have authority over men; she is to keep silent. For Adam was formed first, then Eve; and Adam was not deceived, but the woman was deceived and became a transgressor. Yet woman will be saved through bearing children, if she continues in faith and love and holiness, with modesty. (1 Tm. 2:11–15)

Judaism also traditionally supports patriarchy. Male Orthodox Jews say the following as part of their daily prayers:

Blessed art thou, O Lord our
    God, King of the Universe, that
    I was not born a gentile.
Blessed art thou, O Lord our
    God, King of the Universe, that
    I was not born a slave.
Blessed art thou, O Lord our
God, King of the Universe, that
I was not born a woman.

Major religions have also excluded women from the clergy. Even today, Islam and the Roman Catholic church ban women from the priesthood, as do about half of Protestant denominations. But a growing number of Protestant religious organizations, including the Church of England, ordain women, who now represent 15 percent of U.S. clergy. Orthodox Judaism upholds the traditional prohibition against women serving as rabbis, but Reform and Conservative Judaism look to both men and women as spiritual leaders. Across the United States, the proportion of women in seminaries has never been higher (now roughly one-third), further evidence that change is ongoing (Chaves, 1996, 1997; Nesbitt, 1997).

Challenges to the patriarchal structure of organized religion—from

ordaining women to gender-neutral language in hymnals and prayers—have sparked heated controversy between progressives and traditionalists. Propelling these developments is a lively feminism in many religious communities. According to feminist Christians, for example, patriarchy in the church stands in stark contrast to the largely feminine image of Jesus Christ in the Scriptures as "nonaggressive, noncompetitive, meek and humble of heart, a nurturer of the weak and a friend of the outcast" (Sandra Schneiders, quoted in Woodward, 1989:61).

Feminists argue that unless traditional notions of gender are removed from our understanding of God, women will never be equal to men in the church. The theologian Mary Daly puts the matter bluntly: "If God is male, then male is God" (quoted in Woodward, 1989:58).

to eternal damnation. Each person's fate, sealed before birth and known only to God, is either eternal glory or endless hellfire.

Driven by anxiety over their fate, Calvinists understandably sought evidence of God's favor and gradually came to regard prosperity as a sign of divine blessing. Religious conviction and a rigid sense of duty led Calvinists to work all the time, and many amassed great wealth. But money was not for self-indulgent spending or for sharing with the poor, whose plight they saw as a mark of God's rejection. As agents of God's work on Earth, Calvinists believed that they best fulfilled their calling by reinvesting profits and reaping ever-greater success in the process.

All the while, Calvinists lived thrifty lives and embraced technological advances, thereby laying the groundwork for the rise of industrial capitalism. In time, the religious fervor that motivated early Calvinists weakened, leaving a profane "Protestant work

ethic." To Max Weber, industrial capitalism was a "disenchanted" religion. Weber's analysis clearly shows the power of religious thinking to alter the basic shape of society.

LIBERATION THEOLOGY

Christianity has a long-standing concern for poor and oppressed people, urging all to strengthen their faith in a better life to come. In recent decades, however, some church leaders and theologians have endorsed **liberation theology,** *a fusion of Christian principles with political activism, often Marxist in character.*

This social movement started in the late 1960s in Latin America's Roman Catholic church and continues today with Christian activists working to liberate people in poor nations from abysmal poverty. The message of liberation theology is simple: Social oppression runs counter to Christian morality, so as a matter of faith and justice, Christians must promote greater social equality.

Despite its Roman Catholic beginnings, Pope John Paul II condemns liberation theology for distorting traditional church doctrine with left-wing politics. But over the pontiff's objections, the liberation theology movement remains powerful in Latin America, where many people find that their Christian faith drives them to improve conditions for the world's poor (Boff & Boff, 1984; Neuhouser, 1989; Rowland, 1999).

TYPES OF RELIGIOUS ORGANIZATION

Sociologists categorize the hundreds of different religious organizations found in the United States along a continuum, with *churches* at one end and *sects* at the other. We can describe any existing religious organization in relation to these two ideal types by locating it on the church-sect continuum.

CHURCH

Drawing on the ideas of his teacher Max Weber, Ernst Troeltsch (1931) defined a **church** as *a type of religious organization that is well integrated into the larger society.* Churchlike organizations usually persist for centuries and include generations of the same families. Churches have well-established rules and regulations and expect their leaders to be formally trained and ordained.

Though concerned with the sacred, a church tries to fit in with the profane world, which gives it broad appeal. The religious doctrine of a church conceives of God in highly intellectualized terms (say, as a force for good), and favors abstract moral standards ("Do unto others as you would have them do unto you") over specific rules for day-to-day living. By teaching morality in safely abstract terms, church leaders avoid social controversy. For example, many congregations may celebrate the unity of all peoples but nevertheless have all-white memberships. Such duality minimizes conflict between a church and political life (Troeltsch, 1931).

December 11, Casablanca, Morocco. The waves of the Atlantic crash along the walls of Casablanca's magnificent coastline mosque, reputedly the largest in the world. From the top of the towering structure, a green laser cuts through the night sky, pointing eastward to Mecca, the holy city of Islam toward which the faithful bow in prayer. To pay for this monumental house of worship, King Hassam II, Morocco's head of state and religious leader, levied a tax on every citizen in his realm, all of whom are officially Muslim. This example of government religion contrasts sharply with our ideas about the separation of church and state.

A church may operate with or apart from the state. A **state church** is *a church formally allied with the state,* as illustrated by Islam in Morocco. State churches have existed throughout human history; for centuries Roman Catholicism was the official religion of the Roman Empire, as was Confucianism in China until early in the twentieth century. Today, the Anglican church is the official Church of England, as Islam is the official religion of Pakistan and Iran. State churches count everyone in the society as members, a practice that severely limits tolerance of religious difference.

A **denomination,** by contrast, is *a church, independent of the state, that accepts religious pluralism.* Denominations exist in nations that formally separate church and state, such as the United States, which has dozens of Christian denominations—including Catholics, Baptists, Methodists, and Lutherans—as well as various categories of Judaism, Islam, and other traditions. Members of a denomination hold to their own beliefs, but they accept the right of others to disagree.

SECT

The second general religious form is the **sect,** *a type of religious organization that stands apart from the larger society.* Sect members have rigid religious convictions and deny the beliefs of others. Generally, to members of a sect, religion is not just one aspect of life but a firm plan for how to live. In some cases, then, members of a sect may withdraw completely from society in order to practice their religion without interference. The Amish are one example of a North American sect that isolates itself (Kraybill, 1994). Because our culture holds up religious tolerance as a virtue, members of sects are sometimes accused of being narrow-minded in insisting that they alone follow the true religion.

In organizational terms, sects are less formal than churches. Thus, sect members are often highly spontaneous and emotional in worship, whereas members of churches tend to listen passively to their leader. Sects also reject the intellectualized religion of churches, stressing instead the personal experience of divine power. Rodney Stark (1985:314) contrasts a church's vision of a distant God ("Our Father, who art in Heaven") with a sect's more immediate God ("Lord, bless this poor sinner kneeling before you now.")

A further distinction between church and sect turns on patterns of leadership. The more churchlike an organization, the more likely that its leaders are formally trained and ordained. Sectlike organizations, which celebrate the personal presence of God, expect their leaders to exhibit divine inspiration in the form of **charisma** (from the Greek term meaning "divine favor"), *extraordinary personal qualities that can turn an audience into followers*, infusing them with an emotional experience.

Sects generally form as breakaway groups from established religious organizations (Stark & Bainbridge, 1979). Their psychic intensity and informal structure render them less stable than churches, and many sects blossom only to disappear soon after. The sects that do endure typically become more like churches, losing fervor as they become more bureaucratic and established.

To sustain their membership, many sects actively recruit, or *proselytize*, new members. Sects highly value the experience of *conversion*, a personal transformation or religious rebirth. Jehovah's Witnesses, for example, eagerly share their faith with others in hopes of attracting new members.

Finally, churches and sects differ in their social composition. Because they are more closely tied to the world, well-established churches tend to include people of high social standing. By contrast, sects attract more disadvantaged people. A sect's openness to new members and its promise of salvation and personal fulfillment appeal to people who may perceive themselves as social outsiders.

CULT

A **cult** is *a religious organization that is largely outside a society's cultural traditions*. Whereas most sects spin off from a conventional religious organization, a cult typically forms around a highly charismatic leader who offers a compelling message of a new and very different way of life. As many as 5,000 cults exist in the United States (Marquand & Wood, 1997).

In global perspective, the range of religious activity is truly astonishing. Members of this Southeast Asian cult show their devotion to God by suspending themselves in the air using ropes and sharp hooks that pierce their skin.

Because some cult principles or practices are unconventional, the popular view is that they are deviant or even evil. The deaths of more than eighty cult members in Waco, Texas, in 1993 and the suicides of thirty-nine members of California's Heaven's Gate cult in 1997—people who claimed that dying was a doorway to a higher existence, perhaps in the company of aliens from outer space—confirmed the public's negative image of most cults. In short, say some scholars, calling any religious community a "cult" amounts to dismissing its members as crazy (Richardson, 1990; Shupe, 1995; Gleick, 1997).

Typically, societies with simple technology are animistic, meaning they recognize divine power in the elements of the natural world, such as the animals they hunt for food. This painting, located in the Lascaux caves in France, was created some 17,000 years ago.

The popular view of cults is unfortunate because there is nothing intrinsically wrong with this kind of religious organization. Many long-standing religions—Christianity, Islam, and Judaism included—began as cults. Of course, not all or even most cults exist for very long. One reason is that they are even more at odds with the larger society than sects. Many cults demand that members not only accept their doctrine but embrace a radically new lifestyle. Such lifestyle changes sometimes prompt others to accuse cults of brainwashing their members, although research suggests that most people who join cults experience no psychological harm (Barker, 1981; Kilbourne, 1983).

RELIGION IN HISTORY

Religion shapes social life everywhere in the world. Like other social institutions, religion shows wide variation both historically and cross-culturally.

RELIGION IN PREINDUSTRIAL SOCIETIES

Religion is older than written history. Archaeological evidence indicates that our human ancestors performed religious rituals some 40,000 years ago. Early hunters and gatherers embraced **animism** (from the Latin term meaning "the breath of life"), *the belief that elements of the natural world are conscious life forms that affect humans.* Animistic people view forests, oceans, mountains, and even the wind as spiritual forces. Many Native American societies are animistic, which accounts for their historical reverence for the natural environment. Although hunters and gatherers might have singled out someone as a *shaman* with special religious skills, there were no full-time religious leaders.

Among pastoral and horticultural people, there arose a belief in a single divine power responsible for creating the world. The popular conception of God as a shepherd should be no surprise because Christianity, Judaism, and Islam had their beginnings among pastoral peoples.

In agrarian societies, religion becomes more important, with a specialized priesthood in charge of religious organizations. The centrality of religion is evident in the huge cathedrals that dominated towns in medieval Europe.

RELIGION IN INDUSTRIAL SOCIETIES

The Industrial Revolution ushered in a growing emphasis on science. More and more, people looked to physicians and scientists for the knowledge and comfort they had sought from priests.

Even so, religion continues because science is powerless to address issues of ultimate meaning in human life. In other words, learning *how* the world works is a matter for scientists, but *why* we and the rest of the universe exist at all is a question for religion to answer.

WINDOW ON THE WORLD

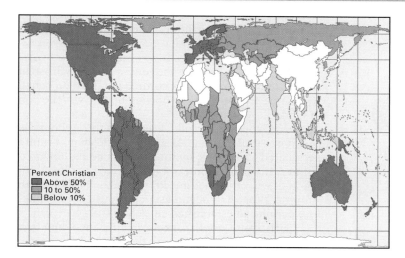

GLOBAL MAP 19–1
Christianity in Global Perspective

Source: *Peters Atlas of the World* (1990).

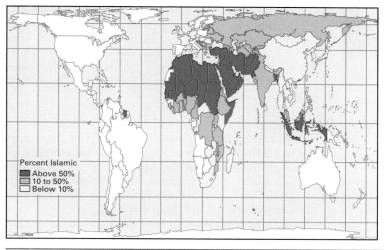

GLOBAL MAP 19–2
Islam in Global Perspective

Source: *Peters Atlas of the World* (1990).

WORLD RELIGIONS

The diversity of religious expression in the world is almost as wide ranging as the diversity of culture itself. Many of the thousands of different religions are highly localized with few followers. *World religions*, by contrast, are widely known and have millions of adherents. We shall briefly describe six world religions, which together claim 4 billion believers, representing fully three-fourths of humanity.

CHRISTIANITY

Christianity is the most widespread religion, with 2 billion followers, roughly one-third of the world's people. Most Christians live in Europe or the Americas; more than 85 percent of the people in the United States and Canada identify with Christianity. Moreover, as shown in Global Map 19–1, people who are at least nominally Christian represent a large share of the population in many other world regions, with the notable exceptions

NOTE: Although Judaism and Christianity are both monotheistic religions, they may have polytheistic origins. In the original Hebrew, the accounts of creation in Genesis used plural pronouns ("Then God said, Let us make man in our image" 1:26), leading scholars to speculate that the religion evolved from polytheistic roots.

NOTE: Literal interpretation of the sacred texts of any religion sharply limits debate among adherents about religious truth, thereby fostering consensus. But literal readings may still reveal inconsistencies; for example, there are *two* creation stories in Genesis.

DIVERSITY: Muslims hold the Qur'an (Koran) to be the literal words of God. For this reason, even translation from Arabic into other languages raises fears of distortion.

RESOURCE: The article by Jane I. Smith, "Women and Islam," is among the cross-cultural selections in the *Seeing Ourselves* reader.

Many religions promote literacy because they demand followers study sacred texts. As part of their upbringing, most Islamic parents teach their children lessons from the Qur'an (Koran); later, the children will do the same to a new generation of believers.

of northern Africa and Asia. European colonization spread Christianity throughout much of the world over the last 500 years. Its dominance in the West is shown by the fact that the calendar begins by marking the birth of Christ.

Christianity originated as a cult, incorporating elements of its much older predecessor, Judaism. Like most cults, Christianity was propelled by the personal charisma of a leader, Jesus of Nazareth, who preached a message of personal salvation. Jesus did not directly challenge the political powers of his day, admonishing his followers to "render therefore to Caesar things that are Caesar's" (Matt. 22:21). But his message was revolutionary nonetheless, promising that faith and love would triumph over sin and death.

Christianity is one example of **monotheism,** *belief in a single divine power,* and it thus broke with the Roman Empire's traditional **polytheism,** *belief in many gods.* Yet

Christianity has a unique vision of the Supreme Being as a sacred Trinity: God the Creator; Jesus Christ, Son of God and Redeemer; and the Holy Spirit, a Christian's personal experience of God's presence.

The claim that Jesus was divine rests on accounts of his final days on Earth. Tried and sentenced to death in Jerusalem on charges that he was a threat to established political leaders, Jesus was executed by crucifixion. Therefore, the cross became a sacred Christian symbol. Three days later, according to Christian belief, Jesus arose from the dead, showing that he was the Son of God.

Jesus' apostles spread Christianity throughout the Mediterranean region. At first, the Roman Empire persecuted Christians; by the fourth century, however, Christianity had become a state church, the official religion of what then became known as the Holy Roman Empire. What had begun as a cult four centuries before became an established church.

Christianity took various forms, including the Roman Catholic church and the Orthodox church, based in Constantinople (now Istanbul, Turkey). Toward the end of the Middle Ages, the Protestant Reformation in Europe created hundreds of new denominations. Dozens of these denominations—the Baptists and Methodists are the two largest—now command large followings in the United States (Smart, 1969; Kaufman, 1976; Jacquet & Jones, 1991).

ISLAM

Islam has some 1.2 billion followers (about 20 percent of humanity); followers of Islam are called Muslims. A majority of people in the Middle East are Muslims, which explains our tendency to associate Islam with Arabs in that region of the world. But most Muslims live elsewhere: Global Map 19–2 on page 499 shows that most people in northern Africa and Indonesia are also Muslims. Moreover, significant concentrations of Muslims are found in Western Asia in Pakistan, India, Bangladesh, and the southern republics of the former Soviet Union. As noted in the opening to this chapter, there are 7 to 10 million Muslims in North America, making Islam a significant part of religious life in the United States (Weeks, 1988; University of Akron Research Center, 1993; Blank, 1998).

Islam is the word of God as revealed to Muhammad, who was born in the city of Mecca (now in Saudi Arabia) about the year 570. To Muslims, Muhammad is a prophet, not a divine being as Jesus is to Christians. The Qur'an (Koran), sacred to Muslims, is the word of God (in Arabic, 'Allah') as transmitted

GLOBAL: Note that religion is a less pronounced element of U.S. culture than it is in an officially Islamic society such as Morocco. (The U.S. is more like Turkey, which has no official religion and, although 98% of the population is Muslim, many are not actively religious.)
Q: "The strong secular bias of the West has made it virtually impossible for it to understand the values of any modern society which is resolutely religious." Roy Enquist de Gruchy

NOTE: Jews also look to the Talmud (composed of the Mishnah [text] and Gemorrah [commentary]) for explicit guidance in everyday life.
NOTE: The ancient Hebrews distinguished the sacred and the secular through keeping the Sabbath, dietary restrictions, and maintaining holy places.

through Muhammad, God's messenger. In Arabic, the word "Islam" means both "submission" and "peace," and the Qur'an urges submission to Allah as the path to inner peace. Muslims express this personal devotion in ritual prayers five times a day.

Islam spread rapidly after the death of Muhammad, although divisions arose, as they did within Christianity. However, all Muslims accept the Five Pillars of Islam: (1) recognizing Allah as the one, true God and Muhammad as God's messenger; (2) ritual prayer; (3) giving alms to the poor; (4) fasting during the month of Ramadan; and (5) making a pilgrimage at least once to the Sacred House of Allah in Mecca (Weeks, 1988; El-Attar, 1991). Like Christianity, Islam holds people accountable to God for their deeds on Earth. Those who live obediently will be rewarded in heaven, and evildoers will suffer unending punishment.

Muslims are also obligated to defend their faith, which has led to holy wars against unbelievers (in roughly the same way that medieval Christians fought in the Crusades). Recently, in Afghanistan, Algeria, Egypt, Iran, and elsewhere, some fundamentalist Muslims have sought to rid their society of Western influences that they consider morally wrong (Martin, 1982; Arjomand, 1988).

To many Westerners, Muslim women are among the most socially oppressed people on Earth. Of course, Muslim nations differ in this regard: For example, Tunisia allows women far more opportunities than, say, Saudi Arabia (Ganley, 1998). In general, however, Muslim women lack many of the personal freedoms enjoyed by Muslim men, yet many—and perhaps most—accept the mandates of their religion and find security in a system that guides the behavior of both women and men (S. Peterson, 1996). Muslims also point out that patriarchy was well established in the Middle East long before the birth of Muhammad, and some defenders argue that Islam actually improved the social position of women by requiring that husbands deal justly with their wives. Furthermore, although Islam permits a man to have up to four wives, it admonishes men to have only one wife if having more would cause him to treat any woman unjustly (Qur'an, "The Women," v. 3).

JUDAISM

Simply in terms of numbers, Judaism's total of 15 million followers worldwide makes it something less than a world religion. Moreover, only in Israel do Jews represent a national majority. But Judaism has special significance to the United States because the largest concentration of Jews (6 million people) is found in North America.

Jews look to the past as a source of guidance in the present and for the future. Judaism has deep historical roots that extend some 4,000 years before the birth of Christ to the ancient cultures of Mesopotamia. At this time, Jews were animistic, but this belief changed after Jacob—grandson of Abraham, the earliest great ancestor—led his people to Egypt.

Jews endured centuries of slavery in Egypt. In the thirteenth century B.C.E., Moses, the adopted son of an Egyptian princess, was called by God to lead the Jews from bondage. This exodus (this word's Latin and Greek roots mean "a marching out") from Egypt is commemorated by Jews today in the annual ritual of Passover. Once liberated, Jews became monotheistic, recognizing a single, all-powerful God.

A distinctive concept of Judaism is the *covenant*, a special relationship with God by which Jews became the "chosen people." The covenant also implies a duty to observe God's law, especially the Ten Commandments as revealed to Moses on Mount Sinai. Jews regard the Old Testament of the Bible as both a record of their history and a statement of the obligations of Jewish life. Of special importance are the Bible's first five books (Genesis, Exodus, Leviticus, Numbers, and Deuteronomy), designated the *Torah* (a word roughly meaning "teaching" and "law"). In contrast to Christianity's central concern with personal salvation, therefore, Judaism emphasizes moral behavior in this world.

Judaism has three main denominations. Orthodox Jews (including more than 1 million people in the United States) strictly observe traditional beliefs and practices, wear traditional dress, segregate men and women at religious services, and eat only kosher foods. Such traditional practices set off Orthodox Jews in the United States as the most sectlike. In the mid-nineteenth century, many Jews sought greater acceptance by the larger society, leading to the formation of more churchlike Reform Judaism (now including more than 1.3 million people in this country). A third segment, Conservative Judaism (with about 2 million adherents), has since established a middle ground between the other two denominations.

Whatever their denomination, Jews share a history of prejudice and discrimination. A collective memory of centuries of slavery in Egypt, conquest by Rome, and persecution in Europe has shaped Jewish identity. It was Jews in Italy who first lived in an urban ghetto (derived from the Italian word *borghetto*, meaning "settlement outside of the city walls"), and this residential segregation soon spread to other parts of Europe.

WINDOW ON THE WORLD

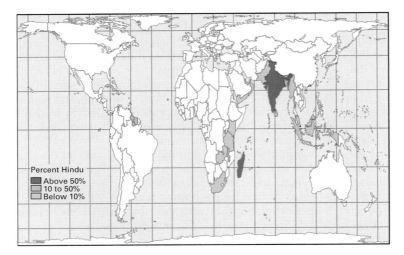

GLOBAL MAP 19–3
Hinduism in Global Perspective

Source: *Peters Atlas of the World* (1990).

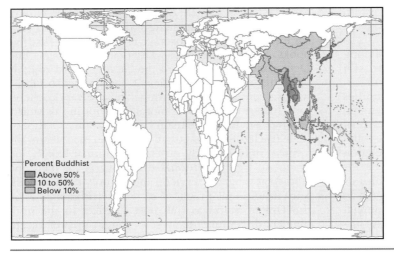

GLOBAL MAP 19–4
Buddhism in Global Perspective

Source: *Peters Atlas of the World* (1990).

Jewish immigration to the United States began in the mid-1600s. Many early immigrants prospered, and many were also assimilated into largely Christian communities. But as larger numbers entered the country toward the end of the nineteenth century, prejudice and discrimination against them—commonly called *anti-Semitism*—increased. During World War II, anti-Semitism reached a vicious peak as the Nazi regime in Germany systematically annihilated 6 million Jews.

On average, Jews have prospered, with social standing well above average. Still, many Jews are concerned about the future of their religion because in recent years more than half the Jews in the United States have married non-Jews. In only a few cases are non-Jewish spouses converting to Judaism. Just as significantly, about half the children raised in Jewish households are not learning Jewish culture and ritual. For the present, such patterns symbolize Jewish success in gaining acceptance into society. At the same

GLOBAL: One could say that, to the Hindu, nothing is sacred or everything is sacred.

NOTE: The diffusion of religious elements usually is selective. For instance, in the 1960s many young people in the U.S. adopted the Hindu concepts of *dharma* (fate) and *karma* (spiritual progression of souls) while scorning the caste system historically associated with Hinduism.

DIVERSITY: By 1990, chaplains in the U.S. armed forces represented 105 religious organizations, including 1 Buddhist chaplain (some 2,500 military personnel are adherents of this religion).

NOTE: Buddhism's "eightfold path" to enlightenment includes proper views, resolve, speech, action, livelihood, effort, mindfulness, and concentration.

time, however, they cast some doubt on the future of Judaism in North America (Bedell, Sandon, & Wellborn, 1975; Holm, 1977; Schmidt, 1980; Seltzer, 1980; B. Wilson, 1982; Eisen, 1983; Dershowitz, 1997; Van Biema, 1997a).

HINDUISM

Hinduism is the oldest of all the world religions, originating in the Indus River valley about 4,500 years ago. Hindus number some 800 million (14 percent of humanity). Global Map 19–3 shows that Hinduism remains an Eastern religion, practiced mostly in India and Pakistan but with a significant presence in southern Africa and Indonesia.

Over the centuries, Hinduism and the culture of India have become intertwined, so that now one is not easily described apart from the other (although India also has a sizable Muslim population). This connection also explains why Hinduism, unlike Christianity, Islam, and Judaism, has not diffused widely to other nations. Nevertheless, with 1.4 million followers in the United States, Hinduism is a significant part of this country's cultural diversity.

Hinduism differs from most other religions by not being linked to the life of any single person. Hinduism also has no sacred writings comparable to the Bible or the Qur'an. Nor does Hinduism envision God as a specific entity. For this reason, Hinduism—like other Eastern religions, as we shall see—is sometimes described as an ethical religion. Hindu beliefs and practices vary widely, but all Hindus recognize a moral force in the universe that presents everyone with responsibilities, called *dharma*. For example, dharma calls people to observe the traditional caste system, described in Chapter 10 ("Social Stratification").

Another Hindu principle, *karma*, is a belief in the spiritual progress of the human soul. To a Hindu, all actions have spiritual consequences, and proper living contributes to moral development. Karma works through *reincarnation*, a cycle of death and rebirth by which the individual is reborn into a spiritual state corresponding to the moral quality of a previous life. Unlike Christianity and Islam, Hinduism proclaims no ultimate judgment at the hands of a supreme god, although in the cycle of rebirth, people reap what they have sown. *Moksha* is the state of spiritual perfection: When a soul reaches this level, it is no longer reborn.

Hinduism stands as evidence that not all religions can be neatly labeled monotheistic or polytheistic. Hinduism is monotheistic insofar as it envisions the universe as a single moral system, yet Hindus see this

The spiritual leader of Tibetan Buddhism is the Dalai Lama, shown here teaching a large assembly of followers. For more information on the Dalai Lama, go to http://www.dalailama.com

moral order at work in every element of nature. Moreover, many Hindus participate in public rituals, such as the *Kumbh Mela*, which every twelve years brings some 20 million pilgrims to the sacred Ganges River to bathe in its purifying waters. At the same time, Hindus practice private devotions, which vary from village to village across the vast nation of India.

Elements of Hindu thought have characterized some cults in the United States over the years, but Hinduism is still unfamiliar to most Westerners. Nonetheless, like religions better known to us, Hinduism is a powerful force offering both explanation and guidance in life (Pitt, 1955; Sen, 1961; Embree, 1972; Kaufman, 1976; Schmidt, 1980).

BUDDHISM

Twenty-five hundred years ago, the rich culture of India also gave rise to Buddhism. Today some 350 million people (6 percent of humanity) are Buddhists,

GLOBAL SNAPSHOT

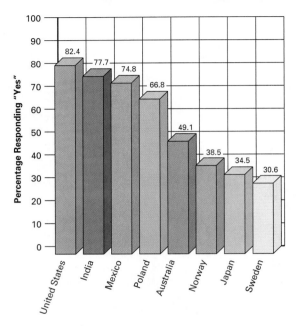

FIGURE 19–1 Religiosity in Global Perspective

Survey Question: "Do you gain comfort and strength from religion?"

Source: Inglehart et al. (2000).

almost all of whom are Asians. As shown in Global Map 19–4, Buddhists make up more than half the populations of Myanmar (Burma), Thailand, Cambodia, and Japan; Buddhism is also widespread in India and the People's Republic of China. Of the world religions considered so far, Buddhism most resembles Hinduism in doctrine, but, like Christianity, its inspiration stems from the life of one person.

Siddhartha Gautama was born to a high-caste family in Nepal about 563 B.C.E. As a young man, he was preoccupied with spiritual matters. At age twenty-nine, he underwent a radical personal transformation and set off for years of travel and meditation. His journey ended when he achieved what Buddhists describe as *bodhi*, or enlightenment. Understanding the essence of life, Gautama became a Buddha.

Energized by his personal charisma, followers spread Buddha's teachings—the *dhamma*—across India.

In the third century B.C.E., the ruler of India became a Buddhist and sent missionaries throughout Asia, making Buddhism a world religion.

Buddhists believe that much of life involves suffering. This idea is rooted in the Buddha's own travels in a society rife with poverty. But the solution to suffering is not wealth, Buddha claimed. On the contrary, materialism limits spiritual development. Instead, Buddha taught that we must transcend our selfish concerns and desires through meditation, with the goal of obtaining *nirvana*, a state of enlightenment and peace.

Buddhism closely parallels Hinduism in recognizing no god of judgment, yet each daily action has spiritual consequences. Another similarity is a belief in reincarnation. Here, again, only enlightenment ends the cycle of death and rebirth and finally liberates a person from the suffering of the world (Schumann, 1974; Thomas, 1975; Van Biema, 1997b).

CONFUCIANISM

From about 200 B.C.E. until the beginning of the twentieth century, Confucianism was a state church, the official religion of China. A dramatic change took place after the 1949 Revolution when the communist government of the new People's Republic of China vigorously repressed religion. Today, although officials provide no precise count, hundreds of millions of Chinese are still influenced by Confucianism. Almost all Confucianists live in China, although Chinese immigration has spread this religion to other nations in Southeast Asia. Perhaps 100,000 followers of Confucius live in North America.

Confucius or, more properly, K'ung Fu-tzu, lived between 551 and 479 B.C.E. Like Buddha, Confucius was deeply concerned about people's suffering. The Buddha's response was a sectlike spiritual withdrawal from the world; By contrast, Confucius instructed his followers to engage the world according to a code of moral conduct. Thus it was that Confucianism became fused with the traditional culture of China. Here we see a second example of what might be called a national religion: As Hinduism has remained largely synonymous with Indian culture, Confucianism is enshrined in the Chinese way of life.

A central concept of Confucianism is *jen*, meaning "humaneness." In practice, this means that we must always subordinate our self-interest to moral principle. In the family, the individual must be loyal and considerate. Families also must remain mindful of their duties toward the larger community. In this way, layer upon layer of moral obligation integrates society as a whole.

SOCIAL SURVEY: "How close do you feel to God most of the time?" (GSS 1989, N = 1,006; *Codebook*, 2001:140)
"Extremely close" 28.9% "Not close at all" 6.4%
"Somewhat close" 52.3% "Does not believe in God" 2.1%
"Not very close" 8.8% DK/NR 1.5%

Most of all, Confucianism stands out as lacking a clear sense of the sacred. Recalling Durkheim's analysis, we might view Confucianism as the celebration of the sacred character of society itself. Or we might argue that Confucianism is less a religion than a model of disciplined living. Certainly the historical dominance of Confucianism helps explain why Chinese culture is skeptical of the supernatural. But even as a disciplined way of life, Confucianism shares with religion a body of beliefs and practices that have as their goal goodness, concern for others, and social harmony (Kaufman, 1976; Schmidt, 1980; McGuire, 1987).

RELIGION: EAST AND WEST

This overview of world religions points up two general differences between the belief systems of Eastern and Western societies. First, Western religions (Christianity, Islam, Judaism) typically are deity-based, with a clear focus on God. However, Eastern religions (Hinduism, Buddhism, Confucianism) tend to be ethical codes; therefore, they make a less clear-cut distinction between what is sacred and what is secular.

Second, believers in Western religions form congregations. That is, people join an organization and worship formally in groups at a specific time and place. By contrast, Eastern religions are informally fused with culture itself. For this reason, for example, a visitor finds a Japanese temple filled with both tourists and worshipers, who come and go as they please and pay little attention to those around them.

But these two distinctions do not overshadow the common element of all religions: a conception of a higher moral force or purpose that transcends individualism and the concerns of everyday life. Although they take different paths, all religions give people a spiritual sense that their lives can serve some larger purpose.

 For information on various religions, visit http://www.adherents.com

RELIGION IN THE UNITED STATES

In global perspective, the United States is a relatively religious nation. As Figure 19–1 shows, eight in ten members of our society say they gain "comfort and strength from religion," a substantially higher share than in most other high-income countries.

That said, scholars debate exactly how religious this nation is. Whereas some claim that religion is central to our way of life, others conclude that a decline

TABLE 19–1 Religious Identification in the United States, 2000	
Religion	**Percentage Indicating Preference**
Protestant denominations	**56.2%**
Baptist	20.6
Methodist	9.3
Lutheran	5.4
Presbyterian	3.4
Episcopalian	1.9
All others or no denomination	15.6
Catholic	**25.1**
Jewish	**2.3**
Other or no answer	**1.7**
No religious preference	**14.7**

Source: *General Social Surveys, 1972–2000: Cumulative Codebook* (Chicago: National Opinion Research Center, 2001), pp. 129–30.

of the traditional family and the advancing role of science and technology are undermining religious commitment and faith (Collins, 1982; Greeley, 1989; Woodward, 1992a; Hadaway, Marler, & Chaves, 1993).

RELIGIOUS AFFILIATION

Most people in the United States identify with a religion. On national surveys, 85 percent of U.S. adults claim a religious preference (NORC, 2001:129). Table 19–1 shows that more than half of U.S. adults consider themselves Protestants, one-fourth are Catholics, and 2 percent Jews. Significant numbers of people also adhere to dozens of other religions, from animism to Zen Buddhism, making our society as religiously diverse as any on Earth.

About 60 percent consider themselves a member of some religious organization, and 90 percent say they had at least some formal religious instruction growing up (NORC, 2001:373–74). National Map 19–1 on page 506 shows the share of people who claim to belong to any church across the United States.

National Map 19–2 takes us one more step, showing that the religion most people identify with varies by region. New England and the Southwest are predominantly Catholic, the South is overwhelmingly Baptist, and in the northern Plains states, Lutherans predominate. In and around Utah, there is a heavy concentration of members of the Church of Jesus Christ of Latter Day Saints (Mormons).

THE MAP1: High church membership characterizes the Mormon region of Utah, the South and Southwest (where fundamentalism and Hispanic immigrants are marked), and the Plains states (where there is a high percentage of small-town elderly people).

THE MAP2: Immigration (of Lutherans to the upper Midwest) and migration (of Mormons to Utah) shaped much of the religious diversity of the U.S.

SOCIAL SURVEY: "Where would you place your feelings about your faith?" (GSS 1988, *N* = 1,481; *Codebook*, 2001:380)
(1) "My faith is completely free of doubts" 27.1%
(2) 18.0%
(3) 15.5%
(4) 16.3%
(5) 9.3%

SEEING OURSELVES

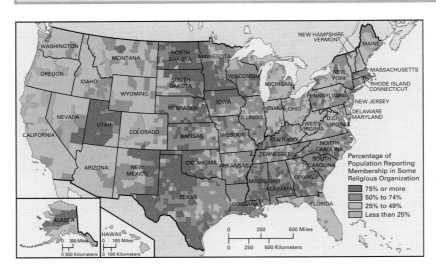

NATIONAL MAP 19–1
Religious Membership across the United States

In general, people in the United States are more religious than people in other high-income nations. Yet membership in a religious organization is more common in some parts of the country than in others. What pattern do you see in the map? Can you explain the pattern?

Source: From Rodger Doyle, *Atlas of Contemporary America*. Map copyright © 1994 by Facts on File, Inc. Reprinted with the permission of Facts on File, Inc.

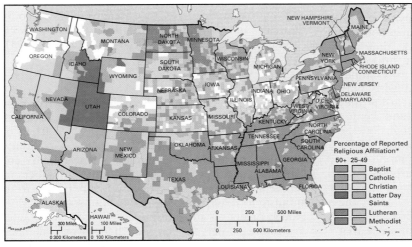

NATIONAL MAP 19–2
Religious Diversity across the United States

In the vast majority of counties, at least 25 percent of people who report having an affiliation are members of the same religious organization. Thus, although the United States is religiously diverse at the national level, most people live in communities where one denomination predominates. What historical facts might account for this pattern?

*When two or more churches have 25 to 49 percent of the membership in a county, the largest is shown. When no church has 25 percent of the membership that county is left blank. A few exceptions include Palm Beach County in southern Florida, which is primarily Jewish, and Holmes County in central Ohio, which is largely Amish.

Source: The Glenmary Research Center, Atlanta, Georgia (1990).

RELIGIOSITY

Religiosity is *the importance of religion in a person's life.* Identifying with a religion is only one measure of religiosity, of course, and a superficial one at that. How religious people turn out to be depends on how we operationalize the concept.

Years ago, Charles Glock (1959, 1962) suggested that we could measure five distinct dimensions of religiosity. *Experiential* religiosity refers to how emotionally tied to a religion someone is. *Ritualistic* religiosity means how often someone prays or goes to church. *Ideological* religiosity describes how much a person believes in religious doctrine. *Consequential* religiosity has to do with how strongly religious beliefs figure in one's daily behavior. Finally, *intellectual* religiosity refers to how much someone knows about the history and doctrines of a religion. Anyone is likely to

(6) 4.9%
(7) "My faith is mixed with doubts" 7.1%
DK/NR 1.8%
SOCIAL SURVEY: "Which of these statements comes closest to describing your feelings about the Bible?" (GSS 2000, *N* = 2,331; *Codebook*, 2001:154)

"The Bible is the actual word of God and is to be taken literally" 33.6%
"The Bible is the inspired word of God but not everything in it should be taken literally, word for word" 46.5%
"The Bible is an ancient book of fables, legends, history, and moral precepts recorded by men" 15.5%
Other/DK/NR 4.4%

be more religious on some dimensions and less on others, so assessing religiosity is a difficult task.

When asked directly, 86 percent of U.S. adults claim to believe in a divine power of some kind, although just 61 percent claim that they "know that God exists and have no doubts about it" (NORC, 2001:375). These measures of experiential religiosity are relatively high.

Measures of ideological religiosity yield lower numbers. Seventy-two percent of U.S. adults report a belief in life after death. And the numbers for ritualistic religiosity drop further: Fifty-five percent of adults say they pray at least once a day, and just 29 percent claim to attend religious services on a weekly or almost-weekly basis (NORC, 2001:133, 138, 131).

Clearly, the question "How religious are we?" offers no easy answers. Keep in mind, too, that many people probably claim to be more religious than they really are. For example, a team of researchers posted observers at every place of worship in Ashtabula County, Ohio, and estimated the number of people attending Sunday services; in a subsequent survey of county residents, twice as many people claimed that they attended church that Sunday than really did. The researchers concluded that no more than 20 percent of people attend church regularly (Hadaway, Marler, & Chaves, 1993). Critics charge that this study may have underestimated the actual number of people attending religious services. Based on all available evidence, it is likely that 25 to 35 percent of the population attends church regularly (Caplow, 1998; Hout & Greeley, 1998; Woodberry, 1998).

Overall, although most people in the United States claim to be at least somewhat religious, probably no more than about one-third actually are. Moreover,

 Access Gallup polls on religion at http://www.gallup.com/poll/indicators/indreligion.asp

religiosity varies among denominations. Members of sects are the most religious of all, followed by Catholics and then "mainstream" Protestants. In general, older people are more religious than younger people, and women are more religious than men (Stark & Glock, 1968; Hadaway, Marler, & Chaves, 1993; Sherkat & Ellison, 1999).

RELIGION AND SOCIAL STRATIFICATION

Sociologists who study religion have found that religious affiliation is related to other familiar social patterns. We shall consider three: social class, race, and ethnicity.

Social Class

A recent study of *Who's Who in America*, which profiles high achievers, showed that 33 percent of the people who gave a religious affiliation were Episcopalians, Presbyterians, and United Church of Christ members, denominations that together account for less than 10 percent of the population. Jews also enjoy high social position, with their 2 percent of the U.S. population accounting for 12 percent of the listings in *Who's Who*.

Research also shows that other denominations—including Congregationalists, Methodists, and Catholics—have a moderate social position. Lower social standing is typical of Baptists, Lutherans, and members of sects. Within all denominations, of course, there is wide variation (Roof, 1979; Davidson, Pyle, & Reyes, 1995; Waters, Heath, & Watson, 1995).

By and large, Protestants with high social standing are people of northern European background whose families came to the United States at least a century ago. They encountered little prejudice and discrimination and have had the longest time to establish themselves socially. Roman Catholics, more recent immigrants to the United States, have faced greater social barriers because of their religion.

Jews command unexpectedly high social standing considering that they often contend with anti-Semitism from the Christian majority. The reason for this achievement is mostly cultural, because Jewish tradition places great value on education and hard work. Although a large proportion of Jews began life in the United States in poverty, many improved their social position in subsequent generations.

Ethnicity and Race

Throughout the world, religion is tied to ethnicity. Many religions predominate in a single nation or geographic region. Islam predominates in the Arab societies of the Middle East, Hinduism is fused with the culture of India, and Confucianism runs deep in Chinese society. Christianity and Judaism do not follow this pattern; although these religions are mostly Western, Christians and Jews are found all over the world.

Religion and national identity come together in the United States as well. For example, we have *Anglo-Saxon* Protestants, *Irish* Catholics, *Russian* Jews, and people who are *Greek* Orthodox. This linking of nation and creed results from the influx of immigrants from nations with a single major religion. Still, nearly every ethnic category displays some religious diversity. For instance, people of English ancestry may be

GLOBAL: A global perspective shows mixed support for the secularization thesis. Religion is declining in importance in some regions (the Scandinavian countries such as Sweden, for example) but rising in others (such as Algeria) (cf. Cox, 1990).
DIVERSITY: David Cone (Alabama State University) describes the black church itself as a variant of liberation theology.

NOTE: One index of secularization is cremations, which are replacing traditional burials as religious and ethnic traditions weaken. They are also most popular in regions of the country—including California and Florida—where the population is most geographically mobile. Four percent of people chose cremation in 1972, according to the Cremation Association of North America; the current figure is 23%.

Protestants, Roman Catholics, Jews, Hindus, Muslims, or followers of other religions.

Historically, the church has been central to the spiritual—and political—lives of African Americans. Transported to the Western Hemisphere in slave ships, most Africans became Christians—the dominant religion in the Americas—but they blended Christian belief with elements of African religions. Guided by this religious mix, Christian people of color therefore have developed rituals that, by European standards, are quite spontaneous and emotional (Frazier, 1965; Roberts, 1980).

When African Americans migrated from the rural South to the industrial cities of the North around 1940, the church played a major role in addressing problems of dislocation, poverty, and prejudice (cf. Pattillo-McCoy, 1998). Furthermore, black churches have provided an important avenue of achievement for talented men and women. The Reverends Ralph Abernathy, Martin Luther King, Jr., and Jesse Jackson have all won recognition as national, even world leaders.

RELIGION IN A CHANGING SOCIETY

June 4, Ticonderoga, New York. Our summer church is small—maybe forty people attend on a Sunday in summer. These days, says long-time member Ed Keller, it's tough for churches to survive, with kids' sports teams scheduling Sunday games, Wal-Mart and the other stores opening early, and many people looking forward to a chance to sleep a little later after a hectic week. The people here seem very committed to the church, but there are not very many of them.

All social institutions evolve over time. Just as the economy, politics, and family have changed over the past century, so has our society's religious life.

SECULARIZATION

Secularization is *the historical decline in the importance of the supernatural and the sacred.* For society as a whole, secularization involves a declining influence of religion in everyday life. For religious organizations, becoming more secular means less focus on otherworldly issues (such as life after death) and more on worldly affairs (such as sheltering the homeless and feeding the hungry). Secularization also means that functions once performed by the church (such as charity) are now primarily the responsibility of nonreligious organizations, such as the United Way and government.

With Latin roots meaning "the present age," secularization is associated with modern, technologically advanced societies in which science is the dominant mode of understanding. Today, for example, people are more likely to experience the transitions of birth, illness, and death in the presence of physicians (with scientific knowledge) than religious leaders (whose knowledge is based on faith). This shift alone suggests that religion's relevance for our everyday lives has declined. Harvey Cox elaborates,

> The world looks less and less to religious rules and rituals for its morality or its meanings. For some, religion provides a hobby, for others a mark of national or ethnic identification, for still others an aesthetic delight. For fewer and fewer does it provide an inclusive and commanding system of personal and cosmic values and explanations. (1971:3; orig. 1965)

If Cox is right, should we expect religion to disappear someday? The consensus among sociologists is "no." The vast majority of people in the United States still profess a belief in God, and as many people claim to pray each day as vote in national elections. In fact, religious affiliation today is higher than it was in 1850. Secularization, then, does not signal the death of religion. For one thing, although some dimensions of religiosity (such as belief in life after death) have declined, others (such as religious affiliation) have increased. Furthermore, while affiliation with some religious organizations is declining, the numbers joining others are increasing. In short, the secularization thesis remains highly controversial among scholars (Hammond, 1985; Hout & Greeley, 1987; McGuire, 1987; Gorski, 2000).

Our society is of two minds as to whether secularization is good or bad. Conservatives take any weakening of religion as a mark of moral decline. Progressives think secularization liberates people from the all-encompassing beliefs of the past, so people can choose what to believe. Secularization has also helped bring some practices (such as ordaining only men) into line with widespread social attitudes (by opening clerical positions to both women and men).

Back in 1963, the U.S. Supreme Court banned prayer in school as violating the Constitutional separation of church and state. In recent years, however, religion has returned to many public schools; the box takes a closer look.

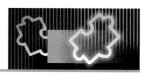

GLOBAL: One measure of the strength of civil religion is the number of national holidays each year: U.S., 32; Japan, 19; Germany, 13; Canada and France, 11; Sweden and Great Britain, 10 (Baker, 1997).

NOTE: Civil religion is evident in the writing of Jean-Jacques Rousseau, who hated the church but wanted to keep a spirit and discipline in citizenship; curiously, secular conservatives, too, wish to maintain religion's capacity to legitimize public order and maintain the social fabric.

SOCIAL SURVEY: "The U.S. Supreme Court has ruled that no state or local government may require the reading of the Lord's Prayer or Bible verses in public schools. What are your views on this?" (GSS 2000, N = 1,877; *Codebook*, 2001:153)
"Approve" 36.7% "Disapprove" 57.9% DK/NR 5.4%

CRITICAL THINKING

Should Students Pray in School?

It is late afternoon on a cloudy spring day in Minneapolis, and two dozen teenagers have come together to pray. They share warm smiles as they enter the room. As soon as everyone is seated, the prayers begin, with one voice following another. One girl prays for her brother, a boy prays for the success of an upcoming food drive, another asks God to comfort a favorite teacher who is having a hard time. Then they join their voices to pray for all the teachers at their school who are not Christians. Following the prayers, the young people sing Christian songs, discuss a Scripture lesson, and bring their meeting to a close with a group hug.

What is so unusual about this prayer meeting is that it is taking place in room 133 of Patrick Henry High School, a *public* institution. Indeed, in public schools from coast to coast, something of a religious revival is taking place as more and more students hold meetings like this one.

You would have to be at least in your mid-forties to remember when it was routine for public school students to begin the day with Bible reading and prayer. In 1963, the Supreme Court ruled that this practice violated the separation of church and state mandated by the U.S. Constitution.

Most school officials took this decision to mean that any religious activity anywhere in public schools was illegal. But from the outset critics charged that by supporting a wide range of other activities and clubs while banning any religious activity, schools were really being *anti*religious. In 1990, the Supreme Court handed down a new ruling, stating that religious groups can meet on school property if group membership is voluntary, meetings are held outside regular class hours, and students rather than adults run them.

Today, student religious groups have formed in perhaps one-fourth of all public schools. Evangelical Christian organizations such as First Priority and National Network of Youth are using the Internet and word of mouth to expand

the place of religion in every public school across the country. However, opponents of school prayer worry that religious zeal may lead some students to pressure others to join their groups, which ensures that the controversy over prayer in public schools will continue.

What do you think?

1. *Do you think that religious clubs should have the same freedom to operate on school grounds as other organizations? Why or why not?*
2. *The writers of our Constitution stated in the First Amendment that Congress should not establish any official religion and also pass no law that would interfere with the free practice of religion. How do you think this amendment applies to prayer in school?*
3. *In 1995, President Bill Clinton said, "Nothing in the First Amendment converts our public schools into religion-free zones." Do you think schools should support spiritual education and development, be neutral to religious activity, or oppose such activity? Why?*

Source: Based on Van Biema (1998, 1999).

CIVIL RELIGION

One dimension of secularization is the rise of what Robert Bellah (1975) calls **civil religion,** *a quasi-religious loyalty binding individuals in a basically secular society.* In other words, although some dimensions of religiosity are weakening, citizenship has taken on religious qualities.

Certainly, most people in the United States consider our way of life a force for moral good in the world. Many people also find religious qualities in political movements, whether liberal or conservative (Williams & Demerath, 1991). Civil religion also involves a range of rituals, from singing the national anthem at sporting events to waving the flag at public parades. At all such events, the U.S. flag serves as a

NOTE: Fundamentalism is, in part, a product of our frontier history, when circuit preachers made dramatic presentations in hopes of prompting an immediate conversion by those attending. Fundamentalism is less pronounced in Europe because European churches are more established and usually linked to the state.
SOCIAL SURVEY: Characterization of religion respondent was raised in. (GSS 2000, N = 2,817; Codebook, 2001:148)

| "Fundamentalist" | 31.9% | "Liberal" | 23.4% |
| "Moderate" | 40.2% | DK/NR | 4.5% |

SOCIAL SURVEY: "Would you say that you have been 'born again,' or have had a 'born again' experience—that is, a turning point in your life when you committed yourself to Christ?" (GSS 1998, N = 1,445; Codebook, 2001:375)

| "Yes" | 37.0% | "No" | 61.7% | DK/NR | 1.2% |

sacred symbol of our national identity, and we expect people to treat it with respect.

Civil religion is not a specific doctrine. However, it does incorporate many elements of traditional religion into the political system of a secular society.

A POST-DENOMINATION SOCIETY

In a society with no formal ties between church and state, religious organizations take the form of denominations. Yet in recent decades, an increasing number of people are pursuing spiritual growth outside established religious organizations. This trend toward spirituality but away from established religious organizations suggests that the United States is becoming a *post-denomination society*. In simple terms, more people seem to be saying that they are interested in spirituality but are "none of the above" in terms of conventional denominations.

Exactly what is the difference between a focus on spirituality and a concern with religion? Spirituality is a form of religious expression that is

> the search for . . . a religion of the heart, not the head. It's a religious expression that downplays doctrine and dogma, and revels in direct experience of the divine—whether it's called the 'holy spirit' or 'divine consciousness' or 'true self.' It's practical and personal, more about stress reduction than salvation, more therapeutic than theological. It's about feeling good rather than being good. It's as much about the body as the soul. (Cimino & Lattin, 1999:62)

From a traditional point of view, this concept of spirituality may seem more like psychology than religion. Yet as seen in the case of civil religion, religious interest in the modern world can take new forms.

Finally, keep in mind the effect of high immigration on religious life in the United States. As people come from Latin America, Asia, and other regions and join the U.S. cultural mix, they are likely to fuse traditional religious ideas with ideas they encounter in their new land. The result is religious innovation (Yang & Ebaugh, 2001).

RELIGIOUS REVIVAL

At the same time that "new age" spirituality is flourishing, a great deal of change has been going on in the world of organized religion. Membership in established, mainstream churches such as the Episcopalian and Presbyterian denominations has plummeted by almost 50 percent since 1960. During the same period, however, affiliation with conservative religious organizations (including the Mormons, Seventh-Day Adventists, and especially Christian sects) has risen just as dramatically. As many churchlike organizations have become more worldly, many people apparently abandon them in favor of more sectlike communities that offer a more intense religious experience (Stark & Bainbridge, 1981; Roof & McKinney, 1987; Jacquet & Jones, 1991; Warner, 1993; Iannaccone, 1994).

Religious Fundamentalism

One of the striking religious trends today is the growth of **fundamentalism,** *a conservative religious doctrine that opposes intellectualism and worldly accommodation in favor of restoring traditional, otherworldly religion.* In the United States, fundamentalism has made the greatest gains among Protestants. Southern Baptists, for example, are the largest religious community in the United States. But fundamentalism has also made gains among Roman Catholics, Jews, and Muslims.

In response to what they see as the growing influence of science and the erosion of the conventional family, religious fundamentalists defend what they call "traditional values." As they see it, liberal churches are simply too open to change. Religious fundamentalism is distinctive in five ways (Hunter, 1983, 1985, 1987):

1. **Fundamentalists interpret sacred texts literally.** Fundamentalists insist on a literal interpretation of the Bible and other sacred texts in order to counter what they consider excessive intellectualism among more liberal religious organizations. For example, fundamentalist Christians believe that God created the world precisely as described in Genesis.

2. **Fundamentalists reject religious pluralism.** Fundamentalists believe that tolerance and relativism water down personal faith. Simply they maintain that their religious beliefs are true and other beliefs are not.

3. **Fundamentalists pursue the personal experience of God's presence.** In contrast to the worldliness and intellectualism of other religious organizations, fundamentalism seeks a return to "good ol' time religion" and spiritual revival. To fundamentalist Christians, being "born again" and having a personal relationship with Jesus Christ should be evident in a person's everyday life.

RESOURCE: The *Seeing Ourselves* reader contains the contemporary selection "Culture Wars," by James Davison Hunter.
DIVERSITY: Among Christians, *evangelism* (with Latin and Greek roots meaning "bring good news") refers to the movement to "spread the word" of the Gospels; most Christian fundamentalists are conservative evangelists. Some fundamentalists are Pentacostals, who stress the personal experience of the Holy Spirit.

NOTE: The U.S. Roman Catholic church has gained membership in the last several decades, mostly through immigration from Catholic countries.
NOTE: In recent decades, members of liberal Protestant churches have moved away from Republican candidates toward more liberal Democrats. Otherwise, there has been little change in political alignments by religion (cf. Manza & Brooks, 1997).

APPLYING SOCIOLOGY

The Cyber-Church: Logging On to Religion

For decades, the bumpy red-clay road was the only link between the outside world and the Monastery of Christ in the Desert. The monastery, a brown adobe structure hidden away at a remote site in northwestern New Mexico, is twenty miles from the nearest power line and maybe fifty from the closest telephone. Anyone making the two-hour auto trek from Albuquerque is greeted by an ancient-looking, hand-carved wooden sign that states simply "Ring this bell."

But in the 1990s, the brothers of the monastery entered the Information Age. On the roof, a dozen solar panels supply power to a personal computer linked to a cellular phone, allowing the monks to spread their message throughout the world on their home page.

What does the sociological perspective tells us about high-tech religion? For one thing, this is not the first time that new technology has changed the face of religion. Six hundred years ago in medieval Europe, face-to-face talk was the way people transmitted religious ideas. Clerics gathered in the universities of the largest cities of the day, and people went to services in churches and other houses of worship across the land. Bibles and other sacred texts were few and far between; monks in monasteries took years to complete the painstaking task of copying them by hand. But

religion changed when Johann Gutenberg, a German inventor (in 1999 named by the Biography channel as the most influential person of the last 1,000 years), built a movable-type press and published the first printed book—a Bible—in 1456. Within fifty years, millions of books were in print across Europe, and most of them were about religious matters. It is no coincidence that the spread of printed books was soon followed by a major religious transformation: the Protestant Reformation. An expanding market of religious ideas prompted people to rethink established principles and practices.

In the twentieth century, radio (beginning in the 1920s) and television (after 1950) extended the reach of religious leaders, who founded "media congregations" no longer confined by the walls of a single building. During the 1990s, the Internet accelerated this trend as hundreds of thousands of Web sites offered messages from established churches, obscure cults, and "new age" groups.

How will computer technology affect religious life? With more information available than ever before, people's religious ideas may not be bound by religious organizations as in the past. Instead, an emphasis on spirituality may give rise to a post-denomination society, as noted earlier. New information technology may also usher in an age of "cyber-churches." Television has already shown that it can transmit the personal charisma and spiritual message of religious leaders to ever-larger audiences. Perhaps the Internet will lead to "virtual congregations," both larger in number and broader in background than any before.

Source: Based on Ramo (1996).

4. **Fundamentalism opposes "secular humanism."** Fundamentalists think accommodation to the changing world undermines religious conviction. *Secular humanism* is a general term that refers to our society's tendency to look to scientific experts rather than God for guidance about how to live.

5. **Many fundamentalists endorse conservative political goals**. Although fundamentalism tends to back away from worldly concerns, some fundamentalist leaders (including Ralph Reed, Pat Robertson, and Gary Bauer) have entered politics to oppose the "liberal agenda" that includes

DISCUSS: In 1999, the Kansas Board of Education decided to discourage the teaching of evolution; similarly, in Alabama, some textbooks carry this statement: "This textbook discusses evolution, a controversial theory some scientists present as a scientific explanation for the origin of living things, such as plants, animals, and humans. No one was present when life first appeared on earth.

Therefore, any statement about life's origins should be considered as theory, not fact" (cf. Johnson, 1999).

SOCIAL SURVEY: "Would you generally favor or oppose teaching creationism along with evolution in public schools?" Favor, 68%; Oppose, 29%; No opinion, 3% (CNN/USA Today/Gallup poll, June 25–27, 1999).

CONTROVERSY & DEBATE

Does Science Threaten Religion?

Some 400 years ago, the Italian physicist and astronomer Galileo (1564–1642) helped start the scientific revolution with a series of startling discoveries. Dropping objects from the Leaning Tower of Pisa, he discovered some of the laws of gravity; fashioning his own telescope, he surveyed the heavens and found that the earth orbited the sun, not the other way around.

For his trouble, Galileo was denounced by the Roman Catholic church, which had preached for centuries that the earth stood motionless at the center of the universe. In response, Galileo only made matters worse by declaring that religious leaders and biblical doctrine had little to say about matters of science. Before long, he found his work banned and himself under house arrest.

From its beginnings, science has had an uneasy relationship with religion. In the twentieth century, clashes arose mainly over the issue of creation. Charles Darwin's masterwork, *On the Origin of Species*, theorizes that humanity evolved from lower forms of life over the course of a billion years. Yet the theory of evolution seems to fly in the face of the biblical account of creation found in Genesis, which states that "God created the heavens and the earth," introducing life on the third day and, on the fifth and sixth days, animal life, including human beings fashioned in God's own image.

Galileo would certainly have been an eager observer of the famous "Scopes monkey trial." In 1925, the state of Tennessee put a small-town science teacher named John Thomas Scopes on trial for teaching evolution in the local high school. State law forbade teaching "any theory that denies the story of the Divine Creation of man as taught in the Bible" and especially the idea that "man descended from a lower order of animals." Scopes was found guilty and fined $100. His conviction was reversed on appeal, which prevented the case reaching the U.S. Supreme Court. The Tennessee law stayed on the books until 1967. A year later, the U.S. Supreme Court (*Epperson* v. *Arkansas*) struck down all such laws as an unconstitutional case of government-supported religion.

Today, almost four centuries after Galileo was silenced, many people still ponder the apparently conflicting claims of science and religion. A third of U.S. adults believe that the Bible is the literal word of God, and many of them reject any scientific findings that run counter to biblical scripture (NORC, 2001:155).

But a middle ground is emerging: Half of U.S. adults (and also many church leaders) say the Bible is a book of truths inspired by God without being correct in a literal, scientific sense. That is, science and religion represent two levels of understanding that respond to different questions. Both Galileo and Darwin devoted their lives to investigating *how* the natural world operates. Yet only religion can address *why* humans and the natural world exist in the first place.

This basic difference between science and religion helps explain why our nation is the most actively scientific but devoutly religious in the world. Moreover, as one scientist recently hypothesized, the mathematical odds that a cosmic "Big Bang" 12 billion years ago created the universe and led to the formation of life as we know it are utterly infinitesimal—smaller than the chance of winning a state lottery twenty weeks in a row. Doesn't such a scientific fact suggest an intelligent and purposeful power in our creation? Can't one be both a religious believer and a scientific investigator?

In 1992, a Vatican commission created by Pope John Paul II concluded that the church's silencing of Galileo was wrong. Today, most scientific and religious leaders agree that science and religion represent important but different truths. Many also believe that in today's rush to scientific discovery, our world has never been more in need of the moral guidance afforded by religion.

Continue the debate . . .

1. *Why do you think some scientific people reject religious accounts of human creation? Why do some religious people reject scientific accounts?*

2. *Do you think the sociological study of religion challenges anyone's faith? Why or why not?*

3. *Does it surprise you that about half of U.S. adults think science is changing our way of life too fast? Do you agree? Why or why not?*

Sources: Based on Gould (1981), Huchingson (1994), and Applebome (1996).

SOCIAL SURVEY: In a recent *Time*/CNN poll, 55% of U.S. adults thought religion would have a greater role in our society after the year 2000; 37% said a lesser role.

DISCUSS: Do colleges discriminate against religious people? A 1995 Supreme Court ruling (5–4) concluded that the University of Virginia violated free-speech guarantees when it failed to fund a Christian magazine along with other student groups.

Q: "We have too many men of science, too few of God. We have grasped the mystery of the atom and rejected the Sermon on the Mount. . . . Ours is a world of nuclear giants and ethical infants. We know more about war than about peace, more about killing than about living." General Omar N. Bradley (1948)

Q: "Science without religion is lame; religion without science is blind." Albert Einstein

feminism and gay rights. Fundamentalists oppose abortion, gay marriages, and liberal bias in the media; they support the traditional two-parent family and seek a return of prayer in schools (Hunter, 1983; Speer, 1984; Ellison & Sherkat, 1993; Green, 1993; Manza & Brooks, 1997; Thomma, 1997; Rozell, Wilcox, & Green, 1998).

Opponents regard fundamentalism as rigid and self-righteous. But many find in fundamentalism—with its greater religious certainty and emphasis on the emotional experience of God's presence—an appealing alternative to the more intellectual, tolerant, and worldly "mainstream" denominations (Marquand, 1997).

Which religions are "fundamentalist"? In the United States, the term is most correctly applied to conservative Christian organizations in the evangelical tradition, including Pentecostals, Southern Baptists, Seventh-Day Adventists, and Assemblies of God. Several national social movements, including Promise Keepers for men and Chosen Women, have a fundamentalist orientation. In national surveys, 32 percent of U.S. adults describe their religious upbringing as "fundamentalist"; 40 percent claim a "moderate" religious background, and 23 percent a liberal background (NORC, 2001:148).

The Electronic Church

In contrast to small village congregations of years past, some religious organizations, especially fundamentalists, have become electronic churches featuring "prime-time preachers" (Hadden & Swain, 1981). Electronic religion, found only in the United States, propelled Billy Graham, Oral Roberts, Pat Robertson, Robert Schuller, and others to greater prominence than all but a few clergy in the past. About 5 percent of the national television audience (some

 Visit the Web site of the Monastery of Christ in the Desert at http://www.christdesert.org

10 million people) regularly view religious television, and perhaps 20 percent (about 40 million) watch some religious program every week (NORC, 2001).

Recently, an increasing number of religious organizations are using computer technology to spread their message, a trend that Pope John Paul II has called the "new evangelism." The box on page 511 offers a sociological look at finding God online.

LOOKING AHEAD: RELIGION IN THE TWENTY-FIRST CENTURY

The popularity of media ministries, the rapid growth of fundamentalism, the flourishing of spiritual movements, and the continuing adherence of millions more people to mainstream churches show that religion will remain a major part of modern society. However, new approaches to religious experience—as well as high levels of immigration from many religious countries (in Latin America and elsewhere)—will continue to diversify the religious character of U.S. society in this new century.

In addition, the world is becoming more complex, and rapid change seems to outstrip our ability to make sense of it all. But rather than undermining religion, this process fires the religious imagination. Tensions between the spiritual realm of religion and the secular world of science and technology will surely continue; the box takes a closer look at this dynamic relationship.

Science is simply unable to provide answers to the most basic human questions about the purpose of our lives. Moreover, new technology that can alter, extend, and even create life confronts us with new and vexing moral dilemmas. Against this backdrop of uncertainty, it is little wonder that many people look to their faith for assurance and hope.

 The first site provides a discussion of creationism; the second offers a critical counterpoint: http://www.creationists.org and http://www.swcp.com/~diamond/cre_answ.shtml

SUMMARY

1. Religion is a major social institution based on the distinction between the sacred and the profane. Religion is a matter of faith, not scientific evidence, which people express through various rituals.

2. Sociology analyzes the consequences of religion for social life, but no scientific research can assess the truth of any religion.

3. Emile Durkheim argued that through religion, individuals experience the power of their society. His structural-functional analysis suggests that religion promotes social cohesion and conformity and confers meaning and purpose on life.

4. Using the symbolic-interaction paradigm, Peter Berger explains that people construct religious

Q: "Atheism is a non-prophet organization."
Q: "If we do discover a complete theory [of physics] . . . it would be the ultimate triumph of human reason—for then we would truly know the mind of God." Stephen Hawking
EXERCISE: Ask students to attend a worship service of an

unfamiliar religious organization; a good discussion will follow. Another idea: Direct students to campus religious leaders to discuss the role of religion in a college education.
Q: "Which is it? Is man one of God's blunders or is God one of man's blunders?" Friedrich Nietzsche

beliefs as a way to respond to life's uncertainties and disruptions.

5. Using the social-conflict paradigm, Karl Marx charged that religion promotes social inequality and the status quo. On the other hand, Max Weber's analysis of Calvinism's contribution to the rise of industrial capitalism demonstrates religion's power to promote social change.

6. Churches, which are religious organizations well integrated into their society, fall into two categories: state churches and denominations.

7. Sects, the result of religious division, are marked by charismatic leadership and suspicion of the larger society.

8. Cults are religious organizations based on new and unconventional beliefs and practices.

9. Technologically simple human societies were generally animistic, with religion incorporated into family life; in more complex societies, religion emerges as a distinct social institution.

10. Followers of six world religions—Christianity, Islam, Judaism, Hinduism, Buddhism, and Confucianism—represent three-fourths of all humanity.

11. In the United States, almost all adults claim a religious preference; 61 percent identify with a religious

organization, with the largest number belonging to various Protestant denominations.

12. How religious we conclude our nation is depends on how we operationalize the concept of religiosity. Most people say they believe in God, but only about one-fifth of the U.S. population attends religious services regularly.

13. Secularization is the diminishing importance of the supernatural and the sacred. In the United States, while some indicators of religiosity (such as membership in mainstream churches) have declined, others (such as membership in sects) are on the rise. Thus, it is doubtful that secularization will bring on the demise of religion.

14. Civil religion is the quasi-religious patriotism that ties people to their society.

15. A post-denomination society recognizes the trend by which people pursue spiritual growth outside established religious organizations.

16. Fundamentalism opposes religious accommodation to the world, favoring an otherworldly focus. Fundamentalist Christianity also advocates literal interpretation of the Bible, rejects religious diversity, and pursues the personal experience of God's presence. Some fundamentalist Christian organizations actively support conservative political goals.

KEY CONCEPTS

profane (p. 491) that which people define as an ordinary element of everyday life

sacred (p. 491) that which people set apart as extraordinary, inspiring a sense of awe and reverence

religion (p. 491) a social institution involving beliefs and practices based on a conception of the sacred

ritual (p. 491) formal, ceremonial behavior

faith (p. 492) belief anchored in conviction rather than scientific evidence

totem (p. 492) an object in the natural world collectively defined as sacred

liberation theology (p. 495) a fusion of Christian principles with political activism, often Marxist in character

church (p. 496) a type of religious organization well integrated into the larger society

state church (p. 496) a church formally allied with the state

denomination (p. 496) a church, independent of the state, that accepts religious pluralism

sect (p. 496) a type of religious organization that stands apart from the larger society

charisma (p. 497) extraordinary personal qualities that can turn an audience into followers

cult (p. 497) a religious organization that is largely outside a society's cultural traditions

animism (p. 498) the belief that elements of the natural world are conscious life forms that affect humans

monotheism (p. 500) belief in a single divine power

polytheism (p. 500) belief in many gods

religiosity (p. 506) the importance of religion in a person's life

secularization (p. 508) the historical decline in the importance of the supernatural and the sacred

civil religion (p. 509) a quasi-religious loyalty binding individuals in a basically secular society

fundamentalism (p. 510) a conservative religious doctrine that opposes intellectualism and worldly accommodation in favor of restoring traditional, otherworldly religion

CTQ1: Durkheim explained that the sacred involves that which is set apart as extraordinary, inspiring awe and reverence.

CTQ2: See discussions on pages 493–95.

CTQ3: The issue here is the degree to which the religious organization is integrated into the larger society. Churches are most integrated; sects, less so; cults are largely outside a society's religious traditions.

CTQ4: Membership in mainline denominations has declined in recent decades, yet membership in fundamentalist religious organizations has risen.

Q: "There is only one religion, although there are a hundred versions of it." George Bernard Shaw

Q: "If God made us in his image, we have certainly returned the compliment." Voltaire

CRITICAL-THINKING QUESTIONS

1. Explain the basic distinction between the sacred and the profane that underlies all religious belief.

2. Explain Karl Marx's argument that religion supports the status quo. Based on Max Weber's analysis of Calvinism, develop a counterargument that religion can be a major force for social change.

3. Distinguish between churches, sects, and cults. Is one type of religious organization inherently better than another? Why or why not?

4. What evidence suggests that religion is experiencing a decline in importance in the United States? In what ways does religion seem to be getting stronger?

APPLICATIONS AND EXERCISES

1. Some colleges are decidedly religious; others are passionately secular. Investigate the place of religion on your campus. Is your school affiliated with a religious organization? Was it ever? Is there a chaplain or other religious official? See if you can learn from sources on campus what share of students regularly attend any religious service.

2. Assessing people's religious commitment is very difficult. Develop five questions measuring religiosity that might be asked on a questionnaire or in an interview. Present them to several people; how well do they seem to work?

3. Is religion getting weaker? To test the secularization thesis, go the library or local newspaper office and obtain an issue of your local newspaper published fifty years ago and, if possible, one hundred years ago. Compare the attention to religious issues then and now.

4. Packaged in the back of this new textbook is an interactive CD-ROM that offers a variety of study and review materials intended to help you better understand the material covered in this chapter. For this chapter, the CD-ROM contains an author's tip video, Real Life Sociology videos, other relevant audio and video, interactive map animations, audio journal entries from the author, Web links, and much more.

SITES TO SEE

http://www.prenhall.com/macionis

Visit the interactive *Companion Website*™ that accompanies this text. Begin by clicking on the cover of your book. You will find a chapter-by-chapter study guide, practice tests, and a significant portion of the text for on-line review, as well as many suggested Web links.

http://www.parishioners.org/

Here is a site offering information on a variety of religious issues, including cults and toleration of religious differences.

http://www.bwanet.org
http://www.churchworldservice.org
http://www.catholicrelief.org
http://www.jdc.org

A number of religious organizations are involved in addressing hunger and other social problems. These are the Web sites that describe the activities of Baptist World Alliance, Church World Service, Catholic Relief Services, and the American Jewish Joint Distribution Committee.

http://www.trinityumc.net/youth/cool.htm

This is a Web site just for fun: Check it out!

INVESTIGATE WITH CONTENTSELECT

Follow the instructions found on page 23 of this textbook to enter this chapter of the book's *Companion Website*™. Once in the chapter, click on the ContentSelect icon at the bottom left of your screen and enter your personal User ID and Password. Enter keywords such as "religion," "spirituality," "cults," and "liberation theology," and the search engine will help you become an effective researcher.

CHAPTER

20

Jacob Lawrence
The Libraries Are Appreciated, 1943

Gouache and watercolor on paper, 14 1/4 × 21 1/4 in. Louis E. Stern Collection, Philadelphia Museum of Art,
Philadelphia, PA, 63-181-40. © Philadelphia Museum of Art/Corbis. © Jacob Lawrence.

EDUCATION

Tony Scalia doesn't know it, but he is getting the short end of the stick. He is a bright boy—teachers say he stands out among all the fourth-graders—but he barely passed the state proficiency tests. Many of his classmates failed the tests, and overall, children who attend Toledo's Warren Elementary School have some of the lowest average test scores in all of Ohio.

Across town, another fourth grader named Sarah Berrick is doing just fine. Most teachers consider Sarah an average student, but her test scores were all quite satisfactory. Indeed, the children who go to Monclova Elementary School have about the highest average test scores in the entire state.

How do we explain the difference in the achievement of these two students? The answer is not so much a matter of the two children as it is of their neighborhoods. Warren Elementary is in one of Toledo's poorest neighborhoods, and the school looks the part, with large classes and a building in obvious need of repair. Monclova Elementary, by contrast, is found in one of Toledo's most affluent communities, where plenty of money from tax revenues ensures that classes are small and facilities are excellent.

In short, as go the schools, so go the children. Throughout Ohio—and indeed across the United States—we find the same pattern repeated: Children who attend schools in high-income neighborhoods perform much better academically than children who attend schools in low-income communities (Troy, 2000).

Why do schools, like Mondova Elementary School, in high-income areas do such a better job of educating young people? This chapter offers some answers by focusing on **education,** *the social institution through which society provides its members with important knowledge, including basic facts, job skills, and cultural norms and values.* In high-income nations such as the United States, education is largely a matter of **schooling,** *formal instruction under the direction of specially trained teachers.*

EDUCATION: A GLOBAL SURVEY

From New England to Hawaii, from Alaska to Texas, people expect children to spend much of their first eighteen years of life in school. A century ago, however, this was not the case, as only a small elite in the United States had the privilege of attending school. In poor countries around the world, even today, most young people receive only a few years of formal schooling.

517

SUPPLEMENTS: An outline for this chapter, supplementary lecture material, and discussion topics are found in the *Data File*.
NOTE: The world's oldest university was founded in Paris early in the 12th century. In England, the oldest is Oxford, also founded in the early 12th century. By the 13th century, historical notes mention "university chests," benefactions for the assistance of poor students— the earliest form of financial aid.

Q: "A human being is not, in any proper sense, a human being until he is educated." Horace Mann
SOCIAL SURVEY: "How important for getting ahead in life is having a good education?" (GSS 1987, *N* = 1,285; *Codebook*, 2001:939)

"Essential"	34.7%	"Not very important"	1.3%
"Very important"	48.2%	"Not important at all"	0%
"Fairly important"	14.3%	DK/NR	1.5%

In the past, young children in poor countries such as India were as likely to work as to attend school. In recent decades, however, India has made great strides toward universal schooling. Still, in a nation that is largely rural, about 40 percent of Indian children receive no more than an elementary education.

SCHOOLING AND ECONOMIC DEVELOPMENT

The extent of schooling in any society is closely tied to its level of economic development. Chapter 4 ("Society") explained that our hunting and gathering ancestors lived a simple life in families without governments, churches, or schools. For these people, "schooling" amounted to the knowledge and skills parents transmitted directly to their children (Nolan & Lenski, 1999).

In low- and middle-income nations, where most of the world's people live, boys and girls spend several years in school, but their learning is limited to the practical knowledge they need to farm or perform other traditional tasks. The opportunity to study literature, art, history, and science generally is available only to the lucky few who are wealthy and do not need to work. It is no surprise, then, that the word "school" has roots in the Greek word for "leisure." In ancient Greece, the students of renowned teachers such as Socrates, Plato, and Aristotle were almost all aristocratic young men. The same was true in ancient China, where the famous philosopher K'ung Fu-tzu (Confucius) shared his wisdom with just a select few. During the Middle Ages in Europe, the first colleges and universities founded by the Roman Catholic church admitted only males who came from privileged families.

Today, schooling in low-income nations is diverse because it reflects the local culture. In Iran, for example, schooling is closely tied to Islam. Similarly, schooling in Bangladesh (Asia), Zambia (Africa), and Nicaragua (Latin America) has been molded by distinctive cultural traditions.

But all low-income countries have one trait in common when it comes to schooling: There is not very much of it. In the world's poorest nations (including several in Central Africa), only half of all elementary-aged children ever get to school; in the world as a whole, just half of all children reach the secondary grades (Najafizadeh & Mennerick, 1992). As a result, 15 percent of Latin Americans, 30 percent of Asians, and 40 percent of Africans are illiterate. Global Map 20–1 shows the extent of illiteracy around the world.

High-income nations endorse the idea that everyone should go to school. For one thing, workers who use machinery or computers need at least basic reading, writing, and arithmetic skills. For high-income nations, literacy is also a necessary condition of political democracy.

The following national comparisons illustrate the link between schooling and economic development. Notice that various high-income nations differ in their approach to educating their populations.

SCHOOLING IN INDIA

India is a poor country. People earn about 7 percent of the income standard in the United States, and poor families often depend on the earnings of children. Thus, even though India has outlawed child labor, many Indian children (especially girls who live in rural

GLOBAL: A classic example of a foreign nation structuring an educational system is the U.S. remaking of Japanese schooling during the occupation after World War II.

NOTE: Since 1970, significant improvements in elementary school enrollment have been reported by most nations in sub-Saharan Africa. Still, many of these societies have a level of schooling that is comparable to that offered in the U.S. in 1850.

RESOURCE: The Macionis and Benokraitis reader, *Seeing Ourselves*, examines "Academic Achievement in Southeast Asian Refugee Families."

GLOBAL: Research explains the U.S.-Asian "math gap" in terms of parental attitudes: Most U.S. parents are satisfied with their children's learning and amount of homework; most Asian parents are not and are more demanding of their children.

WINDOW ON THE WORLD

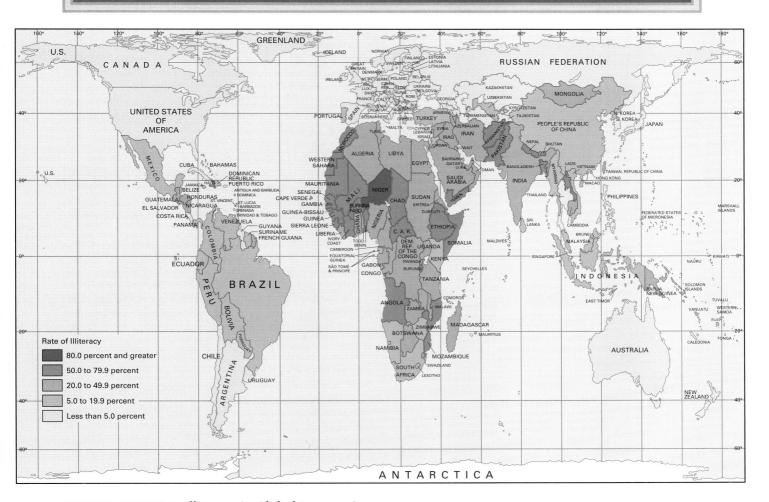

GLOBAL MAP 20–1 Illiteracy in Global Perspective

Reading and writing skills are widespread in high-income countries, with illiteracy rates generally below 5 percent. In much of Latin America, however, illiteracy is more common, one consequence of limited economic development. In twenty-seven nations—twenty of them in Africa—illiteracy is the rule rather than the exception; there, people rely on "the oral tradition" of face-to-face communication rather than the written word.

Sources: United Nations Development Programme (2001); map projection from *Peters Atlas of the World* (1990).

areas) work in factories—weaving rugs or making handicrafts—up to sixty hours per week, which greatly limits their opportunity for schooling.

In recent decades, schooling in India has increased. Most children now receive some primary education, typically in crowded schoolrooms where one teacher attends to perhaps sixty children (more than twice as many as in the average U.S. classroom). This is all the schooling most Indians ever acquire because less than half enter secondary school and

DIVERSITY: College completion (in 2000, aged 25 and over), as in Table 20–1, by sex: 27.8% for men, 23.6% for women; African American men, 16.4%, African American women, 16.8%; Hispanic men, 10.7%, Hispanic women, 10.6%.
GLOBAL: One key to Japanese educational achievement is powerful cultural discipline. Such collective pressure generates collective distinction but produces fewer highly innovative individuals. To illustrate,

U.S. men and women have received proportionately more Nobel Prizes than have the Japanese.
GLOBAL: British "public" schools number about 1,000 and cost roughly $20,000 a year. Their popularity has dropped in recent years, perhaps because of the high cost and growing opposition by parents to sending off their young children to fend for themselves.

TABLE 20–1 Educational Achievement in the United States, 1910–2000*

Year	High School Graduates	College Graduates	Median Years of Schooling
1910	13.5%	2.7%	8.1
1920	16.4	3.3	8.2
1930	19.1	3.9	8.4
1940	24.1	4.6	8.6
1950	33.4	6.0	9.3
1960	41.1	7.7	10.5
1970	55.2	11.0	12.2
1980	68.7	17.0	12.5
1990	77.6	21.3	12.4
2000	84.1	25.6	12.7

*For people twenty-five years of age and over. Percentage of high school graduates includes those who go on to college. Percentage of high school dropouts can be calculated by subtracting percentage of high school graduates from 100 percent.

Source: U.S. Census Bureau (2000).

very few go to college. The result is that only slightly more than half of the people in this vast country are literate.

Patriarchy also shapes Indian education. Indian parents are joyful at the birth of a boy because he and his future wife will contribute income to the family. By contrast, girls are a financial liability because parents must provide a dowry at the time of marriage, and, after her marriage, a daughter's work benefits her husband's family. Therefore, many Indians see less reason to invest in the schooling of girls, so only 30 percent of girls (compared to 45 percent of boys) reach the secondary grades. The flipside of this pattern is that a large majority of the children working in Indian factories are girls—a family's way of benefitting from a daughter while they can (United Nations Development Programme, 1995).

SCHOOLING IN JAPAN

September 30, Kobe, Japan. Compared with people in the United States, the Japanese are, above all, orderly. Young boys and girls on their way to school stand out with their uniforms, an armload of books, and a look of seriousness and purpose.

Schooling has not always been part of the Japanese way of life. Before industrialization brought

mandatory education in 1872, only a privileged few attended school. Today, Japan's educational system is widely praised for producing some of the world's highest achievers.

The early grades concentrate on transmitting Japanese traditions, especially obligation to family. By their early teens, however, students encounter Japan's system of rigorous and competitive examinations. These written tests, which resemble the Scholastic Aptitude Tests (SATs) used for college admissions in the United States, make all the difference in the future of each Japanese student.

In Japan, schooling reflects personal ability more than it does in the United States, where family income plays a greater part in a student's college plans. The Japanese government pays much of the costs of higher education. But without high examination scores, even the richest families cannot get their children into a good university.

More men and women graduate from high school in Japan (90 percent) than in the United States (84 percent). But because of competitive examinations, only about 45 percent of high school graduates—compared to 63 percent in the United States—enter college. Understandably, then, Japanese students take entrance examinations very seriously, and about half attend "cram schools" after their regular school day ends to prepare for these exams. Because most Japanese women are not in the labor force, many mothers devote themselves to their children's success in school.

Because of the pressure it places on students, Japanese schooling produces impressive results. In a number of fields, notably mathematics and science, young Japanese students outperform students in every other high-income nation, including the United States (Hayneman & Loxley, 1983; Rohlen, 1983; Brinton, 1988; Simons, 1989).

SCHOOLING IN GREAT BRITAIN

During the Middle Ages, schooling was a privilege of the British nobility, who studied classical subjects because they had little interest in the practical skills related to earning a living. But as the Industrial Revolution created a need for an educated labor force and working-class people demanded access to schools, a rising share of the population entered the classroom. British law now requires every British child to attend school until age sixteen.

However, traditional social distinctions persist in British education. Most wealthy families send their children to what the British call *public schools*, the equivalent of U.S. private boarding schools. These elite schools, which enroll about 7 percent of British students, not only teach academic subjects but also convey to children from wealthy (especially newly rich) families the distinctive patterns of speech, mannerisms, and social graces of the British upper class. These academies are far too expensive for most students, however, who attend state-supported day schools (Ambler & Neathery, 1999).

Since 1960, the British have deemphasized the importance of social background in schooling by expanding their university system and using competitive entrance examinations. For those who score the highest, the government pays most of college costs. But these exams are less important than those in Japan because many well-to-do children who do not score well still manage to attend Oxford or Cambridge, the most prestigious British universities, on a par with Yale, Harvard, and Princeton in the United States. "Oxbridge" graduates go on to take their place among the British power elite: More than two-thirds of the top members of the British government have "Oxbridge" degrees (Sampson, 1982; Gamble, Ludlam, & Baker, 1993).

These brief sketches of schooling in India, Japan, and Great Britain show the crucial importance of economic development. In poor countries, many children, especially girls, work rather than go to school. Rich nations adopt mandatory education laws to create an industrial work force as well as to satisfy demands for greater equality. But rich nations vary among themselves, as we see in the intense competition of Japanese schools, the traditional social stratification that shapes schools in Great Britain, and the practical emphasis found in the schools of the United States.

SCHOOLING IN THE UNITED STATES

The United States was among the first countries to set a goal of mass education. By 1850, about half the young people between ages five and nineteen were enrolled in school. In 1918, the last of the states passed a *mandatory education law* requiring children to attend school until age sixteen or completion of the eighth grade. Table 20–1 shows that a milestone was reached in the mid-1960s when, for the first time, a majority of U.S. adults had high school diplomas. Today, more than four out of five have a high school education, and one in four have a four-year college degree.

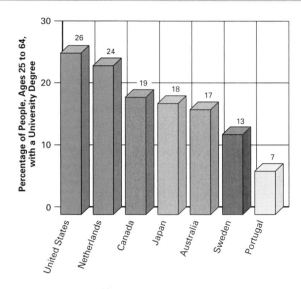

GLOBAL SNAPSHOT

FIGURE 20–1 College Degrees in Global Perspective

Source: U.S. Census Bureau (2000).

The educational system in the United States has been shaped by both affluence and democratic principles. Thomas Jefferson thought the new nation could become democratic only if people "read and understand what is going on in the world" (quoted in Honeywell, 1931:13). As Figure 20–1 shows, the United States has an outstanding record of higher education for its people: No other country has as large a share of adults with a university degree (U.S. Census Bureau, 2000).

Schooling in the United States also tries to promote *equal opportunity*. National surveys show that most people think schooling is crucial to success, and a majority also believe that everyone has the chance to get an education consistent with personal ability and talent (NORC, 2001). In truth, this opinion better expresses our aspirations than our achievement. In the early twentieth century, for example, women were all but excluded from higher

 For a Census Bureau report on educational degrees and average salaries, see http://www.census.gov/population/www/socdemo/fld-of-trn.html

APPLYING SOCIOLOGY

Following the Jobs: Trends in Bachelor's Degrees

ollege attendance in the United States has never been higher, especially among women. However, both sexes see college education in practical terms and pursue degrees in fields where they think jobs are plentiful.

In the postindustrial economy, the greatest surge in bachelor's degrees is in parks, recreation, fitness, and leisure studies, as the figure shows. The number of degrees in the health sciences, environmental studies, and ethnic and cultural studies are also up sharply. On the other hand, ROTC and military technologies heads the list of fields posting reductions, followed by library science, communications technologies, and engineering-related technologies.

Source: U.S. National Center for Education Statistics (2001).

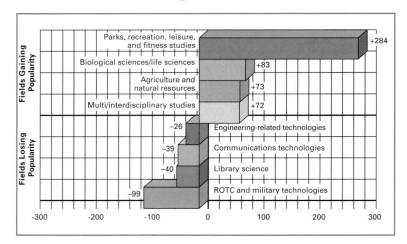

Percentage Changes in Bachelor's Degrees Earned, 1988–1998

---

education, and even today most people who attend college come from families with above-average incomes.

In the United States, the educational system stresses the value of *practical* learning, that is, knowledge that has a direct bearing on individuals' work and interests. Educational philosopher John Dewey (1859–1952) championed *progressive education*, constantly updating what our schools teach to make learning relevant to people's lives.

Reflecting this pragmatism, today's college students select their major area of study with an eye toward future jobs. The box takes a closer look at the changing interests of college students.

THE FUNCTIONS OF SCHOOLING

Structural-functional analysis looks at how formal education contributes to the operation of society. One of the most important functions is socialization. Schooling provides a cultural lifeline that links the generations.

SOCIALIZATION

Technologically simple societies transmit their way of life informally from parents to children. As societies develop complex technology, however, kin can no longer stay abreast of rapidly expanding information and skills. Thus, schooling gradually emerges as a distinctive social institution employing specially trained personnel to convey the knowledge needed for adult roles.

In primary school, children learn basic language and mathematical skills. Secondary school builds on this foundation, and, for many, college allows further specialization. In addition, schools transmit cultural values and norms. For example, civics classes explicitly instruct students in our political way of life. Sometimes the operation of the classroom itself teaches important cultural lessons. From the earliest grades, rituals such as saluting the flag and singing "The Star-Spangled Banner" foster patriotism. Likewise, spelling bees and classroom drills develop competitive individualism, respect for authority, and a sense of fair play.

DISCUSS: Discuss the cultural values implicit in the classroom spelling bee (including competition, individual performance, specific standards of achievement).

DIVERSITY: Dovetailing with the social integration function of schooling is the multiculturalism debate, examined in Chapter 3 ("Culture").

DISCUSS: Discuss Herrnstein and Murray's contention in *The Bell Curve* that higher education became more meritocratic across the 20th century, with the effect of segregating an emerging "cognitive elite."

Q: "Education, then, beyond all other devices of human origin, is a great equalizer of conditions of men—the balance wheel of the social machinery." Horace Mann (1948)

CULTURAL INNOVATION

Education creates as well as transmits culture. Schools stimulate intellectual inquiry and critical thinking, sparking the development of new ideas.

Today, for example, college professors throughout the country are conducting research to expand our knowledge in countless areas. Medical research carried on at major universities over the years has increased life expectancy, just as research by sociologists and psychologists helps us take advantage of our longevity.

SOCIAL INTEGRATION

Schooling helps forge a mass of people into a unified society. This integrative function is especially important in nations with pronounced social diversity, where various cultures know little about—or may even be hostile to—one another. In the past, the Soviet Union and Yugoslavia relied on schools to unite their disparate peoples, without ultimately succeeding.

One basic way schools integrate culturally diverse people is by teaching a common language that encourages broad communication and builds a national identity. Of course, some ethnic minorities resist state-sponsored schooling for exactly this reason. In the former Soviet Union, for example, Lithuanians, Ukrainians, and Azerbaijanis objected to learning Russian because they saw it as a threat to their own traditions and emblematic of their domination by others. The Amish, a culturally distinctive people in the United States, historically fought to keep their children out of public schools in order to preserve their cultural traditions.

A century ago, mandatory education laws in the United States coincided with the arrival of millions of European immigrants, helping to integrate society. Today as well, formal education helps integrate large numbers of immigrants from Latin America and Asia, who, in turn, add their traditions to our ever-changing cultural mix. At the same time, as racial and ethnic minorities have become a numerical majority in many of the largest school districts, the debate over multicultural education has grown (see Chapter 3, "Culture").

SOCIAL PLACEMENT

Formal education helps young people assume culturally approved statuses and perform roles that contribute to the ongoing life of society. Ideally, schools accomplish this by identifying and developing each individual's aptitudes and abilities and then evaluating the student's performance in terms of achievement rather than social background.

In principle, however, teachers encourage the "best and the brightest" to pursue the most challenging and advanced studies while guiding students with more ordinary ability into educational programs suited to their talents. In short, schooling enhances meritocracy by making personal merit a foundation of future social position.

LATENT FUNCTIONS OF SCHOOLING

Besides these manifest functions of formal education, a number of latent functions are less widely recognized. One is child care. As the number of one-parent families and two-career couples rises, schools have become vital to relieving parents of some child-care responsibilities.

For teenagers, schooling consumes considerable time and energy, often fostering conformity at a time of life when the risk of unlawful behavior is high. Also, because many students attend school well into their twenties, education engages thousands of young people, especially during times when jobs are not readily available.

Another latent function of schools is establishing relationships and networks. Many people form lifelong friendships and even meet their future spouses in high school and college. Affiliation with a particular school also can create valuable career opportunities.

Critical evaluation. Structural-functional analysis of formal education identifies both manifest and latent contributions of this social institution to a modern way of life. But it overlooks the core truth noted in the opening to this chapter: The quality of schooling is far greater for some than for others. Indeed, critics of the U.S. educational system maintain that schooling reproduces the class structure in each generation. In the next section, social-conflict analysis takes up precisely this issue.

SCHOOLING AND SOCIAL INEQUALITY

Social-conflict analysis counters the functionalist view that schooling is a meritocratic strategy for developing people's talents and abilities. Rather, this approach argues that schools routinely provide learning according to students' social background, thereby perpetuating social inequality.

Q: "A classification scheme is meant to provide ways of grouping learners for instructional purposes through a series of labels such as slow learner, underachiever, late bloomer, disadvantaged, and deprived. These labels become an intrinsic part of the normal operation of the organization. Teachers, administrators, and counselors use these labels. However, labeling human beings is a way of limiting them. We traditionally do not expect as much from those who

are classified as slow as we do from those who are classified as fast." Mario D. Fantini

Q: "And then in high school, they sorted us into college prep and vocational ed types, sorted us like apples, some mashed into cider and applesauce, others polished, wrapped in tissue paper, crated and marked for export." P.F. Kluge

Q: "In education, there should be no class distinction." Confucius

Many of the world's societies consider schooling more important for males than for females. Although the U.S. education gap between women and men has largely closed in recent decades, many women still study conventionally "feminine" subjects such as literature, whereas men pursue mathematics and engineering. And by stressing the experiences of some types of people (say, military generals) while ignoring the lives of others (such as farm women), schools reinforce the values and importance of dominant categories of people. Finally, as we shall see later, affluent people have much more educational opportunity than poor people.

SOCIAL CONTROL

Social-conflict analysis contends that schooling is a means of social control, reinforcing acceptance of the status quo. In various, sometimes subtle ways, schools reproduce the status hierarchy.

Samuel Bowles and Herbert Gintis (1976) point out that the clamor for public education in the late nineteenth century arose at precisely the time that capitalists were seeking a literate, docile, and disciplined work force. Mandatory education laws ensured that schools would teach immigrants not only English but also cultural values that support capitalism. Compliance, punctuality, and discipline were—and still are—part of what conflict theorists call the **hidden curriculum,** *subtle presentations of political or cultural ideas in the classroom.*

STANDARDIZED TESTING

Here is a question of the kind historically used to measure academic ability of school-age children in the United States:

> Painter is to painting as _____ is to sonnet.
> *Answer:*
> a. driver   c. priest
> b. poet   d. carpenter

The correct answer is (b) *poet:* A painter creates a painting just as a poet creates a sonnet. This question supposedly measures logical reasoning, but demonstrating this skill depends on knowing what each term means. Unless students are familiar with sonnets as a Western European form of written verse, they are not likely to answer the question correctly.

Educational specialists claim that bias of this kind has been all but eliminated from standardized tests; testing organizations carefully study response patterns and drop any question that favors one racial or ethnic category over another. However, critics maintain that some bias based on class, race, or ethnicity is inherent in any formal testing because questions inevitably reflect our society's dominant culture and thereby put minorities at a disadvantage (Owen, 1985; Crouse & Trusheim, 1988; Putka, 1990).

SCHOOL TRACKING

Despite continuing controversy over standardized tests, most schools in the United States use them as the basis for **tracking,** *assigning students to different types of educational programs.* Tracking is also a common practice in many other high-income nations, including Great Britain, France, and Japan.

The official justification for tracking is to give students the kind of learning that fits their abilities and motivation. Young people have different interests, with some drawn to, say, the study of languages and others to art or physical education. Given disparate talents and goals, no single program for all students would serve any of them well.

Critics counter that by tracking students, our schools sort out children as either winners or losers, based as much on their social background as their personal aptitude. Most students from affluent families do well on standardized tests, so schools place them in college-bound tracks; students from modest backgrounds typically do less well on tests and end up in tracks that teach only technical trades. Thus, tracking effectively segregates students—academically and socially—into different worlds.

Furthermore, most schools reserve their best teachers for students in the top tracks. These teachers put more effort into teaching, show more respect to students, and expect more from them. By contrast, teachers in low tracks use more memorization, classroom drill, and other unstimulating techniques. They also emphasize regimentation, punctuality, and respect for authority figures.

In light of these criticisms, schools across the United States are now cautious about making tracking assignments and allow more mobility between tracks. Some schools have even moved away from the practice entirely. Although limited tracking seems to be necessary to match instruction with student abilities, rigid tracking has a powerful impact on students' learning and self-concept. Young people who spend years in higher tracks tend to see themselves as bright and able, whereas students in lower tracks have less ambition and low self-esteem (Bowles & Gintis, 1976;

DIVERSITY: On average, men outperform women on both verbal and math SATs. Verbal scores, *1967:* men, 540; women, 545. Math scores: men, 535; women, 495. Verbal scores, *2001:* men, 509; women, 502. Math: men, 533; women, 498.

RESOURCE: Among the classics in the Macionis and Benokraitis reader is "Education and Inequality," by Samuel Bowles and Herbert Gintis.

Q: "The [private] school—rather than the upper-class family—is the most important agency for transmitting the traditions of the upper classes, and regulating the admission of new wealth and talent. . . . It is by means of these schools more than by any other single agency that the older and the newer families . . . become members of a self-conscious upper class." C. Wright Mills (1959:64–65)

Sociological research has documented the fact that young people living in low-income communities suffer in school due to large class sizes, poor quality teaching, and insufficient budgets for technology and other instructional materials. In a nation where people believe that schools should give everyone a chance to develop talents and abilities, should such inequalities exist?

Oakes, 1982, 1985; Hallinan & Williams, 1989; Kilgore, 1991; Gamoran, 1992; Kozol, 1992).

INEQUALITY BETWEEN SCHOOLS

Just as students are treated differently within schools, schools themselves differ in fundamental ways. The biggest difference is between public and private schools.

Public and Private Schools

In 1998, 90 percent of the 51 million U.S. school-aged children attended state-funded public schools. The remainder were in private schools.

Most private school students attend one of the 8,000 *parochial schools* (from Latin, meaning "of the parish") operated by the Roman Catholic church. The Catholic school system grew rapidly a century ago as cities swelled with millions of Catholic immigrants and their children. These schools helped the new arrivals maintain their religious heritage in the midst of a predominantly Protestant society. Today, after decades of flight from the city by white people, many parochial schools enroll non-Catholics, including a growing number of

African Americans whose families seek an alternative to the local public schools.

Protestants, especially in fundamentalist denominations, also have private schools or Christian academies. These Christian schools are favored by parents who want their children to receive religious instruction or who seek higher academic and disciplinary standards. Some white parents turn to Christian schools to provide a racially homogeneous environment for their children in the face of school desegregation mandates. In recent years, African Americans also have sought out Christian schools as an alternative to public education (James, 1989; Dent, 1996).

Some 6,000 nonreligious private schools in the United States also enroll students. Many of these schools are prestigious and expensive preparatory schools and are especially favored by "newly rich" parents eager for their daughters and sons to rub elbows with children from "old money." These institutions, many modeled on boarding schools in Great Britain, are academically outstanding and send many graduates to equally prestigious and expensive private universities. After learning the mannerisms and social graces of the elite, many "preppies" maintain lifelong school-based networks that provide numerous social advantages.

NOTE: Stanford, Calif., is the most educated town in the U.S.; 90% of adult residents have a BA degree or higher.

Q: "Children in one set of schools are trained to be governors; children in the other set are trained to be governed." Jonathan Kozol

RESOURCE: An excerpt by Jonathan Kozol, "Savage Inequalities: Children in U.S. Schools," is included in the Macionis and Benokraitis reader, *Seeing Ourselves*.

DIVERSITY: The Department of Education reports that 18% of U.S. students repeat at least one grade before completing the 8th grade. Categories of students more likely to repeat a grade: boys vs. girls; public school students vs. those in private or parochial schools; children with single parents vs. those living with father and mother; Hispanics, African Americans, and Native Americans vs. Asian Americans and whites.

DIVERSITY: RACE, CLASS, AND GENDER

Schooling in the United States: Savage Inequality

"Public School 261? Head down Jerome Avenue and look for the mortician's office." On his way to doing fieldwork for his study of New York City schools, Jonathan Kozol parks his car and walks toward PS 261. Finding PS 261 is not so easy because the school has no sign. In fact, the building is a former roller rink and doesn't look much like a school at all.

The principal explains that PS 261 is in a minority area of the North Bronx, so the school population is 90 percent African American and Hispanic. Officially, the school should serve 900 students but actually enrolls 1,300. The rules say class size should not exceed 32, but later Kozol notes that it sometimes approaches 40. Because of the small cafeteria, the children must eat in three shifts. After lunch because there is no place to play, students just squirm in their seats until told to return to their classrooms. Only one classroom in the entire school has a window to the world outside.

Toward the end of the day, Kozol asks a teacher about the overcrowding and the poor condition of the building. She sums up her thoughts: "I had an awful room last year. In the winter, it was 56 degrees. In the summer, it was up to 90." "Do the children ever comment on the building?" Kozol asks. "They don't say," she responds, "but they know. All these kids see TV. They know what suburban schools are like. Then they look around them at their school. They don't comment on it, but you see it in their eyes. They understand."

Several months later, Kozol visits PS 24, in the affluent Riverdale section of New York. This school is set back from the road, beyond a lawn planted with magnolia and dogwood trees that are in full bloom. On one side of the building is a playground for the youngest children; behind the school are playing fields for the older kids. Many people buy expensive homes in Riverdale because the local schools have an excellent reputation. There are 825 children here; most are white and a few are Asian, Hispanic, or black. The building is in good repair and has a large library and even a planetarium. All the classrooms have windows with bright curtains.

Entering one of the many classes for gifted students, Kozol asks the children what they are doing. A young girl answers confidently, "My name is Laurie, and we're doing problem solving." A tall, good-natured boy continues: "I'm David. One thing that we do is logical thinking. Some problems, we find, have more than one good answer." Kozol asks whether such reasoning is innate or something a child learns. Susan, whose smile reveals her braces, responds, "You know some things to start with when you enter school. But we learn some things that other children don't. We learn certain things that other children don't know because we're *taught* them."

Source: Adapted from Kozol (1992:85–88, 92–96).

Are private schools better than public schools? Research indicates that, given similar backgrounds, students in private schools achieve more than students in public schools. Private schools seem to generate greater interest in learning, probably because of smaller class size and more student-teacher contact. Furthermore, private schools are more academically demanding and enforce stringent disciplinary policies, resulting in a safer, more orderly environment. With everything else equal, graduates of private schools are more likely to complete college and enter high-paying occupations (Coleman, Hoffer, & Kilgore, 1981; Coleman & Hoffer, 1987).

Inequality in Public Schooling

But as the description of two Toledo, Ohio, schools in the opening to this chapter suggests, even the public schools are not all the same. Across the country, Winnetka, Illinois, one of the richest suburbs in the United States, spends more than $8,000 annually per student, compared to less than $3,000 in a poor area such as Socorro, Texas. And even within states, as the opening to this chapter explained, some school districts have far more money per student than others (Carroll, 1990; Edwards, 1998). The box takes a closer look at differences in school quality within New York City.

THE MAP: Relatively affluent regions of the U.S. have a higher share of young people enrolled in college; in addition, high-enrollment counties are those where people endorse greater opportunities for women (compare with National Map 13–1).

NOTE: Catholic schools generally outperform public schools, despite spending only about one-third as much per student (Stern, 1996).

NOTE: The American Federation of Teachers (AFT) put the median U.S. public school teacher's salary at $41,820 in 2000; by state, Connecticut was highest ($52,410 median); lowest was South Dakota ($29,072).

DIVERSITY: The largest historically black colleges in the U.S. are Southern (Baton Rouge, La.) with 15,000 students; Texas Southern (Houston), 10,000; and Florida A&M (Tallahassee), 9,200.

SEEING OURSELVES

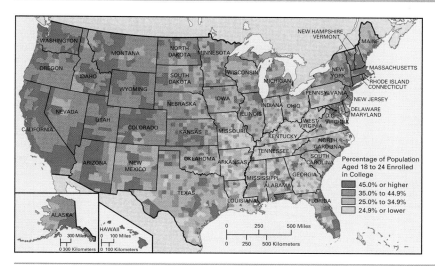

NATIONAL MAP 20–1
College Attendance across the United States

Generally speaking, college attendance is highest among adults along the Northeast and West coasts. By contrast, adults in the Midwest and the South (especially the Appalachian region) are the least likely members of our society to attend college. How would you explain this pattern? (Income is one obvious consideration. Would people's ideas about gender equality be another?)

Source: *American Demographics* magazine, April 1993, p. 60. Reprinted with permission. ©1993 *American Demographics* magazine.

Percentage of Population Aged 18 to 24 Enrolled in College
- 45.0% or higher
- 35.0% to 44.9%
- 25.0% to 34.9%
- 24.9% or lower

Beyond the city limits, affluent suburban school districts offer better schooling than less well-funded systems in central cities. This disparity—which benefits whites—led to *busing*, or transporting students to achieve racial balance and equal opportunity in schools. Although only 5 percent of U.S. schoolchildren are bused to schools outside their neighborhoods, this policy has generated heated controversy. Busing advocates claim that the only way government will adequately fund schools in poor, minority neighborhoods is if white children from richer neighborhoods attend them. Critics respond that busing is expensive and undermines the concept of neighborhood schools. But both sides acknowledge that given the racial imbalance of our nation's urban areas, an effective busing scheme would have to join inner cities and suburbs, a plan that is almost never politically feasible.

A classic report by a research team headed by James Coleman (1966) confirmed that predominantly minority schools suffer more problems, ranging from larger class size to insufficient libraries and fewer science labs. But the Coleman report cautioned that money will not magically improve academic quality. Even more important are the cooperative efforts and enthusiasm of teachers, parents, and the students themselves. In other words, even if school funding were exactly the same everywhere, students who benefit from more *social*

capital—that is, those whose parents value schooling, read to their children, and encourage the development of imagination—would still perform better. Reacting to differences in Ohio schools, state governor Bob Taft (cited in Troy, 2000:A1) put it, "Some children may have been read to 1,000 hours before they come to school. Some children have parents who cannot read themselves." Thus, we should not expect schools alone to overcome marked social inequality in the United States (Schneider et al., 1998; Israel, Beaulieu, & Hartless, 2001).

ACCESS TO HIGHER EDUCATION

In industrial societies, higher education is the main path to occupational achievement. In the United States, 63 percent of high school graduates enroll in college the following fall (U.S. National Center for Education Statistics, 2001). Moreover, among young people eighteen to twenty-four years old, about 33 percent are enrolled in college: National Map 20–1 shows where in the United States college attendance is most and least likely.

The most crucial factor affecting access to U.S. higher education is money. College is expensive, and the cost is rising rapidly. Even at state-supported institutions, annual tuition averages about $3,000, and

DIVERSITY SNAPSHOT

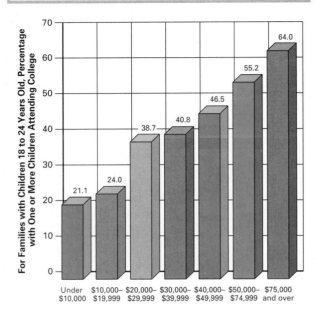

FIGURE 20–2 College Attendance and Family Income, 2000

Source: U.S. Census Bureau (2001).

admission to the most exclusive private colleges and universities exceeds $30,000 a year. As shown in Figure 20–2, families with incomes above $75,000 annually (roughly the richest 20 percent, who fall within the upper and upper-middle classes) send two-thirds of their children to college because they can afford to, but fewer than one-fourth of young people from families earning less than $20,000 each year reach college.

The cost of higher education prevents many minorities, typically with below-average incomes, from attending college. As Figure 20–3 shows, whites are more likely than African Americans and Hispanics to complete high school, and this disparity remains with each step up in the educational system. For some, schooling is a path to social mobility, but it has not overcome persistent racial inequality in the United States (Epps, 1995).

Completing college carries numerous rewards, including intellectual and personal growth as well as higher income. Over a person's working lifetime, a college degree adds almost $500,000 to income (Speer, 1994). Table 20–2 shows why. In 1999, women with an eighth-grade education typically earned $14,375, high school graduates averaged $21,970, and college graduates averaged $36,340. The ratios in parentheses show that a woman with a bachelor's degree earns two-and-one-half times as much as a woman with eight or fewer years of schooling. Across the board, men earn considerably more than women; moreover, more schooling boosts income faster for men than for women. Finally, for both men and women, some of the greater earnings that come with more schooling have to do with social background, because the people with the most schooling are likely to come from upper-class families to begin with.

CREDENTIALISM

Sociologist Randall Collins (1979) calls the United States a *credential society* because people regard diplomas and degrees highly. In modern, technologically advanced societies, credentials say "who you are" as much as family background.

Credentialism, then, is *evaluating a person on the basis of educational degrees.* On one hand, credentialism is simply the way our modern society goes about filling jobs with well-trained people. On the other hand, Collins explains that credentials often bear little relation to the responsibilities of a specific job. In reality, advanced degrees often are an easy way to sort out the people with the manners, attitudes, and even skin color many employers are looking for. Credentialism thus is a gatekeeping strategy that restricts important occupations to a small segment of the population.

PRIVILEGE AND PERSONAL MERIT

If attending college is a rite of passage for affluent men and women, as social-conflict analysis suggests, then *schooling transforms social privilege into personal merit.* But given our cultural emphasis on individualism, we tend to see credentials as "badges of ability" rather than as symbols of family affluence (Sennett & Cobb, 1973). When we congratulate the new graduate, we rarely recognize the resources—both financial and cultural—that made this achievement possible. Yet the fact is that young people from families with incomes exceeding $100,000 a year average 1,130 on college board exams—more than 200 points higher than young people from families with $15,000 income.

DIVERSITY: Race and ethnicity continue to account for significant differences in SAT performance. Combined math/verbal scores in 2000: Asian, Asian American, Pacific Islander: 1,064; white, 1,058; Hispanic/Latino, 928; African American, 860.
NOTE: Another angle on earnings and education: A male high school graduate earns 63% as much as a male with a college degree, and this gap is increasing.

Q: "Discipline is the ultimate tenet of education. Discipline establishes the format, the environment for academic achievement to occur." Joe Clark, controversial principal of Paterson, N.J.'s, Eastside High School
NOTE: Recent research suggests that one-third of parents are "seriously disengaged" from their adolescent children's lives (Steinberg, 1996).

In the same way, we are quick to label the high school dropout as personally deficient, giving little thought to the social circumstances of that person's life. The box on page 530 illustrates this process with the words of one bright but disillusioned boy.

Critical evaluation. Social-conflict analysis links formal education and social inequality to show how schooling transforms privilege into personal worthiness and social disadvantage into personal deficiency. However, critics say that social-conflict analysis minimizes the extent to which schooling provides upward social mobility for talented men and women from all backgrounds. Furthermore, despite the claims that schooling supports the status quo, today's college curricula (including courses in sociology) challenge social inequality on many fronts.

PROBLEMS IN THE SCHOOLS

An intense debate revolves around schooling in the United States today. Perhaps because we expect our schools to do so much—equalize opportunity, instill discipline, and fire the individual imagination—many

 For the full results of this national poll, go to http://www.pdkintl.org

people do not think that public schools are doing a good job. Table 20–3 on page 531 shows that half of all adults give our schools a grade of A or B, but almost as many give our schools a grade of C or below (Phi Delta Kappa International, 2001).

DISCIPLINE AND VIOLENCE

When many of today's older teachers think back to their own days as students, school "problems" consisted of talking out of turn, chewing gum, violating the dress code, and cutting class. But today, schools are grappling with issues such as drug and alcohol abuse, teenage pregnancy, and—as deadly incidents in a number of schools illustrate—outright violence. It is little wonder that although almost everyone agrees that schools should teach personal discipline, few think schools are getting the job done (NORC, 2001:884).

In recent years, violence has claimed the lives of students and teachers in high schools across the United States. Moreover, in national surveys, about one-fourth of students and 11 percent of teachers report being victims of violence in and around schools (Arnette & Walsleben, 1998).

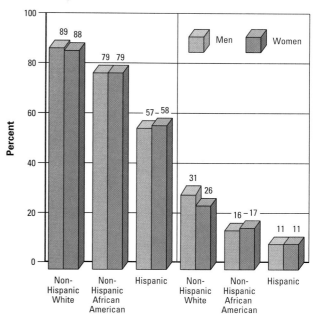

DIVERSITY SNAPSHOT

FIGURE 20–3 Educational Achievement for Various Categories of People, Aged 25 Years and Over, 2000

Source: U.S. Census Bureau (2000).

TABLE 20–2 Median Income by Sex and Educational Attainment*

Education	Men	Women
Professional degree	$96,275 (4.9)	$56,726 (3.9)
Doctorate	76,858 (3.9)	56,345 (3.9)
Master's	61,776 (3.1)	45,345 (3.2)
Bachelor's	51,005 (2.6)	36,340 (2.5)
1–3 years of college	37,245 (1.9)	26,456 (1.8)
4 years of high school	32,098 (1.6)	21,970 (1.5)
9–11 years of school	24,279 (1.2)	16,330 (1.1)
0–8 years of school	19,757 (1.0)	14,375 (1.0)

*Persons aged twenty-five years and over working full time, 1999. The earnings ratio, in parentheses, indicates how many times the lower income level an individual with additional schooling earns.
Source: U.S. Census Bureau (2000).

Q: "Don't let school interfere with your education." Mark Twain
DISCUSS: How might the following factors correlate with the recent rise in school violence? Compared to 1960, the average child spends 11 fewer hours with parents each week, depression among children has increased tenfold, and teen suicide has risen fourfold. Between 1993 and 1996, news coverage of homicide increased eightfold (Cloud, 1999).

SOCIAL SURVEY: In national surveys, about 12% of high school students reported carrying a weapon to school during the previous 30 days (cf. Arnette & Walsleben, 1998).
Q: "There has come to be a recognition that many of the issues in education today are not in the domain of educational psychologists, but have to do with the social structure of the school and the world outside the school." James S. Coleman

DIVERSITY: RACE, CLASS, AND GENDER

"Cooling Out" the Poor: Transforming Disadvantage into Deficiency

If schools paint disadvantaged students as "dumb," over time some of them come to believe it. This process of "cooling out" their ambitions sets into motion a self-fulfilling prophecy by which many poor students end up settling for no more than what society handed them when they were born. Eleven-year-old Ollie Taylor describes the experience in these words:

> The only thing that matters in my life is school and there they think I'm dumb and always will be. I'm starting to think they're right. Hell, I know they put all the black kids together in one group if they can, but that doesn't make any difference either. I'm still dumb. Even if I look

around and know that I'm the smartest in my group, all that means is that I'm the smartest of the dumbest, so I haven't got anywhere at all, have I? I'm right where I always was. Every word those teachers tell me, even the ones I like most, I can hear in their voice that what they're really saying is "All right you dumb kids. I'll make it as easy as I can, and if you don't get it then, you'll never get it. Ever." That's what I hear every day, man. From every one of them. Even the other kids talk that way to me too.

Source: Cottle (1974:22–24).

As most people see it, schools themselves do not create the violence; rather, disorder spills into schools from the surrounding society. But in recent decades, teachers have lost much of their authority in dealing with troublemakers, especially young people who have little interest in school in the first place (Toby, 1998). Nevertheless, schools have it in their power to effect change for the better. The key is to set and enforce firm disciplinary policies, with school personnel supported by parents and, if necessary, police. Violence may be a problem deeply engrained in society itself, but schools can protect teachers and students by forging alliances with parents and community leaders (Gup, 1992).

STUDENT PASSIVITY

If some schools are plagued by violence, many more are afflicted with passive, bored students. Some of the blame for passivity can be placed on television (which

now consumes more of young people's time than school), on parents (who are not involved enough with their children), and on the students themselves. But schools also play a part: Our educational system itself generates student passivity (Coleman, Hoffer, & Kilgore, 1981).

Bureaucracy

The small, personal schools that served countless local communities a century ago have evolved into huge educational factories. In a study of high schools across the United States, Theodore Sizer (1984:207–9) identified five ways in which large, bureaucratic schools undermine education:

1. **Rigid uniformity.** Bureaucratic schools run by outsider specialists (such as state education officials) generally ignore the cultural character of local communities and the personal needs of their children.

2. **Numerical ratings.** School officials define success in terms of numerical attendance records, dropout rates, and achievement test scores. Therefore, they overlook dimensions of schooling that are difficult to quantify, such as the creativity of students and the energy and enthusiasm of teachers.

3. **Rigid expectations.** Officials expect fifteen-year-olds to be in the tenth grade and eleventh-graders to score at a certain level on a standardized verbal achievement test. Rarely are exceptionally bright and motivated students permitted to graduate early. Likewise, the system pushes students from grade to grade whether they have learned anything or not.

4. **Specialization.** High school students learn Spanish from one teacher, receive guidance from another, and are coached in sports by still others. Although specialized teachers may know more about their subjects, no school employee comes to know and appreciate the "complete" student. Students experience this division of labor as a continual shuffling from one fifty-minute period to another throughout the school day.

5. **Little individual responsibility.** Highly bureaucratic schools do not empower students to learn on their own. Similarly, teachers have little latitude in what and how they teach their classes; they dare not accelerate learning for fear of disrupting "the system."

Of course, with more than 50 million schoolchildren in the United States, schools have to be bureaucratic to get the job done. But we can humanize schools to make them more responsive to the students they claim to serve, Sizer maintains. He recommends eliminating rigid class schedules, reducing class size, and training teachers more broadly to help them become more involved in the lives of their students. Overall, as James Coleman (1993) suggested, schools need to be less "administratively driven" and more "output-driven." Perhaps this transformation could begin by ensuring that graduation from high school depends on what students have learned rather than simply on the number of years spent in the building.

College: The Silent Classroom

Here are the observations of a bright and highly motivated first-year student at a high-quality four-year college. Do they strike a familiar chord?

TABLE 20–3 Grading Public Schools in the United States, 2001	
Rating*	**Proportion of Respondents**
A	11%
B	40
C	30
D	8
FAIL	5
Don't know	6

*These figures reflect the responses of a national sample of U.S. adults who were posed the following question: "Students are often given the grades A, B, C, D, and FAIL to denote the quality of their work. Suppose the public schools themselves, in this community, were graded in the same way. What grade would you give the public schools here—A, B, C, D, or FAIL?"

Source: Phi Delta Kappa International/Gallup Poll. [Online] Available http://www.pdkintl.org/kappan/k0109gal.htm, September 24, 2001.

I have been disappointed in my first year at college. Too many students do as little work as they can get away with, take courses that are recommended by other students as being "gut" classes, and never challenge themselves past what is absolutely necessary. It's almost like thinking that we don't watch professors but we watch television. (Forrest, 1984:10)

Passivity is common in colleges and universities. Martha E. Gimenez (1989) describes college as the "silent classroom" because usually the only voice heard is the teacher's. Sociologists tend not to conduct research on the college classroom—a curious fact considering how much time they spend there. An exception is a study at a coeducational university where David Karp and William Yoels (1976) found that—even in small classes—only a handful of students said anything at all during the typical class period. Karp and Yoels concluded that passivity is a classroom norm, and students even become irritated if one of their number is especially talkative.

Students offered Karp and Yoels various explanations for classroom passivity, including not having done the assigned reading or fearing that they might sound unintelligent to teachers and other students. To them, passivity is mostly their own fault. Yet long before they reach college, Karp and Yoels point out, students learn to view instructors as "experts" who serve up "truth." Thus they find little value in classroom discussion and perceive that their proper role is to listen quietly and take notes. As a result, the researchers

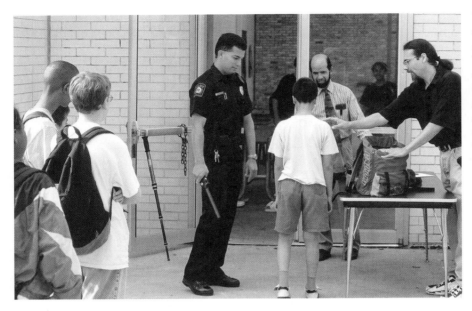

We are all too familiar with the school shootings that have made headlines in recent years. Fear of violence has led many schools to adopt security procedures that seem more appropriate for prisons than places of learning. Here, in the presence of police, officials direct students through a metal detector in an effort to prevent weapons from entering the school.

estimate, just 10 percent of college class time is used for student-led discussion.

Students also realize that instructors generally come to class ready to deliver a prepared lecture. The lecture allows teachers to present a great deal of material in each class, but only to the extent that they avoid being sidetracked by student questions or comments (Boyer, 1987). Early in each course, most instructors single out a few students who are willing and able to provide the occasional, limited comments they desire. Taken together, such patterns form a recipe for passivity on the part of most college students.

Yet faculty can bring students to life in their classrooms by actively involving them in learning. One recent study of classroom dynamics linked higher levels of student participation to four teaching strategies: (1) calling on students by name when they volunteer; (2) positively reinforcing student participation; (3) asking analytical rather than factual questions and giving students time to answer; and (4) asking for student opinions even when there are no volunteers (Auster & MacRone, 1994).

DROPPING OUT

If many students are passive in class, others are not there at all. The problem of *dropping out*—quitting school before earning a high school diploma—leaves young people (many of whom are disadvantaged to

begin with) ill-equipped for the world of work and at high risk for poverty.

The dropout rate has eased slightly in recent decades; currently about 12 percent of people between ages sixteen and twenty-four have dropped out of school, a total of 3.6 million young women and men. Dropping out is least pronounced among non-Hispanic whites (8 percent), higher among non-Hispanic African Americans (14 percent), and highest of all among Hispanics (30 percent) (U.S. National Center for Education Statistics, 2001). National Map 20–2 shows the dropout rate for counties across the United States.

Some students drop out because of problems with the English language or because of pregnancy; others, whose families are poor, must go to work. The dropout rate (12.3 percent) among children growing up in the bottom 20 percent of households is seven times higher than that (1.8 percent) for youngsters whose households fall in the top 20 percent by income (U.S. National Center for Education Statistics, 2001). These data point to the fact that many dropouts are young people whose parents also have little schooling, creating a multigenerational cycle of disadvantage (Pirog & Magee, 1997).

The United States was once the world leader in high school graduation rates. In recent years, however, many other countries have greatly improved their performance, while there has been little change here. As a

THE MAP: High dropout rates across the South are explained by high rates of poverty: Young people in poor families are roughly 10 times more likely to drop out of school than children in affluent families. In the Southwest, the high concentration of Hispanic people helps explain the high dropout rates.

Q: "I am always ready to learn, although I do not always like being taught." Winston Churchill

NOTE: Dropout rates are extremely high for large, urban school systems in the U.S. Examples: Boston, 46%; Chicago, 45%; Los Angeles, 45%; New York, 34%; St. Louis, 30%.

DIVERSITY: In 1998, Hispanics accounted for 56% of U.S. immigrants but 90% of immigrant school dropouts (Department of Education).

SEEING OURSELVES

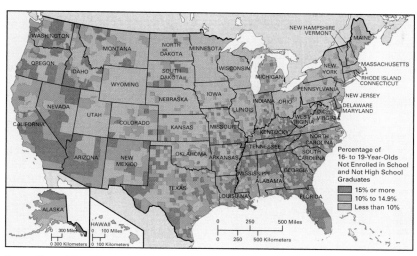

NATIONAL MAP 20–2
High School Dropouts across the United States

Across the United States, the highest dropout rate is found in Holmes County, Ohio, where more than half of young people are not enrolled in school or high school graduates. This county has a largely Amish population, and young people leave school to work on farms. Regionally, dropout rates are high across the South—from West Virginia down to Florida and from the Carolinas to Louisiana and east Texas. Rates are also high in the Southwest. What factors do you think account for this pattern?

Percentage of 16- to 19-Year-Olds Not Enrolled in School and Not High School Graduates
- 15% or more
- 10% to 14.9%
- Less than 10%

Source: From *Atlas of Contemporary America* by Rodger Doyle. Map copyright © 1994 by Facts on File, Inc. Reprinted with permission of Facts on File, Inc.

result, this country now ranks twenty-third in high school graduation rates, lagging behind Canada, Japan, and most of the nations of Western Europe (Desruisseaux, 1998).

ACADEMIC STANDARDS

Perhaps the most serious educational issue confronting our society is the quality of schooling. *A Nation at Risk*, a comprehensive report on the quality of U.S. schools published in 1983 by the National Commission on Excellence in Education, begins with this alarming statement:

> If an unfriendly foreign power had attempted to impose on America the mediocre educational performance that exists today, we might well have viewed it as an act of war. As it stands, we have allowed this to happen to ourselves. (1983:5)

Supporting this conclusion, the report notes that "nearly 40 percent of seventeen-year-olds cannot draw inferences from written material; only one-fifth can write a persuasive essay; and only one-third can solve mathematical problems requiring several steps" (1983:9). Furthermore, scores on the Scholastic Aptitude Test

(SAT) have declined in recent decades. In 1967, median scores for students were 516 on the mathematical test and 543 on the verbal test; by 2000, despite a recovery during the last few years, the averages were 514 and 505, respectively. Nationwide, about one-third of high school students—and more than half in urban schools—fail to master even the basics in reading, math, and science on the National Assessment of Education Progress examination (Sanchez, 1998; Marklein, 2000).

For many, even basic literacy is at issue. **Functional illiteracy,** *a lack of reading and writing skills needed for everyday living*, is a problem for one in eight children who leave U.S. secondary schools. For older people, the problem is even worse, so that, overall, some 40 million U.S. adults (roughly 20 percent of the total) read and write at an eighth-grade level or below. As Figure 20–4 on page 534 shows, the extent of functional illiteracy in the United States is below that of middle-income nations (such as Poland) but higher than in other high-income countries (such as Canada and Sweden).

To improve our educational system, *A Nation at Risk* called for drastic measures. First, all schools should require students to complete several years of English, mathematics, social studies, general science,

NOTE: Federal literacy programs enroll several million adults each year, a small proportion of those who are functionally illiterate.

NOTE: One study of the mathematical skills of 12th graders concluded that 48.2% knew the basics, 35.6% were below "basics" level, 13.6% were "proficient," and 2.6% were "advanced" (National Assessment of Educational Progress).

NOTE: Edison Schools is the largest for-profit school company; they claim to spend less than 15% of their costs on administration, compared to about 30% in regular public schools.

NOTE: The most powerful opponent of school choice programs is the National Education Association (NEA), with more than 2 million members, mostly teachers.

GLOBAL SNAPSHOT

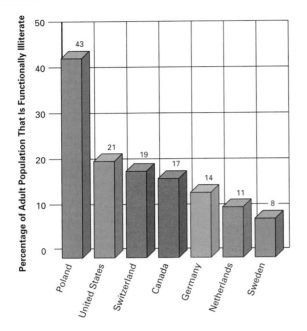

FIGURE 20–4 Functional Illiteracy in Global Perspective

Source: Fiske (1997).

and computer science courses. Second, schools should not promote failing students from grade to grade; instead, students should remain in the classroom as long as necessary to learn basic skills. Third, teacher training must improve, and teachers' salaries should rise to attract talent into the profession. *A Nation at Risk* concluded that educators must ensure that schools meet public expectations and that citizens must be prepared to bear the costs of good schools.

What has happened in the years since this report was issued? In some respects, schools have improved. A report by the Center on Education Policy (2000) noted a decline in the dropout rate, a trend toward schools offering more challenging courses, and a larger share of high school graduates going on to college. Despite several tragic cases of shootings, overall school violence was down during the 1990s. At the same time, the evidence suggests that a majority of

elementary school students are falling below standards in reading; in many cases, they can't read at all. In short, although some improvement is evident, there remains much to be done.

A final concern is the low performance of U.S. students in a global context. Although per-student spending is greater in this country than almost anywhere else, U.S. eighth graders still place seventeenth in the world in science achievement and twenty-eighth in mathematics (Bennett, 1997; Finn & Walberg, 1998). Cultural values play a big part in international comparisons. For example, U.S. students generally are less motivated than their counterparts in Japan and also do less homework. Moreover, Japanese young people spend sixty more days in school each year than U.S. students. Perhaps one approach to improving schools is simply to have students spend more time there.

RECENT ISSUES IN U.S. EDUCATION

Our society's schools continuously confront new challenges. This final section explores several recent and important educational issues.

SCHOOL CHOICE

Some analysts claim that the reason our schools do not teach very well is that they have no competition. Thus, giving parents options for schooling their children might force all schools to do a better job. This is the essence of a policy called *school choice*.

Proponents of school choice advocate creating a market for schooling so that parents and students can shop for the best value. According to the most sweeping proposal, the government would give vouchers to families with school-aged children and allow them to spend that money at public, private, or parochial schools. During the 1990s, Indianapolis, Minneapolis, Milwaukee, Cleveland, and the state of Florida experimented with choice plans aimed at making public schools perform better to win the confidence of families. In addition, the Children's Scholarship Fund, a privately funded charity, has supported 40,000 children who want to attend nonpublic schools and has more than 1 million children on its waiting list.

Supporters claim that giving parents a choice about where to enroll their children is the only sure way to improve all schools. But critics (including teachers' unions) charge that school choice has yet to prove itself. Moreover, they believe these programs

DISCUSS: The Children's Scholarship Fund (1-800-805-KIDS) is a private charity that distributes scholarships worth $170 million to 40,000 low-income U.S. children. Is this charity—funded by rich businesspeople—a good way to help poor children afford better schooling? Or a strategy to increase demand for school choice programs and weaken public education? (cf. Rhodes, 1999)

NOTE: Since 1970, the number of U.S. students with "specific learning disabilities" has increased rapidly from 796,000 to 2.7 million, which is now 6% of public school students.
NOTE: With greater resources going to gifted and learning disabled students, the share of budgets going to "ordinary students" fell from 80% in 1967 to 59% in 1998 (Ratnesar, 1998).

erode our nation's commitment to public education, especially in the central cities, where the need is greatest (Martinez et al., 1995; Godwin et al., 1998; Cohen, 1999; Forstmann, 1999). Despite pressure from the Bush administration, Congress has so far resisted enacting any voucher system.

A more modest form of school choice involves *magnet schools*, 1,000 of which now exist across the country. Magnet schools offer special facilities and programs to promote educational excellence in a particular area, such as computer science, foreign languages, science, mathematics, or the arts. In school districts with magnet schools, parents can choose the one best suited to their child's particular talents and interests.

Another successful choice program involves *charter schools*, public schools that are given more freedom to operate in order to try out new policies and programs. There are about 1,500 such schools in the United States. In many of these schools, students demonstrate high academic achievement—a necessary condition for the charter to be renewed.

A final development in the school choice movement is *schooling for profit*. Advocates of this plan say school systems operated by private profit-making companies would be more efficient than schools run by local governments. Private schooling is nothing new; across the United States, more than 25,000 schools are run by private organizations and religious groups. What is new, however, is the small number of public schools—about 250 in 2000 enrolling some 120,000 students—that are run by private businesses for profit (Greenwald, 2000).

Research confirms that many public school systems suffer from bureaucratic bloat, spending too much and teaching too little. And our society has long looked to competition and private initiative to improve quality and cut costs. Evidence suggests that for-profit schools have reduced administrative costs far below those of regular public schools. But the educational results of schooling for profit appear mixed. Several companies claim to have improved student learning, yet some cities have cut back on business-run schools. In 1995, for example, Baltimore canceled the contract of the corporation that had taken over nine of its schools in 1992; school boards in Miami and Hartford, Connecticut, have also canceled contracts. In short, public school systems perform poorly in many cities; but whether private business can improve on their record remains unclear (Putka & Stecklow, 1994; Kanamine, 1995; Ravitch & Viteritti, 1996; Bennett, 1997; Toch, 1998).

Educators have long debated the proper manner in which to school children with disabilities. On one hand, such children may benefit from distinctive facilities and specially trained teachers. On the other hand, they are less likely to be stigmatized as "different" if included in regular classroom settings. What do you consider to be the ramifications of the "special education" versus "inclusive education" debate for the classroom experience of all *children, not only those who have disabilities?*

SCHOOLING PEOPLE WITH DISABILITIES

Bureaucratic schools do not readily meet the special needs of some people, including many of the 5 million U.S. children with physical impairments. Many children with disabilities have difficulty getting to and from school, and many with crutches or wheelchairs cannot negotiate stairs and other obstacles inside school buildings. Children with developmental disabilities such as mental retardation require extensive personal attention from specially trained teachers. As a result, many children with mental and physical disabilities have received a public education only because of persistent efforts by parents and other concerned citizens.

About one-fourth of children with disabilities are schooled in special facilities; the rest attend public schools, many participating in regular classes. Thus, most schools avoid expensive "special education" in favor of **mainstreaming,** *integrating special students into the overall educational program.* Mainstreaming is a form of *inclusive education* that works best for physically impaired students who have no difficulty keeping up with the rest of the class. Moreover, putting children with and without disabilities in the same classroom allows everyone to learn more about interacting with people who differ from themselves.

ADULT EDUCATION

Most schooling involves young people. However, the share of U.S. students aged twenty-five and older has risen sharply in recent years and now accounts for 36 percent of people in the classroom.

In 1999, more than 76 million U.S. adults enrolled in some type of schooling. These older students range in age from the mid-twenties to the seventies and beyond. Adults in school are twice as likely to be women as men and generally have above-average incomes. Some are people who dropped out of high school in the past; others are part-time students completing college degrees. Still others already have a college diploma and other advanced degrees and are trying to advance their careers or are simply returning to the classroom to experience the joy of learning (Speer, 1996; Miller, 1997a).

THE TEACHER SHORTAGE

A final challenge for U.S. schools is hiring enough teachers to fill the classrooms. A number of factors— including low salaries, frustration, and retirement, as well as rising enrollment and reductions in class size— have combined to create more than 200,000 teaching vacancies in the United States each year.

How will these slots be filled? About the same number of people graduate with education degrees annually, but most lack a degree in a specific field (such as mathematics, biology, or English). In fact, many have trouble passing state certification tests in the area they wish to teach.

As a result, schools have adopted new recruitment strategies. One is to encourage more people who have already established successful careers to switch to teaching. To attract people, schools are making it easier to obtain teaching certification, offering higher salaries and signing bonuses, and pointing out that there is probably no work more important than training our children. In addition, many school districts are going

 For a National Center for Education Statistics (NCES) report titled "Trends in Educational Equity of Girls & Women," go to http://nces.ed.gov/pubs2000/2000030.pdf

global, actively recruiting in countries such as Spain, India, and the Philippines to bring talented women and men to U.S. classrooms (Dervarics, 1999; Lord, 2001; Philadelphia, 2001).

Of course, the debates about education in the United States spread beyond the issues noted here. The final box takes a look at the recent trend by which men represent a declining share of students on college campuses.

LOOKING AHEAD: SCHOOLING IN THE TWENTY-FIRST CENTURY

Despite the fact that the United States leads the world in providing a college education to its people, our public school system continues to struggle with serious problems, many of which have their roots in the larger society. Thus, during this new century, we cannot expect schools *by themselves* to improve the quality of education. Schools will improve only to the extent to which students, teachers, parents, and local communities commit to educational excellence. In short, educational dilemmas are *social* problems, and there is no quick fix.

For much of the twentieth century, there were just two models for education in the United States: public schools run by the government and private schools operated by nongovernment organizations. In the last decade, however, many new ideas about schooling have come on the scene, including schooling for profit and a wide range of "choice" programs (Finn & Gau, 1998). In the decades ahead, we will probably see some significant changes in mass education, guided in part by social science research on the consequences of different strategies.

Whatever decisions are made about who controls education, one factor that will continue to re-shape schools is new information technology. Today, 97 percent of conventional primary and secondary schools have instructional computers. The promise of this new technology goes beyond helping students learn basic skills; computers can improve the overall quality of learning. Computers help students be more active learners and allow them to progress at their own pace. For students with disabilities who cannot write using a pencil, computers permit easier self-expression. For all students, using computers in schools—in some cases as early as kindergarten— appears to increase significantly how fast students learn and helps prepare them for the workplace of the twenty-first century.

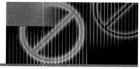

CONTROVERSY & DEBATE

The Twenty-First Century Campus: Where Are the Men?

A century ago, the campuses of colleges and universities across the United States might as well have hung out a sign that read "Men Only!" Almost all of the students and faculty were male. Although there were a number of women's colleges, many more schools, including some of the best-known U.S. universities (such as Yale, Harvard, and Princeton), barred women outright.

As the twentieth century proceeded, however, women won greater social equality. Therefore, few people were surprised when, in 1980, the number of women enrolled at U.S. colleges finally matched the number of men.

What is surprising is what has happened since then: The share of women on the campus has continued to increase. As a result, in 2000 men accounted for only 44 percent of all U.S. undergraduates. Student Meg DeLong noticed the gender imbalance right away when she moved into her dorm at the University of Georgia at Athens. In fact, 39 percent of the first-year students were men. In classes, DeLong found there were few men, and women dominated discussions. Out of class, she and many other women complained that having so few men on campus was

hurting their social life (not surprisingly, the men felt otherwise about their own social life).

Why the shifting gender balance on U.S. campuses? No one knows for sure, but several theories have been put forward. Some suggest that young men are drawn away from college by the lure of jobs, especially in high technology. This pattern is sometimes called the "Bill Gates syndrome," after the Microsoft founder who dropped out of college to become the world's richest person. In addition, analysts point to an anti-intellectual male culture. That is, whereas young women are drawn to learning and seek to do well in school, young men are more likely to consider studying and schoolwork as "something for girls." In short, rightly or wrongly, more men seem to think they can get a good job without investing years of their lives and a lot of money to get a college degree.

The gender gap is evident among all racial and ethnic categories. In fact, only 37 percent of African American college students are men. It is also found at all class levels. Indeed, the lower the income level, the greater the gender gap in college attendance.

Many college officials are concerned about this trend. In an effort to attract

more balanced enrollments, some colleges adopted what amounts to affirmative action programs that favor males. In several states, however, courts have ruled that such policies are illegal. Therefore, many colleges are turning to more vigorous recruitment, having admission officers pay special attention to male applicants and stressing a college's strength in mathematics and science—areas that traditionally have attracted men. Although colleges across the country are striving to increase their number of minority students, the hope is that they can also succeed in attracting more men.

Continue the debate . . .

1. *Do you think that among high school students, men are less concerned than women with academic achievement? Why?*

2. *Is there a lack of males on your campus? Does it create problems? What problems? For whom?*

3. *What programs or policies do you think might increase the number of men going to college?*

Source: Based on Fonda (2000).

The numerous benefits of computers should not blind us to their limitations, however. Computers will never bring to the educational process the personal insight or imagination of a motivated teacher. Nor can computers tap what one teacher calls the "springs of human identity and creativity" that we discover by exploring literature and language rather than simply manipulating mathematical codes. Indeed, despite their proliferation in the classroom, computers have yet to

change teaching and learning in any fundamental sense or even replace the traditional blackboard (Berger, 1991; Elmer-DeWitt, 1991; Skinner, 1997). Therefore, we should not look to technology to solve the problems—including violence and rigid bureaucracy—that plague our schools. What we need is a broad plan for social change that refires this country's early ambition to provide high-quality universal schooling—a goal that has so far eluded us.

SUMMARY

1. Education is the major social institution for transmitting knowledge and skills and teaching cultural norms and values. In preindustrial societies, education occurs informally within the family; industrial societies develop formal systems of schooling.

2. The United States was among the first countries to institute compulsory mass education, reflecting both democratic political ideals and the needs of the industrial-capitalist economy.

3. Structural-functional analysis highlights major functions of schooling, including socialization, cultural innovation, social integration, and perpetuation of the social hierarchy. Latent functions of schooling include providing child care and building social networks.

4. Social-conflict analysis links schooling to hierarchy involving class, race, and gender. Formal education also promotes conformity to produce compliant adult workers.

5. Standardized achievement tests are controversial. Some see them as a reasonable measure of academic aptitude and learning; others say they are culturally biased tools used to label less privileged students as personally deficient.

6. Tracking also is controversial. Some see tracking as the way schools provide appropriate instruction for students with different interests and aptitudes; others say tracking gives privileged youngsters a richer education.

7. Most young people in the United States attend state-funded public schools. Most private schools offer a religious education. A small proportion of students, usually well-to-do, attend elite, private preparatory schools.

8. One-fourth of U.S. adults over age twenty-five are college graduates, marking the emergence of a "credential society." People with college degrees enjoy much higher lifetime earnings.

9. Most adults in the United States are critical of public schools. Violence permeates many schools, especially those in poor neighborhoods. The bureaucratic character of schools also fosters high dropout rates and student passivity.

10. Declining academic standards are reflected in today's lower average scores on achievement tests and the functional illiteracy of a significant proportion of high school graduates.

11. The school choice movement seeks to make schools more responsive to the public. Innovative options include magnet schools, schooling for profit, and charter schools, all of which are topics of continuing policy debate.

12. Children with mental or physical disabilities historically have been schooled in special classes or not at all. Mainstreaming affords them broader opportunities.

13. Adults are a growing proportion of students in the United States. Most older learners are women who are engaged in job-related study.

14. The Information Revolution is changing schooling through increasing use of computers. Although computers permit interactive, self-paced learning, they are not suitable for teaching every subject.

KEY CONCEPTS

education (p. 517) the social institution through which society provides its members with important knowledge, including basic facts, job skills, and cultural norms and values

schooling (p. 517) formal instruction under the direction of specially trained teachers

hidden curriculum (p. 524) subtle presentations of political or cultural ideas in the classroom

tracking (p. 524) assigning students to different types of educational programs

credentialism (p. 528) evaluating a person on the basis of educational degrees

functional illiteracy (p. 533) a lack of reading and writing skills needed for everyday living

mainstreaming (p. 535) integrating special students into the overall educational program

CRITICAL-THINKING QUESTIONS

1. Why does industrialization lead societies to expand their systems of schooling?

2. In what ways is schooling in the United States shaped by our economic, political, and cultural systems?

CTQ4: Many good college professors do motivate students to become active learners using various classroom techniques; still, the norm of educational passivity is established much earlier.

NOTE: Higher education institutions offering the top average salaries for full professor include Harvard (number one at $104,000), Rutgers, Princeton, and Yale, ranging from $96,500 to $99,300. National averages: full, $63,450 (men, $64,560; women, $57,160); associate, $47,040; assistant, $39,050; instructor, $29,680; lecturer, $32,600; overall average, $49,500. Average at doctorate-granting institutions, $71,290; community colleges, $51,790; private colleges, $84,790; public colleges, $67,560. Forty percent of all faculty are part timers who earn much less than these figures. Lawyers earn 70% more than professors, on average (AAUP).

3. From a structural-functional perspective, why is schooling important to the operation of society? From a social-conflict point of view, how does formal education reproduce social inequality in each generation?

4. Do you agree with research findings presented in this chapter that college students generally are passive in class? If so, what do you think colleges can do to make everyone more active participants in learning?

APPLICATIONS AND EXERCISES

1. Arrange to visit a secondary school near your college or home. Does it have a tracking policy? If so, find out how it works. How much importance does a student's social background have in making a track assignment?

2. Most people agree that teaching our children is a vital task. Yet most teachers earn relatively low salaries. Check the prestige ranking for teachers back in Table 11–2. See what you can learn about the average salaries of teachers compared to those of other workers. Can you explain this pattern?

3. After the passage of the Americans with Disabilities Act in 1990, schools have sought to "accommodate" students with a broader range of physical and mental disabilities. Do some research or contact officials on your campus to learn how laws of this kind are changing education.

4. Packaged in the back of this new textbook is an interactive CD-ROM that offers a variety of study and review materials intended to help you better understand the material covered in this chapter. For this chapter, the CD-ROM contains an author's tip video, Real Life Sociology videos, other relevant audio and video, interactive map animations, audio journal entries from the author, Web links, and much more.

 ## SITES TO SEE

http://www.prenhall.com/macionis

Visit the interactive *Companion Website*™ that accompanies this text. Begin by clicking on the cover of your book. You will find a chapter-by-chapter study guide, practice tests, and a significant portion of the text for on-line review, as well as many suggested Web links.

http://nces.ed.gov/

The National Center for Education Statistics provides data about U.S. education, including a profile of those who have earned various degrees by gender and race.

http://www.acpe.asu.edu/VirtualU/

To explore how new information technology is reshaping education, read about the founding of Western Virtual University, this country's first "cyber-college." Think about the advantages and disadvantages of this type of schooling.

http://www2.kenyon.edu/projects/famfarm/

Visit the Family Farm Web site at Kenyon College. This site was created by students to share what they have learned about farming and rural life in a rural county in central Ohio.

http://www.nces.ed.gov/pubs98/violence/index.html

The issue of school violence is the focus of this government Web site.

http://www.chronicle.com

This site provides general news and information about higher education.

 INVESTIGATE WITH CONTENTSELECT

Follow the instructions found on page 23 of this textbook to enter this chapter of the book's *Companion Website*™. Once in the chapter, click on the ContentSelect icon at the bottom left of your screen and enter your personal User ID and Password. Enter keywords such as "tracking," "functional illiteracy," and "charter schools," and the search engine will help you become an effective researcher.

CHAPTER

21

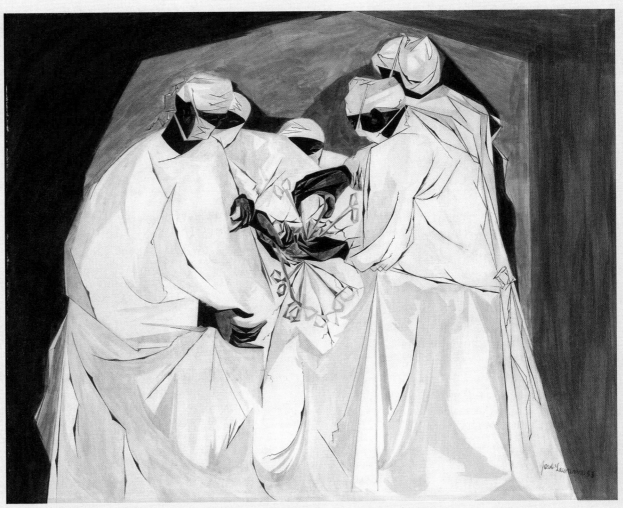

Jacob Lawrence (b. 1917)
Harlem Hospital Surgery, 1953

Tempera on masonite, 20 × 24 in., signed and dated.
Courtesy of Michael Rosenfeld Gallery, New York. © Jacob Lawrence.

HEALTH AND MEDICINE

I n 1995, television came to Fiji, a small island in the South Seas of the Pacific Ocean. A single cable channel carried programming from the United States, Great Britain, and Australia. When Anne Becker, a Harvard researcher specializing in eating disorders, read the news, her sociological imagination led her to wonder what effect watching television would have on young women there.

Becker knew that Fijian culture emphasized good nutrition and

looking strong and healthy. Dieting to look very thin had never been common in Fiji. Indeed, in 1995, Becker found, just 3 percent of teenage girls reported ever vomiting to control their weight. By 1998, however, a striking change was evident: Fifteen percent of teenage girls—a fivefold increase—reported this practice. Moreover, Becker found that 62 percent of girls said they had dieted during the previous month, and 74 percent reported feeling "too big" or "fat" (Becker, 1999).

The rapid rise in eating disorders in Fiji after television was introduced shows the power of society to shape patterns of health. Eating disorders, including anorexia nervosa (medically, a practice of severe caloric restriction, commonly understood as compulsive dieting) and bulimia (binge eating followed by vomiting), are even more common in the United States. In fact, about half of college women report engaging in such behavior, even though most, medically speaking, are not overweight.

Consider, too, that 95 percent of people with an eating disorder are female. Why? Because weight control is part of our cultural definition of femininity: As the Duchess of Windsor once put it, "A woman cannot be too rich or too thin." In the United States— and now Fiji as well—society teaches young women that they are "never too thin to feel fat" (Wooley, Wooley, & Dyrenforth, 1979; Levine, 1987; Parrott, 1987; Robinson, 1987).

WHAT IS HEALTH?

The World Health Organization defines **health** as *a state of complete physical, mental, and social well-being* (1946:3). This definition underscores the major theme of this chapter: *Health is as much a social as a biological issue because well-being and illness have their roots in the organization of society.*

For the Web site of the World Health Organization, go to http://www.who.int

HEALTH AND SOCIETY

Society shapes people's health in five major ways:

1. **Cultural patterns define health**. Standards of health vary from society to society. Early in the twentieth century, yaws, a contagious skin disease, was so common in sub-Saharan Africa that people there considered it normal. Similarly, according to the U.S. Centers for Disease Control and Prevention (2000), the rich foods that people in the United States consume are responsible for almost two-thirds of adults being overweight. "Health" is sometimes a matter of having the same disease as one's neighbors (Dubos, 1980; Pinhey, Rubinstein, & Colfax, 1997).

2. **What is considered healthy often is the same as what people define as morally good.** Members of our society (especially men) think a competitive way of life is healthy because it fits our cultural mores. This is so even though stress contributes to heart disease and many other illnesses. On the other hand, some people who object to homosexuality on moral grounds call this sexual orientation "sick," even though it is natural from a biological point of view. Thus, ideas about good health amount to a form of social control that encourages conformity to cultural norms.

541

SUPPLEMENTS: An outline of this chapter, supplementary lecture material, and suggested discussion topics are included in the *Data File*.
Q: "Medicine and biology were of crucial importance, providing the basic concepts through which the class and sexual divisions of Victorian society were expressed and ultimately justified." Lesley Doyal (1981:141)

THEN AND NOW: Technology has rapidly changed the character of modern medicine. The first map of the circulatory system was made in 1628. The first heart transplant was done in 1961; for several years thereafter, each transplant was a major media event. Today, such procedures are common (about 1,500 performed annually) and are covered (with special provisions) by Medicare.

The profession of surgery has existed only for several centuries. Before that, barbers offered their services to the very sick, often cutting the skin to "bleed" a patient. Of course, this "treatment" was rarely effective, but it did produce plenty of bloody bandages, which practitioners hung out to dry. This practice identifies the origin of the red and white barber poles we see today.

Lucas van Leyden, *The Surgeon and the Peasant*, Rijksmuseum, Amsterdam.

3. **Cultural standards of health change over time**. In the early twentieth century, some physicians warned women not to go to college because higher education strained the female brain. Others denounced masturbation as a danger to health. Today, on both counts, we know differently. Similarly, in 1950, about 30 percent of U.S. adults reported bathing every day, compared to about 75 percent in 2000 (Gallup, 2000).

4. **A society's technology affects people's health.** In poor societies, infectious diseases are rampant because of malnutrition and poor sanitation. As industrialization raises living standards, people become more healthy. But industrial technology also creates new threats to health. As Chapter 22 ("Population, Urbanization, and Environment") explains, high-income countries threaten human health by overtaxing the world's resources and creating pollution.

5. **Social inequality affects people's health.** All societies distribute resources unequally. Therefore, some people are healthier than others. This pattern starts at birth, with infant mortality highest among the poor. Poor people also live fewer years than rich people.

HEALTH: A GLOBAL SURVEY

Because health is closely linked to social life, we find that humans have fared better and better over the long course of history. For the same reason, we see striking differences in health around the world today.

HEALTH IN HISTORY

Many hunting and gathering people had fairly healthful diets, eating a range of vegetation and, when available, lean meat. With only simple technology, however, our ancestors were vulnerable to drought and other natural events that could cause widespread hunger. In addition, they faced injuries and illnesses for which there was little or no treatment. Thus, in these societies, few people lived to age forty, and about half never made it to twenty (Nolan & Lenski, 1999; Scupin, 2000).

With the discovery of agriculture, food became more plentiful. At the same time, many societies began to rely on single crops, which led to a less nutritious diet. Moreover, social inequality increased, so that elites enjoyed better health and peasants and slaves lived in crowded, unsanitary shelters and often went hungry. In the growing cities of medieval Europe, human waste and other refuse piled up in the streets, spreading infectious diseases and plagues that periodically wiped out entire towns (Mumford, 1961).

HEALTH IN LOW-INCOME COUNTRIES

November 1, central India. Poverty is not just a matter of what you have; it shapes what you are. Probably most of the people we see in the villages here

Q: "Hunger may have been the human race's constant companion, and 'the poor may always be with us,' but in the twentieth century, one cannot take this fatalistic view of the destiny of millions of fellow creatures. Their condition is not inevitable but is caused by identifiable forces within the province of rational, human control." Susan George

Q: "The ways in which the poor die reflect the conditions of their lives." Carol Stack (1975)

NOTE: The terms "healthful" and "wholesome" are used to refer to what is both medically and morally desirable.

NOTE: One sign of long-term improvement in nutrition: Lucy, the 3-million-year-old adult fossilized skeleton found in Ethiopia, stood only about 3 feet 6 inches tall; she would have weighed 65 pounds.

GLOBAL SOCIOLOGY

Killer Poverty: A Report from Africa

The television images of famine in Africa bring home to people in the United States the horror of starving children. Some of the children appear bloated, while others seem to have shriveled to little more than skin drawn tightly over bones. Both of these deadly conditions are direct results of poverty, Susan George (1977) explains.

The bloated bodies of some children are caused by protein deficiency. In west Africa this condition is known as *kwashiorkor*, which means literally "one-two." The term comes from the common practice among mothers of abruptly weaning a first child upon the birth of a second. Deprived of mother's milk, a baby may receive no protein at all.

The shriveled bodies of other children come from a lack of both protein and calories. These children have too little food of any kind.

Strictly speaking, only rarely does starvation kill children. Hunger weakens children, leaving them vulnerable to stomach ailments such as gastroenteritis, or diseases such as measles. For

example, the death rate from measles is a thousand times greater in parts of Africa than in North America.

Eating just a single food also makes for poor nutrition, providing too little protein, vitamins, and minerals. Millions of people in low-income countries suffer from goiter, a debilitating, diet-related disease of the thyroid gland.

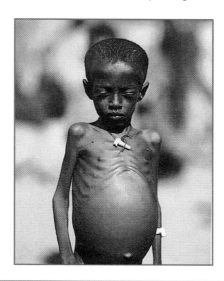

Pellagra, common among people who consume mostly corn, is a serious disease that can lead to insanity. Similarly, people who eat only processed rice are prone to beriberi.

Health is obviously a social issue because diseases that are virtually unknown to people in rich countries are common in poor nations around the world.

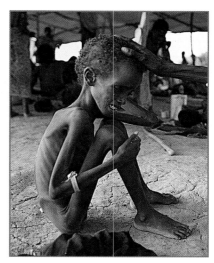

have never had the benefit of a doctor or a dentist. The result is easy to see: People look old before their time.

Severe poverty in much of the world cuts life expectancy far below the seventy or more years typical of rich societies. A look back at Global Map 15–2, on page 389, shows that people in most parts of Africa have a life expectancy of barely fifty, and in the world's poorest nations, such as Ethiopia and Rwanda, the figure falls to forty.

The World Health Organization reports that 1 billion people around the world—one in six—suffer from serious illness caused by poverty. Poor sanitation and malnutrition kill people of all ages but especially children. Bad health results not just from having too little to eat but also from consuming only one kind of food, as the box explains.

In impoverished countries, sanitary drinking water is as hard to come by as a balanced diet. Unsafe water is a major cause of the infectious diseases that imperil both adults and children. The leading causes of death in the United States a century ago, including

GLOBAL: Only about one-third of the world's people tap into a safe water supply. Worldwide, more than 500,000 women, almost all in poor countries, die each year from pregnancy-related causes.

NOTE: Until the end of the 19th century, Philadelphia drew water from the Delaware River at one point while discharging sewage at another. Such practices were common until the germ theory of disease led to programs to improve environmental quality.

GLOBAL: Illustrating high mortality from infectious disease early in the 20th century, a 1918 flu epidemic killed millions worldwide, including 500,000 in the U.S.

Q: "Less access to the present health system would, contrary to popular rhetoric, *benefit* the poor." Ivan Illich

GLOBAL: Physicians in most poor societies of the world do not share diagnostic information freely with patients.

WINDOW ON THE WORLD

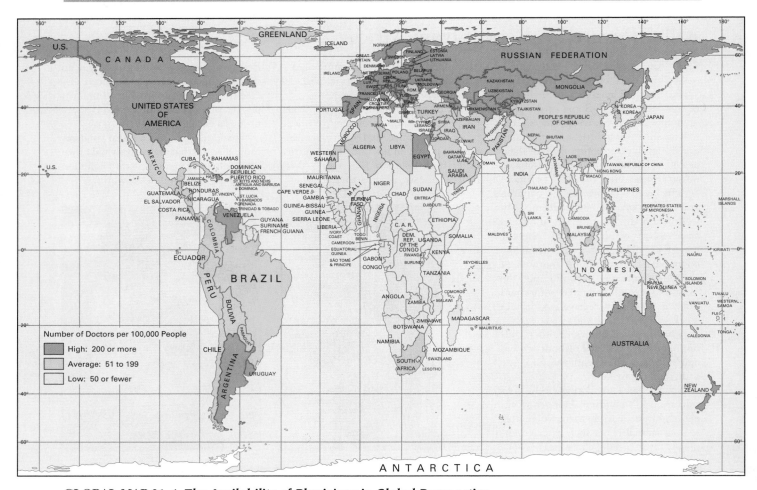

GLOBAL MAP 21–1 The Availability of Physicians in Global Perspective

Medical doctors, widely available to people in rich nations, are perilously scarce in poor societies. Although traditional forms of healing do improve health, antibiotics and vaccines—vital for controlling infectious diseases—often are in short supply. In poor countries, therefore, death rates are high, especially among infants.

Source: United Nations Development Programme (2001); map projection from *Peters Atlas of the World* (1990).

influenza, pneumonia, and tuberculosis, are widespread killers in poor societies today.

To make matters worse, medical personnel are few and far between, so that the world's poorest people, many of whom live in central Africa, never see a physician. Global Map 21–1 shows the availability of doctors throughout the world.

In poor nations with minimal medical care, 10 percent of children die within a year of their birth. In some countries, half the children never reach adulthood—a pattern that parallels the death rates in Europe two centuries ago (George, 1977; Harrison, 1984; United Nations Development Programme, 2001).

In much of the world, illness and poverty form a vicious circle: Poverty breeds disease, which in turn, undermines people's ability to work. Moreover, when medical technology curbs infectious disease, the populations of poor nations soar. Without resources to ensure the well-being of the people they have now, poor societies can ill afford large populations. Ultimately, programs to lower death rates in poor countries will succeed only if they are coupled with programs to reduce birth rates.

HEALTH IN HIGH-INCOME COUNTRIES

Industrialization dramatically changed patterns of human health in Europe, although at first not for the better. By 1800, as the Industrial Revolution took hold, factories offered jobs that drew people from all over the countryside. Cities quickly became overcrowded, creating serious sanitation problems. Moreover, factories fouled the air with smoke, which few saw as a threat to health until well into the twentieth century. And accidents in the workplace were common.

But industrialization gradually improved health in Western Europe and North America as rising living standards translated into better nutrition and safer housing for most people. After 1850, medical advances also improved health, primarily by controlling infectious diseases. In 1854, for example, John Snow mapped the street addresses of London's cholera victims and found they all had drunk contaminated water from the well in Golden Square (Rockett, 1994). Not long afterward, scientists linked cholera to a specific bacterium and developed a vaccine against the deadly disease. Armed with scientific knowledge, early environmentalists campaigned against age-old practices such as discharging raw sewage into rivers used for drinking water. By the early twentieth century, death rates from infectious diseases had fallen sharply.

Over the long term, then, industrialization has dramatically improved human health. In 1900, influenza and pneumonia caused one-fourth of all deaths in the United States. By 2000, these diseases caused fewer than 3 percent of deaths.

 Visit the Web site for the U.S. National Center for Health Statistics: http://www.cdc.gov/nchs/

As Table 21–1 indicates, other infectious diseases that were once major killers now rarely threaten our health.

With infectious diseases less of a threat, it is now chronic illnesses such as heart disease, cancer, and stroke that claim most people in the United States. Nothing alters the reality of death, but industrial societies manage to delay death until old age (Edmondson, 1997a).

TABLE 21–1 The Leading Causes of Death in the United States, 1900 and 2000	
1900	**2000**
1. Influenza and pneumonia	1. Heart disease
2. Tuberculosis	2. Cancer
3. Stomach and intestinal diseases	3. Stroke
4. Heart disease	4. Lung disease (noncancerous)
5. Cerebral hemorrhage	5. Accidents
6. Kidney disease	6. Diabetes
7. Accidents	7. Pneumonia and influenza
8. Cancer	8. Alzheimer's disease
9. Diseases in early infancy	9. Kidney disease
10. Diphtheria	10. Blood disease

Sources: Information for 1990 is from William C. Cockerham, *Medical Sociology*, 2d ed. (Englewood Cliffs, N.J.: Prentice Hall, 1986), p. 24; information for 2000 is from U.S. National Center for Health Statistics, *National Vital Statistics Report* (Hyattsville, Md.: The Center, 2001), vol. 49, no. 12 (October 9, 2001).

HEALTH IN THE UNITED STATES

In the United States, well-off people are among the healthiest in the world. However, the poorest in this country are no better off than people living in low-income countries.

WHO IS HEALTHY?
AGE, GENDER, CLASS, AND RACE

Social epidemiology is *the study of how health and disease are distributed throughout a society's population.* Just as early social epidemiologists traced the origin and spread of epidemic diseases, researchers today examine the connection between health and our physical and social environments. National Map 21–1 on page 546 surveys the health of women and men across the United States. Note that there is as much as a twenty-year difference in average life expectancy between the richest and poorest communities. The following sections explain this difference in terms of age and gender, social class, and race.

Age and Gender

Death is now rare among young people, with two notable exceptions. Many young people fall victim to accidents and, more recently, to acquired immune deficiency syndrome (AIDS).

THE MAP: One component of health differences is income: People living in Fairfax County, Va. (a Washington, D.C., suburb), live about 15 years longer than people living in the downtown capital, 12 miles away. Race, also is at work, with African Americans and Native Americans worse off than whites, even controlling for income.

NOTE: The Harvard School of Public Health's projections of the top 10 killers of the U.S. population in 2020: (1) heart disease, (2) severe depression, (3) traffic accidents, (4) stroke, (5) chronic pulmonary disease, (6) respiratory infections, (7) tuberculosis, (8) war injuries, (9) diarrheal infections, (10) HIV/AIDS.

NOTE: Just as income shapes health, so does health affect income: On average, members of low-income families miss four days of school or work each year due to illness, whereas higher-income people lose only three (U.S. National Center for Health Statistics, 1999).

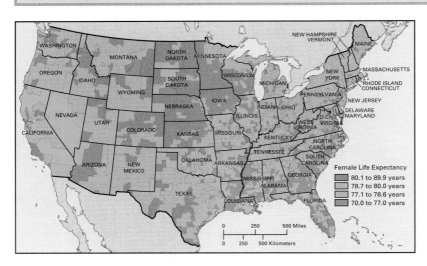

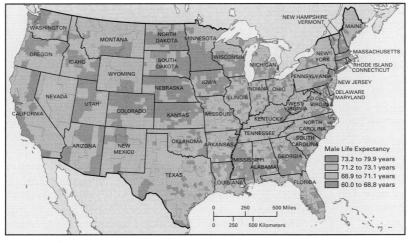

NATIONAL MAP 21–1
Life Expectancy across the United States

These two maps show that, on average, women live longer than men. Yet a gap of roughly twenty years separates people in the healthiest counties of the United States and those in the least healthy counties. Looking over the maps, in which regions of the country is health the best, and the worst? Compare these maps with the income distribution shown in National Map 11–3, on page 289, and the racial distribution shown in National Map 14–4, on page 374. Can you offer an explanation for the differences in health found here?

Source: C. J. L. Murray, C. M. Michand, M. McKenna, and J. Marks, "U.S. County Patterns of Mortality by Race, 1965–1994" (Boston: Harvard School of Public Health, 1997).

Across the life course, women fare better in terms of health than men. They have a slight biological advantage that renders them less likely than men to die before or immediately after birth. Then, as socialization takes over, men become more aggressive and individualistic, which results in higher rates of accidents, violence, and suicide. Our cultural conception of masculinity also pressures adult men to be more competitive, to repress their emotions, and to take up hazardous behaviors such as smoking cigarettes and drinking alcohol to excess. As the box explains, what doctors call "coronary-prone behavior" is really a fairly accurate description of what our culture defines as masculinity.

Social Class and Race

Infant mortality—the death rate among children under one year of age—is twice as high for poor children as for children in wealthy families. The health of

DISCUSS: Is competition "natural," even though high levels of stress contribute to heart disease, which is the leading killer in the U.S. (see Table 21–1)? Heart disease kills about 1 million people annually, more than the total killed in all U.S. wars over the course of the 20th century.

NOTE: The importance of the natural environment to health is addressed in Chapter 22 ("Population, Urbanization, and Environment").

DIVERSITY: Leading causes of death among 15- to 24-year-olds by sex and race (U.S. National Center for Health Statistics):
Af. Amer. females: accidents, homicide, heart disease, cancer, AIDS
Af. Amer. males: homicide, accidents, suicide, heart disease, cancer
White females: accidents, suicide, cancer, homicide, heart disease
White males: accidents, suicide, homicide, cancer, heart disease

DIVERSITY: RACE, CLASS, AND GENDER

Masculinity: A Threat to Health?

Doctors call it "coronary-prone behavior." Psychologists call it the "type A personality." Almost everyone recognizes it as our culture's concept of masculinity. This pattern of attitudes and behavior, common among men in our society, includes (1) chronic impatience ("C'mon! Go faster or get outta my way!"), (2) uncontrolled ambition ("I've gotta have it. I *need* that!"), and (3) free-floating hostility ("Why are so many people *such idiots!?*").

This pattern, although normal from a cultural point of view, is one major reason that men who are driven to succeed are at high risk for heart disease. By acting out the Type-A personality, we may get the job done, but we set in motion complex biochemical processes that are very hard on the human heart.

Here are a few questions to help you assess your own degree of risk (or that of someone important to you):

1. *Do you believe that a person has to be aggressive to succeed? For you,*

do *"nice guys finish last"?* For your heart's sake, try to remove hostility from your life. One starting point: How about eliminating profanity from your speech? Try replacing aggression with compassion, which can be surprisingly effective in dealing with other people. Medically speaking, compassion and humor—rather than irritation and aggravation—will enhance your life.

2. *How well do you handle uncertainty and opposition?* Do you have moments when you fume "Why won't the

waiter take my order?" or "Environmentalists are plain nuts!"? We all like to know what's going on, and we like others to agree with us. But the world often doesn't work this way. Accepting uncertainty and opposition makes us more mature and certainly healthier.

3. *Are you uneasy showing positive emotion?* Many men think giving and accepting love—from women, from children, and from other men—is a sign of weakness. But the medical truth is that love supports health and hate damages it.

As human beings, we have a great deal of choice about how to live. Think about the choices you make, and reflect on how our society's idea of masculinity often makes us hard on others (including those we love) and—just as important—hard on ourselves.

Sources: Based on Friedman & Rosenman (1974) and Levine (1990).

the richest children in our nation is the best in the world, but our poorest children are as vulnerable as those in many poor countries, including Lebanon and Vietnam. Furthermore, research indicates that the negative effects of childhood poverty on well-being continue into adult life (Reynolds & Ross, 1998).

Table 21–2 on page 548 shows that 78 percent of adults in families with incomes over $35,000 think their health is very good or excellent, but only 48 percent of adults in families earning less than $10,000 say the same. Conversely, whereas only about 4 percent of high-income people describe their health as fair or

poor, almost one-fourth of low-income people respond this way (U.S. National Center for Health Statistics, 1999). Higher income boosts people's health in a number of obvious ways, including better food and better heath care. At the same time, researchers have found that simply living in a more affluent community has positive effects on health (Robert, 1999).

Poverty among African Americans—currently three times the rate of whites—helps explain why black people are more likely to die in infancy and, as adults, are more likely to suffer the effects of violence, drug abuse, and poor health (Hayward et al., 2000).

TABLE 21–2 Assessment of Personal Health by Income, 1996

Family Income	Excellent	Very Good	Good	Fair	Poor
$35,000 and over	47.2%	30.6%	17.8%	3.5%	0.9%
$20,000–$34,999	34.6	31.2	24.8	7.1	2.4
$10,000–$19,999	27.7	25.7	29.3	12.8	4.6
Under $10,000	24.1	23.9	28.3	16.5	7.2

Source: U.S. National Center for Health Statistics, *Current Estimates from the National Health Interview Survey, 1996*, series 10, no. 200 (Washington, D.C.: U.S. Government Printing Office, 1999).

Figure 21–1 shows that life expectancy for white children born in 2000 is almost six years greater than for African Americans (77.4 years compared to 71.8). Gender is an even stronger predictor of health than race because African American females outlive males of either race. From another angle, 79 percent of white men—but just 62 percent of African American men—will live to age sixty-five. The comparable figures for women are 87 percent for whites and 77 percent for African Americans.

Poverty condemns people to crowded, unsanitary living conditions that breed infectious diseases. With a higher risk of poverty, African Americans are four times as likely as whites to die of tuberculosis. Poor people of all races also suffer from nutritional deficiencies. About 20 percent of the U.S. population—more than 50 million people—cannot afford a healthful diet or adequate medical care. As a result, whereas wealthy people can expect to die in old age of chronic illnesses such as heart disease and cancer, poor people are likely to die younger from infectious diseases such as pneumonia.

Poverty also breeds stress and violence. The leading cause of death among African American men age fifteen to twenty-four, who figure prominently in the urban underclass, is homicide. In 1999 alone, 2,674 African Americans were killed by others of their race—one-third the number of black soldiers killed in the entire Vietnam War.

CIGARETTE SMOKING

Cigarette smoking, which tops the list of preventable health hazards, has a definite cultural dimension. Only after World War I did smoking become popular in the United States, and despite growing evidence of its dangers, smoking remained fashionable even a generation ago. Today, however, most adults consider smoking a mild form of social deviance.

The popularity of cigarettes peaked in 1960, when almost 45 percent of U.S. adults smoked. By 1999, only 24 percent were still lighting up (U.S. Centers for Disease Control and Prevention, 2001). Quitting is difficult because cigarette smoke contains nicotine, a physically addictive drug. But people also smoke to cope with stress: Divorced and separated people are likely to smoke, as are the unemployed and people in the armed forces.

Generally speaking, the less schooling people have, the greater their chances of smoking. A slightly larger share of men (26 percent) than women (22 percent) smoke. But cigarettes, the only form of tobacco popular with women, have taken a toll on women's health. Since 1990, lung cancer has surpassed breast cancer as a cause of death among women in the United States.

Some 430,000 men and women die prematurely each year as a direct result of cigarette smoking, which exceeds the combined death toll from alcohol, cocaine, heroin, homicide, suicide, automobile accidents, and AIDS (Mosley & Cowley, 1991; U.S. Centers for Disease Control and Prevention, 2000). Smokers also suffer more frequently from minor illnesses such as the flu, and pregnant women who smoke increase the likelihood of spontaneous abortion, prenatal death, and low-birthweight babies. Even nonsmokers exposed to cigarette smoke have a higher risk of smoking-related diseases.

Tobacco is a $34-billion industry in the United States. In 1997, the tobacco industry conceded that cigarette smoking is harmful to health and agreed to end marketing strategies that targeted young people. But despite the antismoking trend in the United States, smoking among college students is on the rise, up from 22 percent in 1992 to 29 percent in 1997 (Neergaard, 1998). In addition, the use of chewing tobacco—also a threat to health—is increasing, especially among the young.

NOTE: Recall from Chapter 13 ("Gender Stratification") that our culture embraces a "beauty myth" that teaches women to exaggerate the importance of physical attractiveness and to orient themselves toward pleasing men (Wolf, 1990).
GLOBAL: Percentage of couples in committed relationships using condoms: U.S., 20%; nations of central Africa, 1% (Mackay, 2000:54–55).

GLOBAL: Experts estimate that 14 million young U.S. children have high cholesterol (over 200) because of a diet of too much junk food and too little exercise. This problem is greater in the U.S. than in any other high-income country. A 1997 study found that the three most advertised products (during the week of June 17th) were (1) McDonald's, (2) Burger King, and (3) Wendy's. (Of the top 10, 7 were fast food.)

Moreover, the tobacco industry is selling more products abroad, especially in low-income societies where there is less regulation of tobacco marketing and sales (Scherer, 1996; Pollack, 1997). Figure 21–2 on page 550 shows that in many countries, especially in Asia, a large majority of men smoke. Worldwide, more than 1 billion adults (about 30 percent of the total) smoke, consuming some 6 trillion cigarettes annually, and the number is increasing. The good news is that about ten years after quitting, an ex-smoker's health is as good as that of someone who never smoked at all.

EATING DISORDERS

An **eating disorder** is *an intense form of dieting or other unhealthy method of weight control driven by the desire to be very thin.* As the opening to this chapter suggests, eating disorders are encouraged by our culture's definition of femininity. Consider, first, that 95 percent of people who suffer from anorexia nervosa or bulimia are women, mostly from white, relatively affluent families. For women, Michael Levine (1987) explains, our culture equates slenderness with success and being attractive to men. On the flip side, we tend to stereotype overweight women (and, to a lesser extent, men) as "lazy," "sloppy," and even "stupid."

Research shows that most college-age women believe (1) "guys like thin girls," (2) being thin is critical to physical attractiveness, and (3) they are not as thin as men would like. In fact, most college women want to be even thinner than college men say women should be. Most men, on the other hand, think their actual body shape is just about what they want it to be; thus, compared with women, men display little dissatisfaction over body shape (Fallon & Rozin, 1985).

Because few women approach our culture's unrealistic standards of beauty, many women develop a low self-image. Moreover, our idealized image of beauty leads many young women to diet to the point of risking their health.

SEXUALLY TRANSMITTED DISEASES

Sexual activity, though pleasurable and vital to reproducing our species, can transmit more than fifty kinds of infections, or *venereal diseases* (from Venus, the Roman goddess of love). Because many people in our culture associate sex with sin, they regard venereal diseases not only as illnesses but also as marks of immorality.

Sexually transmitted diseases (STDs) grabbed national attention during the "sexual revolution" of the

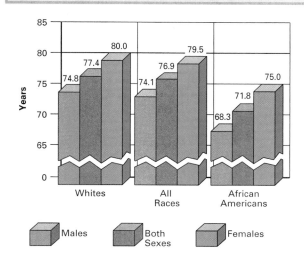

DIVERSITY SNAPSHOT

FIGURE 21–1 Life Expectancy for U.S. Children Born in 2000

Source: U.S. National Center for Health Statistics (2001).

1960s, when infection rates rose as people began sexual activity earlier and had a greater number of partners. As a result, STDs are an exception to the general decline of infectious diseases during the twentieth century. By the late 1980s, however, the rising dangers of STDs—especially AIDS—generated a sexual counter-revolution that discouraged casual sex (Kain, 1987; Kain & Hart, 1987; Laumann et al., 1994). The following sections briefly describe several common STDs.

Gonorrhea and Syphilis

Gonorrhea and syphilis are caused by microscopic organisms that are almost always transmitted by sexual contact. Untreated, gonorrhea causes sterility; syphilis damages major organs and can result in blindness, mental disorders, and death.

About 360,000 cases of gonorrhea and 36,000 cases of syphilis were recorded in 1999, although the actual numbers may be several times higher. Most cases are contracted by non-Hispanic African Americans (77 percent), with lower numbers among non-Hispanic whites (15 percent), Latinos (6 percent), and Asian Americans and Native Americans (less than

GLOBAL SNAPSHOT

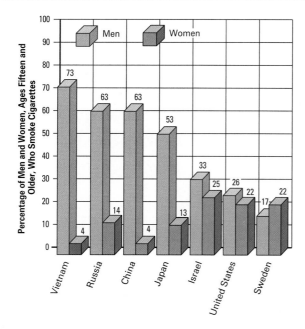

FIGURE 21–2 Cigarette Smoking in Selected Countries

Sources: U.S. Centers for Disease Control and Prevention (2001) and The World Bank (2001).

1 percent) (Masters, Johnson, & Kolodny, 1988; Moran et al., 1989; U.S. Centers for Disease Control and Prevention, 2000).

Gonorrhea and syphilis can be cured easily with antibiotics such as penicillin. Therefore, neither disease is currently a major health problem in the United States.

Genital Herpes

Genital herpes is a virus that infects as many as 45 million adults in the United States (one in seven). Though far less dangerous than gonorrhea and syphilis, herpes is incurable. People with genital herpes may exhibit no symptoms or they may experience periodic, painful blisters on the genitals accompanied by fever and headache. Although not fatal to adults, it

can be deadly to newborns, and a woman with active genital herpes can transmit the disease during a vaginal delivery. Therefore, such women usually give birth by Cesarean section.

AIDS

The most serious of all sexually transmitted diseases is acquired immune deficiency syndrome, or AIDS. Identified in 1981, it is incurable and almost always fatal. AIDS is caused by the human immunodeficiency virus (HIV), which attacks white blood cells, the core of the immune system. AIDS thus renders a person vulnerable to a wide range of other diseases that eventually cause death.

AIDS deaths in the United States deaths dropped to 15,254 in 2000, the lowest number in a decade. But officials recorded some 42,000 new cases in the United States that year, raising the total number of cases on record to more than 774,000. Of these, about 450,000 have died (U.S. Centers for Disease Control and Prevention, 2001).

Globally, HIV infects some 36 million people—half of them under age twenty-five—and the number is rising rapidly. By 2001, the global AIDS death toll had reached 22 million, with about 2 percent of all cases in the United States. Global Map 21–2 shows that Africa (more specifically, countries south of the Sahara Desert) has the highest HIV infection rate and accounts for about 70 percent of global AIDS cases. A recent United Nations study found that across much of sub-Saharan Africa, fifteen-year-olds face a 50 percent chance of becoming infected with HIV. Thus, some analysts believe that AIDS threatens the political and economic security of Africa and, indeed, the entire world (Dowell, 2000; Park, 2000; United Nations, 2001).

Upon infection, people with HIV display no symptoms at all, so most are unaware of their condition. Not for a year or more do symptoms of HIV infection appear. Within five years, one-third of infected people develop full-blown AIDS, half develop AIDS within ten years, and almost all become sick within twenty years.

 For information about United Nations efforts to combat AIDS, go to http://www.unaids.org

HIV is infectious but not contagious. In other words, HIV is transmitted from person to person through blood, semen, or breast milk but *not* through casual contact such as shaking hands, hugging, sharing towels or dishes, swimming together, or even by coughing and sneezing. The risk of transmitting the

WINDOW ON THE WORLD

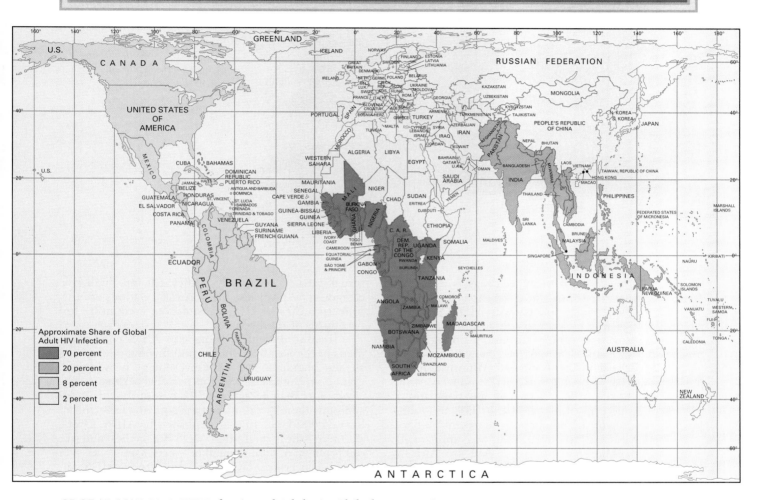

GLOBAL MAP 21–2 HIV Infection of Adults in Global Perspective

Almost 70 percent of all global HIV cases are recorded in sub-Saharan Africa. This high infection rate reflects the prevalence of other sexually transmitted diseases and infrequent use of condoms, factors that promote heterosexual transmission of HIV. Southeast Asia, where HIV is spreading most rapidly, accounts for another 20 percent of infections. South and North America together account for 8 percent of all cases. The incidence of infection is still low in the remaining regions of the world.

Sources: Population Reference Bureau (2000); map projection from *Peters Atlas of the World* (1990).

virus through saliva (as in kissing) is extremely low. Moreover, the chance of passing HIV through sexual activity is greatly reduced by the use of latex condoms. But in the age of AIDS, abstinence or an exclusive relationship with an uninfected person is the only sure way to avoid infection.

Specific behaviors put people at high risk for HIV infection. The first is *anal sex*, which can cause rectal bleeding, allowing easy transmission of HIV from one person to another. The practice of anal sex explains why homosexual and bisexual men account for 46 percent of AIDS cases in the United States.

NOTE: The term "a negotiated death" has emerged to indicate the decision by family members, medical, legal, religious, and ethical specialists, and sometimes patients themselves about how and when death should occur. Such negotiation often results in a doctor issuing a "Do Not Resuscitate" order for a terminally ill patient.

NOTE: Oregon's physician-assisted suicide Proposal 16, the first of its kind in the U.S., passed narrowly in November 1994. A patient wanting to die must obtain statements from two physicians confirming the terminal illness and two other witnesses stating that the patient really wants to die and rationally understands that decision. Then a physician may prescribe a lethal dose of medication, which the patient may decide to take. The policy was reaffirmed in 1997, when voters passed Measure 51.

While the three wars noted on the billboard claimed 112,171 lives, the death toll from AIDS has reached 450,000. As serious as this disease is here in the United States, in some world regions (especially sub-Saharan Africa) AIDS deaths are mounting so quickly that entire societies could collapse.

Sharing needles used to inject drugs is a second high-risk behavior. At present, intravenous drug users account for 25 percent of people with AIDS. Sex with an intravenous drug user is also very risky. Because intravenous drug use is more common among poor people in the United States, AIDS is now becoming a disease of the socially disadvantaged. Minorities make up the majority of people with AIDS: non-Hispanic African Americans (12 percent of the population) represent 38 percent of people with AIDS, and Latinos (13 percent of the population) represent 18 percent of AIDS cases. Moreover, about two-thirds of all women and children with the disease are African American or Latino. By contrast, Asian Americans and Native Americans together account for about 1 percent of people with AIDS (Huber & Schneider, 1992; U.S. Centers for Disease Control and Prevention, 2001).

Using any drug, including alcohol, also increases the risk of HIV infection to the extent that it impairs one's judgment. In other words, even people who understand what places them at risk of infection may not act responsibly if they are under the influence of alcohol, marijuana, or some other drug.

As Figure 21–3 shows, only 11 percent of people with AIDS in the United States became infected through heterosexual contact (although heterosexuals, infected in various ways, account for more than 30 percent of AIDS cases). But heterosexual activity does transmit HIV, and the danger rises with the number of sexual partners, especially if they fall into high-risk categories. Worldwide, heterosexual relations are the primary means of HIV transmission, accounting for two-thirds of all infections.

Treating a single person with AIDS costs hundreds of thousands of dollars, and this figure may rise as new therapies appear. Government health programs, private insurance, and personal savings rarely cover more than a fraction of the cost of treatment. In addition, there is the mounting cost of caring for at least 75,000 U.S. children orphaned by AIDS. Overall, there is little doubt that AIDS is a medical and social problem of monumental proportions.

The government responded slowly to the AIDS crisis, largely because gays and intravenous drug users are widely viewed as deviant. But funds allocated for AIDS research have increased rapidly (now totaling some $7 billion annually), and researchers have identified some drugs, including protease inhibitors, that suppress the symptoms of the disease. But educational programs remain the most effective weapon against AIDS because prevention is the only way to stop a disease that currently has no cure.

ETHICAL ISSUES SURROUNDING DEATH

Another social dimension of health and illness involves ethics. Now that technological advances give human beings the power to draw the line separating

DISCUSS: Some proponents of euthanasia claim we are more humane to dying pets than to dying parents. Ask the class to consider why we should or should not treat dying people and pets in the same way.

GLOBAL: Has the spread of euthanasia led to higher general suicide in the Netherlands? No, according to a study by Marvin Zalman and Steven Stack (1996).

NOTE: In August 1986, Jacqueline Cole lay in a coma brought on by a cerebral hemorrhage. She had previously instructed her husband, Harry Cole (a minister), to "pull the plug" if she ever was dependent on life support. Harry Cole waited 41 days and then asked a judge to order the machines turned off. The judge refused, claiming more time was needed. Six days later, Jacqueline Cole awoke and is now in good health.

life and death, we must decide how and when to do so.

When Does Death Occur?

Common sense suggests that life ceases when breathing and heartbeat stop. But the ability to replace a heart and artificially sustain respiration makes such a definition of death obsolete. Medical and legal experts in the United States now define death as an *irreversible* state involving no response to stimulation, no movement or breathing, no reflexes, and no indication of brain activity (Ladd, 1979; Wall, 1980).

Do People Have a Right to Die?

Today, medical personnel, family members, and patients themselves face the agonizing burden of deciding when a terminally ill person should die. Among the most difficult cases are the roughly 10,000 people in the United States in a permanent vegetative state who cannot express their desires about life and death. Generally speaking, the first duty of physicians and hospitals is to protect a patient's life. Even so, a mentally competent person in the process of dying may refuse medical treatment and even nutrition. Moreover, federal law requires hospitals, nursing homes, and other medical facilities to honor a patient's desire if spelled out in advance in a document called a "living will."

What about Mercy Killing?

Mercy killing is the common term for **euthanasia,** *assisting in the death of a person suffering from an incurable disease.* Euthanasia (from the Greek term meaning "a good death") poses an ethical dilemma, being at the same time an act of kindness and a form of killing.

Whether there is a "right to die" is one of today's most difficult questions. All people with incurable diseases have a right to forgo treatment that might prolong their lives. But whether a doctor should be allowed to help bring about death is the heart of the debate. In 1994, two states—Washington and California—placed before voters propositions that stated physicians should be able to help people who wanted to die; in both cases, the initiatives were defeated. The same year, however, voters in Oregon approved such a measure. This law remained tied up in state court until 1997, when voters again endorsed it.

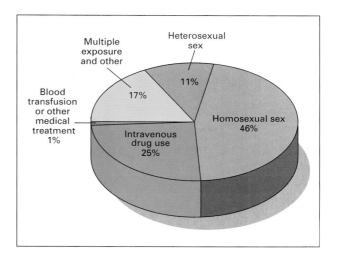

FIGURE 21–3 Types of Transmission for Reported U.S. AIDS Cases as of 2000

Source: U.S. Centers for Disease Control and Prevention (2001).

Since then, Oregon doctors have legally assisted in the death of terminally ill patients. In 1997, however, the U.S. Supreme Court decided that under the U.S. Constitution, there is no "right to die," and this has slowed the spread of such laws. Moreover, in 1999 Congress began debating whether to pass a law that would prohibit states from adopting laws similar to the one in Oregon.

Supporters of *active* euthanasia—allowing a dying person to enlist the services of a physician to bring on a quick death—argue that there are circumstances (such as when a dying person suffers from great pain) that make death preferable to life. However, critics counter that permitting active euthanasia invites abuse (see Chapter 15, "Aging and the Elderly"). They fear that patients will be pressured to end their lives in order to spare family members the burden of caring for them or the high cost of hospitalization. Furthermore, research in the Netherlands, where physician-assisted suicide is legal, indicates that about one-fifth of all deaths occurred without a patient explicitly requesting to die (Gillon, 1999).

In the United States, a majority of adults express support for giving dying people the right to choose to die with a doctor's help (Rosenbaum, 1997; NORC, 2001). Therefore, the "right to die" debate is sure to continue.

Q: "Medicine, a synthesis of many disciplines, is essentially the practice of knowledge and skills and attitudes helpful in the care of the sick." Patricia L. Kendall and George G. Reader

Q: "Physicians have exceedingly high prestige in American society. . . . Medicine thus attracts those who value status and income, who seek a challenging and interesting occupation, who enjoy exercising judgment, and who seek to do good." David Mechanic

NOTE: A problem with the medical establishment has been research that focuses only on males. The famous 1981 study examining whether aspirin reduces heart attacks, for example, used 22,000 subjects, all men. In 1990, however, the National Institutes of Health opened an Office of Research on Women's Health.

Q: "Proper treatment will cure a cold in seven days; left to its own, however, a cold will hang on for a week." Henry G. Felson

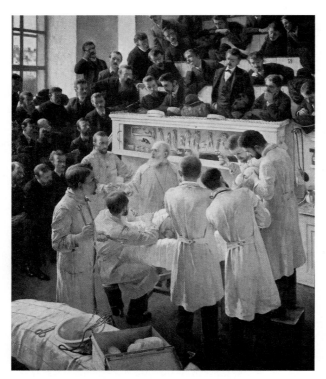

The rise of scientific medicine during the nineteenth century resulted in new skills and technology for treating many common ailments that had afflicted humanity for centuries. At the same time, however, scientific medicine pushed forms of health care involving women to the margins, and placed medicine under the control of men living in cities. We see this pattern in the A. F. Seligmann painting General Hospital, *showing an obviously all-male medical school class in Vienna in 1880.*

THE MEDICAL ESTABLISHMENT

Medicine is *the social institution that focuses on combating disease and improving health.* Through most of human history, health care was entirely the responsibility of individuals and their families. Medicine emerges as a social institution only as societies become more productive and people take on specialized work.

In agrarian societies, health practitioners, including herbalists and acupuncturists, play a central part in improving health. In industrial societies, medical care falls to specially trained and licensed healers, from anesthesiologists to X-ray technicians. Today's

medical establishment in the United States took form over the last 150 years.

THE RISE OF SCIENTIFIC MEDICINE

In colonial times, doctors, herbalists, druggists, midwives, and ministers all engaged in various healing arts. But not all were effective: Unsanitary instruments, no anesthesia, and simple ignorance made surgery a terrible ordeal, and doctors probably killed as many patients as they saved.

But by studying human anatomy and physiology, doctors gradually established themselves as self-regulating professionals with medical degrees. The American Medical Association (AMA) was founded in 1847 and symbolized the growing acceptance of a scientific model of medicine.

Still, traditional approaches to health care, such as a focus on nutrition, had their defenders. The AMA responded boldly—some thought arrogantly—by criticizing these alternative ideas about health. In the early 1900s, state licensing boards agreed to certify only physicians trained in scientific programs approved by the AMA. With control of the certification process, the AMA began closing down schools teaching other healing skills, which limited the practice of medicine to those with an M.D. degree. In the process, both the prestige and income of physicians rose dramatically; today, men and women with M.D. degrees earn, on average, almost $200,000 annually.

Practitioners of other approaches, such as osteopathic physicians, concluded that they had no choice but to fall in line with AMA standards. Most osteopaths (with D.O. degrees), who originally manipulated the skeleton and muscles, today treat illness with drugs in much the same way as medical doctors (with M.D. degrees). Other practitioners—such as chiropractors, herbal healers, and midwives—have held to traditional roles but at the cost of being relegated to the fringe of the medical profession.

Scientific medicine, taught in expensive, urban medical schools, also changed the social profile of doctors. After the AMA standards were adopted, most physicians came from privileged backgrounds and practiced in cities. Furthermore, women, who had figured in many fields of healing, were scorned by the AMA. Some early medical schools did train women and African Americans, but faced with declining financial resources, most of these schools eventually closed. Only in recent decades has the social diversity of medical doctors increased, with women and African Americans representing 28 percent and 6 percent, respectively, of

NOTE: The American Medical Association (AMA) has been losing clout. By 1999, just 30% of physicians belonged to the organization, down from 70% in 1960.

NOTE: There are some 720,000 physicians in the U.S., about 75% of whom are men (93% of all nurses are women). Men now receive 59% of medical degrees, so their representation in the profession is declining.

Q: "One must ask whether the medical intellect functions only or even best solely on a foundation of natural science." John H. Knowles

NOTE: M.D. income varies significantly by specialty and level of experience. Doctors in training earn about $30,000 annually, says the AMA; physicians in family practice average $141,000, and radiologists top the list at $273,000 annually.

all physicians (Gordon, 1980; Starr, 1982; Huet-Cox, 1984; U.S. Department of Labor, 2001).

HOLISTIC MEDICINE

The scientific model of medicine has recently been tempered by the more traditional model of **holistic medicine,** *an approach to health care that emphasizes prevention of illness and takes into account a person's entire physical and social environment.*

Holistic practitioners agree on the need for drugs, surgery, artificial organs, and high technology. At the same time, they don't want technological advances to turn medicine into narrow specialties concerned with symptoms rather than people and with disease instead of health. Here are three foundations of holistic health care (Duhl, 1980; Ferguson, 1980; Gordon, 1980):

1. **Patients are people**. Holistic practitioners are concerned not only with symptoms but with how people's environment and lifestyle affect health. Holistic practitioners extend the bounds of conventional medicine, taking an active role in combating poverty, environmental pollution, and other dangers to public health.

2. **Responsibility, not dependency.** In the scientific model, patients are dependent on physicians. Holistic medicine tries to shift some responsibility for health from physicians to people themselves by encouraging health-promoting behavior. Holistic medicine thus favors an *active* approach to *health* rather than a *reactive* approach to *illness*.

3. **Personal treatment.** Conventional medicine locates medical care in impersonal offices and hospitals, which are disease-centered settings. By contrast, holistic practitioners favor, as much as possible, a personal and relaxed environment such as the home.

In sum, holistic care does not oppose scientific medicine but shifts the emphasis from treating disease toward achieving the greatest well-being for everyone. Because the AMA currently recognizes more than fifty medical specialties, there is a need for practitioners who are concerned with the whole patient.

PAYING FOR HEALTH: A GLOBAL SURVEY

As medicine has come to rely on high technology, the cost of health care in industrial societies has skyrocketed. To meet these costs, countries have adopted various strategies.

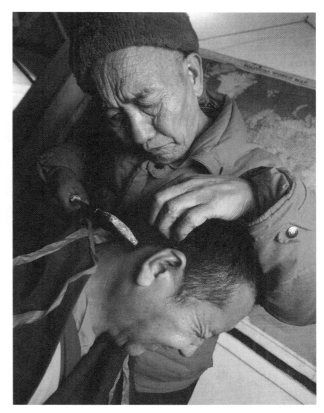

Traditional healers work to improve people's health throughout the world, especially in low-income nations. Here, a Chinese practitioner treats a patient by burning rolled herbs into his scalp.

Medicine in Socialist Societies

In societies with mostly socialist economies, the government provides medical care directly to the people. These nations hold that all citizens have the right to basic medical care. In practice, then, people do not pay physicians and hospitals on their own; instead, the government uses public funds to pay medical costs. The state owns and operates medical facilities and pays salaries to practitioners, who are government employees.

The People's Republic of China. As a poor, agrarian society in the process of industrializing, the People's Republic of China faces the daunting task of providing for the health of more than 1 billion people. China has experimented with private medicine, but the government controls most health care.

DISCUSS: Another way in which the Russian Federation stands out is its low use of effective birth control and its very high rate of abortion. A recent report of the International Planned Parenthood Federation claims there are 9 million abortions there per year, which is 25,000 per day and more than 1,000 per hour.

GLOBAL: Costs for health care in Great Britain and other European countries are rising as their populations age.

NOTE: Several European countries, including the U.K. and France, have enacted laws prohibiting the genital mutilation of women; to date, Minnesota and North Dakota have as well.

RESOURCE: Efua Dorkenoo and Scilla Elworthy's article "Female Genital Mutilation" is included in the Macionis and Benokraitis reader, *Seeing Ourselves*, 5th ed.

GLOBAL SOCIOLOGY

When Health Fails: A Report from Russia

Night is falling in Pitkyaranta, a small town on the western edge of Russia, near the Finnish border. Andrei, a thirty-year-old man with a round face and a long ponytail, weaves his way through the deepening shadows along a busy street. He has spent much of the afternoon in a bar with friends watching music videos, drinking vodka, and smoking cigarettes. Andrei is a railroad worker, but several months ago he was laid off. "Now," he explains bitterly, "I have nothing to do but drink and smoke." Andrei shrugs off a question about his health. "The only thing I care about is finding a job. I am a grown man. I don't want to be supported by my mother and father." Andrei still thinks of himself as young, yet according to current health patterns in Russia, for a man of thirty life is half over.

After the collapse of the Soviet Union in 1991, living conditions worsened every year. One result, say doctors, is increased stress, especially on men who earn too little to support their families or are out of work entirely. Few people eat well any more, and Russian men now drink and smoke as heavily as people anywhere in the world. The World Health Organization reports that alcohol abuse is Russia's number one killer, with cigarette smoking not far behind.

In towns like Pitkyaranta, the signs of poor health are everywhere: Women no longer breast-feed their babies, adults suffer higher rates of accidents and illness, and people look old before their time. Doctors are struggling to stop the health slide, but with poorly equipped hospitals, they are simply overwhelmed. Statistically, while life ex-

pectancy has dropped several years for women, it has gone into free-fall for men and now stands at just fifty-nine years, about where it was half a century ago. Just 100 miles to the west in Finland, where economic trends are far better, life expectancy for men is seventy-four years. In global context, life expectancy for Russian women has fallen below that in rich countries to the West; for Russian men, life expectancy is now the same as in some of the world's lowest-income nations.

A joke is making the rounds among young Russian men. Their health may be failing, they say, but this cloud has a silver lining: At least they no longer have to worry about retirement.

Source: Adapted from Landsberg (1998).

China's famed "barefoot doctors," roughly comparable to U.S. paramedics, bring some modern methods of medical care to millions of peasants in remote rural villages. Otherwise, traditional healing arts, including acupuncture and the use of medicinal herbs, are still widely practiced in China. In addition, the Chinese approach to health is based on a holistic concern for the well-being of both mind and body (Sidel & Sidel, 1982b; Kaptchuk, 1985).

The Russian Federation. The Russian Federation is struggling to transform a state-dominated economy into more of a market system. For this reason, medical care is in transition. Nonetheless, the idea that everyone has a right to basic medical care remains widespread.

As in China, people do not choose a physician but report to a local government-operated health facility.

Physicians in the Russian Federation have lower income than their counterparts in the United States, earning about the same salary as skilled industrial workers (compared to roughly a five-to-one ratio in this country). Worth noting, too, is that about 70 percent of physicians in the Russian Federation are women, compared with about 28 percent in the United States. As in our society, occupations dominated by women yield fewer financial rewards.

Currently, the government uses tax funds to provide medical care. But in recent years, the Russian Federation has suffered setbacks in health care, partly because of a falling standard of living, as the box explains. Moreover, a rising demand for medical care has strained a bureaucratic system that, at best, provides highly standardized and impersonal care. The optimistic view is that as market reforms proceed, both living standards and the quality of medical service will improve. In any case, what seems certain is that disparities in the medical care among various segments of the Russian population will increase (Specter, 1995; Landsberg, 1998).

Medicine in Capitalist Societies

People living in nations with mostly capitalist economies usually pay for their own health care. However, because high cost puts medical care beyond the reach of many people, government programs underwrite a considerable share of the expense.

Sweden. In 1891, Sweden instituted a compulsory, comprehensive system of government medical care. Citizens pay for this program with their taxes, which are among the highest in the world. Typically physicians receive salaries from the government rather than fees from patients, and government officials manage most hospitals. Because this medical system resembles the system found in socialist societies, it is often described as **socialized medicine,** *a medical care system in which the government owns and operates most medical facilities and employs most physicians.*

Great Britain. In 1948, Great Britain, too, established socialized medicine. The British did not do away with private care, however; instead, they created a dual system of medical service. All British citizens are entitled to medical care provided by the National Health Service, but those who can afford to may also purchase care from doctors and hospitals that operate privately.

Canada. Since 1972, Canada has had a single-payer model of medical care that provides care to all Canadians. Like a vast insurance company, the Canadian government pays doctors and hospitals according to a set schedule of fees. But Canada also has a two-tiered system like Great Britain's, with some physicians working outside the government-funded system and setting their own fees.

Canada boasts of providing care for everyone at a lower cost than the (nonuniversal) medical system in the United States. However, the Canadian system uses less advanced technology and responds slowly to people's needs, so that people may wait months for major surgery. At the same time, Canadians point out that lower-income people are not denied medical care, as is the case in the United States (Grant, 1984; Vayda & Deber, 1984; Rosenthal, 1991; Macionis & Gerber, 2002).

Japan. Physicians in Japan have private practices, but a combination of government programs and private

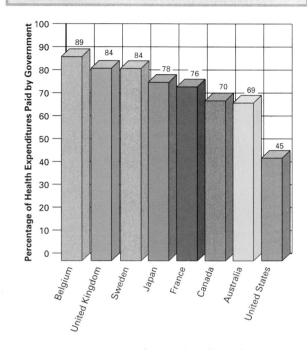

GLOBAL SNAPSHOT

FIGURE 21–4 Extent of Socialized Medicine in Selected Countries
Sources: U.S. Census Bureau (2000) and The World Bank (2001).

insurance pays medical costs. As shown in Figure 21–4, the Japanese approach health care much as the Europeans do, with most medical expenses paid through government.

MEDICINE IN THE UNITED STATES

With our primarily private system of medical care, the United States stands alone among industrialized societies in having no government-sponsored medical system that provides for every citizen. Called a **direct-fee system,** ours is *a medical care system in which patients pay directly for the services of physicians and hospitals.* Thus, while Europeans look to government to fund about 80 percent of their medical costs (paid for through taxation), the U.S. government pays less than half of this country's medical costs (Lohr, 1988; U.S. Census Bureau, 2000).

In the United States, rich people can purchase the best medical care in the world. Yet the poor fare worse than their counterparts in Europe. This disparity explains the relatively high death rates among both infants and adults in the United States compared with those of many European countries (United Nations Development Programme, 2001).

Why does the United States have no national medical care program? First, our society historically has limited government in the interest of greater personal liberty. Second, political support for a national medical program has not been strong, even among labor unions, which have concentrated on winning medical care benefits from employers. Third, the AMA and the health insurance industry have strongly and consistently opposed national medical care proposals (Starr, 1982).

Expenditures for medical care in the United States have increased dramatically, from $12 billion in 1950 to more than $1 trillion in 2000. This amounts to more than $4,000 per person, which is more than any other nation in the world spends for medical care. Who pays the medical bills?

Private insurance programs. In 1999, 172 million people (63 percent) received some medical care benefits from a family member's employer or labor union. Another 23 million people (8 percent) purchased private coverage on their own. Seventy percent of our population, then, has private insurance, although few such programs pay all medical costs (U.S. Census Bureau, 2000).

Public insurance programs. In 1965, Congress created Medicare and Medicaid. Medicare pays a portion of the medical costs of men and women over sixty-five; in 1999, it covered 36 million women and men, 13 percent of the population. During the same year, Medicaid, a medical insurance program for the poor, provided benefits to 28 million people, about 10 percent of the population. An additional 9 million veterans (3 percent of the population) can obtain free care in government-operated hospitals. In all, and allowing for some overlap, 24 percent of this country's people enjoy some medical care benefits from the government, but most also have private insurance.

Health maintenance organizations. About 81 million people (30 percent) in the United States belong to a **health maintenance organization (HMO),** *an*

organization that provides comprehensive medical care to subscribers for a fixed fee. HMOs vary in their costs and benefits, and none provides full coverage. Fixed fees make these organizations profitable to the extent that their subscribers stay healthy; therefore, many take a preventive approach to health. At the same time, HMOs have come under fire for refusing to pay for medical procedures that they consider unnecessary. Therefore, Congress is currently debating the extent to which patients can sue HMOs to obtain better care.

In all, 86 percent of the U.S. population has some medical care coverage, either private or public. But most plans do not provide full coverage, so serious illness threatens even middle-class people with financial hardship. Most programs also exclude certain medical services, such as dental care and treatment for mental health problems. Worse, 39 million people (about 14 percent of the population) have no medical insurance at all. Almost as many lose their medical coverage temporarily each year because of layoffs or job changes. Some of these people choose to forgo medical coverage (especially young people who take good health for granted), but most are part-time or full-time workers who receive no health care benefits. As a result, many low- and moderate-income people cannot afford to become ill and cannot afford to pay for the preventive medical care they need to remain healthy (Altman et al., 1989; Hersch & White-Means, 1993; Smith, 1993; U.S. Census Bureau, 2000).

THEORETICAL ANALYSIS OF HEALTH AND MEDICINE

Each of the major theoretical paradigms in sociology offers a way to organize and interpret the facts and issues presented in this chapter.

STRUCTURAL-FUNCTIONAL ANALYSIS

Talcott Parsons (1964; orig. 1951) viewed medicine as society's strategy to keep its members healthy. In this scheme, illness is dysfunctional because it undermines people's abilities to perform their roles.

The Sick Role

Society responds to sickness, Parsons argued, by providing a **sick role,** *patterns of behavior defined as appropriate*

Q: "We may say that illness is a state of disturbance in the 'normal' functioning of the total human individual, including both the state of the organism as a biological system and of his personal and social adjustments. It is thus partly biological and partly socially defined." Talcott Parsons (1951)

Q: "If you treat a sick child like an adult, and a sick adult like a child, everything usually works out pretty well." Ruth Carlisle

THEN AND NOW: In 1975, the average length of hospital stay for maternity visits was four days; today, it is two days. Among the reasons: drugs, better equipment, and cost pressures from insurance companies.

RESOURCE: A discussion of the sick role by Talcott Parsons is included among the classics in the Macionis and Benokraitis reader, *Seeing Ourselves*.

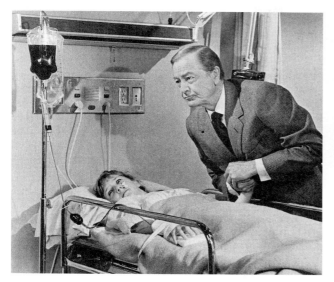
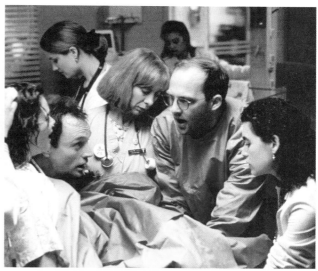

Our national view of medicine has changed during the last several decades. Television viewers in the 1970s watched doctors like Marcus Welby, M.D., confidently take charge of situations in a fatherly— and almost godlike—manner. By the 1990s, programs like E.R. *gave a more realistic view of the limitations of medicine to address illness, as well as the violence that wracks our society.*

for people who are ill. According to Parsons, the sick role has three characteristics:

1. **Illness exempts people from routine responsibilities.** Serious illness relaxes or suspends normal obligations such as going to work or attending school. To prevent abuse of this privilege, however, people do not simply declare themselves ill; they must enlist the support of others—especially a recognized medical expert— before assuming the sick role.

2. **A sick person must want to be well.** We assume that no one wants to be sick, and we withdraw the benefits of the sick role when someone feigns illness in order to avoid responsibility or get attention.

3. **A sick person must seek competent help.** People who are ill must seek out and cooperate with medical care practitioners. By failing to get medical help or to follow doctor's orders, a person risks losing the benefits of the sick role.

The Physician's Role

Physicians evaluate people's claims of sickness and try to restore the sick to normal routines. To do this,

Parsons explained, physicians use their specialized knowledge. Physicians expect patients to provide whatever personal information may assist their efforts and to follow doctor's orders in completing treatment.

Parsons saw the doctor-patient relationship as hierarchical. Yet this pattern varies from society to society. For example, Japanese tradition gives physicians great authority over their patients. Japanese physicians even take it upon themselves to decide how much information about the seriousness of an illness they will share with the patient (Darnton & Hoshia, 1989). Until about thirty years ago, physicians in the United States made similar decisions. But the patient's rights movement embodies the public demand that physicians readily share medical information, and a more equal relationship between doctor and patient, now commonplace in the United States, is developing also in Europe and even in Japan.

Critical evaluation. Parsons's analysis links illness and medicine to the broader organization of society. Others have usefully extended the concept of the sick role to some nonillness situations such as pregnancy (Myers & Grasmick, 1989).

One limitation of the sick role concept is that it applies to acute conditions (such as the flu or a broken leg) better than chronic illnesses (like heart disease), which may not be reversible. Moreover, a sick person's ability to regain health depends on available resources. Many poor people simply cannot afford either medical care or time off from work.

Finally, critics point out that Parsons's analysis implies that doctors—rather than people themselves—bear the primary responsibility for health. A more prevention-oriented approach makes physicians and patients equal partners in the pursuit of health.

SYMBOLIC-INTERACTION ANALYSIS

According to the symbolic-interaction paradigm, society is less a grand system than a series of complex and changing realities. Health and medical care, therefore, are socially constructed by people in everyday interaction.

The Social Construction of Illness

If we socially construct our ideas of health and illness, it follows that members of a very poor society may view hunger and malnutrition as normal. Similarly, people in rich nations, such as our own, may give little thought to the harmful effects of a rich diet.

How we respond to illness, too, is based on social definitions that may or may not square with medical facts. For instance, people with AIDS contend with fear and sometimes outright bigotry that have no medical basis. Likewise, students may pay no attention to signs of illness on the eve of a vacation, but they dutifully report to the infirmary hours before a midterm examination. In short, health is less an objective commodity than a negotiated outcome.

Indeed, how people define a medical situation may actually affect how they feel. Medical experts marvel at *psychosomatic* disorders (a fusion of Greek words for "mind" and "body"), when state of mind guides physical sensations (Hamrick, Anspaugh, & Ezell, 1986). Applying sociologist W. I. Thomas's theorem (1931), we can say that when health or illness is defined as real, it becomes real in its consequences.

The Social Construction of Treatment

In Chapter 6 ("Social Interaction in Everyday Life"), we used Erving Goffman's dramaturgical approach to explain how physicians tailor their physical surroundings ("the office") and their behavior ("the presentation of self") so that others see them as competent and in charge.

Sociologist Joan Emerson (1970) further illustrates this process of constructing reality in her analysis of the gynecological examination carried out by a male doctor. This situation is vulnerable to serious misinterpretation because a man touching a woman's genitals is conventionally viewed as a sexual act or possibly even an assault.

To ensure that people define the situation as impersonal and professional, the medical staff wear uniforms and furnish the examination room with nothing but medical equipment. The doctor's manner and overall performance are designed to make the patient feel that, to him, examining the genital area is no different from treating any other part of the body. A female nurse usually is present during the examination not only to assist the physician but also to dispel any impression that a man and woman are "alone in a room."

Managing situational definitions in this way is rarely taught in medical schools. The oversight is unfortunate because, as Emerson's analysis shows, understanding how people construct reality in the examination room is as important as mastering the medical skills required for treatment.

Critical evaluation. A strength of the symbolic-interaction paradigm lies in revealing that what people view as healthful or harmful depends on numerous factors, many of which are not, strictly speaking, medical. This approach also shows that in any medical procedure, both patient and medical staff engage in a subtle process of reality construction.

Critics fault this approach, however, for implying that there are no objective standards of well-being. Certain physical conditions do indeed cause definite changes in people, regardless of how we view those conditions. For example, people who lack sufficient nutrition and safe water suffer from their unhealthy environment, whether they define their surroundings as normal or not.

SOCIAL-CONFLICT ANALYSIS

Social-conflict analysis draws a connection between health and social inequality and, taking a cue from Karl Marx, ties medicine to the operation of capitalism. Researchers have focused on three main issues: access to medical care, the effects of the profit motive, and the politics of medicine.

Q: "In the USA—the richest country in the world—even the relatively affluent are now concerned about their ability to pay for medical care, while the poor have always been acutely aware of the gross deficiencies in the medical facilities available to them." Lesley Doyal
NOTE: Settling the breast implant class-action suit, three companies—Dow Corning, Bristol-Myers Squibb, and Baxter Healthcare—agreed to pay $3.7 billion over 30 years to women claiming injuries. Dow subsequently filed for bankruptcy, raising doubts about eventual payments.
DIVERSITY: As late as 1969, some localities in the U.S. legally required blood products to be labeled with the race of the donor; recipients were able to refuse blood on these grounds.

Access to Care

Personal health is the foundation of social life. Yet by making health a commodity, capitalist societies allow health to follow wealth. The access problem is more serious in the United States than in other high-income nations because our country has no universal medical care system.

Conflict theorists concede that capitalism provides excellent medical care for the rich, but it does not provide very well for the rest of the population. Most of the 39 million people who lack medical care coverage at present have low incomes.

The Profit Motive

Some conflict analysts go further, arguing that the real problem is not access to medical care but the character of capitalist medicine itself. The profit motive turns physicians, hospitals, and the pharmaceutical industry into multibillion-dollar corporations. The quest for higher profits encourages unnecessary tests and surgery as well as an overreliance on drugs (Ehrenreich, 1978; Kaplan et al., 1985).

Of some 24 million surgical operations performed in the United States each year, three-fourths are "elective," meaning that they promote long-term health and are not prompted by a medical emergency. In addition, of course, any medical procedure or use of drugs is risky and harms between 5 and 10 percent of patients. Therefore, social-conflict theorists contend that surgery probably reflects the financial interests of surgeons and hospitals as much as the medical needs of patients (Illich, 1976; Sidel & Sidel, 1982a; Cowley, 1995).

Finally, say social-conflict analysts, our society is all too tolerant of physicians having a direct financial interest in the tests and procedures they order for their patients (Pear & Eckholm, 1991). Medical care should be motivated by a concern for people, not profits.

Medicine as Politics

Although science declares itself politically neutral, scientific medicine frequently takes sides on significant social issues. For example, the medical establishment opposes government regulation of fees and services and has always campaigned against proposals for government medical care programs. Moreover, the history of medicine itself shows how racial and sexual discrimination has been supported by "scientific" opinions (Leavitt, 1984). Consider the diagnosis of "hysteria," a term that has its origins in the Greek

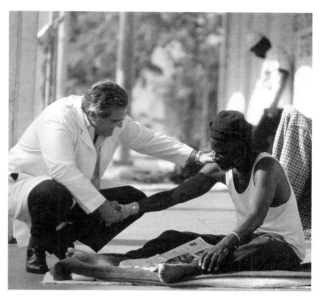

Despite the efforts of exemplary physicians such as Dr. Joe Greer, homeless people throughout the United States have a great need for medical support but receive little health care. In your opinion, what changes are needed to meet the needs of society's most vulnerable members?

word *hyster*, meaning "uterus." In choosing this word to describe a wild, emotional state, the medical profession suggested that being a woman is somehow the same as being irrational.

Even today, according to conflict theory, scientific medicine explains illness exclusively in terms of bacteria and viruses and ignores the damaging effects of social inequality. From a scientific perspective, in other words, a lack of sanitation and an unhealthy diet make poor people sick, but what about asking why people are poor in the first place? In this way, scientific medicine depoliticizes health by reducing social issues to simple biology.

Critical evaluation. Social-conflict analysis provides still another view of the relationships between health, medicine, and our society. According to this paradigm, social inequality is the reason some people have better health than others.

The most common objection to the conflict approach is that it minimizes the gains in U.S. health brought about by scientific medicine and higher living standards. Although there is plenty of room for improvement, health indicators for our population as a

CONTROVERSY & DEBATE

The Genetic Crystal Ball: Do We Really Want to Look?

The liquid in the laboratory test tube seems ordinary enough, rather like a syrupy form of water. But this liquid represents one of the greatest medical breakthroughs of all time; it may even be the key to life itself. The liquid is deoxyribonucleic acid, or DNA, the spiraling molecule found in cells of the human body. DNA contains the blueprint for making each one of us a unique human being.

The human body is composed of some 100 trillion cells, most of which contain a nucleus of twenty-three pairs of chromosomes (one of each pair comes from each parent). Each chromosome is packed with DNA in segments called genes. Genes guide the production of protein, the building block of the human body.

If genetics sounds complicated (and it is), the social implications of genetic knowledge are even more complex. Scientists discovered DNA in 1952, and in 2000 scientists reported that they were nearing the goal of "mapping" our genetic landscape. The ultimate goal of the Human Genome Project is to understand how each bit of DNA shapes our being. But do we really want to turn the key to understand life itself?

In the Human Genome Project, many scientists see a completely new approach to medicine that, instead of treating symptoms, aims to stop illness before it begins. Research already has identified genetic abnormalities that cause some forms of cancer, sickle cell anemia, muscular dystrophy, Huntington's disease, cystic fibrosis, and other crippling and deadly afflictions. During this century, genetic screening—a scientific "crystal ball"—could let people

know their medical destiny and allow doctors to manipulate segments of DNA to prevent diseases before they appear.

But many people urge caution in such research, warning that genetic information could easily be abused. At its worst, genetic mapping opens the door to Nazi-like efforts to breed a super-race. Indeed, in 1994, the People's Republic of China began to regulate marriage and childbirth for the purpose of avoiding "new births of inferior quality."

It seems inevitable that some parents will want to use genetic testing to evaluate the health (or even the eye and hair color) of their future child. What if they want to abort a fetus because, though perfectly healthy, it falls short of their expectations? Or when genetic

manipulations eventually become possible, should parents be able to create "designer children"?

Then there is the issue of "genetic privacy": Can a prospective spouse request a genetic evaluation of her fiancé before agreeing to marry? Can life insurance companies demand genetic testing before issuing policies? Can an employer screen job applicants to weed out those whose future illnesses might drain medical care funds? Clearly, what is scientifically possible is not always morally desirable. Society is already grappling with questions about the proper use of our expanding knowledge about human genetics. Such ethical dilemmas will only mount as genetic research moves forward in the years to come.

Continue the debate . . .

1. *Traditional wedding vows join couples "in sickness and in health." Do you think individuals have a right to know the future health of their potential partner before tying the knot?*

2. *What do you think about the desire of some parents to genetically design their children?*

3. *Is it right that private companies doing genetic research are able to patent their work so that they alone can profit from the results?*

Scientists are learning more and more about the genetic factors that prompt the eventual development of serious diseases. If offered the opportunity, would you want to undergo a genetic screening that would predict the long-term future of your own health?

Sources: Nash (1995), Thompson (1999), and Golden & Lemonick (2000).

NOTE: The fact that 34% of U.S. children born today can expect to live to age 85 is one component of "the graying of the United States," highlighted in Chapter 15.
NOTE: Health costs are daunting, even to corporations. For example, General Motors spends some $3 billion per year to provide health care to workers, retirees, and their families, adding hundreds of dollars to the price of the average car.

THEN AND NOW: In the past, urban living was less healthful than rural living because cities had no sanitation and many urban residents faced extreme poverty. Gradually, however, the quality of urban life improved. Today, cities pose some risks to health (air pollution, crime, high stress) but also offer extensive medical care.
RESOURCE: A survey of "The Health of Latino Families" is included in the new edition of the *Seeing Ourselves* reader.

whole rose steadily over the course of the twentieth century.

In sum, sociology's three major theoretical paradigms convincingly argue that health and medicine are social issues. Indeed, as the final box explains, advancing technology is making it more and more true as time goes on. The renowned French scientist Louis Pasteur (1822–1895), who spent much of his life studying how bacteria cause disease, said just before he died that health depends much less on bacteria than on the social environment in which the bacteria are found (Gordon, 1980:7). Explaining Pasteur's insight is sociology's contribution to human health.

LOOKING AHEAD: HEALTH AND MEDICINE IN THE TWENTY-FIRST CENTURY

At the beginning of the twentieth century, deaths from infectious diseases such as diphtheria and measles were widespread, and scientists had yet to develop penicillin and other antibiotics. Even a simple infection from a minor wound could be life-threatening. Today, a century later, most members of our society take good health and long life for granted. It seems reasonable to expect the improvements in U.S. medical care to continue throughout the twenty-first century.

Another encouraging trend is that more people are taking responsibility for their own health (Caplow

et al., 1991). Every one of us can live better and longer if we avoid tobacco, eat sensibly and in moderation, and exercise regularly.

Yet health problems will continue to plague U.S. society in the decades to come. The biggest problem, discussed throughout this chapter, is this nation's double standard in health: well-being for the rich but higher rates of disease for the poor. International comparisons reveal that the United States lags in many measures of human health because we neglect those at the margins of our society. An important question for this new century: How can a rich society afford to let millions of people live without the security of medical care?

 For a World Health Organization report on health habits of young people in twenty-eight countries including the United States, go to http://www.ruhbc.ed.ac.uk/hbsc/download/hbsc.pdf

Finally, repeating a pattern seen in earlier chapters, we find that health problems are far greater in low-income nations than in the United States. The good news is that life expectancy for the world as a whole has been rising—from forty-eight years in 1950 to sixty-seven years today—and the biggest gains have been in poor countries (Population Reference Bureau, 2001). But in much of Latin America, Asia, and especially Africa, hundreds of millions of adults and children lack not only medical attention but also adequate food and safe water. Improving the health of the world's poorest people is a critical challenge in the twenty-first century.

SUMMARY

1. Health is a social as well as a biological issue, and well-being depends on the extent and distribution of a society's resources. Culture shapes definitions of health and patterns of health care.

2. Throughout human history, health was poor by today's standards. Health improved dramatically in Western Europe and North America over the course of the nineteenth century, first as industrialization contributed to higher living standards and later as developments in medical technology helped control infectious diseases.

3. Health in low-income countries is undermined by inadequate sanitation and hunger. Average life expectancy is about twenty years less than in the United States; in the poorest nations, half the children do not survive to adulthood.

4. Infectious diseases were the major killers at the beginning of the twentieth century. Today most people in the United States die in old age of heart disease, cancer, or stroke.

5. In the United States, more than three-fourths of children born today will live to at least age sixty-five. Throughout the life course, however, people of high social position enjoy better health than the poor.

6. Cigarette smoking increased during the twentieth century to become the greatest preventable cause of death in the United States. Now that the health hazards of smoking are known, social tolerance for using tobacco products is declining.

7. The incidence of sexually transmitted diseases has risen since 1960, an exception to the general decline in infectious disease.

CTQ1: This chapter explains that patterns of health relate to a society's level of technological development, its cultural conceptions of "goodness," and its degree of social inequality.
CTQ2: Generally, acute infectious diseases such as influenza are leading killers in poor countries; chronic conditions such as heart disease are leading killers in rich countries.

Q: "A great doctor kills more people than a great general." G.W. Leibniz
CTQ3: Issues such as diet, exercise, and smoking involve choices; even so, our culture encourages a rich diet and little exercise and, despite recent declines, still supports cigarette smoking. Moreover, some categories of people are healthier than others, which also shows the power of society to shape health.

8. The ability to prolong the lives of terminally ill people is forcing us to confront a number of ethical issues surrounding death and the rights of the dying.

9. Historically a family concern, health care is now the responsibility of trained specialists. In this country, the dominant model is scientific medicine.

10. Holistic healing encourages people to assume greater responsibility for their own health and well-being; it also urges professional healers to get to know patients personally and become familiar with their environment.

11. Socialist societies define medical care as a right that governments offer equally to everyone. Capitalist societies view medical care as a commodity to be purchased, although most capitalist governments support medical care through socialized medicine or national health insurance.

12. With a direct-fee system, the United States is the only high-income nation with no comprehensive medical care program. Most people have private health insurance or government insurance or belong to a health maintenance organization. One in seven adults in the United States cannot afford to pay for medical care.

13. Structural-functional analysis links health and medicine to other social structures. Central to structural-functional analysis is the concept of the sick role, which excuses the ill person from routine social responsibilities.

14. The symbolic-interaction paradigm investigates how health and medical treatments are largely matters of socially constructed definitions.

15. Social-conflict analysis focuses on the unequal distribution of health and medical care. It criticizes the U.S. medical establishment for overrelying on drugs and surgery, giving free rein to the profit motive in medicine, and overemphasizing the biological rather than the social causes of illness.

KEY CONCEPTS

health (p. 541) a state of complete physical, mental, and social well-being

social epidemiology (p. 545) the study of how health and disease are distributed throughout a society's population

eating disorder (p. 549) an intense form of dieting or other unhealthy method of weight control driven by the desire to be very thin

euthanasia (mercy killing) (p. 553) assisting in the death of a person suffering from an incurable disease

medicine (p. 554) the social institution that focuses on combating disease and improving health

holistic medicine (p. 555) an approach to health care that emphasizes prevention of illness and takes into account a person's entire physical and social environment

socialized medicine (p. 557) a medical care system in which the government owns and operates most medical facilities and employs most physicians

direct-fee system (p. 557) a medical care system in which patients pay directly for the services of physicians and hospitals

health maintenance organization (HMO) (p. 558) an organization that provides comprehensive medical care to subscribers for a fixed fee

sick role (p. 558) patterns of behavior defined as appropriate for those who are ill

CRITICAL–THINKING QUESTIONS

1. Why is health as much a social as a biological issue?

2. What are the "diseases of poverty" that kill people in low-income nations? What are the "diseases of affluence," the leading killers in high-income countries?

3. Can you point to ways in which people can take responsibility for the state of their own health? What about ways in which societal factors affect patterns of health?

4. Should the United States follow the lead of other high-income countries and enact a government program of medical care for everyone? Why or why not?

THEN AND NOW: Share of U.S. physicians who are women: *1960, 7%; 2000, 28%.*

CTQ4: Our nation's historical concerns about "big government" and active opposition to universal health programs by the insurance industry and medical establishment play a part here. But the U.S. remains the only nation without a universal program to help pay for medical care.

NOTE: The National Council on Alcoholism estimates that, by age 18, young people in the U.S. have viewed 100,000 beer ads in the various media.

CYBER: Given that social interaction helps prevent and heal illness, the cyber-world's potential to isolate us in self-designed virtual worlds could have negative effects on health, especially for those who become chair potatoes rather than getting outside and walking.

APPLICATIONS AND EXERCISES

1. In most communities, a trip to the local courthouse or city hall is all it takes to find public records showing people's cause of death. Take a look at such records for people a century ago and recently. What patterns of life expectancy emerge? How do causes of death differ?

2. Is there a medical school on or near your campus? If so, obtain a course catalog and see how much (if any) of the medical curriculum involves the social dimensions of medical care.

3. Arrange to speak with a midwife (many list their services in the Yellow Pages) about her work helping women bear their babies. How do midwives differ from medical obstetricians?

4. Packaged in the back of this new textbook is an interactive CD-ROM that offers a variety of study and review materials intended to help you better understand the material covered in this chapter. For this chapter, the CD-ROM contains an author's tip video, Real Life Sociology videos, other relevant audio and video, interactive map animations, audio journal entries from the author, Web links, and much more.

 ## SITES TO SEE

http://www.prenhall.com/macionis

Visit the interactive *Companion Website*™ that accompanies this text. Begin by clicking on the cover of your book. You will find a chapter-by-chapter study guide, practice tests, and a significant portion of the text for on-line review, as well as many suggested Web links.

http://www.cdc.gov

Visit the Web site for the Centers for Disease Control and Prevention. Here you will find information about this organization, health news, statistical data, and even travelers' health advisories. This site offers much evidence of the social dimensions of health.

http://www.who.int/whosis/statistics/menu.cfm

Visit the Web site of the World Health Organization to find basic health indicators for many of the world's nations and data profiling the health of the U.S. population.

http://www.aegis.org
http://www.nlm.nih.gov/

These sites provide an enormous database of articles and information on HIV and AIDS.

http://www.time.com/time/2001/aidsinafrica/

Read this dramatic photojournalism account of AIDS in Africa.

http://www.doctorsoftheworld.org
http://www.imc-la.org
http://www.dwb.org

Here are Web sites for several physicians' organizations dedicated to improving health around the world. The first is operated by Doctors of the World, the second by the International Medical Corps, and the third by Doctors without Borders.

 ## INVESTIGATE WITH CONTENTSELECT

Follow the instructions found on page 23 of this textbook to enter this chapter of the book's *Companion Website*™. Once in the chapter, click on the ContentSelect icon at the bottom left of your screen and enter your personal User ID and Password. Enter keywords such as "health," "AIDS," "cigarette smoking," and "right to die," and the search engine will help you become an effective researcher.

NEW INFORMATION TECHNOLOGY AND SOCIAL INSTITUTIONS

Social institutions change over time for many reasons. One source of change, highlighted in Chapters 16 through 21, is societal conflict over how social institutions ought to operate. We have highlighted debates, for example, about what kind of economy works best, how democratic our political system really is, the meaning of "the family," the role of religion in the modern world, the ways schools go about doing the job of teaching young people, and how nations provide health care to their people.

Another source of change is technology. In the information age, all social institutions are in transition as computers and other communication technologies play a greater role in our lives. This fourth cyber.scope briefly reviews ways in which computer technology is reshaping several of the major social institutions.

The Symbolic Economy

The computer is at the center of the new postindustrial economy. As Chapter 16 ("The Economy and Work") explained, work in the post-industrial economy is less likely to involve making *things* and more likely to involve manipulating *symbols*. Thus, gaining literacy skills is as crucial to success in the twenty-first century as learning mechanical skills was to workers a century ago.

As the industrial age progressed, machines took over more and more of the manual skills performed by human workers. Therefore, we might wonder whether computers are destined to replace humans to perform many of the tasks that involve *thinking*. After all, the human brain is capable of only 100 calculations per second; the most powerful computers process information a billion times faster.

Also, the expanding array of information available through the Internet to people with computer access may make many traditional jobs obsolete. Will we need as many librarians when people can browse online catalogs of books? (Indeed, will we even need libraries as we have known them in the past?) Will there still be travel agents when anyone can readily access flight schedules, shop for good fares, purchase tickets, and reserve hotel rooms and rental cars on the 'Net? Even shopping is beginning to lose some of its popularity as consumers purchase more products from online vendors.

A century ago, shopping meant walking down Main Street, the familiar business district at the center of countless cities and small towns. Fifty years ago, shopping took people to the suburban malls, larger and more impersonal retail centers. Today, commerce is moving to cyberspace, where people can find even more products—but in a totally impersonal environment.

Finally, computer technology seems sure to accelerate the expansion of a global economy as the Internet draws together businesses and consumers into a worldwide market. Perhaps, in the computer-based economy of the twenty-first century, more and more transactions will involve "virtual currency" that will gradually replace conventional paper money.

Politics in the Information Age

By its very nature, cyberspace is both global and without centralized control. In the emerging information age, it is likely that the current system of dividing humanity into 192 distinct nation-states will evolve into a new form. In other words, because the flow of information is unaffected by national boundaries, it makes less and less sense to think of people—who may work, shop, and communicate with others all over the world—as citizens of one geographically bounded nation. Certainly, this is the idea behind the recent merging of fifteen nations in Western Europe into the European Union (EU) and the growing significance of the World Trade Organization (see the opening to Chapter 23).

What effect will the global flow of information have on politics? By increasing the amount of available information and helping people to communicate more easily, cyber-technology undoubtedly will be a force for political democracy. As long as computer-based communication remains free of government control, how can a totalitarian political order persist?

On the other hand, if governments gain control of computer-based communication, they will have a powerful new tool for spreading propaganda and manipulating their populations. Governments bent on tyranny may not be able to control the global Internet, but they may try to control access to computer technology within their borders. Such regulation of information would be a blow to democracy, of course. At the same time, however, any nation would pay a high price for isolating itself from the expanding world of computer-based information and trade.

New information technology is spreading ideas and images around the world as never before. These young women live in Malaysia, a relatively traditional society. How do you think the spread of culture via the Internet from the United States and other rich countries will affect the labor force, family patterns, and the desire for education in societies like this one? Will changes be for the better or worse? Why?

Families of the Future

Over the centuries, new technology has shaped and reshaped the family. The Industrial Revolution moved work from farm and home to factories, making the job and the family separate spheres of life.

More recently, the Information Revolution is creating the opposite effect as new communication technology allows people to work at home (or, with portable computers and telephones, to work almost anywhere). The trend toward *decentralizing* work means that, for more and more people, the line between the office and the home is disappearing.

In some respects, this trend should strengthen families, allowing parents to create more flexible work schedules and placing both fathers and mothers closer to children. Yet in the cyber-age, televisions and computers are playing a larger role in socializing the young. In short, families may be able to spend more time together in this new century, but whether they will actually do so is less certain.

Medicine and the Pursuit of Health

Just as computer technology is decentralizing work, it is making medical care more readily available. In the years to come, many routine health checks (pulse rate, blood pressure, and heart function) will be performed at home by people with computer access who transmit data via modem to personnel at medical centers.

Around the world, new information technology is making better health care available to more and more people. In the United States, hospitals rely on Internet sites to match patients and available organs, saving lives. In villages throughout poor nations, practitioners in clinics can log on to computers to consult with specialists in medical centers in the world's largest cities, gaining the information they need to provide more effective treatments. In recent years, for example, computer links have been vital in helping physicians in central Africa share news, skills, and equipment while fighting the outbreak of the deadly Ebola virus.

New information technology is also making an important contribution to the lives of people with mental and physical disabilities. On one level, new computer programs allow officials to determine whether plans for new public buildings and private homes will include sufficient access for people with disabilities. On another level, specialists at numerous universities and hospitals use computer simulations to train children to operate wheelchairs and to teach mentally retarded adults to ride the train or bus. More broadly, computers now allow people with various physical and mental limitations to enjoy and learn from virtual experiences, including travel, skiing, and even hang-gliding, that seemed impossible a generation ago (Biggs, 1996).

Institutions and Technology: Each Shaping the Other

New technology is bringing changes to all aspects of our lives. But although technology is a powerful agent of change, it does not determine the shape of society. On the contrary, technology alters the boundaries of what is possible. Therefore, *how* and even *if* we employ new information technology is an important decision that societies must make. How we decide these questions comes back to our social institutions, which, after all, define *for whom* society should operate in the first place.

CHAPTER
22

W. Louis Sonntag, Jr.
The Bowery at Night, 1895

Copyright Museum of the City of New York.
32.275.2

POPULATION, URBANIZATION, AND ENVIRONMENT

The old tractors chug down the center of Main Street—part of the Clinton County Corn Festival parade. Once a year almost everyone in this small, southern Ohio town gathers to see neighbors driving McCormick Farmalls, Ford 9Ns, Oliver Super 55s, and even one or two Minneapolis Molines. Parade drivers wave as they pass by in this celebration of rural life.

Jack and Kathy Williams stand in the crowd smiling broadly and snapping pictures. The Williamses were not born in Clinton County; in fact, until two years ago they had never seen a farm tractor up close. Natives of Los Angeles, Jack and Kathy never

quite got used to the crime, the noise, the traffic, or the high cost of living. They were convinced that there had to be a better way to live. The couple discovered the slower rhythms of rural Ohio while visiting friends, and after fifteen years of living in L.A., they decided to relocate. Kathy does freelance editing from their home, and Jack has a job with a local film distribution company. They have never been happier. "If you had asked me about living in this little town ten years ago, I would have laughed. Now it's where I feel at home. The quality of life is far better than in the big cities" (Pooley, 1997).

Kathy and Jack Williams are not alone. During the 1990s, millions of people left big cities for life in rural communities. This chapter investigates such patterns, discussing how the population of the United States is changing, how cities grew, and why some people love them while others decide to leave them. Finally, we look at how population and other factors affect the natural environment. We begin with population.

DEMOGRAPHY: THE STUDY OF POPULATION

From the time people first walked the Earth some 250,000 years ago, until just 250 years ago, the Earth's population hovered around 500 million—about the number of people in Latin America and the Caribbean today. Life for our ancestors often was brutal and usually short; people fell victim to countless diseases, frequent injuries, and periodic natural disasters.

But about 1750, world population began to spike upward. We now add 77 million people to the planet each year, so that in the fall of 1999, the number of people living on the Earth passed the 6 billion mark and reached 6.2 billion in 2002.

The causes and consequences of this drama are the basis of **demography,** *the study of human population.* Demography (from the Greek term meaning "description of people") is a specialty within sociology that analyzes the size and composition of a population and studies how people move from place to place. Demographers not only collect statistics but also pose important questions about the effects of population growth and how population might be controlled. The following sections present basic demographic concepts.

SUPPLEMENTS: An outline of this chapter, supplementary lecture material, and suggested discussion topics are found in the *Data File*.

NOTE: *Life expectancy* is calculated at birth for people born in a given year. Because it is reduced by infant mortality, this term should be distinguished from *longevity*, or how long people can live. For example, when the U.S. was founded, life expectancy was about 35 years because of high death rates from infectious diseases, although living to 65 and beyond was not unheard of. (George Washington died at age 67, Martha Washington at age 70.)

DIVERSITY: Number of birth per woman, by category, for 1998: non-Hispanic white, 1.8; Asian and Pacific Islander, 1.9; American Indian, Eskimo, and Aleut, 2.1; non-Hispanic black, 2.2; Hispanic, 2.9 (U.S. National Center for Health Statistics, 2000).

GLOBAL SNAPSHOT

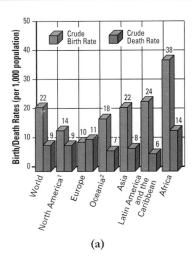

(a)

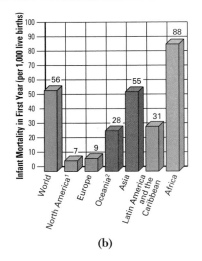

(b)

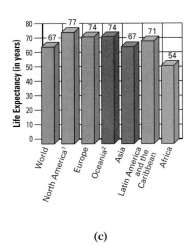

(c)

FIGURE 22–1 (a) Crude Birth Rates and Crude Death Rates;
(b) Infant Mortality Rates; (c) Life Expectancy, 2000

[1]United States and Canada
[2]Australia, New Zealand, and South Pacific Islands
Source: Population Reference Bureau (2001).

FERTILITY

The study of human population begins with how many people are born. **Fertility** is *the incidence of childbearing in a country's population*. During her childbearing years, from the onset of menstruation (typically in the early teens) to menopause (usually in the late forties), a woman is capable of bearing more than twenty children. But *fecundity*, or maximum possible childbearing, is sharply reduced by cultural norms, finances, and personal choice.

Demographers gauge fertility using the **crude birth rate,** *the number of live births in a given year for every thousand people in a population*. To calculate a crude birth rate, divide the number of live births in a year by the society's total population and multiply the result by 1,000. In the United States in 2000, there were 4.1 million live births in a population of 281.4 million (U.S. National Center for Health Statistics, 2001). That yields a crude birth rate of 14.6.

This birth rate is "crude" because it is based on the entire population, not just women in their childbearing years. Comparing crude birth rates for various countries can be misleading, then, if one society has a larger share of women of childbearing age than another. A crude birth rate also ignores differences between various racial and ethnic categories. But this statistic is easy to calculate and gives a good estimate of a society's overall fertility. Figure 22–1(a) shows that in global perspective, the crude birth rate of North Americans is low.

MORTALITY

Population size also reflects **mortality,** *the incidence of death in a country's population*. To measure mortality, demographers use a **crude death rate,** *the number of deaths in a given year for every thousand people in a population*. This time, we take the number of deaths in a year, divide by the total population, and multiply the result by 1,000. In 2000, there were 2.4 million deaths in the U.S. population of 281.4 million, yielding a crude death rate of 8.5. Figure 22–1(a) shows that in global context, this rate is about average.

THE MAP: The main reason for internal migration is the search for economic opportunity. People leave economically depressed areas for those that promise better jobs. Migrants tend to be younger people; those who remain are older, on average, and have less schooling.

NOTE: Fertility in the U.S. has declined despite rising tax deductions for children.

DISCUSS: Ask students to account for an annual trend: U.S. death rates peak in January (just after the holidays) and remain high through April; birth rates rise in May and remain high through October.

EXERCISE: Trace the regional migration of the U.S. population by looking at the shifting location of major league baseball teams. (In 1956, all but 2 of 16 teams were in the Northeast or Midwest; in 1997, the South and West had 12 of 26 teams; see Pollard, 1996a).

SEEING OURSELVES

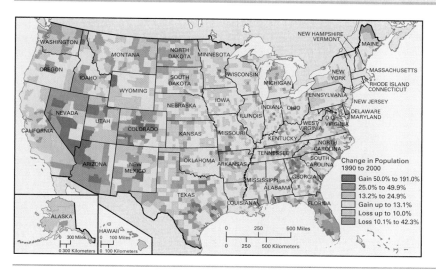

NATIONAL MAP 22–1
Population Change across the United States

This map, based on results of the 2000 census, shows that population is moving from the heartland of the United States toward the coasts. What do you think is causing this internal migration? Can you offer a demographic profile of the people who remain in counties that are losing population?

Source: U.S. Census Bureau (2001).

A third useful demographic measure is the **infant mortality rate,** *the number of deaths among infants under one year of age for each thousand live births in a given year.* To compute infant mortality, divide the number of deaths of children under one year of age by the number of live births during the same year and multiply the result by 1,000. In 2000 there were 28,000 infant deaths and 4.1 million live births in the United States. Dividing the first number by the second and multiplying the result by 1,000 yields an infant mortality rate of 6.8. As Figure 22–1(b) indicates, by world standards North American infant mortality is low.

But remember the differences between various categories of people. For example, African Americans, with nearly three times the burden of poverty as whites, have an infant mortality rate of 14.0—more than twice the white rate of 5.7.

Low infant mortality greatly raises **life expectancy,** *the average life span of a country's population.* U.S. males born in 2000 can expect to live 74.1 years, and females can expect to live 79.5 years. Figure 22–1(c) shows that life expectancy in North America is twenty-three years greater than in low-income countries of Africa.

MIGRATION

Population size is also affected by **migration,** *the movement of people into and out of a specified territory.* Migration

sometimes is involuntary, such as the forced transport of 10 million Africans to the Western Hemisphere as slaves. More recently, Serb soldiers forced ethnic Albanians to flee their homes in Kosovo (Reed, 1999). However, voluntary migration usually results from several "push-pull" factors. Dissatisfaction with life in a large city, as in the opening to this chapter, may "push" people to move, and the more peaceful life in a small town may "pull" them there.

Movement into a territory—or *immigration*—is measured as an *in-migration rate,* calculated as the number of people entering an area for every thousand people in the population. Movement out of a territory—or *emigration*—is measured in terms of an *out-migration rate,* the number leaving for every thousand people. Both types of migration usually occur at once; the difference is the *net-migration rate.*

All nations also experience internal migration, that is, movement within their border from one region to another. National Map 22–1 shows where the U.S. population is moving and the places left behind.

POPULATION GROWTH

Fertility, mortality, and migration all affect the size of a society's population. In general, rich nations (such as the United States) grow as much from immigration as from

NOTE: The table in the end-of-chapter box sketches global birth, death, and natural increase rates over time.

GLOBAL: Examples of falling infant mortality rates:

	1975	2001
India	130	70
Vietnam	106	37
Mexico	60	25

GLOBAL: Median age in Europe has risen from 30 in 1950 to about 36 today and will probably reach 40 by 2025. This suggests little overall growth due to natural increase. In Africa, by comparison, during the same period, median age has fallen from about 18 to 17, indicating high population growth.

GLOBAL: Currently, China (25%) and India (16%) together make up more than 40% of humanity.

WINDOW ON THE WORLD

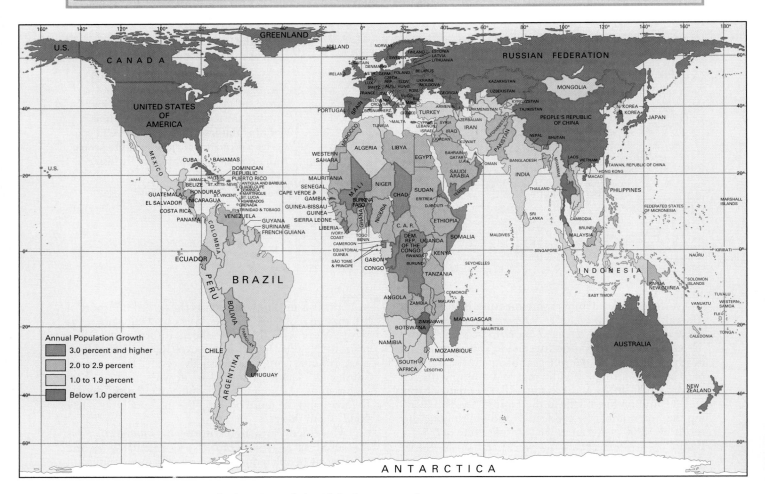

GLOBAL MAP 22–1 Population Growth in Global Perspective

The richest countries of the world—including the United States, Canada, and the nations of Europe—have growth rates below 1 percent. The nations of Latin America and Asia typically have growth rates around 1.6 percent, which double a population in forty-four years. Africa has an overall growth rate of 2.4 percent, which cuts the doubling time to twenty-nine years. In global perspective, we see that a society's standard of living is closely related to its rate of population growth: Population is rising fastest in the world regions that can least afford to support more people.

Source: Population Reference Bureau (2001); map projection from *Peters Atlas of the World* (1990).

natural increase; indeed, a high rate of immigration gives the United States the highest fertility rate of all high-income nations. By contrast, poor nations (such as India) grow almost entirely from natural increase.

To calculate a population's natural growth rate, demographers subtract the crude death rate from the crude birth rate. The natural growth rate of the U.S. population in 2000 was 6.1 per thousand (the crude

NOTE: Ronald Lee, University of California at Berkeley demographer, estimates that 110 billion people have ever lived on Earth; the 6.2 billion people living now are 5.5% of the historical total.
GLOBAL: Sex-ratio imbalance in Asia is especially high for second and third births. In South Korea, for example, 115 boys are born for every 100 girls as second children; for third children, the figure soars to 190 boys for every 100 girls.

DIVERSITY: An imbalance in the sex ratio tends to give the less numerous category more relative power. Historically, men outnumbered women in the western states, so that women had more power than their counterparts in the east. This may have contributed to the fact that many of the first women to gain state and national office were from western states (see Table 13–4 on page 338).
Q: "Children are poor men's riches." Old proverb

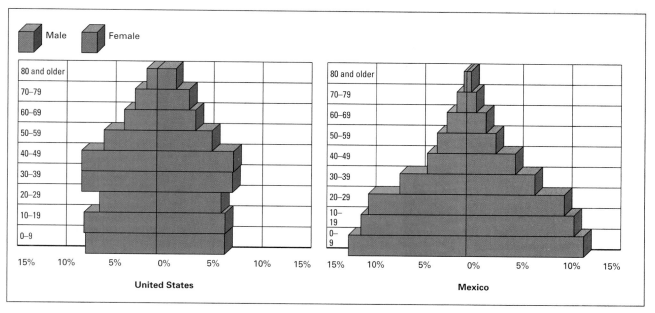

FIGURE 22–2 Age-Sex Population Pyramids for the United States and Mexico, 2000
Source: U.S. Census Bureau (2000).

birth rate of 14.6 minus the crude death rate of 8.5), or about 0.61 percent annual growth.

Global Map 22–1 shows that population growth in the United States and other high-income nations is well below the world average of 1.3 percent. The earth's low-growth continents are Europe (currently posting a slight decline, expressed as −0.1 percent annual growth), North America (0.5 percent), and Oceania (1.1 percent). Close to the global average are Asia (1.4 percent) and Latin America (1.7 percent). The highest-growth region in the world is Africa (2.4 percent).

A handy rule of thumb for estimating population growth is to divide a society's population growth rate into the number 70 to calculate the *doubling time* in years. Thus, an annual growth rate of 2 percent (common in parts of Latin America) doubles a population in thirty-five years, and a 3 percent growth rate (found in some of Africa) drops the doubling time to just twenty-four years. The rapid population growth of the poorest countries is deeply troubling because they can barely support the populations they have now.

POPULATION COMPOSITION

Demographers also study the makeup of a society's population at a given point in time. One variable is the **sex ratio,** *the number of males for every hundred females in a nation's population.* In 2000, the sex ratio in the United States was 96, or 96 males for every 100 females. Sex ratios usually are below 100 because, on average, women outlive men. In India, however, the sex ratio is 107 because parents value sons more than daughters and may either abort a female fetus or, after birth, give more care to a male infant, raising the odds that a female child will die.

A more complex measure is the **age-sex pyramid,** *a graphic representation of the age and sex of a population.* Figure 22–2 presents the age-sex pyramids for the populations of the United States and Mexico. Higher mortality with advancing age gives these figures a roughly pyramidal shape. In the U.S. pyramid, the bulge corresponding to ages thirty through the mid-fifties reflects high birth rates during the *baby boom* from the mid-1940s to 1970. The contraction just below—that is, people under thirty—reflects the subsequent *baby bust* as the birth rate dipped from 25.3 in 1957 to 14.6 in 2000.

Comparing the U.S. and Mexican age-sex pyramids shows different demographic trends. The age-sex pyramid for Mexico, like that of other low-income nations, is wide at the bottom (reflecting higher birth rates) and narrows quickly by what we would call

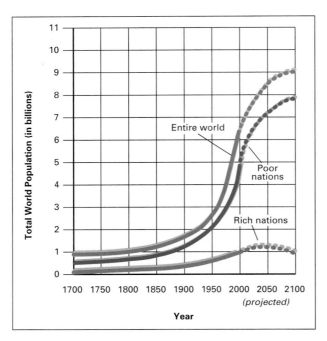

FIGURE 22–3 The Increase in World Population, 1700–2100

middle age (because of higher mortality). In short, Mexico is a much younger society, with a median age of twenty compared to thirty-five in the United States.

 To find out more about U.S. demography, go to http://www.census.gov

With a larger share of females still in their childbearing years, therefore, Mexico's crude birth rate (24) is nearly twice our own (14.6), and its annual rate of population growth (1.9 percent) is four times the U.S. rate (0.61 percent).

HISTORY AND THEORY OF POPULATION GROWTH

In the past, people favored large families because human labor was the key to productivity. Moreover, until rubber condoms appeared 150 years ago, preventing pregnancy was an uncertain proposition at best. But high death rates from widespread infectious diseases put a constant brake on population growth.

However, as shown in Figure 22–3, a major demographic shift began about 1750 as the world's population turned upward, reaching the 1 billion mark by 1800. This milestone (which took all of human history

up to this point) was repeated by 1930—barely a century later—when a second billion people were added to the planet. In other words, not only was population increasing but the *rate* of growth was accelerating. Global population reached 3 billion by 1962 (just thirty-two years later) and 4 billion by 1974 (a scant twelve years later). The rate of world population increase has slowed recently, but our planet passed the 5 billion mark in 1987 and the 6 billion mark late in 1999. In no previous century did the world's population even double. In the twentieth century, it quadrupled.

Currently, the world is gaining 77 million people each year, with 96 percent of this increase in poor countries. Experts predict that the Earth's population will reach between 8 billion and 9 billion by 2050 (Wattenberg, 1997; Thirunarayanapuram, 1998). Given the world's troubles in feeding the present population, such an increase is a matter of urgent concern.

MALTHUSIAN THEORY

It was the sudden population growth 250 years ago that sparked the development of demography. Thomas Robert Malthus (1766–1834), an English economist and clergyman, warned that population increase would soon lead to social chaos. Malthus (1926; orig. 1798) calculated that population would increase by what mathematicians call a *geometric progression,* illustrated by the series of numbers 2, 4, 8, 16, 32, and so on. At such a rate, Malthus concluded, world population would soon soar out of control.

Food production would also increase, Malthus explained, but only in *arithmetic progression* (as in the series 2, 3, 4, 5, 6) because even with new agricultural technology, farmland is limited. Thus, Malthus presented a distressing vision of the future: people reproducing beyond what the planet could feed, leading ultimately to widespread starvation.

Malthus recognized that artificial birth control or abstinence might change the equation. But he found one morally wrong and the other quite unlikely. Thus, famine and war stalked humanity in Malthus's scheme, and he was justly known as "the dismal parson."

Critical evaluation. Fortunately, Malthus's prediction was flawed. First, by 1850, the European birth rate began to drop, partly because children were becoming an economic liability rather than an asset and partly because people began using artificial birth control. Second, Malthus underestimated human ingenuity: Irrigation, fertilizers, and pesticides have increased farm production far more than he imagined.

NOTE: A greater proportion of U.S. babies born today will reach age 65 than survived a single year in 1900.

NOTE: Demographic transition theory is one element of modernization theory, discussed in Chapter 12, "Global Stratification."

GLOBAL: China has a legal minimum age of marriage: 22 years for men and 20 for women. In some cities, such as Beijing, the ages are higher: 28 and 25, respectively.

GLOBAL: A population control success story in Africa is Kenya, where lifetime average births dropped from 6.7 per woman in 1989 to 2.1 in 1999. Even so, population is growing rapidly.

GLOBAL: In rich societies, women average just under one child during their reproductive lifetimes (counting only those who have children, the median is just under two). In poor societies, almost all women have children, averaging almost five.

FIGURE 22–4
Demographic Transition Theory

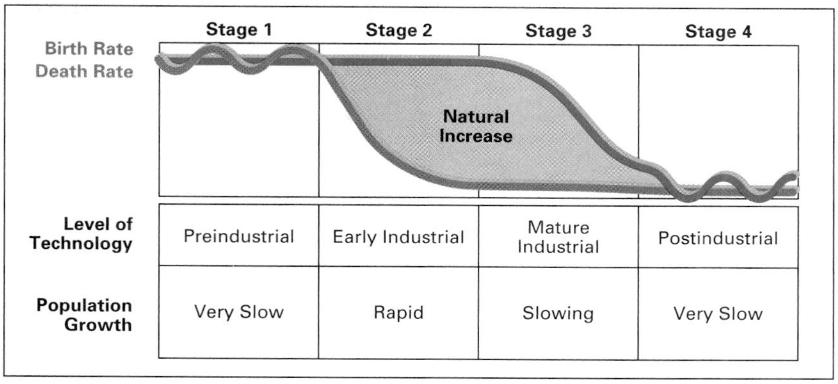

Some criticized Malthus for ignoring the role of social inequality in world abundance and famine. Karl Marx (1967; orig. 1867), for one, objected to viewing suffering as a "law of nature" rather than the curse of capitalism. More recently, "critical demographers" claim that saying the high birth rate in low-income countries is responsible for poverty amounts to blaming the victims. On the contrary, they continue, global inequality is the real problem that is yet to be addressed (Horton, 1999; Kuumba, 1999).

Still, Malthus offers an important lesson. Habitable land, clean water, and fresh air are limited resources, and as we explain presently, greater economic productivity has taken a heavy toll on the natural environment. In addition, medical advances have lowered death rates, pushing up world population. Common sense tells us that no level of population growth can go on forever. Therefore, people everywhere must become aware of the dangers of population increase.

DEMOGRAPHIC TRANSITION THEORY

Malthusian theory has been superseded by **demographic transition theory,** *the thesis that population patterns reflect a society's level of technological development.* Figure 22–4 shows the demographic consequences at four levels of technological development. Preindustrial, agrarian societies—those at Stage 1—have high birth rates because of the economic value of children and the absence of birth control. Death rates are also high because of low living standards and little medical technology. Outbreaks of disease neutralize births, so population rises and falls with only a modest overall increase. This was the case for thousands of years in Europe before the Industrial Revolution.

Stage 2—the onset of industrialization—brings a demographic transition as death rates fall because of greater food supplies and scientific medicine. But birth rates remain high, resulting in rapid population growth. It was during Europe's Stage 2 that Malthus formulated his ideas, which explains his pessimistic view of the future. The world's poorest countries today are in this high-growth stage.

In Stage 3—a mature industrial economy—the birth rate drops, curbing population growth once again. Fertility falls because most children survive to adulthood and because high living standards make raising children expensive. In short, affluence transforms children from economic assets into economic liabilities. Smaller families, made possible by effective birth control, are also favored by women working outside the home. As birth rates follow death rates downward, population growth slows further.

In Stage 4—a postindustrial economy—the demographic transition is complete. The birth rate keeps falling, partly because dual-income couples gradually become the norm and partly because the cost of raising children continues to rise. This trend, coupled with steady death rates, means that at best, population grows only very slowly or even decreases. This is the case now in Japan, Europe, and the United States.

Critical evaluation. Demographic transition theory suggests that the key to population control lies in technology. Instead of the runaway population increase feared by Malthus, this theory sees technology reining in growth and spreading material plenty.

Demographic transition theory dovetails with modernization theory, one approach to global development discussed in Chapter 12 ("Global Stratification").

The Getu family, on the left, lives in the low-income African nation of Ethiopia. The de Frutos family, to the right, lives in the high-income European nation of Spain. Comparing the two photographs, what can you learn about the relationship between a society's level of material affluence and family size? In fact, the fertility rate in Ethiopia is about five times higher than in Spain. Thus, while population levels are stable or declining in most of the world's richest countries, they are increasing in the world's poorest nations. This is why poor countries now account for 96 percent of global population increase.

Modernization theorists are optimistic that poor countries will solve their population problems as they industrialize. But critics—notably dependency theorists—strongly disagree. Unless there is a significant redistribution of global resources, they maintain, our planet will become increasingly divided into industrialized "haves," enjoying low population growth, and nonindustrialized "have-nots," struggling in vain to feed more and more people.

GLOBAL POPULATION TODAY: A BRIEF SURVEY

What can we say about population in today's world? Drawing on the discussion so far, we can reach several conclusions.

The Low-Growth North

When the Industrial Revolution began, population growth in Western Europe and North America peaked at 3 percent annually. But in the centuries since, the growth rate steadily declined and, in 1970, fell below 1 percent. As our postindustrial society enters Stage 4, the U.S. birth rate is less than the replacement level of 2.1 children per woman, a point demographers term **zero population growth**: *the level of reproduction that maintains population at a steady state.* Some fifty nations, almost all of them rich, have passed the point of zero population growth (Wattenberg, 1997).

 To find out more about zero population growth, go to http://www.zpg.org

Factors holding down population in these postindustrial societies include a high proportion of men and women in the labor force, rising costs of raising children, trends toward later marriage and singlehood, and widespread use of contraceptives and abortion.

In postindustrial nations, therefore, population increase is not the pressing problem that it is in poor countries. Indeed, some analysts point to a future problem of *underpopulation* in countries such as Japan, Italy, and the United States, where the swelling ranks of the elderly have fewer and fewer young people to support them in old age (Chesnais, 1997).

The High-Growth South

Population is a critical problem in poor nations of the Southern Hemisphere. No nation in the world lacks industrial technology entirely; demographic transition

Q: "Although individual women [worldwide] are having fewer children, on average, than their mothers there are simply more women having children, resulting in continuing increases in additions to world population." Population Reference Bureau

GLOBAL: In Islamic nations high fertility and low contraception use rates are the norm. Yet fertility is falling in these societies. Morocco is a case in point: It has a 2.0% growth rate, but its fertility has

fallen in recent decades from seven births per woman to about three. Contraceptive use among women of childbearing age has risen from about 25% to nearly 60%.

GLOBAL: One key predictor of fertility is women's income. As wages and salaries rise, fertility falls, and vice versa.

GLOBAL: In China, the average number of births per woman has dropped to about 1.8.

DIVERSITY: RACE, CLASS, AND GENDER

Empowering Women: The Key to Controlling Population Growth

Sohad Ahmad lives with her husband in a farming village fifty miles south of Cairo, Egypt's capital. Ahmad lives a poor life, like hundreds of millions of other women in the world. Yet her situation differs in an important respect: She has had only two children and will have no more.

Why do Ahmad and her husband reject the conventional wisdom that children are an economic asset? One part of the answer is that Egypt's growing population has already created such a demand for land that Ahmad's family could not afford more even if they had the children to farm it. But the main reason is that she does not want her life defined only by childbearing.

Like Ahmad, more women in Egypt are taking control of their fertility and seeking more opportunities. Indeed, this country has made great progress in reducing its annual population growth from 3.0 percent just ten years ago to 2.1 percent today.

With its focus on raising the standing of women, the 1994 Cairo conference broke new ground. Past population control programs simply tried to make birth control technology available to women. This is vital because only half the world's married women use effective birth control. But even with available birth

A simple truth: Women who have more opportunity for schooling and paid work have fewer children. As more women attend school in traditional societies, the fertility rate in these countries is falling.

control, population continues to expand in societies that define women's primary responsibility as raising children.

Dr. Nafis Sadik, an Egyptian woman who heads the United Nations efforts at population control, sums up the new approach to lowering birth rates this way: *Give women more life choices and they will have fewer children.* In other words, women with access to schooling and jobs, who can decide when and whether to marry, and who bear children as a matter of choice, will limit their own fertility. Schooling must be available to older women, too, Sadik adds, because they exercise great influence in local communities.

Evidence from countries around the world shows that controlling population and raising the social standing of women are one and the same.

Sources: Linden (1994), Ashford (1995), and Population Reference Bureau (2001).

theory's Stage 1, therefore, applies just to remote rural areas of low-income nations. In Latin America, Africa, and Asia, many low-income nations are at Stage 2, with a mix of agrarian and industrial economies. Advanced medical technology, supplied by rich societies, has sharply reduced death rates, but birth rates remain high. This is why poor societies now account for two-thirds of the Earth's people and 96 percent of global population increase.

In the last decade, the world has made significant progress in lowering fertility. In poor countries throughout the world, birth rates have fallen from an

average of about six children per woman in 1950 to about four today. But fertility this high will still intensify global poverty. At a 1994 global population conference in Cairo, delegates from 180 nations agreed that a critical element in controlling world population growth is improving the status of women. The box takes a closer look.

Mortality also has fallen significantly over the last several decades. Although no one would oppose medical programs that save lives—mostly of children—lower death rates mean rising population. In fact, population growth in most low-income regions of the

Q: "The central problem of the sociologist of the city is to discover the forms of social action and organization that typically emerge in relatively permanent, compact settlements of large numbers of heterogeneous individuals." Louis Wirth (1938)

Q: "The bourgeoisie has subjected the country to the rule of the towns. It has created enormous cities, has greatly increased the urban population as compared to the rural, and has thus rescued a considerable part of the population from the idiocy of rural life." Karl Marx and Friedrich Engels

Q: "The main population of the city that boasted its world conquests lived in cramped, noisy, airless, foul smelling, infected quarters, paying extortionate rents to merciless landlords, undergoing daily indignities and terrors that coarsened and brutalized them." Lewis Mumford (1961:221)

world results *mostly* from falling death rates. Around 1920, medical and health advances began spreading from Europe and North America around the world. Since then, inoculations against infectious diseases and the use of antibiotics and insecticides have pushed down death rates. For example, in Sri Lanka, malaria caused half of all deaths in the 1930s; a decade later, use of insecticides to kill malaria-carrying mosquitoes cut the death toll in half. As a result of this medical achievement, Sri Lanka's population began to soar. Similarly, India's infant mortality rate slid from 130 in 1975 to 70 in 2001, and its population rose over the 1 billion mark.

In short, in much of the world mortality is falling,

Read about efforts to control population increase in South Asia at http://www.asia-initiative.org/

especially among children. Now we must control birth in poor countries as successfully as we are fending off death.

URBANIZATION: THE GROWTH OF CITIES

```
October 8, Hong Kong. The cable train
grinds to the top of Victoria Peak,
where we behold one of the world's most
spectacular vistas: the city of Hong
Kong at night! A million bright, color-
ful lights ring the harbor as ships,
ferries, and traditional Chinese
"junks" churn by. Few places match Hong
Kong for sheer energy. This small city
is as economically productive as the
state of Wisconsin or the nation of Fin-
land. One could sit here for hours en-
tranced by the spectacle of Hong Kong.
```

For most of human history, the sights and sounds of great cities such as Hong Kong, New York, and Los Angeles were simply unimaginable. Our distant ancestors lived in small, nomadic groups, moving as they depleted vegetation or hunted migratory game. The tiny settlements that marked the emergence of civilization in the Middle East some 12,000 years ago held only a small fraction of the Earth's people. Today the largest three or four cities of the world hold as many people as the entire planet did back then.

Urbanization is *the concentration of humanity into cities.* Urbanization redistributes population within a society and transforms many patterns of social life. We will trace these changes in terms of three urban

revolutions: the emergence of cities 10,000 years ago, the development of industrial cities after 1750, and the explosive growth of cities in poor countries today.

THE EVOLUTION OF CITIES

Cities are a relatively new development in human history. Only about 12,000 years ago did our ancestors begin founding permanent settlements, launching the *first urban revolution.*

The First Cities

Before humans could build permanent settlements, they had to discover how to domesticate animals and cultivate crops. As explained in Chapter 4 ("Society"), hunting and gathering forced people to move all the time; raising food, however, required people to stay in one place (Nolan & Lenski, 1999). Raising their own food also created a material surplus, which freed some people from food production and allowed them to build shelter, make tools, weave cloth, and take part in religious rituals. The emergence of cities, then, led to specialization and higher living standards.

The first city—Jericho, which lies to the north of the Dead Sea and dates back some 10,000 years—was home to only around 600 people. But as the centuries passed, cities grew to tens of thousands of people and became the centers of vast empires. By 3000 B.C.E., Egyptian cities flourished, as did cities in China about 2000 B.C.E. and in Central and South America about 1500 B.C.E. In North America, however, only a few Native American societies formed settlements, which meant widespread urbanization had to await the arrival of European settlers in the seventeenth century (Lamberg-Karlovsky & Lamberg-Karlovsky, 1973; Change, 1977; Coe & Diehl, 1980).

Preindustrial European Cities

European cities date back some 5,000 years to the Greeks and, later, the Romans. Both created great empires and founded cities across Europe, including Vienna, Paris, and London. After the fall of the Roman Empire, people withdrew to defensive walled settlements and warlords battled for territory, beginning a period known as the Dark Ages. Only in the eleventh century did trade flourish once again, allowing cities to grow.

Medieval cities were very different from today's cities. Beneath towering cathedrals, the narrow and winding streets of London, Brussels, and Florence

Q: "In Europe, the modern European community emerged by gradual stages out of the simple town economy of the Middle Ages; by comparison, the American city leaped into being with breathtaking speed." Arthur M. Schlesinger, Jr.

NOTE: Cities grew upward, propelled by advances in building technology. In 1848, 5-story iron frame buildings were big news; by 1884, a steel structure in Chicago reached 10 stories, and buildings began to use elevators (devised in the 1850s). By 1900, skylines reached 30 stories and, on the eve of World War I, New York had 61 buildings more than 20 stories tall. Today, Kuala Lumpur's Petronas Towers are the world's tallest (1,482 feet). The technology exists to raise towers to a mile or more, restrained by high cost, the inability to control fire, and people's general reluctance to live that high above the ground.

teemed with merchants, artisans, priests, peddlers, jugglers, nobles, and servants. Occupational groups such as bakers, carpenters, and metalworkers clustered together in distinct sections, or "quarters." Ethnicity also defined communities as residents sought to keep out people who differed from themselves. The term "ghetto" (from the Italian *borghetto*, meaning "outside the city walls") first described the segregation of Jews in Venice.

Industrial European Cities

As the Middle Ages came to a close, steadily increasing commerce enriched a new urban middle class or *bourgeoisie* (French, meaning "of the town"). With more and more money, the *bourgeoisie* soon rivaled the hereditary nobility.

By about 1750, the Industrial Revolution triggered a *second urban revolution*, first in Europe and then in North America. Factories unleashed tremendous productive power, causing cities to grow to unprecedented size. London, the largest European city, reached 550,000 people by 1700 and exploded to 6.5 million by 1900 (A. Weber, 1963, orig. 1899; Chandler & Fox, 1974).

Cities not only grew but also changed shape. Older winding streets gave way to broad, straight boulevards to accommodate the flow of commercial traffic and, eventually, motor vehicles. Steam and electric trolleys crisscrossed the expanding cities. Because land came to be seen as a commodity to be bought and sold, developers divided cities into regular-sized lots (Mumford, 1961). The center of the city was no longer the cathedral but a bustling central business district, filled with banks, retail stores, and tall office buildings.

With the new focus on business, cities became crowded and impersonal. Crime rates rose. Especially at the outset, a few industrialists lived in grand style, but most men, women, and children worked in factories for bare subsistence.

Organized efforts by workers to improve their lives eventually brought changes to the workplace, better housing, and the right to vote. Public services such as water, sewerage, and electricity further improved urban living. Today, some urbanites still live in poverty, but a rising standard of living has partly fulfilled the city's historical promise of a better life.

THE GROWTH OF U.S. CITIES

Most of the Native Americans who inhabited North America for thousands of years before the arrival of Europeans were migratory people who formed few permanent settlements. The spread of villages and towns came after European colonization.

TABLE 22–1 The Urban Population of the United States, 1790–2000

Year	Population (in millions)	Percentage Urban
1790	3.9	5.1%
1800	5.3	6.1
1820	9.6	7.3
1840	17.1	10.5
1860	31.4	19.7
1880	50.2	28.1
1900	76.0	39.7
1920	105.7	51.3
1940	131.7	56.5
1960	179.3	69.9
1980	226.5	73.7
1990	253.0	75.2
2000	281.4	80.3

Source: U.S. Census Bureau (2001).

Colonial Settlement: 1565–1800

In 1565, the Spanish built a settlement at St. Augustine, Florida, and in 1607 the English founded Jamestown, Virginia. The first lasting settlement came in 1624, when the Dutch established New Amsterdam, later called New York.

New York and Boston (founded by the English in 1630) started out as tiny villages in a vast wilderness. They resembled medieval towns in Europe, with narrow, winding streets, some of which still curve through lower Manhattan and downtown Boston. But economic growth soon transformed these quiet villages into thriving towns with new, wide streets, usually built on a grid pattern. Even so, when the first census was completed in 1790, as Table 22–1 shows, just 5 percent of the nation's people lived in cities.

Urban Expansion: 1800–1860

Early in the nineteenth century, towns sprang up along the transportation routes that opened the American West. By 1860, Buffalo, Cleveland, Detroit, and Chicago were changing the face of the Midwest, and about one-fifth of the U.S. population lived in cities.

Urban expansion was greatest in the northern states; New York City, for example, had ten times the population of Charleston, South Carolina. The division of the United States into the industrial-urban

Q: "Cities have been *delocalized*." Jean Gottman

GLOBAL: In 2001, the world's urban population was about 2.8 billion, approaching half of humanity.

GLOBAL: London was the first city to reach 2 million, about 1840; by 1900, only 4 cities had this number of people (Berlin, Paris, and New York). In 1985, there were 85 cities with 2 million or more people; by 2000, 170 cities were over this mark.

NOTE: Urban growth late in the 19th century was nothing less than staggering, contributing to the birth of urban sociology. Chicago, the first city of urban sociology, grew 12 times over between 1870 and 1920.

RESOURCE: Joe Feagin and Robert Parker take a critical look at U.S. cities in their article "The Urban Real Estate Game," included in the Macionis and Benokraitis reader.

North and the agrarian-rural South was one major cause of the Civil War (Schlesinger, 1969).

The Metropolitan Era: 1860–1950

The Civil War (1861–1865) gave an enormous boost to urbanization, as factories strained to produce weapons. Waves of people deserted the countryside for cities in hopes of obtaining better jobs. Joining them were tens of millions of immigrants, mostly from Europe, forming a culturally diverse urban mix.

In 1900, New York's population passed the 4 million mark, and Chicago—a city of scarcely 100,000 people in 1860—was closing in on 2 million. Such growth marked the era of the **metropolis** (from Greek, meaning "mother city"), *a large city that socially and economically dominates an urban area.* Metropolises became the economic centers of the United States. By 1920, cities were home to a majority of the U.S. population as well.

Industrial technology pushed the urban skyline ever higher. In the 1880s, steel girders and mechanical elevators raised structures more than ten stories high. In 1930, New York's Empire State Building became an urban wonder, a "skyscraper" stretching 102 stories into the clouds.

Urban Decentralization: 1950–Present

The industrial metropolis reached its peak about 1950. Since then, something of a turnaround—called *urban decentralization*—has occurred as people have deserted downtown areas for outlying **suburbs**, *urban areas beyond the political boundaries of a city.* Thus, the old industrial cities of the Northeast and Midwest stopped growing—and some lost considerable population—in the decades after 1950. The urban landscape of densely packed central cities evolved into sprawling suburban regions.

SUBURBS AND URBAN DECLINE

Imitating European nobility, some of the rich always lived beyond the city limits or, more precisely, kept both "town" and "country" houses (Baltzell, 1979a). It was not until after World War II that ordinary people found a suburban home within their reach. With more and more cars, new four-lane highways, government-backed mortgages, and inexpensive tract homes, the suburbs grew rapidly. By 1999, most of the U.S. population lived in the suburbs, and they frequented nearby shopping malls rather than the older downtown shopping

districts in the cities (Rosenthal, 1974; Tobin, 1976; Geist, 1985; Palen, 1995; Peterson, 1999).

Suburban growth threw many older cities of the Snowbelt—the Northeast and Midwest—into financial crisis. Cities lost affluent taxpayers to the suburbs and were left with the burden of funding expensive social programs for the poor who stayed behind. And so inner-city decay began to scar cities throughout the Northeast and Midwest. Especially to white people, the inner cities became synonymous with slums, crime, drugs, unemployment, the poor, and minorities (Sternlieb & Hughes, 1983; Logan & Schneider, 1984; Stahura, 1986; Galster, 1991).

POSTINDUSTRIAL SUNBELT CITIES

The picture is different in the Sunbelt: the South and West. Gradually, population has shifted to the Sunbelt, where 60 percent of people now live. In 1950, nine of the ten biggest U.S. cities were in the Snowbelt; by 2000, six of the top ten were in the Sunbelt (U.S. Census Bureau, 2001).

Why are Sunbelt cities growing so large? Unlike their colder counterparts, these cities came of age *after* urban decentralization began. So whereas Snowbelt cities have long been enclosed by a ring of politically independent suburbs, Sunbelt cities have pushed their boundaries outward, along with the population flow. Houston, for example, covers more than 550 square miles, compared to Chicago's 227.

The great sprawl of Sunbelt cities has drawbacks, however. Many people in cities like Atlanta, Dallas, Phoenix, and Los Angeles argue that the growth follows no plan and ends up with clogged roads leading to slapdash developments. It was a sign of the times that in the 1998 national elections, no fewer than 240 anti-sprawl initiatives were on the ballot across the United States, and voters passed most of them (Lacayo, 1999).

MEGALOPOLIS: REGIONAL CITIES

Another result of urban decentralization is urban regions. The U.S. Census Bureau (2001) recognizes 276 metropolitan areas, which are classified as *metropolitan statistical areas (MSAs)* or *consolidated metropolitan statistical areas (CMSAs).* An MSA includes at least one city with 50,000 or more people plus densely populated surrounding counties. Almost all of the fifty fastest-growing MSAs are in the Sunbelt.

The biggest MSAs with more than 1 million people, are designated CMSAs; in 2000, there were

The rural rebound has been most pronounced in towns that offer spectacular natural beauty. There are times when people living in the scenic town of Park City, Utah, cannot even find a parking space.

eighteen. Heading the list is New York and adjacent urban areas in Long Island, western Connecticut, and northern New Jersey, with a total population of more than 21 million. Next in size is the CMSA in southern California that includes Los Angeles, Riverside, and Anaheim, with a population of more than 16 million.

As regional cities grow, they begin to overlap each other. For example, along the East Coast a 400-mile supercity stretches all the way from New England to Virginia. In the early 1960s, French geographer Jean Gottmann (1961) coined the term **megalopolis** to designate *a vast urban region containing a number of cities and their surrounding suburbs.* Other supercities cover the eastern coast of Florida and stretch from Cleveland west to Chicago. More megalopolises undoubtedly will emerge, especially in the fast-growing Sunbelt.

EDGE CITIES

Urban decentralization has also created *edge cities*, business centers some distance from the old downtowns. Edge cities—a mix of corporate office buildings, shopping malls, hotels, and entertainment complexes—differ from suburbs, which contain mostly homes. Thus, whereas the population of suburbs peaks at night, the population of edge cities peaks during the work day.

As part of expanding urban regions, most edge cities have no clear physical boundaries. Some have

names, including Los Colinas (near the Dallas–Fort Worth airport), Tyson's Corner (in Virginia, near Washington, D.C.), and King of Prussia (northwest of Philadelphia). Other edge cities are known only by the major highways that flow through them, including Route 1 in Princeton, New Jersey, and Route 128 near Boston (Garreau, 1991; Macionis & Parrillo, 2001).

THE RURAL REBOUND

Over the course of U.S. history, as the data in Table 22–1 show, the urban population has steadily increased. Immigration has played a part in the increase because most newcomers settle in cities. Urban growth can also be traced to migration from rural areas, typically by people seeking more economic opportunity.

Even so, since 1990 rural areas have been gaining population, a trend analysts call the "rural rebound." During the 1990s, three-fourths of the rural counties across the United States added population. Most of this increase resulted from migration of people from urban areas, as illustrated by the family in the chapter opening. This trend has not affected all rural places, however; for example, the Great Plains and the Mississippi Delta still show losses, as you can see by looking back at National Map 22–1. But even those losses are smaller than those during previous decades (Johnson, 1999).

Q: "In *Gemeinschaft* [people] remain essentially united in spite of all separating factors, whereas in *Gesellschaft* they are essentially separated in spite of all uniting factors." Ferdinand Tönnies

Q: "Empirically, pure *Gemeinschaft* is impossible, because all *Gemeinschaften* have rational aspects; likewise, pure *Gesellschaft* is impossible, because man's social conduct can never be entirely determined by intellect and reason." Rudolf Heberle

RESOURCE: The Macionis and Benokraitis reader, *Seeing Ourselves*, includes three urban classics: Ferdinand Tönnies's "*Gemeinschaft* and *Gesellschaft*," Georg Simmel's "The Metropolis and Mental Life," and Louis Wirth's "Urbanism as a Way of Life."

Q: "Urban life brings physical proximity but social distance among its inhabitants. In rural life, the people are physically far apart but socially together." L.G. Bonald

Peasant Dance *(above, c. 1565), by Pieter Breughel the Elder, conveys the essential unity of rural life forged by generations of kinship and neighborhood. By contrast, Ernest Fiene's* Nocturne *(left) communicates the impersonality common to urban areas. Taken together, these paintings capture Tönnies's distinction between* Gemeinschaft *and* Gesellschaft.

Pieter Breughel the Elder (c. 1525/30–1569), *Peasant Dance*, c. 1565, Kunsthistorisches Museum, Vienna/Superstock. Ernest Fiene (1894–1965), *Nocturne*. Photograph © Christie's Images.

The rural rebound has been especially marked in rural communities that offer scenic and recreational attractions such as lakes, mountains, and ski areas. But the trend to live in rural communities has become widespread and reflects both decisions by urban people to relocate and decisions by rural people to stay where they are. In most cases, lifestyle is the impetus, with people preferring the slower pace, less traffic, less crime, and cleaner air found in the country and small towns. An increasing number of companies have also relocated to rural counties, which has increased economic opportunity for the rural population (Baldauf, 1996; Johnson, 1999; Johnson & Fuguitt, 2000).

URBANISM AS A WAY OF LIFE

How does rural life differ from urban life? This question has long attracted the attention of sociologists both in Europe and the United States. Here, we survey the ideas of a number of people who sought to answer this question.

FERDINAND TÖNNIES: *GEMEINSCHAFT* AND *GESELLSCHAFT*

In the late nineteenth century, the German sociologist Ferdinand Tönnies (1855–1937) studied how life in the new industrial metropolis differed from life in rural villages. From this contrast, he developed two concepts that have become a lasting part of sociology's terminology.

Tönnies (1963; orig. 1887) used the German word ***Gemeinschaft*** (meaning roughly "community") to refer to *a type of social organization by which people are closely tied by kinship and tradition.* The *Gemeinschaft* of the rural village joins people in what amounts to a single primary group.

By and large, argued Tönnies, *Gemeinschaft* is absent in the modern city. On the contrary, urbanization fosters ***Gesellschaft*** (a German word meaning roughly "association"), *a type of social organization by which people come together only on the basis of individual self-interest.* In the *Gesellschaft* way of life, individuals are motivated by their own needs rather than a drive to

Q: "Thus the metropolitan type of man . . . develops an organ protecting him against the threatening currents and discrepancies of his external environment which would uproot him. He reacts with his head instead of his heart." Georg Simmel

Q: "The city, and particularly the great city, is . . . where human relationships are likely to be impersonal and rational, defined in terms of interest and in terms of cash." Robert Park

Q: "Having seen it, I urgently desire never to see it again. It is inhabited by savages." Rudyard Kipling, on Chicago

Q: "We must restore to the city the maternal, life-nurturing functions, the autonomous activities, the symbiotic associations that have been neglected or suppressed. For the city should be an organ of love." Lewis Mumford (1961:575)

enhance the well-being of everyone. City dwellers display little sense of community or common identity and look to others mostly as a means of advancing their individual goals. Thus, Tönnies saw in urbanization the erosion of close, enduring social relations in favor of the fleeting and impersonal ties typical of business.

EMILE DURKHEIM: MECHANICAL AND ORGANIC SOLIDARITY

The French sociologist Emile Durkheim (see Chapter 4, "Society") agreed with much of Tönnies's thinking about cities. But, Durkheim countered, urbanites do not lack social bonds; they simply organize social life differently than rural people.

Durkheim described traditional, rural life as *mechanical solidarity*, social bonds based on common sentiments and shared moral values. With its emphasis on tradition, Durkheim's concept of mechanical solidarity bears a striking similarity to Tönnies's *Gemeinschaft*. Urbanization erodes mechanical solidarity, Durkheim explained, but it also generates a new type of bonding, which he called *organic solidarity*, social bonds based on specialization and interdependence. This concept, which parallels Tönnies's *Gesellschaft*, reveals an important difference between the two thinkers. Both thought the growth of industrial cities undermined tradition, but Durkheim optimistically pointed to a new kind of solidarity. Where societies had been built on *likeness*, Durkheim now saw social life based on *difference*.

For Durkheim, urban society offers more individual choice, moral tolerance, and personal privacy than people find in rural villages. In sum, something is lost in the process of urbanization, but much is gained.

GEORG SIMMEL: THE BLASÉ URBANITE

The German sociologist Georg Simmel (1858–1918) offered a micro-analysis of cities, studying how urban life shapes individual experience. According to Simmel, individuals perceive the city as a crush of people, objects, and events. To prevent being overwhelmed by all this stimulation, urbanites develop a *blasé attitude*, tuning out much of what goes on around them. Such detachment does not mean that city dwellers lack compassion for others; they simply keep their distance as a survival strategy so they can focus their time and energy on those who really matter to them.

THE CHICAGO SCHOOL: ROBERT PARK AND LOUIS WIRTH

Sociologists in the United States soon joined the study of rapidly growing cities. Robert Park, a leader of the first U.S. sociology program at the University of Chicago, sought to add a street-level perspective by getting out and studying real cities. As he said of himself,

> I suspect that I have actually covered more ground, tramping about in cities in different parts of the world, than any other living man. (1950:viii)

Walking the streets, Park found the city to be an organized mosaic of distinctive ethnic communities, commercial centers, and industrial districts. Over time, he observed, these "natural areas" develop and change in relation to each other. To Park, then, the city was a living organism—a human kaleidoscope.

Another major figure in the Chicago School of urban sociology was Louis Wirth (1897–1952). Wirth (1938) is best known for blending the ideas of Tönnies, Durkheim, Simmel, and Park into a comprehensive theory of urban life.

Wirth began by defining the city as a setting with a large, dense, and socially diverse population. These traits result in an impersonal, superficial, and transitory way of life. Living among millions of others, urbanites come into contact with many more people than rural residents. Thus, when city people notice others at all, they usually know them not in terms of *who they are* but *what they do*—as the bus driver, florist, or grocery store clerk, for instance. Specialized, urban relationships can be pleasant for all concerned. But we should remember that self-interest rather than friendship is the main reason for the interaction.

Finally, limited social involvement and great social diversity make city dwellers more tolerant than rural villagers. Rural communities often jealously enforce their narrow traditions, but the heterogeneous population of a city rarely shares any single code of moral conduct (T. Wilson, 1985, 1995).

Critical evaluation. Both in Europe and in the United States, early sociologists presented a mixed view of urban living. On one hand, rapid urbanization was troubling. Tönnies and Wirth saw personal ties and traditional morality lost in the anonymous rush of the city. On the other hand, Durkheim and Park emphasized urbanism's positive face, pointing to greater autonomy and personal choice.

DIVERSITY: RACE, CLASS, AND GENDER

Census 2000: The Minority Majority in the Largest U.S. Cities

According to the results of the 2000 census, minorities—Hispanics, African Americans, and Asians—are now a majority of the population of the 100 largest U.S. cities. In 1990, non-Hispanic whites were a majority in 70 of the largest 100 cities; in 2000, this number had fallen to 52.

Why the change? One reason is that large cities have been losing their non-Hispanic white population. Santa Ana, California, for example, lost 38 percent of its 1990 white population; the drop was 40 percent in Birmingham, Alabama, and a whopping 53 percent in Detroit, Michigan. For all 100 of the largest cities, the white share of population fell from 52 percent in 1990 to 44 percent in 2000.

But perhaps the biggest reason for the minority-majority trend is the increase in immigration. Immigration, coupled with higher birth rates among new immigrants, resulted in a 43 percent gain in the Hispanic population (almost 4 million people) of the largest 100 cities between 1990 and 2000. The Asian population also surged by 40 percent (more than 1.1 million people). The African American population held steady over the course of the last decade.

Political officials and other policy makers are taking a close look at these figures. Clearly, the future vitality of the largest U.S. cities depends on meeting the needs and taking advantage of the contributions of the swelling minority population.

Sources: Based on Schmitt (2001) and U.S. Census Bureau (2001).

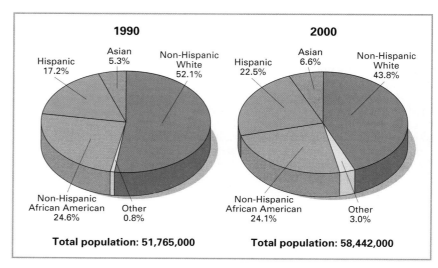

Total population: 51,765,000   **Total population: 58,442,000**

Minority Population Change in the 100 Largest U.S. Cities

One problem is that Wirth and others painted urbanism in broad strokes that overlook the effects of class, race, and gender. There are many kinds of urbanites—rich and poor, black and white, Anglo and Latino, women and men—all leading distinctive lives (Gans, 1968). Indeed, as the box explains, the share of minorities in the largest U.S. cities increased sharply during the 1990s. Furthermore, cities intensify social differences. That is, because various categories of people can form "critical masses," we see the extent of social diversity most clearly in cities (Macionis & Parrillo, 2001).

URBAN ECOLOGY

Sociologists (especially members of the Chicago School) also developed **urban ecology,** *the study of the link between the physical and social dimensions of cities.* Consider, for example, why cities are located where they are. The first cities emerged in fertile regions where the ecology favored raising crops. Preindustrial people, concerned with defense, built their cities on mountains (ancient Athens was perched on an outcropping of rock) or in areas surrounded by water (Paris and Mexico City were founded on islands).

THEN AND NOW: Share of U.S. population by region, *1900:* Northeast, 28%; Midwest, 34%; South, 32%; West, 6%; *2000:* Northeast, 19%; Midwest, 23%; South, 36%; West, 22% (U.S. Census Bureau).
NOTE: The criticism that urban ecology ignores the role of political and economic elites stands at the core of what has become known as the "new" urban sociology.

GLOBAL: The population density of the U.S. (2001) is 77 people per square mile. The world average is 118. By region: Asia, 303; Africa, 70; Latin America, 66; North America, 41; Europe, 82; Oceania, 9 (Population Reference Bureau, 2001).
GLOBAL: In the U.S., "urban" means living in a settlement of at least 2,500 people; in some nations, "urban" refers to smaller villages. In Columbia, for example, urban places are as small as 1,500 people.

With the Industrial Revolution, economic considerations situated all the major U.S. cities near rivers and natural harbors that facilitated trade.

Urban ecologists also study the physical design of cities. In 1925, Ernest W. Burgess, a student and colleague of Robert Park, described land use in Chicago in terms of *concentric zones.* City centers, Burgess observed, are business districts bordered by a ring of factories, followed by residential rings with housing that becomes more expensive the farther it is from the noise and pollution of the city's center.

Homer Hoyt (1939) refined Burgess's observations, noting that distinctive districts sometimes form *wedge-shaped sectors.* For example, one fashionable area may develop next to another, or an industrial district may extend outward from a city's center along a train or trolley line.

Chauncy Harris and Edward Ullman (1945) added yet another insight: As cities decentralize, they lose their single-center form in favor of a *multicentered model.* As cities grow, residential areas, industrial parks, and shopping districts typically push away from one another. Few people want to live close to industrial areas, for example, so the city becomes a mosaic of distinct districts.

Social area analysis investigates what people in particular neighborhoods have in common. Three factors seem to explain most of the variation—family patterns, social class, and race and ethnicity (Shevky & Bell, 1955; Johnston, 1976). Families with children gravitate to areas with large apartments or single-family homes and good schools. The rich seek high-prestige neighborhoods, often in the central city near cultural attractions. People with a common social heritage cluster in distinctive communities.

Finally, Brian Berry and Philip Rees (1969) tie together many of these insights. They explain that distinct family types tend to settle in the concentric zones described by Ernest Burgess. Specifically, households with few children tend to cluster toward the city's center, while those with more children live farther away. Social class differences are primarily responsible for the sector-shaped districts described by Homer Hoyt as, for instance, the rich occupy one "side of the tracks" and the poor the other. And racial and ethnic neighborhoods are found at various points throughout the city, consistent with Harris and Ullman's multicentered model.

URBAN POLITICAL ECONOMY

After the urban rioting of the 1960s, some analysts turned away from the ecological approach to a social-conflict understanding of city life. The *urban political economy* model applies Karl Marx's analysis of conflict in the workplace to conflict in the city (Lindstrom, 1995).

The ecological approach sees the city as a "natural" organism, with particular districts and neighborhoods developing according to an internal logic. Political economists disagree. They believe city life is defined by people with power: corporate leaders and political officials. Capitalism, which transforms the city into "real estate" traded for profit and concentrates wealth in the hands of a few, is the key to understanding city life. From this point of view, for example, the decline in industrial Snowbelt cities after 1950 was the result of deliberate decisions by the corporate elite to move their production facilities to the Sunbelt (where labor is cheaper and less likely to be unionized) or move them out of the country entirely to low-income nations (Harvey, 1976; Molotch, 1976; Castells, 1977, 1983; Feagin, 1983; Lefebvre, 1991; Jones & Wilson, 1999).

Critical evaluation. Compared with the older urban ecology approach, the political economy view seems better able to address the fact that many U.S. cities are in *crisis*, with widespread poverty, high crime, and barely functioning schools. But one criticism applies to both approaches: They focus on U.S. cities during a limited period of history. Much of what we know about industrial cities does not apply to preindustrial towns in our own past or the rapidly growing cities in many poor nations today. Therefore, it is unlikely that any single model of cities can account for the full range of urban diversity that we find in the world today.

URBANIZATION IN POOR SOCIETIES

`November 16, Cairo, Egypt.` People call the vast Muslim cemetery in Old Cairo, the City of the Dead. In truth, it is very much alive: Tens of thousands of squatters have moved into the mausoleums, making this place an eerie mix of life and death. Children run across the stone floors, clotheslines stretch between the monuments, and an occasional television antenna protrudes from a tomb roof. With Cairo growing by 1,000 people a day, families live where they can.

Q: "In the course of my own lifetime, the Earth's population has increased two-and-a-half times, and most of this increase is now to be found in the exploding urban centers, especially in the slums and shantytowns, of Africa, Asia, and Latin America." Isaac Asimov

NOTE: Population "conservatives" tend to argue that rising populations reflect *success* in combating death rates; population "liberals" claim that rising population results from *failure* to control births.

GLOBAL: Selected population densities (people per square mile): Macao, 56,721; Hong Kong, 16,743; Taiwan, 1,608; Lebanon, 1,061; Japan, 872; India, 814; Israel, 791; Haiti, 650; U.K., 635; PRC, 344; Mexico, 132; U.S., 77; Brazil, 52; Canada, 8 (Population Reference Bureau, 2001).

Q: "The crisis of civilization that we see today is a crisis of the naive belief in the omnipotence of humanity." Mikhail Gorbachev

Twice in human history the world has experienced a revolutionary expansion of cities. The first urban revolution began about 8000 B.C.E. with the first urban settlements and continued until permanent settlements were in place on several continents. Then, about 1750, the second urban revolution took off and lasted for two centuries as the Industrial Revolution led to rapid growth of cities in Europe and North America.

A third urban revolution is now underway. Today, 75 percent of people in high-income countries are already city dwellers. But extraordinary urban growth is occurring in low-income nations. In 1950, about 25 percent of the people in poor countries lived in cities; by 2010, the figure will exceed 50 percent. Moreover, in 1950, only seven cities in the world had populations over 5 million, and only two of these were in low-income countries. By 2000, forty-eight cities had passed this mark, and thirty-two of them were in less developed nations (Brockerhoff, 2000; *Time Almanac 2001*, 2000).

A third urban revolution is taking place because many poor nations have entered the high-growth Stage 2 of demographic transition theory. Falling death rates have fueled population increase in Latin America, Asia, and, especially, Africa. For urban areas, the rate of increase is *twice* as high because, in addition to natural increase, millions of people leave the countryside each year in search of jobs, health care, education, and conveniences such as running water and electricity.

Cities do offer more opportunities than rural areas, but they provide no quick fix for the massive problems of escalating population and grinding poverty. Many cities in less developed nations—including Mexico City, Egypt's Cairo, India's Calcutta, and Manila in the Philippines—are simply unable to meet the basic needs of much of their population. All these cities are surrounded by wretched shantytowns, settlements of makeshift homes built from discarded materials. As noted in Chapter 12 ("Global Stratification"), even city dumps are home to thousands of poor people, who pick through the waste hoping to find enough to survive for another day.

ENVIRONMENT AND SOCIETY

Our species has prospered, rapidly increasing the population of the planet. Moreover, within the next twenty-five years, most people will live in cities, which promise a better life than that found in rural villages.

But these advances come at a high price. Never before in history have human beings placed such demands on the Earth. This disturbing development brings us to the final section of this chapter: the interplay between the natural environment and society. Like demography, **ecology** is another cousin of sociology; it is *the study of the interaction of living organisms and the natural environment.* Ecology rests on the research of both social scientists and natural scientists. Here, however, we focus on the aspects of ecology that involve sociological concepts and issues.

The **natural environment** is *the Earth's surface and atmosphere, including living organisms, air, water, soil, and other resources necessary to sustain life.* Like every other species, humans depend on the natural environment to live. Yet with our capacity for culture, humans stand apart from other species. We alone take deliberate action to remake the world according to our own interests and desires—for better *and* for worse.

Why is the environment of interest to sociologists? Simply because environmental problems—from pollution to acid rain to global warming—do not arise from the natural world operating on its own. Rather, as we shall explain, such problems result from the specific actions of human beings, making them *social* problems (Marx, 1994).

THE GLOBAL DIMENSION

The study of the natural environment must take a global perspective. The reason is simple: Regardless of political divisions between nations, the planet is a single **ecosystem,** *a system composed of the interaction of all living organisms and their natural environment.*

The Greek meaning of *eco* is "house," reminding us that this planet is our home and that all living things and their natural environment are *interrelated.* In practice, change in any part of the natural environment ripples throughout the entire global ecosystem.

Consider, from an ecological point of view, our national love of hamburgers. People in North America (and, increasingly, around the world) have created a huge demand for beef, which has greatly expanded the ranching industry in Brazil, Costa Rica, and other Latin American nations. To produce the lean meat sought by fast-food corporations, cattle in Latin America feed on grass, which uses a great deal of land. Latin American ranchers get the land for grazing by clearing thousands of square miles of forests each year. These tropical forests are vital to maintaining the Earth's atmosphere. Deforestation ends up threatening everyone, including people in the United States who enjoy hamburgers without a thought to the environment (Myers, 1984a).

Q: "Technology has not only failed to ease the conflict between man and nature, it has aggravated that conflict." Mikhail Gorbachev
DIVERSITY: Cultures vary with regard to their views of the environment. Whereas most Western cultures are materialistic and aggressive toward the environment, some (the North American Hopi and the Hindu, for example) see humans and the environment as linked.

DISCUSS: A widespread view holds that only "modern" people are concerned about the environment. Do students agree? The conventional view is challenged by Brechin and Kempton (1994), who argue that "folk societies" typically are environmentally aware.
NOTE: Environmentalists use the term "overshoot" to refer to exceeding the carrying capacity of an environment (intentionally or otherwise).

TECHNOLOGY AND THE ENVIRONMENTAL DEFICIT

As humans have developed more powerful technology, we have increasingly remade the world as we choose. Members of societies with simple technology—the hunters and gatherers described in Chapter 4 ("Society")—have scarcely any ability to affect the environment. On the contrary, members of such societies are keenly dependent on nature, so that their lives are defined by the migration of game and the rhythm of the seasons. They are especially vulnerable to natural catastrophes, such as fires, floods, droughts, and storms.

Societies at intermediate stages of technological development have a somewhat greater capacity to affect the environment. But the environmental impact of horticulture (small-scale farming), pastoralism (the herding of animals), and even agriculture (the use of animal-drawn plows) is limited because people still rely on muscle power to produce food and other goods.

Human control of the natural environment grew dramatically with the Industrial Revolution. Muscle power gave way to engines that burn fossil fuels, coal at first and then oil. Such machinery affects the environment in two ways: by consuming natural resources and by releasing pollutants into the atmosphere. Even more important, humans armed with industrial technology are able to bend nature to their will, tunneling through mountains, damming rivers, irrigating deserts, and drilling for oil on the ocean floor. This is why people in rich nations, who represent just 18 percent of humanity, use 80 percent of the world's energy (Connett, 1991; Miller, 1992).

The environmental impact of industrial technology goes beyond energy consumption. Just as important is the fact that members of industrial societies produce 100 times more goods than people in agrarian societies. Higher living standards, in turn, increase the problem of solid waste (because people ultimately throw away most of what they produce) and pollution (because industrial production generates smoke and other toxic substances).

From the start, people recognized the material benefits of industrial technology. But only a century later did they begin to see the long-term effects on the natural environment. Indeed, one trait of the recent postindustrial era is a growing concern for environmental quality (Abrahamson, 1997; Kidd & Lee, 1997). Today, we realize that the technological power to make our lives better can also put the lives of future generations in jeopardy (Voight, cited in Bormann & Kellert, 1991:ix–x).

Many environmentalists believe that our planet is in danger. The importance of sociology in understanding environmental issues stems from the fact that problems are not caused by the natural world operating on its own. Rather, they result from the way humans organize social life.

Evidence is mounting that we are running up an **environmental deficit,** *profound and long-term harm to the natural environment caused by humanity's focus on short-term material affluence* (Bormann, 1990). The concept of environmental deficit is important for three reasons. First, it reminds us that the state of the environment is a *social issue*, reflecting choices people make about how to live. Second, it suggests that much environmental damage—to the air, land, and water—is *unintended*. By focusing on the short-term benefits of, say, cutting down forests, strip mining, or using throw-away packaging, we fail to see their long-term environmental effects. Third, in some respects, the environmental deficit is *reversible*. Inasmuch as societies have created environmental problems, in other words, societies can undo many of them.

CULTURE: GROWTH AND LIMITS

Whether we recognize environmental dangers and decide to do something about them is a cultural matter. Thus, along with technology, culture has powerful environmental consequences.

RESOURCE: Lester Brown's essay "The State of the World's Natural Environment" is one of the contemporary selections in the companion reader, *Seeing Ourselves*.

NOTE: *The Limits to Growth* authors called themselves the "Club of Rome." Their arguments bring to mind the earlier contentions of Thomas Robert Malthus; thus, they are also known as neo-Malthusians.

NOTE: The first Earth Day was in 1970, marking the onset of the environmental movement.

NOTE: The book *The Limits to Growth* largely set in motion the environmental movement; some 3 million copies of the book, published in 27 languages, have been sold.

Q: "When the well is dry, we know the worth of water." Benjamin Franklin

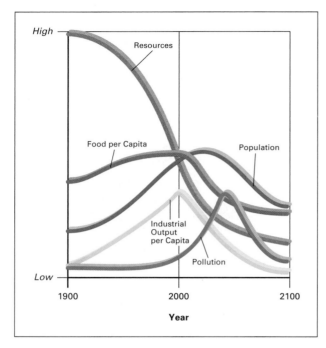

FIGURE 22–5 The Limits to Growth: Projections

Source: Based on Meadows et al. (1972).

The Logic of Growth

Why does our nation set aside specific areas as "parks" and "game preserves"? Doing this seems to indicate that, except for these special areas, people can freely use natural resources for their own purposes (Myers, 1991). This aggressive approach to the natural environment has long been central to our way of life.

Chapter 3 ("Culture") described the core values that underlie social life in the United States. One of these is *material comfort*, the belief that money and the things it buys enrich our lives. We also believe in the idea of *progress*, thinking that the future will be better than the present. Moreover, we look to *science* to make our lives easier and more rewarding. Taken together, such cultural values form *the logic of growth*.

The logic of growth is an optimistic view of the world. It holds that more powerful technology has improved our lives and new discoveries will make the future better still. In simple terms, the logic of growth asserts that "people are clever," "having things is good," and "life gets better." A powerful force throughout the history of the United States and other high-income nations, the logic of growth is the driving force behind settling the wilderness, building towns and roads, and pursuing material affluence.

Even so, "progress" can lead to unexpected problems, including harming the environment. The logic of growth responds by arguing that people (especially scientists and other technology experts) will find a way out of any problem that growth places in our path. If one resource becomes inadequate, we will come up with other, new resources that will do the job just as well. For example, by the time the growing number of cars in the world depletes the planet's oil reserves, scientists will have come up with electric, solar, or nuclear engines or some as yet unknown technology to free us from dependence on oil.

But environmentalists counter that the logic of growth is flawed in assuming that natural resources such as oil, clean air, fresh water, and topsoil will always be plentiful. On the contrary, they point out, these are *finite* resources that we can and will exhaust if we continue to pursue growth at any cost. Echoing Malthus, environmentalists warn that if we call on the Earth to support increasing numbers of people, we will surely deplete finite resources, destroying the environment—and ourselves—in the process (Milbrath, 1989; Livernash & Rodenburg, 1998).

The Limits to Growth

If we cannot invent our way out of the problems created by the logic of growth, perhaps we need another way of thinking about the world. Environmentalists therefore counter that growth must have limits. Stated simply, the *limits to growth thesis* is that humanity must implement policies to control the growth of population, production, and use of resources to avoid environmental collapse.

In *The Limits to Growth*, a controversial book that was influential in launching the environmental movement, Donella Meadows and her colleagues (1972) used a computer model to calculate the planet's available resources, rates of population growth, amount of land available for cultivation, levels of industrial and food production, and amount of pollutants released into the atmosphere. The model reflects changes that have occurred since 1900 and then projects forward to the end of the twenty-first century. Although—so far—most of the predictions seem on track, the authors concede that such long-range projections are speculative. Moreover, some critics think they will turn out to be wrong (Simon, 1981). But right or wrong, the general conclusions of the study, shown in Figure 22–5, call for serious consideration.

GLOBAL: Heavy reliance on landfills is typical of some industrial nations (U.S., U.K., Australia, Canada) but not others, where incineration is the favored means of disposal (Japan, Sweden, Switzerland, Luxembourg).
GLOBAL: In global perspective, we in the U.S. create about one-fifth of all the world's trash. In general, the richer the nation, the more materials it consumes and the more it ends up throwing away.

Q: "We all live downwind." Bumper sticker
SOCIAL SURVEY: "It is just too difficult for someone like me to do much about the environment." (GSS 2000, N = 1,276; *Codebook,* 2001:1073)
"Strongly agree"   5.6%   "Disagree"   40.4%
"Agree"   21.1%   "Strongly disagree"   7.2%
"Neither agree nor disagree" 18.9%   DK/NR   6.8%

According to the limits to growth thesis, we are quickly consuming the Earth's finite resources. Supplies of oil, natural gas, and other energy sources are already falling sharply and will continue to drop, a little faster or slower depending on conservation policies in rich nations and industrialization in other nations. Although food production per person will continue to rise during this century, world hunger will persist because existing food supplies are so unequally distributed. By 2050, the model predicts, hunger will reach a crisis level, first stabilizing population and then sending it back downward. Eventually, depleted resources will cripple industrial output as well. Only then will pollution rates fall.

Limits to growth theorists are also known as neo-Malthusians because they share Malthus's pessimism about the future. They doubt that current patterns of life are sustainable for even another century. If so, we face a fundamental choice: Either we make deliberate changes in how we live, or widespread calamity will force change upon us.

SOLID WASTE: THE DISPOSABLE SOCIETY

As an interesting exercise, carry a trash bag around for a single day and collect everything you throw away. Most people are surprised to find that the average person in the United States discards close to five pounds of paper, metal, plastic, and other materials daily (over a lifetime, that's about 50 tons!). For the country as a whole, this amounts to about 1 billion pounds of solid waste *every day*. Figure 22–6 shows the composition of a normal household's trash.

As a rich nation of people who value convenience, the United States has become a *disposable society*. We consume more products than virtually any other nation, and many of these products have throwaway packaging. The most familiar case is fast food, served with cardboard, plastic, and Styrofoam containers that we discard within minutes. And countless other products, from film to fishhooks, are elaborately packaged to make the product more attractive to the customer and to discourage tampering and theft.

Consider, too, that manufacturers market soft drinks, beer, and fruit juices in aluminum cans, glass jars, and plastic containers, which not only consume finite resources but also generate mountains of solid waste. Then there are countless items intentionally designed to be disposable: pens, razors, flashlights, batteries, even cameras. Other products—from light bulbs to automobiles—are designed to have a limited useful life and then become unwanted junk. As Paul Connett (1991) points out, even the words we use to

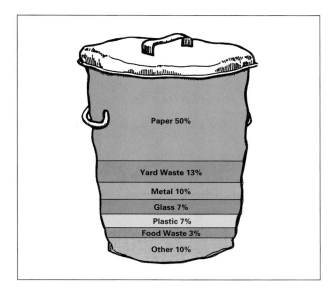

FIGURE 22–6 Composition of Household Trash
Source: Based on Franklin Associates (1986) and Corley et al. (1993).

describe what we throw away—*waste, litter, trash, refuse, garbage, rubbish*—show how little we value what we cannot immediately use. But this was not always the case, as the box on page 590 explains.

Living in a rich society, the average person in the United States consumes 50 times more steel, 170 times more newspaper, 250 times more gasoline, and 300 times more plastic each year than the typical person in India (Miller, 1992). This high level of consumption means that we in the United States not only use a disproportionate share of the planet's natural resources but also generate most of the world's refuse.

We like to say that we "throw things away." But 80 percent of our solid waste is not burned or recycled and never "goes away." Rather, it ends up in landfills. One problem with landfills is that across the country they are filling up. Second, material in landfills can pollute groundwater. Although in most places laws now regulate what can be discarded in a landfill, the Environmental Protection Agency has identified 30,000 dump sites across the United States containing hazardous materials that are polluting water both above and below the ground. Third, what goes into landfills all too often stays there—sometimes for centuries. Tens of millions of tires, diapers, and other items that we bury in landfills each year do not decompose and will be an unwelcome legacy for future generations.

Q: "Man has lost the capacity to foresee and to forestall. He will end by destroying the Earth." Albert Schweitzer

NOTE: In 1993, the space shuttle *Endeavour* had to change course quickly to avoid a large piece of space junk (an old U.S.S.R. rocket). This near-collision raises the specter of future space pollution. Currently, more than 1,000 pieces of space junk can be seen from Earth; the oldest being tracked is the remains of the 1958 *Vanguard I* satellite.

DISCUSS: What do people think about junk mail? The U.S. Postal Service delivers about 65 billion pieces annually; 10 billion are thrown out without even being opened. The paper in a year's junk mail represents almost 10 million trees.

DISCUSS: Some conflict theorists note that recycling is popular because it demands little or no change in the basic character of capitalist production (cf. Schnaiberg & Gould, 1994).

APPLYING SOCIOLOGY

Why Grandmother Had No Trash

Grandma Macionis, we always used to say, never threw away anything. She was born and raised in Lithuania—the "old country"—where life in a poor village shaped her in ways that never changed, even after she immigrated to the United States as a young woman and settled in Philadelphia.

After opening a birthday present, she would carefully save the box, wrapping paper, and ribbon, which meant as much to her as the gift they contained. Grandma never wore new clothes, her kitchen knives were worn narrow from decades of sharpening, and all her garbage was recycled as compost for her vegetable garden.

As strange as Grandma seemed to her grandchildren, she was a product of her culture. A century ago, in fact, there was little "trash." If a pair of socks wore thin, Grandma mended them, probably more than once. When they were beyond repair, she used them as a rag for cleaning or sewed them (with other old clothing) into a quilt. For her, everything had value—if not in one way, then in another.

During the twentieth century, as women joined men in working outside the home, income went up and families began buying more and more "time-saving" products. Before long, few people cared about the home recycling that Grandma practiced. Soon, cities sent crews from block to block to pick up truckloads of discarded material. The era of "trash" had begun.

Environmentalists argue that we should address the problem of solid waste by doing what many of our grandparents did: turn waste into a resource. One way to do this is through *recycling*, reusing resources we would otherwise discard. Recycling is a routine practice in Japan and many other nations, and it is becoming more common in the United States, where we now reuse about one-third of waste materials. The share is increasing as laws mandate reuse of certain materials such as glass bottles and aluminum cans. In addition, because our nation has a market-based economy, recycling is bound to increase as it becomes more profitable.

WATER AND AIR

Oceans, lakes, and streams are the lifeblood of the global ecosystem. Humans depend on water for drinking, bathing, cooling, and cooking, for recreation, and for a host of other activities.

Through the *hydrologic cycle*, the Earth naturally recycles water and refreshes the land. The process begins as heat from the sun causes the Earth's water, 97 percent of which is in the oceans, to evaporate and

form clouds. Because water evaporates at lower temperatures than most pollutants, the water vapor that rises from the seas is relatively pure, leaving various contaminants behind. Water then falls to the Earth as rain, which drains into streams and rivers and, finally, returns to the sea. Two major concerns about water, then, are supply and pollution.

Water Supply

For thousands of years, since the time of the ancient civilizations of China, Egypt, and Rome, water rights have figured prominently in codes of law. Today, as Global Map 22–2 shows, some regions of the world, especially the tropics, enjoy a plentiful supply of water. But high demand, coupled with modest reserves, makes water supply a matter of concern in much of North America and Asia, where people look to rivers rather than rainfall for their water. In the Middle East, water supply has already reached a critical level. In Egypt, for instance, an arid region of the world, people depend on the Nile River for most of their water. As the Egyptian population increases, however, shortages

WINDOW ON THE WORLD

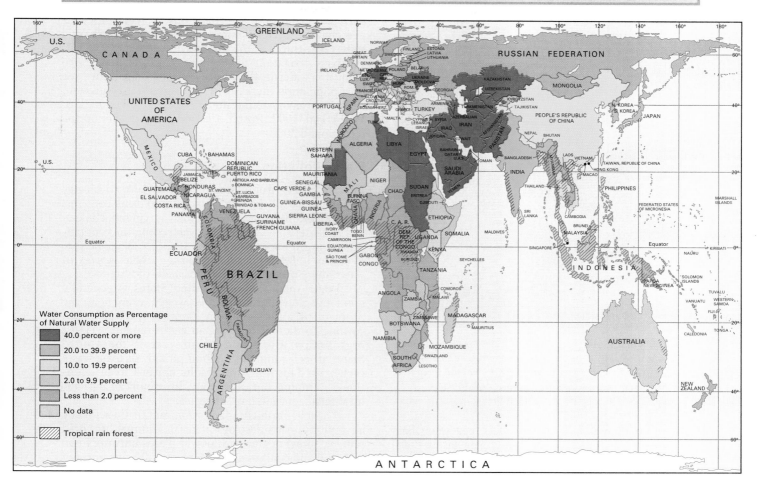

GLOBAL MAP 22–2 Water Consumption in Global Perspective

This map shows water consumption as a percentage of each country's renewable water resources. Nations near the equator consume only a tiny share of their available resources; indeed, much of this region is covered with rain forest. Northern Africa and the Middle East are a different story, however, with dense populations drawing on very limited water resources. As a result, in countries like Libya, Egypt, and Saudi Arabia, people (especially the poor) do not have as much water as they would like or, often, as they need.

Source: United Nations Development Programme (2000).

are becoming frequent. Egyptians today must make do with one-sixth the amount of water per person from the Nile compared to 1900. Furthermore, experts predict that within thirty years, as many as 1 billion people in northern Africa and the Middle East may lack the water they need for irrigation and drinking (Myers, 1984c; Postel, 1993).

Throughout the world, soaring population and complex technology have greatly increased societies' appetite for water. The global consumption of water

GLOBAL: In the former Soviet Union, the Aral Sea is disappearing because of shortsighted irrigation projects. It is now almost half its original size.

NOTE: The federal government's Clean Water Act of 1972 was a first step toward improving this country's water. Before then, many urban rivers were so polluted that the water was dangerous for drinking or even for bathing. In one of the most egregious examples,

Cleveland's Cuyahoga River became so choked with oil and other toxic substances that it actually caught fire.

SOCIAL SURVEY: "Are we spending too much money, too little money, or about the right amount on improving and protecting the environment?" (GSS 2000, N = 1,409; Codebook, 2001:98)

"Too little"   60.9%   "Too much"   7.9%
"About right"   27.3%   DK/NR   3.8%

In the United States, most of us take safe water for granted. But people, and especially children, in poor countries around the world are at high risk from infectious diseases that are spread by unclean water used for bathing, cooking, and drinking.

(now more than 6 billion cubic feet per year) has tripled since 1950 and is expanding even faster than the world's population. As a result, even in the parts of the world that receive plenty of rainfall, people are using groundwater faster than it can be naturally replenished. In the Tamil Nadu region of southern India, for example, so much groundwater is being used that the water table has fallen 100 feet over the last several decades. Mexico City—which has sprawled to some 1,400 square miles—has pumped so much water from its underground aquifer that the city has sunk thirty feet during the last century and is dropping about two inches per year. Farther north in the United States, pumping from the Ogallala aquifer, which lies below seven states from South Dakota to Texas, is now so rapid that some experts fear it could run dry within several decades.

In light of such developments, we must face the reality that water is a valuable, finite resource. Greater conservation of water by individuals (the average person consumes 10 million gallons in a lifetime) is part of the answer. However, households around the world account for just 10 percent of water use. We need to curb water consumption by industry, which uses 25 percent of the global total, and farming, which consumes two-thirds of the total for irrigation.

New irrigation technology may reduce the demand for water in the future. But, here again, we see how population increase, as well as economic growth, strains our ecosystem (Goldfarb, 1991; Falkenmark & Widstrand, 1992; Postel, 1993; Population Action International, 2000).

Water Pollution

In large cities—from Mexico City to Cairo to Shanghai—many people have no choice but to drink contaminated water. Infectious diseases such as typhoid, cholera, and dysentery—all caused by waterborne microorganisms—spread rapidly (Clarke, 1984b; Falkenmark & Widstrand, 1992). Besides ensuring ample *supplies* of water, then, we must protect the *quality* of water.

Water quality in the United States is generally good by global standards. However, even here the problem of water pollution is growing steadily. According to the Sierra Club, an environmental activist organization, rivers and streams across the United States absorb some 500 million pounds of toxic waste each year. This pollution results not just from intentional dumping but also from the runoff of agricultural fertilizers and lawn chemicals.

A special problem is *acid rain*, rain made acidic by air pollution that destroys plant and animal life. Acid rain (or snow) begins with power plants burning fossil fuels (oil and coal) to generate electricity; this burning releases sulfuric and nitrous oxides into the air. As the wind sweeps these gases into the atmosphere, they react with the air to form sulfuric and nitric acids, which turns atmospheric moisture acidic.

This is a clear case of one type of pollution causing another: Air pollution (from smokestacks) ends up contaminating water (in lakes and streams that collect acid rain). Moreover, acid rain is truly a global phenomenon because the regions that suffer the harmful effects may be thousands of miles from the original pollution. For instance, British power plants have caused acid rain that has devastated forests and fish in Norway and Sweden, up to a thousand miles to the northeast. In the United States, we see a similar pattern as midwestern smokestacks have harmed the natural environment of New England.

GLOBAL: Some 1.4 billion people on Earth (22%) breathe air that threatens their health. China has 2 million deaths per year due to bad air; there are another 2 million around the world, caused mostly by toxic fumes from cooking and heating with poor-quality fuels and by a congested environment (Kemp, 1998).
NOTE: Reforestation programs can significantly help in reducing the buildup of atmospheric carbon dioxide.

NOTE: Although the U.S. accounts for scarcely 5% of the planet's population, it consumes one-third of the world's energy.
NOTE: A significant forest region, which contains substantial biological diversity, is found in the temperate climate of the Pacific Northwest in the U.S.
NOTE: Given global connections, argues Lester Milbrath, one principle of environmentalism is that "We can never do just one thing."

Air Pollution

Because we are surrounded by air, most people in the United States are more aware of air pollution than contaminated water. One of the unexpected consequences of industrial technology, especially the factory and the motor vehicle, has been a decline in air quality. In 1950, exhaust fumes from automobiles shrouded cities such as Los Angeles. In London, factory smokestacks, automobiles, and coal fires used to heat households all added to what was probably the worst urban air quality of the last century. What some British jokingly called "pea soup" was, in reality, a deadly mix of pollution. For five days in 1952, an especially thick haze that hung over London killed 4,000 people (Clarke, 1984a).

In the final decades of the twentieth century air quality improved. Rich nations passed laws that banned high-pollution heating, including the coal fires that choked London fifty years ago. In addition, scientists devised ways to reduce the noxious output of factories and the growing numbers of automobiles and trucks.

If high-income countries can breathe a bit more easily than they once did, the problem of air pollution in poor societies is becoming more serious. One reason is that people in low-income countries still rely on wood, coal, peat, and other "dirty" fuels to cook and to heat their homes. Moreover, nations eager to encourage short-term industrial development often pay little heed to the longer-term dangers of air pollution. As a result, many cities in Latin America, Eastern Europe, and Asia are plagued by air pollution as bad as London's fifty years ago.

THE RAIN FORESTS

Rain forests are *regions of dense forestation, most of which circle the globe close to the equator.* A glance back at Global Map 22–2, on page 591, shows that the largest tropical rain forests are in South America (notably Brazil), west central Africa, and Southeast Asia. In all, the world's rain forests cover some 2 billion acres, or 7 percent of the Earth's total land surface.

Like other global resources, rain forests are falling victim to the needs and appetites of the surging world population. As noted earlier, to meet the demand for beef, ranchers in Latin America burn forested areas to increase their supply of grazing land. We are also losing rain forests to the hardwood trade. People in rich nations pay high prices for mahogany and other woods because, as environmentalist Norman Myers (1984b:88) puts it, they have "a penchant for parquet floors, fine furniture, fancy paneling, weekend yachts,

and high-grade coffins." Under such economic pressure, the world's rain forests are now just half their original size, and they continue to shrink by about 1 percent (65,000 square miles) annually. Unless we stop this loss, the rain forests will vanish before the end of the twenty-first century, and with them will go protection for the earth's biodiversity and climate.

Global Warming

Why are rain forests so important? One reason is that they cleanse the atmosphere of carbon dioxide (CO_2). Since the beginning of the Industrial Revolution, the amount of carbon dioxide produced by humans (mostly from factories and automobiles) has risen tenfold. Much of this carbon dioxide is absorbed by the oceans. But plants take in carbon dioxide and expel oxygen. This is why rain forests are vital to maintaining the chemical balance of the atmosphere.

The problem, then, is that carbon dioxide production is rising while the amount of plant life on the Earth is shrinking. To make matters worse, rain forests are being destroyed mostly by burning, which releases even more carbon dioxide into the atmosphere. Experts estimate that the atmospheric concentration of carbon dioxide is now 20 to 30 percent higher than it was 150 years ago.

High above the Earth, carbon dioxide acts like the glass roof of a greenhouse, letting heat from the sun pass through to the Earth while preventing much of it from escaping back into outer space. The result of this *greenhouse effect*, say ecologists, is **global warming**, *a rise in the Earth's average temperature caused by an increasing concentration of carbon dioxide and other gases in the atmosphere.* Over the last century, the global temperature has risen about 1.0° Fahrenheit (to an average of 58°F). And scientists warn that it could rise by 5° to 10° during this century, which would melt vast areas of the polar ice caps and raise the sea level to cover low-lying land around the world. Were this to happen,

 A FEMA study (2000) claims that one in four houses within 500 feet of a shoreline is in danger over the next 60 years: http://www.heinzcenter.org

water would cover all of Bangladesh, for example, and much of the coastal United States, including Washington, D.C., right up to the steps of the White House. On the other hand, the U.S. Midwest, currently one of the most productive agricultural regions in the world, probably would become arid.

Mounting evidence suggests that the danger of global warming is real. Even so, some scientists point out that global temperature changes have been taking

GLOBAL: The planet has already lost more than half the forest area that existed in 1950.

GLOBAL: Costa Rica leads the world's tropical countries in the rate at which it is cutting its rain forest: 7% annually. However, Brazil is cutting the most forest in absolute terms, about 8 million hectares (3.2 million acres) annually.

DISCUSS: The biodiversity debate also involves the ethical question

of whether all forms of life have a basic right to exist. Are actions by one species that threaten the existence of other species inherently unethical?

NOTE: Environmentalism has spawned various acronyms, including NIMBY (not in my back yard), BANANA (build absolutely nothing anywhere near anything), LULUs (locally unwanted land uses), and NOPE (not on planet Earth).

Members of small, simple societies, such as the Tan't Batu, who thrive in the Philippines, live in harmony with nature; such people do not have the technological means to greatly affect the natural world. Although we in complex societies like to think of ourselves as superior to such people, the truth is that there is much we can—and must—learn from them.

place throughout history, apparently with little or nothing to do with rain forests. Moreover, higher concentrations of carbon dioxide in the atmosphere might speed up plant growth (because plants thrive on this gas), which would correct the imbalance and nudge the Earth's temperature downward once again. Still other scientists think global warming might even have benefits, including longer growing seasons and lower food prices (Silverberg, 1991; Moore, 1995; Begley, 1997; McDonald, 1999).

Declining Biodiversity

Destroying rain forests also reduces the Earth's *biodiversity*. This is because rain forests are home to almost half of this planet's living species.

On Earth, there are as many as 30 million species of animals, plants, and microorganisms. Several dozen unique species of plants and animals cease to exist each day, but given the vast number of living species, why should we be concerned? Environmentalists give three reasons. First, our planet's biodiversity provides a varied

source of human food. Using agricultural technology, scientists can interbreed or genetically combine familiar crops with more exotic plant life, making food more bountiful and more resistant to insects and disease. Thus, biodiversity is needed to feed our planet's rapidly increasing population.

Second, the Earth's biodiversity is a vital genetic resource. Medical and pharmaceutical researchers look to animal and plant biodiversity for new compounds that cure disease and improve our lives. For example, children in the United States now have a good chance of surviving leukemia, a disease that was almost a sure killer two generations ago, because of a compound derived from a pretty tropical flower called the rosy periwinkle. The oral birth control pill, used by tens of millions of women in this country, is another product of plant research, this time involving the Mexican forest yam.

Third, with the loss of any species of life—whether it is the magnificent California condor, the famed Chinese panda, the spotted owl, or even one variety of ant—the beauty and complexity of our natural environment are diminished. And there are clear warning signs of such loss: Three-fourths of the world's 9,000 species of birds are declining in number.

Finally, note that, unlike pollution, the extinction of any species is irreversible and final. An important ethical question, then, is whether we who live today have the right to impoverish the world for those who live tomorrow (Myers, 1984b, 1991; E. Wilson, 1991; Brown et al., 1993).

ENVIRONMENTAL RACISM

Conflict theory has given rise to the concept of **environmental racism,** *the pattern by which environmental hazards are greatest for poor people, especially minorities.* Historically, factories that spew pollution stand near neighborhoods of the poor and people of color. Why? In part because the poor themselves were drawn to factories in search of work, and their low incomes often meant they could afford housing only in undesirable neighborhoods. Sometimes the only housing that fit their budgets stood in the very shadow of the plants and mills where they worked.

Nobody wants a "locally undesirable land use" (LULU) such as a factory or dump nearby, but communities face proposals for such development all the time. When businesses or other large organizations seek to establish a LULU, poor communities often have little power to resist. Through the years, then, the most serious environmental hazards have

NOTE: Members of our society have always tended to treat "growth" as synonymous with "progress," with both viewed as "better" than the alternatives.

DIVERSITY: The concept of "environmental racism" partly reflects the movement's concern over its largely white, middle-class membership. (One recent survey found that 43% of readers of the Sierra Club's magazine have postgraduate degrees.)

SOCIAL SURVEY: "Modern science will solve our environmental problems with little change to our way of life." (GSS 2000, N = 1,276; Codebook, 2001:1068)

"Strongly agree"	2.7%	"Disagree"	35.0%
"Agree"	17.2%	"Strongly disagree"	8.2%
"Neither agree nor disagree"	26.3%	DK/NR	10.7%

been located near Newark, New Jersey (not in upscale Bergen County), in southside Chicago (not wealthy Lake Forest), or on Native American reservations in the West (not in affluent suburbs of Denver or Phoenix) (Perrolle, 1993; Commission for Racial Justice, United Church of Christ, 1994; Szasz, 1994; Pollock & Vittas, 1995; Bohon & Humphrey, 2000).

LOOKING AHEAD: TOWARD A SUSTAINABLE WORLD

The demographic analysis presented in this chapter points to some disturbing trends. We see, first, that Earth's population has reached record levels because birth rates remain high in poor nations and death rates have fallen just about everywhere. Lowering fertility will remain a pressing problem throughout this century. Even with some recent decline in population increase, the nightmare Thomas Malthus described is still a real possibility, as the box on page 596 explains.

Furthermore, population growth remains greatest in the poorest countries of the world, those without the means to support their present populations, much less their future ones. Supporting 77 million additional people on our planet each year—almost 74 million of whom are in low-income societies—will require a global commitment to provide not only food but housing, schools, and employment. The well-being of the entire world may ultimately depend on resolving the economic and social problems of poor, overly populated countries and bridging the widening gulf between "have" and "have-not" societies.

Urbanization, too, is continuing, especially in poor countries. Throughout human history, people have sought out cities with the hope of finding a better life. But the sheer numbers of people who live in the emerging global supercities—Mexico City, São Paulo (Brazil), Kinshasa (Democratic Republic of the Congo), Bombay (India), and Manila (the Philippines)—have created urban problems on a massive scale.

Throughout the entire world, humanity is facing a serious environmental challenge. Part of this problem is population increase, which is greatest in poor societies. But another part of the problem is the high levels of consumption typical of rich nations such as our own. By increasing the planet's environmental deficit, our present way of life is borrowing against the well-being of our children and their children. Globally, members of rich societies, who currently consume so much of the Earth's resources, are mortgaging the future security of the poor countries of the world.

The answer, in principle, is to form an **ecologically sustainable culture,** *a way of life that meets the needs of the present generation without threatening the environmental legacy of future generations.* Sustainable living depends on three strategies.

First, the world needs to bring population growth under control. The current population of more than 6 billion is already straining the natural environment. Clearly, the higher the world's population climbs, the more difficult environmental problems will become. Even if the recent slowing of population growth continues, the world will have 8 billion people by 2050. Few analysts think that the Earth can support this many people; most argue that we must hold the line at about 7 billion, and some argue that we must *decrease* population in the coming decades (Smail, 1997).

A second strategy is *conservation of finite resources.* This means meeting our needs with a responsible eye toward the future by using resources efficiently, seeking alternative sources of energy, and, in some cases, learning to live with less.

A third strategy is *reducing waste.* Whenever possible, simply using less is the best solution. But recycling programs also are part of the answer.

In the end, making all these strategies work depends on a more basic change in the way we think about ourselves and our world. Our *egocentric* outlook sets our own interests as standards for how to live, but a sustainable environment demands an *ecocentric* outlook that helps us see how the present is tied to the future and why everyone must work together. Most nations in the southern half of the world are *underdeveloped,* unable to meet the basic needs of their people. At the same time, most countries in the northern half of the world are *overdeveloped,* using more resources than the Earth can sustain over time. Changes needed to create a sustainable ecosystem will not come easily. But the cost of not responding to the growing environmental deficit will certainly be greater (Humphrey & Buttel, 1982; Burke, 1984; Kellert & Bormann, 1991; Brown et al., 1993; Population Action International, 2000).

In closing, consider that the great dinosaurs dominated this planet for some 160 million years and then perished forever. Humanity is far younger, having existed for a mere 250,000 years. Compared to the dim-witted dinosaurs, our species has the gift of great intelligence. But how will we use this ability? What are the chances that our species will continue to flourish 160 million years—or even 1,000 years—from now? The shape of tomorrow's world depends on the choices we make today.

GLOBAL: As a personal solution to the myriad problems of poor nations, tens of millions of people are migrating toward richer, northern countries. In response, many rich societies are tightening restrictions on immigration.

GLOBAL: A study by the Pakistani government concludes that new technology and other innovations will allow that nation to support some 200 million people—up from the present 145 million.

But the study foresees no way to support 400 million people, the population level Pakistan will reach (assuming today's trends continue) by 2040.

NOTE: The neo-Malthusians fall within the environmental movement, arguing that growth is a social danger. The anti-Malthusians tend to be economists who follow Adam Smith in viewing growth as good.

CONTROVERSY & DEBATE

Apocalypse: Will People Overwhelm the Earth?

Are you worried about the world's increasing population? Think about this: By the time you finish reading this box, more than 1,000 people will be added to our planet. By this time tomorrow, global population will rise by 210,000. Currently, as the following table shows, there are about four births for every two deaths on the planet, pushing the world's population upward by 77 million annually. Put another way, global population growth amounts to adding another Philippines to the world every year.

It is no wonder that demographers and environmentalists are deeply concerned about the future. The Earth has an unprecedented population: The 2 billion people we have *added* since 1974 alone exceeds the planet's total in 1900.

neo-Malthusians by predicting an apocalypse if we do not change our ways. Brown concedes that Malthus failed to imagine how much technology (especially fertilizers and genetically modified plants) could boost agricultural output. But he maintains that the Earth's rising population is nevertheless rapidly outstripping its finite resources. Families in many poor countries can find little firewood, members of rich societies are depleting the oil reserves, and everyone is draining our supply of clean water.

Moreover, according to the neo-Malthusians, we are steadily poisoning the planet with waste. There is a limit to the Earth's capacity to absorb pollution, they warn, and as the number of people continues to increase, the quality of life will decline. Some analysts, in

as many people who, on average, live longer, healthier lives than ever before. As Simon sees it, the current state of the planet is cause for celebration.

The mistake of the neo-Malthusians, Simon argues, is assuming the world has finite resources that are spread thinner and thinner as population increases. Rather, people have the ability to control population growth and to improve their lives in many ways. Furthermore, we do not know what number of people the Earth can support because humans keep rewriting the rules, in effect, by developing new fertilizers, new crops, and new forms of energy. Simon notes that today's global economy makes available more resources than ever (including energy and consumer goods) at increasingly low prices. He looks optimistically to the future because technology, economic investment, and, above all, human ingenuity have consistently proven the doomsayers wrong. And he is betting they will continue to do so.

Global Population Increase			
	Births	**Deaths**	**Net Increase**
Per Year	131,571,719	55,001,289	76,570,430
Per Month	10,964,310	4,583,441	6,380,869
Per Day	360,470	150,688	209,782
Per Hour	15,020	6,279	8,741
Per Minute	250	105	146
Per Second	4.2	1.7	2.4

Might Thomas Robert Malthus—who predicted that population would outstrip the Earth's resources and plunge humanity into war and suffering—be right after all?

Lester Brown, a population and environmental activist, speaks for the

Explore connections between population increase, global inequality, and the natural environment at http://www. peopleandtheplanet.net

fact, argue that we have already passed the Earth's "carrying capacity" for population. Holding the line will not be enough; as they see it, we need to *reduce* global population to perhaps half of what it is today (Smail, 1997).

But other analysts, the *anti-Malthusians*, sharply disagree. Asks Julian Simon, "Why the doom and gloom?" More than two centuries ago, he points out, Malthus predicted catastrophe. But today the Earth supports almost six times

Continue the debate . . .

1. *Where do you place your bet? Do you think the Earth can support 4, 6, 8, or 10 billion people? Why?*

2. *Ninety-six percent of current population growth is in poor countries. What does this mean for the future of rich nations? For the future of poor ones?*

3. *What should people in rich countries do to ensure the future of children everywhere?*

Sources: Based, in part, on Brown et al. (1993), Brown (1995), Simon (1995), and Smail (1997).

Q: "We stand where two roads diverge. But unlike the roads in Robert Frost's poem, they are not equally fair. The road we have long been traveling is deceptively easy, a smooth superhighway on which we progress with great speed, but at its end lies disaster. The other fork in the road, the one 'less traveled by,' offers our last, and only, chance to reach a destination that assures the preservation of our earth." Rachel Carson (1962:277)

SUMMARY

Population

1. Fertility and mortality, measured as crude birth and death rates, are major factors affecting population size. In global terms, U.S. population growth is low.

2. Migration, another key demographic concept, has special importance to the historical growth of the United States and to cities everywhere.

3. Age-sex pyramids show graphically the composition of a population and project population trends. Sex ratio is a society's balance of females and males.

4. Historically, world population grew slowly because high birth rates were offset by high death rates. About 1750, a demographic transition began as world population rose sharply, mainly due to falling death rates.

5. Malthus warned that population growth would outpace food production, threatening society. Demographic transition theory counters that technological advances gradually slow population increase.

6. World population is expected to reach between 8 billion and 9 billion by 2050, with most of the increase in poor societies.

Urbanization

1. The first urban revolution began with the appearance of cities about 8000 B.C.E.. By the start of the common era, cities had emerged in most regions of the world except for North America.

2. Preindustrial cities have low-rise buildings, narrow, winding streets, and personal social ties.

3. A second urban revolution began about 1750 with the Industrial Revolution in Europe. An emphasis on commerce, as well as the increasing size of cities, made urban life more anonymous.

4. Urbanism came to North America with Europeans, who settled in a string of colonial towns along the Atlantic coastline. By 1850, hundreds of new cities were founded from coast to coast.

5. By 1920, a majority of the U.S. population lived in urban areas, and the largest metropolises were home to millions of people.

6. About 1950, cities began to decentralize with the growth of suburbs and edge cities. Nationally, Sunbelt cities—but not the older Snowbelt cities—are increasing in size and population.

7. Rapid urbanization in Europe during the nineteenth century led early sociologists to contrast rural and urban life. Ferdinand Tönnies built his analysis on the concepts of *Gemeinshaft* and *Gesellschaft*, and Emile Durkheim proposed parallel concepts of mechanical solidarity and organic solidarity. Georg Simmel claimed that the overstimulation of city life produced a blasé attitude in urbanites.

8. Robert Park believed cities permit greater social freedom. Louis Wirth saw large, dense, heterogeneous populations creating an impersonal and self-interested, though tolerant, way of life. Other researchers have explored urban ecology and urban political economy.

9. A third urban revolution is occurring in poor countries, where most of the world's largest cities will soon be found.

Environment

1. How human beings organize social life has the greatest effect on the natural environment.

2. Societies increase the environmental deficit by focusing on short-term benefits and ignoring the long-term consequences of their way of life.

3. Our ability to alter the natural world lies in our capacity for culture. Humanity's effect on the environment has increased along with the development of complex technology.

4. The "logic of growth" thesis supports economic development, stating that people can solve environmental problems as they arise. The opposing "limits to growth" thesis states that societies must curb development to prevent eventual environmental collapse.

5. Environmental issues include disposing of solid waste and protecting the quality of air and water. The supply of clean water is already low in some parts of the world.

6. Rain forests help remove carbon dioxide from the atmosphere and are home to a large share of this planet's living species. Under pressure from commercial interests, the world's rain forests are now half their original size and are shrinking by about 1 percent annually.

7. Environmental racism is the pattern by which the poor, especially minorities, suffer most from environmental hazards.

8. To achieve a sustainable environment that does not threaten the well-being of future generations, we must control world population, conserve finite resources, and reduce waste and pollution.

KEY CONCEPTS

Population

demography (p. 569) the study of human population

fertility (p. 570) the incidence of childbearing in a country's population

crude birth rate (p. 570) the number of live births in a given year for every thousand people in a population

mortality (p. 570) the incidence of death in a country's population

crude death rate (p. 570) the number of deaths in a given year for every thousand people in a population

infant mortality rate (p. 571) the number of deaths among infants under one year of age for each thousand live births in a given year

life expectancy (p. 571) the average life span of a country's population

migration (p. 571) the movement of people into and out of a specified territory

sex ratio (p. 573) the number of males for every hundred females in a nation's population

age-sex pyramid (p. 573) a graphic representation of the age and sex of a population

demographic transition theory (p. 575) the thesis that population patterns reflect a society's level of technological development

zero population growth (p. 576) the level of reproduction that maintains population at a steady state

Urbanization

urbanization (p. 578) the concentration of humanity into cities

metropolis (p. 580) a large city that socially and economically dominates an urban area

suburbs (p. 580) urban areas beyond the political boundaries of a city

megalopolis (p. 581) a vast urban region containing a number of cities and their surrounding suburbs

Gemeinschaft (p. 582) a type of social organization by which people are closely tied by kinship and tradition

Gesellschaft (p. 582) a type of social organization by which people come together only on the basis of self-interest

urban ecology (p. 584) the study of the link between the physical and social dimensions of cities

Environment

ecology (p. 586) the study of the interaction of living organisms and the natural environment

natural environment (p. 586) the Earth's surface and atmosphere, including living organisms, air, water, soil, and other resources necessary to sustain life

ecosystem (p. 586) a system composed of the interaction of all living organisms and their natural environment

environmental deficit (p. 587) profound and long-term harm to the natural environment caused by humanity's focus on short-term material affluence

rain forests (p. 593) regions of dense forestation, most of which circle the globe close to the equator

global warming (p. 593) a rise in the Earth's average temperature caused by an increasing concentration of carbon dioxide and other gases in the atmosphere

environmental racism (p. 594) the pattern by which environmental hazards are greatest for poor people, especially minorities

ecologically sustainable culture (p. 595) a way of life that meets the needs of the present generation without threatening the environmental legacy of future generations

CRITICAL-THINKING QUESTIONS

1. What are fertility and mortality rates? Which one has been more important in increasing global population?

2. Evaluate the environmental prediction of Thomas Robert Malthus. On balance, do you think he was more wrong or more right? Why?

3. How does demographic transition theory explain population patterns in terms of technological development?

4. According to Ferdinand Tönnies, Emile Durkheim, Georg Simmel, and Louis Wirth, what characterizes urbanism as a way of life? Note several differences in the ideas of these thinkers.

APPLICATIONS AND EXERCISES

1. Here is an illustration of the problem of runaway growth (Milbrath, 1989:10): *A pond has a single water lily growing on it. The lily doubles in size each day. In thirty days, it covers the entire pond. On which day does it cover half the pond?* When you realize the answer, discuss the implications of this example for population increase.

2. Draw a mental map of a city familiar to you with as much detail of specific places, districts, roads, and transportation facilities as you can. Compare your map with a commercially published one or, better yet, a map drawn by a classmate. Try to account for the differences.

3. Carry a plastic trash bag around with you for one full day. Put everything you throw away in the bag. Afterward, weigh what you have; multiply this amount by 365 to estimate your yearly "trash factor." Multiply this amount by 281 million to estimate the annual waste of the entire U.S. population.

4. In the Bible, read Genesis, chapter 1, especially verses 28–31. According to this account of creation, are humans empowered to do what we want to the Earth? Or are we charged to care for the Earth? For more on this idea, see Wolkomir et al. (1997).

5. Packaged in the back of this new textbook is an interactive CD-ROM that offers a variety of study and review materials intended to help you better understand the material covered in this chapter. For this chapter, the CD-ROM contains an author's tip video, Real Life Sociology videos, other relevant audio and video, interactive map animations, audio journal entries from the author, Web links, and much more.

SITES TO SEE

http://www.prenhall.com/macionis

Visit the interactive *Companion Website*™ that accompanies this text. Begin by clicking on the cover of your book. You will find a chapter-by-chapter study guide, practice tests, and a significant portion of the text for on-line review, as well as many suggested Web links.

http://www.eclac.org

This site, created by the Economic Commission for Latin America and the Caribbean (part of the United Nations), allows country-by-country analysis of population patterns for this region of the world. Most of the site is available in both English and Spanish.

http://www.niehs.nih.gov

Visit the site for the National Institute of Environmental Health Sciences.

http://www.hud.gov

This is the Web site for the government's Department of Housing and Urban Development.

http://www.mte.com/riot_site/webcam.html

Watch big-city life from the comfort of your own home: This site uses a Web camera showing the action on New

York City's Fifth Avenue and Forty-Fifth Street. What can you learn from people-watching in this way? What does this observation *not* tell you about urban life?

http://www.sierraclub.org
http://www.greenpeace.org

These two environmental sites are maintained by the Sierra Club and Greenpeace. Visit the sites to see how these two organizations are similar and how are they different.

http://www2.kenyon.edu/projects/agri/

This site, constructed by college students, investigates how the way we live affects the planet and how the state of our planet affects our lives.

http://www.info.gov.hk/index_e.htm

This site explores the city of Hong Kong.

http://www.urban.nyu.edu/

New York University's Taub Urban Research Center is on the Internet. Visit this site to survey recent research on urban issues.

INVESTIGATE WITH CONTENTSELECT

Follow the instructions found on page 23 of this textbook to enter this chapter of the book's *Companion Website*™. Once in the chapter, click on the ContentSelect icon at the bottom left of your screen and enter your personal

User ID and Password. Enter keywords such as "zero population growth," "cities," and "global warming," and the search engine will help you become an effective researcher.

CHAPTER

23

COLLECTIVE BEHAVIOR
AND SOCIAL MOVEMENTS

Seattle has the reputation of being a hip, laid-back, and progressive town—a mix of the 1960s "peace and love" and twenty-first century high-technology. Seattle is also a popular convention city, which is one reason that representatives of the World Trade Organization (WTO) gathered there at the end of 1999 to discuss the expanding global economy. The WTO is the international organization that develops rules for trade between the various nations of the world.

Other people showed up, too—some 40,000 people, in fact, who had their own ideas about the WTO globalization. These people—representing labor unions, environmental groups, human rights organizations—as well as student

activists gathered in common opposition to the World Trade Organization. As they see it, the WTO puts economic interests above concern for the environment and social justice. In practice, activists claim, the WTO promotes the power of giant corporations to run the entire world.

During the four-day meeting, the broad-based alliance of protesters managed to command more attention from the media than the conference itself. Sometimes peacefully, and sometimes violently, they made their case that increasing corporate power threatens not only the state of environment but also the future well-being of "ordinary" people in rich and poor nations (Kirn, 2000).

This groundswell of action in response to Seattle's WTO conference is an example of **collective behavior,** *activity involving a large number of people, often spontaneous and sometimes controversial.* This chapter investigates various forms of collective behavior, ranging from crowds, mobs and riots, rumor and gossip, public opinion, panic and mass hysteria, and fashions and fads to social movements aimed at changing the course of people's lives around the world.

For much of the twentieth century, sociologists focused on established social patterns such as the family and social stratification. They paid less attention to cases of collective behavior, considering most of it trivial, unusual, or even deviant. But numerous social movements characterized the tumultuous 1960s, and many are still

To find out more about the World Trade Organization, go to http://www.wto.org

changing society today. Therefore, in recent decades sociological interest in all types of collective behavior has increased (Weller & Quarantelli, 1973; G. Marx & Wood, 1975; Aguirre & Quarantelli, 1983; McAdam, McCarthy, & Zald, 1988; Turner & Killian, 1993).

STUDYING COLLECTIVE BEHAVIOR

Despite its importance, collective behavior is difficult for sociologists to study for three main reasons.

1. **Collective behavior is wide ranging.** Collective behavior involves a bewildering array of human action. The traits common to fads, rumors, and mob behavior, for example, are far from obvious.

2. **Collective behavior is complex.** A rumor seems to come out of nowhere and circulates in

SUPPLEMENTS: An outline of this chapter, suggested discussion topics, and supplementary lecture material are found in the *Data File*.
NOTE: Peter Dahlgren characterizes collective behavior as the breakdown of "the smooth rationality upon which the social order rests." Enrico Quarantelli, by contrast, counters that most collective behavior is both continuous and rational.

Q: "Never confuse motion with action." Ernest Hemingway
NOTE: The term "collective behavior" was coined by Robert E. Park; in fact, Park defined sociology as "the science of collective behavior," suggesting a focus on dynamic rather than stable social patterns. (See Ralph Turner's introduction to *Robert E. Park: On Social Control and Collective Behavior*, University of Chicago Press, 1967.)

Sometimes people come together to make events happen; sometimes it is events that bring people together. In the wake of the September 11, 2001, terrorist attacks, people all across the United States came together—as family members, co-workers, neighbors, and friends—to offer support and comfort in the face of fear and loss.

countless different settings. For no apparent reason, one new form of dress catches on and another does not. Why, over the course of this nation's history, would millions of African Americans patiently endure second-class standing for so long and then begin a civil rights movement in the mid-1950s?

3. **Much collective behavior is transitory.** Sociologists can readily study the family because it is a continuing element of social life. However, fashions, rumors, and riots arise and dissipate quickly, making them difficult to study.

Some researchers point out that these problems apply not just to collective behavior but to *most* forms of human behavior (Aguirre & Quarantelli, 1983). Moreover, collective behavior is not always so surprising; anyone can predict that crowds will form at sports events and music festivals, and sociologists can study these gatherings firsthand or record them on videotape to study later. Researchers can even anticipate natural disasters and study the human responses they provoke. For example, each year about sixty major tornadoes occur in particular regions of the United States; sociologists interested in how disasters affect behavior can be prepared to begin research on short notice (Miller, 1985). A number of researchers are now at work studying how the terrorist attacks of September 11, 2001 have affected U.S. society.

Sociologists know a great deal about collective behavior, but they still have much to learn. The most se-

rious shortcoming, according to Benigno Aguirre and E. L. Quarantelli (1983), is that sociologists have yet to develop a theory that ties together all the different actions called "collective behavior."

At the least, all collective behavior involves the action of some **collectivity,** *a large number of people whose minimal interaction occurs in the absence of well-defined and conventional norms.* Collectivities are of two kinds. A *localized collectivity* refers to people in physical proximity to one another; this first type is illustrated by crowds and riots. A *dispersed collectivity* or *mass behavior* involves people who influence one another even though they are separated by great distances; examples here include rumors, public opinion, and fashion (Turner & Killian, 1993).

It is important to distinguish collectivities from the already familiar concept of social groups (see Chapter 7, "Groups and Organizations"). Here are three key differences:

1. **Collectivities are based on limited social interaction.** Group members interact frequently and directly. People in mobs or other localized collectivities interact very little. Most people taking part in dispersed collectivities, such as a fad, do not interact at all.

2. **Collectivities have no clear social boundaries.** Group members share a sense of identity that is usually missing among people engaged in collective behavior. Localized crowds may have a common object of attention (such as someone on a ledge

threatening to jump), but they show little sense of unity. Individuals involved in dispersed collectivities, such as the "public" that is alarmed by the threat of anthrax, have almost no awareness of shared membership. Of course, some issues divide the public into well-defined factions, but often it is difficult to say who falls within the ranks of a particular group, as, for example, the environmentalist or the feminist movements.

3. **Collectivities generate weak and unconventional norms** Conventional cultural norms usually regulate the behavior of group members. Some collectivities, such as people traveling on an airplane, observe conventional norms, but their interaction usually is limited to polite smalltalk in an effort to respect the privacy of people sitting nearby. Other collectivities—such as excited soccer fans who destroy property as they leave a stadium—spontaneously develop very unconventional norms (Weller & Quarantelli, 1973; Turner & Killian, 1993).

LOCALIZED COLLECTIVITIES: CROWDS

One major form of collective behavior is the **crowd,** *a temporary gathering of people who share a common focus of attention and who influence one another*. Historian Peter Laslett (1984) points out that crowds are a modern development; in medieval Europe, about the only time large numbers of people gathered in one place was when armies faced off on the battlefield. Today, however, crowds of 25,000 or more are common at sporting events, rock concerts, and even the registration halls of large universities.

But all crowds are not alike. Herbert Blumer (1969) identified four categories of crowds.

A *casual crowd* is a loose collection of people who interact little, if at all. People at the beach or at the scene of an automobile accident have only a passing awareness of one another.

A *conventional crowd* results from deliberate planning, as illustrated by a country auction, a college lecture, or a family funeral. In each case, interaction conforms to norms appropriate to the situation.

An *expressive crowd* forms around an event with emotional appeal, such as a religious revival, a professional wrestling match, or a New Year's Eve celebration in New York's Times Square. Excitement is the main reason people join expressive crowds, which makes this experience spontaneous and exhilarating.

An *acting crowd* is a collectivity motivated by an intense, single-minded purpose, such as an audience rushing the doors of a concert hall or fleeing from a burning theater. Acting crowds are ignited by very powerful emotions, which can reach a feverish intensity and sometimes erupt into mob violence.

Any crowd can change from one type to another. In 2001, for example, a conventional crowd of more than 10,000 fans filed into a soccer stadium in Johannesburg, South Africa, to watch a match between two rival teams. After a goal was scored, the crowd erupted and people began to push toward the field. Within seconds the stampede crushed forty-seven people to death. By the time order was restored, the dead lay in the stands and across the playing field as if a battle rather than a sporting event had taken place (Nessman, 2001).

Deliberate action by a crowd is not simply the product of rising emotions. Participants in *protest crowds*—a fifth category we can add to Blumer's list—may stage strikes, boycotts, sit-ins, and marches for political purposes (McPhail & Wohlstein, 1983). An example of a protest crowd is the 1999 demonstration at the World Trade

 To find out more about activist opposition to the World Trade Organization, go to http://www.ifg.org

Organization meeting in Seattle described in the opening to this chapter. In such crowds, some participants display the low-level energy characteristic of a conventional crowd, whereas others are emotional enough to be in an acting crowd. Sometimes, too, a protest begins peacefully, but people become aggressive when police or counterdemonstrators appear or when they are intent on disrupting "business as usual."

MOBS AND RIOTS

When an acting crowd turns violent, we may witness the birth of a **mob,** *a highly emotional crowd that pursues a violent or destructive goal*. Despite, or perhaps because of, their intense emotion, mobs tend to dissipate quickly. How long a mob exists often depends on its precise goals and whether its leadership tries to inflame or stabilize the crowd.

Lynching is the most notorious example of mob behavior in the United States. The term is derived from Charles Lynch, a Virginia colonist who sought to maintain law and order in his own way before formal courts were established. The word soon became synonymous with violence and murder outside the law.

Q: "Interest in the field [of collective behavior and social movements] has hardly been constant, tending instead to wax and wane partly in response to the level of movement activity in society." Doug McAdam, John D. McCarthy, and Mayer N. Zald
NOTE: The word "riot" was used in medieval Europe to refer to a dispute or quarrel; its likely Latin root is *rugire*, meaning "to roar."

Q: "For freedom and justice and so the troopers can't hit us anymore." An African American school girl explaining why she was joining the Selma march (1965)
DIVERSITY: Racial violence has a long history in the U.S. Most common were white attacks on black people, Asians, and Native Americans. The pattern of African Americans rioting against whites emerged later, in the 1960s.

Lynching has always been colored by race. After the Civil War, lynch mobs became a terrorist form of social control over emancipated African Americans. An African American who challenged white superiority risked hanging or being burned alive by hateful whites.

Lynch mobs, typically composed of poor whites threatened by competition from freed slaves, reached their peak between 1880 and 1930. Police recorded some 5,000 lynchings in that period, although no doubt many more occurred. Most of these killings were committed in the Deep South, where a farming economy depended on a cheap and docile labor force. On the western frontier, lynch mobs targeted people of Mexican and Asian descent. In about 25 percent of known cases, whites lynched other whites. Lynching women was rare; only about 100 such instances are known, almost all involving women of color (White, 1969, orig. 1929; Grant, 1975).

A frenzied crowd without any particular purpose is a **riot**, *a social eruption that is highly emotional, violent, and undirected*. Unlike the action of a mob, a riot usually has no clear goal, except perhaps to express dissatisfaction. Underlying most riots is long-standing anger that is ignited by some minor incident so that participants become violent, destroying property or harming other people (Smelser, 1962; M. Rosenfeld, 1997). Whereas a mob action usually ends when a specific goal has been achieved (or decisively blocked), a riot tends to disperse only as participants run out of steam or police and community leaders gradually bring them under control.

Throughout our nation's history, riots have erupted as a reaction to social injustice. For example, industrial workers have rioted to vent rage at their working conditions. In 1886, a bitter struggle by Chicago factory workers for an eight-hour workday led to the explosive Haymarket Riot, which left eleven dead and scores injured. Rioting born of anger and despair also takes place frequently in prisons.

In addition, race riots have occurred in this country with striking regularity. Early in this century, crowds of whites attacked African Americans in Chicago, Detroit, and other cities. In the 1960s, riots rocked numerous inner-city ghettos when seemingly trivial events sparked rage at continuing prejudice and discrimination. In Los Angeles in 1992, the acquittal of police officers involved in the beating of motorist Rodney King set off an explosive riot. Violence and fires killed more than fifty people, injured thousands, and destroyed property worth hundreds of millions of dollars.

Riots are not always fired by hate. They can also begin with very positive feelings. In 2000, for example, young men attending New York City's National Puerto Rican Day Parade began spraying water on young women in their midst. Over the next few hours, dozens of women reported being groped, stripped, and assaulted, apparently resulting, as one report put it, from a mixture of "marijuana, alcohol, hot weather, testosterone idiocy, and lapses in police [protection]" (Barstow & Chivers, 2000). Similarly, after a win by the Los Angeles Lakers basketball team a few days later, hundreds of young people went on a jubilant rampage, turning over cars, breaking windows, starting fires, and injuring several dozen people. As one analyst put it, in an "anything goes" culture, people think they can do whatever they feel like doing (Pitts, 2000).

CROWDS, MOBS, AND SOCIAL CHANGE

```
April 13, 2001, Cincinnati, Ohio. The
city has been under siege all week by
African American demonstrators enraged
by the police shooting of an unarmed
black man. In the mayhem, dozens of in-
nocent people—both black and white—
have been seriously hurt by flying
bricks and swinging baseball bats.
Does such violence bring attention to
a just cause, or does it obscure it?
```

What does a riot accomplish? Ordinary people can gain power by acting collectively. The power of the crowd to force some social change—beginning by disrupting the routine social order—makes crowds controversial. Throughout history, defenders of the status quo have feared "the mob" as a threat. By contrast, those seeking change have viewed mobs as rightful protest.

Moreover, crowds share no single political cast. Demonstrators and counterdemonstrators shout slogans for and against abortion, for example, displaying objectives that reflect all positions along the political spectrum (Rudé, 1964; Canetti, 1978; Tarrow, 1994).

EXPLAINING CROWD BEHAVIOR

What accounts for the behavior of crowds? Social scientists have developed several different explanations.

Contagion Theory

An early explanation of collective behavior was formulated by French sociologist Gustave Le Bon

Q: "The age we are about to enter will in truth be the era of crowds." Gustave Le Bon

Q: Gustave Le Bon, himself an aristocrat, denounced crowds as "only powerful for destruction" (1960:18; orig. 1895).

Q: "What constituted a people, a unity, a whole, becomes in the end an agglomeration of individualities lacking cohesion." Gustave Le Bon (1895)

Q: "The nearer the people are drawn to the common level of an equal and similar condition, the less prone does each man become to place implicit faith in a certain man or a certain class of men. But his readiness to believe the multitude increases, and opinion is more than ever the mistress of the world." Alexis de Tocqueville

Q: "The public is the only critic whose opinion is worth anything at all." Mark Twain

Some have claimed that crowds swell with unrestrained emotion as if they have a mind of their own. But in most cases, crowds come into being as people with a sense of injustice join together to express their anger and oppose the powers that be. Thus, although some individuals may act in ways that appear irrational, social unrest is usually a matter of broader political issues (in this case, an unpopular tax that brought more than 200,000 Britons into the streets of London in March, 1990).

(1841–1931). According to Le Bon's *contagion theory* (1960; orig. 1895), crowds exert a hypnotic influence over their members. Shielded by the anonymity afforded by large numbers of people, people abandon personal responsibility and surrender to the contagious emotions of the crowd. A crowd thus assumes a life of its own, stirring up emotions and driving people toward irrational, even violent, action.

Critical evaluation. Le Bon's idea that crowds foster anonymity and sometimes generate strong emotions is surely true. Yet as Clark McPhail (1991) points out, a large body of research shows that "the madding crowd" does not take on a life of its own: Its actions result from the intentions and decisions of specific individuals. In the case of the 2001 soccer stampede in Johannesburg, South Africa, for example, the crowd did not simply "go wild." Investigation showed that promoters had sold far too many tickets to the game, filling the stadium to the point that there was no room even to stand. As more people tried to push in to see the action, a fence collapsed, causing the "stampede" (Nessman, 2001).

Furthermore, although collective behavior may involve strong emotions, such feelings are not necessarily irrational, as contagion theory suggests. On the contrary, emotions—as well as action—can be the product of a well-developed sense of injustice (Jasper, 1998).

Convergence Theory

Convergence theory holds that crowd behavior is not a product of the crowd itself but is carried into the crowd by particular individuals. That is, a crowd is a convergence of like-minded individuals. In other words, whereas contagion theory states that crowds cause people to act in a certain way, convergence theory says the opposite: that people who want to act in a certain way come together to form crowds.

From time to time, news stories describe white people banding together to threaten African Americans who try to move into their neighborhood. In such cases, convergence theorists contend, the crowd itself does not generate racial hatred or violence. On the contrary, hostility has been simmering for some time among many local people. A crowd then arises from a convergence of people who oppose the presence of black neighbors.

Critical evaluation. By linking crowds to broader social forces, convergence theory claims that crowd behavior is not irrational, as Le Bon maintained. Rather, people in crowds express existing beliefs and values (Berk, 1974). But in fairness to Le Bon, people sometimes do things in a crowd that they would not have the courage to do alone, because crowds can diffuse responsibility. In addition, crowds can intensify a sentiment simply by creating a critical mass of like-minded people.

CRITICAL THINKING

The Rumor Mill: Paul Is Dead!

Everyone knows the Beatles. The music of John Lennon, Paul McCartney, George Harrison, and Ringo Starr caused a cultural revolution in the 1960s. However, not everyone today knows the rumor that circulated about Paul McCartney at the height of the group's popularity.

On October 12, 1969, a young man telephoned a Detroit disk jockey to say that he had discovered "evidence" that Paul McCartney was dead:

1. At the end of the song "Strawberry Fields Forever" on the *Magical Mystery Tour* album, filtering out background noise allows the listener to hear a voice saying, "I buried Paul!"

2. The phrase "Number 9, Number 9, Number 9" from the song "Revolution 9" on the *White Album*, when played backward, seems to intone, "Turn me on, dead man!"

Two days later, the University of Michigan student newspaper ran a story titled "McCartney Is Dead: Further Clues Found." It sent millions of Beatles fans scurrying for their albums.

3. A picture inside the *Magical Mystery Tour* album shows John, George, and Ringo wearing red carnations, but Paul is wearing a black flower.

4. The cover of the *Sergeant Pepper's Lonely Hearts Club Band* album shows a grave with yellow flowers arranged in the shape of Paul's bass guitar.

5. On the inside of that album, McCartney wears an armpatch with the letters "OPD." Is this the insignia of some police department or confirmation that Paul had been "Officially Pronounced Dead"?

6. On the back cover of the same album, the other three Beatles are facing forward but McCartney has his back to the camera.

7. On the album cover of *Abbey Road*, John Lennon is clothed as a clergyman, Ringo Starr wears an undertaker's black tie, and George Harrison is clad in workman's attire as if ready to dig a grave. For his

Emergent-Norm Theory

Ralph Turner and Lewis Killian (1993) developed the *emergent-norm theory* of crowd dynamics. These researchers concede that social behavior is never entirely predictable, but if similar interests draw people together, distinctive patterns of behavior may emerge in the crowd.

According to Turner and Killian, crowds begin as collectivities containing people with mixed interests and motives. Especially in the case of less stable crowds—expressive, acting, and protest crowds—norms may be vague and changing, as when one person decides to break a store window and others join in and begin looting merchandise. In short, people in crowds make their own rules as they go along.

Critical evaluation. Emergent-norm theory represents a symbolic-interaction approach to crowd dynamics. Turner and Killian (1972:10) explain that crowd behavior is neither as irrational as contagion theory suggests nor as deliberate as convergence theory implies. Certainly, crowd behavior reflects the desires of participants, but it is also guided by norms that emerge as the situation unfolds.

Thus, decision making plays a major role in crowd behavior, although casual observers of the crowd may not realize it. For example, frightened people clogging the exits of a burning theater may appear to be victims of irrational panic, but from their point of view, fleeing a life-threatening situation makes a lot of sense.

Furthermore, emergent-norm theory points out that people in a crowd take on different roles. Some step forward as leaders, others become lieutenants, rank-and-file followers, inactive bystanders, or even opponents (Weller & Quarantelli, 1973; Zurcher & Snow, 1981).

DISPERSED COLLECTIVITIES: MASS BEHAVIOR

It is not just people clustered together in crowds who participate in collective behavior. **Mass behavior** is

NOTE: Delbert Miller claimed that in 1945 only a small number of people on his campus learned of the death of President Roosevelt directly from radio reports. Within 30 minutes, however, about 90% of the people had been informed by word of mouth (*American Sociological Review* 10:691-94). Obviously, today's more powerful mass media reduce the significance of word of mouth in spreading national rumor.

NOTE: Levin and Arluke spread a rumor on their campus by widely distributing flyers announcing a fictitious wedding. The flyers were not circulated until a day before the supposed event. Still, the researchers found that, one week later, 52% of a campus sample had heard about the wedding, and 12% claimed to have attended it (1987:14–15).

part, McCartney is barefoot, which is how Tibetan ritual prepares a corpse for burial. Behind Paul, a Volkswagen nearby displays the license plate "28 IF," apparently stating that McCartney would be 28 *if* he were alive.

The rumor explained that McCartney had died of head injuries suffered in an automobile accident in November 1966. After the accident, record company executives had secretly replaced Paul with a double.

Of course, Paul McCartney is very much alive and still jokes about the episode. Few doubt that Paul himself dreamed up some of the details of his "death" with a little help from his friends to encourage the interest of their fans. But the incident has a serious side,

showing how quickly rumors can arise and persist in a climate of distrust. In the late 1960s, many disaffected young people were quite ready to believe that the media and other powerful interests were concealing McCartney's death.

In 1969, McCartney himself denied the rumor in a *Life* magazine story. But thousands of suspicious readers noticed that on the other side of the page with McCartney's picture was an ad for an automobile: If one held this page up to the light, the car lay across McCartney's chest and blocked his head. Another clue!

What do you think?

1. *What can we say about the kind of issues that give rise to rumors?*

2. *Have there been rumors this year on your campus? About what?*

3. *On balance, do you think rumors are helpful or harmful? Why?*

Sources: Based on Rosnow & Fine (1976) and Kapferer (1992).

collective behavior among people dispersed over a wide geographical area.

RUMOR AND GOSSIP

A common type of mass behavior is **rumor**, *unsubstantiated information spread informally, often by word of mouth*. People pass along rumors through face-to-face communication, of course, but today's modern technology—including telephones, the mass media, and now the Internet—spreads rumors faster and farther than ever before.

Rumor has three essential characteristics.

1. **Rumor thrives in a climate of ambiguity.** Rumors arise when people lack definitive information about an important issue. A lack of knowledge about terrorism and the threat of catching anthrax from the mail led to widespread fear in the wake of the September 11, 2001, attacks (Kaplan, 2001).

2. **Rumor is unstable.** People change a rumor as they pass it along, usually giving it a "spin" that serves their own interests. Before long, many competing versions exist.

3. **Rumor is difficult to stop.** The number of people aware of a rumor increases exponentially as each person spreads information to several others. Rumors dissipate with time, but the only way to control rumors is for a believable source to issue a clear and convincing statement of the facts.

 To check the truth about recent rumors making the rounds on the Internet, visit http://www. nonprofit.net/hoax/

Rumor can trigger the formation of crowds or other collective behavior. For this reason, officials establish rumor control centers during a crisis in order to manage information. Yet some rumors persist for years, perhaps just because people enjoy them; the box gives one notable example.

SEEING OURSELVES

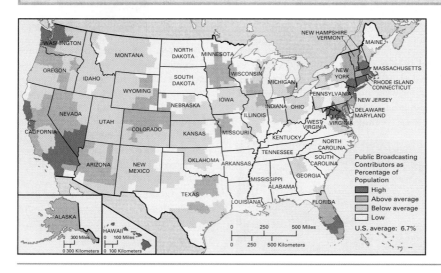

NATIONAL MAP 23–1
Support for Public Broadcasting across the United States

About 7 percent of people in the United States pledge money to support the Public Broadcasting System (PBS). As the map shows, PBS supporters are concentrated in particular regions of the country. What do you think accounts for this pattern?

Source: *Time* (January 16, 1995). Copyright © 1995 Time, Inc. Reprinted by permission.

Public Broadcasting Contributors as Percentage of Population
- High
- Above average
- Below average
- Low

U.S. average: 6.7%

Gossip is *rumor about people's personal affairs.* According to Charles Horton Cooley (1962; orig. 1909), rumor involves an issue of concern to a large audience, but gossip interests only a small circle of people who know a particular person. Rumors therefore spread widely, whereas gossip tends to be more localized.

Communities use gossip as a means of social control, praising or scorning someone to encourage conformity to local norms. Moreover, people gossip about others to raise their own standing as social "insiders," just as more powerful people use gossip to keep those who are socially marginal "in their place" (Baumgartner, 1998; Nicholson, 2001). Yet no community wants gossip to get out of control, which may be the reason people who gossip *too* much are criticized as "busybodies."

PUBLIC OPINION AND PROPAGANDA

Another form of dispersed collective behavior is **public opinion,** *widespread attitudes about controversial issues.* Exactly who is or is not included in any "public" depends on the issue involved. Over the years in the United States, "publics" have formed over numerous controversial issues, from water fluoridation, air pollution, and the social standing of women to handguns and health care (Lang & Lang, 1961; Turner, Killian, & Sow, 2001). More recently, the public has debated

affirmative action, welfare reform, and government funding of public radio and television. National Map 23–1 shows where supporters of public broadcasting reside.

On any given issue, anywhere from 2 to 10 percent of people offer no opinion at all because of ignorance or indifference. Moreover, over time, public interest in issues rises and falls. For example, interest in the social position of women in the United States ran high a century ago during the women's suffrage movement but declined after 1920 when women gained the right to vote. Since the 1960s, a second wave of feminism has again created a public with strong opinions on gender-related issues.

Also, keep in mind that on any issue, not everyone's opinion carries the same weight. Some categories of people have more clout because they are better educated, wealthier, or better connected. As Chapter 17 ("Politics and Government") explained, many special interest groups shape public policy in the United States even though they represent just a small fraction of the population. For example, physicians are a well-organized and well-funded interest group that greatly influences U.S. health care policy, just as members of the National Education Association have a great deal to say about public education in the United States.

Special interest groups and political leaders all try to shape public tastes and attitudes by using

propaganda, *information presented with the intention of shaping public opinion.* Although the term has negative connotations, propaganda is not necessarily false. A thin line separates information from propaganda; the difference depends mostly on the presenter's intention. We offer *information* to enlighten others; we use *propaganda* to sway an audience toward some viewpoint. Political speeches, commercial advertising, and even some college lectures may disseminate propaganda in an effort to steer people toward thinking or acting in some specific way.

PANIC AND MASS HYSTERIA

A **panic** is *a form of localized collective behavior by which people react to a threat or other stimulus with irrational, frantic, and often self-destructive behavior.* The classic illustration of a panic is people streaming toward exits of a crowded theater after someone yells "Fire!" As they flee, they trample one another, blocking exits so that few actually escape.

Closely related to panic is **mass hysteria** or **moral panic,** *a form of dispersed collective behavior by which people react to a real or imagined event with irrational and even frantic fear.* Whether the cause of the hysteria is real or not, a large number of people certainly take it very seriously.

Some causes of mass hysteria or moral panic emerge within popular culture. In recent years, moral panics have centered on fear of AIDS (or people with AIDS), concern about missing children (whose numbers were greatly exaggerated during the 1980s), cybersmut (that is, pornography widely available to young people via the Internet), and political correctness (a liberal viewpoint that allegedly dominates academia and the media).

As these examples suggest, the real danger involved in such cases is debatable. Why, then, are these concerns widespread? As Erich Goode (2000:549) puts it, "the mass media *thrives* on scares; contributing to moral panics is the media's stock in trade." Therefore, many people become fearful about issues that are not really so dangerous because of what they learn about them from the mass media (Glassner, 1999).

Mass hysteria can be triggered by an event, which, at the extreme, sends people into chaotic flight. Of course, people who see others overcome by fear may become more afraid themselves, so that hysteria feeds on itself. So it was on the morning or September 11, 2001, in the wake of terrorist attacks. Although there were countless acts of heroism, panic was also widespread, especially in Washington, D.C., after a plane crashed into the Pentagon. Within an hour and a half, evacuation orders had been given and the streets of the city were choked with cars trying to get out. Yet the city's main bridges had been closed, which soon led to a citywide gridlock. People thought they were in danger, they found that they were unable to escape, and fear built on itself. Because no one knew what might happen next, rumors were everywhere: More attacks were coming, and even the city's water had been poisoned (Gibbs, 2001).

FASHIONS AND FADS

Two more kinds of collective behavior—fashions and fads—involve people spread over a large area. A **fashion** is *a social pattern favored by a large number of people.* Some fashions last for years, whereas others change after just a few months. The arts (including painting, music, drama, and literature), the shape of buildings, automobiles, clothes, our use of language, and public opinion all change as ideas go in and out of fashion.

Lyn Lofland (1973) explains that in preindustrial societies, clothing and personal appearance reflect traditional *style,* which changes very little. Women and men, the rich and the poor, lawyers and carpenters wear distinctive clothes and hairstyles that indicate their occupations and social standing.

In industrial societies, however, established style gives way to changing fashion. For one thing, modern people care less about tradition and often eagerly embrace new ways of living. Also, high social mobility means that people use their looks to make statements about themselves. German sociologist Georg Simmel (1971; orig. 1904) explained that affluent people usually are the trendsetters because people look to them and because they have the money to spend on luxuries. Or as U.S. sociologist Thorstein Veblen (1953; orig. 1899) put it, fashion involves *conspicuous consumption,* as people buy expensive products (from bottled water to Range Rovers) simply to show off their wealth.

Ordinary people who want to appear wealthy often snap up less expensive copies of what the rich make fashionable. In this way, a fashion trickles downward through the class structure. But before long, the fashion loses its prestige when too many average people share "the look," so the rich move on to something new. In short, fashions are born along the Fifth Avenues and Rodeo Drives of the rich but reach mass popularity in discount stores across the country.

Because change in high-income societies is so rapid, we see differences in personal appearance—one important element of fashion—over relatively short periods of time. These six photographs (beginning at the top, left) show hair styles commonly worn by women in the 1950s, 1960s, 1970s, 1980s, 1990s, and since 2000.

A reversal of this pattern has been occurring since the 1960s, as better-off people mimic fashions found among people of lower social position. This pattern began when affluent college students began buying blue jeans, or dungarees (from a Hindi word for a coarse fabric). For decades, manual laborers had worn blue jeans. But in the era of civil rights and antiwar movements, jeans became the uniform of liberal political activists and soon were popular on college campuses across the country. Cargo pants and other emblems of the hip-hop culture do much the same today, allowing even the most affluent entertainers and celebrities to mimic the styles of those with much less.

A **fad** is *an unconventional social pattern that people embrace briefly but enthusiastically*. Fads, sometimes called *crazes*, are common in high-income societies, where many people have the money to spend on amusing, if often frivolous, products. During the 1950s, two young entrepreneurs in California produced a brightly colored plastic version of a popular Australian toy, a three-foot-diameter hoop that one could swing around the waist by gyrating the hips. In no time, the "hula hoop" was a national craze. But in less than a year, hula hoops vanished from the scene.

In recent years, collecting Pokémon cards has been a fad among young people. But Pokémon's popularity already has begun to fade, showing that fads enter and depart from our culture all the time (Aguirre, Quarantelli, & Mendoza, 1988).

How do fads differ from fashions? Fads are passing fancies that capture the mass imagination but quickly burn out. Fashions, by contrast, reflect basic cultural values such as individuality and sexual attractiveness and tend to evolve over time. Therefore, a fashion—but rarely a fad—is incorporated into a society's culture. For instance, the fad of streaking came out of nowhere and soon vanished; the fashion of wearing blue jeans, on the other hand, originated in the rough mining camps of Gold Rush California more than a century ago and still influences clothing designs today. This "staying power" explains why we are happy to be called "fashionable" but put off by being called "faddish" (Blumer, 1968; Turner & Killian, 1993).

SOCIAL MOVEMENTS

A **social movement** is *an organized activity that encourages or discourages social change*. Social movements may be the most important type of collective behavior

NOTE: Contrast transient *fads* with more lasting *trends*, which are rooted in a basic cultural pattern. A recent marketing trend is "value pricing" in fast food, automobiles, and even textbooks, which caught on as the economy sagged in the late 1980s. Another example is the McDonaldization trend, discussed in Chapter 7, involving fast food, fast oil changes, and packaged vacations, which responds to our need for quick products on the go (Letscher, 1994).

NOTE: Say what you will about the faddish "Wacky Wall Walker," it sold some 250 million units during its short life.
DISCUSS: Why do some fads (Cabbage Patch dolls or Teletubby dolls) fade away quickly whereas others (Koosh balls) stay around for a number of years? What do students expect to be the future of Pokémon?

because they are deliberately organized and often have lasting effects on the shape of our society.

Social movements occur more frequently in today's world than in the past. Preindustrial societies are tightly bound by tradition, making social movements extremely rare. However, industrial and post-industrial societies foster diverse subcultures and countercultures so that social movements develop around a wide range of public issues. In recent decades, for example, the gay rights movement has won legal changes in numerous cities and several states, forbidding discrimination based on sexual orientation and allowing formal domestic partnership. Like any social movement that seeks change, the gay rights movement has prompted a countermovement made up of traditionalists who want to limit social acceptance of homosexuality. In today's society, almost every important public issue gives rise to a social movement favoring change and an opposing countermovement resisting it (Lo, 1982; Meyer & Staggenborg, 1996).

TYPES OF SOCIAL MOVEMENTS

Sociologists classify social movements according to two variables (Aberle, 1966; Cameron, 1966; Blumer, 1969). One variable asks *who is changed?* Some movements target selected people, and others try to change everyone. A second variable asks *how much change?* Some movements seek only limited change in our lives, and others are radical. Combining these variables results in four types of social movements, shown in Figure 23–1.

Alternative social movements are least threatening to the status quo because they seek limited change in only a part of the population. Promise Keepers, one example of an alternative social movement, encourages men to be more spiritual and supportive of their families.

Visit the Promise Keepers Web site at http://www.promisekeepers.org

Redemptive social movements also have a selective focus, but they seek radical change in those they engage. For example, Alcoholics Anonymous is an organization that helps alcoholics achieve a sober life.

Reformative social movements aim for only limited social change but target everyone. Multiculturalism, described in Chapter 3 ("Culture"), is an educational and political movement that advocates working toward social equality for people of all races and ethnicities. Reformative social movements generally work inside the existing political system. Some are *progressive*

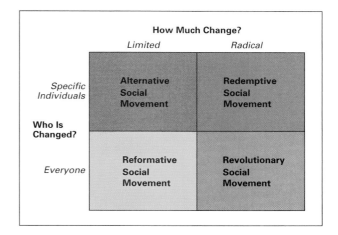

FIGURE 23–1 Four Types of Social Movements
Source: Based on Aberle (1966).

(promoting a new social pattern), whereas others are *reactionary* (countermovements trying to preserve the status quo or to revive past social patterns). Thus, just as multiculturalists push for greater racial equality, white supremacist organizations try to maintain the historical dominance of white people.

Revolutionary social movements are the most extreme of all, striving for basic transformation of an entire society. Sometimes pursuing specific goals, sometimes spinning utopian dreams, these social movements reject existing social institutions as flawed while promoting radically new alternatives. Both the left-wing Communist Party (pushing for government control of the economy) and right-wing militia groups (advocating the destruction of "big government") seek to radically change our way of life.

EXPLAINING SOCIAL MOVEMENTS

Because social movements are intentional and long-lasting, sociologists find this type of collective behavior easier to explain than fleeting incidents of mob behavior or mass hysteria. Several theories have come to the fore.

Deprivation Theory

Deprivation theory holds that social movements arise among people who feel deprived. People who feel they lack enough income, safe working conditions, basic political rights, or plain human dignity may organize a

Q: "Public opinion in this country is everything." Abraham Lincoln

Q: "Social movements and their goals represent, respectively, actual and potential social changes." C. Wendell King

RESOURCE: Jo Freeman's article "On the Origins of Social Movements" is among the classics included in the 5th edition of the Macionis and Benokraitis reader, *Seeing Ourselves*.

SOCIAL SURVEY: "What are your personal feelings about people who organize protests against a government action they strongly oppose?" (GSS 1990, *N* = 1,217; *Codebook*, 2001:900)

"Extremely favorable"	8.8%	"Unfavorable"	14.2%
"Favorable"	26.5%	"Extremely unfavorable"	5.7%
"Neutral"	33.9%	DK/NR	11.0%

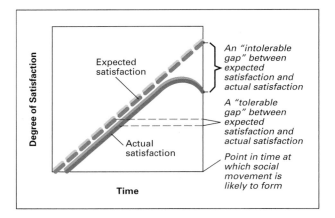

FIGURE 23–2 Relative Deprivation and Social Movements

In this diagram, the solid line represents a rising standard of living over time. The dotted line indicates the expected standard of living, which is typically somewhat higher. James C. Davies describes the difference between the two as "a tolerable gap between what people want and what they get." If the standard of living suddenly drops in the midst of rising expectations, however, the gap becomes intolerable. At this point, we can expect social movements to form.

Source: Davies (1962).

social movement to bring about a more just state of affairs (Morrison, 1978; Rose, 1982).

The rise of the Ku Klux Klan and passage of Jim Crow laws by whites intent on enforcing segregation in the South after the Civil War illustrate deprivation theory. With the end of slavery, white people lost a source of free labor and the claim that they were socially superior to African Americans. Many whites reacted to their sense of deprivation by trying to keep all people of color "in their place" (Dollard et al., 1939). African Americans had experienced much greater deprivation, of course, but as slaves they had little opportunity to organize. During the twentieth century, however, African Americans organized successfully in pursuit of racial equality.

As Chapter 7 ("Groups and Organizations") explained, deprivation is a relative concept. Regardless of anyone's absolute amount of money and power, people feel either better or worse off than some category of

For information on the Ku Klux Klan and other hate groups, visit http://www.splcenter.org/intelligenceproject/ip-index.html

others. **Relative deprivation,** then, is *a perceived disadvantage arising from some specific comparison* (Stouffer et al., 1949; Merton, 1968).

More than a century ago, Alexis de Tocqueville (1955; orig. 1856) studied the French Revolution. Why, he asked, did rebellion occur in progressive France rather than in more traditional Germany, where peasants were, by any objective measure, worse off? Tocqueville's answer was that as bad as their condition was, German peasants had known nothing but feudal servitude and thus had no basis for feeling deprived. French peasants, on the other hand, had seen improvements in their lives that whetted their appetites for more. Thus the French—not the Germans—felt a keen sense of relative deprivation. The irony, as Tocqueville saw it, was that increasing freedom and prosperity did not satisfy people as much as stimulate their desire for an even better life (1955:175; orig. 1856).

Closer to home, Tocqueville's insight helps explain patterns of rioting during the 1960s. Protest riots involving African Americans began not in the South, where many black people lived in miserable poverty and most were not even registered to vote, but in Detroit, where the auto industry was booming, black unemployment was low, and black home ownership was the highest in the country (Thernstrom & Thernstrom, 1998).

James C. Davies (1962) agrees that as life gets better, people take their rising fortunes for granted and expect even more. But what happens if the standard of living suddenly stops improving or begins to drop? As Figure 23–2 illustrates, relative deprivation is the result, generating unrest and social movements aimed at change.

Critical evaluation. Deprivation theory challenges our common-sense assumption that the worst-off people are the most likely to organize for change. People do not organize simply because they suffer in an absolute sense; rather, they form social movements because of *relative* deprivation. Indeed, both Tocqueville and Marx—as different as they were in many ways—agreed on the importance of relative deprivation in the formation of social movements.

But most people experience some discontent all the time, so deprivation theory leaves us wondering why social movements arise among some categories of people and not others. A second problem is that deprivation theory suffers from circular reasoning: We assume that deprivation causes social movements, but often the only evidence of deprivation is the social

NOTE: Mass-society theory has much in common with Hirschi's control theory of deviance (see Chapter 8, "Deviance"): Both suggest that the behavior in question arises among those with few social attachments.

Q: "Psychological attributes of individuals, such as frustration and alienation, have minimal direct impact for explaining the occurrence of rebellion and revolution per se." Carol Mueller

NOTE: The conservative character of mass-society theory stems from the implication that it is the loss of traditional social ties (and not social inequality) that leads to social movements. Kornhauser follows Tocqueville rather than Marx in focusing on mass movements rather than on class movements. The distinction between mass society and class society is developed further in Chapter 24.

movement itself (Jenkins & Perrow, 1977). A third limitation of this approach is that it focuses exclusively on the cause of a social movement and tells us little about movements themselves (McAdam, McCarthy, & Zald, 1988).

Mass-Society Theory

William Kornhauser's mass-society theory (1959) argues that social movements attract socially isolated people who feel personally insignificant. From this point of view, social movements occur in large *mass* societies. Social movements are *personal* as well as *political* in that they offer a sense of purpose and belonging to people otherwise adrift in society (Melucci, 1989).

It follows, says Kornhauser, that categories of people with weak social ties are those who most readily join a social movement. People who are well integrated socially, by contrast, are unlikely to seek membership in a social movement.

Like Gustave Le Bon, discussed earlier, Kornhauser offers a conservative view of social movements. Activists tend to be psychologically vulnerable people who eagerly join groups and often are manipulated by group leaders. In Kornhauser's view, social movements are unlikely to be very democratic.

Critical evaluation. To Kornhauser's credit, his theory focuses on both the kind of society that produces social movements and the kinds of people who join them. But one criticism is that if we try to test the idea that mass societies foster social movements, we run up against the problem of having no clear standard for measuring the extent to which we live in a "mass society."

A second criticism is that explaining social movements in terms of people hungry to belong belittles the social justice issues that movements address. Put otherwise, mass society theory suggests that flawed people—rather than a flawed society—are responsible for social movements.

What does research show about mass society theory? The record is mixed. On the down side, some studies conclude that the Nazi movement in Germany did not draw heavily from socially isolated people (Lipset, 1963; Oberschall, 1973). Similarly, many of the people who took part in urban riots during the 1960s had strong ties to their communities (Sears & McConahay, 1973). Evidence also suggests that most young people who join religious movements have fairly normal family ties (Wright & Piper, 1986).

Finally, researchers who have examined the biographies of 1960s political activists find evidence of deep and continuing commitment to political goals rather than isolation from society (McAdam, 1988, 1989; Whalen & Flacks, 1989).

On the up side, research by Frances Piven and Richard Cloward (1977) supports mass-society theory. Piven and Cloward found that a breakdown of routine social patterns encourages poor people to form social movements. Also, in a study of the New Mexico State Penitentiary, Bert Useem (1985) found that when prison programs promoting social ties between inmates were suspended, inmates were more likely to protest their conditions.

Structural-Strain Theory

One of the most influential theories about social movements was developed by Neil Smelser (1962). *Structural-strain theory* identifies six factors that encourage the development of social movements. Smelser's theory also suggests which kinds of situations lead to unorganized mobs or riots and which to highly organized social movements. We will use the prodemocracy movement that transformed Eastern Europe during the late 1980s to illustrate Smelser's theory.

1. **Structural conduciveness.** Social movements arise as people come to think their society has some serious problems. In Eastern Europe, these problems included low living standards and political repression by national governments.

2. **Structural strain.** People begin to experience relative deprivation when their society fails to meet their expectations. Eastern Europeans joined the prodemocracy movement because they knew their living standards were far lower than living standards in Western Europe and much below what years of propaganda about prosperous socialism had led them to expect.

3. **Growth and spread of an explanation.** Forming a well-organized social movement requires a clear statement of a problem, its causes, and its solutions. If people are confused about their suffering, they are likely to express their dissatisfaction in an unorganized way such as rioting. In the case of Eastern Europe, intellectuals played a key role in the prodemocracy movement by pointing out economic and political flaws in the system and proposing strategies to increase democracy.

DISCUSS: The women's movement illustrates the stages of Smelser's theory. (1) Historical pattern of patriarchy; women can organize in opposition. (2) Strain between U.S. ideal of equality and reality of patriarchy. (3) Early feminist scholarship and organization. (4) First wave of feminism—passage of 13th, 14th, and 15th amendments extended rights to African American men but ignored women of both races; second wave of feminism—African American civil rights movement (led predominantly by men) and the increasing proportion of women in the labor force. (5) Mobilization spearheaded by organizations such as the National Organization for Women (NOW); widespread publication of feminist ideas (e.g., *Ms.* magazine). (6) Passage of 19th Amendment slowed the women's movement; ERA remains unratified, but legislation has advanced women's social and economic rights.

4. **Precipitating factors.** Discontent often festers for a long time, only to be transformed into collective action by a specific event. In Eastern Europe, such an event occurred in 1985 when Mikhail Gorbachev came to power in the Soviet Union and began his program of *perestroika* (restructuring). As Moscow relaxed its rigid control over Eastern Europe, people there saw a historic opportunity to reorganize political and economic life and claim greater freedom.

5. **Mobilization for action.** Once people share a concern about some public issue, they are ready to take action—to distribute leaflets, stage protest rallies, and build alliances with sympathetic organizations. The initial success of the Solidarity movement in Poland—covertly aided by the Reagan administration in the United States and by Pope John Paul II in the Vatican—mobilized people throughout Eastern Europe to press for change. The rate of change accelerated as reform movements gained strength: What had taken a decade in Poland took only months in Hungary and only weeks in other Eastern European nations.

6. **Lack of social control.** The success of any social movement depends, in large part, on how political officials, police, and the military respond. Sometimes the state moves swiftly to crush a social movement, as happened to the prodemocracy forces in the People's Republic of China. But Gorbachev adopted a policy of nonintervention in Eastern Europe, thereby opening the door for change. Ironically, the movements that began in Eastern Europe soon spread to the Soviet Union itself, ending the historic domination of the Communist party and producing a new political confederation in 1992.

Critical evaluation. Smelser's analysis recognizes the complexity of social movements and suggests how various factors encourage or inhibit their development. Structural-strain theory also explains why people may respond to their problems either by forming organized social movements or participating in spontaneous mob action or rioting.

Yet Smelser's theory contains some of the same circularity of argument found in Kornhauser's analysis. A social movement is caused by strain, says Smelser, but the only evidence of underlying strain appears to be the social movement itself. Finally, structural-strain theory is incomplete, overlooking the important role that resources such as the mass media or international alliances play in the success or failure of a social movement (Oberschall, 1973; Jenkins & Perrow, 1977; McCarthy & Zald, 1977; Olzak & West, 1991).

Resource-Mobilization Theory

Resource-mobilization theory points out that no social movement is likely to succeed—or even get off the ground—without substantial resources, including money, human labor, office and communication facilities, access to the mass media, and a positive public image. In short, any social movement rises or falls on its ability to attract resources, mobilize people, and forge alliances. The 1989 prodemocracy movement in China was fueled by students whose location on campuses clustered together in Beijing allowed them to build networks and recruit new members (Zhao, 1998). Similarly, to challenge socialism in Eastern Europe, Poles and others needed fax machines, copiers, telecommunication gear, money, and moral support provided by other nations. In recent years, the Internet has been a vital resource enabling organizations to link tens of thousands of people across the United States and to draw large numbers of demonstrators to Washington, D.C., or cities such as Seattle in order to stage protests.

According to resource mobilization theory, outsiders can be just as important as insiders in affecting the outcome of a social movement. Because socially disadvantaged people, by definition, lack the money, contacts, leadership skills, and organizational know-how that a successful movement requires, sympathetic outsiders fill the resource gap. In U.S. history, well-to-do white people, including college students, performed a vital service to the black civil rights movement in the 1960s, and affluent men have joined women as leaders of the current women's movement (Snow, Zurcher, & Ekland-Olson, 1980; Killian, 1984; Snow et al., 1986; Baron, Mittman, & Newman, 1991; Burstein, 1991; Meyer & Whittier, 1994; Valocchi, 1996).

On the other side of the coin, a lack of resources limits efforts to bring about change. The history of the AIDS epidemic is a case in point. Initially, in the early 1980s, the government paid little attention to the rising incidence of AIDS, leaving gay communities in San Francisco, New York, and other cities to shoulder the responsibility for treatment and educational programs. Gradually, as more people began to grasp the scope of the problem, public pressure prompted local, state, and federal governments to allocate more

DISCUSS: Illustrating the importance of resources to social movements, consider the contribution academics have made to the growing success of the feminist movement.
RESOURCE: One of the cross-cultural selections in the Macionis and Benokraitis reader, *Seeing Ourselves*, is Janet Hadley's "Abortion Movements in Poland, Great Britain, and the United States."

Q: "Do not make the mistake of thinking that a concerned group of people cannot change the world; it's the only thing that ever has." Margaret Mead
NOTE: The importance of coming forward with personal testimonies within the movement to end sexual violence can be used to illustrate culture theory. Key terms and phrases ("glass ceiling" or "date rape") are important in focusing a social movement.

The mass media often play an important part in guiding public opinion toward or away from change. Media performances do this by providing symbols that mobilize support for some point of view. Soviet-backed governments throughout Eastern Europe were collapsing, one after another, during the early 1990s; Roger Waters (former member of Pink Floyd) performed "The Wall" at the site of the Berlin Wall, celebrating the fact that this barrier was finally coming down.

resources for research, education, and treatment. Members of the Hollywood-based entertainment industry in particular lent their money, visibility, and prestige to the movement. These resources were crucial in transforming a fledgling social movement into a well-organized, global coalition of political leaders, educators, and medical specialists.

Critical evaluation. Resource-mobilization theory recognizes that both resources and discontent are necessary to the success of a social movement. Research confirms that forging alliances to gain resources is especially important and notes that movements with few resources may, in desperation, turn to violence to call attention to their cause (Grant & Wallace, 1991).

Critics of this theory counter that even relatively powerless segments of a population can promote change if they are able to organize effectively and have strongly committed members (Donnelly & Majka, 1998). Research by Aldon Morris (1981) shows that people of color drew largely on their own skills and resources to fuel the civil rights movement of the 1950s and 1960s. A second problem with this theory is that it overstates the extent to which powerful people are willing to challenge the status quo. Some rich white people did provide valuable resources to the black civil rights movement, but probably more often, elites were indifferent or opposed to significant change (McAdam, 1982, 1983; Pichardo, 1995).

Overall, the success or failure of a social movement is determined by political struggle. A strong and united establishment (perhaps aided by a countermovement) reduces the odds that a social movement will succeed. However, if the established powers are divided, the movement's chances of success improve.

Culture Theory

In recent years, sociologists have recognized that social movements depend not only on material resources and the structure of political power but also on cultural symbols. That is, people in any particular situation are likely to mobilize to form a social movement only to the extent that they develop "shared understandings of the world that legitimate and motivate collective action" (McAdam, McCarthy, & Zald, 1996:6).

In part, mobilization depends on a sense of injustice, as suggested by deprivation theory. In addition, people must come to believe that they are not able to respond to their situation effectively acting as individuals. Finally, social movements gain strength as they develop symbols and a sense of community that both generate strong feelings and direct this emotional energy into organized action. News photographs of children harmed by bombing during the Vietnam War, for example, bolstered the antiwar movement. Likewise, the media presentation of the attack on the World Trade Center in 2001 (a site later referred to simply as "ground zero") helped mobilize public support for a military response against terrorists in Afghanistan (Morris & Mueller, 1992; Giugni, 1998; Staggenborg, 1998; Gibbs, 2001).

NOTE: A Marxist view of new social movements sees people and the state as entering more and more areas of private life in an effort to resolve the contradictions of late-20th-century capitalist economies.

Q: "You cannot put a rope around the neck of an idea." Sean O'Casey

NOTE: A key contention of new social movements theory is that recruitment into social movements is based more on symbolism (in Weberian terms) than on class interests (in Marxist terms). Indeed, Stanley Aronowitz (1992) suggests that minorities, lesbians, and environmentalists—adherents of the new social movements of the left—may take over the working classes' historic mission to overthrow capitalism. New social movements are found in postindustrial societies, conventional social movements in industrial societies.

One example of a new social movement is the worldwide effort to eliminate land mines. Years after hostilities cease, these mines remain in place and take a staggering toll in civilian lives. At a protest in Berlin, Germany, a mountain of shoes stands as a memorial to the tens of thousands of people who have been crippled or died as a result of stepping on underground mines.

Critical evaluation. This approach reminds us that not just material resources but also cultural symbols form the foundation of social movements. At the same time, powerful symbols (such as the flag and ideas about patriotism and respecting our leaders) help support the status quo. How and when symbols turn people from supporting the system toward protest are questions that warrant further research.

New Social Movements Theory

A final, more recent theoretical approach addresses the changing character of social movements. *New social movements theory* emphasizes the distinctive features of recent social movements in postindustrial societies of North America and Western Europe (Melucci, 1980; McAdam, McCarthy, & Zald, 1988; Kriesi, 1989; Pakulski, 1993).

First, most of today's social movements are international, focusing on global ecology, the social standing of women and gay people, animal rights, and the

risks of terrorism. As the process of globalization con-

For information on laws involving animal rights, see http://www.animal-law.org

nects the world's nations in more and more ways, in other words, social movements are becoming global.

Second, whereas traditional social movements such as labor organizations are concerned mostly with economic issues, new social movements tend to focus on cultural change and improving our social and physical surroundings. The international environmental movement, for example, opposes practices that aggravate global warming and other environmental dangers.

Third, whereas most social movements of the past drew strong support from working-class people, new social movements, with their noneconomic agendas, usually draw support from the middle and upper-middle classes. This is because, as discussed in Chapter 17 ("Politics and Government"), more affluent people tend to be more conservative on economic issues (because they have wealth to protect) but more liberal on social issues (partly as a result of extended education). Furthermore, in the United States and other rich nations, the number of highly educated professionals—the people who most support new social movements—is increasing, which suggests that these movements will grow (Jenkins & Wallace, 1996; Rose, 1997).

Critical evaluation. One clear strength of this theory is its recognition that social movements have increased in scale in response to the development of a global economy and international political connections. This theory also highlights the power of the mass media and new information technology to unite people around the world in pursuit of political goals.

However, critics claim that this approach exaggerates the differences between past and present social movements. The women's movement, for example, focuses on many of the same issues—workplace conditions and pay—that have concerned labor organizations for decades. Similarly, many of those protesting the rising power of the World Trade Organization (described in the opening to this chapter) consider economic equality around the world their primary goal.

Each of the five theories we have presented offers some explanation for the emergence of social movements; no single theory can stand alone (Kowalewski & Porter, 1992). Table 23–1 summarizes the theories.

NOTE: Since 1975, women have been overly represented as candidates for offices in the American Sociological Association and also have had higher odds of winning than men, holding constant qualifications. Organizations such as Sociologists for Women in Society (SWS) have played a part in boosting women's power in the ASA (Rosenfeld, Cunningham, & Schmidt, 1997).

SOCIAL SURVEY: "Should organizing a nationwide strike of all workers against the government be allowed or not?" (GSS 1996, N = 1,332; *Codebook*, 2001:874)
"Definitely allowed"   16.4%   "Definitely not allowed" 27.6%
"Probably allowed"   20.4%   DK/NR   8.6%
"Probably not allowed" 27.0%

TABLE 23–1 Theories of Social Movements: A Summary

Deprivation Theory	People experiencing relative deprivation begin social movements. The social movement is a means of seeking change that brings participants greater benefits. Social movements are especially likely when rising expectations are frustrated.
Mass-Society Theory	People who lack established social ties are mobilized into social movements. Periods of social breakdown are likely to spawn social movements. The social movement gives members a sense of belonging and social participation.
Structural-Strain theory	People come together because of their shared concern about the inability of society to operate as they believe it should. The growth of a social movement reflects many factors, including a belief in its legitimacy and some precipitating event that provokes action.
Resource-Mobilization Theory	People may join for all the reasons noted above and also because of social ties to existing members. But the success or failure of a social movement depends largely on the resources available to it. Also important is the extent of opposition within the larger society.
Culture Theory	People are drawn to a social movement by cultural symbols that define some cause as just. The movement itself usually becomes a symbol of power and justice.
New Social Movements Theory	People who become part of social movements are motivated by quality-of-life issues, not necessarily economic concerns. Mobilization is national or international in scope. New social movements arise in response to the expansion of the mass media and new information technology.

GENDER AND SOCIAL MOVEMENTS

Gender figures prominently in the operation of social movements. In keeping with traditional ideas about gender in the United States, men more than women tend to take part in public life, including spearheading social movements.

Investigating "Freedom Summer," a 1964 voter registration project in Mississippi, Doug McAdam (1992) found that most people believed registering African-American voters in the midst of considerable hostility from whites was dangerous and therefore "men's work" unsuitable for women. He also discovered that project leaders were likely to assign women volunteers to clerical and teaching assignments, leaving the field activities to men. This was so even though women who participated in Freedom Summer were more qualified than their male counterparts in terms of years of activism and organizational affiliations. McAdam concluded that only the most committed women were able to overcome the movement's gender barriers. In short, although women have played leading roles in many social movements (including the abolitionist and feminist movements in the United States), male dominance has been the norm even in social movements that otherwise oppose the status quo (Herda-Rapp, 1998).

STAGES IN SOCIAL MOVEMENTS

Despite the many differences that set one social movement off from another, all unfold in roughly the same way, as shown in Figure 23–3 on page 618. Researchers have identified four stages in the life of the typical social movement (Blumer, 1969; Mauss, 1975; Tilly, 1978).

Stage 1: Emergence. Social movements are driven by the perception that all is not well. Some, such as the civil rights and women's movements, are born of widespread dissatisfaction. Others emerge only as a small vanguard group increases public awareness of some issue. Gay activists, for example, initially raised public concern about the threat posed by AIDS.

Stage 2: Coalescence. After emerging, a social movement must define itself and develop a strategy for "going public." Leaders must determine policies, decide on tactics, build morale, and recruit new members. At this stage, the movement may engage in collective action such as rallies or demonstrations to attract media attention and thereby public notice. The movement may also form alliances with other organizations to acquire necessary resources.

Q: "Mass movements can rise and spread without belief in a God, but never without belief in a devil." Eric Hoffer

NOTE: In some cases, the failure of a social movement to establish and sustain a social identity leads to its demise. For example, the American Indian movement, which lasted from about 1968 to 1973, never succeeded in fostering a pan-tribal identity (Stotok, Shriver, & Cable, 1994).

Q: "Anyone who can remember the '60s probably wasn't there." Robin Williams

NOTE: Many social movements fall into one of two categories: *equality movements* seeking social equality for various categories of people (based on class, race, sexual orientation, etc.) and specific *protest movements* targeting gun control, nuclear power, animal experimentation, etc. (Caplow, 1991).

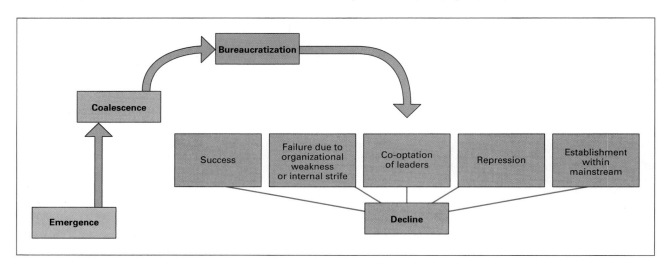

FIGURE 23–3 Stages in the Lives of Social Movements

Stage 3: Bureaucratization. To become a political force, a social movement must take on bureaucratic traits, described in Chapter 7 ("Groups and Organizations"). Thus, as it becomes established, the social movement depends less on the charisma and talents of a few leaders and more on a capable staff. When social movements do not become established in this way, they risk dissolving. For example, many activist organizations on college campuses during the late 1960s were energized by a single charismatic leader and consequently did not last long. On the other hand, the National Organization for Women (NOW), despite its changing leadership, is well established and can be counted on to speak for feminists.

Even so, bureaucratization can sometimes hinder a social movement. In reviewing social movements in U.S. history, Frances Piven and Richard Cloward (1977) found that leaders can become so engrossed in building an organization that they neglect the need to keep people fired up for change. In such cases, the radical edge of protest is lost.

Stage 4: Decline. Eventually, most social movements begin to decline. Frederick Miller (1983) suggests four reasons that this can occur.

First, if members have met their goals, decline may simply signal success. For example, the women's suffrage movement disbanded after it won women in the United States the right to vote. Such clear-cut successes are rare, however, because few social movements have a single goal. More commonly, winning one victory leads to new campaigns. Because issues related to gender extend far beyond voting, the women's movement has recast itself time and again.

Second, a social movement may fold because of organizational factors, such as poor leadership, loss of interest among members, insufficient funds, or repression by authorities. Some people lose interest when the excitement of early efforts is replaced by day-to-day routine. Fragmentation by internal conflicts over goals and strategies is another common problem. Students for a Democratic Society (SDS), a student movement promoting participatory democracy and opposing the war in Vietnam, splintered into several small factions by the end of the 1960s as members disagreed over strategies for social change.

Third, a social movement can fall apart if the established power structure, through offers of money, prestige, and other rewards, diverts leaders from their goals. "Selling out" is one facet of the iron law of oligarchy, discussed in Chapter 7 ("Groups and Organizations"). That is, organizational leaders use their positions to enrich themselves. For example, Vernon Jordan, once head of the National Urban League became a close advisor to President Clinton and a rich and powerful Washington "insider" as a result. But this process can also work the other way: Some people leave lucrative, high-prestige occupations to become activists. Cat Stevens, a rock star of the 1970s, became a Muslim, changed his name to Yusuf

NOTE: Joan Fitzgerald and Louise Simmons (1991) point out that to evaluate the success of any social movement, we must look beyond *immediate* effects to assess the movement's contribution to *future* social change.

Q: "All previous historical movements were movements of minorities, or in the interests of minorities. The proletarian movement is the self-conscious, independent movement of the immense majority, in the interest of the immense majority." Karl Marx and Friedrich Engels

DIVERSITY: Although some social movements that challenge the status quo have been dominated by men, not all have; the abolition, suffrage, child-care, and anti–drunk driving movements are only a few examples.

Islam, and has devoted himself in recent decades to spreading his religion.

Fourth and finally, a social movement can collapse because of repression. Officials may crush a social movement by frightening away participants, discouraging new recruits, and even imprisoning leaders. In general, the more revolutionary the social movement, the more officials try to repress it. Until 1990, the government of South Africa banned the African National Congress (ANC), a political organization seeking to overthrow the state-supported system of apartheid. Even suspected members of the ANC were subject to arrest. In 1990, the government lifted the decades-old ban and released ANC leader Nelson Mandela from prison; in 1994, the South African people elected Mandela president and began the journey away from apartheid.

Beyond the reasons noted by Miller, a fifth cause of decline is that a social movement may "go mainstream." Some movements become an accepted part of the system—typically after realizing some of their goals—so that although they continue to flourish, they no longer challenge the status quo. For example, the U.S. labor movement is now well established; its leaders control vast sums of money and, according to some critics, now have more in common with the business tycoons they opposed in the past than with rank-and-file workers.

SOCIAL MOVEMENTS AND SOCIAL CHANGE

Social movements exist to encourage—or to resist—social change. Whatever the intention, their success varies from case to case. The civil rights movement has certainly pushed this country toward racial equality, despite opposition from a handful of white supremacist countermovements such as the Aryan Nation and what's left of the Ku Klux Klan.

Sometimes we overlook the success of past social movements and take for granted the changes other people struggled so hard to win. Beginning a century ago, workers' movements in the United States fought to end child labor in factories, limit working hours, make the workplace safer, and establish the right to bargain collectively with employers. Laws protecting the environment are another product of successful social movements during this century. In addition, women today have greater legal rights and economic opportunities because of the efforts of earlier generations of women.

Seen one way, major social transformations such as the Industrial Revolution and capitalism give rise to social movements, including those involving workers and women. On the other hand, the efforts of workers, women, racial and ethnic minorities, and gay people have sent ripples of change throughout our society. In short, social change is both the cause and the consequence of social movements.

LOOKING AHEAD: SOCIAL MOVEMENTS IN THE TWENTY-FIRST CENTURY

Especially since the turbulent 1960s, a decade marked by widespread social protests, U.S. society has been pushed and pulled by many social movements and countermovements. Sometimes tension explodes into violence, as when demonstrators faced off against police at meetings of world leaders in Seattle in 1999, Washington, DC, in 2000, and Stockholm, Sweden, in 2001. In other cases, the struggles are more restrained, as with political debate between congressional Democrats supporting greater social "safety nets" and Republicans opposed to "big government." Yet people on all sides agree that this nation faces a number of pressing issues, including poor public schools, racial tension, the soaring costs of political campaigns, and tens of millions of people without health care insurance. Of course, different people define the problems in different ways, just as they are likely to settle on different policies as solutions. In short, social movements and the problems they address are always *political* (Macionis, 2002).

Just as social movements have always been part of U.S. society, there is little doubt that they will continue to shape our way of life throughout the twenty-first century. Indeed, for three reasons, the scope of social movements is likely to increase. First, protest should increase as women, African Americans, and other historically marginalized categories of people gain a greater political voice. Second, at a global level, the technology of the Information Revolution means that anyone with a cable or satellite television or a personal computer can stay abreast of political events, often as they happen. Third, new technology and the emerging global economy mean that social movements are now uniting people throughout the entire world. Moreover, because many problems are global in scope, only international cooperation can solve them.

SOCIAL SURVEY: "In general, would you say that people should obey the law without exception, or are there exceptional occasions on which people should follow their consciences even if it means breaking the law?" (GSS 1996, N = 1,332; *Codebook*, 2001:872)
"Obey the law" 40.2%   "Follow conscience" 53.8%   DK/NR 6.0%

SOCIAL SURVEY: "Should organizing protest marches and demonstrations against the government be allowed?" (GSS 1996, N = 1,332; *Codebook*, 2001:873)
"Definitely allowed"   45.9%   "Definitely not allowed"   8.2%
"Probably allowed"   29.9%   DK/NR   5.6%
"Probably not allowed"   10.5%

CONTROVERSY & DEBATE

Are You Willing to Take a Stand?

Are you satisfied with our society as it is? Surely, everyone would change some things about our way of life. And surveys show just that: If they could, a lot of people would change plenty! There is considerable pessimism about the state of U.S. society. Two-thirds of U.S. adults think that the average person's situation "is getting worse, not better," and three-fourths of respondents state that most government officials are "not interested" in the average person's problems (NORC, 2001:210–11).

But in light of such concerns, few people are willing to stand up and try to bring about change. Only 10 percent of

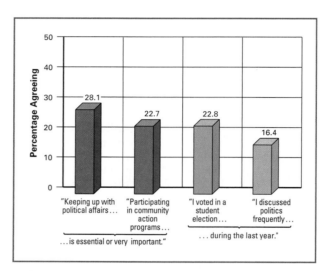

Political Involvement of Students Entering College in 2000: A Survey

Source: Sax et al. (2000).

U.S. adults have ever picketed during a labor strike; just 5 percent say they have ever taken part in any other kind of demonstration (NORC, 2001:249–50).

Many college students probably suspect age has something to do with such apathy. That is, young people have the interest and idealism to challenge the status quo, whereas older adults worry only about their families and their jobs. Indeed, one of the popular sayings of the activist 1960s was "You can't trust people over thirty!" But the facts are otherwise: Students entering college in 2000 expressed less interest in political issues than their parents.

SUMMARY

1. Collective behavior differs from group behavior because it involves limited social interaction within vague social boundaries and also weak and often unconventional norms.

2. Crowds, an important type of collective behavior, take various forms: casual crowds, conventional crowds, expressive crowds, acting crowds, and protest crowds.

3. Crowds that become emotionally intense spawn violence in the form of mobs and riots. Mobs pursue a specific goal; rioting involves undirected destructiveness.

4. Crowds have figured heavily in social change throughout history, although the value of their action depends on one's political outlook.

5. Contagion theory views crowds as anonymous, suggestible, and subject to rising emotions. Convergence theory links crowd behavior to the traits of participants. Emergent-norm theory suggests that crowds develop their own behavioral norms.

6. One form of mass behavior is rumor, which thrives in a climate of ambiguity. Whereas rumor involves public issues, gossip deals with personal issues.

7. Public opinion consists of people's positions on important, controversial issues. Public attitudes change over time; at any time on any given issue, a small share of people hold no opinion at all.

8. Panic (in a local area) and mass hysteria (across an entire society) are types of collective behavior by which people respond to a significant event, real or

THEN AND NOW: Percentage of first-year college students who claim to "frequently discuss politics": *1968*, 30%; *2000*, 16%. Percentage who view "keeping up with political affairs" as an important life goal: *1966*, 58%; *2000*, 28%. Percentage who identify "being very well off financially" as an important life goal: *1968*, 38%; *2000*, 73% (Sax et al., 2000).
SOCIAL SURVEY: In 1973, the following proportion of adults responded that they had taken part in various kinds of protest actions: (GSS 1973, N = 1,504; *Codebook*, 2001:249–50)
Picketing for a labor strike, 9.5%
A civil rights demonstration, 4.3%
An anti-war demonstration, 4.9%
A pro-war demonstration, 0.4%
A school-related demonstration, 5.3%

Asked to select important goals in life from a list, 28 percent of first-year students included "keeping up with political affairs," and just 22 percent checked off "participating in community action programs." As the figure shows, only a handful of students (22 percent) say they voted in a student election during the past year. An even smaller share (16 percent) claimed to discuss politics frequently in the past year.

Certainly, people cite some good reasons to avoid political controversy. Anytime we challenge the system—whether on campus or in the national political arena—we risk making enemies, losing a job, or perhaps even sustaining physical injury.

But the most important reason that people in the United States avoid joining in social movements may have to do with cultural norms about how change should occur. In our individualistic culture, people favor taking personal responsibility over collective action as a means of addressing social problems. For example, when asked about the best way for women or African Americans to improve their social position, most U.S. adults say that individuals should rely on their own efforts. Only a few point to women's groups or civil rights activism as the best way to bring about change (NORC, 2001:228, 362, 364). This individualistic orientation explains why U.S. adults are half as likely as their European counterparts to join in lawful demonstrations (Inglehart et al., 2000).

Of course, sociology poses a counterpoint to our cultural individualism. As C. Wright Mills (1959) explained decades ago, many of the problems we encounter as individuals are caused by the structure of society. Thus, said Mills, solutions to many of life's problems depend on collective effort—that is, people willing to take a stand for what they believe.

Continue the debate . . .

1. *Do you think the reluctance of people in the United States to address problems through collective action shows that they are basically satisfied with their lives? Or that they think individuals acting together can't make a difference?*

2. *Have you ever participated in a political demonstration? What were its goals? What did it accomplish?*

3. *Identify ways in which life today has been affected by people who took a stand in the past (think about race relations, animal welfare, the state of the environment, the standing of women and other issues).*

imagined, with irrational, frantic, and often self-destructive behavior.

9. In industrial societies, people use fashion as a source of social prestige. A fad is more unconventional than a fashion and also of shorter duration, although people embrace fads with greater enthusiasm.

10. Social movements exist to promote or discourage change. Sociologists classify social movements according to the range of people they seek to involve and the extent of the change they seek.

11. According to deprivation theory, social movements arise as people feel deprived in relation to some standard of well-being.

12. Mass-society theory holds that people join social movements to gain a sense of belonging and moral direction.

13. Structural-strain theory explains the development of a social movement as a cumulative effect of six factors. Well-formulated grievances and goals encourage the formation of social movements; undirected anger, by contrast, promotes rioting.

14. Resource-mobilization theory ties the success or failure of a social movement to the availability of resources such as money, human labor, and alliances with other organizations.

15. Culture theory notes the importance of symbols and material resources to the success of a social movement.

16. New social movements theory focuses on quality-of-life issues that are usually international in scope.

17. A typical social movement proceeds through consecutive stages: emergence (defining the public issue),

EXERCISE: Talk radio listeners sometimes form political networks that support or oppose various social movements by encouraging voting, contributions to campaigns, and letters to political officials. Tune in to a locally broadcast talk radio show (Rush Limbaugh's show is just one example) and see how such shows attempt to mobilize an audience (cf. Barker, 1998).

RESOURCE: The *Seeing Ourselves* reader includes the contemporary selection "The Animal Rights Movement as a Moral Crusade" by James M. Jasper and Dorothy Nelkin.

CTQ1: The chapter discusses crowds, mobs, riots, rumor, gossip, panics, fashions, and fads. All have a transitory character. The exception is social movements, which are sometimes long-lasting; this is why we treat that topic separately and at length.

coalescence (entering the public arena), bureaucratization (becoming formally organized), and decline (caused by failure or, sometimes, success).

18. Past social movements have shaped society in ways that people now take for granted. Just as movements produce change, change itself causes social movements.

KEY CONCEPTS

collective behavior (p. 601) activity involving a large number of people, often spontaneous and sometimes controversial

collectivity (p. 602) a large number of people whose minimal interaction occurs in the absence of well-defined and conventional norms

crowd (p. 603) a temporary gathering of people who share a common focus of attention and who influence one another

mob (p. 603) a highly emotional crowd that pursues a violent or destructive goal

riot (p. 604) a social eruption that is highly emotional, violent, and undirected

mass behavior (p. 606) collective behavior among people dispersed over a wide geographical area

rumor (p. 607) unsubstantiated information spread informally, often by word of mouth

gossip (p. 608) rumor about people's personal affairs

public opinion (p. 608) widespread attitudes about controversial issues

propaganda (p. 609) information presented with the intention of shaping public opinion

panic (p. 609) a form of localized collective behavior by which people react to a threat or other stimulus with irrational, frantic, and often self-destructive behavior

mass hysteria or **moral panic** (p. 609) a form of dispersed collective behavior by which people react to a real or imagined event with irrational and even frantic fear

fashion (p. 609) a social pattern favored by a large number of people

fad (p. 610) an unconventional social pattern that people embrace briefly but enthusiastically

social movement (p. 610) organized activity that encourages or discourages social change

relative deprivation (p. 612) a perceived disadvantage arising from a specific comparison

CRITICAL-THINKING QUESTIONS

1. The concept of collective behavior encompasses a broad range of social patterns. List some of these patterns. What traits do they all have in common?

2. Imagine the aftermath of a football game when the revelry turns into a destructive rampage. How might contagion theory, convergence theory, and emergent-norm theory explain such behavior?

3. The 1960s were a decade of both great affluence and widespread social protest. What sociological insights help explain this apparent paradox?

4. In what respects do some recent social movements (those concerned with the environment, animal rights, and gun control) differ from much earlier crusades (focusing on, say, the right of workers to form unions or the right of women to vote)?

CTQ2: Contagion theory highlights the spread of emotional energy through the crowd; convergence theory suggests that people deciding to join such a crowd were predisposed to act in a particular way; emergent norm theory suggests that crowds generate their own norms and actions as they go along.

CTQ3: Relative deprivation theory argues that people assess reality against their expectations. Thus rising affluence extends expectations, which can lead to unrest if the expectations are not met.

CTQ4: Recent movements tend to involve social or cultural issues rather than economic issues. They also tend to draw more support from the middle and upper middle classes and are likely to be international in scope (e.g., women's rights, gay rights, animal rights, environmentalism).

APPLICATIONS AND EXERCISES

1. With ten friends, try this experiment: One person writes down a detailed rumor about someone important and then whispers it to the second person, who whispers it to a third, and so on. The last person to hear the rumor writes it down again. Compare the two versions of the rumor.

2. With other members of the class, identify recent fad products. What makes people want them? Why do they drop from favor so quickly?

3. What social movements are represented by organizations on your campus? Your class might invite several leaders to describe their groups' goals and strategies.

4. Packaged in the back of this new textbook is an interactive CD-ROM that offers a variety of study and review materials intended to help you better understand the material covered in this chapter. For this chapter, the CD-ROM contains an author's tip video, *Real Life Sociology* videos, other relevant audio and video, interactive map animations, audio journal entries from the author, Web links, and much more.

 ## SITES TO SEE

http://www.prenhall.com/macionis

Visit the interactive *Companion Website*™ that accompanies this text. Begin by clicking on the cover of your book. You will find a chapter-by-chapter study guide, practice tests, and a significant portion of the text for online review, as well as many suggested Web links.

http://www.gallup.com

Tracking trends in public opinion is the job of various pollsters, including the Gallup Organization. Visit the Gallup site to see what they do and read about some of their recent surveys.

http://www.ippn.org/ORCCO.htm

Organizing in support of various social movements has long been a characteristic of college campuses across the United States. This site describes the Center for Campus Organizing which provides information on campus-based social movements.

http://www.natlnorml.org

Visit the Web site for the National Organization for the Reform of Marijuana Laws. What are the goals of this organization? How is it trying to expand the social movement in favor of legalizing marijuana use?

 INVESTIGATE WITH CONTENTSELECT

Follow the instructions found on page 23 of this textbook to enter this chapter of the book's *Companion Website*™. Once in the chapter, click on the ContentSelect icon at the bottom left of your screen and enter your personal User ID and Password. Enter keywords such as "lynching," "riots," and "animal rights," and the search engine will help you become an effective researcher.

CHAPTER

24

SOCIAL CHANGE: TRADITIONAL, MODERN, AND POSTMODERN SOCIETIES

The five-story, red brick apartment building at 253 E. 10th Street in New York has been standing for more than a century. In 1900, one of the twenty small apartments in the building was occupied by thirty-nine-year-old Julius Streicher and his thirty-three-year-old wife, Christine—both of whom had immigrated from Germany in 1885—and their four young children.

The Streichers probably considered themselves successful. Julius operated a small clothing shop a few blocks from the apartment; Christine stayed at home,

raised the children, and did the housework. Like most people in the country at that time, neither Julius nor Christine graduated from high school, and they worked for ten to twelve hours, six days a week. Their income—average for that time—was about $35 a month, or about $425 a year. (In today's dollars that would be slightly more than $8,000, but still well below today's poverty line.) They spent almost half of their income for food; most of the rest went for rent.

Today, Dorothy Sabo resides at 253 E. 10th Street, living alone in the same apartment where the Streichers spent much of their lives. Now eighty-seven, she is retired from a career teaching art at a nearby museum. In many respects, Sabo's life has been far easier than the life the Streichers knew. For one thing, when the Streichers lived there, the building had no electricity (people used kerosene lamps and candles) and no running water (Christine Streicher spent Mondays doing laundry with water she carried from a public fountain at the end of the block). There were no telephones, no televisions, and, of course, no computers. Today, Dorothy Sabo takes such conveniences for granted. Although she is hardly rich, her pension and Social Security are several times as much as the Streichers earned.

Sabo has her own worries. She is concerned about the environment and often speaks out about global warming. Here again, a look back in time is instructive. A century ago, if the Streichers and their neighbors thought about "the environment," they would probably have winced at the smell coming up from the street. At a time when motor vehicles were just beginning to appear in New York City, carriages, trucks, and trolleys were all pulled by horses—thousands of them. These animals dumped 60,000 gallons of urine and 2.5 million pounds of manure on the city's streets every day (based on Simon & Cannon, 2001).

SUPPLEMENTS: An outline of this chapter, supplementary lecture material, and suggested discussion topics are included in the *Data File*.

SOCIAL SURVEY: "One trouble with science is that it makes our way of life change too fast." (GSS 1988, *N* = 1,481; *Codebook*, 2001:365)

"Agree"   40.2%   "Disagree"   57.7%   DK/NR   2.1%

DISCUSS: Consider ways in which the university diffuses knowledge, thereby promoting social change (cf. Wilkinson, 1994).

DISCUSS: Are "great people" or "average people" primarily responsible for social change? Historically, conservatives argued the former because this individualistic position favored traditional hierarchy and elites. Liberals tended toward the more egalitarian, collectivist view.

It is scarcely possible for most people today to imagine how different life was a century ago. Not only was life much harder back then, but it was also much shorter. Statistical records show that life expectancy was just forty-six years for men and forty-eight years for women, compared with seventy-four and seventy-nine years today.

Certainly, over the course of the last century, much has changed for the better. Yet as this chapter explains, social change is not all for the better. On the contrary, change has negative consequences, too, creating unexpected new problems. As we shall see, early sociologists were mixed in their assessment of *modernity*, changes brought about by the Industrial Revolution. Likewise, today's sociologists point to both good and bad aspects of *postmodernity*, the recent transformations caused by the Information Revolution and the postindustrial economy. The one thing that is clear is that—for better and worse—the rate of change has never been faster than it is now.

Examine the lives of men and women, black and white, living in New York City between 1900 and 1920: http://www.albany.edu/mumford/1920/groups.html

WHAT IS SOCIAL CHANGE?

In earlier chapters, we examined relatively *static* social patterns, including status and role, social stratification, and social institutions. The *dynamic* forces that have shaped our way of life range from innovations in technology to the expansion of cities and the growth of bureaucracy. These are all dimensions of **social change,** *the transformation of culture and social institutions over time.* The process of social change has four major characteristics:

1. **Social change is inevitable.** "Nothing is certain except death and taxes" goes the old saying. Yet even our thoughts about death have changed dramatically as life expectancy in the United States has nearly doubled, as indicated in the opening to this chapter. Back in 1900, the Streichers and almost all other people in the United States paid little or no tax on their earnings; taxes have increased dramatically over the course of the last century, along with the size and scope of various levels of government. In short, virtually everything is subject to the twists and turns of change.

   Still, some societies change faster than others. As Chapter 4 ("Society") explained, hunting and gathering societies change quite slowly; members of today's high-income societies, on the other hand, experience significant change in a single lifetime.

   Moreover, in any society, some cultural elements change faster than others. William Ogburn's (1964) theory of *cultural lag* (see Chapter 3, "Culture") states that material culture (that is, things) usually changes faster than nonmaterial culture (ideas and attitudes). For example, genetic technology that allows scientists to alter and perhaps even create life has developed more rapidly than ethical standards for deciding when and how to use it.

For an introduction to the recent controversy over stem cell research, visit http://www.nih.gov/news/stemcell/primer.htm

2. **Social change sometimes is intentional but often is unplanned.** Industrial societies actively encourage many kinds of change. For example, scientists seek more efficient forms of energy, and advertisers try to convince us that life is incomplete without this or that new gadget. Yet rarely can anyone envision all the consequences of the changes that are set in motion.

   In 1900, when the country still relied on horses for transportation, people looked ahead to motor vehicles traveling in a single day distances that had taken weeks or months in the past. But no one could see how profoundly the mobility provided by automobiles would alter life in the United States, scattering family members, reshaping cities and suburbs, and threatening the natural environment. In 1900, the entire nation recorded just thirty-eight automobile fatalities (there were only 8,000 "horseless carriages" in the whole country). Few could foresee that in the years that followed, the number of auto-related deaths would soar and now exceed 40,000 each year.

3. **Social change is controversial.** The history of the automobile shows that social change brings both good and bad consequences. The Industrial Revolution that led to the invention of the automobile was itself controversial. Capitalists celebrated the new technology that increased productivity and swelled profits. However, many workers feared that machines would make their skills obsolete and resisted the push toward "progress."

   Today, as in the past, changing social patterns—between black people and white people, women and men, and homosexuals and

NOTE: In modern, rapidly changing societies, the origins of cultural elements often are forgotten. Lucky Strike cigarettes were named for a California gold strike; Baby Ruth candy bars were named for the birth of Grover Cleveland's daughter.

NOTE: In light of how quickly today's information becomes obsolete, note that Euclidian mathematics texts remained up to date and largely unchanged for 23 centuries.

Q: "All of us are taking a journey into the future that will last every day of our lives. What will we be seeing and doing? How will we live?" Isaac Asimov

Q: "The philosophers have attempted to understand the world. The point, however, is to change it." Karl Marx

NOTE: Two sections of Chapter 4 ("Society") introduced Marx's materialist analysis of change and Weber's idealist analysis.

heterosexuals—still create controversy as people disagree about how we ought to live.

4. **Some changes matter more than others.** Some changes (such as clothing fads) have only passing significance, whereas others (such as computers) last a long time and may end up transforming the entire world. Looking ahead, will the Information Revolution turn out to be as pivotal as the Industrial Revolution? Like the automobile and television, the computer has both positive and negative effects, providing new kinds of jobs while eliminating old ones, isolating people in offices while linking people in global electronic networks, offering vast amounts of information while threatening personal privacy.

CAUSES OF SOCIAL CHANGE

Social change has many causes. Then, too, in a world linked by sophisticated communication and transportation technology, change in one place often begets change elsewhere.

CULTURE AND CHANGE

Chapter 3 ("Culture") identified three important sources of cultural change. First, *invention* produces new objects, ideas, and social patterns. Rocket propulsion research, which began in the 1940s, has produced spacecraft that reach toward the stars. Today we take such technology for granted; during the twenty-first century a significant number of people may well travel in space.

Second, *discovery* occurs when people take note of existing elements of the world. For example, medical advances offer a growing understanding of the human body. Beyond the direct effects on human health, medical discoveries have stretched life expectancy, setting in motion the "graying" of the United States and other high-income nations (see Chapter 15, "Aging and the Elderly").

Third, *diffusion* creates change as products, people, and information spread from one culture to another. Ralph Linton (1937a) recognized that many familiar elements of our culture came from other lands. Cloth (first made in Asia), clocks (invented in Europe), and coins (introduced in Turkey) are all part of our way of life. In general, material objects diffuse more readily than cultural ideas. That is, new breakthroughs (such as the science of cloning) occur faster than our understanding of when—and even whether—they are morally desirable.

Today, most of the people with access to computers live in rich countries such as the United States. But the number of people in low-income nations going "online" is on the rise. How do you think the introduction of new information technology will change more traditional societies? Are all the changes likely to be for the good?

Today, as throughout our entire history as a nation, immigrants bring change to the United States. In recent decades, people from Latin America and Asia have introduced new cultural patterns, clearly evident in the sights, smells, and sounds of cities across the country. Conversely, the global power of the United States ensures that much of our culture—from cheeseburgers to hip hop to M.B.A. degrees—is being diffused to other societies.

CONFLICT AND CHANGE

Tension and conflict in a society also produce change. Karl Marx saw class conflict as the engine that drives societies from one historical era to another (see Chapter 4, "Society," and Chapter 10, "Social Stratification"). In industrial-capitalist societies, he predicted, struggle between capitalists and workers would propel society toward a socialist system of production.

In the century since Marx's death, this model has proven simplistic. Yet Marx correctly foresaw that

THE MAP: Signaling the mobility and growth of U.S. society: The average age of housing stock is 30 years—below the median age of the population (36 years). The counties with more long-term residents typically have an older population, and they are also places where economic growth is limited or stagnant. Many of them have lost young people to urban areas offering greater economic prospects. Thus few counties have escaped change of one kind or another. The trend from 1985 to 1995 was toward less moving.

NOTE: Census data point to Johnstown, Pa., as the most settled U.S. community, where 25% of residents have not moved since 1959 (U.S. average: 8.4%); Bryan-College Station, Tex., is the most mobile: 41% moved in the 18 months before the data were collected (U.S. average: 21.7%).

SEEING OURSELVES

NATIONAL MAP 24–1
Who Stays Put?
Residential Stability across the United States

Overall, only about 9 percent of U.S. residents have not moved during the last thirty years. Counties with a higher proportion of "long-termers" typically have experienced less change over recent decades: Many neighborhoods have been in place since before World War II, and many of the same families live in them. Looking at the map, what can you say about these stable areas? Why are most of these counties rural and some distance from the coasts?

Source: U.S. Census Bureau (1996).

social conflict arising from inequality (involving not just class but also race and gender) would force changes in every society, including our own.

IDEAS AND CHANGE

Max Weber also contributed to our understanding of social change. Weber acknowledged that conflict could bring about change, but he traced the roots of most social change to ideas. For example, people with charisma can carry a message that sometimes changes the world.

Weber also highlighted the importance of ideas by showing how the religious beliefs of early Protestants set the stage for the spread of industrial capitalism (see Chapter 4, "Society"). The fact that industrial capitalism developed primarily in areas of Western Europe where the Protestant work ethic was strong proved to Weber the power of ideas to bring about change (1958; orig. 1904–5).

Ideas also direct social movements. Chapter 23 ("Collective Behavior and Social Movements") explained how change comes from the determination of people acting together to, say, clean up the environment or make the world more just by improving the lives of oppressed people. For example, the gay rights movement draws strength from people who believe that lesbians and gay men should enjoy the same rights and opportunities as the heterosexual majority.

DEMOGRAPHIC CHANGE

Population patterns also transform a society. A century ago, as the chapter opening suggested, the typical household (4.8 people) was far larger than it is today (2.6 people). Women are having fewer children, for one thing, and more people are living alone. In addition, change is taking place as our population, collectively speaking, grows older. As Chapter 15 ("Aging and the Elderly") explained, 12 percent of the U.S. population was over age sixty-five in 2000, three times the proportion back in 1900. By the year 2030, seniors will account for 20 percent of the total (U.S. Census Bureau, 2001). Medical research and health care services already focus extensively on the elderly. But life will change in countless additional ways as homes and household products are redesigned to meet the needs of the growing ranks of older consumers.

Migration within and between societies is another demographic factor that promotes change. Between 1870 and 1930, tens of millions of immigrants entered the industrial cities in the United States. Millions more from rural areas joined the rush. As a result, farm communities declined, cities expanded, and by 1920, the United States had become a predominantly urban nation. Similarly, changes are taking place today as people move from the Snowbelt to the Sunbelt and mix with new immigrants from Latin America and Asia.

In response to the accelerating pace of change in the nineteenth century, Paul Gauguin left his native France for the South Seas where he was captivated by a simpler and seemingly timeless way of life. He romanticized this environment in his painting, Les trois huttes Tahiti.

Paul Gauguin (1848–1903), *Les trois huttes Tahiti.*
Photo © Christie's Images.

Where in the United States have demographic changes been greatest, and which areas have been least affected? National Map 24–1 provides one answer, showing counties where the largest share of people have lived in their present homes for thirty years or more.

MODERNITY

A central concept in the study of social change is **modernity,** *social patterns resulting from industrialization.* In everyday usage, modernity (its Latin root means "lately") designates the present in relation to the past. Sociologists include in this catchall concept the social patterns set in motion by the Industrial Revolution, which began in Western Europe in the mid-eighteenth century and spread to the United States in about fifty years. **Modernization,** then, is *the process of social change begun by industrialization.* The time line inside the front cover of the text highlights important events that mark the emergence of modernity. Table 24–1 on page 630 provides a snapshot of change over the course of the last century. The United States became a larger, more urban, and far more prosperous nation. At the same time, traditional families underwent significant change. Industrial technology put the country on wheels and in the air but this technology also placed greater stress on the natural environment.

FOUR DIMENSIONS OF MODERNIZATION

In his influential study of social change, Peter Berger (1977) identified four characteristics of modernization:

1. **The decline of small, traditional communities.** Modernity involves "the progressive weakening, if not destruction, of the . . . relatively cohesive communities in which human beings have found solidarity and meaning throughout most of history" (Berger 1977:72). For thousands of years, in hunting and gathering camps and the agrarian villages of Europe and North America, people lived in small communities where social life revolved around family and neighborhood. Such traditional worlds gave each person a well-defined place that, although limiting the range of choice, offered a strong sense of identity, belonging, and purpose.

   Small, isolated communities still exist in remote corners of the United States, of course, but they are home to only a small percentage of our nation's people. And their isolation is little more than geographic. Cars, telephones, television, and, increasingly, computers give rural families the pulse of the larger society and connect them to the entire world.

2. **The expansion of personal choice.** Members of traditional, preindustrial societies view their lives as shaped by forces beyond human control: gods, spirits, or simply fate. But as the power of tradition erodes, people come to see their lives as a series of options, a process Berger calls *individualization.* For example, many people in the United States choose a particular "lifestyle" (sometimes adopting one after another), showing an openness to change.

CHAPTER 24 Social Change: Traditional, Modern, and Postmodern Societies **629**

GLOBAL: Most of humanity still lives in powerful, ascriptive communities, thinking of themselves as embedded in kinship, locality, and tradition. From the standpoint of such people throughout the world, we in the U.S. seem not only affluent but highly individualistic. From our perspective, behavior based on ascriptive solidarities (that is, reflecting categories rather than individual traits) seems wrongheaded and discriminatory.

SOCIAL SURVEY: "How important is each of the following in helping you to make decisions about your life?" (GSS 1988, N = 1,481; *Codebook*, 2001:378–79) (Percentage saying "very important"):
Your own personal judgment, 71.0%
Family and friends, 48.2%
The Bible, 34.1%
The teachings of your church or synagogue, 28.6%

TABLE 24–1 The United States: A Century of Change

	1900	2000
National population	76,000,000	281,000,000
Percentage urban	40%	80%
Life expectancy	46 years (men); 48 years (women)	74 years (men); 79 years (women)
Median age	22.9 years	35.3 years
Average household income	$8,000 (in 2000 dollars)	$40,000 (in 2000 dollars)
Share of income spent on food	43%	15%
Share of homes with flush toilets	10%	98%
Average number of cars	1 car for every 2,000 households	1.3 cars for every household
Divorce rate	About 1 in 20 marriages ends in divorce	About 8 in 20 marriages end in divorce
Average gallons of petroleum products consumed per person per year	34	1,100

3. **Increasing social diversity.** In preindustrial societies, strong family ties and powerful religious beliefs enforce conformity while discouraging diversity and change. Modernization promotes a more rational, scientific worldview as tradition loses its hold and people gain more and more individual choice. The growth of cities, expansion of impersonal bureaucracy, and social mix of people from various backgrounds combine to foster diverse beliefs and behavior.

4. **Future orientation and growing awareness of time.** Whereas premodern people focus on the past, people in modern societies think more about the future. Modern people are forward looking and optimistic that new inventions and discoveries will improve their lives.

Modern people also organize their daily routines down to the very minute. With the introduction of clocks in the late Middle Ages, Europeans began to think not in terms of sunlight and seasons but in terms of hours and minutes. Preoccupied with personal gain, modern people demand precise measurement of time and are likely to agree that "Time is money." Berger points out that one good indicator of a society's degree of modernization is the proportion of people who wear wristwatches.

Finally, recall that modernization touched off the development of sociology itself. As Chapter 1 ("The Sociological Perspective") explained, the discipline originated in the wake of the Industrial Revolution in Western Europe, where social change was proceeding most rapidly. Early European and U.S. sociologists set out to analyze the rise of modern society and its consequences—both good and bad—for human beings.

FERDINAND TÖNNIES: THE LOSS OF COMMUNITY

The German sociologist Ferdinand Tönnies (1855–1937) produced a lasting account of modernization in his theory of *Gemeinschaft* and *Gesellschaft* (see Chapter 22, "Population, Urbanization, and Environment"). Like Peter Berger, whose work he influenced, Tönnies (1963; orig. 1887) viewed modernization as the progressive loss of *Gemeinschaft*, or human community. As Tönnies saw it, the Industrial Revolution weakened the social fabric of family and tradition by introducing a businesslike emphasis on facts, efficiency, and money. European and North American societies gradually became rootless and impersonal as people came to associate mostly on the basis of self-interest—the state Tönnies called *Gesellschaft*.

 For a short biography of Ferdinand Tönnies, visit the Gallery of Sociologists at http://www.TheSociologyPage.com

Early in the twentieth century, at least some areas of the United States approached Tönnies's concept of *Gemeinschaft*. Families that had lived for generations in small villages and towns were bound together in a hardworking, slow-moving way of life. Telephones (invented in 1876) were rare; it wasn't until 1915 that someone placed the first coast-to-coast call (see the time line inside the front cover of this book). Living without television (introduced in 1939 and not widespread until after 1950), families entertained themselves, often gathering with friends in the evening to share stories, sorrows, or song. Without rapid transportation (Henry Ford's assembly line began in 1908, but cars became common only after World War II), people lived their whole lives in one small town, which was their entire world.

Q: "We must become the change we want to see." Mahatma Gandhi
NOTE: A characteristic of modernity is the rise of tolerance (from the Latin *tolerare*, meaning "to bear"). For most of us, the virtues of tolerance are easy to enumerate if not always to act on. Contemporary people tend to embrace cultural relativism (especially as their schooling increases); traditional people (and those with less schooling) generally adopt a more ethnocentric, absolutist worldview.

Q: "With the loss of tradition we have lost the thread that safely guided us through the vast realms of the past." Hannah Arendt
NOTE: Durkheim's concept of "mechanical solidarity" implies that we can learn the workings of an entire society by examining any one component of it, just as we can understand a physical substance through analysis of a single molecule. This is not true of internally differentiated, organic bodies.

George Tooker's 1950 painting The Subway *depicts a common problem of modern life: Weakening social ties and eroding traditions create a generic humanity in which everyone is alike yet each person is an anxious stranger in the midst of others.*

George Tooker, *The Subway*, 1950, egg tempera on gesso panel, 18⅛ × 36⅛", Whitney Museum of American Art, New York. Purchased with funds from the Julianna Force Purchase Award, 50.23. Photograph © 2000 Whitney Museum of American Art.

Inevitable tensions and conflicts—sometimes based on race, ethnicity, or religion—divided these small communities. But according to Tönnies, because of the traditional spirit of *Gemeinschaft*, people were "essentially united in spite of all separating factors" (1963:65; orig. 1887).

Modernity turns societies inside out so that, as Tönnies put it, people are "essentially separated in spite of uniting factors" (1963:65; orig. 1887). This is the world of *Gesellschaft*, where, especially in large cities, most people live among strangers and ignore others they pass on the street. Trust is hard to come by in a mobile and anonymous society; people tend to put their personal needs ahead of group loyalty, and a majority of adults believe "you can't be too careful" in dealing with people (NORC, 2001:178). No wonder that millions of men and women attend weekly support groups (also made up of strangers) to establish even temporary emotional ties and find someone who is willing simply to listen (Leerhsen, 1990).

Critical evaluation. Tönnies's theory of *Gemeinschaft* and *Gesellschaft* is the most widely cited model of modernization. The theory's strength lies in its synthesis of various dimensions of change: growing population, the rise of cities, increasing impersonality in social interaction.

One problem with Tönnies's theory is that modern life, though often impersonal, is not completely devoid of *Gemeinschaft*. Even in a world of strangers, friendships can be strong and lasting. Traditions are especially pronounced in many ethnic neighborhoods, where residents maintain close community ties.

Another criticism is that Tönnies said little about which factors (industrialization, urbanization, weakening of families) are cause and which are effect. Some analysts also think that Tönnies favored—perhaps even romanticized—traditional societies while overlooking bonds of family, neighborhood, and friendship in modern societies.

EMILE DURKHEIM: THE DIVISION OF LABOR

The French sociologist Emile Durkheim, whose work is discussed in Chapter 4 ("Society"), shared Tönnies's interest in the profound social changes wrought by the Industrial Revolution. For Durkheim, modernization is defined by an increasing *division of labor*, or specialized economic activity (1964a; orig. 1893). Whereas all members of a traditional society usually perform the same daily round of activities, modern societies function by having people perform highly specific roles.

Durkheim explained that preindustrial societies are held together by *mechanical solidarity*, or shared moral sentiments. In other words, members of preindustrial societies view everyone as basically alike, doing the same kind of work and belonging together. Durkheim's concept of mechanical solidarity is virtually the same as Tönnies's *Gemeinschaft*.

With modernization, the division of labor becomes more and more pronounced. To Durkheim, this change means less mechanical solidarity but more of another kind of tie: *organic solidarity*, or the mutual dependency of people engaged in specialized work. Put simply, modern societies are held together not by likeness but by difference: All of us must depend on others to meet most of our needs. Organic solidarity corresponds to Tönnies's concept of *Gesellschaft*.

RESOURCE: Emile Durkheim's "Anomy and Modern Life" and Max Weber's "The Disenchantment of Modern Life" are among the classics in the 5th edition of *Seeing Ourselves*.

DISCUSS: Consider the limits of science implied by Leo Tolstoy's observation that "Science is meaningless because it gives no answer to the question, the only question of importance for us: 'What shall we do and how shall we live?'"

DISCUSS: Pose to the class the Weberian irony that the more we learn about the natural world, the more uncertainty we feel about ultimate cause and meaning.

Q: "The bourgeoisie, during its rule of scarcely one hundred years, has created more massive and more colossal productive forces than have all preceding generations together." Karl Marx and Friedrich Engels

Max Weber maintained that the distinctive character of modern society was its rational worldview. Virtually all of Weber's work on modernity centered on types of people he considered typical of their age: the scientist, the capitalist, and the bureaucrat. Each is rational to the core: The scientist is committed to the orderly discovery of truth, the capitalist to the orderly pursuit of profit, and the bureaucrat to orderly conformity to a system of rules.

Despite obvious similarities in their thinking, Durkheim and Tönnies viewed modernity somewhat differently. To Tönnies, the change from *Gemeinschaft* to *Gesellschaft* amounts to the loss of social solidarity because modern people lose the "natural" and "organic" bonds of the rural village, leaving only the "artificial" and "mechanical" ties of the big city. Durkheim had a different take on modernity, even reversing Tönnies's language to bring home the point. Durkheim labeled modern society "organic," arguing that modern society is no less natural than any other, and he described traditional societies as "mechanical" because they are so regimented. Thus Durkheim viewed modernization not as the loss of community but as a change from community based on bonds of likeness (kinship and neighborhood) to community based on economic interdependence (the division of labor). Durkheim's view of modernity is both more complex and more positive than Tönnies's.

Critical evaluation. Durkheim's ideas stand alongside those of Tönnies as a highly influential analysis of modernity. Of the two thinkers, Durkheim is the more optimistic; still, he feared that modern societies might become so diverse that they would collapse into a state of *anomie*, a condition in which norms and values are so weak and inconsistent that society provides little moral guidance to individuals. Without strong moral ties to society, modern people become egocentric and find little purpose in life.

The suicide rate—which Durkheim considered a good index of anomie—has increased in the United States over the twentieth century. Moreover, in a recent survey, the vast majority of U.S. adults reported that they see moral questions not in clear terms of right and wrong but in confusing "shades of gray" (NORC, 2001:377).

Even so, in modern societies, shared norms and values are still strong enough to give most people some sense of meaning and purpose. Moreover, whatever the hazards of anomie, most people seem to value the personal freedom modern society affords.

MAX WEBER: RATIONALIZATION

For Max Weber, whose work is also discussed in Chapter 4 ("Society"), modernity means replacing a traditional worldview with a rational way of thinking. In preindustrial societies, tradition acts as a constant brake on change. To traditional people, "truth" is roughly the same as "what has always been" (1978:36; orig. 1921). To modern people, however, "truth" is the result of rational calculation. Because they value efficiency and have little reverence for the past, modern people adopt whatever social patterns allow them to achieve their goals.

Q: "Our lives make sense in a thousand ways, most of which we are unaware of, because of traditions that are centuries, if not millennia, old." Robert N. Bellah et al. (1985:282)

RESOURCE: An excerpt from Robert Bellah's *Habits of the Heart* is included in the Macionis and Benokraitis reader, *Seeing Ourselves*.

Q: "As habit is essential to vice, it is essential to virtue as well." Ferdinand Tönnies

Q: "Only the wisest and the stupidest do not change." Confucius

Q: "One of the most fundamental traits of modernization is a vast movement from fate to choice in human affairs." Peter Berger

Q: "A case can be made that the central question of sociology, from its inception in the rather fanciful philosophy of Auguste Comte, has been the question about the nature of modernity." Peter Berger (1986:28)

Echoing Tönnies and Durkheim, who held that industrialization weakens tradition, Weber declared that modern society is "disenchanted." The unquestioned truths of an earlier time have been challenged by rational, scientific thinking. In short, modern society turns away from the gods. Throughout his life, Weber studied various modern "types"—the capitalist, the scientist, the bureaucrat—all of whom share the rational worldview that Weber believed was coming to characterize modern society.

Critical evaluation. Compared with Tönnies and especially Durkheim, Weber was critical of modern society. He knew that science could produce technological and organizational wonders but worried that science was turning us away from more basic questions about the meaning and purpose of human existence. Weber feared that rationalization, especially in bureaucracies, would erode the human spirit with endless rules and regulations.

Finally, some of Weber's critics think that the alienation he attributed to bureaucracy actually stemmed from social inequality. That criticism leads us to the ideas of Karl Marx.

KARL MARX: CAPITALISM

For Karl Marx, modern society was synonymous with capitalism; he saw the Industrial Revolution as primarily a *capitalist revolution*. Marx traced the emergence of the bourgeoisie in medieval Europe to the expansion of commerce. The bourgeoisie gradually displaced the feudal aristocracy as the Industrial Revolution placed a powerful new system of production under their control.

Marx agreed that modernity weakened small communities (as described by Tönnies), sharpened the division of labor (as noted by Durkheim), and fostered a rational worldview (as Weber believed). But he saw all these simply as conditions necessary for capitalism to flourish. According to Marx, capitalism draws people from farms and small towns into an ever-expanding market system centered in cities; specialization is needed for efficient factories; and rationality is exemplified by the capitalists' relentless pursuit of profit.

Earlier chapters have painted Marx as a spirited critic of capitalist society, but his vision of modernity also is optimistic. Unlike Weber, who viewed modern society as an "iron cage" of bureaucracy, Marx believed that social conflict in capitalist societies would sow seeds of revolution, leading to an

For more on Durkheim, Weber, and Marx, visit the Gallery of Sociologists at http://www.TheSociologyPage.com

egalitarian socialism. As he saw it, such a society would harness industrial technology to enrich people's lives and wipe out social class, the source of social conflict and dehumanization. Although Marx was an outspoken critic of modern society, he nevertheless imagined a future of human freedom, creativity, and community.

Critical evaluation. Marx's theory of modernization is a complex theory of capitalism. But Marx underestimated the dominance of bureaucracy in modern societies. In socialist societies, in particular, the stifling effects of bureaucracy turned out to be as bad as, or even worse than, the dehumanizing aspects of capitalism. The political upheavals that swept Eastern Europe and the former Soviet Union in the 1990s reveal the depth of popular opposition to oppressive state bureaucracies.

THEORETICAL ANALYSIS OF MODERNITY

The rise of modernity is a complex process involving many dimensions of change, as described in previous chapters and summarized in Table 24–2 on page 634. How can we make sense of so many changes going on all at once? Sociologists have developed two broad explanations of modern society: One is guided by the structural-functional paradigm and one is based on social-conflict theory.

STRUCTURAL-FUNCTIONAL THEORY: MODERNITY AS MASS SOCIETY

November 11, on the Interstate 275 outerbelt. From the car, we see a BP and a Sunoco station, K-Mart and Wal-Mart, AmeriSuites hotel, a Bob Evans, a Chi Chi's Mexican restaurant, and a McDonald's. This road happens to circle Cincinnati. But it could be almost anywhere in the United States.

One broad approach—drawing on the ideas of Ferdinand Tönnies, Emile Durkheim, and Max Weber—depicts modernization as the emergence of *mass society* (Dahrendorf, 1959; Kornhauser, 1959; Nisbet, 1966, 1969; Stein, 1972; Berger, Berger, & Kellner, 1974; Pearson, 1993). A **mass society** is *a society in which prosperity and bureaucracy have eroded traditional social ties*. A mass society is highly productive; on average, people have more income than ever. At

SOCIAL SURVEY: "Morality is a personal matter and society should not force everyone to follow one standard." (GSS 1988, N = 1,481; Codebook, 2001:377)

"Agree strongly"   31.7%   "Disagree strongly" 7.6%
"Agree somewhat"   38.8%   DK/NR   4.4%
"Disagree somewhat"   17.5%

NOTE: The term "individual," with a Latin root meaning "indivisible," first became widely used in early 19th-century Europe, at a time when traditional social ties were weakening.

DISCUSS: Graphically contrast traditional society (strong social surroundings, weak individualism) with modern society (opposite pattern) using these figures: (from E. Digby Baltzell).

Q: "Things do not change; we change." Henry David Thoreau

TABLE 24–2 Traditional and Modern Societies: The Big Picture

Elements of Society	Traditional Societies	Modern Societies
Cultural Patterns		
Values	Homogeneous; sacred character; few subcultures and countercultures	Heterogeneous; secular character; many subcultures and countercultures
Norms	High moral significance; little tolerance of diversity	Variable moral significance; high tolerance of diversity
Time orientation	Present linked to past	Present linked to future
Technology	Preindustrial; human and animal energy	Industrial; advanced energy sources
Social Structure		
Status and role	Few statuses, most ascribed; few specialized roles	Many statuses, some ascribed and some achieved; many specialized roles
Relationships	Typically primary; little anonymity or privacy	Typically secondary; considerable anonymity and privacy
Communication	Face to face	Face-to-face communication supplemented by mass media
Social control	Informal gossip	Formal police and legal system
Social stratification	Rigid patterns of social inequality; little mobility	Fluid patterns of social inequality; considerable mobility
Gender patterns	Pronounced patriarchy; women's lives centered on the home	Declining patriarchy; increasing number of women in the paid labor force
Settlement patterns	Small scale; population typically small and widely dispersed in rural villages and small towns	Large scale; population typically large and concentrated in cities
Social Institutions		
Economy	Based on agriculture; much manufacturing in the home; little white-collar work	Based on industrial mass production; factories become centers of production; increasing white-collar work
State	Small-scale government; little state intervention in society	Large-scale government; considerable state intervention in society
Family	Extended family as the primary means of socialization and economic production	Nuclear family retains some socialization functions but is more a unit of consumption than of production
Religion	Religion guides worldview; little religious pluralism	Religion weakens with the rise of science; extensive religious pluralism
Education	Formal schooling limited to elites	Basic schooling becomes universal, with growing proportion receiving advanced education
Health	High birth and death rates; short life expectancy because of low standard of living and simple medical technology	Low birth and death rates; longer life expectancy because of higher standard of living and sophisticated medical technology
Social Change	Slow; change evident over many generations	Rapid; change evident within a single generation

the same time, it is marked by weak kinship and impersonal neighborhoods, so people often feel socially isolated. Although many people have material plenty, they are spiritually weak and often experience moral uncertainty about how to live.

The Mass Scale of Modern Life

Mass-society theory argues, first, that the scale of modern life has greatly increased. Before the Industrial Revolution, Europe and North America formed a mosaic of countless rural villages and small towns. In these small communities, which inspired Tönnies's concept of Gemeinschaft, people lived out their lives surrounded by kin and guided by a shared heritage. Gossip was an informal yet highly effective way to ensure conformity to community standards. These small communities, with their strong moral values, tolerated little social diversity—the state of mechanical solidarity described by Durkheim.

For example, before 1690, English law demanded that everyone regularly participate in the Christian ritual of Holy Communion (Laslett, 1984). On this continent, only Rhode Island among the New England

DISCUSS: Leaving home—presumably in search of a better life—has long been a measure of success in the U.S. Ask the class about their aspirations in this regard.

DISCUSS: What does "success" mean? We have come to use the word "success" in a notably nonspecific manner. Its traditional meaning—to follow or replace another by descent—made sense in a fixed social order with strong social ties. The term's contemporary

meaning of achieving individual goals (whatever they may be) suggests a far more fluid social order.

Q: "While I take inspiration from the past, like most Americans, I live for the future." Former President Ronald Reagan (1992)

NOTE: The conservative implication of mass-society theory is that social inequality still persists, but it is not as severe a problem as it was in the 19th century. Instead, the growing state is problematic.

colonies tolerated any religious dissent. Because social differences were repressed, subcultures and counter-cultures rarely arose and change proceeded slowly.

Increasing population, the growth of cities, and specialized economic activity driven by the Industrial Revolution gradually altered this pattern. People came to know one another by their jobs (for example, as "the doctor" or "the bank teller") rather than by their kinship group or hometown. People looked on most others simply as strangers. The face-to-face communication of the village eventually was replaced by the mass media—newspapers, radio, television, and more recently, computer networks—furthering the process of social atomization. Large organizations steadily assumed more and more responsibility for seeing to the daily tasks that had once been carried out by family, friends, and neighbors; public education drew more and more people to schools; police, lawyers, and courts supervised a formal criminal justice system. Even charity became the work not of family members and neighbors but of faceless bureaucrats working for various social welfare agencies.

Geographic mobility and exposure to diverse ways of life erode traditional values. People become more tolerant of social diversity, defending individual rights and freedom of choice. Treating people differently—based on their race, sex, or religion—comes to be defined as backward and unjust. In the process, minorities at the margin of society acquire greater power and broader participation in public life.

Greater personal freedom permits the development of more subcultures. At the same time, the mass media foster a national culture that washes over traditional differences that set off one region from another. As one analyst put it, "Even in Baton Rouge, La., the local kids don't say 'y'all' anymore; they say 'you guys' just like on TV" (Gibbs, 2000:42). Yet mass-society theorists fear that transforming people of various backgrounds into a generic mass may end up dehumanizing everyone.

The Ever-Expanding State

In the small-scale, preindustrial societies of Europe, government amounted to little more than a local noble. A royal family formally reigned over an entire nation, but without efficient transportation or communication, the power of even absolute monarchs fell far short of the power wielded by today's political leaders.

As technological innovation allowed government to expand, the centralized state grew in size and importance. At the time the United States gained independence from Great Britain, the federal government was

a tiny organization whose prime function was national defense. Since then, government has entered more and more areas of social life: schooling the population, regulating wages and working conditions, establishing standards for products of all sorts, and offering financial assistance to the ill and the unemployed. To pay for such programs, taxes have soared: Today's average worker labors five months each year to pay for the broad array of services that government provides.

In a mass society, power resides in large bureaucracies, leaving people in local communities little control over their lives. For example, state officials mandate that local schools must have a standardized educational program, local products must be government certified, and every citizen must maintain extensive tax records. Although such regulations may protect people and advance social equality, they also force us to deal more and more with nameless officials in distant and often unresponsive bureaucracies, and they undermine the autonomy of families and neighborhoods.

Critical evaluation. The theory of mass society concedes that the transformation of small communities has positive aspects but only at the cost of losing at least some of our cultural heritage. Modern societies increase individual rights, tolerate greater social differences, and raise standards of living (Inglehart & Baker, 2000). But they are prone to what Weber feared most—excessive bureaucracy—as well as Tönnies's self-centeredness and Durkheim's anomie. Their size, complexity, and tolerance of diversity all but doom traditional values and family patterns, leaving individuals isolated, powerless, and materialistic. As Chapter 17 ("Politics and Government") noted, voter apathy is a serious problem in the United States. But should we be surprised that people in vast, impersonal societies think no one person can make a difference?

Critics contend that mass-society theory romanticizes the past. They remind us that many people in small towns were eager to set out for the excitement and higher standard of living found in cities. Moreover, mass-society theory ignores problems of social inequality. Critics say this theory attracts social and economic conservatives who defend conventional morality and are indifferent to the historical plight of women and other minorities.

SOCIAL-CONFLICT THEORY: MODERNITY AS CLASS SOCIETY

The second interpretation of modernity derives largely from the ideas of Karl Marx. From a social-conflict

Many people marveled at the industrial technology that was changing the world a century ago. But some critics pointed out that the social consequences of the Industrial Revolution were not all positive. The painting Trabajadores *(Workers) by Mirta Cerra portrays the exhausting and mind-numbing routines of manual workers.*

Mirta Cerra (1904–1986), *Trabajadores*, oil on canvas laid down on panel, 46 × 62 in. (107.3 × 157.5 cm). © Christie's Images.

perspective, modernity takes the form of a **class society,** *a capitalist society with pronounced social stratification.* That is, while agreeing that modern societies have expanded to a mass scale, this approach views the heart of modernization as an expanding capitalist economy, rife with inequality (Miliband, 1969; Habermas, 1970; Polenberg, 1980; Blumberg, 1981; Harrington, 1984).

Capitalism

Class-society theory follows Marx in claiming that the increasing scale of social life in modern society results from the insatiable appetite of capitalism. Because a capitalist economy pursues ever-greater profits, both production and consumption steadily increase.

According to Marx, capitalism rests on "naked self-interest" (Marx & Engels, 1972:337; orig. 1848). This self-centeredness erodes the social ties that once cemented small communities. Capitalism also treats people as commodities: a source of labor and a market for capitalist products.

Capitalism supports science not just as the key to greater productivity but as an ideology that justifies the status quo. That is, modern societies encourage people to view human well-being as a *technical* puzzle to be solved by engineers and other experts rather than as a moral issue to be realized through the pursuit of *social* justice (Habermas, 1970). For example, a capitalist culture seeks to improve health through scientific medicine rather than by eliminating poverty, which threatens many people's health.

Business also raises the banner of scientific logic, trying to increase profits through greater efficiency. As Chapter 16 ("The Economy and Work") explains, today's capitalist corporations are enormous and control unimaginable wealth as a result of "going global" and becoming multinationals. From the class-society point of view, then, the expanding scale of life is less a function of *Gesellschaft* than the inevitable and destructive consequence of capitalism.

Persistent Inequality

Modernity has gradually worn away the rigid categories that set nobles apart from commoners in preindustrial societies. But class-society theory maintains that elites persist, albeit now as capitalist millionaires rather than nobles born to wealth and power. In the United States, we may have no hereditary monarchy, but the richest 5 percent of the population nevertheless controls about 60 percent of all privately held property.

What of the state? Mass-society theorists contend that the state works to increase equality and combat social problems. Marx was skeptical that the state could accomplish more than minor reforms because, as he saw it, the real power lies in the hands of capitalists who control the economy. Other class-society theorists add that to the extent that working people and minorities have greater political rights and enjoy a higher standard of living today, these changes are the fruit of political struggle, not expressions of government goodwill. In

Q: "We know that we are in motion but do not know where we are going, and hence cannot predict the values of our children." Allen Wheelis (1958:23)

Q: "Identity is a coherent sense of self. It depends upon the awareness that one's endeavors and one's life make sense, that they are meaningful in the context in which life is lived. It depends also upon stable values, and upon the conviction that one's actions and values

are harmoniously related. It is a sense of wholeness, of integration, of knowing what is right and what is wrong and of being able to choose." Allen Wheelis (1958:18)

NOTE: Following Wheelis's argument, we might say that conformity in traditional societies reflects unchanging morality; what we call morality in modern societies is more a matter of conformity to changing public opinion.

short, they conclude, despite our pretensions of democracy, most people are all but powerless in the face of wealthy elites.

Critical evaluation. Table 24–3 summarizes the interpretations of modernity offered by mass-society theory and class-society theory. Whereas the former focuses on the increasing scale of life and the growth of government, the latter stresses the expansion of capitalism and the persistence of inequality.

Class-society theory also dismisses Durkheim's argument that people in modern societies suffer from anomie, claiming instead that they suffer from alienation and powerlessness. Not surprisingly, then, the class-society interpretation of modernity enjoys widespread support among liberals (and radicals) who favor greater equality and call for extensive regulation (or abolition) of the capitalist marketplace.

A basic criticism of class-society theory is that it overlooks the many ways in which equality in modern societies has increased. For example, discrimination based on race, ethnicity, and gender is now illegal and widely regarded as a social problem. Tolerance for people with same-sex orientation has increased dramatically, and people with disabilities have more rights and opportunities than ever before. It is true that differences in income remain large; however, most people in the United States favor unequal rewards, at least insofar as they reflect differences in personal talent and effort.

Moreover, few observers think a centralized economy would cure the ills of modernity in light of socialism's failure to generate a high overall standard of living. Many other problems in the United States—from unemployment, homelessness, and industrial pollution to unresponsive government—are also found in socialist nations such as the former Soviet Union.

MODERNITY AND THE INDIVIDUAL

Both mass- and class-society theories look at the broad societal changes that have taken place since the Industrial Revolution. But from these macro-level approaches we can also draw micro-level insights into how modernity shapes individual lives.

Mass Society: Problems of Identity

Modernity liberated individuals from small, tightly knit communities of the past. Most people in modern societies, therefore, have the privacy and freedom to express their individuality. However, mass-society theory suggests that so much social diversity, widespread

TABLE 24–3 Two Interpretations of Modernity: A Summary		
	Mass Society	Class Society
Process of Modernization	Industrialization; growth of bureaucracy	Rise of capitalism
Effects of Modernization	Increasing scale of life; rise of the state and other formal organizations	Expansion of the capitalist economy; persistence of social inequality

isolation, and rapid social change make it difficult to establish a coherent identity (Wheelis, 1958; Riesman, 1970; Berger, Berger, & Kellner, 1974).

Chapter 5 ("Socialization") explained that a person's personality is largely a product of social experience. The small, homogeneous, and slowly changing societies of the past provided a firm, if narrow, foundation for building a meaningful identity. Even today, the Amish communities that flourish in the United States and Canada teach young men and women "correct" ways to think and behave. Not everyone born into an Amish community can tolerate strict demands for conformity, but most members establish a well-integrated and satisfying personal identity (cf. Hostetler, 1980; Kraybill & Olshan, 1994).

Mass societies are quite another story. Socially diverse and rapidly changing, they offer only shifting sands on which to build a personal identity. Left to make many life decisions on our own, many people—especially those with greater affluence and thus more freedom—face a bewildering range of options. Choice has little value without standards to guide our selections, and in a tolerant mass society, people may find one path no more compelling than the next. Not surprisingly, many people shuttle from one identity to another, changing their lifestyles, relationships, and even religions in search of an elusive "true self." Beset by the widespread "relativism" of modern societies, people without a moral compass lack the security and certainty once provided by tradition.

To David Riesman (1970; orig. 1950), modernization brings changes in **social character,** *personality patterns common to members of a particular society.* Preindustrial societies foster what Riesman calls **tradition-directedness,** *rigid conformity to time-honored ways of living.* Members of traditional societies model their lives on those of their ancestors, so that "living a good

NOTE: David Reisman used the term "social character" to mean "mode of conformity." Tradition direction is conformity based on categorical memberships; inner direction (not addressed in this chapter) is conformity to inwardly held values in the absence of strong tradition; other direction is conformity to one's contemporaries.
NOTE: The "lonely crowd" thesis includes the argument that the family has lost its socialization function to schools, various specialists, and the mass media, prompting more other-direction in children.
DISCUSS: Most psychiatrists and psychologists agree that our society is witnessing a rise in mild personality disorders. Do you think that the weaker moral structure of today's society, which fails to provide the guidance and support found in earlier times, plays a part in this rise?

Mass-society theory attributes feelings of anxiety, isolation, and lack of meaning in the modern world to rapid social change that washes away tradition. Edvard Munch captured this vision of modern emptiness in his painting The Scream *(left). Class-society theory, by contrast, ties such feelings to social inequality, by which some categories of people are made into second-class citizens (or not made citizens at all). Paul Marcus portrays modern injustice in the painting* Crossing the Rio Grande *(right).*

Edvard Munch, *The Scream,* Oslo, National Gallery, Scala/Art Resource, NY. © 1998 Artists Rights Society (ARS), NY/ADAGP, Paris. © Paul Marcus, *Crossing the Rio Grande,* 1999, oil painting on canvas, 63 × 72 in. Studio SPM Inc.

life" amounts to "doing what our people have always done."

Tradition-directedness corresponds to Tönnies's *Gemeinschaft* and Durkheim's mechanical solidarity. Culturally conservative, tradition-directed people think and act alike. Unlike the conformity sometimes found in modern societies, the uniformity of tradition-directedness is not an effort to mimic one another. Instead, people are alike because they all draw on the same solid cultural foundation. Amish women and men exemplify tradition-directedness; in Amish culture, tradition ties everyone to ancestors and descendants in an unbroken chain of righteous living.

Members of diverse and rapidly changing societies consider a tradition-directed personality deviant because it seems so rigid. Modern people prize personal flexibility and sensitivity to others, what Riesman describes as **other-directedness,** *a receptiveness to the latest trends and fashions, often expressed by imitating others.* Because their socialization occurs in societies that are constantly in flux, other-directed people develop fluid identities marked by superficiality, inconsistency, and change. They try on different "selves," almost like new pieces of clothing. They seek out role models, try to maintain self-esteem, and engage in varied performances as they move from setting to setting (Goffman, 1959). In a traditional society, such "shiftiness" makes a person untrustworthy, but in a changing, modern society, the chameleon-like ability to fit in virtually anywhere is very useful.

In societies that value the up-to-date rather than the traditional, people anxiously solicit the approval of others, looking to members of their own generation rather than to elders as significant role models. Peer pressure can be irresistible to people with no enduring standards to guide them. Our society urges individuals to be true to themselves. But when social surroundings change so rapidly, how can people develop the self to which they should be true? This problem lies at the root of the identity crisis so widespread in industrial societies today. "Who am I?" is a nagging question that many of us struggle to answer. In truth, this problem is not so much us as the society in which we live, that is, the inherent instability of modern mass society.

GLOBAL: "Honor" in medieval Europe, "wa" in Japan, and "dharma" in India all express the power of the community to direct the thoughts and behavior of individuals. With modernization, all have eroded in favor of "dignity," "choice," and "individual rights."
DISCUSS: Honor is a matter of specific status; dignity is generically human. One loses honor by violating normative roles; one loses dignity by giving up (or giving away) autonomy. Discuss the differences between "dying with honor" and "dying with dignity."
NOTE: Another implication of the loss of traditional honor in modern societies is the decline of public civility.
Q: "I never met a man I didn't like." Will Rogers, speaking as the typical other-directed American. A more recent study of other-direction is Woody Allen's Zelig, featuring a character whose personality is determined by his surroundings.

Class Society: Problems of Powerlessness

Class-society theory paints a different picture of modernity's effects on individuals. This approach maintains that persistent social inequality undermines modern society's promise of individual freedom. For some, modernity serves up great privilege, but for many, everyday life means coping with economic uncertainty and a gnawing sense of powerlessness (Newman, 1993).

For minorities, the problem of relative disadvantage looms even larger. Similarly, although women enjoy increasing participation in modern societies, they continue to run up against traditional barriers of sexism. In short, this approach rejects mass-society theory's claim that people suffer from too much freedom. Instead, class-society theory holds that our society still denies a majority of people full participation in social life.

On a global scale, as Chapter 12 ("Global Stratification") explained, the expanding scope of world capitalism has placed a large part of the earth's population in the shadow of multinational corporations. As a result, about two-thirds of the world's income is concentrated in the high-income nations where only 18 percent of its people live. Is it any wonder, class-society theorists ask, that people in poor nations seek greater power to shape their own lives?

The problem of widespread powerlessness led Herbert Marcuse (1964) to challenge Max Weber's statement that modern society is rational. Marcuse condemned modern society as irrational for failing to meet the needs of so many people. Although modern capitalist societies produce unparalleled wealth, poverty remains the daily plight of more than a billion people. Moreover, Marcuse argues, advancing technology reduces people's control over their own lives. High technology confers great power on a core of specialists—not the majority of people—who control events and dominate the public agenda, whether the issue is computing, energy production, or health care. Countering the common view that technology *solves* the world's problems, Marcuse believed that science actually *causes* them. In sum, class-society theory claims that people suffer because modern, scientific societies concentrate both wealth and power in the hands of a privileged few.

MODERNITY AND PROGRESS

In modern societies, most people expect—and applaud—social change. We link modernity to the idea

We tend to view tradition and modernity as opposites—the more of one found in a society, the less there is of the other. In reality, these concepts can operate independently, as we see in Japan, where traditional and modern aspects of life are often seen side by side.

of *progress* (from Latin, meaning "moving forward"), a state of continual improvement. At the same time, we see stability as stagnation.

Given our bias in favor of change, members of our society tend to see traditional cultures as backward. But change, particularly toward material affluence, is a mixed blessing. As the box shows, social change is too complex simply to equate with progress.

Even getting rich has its advantages and disadvantages, as the case of the Kaiapo shows. Historically, among people in the United States, a rising standard of living made lives longer and, in a material sense, more comfortable. At the same time, many people wonder whether today's routines are too stressful, with families often having little time for relaxation or simply spending time together.

RESOURCE: Marlise Simons describes the Kaiapo in more detail in a cross-cultural selection in the Macionis and Benokraitis reader, *Seeing Ourselves.*

NOTE: The saying "You can't argue with progress" suggests the inevitable and linear nature of change as our culture sees it.

NOTE: Humorist Mark Twain claimed the opposite of progress was Congress.

Q: "Man will never fly. Not in a thousand years." Wilbur Wright (1901)

Q: "The major advances in civilization are processes that all but wreck the societies in which they occur." Alfred North Whitehead

NOTE: Maureen T. Hallinan (1997) suggests thinking about social change without assuming that trends are continuous and linear in an effort to better explain "dramatic social upheavals."

GLOBAL SOCIOLOGY

Does "Modern" Mean "Progress"? The Case of Brazil's Kaiapo

The firelight flickers in the gathering darkness. Chief Kanhonk sits, as he has done at the end of the day for many years, ready to begin an evening of animated talk and storytelling (Simons, 2001). This is the hour when the Kaiapo, a small society in Brazil's lush Amazon region, celebrate their heritage. Because the Kaiapo are a traditional people with no written language, the elders rely on evenings by the fire to pass along their culture to their children and grandchildren. In the past, evenings like this have been filled with tales of brave Kaiapo warriors fighting off Portuguese traders in pursuit of slaves and gold.

But as the minutes pass, only a few older villagers assemble for the evening ritual. "It is the Big Ghost," one man grumbles, explaining the poor turnout. The "Big Ghost" has indeed descended upon them; its bluish glow spills from windows throughout the village. The Kaiapo children—and many adults as well—are watching sitcoms on television. The installation of a satellite dish in the village several years ago has had consequences far

greater than anyone imagined. In the end, what their enemies failed to do with guns, the Kaiapo may well do to themselves with prime-time programming.

The Kaiapo are among the 230,000 native peoples who inhabit Brazil. They stand out because of their striking body paint and ornate ceremonial dress. During the 1980s, they became rich from gold mining and harvesting mahogany trees. Now they must decide whether their newfound fortune is a blessing or a curse.

To some, affluence means the opportunity to learn about the outside world through travel and television. Others, such as Chief Kanhonk, are not so sure. Sitting by the fire, he thinks aloud, "I have been saying that people

must buy useful things like knives and fishing hooks. Television does not fill the stomach. It only shows our children and grandchildren white people's things." Bebtopup, the oldest priest, nods in agreement: "The night is the time the old people teach the young people. Television has stolen the night" (Simons, 2001:497).

The Kaiapo story shows us that change is not a simple path toward "progress." The Kaiapo are moving toward modernity, but this process will have both positive and negative consequences. On one hand, they now enjoy a higher standard of living with better shelter, more clothing, and new technology such as television to connect to the larger world. On the other hand, this new affluence has greatly weakened Kaiapo traditions, so that many of their number now wonder—and with good reason—who or what they have become. The drama of the Kaiapo is being played out around the world as more and more traditional cultures are lured away from their heritage by the affluence and materialism of rich societies.

For more on Brazil's Kaiapo, go to http://www.uwgb.edu/galta/mrr/kayapo/page7.htm

Source: Based on Simons (2001).

Science also has its pluses and minuses. A recent survey showed that people in the United States have great confidence—more than those in most other societies—that science improves our lives (Inglehart et al., 2000). But surveys also show that many adults in the United States feel that science "makes our way of life change too fast" (NORC, 2001:365).

New technology has always sparked controversy. A century ago, the introduction of automobiles and

telephones allowed more rapid transportation and more efficient communication. But at the same time, such technology weakened traditional attachments to hometowns and even to families. Today, people might wonder whether computer technology will do the same thing: give us access to people around the world but disconnect us from the community right outside our doors, providing more information than ever before but, in the process, threatening personal privacy.

Q: "'Postmodernism' usually refers to a certain constellation of styles and tones in cultural works: pastiche; blankness; a sense of exhaustion; a mixture of levels, forms, styles; a relish for copies and repetitions; a knowingness that dissolves commitment into irony; acute self-consciousness about the constructed nature of the work; pleasure in the play of surfaces; a rejection of history." Todd Gitlin ("Postmodernism: Roots and Politics," *Dissent*, Winter 1989:100-8)

NOTE: Postmodernism recognizes that, with the onset of the Information Revolution, ideas are gaining in importance as things decline in significance (New Age thinking and fundamentalist religious revivals are examples). Such a change prompts us to look critically at the emphasis on material possessions that came with modern, industrial culture.

Q: "Humility is the final achievement." Anonymous

In short, we all realize that social change comes faster all the time, but we may disagree about whether a particular change is progress or a step backwards.

MODERNITY: GLOBAL VARIATION

`October 1, Kobe, Japan.` Riding the computer-controlled monorail high above the streets of Kobe or the 200-mile-per-hour bullet train to Tokyo, we see Japan as the high-technology society of the future. Yet Japan remains strikingly traditional in other respects: Few corporate executives and almost no senior politicians are women; young people still accord their elders great respect; and public orderliness contrasts with the turmoil of U.S. cities.

Japan is a nation at once traditional and modern. This contradiction reminds us that although it is useful to contrast traditional and modern societies, the old and the new often coexist in unexpected ways. In the People's Republic of China, ancient Confucian principles are mixed with contemporary socialist thinking. Similarly, in Mexico and much of Latin America, people observe centuries-old Christian rituals even as they struggle to move ahead economically. In short, combinations of traditional and modern are far from unusual—indeed, they are found throughout the world.

POSTMODERNITY

If modernity was the product of the Industrial Revolution, is the Information Revolution creating a postmodern era? A number of scholars think so, and use the term **postmodernity** to refer to *social patterns characteristic of postindustrial societies.*

Precisely what postmodernism is remains a matter of debate. The term has been used for decades in literary, philosophical, and even architectural circles. It moved into sociology on a wave of social criticism that has been building since the spread of left-leaning politics in the 1960s. Although there are many variants of postmodern thinking, all share the following five themes (Bernstein, 1992; Borgmann, 1992; Crook, Pakulski, & Waters, 1992; Hall & Neitz, 1993; Inglehart, 1997; Rudel & Gerson, 1999):

1. **In important respects, modernity has failed.** The promise of modernity was a life free from want. As postmodernist critics see it, however, the twentieth century was unsuccessful in solving social problems such as poverty because many people still lack financial security.

2. **The bright light of "progress" is fading.** Modern people look to the future, expecting that their lives will improve in significant ways. Members (even leaders) of postmodern societies, however, are less confident about what the future holds. Furthermore, the buoyant optimism that carried society into the modern era more than a century ago has given way to stark pessimism; most U.S. adults believe that life is getting worse (NORC, 2001:210).

3. **Science no longer holds the answers.** The defining trait of the modern era was a scientific outlook and a confident belief that technology would make life better. But postmodern critics contend that science has not solved many old problems (such as poor health) and has even created new problems (such as environmental degradation).

   More generally, postmodernist thinkers discredit science as a "metanarrative" that implies a singular truth. On the contrary, they maintain, objective reality and truth do not exist at all. Reality amounts to "social construction," they say; moreover, we can "deconstruct" science to see how it has been widely used for political purposes, especially by powerful segments of society.

4. **Cultural debates are intensifying.** Modernity was to be an era of individuality and tolerance. But it has fallen short here as well. Feminism points out that patriarchy still limits the lives of women, and multiculturalism seeks to empower minorities who remain at the margins of social life.

   Moreover, now that more people have all the material things they need, ideas are taking on more importance. Thus, postmodernity is also a postmaterialist era in which issues like social justice, the environment, and gay rights command more public attention.

5. **Social institutions are changing.** Just as industrialization brought sweeping transformation to social institutions, the rise of a postindustrial society is remaking society all over again. For example, just as the Industrial Revolution placed *material things* at the center of productive life, now the Information Revolution emphasizes *ideas.* Similarly, the postmodern family no longer conforms to any singular pattern; on the contrary, people are choosing between many new family forms.

CRITICAL THINKING

Tracking Change: Is Life in the United States Getting Better or Worse?

We began this chapter with a look at what life was like in a large U.S. city in 1900, more than a century ago. It is easy to see that in many ways life is far better for us than it was for our grandparents and great-grandparents. In recent decades, however, not all indicators have been good.

Here is a look at some trends shaping the United States since 1970.

First, the good news: By some measures—shown in the first set of figures—life is clearly improving. Infant mortality has fallen steadily, meaning that fewer and fewer children die soon after birth. More people are reaching old age,

and after reaching sixty-five, they are living longer than ever. More good news: The poverty rate among the elderly is well below what it was in 1970. Schooling is another area of improvement: The share of people dropping out of high school is down, and the share completing college is up.

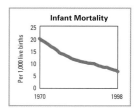

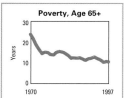
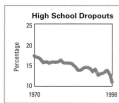

Second, some "no-news" results: A number of indicators show that life is about the same as it was in the 1970s. For

example, teenage drug use was about the same in 1996 as a generation before. Likewise, alcohol-related traffic deaths

show only a slight decline. Unemployment has had its ups and downs, but the overall level has stayed about the same.

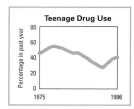
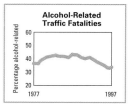
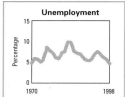

Critical evaluation. Analysts who claim that high-income societies are entering a postmodern era criticize modernity for failing to meet human needs. Yet few think that modernity has failed completely; after all, we have seen marked increases in longevity and living standards over the course of this century. Moreover, even if we accept postmodernist views that science is bankrupt and progress is a sham, what are the alternatives?

Finally, many voices offer very different understandings of recent social trends. The box provides one case in point.

LOOKING AHEAD: MODERNIZATION AND OUR GLOBAL FUTURE

In Chapter 1, we imagined the entire world reduced to a village of 1,000 people. About 175 residents of this "global village" come from high-income countries. At the same time, 200 people are so poor that their lives are at risk.

The tragic plight of the world's poor shows that some desperately needed change has not yet occurred. Chapter 12 ("Global Stratification") presented two

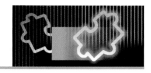

Finally, there was about the same amount of affordable housing in the United States in 1996 as there was in 1970.

Third, the bad news: By some measures, several having to do with children, the quality of life in the United States has fallen. The official rate of child abuse is up, as is the level of child poverty and the rate of suicide among youths. Although the level of violent crime fell through the 1990s, it is still above the 1970 level. Average weekly wages—one measure of economic security—show a downward trend, so that families have had to rely

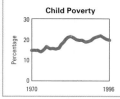

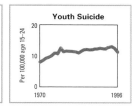

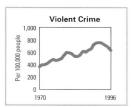

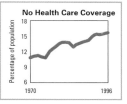

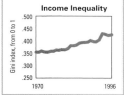

on two or more earners to maintain family income. The number of people without health insurance is also on the rise. Finally, economic inequality in this country has been increasing.

Overall, then, the evidence does not support any simple ideas about "progress over time." Social change has been—and probably will continue to be—a complex process that reflects the kinds of priorities we set for this nation as well as our will to achieve them.

What do you think?

1. *Based on material from earlier chapters, can you explain any of the trends shown here? Which ones?*

2. *Which of the trends do you find most important? Why?*

3. *On balance, do you think the quality of life in the United States is improving or not? Why?*

Source: Miringoff & Miringoff (1999).

competing views of why 1 billion people around the world are poor. *Modernization theory* claims that in the past the entire world was poor and that technological change, especially the Industrial Revolution, enhanced human productivity and raised living standards in some nations. From this point of view, the solution to global poverty is to promote technological development around the world.

For reasons suggested earlier, however, global modernization may be difficult. Recall that David Riesman portrayed preindustrial people as *tradition-directed*

and likely to resist change. So modernization theorists advocate that the world's rich societies help poor countries grow economically. Specifically, industrial nations should export technology to poor regions, welcome students from abroad, and provide foreign aid to stimulate economic growth.

The review of modernization theory in Chapter 12 points to some success with policies in Latin America and greater success in the small Asian countries of Taiwan, South Korea, Singapore, and Hong Kong. But jump-starting development in the poorest countries of

NOTE: For a summary of the proliferation of rights, look back at the box about the culture of victimization in Chapter 3.
DISCUSS: Etzioni maintains that U.S. moral revival is possible without the new puritanism of the right or the danger of totalitarianism from the left. Although he believes that family is vital, he supports women's equal access to the workplace. He also proposes that schools teach morality but with no indoctrination.

Q: Communitarians are "people committed to creating a new moral, social, and political order based on restored communities, without allowing puritanism or oppression." Amitai Etzioni
Q: Mahatma Gandhi notes seven great dangers to human virtue: wealth without work, pleasure without conscience, knowledge without character, business without ethics, science without humanity, religion without sacrifice, and politics without principle.

CONTROVERSY & DEBATE

Personal Freedom and Social Responsibility: Can We Have It Both Ways?

Shortly after midnight on a crisp March evening in 1964, a car pulled to a stop in the parking lot of a New York apartment complex. Kitty Genovese turned off the headlights, locked the doors of her vehicle, and headed across the blacktop toward the entrance to her building. Moments from safety, she was attacked by a man wielding a knife; as she shrieked in terror, he stabbed her again and again. Windows opened above as curious neighbors looked down for the cause of the commotion. But the attack continued for more than thirty minutes, until Genovese lay dead in the doorway. The police never identified her assailant, but they did discover a stunning fact: *Not one of dozens of neighbors who witnessed the attack on Kitty Genovese went to her aid or even called police.*

More than any other event in recent decades, the Genovese tragedy forced people to confront the question of what we owe others. Members of modern societies prize their individual rights and personal privacy, sometimes to the point of withdrawing from public responsibility and turning a cold shoulder to people in need. When a cry for help is met with indifference, have we pushed our modern idea of personal autonomy too far? In a cultural climate of expanding individual rights, can we keep a sense of human community?

These questions point up the tension between traditional and modern social systems, which we can see in the writings of all the sociologists discussed in this chapter. Tönnies, Durkheim, and others concluded that, in some respects, traditional community and modern individualism are at odds. That is, society can unite its members in a moral community but only to the extent that it limits their range of personal choice about how to live. In short, we value both community and autonomy, but we can't have it both ways.

In recent years, sociologist Amitai Etzioni (1993, 1996) has tried to strike a middle ground. The *communitarian movement* rests on the simple premise that "strong rights presume strong responsibilities." Or, put another way, an individual's pursuit of self-interest must be balanced by a commitment to the larger community.

As Etzioni sees it, modern people have become too concerned with individual rights. That is, people expect the system to work for them, but they are reluctant to support the system. For example, although we believe in the principle of trial by a jury of one's peers, fewer and fewer people today are willing to perform jury duty; similarly, the public is quick to accept government services but reluctant to pay for these services with taxes.

---

the world poses greater challenges. And even where dramatic change has occurred, modernization entails a tradeoff. Traditional people, such as Brazil's Kaiapo, may acquire wealth through economic development, but they lose their cultural identity and values as they are drawn into global "McCulture," which is based on Western materialism, pop music, trendy clothes, and fast food. One Brazilian anthropologist expressed hope about the future of the Kaiapo: "At least they quickly understood the consequences of watching television. . . . Now [they] can make a choice" (Simons, 2001:497).

But not everyone thinks that modernization is really an option. According to a second approach to global stratification, *dependency theory*, today's poor societies have little ability to modernize, even if they want to. From this point of view, the major barrier to economic development is not traditionalism but the global domination of rich, capitalist societies. Initially, domination took the form of colonialism, whereby European societies seized much of Latin America, Africa, and Asia. Trading relationships soon enriched England, Spain, and other colonial powers, and their colonies became poorer and poorer. Almost all societies that were colonized are now politically independent, but colonial-style ties continue in the form of multinational corporations operating throughout the world.

In effect, dependency theory asserts that rich nations achieved their modernization at the expense of poor ones, plundering poor nations' natural resources

NOTE: After the Genovese murder, the *New York Times* asked, "Does residence in a great city destroy all sense of personal responsibility for one's neighbors?"

DISCUSS: What do changes in popular magazines suggest about social change? In the 1950s, *Life* was big; by 1974, *People* was out; by 1979, *Self* was launched; in 1986, *Child.* Does this trend show a narrowing of our interests?

Q: "Change is one thing, progress is another. Change is scientific; progress is ethical; change is indubitable, whereas progress is a matter of controversy." Bertrand Russell

Q: "A man cannot get rich if he takes care of his family." Navaho saying

Q: "And, in the end, the love you take is equal to the love you make." The Beatles

Specifically, the communitarians advance four proposals to balance individual rights and public responsibilities. First, our society should halt the expanding "culture of rights" by which people put their own interests ahead of social responsibility (after all, nothing in the Constitution allows us to do whatever we want to). Second, communitarians remind us, all rights involve responsibilities (we cannot simply take from society without giving something back). Third, there are certain responsibilities that no one is free to ignore (such as upholding the law and protecting the natural environment). And, fourth, defending some community interests may require limiting individual rights (for example, protecting public safety might mean subjecting workers to drug tests).

The communitarian movement appeals to many people who, along with Etzioni, seek to balance personal freedom with social responsibility. But critics have attacked this initiative from both sides of the political spectrum. To those on the left, problems such as voter apathy and street crime cannot be solved with some vague notion of "social reintegration." Instead, we need expanded government programs to ensure equality in U.S. society. Specifically, these critics say, we must curb the political influence of the rich and actively combat racism and sexism.

Conservatives on the political right also find fault with Etzioni's proposals, but for different reasons (cf. Pearson, 1995). To these critics, the communitarian movement amounts to little more than a rerun of the 1960s leftist agenda. That is, the communitarian vision of a good society favors liberal goals (such as protecting the environment) but ignores conservative goals such as allowing prayer in school or restoring the strength of traditional families. Moreover, conservatives ask whether a free society should permit the kind of social engineering that Etzioni advocates to build social responsibility (such as institutionalizing antiprejudice programs in schools and requiring people to perform a year of national service).

Perhaps, as Etzioni himself has suggested, the fact that both the left and the right find fault with his views shows that he has found a moderate, sensible answer to a serious problem. But it may also be that, in a society as diverse as the United States, people will not readily agree on what they owe to themselves—or each other.

Continue the debate . . .

1. *Have you ever failed to come to the aid of someone in need or danger? Why?*

2. *President Kennedy admonished us, "Ask not what your country can do for you; ask what you can do for your country." Do you think people today support this idea? What makes you think so?*

3. *Do you agree or disagree that our society needs to balance rights with more responsibility? Explain your position.*

and exploiting their human labor. Even today, the world's poorest countries remain locked in a disadvantageous economic relationship with rich nations, dependent on wealthy countries to buy their raw materials and in return provide them with whatever manufactured products they can afford. Overall, dependency theorists conclude, ties with rich societies only perpetuate current patterns of global inequality.

Whichever approach one finds more convincing, we can no longer isolate change in the United States from change in the rest of the world. At the beginning of the twentieth century, most people in today's high-income countries lived in small settlements with limited awareness of the larger world. Now, early in the twenty-first century, the entire world has become one huge village because the lives of all people are increasingly linked.

The last century witnessed unprecedented human achievement. Yet solutions to many problems of human existence—including finding meaning in life, resolving conflicts between nations, and eradicating poverty—have eluded us. To this list of pressing matters new concerns have been added, such as controlling population growth and establishing a sustainable society by living in harmony with the natural environment. In the next hundred years, we must be prepared to tackle such problems with imagination, compassion, and determination. Our unprecedented understanding of human society gives us reason to look to the task ahead with optimism.

CHAPTER 24 Social Change: Traditional, Modern, and Postmodern Societies **645**

Q: "Let us not look backward in anger or forward in fear, but around in awareness." James Thurber

Q: Somewhere ages and ages hence:
 Two roads diverged in a wood, and I—
 I took the one less traveled by,
 And that has made all the difffference.
 Robert Frost

CTQ1: The four theorists agreed that modernity is distinctive. Tönnies envisioned modernity as *Gesellschaft*, Durkheim as organic solidarity marked by anomie, Weber as a rational worldview marked by alienation (excessive formalization), Marx as capitalism marked by alienation (powerlessness).

Q: "Nobody makes a greater mistake than he who does nothing because he could only do a little." Edmund Burke

SUMMARY

1. Every society changes continuously, although at varying speeds. Social change often generates controversy.

2. Social change results from invention, discovery, and diffusion, as well as social conflict.

3. Modernity refers to the social consequences of industrialization, which, according to Peter Berger, include the erosion of traditional communities, expanding personal choice, increasingly diverse beliefs, and a keen awareness of the future.

4. Ferdinand Tönnies described modernization as the transition from *Gemeinschaft* to *Gesellschaft*, which signifies the progressive loss of community amid growing individualism.

5. Emile Durkheim saw modernization as a function of a society's expanding division of labor. Mechanical solidarity, based on shared activities and beliefs, gradually gives way to organic solidarity, in which specialization makes people interdependent.

6. According to Max Weber, modernity replaces tradition with a rational worldview. Weber feared the dehumanizing effects of rational organization.

7. Karl Marx saw modernity as the triumph of capitalism over feudalism. Viewing capitalist societies as fraught with social conflict, Marx advocated revolutionary change to achieve a more egalitarian, socialist society.

8. According to mass-society theory, modernity increases the scale of life, enlarging the role of government and other formal organizations in carrying out tasks previously performed by family members and neighbors. Cultural diversity and rapid social change make it difficult for people in modern societies to develop stable identities and to find meaning in their lives.

9. Class-society theory states that capitalism is central to Western modernization. This approach charges that by concentrating wealth in the hands of a few, capitalism generates widespread feelings of powerlessness.

10. Social change is too complex and controversial simply to be equated with social progress.

11. "Postmodernity" refers to cultural traits of postindustrial societies. Postmodern criticism of society centers on the failure of modernity, and specifically science, to fulfill its promise of prosperity and well-being.

12. In a global context, modernization theory links global poverty to the power of tradition. Therefore, some modernization theorists advocate that rich societies intervene to stimulate economic development in poor nations.

13. Dependency theory explains global poverty as the product of the world economic system. The operation of multinational corporations ensures that poor nations will remain economically dependent on rich nations.

KEY CONCEPTS

social change (p. 626) the transformation of culture and social institutions over time

modernity (p. 629) social patterns resulting from industrialization

modernization (p. 629) the process of social change begun by industrialization

mass society (p. 633) a society in which industry and bureaucracy have eroded traditional social ties

class society (p. 636) a capitalist society with pronounced social stratification

social character (p. 637) personality patterns common to members of a particular society

tradition-directedness (p. 637) rigid conformity to time-honored ways of living

other-directedness (p. 638) a receptiveness to the latest trends and fashions, often expressed by imitating others

postmodernity (p. 641) social patterns characteristic of postindustrial societies

CTQ2: Large-scale, impersonal living is the essence of mass society; trace this idea in the work of Tönnies, Durkheim, and Weber. Marked inequality is the basis of a class society; see this idea in the work of Marx and later neo-Marxist thinkers.
CTQ3: Durkheim's *anomie* should be pronounced among affluent, "free" people. Marx's *alienation* should be pronounced among poor,

powerless people. (Weber's alienation, by contrast, should be found among everyone.)
CTQ4: Postmodern society, roughly synonymous with postindustrial society, refers to the social and cultural traits that accompany a transformation from an industrial to an information-based economy. See the discussion near the end of this chapter.

CRITICAL-THINKING QUESTIONS

1. How well do you think Tönnies, Durkheim, Weber, and Marx predicted the character of modern society? How are their visions of modernity the same? How do they differ?

2. What traits lead some to call the United States a "mass society"? Why do other analysts describe the United States as a "class society"?

3. What is the difference between *anomie* (a trait of mass society) and *alienation* (a characteristic of class society)? In which categories of the U.S. population would you expect each to be pronounced?

4. Why do some analysts see the United States as a postmodern society? Do you agree? Why or why not?

APPLICATIONS AND EXERCISES

1. Do you have an elderly relative or friend? Most older people will be happy to tell you about the social changes they have seen in their lifetimes.

2. Ask people in your class or your friends to make five predictions about U.S. society in the year 2050, when today's twenty-year-olds will be senior citizens. Compare notes: On what issues is there agreement?

3. Has the rate of social change been increasing? Do some research about inventions over time and see for yourself. For example, consider modes of travel, including walking, riding animals, trains, cars, airplanes,

and rockets in space. The first two characterized society for tens of thousands of years; the last four emerged in barely two centuries.

4. Packaged in the back of this new textbook is an interactive CD-ROM that offers a variety of study and review materials intended to help you better understand the material covered in this chapter. For this chapter, the CD-ROM contains an author's tip video, Real Life Sociology videos, other relevant audio and video, interactive map animations, audio journal entries from the author, Web links, and much more.

 ## SITES TO SEE

http://www.prenhall.com/macionis

Visit the interactive *Companion Website*™ that accompanies this text. Begin by clicking on the cover of your book. You will find a chapter-by-chapter study guide, practice tests, and a significant portion of the text for on-line review, as well as many suggested Web links.

http://www.gwu.edu/~ccps/

This Web site describes the Communitarian Network, including its goals and how it proposes to achieve them.

http://www.utoronto.ca/utopia/

Deliberate change sometimes is inspired by visions of

utopia, ideal societies that exist nowhere. Read about the Society for Utopian Studies at this Web site.

http://www.TheSociologyPage.com or http://www.macionis.com

Finally, on a personal note, I hope this book has helped you and will be a useful resource for courses later on. Please visit my Web page, and send an e-mail message (macionis@kenyon.edu) with your thoughts and suggestions. And, yes, I *will* write back!

John J. Macionis

 INVESTIGATE WITH CONTENTSELECT

Follow the instructions found on page 23 of this textbook to enter this chapter of the book's *Companion Website*™. Once in the chapter, click on the ContentSelect icon at the bottom left of your screen and enter your personal

User ID and Password. Enter keywords such as "social change," "mass society," and "postmodernity," and the search engine will help you become an effective researcher.

cyber.scope

NEW INFORMATION TECHNOLOGY AND SOCIAL CHANGE

Chapter 3 ("Culture") presented William Ogburn's (1964) concept of *cultural lag*, the pattern by which some elements of culture change faster than others. Usually, Ogburn explained, technology changes quickly; getting used to new technology, on the other hand, takes people much longer. This cultural pattern of lagging behind probably explains why we use old terminology to describe new developments, such as measuring the "horsepower" of gasoline engines or, more recently, exploring the "superhighway" of cyberspace.

The fact that developments in science and technology outpace our ability to comprehend them makes many people uneasy about social change. In a national survey, about 40 percent of U.S. adults agreed with the statement, "One trouble with science is that it makes our way of life change too fast" (NORC, 2001:365). But the majority of people are more optimistic, expecting that new technology will improve our lives. This final cyber.scope highlights how the age of computers is altering the shape of cities, forming new kinds of human communities, and bringing people together in new ways to form social movements.

The New Shape of Cities

As Chapter 22 ("Population, Urbanization, and Environment") explains, the metropolis stands as the greatest monument to the industrial era. A century ago, factories full of huge machines offered jobs that drew people from across the countryside to form cities of unprecedented size. Industrial

metropolises such as New York, Chicago, Philadelphia, and Detroit churned with activity, and new buildings of mortar, steel, and glass stretched skyward.

These cities became busier and denser as industrial technology centralized people. Businesses fused together into a central business district, where executives and managers could easily establish face-to-face communication. Factories were situated together near rivers and railroads, which brought them fuel and raw materials and took away their finished products.

The industrial cities of the United States reached their peak populations about 1950, just as scientists were building their first computers. Computer technology helped push the economy from industry to service and information work, and this shift spurred the decentralization of cities. Population began radiating farther away from the central city so that, by 1970, most city dwellers were actually living in suburbs miles from the central city. Businesses followed suit, deserting the downtowns for industrial parks and outlying shopping malls. Today's urban sprawl is the result.

Why have the old central cities lost much of their attraction? One reason is that in the business world, having a central city address is no longer so important. That is, with new information technology, people can communicate efficiently without working in the same area. Thus, today's cities are growing "out" more than they are growing "up." The urban scene early in the twenty-first century shows steady central city populations surrounded

by swelling suburbs and rapidly growing "edge cities"—clusters of office buildings, shopping malls, hotels, and entertainment complexes miles from the old "downtowns."

Change in the shape of cities highlights, once again, one of the most important consequences of new information technology: Physical distance no longer separates people the way it used to. Thus, people who work together do not need to share an office building or even live in the same city. The other side of the same coin is that in the cyber-age, we may not pay very much attention to the people who are—physically speaking—all around us. In short, new information technology is forming new kinds of human communities while eroding older ones.

The Rise of Virtual Communities

Consider some dramatic changes taking place at Dartmouth College, in Hanover, New Hampshire, one of the country's most academically competitive schools and a college at the forefront of the Information Revolution. Since the college wired all dormitories—sometimes called the "one plug per pillow" model—life on campus has not been the same. In the cyber-age, students such as Arthur Desrosiers have discovered that they have fewer and fewer reasons to leave their rooms. Desrosiers, a Dartmouth sophomore, relies on his computer to browse the college library, write papers, ask questions of his professors, send notes to his girlfriend, keep up with old high school friends, and even order pizza while joining in 2:00 A.M.

NOTE: Sunbelt cities, which came of age in the postindustrial era, continue to increase in population.

DISCUSS: Does e-mail allow students more access to faculty? Or less because face-to-face contact is less common? What differences can students see in the range and content of personal conversations versus cyber-conversations?

Q: "Computers are useless. They can only give you answers." Pablo Picasso

CYBER: Computer technology has made many recent social movements global in scope. By contrast, the French Revolution of 1789 was limited to people in personal contact with one another and was carried out entirely within the city of Paris.

online chat sessions. Perhaps strangest of all, Desrosiers often fires messages back and forth to his two roommates, even though they are silently staring at screens of their own just a few feet away in the same room.

It may be a sign of the times that a once-popular restaurant just down the street from dorms that house 3,000 students has closed its doors. Similarly, the student union is far less busy that it was just a few years ago. There, some of the space once used for socializing now accommodates—you guessed it—computer terminals for students who want to check their e-mail between classes.

At Dartmouth, computers have never been more popular. All together, the 8,000 students, faculty, and staff send and receive some 250,000 messages each day. No one doubts that new information technology has opened up more possibilities for accessing more information than ever before and contacting people almost anywhere in the world. But some people are beginning to see that an older form of local community is being lost in the process. Some faculty worry that they see less and less of their students. Some students, too, are beginning to think that they ought to see more of each other. As senior Abigail Butler puts it, "I know people who sit home Friday and Saturday night and e-mail back and forth to people they only know by nicknames, while the rest of the world is going by. After a while it starts to be really unfulfilling. It's easier to just meet someone in

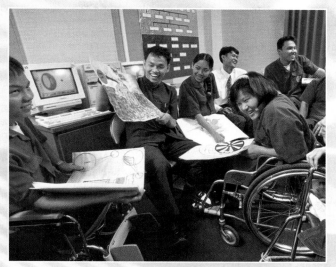

With access to the Internet, these Thai students have joined an international social movement to advance the opportunities of people with disabilities.

person and actually talk" (Gabriel, 1996).

Social Movements: New Ways to Connect

New ways to connect with people means a rising potential for starting and expanding social movements. Today, anyone with an interest in some issue and a computer can make contact, ask questions, and spread ideas—in short, play a role in intentional social change. In addition, computers offer access to almost unlimited information by accessing the Web pages of countless organizations and individuals with programs for change.

Perhaps most important, computer technology has made it easy to make connections on a global scale. Take the students at the Redemptorist Vocational School in Pattaya, Thailand. These young men and women have physical disabilities, which, before the information age, might have kept them

from learning at all. But using their school's computers, the students have established contact with hundreds of other people with disabilities in dozens of countries, including the United States. From these contacts and from visiting the Web sites of national and international organizations representing people with disabilities, the students have received a rich education indeed. They have been surprised to learn that many countries have laws that protect people with disabilities from discrimination and that mandate access ramps for sidewalks and buildings; they have discovered that cities abroad feature buses that "kneel" to permit entry by people in wheelchairs, as well as public restrooms designed to accommodate everyone. Armed with their new knowledge, the students at the Redemptorist Vocational School are now taking the lead in their own country, using the Internet to educate people about disabilities and lobbying government officials to make changes in Thailand's laws.

The Internet is a powerful communication resource for anyone. But it is especially important for people whose ability to make contact with others is otherwise limited, including people with disabilities. As one Thai student reports, "On the 'Net, I don't feel like a handicapped person" (Smolan & Erwitt, 1996:150). Even though computer access is far from equal around the world, the Internet is providing more and more people in poor countries with the power of a global reach.

GLOSSARY

abortion the deliberate termination of a pregnancy

absolute poverty a deprivation of resources that is life-threatening

achieved status a social position a person assumes voluntarily that reflects personal ability and effort

activity theory the idea that a high level of activity enhances personal satisfaction in old age

Afrocentrism the dominance of African cultural patterns

ageism prejudice and discrimination against the elderly

age-sex pyramid a graphic representation of the age and sex of a population

age stratification the unequal distribution of wealth, power, and privilege among people at different stages of the life course

agriculture large-scale cultivation using plows harnessed to animals or more powerful energy sources

alienation the experience of isolation and misery resulting from powerlessness

animism the belief that elements of the natural world are conscious life forms that affect humans

anomie Durkheim's term for a condition in which society provides little moral guidance to individuals

anticipatory socialization learning that helps a person achieve a desired position

ascribed status a social position a person receives at birth or assumes involuntarily later in life

asexuality a sexual orientation in which a person is not attracted to people of either sex

assimilation the process by which minorities gradually adopt patterns of the dominant culture

authoritarianism a political system that denies popular participation in government

authority power that people perceive as legitimate rather than coercive

beliefs specific statements that people hold to be true

bilateral descent a system tracing kinship through both men and women

bisexuality a sexual orientation in which a person is attracted to people of both sexes

blue-collar occupations lower-prestige work that involves mostly manual labor

bureaucracy an organizational model rationally designed to perform tasks efficiently

bureaucratic inertia the tendency of bureaucratic organizations to perpetuate themselves

bureaucratic ritualism a preoccupation with rules and regulations to the point of thwarting an organization's goals

capitalism an economic system in which natural resources and the means of producing goods and services are privately owned

capitalists people who own and operate factories and other businesses in pursuit of profits

caregiving informal and unpaid care provided to a dependent person by family members, other relatives, or friends

caste system social stratification based on ascription

cause and effect a relationship in which change in one variable (the independent variable) causes change in another (the dependent variable)

charisma extraordinary personal qualities that can turn an audience into followers

charismatic authority power legitimized through extraordinary personal abilities that inspire devotion and obedience

church a type of religious organization well integrated into the larger society

civil religion a quasi-religious loyalty binding citizens in a basically secular society

class conflict conflict between entire classes over the distribution of a society's wealth and power

class consciousness Marx's term for workers' recognition of themselves as a class united in opposition to capitalists and, ultimately, to capitalism itself

class society a capitalist society with pronounced social stratification

class system social stratification based on both birth and individual achievement

cohabitation the sharing of a household by an unmarried couple

cohort a category of people who share some trait, usually their age

collective behavior activity involving a large number of people, often spontaneous and sometimes controversial

collectivity a large number of people whose minimal interaction occurs in the absence of well-defined and conventional norms

colonialism the process by which some nations enrich themselves through political and economic control of other nations

communism a hypothetical economic and political system in which all members of a society are socially equal

concept a mental construct that represents some part of the world, inevitably in a simplified form

concrete operational stage Piaget's term for the level of human development at which individuals first perceive causal connections in their surroundings

conglomerate a giant corporation composed of many smaller corporations

control holding constant all variables except one to see clearly the effect of that variable

corporate crime the illegal actions of a corporation or people acting on its behalf

corporation an organization with a legal existence, including rights and liabilities, apart from those of its members

correlation a relationship by which two (or more) variables change together

counterculture cultural patterns that strongly oppose those widely accepted within a society

credentialism evaluating a person on the basis of educational degrees

crime the violation of society's formally enacted criminal law

crimes against the person (violent crimes) crimes that direct violence or the threat of violence against others

crimes against property (property crimes) crimes that involve theft of property belonging to others

criminal justice system a formal response by police, courts, and prison officials to alleged violations of the law

criminal recidivism subsequent offenses by people convicted of crimes

critical sociology the study of society that focuses on the need for social change

crowd a temporary gathering of people who share a common focus of attention and who influence one another

crude birth rate the number of live births in a given year for every thousand people in a population

crude death rate the number of deaths in a given year for every thousand people in a population

cult a religious organization that is largely outside a society's cultural traditions

cultural integration the close relationship between various elements of a cultural system

cultural lag the fact that some cultural elements change more quickly than others, which may disrupt a cultural system

cultural relativism the practice of evaluating a culture by its own standards

cultural transmission the process by which one generation passes culture to the next

cultural universals traits that are part of every known culture

culture the values, beliefs, behavior, and material objects that, together, form a people's way of life

culture shock personal disorientation when experiencing an unfamiliar way of life

Davis-Moore thesis the assertion that social stratification has beneficial consequences for the operation of a society

deductive logical thought reasoning that transforms general theory into specific hypotheses suitable for testing

democracy a type of political system in which power is exercised by the people as a whole

demographic transition theory the thesis that population patterns reflect a society's level of technological development

demography the study of human population

denomination a church, independent of the state, that accepts religious pluralism

dependency theory a model of economic development that explains global inequality in terms of the historical exploitation of poor societies by rich ones

dependent variable a variable that is changed by another (independent) variable

descent the system by which members of a society trace kinship over generations

deterrence the attempt to discourage criminality through punishment

deviance the recognized violation of cultural norms

direct-fee system a medical care system in which patients pay directly for the services of physicians and hospitals

discrimination any action that involves treating various categories of people unequally

disengagement theory the idea that society enhances its orderly operation by disengaging people from positions of responsibility as they reach old age

division of labor specialization of economic activity

dramaturgical analysis Erving Goffman's term for the study of social interaction in terms of theatrical performance

dyad a social group with two members

dysfunction (*see* social dysfunction)

eating disorder an intense form of dieting or other unhealthy method of weight control driven by the desire to be very thin

ecologically sustainable culture a way of life that meets the needs of the present generation without threatening the environmental legacy of future generations

ecology the study of the interaction of living organisms and the natural environment

economy the social institution that organizes a society's production, distribution, and consumption of goods and services

ecosystem a system composed of the interaction of all living organisms and their natural environment

education the social institution through which society provides its members with important knowledge, including basic facts, job skills, and cultural norms and values

ego Freud's designation for a person's conscious efforts to balance innate pleasure-seeking drives with the demands of society

empirical evidence information we can verify with our senses

endogamy marriage between people of the same social category

environmental deficit profound and long-term harm to the natural environment caused by humanity's focus on short-term material affluence

environmental racism the pattern by which environmental hazards are greatest for poor people, especially minorities

ethnicity a shared cultural heritage

ethnocentrism the practice of judging another culture by the standards of one's own culture

ethnomethodology Harold Garfinkel's term for the study of the way people make sense of their everyday surroundings

Eurocentrism the dominance of European (especially English) cultural patterns

euthanasia (mercy killing) assisting in the death of a person suffering from an incurable disease

exogamy marriage between people of different social categories

experiment a research method for investigating cause and effect under highly controlled conditions

expressive leadership group direction that focuses on collective well-being

extended family (consanguine family) a family unit that includes parents and children as well as other kin

fad an unconventional social pattern that people embrace briefly but enthusiastically

faith belief anchored in conviction rather than scientific evidence

false consciousness Marx's term for explanations of social problems as the shortcomings of individuals rather than the flaws of society

family a social institution found in all societies that unites people into cooperative groups to oversee the bearing and raising of children

family unit a social group of two or more people, related by blood, marriage, or adoption, who usually live together

family violence emotional, physical, or sexual abuse of one family member by another

fashion a social pattern favored by a large number of people

feminism the advocacy of social equality for men and women, in opposition to patriarchy and sexism

feminization of poverty the trend by which women represent an increasing proportion of the poor

fertility the incidence of childbearing in a country's population

folkways norms for routine, casual interaction

formal operational stage Piaget's term for the level of human development at which individuals think abstractly and critically

formal organization a large secondary group organized to achieve its goals efficiently

functional illiteracy a lack of reading and writing skills needed for everyday living

fundamentalism a conservative religious doctrine that opposes intellectualism and worldly accommodation in favor of restoring traditional, otherworldly religion

Gemeinschaft a type of social organization by which people are closely tied by kinship and tradition

gender the personal traits and social positions that members of a society attach to being female and male

gender roles (sex roles) attitudes and activities that a society links to each sex

gender stratification the unequal distribution of wealth, power, and privilege between men and women

generalized other George Herbert Mead's term for the widespread cultural norms and values we use as a reference in evaluating ourselves

genocide the systematic annihilation of one category of people by another

gerontocracy a form of social organization in which the elderly have the most wealth, power, and prestige

gerontology the study of aging and the elderly

Gesellschaft a type of social organization by which people come together only on the basis of individual self-interest

global economy expanding economic activity with little regard for national borders

global perspective the study of the larger world and our society's place in it

global warming a rise in the Earth's average temperature caused by an increasing concentration of carbon dioxide and other gases in the atmosphere

gossip rumor about people's personal affairs

government a formal organization that directs the political life of a society

groupthink the tendency of group members to conform, resulting in a narrow view of some issue

hate crime a criminal act against a person or person's property by an offender motivated by racial or other bias

Hawthorne effect a change in a subject's behavior caused simply by the awareness of being studied

health a state of complete physical, mental, and social well-being

health maintenance organization (HMO) an organization that provides comprehensive medical care to subscribers for a fixed fee

hermaphrodite a human being with some combination of female and male genitalia

heterosexism a view stigmatizing anyone who is not heterosexual as "queer"

heterosexuality a sexual orientation in which a person is attracted to someone of the other sex

hidden curriculum subtle presentations of political or cultural ideas in the classroom

high culture cultural patterns that distinguish a society's elite

high-income countries nations with very productive economic systems in which most people have high incomes

holistic medicine an approach to health care that emphasizes prevention of illness and takes into account the person's entire physical and social environment

homogamy marriage between people with the same social characteristics

homophobia the dread of close personal interaction with people thought to be gay, lesbian, or bisexual

homosexuality a sexual orientation in which a person is attracted to someone of the same sex

horticulture the use of hand tools to raise crops

hunting and gathering the use of simple tools to hunt animals and gather vegetation

hypothesis an unverified statement of a relationship between variables

id Freud's designation for the human being's basic drives

ideal type an abstract statement of the essential characteristics of any social phenomenon

ideology cultural beliefs that justify social stratification

incest taboo a cultural norm forbidding sexual relations or marriage between certain relatives

income wages or salary from work and earnings from investments

independent variable a variable that causes change in another (dependent) variable

inductive logical thought reasoning that transforms specific observations into general theory

industrialism the production of goods using advanced sources of energy to drive large machinery

infant mortality rate the number of deaths among infants under one year of age for each thousand live births in a given year

infidelity sexual activity outside marriage

ingroup a social group commanding a member's esteem and loyalty

institutional prejudice and discrimination bias inherent in the operation of society's institutions

instrumental leadership group direction that emphasizes the completion of tasks

intergenerational social mobility upward or downward social mobility of children in relation to their parents

interpretive sociology the study of society that focuses on the meanings people attach to their social world

interview a series of questions a researcher administers in person to respondents

intragenerational social mobility a change in social position occurring during a person's lifetime

kinship a social bond based on blood, marriage, or adoption

labeling theory the assertion that deviance and conformity result not so much from what people do as from how others respond to those actions

labor unions organizations of workers that seek to improve wages and working conditions through various strategies, including negotiations and strikes

language a system of symbols that allows people to communicate with one another

latent functions the unrecognized and unintended consequences of any social pattern

liberation theology a fusion of Christian principles with political activism, often Marxist in character

life expectancy the average life span of a country's population

looking-glass self Cooley's term for a self-image based on how we think others see us

low-income countries nations with less productive economic systems in which most people are poor

macro-level orientation a broad focus on social structures that shape society as a whole

mainstreaming integrating special students into the overall educational program

manifest functions the recognized and intended consequences of any social pattern

marriage a legally sanctioned relationship, usually involving economic cooperation as well as sexual activity and childbearing, that people expect to be enduring

Marxist political-economy model an analysis that explains politics in terms of the operation of a society's economic system

mass behavior collective behavior among people dispersed over a wide geographic area

mass hysteria a form of dispersed collective behavior by which people react to a real or imagined event with irrational and even frantic fear

mass media impersonal communications aimed at a vast audience

mass society a society in which industry and bureaucracy have eroded traditional social ties

master status a status that has special importance for social identity, often shaping a person's entire life

material culture the tangible things created by members of a society

matriarchy a form of social organization in which females dominate males

matrilineal descent a system tracing kinship through women

matrilocality a residential pattern in which a married couple lives with or near the wife's family

measurement the process of determining the value of a variable in a specific case

mechanical solidarity Durkheim's term for social bonds, based on common sentiments and shared moral values, that are strong among members of preindustrial societies

medicalization of deviance the transformation of moral and legal deviance into a medical condition

medicine the social institution that focuses on combating disease and improving health

megalopolis a vast urban region containing a number of cities and their surrounding suburbs

meritocracy social stratification based on personal merit

metropolis a large city that socially and economically dominates an urban area

micro-level orientation a close-up focus on social interaction in specific situations

middle-income countries nations with moderately productive economic systems in which personal income is about the global average

migration the movement of people into and out of a specified territory

military-industrial complex the close association of the federal government, the military, and defense industries

minority any category of people, distinguished by physical or cultural difference, that a society sets apart and subordinates

miscegenation biological reproduction by partners of different racial categories

mob a highly emotional crowd that pursues a violent or destructive goal

modernity social patterns resulting from industrialization

modernization the process of social change begun by industrialization

modernization theory a model of economic and social development that explains global inequality in terms of technological and cultural differences between societies

monarchy a type of political system in which a single family rules from generation to generation

monogamy marriage uniting two partners

monopoly domination of a market by a single producer

monotheism belief in a single divine power

mores norms that are widely observed and have great moral significance

mortality the incidence of death in a country's population

multiculturalism an educational program recognizing the cultural diversity of the United States and promoting the equality of all cultural traditions

multinational corporation a large business that operates in many countries

natural environment the Earth's surface and atmosphere, including living organisms as well as the air, water, soil, and other resources necessary to sustain life

neocolonialism a new form of global power relationships that involves not direct political control but economic exploitation by multinational corporations

neolocality a residential pattern in which a married couple lives apart from both sets of parents

network a web of weak social ties

nonmaterial culture the intangible world of ideas created by members of a society

nonverbal communication communication using body movements, gestures, and facial expressions rather than speech

norms rules and expectations by which a society guides the behavior of its members

nuclear family (conjugal family) a family unit composed of one or two parents and their children

nuclear proliferation the acquisition of nuclear-weapons technology by more and more nations

objectivity a state of personal neutrality in conducting research

oligarchy the rule of the many by the few

oligopoly domination of a market by a few producers

operationalizing a variable specifying exactly what one is to measure before assigning a value to a variable

organic solidarity Durkheim's term for social bonds based on specialization and interdependence that are strong among members of industrial societies

organizational environment a range of factors outside an organization that affect its operation

organized crime a business supplying illegal goods or services

other-directedness a receptiveness to the latest trends and fashions, often expressed by imitating others

outgroup a social group toward which one feels competition or opposition

panic a form of localized collective behavior by which people react to a threat or other stimulus with irrational, frantic, and often self-destructive behavior

paradigm (*see* theoretical paradigm)

participant observation a method in which investigators systematically observe people while joining in their routine activities

pastoralism the domestication of animals

patriarchy a form of social organization in which males dominate females

patrilineal descent a system tracing kinship through men

patrilocality a residential pattern in which a married couple lives with or near the husband's family

peer group a social group whose members have interests, social position, and age in common

personality a person's fairly consistent patterns of acting, thinking, and feeling

personal space the surrounding area over which a person makes some claim to privacy

plea bargaining a legal negotiation in which a prosecutor reduces a charge in exchange for a defendant's guilty plea

pluralism a state in which racial and ethnic minorities are distinct but have social parity

pluralist model an analysis of politics that sees power as dispersed among many competing interest groups

political action committee (PAC) an organization formed by a special-interest group, independent of political parties, to pursue political aims by raising and spending money

political revolution the overthrow of one political system in order to establish another

politics the social institution that distributes power, sets a society's agenda, and makes decisions

polyandry marriage uniting one female and two or more males

polygamy marriage uniting three or more people

polygyny marriage uniting one male and two or more females

polytheism belief in many gods

popular culture cultural patterns that are widespread among a society's population

population the people who are the focus of research

pornography sexually explicit material that causes sexual arousal

positivism a way of understanding based on science

postindustrial economy a productive system based on service work and high technology

postindustrialism technology that supports an information-based economy

postmodernity social patterns characteristic of postindustrial societies

power the ability to achieve desired ends despite resistance from others

power-elite model an analysis of politics that sees power as concentrated among the rich

prejudice a rigid and irrational generalization about an entire category of people

preoperational stage Piaget's term for the level of human development at which individuals first use language and other symbols

presentation of self an individual's effort to create specific impressions in the minds of others

primary group a small social group whose members share personal and enduring relationships

primary labor market jobs that provide extensive benefits to workers

primary sector the part of the economy that draws raw materials from the natural environment

primary sex characteristics the genitals, organs used for reproduction

profane that which people define as an ordinary element of everyday life

profession a prestigious, white-collar occupation that requires extensive formal education

proletarians people who sell their productive labor for wages

propaganda information presented with the intention of shaping public opinion

prostitution the selling of sexual services

public opinion widespread attitudes about controversial issues

queer theory a growing body of knowledge that challenges a perceived heterosexual bias in sociology

questionnaire a series of written questions a researcher presents to subjects

race a socially constructed category composed of people who share biologically transmitted traits that members of a society consider important

racism the belief that one racial category is innately superior or inferior to another

rain forests regions of dense forestation, most of which circle the globe close to the equator

rationality deliberate, matter-of-fact calculation of the most efficient means to accomplish a particular task

rationalization of society Weber's term for the historical change from tradition to rationality as the dominant mode of human thought

rational-legal authority (also **bureaucratic authority**) power legitimized by legally enacted rules and regulations

reference group a social group that serves as a point of reference in making evaluations and decisions

rehabilitation a program for reforming the offender to prevent subsequent offenses

relative deprivation a perceived disadvantage arising from a specific comparison

relative poverty the deprivation of some people in relation to those who have more

reliability consistency in measurement

religion a social institution involving beliefs and practices based on a conception of the sacred

religiosity the importance of religion in a person's life

replication repetition of research by other investigators

research method a systematic plan for conducting research

resocialization radically changing an inmate's personality by carefully controlling the environment

retribution an act of moral vengeance by which society inflicts suffering on an offender comparable to that caused by the offense

riot a social eruption that is highly emotional, violent, and undirected

ritual formal, ceremonial behavior

role behavior expected of someone who holds a particular status

role conflict conflict between the roles corresponding to two or more statuses

role set a number of roles attached to a single status

role strain tension between roles connected to a single status

routinization of charisma the transformation of charismatic authority into some combination of traditional and bureaucratic authority

rumor unsubstantiated information spread informally, often by word of mouth

sacred that which people set apart as extraordinary, inspiring a sense of awe and reverence

sample a part of a population that represents the whole

Sapir-Whorf thesis the thesis that people perceive the world through the cultural lens of language

scapegoat a person or category of people, typically with little power, whom people unfairly blame for their own troubles

schooling formal instruction under the direction of specially trained teachers

science a logical system that bases knowledge on direct, systematic observation

scientific management Frederick Taylor's term for the application of scientific principles to the operation of a business or other large organization

scientific sociology the study of society based on systematic observation of social behavior

secondary analysis a research method in which a researcher uses data collected by others

secondary group a large and impersonal social group whose members pursue a specific goal or activity

secondary labor market jobs that provide minimal benefits to workers

secondary sector the part of the economy that transforms raw materials into manufactured goods

secondary sex characteristics bodily differences, apart from the genitals, that distinguish biologically mature females and males

sect a type of religious organization that stands apart from the larger society

secularization the historical decline in the importance of the supernatural and the sacred

segregation the physical and social separation of categories of people

self George Herbert Mead's term for the part of an individual's personality composed of self-awareness and self-image

sensorimotor stage Piaget's term for the level of human development at which individuals experience the world only through their senses

sex the biological distinction between females and males

sexism the belief that one sex is innately superior to the other

sex ratio the number of males for every hundred females in a nation's population

sexual harassment comments, gestures, or physical contact of a sexual nature that are deliberate, repeated, and unwelcome

sexual orientation a person's preference in terms of sexual partners: same sex, other sex, either sex, neither sex

sick role patterns of behavior defined as appropriate for those who are ill

social change the transformation of culture and social institutions over time

social character personality patterns common to members of a particular society

social conflict struggle between segments of society over valued resources

social-conflict paradigm a framework for building theory that sees society as an arena of inequality that generates conflict and change

social construction of reality the process by which people creatively shape reality through social interaction

social control various means by which members of society encourage conformity to norms; attempts by society to regulate people's thought and behavior

social dysfunctions the undesirable consequences of any social pattern for the operation of society

social epidemiology the study of how health and disease are distributed throughout a society's population

social functions the consequences of a social pattern for the operation of society as a whole

social group two or more people who identify and interact with one another

social institutions major spheres of social life, or societal subsystem, organized to meet human needs

social interaction the process by which people act and react in relation to others

socialism an economic system in which natural resources and the means of producing goods and services are collectively owned

socialization the lifelong social experience by which individuals develop their human potential and learn culture

socialized medicine a health care system in which the government owns and operates most medical facilities and employs most physicians

social mobility change in one's position in the social hierarchy

social movement organized activity that encourages or discourages social change

social stratification a system by which a society ranks categories of people in a hierarchy

social structure any stable pattern of social behavior

societal protection a means by which society renders an offender incapable of further offenses temporarily through incarceration or permanently by execution

society people who interact in a defined territory and share culture

sociobiology a theoretical paradigm that explores ways in which human biology affects how we create culture

sociocultural evolution Lenski's term for the changes that occur as a society acquires new technology

socioeconomic status (SES) a composite ranking based on various dimensions of social inequality

sociology the systematic study of human society

special-interest group a political alliance of people interested in some economic or social issue

spurious correlation an apparent, although false, relationship between two (or more) variables caused by some other variable

state capitalism an economic and political system in which companies are privately owned but cooperate closely with the government

state church a church formally allied with the state

status a social position that an individual occupies

status consistency the degree of consistency in a person's social standing across various dimensions of social inequality

status set all the statuses a person holds at a given time

stereotypes exaggerated descriptions applied to every person in some category

stigma a powerfully negative label that greatly changes a person's self-concept and social identity

structural-functional paradigm a framework for building theory that sees society as a complex system whose parts work together to promote solidarity and stability

structural social mobility a shift in the social position of large numbers of people due more to changes in society itself than to individual efforts

subculture cultural patterns that set apart some segment of a society's population

suburbs urban areas beyond the political boundaries of a city

superego Freud's term for the cultural values and norms internalized by an individual

survey a research method in which subjects respond to a series of statements or questions in a questionnaire or an interview

symbolic-interaction paradigm a framework for building theory that sees society as the product of the everyday interactions of individuals

symbols anything that carries a particular meaning recognized by people who share culture

technology knowledge that people use to make a way of life in their surroundings

terrorism random acts of violence or the threat of such violence used by an individual or group as a political strategy

tertiary sector the part of the economy involving services rather than goods

theoretical paradigm a basic image of society that guides thinking and research

theory a statement of how and why specific facts are related

Thomas theorem W. I. Thomas's assertion that situations that are defined as real are real in their consequences

total institution a setting in which people are isolated from the rest of society and manipulated by an administrative staff

totalitarianism a political system that extensively regulates people's lives

totem an object in the natural world collectively defined as sacred

tracking the assignment of students to different types of educational programs

tradition sentiments and beliefs passed from generation to generation

traditional authority power legitimized through respect for long-established cultural patterns

tradition-directedness rigid conformity to time-honored ways of living

transsexuals people who feel they are one sex even though biologically they are the other

triad a social group with three members

underground economy economic activity involving income unreported to the government as required by law

urban ecology the study of the link between the physical and social dimensions of cities

urbanization the concentration of humanity into cities

validity precision in measuring exactly what one intends to measure

values culturally defined standards by which people assess desirability, goodness, and beauty and that serve as broad guidelines for social living

variable a concept whose value changes from case to case

victimless crimes violations of law in which there are no readily apparent victims

war organized, armed conflict between the people of various societies, directed by their governments

wealth the total value of money and other assets, minus outstanding debts

welfare capitalism an economic and political system that combines a mostly market-based economy with extensive social welfare programs

welfare state a range of government agencies and programs that provides benefits to the population

white-collar crime crime committed by people of high social position in the course of their occupations

white-collar occupations higher-prestige work that involves mostly mental activity

zero population growth the level of reproduction that maintains population at a steady state

REFERENCES

ABBOTT, ANDREW. *The System of Professions: An Essay on the Division of Expert Labor.* Chicago: University of Chicago Press, 1988.

ABERLE, DAVID F. *The Peyote Religion among the Navaho.* Chicago: Aldine, 1966.

ABRAHAMSON, PAUL R. "Postmaterialism and Environmentalism: A Comment on an Analysis and a Reappraisal." *Social Science Quarterly.* Vol. 78, No. 1 (March 1997):21–23.

ADELSON, JOSEPH. "Splitting Up." *Commentary* (September 1996).

ADLER, JERRY. "When Harry Called Sally . . ." *Newsweek* (October 1, 1990):74.

ADORNO, T. W., et al. *The Authoritarian Personality.* New York: Harper & Brothers, 1950.

AGUIRRE, BENIGNO E., and E. L. QUARANTELLI. "Methodological, Ideological, and Conceptual-Theoretical Criticisms of Collective Behavior: A Critical Evaluation and Implications for Future Study." *Sociological Focus.* Vol. 16, No. 3 (August 1983):195–216.

AGUIRRE, BENIGNO E., E. L. QUARANTELLI, and JORGE L. MENDOZA. "The Collective Behavior of Fads: Characteristics, Effects, and Career of Streaking." *American Sociological Review.* Vol. 53, No. 4 (August 1988):569–84.

AKERS, RONALD L., MARVIN D. KROHN, LONN LANZA-KADUCE, and MARCIA RADOSEVICH. "Social Learning and Deviant Behavior." *American Sociological Review.* Vol. 44, No. 4 (August 1979):636–55.

ALAM, SULTANA. "Women and Poverty in Bangladesh." *Women's Studies International Forum.* Vol. 8, No. 4 (1985):361–71.

ALBA, RICHARD D. *Ethnic Identity: The Transformation of White America.* Chicago: University of Chicago Press, 1990.

ALBON, JOAN. "Retention of Cultural Values and Differential Urban Adaptation: Samoans and American Indians in a West Coast City." *Social Forces.* Vol. 49, No. 3 (March 1971):385–93.

ALFORD, RICHARD. "The Structure of Human Experience: Expectancy and Affect; The Case of Humor." Unpublished paper, Department of Sociology, University of Wyoming, 1979.

ALLAN, EMILIE ANDERSEN, and DARRELL J. STEFFENSMEIER. "Youth, Underemployment, and Property Crime: Differential Effects of Job Availability and Job Quality on Juvenile and Young Adult Arrest Rates." *American Sociological Review.* Vol. 54, No. 1 (February 1989):107–23.

ALLEN, MICHAEL PATRICK, and PHILIP BROYLES. "Campaign Finance Reforms and the Presidential Campaign Contributions of Wealthy Capitalist Families." *Social Science Quarterly.* Vol. 72, No. 4 (December 1991):738–50.

ALLEN, WALTER R. "African American Family Life in Social Context: Crisis and Hope." *Sociological Forum.* Vol. 10, No. 4 (December 1995):569–92.

ALLSOP, KENNETH. *The Bootleggers.* London: Hutchinson, 1961.

ALTER, JONATHAN. "Down to Business." *Newsweek* (May 12, 1997):58–60.

———. "The Death Penalty on Trial." *Newsweek* (June 12, 2000):24–34.

ALTMAN, DREW, et al. "Health Care for the Homeless." *Society.* Vol. 26, No. 4 (May–June 1989):4–5.

ALTONJI, JOSEPH G., ULRICH DORASZELSKI, and LEWIS SEGAL. "Black/White Differences in Wealth." *Economic Perspectives.* Vol. 24, No. 1 (First Quarter, 2000):38–50.

AMATO, PAUL R. "What Children Learn from Divorce." *Population Today.* Vol. 29, No. 1 (January 2001):1, 4.

AMBLER, JOHN S., and JODY NEATHERY. "Education Policy and Equality: Some Evidence from Europe." *Social Science Quarterly.* Vol. 80, No. 3 (September 1999):437–56.

American Demographics. Zandi Group survey. Vol. 20 (March 3, 1998):38.

AMERICAN SOCIOLOGICAL ASSOCIATION. "Code of Ethics." Washington, D.C.: 1997.

AMNESTY INTERNATIONAL. *Website against the Death Penalty.* [Online] Available September 20, 2001, at http://www.web.amnesty.org/

ANDERSON, ELIJAH. "The Code of the Streets." *Atlantic Monthly.* Vol. 273 (May 1994):81–94.

ANDERSON, JOHN WARD. "Early to Wed: The Child Brides of India." *Washington Post* (May 24, 1995):A27, A30.

ANDO, FAITH H. "Women in Business." In Sara E. Rix, ed., *The American Woman: A Status Report 1990–91.* New York: Norton, 1990:222–30.

ANG, IEN. *Watching Dallas: Soap Opera and the Melodramatic Imagination.* London: Methuen, 1985.

ANGIER, NATALIE. "Scientists, Finding Second Idiosyncrasy in Homosexuals' Brains, Suggest Orientation Is Physiological." *New York Times* (August 1, 1992):A7.

ANNAN, KOFI. "Astonishing Facts." *New York Times* (September 27, 1998):16.

APA. *Violence and Youth: Psychology's Response.* Washington, D.C.: American Psychological Association, 1993.

APPLEBOME, PETER. "70 Years after Scopes Trial, Creation Debate Lives." *New York Times* (March 10, 1996):1, 10.

ARCHER, DANE, and ROSEMARY GARTNER. *Violence and Crime in Cross-National Perspective.* New Haven, Conn.: Yale University Press, 1987.

ARENDT, HANNAH. *The Origins of Totalitarianism.* Cleveland, Ohio: Meridian Books, 1958.

———. *Between Past and Future: Six Exercises in Political Thought.* Cleveland, Ohio: Meridian Books, 1963.

ARIÈS, PHILIPPE. *Centuries of Childhood: A Social History of Family Life.* New York: Vintage Books, 1965.

———. *Western Attitudes toward Death: From the Middle Ages to the Present.* Baltimore: Johns Hopkins University Press, 1974.

ARJOMAND, SAID AMIR. *The Turban for the Crown: The Islamic Revolution in Iran.* New York: Oxford University Press, 1988.

ARNETTE, JUNE L., and MARJORIE C. WALSLEBEN. "Combating Fear and Restoring Safety in Schools." *Juvenile Justice Bulletin* (April 1998). Washington, D.C.: U.S. Department of Justice.

ARONOWITZ, STANLEY. *The Politics of Identity: Class, Culture, and Social Movements.* New York: Routledge, 1992.

ASANTE, MOLEFI KETE. *Afrocentricity.* Trenton, N.J.: Africa World Press, 1988.

ASCH, SOLOMON. *Social Psychology.* Englewood Cliffs, N.J.: Prentice Hall, 1952.

ASHFORD, LORI S. "New Perspectives on Population: Lessons from Cairo." *Population Bulletin.* Vol. 50, No. 1 (March 1995).

ASSOCIATED PRESS. "Death Toll Grows from Collapsed Garbage." July 11, 2000.

ASTONE, NAN MARIE, and SARA S. MCLANAHAN. "Family Structure, Parental Practices and High School Completion." *American Sociological Review.* Vol. 56, No. 3 (June 1991):309–20.

ATCHLEY, ROBERT C. "Retirement as a Social Institution." *Annual Review of Sociology.* Vol. 8. Palo Alto, Calif.: Annual Reviews, 1982:263–87.

———. *Aging: Continuity and Change.* Belmont, Calif.: Wadsworth, 1983; 2d ed., 1987.

AUSTER, CAROL J., and MINDY MACRONE. "The Classroom as a Negotiated Social Setting: An Empirical Study of the Effects of Faculty Members' Behavior on Students' Participation." *Teaching Sociology.* Vol. 22, No. 4 (October 1994):289–300.

BACHRACH, PETER, and MORTON S. BARATZ. *Power and Poverty.* New York: Oxford University Press, 1970.

BACKMAN, CARL B., and MURRAY C. ADAMS. "Self-Perceived Physical Attractiveness, Self-Esteem, Race, and Gender." *Sociological Focus.* Vol. 24, No. 4 (October 1991):283–90.

BAILEY, WILLIAM C. "Murder, Capital Punishment, and Television: Execution Publicity and Homicide Rates." *American Sociological Review.* Vol. 55, No. 5 (October 1990):628–33.

BAILEY, WILLIAM C., and RUTH D. PETERSON. "Murder and Capital Punishment: A Monthly Time-Series Analysis of Execution Publicity." *American Sociological Review.* Vol. 54, No. 5 (October 1989):722–43.

BAKER, MARY ANNE, CATHERINE WHITE BERHEIDE, FAY ROSS GRECKEL, LINDA CARSTARPHEN GUGIN, MARCIA J. LIPETZ, and MARCIA TEXLER SEGAL. *Women Today: A Multidisciplinary Approach to Women's Studies.* Monterey, Calif.: Brooks/Cole, 1980.

BAKER, PATRICIA S., WILLIAM C. YOELS, JEFFREY M. CLAIR, and RICHARD M. ALLMAN. "Laughter in the Triadic Geriatric Encounters: A Transcript-Based Analysis." In Rebecca J. Erikson and Beverly Cuthbertson-Johnson, eds., *Social Perspectives on Emotion.* Vol. 4. Greenwich, Conn.: JAI Press, 1997:179–207.

BALDAUF, SCOTT. "More Americans Move Off the Beaten Path." *Christian Science Monitor* (August 7, 1996):1, 4.

BALTES, PAUL B., and K. WARNER SCHAIE. "The Myth of the Twilight Years." *Psychology Today.* Vol. 7, No. 10 (March 1974):35–39.

BALTZELL, E. DIGBY. *The Protestant Establishment: Aristocracy and Caste in America.* New York: Vintage Books, 1964.

———. "Introduction to the 1967 Edition." In W. E. B. Du Bois, *The Philadelphia Negro: A Social Study.* New York: Schocken Books, 1967; orig. 1899.

———. "The Protestant Establishment Revisited." *The American Scholar.* Vol. 45, No. 4 (Autumn 1976):499–518.

———. *Philadelphia Gentlemen: The Making of a National Upper Class.* Philadelphia: University of Pennsylvania Press, 1979a; orig. 1958.

———. *Puritan Boston and Quaker Philadelphia.* New York: Free Press, 1979b.

———. "The WASP's Last Gasp." *Philadelphia Magazine.* Vol. 79 (September 1988):104–7, 184, 186, 188.

———. *Sporting Gentlemen: From the Age of Honor to the Cult of the Superstar.* New York: Free Press, 1995.

BANFIELD, EDWARD C. *The Unheavenly City Revisited.* Boston: Little, Brown, 1974.

BARASH, DAVID. *The Whispering Within.* New York: Penguin Books, 1981.

BARKER, EILEEN. "Who'd Be a Moonie? A Comparative Study of Those Who Join the Unification Church in Britain." In Bryan Wilson, ed., *The Social Impact of New Religious Movements.* New York: Rose of Sharon Press, 1981:59–96.

BARON, JAMES N., MICHAEL T. HANNAN, and M. DIANE BURTON. "Building the Iron Cage: Determinants of Managerial Intensity in the Early Years of Organizations." *American Sociological Review.* Vol. 64, No. 4 (August 1999):527–47.

BARON, JAMES N., BRIAN S. MITTMAN, and ANDREW E. NEWMAN. "Targets of Opportunity: Organizational and Environmental Determinants of Gender Integration within the California Civil Service, 1979–1985." *American Journal of Sociology.* Vol. 96, No. 6 (May 1991):1362–401.

BARONE, MICHAEL, and GRANT UJIFUSA. *The Almanac of American Politics.* Washington, D.C.: Barone and Co., 1981.

BARRY, KATHLEEN. "Feminist Theory: The Meaning of Women's Liberation." In Barbara Haber, ed., *The Women's Annual 1982–1983.* Boston: G.K. Hall, 1983:35–78.

BARTLETT, BRUCE. "Death, Wealth, and Taxes." *The Public Interest.* Vol. 141, (Fall 2000):55–67.

BARTLETT, DONALD L., and JAMES B. STEELE. "Corporate Welfare." *Time.* Vol. 152, No. 19 (November 9, 1998):36–54.

———. "How the Little Guy Gets Crunched." *Time.* Vol. 155, No. 5 (February 7, 2000):38–41.

BASSUK, ELLEN J. "The Homelessness Problem." *Scientific American.* Vol. 251, No. 1 (July 1984):40–45.

BAUER, P. T. *Equality, the Third World, and Economic Delusion.* Cambridge, Mass.: Harvard University Press, 1981.

BAUMGARTNER, M. P. "Introduction: The Moral Voice of the Community." *Sociological Focus.* Vol. 31, No. 2 (May 1998):105–17.

BAYDAR, NAZLI, and JEANNE BROOKS-GUNN. "Effect of Maternal Employment and Child-Care Arrangements on Preschoolers' Cognitive and Behavioral Outcomes: Evidence from Children from the National Longitudinal Survey of Youth." *Developmental Psychology.* Vol. 27 (1991):932–35.

BAYLEY, DAVID H. "Policing in America." *Society.* Vol. 36, No. 1 (November–December 1998):16–19.

BECKER, ANNE. Paper presented at the annual meeting of the American Psychiatric Association, Washington, D.C., May 19, 1999. Reported in "Eating Disorders Jump When Fiji Gets Television." *Toledo Blade* (May 20, 1999):12.

BECKER, HOWARD S. *Outside: Studies in the Sociology of Deviance.* New York: Free Press, 1966.

BEDELL, GEORGE C., LEO SANDON, JR., and CHARLES T. WELLBORN. *Religion in America.* New York: Macmillan, 1975.

BEEGHLEY, LEONARD. *The Structure of Social Stratification in the United States.* Needham Heights, Mass.: Allyn & Bacon, 1989.

BEGLEY, SHARON. "Gray Matters." *Newsweek* (March 7, 1995):48–54.

———. "How to Beat the Heat." *Newsweek* (December 8, 1997):34–38.

BEINS, BARNEY, cited in "Examples of Spuriousness." *Teaching Methods.* No. 2 (Fall 1993):3.

BELL, ALAN P., MARTIN S. WEINBERG, and SUE KIEFER-HAMMERSMITH. *Sexual Preference: Its Development in Men and Women.* Bloomington: Indiana University Press, 1981.

BELL, DANIEL. *The Coming of Post-Industrial Society: A Venture in Social Forecasting.* New York: Basic Books, 1973.

BELLAH, ROBERT N. *The Broken Covenant.* New York: Seabury Press, 1975.

BELLAH, ROBERT N., RICHARD MADSEN, WILLIAM M. SULLIVAN, ANN SWIDLER, and STEVEN M. TIPTON. *Habits of the Heart: Individualism and Commitment in American Life.* New York: Harper & Row, 1985.

BELLAS, MARCIA L. "Comparable Worth in Academia: The Effects on Faculty Salaries of the Sex Composition and Labor-Market Conditions of Academic Disciplines." *American Sociological Review.* Vol. 59, No. 6 (December 1994):807–21.

BELLUCK, PAM. "Black Youths' Rate of Suicide Rising Sharply." *New York Times* (March 20, 1998):A1, A18.

BEM, SANDRA LIPSITZ. *The Lenses of Gender: Transforming the Debate on Sexual Inequality.* New Haven, Conn.: Yale University Press, 1993.

BENEDICT, RUTH. "Continuities and Discontinuities in Cultural Conditioning." *Psychiatry.* Vol. 1 (May 1938):161–67.

BENET, SULA. "Why They Live to Be 100, or Even Older, in Abkhasia." *New York Times Magazine* (December 26, 1971):3, 28–29, 31–34.

BENJAMIN, LOIS. *The Black Elite: Facing the Color Line in the Twilight of the Twentieth Century.* Chicago: Nelson-Hall, 1991.

BENNETT, NEIL G., DAVID E. BLOOM, and PATRICIA H. CRAIG. "The Divergence of Black and White Marriage Patterns." *American Journal of Sociology.* Vol. 95, No. 3 (November 1989):692–722.

BENNETT, WILLIAM J. "School Reform: What Remains to Be Done." *Wall Street Journal* (September 2, 1997):A18.

BENOKRAITIS, NIJOLE, and JOE FEAGIN. *Modern Sexism: Blatant, Subtle, and Overt Discrimination.* 2d ed. Englewood Cliffs, N.J.: Prentice Hall, 1995.

BENSON, MICHAEL L., and FRANCIS T. CULLEN. *Combating Corporate Crime.* Boston: Northeastern University Press, 1998.

BERGAMO, MONICA, and GERSON CAMAROTTI. "Brazil's Landless Millions." *World Press Review.* Vol. 43, No. 7 (July 1996):46–47.

BERGEN, RAQUEL KENNEDY. "Interviewing Survivors of Marital Rape: Doing Feminist Research on Sensitive Topics." In Claire M. Renzetti and Raymond M. Lee, eds., *Researching Sensitive Topics.* Thousand Oaks, Calif.: Sage, 1993.

BERGER, PETER L. *Invitation to Sociology.* New York: Anchor Books, 1963.

———. *The Sacred Canopy: Elements of a Sociological Theory of Religion.* Garden City, N.Y.: Doubleday, 1967.

———. *Facing Up to Modernity: Excursions in Society, Politics, and Religion.* New York: Basic Books, 1977.

———. *The Capitalist Revolution: Fifty Propositions about Prosperity, Equality, and Liberty.* New York: Basic Books, 1986.

———. "Sociology: A Disinvitation?" *Society.* Vol. 30, No. 1 (November–December 1992):12–18.

BERGER, PETER, BRIGITTE BERGER, and HANSFRIED KELLNER. *The Homeless Mind: Modernization and Consciousness.* New York: Vintage Books, 1974.

BERGER, PETER L., and HANSFRIED KELLNER. *Sociology Reinterpreted: An Essay on Method and Vocation.* Garden City, N.Y.: Anchor Books, 1981.

BERGER, PETER L., and THOMAS LUCKMANN. *The Social Construction of Reality.* Garden City, N.J.: Doubleday, 1966.

BERGESEN, ALBERT, ed. *Crises in the World-System.* Beverly Hills, Calif.: Sage, 1983.

BERK, RICHARD A. *Collective Behavior.* Dubuque, Iowa: Wm. C. Brown, 1974.

BERNARD, JESSIE. *The Female World.* New York: Free Press, 1981.

———. *The Future of Marriage.* New Haven, Conn.: Yale University Press, 1982; orig. 1973.

BERNARD, LARRY CRAIG. "Multivariate Analysis of New Sex Role Formulations and Personality." *Journal of Personality and Social Psychology.* Vol. 38, No. 2 (February 1980):323–36.

BERNSTEIN, NINA. "On Frontier of Cyberspace, Data Is Money, and a Threat." *New York Times* (June 12, 1997):A1, B14–15.

BERNSTEIN, RICHARD J. *The New Constellation: The Ethical-Political Horizons of Modernity/Postmodernity.* Cambridge, Mass.: MIT Press, 1992.

BERRILL, KEVIN T. "Anti-Gay Violence and Victimization in the United States: An Overview." In Gregory M. Herek and Kevin T. Berrill, *Hate Crimes: Confronting Violence against Lesbians and Gay Men.* Newbury Park, Calif.: Sage, 1992:19–45.

BERRY, BRIAN L., and PHILIP H. REES. "The Factorial Ecology of Calcutta." *American Journal of Sociology.* Vol. 74, No. 5 (March 1969):445–91.

BERSCHEID, ELLEN, and ELAINE HATFIELD. *Interpersonal Attraction.* 2d ed. Reading, Mass.: Addison-Wesley, 1983.

BESHAROV, DOUGLAS J. and PETER GERMANIS. "Welfare Reform: Four Years Later." *The Public Interest.* Vol. 140 (Summer 2000):17–35.

BESHAROV, DOUGLAS J., and LISA A. LAUMANN. "Child Abuse Reporting." *Society.* Vol. 34, No. 4 (May/June 1996):40–46.

BESSER, TERRY L. "The Commitment of Japanese Workers and U.S. Workers: A Reassessment of the Literature." *American Sociological Review.* Vol. 58, No. 6 (December 1993):873–81.

BEST, JOEL. "Victimization and the Victim Industry." *Society.* Vol. 34, No. 2 (May/June 1997):9–17.

BEST, RAPHAELA. *We've All Got Scars: What Boys and Girls Learn in Elementary School.* Bloomington: Indiana University Press, 1983.

BEUTEL, ANN M., and MARGARET MOONEY MARINI. "Gender and Values." *American Sociological Review.* Vol. 60 (June 1995):436–48.

BIANCHI, SUZANNE M., and LYNNE M. CASPER. "American Families." *Population Bulletin.* Vol. 55, No. 4 (December 2000).

BIANCHI, SUZANNE M., and DAPHNE SPAIN. "Women, Work, and Family in America." *Population Bulletin.* Vol. 51, No. 3 (December 1996).

BIBLARZ, TIMOTHY J., and ADRIAN E. RAFTERY. "The Effects of Family Disruption on Social Mobility." *American Sociological Review.* Vol. 58, No. 1 (February 1993):97–109.

BILLSON, JANET MANCINI, and BETTINA J. HUBER. *Embarking upon a Career with an Undergraduate Degree in Sociology.* 2d ed. Washington, D.C.: American Sociological Association, 1993.

BLANK, JONAH. "The Muslim Mainstream." *U.S. News & World Report.* Vol. 125, No. 3 (July 20, 1998):22–25.

BLANKENHORN, DAVID. *Fatherless America: Confronting Our Most Urgent Social Problem.* New York: HarperCollins, 1995.

BLAU, JUDITH R., and PETER M. BLAU. "The Cost of Inequality: Metropolitan Structure and Violent Crime." *American Sociological Review.* Vol. 47, No. 1 (February 1982):114–29.

BLAU, PETER M. *Exchange and Power in Social Life.* New York: Wiley, 1964.

———. *Inequality and Heterogeneity: A Primitive Theory of Social Structure.* New York: Free Press, 1977.

BLAU, PETER M., TERRY C. BLUM, and JOSEPH E. SCHWARTZ. "Heterogeneity and Intermarriage." *American Sociological Review.* Vol. 47, No. 1 (February 1982):45–62.

BLAU, PETER M., and OTIS DUDLEY DUNCAN. *The American Occupational Structure.* New York: Wiley, 1967.

BLAUSTEIN, ALBERT P., and ROBERT L. ZANGRANDO. *Civil Rights and the Black American.* New York: Washington Square Press, 1968.

BLOOM, LEONARD. "Familial Adjustments of Japanese-Americans to Relocation: First Phase." In Thomas F. Pettigrew, ed., *The Sociology of Race Relations.* New York: Free Press, 1980:163–67.

BLUM, LINDA M. *Between Feminism and Labor: The Significance of the Comparable Worth Movement.* Berkeley: University of California Press, 1991.

BLUMBERG, PAUL. *Inequality in an Age of Decline.* New York: Oxford University Press, 1981.

BLUMER, HERBERT G. "Fashion." In David L. Sills, ed., *International Encyclopedia of the Social Sciences.* Vol. 5. New York: Macmillan and Free Press, 1968:341–45.

———. "Collective Behavior." In Alfred McClung Lee, ed., *Principles of Sociology.* 3d ed. New York: Barnes & Noble Books, 1969:65–121.

BLUMSTEIN, ALFRED, and RICHARD ROSENFELD. "Assessing the Recent Ups and Downs in U.S. Homicide Rates." *National Institute of Justice Journal.* Vol. 237 (October 1998):9–11.

BLUMSTEIN, PHILIP, and PEPPER SCHWARTZ. *American Couples.* New York: William Morrow, 1983.

BOBO, LAWRENCE, and VINCENT L. HUTCHINGS. "Perceptions of Racial Group Competition: Extending Blumer's Theory of Group Position to a Multiracial Social Context." *American Sociological Review.* Vol. 61, No. 6 (December 1996):951–72.

BOFF, LEONARD and CLODOVIS. *Salvation and Liberation: In Search of a Balance between Faith and Politics.* Maryknoll, N.Y.: Orbis Books, 1984.

BOGARDUS, EMORY S. "Comparing Racial Distance in Ethiopia, South Africa, and the United States." *Sociology and Social Research.* Vol. 52, No. 2 (January 1968):149–56.

BOGGESS, SCOTT, and JOHN BOUND. "Did Criminal Activity Increase during the 1980s? Comparisons across Data Sources." *Social Science Quarterly.* Vol. 78, No. 3 (September 1997):725–39.

BOHANNAN, CECIL. "The Economic Correlates of Homelessness in Sixty Cities." *Social Science Quarterly.* Vol. 72, No. 4 (December 1991):817–25.

BOHLEN, CELESTINE. "Facing Oblivion, Rust-Belt Giants Top Russian List of Vexing Crises." *New York Times* (November 8, 1998):1, 6.

BOHM, ROBERT M. "American Death Penalty Opinion, 1936–1986: A Critical Examination of the Gallup Polls." In Robert M. Bohm, ed., *The Death Penalty in America: Current Research*. Cincinnati: Anderson Publishing Co., 1991:113–45.

BOHON, STEPHANIE A., and CRAIG R. HUMPHREY. "Courting LULUs: Characteristic of Suitor and Objector Communities." *Rural Sociology*. Vol. 65, No. 3 (September 2000):376–95.

BOLI, JOHN, and GEORGE M. THOMAS. "World Culture in the World Polity: A Century of International Non-Governmental Organization." *American Sociological Review*. Vol. 62, No. 2 (April 1997):171–90.

BONANNO, ALESSANDRO, DOUGLAS H. CONSTANCE, and HEATHER LORENZ. "Powers and Limits of Transnational Corporations: The Case of ADM." *Rural Sociology*. Vol. 65, No. 3 (September, 2000):440–60.

BONCZAR, THOMAS P., and ALLAN J. BECK. *Lifetime Likelihood of Going to State or Federal Prison*. Washington, D.C.: U.S. Bureau of Justice Statistics, 1997.

BONILLA-SANTIAGO, GLORIA. "A Portrait of Hispanic Women in the United States." In Sara E. Rix, ed., *The American Woman 1990–91: A Status Report*. New York: Norton, 1990:249–57.

BONNER, JANE. Research presented in *The Two Brains*. Public Broadcasting System telecast, 1984.

BOOTH, ALAN, and JAMES DABBS. "Male Hormone Is Linked to Marital Problems." *Wall Street Journal* (August 19, 1992):B1.

BOOTH, ALAN, and LYNN WHITE. "Thinking about Divorce." *Journal of Marriage and the Family*. Vol. 42, No. 3 (August 1980):605–16.

BOOTH, WILLIAM. "By the Sweat of Their Brows: A New Economy." *The Washington Post* (July 13, 1998):A1, A10–A11.

BORGMANN, ALBERT. *Crossing the Postmodern Divide*. Chicago: University of Chicago Press, 1992.

BORMANN, F. HERBERT. "The Global Environmental Deficit." *BioScience*. Vol. 40 (1990):74.

BORMANN, F. HERBERT, and STEPHEN R. KELLERT. "The Global Environmental Deficit." In Herbert F. Bormann and Stephen R. Kellert, eds., *Ecology, Economics, and Ethics: The Broken Circle*. New Haven, Conn.: Yale University Press, 1991:ix–xviii.

BOSWELL, TERRY E. "A Split Labor Market Analysis of Discrimination against Chinese Immigrants, 1850–1882." *American Sociological Review*. Vol. 51, No. 3 (June 1986):352–71.

BOSWELL, TERRY E., and WILLIAM J. DIXON. "Marx's Theory of Rebellion: A Cross-National Analysis of Class Exploitation, Economic Development, and Violent Revolt." *American Sociological Review*. Vol. 58, No. 5 (October 1993):681–702.

BOTT, ELIZABETH. *Family and Social Network*. New York: Free Press, 1971; orig. 1957.

BOULDING, ELISE. *The Underside of History*. Boulder, Colo.: Westview Press, 1976.

BOWEN, WILLIAM G., and DEREK K. BOK. *The Shape of the River: Long-Term Consequences of Considering Race in College and University Admissions*. Princeton, N.J.: Princeton University Press, 1999.

BOWLES, SAMUEL, and HERBERT GINTIS. *Schooling in Capitalist America: Educational Reform and the Contradictions of Economic Life*. New York: Basic Books, 1976.

BOYER, DEBRA. "Male Prostitution and Homosexual Identity." *Journal of Homosexuality*. Vol. 17, Nos. 1–2 (1989):151–84.

BOYER, ERNEST L. *College: The Undergraduate Experience in America*. Prepared by the Carnegie Foundation for the Advancement of Teaching. New York: Harper & Row, 1987.

BRAITHWAITE, JOHN. "The Myth of Social Class and Criminality Reconsidered." *American Sociological Review*. Vol. 46, No. 1 (February 1981):36–57.

BRANEGAN, JAY. "Is Singapore a Model for the West?" *Time*. Vol. 141, No. 3 (January 18, 1993):36–37.

BRECHIN, STEVEN R., and WILLETT KEMPTON. "Global Environmentalism: A Challenge to the Postmaterialism Thesis." *Social Science Quarterly*. Vol. 75, No. 2 (June 1994):245–69.

BREEN, LEONARD Z. "The Aging Individual." In Clark Tibbitts, ed., *Handbook of Social Gerontology*. Chicago: University of Chicago Press, 1960:145–62.

BRIANS, CRAIG LEONARD, and BERNARD GROFMAN. "Election Day Registration's Effect on U.S. Voter Turnout." *Social Science Quarterly*. Vol. 82, No. 1 (March 2001):170–83.

BRIGHTMAN, JOAN. "Yellow Pages Change with the Times." *American Demographics*. Vol. 17, No. 3 (March 1995):16–18.

BRINES, JULIE, and KARA JOYNER. "The Ties That Bind: Principles of Cohesion in Cohabitation and Marriage." *American Sociological Review*. Vol. 64, No. 3 (June 1999):333–55.

BRINTON, CRANE. *The Anatomy of Revolution*. New York: Vintage Books, 1965.

BRINTON, MARY C. "The Social-Institutional Bases of Gender Stratification: Japan as an Illustrative Case." *American Journal of Sociology*. Vol. 94, No. 2 (September 1988):300–34.

BROCKERHOFF, MARTIN P. "An Urbanizing World." *Population Bulletin*. Vol. 55, No. 3 (September 2000).

BRODER, JOHN M. "Big Social Changes Revive False God of Numbers." *New York Times* (August 17, 1997): section 4, pp. 1, 4.

BRODKIN, KAREN. "How Jews Became White Folks." In Paula S. Rothenberg, ed., *White Privilege*. New York: Worth, 2001.

BROUGHTON, PHILIP DELVES. "Mississippi Vote to Keep Confederate Flag Symbol." *Electronic Telegraph*. Issue 2155 (April 19, 2001).

BROWN, LESTER R. "Reassessing the Earth's Population." *Society*. Vol. 32, No. 4 (May–June 1995):7–10.

BROWN, LESTER R., et al., eds. *State of the World 1993: A Worldwatch Institute Report on Progress toward a Sustainable Society*. New York: Norton, 1993.

BROWN, MARY ELLEN, ed. *Television and Women's Culture: The Politics of the Popular*. Newbury Park, Calif.: Sage, 1990.

BROWNING, CHRISTOPHER R., and EDWARD O. LAUMANN. "Sexual Contact between Children and Adults: A Life Course Perspective." *American Sociological Review*. Vol. 62, No. 5 (August 1997):540–60.

BRUNO, MARY. "Abusing the Elderly." *Newsweek* (September 23, 1985):75–76.

BUCHANAN, PATRICK J. "Why Conservatives Cannot Quit the Culture War." *New York Post* (February 20, 1999):15.

BUCKLEY, STEPHEN. "A Spare and Separate Way of Life." *Washington Post* (December 18, 1996):A1, A32–33.

Bulletin of the Atomic Scientists. Data on the doomsday clock. [Online] Available February 12, 2000, at http://www.bullatomsci.org/clock/pressrelease9.html

BUMPASS, LARRY, and JAMES A. SWEET. *1992–1994 National Survey of Families and Households*. Reported in "Report from PPA." *Population Today*. Vol. 23, No. 6 (June 1995):3.

BUNZEL, JOHN H. "Black and White at Stanford." *The Public Interest*. Vol. 105 (Fall 1991):61–77.

BURAWAY, MICHAEL. "Review Essay: The Soviet Descent into Capitalism." *American Journal of Sociology*. Vol. 102, No. 5 (March 1997):1430–44.

BURCH, ROBERT. Testimony to House of Representatives Hearing in "Review: The World Hunger Problem." October 25, 1983, Serial 98–38.

BURKE, TOM. "The Future." In Sir Edmund Hillary, ed., *Ecology 2000: The Changing Face of the Earth*. New York: Beaufort Books, 1984:227–41.

BURKETT, ELINOR. "God Created Me to Be a Slave." *New York Times* Sunday Magazine (October 12, 1997):56–60.

BURKHAUSER, RICHARD. "The Value of a Dollar." *Cornell Magazine* (March/April 2000):12–13.

BURNS, PETER F., PETER L. FRANCIA, and PAUL S. HERRNSON. "Labor at Work: Union Campaign Activities and Legislative Payoffs in the U.S. House of Representatives." *Social Science Quarterly*. Vol. 81, No. 2 (June 2000):507–22.

BURSTEIN, PAUL. "Legal Mobilization as a Social Movement Tactic: The Struggle for Equal Employment Opportunity." *American Journal of Sociology*. Vol. 96, No. 5 (March 1991):1201–25.

Business Week. "Online Privacy: It's Time for Rules in Wonderland." (March 20, 2000):82–96.

BUTLER, ROBERT N. *Why Survive? Being Old in America*. New York: Harper & Row, 1975.

BUTTERFIELD, FOX. "Prison: Where the Money Is." *New York Times* (June 2, 1996):E16.

CALLAHAN, DANIEL. *Setting Limits: Medical Goals in an Aging Society*. New York: Simon & Schuster, 1987.

CAMERON, WILLIAM BRUCE. *Modern Social Movements: A Sociological Outline*. New York: Random House, 1966.

CANETTI, ELIAS. *Crowds and Power*. New York: Seabury Press, 1978.

CANTOR, MURIAL G., and SUZANNE PINGREE. *The Soap Opera*. Beverly Hills, Calif.: Sage, 1983.

CAPEK, STELLA A. "The 'Environmental Justice' Frame: A Conceptual Discussion and an Application." *Social Problems*. Vol. 40, No. 1 (February 1993):5–24.

CAPIZANO, JEFFREY, GINA ADAMS, and FREYA SONENSTEIN. *Child Care Arrangements for Children under Five: Variation across States*. Report of the Urban Institute. [Online] Available February 14, 2001, at http://www.newfederalism. urban.org/html/series–b/b7.html

CAPIZANO, JEFFREY, KATHRYN TOUT, and GINA ADAMS. *Child Care Patterns of School-Age Children with Employed Mothers*. Report of the Urban Institute. [Online] Available February 14, 2001, at http://www.newfederalism. urban.org/html/op41/occa41.html#childcare

CAPLOW, THEODORE. "The Case of the Phantom Episcopalians." *American Sociological Review*. Vol. 63, No. 1 (February 1998):112–13.

CAPLOW, THEODORE, et al. *Middletown Families*. Minneapolis: University of Minnesota Press, 1982.

CAPLOW, THEODORE, HOWARD M. BAHR, JOHN MODELL, and BRUCE A. CHADWICK. *Recent Social Trends in the United States, 1960–1990*. Montreal: McGill-Queen's University Press, 1991.

CARLEY, KATHLEEN. "A Theory of Group Stability." *American Sociological Review*. Vol. 56, No. 3 (June 1991):331–54.

CARLSON, NORMAN A. "Corrections in the United States Today: A Balance Has Been Struck." *The American Criminal Law Review*. Vol. 13, No. 4 (Spring 1976):615–47.

CARMICHAEL, STOKELY, and CHARLES V. HAMILTON. *Black Power: The Politics of Liberation in America*. New York: Vintage Books, 1967.

CARR, LESLIE G. "Colorblindness and the New Racism." Paper presented at the annual meeting, American Sociological Association, Washington, D.C., 1995.

CARROLL, GINNY. "Who Foots the Bill?" *Newsweek*. Special Issue (Fall–Winter 1990):81–85.

CARROLL, JAMES R. "Congress Is Told of Coal-Dust Fraud UMW; Senator from Minnesota Rebukes Industry." *Louisville Courier Journal* (Thursday, May 27, 1999):1A.

CARSON, RACHEL. *Silent Spring*. Boston: Houghton Mifflin, 1962.

CASTELLS, MANUEL. *The Urban Question*. Cambridge, Mass.: MIT Press, 1977.

———. *The City and the Grass Roots*. Berkeley: University of California Press, 1983.

CATALYST. *1999 Catalyst Census of Women Corporate Officers and Top Earners*. [Online] Available April 18, 2000, at http://www.catalystwomen.org/press/factscote99.html

——— *Infobrief: Women CEOs*. [Online] Available April 18, 2000, at http://www.catalystwomen.org/press.html

——— *Infobrief: Women in Corporate Leadership*. [Online] Available April 18, 2000, at http://www.catalystwomen.org/press.html

————. *Women CEOs*. [Online] Available February 2, 2001, at http://www.catalystwomen.org/press/infobriefs/infobrief2.html

————. *Women Corporate Officers and Top Earners*. [Online] Available February 2, 2001, at http://www.catalystwomen.org/press/infobriefs/infocote.html

CENTER ON EDUCATION POLICY. "The Good News about American Education." Reported in Brigette Greenberg, "Report Finds America's Public Schools Showing Improvement." *Naples Daily News* (January 8, 2000):4a.

CENTER FOR RESPONSIVE POLITICS. *The Big Picture*. [Online] Available February 12, 1998, at http://www.crp.org/crpdocs/bigpicture/default.htm

————. *The Big Picture: The Money behind the 1998 Elections*. [Online] Available March 30, 2000, at http://www.opensecrets.org/pubs/bigpicture2000/index.htm

CENTER FOR THE STUDY OF SPORT IN SOCIETY. *2001 Racial and Gender Report Card*. Boston, Mass.: Northeastern University, 2001.

CERE, DANIEL. "Courtship Today: The View from Academia." *The Public Interest*. Vol. 143 (Spring 2001):53–71.

CHAGNON, NAPOLEON A. *Yanomamö: The Fierce People*. 4th ed. New York: Holt, Rinehart & Winston, 1992.

CHANDLER, TERTIUS, and GERALD FOX. *3000 Years of Urban History*. New York: Academic Press, 1974.

CHANDLER, TIMOTHY D., YOSHINORI KAMO, and JAMES D. WERBEL. "Do Delays in Marriage and Childbirth Affect Earnings?" *Social Science Quarterly*. Vol. 75, No. 4 (December 1994):838–53.

CHANGE, KWANG-CHIH. *The Archaeology of Ancient China*. New Haven, Conn.: Yale University Press, 1977.

CHAPPELL, NEENA L., and BETTY HAVENS. "Old and Female: Testing the Double Jeopardy Hypothesis." *The Sociological Quarterly*. Vol. 21, No. 2 (Spring 1980):157–71.

CHARLES, MARIA. "Cross-National Variation in Occupational Segregation." *American Sociological Review*. Vol. 57, No. 4 (August 1992):483–502.

CHAUNCEY, GEORGE. *Gay New York: Gender, Urban Culture, and the Making of the Gay Male World 1890–1940*. New York: Basic Books, 1994.

CHAVES, MARK. "Ordaining Women: The Diffusion of an Organizational Innovation." *American Journal of Sociology*. Vol. 101, No. 4 (January 1996):840–73.

————. *Ordaining Women: Culture and Conflict in Religious Organizations*. Cambridge, Mass.: Harvard University Press, 1997.

CHERLIN, ANDREW J., P. LINDSAY CHASE-LANSDALE, and CHRISTINE MCRAE. "Effects of Parental Divorce on Mental Health throughout the Life Course." *American Sociological Review*. Vol. 63, No. 2 (April 1998):239–49.

CHESNAIS, JEAN-CLAUDE. "The Demographic Sunset of the West?" *Population Today*. Vol. 25, No. 1 (January 1997):4–5.

CHILDREN'S DEFENSE FUND. *The State of America's Children Yearbook, 1995*. Washington, D.C.: Children's Defense Fund, 1995.

CHOLDIN, HARVEY M. "How Sampling Will Help Defeat the Undercount." *Society*. Vol. 34, No. 3 (March/April 1997):27–30.

CHUA-EOAN, HOWARD. "Profiles in Outrage." *Time*. Vol. 156, No. 13 (September 25, 2000):38–39.

CHURCH, GEORGE J. "Unions Arise—with New Tricks." *Time*. Vol. 143, No. 24 (June 13, 1994):56–58.

————. "Ripping Up Welfare." *Time*. Vol. 148, No. 8 (August 12, 1996):18–22.

CIMINO, RICHARD, and DON LATTIN. "Choosing My Religion." *American Demographics*. Vol. 21, No. 4 (April 1999):60–65.

CLARK, CURTIS B. "Geriatric Abuse: Out of the Closet." In *The Tragedy of Elder Abuse: The Problem and the Response*. Hearings before the Select Committee on Aging, House of Representatives (July 1, 1986):49–50.

CLARK, MARGARET S., ed. *Prosocial Behavior*. Newbury Park, Calif.: Sage, 1991.

CLARKE, ROBIN. "Atmospheric Pollution." In Sir Edmund Hillary, ed., *Ecology 2000: The Changing Face of the Earth*. New York: Beaufort Books, 1984a:130–48.

————. "What's Happening to Our Water?" In Sir Edmund Hillary, ed., *Ecology 2000: The Changing Face of the Earth*. New York: Beaufort Books, 1984b:108–29.

CLAWSON, DAN, and MARY ANN CLAWSON. "What Has Happened to the U.S. Labor Movement? Union Decline and Renewal." *Annual Review of Sociology*. Vol. 25 (1999):95–119.

CLEMETSON, LYNETTE. "Grandma Knows Best." *Newsweek* (June 12, 2000):60–61.

CLINARD, MARSHALL, and DANIEL ABBOTT. *Crime in Developing Countries*. New York: Wiley, 1973.

CLOUD, JOHN. "What Can the Schools Do?" *Time*. Vol. 153, No. 17 (May 3, 1999):38–40.

CLOWARD, RICHARD A., and LLOYD E. OHLIN. *Delinquency and Opportunity: A Theory of Delinquent Gangs*. New York: Free Press, 1966.

COE, MICHAEL D., and RICHARD A. DIEHL. *In the Land of the Olmec*. Austin: University of Texas Press, 1980.

COHEN, ADAM. "A New Push for Blind Justice." *Time*. Vol. 145, No. 7 (February 20, 1995):39–40.

————. "Test-Tube Tug-of-War." *Time*. Vol. 151, No. 13 (April 6, 1998):65.

————. "A First Report Card on Vouchers." *Time*. Vol. 153, No. 16 (April 26, 1999):36–38.

COHEN, ALBERT K. *Delinquent Boys: The Culture of the Gang*. New York: Free Press, 1971; orig. 1955.

COHEN, LLOYD R. "Sexual Harassment and the Law." *Society*. Vol. 28, No. 4 (May–June 1991):8–13.

COHN, RICHARD M. "Economic Development and Status Change of the Aged." *American Journal of Sociology*. Vol. 87, No. 2 (March 1982):1150–61.

COLEMAN, JAMES S. "Rational Organization." *Rationality and Society*. Vol. 2, (1990):94–105.

————. "The Design of Organizations and the Right to Act." *Sociological Forum*. Vol. 8, No. 4 (December 1993):527–46.

COLEMAN, JAMES S., and THOMAS HOFFER. *Public and Private High Schools: The Impact of Communities*. New York: Basic Books, 1987.

COLEMAN, JAMES, THOMAS HOFFER, and SALLY KILGORE. *Public and Private Schools: An Analysis of Public Schools and Beyond*. Washington, D.C.: National Center for Education Statistics, 1981.

COLEMAN, RICHARD P., and BERNICE L. NEUGARTEN. *Social Status in the City*. San Francisco: Jossey-Bass, 1971.

COLEMAN, RICHARD P., and LEE RAINWATER. *Social Standing in America*. New York: Basic Books, 1978.

COLLINS, RANDALL. "A Conflict Theory of Sexual Stratification." *Social Problems*. Vol. 19, No. 1 (Summer 1971):3–21.

————. *The Credential Society: An Historical Sociology of Education and Stratification*. New York: Academic Press, 1979.

————. *Sociological Insight: An Introduction to Nonobvious Sociology*. New York: Oxford University Press, 1982.

COLLOWAY, N. O., and PAULA L. DOLLEVOET. "Selected Tabular Material on Aging." In Caleb Finch and Leonard Hayflick, eds., *Handbook of the Biology of Aging*. New York: Van Nostrand Reinhold, 1977:666–708.

COLTON, HELEN. *The Gift of Touch: How Physical Contact Improves Communication, Pleasure, and Health*. New York: Seaview/Putnam, 1983.

COMMISSION FOR RACIAL JUSTICE, UNITED CHURCH OF CHRIST. *CRJ Reporter*. New York: Commission for Racial Justice, the United Church of Christ, 1994.

COMTE, AUGUSTE. *Auguste Comte and Positivism: The Essential Writings*. Gertrud Lenzer, ed. New York: Harper Torchbooks, 1975.

CONNETT, PAUL H. "The Disposable Society." In F. Herbert Bormann and Stephen R. Kellert, eds., *Ecology, Economics, and Ethics: The Broken Circle*. New Haven, Conn.: Yale University Press, 1991:99–122.

COOK, RHODES. "House Republicans Scored a Quiet Victory in '92." *Congressional Quarterly Weekly Report*. Vol. 51, No. 16 (April 17, 1993):965–68.

COOLEY, CHARLES HORTON. *Social Organization*. New York: Schocken Books, 1962; orig. 1909.

————. *Human Nature and the Social Order*. New York: Schocken Books, 1964; orig. 1902.

COONEY, MARK. "From Warfare to Tyranny: Lethal Conflict and the State." *American Sociological Review*. Vol. 62, No. 2 (April 1997):316–38.

CORCORAN, MARY, SANDRA K. DANZIGER, ARIEL KALIL, and KRISTIN S. SEEFELDT. "How Welfare Reform Is Affecting Women's Work." *Annual Review of Sociology*. Vol. 26 (2000):241–69.

CORLEY, ROBERT N., O. LEE REED, PETER J. SHEDD, and JERE W. MOREHEAD. *The Legal and Regulatory Environment of Business*. 9th ed. New York: McGraw-Hill, 1993.

CORNELL, BARBARA. "Pulling the Plug on TV." *Time*. Vol. 152, No. 16 (October 16, 2000):F16.

COSE, ELLIS. "Census and the Complex Issue of Race." *Society*. Vol. 34, No. 6 (September/October, 1997):9–13.

————. "The Good News about Black America." *Newsweek* (June 7, 1999):28–40.

COSER, LEWIS. *The Functions of Social Conflict*. New York: Free Press, 1956.

————. *Masters of Sociological Thought: Ideas in Historical and Social Context*. New York: Harcourt Brace Jovanovich, 1971.

COTTLE, THOMAS J. "What Tracking Did to Ollie Taylor." *Social Policy*. Vol. 5, No. 2 (July–August 1974):22–24.

COUNCIL ON FAMILIES IN AMERICA. *Marriage in America: A Report to the Nation*. New York: Institute for American Values, 1995.

COUNTS, G. S. "The Social Status of Occupations: A Problem in Vocational Guidance." *School Review*. Vol. 33 (January 1925):16–27.

COURTNEY, ALICE E., and THOMAS W. WHIPPLE. *Sex Stereotyping in Advertising*. Lexington, Mass.: D.C. Heath, 1983.

COURTWRIGHT, DAVID T. *Violent Land: Single Men and Social Disorder from the Frontier to the Inner City*. Cambridge, Mass.: Harvard University Press, 1996.

COVINGTON, JEANETTE. "Racial Classification in Criminology: The Reproduction of Racialized Crime." *Sociological Forum*. Vol. 10, No. 4 (December 1995):547–68.

COWAN, CAROLYN POPE. *When Partners Become Parents*. New York: Basic Books, 1992.

COWGILL, DONALD, and LOWELL HOLMES. *Aging and Modernization*. New York: Appleton-Century-Crofts, 1972.

COWLEY, GEOFFREY. "The Prescription That Kills." *Newsweek* (July 17, 1995):54.

COX, HARVEY. *The Secular City*. Rev. ed. New York: Macmillan, 1971; orig. 1965.

————. "Church and Believers: Always Strangers?" In Thomas Robbins and Dick Anthony, *In Gods We Trust: New Patterns of Religious Pluralism in America*. 2d ed. New Brunswick, N.J.: Transaction, 1990:449–62.

COYOTE (Call Off Your Old Tired Ethics). [Online] Available April 2, 2000, at http://www.freedomusa.org/coyotela/what–is.html

CRISPELL, DIANE. "Grandparents Galore." *American Demographics*. Vol. 15, No. 10 (October 1993):63.

————. "Speaking in Other Tongues." *American Demographics*. Vol. 19, No. 1 (January 1997a):12–15.

————. "Lucky to Be Alive." *American Demographics*. Vol. 19, No. 4 (April 1997b):25.

CROOK, STEPHAN, JAN PAKULSKI, and MALCOLM WATERS. *Postmodernity: Change in Advanced Society*. Newbury Park, Calif.: Sage, 1992.

CROSSEN, CYNTHIA, and ELLEN GRAHAM. "Good News—and Bad—about America's Health." *Wall Street Journal* (June 28, 1996):R1.

CROSSETTE, BARBARA. "Female Genital Mutilation by Immigrants Is Becoming Cause for Concern in the U.S." *New York Times International* (December 10, 1995):11.

CROUSE, JAMES, and DALE TRUSHEIM. *The Case against the SAT.* Chicago: University of Chicago Press, 1988.

CUFF, E. C., and G. C. F. PAYNE, eds. *Perspectives in Sociology.* London: Allen & Unwin, 1979.

CUMMING, ELAINE, and WILLIAM E. HENRY. *Growing Old: The Process of Disengagement.* New York: Basic Books, 1961.

CUMMINGS, SCOTT, and THOMAS LAMBERT. "Anti-Hispanic and Anti-Asian Sentiments among African Americans." *Social Science Quarterly.* Vol. 78, No. 2 (June 1997):338–53.

CURRIE, ELLIOTT. *Confronting Crime: An American Challenge.* New York: Pantheon Books, 1985.

CURRY, GEORGE E., ed. *The Affirmative Action Debate.* Reading, Mass.: Addison-Wesley, 1996.

CURTIS, JAMES E., EDWARD G. GRABB, and DOUGLAS BAER. "Voluntary Association Membership in Fifteen Countries: A Comparative Analysis." *American Sociological Review.* Vol. 57, No. 2 (April 1992):139–52.

CURTISS, SUSAN. *Genie: A Psycholinguistic Study of a Modern-Day "Wild Child."* New York: Academic Press, 1977.

CUTRIGHT, PHILLIP. "Occupational Inheritance: A Cross-National Analysis." *American Journal of Sociology.* Vol. 73, No. 4 (January 1968):400–16.

DAHL, ROBERT A. *Who Governs?* New Haven, Conn.: Yale University Press, 1961.

———. *Dilemmas of Pluralist Democracy: Autonomy vs. Control.* New Haven, Conn.: Yale University Press, 1982.

DAHRENDORF, RALF. *Class and Class Conflict in Industrial Society.* Stanford, Calif.: Stanford University Press, 1959.

DALY, MARTIN, and MARGO WILSON. *Homicide.* New York: Aldine, 1988.

DANIELS, ROGER. "The Issei Generation." In Amy Tachiki et al., eds., *Roots: An Asian American Reader.* Los Angeles: UCLA Asian American Studies Center, 1971:138–49.

DARNTON, NINA, and YURIKO HOSHIA. "Whose Life Is It, Anyway?" *Newsweek.* Vol. 113, No. 4 (January 13, 1989):61.

DAVIDSON, JAMES D., RALPH E. PYLE, and DAVID V. REYES. "Persistence and Change in the Protestant Establishment, 1930–1992." *Social Forces.* Vol. 74, No. 1 (September 1995):157–75.

DAVIDSON, JULIA O'CONNELL. *Prostitution, Power, and Freedom.* Ann Arbor: University of Michigan Press, 1998.

DAVIES, CHRISTIE. *Ethnic Humor around the World: A Comparative Analysis.* Bloomington: Indiana University Press, 1990.

DAVIES, JAMES C. "Toward a Theory of Revolution." *American Sociological Review.* Vol. 27, No. 1 (February 1962):5–19.

DAVIES, MARK, and DENISE B. KANDEL. "Parental and Peer Influences on Adolescents' Educational Plans: Some Further Evidence." *American Journal of Sociology.* Vol. 87, No. 2 (September 1981):363–87.

DAVIS, BYRON BRADLEY. "Sports World." *Christian Science Monitor* (September 9, 1997):11.

DAVIS, DONALD M., cited in "T.V. Is a Blonde, Blonde World." *American Demographics,* special issue: *Women Change Places.* Ithaca, N.Y.: 1993.

DAVIS, KINGSLEY. "Extreme Social Isolation of a Child." *American Journal of Sociology.* Vol. 45, No. 4 (January 1940):554–65.

———. "Final Note on a Case of Extreme Isolation." *American Journal of Sociology.* Vol. 52, No. 5 (March 1947):432–37.

———. "The Myth of Functional Analysis as a Special Method in Sociology and Anthropology." *American Sociological Review.* Vol. 24, No. 1 (February 1959):75ff.

———. "Sexual Behavior." In Robert K. Merton and Robert Nisbet, eds., *Contemporary Social Problems.* 3d ed. New York: Harcourt Brace Jovanovich, 1971:313–60.

DAVIS, KINGSLEY, and WILBERT MOORE. "Some Principles of Stratification." *American Sociological Review.* Vol. 10, No. 2 (April 1945):242–49.

DECKARD, BARBARA SINCLAIR. *The Women's Movement: Political, Socioeconomic, and Psychological Issues.* 2d ed. New York: Harper & Row, 1979.

DEDRICK, DENNIS K., and RICHARD E. YINGER. "MAD, SDI, and the Nuclear Arms Race." Manuscript in development. Georgetown, Ky.: Georgetown College, 1990.

DEJONG, GORDON F., and ANNA B. MADAMBA. "A Double Disadvantage? Minority Group, Immigrant Status, and Underemployment in the United States." *Social Science Quarterly.* Vol. 82, No. 1 (March 2001):117–30.

DELACROIX, JACQUES, and CHARLES C. RAGIN. "Structural Blockage: A Crossnational Study of Economic Dependency, State Efficacy, and Underdevelopment." *American Journal of Sociology.* Vol. 86, No. 6 (May 1981):1311–47.

DELLA CAVA, MARCO R. "For Dutch, It's as Easy as Asking a Doctor." *USA Today* (January 7, 1997):4A.

DELUCA, TOM. "Joe the Bookie and the Class Voting Gap." *American Demographics.* Vol. 20, No. 11 (November 1998):26–29.

DE MENTE, BOYE. *Japanese Etiquette and Ethics in Business.* 5th ed. Lincolnwood, Ill.: NTC Business Books, 1987.

DEMERATH, N. J., III. "Who Now Debates Functionalism? From *System, Change, and Conflict* to 'Culture, Choice, and Praxis.'" *Sociological Forum.* Vol. 11, No. 2 (June 1996):333–45.

DENT, DAVID J. "African-Americans Turning to Christian Academies." *New York Times,* Education Life supplement (August 4, 1996):26–29.

DERSHOWITZ, ALAN. *The Vanishing American Jew.* Boston: Little, Brown, 1997.

Der Spiegel. "Third World Metropolises Are Becoming Monsters; Rural Poverty Drives Millions to the Slums." In *World Press Review* (October 1989).

DERVARICS, CHARLES. "Is Welfare Reform Reforming Welfare?" *Population Today.* Vol. 26, No. 10 (October 1998):1–2.

———. "The Coming Age of Older Women." *Population Today.* Vol. 27, No. 2 (February 1999):2–3.

———. "Is There a Teacher Shortage?" *Population Today.* Vol. 27, No. 11 (November 1999):1–2.

DESRUISSEAUX, PAUL. "U.S. Trails 22 Nations in High-School Completion." *Chronicle of Higher Education.* Vol. 45, No. 15 (December 4, 1998):A45.

DEUTSCHER, IRWIN. *Making a Difference: The Practice of Sociology.* New Brunswick, N.J.: Transaction, 1999.

DEVINE, JOEL A. "State and State Expenditure: Determinants of Social Investment and Social Consumption Spending in the Postwar United States." *American Sociological Review.* Vol. 50, No. 2 (April 1985):150–65.

DIIULIO, JOHN J., JR. "Broken Streets, Broken Lives." *The Public Interest.* Vol. 139 (Spring 2000):106–10.

DIXON, WILLIAM J., and TERRY BOSWELL. "Dependency, Disarticulation, and Denominator Effects: Another Look at Foreign Capital Penetration." *American Journal of Sociology.* Vol. 102, No. 2 (September 1996):543–62.

DIZARD, JAN E., and HOWARD GADLIN. *The Minimal Family.* Amherst: The University of Massachusetts Press, 1990.

DOBSON, RICHARD B. "Mobility and Stratification in the Soviet Union." *Annual Review of Sociology.* Vol. 3. Palo Alto, Calif.: Annual Reviews, 1977:297–329.

DOBYNS, HENRY F. "An Appraisal of Techniques with a New Hemispheric Estimate." *Current Anthropology.* Vol. 7, No. 4 (October 1966):395–446.

DOLLARD, JOHN, et al. *Frustration and Aggression.* New Haven, Conn.: Yale University Press, 1939.

DOMHOFF, G. WILLIAM. *Who Rules America Now? A View of the '80s.* Englewood Cliffs, N.J.: Prentice Hall, 1983.

DONAHUE, JOHN J. III, and STEVEN D. LEAVITT. Research cited in "New Study Claims Abortion Is Behind Decrease in Crime." *Population Today.* Vol. 28, No. 1 (January 2000):1, 4.

DONNELLY, PATRICK G., and THEO J. MAJKA. "Residents' Efforts at Neighborhood Stabilization: Facing the Challenges of Inner-City Neighborhoods." *Sociological Forum.* Vol. 13, No. 2 (June 1998):189–213.

DONOVAN, VIRGINIA K., and RONNIE LITTENBERG. "Psychology of Women: Feminist Therapy." In Barbara Haber, ed., *The Women's Annual 1981: The Year in Review.* Boston: G.K. Hall, 1982:211–35.

DOWELL, WILLIAM. "Addressing Africa's Agony." *Time.* Vol. 155, No. 3 (January 24, 2000):36.

DOYAL, LESLEY, and IMOGEN PENNELL. *The Political Economy of Health.* London: Pluto Press, 1981.

DOYLE, JAMES A. *The Male Experience.* Dubuque, Iowa: Wm. C. Brown, 1983.

DOYLE, RICHARD F. *A Manifesto of Men's Liberation.* 2d ed. Forest Lake, Minn.: Men's Rights Association, 1980.

D'SOUZA, DINESH. "The Billionaire Next Door." *Forbes.* Vol. 164, No. 9 (October 11, 1999):50–62.

DU BOIS, W. E. B. *The Philadelphia Negro: A Social Study.* New York: Schocken Books, 1967; orig. 1899.

DUBOS, RENÉ. *Man Adapting.* New Haven, Conn.: Yale University Press, 1980; orig. 1965.

DUHL, LEONARD J. "The Social Context of Health." In Arthur C. Hastings et al., eds., *Health for the Whole Person: The Complete Guide to Holistic Medicine.* Boulder, Colo.: Westview Press, 1980:39–48.

DUNBAR, LESLIE. *The Common Interest: How Our Social Welfare Policies Don't Work and What We Can Do about Them.* New York: Pantheon, 1988.

DUNCAN, CYNTHIA M. *Worlds Apart: Why Poverty Persists in Rural America.* New Haven, CT: Yale University Press, 1999.

DUNCAN, GREG J., W. JEAN YEUNG, JEANNE BROOKS-GUNN, and JUDITH R. SMITH. "How Much Does Childhood Poverty Affect the Life Chances of Children?" *American Sociological Review.* Vol. 63, No. 3 (June 1998):406–23.

DURKHEIM, EMILE. *Moral Education.* New York: Free Press, 1961; orig. 1902–3.

———. *The Division of Labor in Society.* New York: Free Press, 1964a; orig. 1893.

———. *The Rules of Sociological Method.* New York: Free Press, 1964b; orig. 1895.

———. *The Elementary Forms of Religious Life.* New York: Free Press, 1965; orig. 1915.

———. *Suicide.* New York: Free Press, 1966; orig. 1897.

———. *Sociology and Philosophy.* New York: Free Press, 1974; orig. 1924.

DURNING, ALAN THEIN. "Supporting Indigenous Peoples." In Lester R. Brown et al., eds., *State of the World 1993: A Worldwatch Institute Report on Progress toward a Sustainable Society.* New York: Norton, 1993:80–100.

DWORKIN, ANDREA. *Intercourse.* New York: Free Press, 1987.

EBAUGH, HELEN ROSE FUCHS. *Becoming an EX: The Process of Role Exit.* Chicago: University of Chicago Press, 1988.

EBERSTADT, NICHOLAS. "What Is Population Policy?" *Society.* Vol. 32, No. 4 (May–June 1995):26–29.

EDIN, KATHRYN, and LAURA LEIN. "Work, Welfare, and Single Mothers' Economic Survival Strategies." *American Sociological Review.* Vol. 62, No. 2 (April 1996):253–66.

EDMONDSON, BRAD. "The Great Money Grab." *American Demographics.* Vol. 17, No. 2 (February 1995):2.

———. "Fountains of Youth." *American Demographics.* Vol. 18, No. 7 (July 1996):60.

———. "The Facts of Death." *American Demographics.* Vol. 49, No. 4 (April 1997a):47–53.

———. "The Wired Bunch." *American Demographics.* Vol. 49, No. 6 (June 1997b):10–15.

EDWARDS, DAVID V. *The American Political Experience.* 3d ed. Englewood Cliffs, N.J.: Prentice Hall, 1985.

EDWARDS, RICHARD. *Contested Terrain: The Transformation of the Workplace in the Twentieth Century.* New York: Basic Books, 1979.

EDWARDS, TAMALA M. "Revolt of the Gentry." *Time.* Vol. 151, No. 23 (June 15, 1998):34–35.

———. "Flying Solo." *Time.* Vol. 156, No. 9 (August 28, 2000):47–55.

EHRENREICH, BARBARA. *The Hearts of Men: American Dreams and the Flight from Commitment.* Garden City, N.Y.: Anchor Books, 1983.
———. "The Real Truth about the Female Body." *Time.* Vol. 153, No. 9 (March 15, 1999):56–65.
EHRENREICH, JOHN. "Introduction." In John Ehrenreich, ed., *The Cultural Crisis of Modern Medicine.* New York: Monthly Review Press, 1978:1–35.
EICHLER, MARGRIT. *Nonsexist Research Methods: A Practical Guide.* Winchester, Mass.: Unwin Hyman, 1988.
EISEN, ARNOLD M. *The Chosen People in America: A Study of Jewish Religious Ideology.* Bloomington: Indiana University Press, 1983.
EISENBERG, DANIEL. "Anatomy of a Recall." *Time.* Vol. 156, No. 11 (September 11, 2000):28–32.
EISENSTEIN, ZILLAH R., ed. *Capitalist Patriarchy and the Case for Socialist Feminism.* New York: Monthly Review Press, 1979.
EISLER, BENITA. *The Lowell Offering: Writings by New England Mill Women 1840–1845.* Philadelphia: J.B. Lippincott, 1977.
EKMAN, PAUL. "Biological and Cultural Contributions to Body and Facial Movements in the Expression of Emotions." In A. Rorty, ed., *Explaining Emotions.* Berkeley: University of California Press, 1980a:73–101.
———. *Face of Man: Universal Expression in a New Guinea Village.* New York: Garland Press, 1980b.
———. *Telling Lies: Clues to Deceit in the Marketplace, Politics, and Marriage.* New York: Norton, 1985.
EL-ATTAR, MOHAMED. Personal communication, 1991.
ELIAS, ROBERT. *The Politics of Victimization: Victims, Victimology and Human Rights.* New York: Oxford University Press, 1986.
ELLIOT, DELBERT S., and SUZANNE S. AGETON. "Reconciling Race and Class Differences in Self-Reported and Official Estimates of Delinquency." *American Sociological Review.* Vol. 45, No. 1 (February 1980):95–110.
ELLISON, CHRISTOPHER G., JOHN P. BARTKOWSKI, and MICHELLE L. SEGAL. "Do Conservative Protestant Parents Spank More Often? Further Evidence from the National Survey of Families and Households." *Social Science Quarterly.* Vol. 77, No. 3 (September 1996):663–73.
ELLISON, CHRISTOPHER G., and DARREN E. SHERKAT. "Conservative Protestantism and Support for Corporal Punishment." *American Sociological Review.* Vol. 58, No. 1 (February 1993):131–44.
ELMER-DEWITT, PHILIP. "The Revolution That Fizzled." *Time.* Vol. 137, No. 20 (May 20, 1991):48–49.
———. "First Nation in Cyberspace." *Time.* Vol. 142, No. 24 (December 6, 1993):62–64.
———. "The Genetic Revolution." *Time.* Vol. 143, No. 3 (January 17, 1994a):46–53.
———. "Battle for the Internet." *Time.* Vol. 144, No. 4 (July 25, 1994b):50–56.
———. "Now for the Truth about Americans and Sex." *Time.* Vol. 144, No. 16 (October 17, 1994c):62–70.
EMBER, MELVIN, and CAROL R. EMBER. "The Conditions Favoring Matrilocal versus Patrilocal Residence." *American Anthropologist.* Vol. 73, No. 3 (June 1971):571–94.
———. *Anthropology.* 6th ed. Englewood Cliffs, N.J.: Prentice Hall, 1991.
EMBREE, AINSLIE T. *The Hindu Tradition.* New York: Vintage Books, 1972.
EMERSON, JOAN P. "Behavior in Private Places: Sustaining Definitions of Reality in Gynecological Examinations." In H. P. Dreitzel, ed., *Recent Sociology.* Vol. 2. New York: Collier, 1970:74–97.
ENDICOTT, KAREN. "Fathering in an Egalitarian Society." In Barry S. Hewlett, ed., *Father-Child Relations: Cultural and Bio-Social Contexts.* New York: Aldine, 1992:281–96.
ENGELS, FRIEDRICH. *The Origin of the Family.* Chicago: Charles H. Kerr & Company, 1902; orig. 1884.
ENGLAND, PAULA. *Comparable Worth: Theories and Evidence.* Hawthorne, N.Y.: Aldine, 1992.
ENGLAND, PAULA, JOAN M. HERMSEN, and DAVID A. COTTER. "The Devaluation of Women's Work: A Comment on Tam." *American Journal of Sociology.* Vol. 105, No. 6 (May 2000):1741–60.
EPPS, EDGAR G. "Race, Class, and Educational Opportunity: Trends in the Sociology of Education." *Sociological Forum.* Vol. 10, No. 4 (December 1995):593–608.
ERBER, ERNEST. "Virtues and Vices of the Market: Balanced Correctives to a Current Craze." *Dissent.* Vol. 37 (Summer 1990):353–60.
ERIKSON, ERIK H. *Childhood and Society.* New York: Norton, 1963; orig. 1950.
———. *Identity and the Life Cycle.* New York: Norton, 1980.
ERIKSON, KAI T. *Wayward Puritans: A Study in the Sociology of Deviance.* New York: Wiley, 1966.
ERIKSON, ROBERT S., NORMAN R. LUTTBEG, and KENT L. TEDIN. *American Public Opinion: Its Origins, Content, and Impact.* 2d ed. New York: Wiley, 1980.
ETZIONI, AMITAI. *A Comparative Analysis of Complex Organization: On Power, Involvement, and Their Correlates.* Rev. and enlarged ed. New York: Free Press, 1975.
———. "Too Many Rights, Too Few Responsibilities." *Society.* Vol. 28, No. 2 (January–February 1991):41–48.
———. "How to Make Marriage Matter." *Time.* Vol. 142, No. 10 (September 6, 1993):76.
———. "The Responsive Community: A Communitarian Perspective." *American Sociological Review.* Vol. 61, No. 1 (February 1996):1–11.
ETZIONI-HALEVY, EVA. *Bureaucracy and Democracy: A Political Dilemma.* Rev. ed. Boston: Routledge & Kegan Paul, 1985.
FAGAN, JEFFREY, FRANKLIN E. ZIMRING, and JUNE KIM. "Declining Homicide in New York City: A Tale of Two Trends." *National Institute of Justice Journal.* Vol. 237 (October 1998):12–13.
FALK, GERHARD. Personal communication, 1987.

FALKENMARK, MALIN, and CARL WIDSTRAND. "Population and Water Resources: A Delicate Balance." *Population Bulletin.* Vol. 47, No. 3 (November 1992). Washington, D.C.: Population Reference Bureau.
FALLON, A. E., and P. ROZIN. "Sex Differences in Perception of Desirable Body Shape." *Journal of Abnormal Psychology.* Vol. 94, No. 1 (1985):100–5.
FALLOWS, JAMES. "Immigration: How It's Affecting Us." *The Atlantic Monthly.* Vol. 252 (November 1983):45–52, 55–62, 66–68, 85–90, 94, 96, 99–106.
FANON, FRANTZ. *The Wretched of the Earth.* New York: Grove Press, 1963.
FARLEY, CHRISTOPHER JOHN. "Winning the Right to Fly." *Time.* Vol. 146, No. 9 (August 28, 1995):62–64.
FARRELL, MICHAEL P., and STANLEY D. ROSENBERG. *Men at Midlife.* Boston: Auburn House, 1981.
FEAGIN, JOE. *The Urban Real Estate Game.* Englewood Cliffs, N.J.: Prentice Hall, 1983.
———. "Death By Discrimination?" *Newsletter, Society for the Study of Social Problems.* Vol. 28, No. 1 (Winter 1997):15–16.
FEATHERMAN, DAVID L., and ROBERT M. HAUSER. *Opportunity and Change.* New York: Academic Press, 1978.
FEATHERSTONE, MIKE, ed. *Global Culture: Nationalism, Globalization, and Modernity.* London: Sage, 1990.
FEDARKO, KEVIN. "Land Mines: Cheap, Deadly, and Cruel." *Time.* Vol. 147, No. 20 (May 13, 1996):54–55.
FELLMAN, BRUCE. "Taking the Measure of Children's T.V." *Yale Alumni Magazine* (April 1995):46–51.
FERGUSON, ANDREW. "Inside the Crazy Culture of Kids' Sports." *Time.* Vol. 154, No. 2 (July 12, 1999):52–60.
FERGUSON, TOM. "Medical Self-Care: Self Responsibility for Health." In Arthur C. Hastings et al., eds., *Health for the Whole Person: The Complete Guide to Holistic Medicine.* Boulder, Colo.: Westview Press, 1980:87–109.
FERNANDEZ, ROBERTO M., and NANCY WEINBERG. "Sifting and Sorting: Personal Contacts and Hiring in a Retail Bank." *American Sociological Review.* Vol. 62, No. 6 (December 1997):883–902.
FERREE, MYRA MARX, and ELAINE J. HALL. "Rethinking Stratification from a Feminist Perspective: Gender, Race, and Class in Mainstream Textbooks." *American Sociological Review.* Vol. 61, No. 6 (December 1996):929–50.
FETTO, JOHN. "Down for the Count." *American Demographics.* Vol. 21, No. 11 (November 1999):46–47.
———. "Lean on Me." *American Demographics.* Vol. 22, No. 12 (December 2000):16–17.
FINE, GARY ALAN. "Nature and the Taming of the Wild: The Problem of 'Overpick' in the Culture of Mushroomers." *Social Problems.* Vol. 44, No. 1 (February 1997):68–88.
FINKELSTEIN, NEAL W., and RON HASKINS. "Kindergarten Children Prefer Same-Color Peers." *Child Development.* Vol. 54, No. 2 (April 1983):502–8.
FINN, CHESTER E., JR., and REBECCA L. GAU. "New Ways of Education." *The Public Interest.* Vol. 130 (Winter 1998):79–92.
FINN, CHESTER E., JR., and HERBERT J. WALBERG. "The World's Least Efficient Schools." *Wall Street Journal* (June 22, 1998):A22.
FIORENTINE, ROBERT. "Men, Women, and the Premed Persistence Gap: A Normative Alternatives Approach." *American Journal of Sociology.* Vol. 92, No. 5 (March 1987):1118–39.
FIORENTINE, ROBERT, and STEPHEN COLE. "Why Fewer Women Become Physicians: Explaining the Premed Persistence Gap." *Sociological Forum.* Vol. 7, No. 3 (September 1992):469–96.
FIREBAUGH, GLENN. "Growth Effects of Foreign and Domestic Investment." *American Journal of Sociology.* Vol. 98, No. 1 (July 1992):105–30.
———. "Does Foreign Capital Harm Poor Nations? New Estimates Based on Dixon and Boswell's Measures of Capital Penetration." *American Journal of Sociology.* Vol. 102, No. 2 (September 1996):563–75.
———. "Empirics of World Income Inequality." *American Journal of Sociology.* Vol. 104, No. 6 (May 1999):1597–1630.
———. "The Trend in Between-Nation Income Inequality." *Annual Review of Sociology.* Vol. 26 (2000):323–39.
FIREBAUGH, GLENN, and FRANK D. BECK. "Does Economic Growth Benefit the Masses? Growth, Dependence, and Welfare in the Third World." *American Sociological Review.* Vol. 59, No. 5 (October 1994):631–53.
FIREBAUGH, GLENN, and KENNETH E. DAVIS. "Trends in Antiblack Prejudice, 1972–1984: Region and Cohort Effects." *American Journal of Sociology.* Vol. 94, No. 2 (September 1988):251–72.
FIREBAUGH, GLENN, and DUMITRU SANDU. "Who Supports Marketization and Democratization in Post-Communist Romania?" *Sociological Forum.* Vol. 13, No. 3 (September 1998):521–41.
FISCHER, CLAUDE W. *The Urban Experience.* 2d ed. New York: Harcourt Brace Jovanovich, 1984.
FISHER, ELIZABETH. *Woman's Creation: Sexual Evolution and the Shaping of Society.* Garden City, N.Y.: Anchor/Doubleday, 1979.
FISHER, ROGER, and WILLIAM URY. "Getting to YES." In William M. Evan and Stephen Hilgartner, eds., *The Arms Race and Nuclear War.* Englewood Cliffs, N.J.: Prentice Hall, 1988:261–68.
FISKE, ALAN PAIGE. "The Cultural Relativity of Selfish Individualism: Anthropological Evidence that Humans Are Inherently Sociable." In Margaret S. Clark, ed., *Prosocial Behavior.* Newbury Park, Calif.: Sage, 1991:176–214.
FISKE, EDWARD B. "Adults: The Forgotten Illiterates." *Christian Science Monitor* (May 30, 1997):18.
FITZGERALD, JOAN, and LOUISE SIMMONS. "From Consumption to Production: Labor Participation in Grass-Roots Movements in Pittsburgh and Hartford." *Urban Affairs Quarterly.* Vol. 26 (June 1991):512–31.
FITZPATRICK, MARY ANNE. *Between Husbands and Wives: Communication in Marriage.* Newbury Park, Calif.: Sage, 1988.

FLAHERTY, MICHAEL G. "A Formal Approach to the Study of Amusement in Social Interaction." *Studies in Symbolic Interaction.* Vol. 5. New York: JAI Press, 1984:71–82.

———. "Two Conceptions of the Social Situation: Some Implications of Humor." *The Sociological Quarterly.* Vol. 31, No. 1 (Spring 1990).

FLORIDA, RICHARD, and MARTIN KENNEY. "Transplanted Organizations: The Transfer of Japanese Industrial Organization to the U.S." *American Sociological Review.* Vol. 56, No. 3 (June 1991):381–98.

FLYNN, PATRICIA. "The Disciplinary Emergence of Bioethics and Bioethics Committees: Moral Ordering and its Legitimation." *Sociological Focus.* Vol. 24, No. 2 (May 1991):145–56.

FOBES, RICHARD. "Creative Problem Solving." *The Futurist.* Vol. 30, No. 1 (January–February 1996):19–22.

FONDA, DAREN. "The Male Minority." *Time.* Vol. 156, No. 24 (December 11, 2000):58–60.

FORBES. "The Forbes Four Hundred." [Online] Available October 6, 2001, at http://www.forbes.com/2001/09/27/400.html

FORD, CLELLAN S., and FRANK A. BEACH. *Patterns of Sexual Behavior.* New York: Harper & Row, 1951.

FORREST, HUGH. "They Are Completely Inactive . . ." *The Gambier Journal.* Vol. 3, No. 4 (February 1984):10–11.

FORSTMANN, THEODORE J. "A Competitive Vision for American Education." *Imprimis.* Vol. 28, No. 9 (September 1999):1–4.

FOST, DAN. "American Indians in the 1990s." *American Demographics.* Vol. 13, No. 12 (December 1991):26–34.

FOUCAULT, MICHEL. *The History of Sexuality: An Introduction.* Vol. 1, trans. Robert Hurley. New York: Vintage, 1990; orig. 1978.

FRANK, ANDRÉ GUNDER. *On Capitalist Underdevelopment.* Bombay: Oxford University Press, 1975.

———. *Crisis: In the World Economy.* New York: Holmes & Meier, 1980.

———. *Reflections on the World Economic Crisis.* New York: Monthly Review Press, 1981.

FRANK, JOHN DAVID, JOHN W. MEYER, and DAVID MIYAHARA. "The Individualist Polity and the Prevalence of a Professionalized Psychology: A Cross-National Study." *American Sociological Review.* Vol. 60, No. 3 (June 1995):360–77.

FRANKLIN, JOHN HOPE. *From Slavery to Freedom: A History of Negro Americans.* 3d ed. New York: Vintage Books, 1967.

FRANKLIN ASSOCIATES. *Characterization of Municipal Solid Waste in the United States, 1960–2000.* Prairie Village, Kans.: Franklin Associates, 1986.

FRAZIER, E. FRANKLIN. *Black Bourgeoisie: The Rise of a New Middle Class.* New York: Free Press, 1965.

FREDRICKSON, GEORGE M. *White Supremacy: A Comparative Study in American and South African History.* New York: Oxford University Press, 1981.

FREE, MARVIN D. "Religious Affiliation, Religiosity, and Impulsive and Intentional Deviance." *Sociological Focus.* Vol. 25, No. 1 (February 1992):77–91.

FREEDOM HOUSE. *Freedom in the World 2000–2001.* New York: Freedom House, 2001.

FRENCH, MARILYN. *Beyond Power: On Women, Men, and Morals.* New York: Summit Books, 1985.

FRIEDAN, BETTY. *The Fountain of Age.* New York: Simon & Schuster, 1993.

FRIEDMAN, MEYER, and RAY H. ROSENMAN. *Type A Behavior and Your Heart.* New York: Fawcett Crest, 1974.

FRIEDMAN, MILTON, and ROSE FRIEDMAN. *Free to Choose: A Personal Statement.* New York: Harcourt Brace Jovanovich, 1980.

FRIEDRICH, CARL J., and ZBIGNIEW BRZEZINSKI. *Totalitarian Dictatorship and Autocracy.* 2d ed. Cambridge, Mass.: Harvard University Press, 1965.

FRUM, DAVID, and FRANK WOLFE. "If You Gotta Get Sued, Get Sued in Utah." *Forbes.* Vol. 153, No. 2 (January 1994):70–73.

FRUMKIN, PETER. "Are Nonprofit CEOs Overpaid?" *The Public Interest.* Vol. 142 (Winter 2001):83–94.

FUCHS, VICTOR R. "Sex Differences in Economic Well-Being." *Science.* Vol. 232 (April 25, 1986):459–64.

FUGITA, STEPHEN S., and DAVID J. O'BRIEN. "Structural Assimilation, Ethnic Group Membership, and Political Participation among Japanese Americans: A Research Note." *Social Forces.* Vol. 63, No. 4 (June 1985):986–95.

FUJIMOTO, ISAO. "The Failure of Democracy in a Time of Crisis." In Amy Tachiki et al., eds., *Roots: An Asian American Reader.* Los Angeles: UCLA Asian American Studies Center, 1971:207–14.

FULLER, REX, and RICHARD SCHOENBERGER. "The Gender Salary Gap: Do Academic Achievement, Intern Experience, and College Major Make a Difference?" *Social Science Quarterly.* Vol. 72, No. 4 (December 1991):715–26.

FUREDI, FRANK. "New Britain: A Nation of Victims." *Society.* Vol. 35, No. 3 (April 1998):80–84.

FURSTENBERG, FRANK F., JR., and ANDREW CHERLIN. *Divided Families: What Happens to Children When Parents Part.* Cambridge, Mass.: Harvard University Press, 1991.

GABRIEL, TRIP. "Computers Help Unite Campuses but Also Drive Some Students Apart." *New York Times* (November 11, 1996).

GAGLIANI, GIORGIO. "How Many Working Classes?" *American Journal of Sociology.* Vol. 87, No. 2 (September 1981):259–85.

GAGNÉ, PATRICIA, and RICHARD TEWKSBURY. "Conformity Pressures and Gender Resistance among Transgendered Individuals." *Social Problems.* Vol. 45, No. 1 (February 1998):81–101.

GAGNÉ, PATRICIA, RICHARD TEWKSBURY, and DEANNA MCGAUGHEY. "Coming Out and Crossing Over: Identity Formation and Proclamation in a Transgender Community." *Gender and Society.* Vol. 11, No. 4 (August 1997):478–508.

GALLAGHER, MAGGIE. "Does Bradley Know What Poverty Is?" *The New York Post* (October 28, 1999):37.

GALLUP. Poll results reported in "Numbers," *Time,* Vol. 155, No. 9 (February 28, 2000):25.

GALSTER, GEORGE. "Black Suburbanization: Has It Changed the Relative Location of Races?" *Urban Affairs Quarterly.* Vol. 26, No. 4 (June 1991):621–28.

GAMBLE, ANDREW, STEVE LUDLAM, and DAVID BAKER. "Britain's Ruling Class." *The Economist.* Vol. 326, No. 7795 (January 23, 1993):10.

GAMORAN, ADAM. "The Variable Effects of High-School Tracking." *American Sociological Review.* Vol. 57, No. 6 (December 1992):812–28.

GAMSON, WILLIAM A. "Beyond the Science-versus-Advocacy Distinction." *Contemporary Sociology.* Vol. 28, No. 1 (January 1999):23–26.

GANLEY, ELAINE. "Among Islamic Countries, Women's Roles Vary Greatly." *The Washington Times* (April 15, 1998):A13.

GANS, HERBERT J. *People and Plans: Essays on Urban Problems and Solutions.* New York: Basic Books, 1968.

———. *Deciding What's News: A Study of CBS Evening News, NBC Nightly News, Newsweek and Time.* New York: Vintage Books, 1980.

GARDNER, MARILYN. "At-Home Dads Give Their New Career High Marks." *Christian Science Monitor* (May 30, 1996):1, 12.

GARDYN, REBECCA. "Retirement Redefined." *American Demographics.* Vol. 22, No. 11 (November 2000):52–57.

GARFINKEL, HAROLD. "Conditions of Successful Degradation Ceremonies." *American Journal of Sociology.* Vol. 61, No. 2 (March 1956):420–24.

———. *Studies in Ethnomethodology.* Cambridge, Mass.: Polity Press, 1967.

GARREAU, JOEL. *Edge City.* New York: Doubleday, 1991.

GEERTZ, CLIFFORD. "Common Sense as a Cultural System." *The Antioch Review.* Vol. 33, No. 1 (Spring 1975):5–26.

GEIST, WILLIAM. *Toward a Safe and Sane Halloween and Other Tales of Suburbia.* New York: Times Books, 1985.

GELLES, RICHARD J., and CLAIRE PEDRICK CORNELL. *Intimate Violence in Families.* 2d ed. Newbury Park, Calif.: Sage, 1990.

GEORGE, SUSAN. *How the Other Half Dies: The Real Reasons for World Hunger.* Totowa, N.J.: Rowman & Allanheld, 1977.

GERBER, THEODORE P., and MICHAEL HOUT. "More Shock Than Therapy: Market Transition, Employment, and Income in Russia, 1991–1995." *American Journal of Sociology.* Vol. 104, No. 1 (July 1998):1–50.

GERLACH, MICHAEL L. *The Social Organization of Japanese Business.* Berkeley: University of California Press, 1992.

GERSTEL, NAOMI. "Divorce and Stigma." *Social Problems.* Vol. 43, No. 2 (April 1987):172–86.

GERTH, H. H., and C. WRIGHT MILLS, eds. *From Max Weber: Essays in Sociology.* New York: Oxford University Press, 1946.

GESCHWENDER, JAMES A. *Racial Stratification in America.* Dubuque, Iowa: Wm. C. Brown, 1978.

GEST, TED. "Law Schools' New Female Face." *U.S. News & World Report.* Vol. 130, No. 14 (April 9, 2001):76–77.

GEWERTZ, DEBORAH. "A Historical Reconsideration of Female Dominance among the Chambri of Papua New Guinea." *American Ethnologist.* Vol. 8, No. 1 (1981):94–106.

GIBBONS, DON C., and MARVIN D. KROHN. *Delinquent Behavior.* 4th ed. Englewood Cliffs, N.J.: Prentice Hall, 1986.

GIBBS, NANCY. "When Is It Rape?" *Time.* Vol. 137, No. 22 (June 3, 1991a):48–54.

———. "The Clamor on Campus." *Time.* Vol. 137, No. 22 (June 3, 1991b):54–55.

———. "How Much Should We Teach Our Children about Sex?" *Time.* Vol. 141, No. 21 (May 24, 1993):60–66.

———. "Cause Celeb." *Time.* Vol. 147, No. 25 (June 17, 1996):28–30.

———. "The Pulse of America Along the River." *Time.* Vol. 156, No. 2 (July 10, 2000):42–46.

———. "What Kids (Really) Need." *Time.* Vol. 157, No. 17 (April 30, 2001):48–49.

———. "If You Want to Humble an Empire." *Time.* September 11, 2001. Special issue.

GIDDENS, ANTHONY. *Sociology: A Brief but Critical Introduction.* New York: Harcourt Brace Jovanovich, 1982.

———. *The Transformation of Intimacy.* Cambridge, UK: Polity Press, 1992.

GIELE, JANET Z. "Gender and Sex Roles." In Neil J. Smelser, ed., *Handbook of Sociology.* Newbury Park, Calif.: Sage, 1988:291–323.

GIGLIOTTI, RICHARD J., and HEATHER K. HUFF. "Role Related Conflicts, Strains, and Stresses of Older-Adult College Students." *Sociological Focus.* Vol. 28, No. 3 (August 1995):329–42.

GILBERT, NEIL. "Realities and Mythologies of Rape." *Society.* Vol. 29, No. 4 (May–June 1992):4–10.

GILBERTSON, GRETA A., and DOUGLAS T. GURAK. "Broadening the Enclave Debate: The Dual Labor Market Experiences of Dominican and Colombian Men in New York City." *Sociological Forum.* Vol. 8, No. 2 (June 1993):205–20.

GILL, RICHARD T. "What Happened to the American Way of Death?" *The Public Interest.* Vol. 127 (Spring 1996):105–17.

GILLIARD, DARRELL K., and ALLEN J. BECK. *Prisoners in 1997.* Washington, D.C.: U.S. Bureau of Justice Statistics, 1998.

GILLIGAN, CAROL. *In a Different Voice: Psychological Theory and Women's Development.* Cambridge, Mass.: Harvard University Press, 1982.

———. *Making Connections: The Relational Worlds of Adolescent Girls at Emma Willard School.* Cambridge, Mass.: Harvard University Press, 1990.

GILLON, RAANAN. "Euthanasia in the Netherlands: Down the Slippery Slope?" *Journal of Medical Ethics.* Vol. 25, No. 1 (February 1999):3–4.

GIMENEZ, MARTHA E. "Silence in the Classroom: Some Thoughts about Teaching in the 1980s." *Teaching Sociology.* Vol. 17, No. 2 (April 1989):184–91.

GINSBURG, FAYE, and ANNA LOWENHAUPT TSING, eds. *Uncertain Terms: Negotiating Gender in American Culture.* Boston: Beacon Press, 1990.

GIOVANNINI, MAUREEN. "Female Anthropologist and Male Informant: Gender Conflict in a Sicilian Town." In John J. Macionis and Nijole V. Benokraitis, eds., *Seeing Ourselves: Classic, Contemporary, and Cross-Cultural Readings in Sociology.* 2d ed. Englewood Cliffs, N.J.: Prentice Hall, 1992:27–32.

GIROUX, GREGORY L. "GOP Maintains Thin Edge." *CQ Weekly.* Vol. 58, No. 44 (November 11, 2000):2652.

GIUGNI, MARCO G. "Structure and Culture in Social Movements Theory." *Sociological Forum.* Vol. 13, No. 2 (June 1998):365–75.

GLADUE, BRIAN A., RICHARD GREEN, and RONALD E. HELLMAN. "Neuroendocrine Response to Estrogen and Sexual Orientation." *Science.* Vol. 225, No. 4669 (September 28, 1984):1496–99.

GLASSNER, BARRY. *The Culture of Fear: Why Americans Are Afraid of the Wrong Things.* New York: Basic Books, 1999.

GLEICK, ELIZABETH. "The Marker We've Been Waiting For." *Time.* Vol. 149, No. 14 (April 7, 1997):28–42.

GLENN, NORVAL D., and BETH ANN SHELTON. "Regional Differences in Divorce in the United States." *Journal of Marriage and the Family.* Vol. 47, No. 3 (August 1985):641–52.

GLOCK, CHARLES Y. "The Religious Revival in America." In Jane Zahn, ed., *Religion and the Face of America.* Berkeley: University of California Press, 1959:25–42.

———. "On the Study of Religious Commitment." *Religious Education.* Vol. 62, No. 4 (1962):98–110.

GLUECK, SHELDON, and ELEANOR GLUECK. *Unraveling Juvenile Delinquency.* New York: Commonwealth Fund, 1950.

GNIDA, JOHN J. "Teaching 'Nature versus Nurture': The Case of African American Athletic Success." *Teaching Sociology.* Vol. 23, No. 4 (October 1995):389–95.

GODWIN, KENNETH, FRANK KEMERER, VALERIE MARTINEZ, and RICHARD RUDERMAN. "Liberal Equity in Education: A Comparison of Choice Options." *Social Science Quarterly.* Vol. 79, No. 3 (September 1998):502–22.

GOETTING, ANN. *Getting Out: Life Stories of Women Who Left Abusive Men.* New York: Columbia University Press, 1999.

GOFFMAN, ERVING. *The Presentation of Self in Everyday Life.* Garden City, N.Y.: Anchor Books, 1959.

———. *Asylums: Essays on the Social Situation of Mental Patients and Other Inmates.* Garden City, N.Y.: Anchor Books, 1961.

———. *Stigma: Notes on the Management of Spoiled Identity.* Englewood Cliffs, N.J.: Prentice Hall, 1963.

———. *Interactional Ritual: Essays on Face to Face Behavior.* Garden City, N.Y.: Anchor Books, 1967.

———. *Gender Advertisements.* New York: Harper Colophon, 1979.

GOLASH, TANYA. From "Proposed American Sociological Association Statement on Race." [Online] Available 2001 at http://www.unc.edu/~tatiana

GOLDBERG, STEVEN. *The Inevitability of Patriarchy.* New York: William Morrow, 1974.

———. Personal communication, 1987.

GOLDEN, FREDERIC. "Good Eggs, Bad Eggs." *Time.* Vol. 153, No. 1 (January 11, 1999a):56–59.

———. "Lying Faces Unmasked." *Time.* Vol. 153, No. 13 (April 5, 1999b):52.

GOLDEN, FREDERIC, and MICHAEL D. LEMONICK. "The Race Is Over." *Time.* Vol. 156, No. 1 (July 3, 2000):18–23.

GOLDFARB, WILLIAM. "Groundwater: The Buried Life." In F. Herbert Bormann and Stephen R. Kellert, eds., *Ecology, Economics, and Ethics: The Broken Circle.* New Haven, Conn.: Yale University Press, 1991:123–35.

GOLDFIELD, MICHAEL. "Rebounding Unions Target Service Sector." *Population Today.* Vol. 28, No. 7 (October 2000):3, 10.

GOLDSMITH, H. H. "Genetic Influences on Personality from Infancy." *Child Development.* Vol. 54, No. 2 (April 1983):331–35.

GOODE, ERICH. "No Need to Panic? A Bumper Crop of Books on Moral Panics." *Sociological Forum.* Vol. 15, No. 3 (September 2000):543–52.

GOODE, WILLIAM J. "The Theoretical Importance of Love." *American Sociological Review.* Vol. 24, No. 1 (February 1959):38–47.

———. "Encroachment, Charlatanism, and the Emerging Profession: Psychology, Sociology and Medicine." *American Sociological Review.* Vol. 25, No. 6 (December 1960):902–14.

GORDON, JAMES S. "The Paradigm of Holistic Medicine." In Arthur C. Hastings et al., eds., *Health for the Whole Person: The Complete Guide to Holistic Medicine.* Boulder, Colo.: Westview Press, 1980:3–27.

GORDON, SOL, and CRAIG W. SNYDER. *Personal Issues in Human Sexuality: A Guidebook for Better Sexual Health.* 2d ed. Boston: Allyn & Bacon, 1989.

GORING, CHARLES BUCKMAN. *The English Convict: A Statistical Study.* Montclair, N.J.: Patterson Smith, 1972; orig. 1913.

GORMAN, CHRISTINE. "Stressed Out Kids." *Time.* Vol. 156, No. 26 (December 25, 2000/January 1, 2001):168.

GORSKI, PHILIP S. "Historicizing the Secularization Debate: Church, State, and Society in Late Medieval and Early Modern Europe, ca. 1300 to 1700." *American Sociological Review.* Vol. 65, No. 1 (February 2000):138–67.

GOTHAM, KEVIN FOX. "Race, Mortgage Lending, and Loan Rejections in a U.S. City." *Sociological Focus.* Vol. 31, No. 4 (October 1998):391–405.

GOTTFREDSON, MICHAEL R., and TRAVIS HIRSCHI. "National Crime Control Policies." *Society.* Vol. 32, No. 2 (January–February 1995):30–36.

GOTTMANN, JEAN. *Megalopolis.* New York: Twentieth Century Fund, 1961.

GOUGH, KATHLEEN. "The Origin of the Family." *Journal of Marriage and the Family.* Vol. 33, No. 4 (November 1971):760–71.

———. "The Origin of the Family." In John J. Macionis and Nijole V. Benokraitis, eds., *Seeing Ourselves: Classic, Contemporary, and Cross-Cultural Readings in Sociology.* Englewood Cliffs, N.J.: Prentice Hall, 1989.

GOULD, STEPHEN J. "Evolution as Fact and Theory." *Discover* (May 1981):35–37.

GOULDNER, ALVIN. *The Coming Crisis of Western Sociology.* New York: Avon Books, 1970.

GRAHAM, JOHN W., and ANDREA H. BELLER. "Child Support in Black and White: Racial Differentials in the Award and Receipt of Child Support during the 1980s." *Social Science Quarterly.* Vol. 77, No. 3 (September 1996):528–42.

GRANT, DON SHERMAN, II, and MICHAEL WALLACE. "Why Do Strikes Turn Violent?" *American Journal of Sociology.* Vol. 96, No. 5 (March 1991):1117–50.

GRANT, DONALD L. *The Anti-Lynching Movement.* San Francisco: R & E Research Associates, 1975.

GRANT, KAREN R. "The Inverse Care Law in the Context of Universal Free Health Insurance in Canada: Toward Meeting Health Needs through Public Policy." *Sociological Focus.* Vol. 17, No. 2 (April 1984):137–55.

GRATETT, RYKEN. "Hate Crimes: Better Data or Increasing Frequency?" *Population Today.* Vol. 28, No. 5 (July 2000):1, 4.

GREELEY, ANDREW M. *Religious Change in America.* Cambridge, Mass.: Harvard University Press, 1989.

GREEN, GARY PAUL, LEANN M. TIGGES, and DANIEL DIAZ. "Racial and Ethnic Differences in Job-Search Strategies In Atlanta, Boston, and Los Angeles." *Social Science Quarterly.* Vol. 80, No. 2 (June 1999):263–90.

GREEN, JOHN C. "Pat Robertson and the Latest Crusade: Resources and the 1988 Presidential Campaign." *Social Sciences Quarterly.* Vol. 74, No. 1 (March 1993):156–68.

GREENBERG, DAVID F. *The Construction of Homosexuality.* Chicago: University of Chicago Press, 1988.

GREENFIELD, LAWRENCE A. *Child Victimizers: Violent Offenders and Their Victims.* Washington, D.C.: U.S. Bureau of Justice Statistics, 1996.

GREENHOUSE, LINDA. "Justices Uphold Stiffer Sentences for Hate Crimes." *New York Times* (June 12, 1993):1, 8.

GREENWALD, JOHN. "The New Service Class." *Time.* Vol. 144, No. 20 (November 14, 1994):72–74.

———. "School for Profit." *Time.* Vol. 155, No. 11 (March 20, 2000):56–57.

GREGORY, PAUL R., and ROBERT C. STUART. *Comparative Economic Systems.* 2d ed. Boston: Houghton Mifflin, 1985.

GROSS, JANE. "New Challenge of Youth: Growing Up in a Gay Home." *New York Times* (February 11, 1991):A1, B7.

GROTH, NICHOLAS A., and H. JEAN BIRNBAUM. *Men Who Rape: The Psychology of the Offender.* New York: Plenum, 1979.

GUP, TED. "What Makes This School Work?" *Time.* Vol. 140, No. 25 (December 21, 1992):63–65.

GURAK, DOUGLAS T., and JOSEPH P. FITZPATRICK. "Intermarriage among Hispanic Ethnic Groups in New York City." *American Journal of Sociology.* Vol. 87, No. 4 (January 1982):921–34.

GURNETT, KATE. "On the Forefront of Feminism." *Albany Times Union* (July 5, 1998):G-1, G-6.

GUSTAFSSON, BJORN, and MATS JOHANSSON. "In Search of Smoking Guns: What Makes Income Inequality Vary over Time in Different Countries?" *American Sociological Review.* Vol. 64, No. 4 (August 1999):585–605.

GWARTNEY-GIBBS, PATRICIA A. "The Institutionalization of Premarital Cohabitation: Estimates from Marriage License Applications, 1970 and 1980." *Journal of Marriage and the Family.* Vol. 48, No. 2 (May 1986):423–34.

GWYNNE, S. C., and JOHN F. DICKERSON. "Lost in the E-Mail." *Time.* Vol. 149, No. 15 (April 21, 1997):88–90.

HABERMAS, JÜRGEN. *Toward a Rational Society: Student Protest, Science, and Politics.* Jeremy J. Shapiro, trans. Boston: Beacon Press, 1970.

HACKER, HELEN MAYER. "Women as a Minority Group." *Social Forces.* Vol. 30 (October 1951):60–69.

———. "Women as a Minority Group: 20 Years Later." In Florence Denmark, ed., *Who Discriminates against Women?* Beverly Hills, Calif.: Sage, 1974:124–34.

HADAWAY, C. KIRK, PENNY LONG MARLER, and MARK CHAVES. "What the Polls Don't Show: A Closer Look at U.S. Church Attendance." *American Sociological Review.* Vol. 58, No. 6 (December 1993):741–52.

HADDEN, JEFFREY K., and CHARLES E. SWAIN. *Prime Time Preachers: The Rising Power of Televangelism.* Reading, Mass.: Addison-Wesley, 1981.

HAFNER, KATIE. "Making Sense of the Internet." *Newsweek* (October 24, 1994):46–48.

HAGAN, JACQUELINE MARIA. "Social Networks, Gender, and Immigrant Incorporation: Resources and Restraints." *American Sociological Review.* Vol. 63, No. 1 (February 1998):55–67.

HAGAN, JOHN, and PATRICIA PARKER. "White-Collar Crime and Punishment: The Class Structure and Legal Sanctioning of Securities Violations." *American Sociological Review.* Vol. 50, No. 3 (June 1985):302–16.

HAIG, ROBIN ANDREW. *The Anatomy of Humor: Biopsychosocial and Therapeutic Perspectives.* Springfield, Ill.: Charles C. Thomas, 1988.

HALBERSTAM, DAVID. *The Reckoning.* New York: Avon Books, 1986.

HALEDJIAN, DEAN. "How to Tell a Businessman from a Businesswoman." Annandale, Va.: Northern Virginia Community College, 1997.

HALL, JOHN R., and MARY JO NEITZ. *Culture: Sociological Perspectives.* Englewood Cliffs, N.J.: Prentice Hall, 1993.

HALL, KELLEY J., and BETSY LUCAL. "Tapping in Parallel Universes: Using Superhero Comic Books in Sociology Courses." *Teaching Sociology.* Vol. 27, No. 1 (January 1999):60–66.

HALLINAN, MAUREEN T. "The Sociological Study of Social Change." *American Sociological Review.* Vol. 62, No. 1 (February 1997):1–11.

HALLINAN, MAUREEN T., and RICHARD A. WILLIAMS. "Interracial Friendship Choices in Secondary Schools." *American Sociological Review.* Vol. 54, No. 1 (February 1989):67–78.

HAMEL, RUTH. "Raging against Aging." *American Demographics*. Vol. 12, No. 3 (March 1990):42–45.

HAMER, DEAN, and PETER COPELAND. *The Science of Desire: The Search for the Gay Gene and the Biology of Behavior*. New York: Simon & Schuster, 1994.

HAMILTON, RICHARD F. "*The Communist Manifesto* at 150." *Society*. Vol. 38, No. 2 (January/February 2001):75–80.

HAMMOND, PHILIP E. "Introduction." In Philip E. Hammond, ed., *The Sacred in a Secular Age: Toward Revision in the Scientific Study of Religion*. Berkeley: University of California Press, 1985:1–6.

HAMRICK, MICHAEL H., DAVID J. ANSPAUGH, and GENE EZELL. *Health*. Columbus, Ohio: Merrill, 1986.

HANDGUN CONTROL, INC. Personal communication, 2001.

HANDLIN, OSCAR. *Boston's Immigrants 1790–1865: A Study in Acculturation*. Cambridge, Mass.: Harvard University Press, 1941.

HANEY, CRAIG, CURTIS BANKS, and PHILIP ZIMBARDO. "Interpersonal Dynamics in a Simulated Prison." *International Journal of Criminology and Penology*. Vol. 1 (1973):69–97.

HARBERT, ANITA A., and LEON H. GINSBERG. *Human Services for Older Adults*. Columbia: University of South Carolina Press, 1991.

HAREVEN, TAMARA K. "The Life Course and Aging in Historical Perspective." In Tamara K. Hareven and Kathleen J. Adams, eds., *Aging and Life Course Transitions: An Interdisciplinary Perspective*. New York: Guilford Press, 1982:1–26.

HARLAN, WILLIAM H. "Social Status of the Aged in Three Indian Villages." In Bernice L. Neugarten, ed., *Middle Age and Aging: A Reader in Social Psychology*. Chicago: University of Chicago Press, 1968:469–75.

HARLOW, HARRY F., and MARGARET KUENNE HARLOW. "Social Deprivation in Monkeys." *Scientific American*. Vol. 207 (November 1962):137–46.

HARPSTER, PAULA, and ELIZABETH MONK-TURNER. "Why Men Do Housework: A Test of Gender Production and the Relative Resources Model." *Sociological Focus*. Vol. 31, No. 1 (February 1998):45–59.

HARRIES, KEITH D. *Serious Violence: Patterns of Homicide and Assault in America*. Springfield, Ill.: Charles C. Thomas, 1990.

HARRINGTON, MICHAEL. *The New American Poverty*. New York: Penguin Books, 1984.

HARRIS, CHAUNCY D., and EDWARD L. ULLMAN. "The Nature of Cities." *The Annals*. Vol. 242 (November 1945):7–17.

HARRIS, JACK DASH. Lecture on cockfighting in the Philippines. Semester at Sea (October 27, 1994).

HARRIS, MARVIN. "Why Men Dominate Women." *New York Times Magazine* (November 13, 1977):46, 115–23.

———. *Cultural Anthropology*. 1st ed., 1983; 2d ed. New York: Harper & Row, 1987.

HARRISON, C. KEITH. "Black Athletes at the Millennium." *Society*. Vol. 37, No. 3 (March/April 2000):35–39.

HARRISON, PAUL. *Inside the Third World: The Anatomy of Poverty*. 2d ed. New York: Penguin Books, 1984.

HARVEY, DAVID. "Labor, Capital, and Class Struggle around the Built Environment." *Politics and Society*. Vol. 6 (1976):265–95.

HAVIGHURST, ROBERT J., BERNICE L. NEUGARTEN, and SHELDON S. TOBIN. "Disengagement and Patterns of Aging." In Bernice L. Neugarten, ed., *Middle Age and Aging: A Reader in Social Psychology*. Chicago: University of Chicago Press, 1968:161–72.

HAWTHORNE, PETER. "South Africa's Makeover." *Time*. Vol. 154, No. 2 (July 12, 1999).

———. "An Epidemic of Rapes." *Time*. Vol. 154, No. 18 (November 1, 1999):59.

HAYNEMAN, STEPHEN P., and WILLIAM A. LOXLEY. "The Effect of Primary-School Quality on Academic Achievement across Twenty-Nine High- and Low-Income Countries." *American Journal of Sociology*. Vol. 88, No. 6 (May 1983):1162–94.

HAYWARD, MARK D., EILEEN M. CRIMMINS, TONI P. MILES, and YU YANG. "The Significance of Socioeconomic Status in Explaining the Racial Gap in Chronic Health Conditions." *American Sociological Review*. Vol. 65, No. 6 (December 2000):910–30.

HEATH, JULIA A., and W. DAVID BOURNE. "Husbands and Housework: Parity or Parody?" *Social Science Quarterly*. Vol. 76, No. 1 (March 1995):195–202.

HELGESEN, SALLY. *The Female Advantage: Women's Ways of Leadership*. New York: Doubleday, 1990.

HELIN, DAVID W. "When Slogans Go Wrong." *American Demographics*. Vol. 14, No. 2 (February 1992):14.

HENLEY, NANCY, MYKOL HAMILTON, and BARRIE THORNE. "Womanspeak and Manspeak: Sex Differences in Communication, Verbal and Nonverbal." In John J. Macionis and Nijole V. Benokraitis, eds., *Seeing Ourselves: Classic, Contemporary, and Cross-Cultural Readings in Sociology*. 2d ed. Englewood Cliffs, N.J.: Prentice Hall, 1992:10–15.

HENRY, WILLIAM A., III. "Gay Parents: Under Fire and On the Rise." *Time*. Vol. 142, No. 12 (September 20, 1993):66–71.

HERDA-RAPP, ANN. "The Power of Informal Leadership: Women Leaders in the Civil Rights Movement." *Sociological Focus*. Vol. 31, No. 4 (October 1998):341–55.

HERDT, GILBERT H. "Semen Transactions in Sambian Culture." In David N. Suggs and Andrew W. Miracle, eds., *Culture and Human Sexuality*. Pacific Grove, Calif.: Brooks Cole, 1993:298–327.

HEREK, GREGORY M. "Myths about Sexual Orientation: A Lawyer's Guide to Social Science Research." *Law and Sexuality*. No. 1 (1991):133–72.

HERMAN, DIANNE. "The Rape Culture." In John J. Macionis and Nijole V. Benokraitis, eds., *Seeing Ourselves: Classic, Contemporary, and Cross-Cultural Readings in Sociology*. 5th ed. Upper Saddle River, N.J.: Prentice Hall, 2001.

HERMAN, EDWARD S. *Corporate Control, Corporate Power: A Twentieth Century Fund Study*. New York: Cambridge University Press, 1981.

HERRNSTEIN, RICHARD J., and CHARLES MURRAY. *The Bell Curve: Intelligence and Class Structure in American Life*. New York: Free Press, 1994.

HERRSTROM, STAFFAN. "Sweden: Pro-Choice on Child Care." *New Perspectives Quarterly*. Vol. 7, No. 1 (Winter 1990):27–28.

HERSCH, JONI, and SHELLY WHITE-MEANS. "Employer-Sponsored Health and Pension Benefits and the Gender/Race Wage Gap." *Social Science Quarterly*. Vol. 74, No. 4 (December 1993):850–66.

HESS, BETH B. "Breaking and Entering the Establishment: Committing Social Change and Confronting the Backlash." *Social Problems*. Vol. 46, No. 1 (February 1999):1–12.

HESS, STEPHEN. "Reporters Who Cover Congress." *Society*. Vol. 28, No. 2 (January–February 1991):60–65.

HEWLETT, BARRY S. "Husband-Wife Reciprocity and the Father-Infant Relationship among Aka Pygmies." In Barry S. Hewlett, ed., *Father-Child Relations: Cultural and Bio-Social Contexts*. New York: Aldine, 1992:153–76.

HIROSHI, MANNARI. *The Japanese Business Leaders*. Tokyo: University of Tokyo Press, 1974.

HIRSCHI, TRAVIS. *Causes of Delinquency*. Berkeley: University of California Press, 1969.

HOBERMAN, JOHN. *Darwin's Athletes: How Sport Has Damaged Black America and Preserved the Myth of Race*. Boston: Houghton Mifflin, 1997.

———. "Response to Three Reviews of Darwin's Athletes." *Social Science Quarterly*. Vol. 79, No. 4 (December 1998):898–903.

HOCHSCHILD, ARLIE, and ANNE MACHUNG. *The Second Shift: Working Parents and the Revolution at Home*. New York: Viking Books, 1989.

HOCKEY, JENNY, and ALLISON JAMES. *Growing Up and Growing Old: Aging and Dependency in the Life Course*. Newbury Park, Calif.: Sage, 1993.

HODGE, ROBERT W., DONALD J. TREIMAN, and PETER H. ROSSI. "A Comparative Study of Occupational Prestige." In Reinhard Bendix and Seymour Martin Lipset, eds., *Class, Status, and Power: Social Stratification in Comparative Perspective*. 2d ed. New York: Free Press, 1966:309–21.

HOERR, JOHN. "The Payoff from Teamwork." *Business Week*. No. 3114 (July 10, 1989):56–62.

HOFFMAN, *Psychology in Action*. 6th ed. New York: Wiley, 2001.

HOGAN, DENNIS P., and EVELYN M. KITAGAWA. "The Impact of Social Status and Neighborhood on the Fertility of Black Adolescents." *American Journal of Sociology*. Vol. 90, No. 4 (January 1985):825–55.

HOGAN, RICHARD, and CAROLYN C. PERRUCCI. "Producing and Reproducing the Class and Status Differences: Racial and Gender Gaps in U.S. Employment and Retirement Income." *Social Problems*. Vol. 45, No. 4 (November 1998):528–49.

HOGGART, RICHARD. "The Abuses of Literacy." *Society*. Vol. 55, No. 3 (March–April 1995):55–62.

HOLLANDER, PAUL. "We Are All (Sniffle, Sniffle) Victims Now." *Wall Street Journal* (January 18, 1995):A14.

HOLM, JEAN. *The Study of Religions*. New York: Seabury Press, 1977.

HOLMES, MALCOLM D., HARMON M. HOSCH, HOWARD C. DAUDISTEL, DOLORES PEREZ, and JOSEPH B. GRAVES. "Judges, Ethnicity and Minority Sentencing: Evidence among Hispanics." *Social Science Quarterly*. Vol. 74, No. 3 (September 1993):496–506.

HOLMES, STEVEN A. "U.S. Reports Drop in Rate of Births to Unwed Women." *New York Times* (October 5, 1996a):1, 9.

———. "For Hispanic Poor, No Silver Lining." *New York Times* (October 13, 1996b): section 4, p. 5.

HOLMES, THOMAS H., and RICHARD H. RAHE. "The Social Readjustment Rating Scale." *Journal of Psychosomatic Research*. Vol. 11 (1967):213–18.

HOLMSTROM, DAVID. "Abuse of Elderly, Even by Adult Children, Gets More Attention and Official Concern." *Christian Science Monitor* (July 28, 1994):1.

HOLTZ, HARVEY, ed. *Education and the American Dream: Conservatives, Liberals, and Radicals Debate the Future of Education*. Granby, Mass.: Bergin & Garvey, 1989.

HONAN, WILLIAM H. "Class Notes: Northwestern University Takes a Lead in Using the Internet to Add Sound and Sight to Courses." *New York Times* (May 28, 1997):B7.

HONEYWELL, ROY J. *The Educational Work of Thomas Jefferson*. Cambridge, Mass.: Harvard University Press, 1931.

HORNBLOWER, MARGOT. "He? She? Whatever!" *Time*. Vol. 154, No. 15 (October 11, 1999):76.

HOROWITZ, IRVING LOUIS. *The Decomposition of Sociology*. New York: Oxford University Press, 1993.

HORTON, HAYWARD DERRICK. "Critical Demography: The Paradigm of the Future?" *Sociological Forum*. Vol. 14, No. 3 (September 1999):363–67.

HORTON, HAYWARD DERRICK, BEVERLY LUNDY ALLEN, CEDRIC HERRING, and MELVIN E. THOMAS. "Lost in the Storm: The Sociology of the Black Working Class, 1850 to 1990." *American Sociological Review*. Vol. 65, No. 1 (February 2000):128–37.

HOSTETLER, JOHN A. *Amish Society*. 3d ed. Baltimore: Johns Hopkins University Press, 1980.

HOUT, MICHAEL. "More Universalism, Less Structural Mobility: The American Occupational Structure in the 1980s." *American Journal of Sociology*. Vol. 95, No. 6 (May 1998):1358–400.

HOUT, MICHAEL, and ANDREW M. GREELEY. "The Center Doesn't Hold: Church Attendance in the United States, 1940–1984." *American Sociological Review*. Vol. 52, No. 3 (June 1987):325–45.

———. "What Church Officials' Reports Don't Show: Another Look at Church Attendance Data." *American Sociological Review*. Vol. 63, No. 1 (February 1998):113–19.

HOUT, MIKE, CLEM BROOKS, and JEFF MANZA. "The Persistence of Classes in Post-Industrial Societies." *International Sociology*. Vol. 8, No. 3 (September 1993):259–77.

HOYT, HOMER. *The Structure and Growth of Residential Neighborhoods in American Cities*. Washington, D.C.: Federal Housing Administration, 1939.

HSU, FRANCIS L. K. *The Challenge of the American Dream: The Chinese in the United States*. Belmont, Calif.: Wadsworth, 1971.

HUBER, JOAN, and BETH E. SCHNEIDER, eds. *The Social Context of AIDS*. Newbury Park, Calif.: Sage, 1992.

HUD. "The Forgotten Americans: Homelessness—Programs and the People They Serve."

HUET-COX, ROCIO. "Medical Education: New Wine in Old Wine Skins." In Victor W. Sidel and Ruth Sidel, eds., *Reforming Medicine: Lessons of the Last Quarter Century*. New York: Pantheon Books, 1984:129–49.

HUFFMAN, KAREN. *Psychology in Action*. New York: Wiley, 2000.

HUFFMAN, MATT L., STEVEN C. VELASCO, and WILLIAM T. BIELBY. "Where Sex Composition Matters Most: Comparing the Effects of Job versus Occupational Sex Composition of Earnings." *Sociological Focus*. Vol. 29, No. 3 (August 1996):189–207.

HUGHES, MICHAEL, and MELVIN E. THOMAS. "The Continuing Significance of Race Revisited: A Study of Race, Class, and Quality of Life in America, 1972 to 1996." *American Sociological Review*. Vol. 63, No. 6 (December 1998):785–95.

HULS, GLENNA. Personal communication, 1987.

HUMMER, ROBERT A., RICHARD G. ROGERS, CHARLES B. NAM, and FELICIA B. LECLERE. "Race/Ethnicity, Nativity, and U.S. Adult Mortality." *Social Science Quarterly*. Vol. 80, No. 1 (March 1999):136–53.

HUMPHREY, CRAIG R., and FREDERICK R. BUTTEL. *Environment, Energy, and Society*. Belmont, Calif.: Wadsworth, 1982.

HUMPHREY, DEREK. *Final Exit: The Practicalities of Self-Deliverance and Assisted Suicide for the Dying*. Eugene, Ore.: The Hemlock Society, 1991.

HUNDLEY, TOM. "UN Convicts Serb in Bosnia Genocide." *Chicago Tribune* (August 3, 2001):1, 23.

HUNNICUT, BENJAMIN K. "Are We All Working Too Hard? No Time for God or Family." *Wall Street Journal* (January 4, 1990).

HUNT, MORTON. *Sexual Behavior in the 1970s*. Chicago: Playboy Press, 1974.

HUNTER, FLOYD. *Community Power Structure*. Garden City, N.Y.: Doubleday, 1963; orig. 1953.

HUNTER, JAMES DAVISON. *American Evangelicalism: Conservative Religion and the Quandary of Modernity*. New Brunswick, N.J.: Rutgers University Press, 1983.

———. "Conservative Protestantism." In Philip E. Hammond, ed., *The Sacred in a Secular Age*. Berkeley: University of California Press, 1985:50–66.

———. *Evangelicalism: The Coming Generation*. Chicago: University of Chicago Press, 1987.

———. *Culture Wars: The Struggle to Define America*. New York: Basic Books, 1991.

HYMOWITZ, CAROL. "World's Poorest Women Advance by Entrepreneurship." *Wall Street Journal* (September 9, 1995):B1.

HYMOWITZ, KAY S. "Kids Today Are Growing Up Way Too Fast." *Wall Street Journal* (October 28, 1998):A22.

IANNACCONE, LAURENCE R. "Why Strict Churches Are Strong." *American Journal of Sociology*. Vol. 99, No. 5 (March 1994):1180–211.

IDE, THOMAS R., and ARTHUR J. CORDELL. "Automating Work." *Society*. Vol. 31, No. 6 (September–October 1994):65–71.

ILLICH, IVAN. *Medical Nemesis: The Expropriation of Health*. New York: Pantheon Books, 1976.

IMIG, DOUGLAS R., and DAVID S. MEYER. "Privacy and Opportunity and Peace and Justice Advocacy in the 1980s: A Tale of Two Sectors." *Social Science Quarterly*. Vol. 74, No. 4 (December 1993):750–70.

INGLEHART, RONALD. *Modernization and Postmodernization: Cultural, Economic, and Political Change in 43 Societies*. Princeton, N.J.: Princeton University Press, 1997.

INGLEHART, RONALD, and WAYNE E. BAKER. "Modernization, Cultural Change, and the Persistence of Traditional Values." *American Sociological Review*. Vol. 65, No. 1 (February 2000):19–51.

INGLEHART, RONALD, et al. *World Values Surveys and European Values Surveys, 1981–1984, 1990–1993, and 1995–1997*. [Computer file] ICPSR version. Ann Arbor, Mich.: Interuniversity Consortium for Political and Social Research, 2000.

INTER-PARLIAMENTARY UNION. *Men and Women in Politics: Democracy in the Making*. Geneva: 1997.

ISAY, RICHARD A. *Being Homosexual: Gay Men and Their Development*. New York: Farrar, Straus, & Giroux, 1989.

ISRAEL, GLENN D., LIONEL J. BEAULIEU, and GLEN HARTLESS. "The Influence of Family and Community Social Capital on Educational Achievement." *Rural Sociology*. Vol. 66, No. 1 (March 2001):43–68.

JACKSON, DAVID S. "Taking CEO Pay to New Heights." *Time*. Vol. 155, No. 4 (January 31, 2000):55.

JACOBS, DAVID, and RONALD E. HELMS. "Toward a Political Model of Incarceration: A Time-Series Examination of Multiple Explanations for Prison Admission Rates." *American Journal of Sociology*. Vol. 102, No. 2 (September 1996):323–57.

JACOBS, DAVID, and ROBERT M. O'BRIEN. "The Determinants of Deadly Force: A Structural Analysis of Police Violence." *American Journal of Sociology*. Vol. 103, No. 4 (January 1998):837–62.

JACOBS, JAMES B. "Should Hate Be a Crime?" *The Public Interest*. No. 113 (Fall 1993):3–14.

JACOBS, JANE. *The Economy of Cities*. New York: Vintage Books, 1970.

JACOBY, RUSSELL, and NAOMI GLAUBERMAN, eds. *The Bell Curve Debate*. New York: Random House, 1995.

JACQUET, CONSTANT H., and ALICE M. JONES. *Yearbook of American and Canadian Churches 1991*. Nashville, Tenn.: Abingdon Press, 1991.

JAGAROWSKY, PAUL A., and MARY JO BANE. *Neighborhood Poverty: Basic Questions*. Discussion paper series H-90–3. John F. Kennedy School of Government. Cambridge, Mass.: Harvard University Press, 1990.

JAGGER, ALISON. "Political Philosophies of Women's Liberation." In Laurel Richardson and Verta Taylor, eds., *Feminist Frontiers: Rethinking Sex, Gender, and Society*. Reading, Mass.: Addison-Wesley, 1983.

JAMES, DAVID R. "City Limits on Racial Equality: The Effects of City-Suburb Boundaries on Public-School Desegregation, 1968–1976." *American Sociological Review*. Vol. 54, No. 6 (December 1989):963–85.

JANIS, IRVING. *Victims of Groupthink*. Boston: Houghton Mifflin, 1972.

———. *Crucial Decisions: Leadership in Policymaking and Crisis Management*. New York: Free Press, 1989.

JANUS, CHRISTOPHER G. "Slavery Abolished? Only Officially." *Christian Science Monitor* (May 17, 1996):18.

JARRETT, ROBIN L. "Living Poor: Family Life among Single Parent, African-American Women." *Social Problems*. Vol. 41, No. 1 (February 1994):30–49.

JASPER, JAMES M. "The Emotions of Protest: Affective and Reactive Emotions in and around Social Movements." *Sociological Forum*. Vol. 13, No. 3 (September 1998):397–424.

JEFFERSON, THOMAS. Letter to James Madison, October 28, 1785. In Julian P. Boyd, ed., *The Papers of Thomas Jefferson*. Princeton, N.J.: Princeton University Press, 1953:681–83; orig. 1785.

JENCKS, CHRISTOPHER. "Genes and Crime." *The New York Review* (February 12, 1987):33–41.

JENKINS, J. CRAIG, and CHARLES PERROW. "Insurgency of the Powerless: Farm Worker Movements (1946–1972)." *American Sociological Review*. Vol. 42, No. 2 (April 1977):249–68.

JENKINS, J. CRAIG, and MICHAEL WALLACE. "The Generalized Action Potential of Protest Movements: The New Class, Social Trends, and Political Exclusion Explanations." *Sociological Forum*. Vol. 11, No. 2 (June 1996):183–207.

JOHNSON, CATHRYN. "Gender, Legitimate Authority, and Leader-Subordinate Conversations." *American Sociological Review*. Vol. 59, No. 1 (February 1994):122–35.

JOHNSON, DIRK. "Census Finds Many Claiming New Identity: Indian." *New York Times* (March 5, 1991):A1, A16.

JOHNSON, GEORGE. "It's a Fact: Faith and Theory Collide over Evolution." *New York Times* (August 15, 1999):Sec. 4; 1, 4.

JOHNSON, JEAN. "Americans' Views on Crime and Law Enforcement." *National Institute of Justice Journal*. Issue 233 (September 1997):9–14.

JOHNSON, KENNETH M. "The Rural Rebound." *Reports on America*. Vol. 1 No. 3 (September 1999). Washington, DC: Population Reference Bureau.

JOHNSON, KENNETH M., and GLENN V. FUGUITT. "Continuity and Change in Rural Migration Patterns, 1950–1995." *Rural Sociology*. Vol. 65, No. 1 (March 2000):27–49.

JOHNSON, PAUL. "The Seven Deadly Sins of Terrorism." In Benjamin Netanyahu, ed., *International Terrorism*. New Brunswick, N.J.: Transaction Books, 1981:12–22.

JOHNSON, ROLAND. [Online] Available in 1996 at http://www.personalwebs.myriad.net/Roland

JOHNSTON, DAVID CAY. "Voting, America's Not Keen On. Coffee Is Another Matter." *New York Times* (November 10, 1996): section 4, p. 2.

JOHNSTON, R. J. "Residential Area Characteristics." In D. T. Herbert and R. J. Johnston, eds., *Social Areas in Cities. Vol. 1: Spatial Processes and Form*. New York: Wiley, 1976:193–235.

JONES, ANDREW E. G., and DAVID WILSON. *The Urban Growth Machine: Critical Perspectives*. Albany: State University of New York Press, 1999.

JONES, ANTHONY. "Soviet Sociology, Past and Present." *Contemporary Sociology*. Vol. 18, No. 3 (May 1989):316–19.

JONES, ARTHUR. "Welfare Reform Makes Children Prime Victims." *National Catholic Reporter* (April 30, 1999a):14–16.

JONES, JUDY. "More Miners Will Be Offered Free X-Rays; Federal Agency Wants to Monitor Black-Lung Cases." *Louisville Courier Journal* (Thursday, May 13, 1999b):1A.

JONES, ROBERT EMMET, and LEWIS F. CARTER. "Concern for the Environment among Black Americans: An Assessment of Common Assumptions." *Social Science Quarterly*. Vol. 75, No. 3 (September 1994):560–79.

JORDAN, MARY. "New Factors Sustain Age-Old Ritual." *Washington Post* (March 31, 1998):A12.

JOSEPHY, ALVIN M., JR. *Now That the Buffalo's Gone: A Study of Today's American Indians*. New York: Alfred A. Knopf, 1982.

JOYNSON, ROBERT B. "Fallible Judgments." *Society*. Vol. 31, No. 3 (March–April 1994):45–52.

KADUSHIN, CHARLES. "Friendship among the French Financial Elite." *American Sociological Review*. Vol. 60, No. 2 (April 1995):202–21.

KAIN, EDWARD L. "A Note on the Integration of AIDS into the Sociology of Human Sexuality." *Teaching Sociology*. Vol. 15, No. 4 (July 1987):320–23.

———. *The Myth of Family Decline: Understanding Families in a World of Rapid Social Change*. Lexington, Mass.: Lexington Books, 1990.

KAIN, EDWARD L., and SHANNON HART. "AIDS and the Family: A Content Analysis of Media Coverage." Presented to National Council on Family Relations, Atlanta, 1987.

KALLEBERG, ARNE, BARBARA F. RESKIN, and KEN HUDSON. "Bad Jobs in America: Standard and Nonstandard Employment Relations and Job Quality in the United States." *American Sociological Review*. Vol. 65, No 2 (April 2000):256–78.

KALLEBERG, ARNE L., and MARK E. VAN BUREN. "Is Bigger Better? Explaining the Relationship between Organization Size and Job Rewards." *American Sociological Review*. Vol. 61, No. 1 (February 1996):47–66.

KAMINER, WENDY. "Volunteers: Who Knows What's in It for Them." *Ms.* (December 1984):93–94, 96, 126–28.

———. "Demasculinizing the Army." *New York Times Review of Books* (June 15, 1997):7.

KANAMINE, LINDA. "School Operation Fails For-Profit Test." *USA Today* (November 24, 1995):6A.

KANE, EMILY W. "Racial and Ethnic Variations in Gender-Related Attitudes." *Annual Review of Sociology*. Vol. 26 (2000):419–39.

KANN, LAURA, et al. "Youth Risk Behavior Surveillance: United States, 1993." *Morbidity and Mortality Weekly Report*. Vol. 44 (S-1), March 24, 1995.

KANTER, ROSABETH MOSS. *Men and Women of the Corporation*. New York: Basic Books, 1977.

KANTER, ROSABETH MOSS, and BARRY A. STEIN. "The Gender Pioneers: Women in an Industrial Sales Force." In R. M. Kanter and B. A. Stein, eds., *Life in Organizations*. New York: Basic Books, 1979:134–60.

KANTROWITZ, BARBARA, and PAT WINGERT. "Unmarried with Children." *Newsweek* (May 28, 2001):46–52.

KAO, GRACE. "Group Images and Possible Selves among Adolescents: Linking Stereotypes to Expectations by Race and Ethnicity." *Sociological Forum*. Vol. 15, No. 3 (September 2000):407–30.

KAPFERER, JEAN-NOEL. "How Rumors Are Born." *Society*. Vol. 29, No. 5 (July–August 1992):53–60.

KAPLAN, DAVID E., and MICHAEL SCHAFFER. "Losing the Psywar." *U.S. News & World Report* (October 8, 2001):46.

KAPLAN, ELAINE BELL. "Black Teenage Mothers and Their Mothers: The Impact of Adolescent Childbearing on Daughters' Relations with Mothers." *Social Problems*. Vol. 43, No. 4 (November 1996):427–43.

KAPLAN, ERIC B., et al. "The Usefulness of Preoperative Laboratory Screening." *Journal of the American Medical Association*. Vol. 253, No. 24 (June 28, 1985):3576–81.

KAPTCHUK, TED. "The Holistic Logic of Chinese Medicine." In Shepard Bliss et al., eds., *The New Holistic Health Handbook*. Lexington, Mass.: The Steven Greene Press/Penguin Books, 1985:41.

KARP, DAVID A., and WILLIAM C. YOELS. "The College Classroom: Some Observations on the Meaning of Student Participation." *Sociology and Social Research*. Vol. 60, No. 4 (July 1976):421–39.

KASINITZ, PHILIP, and JAN ROSENBERG. "Missing the Connection: Social Isolation and Employment on the Brooklyn Waterfront." *Social Problems*. Vol. 43, No. 2 (May 1966):180–96.

KATES, ROBERT W. "Ending Hunger: Current Status and Future Prospects." *Consequences*. Vol. 2, No. 2 (1996):3–11.

KATZ, MICHAEL B. *In the Shadow of the Poorhouse*. New York: Basic Books, 1986.

KAUFMAN, MARC. "Becoming 'Old Old.'" *Philadelphia Inquirer* (October 28, 1990):1-A, 10-A.

KAUFMAN, ROBERT L., and SEYMOUR SPILERMAN. "The Age Structures of Occupations and Jobs." *American Journal of Sociology*. Vol. 87, No. 4 (January 1982):827–51.

KAUFMAN, WALTER. *Religions in Four Dimensions: Existential, Aesthetic, Historical and Comparative*. New York: Reader's Digest Press, 1976.

KEISTER, LISA. *Wealth in America: Trends in Wealth Inequality*. Cambridge, UK: Cambridge University Press, 2000.

KEISTER, LISA A., and STEPHANIE MOLLER. "Wealth Inequality in the United States." *Annual Review of Sociology*. Vol. 26 (2000):63–81.

KEITH, PAT M., and ROBERT B. SCHAFER. "They Hate to Cook: Patterns of Distress in an Ordinary Role." *Sociological Focus*. Vol. 27, No. 4 (October 1994):289–301.

KELLER, HELEN. *The Story of My Life*. New York: Doubleday, Page, 1903.

KELLERT, STEPHEN R., and F. HERBERT BORMANN. "Closing the Circle: Weaving Strands among Ecology, Economics, and Ethics." In F. Herbert Bormann and Stephen R. Kellert, eds., *Ecology, Economics, and Ethics: The Broken Circle*. New Haven, Conn.: Yale University Press, 1991:205–10.

KELLEY, JONATHAN, and M. D. R. EVANS. "Class and Class Conflict in Six Western Nations." *American Sociological Review*. Vol. 60, No. 2 (April 1995):157–78.

KEMP, DOMINIC. "Deaths, Diseases Traced to Environment" *Popline*. Vol. 20 (May/June 1998):3.

KENNICKELL, ARTHUR B., MARTHA STARR-MCCLUER, and BRIAN J. SURETTE. "Recent Changes in U.S. Family Finances: Results from the 1998 Survey of Consumer Finances." [Online] Available April 7, 2000, at http://www.federalreserve.gov/pubs/bulletin/2000/0100lead.pdf

KENTOR, JEFFREY. "The Long-Term Effects of Foreign Investment Dependence on Economic Growth, 1940–1990." *American Journal of Sociology*. Vol. 103, No. 4 (January 1998):1024–46.

KERCKHOFF, ALAN C., RICHARD T. CAMPBELL, and IDEE WINFIELD-LAIRD. "Social Mobility in Great Britain and the United States." *American Journal of Sociology*. Vol. 91, No. 2 (September 1985):281–308.

KIDD, QUENTIN, and AIE-RIE LEE. "Postmaterialist Values and the Environment: A Critique and Reappraisal." *Social Science Quarterly*. Vol. 78, No. 1 (March 1997):1–15.

KIDRON, MICHAEL, and RONALD SEGAL. *The New State of the World Atlas*. New York: Simon & Schuster, 1991.

KILBOURNE, BROCK K. "The Conway and Siegelman Claims against Religious Cults: An Assessment of Their Data." *Journal for the Scientific Study of Religion*. Vol. 22, No. 4 (December 1983):380–85.

KILGORE, SALLY B. "The Organizational Context of Tracking in Schools." *American Sociological Review*. Vol. 56, No. 2 (April 1991):189–203.

KILLIAN, LEWIS M. "Organization, Rationality and Spontaneity in the Civil Rights Movement." *American Sociological Review*. Vol. 49, No. 6 (December 1984):770–83.

KING, KATHLEEN PIKER, and DENNIS E. CLAYSON. "The Differential Perceptions of Male and Female Deviants." *Sociological Focus*. Vol. 21, No. 2 (April 1988):153–64.

KING, MARTIN LUTHER, JR. "The Montgomery Bus Boycott." In Walt Anderson, ed., *The Age of Protest*. Pacific Palisades, Calif.: Goodyear, 1969:81–91.

KINKEAD, GWEN. *Chinatown: A Portrait of a Closed Society*. New York: Harper-Collins, 1992.

KINSEY, ALFRED, et al. *Sexual Behavior in the Human Male*. Philadelphia: Saunders, 1948.

———. *Sexual Behavior in the Human Female*. Philadelphia: Saunders, 1953.

KIRN, WALTER. "The New Radicals." *Time*. Vol. 155, No. 16 (April 24, 2000):42–46.

KISER, EDGAR, and JOACHIM SCHNEIDER. "Bureaucracy and Efficiency: An Analysis of Taxation in Early Modern Prussia." *American Sociological Review*. Vol. 59, No. 2 (April 1994):187–204.

KITTRIE, NICHOLAS N. *The Right to Be Different: Deviance and Enforced Therapy*. Baltimore: Johns Hopkins University Press, 1971.

KLEIN, J. D. "The National Longitudinal Study on Adolescent Health: Preliminary Results: Great Expectations." *JAMA: The Journal of the American Medical Association*. Vol. 278, No. 10 (1997):864.

KLEINFELD, JUDITH. "Student Performance: Males versus Females." *The Public Interest*. No. 134 (Winter 1999):3–20.

KLUCKHOHN, CLYDE. "As an Anthropologist Views It." In Albert Deuth, ed., *Sex Habits of American Men*. New York: Prentice Hall, 1948.

KOELLN, KENNETH, ROSE M. RUBIN, and MARION SMITH PICARD. "Vulnerable Elderly Households: Expenditures on Necessities by Older Americans." *Social Science Quarterly*. Vol. 76, No. 3 (September 1995):619–33.

KOHLBERG, LAWRENCE, and CAROL GILLIGAN. "The Adolescent as Philosopher: The Discovery of Self in a Postconventional World." *Daedalus*. Vol. 100 (Fall 1971):1051–86.

KOHN, MELVIN L. *Class and Conformity: A Study in Values*. 2d ed. Homewood, Ill.: Dorsey Press, 1977.

———. "The 'Bell Curve' from the Perspective of Research on Social Structure and Personality." *Sociological Forum*. Vol. 11, No. 2 (1996):395.

KOLATA, GINA. "When Grandmother Is the Mother, Until Birth." *New York Times* (August 5, 1991):1, 11.

KOMAROVSKY, MIRRA. *Blue Collar Marriage*. New York: Vintage Books, 1967.

KONO, CLIFFORD, DONALD PALMER, ROGER FRIEDLAND, and MATTHEW ZAFONTE. "Lost in Space: The Geography of Corporate Interlocking Directorates." *American Journal of Sociology*. Vol. 103, No. 4 (January 1998):863–911.

KORNHAUSER, WILLIAM. *The Politics of Mass Society*. New York: Free Press, 1959.

KORPI, WALTER, and JOAKIM PALME. "The Paradox of Redistribution and Strategies of Equality: Welfare State Institutions, Inequality, and Poverty in the Western Countries." *American Sociological Review*. Vol. 65, No. 5 (October 1998):661–87.

KORZENIEWICZ, ROBERTO P., and KIMBERLY AWBREY. "Democratic Transitions and the Semiperiphery of the World Economy." *Sociological Forum*. Vol. 7, No. 4 (December 1992):609–40.

KOSTERS, MARVIN. "Looking for Jobs in All the Wrong Places." *The Public Interest*. Vol. 125 (Fall 1996):125–31.

KOUSHA, MAHNAZ. "Review of *Modernizing Women* by Valentine M. Moghadam." In *Gender and Society*. Vol. 8 (December 1994):624–26.

KOWALEWSKI, DAVID, and KAREN L. PORTER. "Ecoprotest: Alienation, Deprivation, or Resources." *Social Sciences Quarterly*. Vol. 73, No. 3 (September 1992):523–34.

KOZOL, JONATHAN. *Rachel and Her Children: Homeless Families in America*. New York: Crown Publishers, 1988.

———. *Savage Inequalities: Children in America's Schools*. New York: Harper Perennial, 1992.

KRAFFT, SUSAN. "¿Quién es Numero Uno?" *American Demographics*. Vol. 15, No. 7 (July 1993):16–17.

KRANTZ, MICHAEL. "Say It with a :-)." *Time*. Vol. 149, No. 15 (1997):29.

KRASKA, PETER B., and VICTOR E. KAPPELER. "Militarizing American Police: The Rise and Normalization of Paramilitary Units." *Social Problems*. Vol. 44, No. 1 (February 1997):1–18.

KRAYBILL, DONALD B. *The Riddle of Amish Culture*. Baltimore: Johns Hopkins University Press, 1989.

———. "The Amish Encounter with Modernity." In Donald B. Kraybill and Marc A. Olshan, eds., *The Amish Struggle with Modernity*. Hanover, N.H.: University Press of New England, 1994:21–33.

KRAYBILL, DONALD B., and MARC A. OLSHAN, eds. *The Amish Struggle with Modernity*. Hanover, N.H.: University Press of New England, 1994.

KRIESI, HANSPETER. "New Social Movements and the New Class in the Netherlands." *American Journal of Sociology*. Vol. 94, No. 5 (March 1989):1078–116.

KRISTOL, IRVING. "Life without Father." *Wall Street Journal* (November 3, 1994):A18.

———. "Age before Politics." *Wall Street Journal* (April 25, 1996):A20.

KRIVO, LAUREN J., RUTH D. PETERSON, HELEN RIZZO, and JOHN R. REYNOLDS. "Race, Segregation, and the Concentration of Disadvantage: 1980–1990." *Social Problems*. Vol. 45, No. 1 (February 1998):61–80.

KRUKS, GABRIEL N. "Gay and Lesbian Homeless/Street Youth: Special Issues and Concerns." *Journal of Adolescent Health*. Special Issue. No. 12 (1991):515–18.

KÜBLER-ROSS, ELISABETH. *On Death and Dying*. New York: Macmillan, 1969.

KUHN, THOMAS. *The Structure of Scientific Revolutions*. 2d ed. Chicago: University of Chicago Press, 1970.

KUUMBA, M. BAHATI. "A Cross-Cultural Race/Class/Gender Critique of Contemporary Population Policy: The Impact of Globalization." *Sociological Forum.* Vol. 14, No. 3 (March 1999):447–63.

KUZNETS, SIMON. "Economic Growth and Income Inequality." *The American Economic Review.* Vol. 14, No. 1 (March 1955):1–28.

———. *Modern Economic Growth: Rate, Structure, and Spread.* New Haven, Conn.: Yale University Press, 1966.

LABOVITZ, PRICISSA. "Immigration: Just the Facts." *New York Times* (March 25, 1996).

LACAYO, RICHARD. "The Brawl over Sprawl." *Time.* Vol. 153, No. 11 (March 22, 1999):44–48.

LACH, JENNIFER. "The Color of Money." *American Demographics.* Vol. 21, No. 2 (February 1999):59–60.

———. "Is It the Flu, or Are You Faking It?" *American Demographics.* Vol. 21, No. 11 (November 1999):10–11.

LADD, JOHN. "The Definition of Death and the Right to Die." In John Ladd, ed., *Ethical Issues Relating to Life and Death.* New York: Oxford University Press, 1979:118–45.

LAI, H. M. "Chinese." In *Harvard Encyclopedia of American Ethnic Groups.* Cambridge, Mass.: Harvard University Press, 1980:217–33.

LAMBERG-KARLOVSKY, C. C., and MARTHA LAMBERG-KARLOVSKY. "An Early City in Iran." In *Cities: Their Origin, Growth, and Human Impact.* San Francisco: Freeman, 1973:28–37.

LANDERS, ANN. Syndicated column: *Dallas Morning News* (July 8, 1984):4F.

LANDERS, RENE M. "Gender, Race, and the State Courts." *Radcliffe Quarterly.* Vol. 76, No. 4 (December 1990):6–9.

LANDSBERG, MITCHELL. "Health Disaster Brings Early Death in Russia." *Washington Times* (March 15, 1998):A8.

LANE, DAVID. "Social Stratification and Class." In Erik P. Hoffman and Robbin F. Laird, eds., *The Soviet Polity in the Modern Era.* New York: Aldine, 1984:563–605.

LANG, KURT, and GLADYS ENGEL LANG. *Collective Dynamics.* New York: Thomas Y. Crowell, 1961.

LANGBEIN, LAURA I. "Politics, Rules, and Death Row: Why States Eschew or Execute Executions." *Social Science Quarterly.* Vol. 80, No. 4 (December 1999):629–47.

LAPPÉ, FRANCES MOORE, and JOSEPH COLLINS. *World Hunger: Twelve Myths.* New York: Grove Press/Food First Books, 1986.

LAPPÉ, FRANCES MOORE, JOSEPH COLLINS, and DAVID KINLEY. *Aid as Obstacle: Twenty Questions about Our Foreign Policy and the Hungry.* San Francisco: Institute for Food and Development Policy, 1981.

LARMER, BROOK. "Dead End Kids." *Newsweek* (May 25, 1992):38–40.

LASLETT, BARBARA. "Family Membership, Past and Present." *Social Problems.* Vol. 25, No. 5 (June 1978):476–90.

LASLETT, PETER. *The World We Have Lost: England before the Industrial Age.* 3d ed. New York: Charles Scribner's Sons, 1984.

LASSWELL, MARK. "A Tribe at War: Not the Yanomami: The Anthropologists." *Wall Street Journal* (November 17, 2000):A17.

LAUMANN, EDWARD O., JOHN H. GAGNON, ROBERT T. MICHAEL, and STUART MICHAELS. *The Social Organization of Sexuality: Sexual Practices in the United States.* Chicago: University of Chicago Press, 1994.

LEACOCK, ELEANOR. "Women's Status in Egalitarian Societies: Implications for Social Evolution." *Current Anthropology.* Vol. 19, No. 2 (June 1978):247–75.

LEAVITT, JUDITH WALZER. "Women and Health in America: An Overview." In Judith Walzer Leavitt, ed., *Women and Health in America.* Madison: University of Wisconsin Press, 1984:3–7.

LE BON, GUSTAVE. *The Crowd: A Study of the Popular Mind.* New York: Viking Press, 1960; orig. 1895.

LEE, SHARON M. "Poverty and the U.S. Asian Population." *Social Science Quarterly.* Vol. 75, No. 3 (September 1994):541–59.

LEERHSEN, CHARLES. "Unite and Conquer." *Newsweek* (February 5, 1990):50–55.

LEFEBVRE, HENRI. *The Production of Space.* Oxford, U.K.: Blackwell, 1991.

LELAND, JOHN. "Bisexuality." *Newsweek* (July 17, 1995):44–49.

LEMERT, EDWIN M. *Social Pathology.* New York: McGraw-Hill, 1951.

———. *Human Deviance, Social Problems, and Social Control.* 2d ed. Englewood Cliffs, N.J.: Prentice Hall, 1972.

LENGERMANN, PATRICIA MADOO, and RUTH A. WALLACE. *Gender in America: Social Control and Social Change.* Englewood Cliffs, N.J.: Prentice Hall, 1985.

LENNON, MARY CLARE, and SARAH ROSENFELD. "Relative Fairness and the Doctrine of Housework: The Importance of Options." *American Journal of Sociology.* Vol. 100, No. 2 (September 1994):506–31.

LENSKI, GERHARD E. *Power and Privilege: A Theory of Social Stratification.* New York: McGraw-Hill, 1966.

LENSKI, GERHARD, PATRICK NOLAN, and JEAN LENSKI. *Human Societies: An Introduction to Macrosociology.* 7th ed. New York: McGraw-Hill, 1995.

LEONARD, EILEEN B. *Women, Crime, and Society: A Critique of Theoretical Criminology.* New York: Longman, 1982.

LERNER, DANIEL. *The Passing of Traditional Society: Modernizing the Middle East.* New York: The Free Press, 1958.

LESLIE, GERALD R., and SHEILA K. KORMAN. *The Family in Social Context.* 7th ed. New York: Oxford University Press, 1989.

LESTER, DAVID. *The Death Penalty: Issues and Answers.* Springfield, Ill.: Charles C. Thomas, 1987.

LETSCHER, MARTIN. "Tell Fads from Trends." *American Demographics.* Vol. 16, No. 12 (December 1994):38–45.

LeVay, SIMON. *The Sexual Brain.* Cambridge, Mass.: MIT Press, 1993.

LEVER, JANET. "Sex Differences in the Complexity of Children's Play and Games." *American Sociological Review.* Vol. 43, No. 4 (August 1978):471–83.

LEVIN, JACK, and ARNOLD ARLUKE. *Gossip: The Inside Scoop.* New York: Plenum, 1987.

LEVINE, MICHAEL. "Reducing Hostility Can Prevent Heart Disease." *Mount Vernon News* (August 7, 1990):4A.

LEVINE, MICHAEL P. *Student Eating Disorders: Anorexia Nervosa and Bulimia.* Washington, D.C.: National Educational Association, 1987.

LEVINE, ROBERT V. "Is Love a Luxury?" *American Demographics.* Vol. 15, No. 2 (February 1993):27–28.

LEVINE, SAMANTHA. "The Price of Child Abuse." *U.S. News & World Report.* Vol. 130, No. 14 (April 9, 2001):58.

LEVINSON, DANIEL J., CHARLOTTE N. DARROW, EDWARD B. KLEIN, MARIA H. LEVINSON, and BRAXTON MCKEE. *The Seasons of a Man's Life.* New York: Alfred A. Knopf, 1978.

LEWIS, FLORA. "The Roots of Revolution." *New York Times Magazine* (November 11, 1984):70–71, 74, 77–78, 82, 84, 86.

LEWIS, OSCAR. *The Children of Sánchez.* New York: Random House, 1961.

LEWIS, PEIRCE, CASEY MCCRACKEN, and ROGER HUNT. "Politics: Who Cares?" *American Demographics.* Vol. 16, No. 10 (October 1994):20–26.

LI, JIANG HONG, and ROGER A. WOJTKIEWICZ. "A New Look at the Effects of Family Structure on Status Attainment." *Social Science Quarterly.* Vol. 73, No. 3 (September 1992):581–95.

LIAZOS, ALEXANDER. "The Poverty of the Sociology of Deviance: Nuts, Sluts and Preverts." *Social Problems.* Vol. 20, No. 1 (Summer 1972):103–20.

———. *People First: An Introduction to Social Problems.* Boston: Allyn and Bacon, 1982.

LICHTER, DANIEL T., DIANE K. MCLAUGHLIN, and DAVID C. RIBAR. "Welfare and the Rise in Female-Headed Families." *American Journal of Sociology.* Vol. 103, No. 1 (July 1997):112–43.

LICHTER, S. ROBERT, STANLEY ROTHMAN, and LINDA S. LICHTER. *The Media Elite: America's New Powerbrokers.* New York: Hastings House, 1990.

LICHTER, S. ROBERT, STANLEY ROTHMAN, and LINDA R. ROTHMAN. *The Media Elite: America's New Powerbrokers.* Bethesda, Md.: Adler & Adler, 1986.

LIEBOW, ELLIOT. *Tally's Corner.* Boston: Little, Brown, 1967.

LIGHT, PAUL C. "Big Government Is Bigger Than You Think." *The Wall Street Journal* (January 13, 1999):A22.

LIN, GE, and PETER ROGERSON. Research reported in Diane Crispell, "Sons and Daughters Who Keep in Touch." *American Demographics.* Vol. 16, No. 8 (August 1994):15–16.

LIN, NAN, and WEN XIE. "Occupational Prestige in Urban China." *American Journal of Sociology.* Vol. 93, No. 4 (January 1988):793–832.

LINDEN, EUGENE. "Can Animals Think?" *Time.* Vol. 141, No. 12 (March 22, 1993):54–61.

———. "More Power to Women, Fewer Mouths to Feed." *Time.* Vol. 144, No. 13 (September 26, 1994):64–65.

LINDSTROM, BONNIE. "Chicago's Post-Industrial Suburbs." *Sociological Focus.* Vol. 28, No. 4 (October 1995):399–412.

LING, PYAU. "Causes of Chinese Emigration." In Amy Tachiki et al., eds., *Roots: An Asian American Reader.* Los Angeles: UCLA Asian American Studies Center, 1971:134–38.

LINN, MICHAEL. Noted in *Cornell Alumni News.* Vol. 99, No. 2 (September 1996):25.

LINO, MARK. *Expenditures on Children by Families, 1999 Annual Report.* Washington, D.C.: U.S. Department of Agriculture, Center for Nutrition Policy and Promotion, 2000.

LINTON, RALPH. "One Hundred Percent American." *The American Mercury.* Vol. 40, No. 160 (April 1937a):427–29.

———. *The Study of Man.* New York: D. Appleton-Century, 1937b.

LIPS, HILARY. *Sex and Gender: An Introduction.* 2d ed. Mountain View, Calif.: Mayfield Publishing Co., 1993.

LIPSET, SEYMOUR MARTIN. *Political Man: The Social Bases of Politics.* Garden City, N.Y.: Anchor/Doubleday, 1963.

———. "Canada and the United States." Charles F. Donan and John H. Sigler, eds. Englewood Cliffs, N.J.: Prentice Hall, 1985.

LIPSET, SEYMOUR MARTIN, and REINHARD BENDIX. *Social Mobility in Industrial Society.* Berkeley: University of California Press, 1967.

LISKA, ALLEN E. *Perspectives on Deviance.* 3d ed. Englewood Cliffs, N.J.: Prentice Hall, 1991.

LISKA, ALLEN E., and MARK TAUSIG. "Theoretical Interpretations of Social Class and Racial Differentials in Legal Decision Making for Juveniles." *Sociological Quarterly.* Vol. 20, No. 2 (Spring 1979):197–207.

LISKA, ALLEN E., and BARBARA D. WARNER. "Functions of Crime: A Paradoxical Process." *American Journal of Sociology.* Vol. 96, No. 6 (May 1991):1441–63.

LITTMAN, DAVID L. "2001: A Farm Odyssey." *Wall Street Journal* (September 14, 1992):A10.

LIVERNASH, ROBERT, and ERIC RODENBURG. "Population Change, Resources, and the Environment." *Population Bulletin.* Vol. 53, No. 1 (March 1998).

LIVINGSTON, KEN. "Politics and Mental Illness." *Public Interest.* Vol. 143 (Winter, 1999):105–9.

LO, CLARENCE Y. H. "Countermovements and Conservative Movements in the Contemporary U.S." *Annual Review of Sociology.* Vol. 8. Palo Alto, Calif.: Annual Reviews, 1982:107–34.

LOFLAND, LYN. *A World of Strangers.* New York: Basic Books, 1973.

LOGAN, JOHN R., and MARK SCHNEIDER. "Racial Segregation and Racial Change in American Suburbs, 1970–1980." *American Journal of Sociology.* Vol. 89, No. 4 (January 1984):874–88.

LOHR, STEVE. "British Health Service Faces a Crisis in Funds and Delays." *New York Times* (August 7, 1988):1, 12.

LONGINO, JR., CHARLES F. "Myths of An Aging America." *American Demographics.* Vol. 16, No. 8 (August 1994):36–42.

LORD, MARY. "Good Teachers, the Newest Imports." *U.S. News & World Report.* Vol. 130, No. 13 (April 9, 2001):54.

LORD, WALTER. *A Night to Remember.* Rev. ed. New York: Holt, Rinehart & Winston, 1976.

LORENZ, FREDERICK O., and BRENT T. BRUTON. "Experiments in Surveys: Linking Mass Class Questionnaires to Introductory Research Methods." *Teaching Sociology.* Vol. 24, No. 3 (July 1996):264–71.

LOVEMAN, MARA. "Is 'Race' Essential?" *American Sociological Review.* Vol. 64, No. 6 (December 1999):890–98.

LOVGREN, STEFEN. "Will All the Blue Men End Up in Timbuktu?" *U.S. News & World Report* (December 7, 1998):40.

LUBLIN, JOANN S. "Pay for No Performance." *Wall Street Journal* (April 22, 1998):R1.

LUKER, KRISTEN. *Abortion and the Politics of Motherhood.* Berkeley: University of California Press, 1984.

LUND, DALE A. "Conclusions about Bereavement in Later Life and Implications for Interventions and Future Research." In Dale A. Lund, ed., *Older Bereaved Spouses: Research with Practical Applications.* London: Taylor-Francis-Hemisphere, 1989:217–31.

———. "Caregiving." *Encyclopedia of Adult Development.* Phoenix, Ariz.: Oryx Press, 1993:57–63.

LUND, DALE A., MICHAEL S. CASERTA, and MARGARET F. DIMOND. "Gender Differences through Two Years of Bereavement among the Elderly." *The Gerontologist.* Vol. 26, No. 3 (1986):314–20.

LUNDMAN, RICHARD L. Correspondence to author, 1999.

LUNSFORD, JACK. Remarks at a meeting of the Arizona Task Force on the Western Virtual University. [Online] Available May 6, 1996, at http://www.acpe.asu.edu/VirtualU/

LUO, JAR-DER. "The Significance of Networks in the Initiation of Small Businesses in Taiwan." *Sociological Focus.* Vol. 12, No. 2 (June 1997):297–317.

LUTZ, CATHERINE A. *Unnatural Emotions: Everyday Sentiments on a Micronesia Atoll and Their Challenge to Western Theory.* Chicago: University of Chicago Press, 1988.

LUTZ, CATHERINE A., and GEOFFREY M. WHITE. "The Anthropology of Emotions." In Bernard J. Siegel, Alan R. Beals, and Stephen A. Tyler, eds., *Annual Review of Anthropology.* Palo Alto, Calif.: Annual Reviews, Vol. 15 (1986):405–36.

LYNCH, MICHAEL, and DAVID BOGEN. "Sociology's Asociological 'Core': An Examination of Textbook Sociology in Light of the Sociology of Scientific Knowledge." *American Sociological Review.* Vol. 62, No. 3 (June 1997):481–93.

LYND, ROBERT S. *Knowledge for What? The Place of Social Science in American Culture.* Princeton, N.J.: Princeton University Press, 1967.

LYND, ROBERT S., and HELEN MERRELL LYND. *Middletown in Transition.* New York: Harcourt, Brace & World, 1937.

LYNOTT, PATRICIA PASSUTH, and BARBARA J. LOGUE. "The 'Hurried Child': The Myth of Lost Childhood in Contemporary American Society." *Sociological Forum.* Vol. 8, No. 3 (September 1993):471–91.

MA, LI-CHEN. Personal communication, 1987.

MABRY, MARCUS. "New Hope for Old Unions?" *Newsweek* (February 24, 1992):39.

MABRY, MARCUS, and TOM MASLAND. "The Man after Mandela." *Newsweek* (June 7, 1999):54–55.

McADAM, DOUG. *Political Process and the Development of Black Insurgency, 1930–1970.* Chicago: University of Chicago Press, 1982.

———. "Tactical Innovation and the Pace of Insurgency." *American Sociological Review.* Vol. 48, No. 6 (December 1983):735–54.

———. *Freedom Summer.* New York: Oxford University Press, 1988.

———. "The Biographical Consequences of Activism." *American Sociological Review.* Vol. 54, No. 5 (October 1989):744–60.

———. "Gender as a Mediator of the Activist Experience: The Case of Freedom Summer." *American Journal of Sociology.* Vol. 97, No. 5 (March 1992):1211–40.

McADAM, DOUG, JOHN D. McCARTHY, and MAYER N. ZALD. "Social Movements." In Neil J. Smelser, ed., *Handbook of Sociology.* Newbury Park, Calif.: Sage, 1988:695–737.

———, eds. *Comparative Perspectives on Social Movements: Political Opportunities, Mobilizing Structures, and Cultural Framings.* Cambridge: Cambridge University Press, 1996.

McALLISTER, J. F. O. "Cinderella, Career Gal." *Time.* Vol. 157, No. 16 (April 23, 2001):8.

McBROOM, WILLIAM H., and FRED W. REED. "Recent Trends in Conservatism: Evidence of Non-Unitary Patterns." *Sociological Focus.* Vol. 23, No. 4 (October 1990):355–65.

McCARTHY, JOHN D., and MAYER N. ZALD. "Resource Mobilization and Social Movements: A Partial Theory." *American Journal of Sociology.* Vol. 82, No. 6 (May 1977):1212–41.

McCARTHY, TERRY. "Give Me Your Tired, Your Poor . . ." *Time.* Vol. 151, No. 4 (February 2, 1998):4.

MACCOBY, ELEANOR EMMONS, and CAROL NAGY JACKLIN. *The Psychology of Sex Differences.* Palo Alto, Calif.: Stanford University Press, 1974.

McCOLM, R. BRUCE, JAMES FINN, DOUGLAS W. PAYNE, JOSEPH E. RYAN, LEONARD R. SUSSMAN, and GEORGE ZARYCKY. *Freedom in the World: Political Rights & Civil Liberties, 1990–1991.* New York: Freedom House, 1991.

McCONNELL, SCOTT. "New Liberal Fear: Hyperdemocracy." *The New York Post* (January 18, 1995):19.

McCORMICK, NAOMI B. *Sexual Salvation.* Westport, Conn.: Praeger, 1994.

MacDONALD, J. FRED. *Blacks and White TV: African Americans in Television since 1948.* Chicago: Nelson-Hall, 1992.

McDONALD, KIM A. "Debate over How to Gauge Global Warming Heats Up Meeting of Climatologists." *Chronicle of Higher Education.* Vol. 45, No. 22 (February 5, 1999):A17.

MACE, DAVID, and VERA MACE. *Marriage East and West.* Garden City, N.Y.: Doubleday (Dolphin), 1960.

McGEARY, JOHANNA. "Nukes . . . They're Back." *Time.* Vol. 151, No. 20 (May 25, 1998):34–42.

McGUIRE, MEREDITH B. *Religion: The Social Context.* 2d ed. Belmont, Calif.: Wadsworth, 1987.

MACIONIS, JOHN J. "Intimacy: Structure and Process in Interpersonal Relationships." *Alternative Lifestyles.* Vol. 1, No. 1 (February 1978):113–30.

———. "A Sociological Analysis of Humor." Presentation to the Texas Junior College Teachers Association, Houston, 1987.

———. "Making Society (and, Increasingly, the World) Visible." In Earl Babbie, ed., *The Spirit of Sociology.* Belmont, Calif.: Wadsworth, 1993:221–24.

———. *Social Problems.* Upper Saddle River, N.J.: Prentice Hall, 2002.

MACIONIS, JOHN J., and LINDA GERBER. *Sociology: Third Canadian Edition.* Scarborough, Ontario: Prentice Hall Allyn & Bacon Canada, 2001.

———. *Sociology: Fourth Canadian Edition.* Scarborough, Ontario: Prentice Hall Allyn & Bacon Canada, 2002.

MACIONIS, JOHN J., and VINCENT R. PARRILLO. *Cities and Urban Life.* 2d ed. Upper Saddle River, N.J.: Prentice Hall, 2001.

MACKAY, JUDITH. *The Penguin Atlas of Human Sexual Behavior.* New York: Penguin Group, 2000.

McKEE, VICTORIA. "Blue Blood and the Color of Money." *New York Times* (June 9, 1996):49–50.

MACKLIN, ELEANOR D. "Nonmarital Heterosexual Cohabitation: An Overview." In Eleanor D. Macklin and Roger H. Rubin, eds., *Contemporary Families and Alternative Lifestyles: Handbook on Research and Theory.* Beverly Hills, Calif.: Sage, 1983:49–74.

McLEOD, JANE D., and MICHAEL J. SHANAHAN. "Poverty, Parenting, and Children's Mental Health." *American Sociological Review.* Vol. 58, No. 3 (June 1993):351–66.

McLEOD, JAY. *Ain't No Makin' It: Aspirations and Attainment in a Low-Income Neighborhood.* Boulder, Colo.: Westview Press, 1995.

McLUHAN, MARSHALL. *The Gutenberg Galaxy.* New York: New American Library, 1969.

McNEIL, DONALD G., JR. "Should Women Be Sent into Combat?" *New York Times* (July 21, 1991):E3.

McNULTY, PAUL J. "Who's in Jail and Why They Belong There." *Wall Street Journal* (November 9, 1994):A23.

McPHAIL, CLARK. *The Myth of the Maddening Crowd.* New York: Aldine, 1991.

McPHAIL, CLARK, and RONALD T. WOHLSTEIN. "Individual and Collective Behaviors within Gatherings, Demonstrations, and Riots." *Annual Review of Sociology.* Vol. 9. Palo Alto, Calif.: Annual Reviews, 1983:579–600.

MacPHERSON, KAREN. "Children Have a Full-Time Media Habit, Study Says." *Toledo Blade* (November 18, 1999):3.

McRAE, SUSAN. *Cross-Class Families: A Study of Wives' Occupational Superiority.* New York: Oxford University Press, 1986.

MADDOX, SETMA. "Organizational Culture and Leadership Style: Factors Affecting Self-Managed Work Team Performance." Paper presented at the annual meeting of the Southwest Social Science Association, Dallas, February 1994.

MADSEN, AXEL. *Private Power: Multinational Corporations for the Survival of Our Planet.* New York: William Morrow, 1980.

MAINES, DAVID R. "Charting Futures for Sociology: Culture and Meaning." *Contemporary Sociology.* Vol. 29, No. 4 (July 2000):577–84.

MALTHUS, THOMAS ROBERT. *First Essay on Population 1798.* London: Macmillan, 1926; orig. 1798.

MANZA, JEFF, and CLEM BROOKS. "The Religious Factor in U.S. Presidential Elections, 1960–1992." *American Journal of Sociology.* Vol. 103, No. 1 (July 1997):38–81.

———. "The Gender Gap in U.S. Presidential Elections: When? Why? Implications?" *American Journal of Sociology.* Vol. 103, No. 5 (March 1998):1235–66.

MARCUSE, HERBERT. *One-Dimensional Man.* Boston: Beacon Press, 1964.

MARE, ROBERT D. "Five Decades of Educational Assortative Mating." *American Sociological Review.* Vol. 56, No. 1 (February 1991):15–32.

MARÍN, GERARDO, and BARBARA VANOSS MARÍN. *Research with Hispanic Populations.* Newbury Park, Calif.: Sage, 1991.

MARINI, MARGARET MOONEY, and PI-LING FAN. "The Gender Gap in Earnings at Career Entry." *American Sociological Review.* Vol. 62, No. 4 (August 1997):588–604.

MARKLEIN, MARY BETH. "Optimism Rises as SAT Math Scores Hit 30-Year High." *USA Today* (August 30, 2000):1A.

MARKOFF, JOHN. "Remember Big Brother? Now He's a Company Man." *New York Times* (March 31, 1991):7.

MARKOVSKY, BARRY, JOHN SKVORETZ, DAVID WILLER, MICHAEL J. LOVAGLIA, and JEFFREY ERGER. "The Seeds of Weak Power: An Extension of Network Exchange Theory." *American Sociological Review.* Vol. 58, No. 2 (April 1993):197–209.

MARKSON, ELIZABETH W. "Moral Dilemmas." *Society.* Vol. 29, No. 5 (July–August 1992):4–6.

MARQUAND, ROBERT. "Worship Shift: Americans Seek Feeling of 'Awe'." *Christian Science Monitor* (May 28, 1997):1, 8.

MARQUAND, ROBERT, and DANIEL B. WOOD. "Rise in Cults as Millennium Approaches." *Christian Science Monitor* (March 28, 1997):1, 18.

MARSHALL, SUSAN E. "Ladies against Women: Mobilization Dilemmas of Antifeminist Movements." *Social Problems.* Vol. 32, No. 4 (April 1985):348–62.

MARTIN, JOHN M., and ANNE T. ROMANO. *Multinational Crime: Terrorism, Espionage, Drug and Arms Trafficking.* Newbury Park, Calif.: Sage, 1992.

MARTIN, RICHARD C. *Islam: A Cultural Perspective.* Englewood Cliffs, N.J.: Prentice Hall, 1982.

MARTINEZ, RAMIRO, JR. "Latinos and Lethal Violence: The Impact of Poverty and Inequality." *Social Problems.* Vol. 43, No. 2 (May 1996):131–46.

MARTINEZ, VALERIE J., R. KENNETH GODWIN, FRANK R. KEMERER, and LAURA PERNA. "The Consequences of School Choice: Who Leaves and Who Stays in the Inner City." *Social Science Quarterly.* Vol. 76, No. 1 (September 1995):485–501.

MARULLO, SAM. "The Functions and Dysfunctions of Preparations for Fighting Nuclear War." *Sociological Focus.* Vol. 20, No. 2 (April 1987):135–53.

MARX, GARY T., and JAMES L. WOOD. "Strands of Theory and Research in Collective Behavior." In Alex Inkeles et al., eds., *Annual Review of Sociology.* Vol. 1. Palo Alto, Calif.: Annual Reviews, 1975:363–428.

MARX, KARL. Excerpt from "A Contribution to the Critique of Political Economy." In Karl Marx and Friedrich Engels, *Marx and Engels: Basic Writings on Politics and Philosophy,* Lewis S. Feurer, ed. Garden City, N.Y.: Anchor Books, 1959:42–46.

———. *Karl Marx: Early Writings.* T. B. Bottomore, ed. New York: McGraw-Hill, 1964a.

———. *Karl Marx: Selected Writings in Sociology and Social Philosophy.* T. B. Bottomore, trans. New York: McGraw-Hill, 1964b.

———. *Capital.* Friedrich Engels, ed. New York: International Publishers, 1967; orig. 1867.

———. "Theses on Feuer." In Robert C. Tucker, ed., *The Marx-Engels Reader.* New York: Norton, 1972:107–9; orig. 1845.

MARX, KARL, and FRIEDRICH ENGELS. "Manifesto of the Communist Party." In Robert C. Tucker, ed., *The Marx-Engels Reader.* New York: Norton, 1972:331–62; orig. 1848.

———. *The Marx-Engels Reader.* 2d ed. Robert C. Tucker, ed. New York: Norton, 1978.

MARX, LEO. "The Environment and the 'Two Cultures' Divide." In James Rodger Fleming and Henry A. Gemery, eds., *Science, Technology, and the Environment: Multidisciplinary Perspectives.* Akron, Ohio: University of Akron Press, 1994:3–21.

MASSEY, DOUGLAS. "Housing Discrimination 101." *Population Today.* Vol. 28, No. 6 (August/September 2000):1, 4.

MASSEY, DOUGLAS S., and NANCY A. DENTON. "Hypersegregation in U.S. Metropolitan Areas: Black and Hispanic Segregation along Five Dimensions." *Demography.* Vol. 26, No. 3 (August 1989):373–91.

MASTERS, WILLIAM H., VIRGINIA E. JOHNSON, and ROBERT C. KOLODNY. *Human Sexuality.* 3d ed. Glenview, Ill.: Scott, Foresman/Little, Brown, 1988.

MATLOFF, JUDITH. "Nomadic 'Blue Men' of the Desert Try to Go Roam Again." *Christian Science Monitor* (September 9, 1997):7.

MATTHIESSEN, PETER. *Indian Country.* New York: Viking Press, 1984.

MAUER, MARC. "Americans behind Bars: U.S. and International Use of Incarceration 1995." [Online] Available April 1, 2000, at http://www.sentencingproject.org/pubs/tsppubs/9030data.html

MAURO, TONY. "Ruling Likely Will Add Fuel to Already Divisive Debate." *USA Today* (January 7, 1997):1A, 2A.

MAUSS, ARMAND L. *Social Problems of Social Movements.* Philadelphia: Lippincott, 1975.

MAYO, KATHERINE. *Mother India.* New York: Harcourt, Brace, 1927.

MEAD, GEORGE HERBERT. *Mind, Self, and Society.* Charles W. Morris, ed. Chicago: University of Chicago Press, 1962; orig. 1934.

MEAD, MARGARET. *Sex and Temperament in Three Primitive Societies.* New York: William Morrow, 1963; orig. 1935.

MEADOWS, DONELLA H., DENNIS L. MEADOWS, JORGAN RANDERS, and WILLIAM W. BEHRENS, III. *The Limits to Growth: A Report on the Club of Rome's Project on the Predicament of Mankind.* New York: Universe, 1972.

MELTZER, BERNARD N. "Mead's Social Psychology." In Jerome G. Manis and Bernard N. Meltzer, eds., *Symbolic Interaction: A Reader in Social Psychology.* 3d ed. Needham Heights, Mass.: Allyn & Bacon, 1978.

MELUCCI, ALBERTO. "The New Social Movements: A Theoretical Approach." *Social Science Information.* Vol. 19, No. 2 (May 1980):199–226.

———. *Nomads of the Present: Social Movements and Individual Needs in Contemporary Society.* Philadelphia: Temple University Press, 1989.

MENCKEN, F. CARSON, and IDEE WINFIELD. "Employer Recruiting and the Gender Composition of Jobs." *Sociological Focus.* Vol. 32, No. 2 (May 1999):210–20.

MENJIVAR, CECILIA. "Immigrant Kinship Networks and the Impact of the Receiving Context: Salvadorans in San Francisco in the Early 1990s." *Social Problems.* Vol. 44, No. 1 (February 1997):104–23.

MERGENHAGEN, PAULA. "Rethinking Retirement." *American Demographics.* Vol. 16, No. 6 (June 1994):28–34.

———. "Black-Owned Businesses." *American Demographics.* Vol. 18, No. 6 (June 1996a):24–27, 30–33.

———. "Sun City Gets Boomerized." *American Demographics.* Vol. 18, No. 8 (August 1996b):16–20.

———. "Her Own Boss." *American Demographics.* Vol. 18, No. 12 (December 1996c):37–41.

MERTON, ROBERT K. "Social Structure and Anomie." *American Sociological Review.* Vol. 3, No. 6 (October 1938):672–82.

———. *Social Theory and Social Structure.* New York: Free Press, 1968.

———. "Discrimination and the American Creed." In *Sociological Ambivalence and Other Essays.* New York: Free Press, 1976:189–216.

MEYER, DAVID S., and SUZANNE STAGGENBORG. "Movements, Countermovements, and the Structure of Political Opportunity." *American Journal of Sociology.* Vol. 101, No. 6 (May 1996):1628–60.

MEYER, DAVIS S., and NANCY WHITTIER. "Social Movement Spillover." *Social Problems.* Vol. 41, No. 2 (May 1994):277–98.

MICHELS, ROBERT. *Political Parties.* Glencoe, Ill.: Free Press, 1949; orig. 1911.

MILBRATH, LESTER W. *Envisioning A Sustainable Society: Learning Our Way Out.* Albany: State University of New York Press, 1989.

MILGRAM, STANLEY. "Behavioral Study of Obedience." *Journal of Abnormal and Social Psychology.* Vol. 67, No. 4 (1963):371–78.

———. "Group Pressure and Action against a Person." *Journal of Abnormal and Social Psychology.* Vol. 69, No. 2 (August 1964):137–43.

———. "Some Conditions of Obedience and Disobedience to Authority." *Human Relations.* Vol. 18 (February 1965):57–76.

———. "The Small World Problem." *Psychology Today.* Vol. 2 (1967):60–67.

MILIBAND, RALPH. *The State in Capitalist Society.* London: Weidenfield & Nicolson, 1969.

MILLER, ARTHUR G. *The Obedience Experiments: A Case of Controversy in Social Science.* New York: Praeger, 1986.

MILLER, BERNA. "The Quest for Lifelong Learning." *American Demographics.* Vol. 19, No. 3 (March 1997a):20, 22.

———. "Population Update for April." *American Demographics.* Vol. 19, No. 4 (April 1997b):18.

MILLER, DAVID L. *Introduction to Collective Behavior.* Belmont, Calif.: Wadsworth, 1985.

MILLER, FREDERICK D. "The End of SDS and the Emergence of Weatherman: Demise through Success." In Jo Freeman, ed., *Social Movements of the Sixties and Seventies.* New York: Longman, 1983:279–97.

MILLER, G. TYLER, JR. *Living in the Environment: An Introduction to Environmental Science.* Belmont, Calif.: Wadsworth, 1992.

MILLER, WALTER B. "Lower Class Culture as a Generating Milieu of Gang Delinquency." In Marvin E. Wolfgang, Leonard Savitz, and Norman Johnston, eds., *The Sociology of Crime and Delinquency.* 2d ed. New York: Wiley, 1970:351–63; orig. 1958.

MILLET, KATE. *Sexual Politics.* Garden City, N.Y.: Doubleday, 1970.

MILLS, C. WRIGHT. *The Power Elite.* New York: Oxford University Press, 1956.

———. *The Sociological Imagination.* New York: Oxford University Press, 1959.

MINK, BARBARA. "How Modernization Affects Women." *Cornell Alumni News.* Vol. 3, No. 3 (April 1989):10–11.

MINTZ, BETH, and MICHAEL SCHWARTZ. "Interlocking Directorates and Interest Group Formation." *American Sociological Review.* Vol. 46, No. 6 (December 1981):851–69.

MIRINGOFF, MARC, and MARQUE-LUISA MIRINGOFF. "The Social Health of the Nation." *The Economist.* Vol. 352, No. 8128 (July 17, 1999):suppl. 6–7.

MIROWSKY, JOHN. "The Psycho-Economics of Feeling Underpaid: Distributive Justice and the Earnings of Husbands and Wives." *American Journal of Sociology.* Vol. 92, No. 6 (May 1987):1404–34.

MIROWSKY, JOHN, and CATHERINE ROSS. "Working Wives and Mental Health." Presentation to the American Association for the Advancement of Science, New York, 1984.

MOEN, PHYLLIS, DONNA DEMPSTER-McCLAIN, and ROBIN M. WILLIAMS. "Successful Aging: A Life-Course Perspective on Women's Multiple Roles and Health." *American Journal of Sociology.* Vol. 97 (May 1992):1612–38.

MOGELONSKY, MARCIA. "Reconfiguring the American Dream (House)." *American Demographics.* Vol. 19, No. 1 (January 1997):31–35.

MOLM, LINDA D. "Risk and Power Use: Constraints on the Use of Coercion in Exchange." *American Sociological Review.* Vol. 62, No. 1 (February 1997):113–33.

MOLOTCH, HARVEY. "The City as a Growth Machine." *American Journal of Sociology.* Vol. 82, No. 2 (September 1976):309–33.

MONTAGU, ASHLEY. *The Nature of Human Aggression.* New York: Oxford University Press, 1976.

MOORE, GWEN. "Structural Determinants of Men's and Women's Personal Networks." *American Sociological Review.* Vol. 55, No. 5 (October 1991):726–35.

———. "Gender and Informal Networks in State Government." *Social Science Quarterly.* Vol. 73, No. 1 (March 1992):46–61.

MOORE, JOAN, and HARRY PACHON. *Hispanics in the United States.* Englewood Cliffs, N.J.: Prentice Hall, 1985.

MOORE, WILBERT E. "Modernization as Rationalization: Processes and Restraints." In Manning Nash, ed., *Essays on Economic Development and Cultural Change in Honor of Bert F. Hoselitz.* Chicago: University of Chicago Press, 1977:29–42.

———. *World Modernization: The Limits of Convergence.* New York: Elsevier, 1979.

MORAN, JOHN S., S. O. ARAL, W. C. JENKINS, T. A. PETERMAN, and E. R. ALEXANDER. "The Impact of Sexually Transmitted Diseases on Minority Populations." *Public Health Reports.* Vol. 104, No. 6 (November–December 1989):560–65.

MORGAN, LAURIE A. "Glass Ceiling or Cohort Effect? A Longitudinal Study of the Gender Earnings Gap for Engineers, 1982 to 1989." *American Sociological Review.* Vol. 63, No. 4 (August 1998):479–93.

MORRIS, ALDON. "Black Southern Sit-In Movement: An Analysis of Internal Organization." *American Sociological Review.* Vol. 46, No. 6 (December 1981):744–67.

MORRIS, JIM, and MARIANNE LAVELLE. "Secret Data Reveal Why Tires Went Bad." *U.S. News & World Report.* Vol. 129, No. 12 (September 25, 2000):42–43.

MORRISON, DENTON E. "Some Notes toward Theory on Relative Deprivation, Social Movements, and Social Change." In Louis E. Genevie, ed., *Collective Behavior and Social Movements.* Itasca, Ill.: Peacock, 1978:202–9.

MOSLEY, W. HENRY, and PETER COWLEY. "The Challenge of World Health." *Population Bulletin.* Vol. 46, No. 4 (December 1991). Washington, D.C.: Population Reference Bureau.

Mouw, Ted. "Job Relocation and the Racial Gap in Unemployment in Detroit and Chicago, 1980 to 1990." *American Sociological Review*. Vol. 65, No. 5 (October 2000):730–53.

Moynihan, Daniel Patrick. "Toward a New Intolerance." *The Public Interest*. No. 112 (Summer 1993):119–22.

Mufson, Steven. "China's Growing Inequality." *Washington Post* (January 1, 1997):A1, A26–A27.

Mulford, Matthew, John Orbell, Catherine Shatto, and Jean Stockard. "Physical Attractiveness, Opportunity, and Success in Everyday Exchange." *American Journal of Sociology*. Vol. 106, No. 6 (May 1998):1565–92.

Mumford, Lewis. *The City in History: Its Origins, Its Transformations, and Its Prospects*. New York: Harcourt, Brace & World, 1961.

Murdock, George Peter. "Comparative Data on the Division of Labor by Sex." *Social Forces*. Vol. 15, No. 4 (May 1937):551–53.

———. "The Common Denominator of Cultures." In Ralph Linton, ed., *The Science of Man in World Crisis*. New York: Columbia University Press, 1945:123–42.

———. *Social Structure*. New York: Free Press, 1965; orig. 1949.

Murray, Charles. *Losing Ground: American Social Policy 1950–1980*. New York: Basic Books, 1984.

———. "Keeping Priorities Straight on Welfare Reform." *Society*. Vol. 33, No. 5 (July/August 1996):10–12.

Murray, Stephen O., and Will Roscoe, eds. *Studies of African Homosexualities*. New York: St. Martin's Press, 1998.

Mutchler, Jan E. "Living Arrangements and Household Transitions among the Unmarried in Later Life." *Social Science Quarterly*. Vol. 73 (Spring 1992):565–80.

Myers, Norman. "Humanity's Growth." In Sir Edmund Hillary, ed., *Ecology 2000: The Changing Face of the Earth*. New York: Beaufort Books, 1984a:16–35.

———. "The Mega-Extinction of Animals and Plants." In Sir Edmund Hillary, ed., *Ecology 2000: The Changing Face of the Earth*. New York: Beaufort Books, 1984b:82–107.

———. "Disappearing Cultures." In Sir Edmund Hillary, ed., *Ecology 2000: The Changing Face of the Earth*. New York: Beaufort Books, 1984c:162–69.

———. "Biological Diversity and Global Security." In F. Herbert Bormann and Stephen R. Kellert, eds., *Ecology, Economics, and Ethics: The Broken Circle*. New Haven, Conn.: Yale University Press, 1991:11–25.

Myers, Sheila, and Harold G. Grasmick. "The Social Rights and Responsibilities of Pregnant Women: An Application of Parsons' Sick Role Model." Paper presented to the Southwestern Sociological Association, Little Rock, Arkansas, March 1989.

Myerson, Allen R. "This Man Wants to Bury You." *New York Times* (August 1, 1993):section 3, pp. 1, 6.

Myrdal, Gunnar. *An American Dilemma: The Negro Problem and Modern Democracy*. New York: Harper & Brothers, 1944.

Nagel, Joane. "Constructing Ethnicity: Creating and Recreating Ethnic Identity and Culture." *Social Problems*. Vol. 41, No. 1 (February 1994):152–76.

———. *American Indian Ethnic Renewal: Red Power and the Resurgence of Identity and Culture*. New York: Oxford University Press, 1996.

Najafizadeh, Mehrangiz, and Lewis A. Mennerick. "Sociology of Education or Sociology of Ethnocentrism: The Portrayal of Education in Introductory Sociology Textbooks." *Teaching Sociology*. Vol. 20, No. 3 (July 1992):215–21.

Nash, J. Madeleine. "To Know Your Own Fate." *Time*. Vol. 145, No. 14 (April 3, 1995):62.

National Commission on Excellence in Education. *A Nation at Risk*. Washington, D.C.: U.S. Government Printing Office, 1983.

Navarro, Mireya. "Puerto Rican Presence Wanes in New York." *The New York Times* (February 28, 2000):A1, A20.

Neergaard, Lauren. "Cigarette Smoking Jumps 28% on Campus." *Bowling Green Sentinel Tribune* (November 18, 1998):9.

Nelan, Bruce W. "Crimes without Punishment." *Time*. Vol. 141, No. 2 (January 11, 1993):21.

Nelson, Amy L. "The Effect of Economic Restructuring on Family Poverty in the Industrial Heartland, 1970–1990." *Sociological Focus*. Vol. 31 No. 2 (May 1998):201–16.

Nelson, Joel I. "Work and Benefits: The Multiple Problems of Service Sector Employment." *Social Problems*. Vol. 42, No. 2 (May 1994):240–55.

Nesbitt, Paula D. *Feminization of the Clergy in America: Occupational and Organizational Perspectives*. New York: Oxford University Press, 1997.

Nessman, Ravi. "Stampede at Soccer Match Kills 47." Associated Press news report, April 11, 2001. [Online]. Accessed at http://www.dailynews.yahoo.com

Neugarten, Bernice L. "Grow Old with Me. The Best Is Yet to Be." *Psychology Today*. Vol. 5 (December 1971):45–48, 79, 81.

———. "Personality and the Aging Process." *The Gerontologist*. Vol. 12, No. 1 (Spring 1972):9–15.

———. "Personality and Aging." In James E. Birren and K. Warner Schaie, eds., *Handbook of the Psychology of Aging*. New York: Van Nostrand Reinhold, 1977:626–49.

Neuhouser, Kevin. "The Radicalization of the Brazilian Catholic Church in Comparative Perspective." *American Sociological Review*. Vol. 54, No. 2 (April 1989):233–44.

Neuman, W. Laurence. *Social Research Methods: Qualitative and Quantitative Approaches*. 3d ed. Boston: Allyn & Bacon, 1997.

Newman, Katherine S. *Declining Fortunes: The Withering of the American Dream*. New York: Basic Books, 1993.

Newman, William M. *American Pluralism: A Study of Minority Groups and Social Theory*. New York: Harper & Row, 1973.

NFWBO. National Foundation for Women Business Owners. "Women Business Owners Economic Impact Re-Affirmed." [Online] Accessed in 1996 at http:www.nfwbo.org/nfwbo

Nielsen, A. C. Survey data cited in *Information Please Almanac 1997*. Boston: Houghton Mifflin, 1997.

Nielsen, Francois, and Arthur S. Alderson. "The Kuznets Curve: The Great U-Turn: Income Inequality in U.S. Counties, 1970 to 1990." *American Sociological Review*. Vol. 62, No. 1 (February 1997):12–33.

Nielsen, Joyce McCarl, ed. *Feminist Research Methods: Exemplary Readings in the Social Sciences*. Boulder, Colo.: Westview Press, 1990.

1991 Green Book. U.S. House of Representatives. Washington, D.C.: U.S. Government Printing Office, 1991.

Nisbet, Robert A. *The Sociological Tradition*. New York: Basic Books, 1966.

———. *The Quest for Community*. New York: Oxford University Press, 1969.

Nock, Steven L., James D. Wright, and Laura Sanchez. "America's Divorce Problem." *Society*. Vol. 36, No. 4 (May/June 1999):43–52.

Nolan, Patrick and Gerhard Lenski. *Human Societies: An Introduction to Macrosociology*. 8th ed. New York: McGraw-Hill, 1999.

Norbeck, Edward. "Class Structure." In *Kodansha Encyclopedia of Japan*. Tokyo: Kodansha, 1983:322–25.

NORC. *General Social Surveys, 1972–2000: Cumulative Codebook*. Chicago: National Opinion Research Center, 2001.

Nord, Mark. "Does It Cost Less to Live in Rural Areas? Evidence from New Data on Food Scarcity and Hunger." *Rural Sociology*. Vol. 65, No. 1 (March 2000):104–25.

Novak, Viveca. "The Cost of Poor Advice." *Time*. Vol. 154, No. 1 (July 5, 1999):38.

Nunn, Clyde Z., Harry J. Crockett, Jr., and J. Allen Williams, Jr. *Tolerance for Nonconformity*. San Francisco: Jossey-Bass, 1978.

Oakes, Jeannie. "Classroom Social Relationships: Exploring the Bowles and Gintis Hypothesis." *Sociology of Education*. Vol. 55, No. 4 (October 1982):197–212.

———. *Keeping Track: How High Schools Structure Inequality*. New Haven, Conn.: Yale University Press, 1985.

Oberschall, Anthony. *Social Conflict and Social Movements*. Englewood Cliffs, N.J.: Prentice Hall, 1973.

O'Brien, David J., Edward W. Hassinger, and Larry Dershem. "Size of Place, Residential Stability, and Personal Social Networks." *Sociological Focus*. Vol. 29, No. 1 (February 1996):61–72.

O'Connor, Rory J. "Internet Declared Protected Speech." *Post-Star* (Glens Fall, N.Y.: June 27, 1997):A1–A2.

Ogburn, William F. *On Culture and Social Change*. Chicago: University of Chicago Press, 1964.

O'Hare, William P. "In the Black." *American Demographics*. Vol. 11, No. 11 (November 1989):25–29.

———. "The Rise of Hispanic Affluence." *American Demographics*. Vol. 12, No. 8 (August 1990):40–43.

———. "Managing Multiple-Race Data." *American Demographics*. Vol. 20, No. 4 (April 1998):42–44.

O'Hare, William P., William H. Frey, and Dan Fost. "Asians in the Suburbs." *American Demographics*. Vol. 16, No. 9 (May 1994):32–38.

O'Hare, William P., and Jan Larson. "Women in Business: Where, What, and Why." *American Demographics*. Vol. 13, No. 7 (July 1991):34–38.

Okrent, Daniel. "Raising Kids Online: What Can Parents Do?" *Time*. Vol. 154, No. 18 (May 10, 1999):38–43.

Olsen, Gregg M. "Re-Modeling Sweden: The Rise and Demise of the Compromise in a Global Economy." *Social Problems*. Vol. 43, No. 1 (February 1996):1–20.

Olzak, Susan. "Labor Unrest, Immigration, and Ethnic Conflict in Urban America, 1880–1914." *American Journal of Sociology*. Vol. 94, No. 6 (May 1989):1303–33.

Olzak, Susan, and Elizabeth West. "Ethnic Conflict and the Rise and Fall of Ethnic Newspapers." *American Sociological Review*. Vol. 56, No. 4 (August 1991):458–74.

Orlansky, Michael D., and William L. Heward. *Voices: Interviews with Handicapped People*. Columbus, Ohio: Merrill, 1981:85, 92, 133–34, 172.

Orshansky, Mollie. "How Poverty Is Measured." *Monthly Labor Review*. Vol. 92, No. 2 (February 1969):37–41.

Orwin, Clifford. "All Quiet on the Western Front?" *The Public Interest*. Vol. 123 (Spring 1996): 3–9.

Osgood, D. Wayne, Janet K. Wilson, Patrick M. O'Malley, Jerald G. Bachman, and Lloyd D. Johnston. "Routine Activities and Individual Deviant Behavior." *American Sociological Review*. Vol. 61, No. 4 (August 1996):635–55.

Ostrander, Susan A. "Upper Class Women: The Feminine Side of Privilege." *Qualitative Sociology*. Vol. 3, No. 1 (Spring 1980):23–44.

———. *Women of the Upper Class*. Philadelphia: Temple University Press, 1984.

Ouchi, William. *Theory Z: How American Business Can Meet the Japanese Challenge*. Reading, Mass.: Addison-Wesley, 1981.

Owen, David. *None of the Above: Behind the Myth of Scholastic Aptitude*. Boston: Houghton Mifflin, 1985.

Page, Susan. "New Tactics Pushed in Terror War." *USA Today* (January 7, 2005):1A.

Pakulski, Jan. "Mass Social Movements and Social Class." *International Sociology*. Vol. 8, No. 2 (June 1993):131–58.

Pallone, Nathaniel J., and James J. Hennessy. "Brain Dysfunction and Criminal Violence." *Society*. Vol. 35, No. 6 (September–October 1998):20–27.

Palmore, Erdman. "Predictors of Successful Aging." *The Gerontologist*. Vol. 19, No. 5 (October 1979):427–31.

———. "What Can the USA Learn from Japan about Aging?" In Steven H. Zarit, ed., *Readings in Aging and Death: Contemporary Perspectives*. New York: Harper & Row, 1982:166–69.

PARCEL, TOBY L., CHARLES W. MUELLER, and STEVEN CUVELIER. "Comparable Worth and Occupational Labor Market: Explanations of Occupational Earnings Differentials." Paper presented to the American Sociological Association, New York, 1986.

PARENTI, MICHAEL. *Inventing Reality: The Politics of the Mass Media*. New York: St. Martin's Press, 1986.

PARINI, JAY. "The Meaning of Emeritus." *Dartmouth Alumni Magazine* (July/August 2001):40–43.

PARK, ALICE. "Suffer the Children." *Time*. Vol. 156, No. 2 (July 10, 2000):99.

PARK, ROBERT E. *Race and Culture*. Glencoe, Ill.: Free Press, 1950.

PARRILLO, VINCENT N. "Diversity in America: A Sociohistorical Analysis." *Sociological Forum*. Vol. 9, No. 4 (December 1994):42–45.

PARROTT, JULIE. "The Effects of Culture on Eating Disorders." Paper presented to Southwestern Social Science Association, Dallas, Texas, March 1987.

PARSONS, TALCOTT. "Age and Sex in the Social Structure of the United States." *American Sociological Review*. Vol. 7, No. 4 (August 1942):604–16.

———. *Essays in Sociological Theory*. New York: Free Press, 1954.

———. *The Social System*. New York: Free Press, 1964; orig. 1951.

———. *Societies: Evolutionary and Comparative Perspectives*. Englewood Cliffs, N.J.: Prentice Hall, 1966.

PARSONS, TALCOTT, and ROBERT F. BALES, eds. *Family, Socialization and Interaction Process*. New York: Free Press, 1955.

PATTILLO-McCOY, MARY. "Church Culture as a Strategy of Action in the Black Community." *American Sociological Review*. Vol. 63, No. 6 (December 1998):767–84.

PAUL, ELLEN FRANKEL. "Bared Buttocks and Federal Cases." *Society*. Vol. 28, No. 4 (May–June, 1991):4–7.

PEAR, ROBERT. "Women Reduce Lag in Earnings, but Disparities with Men Remain." *New York Times* (September 4, 1987):1, 7.

PEAR, ROBERT, and ERIK ECKHOLM. "When Healers Are Entrepreneurs: A Debate over Costs and Ethics." *New York Times* (June 2, 1991):1, 17.

PEARSON, DAVID E. "Post-Mass Culture." *Society*. Vol. 30, No. 5 (July–August 1993):17–22.

———. "Community and Sociology." *Society*. Vol. 32, No. 5 (July–August 1995):44–50.

PEASE, JOHN, and LEE MARTIN. "Want Ads and Jobs for the Poor: A Glaring Mismatch." *Sociological Forum*. Vol. 12. No. 4 (December 1997):545–64.

PERROLLE, JUDITH A. "Comments from the Special Issue Editor: The Emerging Dialogue on Environmental Justice." *Social Problems*. Vol. 40, No. 1 (February 1993):1–4.

PERSELL, CAROLINE HODGES. "The Interdependence of Social Justice and Civil Society." *Sociological Forum*. Vol. 12, No. 2 (June 1997):149–72.

PESSEN, EDWARD. *Riches, Class, and Power: America before the Civil War*. New Brunswick, N.J.: Transaction Books, 1990.

PETERS, TOM. "What Will We Do for Work?" *Time*. Vol. 155, No. 21 (May 22, 2000):68–71.

Peters Atlas of the World. New York: Harper & Row, 1990.

PETERSEN, TROND, ISHAK SAPORTA, and MARC-DAVID L. SEIDEL. "Offering a Job: Meritocracy and Social Networks." *American Journal of Sociology*. Vol. 106, No. 3 (November 2000):763–816.

PETERSILIA, JOAN. "Probation in the United States: Practices and Challenges." *National Institute of Justice Journal*. No. 233 (September 1997):4.

PETERSON, SCOTT. "Women Live on Own Terms behind the Veil." *Christian Science Monitor* (July 31, 1991):1, 10.

PHELAN, JO, BRUCE G. LINK, ANN STUEVE, and ROBERT E. MOORE. "Education, Social Liberalism, and Economic Conservatism: Attitudes toward Homeless People." *American Sociological Review*. Vol. 60, No. 1 (February 1995):126–40.

PHILADELPHIA, DESA. "Rookie Teacher, Age 50." *Time*. Vol. 157, No. 14 (April 9, 2001):66–68.

PHILIPSON, ILENE J., and KAREN V. HANSEN. "Women, Class, and the Feminist Imagination." In Karen V. Hansen and Ilene J. Philipson, eds., *Women, Class, and the Feminist Imagination: A Socialist-Feminist Reader*. Philadelphia: Temple University Press, 1992:3–40.

PHILLIPSON, CHRIS. *Capitalism and the Construction of Old Age*. London: Macmillan, 1982.

PICHARDO, NELSON A. "The Power Elite and Elite-Driven Countermovements: The Associated Farmers of California during the 1930s." *Sociological Forum*. Vol. 10, No. 1 (March 1995):21–49.

PIERCE, EMILY. "Momentum Swing." *C Q Weekly*. Vol. 58, No. 44 (Nov. 11, 2000):2646.

PILLEMER, KARL. "Maltreatment of the Elderly at Home and in Institutions: Extent, Risk Factors, and Policy Recommendations." In U.S. Congress. House, Select Committee on Aging and Senate, Special Committee on Aging. *Legislative Agenda for an Aging Society: 1988 and Beyond*. Washington, D.C.: U.S. Government Printing Office, 1988.

PINCHOT, GIFFORD, and ELIZABETH PINCHOT. *The End of Bureaucracy and the Rise of the Intelligent Organization*. San Francisco: Berrett-Koehler, 1993.

PINES, MAYA. "The Civilization of Genie." *Psychology Today*. Vol. 15 (September 1981):28–34.

PINHEY, THOMAS K., DONALD H. RUBINSTEIN, and RICHARD S. COLFAX. "Overweight and Happiness: The Reflected Self-Appraisal Hypothesis Reconsidered." *Social Science Quarterly*. Vol. 78, No. 3 (September 1997):747–55.

PIRANDELLO, LUIGI. "The Pleasure of Honesty." In *To Clothe the Naked and Two Other Plays*. New York: Dutton, 1962:143–98.

PIROG, MAUREEN A., and CHRIS MAGEE. "High School Completion: The Influence of Schools, Families, and Adolescent Parenting." *Social Science Quarterly*. Vol. 78, No. 3 (September 1997):710–24.

PITNEY, JOHN J., JR. "What Scholars Don't Know about Term Limits." *The Chronicle of Higher Education*. Vol. 41, No. 33 (April 28, 1995):A76.

PITT, MALCOLM. *Introducing Hinduism*. New York: Friendship Press, 1955.

PITTS, LEONARD, JR. "When a Win Sparks a Riot." *The Philadelphia Inquirer* (June 26, 2000):A11.

PIVEN, FRANCES FOX, and RICHARD A. CLOWARD. *Poor People's Movements: Why They Succeed, How They Fail*. New York: Pantheon Books, 1977.

PLOMIN, ROBERT, and TERRYL T. FOCH. "A Twin Study of Objectively Assessed Personality in Childhood." *Journal of Personality and Social Psychology*. Vol. 39, No. 4 (October 1980):680–88.

PODOLNY, JOEL M., and JAMES N. BARON. "Resources and Relationships: Social Networks and Mobility in the Workplace." *American Sociological Review*. Vol. 62, No. 5 (October 1997):673–93.

POHL, RUDIGER. "The Transition from Communism to Capitalism in East Germany." *Society*. Vol. 33, No. 4 (June 1996):62–65.

POLENBERG, RICHARD. *One Nation Divisible: Class, Race, and Ethnicity in the United States since 1938*. New York: Pelican Books, 1980.

POLLACK, ANDREW. "Happy in the East (^-^) or Smiling :-) in the West." *New York Times* (August 12, 1996).

———. "Overseas, Smoking Is One of Life's Small Pleasures." *New York Times* (August 17, 1997):E5.

POLLARD, KELVIN. "Play Ball! Demographics and Major League Baseball." *Population Today*. Vol. 24, No. 4 (April 1996a):3.

———. "Speaking Graphically: Per Capita Fresh Water Availability . . ." *Population Today*. Vol. 24, No. 12 (December 1996b):6.

POLLOCK, PHILIP H., III, and M. ELLIOT VITTAS. "Who Bears the Burdens of Environmental Pollution: Race, Ethnicity, and Environmental Equity in Florida." *Social Science Quarterly*. Vol. 76, No. 2 (June 1995):294–310.

POLSBY, NELSON W. "Three Problems in the Analysis of Community Power." *American Sociological Review*. Vol. 24, No. 6 (December 1959):796–803.

POMER, MARSHALL I. "Labor Market Structure, Intragenerational Mobility, and Discrimination: Black Male Advancement out of Low-Paying Occupations, 1962–1973." *American Sociological Review*. Vol. 51, No. 5 (October 1986):650–59.

PONIEWOZIK, JAMES. "Postnuclear Explosion." *Time*. Vol. 156, No. 19 (November 6, 2000):110–11.

POOLEY, ERIC. "The Great Escape." *Time*. Vol. 150, No. 24 (December 8, 1997):52–64.

POPENOE, DAVID. *Disturbing the Nest: Family Change and Decline in Modern Societies*. New York: Aldine, 1988.

———. "Family Decline in the Swedish Welfare State." *The Public Interest*. No. 102 (Winter 1991):65–77.

———. "The Controversial Truth: Two-Parent Families Are Better." *New York Times* (December 26, 1992):21.

———. "American Family Decline, 1960–1990: A Review and Appraisal." *Journal of Marriage and the Family*. Vol. 55, No. 3 (August 1993a):527–55.

———. "Parental Androgyny." *Society*. Vol. 30, No. 6 (September–October 1993b):5–11.

———. "Scandinavian Welfare." *Society*. Vol. 31, No. 6 (September–October, 1994):78–81.

———. "Can the Nuclear Family Be Revived?" *Society*. Vol. 36, No. 5 (July/August 1999):28–30.

POPENOE, DAVID, and BARBARA DAFOE WHITEHEAD. *Should We Live Together? What Young Adults Need to Know about Cohabitation before Marriage*. New Brunswick, N.J.: The National Marriage Project, 1999.

POPKIN, SUSAN J. "Welfare: Views from the Bottom." *Social Problems*. Vol. 17, No. 1 (February 1990):64–79.

POPULATION ACTION INTERNATIONAL. *People in the Balance: Population and Resources at the Turn of the Millennium*. Washington, D.C.: PAI, 2000.

POPULATION REFERENCE BUREAU. *2000 World Population Data Sheet*. Washington, D.C.: Population Reference Bureau, 2000.

———. *2001 World Population Data Sheet*. Washington, D.C.: Population Reference Bureau, 2001.

Population Today. "Majority of Children in Poverty Live with Parents Who Work." Vol. 23, No. 4 (April 1995):6.

PORTER, EDUARDO. "Even 126 Sizes Do Not Fit All." *The Wall Street Journal* (March 2, 2001):B1.

PORTES, ALEJANDRO, and LEIF JENSEN. "The Enclave and the Entrants: Patterns of Ethnic Enterprise in Miami before and after Mariel." *American Sociological Review*. Vol. 54, No. 6 (December 1989):929–49.

POSTEL, SANDRA. "Facing Water Scarcity." In Lester R. Brown et al., eds., *State of the World 1993: A Worldwatch Institute Report on Progress toward a Sustainable Society*. New York: Norton, 1993:22–41.

POWELL, CHRIS, and GEORGE E. C. PATON, eds. *Humour in Society: Resistance and Control*. New York: St. Martin's Press, 1988.

PRESS, ANDREA L. Review of *Enlightened Racism: "The Cosby Show," Audiences, and the Myth of the American Dream*, by Sut Jhally and Justin Lewis. *American Journal of Sociology*. Vol. 99, No. 1 (July 1993):219–21.

PRESSER, HARRIET B. "The Housework Gender Gap." *Population Today*. Vol. 21, No. 7/8 (July–August 1993):5.

PRESSLEY, SUE ANNE, and NANCY ANDREWS. "For Gay Couples, the Nursery Becomes the New Frontier." *Washington Post* (December 20, 1992):A1, A22–23.

PRESTON, LEE E. "Corporate Boards and Corporate Governance." *Society*. Vol. 32, No. 3 (March–April 1995):17–20.

PRIMEGGIA, SALVATORE, and JOSEPH A. VARACALLI. "Southern Italian Comedy: Old to New World." In Joseph V. Scelsa, Salvatore J. LaGumina, and Lydio Tomasi, eds., *Italian Americans in Transition*. New York: The American Italian Historical Association, 1990:241–52.

PRINDLE, DAVID F. *Risky Business: The Political Economy of Hollywood*. Boulder, Colo.: Westview Press, 1993.

PRINDLE, DAVID F., and JAMES W. ENDERSBY. "Hollywood Liberalism." *Social Science Quarterly*. Vol. 74, No. 1 (March 1993):136–49.

PUTERBAUGH, GEOFF, ed. *Twins and Homosexuality: A Casebook*. New York: Garland, 1990.

PUTKA, GARY. "SAT to Become a Better Gauge." *Wall Street Journal* (November 1, 1990):B1.

PUTKA, GARY, and STEVE STECKLOW. "Do For-Profit Schools Work? These Seem to for One Entrepreneur." *Wall Street Journal* (June 8, 1994):A1, A4.

QUEENAN, JOE. "The Many Paths to Riches." *Forbes*. Vol. 144, No. 9 (October 23, 1989):149–67.

QUINNEY, RICHARD. *Class, State and Crime: On the Theory and Practice of Criminal Justice*. New York: David McKay, 1977.

RABKIN, JEREMY. "The Supreme Court in the Culture Wars." *The Public Interest*. Vol. 125 (Fall 1996):3–26.

RALEY, R. KELLY. "A Shortage of Marriageable Men? A Note on the Role of Cohabitation in Black-White Differences in Marriage Rates." *American Journal of Sociology*. Vol. 61, No. 6 (December 1996):973–83.

RAMO, JOSHUA COOPER. "Finding God on the Web." *Time* (December 16, 1996):60–67.

RAPHAEL, RAY. *The Men from the Boys: Rites of Passage in Male America*. Lincoln: University of Nebraska Press, 1988.

RATAN, SUNEEL. "A New Divide between Haves and Have-Nots?" *Time*. Special Issue. Vol. 145, No. 12 (Spring 1995):25–26.

RATNESAR, ROMESH. "Lost in the Middle." *Time*. Vol. 152, No. 17 (September 14, 1998):60–62.

———. "Not Gone, but Forgotten?" *Time*. Vol. 153, No. 15 (February 8, 1999):30–31.

RAVITCH, DIANE, and JOSEPH VITERITTI. "A New Vision for City Schools." *The Public Interest*. Vol. 122 (Winter 1996):3–16.

RAY, PAUL H. "The Emerging Culture." *American Demographics*. Vol. 19, No. 2 (February 1997):29–34, 56.

RECKLESS, WALTER C., and SIMON DINITZ. "Pioneering with Self-Concept as a Vulnerability Factor in Delinquency." *Journal of Criminal Law, Criminology, and Police Science*. Vol. 58, No. 4 (December 1967):515–23.

RECTOR, ROBERT. "America Has the World's Richest Poor People." *Wall Street Journal* (September 24, 1998):A18.

REED, HOLLY E. "Kosovo and the Demography of Forced Migration." *Population Today*. Vol. 27, No. 6 (June 1999):4.

REICH, ROBERT B. "As the World Turns." *The New Republic* (May 1, 1989):23, 26–28.

———. *The Work of Nations: Preparing Ourselves for 21st-Century Capitalism*. New York: Alfred A. Knopf, 1991.

REIMAN, JEFFREY. *The Rich Get Richer and the Poor Get Prison: Ideology, Class, and Criminal Justice*. Boston: Allyn & Bacon, 1998.

REINGOLD, BETH, and RICHARD S. WIKE. "Confederate Symbols, Southern Identity, and Racial Attitudes: The Case of the Georgia State Flag." *Social Science Quarterly*. Vol. 79, No. 3 (September 1998):568–80.

REINHARZ, SHULAMIT. *Feminist Methods in Social Research*. New York: Oxford University Press, 1992.

REITZES, DONALD C., ELIZABETH J. MUTRAN, and MARIA E. FERNANDEZ. "The Decision to Retire: A Career Perspective." *Social Science Quarterly*. Vol. 79, No. 3 (September 1998):607–19.

REMOFF, HEATHER TREXLER. *Sexual Choice: A Woman's Decision*. New York: Dutton/Lewis, 1984.

REMY, JACQUELINE. "Interview with Agnes Fournier de Saint-Maur, Interpol Police Lieutenant." For *L'Express*. Reprinted in *World Press Review* (November 1996):7.

RESKIN, BARBARA F., and DEBRA BRANCH MCBRIER. "Why Not Ascription? Organizations' Employment of Male and Female Managers." *American Sociological Review*. Vol. 65, No. 2 (April 2000):210–33.

REYNOLDS, JOHN R., and CATHERINE E. ROSS. "Social Stratification and Health: Education's Benefit beyond Economic Status and Social Origins." *Social Problems*. Vol. 45, No. 2 (May 1998):221–45.

RHODES, STEVE. "The Luck of the Draw." *Newsweek* (April 26, 1999):41.

RICHARDSON, JAMES T. "Definitions of Cult: From Sociological-Technical to Popular Negative." Paper presented to the American Psychological Association, Boston, August 1990.

RICHE, MARTHA FARNSWORTH. "America's Diversity and Growth: Signposts for the 21st Century." *Population Bulletin*. Vol. 55, No. 2 (June 2000).

RIDDLE, JOHN M., J. WORTH ESTES, and JOSIAH C. RUSSELL. "Ever since Eve: Birth Control in the Ancient World." *Archaeology*. Vol. 47, No. 2 (March/April 1994):29–35.

RIDGEWAY, CECILIA L. *The Dynamics of Small Groups*. New York: St. Martin's Press, 1983.

RIDGEWAY, CECILIA L. and KRISTAN GLASGOW ERICKSON. "Creating and Spreading Status Beliefs." *American Journal of Sociology*. Vol. 106, No. 3 (November 2000):579–615.

RIESMAN, DAVID. *The Lonely Crowd: A Study of the Changing American Character*. New Haven, Conn.: Yale University Press, 1970; orig. 1950.

RILEY, MATILDA WHITE, ANNE FONER, and JOAN WARING. "Sociology of Age." In Neil J. Smelser, ed., *Handbook of Sociology*. Newbury Park, Calif.: Sage, 1988:243–90.

RILEY, NANCY E. "Gender, Power, and Population Change." *Population Bulletin*. Vol. 52, No. 1 (May 1997).

RIMER, SARA. "Blacks Carry Load of Care for Their Elderly." *The New York Times* (March 15, 1998):1, 22.

RITZER, GEORGE. *The McDonaldization of Society: An Investigation into the Changing Character of Contemporary Social Life*. Thousand Oaks, Calif.: Pine Forge Press, 1993.

———. *The McDonaldization of Society*. Revised ed. Thousand Oaks, Calif.: Sage, 1996.

———. *The McDonaldization Thesis: Explorations and Extensions*. Thousand Oaks, Calif.: Sage, 1998.

———. "The Globalization of McDonaldization." *The Spark* (February 2000):8–9.

RITZER, GEORGE, and DAVID WALCZAK. *Working: Conflict and Change*. 4th ed. Englewood Cliffs, N.J.: Prentice Hall, 1990.

RIVERA-BATIZ, FRANCISCO L., and CARLOS SANTIAGO, cited in Sam Roberts, "Puerto Ricans on Mainland Making Gains, Study Finds." *New York Times* (October 19, 1994):A20.

ROBERT, STEPHANIE A. "Socioeconomic Position and Health: The Independent Contribution of Community Socioeconomic Context." *Annual Review of Sociology*. Vol. 25 (1999):489–516.

ROBERTS, J. DEOTIS. *Roots of a Black Future: Family and Church*. Philadelphia: Westminster Press, 1980.

ROBERTS, STEVEN V. "Open Arms for Online Democracy." *U.S. News & World Report*. Vol. 118, No. 2 (January 16, 1995):10.

ROBINSON, DAWN. "Toward a Synthesis of Sociological and Psychological Theories of Eating Disorders." Paper presented to Southwestern Social Science Association, Dallas, Texas, March 1987.

ROBINSON, JOHN P., PERLA WERNER, and GEOFFREY GODBEY. "Freeing Up the Golden Years." *American Demographics*. Vol. 19, No. 10 (October 1997):20–24.

ROBINSON, JOYCE, and GLENNA SPITZE. "Whistle While You Work? The Effect of Household Task Performance on Women's and Men's Well-Being." *Social Science Quarterly*. Vol. 73, No. 4 (December 1992):844–61.

ROBINSON, THOMAS N., MARTA L. WILDE, LISA C. NAVRACRUZ, K. FARISH HAYDEL, and ANN VARADY. "Effects of Reducing Children's Television and Video Game Use on Aggressive Behavior." *Archives of Pediatrics and Adolescent Medicine*. Vol. 155 (January 2001):17–23.

ROBINSON, VERA M. "Humor and Health." In Paul E. McGhee and Jeffrey H. Goldstein, eds., *Handbook of Humor Research, Vol. II, Applied Studies*. New York: Springer-Verlag, 1983:109–28.

ROCHE, TIMOTHY. "A Psychotic Killer Sues His Psychiatrist." *Time*. Vol. 153, No. 15 (April 19, 1999):8.

ROCKETT, IAN R. H. "Population and Health: An Introduction to Epidemiology." *Population Bulletin*. Vol. 49, No. 3 (November 1994). Washington, D.C.: Population Reference Bureau.

RODGERS, JOAN R. "An Empirical Study of Intergenerational Transmission of Poverty in the United States." *Social Science Quarterly*. Vol. 76, No. 1 (March 1995):178–94.

ROESCH, ROBERTA. "Violent Families." *Parents*. Vol. 59, No. 9 (September 1984):74–76, 150–52.

ROETHLISBERGER, F. J., and WILLIAM J. DICKSON. *Management and the Worker*. Cambridge, Mass.: Harvard University Press, 1939.

ROGERS-DILLON, ROBIN H. "What Do We Really Know about Welfare Reform?" *Society*. Vol. 38, No. 2 (January/February 2001):7–15.

ROHLEN, THOMAS P. *Japan's High Schools*. Berkeley: University of California Press, 1983.

ROMAINE, SUZANNE. *Communicating Gender*. Mahwah, NJ: Erlbaum, 1999.

RÓNA-TAS, ÁKOS. "The First Shall Be Last? Entrepreneurship and Communist Cadres in the Transition from Socialism." *American Journal of Sociology*. Vol. 100, No. 1 (July 1994):40–69.

ROOF, WADE CLARK. "Socioeconomic Differentials among White Socioreligious Groups in the United States." *Social Forces*. Vol. 58, No. 1 (September 1979):280–89.

ROOF, WADE CLARK, and WILLIAM MCKINNEY. *American Mainline Religion: Its Changing Shape and Future*. New Brunswick, N.J.: Rutgers University Press, 1987.

ROSE, FRED. "Toward a Class-Cultural Theory of Social Movements: Reinterpreting New Social Movements." *Sociological Forum*. Vol. 12, No. 3 (September 1997):461–94.

ROSE, JERRY D. *Outbreaks*. New York: Free Press, 1982.

ROSEN, ELLEN ISRAEL. *Bitter Choices: Blue-Collar Women In and Out of Work*. Chicago: University of Chicago Press, 1987.

ROSEN, JEFFREY. *The Unwanted Gaze*. New York: Random House, 2000.

ROSENBAUM, DAVID E. "Americans Want a Right to Die. Or So They Think." *New York Times* (June 8, 1997):E3.

ROSENDAHL, MONA. *Inside the Revolution: Everyday Life in Socialist Cuba*. Ithaca, N.Y.: Cornell University Press, 1997.

ROSENFELD, MEGAN. "Little Boys Blue: Reexamining the Plight of Young Males." *Washington Post* (March 26, 1998):A1, A17–A18.

ROSENFELD, MICHAEL J. "Celebration, Politics, and Selective Looting and Riots: A Micro-Level Study of the Bulls Riot of 1992 in Chicago." *Social Problems*. Vol. 44, No. 4 (November 1997):483–502.

ROSENFELD, SARAH. "Labeling Mental Illness: The Effects of Received Services and Perceived Stigma on Life Satisfaction." *American Sociological Review*. Vol. 62, No. 4 (August 1997):660–72.

ROSENTHAL, ELIZABETH. "Canada's National Health Plan Gives Care to All, with Limits." *New York Times* (April 30, 1991):A1, A16.

ROSENTHAL, JACK. "The Rapid Growth of Suburban Employment." In Lois H. Masotti and Jeffrey K. Hadden, eds., *Suburbia in Transition*. New York: New York Times Books, 1974:95–100.

ROSNOW, RALPH L., and GARY ALAN FINE. *Rumor and Gossip: The Social Psychology of Hearsay.* New York: Elsevier, 1976.

ROSS, CATHERINE E., JOHN MIROWSKY, and JOAN HUBER. "Dividing Work, Sharing Work, and In-Between: Marriage Patterns and Depression." *American Sociological Review.* Vol. 48, No. 6 (December 1983):809–23.

ROSS, JOHN. "To Die in the Street: Mexico City's Homeless Population Boom as Economic Crisis Shakes Social Protections." *SSSP Newsletter.* Vol. 27, No. 2 (Summer 1996):14–15.

ROSSI, ALICE S. "Gender and Parenthood." In Alice S. Rossi, ed., *Gender and the Life Course.* New York: Aldine, 1985:161–91.

ROSSI, PETER H. Review of Christopher Jencks, *The Homeless* (Cambridge, Mass.: Harvard University Press). *Society.* Vol. 32, No. 4 (May–June 1995):80–81.

ROSTOW, WALT W. *The Stages of Economic Growth: A Non-Communist Manifesto.* Cambridge, U.K.: Cambridge University Press, 1960.

———. *The World Economy: History and Prospect.* Austin: University of Texas Press, 1978.

ROSZAK, THEODORE. *The Cult of Information: The Folklore of Computers and the True Art of Thinking.* New York: Pantheon Books, 1986.

ROTHMAN, BARBARA KATZ. "Of Maps and Imaginations: Sociology Confronts the Genome." *Social Problems.* Vol. 42, No. 1 (February 1995):1–10.

ROTHMAN, STANLEY, and AMY E. BLACK. "Who Rules Now? American Elites in the 1990s." *Society.* Vol. 35, No. 6 (September–October 1998):17–20.

ROTHMAN, STANLEY, and S. ROBERT LICHTER. "Social Science and Ideology: A Reply to Prindle, Endersby, and Gans." *Social Science Quarterly.* Vol. 75 (June 1994):455–57.

ROTHMAN, STANLEY, STEPHEN POWERS, and DAVID ROTHMAN. "Feminism in Films." *Society.* Vol. 30, No. 3 (March–April 1993):66–72.

ROWE, DAVID C. "Biometrical Genetic Models of Self-Reported Delinquent Behavior: A Twin Study." *Behavior Genetics.* Vol. 13, No. 5 (1983):473–89.

ROWE, DAVID C., and D. WAYNE OSGOOD. "Heredity and Sociological Theories of Delinquency: A Reconsideration." *American Sociological Review.* Vol. 49, No. 4 (August 1984):526–40.

ROWLAND, CHRISTOPHER, ed. *The Cambridge Companion to Liberation Theology.* Cambridge, U.K.: Cambridge University Press, 1999.

ROZELL, MARK J., CLYDE WILCOX, and JOHN C. GREEN. "Religious Constituencies and Support for the Christian Right in the 1990s." *Social Science Quarterly.* Vol. 79, No. 4 (December 1998):815–27.

RUBENSTEIN, ELI A. "The Not So Golden Years." *Newsweek* (October 7, 1991):13.

RUBIN, LILLIAN BRESLOW. *Worlds of Pain: Life in the Working-Class Family.* New York: Basic Books, 1976.

RUDÉ, GEORGE. *The Crowd in History: A Study of Popular Disturbances in France and England, 1730–1848.* New York: Wiley, 1964.

RUDEL, THOMAS K., and JUDITH M. GERSON. "Postmodernism, Institutional Change, and Academic Workers: A Sociology of Knowledge." *Social Science Quarterly.* Vol. 80, No. 2 (June 1999):213–28.

RUDOLPH, ELLEN. "Women's Talk: Japanese Women." *New York Times Magazine* (September 1, 1991).

RULE, JAMES, and PETER BRANTLEY. "Computerized Surveillance in the Workplace: Forms and Delusions." *Sociological Forum.* Vol. 7, No. 3 (September 1992):405–23.

RUSSELL, CHERYL. "Are We in the Dumps?" *American Demographics.* Vol. 17, No. 1 (January 1995a):6.

———. "True Crime." *American Demographics.* Vol. 17, No. 8 (August 1995b):22–31.

RUSSELL, CHERYL, and MARCIA MOGELONSKY. "Riding High on the Market." *American Demographics.* Vol. 22, No. 4 (April 2000):44–54.

RUTHERFORD, MEGAN. "Women Run the World." *Time.* Vol. 153, No. 25 (June 28, 1999):72.

———. "Simply Grand." *Time.* Vol. 154, No. 15 (October 11, 1999). Special section.

RYAN, WILLIAM. *Blaming the Victim.* Rev. ed. New York: Vintage Books, 1976.

RYMER, RUSS. *Genie.* New York: HarperPerennial, 1994.

SACHS, JEFFREY. "The Real Causes of Famine." *Time.* Vol. 152, No. 17 (October 26, 1998):69.

SADIK, NAFIS, ed. *Population Policies and Programmes: Lessons Learned from Two Decades of Experience.* New York: New York University Press, 1991.

ST. JEAN, YANICK, and JOE R. FEAGIN. *Double Burden: Black Women and Everyday Racism.* Armonk, N.Y.: M. E. Sharpe, 1998.

SALE, KIRKPATRICK. *The Conquest of Paradise: Christopher Columbus and the Columbian Legacy.* New York: Alfred A. Knopf, 1990.

SAMPSON, ANTHONY. *The Changing Anatomy of Britain.* New York: Random House, 1982.

SAMPSON, ROBERT J. "Urban Black Violence: The Effects of Male Joblessness and Family Disruption." *American Journal of Sociology.* Vol. 93, No. 2 (September 1987):348–82.

SAMPSON, ROBERT J., and JOHN H. LAUB. "Crime and Deviance over the Life Course: The Salience of Adult Social Bonds." *American Sociological Review.* Vol. 55, No. 5 (October 1990):609–27.

SANCHEZ, RENE. "Urban Students Not Making the Mark." *Washington Post* (January 8, 1998):A18.

SANTOLI, AL. "Fighting Child Prostitution." *Freedom Review.* Vol. 25, No. 5 (September–October 1994):5–8.

SAPIR, EDWARD. "The Status of Linguistics as a Science." *Language.* Vol. 5 (1929):207–14.

———. *Selected Writings of Edward Sapir in Language, Culture, and Personality.* David G. Mandelbaum, ed. Berkeley: University of California Press, 1949.

SAX, LINDA J., ALEXANDER W. ASTIN, WILLIAM S. KORN, and KATHRYN M. MAHONEY. *The American Freshman: National Norms for Fall 1999.* Los Angeles: UCLA Higher Education Research Institute, 1999.

SCAFF, LAWRENCE A. "Max Weber and Robert Michels." *American Journal of Sociology.* Vol. 86, No. 6 (May 1981):1269–86.

SCANLON, JAMES P. "The Curious Case of Affirmative Action for Women." *Society.* Vol. 29, No. 2 (January–February 1992):36–42.

SCHAIE, K. WARNER. "Intelligence and Problem Solving." In James E. Birren and R. Bruce Sloane, eds., *Handbook of Mental Health and Aging.* Englewood Cliffs, N.J.: Prentice Hall, 1980:262–84.

SCHAUB, DIANA. "From Boys to Men." *The Public Interest.* No. 127 (Spring 1997):108–14.

SCHEFF, THOMAS J. *Being Mentally Ill: A Sociological Theory.* 2d ed. New York: Aldine, 1984.

SCHERER, RON. "Worldwide Trend: Tobacco Use Grows." *Christian Science Monitor* (July 17, 1996):4, 8.

SCHILLER, BRADLEY. "Who Are the Working Poor?" *The Public Interest.* Vol. 155 (Spring 1994):61–71.

SCHLESINGER, ARTHUR. "The City in American Civilization." In A. B. Callow, Jr., ed., *American Urban History.* New York: Oxford University Press, 1969:25–41.

SCHLESINGER, ARTHUR, JR. "The Cult of Ethnicity: Good and Bad." *Time.* Vol. 137, No. 27 (July 8, 1991):21.

SCHLESINGER, JACOB M. "Finally, U.S. Median Income Approaches Old Heights." *Wall Street Journal* (September 25, 1998):B1.

SCHMIDT, ROGER. *Exploring Religion.* Belmont, Calif.: Wadsworth, 1980.

SCHMITT, ERIC. "Whites in Minority in Largest Cities, the Census Shows." *New York Times* (April 30, 2001):A1, A12.

SCHNAIBERG, ALLAN, and KENNETH ALAN GOULD. *Environment and Society: The Enduring Conflict.* New York: St. Martin's Press, 1994.

SCHNEIDER, MARK, MELISSA MARSCHALL, PAUL TESKE, and CHRISTINE ROCH. "School Choice and Culture Wars in the Classroom: What Different Parents Seek from Education." *Social Science Quarterly.* Vol. 79, No. 3 (September 1998):489–501.

SCHOR, JUDITH B. Cited in Cheryl Russell, "Overworked? Overwhelmed?" *American Demographics.* Vol. 17, No. 3 (March 1995):8.

SCHULTZ, T. PAUL. "Inequality in the Distribution of Personal Income in the World: How It Is Changing and Why." *Journal of Population Economics.* Vol. 11, No. 2 (1998):307–44.

SCHULTZ & HECKHAUSEN, 1996.

SCHUMAN, HOWARD, and MARIA KRYSAN. "A Historical Note on Whites' Beliefs about Racial Inequality." *American Sociological Review.* Vol. 64, No. 6 (December 1999):847–55.

SCHUMANN, HANS WOLFGANG. *Buddhism: An Outline of Its Teachings and Schools.* Wheaton, Ill.: The Theosophical Publishing House/Quest Books, 1974.

SCHUR, LISA A., and DOUGLAS L. KRUSE. "What Determines Voter Turnout? Lessons from Citizens with Disabilities." *Social Science Quarterly.* Vol. 81, No. 2 (June 2000): 571–87.

SCHUTT, RUSSELL K. "Objectivity versus Outrage." *Society.* Vol. 26, No. 4 (May–June 1989):14–16.

SCHWARTZ, BARRY. "Memory as a Cultural System: Abraham Lincoln in World War II." *American Sociological Review.* Vol. 61, No. 5 (October 1996):908–27.

SCHWARTZ, FELICE N. "Management, Women, and the New Facts of Life." *Harvard Business Review.* Vol. 89, No. 1 (January–February 1989):65–76.

SCHWARTZ, MARTIN D. "Gender and Injury in Spousal Assault." *Sociological Focus.* Vol. 20, No. 1 (January 1987):61–75.

SCHWARZ, JOHN E., and THOMAS J. VOLGY. *The Forgotten Americans: Thirty Million Working Poor in the Land of Opportunity.* New York: Norton, 1992.

SCOTT, JOHN, and CATHERINE GRIFF. *Directors of Industry: The British Corporate Network, 1904–1976.* New York: Blackwell, 1985.

SCOTT, JOSEPH E., and J. CUVELIER. "Violence in *Playboy* Magazine: A Longitudinal Analysis." *Archives of Sexual Behavior.* Vol. 16 (1987):279–88.

SCOTT, W. RICHARD. *Organizations: Rational, Natural, and Open Systems.* Englewood Cliffs, N.J.: Prentice Hall, 1981.

SCUPIN, RAY. Personal communication, 2000.

SEAGER, JONI. *The State of Women in the World Atlas.* New revised 2d ed. New York: Penguin Group, 2000.

SEARS, DAVID O., and JOHN B. McCONAHAY. *The Politics of Violence: The New Urban Blacks and the Watts Riot.* Boston: Houghton Mifflin, 1973.

SEBASTIAN, TIM. "Massacred: 1,000; Tried, 0." *World Press Review* (June 1996):6–10.

SEIDMAN, STEVEN. *Queer Theory/Sociology.* Oxford, U.K.: Blackwell, 1996.

SEKULIC, DUSKO, GARTH MASSEY, and RANDY HODSON. "Who Were the Yugoslavs? Failed Sources of Common Identity in the Former Yugoslavia." *American Sociological Review.* Vol. 59, No. 1 (February 1994):83–97.

SELLIN, THORSTEN. *The Penalty of Death.* Beverly Hills, Calif.: Sage, 1980.

SELTZER, ROBERT M. *Jewish People, Jewish Thought: The Jewish Experience in History.* New York: Macmillan, 1980.

SEN, K. M. *Hinduism.* Baltimore: Penguin Books, 1961.

SENNETT, RICHARD. *The Corrosion of Character: The Personal Consequences of Work in the New Capitalism.* New York: Norton, 1998.

SENNETT, RICHARD, and JONATHAN COBB. *The Hidden Injuries of Class.* New York: Vintage Books, 1973.

THE SENTENCING PROJECT. [Online] Available October 18, 2000, at http://www.sentencingproject.org/brief/facts-pp.pdf

SEPLOW, STEPHEN, and JONATHAN STORM. "How TV Defined Our Lives." *Philadelphia Inquirer* (November 30, 1997):A1, A16–17.

SHAPIRO, JOSEPH P., and JOANNIE M. SCHROF. "Honor Thy Children." *U.S. News & World Report.* Vol. 118, No. 8 (February 27, 1995):39–49.

SHARPE, ANITA. "The Rich Aren't So Different After All." *Wall Street Journal* (November 12, 1996):B1, B10.

SHAWCROSS, WILLIAM. *Sideshow: Kissinger, Nixon and the Destruction of Cambodia.* New York: Pocket Books, 1979.

SHEEHAN, TOM. "Senior Esteem as a Factor in Socioeconomic Complexity." *The Gerontologist*. Vol. 16, No. 5 (October 1976):433–40.

SHELDON, WILLIAM H., EMIL M. HARTL, and EUGENE MCDERMOTT. *Varieties of Delinquent Youth*. New York: Harper, 1949.

SHELEY, JAMES F., JOSHUA ZHANG, CHARLES J. BRODY, and JAMES D. WRIGHT. "Gang Organization, Gang Criminal Activity, and Individual Gang Members' Criminal Behavior." *Social Science Quarterly*. Vol. 76, No. 1 (March 1995):53–68.

SHERKAT, DARREN E., and CHRISTOPHER G. ELLISON. "Recent Developments and Current Controversies in the Sociology of Religion." *Annual Review of Sociology*. Vol. 25 (1999):363–94.

SHERMAN, LAWRENCE W., and DOUGLAS A. SMITH. "Crime, Punishment, and Stake in Conformity: Legal and Informal Control of Domestic Violence." *American Sociological Review*. Vol. 57, No. 5 (October 1992):680–90.

SHEVKY, ESHREF, and WENDELL BELL. *Social Area Analysis*. Stanford, Calif.: Stanford University Press, 1955.

SHIPLER, DAVID K. *Russia: Broken Idols, Solemn Dreams*. New York: Penguin Books, 1984.

SHIPLEY, JOSEPH T. *Dictionary of Word Origins*. Totowa, N.J.: Roman & Allanheld, 1985.

SHIVELY, JOELLEN. "Cowboys and Indians: Perceptions of Western Films among American Indians and Anglos." *American Sociological Review*. Vol. 57, No. 6 (December 1992):725–34.

SHUPE, ANSON. *In the Name of All That's Holy: A Theory of Clergy Malfeasance*. Westport, Conn.: Praeger, 1995.

SHUPE, ANSON, WILLIAM A. STACEY, and LONNIE R. HAZLEWOOD. *Violent Men, Violent Couples: The Dynamics of Domestic Violence*. Lexington, Mass.: Lexington Books, 1987.

SIDEL, RUTH, and VICTOR W. SIDEL. *A Healthy State: An International Perspective on the Crisis in United States Medical Care*. Rev. ed. New York: Pantheon Books, 1982a.

———. *The Health Care of China*. Boston: Beacon Press, 1982b.

SILVERBERG, ROBERT. "The Greenhouse Effect: Apocalypse Now or Chicken Little?" *Omni* (July 1991):50–54.

SILVERSTEIN, MICHAEL. In Jon Snodgrass, ed., *A Book of Readings for Men against Sexism*. Albion, Calif.: Times Change Press, 1977:178–79.

SIMMEL, GEORG. *The Sociology of Georg Simmel*. Kurt Wolff, ed. New York: Free Press, 1950:118–69; orig. 1902.

———. "Fashion." In Donald N. Levine, ed., *Georg Simmel: On Individuality and Social Forms*. Chicago: University of Chicago Press, 1971; orig. 1904.

SIMON, JULIAN. *The Ultimate Resource*. Princeton, N.J.: Princeton University Press, 1981.

———. "More People, Greater Wealth, More Resources, Healthier Environment." In Theodore D. Goldfarb, ed., *Taking Sides: Clashing Views on Controversial Environmental Issues*. 6th ed. Guilford, Conn.: The Dushkin Publishing Group, 1995.

SIMON, ROGER. "The Dems' New Tune: Tryin' to Go Country." *U.S. News & World Report*. Vol. 130, No. 23 (June 11, 2001):22–23.

SIMON, ROGER, and ANGIE CANNON. "An Amazing Journey." *U.S. News & World Report*. Vol. 131, No. 5 (August 6, 2001):10–19.

SIMONS, CAROL. "Japan's *Kyoiku* Mamas." In John J. Macionis and Nijole V. Benokraitis, eds., *Seeing Ourselves: Classic, Contemporary, and Cross-Cultural Readings in Sociology*. Englewood Cliffs, N.J.: Prentice Hall, 1989:281–86.

SIMONS, MARLISE. "The Price of Modernization: The Case of Brazil's Kaiapo Indians." In John J. Macionis and Nijole V. Benokraitis, eds., *Seeing Ourselves: Classic, Contemporary, and Cross-Cultural Readings in Sociology*. 5th ed. Upper Saddle River, N.J.: Prentice Hall, 2001:496–502.

SIMPSON, GEORGE EATON, and J. MILTON YINGER. *Racial and Cultural Minorities: An Analysis of Prejudice and Discrimination*. 4th ed. New York: Harper & Row, 1972.

SINGER, JEROME L., and DOROTHY G. SINGER. "Psychologists Look at Television: Cognitive, Developmental, Personality, and Social Policy Implications." *American Psychologist*. Vol. 38, No. 7 (July 1983):826–34.

SIPES, RICHARD G. "War, Sports and Aggression: An Empirical Test of Two Rival Theories." *American Anthropologist*. Vol. 75, No. 1 (January 1973):64–86.

SIVARD, RUTH LEGER. *World Military and Social Expenditures, 1987–88*. 12th ed. Washington, D.C.: World Priorities, 1988.

———. *World Military and Social Expenditures, 1992–93*. 17th ed. Washington, D.C.: World Priorities, 1993.

SIZER, THEODORE R. *Horace's Compromise: The Dilemma of the American High School*. Boston: Houghton Mifflin, 1984.

SKINNER, DAVID. "Computers: Good for Education?" *The Public Interest*. No. 128 (Summer 1997):98–109.

SKOCPOL, THEDA. *States and Social Revolutions: A Comparative Analysis of France, Russia, and China*. Cambridge, U.K.: Cambridge University Press, 1979.

SMAIL, J. KENNETH. "Beyond Population Stabilization: The Case for Dramatically Reducing Global Human Numbers." Roundtable: World Population Policy commentary and responses. *Politics and the Life Sciences*. Vol. 16, No. 2 (September 1997):183–236.

SMALL BUSINESS ADMINISTRATION. *The Facts about Small Business 1999*. U.S. Small Business Administration, Office of Advocacy. [Online] Available February 13, 2001, at http://www.sba.gov/ADVO/stats/facts99.pdf

SMART, NINIAN. *The Religious Experience of Mankind*. New York: Charles Scribner's Sons, 1969.

SMELSER, NEIL J. *Theory of Collective Behavior*. New York: Free Press, 1962.

SMITH, ADAM. *An Inquiry into the Nature and Causes of the Wealth of Nations*. New York: The Modern Library, 1937; orig. 1776.

SMITH, CRAIG S. "Authorities Took Victim's Organs, His Brother Says." *Columbus Dispatch* (March 11, 2001):A3.

SMITH, DOUGLAS A. "Police Response to Interpersonal Violence: Defining the Parameters of Legal Control." *Social Forces*. Vol. 65, No. 3 (March 1987):767–82.

SMITH, DOUGLAS A., and PATRICK R. GARTIN. "Specifying Specific Deterrence: The Influence of Arrest on Future Criminal Activity." *American Sociological Review*. Vol. 54, No. 1 (February 1989):94–105.

SMITH, DOUGLAS A., and CHRISTY A. VISHER. "Street-Level Justice: Situational Determinants of Police Arrest Decisions." *Social Problems*. Vol. 29, No. 2 (December 1981):167–77.

SMITH, EARL, and WILBERT M. LEONARD II. "Twenty-Five Years of Stacking Research in Major League Baseball: An Attempt at Explaining This Re-Occurring Phenomenon." *Sociological Focus*. Vol. 30, No. 4 (October 1997):321–31.

SMITH, ROBERT B. "Health Care Reform Now." *Society*. Vol. 30, No. 3 (March–April 1993):56–65.

SMITH, TOM W. Research results reported in "Anti-Semitism Decreases but Persists." *Society*. Vol. 33, No. 3 (March/April 1996):2.

SMITH-LOVIN, LYNN, and CHARLES BRODY. "Interruptions in Group Discussions: The Effects of Gender and Group Composition." *American Journal of Sociology*. Vol. 54, No. 3 (June 1989):424–35.

SMOCK, PAMELA J. "Cohabitation in the United States: An Appraisal of Research Themes, Findings, and Implications." *Annual Review of Sociology*. Vol. 26 (2000):1–20.

SMOLAN, RICK, and JENNIFER ERWITT. *24 Hours in Cyberspace*. New York: Macmillan, 1996.

SMOLOWE, JILL. "When Violence Hits Home." *Time*. Vol. 144, No. 1 (July 4, 1994):18–25.

SNELL, MARILYN BERLIN. "The Purge of Nurture." *New Perspectives Quarterly*. Vol. 7, No. 1 (Winter 1990):1–2.

SNOW, DAVID A., E. BURKE ROCHFORD, JR., STEVEN K. WORDEN, and ROBERT D. BENFORD. "Frame Alignment Processes, Micromobilization, and Movement Participation." *American Sociological Review*. Vol. 51, No. 4 (August 1986):464–81.

SNOW, DAVID A., LOUIS A. ZURCHER, JR., and SHELDON EKLAND-OLSON. "Social Networks and Social Movements: A Macrostructural Approach to Differential Recruitment." *American Sociological Review*. Vol. 45, No. 5 (October 1980):787–801.

SOUTH, SCOTT J., and KIM L. LLOYD. "Spousal Alternatives and Marital Dissolution." *American Sociological Review*. Vol. 60, No. 1 (February 1995):21–35.

SOUTH, SCOTT J., and STEVEN F. MESSNER. "Structural Determinants of Intergroup Association: Interracial Marriage and Crime." *American Journal of Sociology*. Vol. 91, No. 6 (May 1986):1409–30.

SOUTH, SCOTT J., and GLENNA SPITZE. "Housework in Marital and Nonmarital Households." *American Sociological Review*. Vol. 59, No. 3 (June 1994):327–47.

SOWELL, THOMAS. *Ethnic America*. New York: Basic Books, 1981.

———. *Race and Culture*. New York: Basic Books, 1994.

———. "Ethnicity and IQ." In Steven Fraser, ed., *The Bell Curve Wars: Race, Intelligence and the Future of America*. New York: Basic Books, 1995:70–79.

SOYINKA, WOLE. "Africa's Culture Producers." *Society*. Vol. 28, No. 2 (January–February 1991):32–40.

SPALTER-ROTH, ROBERTA, FELICE J. LEVINE, and ANDREW SUTTER. "The Pipeline of Faculty of Color in Sociology." *Footnotes*. Vol. 27, No. 4 (April 1999):4–5.

SPATES, JAMES L. "Counterculture and Dominant Culture Values: A Cross-National Analysis of the Underground Press and Dominant Culture Magazines." *American Sociological Review*. Vol. 41, No. 5 (October 1976):868–83.

———. "The Sociology of Values." In Ralph Turner, ed., *Annual Review of Sociology*. Vol. 9. Palo Alto, Calif.: Annual Reviews, 1983:27–49.

SPATES, JAMES L., and H. WESLEY PERKINS. "American and English Student Values." *Comparative Social Research*. Vol. 5. Greenwich, Conn.: JAI Press, 1982:245–68.

SPECTER, MICHAEL. "Plunging Life Expectancy Puzzles Russia." *New York Times* (August 2, 1995):A1, A2.

———. "Deep in the Russian Soul, a Lethal Darkness." *New York Times* (June 8, 1997a): section 4, pp. 1, 5.

———. "Moscow on the Make." *New York Times Magazine* (June 1, 1997b):48–55, 72, 75, 80, 84.

———. "Yogurt? Caucasus Centenarians 'Never Eat It.'" *New York Times* (March 14, 1998):A1, A4.

SPEER, JAMES A. "The New Christian Right and Its Parent Company: A Study in Political Contrasts." In David G. Bromley and Anson Shupe, eds., *New Christian Politics*. Macon, Ga.: Mercer University Press, 1984:19–40.

SPEER, TIBBETT L. "Are College Costs Cutting Enrollment?" *American Demographics*. Vol. 16, No. 11 (November 1994):9–10.

———. "Digging Into the Underground Economy." *American Demographics*. Vol. 17, No. 2 (February 1995):15–16.

———. "A Nation of Students." *American Demographics*. Vol. 48, No. 8 (August 1996):32–39.

SPEIER, HANS. "Wit and Politics: An Essay on Laughter and Power." Ed. and trans. by Robert Jackall. *American Journal of Sociology*. Vol. 103, No. 5 (March 1998):1352–1401.

SPENCER, MARTIN E. "Multiculturalism, 'Political Correctness,' and the Politics of Identity." *Sociological Forum*. Vol. 9, No. 4 (December 1994):547–67.

SPITZER, STEVEN. "Toward a Marxian Theory of Deviance." In Delos H. Kelly, ed., *Criminal Behavior: Readings in Criminology*. New York: St. Martin's Press, 1980:175–91.

SPLAIN, CHERYL S. "Homeless Problem Not Just in Big Cities." *Mount Vernon News* (March 6, 2000):1A, 3A.

STACEY, JUDITH. *Patriarchy and Socialist Revolution in China*. Berkeley: University of California Press, 1983.

————. *Brave New Families: Stories of Domestic Upheaval in Late Twentieth-Century America.* New York: Basic Books, 1990.

————. "Good Riddance to 'The Family': A Response to David Popenoe." *Journal of Marriage and the Family.* Vol. 55, No. 3 (August 1993):545–47.

STACK, CAROL B. *All Our Kin: Strategies for Survival in a Black Community.* New York: Harper & Row, 1975.

STAGGENBORG, SUZANNE. "Social Movement Communities and Cycles of Protest: The Emergence and Maintenance of a Local Women's Movement." *Social Problems.* Vol. 45, No. 2 (May 1998):180–204.

STAHURA, JOHN M. "Suburban Development, Black Suburbanization and the Black Civil Rights Movement since World War II." *American Sociological Review.* Vol. 51, No. 1 (February 1986):131–44.

STANLEY, LIZ, ed. *Feminist Praxis: Research, Theory, and Epistemology in Feminist Sociology.* London: Routledge & Kegan Paul, 1990.

STAPINSKI, HELENE. "Let's Talk Dirty." *American Demographics.* Vol. 20, No. 11 (November 1998):50–56.

STARK, RODNEY. *Sociology.* Belmont, Calif.: Wadsworth, 1985.

STARK, RODNEY, and WILLIAM SIMS BAINBRIDGE. "Of Churches, Sects, and Cults: Preliminary Concepts for a Theory of Religious Movements." *Journal for the Scientific Study of Religion.* Vol. 18, No. 2 (June 1979):117–31.

————. "Secularization and Cult Formation in the Jazz Age." *Journal for the Scientific Study of Religion.* Vol. 20, No. 4 (December 1981):360–73.

STARK, RODNEY, and CHARLES Y. GLOCK. *American Piety: The Nature of Religious Commitment.* Berkeley: University of California Press, 1968.

STARR, PAUL. *The Social Transformation of American Medicine.* New York: Basic Books, 1982.

STAVRIANOS, L. S. *A Global History: The Human Heritage.* 3d ed. Englewood Cliffs, N.J.: Prentice Hall, 1983.

STEELE, RANDY. "Awful but Lawful." *Boating* (June 2000):36.

STEELE, SHELBY. *The Content of Our Character: A New Vision of Race in America.* New York: St. Martin's Press, 1990.

STEIN, MAURICE R. *The Eclipse of Community: An Interpretation of American Studies.* Princeton, N.J.: Princeton University Press, 1972.

STEINBERG, LAURENCE. "Failure outside the Classroom." *Wall Street Journal* (July 11, 1996):A14.

STEPHENS, JOHN D. *The Transition from Capitalism to Socialism.* Urbana: University of Illinois Press, 1986.

STERN, LARRY. Personal communication, 1998.

STERNLIEB, GEORGE, and JAMES W. HUGHES. "The Uncertain Future of the Central City." *Urban Affairs Quarterly.* Vol. 18, No. 4 (June 1983):455–72.

STEVENS, GILLIAN, and GRAY SWICEGOOD. "The Linguistic Context of Ethnic Endogamy." *American Sociological Review.* Vol. 52, No. 1 (February 1987):73–82.

STIER, HAYA. "Continuity and Change in Women's Occupations following First Childbirth." *Social Science Quarterly.* Vol. 77, No. 1 (March 1996):60–75.

STODGHILL, RON, II. "Where'd You Learn That?" *Time.* Vol. 151, No. 23 (1998).

STOFFERAHN, CURTIS W. "Underemployment: Social Fact or Socially Constructed Reality?" *Rural Sociology.* Vol. 65, No. 2 (June 2000):311–30.

STOHL, MICHAEL, and GEORGE A. LOPEZ. *The State as Terrorist: The Dynamics of Government Violence and Repression.* Westport, Conn.: Greenwood Press, 1984.

STONE, LAWRENCE. *The Family, Sex and Marriage in England 1500–1800.* New York: Harper & Row, 1977.

STONE, ROBYN, GAIL LEE CAFFERATA, and JUDITH SANGL. *Caregivers of the Frail Elderly: A National Profile.* Washington, D.C.: U.S. Department of Health and Human Services, 1987.

STOUFFER, SAMUEL A., et al. *The American Soldier: Adjustment during Army Life.* Princeton, N.J.: Princeton University Press, 1949.

STRATTON, LESLIE S. "Why Does More Housework Lower Women's Wages? Testing Hypotheses Involving Job Effort and Hours Flexibility." *Social Sciences Quarterly.* Vol. 82, No. 1 (March 2001):67–76.

STRAUS, MURRAY A., and RICHARD J. GELLES. "Societal Change and Change in Family Violence from 1975 to 1985 as Revealed by Two National Surveys." *Journal of Marriage and the Family.* Vol. 48, No. 4 (August 1986):465–79.

STREIB, GORDON F. "Are the Aged a Minority Group?" In Bernice L. Neugarten, ed., *Middle Age and Aging: A Reader in Social Psychology.* Chicago: University of Chicago Press, 1968:35–46.

SUDNOW, DAVID N. *Passing On: The Social Organization of Dying.* Englewood Cliffs, N.J.: Prentice Hall, 1967.

SULLIVAN, BARBARA. "McDonald's Sees India as Golden Opportunity." *Chicago Tribune.* Business section (April 5, 1995):1.

SUMNER, WILLIAM GRAHAM. *Folkways.* New York: Dover, 1959; orig. 1906.

SUN, LENA H. "WWII's Forgotten Internees Await Apology." *The Washington Post* (March 9, 1998):A1, A5, A6.

SUNG, BETTY LEE. *Mountains of Gold: The Story of the Chinese in America.* New York: Macmillan, 1967.

SUPLEE, CURT. "1 in 8 Plants in Global Study Threatened." *Washington Post* (April 8, 1998):A1, A8.

SUTHERLAND, EDWIN H. "White Collar Criminality." *American Sociological Review.* Vol. 5, No. 1 (February 1940):1–12.

SUTHERLAND, EDWIN H., and DONALD R. CRESSEY. *Criminology.* 10th ed. Philadelphia: J.B. Lippincott, 1978.

SUTTON, JOHN R. "Imprisonment and Social Classification in Five Common-Law Democracies: 1955–1985." *American Journal of Sociology.* Vol. 106, No. 2 (September 2000):350–86.

SWARTZ, STEVE. "Why Michael Milken Stands to Qualify for Guinness Book." *Wall Street Journal.* Vol. 70, No. 117 (March 31, 1989):1, 4.

SZASZ, THOMAS S. *The Manufacturer of Madness: A Comparative Study of the Inquisition and the Mental Health Movement.* New York: Dell, 1961.

————. *The Myth of Mental Illness: Foundations of a Theory of Personal Conduct.* New York: Harper & Row, 1970; orig. 1961.

————. "Mental Illness Is Still a Myth." *Society.* Vol. 31, No. 4 (May–June 1994):34–39.

————. "Idleness and Lawlessness in the Therapeutic State." *Society.* Vol. 32, No. 4 (May–June 1995):30–35.

TAJFEL, HENRI. "Social Psychology of Intergroup Relations." *Annual Review of Psychology.* Palo Alto, Calif.: Annual Reviews, 1982:1–39.

TALLICHET, SUZANNE E. "Barriers to Women's Advancement in Underground Coal Mining." *Rural Sociology.* Vol. 65, No. 2 (June 2000):234–52.

TANBER, GEORGE J. "Freed from Death Row." *Toledo Blade* (November 22, 1998):B1, B2.

TANNAHILL, REAY. *Sex in History.* Scarborough House Publishers, 1992.

TANNEN, DEBORAH. *You Just Don't Understand: Women and Men in Conversation.* New York: Wm. Morrow, 1990.

————. *Talking from 9 to 5: How Women's and Men's Conversational Styles Affect Who Gets Heard, Who Gets Credit, and What Gets Done at Work.* New York: Wm. Morrow, 1994.

TANNENBAUM, FRANK. *Slave and Citizen: The Negro in the Americas.* New York: Vintage Books, 1946.

TANNER, MICHAEL, and STEPHEN MOORE. "Why Welfare Pays." *Wall Street Journal* (September 28, 1995):A20.

TARROW, SIDNEY. *Social Movements, Collective Action and Politics.* New York: Cambridge University Press, 1994.

TAVRIS, CAROL, and SUSAN SADD. *The Redbook Report on Female Sexuality.* New York: Delacorte Press, 1977.

TAX FOUNDATION. [Online] Available March 30, 2000, at http://www.taxfoundation.org

TAYLOR, JOHN. "Don't Blame Me: The New Culture of Victimization." *New York Magazine* (June 3, 1991):26–34.

TERKEL, STUDS. *Working.* New York: Pantheon Books, 1974:1–2, 57–59, 65, 66, 69, 221–22.

TERRY, DON. "In Crackdown on Bias, A New Tool." *New York Times* (June 12, 1993):8.

TEWKSBURY, RICHARD, and PATRICIA GAGNÉ. "Transgenderists: Products of Non-normative Intersections of Sex, Gender, and Sexuality." *The Journal of Men's Studies.* Vol. 5, No. 2 (November 1996):105–29.

THERNSTROM, ABIGAIL, and STEPHAN THERNSTROM. "American Apartheid? Don't Believe It." *Wall Street Journal* (March 2, 1998):A18.

THIRUNARAYANAPURAM, DESIKAN. "Population Explosion Is Far from Over." *Popline.* Vol. 20 (January–February, 1998):1, 4.

THOMAS, EDWARD J. *The Life of Buddha as Legend and History.* London: Routledge & Kegan Paul, 1975.

THOMAS, EVAN, JOHN BARRY, and MELINDA LIU. "Ground Zero." *Newsweek* (May 25, 1998):28–32A.

THOMAS, PAULETTE. "Success at a Huge Personal Cost." *Wall Street Journal* (July 26, 1995):B1, B6.

THOMAS, PIRI. *Down These Mean Streets.* New York: Signet, 1967.

THOMAS, W. I. "The Relation of Research to the Social Process." In Morris Janowitz, ed., *W. I. Thomas on Social Organization and Social Personality.* Chicago: University of Chicago Press, 1966:289–305; orig. 1931.

————. *The Unadjusted Girl.* New York: Harper & Row, 1967:42; orig. 1923.

THOMMA, STEVEN. "Christian Coalition Demands Action from GOP." *Philadelphia Inquirer* (September 14, 1997):A2.

THOMPSON, DICK. "Gene Maverick." *Time.* Vol. 153, No. 1 (January 11, 1999):54–55.

THOMPSON, LARRY. "Fertility with Less Fuss." *Time.* Vol. 144, No. 20 (November 14, 1994):79.

THOMPSON, MARK. "Fatal Neglect." *Time.* Vol. 150, No. 17 (October 27, 1997):34–38.

————. "Shining a Light on Abuse." *Time.* Vol. 152, No. 5 (August 3, 1998):42–43.

THOMPSON, MARK, and DOUGLAS WALLER. "Shield of Dreams." *Time.* Vol. 155, No. 19 (May 8, 2001):45–47.

THORLINDSSON, THOROLFUR, and THORODDUR BJARNASON. "Modeling Durkheim on the Micro Level: A Study of Youth Suicidality." *American Sociological Review.* Vol. 63, No. 1 (February 1998):94–110.

THORNBERRY, TERRANCE, and MARGARET FARNSWORTH. "Social Correlates of Criminal Involvement: Further Evidence on the Relationship between Social Status and Criminal Behavior." *American Sociological Review.* Vol. 47, No. 4 (August 1982):505–18.

THORNE, BARRIE, CHERIS KRAMARAE, and NANCY HENLEY, eds. *Language, Gender and Society.* Rowley, Mass.: Newbury House, 1983.

THORNTON, ARLAND. "Changing Attitudes toward Separation and Divorce: Causes and Consequences." *American Journal of Sociology.* Vol. 90, No. 4 (January 1985):856–72.

THORNTON, ARLAND, WILLIAM G. AXINN, and DANIEL H. HILL. "Reciprocal Effects of Religiosity, Cohabitation, and Marriage." *American Journal of Sociology.* Vol. 98, No. 3 (November 1992):628–51.

THUROW, LESTER C. "A Surge in Inequality." *Scientific American.* Vol. 256, No. 5 (May 1987):30–37.

TILLY, CHARLES. *From Mobilization to Revolution.* Reading, Mass.: Addison-Wesley, 1978.

————. "Does Modernization Breed Revolution?" In Jack A. Goldstone, ed., *Revolutions: Theoretical, Comparative, and Historical Studies.* New York: Harcourt Brace Jovanovich, 1986:47–57.

Time Almanac 2001. Boston: Information Please, 2000.

TIRYAKIAN, EDWARD A. "Revisiting Sociology's First Classic: The Division of Labor in Society and Its Actuality." *Sociological Forum.* Vol. 9, No. 1 (March 1994):3–16.

TITTLE, CHARLES R., and WAYNE J. VILLEMEZ. "Social Class and Criminality." *Social Forces.* Vol. 56, No. 22 (December 1977):474–502.

TITTLE, CHARLES R., WAYNE J. VILLEMEZ, and DOUGLAS A. SMITH. "The Myth of Social Class and Criminality: An Empirical Assessment of the Empirical Evidence." *American Sociological Review.* Vol. 43, No. 5 (October 1978):643–56.

TOBIN, GARY. "Suburbanization and the Development of Motor Transportation: Transportation Technology and the Suburbanization Process." In Barry Schwartz, ed., *The Changing Face of the Suburbs.* Chicago: University of Chicago Press, 1976.

TOBY, JACKSON. "Getting Serious about School Discipline." *The Public Interest.* Vol. 133 (Fall 1998):68–83.

TOCH, THOMAS. "The New Educational Bazaar." *U.S. News & World Report* (April 27, 1998):35–45.

TOCQUEVILLE, ALEXIS DE. *The Old Regime and the French Revolution.* Stuart Gilbert, trans. Garden City, N.Y.: Anchor/Doubleday Books, 1955; orig. 1856.

TOFFLER, ALVIN, and HEIDI TOFFLER. *War and Anti-War: Survival at the Dawn of the 21st Century.* Boston: Little, Brown, 1993.

TOLSON, JAY. "The Trouble with Elites." *The Wilson Quarterly.* Vol. 19, No. 1 (Winter 1995):6–8.

TÖNNIES, FERDINAND. *Community and Society (Gemeinschaft und Gesellschaft).* New York: Harper & Row, 1963; orig. 1887.

TREAS, JUDITH. "Socialist Organization and Economic Development in China: Latent Consequences for the Aged." *The Gerontologist.* Vol. 19, No. 1 (February 1979):34–43.

———. "Older Americans in the 1990s and Beyond." *Population Bulletin.* Vol. 50, No. 2 (May 1995). Washington, D.C.: Population Reference Bureau.

TREIMAN, DONALD J. "Industrialization and Social Stratification." In Edward O. Laumann, ed., *Social Stratification: Research and Theory for the 1970s.* Indianapolis: Bobbs-Merrill, 1970.

TRENT, KATHERINE. "Family Context and Adolescents' Expectations about Marriage, Fertility, and Nonmarital Childbearing." *Social Science Quarterly.* Vol. 75, No. 2 (June 1994):319–39.

TROELTSCH, ERNST. *The Social Teaching of the Christian Churches.* New York: Macmillan, 1931.

TROIDEN, RICHARD R. *Gay and Lesbian Identity: A Sociological Analysis.* Dix Hills, N.Y.: General Hall, 1988.

TROY, TOM. "Money Does Matter." *Toledo Blade* (October 23, 2000):A1, 5, 7.

TUMIN, MELVIN M. "Some Principles of Stratification: A Critical Analysis." *American Sociological Review.* Vol. 18, No. 4 (August 1953):387–94.

———. *Social Stratification: The Forms and Functions of Inequality.* 2d ed. Englewood Cliffs, N.J.: Prentice Hall, 1985.

TURNER, RALPH H., and LEWIS M. KILLIAN. *Collective Behavior.* 2d ed. Englewood Cliffs, N.J.: Prentice Hall, 1972; 3d ed., 1987; 4th ed., 1993.

TYLER, S. LYMAN. *A History of Indian Policy.* Washington, D.C.: United States Department of the Interior, Bureau of Indian Affairs, 1973.

TYREE, ANDREA, MOSHE SEMYONOV, and ROBERT W. HODGE. "Gaps and Glissandos: Inequality, Economic Development, and Social Mobility in 24 Countries." *American Sociological Review.* Vol. 44, No. 3 (June 1979):410–24.

UDRY, J. RICHARD. "Biological Limitations of Gender Construction." *American Sociological Review.* Vol. 65, No. 3 (June 2000):443–57.

UGGEN, CHRISTOPHER. "Ex-Offenders and the Conformist Alternative: A Job-Quality Model of Work and Crime." *Social Problems.* Vol. 46, No. 1 (February 1999):127–51.

UNITED NATIONS. "AIDS Epidemic Update: December 2000." [Online] Available October 22, 2001, at http://www.unaids.org/wac/2000/wad00/files/WAD–epidemic–report.PDF

UNITED NATIONS DEVELOPMENT PROGRAMME. *Human Development Report 1990.* New York: Oxford University Press, 1990.

———. *Human Development Report 1994.* New York: Oxford University Press, 1994.

———. *Human Development Report 1995.* New York: Oxford University Press, 1995.

———. *Human Development Report 1996.* New York: Oxford University Press, 1996.

———. *Human Development Report 1997.* New York: Oxford University Press, 1997.

———. *Human Development Report 1998.* New York: Oxford University Press, 1998.

———. *Human Development Report 1999.* New York: Oxford University Press, 1999.

———. *Human Development Report 2000.* New York: Oxford University Press, 2000.

———. *Human Development Report 2001.* New York: Oxford University Press, 2001.

UNITED NATIONS POPULATION DIVISION. *Population Aging, 1999.* New York: United Nations, 1999.

UNIVERSITY OF AKRON RESEARCH CENTER. *National Survey of Religion and Politics 1992.* Akron, Ohio: University of Akron Research Center, 1993.

UNNEVER, JAMES D., CHARLES E. FRAZIER, and JOHN C. HENRETTA. "Race Differences in Criminal Sentencing." *The Sociological Quarterly.* Vol. 21, No. 2 (Spring 1980):197–205.

UNRUH, JOHN D., JR. *The Plains Across.* Urbana: University of Illinois Press, 1979.

UPTHEGROVE, TAYNA R., VINCENT J. ROSCIGNO, and CAMILLE ZUBRINSKY CHARLES. "Big Money Collegiate Sports: Racial Concentration, Contradictory Pressures, and Academic Performance." *Social Science Quarterly.* Vol. 80, No. 4 (December 1999):718–37.

U.S. BUREAU OF ECONOMIC ANALYSIS. *Foreign Direct Investment in the United States. Country Detail for Selected Items.* Washington, D.C.: The Bureau, 1999.

U.S. BUREAU OF JUSTICE STATISTICS. *Violence against Women.* Washington, D.C.: U.S. Government Printing Office, 1994.

———. *Criminal Victimization 1994.* Washington, D.C.: U.S. Government Printing Office, 1996.

———. *Violence by Intimates.* Washington, D.C.: The Bureau, 1998.

———. *Criminal Victimization 1998: Changes 1997–98 with Trends 1993–98.* Washington, D.C.: The Bureau, 1999.

———. *Sourcebook of Criminal Justice Statistics 1998.* Washington, D.C.: The Bureau, 1999.

———. *Capital Punishment 1999.* Washington, D.C.: The Bureau, 2000.

———. *Criminal Victimization 1999: Changes 1998–99 with Trends 1993–99.* Washington, D.C.: The Bureau, 2000.

———. *Sourcebook of Criminal Justice Statistics 1999.* Washington, D.C.: The Bureau, 2000.

———. *Intimate Partner Violence and Age of Victim, 1993–99.* Washington, D.C.: The Bureau, 2001. [Online] Available December 4, 2001, at http://www.ojp.usdoj.gov/bjs/pub/pdf/ipva99.pdf

———. *Sourcebook of Criminal Justice Statistics Online.* [Online] Available November 11, 2001, at http://www.albany.edu/sourcebook/1995/pdf/

U.S. CENSUS BUREAU. *Asset Ownership of Households: 1993.* Current Population Reports, Series P-70, No. 47. Washington, D.C.: U.S. Government Printing Office, 1995.

———. *Household and Family Characteristics: March 1994.* Current Population Reports, Series P-20, No. 483, Washington, D.C.: U.S. Government Printing Office, 1995.

———. *Income, Poverty, and Valuation of Noncash Benefits: 1993.* Current Population Reports, Series P-60, No. 188. Washington, D.C.: U.S. Government Printing Office, 1995.

———. *Marital Status and Living Arrangements:* March 1995. PPL-52. Washington, D.C.: U.C. Government Printing Office, 1996.

———. *School Enrollment: Social and Economic Characteristics of Students: October 1995 (Update).* PPL-55: The Bureau, 1997.

———. "Who's Minding Our Preschoolers?" Fall 1994 (Update). P70–62. Washington, D.C.: U.S. Government Printing Office, 1997.

———. *Educational Achievement in the United States: March 1998 (Update).* Current Population Reports, P20-515. Washington, D.C.: U.S. Government Printing Office, 1998.

———. *Educational Attainment in the United States: March 1998 (Update).* Current Population Reports, P20-513. Washington, D.C.: U.S. Government Printing Office, 1998.

———. *Household and Family Characteristics: March 1998 (Update).* Current Population Reports, P20-515. Washington, D.C.: U.S. Government Printing Office, 1998.

———. *Poverty in the United States 1997.* Current Population Reports, P60-201. Washington, D.C.: U.S. Government Printing Office, 1998.

———. *Statistical Abstract of the United States 1998.* Washington, D.C.: U.S. Government Printing Office, 1998.

———. *Educational Attainment in the United States: March 1998 (Update).* Washington, D.C.: U.S. Government Printing Office, 1999.

———. *Grandchildren Living in the Home of Their Grandparents: 1970 to Present* (CH-7). Washington, D.C.: The Bureau, 1999.

———. *Health Insurance Coverage* (P60-208). Washington, D.C.: The Bureau, 1999.

———. *Household and Family Characteristics: March 1998 (Update).* Washington, D.C.: The Bureau, 1999.

———. *Metropolitan Area Population Estimates for July 1, 1998, and Population Change for April 1, 1990, to July 1, 1998.* Washington, D.C.: The Bureau, 1999.

———. *Money Income in the United States 1998* (P60-206). Washington, D.C.: U.S. Government Printing Office, 1999.

———. *Population Estimates for Cities with Populations of 100,000 and Greater (Sorted by 1998 Population Size Rank in U.S.).* Washington, D.C.: The Bureau, 1999.

———. *Poverty in the United States 1998* (P60-207). Washington, D.C.: U.S. Government Printing Office, 1999.

———. *School Enrollment—Social and Economic Characteristics of Students: October 1998 (Update).* Current Population Report, P20-521. Washington, D.C.: The Bureau, 1999.

———. *Statistical Abstract of the United States 1999.* Washington, D.C.: U.S. Government Printing Office, 1999.

———. *Educational Attainment in the United States: March 1998 (Update).* [Online] Available March 21, 2000, at http://www.census.gov/prod/3/98pubs/p20-513u.pdf

———. *Educational Attainment in the United States: March 2000 (Update).* Current Population Reports, P20–536. Washington, D.C.: U.S. Government Printing Office, 2000.

———. *Health Insurance Coverage 1999* (P60–211). Washington, D.C.: The Bureau, 2000.

———. *Historical Income Tables: Families,* Tables F-1, F-2, and F-3. [Online] Available March 21, 2000, at http://www.census.gov/hhes/income/histinc/f02.html

———. Vols. Table F-3, "Mean Income Received by Each Fifth and Top 5 Percent of Families (All Races): 1966 to 1999." [Online] Available December 6, 2000, at http://www.census.gov/hhes/income/histinc/f03.html

————. *Housing Vacancies and Home Ownership: Annual Statistics: 1998.* Table 20. [Online] Available March 21, 2000, at http://www.census.gov/hhes/www/housing/hvs/annual98/ann98t20.html

————. *International Data Base.* [Online] Available February 24, 2000, at http://www.census.gov/ipc/www/idbprint.html

————. *Metropolitan Area Population Estimates for July 1, 1999, and Population Change for April 1, 1990, to July 1, 1999.* Washington, D.C.: The Bureau, 2000.

————. *Money Income in the United States 1999.* Current Population Reports (P60–209). Washington, D.C.: U.S. Government Printing Office, 2000.

————. *Poverty in the United States 1999.* Current Population Reports (P60–210). Washington, D.C.: U.S. Government Printing Office, 2000.

————. *Projections of the Total Resident Population by 5-Year Age Groups and Sex with Special Age Categories: Middle Series.* [Online] Available February 24, 2000, at http://www.census.gov/population/projections/nation/summary/np-t3-?.pdf

————. *Projections of the Total Resident Population by 5-Year Age Groups and Sex with Special Age Categories: Middle Series 2050 to 2070.* [Online] Available February 24, 2000, at http://www.census.gov/population/projections/nation/summary/np-t-g.pdf

————. *Resident Estimates of the United States by Age and Sex: April 1, 1990 to November 1, 1999.* [Online] Available February 24, 2000, at http://www.census.gov/population/estimates/nation/intfile2-1.txt

————. *Resident Population Estimates of the United States by Sex, Race, and Hispanic Origin: April 1, 1990 to November 1, 1999.* [Online] Available April 22, 2000, at http://www.census.gov/population/estimates/nation/intfile3-1.txt

————. *Statistical Abstract of the United States 2000.* Washington, D.C.: U.S. Government Printing Office, 2000.

————. Table F-1, "Income Limits for Each Fifth and Top 5 Percent of Families (All Races): 1947 to 1999." [Online] Available December 6, 2000, at http://www.census.gov/hhes/income/histinc/f01.html

————. Table F-2, "Share of Aggregate Income Received by Each Fifth and Top 5 Percent of Families (All Races): 1947 to 1999." [Online] Available December 6, 2000, at http://www.census.gov/hhes/income/histinc/f02.html

————. Table F-7, "Type of Family (All Races) by Median and Mean Income: 1947 to 1998." [Online] Available March 21, 2000, at http://www.census.gov/hhes/income/histinc/f07.html

————. Table P-10, "Age—People (Both Sexes Combined—All Races) by Median and Mean Income: 1974 to 1998." [Online] Available January 28, 2000, at http://www.census.gov/hhes/income/histinc/p10.html

————. Table P-28, "Years of School Completed: Workers 18 Years Old and Over by Mean Earnings, Age, and Sex: 1991 to 1998." [Online] Available December 6, 2000, at http://www.census.gov/hhes/income/histinc/p28.html

————. Table P-31, "Years of School Completed: Workers 18 Years Old and Over by Mean Earnings, Age, and Sex: 1974 to 1979." [Online] Available December 6, 2000, at http://www.census.gov/hhes/income/histinc/p31.html

————. *Age: 2000.* Census 2000 Brief, C2KBR/01-12. [Online] Available September 2001 at http://www.census.gov/population/www/cen2000/briefs.html

————. *America's Families and Living Arrangements: March 2000.* Current Population Reports, P20-537. [Online] Available December 6, 2001, at http://www.census.gov/population/www/socdemo/hh-fam/p20-537-00.html

————. *The Black Population: 2000.* Census 2000 Brief, C2KBR/01-5. [Online] Available August 2001 at http://www.census.gov/population/www/cen2000/briefs.html

————. *Census 2000 PHC-T-5. Ranking Tables for Incorporated Places of 100,000 or More: 1990 and 2000.* [Online] Available October 24, 2001, at http://www.census.gov/population/cen2000/phc-t5/tab02.pdf

————. *Census 2000 PHC-T-15. General Demographic Characteristics by Race for the United States: 2000.* [Online] Available October 10, 2001, at http://www.census.gov/population/www/cen2000/phc-t15.html

————. *Census 2000 Supplementary Survey Summary Tables.* Tables QT-01, QT-02, and QT-03. [Online] Available September 12, 2001, at http://factfinder.census.gov/

————. *CPS Annual Demographic Survey, March Supplement.* [Online] Available March 2001 at http://ferret.bls.census.gov/macro/032001/perinc/new06-000.htm

————. *Child Support 1997.* [Online] Revised version, October 13, 2000. Available December 4, 2001, at http://www.census.gov/hhes/www/childsupport/97tables/tab4.html

————. *Gender: 2000.* Census 2000 Brief, C2KBR/01-9. [Online] Available September 2001 at http://www.census.gov/population/www/cen2000/briefs.html

————. *The Hispanic Population: 2000.* Census 2000 Brief, C2KBR/01-3. [Online] Available May 2001 at http://www.census.gov/population/www/cen2000/briefs.html

————. *Hispanic Population of the United States.* Current Population Survey, March 2000. Washington, D.C.: U.S. Government Printing Office, 2001. [Online] Available November 28, 2001, at http://www.census.gov/population/www/socdemo/hispanic/ho00-04.html

————. *Historical Income Tables: Families.* [Online] Available October 6, 2001, at http://www.census.gov/hhes/income/histinc/

————. *Historical Income Tables: People,* Table P-10. [Online] Available March 1, 2001, at http://www.census.gov/hhes/income/histinc/p10.html

————. *Households and Families: 2000.* Census 2000 Brief, C2KBR/01-8. [Online] Available September 2001 at http://www.census.gov/population/www/cen2000/briefs.html

————. *Interracial Tables.* Table 2, "Race of Couples: 1990." [Online] Available December 4, 2001, at http://www.census.gov/population/socdemo/race/interractab2.txt

————. *Mapping Census 2000: The Geography of U.S. Diversity.* Census Special Reports, Series CENSR/01-1. Washington, D.C.: U.S. Government Printing Office, 2001.

————. *Money Income in the United States: 2000.* Current Population Reports, P60-213. Washington, D.C.: U.S. Government Printing Office, 2001.

————. *Overview of Race and Hispanic Origin: 2000.* Census 2000 Brief, C2KBR/01-1. [Online] Available March 2001 at http://www.census.gov/population/www/cen2000/briefs.html

————. *Population Change and Distribution: 1990 to 2000.* Census 2000 Brief, C2KBR/01-2. [Online] Available April 2001 at http://www.census.gov/population/www/cen2000/briefs.html

————. *Poverty in the United States: 2000.* Current Population Reports, P60-214. Washington, D.C.: U.S. Government Printing Office, 2001.

————. *Resident Population Estimates of the United States by Sex, Race, and Hispanic Origin: April 1, 1990 to July 1, 1999, with Short-Term Projection to November 1, 2000.* [Online] Available September 19, 2001, at http://www.census.gov/population/estimates/nation/intfile3-1.txt

————. *School Enrollment: Social and Economic Characteristics of Students: October 2000.* PPL-148. Washington, D.C.: The Bureau, 2001. [Online] Available October 17, 2001, at http://www.census.gov/population/socdemo/school/ppl-148/

————. *The 65 Years and Over Population: 2000.* Census 2000 Brief, C2KBR/01-10. [Online] Available October 2001 at http://www.census.gov/population/www/cen2000/briefs.html

————. Table DP-1, "Profile of General Demographic Characteristics: 2000." [Online] Available November 21, 2001, at http://www.census.gov/prod/cen2000/dp1/2khus.pdf

————. *The White Population: 2000.* Census 2000 Brief, C2KBR/01-4. [Online] Available August 2001 at http://www.census.gov/population/www/cen2000/briefs.html

U.S. CENSUS OFFICE. *Census of the United States (1900).* Vol. II: Population. Washington, D.C.: The Office, 1902.

U.S. CENTERS FOR DISEASE CONTROL AND PREVENTION. *Morbidity and Mortality Weekly Report.* Vol. 46, No. 51 (December 26, 1997).

————. *HIV/AIDS Surveillance Report.* Vol. 11, No. 1 (Midyear 1999).

————. *Sexually Transmitted Disease Surveillance 1998.* Atlanta, Ga.: The Centers, 1999.

————. *HIV/AIDS Surveillance Report.* Vol. 12, No. 1 (Midyear 2000).

————. *Morbidity and Mortality Weekly Report.* Vol. 49, No. 43 (November 3, 2000):978–82. [Online] Available http://www.cdc.gov/mmwr/preview/mmwrhtml/mm4943a2.htm

————. *Sexually Transmitted Disease Surveillance 1999.* Atlanta, Ga.: The Centers, 2000.

————. *HIV/AIDS Surveillance Report.* Vol. 12, No. 2 (December 2000 Year-end edition), 2001).

————. *Morbidity and Mortality Weekly Report.* Vol. 50, No. 40 (October 12, 2001).

U.S. DEPARTMENT OF HEALTH AND HUMAN SERVICES. Administration for Children and Families. *Temporary Assistance for Needy Families (TANF) Program;* Third Annual Report to Congress, August 2000. Washington, D.C.: The Administration, 2000.

U.S. DEPARTMENT OF JUSTICE. "Nearly Three Percent of College Women Experienced a Completed Rape or Attempted Rape During the College Year, According to a New Justice Department Report." [Online]. Accessed February 15, 2001, at http://www.ojp.usdoj.gov/bjs/pub/press/scvw.pr

U.S. DEPARTMENT OF LABOR. Bureau of Labor Statistics. *Employment and Earnings.* Vol. 46, No. 1 (January 1999).

————. Bureau of Labor Statistics. *Employment Projections.* Table 5, "Civilian Labor Force by Sex, Age, Race, and Hispanic Origin, 1978, 1988, 1998, and Projected 2008." Washington, D.C.: The Bureau, 1999.

————. Bureau of Labor Statistics. *Employment and Earnings.* Vol. 47, No. 1 (January 2000).

————. *International Comparisons of Hourly Compensation Costs for Production Workers in Manufacturing, 1975–1998.* Supplementary tables for BLS News Release USDL 00–07, January 11, 2000. Washington, D.C.: The Bureau, 2000.

————. *International Comparisons of Hourly Compensation Costs for Production Workers in Manufacturing, 1975–1999.* Supplementary tables for BLS News Release USDL 00-254, September 7, 2000. Washington, D.C.: The Bureau, 2000.

————. Women's Bureau. *Women Business Owners: 1999.* [Online] Available February 12, 2000, at http://www.dol.gov/dol/wb/public/wb-pubs/wbo.htm

————. *Employment and Earnings.* Vol. 48, No. 1 (January 2001).

U.S. DEPARTMENT OF STATE. Bureau of Arms Control. *World Military Expenditures and Arms Transfers 1998.* Washington, D.C.: The Bureau, 1999.

————. *Patterns of Global Terrorism 1998.* Washington, D.C.: The Department, 1999.

————. *Patterns of Global Terrorism 1999.* Washington, D.C.: The Department, 2000.

————. *Patterns of Global Terrorism 2000.* [Online] Available July 8, 2001, at http://www.usis.usemb.se/terror/rpt2000/index.html

USEEM, BERT. "Disorganization and the New Mexico Prison Riot of 1980." *American Sociological Review.* Vol. 50, No. 5 (October 1985):677–88.

U.S. EQUAL EMPLOYMENT OPPORTUNITY COMMISSION. *Job Patterns for Minorities and Women in Private Industry, 1996.* Washington, D.C.: The Commission, 1997.

————. *Job Patterns for Minorities and Women in Private Industry 1997.* Washington, D.C.: The Commission, 1998.

——. *Job Patterns for Minorities and Women in Private Industry, 1998.* Washington, D.C.: The Commission, 2000.

——. Table 1, "Occupational Employment in Private Industry by Race/Ethnic Group/Sex, United States, 1998." [Online] Available October 18, 2000, at http://www.eeoc.gov/stats/jobpat/tables-1.html

——. *Job Patterns for Minorities and Women in Private Industry 1999.* [Online] Available September 19, 2001, at http://www.eeoc.gov/stats/jobpat/1999/national.html

U.S. FEDERAL BUREAU OF INVESTIGATION. *Crime in the United States 1998.* Washington, D.C.: The Bureau, 1999.

——. *Crime in the United States 1999.* Washington, D.C.: The Bureau, 2000.

——. *Crime in the United States 2000.* Washington, D.C.: The Bureau, 2001. [Online] Available November 11, 2001, at http://www.fbi.gov/ucr/cius-00/

U.S. FEDERAL ELECTION COMMISSION. "18-Month Summary on Political Action Committees." News release, September 27, 2000. [Online] Available http://www.fec.gov

U.S. HOUSE OF REPRESENTATIVES. "Street Children: A Global Disgrace." Hearing on November 7, 1991. Washington, D.C.: U.S. Government Printing Office, 1992.

U.S. IMMIGRATION AND NATURALIZATION SERVICE. Table 3, "Immigrants Admitted by Region and Selected Country of Birth, Fiscal Years 1984–94." Fax received from INS January 1996.

——. Table 5, "Immigrants Admitted by Region and Selected Country of Birth, Fiscal Years 1994–96." [Online] Available December 5, 1997, at http://www.ins.doj.gov/stats/annual/fy96/1005.htm

——. *Legal Immigration, Fiscal Year 1998.* Washington, D.C.: The Service, 1999.

U.S. INTERNAL REVENUE SERVICE. *Statistics of Income Bulletin* (Spring 1993).

——. *Statistics of Income Bulletin.* Winter 1999/2000. Publication 1136, Rev. 2/00.

U.S. NATIONAL CENTER FOR EDUCATION STATISTICS. *Digest of Education Statistics 1998.* Washington, D.C.: U.S. Government Printing Office, 1999.

——. *Dropout Rates in the United States: 1997.* Washington, D.C.: The Center, 1999.

——. *Digest of Education Statistics 2000.* Washington, D.C.: U.S. Government Printing Office, 2001.

U.S. NATIONAL CENTER FOR HEALTH STATISTICS. *National Vital Statistics Report.* Vol. 47, No. 4 (October 7, 1998).

——. *Current Estimates from the National Health Interview Survey 1996.* Series 10, No. 200. Hyattsville, Md.: The Center, 1999.

——. *National Vital Statistics Report.* Vol. 47, No. 18 (April 29, 1999).

——. *National Vital Statistics Report.* Vol. 47, No. 19 (June 30, 1999).

——. *National Vital Statistics Report.* Vol. 47, No. 21 (July 6, 1999).

——. *National Vital Statistics Report.* Vol. 47, No. 25 (October 5, 1999).

——. "Births, Marriages, Divorces, and Deaths: Provisional Data for November 1999." *National Vital Statistics Report.* Vol. 48, No. 17 (October 31, 2000).

——. *National Vital Statistics Report.* Vol. 48, No. 11 (July 24, 2000). [Online] Available http://www.cdc.gov/nchs/data/nvs48-11.pdf

——. "Nonmarital Childbearing in the United States, 1940–99." *National Vital Statistics Report.* Vol. 48, No. 16 (revised) (October 18, 2000). [Online] Available http://www.cdc.gov/nchs/data/nvs48-16.pdf

——. *National Vital Statistics Report.* Vol. 48, No. 18 (February 7, 2001). [Online] Available February 6, 2001, at http://www.cdc.gov/nchs/data/nvsr/nvsr48/nvs48-18.pdf

——. *National Vital Statistics Report.* Vol. 49, No. 1 (April 17, 2001).

——. *National Vital Statistics Report.* Vol. 49, No. 6 (August 22, 2001).

——. *National Vital Statistics Report.* Vol. 49, No. 12 (October 9, 2001).

——. News release. October 10, 2001.

U.S. NATIONAL CLEARINGHOUSE ON CHILD ABUSE AND NEGLECT. *Child Maltreatment 1996.* Washington, D.C.: The Clearinghouse, 1998.

——. *Child Abuse and Neglect National Statistics* (April 2000). Washington, D.C.: The Clearinghouse, 2000.

VALDEZ, A. "In the Hood: Street Gangs Discover White-Collar Crime." *Police.* Vol. 21, No. 5 (May 1997):49–50, 56.

VALLAS, STEPHEN P., and JOHN P. BECK. "The Transformation of Work Revisited: The Limits of Flexibility in American Manufacturing." *Social Problems.* Vol. 43, No. 3 (August 1996):339–61.

VALOCCHI, STEVE. "The Emergence of the Integrationist Ideology in the Civil Rights Movement." *Social Problems.* Vol. 43, No. 1 (February 1996):116–30.

VAN BIEMA, DAVID. "Parents Who Kill." *Time.* Vol. 144, No. 20 (November 14, 1994):50–51.

——. "Sparse at Seder?" *Time.* Vol. 149, No. 17 (April 28, 1997a):67.

——. "Buddhism in America." *Time.* Vol. 150, No. 15 (October 13, 1997b):71–81.

——. "Spiriting Prayer into School." *Time.* Vol. 152, No. 20 (April 27, 1998):38–41.

——. "A Surge of Teen Spirit." *Time.* Vol. 153, No. 20 (May 31, 1999):58–59.

——. "Strangers in a Land of Strange Mountains." *Time.* Vol. 156, No. 11 (September 11, 2000):7.

VAN DEN HAAG, ERNEST, and JOHN P. CONRAD. *The Death Penalty: A Debate.* New York: Plenum Press, 1983.

VAUGHAN, MARY KAY. "Multinational Corporations: The World as a Company Town." In Ahamed Idris-Soven et al., eds., *The World as a Company Town: Multinational Corporations and Social Change.* The Hague: Mouton Publishers, 1978:15–35.

VAYDA, EUGENE, and RAISA B. DEBER. "The Canadian Health Care System: An Overview." *Social Science and Medicine.* Vol. 18, No. 3 (1984):191–97.

VEBLEN, THORSTEIN. *The Theory of the Leisure Class.* New York: The New American Library, 1953; orig. 1899.

VEDDER, RICHARD, and LOWELL GALLAWAY. "Declining Black Employment." *Society.* Vol. 30, No. 5 (July–August 1993):56–63.

VINOVSKIS, MARIS A. "Have Social Historians Lost the Civil War? Some Preliminary Demographic Speculations." *Journal of American History.* Vol. 76, No. 1 (June 1989):34–58.

VOGEL, EZRA F. *The Four Little Dragons: The Spread of Industrialization in East Asia.* Cambridge, Mass.: Harvard University Press, 1991.

VOGEL, LISE. *Marxism and the Oppression of Women: Toward a Unitary Theory.* New Brunswick, N.J.: Rutgers University Press, 1983.

VOLD, GEORGE B., and THOMAS J. BERNARD. *Theoretical Criminology.* 3d ed. New York: Oxford University Press, 1986.

VON HIRSH, ANDREW. *Past or Future Crimes: Deservedness and Dangerousness in the Sentencing of Criminals.* New Brunswick, N.J.: Rutgers University Press, 1986.

VOSS, JACQUELINE, and LORI KOGAN. Research reported in Keith Mulvihill, "Sex Education Does Not Up Sexual Activity: Study." Accessed at http://dailynews.yahoo.com (May 1, 2001).

VOYDANOFF, PATRICIA., and BRENDA W. DONNELLY. *Adolescent Sexuality and Pregnancy.* Newbury Park, Calif.: Sage, 1990.

WAITE, LINDA J., GUS W. HAGGSTROM, and DAVID I. KANOUSE. "The Consequences of Parenthood for the Marital Stability of Young Adults." *American Sociological Review.* Vol. 50, No. 6 (December 1985):850–57.

WALDER, ANDREW G. "Career Mobility and the Communist Political Order." *American Sociological Review.* Vol. 60, No. 3 (June 1995):309–28.

WALDFOGEL, JANE. "The Effect of Children on Women's Wages." *American Sociological Review.* Vol. 62, No. 2 (April 1997):209–17.

WALDMAN, STEVEN. "Deadbeat Dads." *Newsweek* (May 4, 1992):46–52.

WALDROP, JUDITH. "Live Long and Prosper." *American Demographics.* Vol. 14 (October 1992):40–45.

WALKER, BOB. "Bob Walker's Official New Orleans Area Wedding Guide: Louisiana's Covenant Marriage Law." [Online] Available August 13, 1998, at http://www.acadiacom.net/walker/covenant–marriage.htm

WALKER, KAREN. "'Always There For Me': Friendship Patterns and Expectations among Middle- and Working-Class Men and Women." *Sociological Forum.* Vol. 10, No. 2 (June 1995):273–96.

WALL, THOMAS F. *Medical Ethics: Basic Moral Issues.* Washington, D.C.: University Press of America, 1980.

WALLER, DOUGLAS. "Onward Cyber Soldiers." *Time.* Vol. 146, No. 8 (August 21, 1995):38–44.

WALLERSTEIN, IMMANUEL. *The Modern World-System: Capitalist Agriculture and the Origins of the European World-Economy in the Sixteenth Century.* New York: Academic Press, 1974.

——. *The Capitalist World-Economy.* New York: Cambridge University Press, 1979.

——. "Crises: The World Economy, the Movements, and the Ideologies." In Albert Bergesen, ed., *Crises in the World-System.* Beverly Hills, Calif.: Sage, 1983:21–36.

——. *The Politics of the World Economy: The States, the Movements, and the Civilizations.* Cambridge, U.K.: Cambridge University Press, 1984.

WALLERSTEIN, JUDITH S., and SANDRA BLAKESLEE. *Second Chances: Men, Women, and Children a Decade after Divorce.* New York: Ticknor & Fields, 1989.

WALLIS, DAVID. "After Cyberoverkill Comes Cyberburnout." *New York Times* (August 4, 1996):43, 46.

WALMSLEY, ROY. *World Prison Population.* 2d ed. United Kingdom Home Office Research, Development, and Statistics Directorate, July 2000.

WALSH, MARY WILLIAMS. "No Time to Put Your Feet Up as Retirement Comes in Stages." *The New York Times* (April 15, 2001):1, 18.

WALTON, JOHN, and CHARLES RAGIN. "Global and National Sources of Political Protest: Third World Responses to the Debt Crisis." *American Sociological Review.* Vol. 55, No. 6 (December 1990):876–90.

WARNER, R. STEPHEN. "Work in Progress toward a New Paradigm for the Sociological Study of Religion in the United States." *American Journal of Sociology.* Vol. 98, No. 5 (March 1993):1044–93.

WARNER, W. LLOYD, and PAUL S. LUNT. *The Social Life of a Modern Community.* New Haven, Conn.: Yale University Press, 1941.

WARR, MARK, and CHRISTOPHER G. ELLISON. "Rethinking Social Reactions to Crime: Personal and Altruistic Fear in Family Households." *American Journal of Sociology.* Vol. 106, No. 3 (November 2000):551–78.

WARREN, JOHN ROBERT, and ROBERT M. HAUSER. "Social Stratification across Three Generations: New Evidence from the Wisconsin Longitudinal Study." *American Sociological Review.* Vol. 62 (August 1997):561–72.

WASKUL, DENNIS. "Selfhood in the Age of Computer Mediated Symbolic Interaction." Paper presented to the annual meeting of the Southwest Social Science Association, New Orleans, La., March 1997.

WATERS, MELISSA S., WILL CARRINGTON HEATH, and JOHN KEITH WATSON. "A Positive Model of the Determination of Religious Affiliation." *Social Science Quarterly.* Vol. 76, No. 1 (March 1995):105–23.

WATSON, RUSSELL. "Milosevic in His Bunker." *Newsweek* (June 7, 1999):49–51.

WATTENBERG, BEN J. "The Attitudes behind American Exceptionalism." *U.S. News & World Report.* Vol. 107, No. 6 (August 7, 1989):25.

——. "The Population Explosion Is Over." *New York Times Magazine* (November 23, 1997):60–63.

WATTS, DUNCAN J. "Networks, Dynamics, and the Small-World Phenomenon." *American Journal of Sociology.* Vol. 105, No. 2 (September 1999):493–527.

WEBER, ADNA FERRIN. *The Growth of Cities.* New York: Columbia University Press, 1963; orig. 1899.

WEBER, MAX. *The Protestant Ethic and the Spirit of Capitalism.* New York: Charles Scribner's Sons, 1958; orig. 1904–5.

———. *Economy and Society*. G. Roth and C. Wittich, eds. Berkeley: University of California Press, 1978; orig. 1921.

WEBSTER, ANDREW. *Introduction to the Sociology of Development*. London: Macmillan, 1984.

WEBSTER, MURRAY, JR., and STUART J. HYSOM. "Creating Status Characteristics." *American Sociological Review*. Vol. 63, No. 3 (June 1998):351–78.

WEBSTER, PAMELA S., TERRI ORBUCH, and JAMES S. HOUSE. "Effects of Childhood Family Background on Adult Marital Quality and Perceived Stability." *American Journal of Sociology*. Vol. 101, No. 2 (September 1995):404–32.

WEEKS, JOHN R. "The Demography of Islamic Nations." *Population Bulletin*. Vol. 43, No. 4 (December 1988). Washington, D.C.: Population Reference Bureau.

WEICHER, JOHN C. "Getting Richer (at Different Rates)." *Wall Street Journal* (June 14, 1995):A18.

WEIDENBAUM, MURRAY. "The Evolving Corporate Board." *Society*. Vol. 32, No. 3 (March/April 1995):9–20.

WEINBERG, GEORGE. *Society and the Healthy Homosexual*. Garden City, N.Y.: Anchor Books, 1973.

WEINER, TIM. "Head of C.I.A. Plans Center to Protect U.S. Cyberspace." *New York Times* (June 26, 1996):B7.

WEINRICH, JAMES D. *Sexual Landscapes: Why We Are What We Are, Why We Love Whom We Love*. New York: Charles Scribner's Sons, 1987.

WEISBERG, D. KELLY. *Children of the Night: A Study of Adolescent Prostitution*. Lexington, Mass.: D.C. Heath, 1985.

WEISBURD, DAVID, STANTON WHEELER, ELIN WARING, and NANCY BODE. *Crimes of the Middle Class: White Collar Defenders in the Courts*. New Haven, Conn.: Yale University Press, 1991.

WEITZMAN, LENORE J. *The Divorce Revolution: The Unexpected Social and Economic Consequences for Women and Children in America*. New York: Free Press, 1985.

———. "The Economic Consequences of Divorce Are Still Unequal: Comment on Peterson." *American Sociological Review*. Vol. 61, No. 3 (June 1996):537–38.

WELLER, JACK M., and E. L. QUARANTELLI. "Neglected Characteristics of Collective Behavior." *American Journal of Sociology*. Vol. 79, No. 3 (November 1973):665–85.

WELLFORD, CHARLES. "Labeling Theory and Criminology: An Assessment." In Delos H. Kelly, ed., *Criminal Behavior: Readings in Criminology*. New York: St. Martin's Press, 1980:234–47.

WELLINGTON, SHEILA. "Cracking the Ceiling." *Time*. Vol. 152, No. 23 (December 7, 1998):187.

WERTHEIMER, BARBARA MAYER. "The Factory Bell." In Linda K. Kerber and Jane De Hart Mathews, eds., *Women's America: Refocusing the Past*. New York: Oxford University Press, 1982:130–40.

WESOLOWSKI, WLODZIMIERZ. "Transition from Authoritarianism to Democracy." *Social Research*. Vol. 57, No. 2 (Summer 1990):435–61.

WESTERN, BRUCE. "Postwar Unionization in Eighteen Advanced Capitalist Countries." *American Sociological Review*. Vol. 58, No. 2 (April 1993):266–82.

———. "A Comparative Study of Working-Class Disorganization: Union Decline in Eighteen Advanced Capitalist Countries." *American Sociological Review*. Vol. 60, No. 2 (April 1995):179–201.

WESTERN, MARK, and ERIK OLIN WRIGHT. "The Permeability of Class Boundaries to Intergenerational Mobility among Men in the United States, Canada, Norway and Sweden." *American Sociological Review*. Vol. 59, No. 4 (August 1994):606–29.

WHALEN, JACK, and RICHARD FLACKS. *Beyond the Barricades: The Sixties Generation Grows Up*. Philadelphia: Temple University Press, 1989.

WHEELIS, ALLEN. *The Quest for Identity*. New York: Norton, 1958.

WHELAN, CHRISTINE B. "No Honeymoon for Covenant Marriage." *Wall Street Journal* (August 17, 1998):A14.

WHITAKER, MARK. "Ten Ways to Fight Terrorism." *Newsweek* (July 1, 1985):26–29.

WHITE, JACK E. "I'm Just Who I Am." *Time*. Vol. 149, No. 18 (May 5, 1997):32–36.

WHITE, RALPH, and RONALD LIPPITT. "Leader Behavior and Member Reaction in Three 'Social Climates.'" In Dorwin Cartwright and Alvin Zander, eds., *Group Dynamics*. Evanston, Ill.: Row, Peterson, 1953:586–611.

WHITE, WALTER. *Rope and Faggot*. New York: Arno Press and *New York Times*, 1969; orig. 1929.

WHITMAN, DAVID. "Shattering Myths about the Homeless." *U.S. News & World Report* (March 20, 1989):26, 28.

WHORF, BENJAMIN LEE. "The Relation of Habitual Thought and Behavior to Language." In *Language, Thought, and Reality*. Cambridge, Mass.: The Technology Press of MIT/New York: Wiley, 1956:134–59; orig. 1941.

WHYTE, WILLIAM FOOTE. *Street Corner Society*. 3d ed. Chicago: University of Chicago Press, 1981; orig. 1943.

WHYTE, WILLIAM H., JR. *The Organization Man*. Garden City, N.Y.: Anchor Books, 1957.

WIARDA, HOWARD J. "Ethnocentrism and Third World Development." *Society*. Vol. 24, No. 6 (September–October 1987):55–64.

WIATROWSKI, MICHAEL A., DAVID B. GRISWOLD, and MARY K. ROBERTS. "Social Control Theory and Delinquency." *American Sociological Review*. Vol. 46, No. 5 (October 1981):525–41.

WICKHAM, DEWAYNE. "Homeless Receive Little Attention from Candidates." Accessed October 24, 2000, at http://www.usatoday.com/usatonline

WIDOM, CATHY SPATZ. "Childhood Sexual Abuse and Its Criminal Consequences." *Society*. Vol. 33, No. 4 (May/June 1996):47–53.

WILCOX, CLYDE. "Race, Gender, and Support for Women in the Military." *Social Science Quarterly*. Vol. 73, No. 2 (June 1992):310–23.

WILES, P. J. D. *Economic Institutions Compared*. New York: Halsted Press, 1977.

WILKINSON, DORIS. "Transforming the Social Order: The Role of the University in Social Change." *Sociological Forum*. Vol. 9, No. 3 (September 1994):325–41.

WILLIAMS, RHYS H., and N. J. DEMERATH, III. "Religion and Political Process in an American City." *American Sociological Review*. Vol. 56, No. 4 (August 1991):417–31.

WILLIAMS, ROBIN M., JR. *American Society: A Sociological Interpretation*. 3d ed. New York: Alfred A. Knopf, 1970.

WILLIAMSON, JEFFREY G., and PETER H. LINDERT. *American Inequality: A Macroeconomic History*. New York: Academic Press, 1980.

WILSON, BARBARA. "National Television Violence Study." Reported by Julia Duin, "Study Finds Cartoon Heroes Initiate Too Much Violence." *Washington Times* (April 17, 1998):A4.

WILSON, BRYAN. *Religion in Sociological Perspective*. New York: Oxford University Press, 1982.

WILSON, EDWARD O. "Biodiversity, Prosperity, and Value." In F. Herbert Bormann and Stephen R. Kellert, eds., *Ecology, Economics, and Ethics: The Broken Circle*. New Haven, Conn.: Yale University Press, 1991:3–10.

WILSON, JAMES Q. *Bureaucracy: What Government Agencies Do and Why They Do It*. New York: Basic Books, 1989.

———. "Crime, Race, and Values." *Society*. Vol. 30, No. 1 (November–December 1992):90–93.

WILSON, JAMES Q., and RICHARD J. HERRNSTEIN. *Crime and Human Nature*. New York: Simon & Schuster, 1985.

WILSON, LOGAN. *American Academics Then and Now*. New York: Oxford University Press, 1979.

WILSON, THOMAS C. "Urbanism and Tolerance: A Test of Some Hypotheses Drawn from Wirth and Stouffer." *American Sociological Review*. Vol. 50, No. 1 (February 1985):117–23.

———. "Urbanism and Unconventionality: The Case of Sexual Behavior." *Social Science Quarterly*. Vol. 76, No. 2 (June 1995):346–63.

WILSON, WILLIAM JULIUS. *The Declining Significance of Race*. Chicago: University of Chicago Press, 1978.

———. *When Work Disappears: The World of the New Urban Poor*. New York: Alfred A. Knopf, 1996a.

———. "Work." *New York Times Magazine* (August 18, 1996b):26–31, 40, 48, 52, 54.

WINKLER, KAREN J. "Scholar Whose Ideas of Female Psychology Stir Debate Modifies Theories, Extends Studies to Young Girls." *Chronicle of Higher Education*. Vol. 36, No. 36 (May 23, 1990):A6–A8.

WINNICK, LOUIS. "America's 'Model Minority.'" *Commentary*. Vol. 90, No. 2 (August 1990):22–29.

WINSHIP, CHRISTOPHER, and JENNY BERRIEN. "Boston Cops and Black Churches." *The Public Interest*. Vol. 136 (Summer 1999):52–68.

WINTERS, REBECCA. "Who Needs an M.B.A.?" *Time Select: Business*. Vol. 153, No. 19 (May 17, 1999).

WIRTH, LOUIS. "Urbanism as a Way of Life." *American Journal of Sociology*. Vol. 44, No. 1 (July 1938):1–24.

WITKIN, GORDON. "The Crime Bust." *U.S. News & World Report*. Vol. 124, No. 20 (May 25, 1998):28–40.

WITKIN-LANOIL, GEORGIA. *The Female Stress Syndrome: How to Recognize and Live with It*. New York: Newmarket Press, 1984.

WITT, G. EVANS. "Say What You Mean." *American Demographics*. Vol. 21, No. 2 (February 1999):23.

WOLF, DIANE L., ed. *Feminist Dilemma of Fieldwork*. Boulder, Colo.: Westview Press, 1996.

WOLF, NAOMI. *The Beauty Myth: How Images of Beauty Are Used against Women*. New York: William Morrow, 1990.

WOLFE, DAVID B. "Targeting the Mature Mind." *American Demographics*. Vol. 16, No. 3 (March 1994):32–36.

WOLFGANG, MARVIN E., ROBERT M. FIGLIO, and THORSTEN SELLIN. *Delinquency in a Birth Cohort*. Chicago: University of Chicago Press, 1972.

WOLFGANG, MARVIN E., TERRENCE P. THORNBERRY, and ROBERT M. FIGLIO. *From Boy to Man, From Delinquency to Crime*. Chicago: University of Chicago Press, 1987.

WOLFSON, ADAM. "Killing Off the Dying?" *The Public Interest*. No. 131 (Spring 1998):50–70.

WOLKOMIR, MICHELLE, MICHAEL FUTREAL, ERIC WOODRUM, and THOMAS HOBAN. "Substantive Religious Belief and Environmentalism." *Social Science Quarterly*. Vol. 78, No. 1 (March 1997):96–108.

WONG, BUCK. "Need for Awareness: An Essay on Chinatown, San Francisco." In Amy Tachiki et al., eds., *Roots: An Asian American Reader*. Los Angeles: UCLA Asian American Studies Center, 1971:265–73.

WOOD, PETER B., and MICHELE CHESSER. "Black Stereotyping in a University Population." *Sociological Focus*. Vol. 27, No. 1 (February 1994):17–34.

WOODBERRY, ROBERT D. "When Surveys Lie and People Tell the Truth: Church Attenders." *American Sociological Review*. Vol. 63, No. 1 (February 1998):119–22.

WOODWARD, KENNETH L. "Feminism and the Churches." *Newsweek*. Vol. 13, No. 7 (February 13, 1989):58–61.

———. "Talking to God." *Newsweek*. Vol. 119, No. 1 (January 6, 1992a):38–44.

———. "The Elite, and How to Avoid It." *Newsweek* (July 20, 1992b):55.

WOOLEY, ORLAND W., SUSAN C. WOOLEY, and SUE R. DYRENFORTH. "Obesity and Women—II: A Neglected Feminist Topic." *Women's Studies International Quarterly*. Vol. 2 (1979):81–92.

THE WORLD BANK. *World Development Report 1993*. New York: Oxford University Press, 1993.

———. *World Development Report 1995: Workers in an Integrating World*. New York: Oxford University Press, 1995.

————. *World Development Report 1997: The State in a Changing World.* New York: Oxford University Press, 1997.

————. *World Development Report: Knowledge for Development.* New York: Oxford University Press, 1999.

————. *Entering the 21st Century: World Development Report 1999/2000.* New York: Oxford University Press, 2000.

————. *World Bank Atlas 2001.* Washington, D.C.: The World Bank, 2001.

————. *World Development Indicators 2001.* Washington, D.C.: The World Bank, 2001.

————. *World Development Report 2000/2001.* Washington, D.C.: The World Bank, 2001.

WORLD HEALTH ORGANIZATION. *Constitution of the World Health Organization.* New York: World Health Organization Interim Commission, 1946.

World Values Survey, 1990–1993. Ann Arbor, Mich.: Interuniversity Consortium for Political and Social Research, 1994.

WORSLEY, PETER. "Models of the World System." In Mike Featherstone, ed., *Global Culture: Nationalism, Globalization, and Modernity.* Newbury Park, Calif.: Sage, 1990:83–95.

WREN, CHRISTOPHER S. "In Soweto-by-the-Sea, Misery Lives on as Apartheid Fades." *New York Times* (June 9, 1991):1, 7.

WRIGHT, ERIK OLIN. "Typologies, Scales, and Class Analysis: A Comment on Halaby and Weakliem." *American Sociological Review.* Vol. 58, No. 1 (February 1993):31–34.

WRIGHT, ERIK OLIN, and BILL MARTIN. "The Transformation of the American Class Structure, 1960–1980." *American Journal of Sociology.* Vol. 93, No. 1 (July 1987):1–29.

WRIGHT, ERIC R. "Personal Networks and Anomie: Exploring the Sources and Significance of Gender Composition." *Sociological Focus.* Vol. 28, No. 3 (August 1995):261–82.

WRIGHT, JAMES D. "Address Unknown: Homelessness in Contemporary America." *Society.* Vol. 26, No. 6 (September–October 1989):45–53.

————. "Ten Essential Observations on Guns in America." *Society.* Vol. 32, No. 3 (March–April 1995):63–68.

WRIGHT, QUINCY. "Causes of War in the Atomic Age." In William M. Evan and Stephen Hilgartner, eds., *The Arms Race and Nuclear War.* Englewood Cliffs, N.J.: Prentice Hall, 1987:7–10.

WRIGHT, RICHARD A. "Curing Doonesbury's Disease: A Prescription for Dialogue in the Classroom." *Quarterly Journal of Ideology.* Vol. 9, No. 4 (1985):3–8.

————. *In Defense of Prisons.* Westport, Conn.: Greenwood Press, 1994.

WRIGHT, ROBERT. "Hyperdemocracy." *Time.* Vol. 145, No. 3 (January 23, 1995):15–21.

————. "Sin in the Global Village." *Time.* Vol. 152, No. 16 (October 19, 1998):130.

WRIGHT, STUART A., and ELIZABETH S. PIPER. "Families and Cults: Familial Factors Related to Youth Leaving or Remaining in Deviant Religious Groups." *Journal of Marriage and the Family.* Vol. 48, No. 1 (February 1986):15–25.

WU, LAWRENCE L. "Effects of Family Instability, Income, and Income Instability on the Risk of a Premarital Birth." *American Sociological Review.* Vol. 61, No. 3 (June 1996):386–406.

WYNTER, LEON E. "Business and Race." *Wall Street Journal* (May 10, 1995):B1.

YAMAGATA, HISASHI, KUANG S. YEH, SHELBY STEWMAN, and HIROKO DODGE. "Sex Segregation and Glass Ceilings: A Comparative Static Model of Women's Career Opportunities in the Federal Government over a Quarter Century." *American Journal of Sociology.* Vol. 103, No. 3 (November 1997):566–632.

YANG, FENGGANG, and HELEN ROSE EBAUGH. "Transformations in New Immigrant Religions and Their Global Implications." *American Sociological Review.* Vol. 66, No. 2 (April 2001):269–88.

YANKELOVICH, DANIEL. "How Changes in the Economy Are Reshaping American Values." In Henry J. Aaron, Thomas E. Mann, and Timothy Taylor, eds., *Values and Public Policy.* Washington, D.C.: The Brookings Institution, 1994:20.

YATES, RONALD E. "Growing Old in Japan; They Ask Gods for a Way Out." *Philadelphia Inquirer* (August 14, 1986):3A.

YEATTS, DALE E. "Self-Managed Work Teams: Innovation in Progress." *Business and Economic Quarterly* (Fall–Winter 1991):2–6.

————. "Creating the High Performance Self-Managed Work Team: A Review of Theoretical Perspectives." Paper presented at the annual meeting of the Southwest Social Science Association, Dallas, February 1994.

YODER, JAN D., and ROBERT C. NICHOLS. "A Life Perspective: Comparison of Married and Divorced Persons." *Journal of Marriage and the Family.* Vol. 42, No. 2 (May 1980):413–19.

YOELS, WILLIAM C., and JEFFREY MICHAEL CLAIR. "Laughter in the Clinic: Humor in Social Organization." *Symbolic Interaction.* Vol. 18, No. 1 (1995):39–58.

YUDELMAN, MONTAGUE, and LAURA J. M. KEALY. "The Graying of Farmers." *Population Today.* Vol. 28, No. 4 (May/June, 2000):6.

ZACHARY, G. PASCAL. "Not So Fast: Neo-Luddites Say an Unexamined Cyberlife Is a Dangerous One." *Wall Street Journal* (June 16, 1997):R18.

ZALMAN, MARVIN, and STEVEN STACK. "The Relationship between Euthanasia and Suicide in the Netherlands: A Time Series Analysis, 1950–1990." *Social Science Quarterly.* Vol. 77, No. 3 (September 1996):576–93.

ZANGWILL, ISRAEL. *The Melting Pot.* Macmillan, 1921; orig. 1909.

ZBOROWSKI, MARK. *People in Pain.* San Francisco: Jossey-Bass, 1969.

ZEITLIN, IRVING M. *The Social Condition of Humanity.* New York: Oxford University Press, 1981.

ZHAO, DINGXIN. "Ecologies of Social Movements: Student Mobilization during the 1989 Prodemocracy Movement in Beijing." *American Journal of Sociology.* Vol. 103, No. 6 (May 1998):1493–1529.

ZHOU, MIN, and JOHN R. LOGAN. "Returns of Human Capital in Ethnic Enclaves: New York City's Chinatown." *American Sociological Review.* Vol. 54, No. 5 (October 1989):809–20.

ZHOU, XUEGUANG, and LIREN HOU. "Children of the Cultural Revolution: The State and the Life Course in the People's Republic of China." *American Sociological Review.* Vol. 64, No. 1 (February 1999):12–36.

ZICKLIN, G. "Re-Biologizing Sexual Orientation: A Critique." Paper presented at the Annual Meeting of the Society for the Study of Social Problems, Pittsburgh, Penn., 1992.

ZIMBARDO, PHILIP G. "Pathology of Imprisonment." *Society.* Vol. 9 (April 1972):4–8.

ZUBOFF, SHOSHANA. "New Worlds of Computer-Mediated Work." *Harvard Business Review.* Vol. 60, No. 5 (September–October 1982):142–52.

ZURCHER, LOUIS A., and DAVID A. SNOW. "Collective Behavior and Social Movements." In Morris Rosenberg and Ralph Turner, eds., *Social Psychology: Sociological Perspectives.* New York: Basic Books, 1981:447–82.

PHOTO CREDITS

Paul W. Liebhardt, *ii*; George Breithaupt, *xxxiii*

CHAPTER 1: Smithsonian American Art Museum/Art Resource, N.Y., *xxxiv*; Ed Bock/Corbis/Stock Market, *1*; Caroline Penn/Corbis, *2 (top, left)*; Paul W. Liebhardt, *2 (top, center; bottom, left; bottom, center; bottom, right)*; Minh-Thu Pham, *2 (top, right)*; Lineair/Peter Arnold, Inc., *7*; Getty Images, Inc., *11 (left)*; Simon Bening, *April: Farmyard with Woman Milking Cow*, from *Da Costa Book of Hours*. Bruges, c. 1515. © The Pierpont Morgan Library, New York. M.399,F.5V/Art Resource, N.Y., *11 (right)*; Private Collection/The Stapleton Collection/The Bridgeman Art Library International Ltd., *12*; Corbis, *13 (left)*; Brown Brothers, *13 (right)*; Janet Marqusee Fine Arts Ltd., *15*; Brown Brothers, *16*; Paul Marcus/Studio SPM Inc., *17*; Christie's Images/The Bridgeman Art Library International Ltd., *18*.

CHAPTER 2: Scala/Art Resource, N.Y., *24*; Photo by Ruben Burrell/Courtesy of Hampton University, *25*; Index/The Bridgeman Art Library. ©2003 Banco de Mexico Diego Rivera & Frida Kahlo Museums Trust. Av. Cinco de Mayo No., 2, Col. Centro, Del. Cuauhtemoc 06059, Mexico, D.F., *27*; John Eastcott/Yva Momatiuk/The Image Works, *28*; Bob Daemmrich/Stock Boston, *30*; Doranne Jacobson/International Images, *32*; Argas/Getty Images, *33 (right)*; Steve McCurry/Magnum Photos, Inc., *33 (left)*; Tony Freeman/PhotoEdit, *37*; Philip G. Zimbardo, Inc., Department of Psychology, Stanford University, *38*; Congressional Black Caucus of the U.S. Congress, *41*; Carol Beckwith and Angela Fisher/Robert Estall Photo Agency, *44 (right)*; David Bradnum/Robert Estall Photo Agency, *44 (left)*.

CYBER.SCOPE PART I: Eugene Fisher Photography Worldwide, *54*; General Electric Company, *55*.

CHAPTER 3: Schalkwijk/Art Resource, N.Y., *58*; Sion Touhig/Corbis/Sygma, *59*; Paul W. Liebhardt, *60 (top, left; middle, left)*; Carlos Humberto/TDC/Contact/Corbis/Stock Market, *60 (top, center)*; Doranne Jacobson/International Images, *60 (top, right)*; David Austen/Stock Boston, *60 (middle, center)*; Getty Images, Inc., *60 (middle, right)*; Doranne Jacobson/International Images, *60 (bottom, left)*; Jack Fields/Photo Researchers, Inc., *60 (bottom, right)*; J. Humer/Getty Images, Inc., *62*; Dimitri Lovetsky/AP/Wide World Photos, *61*; Jeff Greenberg/Index Stock Imagery, Inc., *64 (left)*; Pedrick/The Image Works, *64 (center)*; CLEO Photo/Jeroboam, Inc., *64 (right)*; *Mrs. Picasso Dusts the Mantlepiece*, from *Great Housewives of Art* by Sally Swain. Copyright ©1988, 1989 by Sally Swain. Used by permission of Viking Penguin, a division of Penguin Putnam, Inc., *67*; Jeff Greenberg/PhotoEdit, *68*; Margaret Courtney-Clarke/Tom Keller and Associates LLC, *70*; Canapress/E.J. Flynn, *75*; Catherine Karnow/Corbis, *76*; J. P. Laffont/Corbis/Sygma, *79*; Jessie Levine, Laguna Sales, Palo Alto, *80*; Photographer Bill Coleman, www.amishphoto.com, (814) 238-8495 #174 *One Day's Work*, *82*; Copyright 1952, 1980 Ruth Orkin/Getty Images, Inc., *83*.

CHAPTER 4: Arnaudet/Art Resource, N.Y., *88*; ©1996, *The Washington Post*, photo by Carol Guzy, reprinted with permission, *89*; Patrick Bordes/Photo Researchers, Inc., *90*; Victor Englebert/Photo Researchers, Inc., *91*; Robert Frerck/Woodfin Camp & Associates, *92*; Getty Images, Inc., *95 (left)*; Corbis/Sygma, *95 (right)*; Corbis, *100*; Norbert Goeneutte *The Paupers' Meal on a Winter Day in Paris*. Waterhouse and Dodd, London. Fine Art Photographic Library, London/Art Resource, N.Y., *98*; Charles Steiner/The Image Works, *102*; The Granger Collection, *103*; D.C. Moore Gallery, *106*; Elliot Landy/Magnum Photos, Inc., *107 (left; center, left; center right)*; Robert Sorbo/AP/Wide World Photos, *107 (right)*; Paul W. Liebhardt, *108*.

CHAPTER 5: The Bridgeman Art Library International Ltd., *114*; Blair Seitz/Photo Researchers, Inc., *115*; Ted Horowitz/ Corbis/Stock Market, *116 (left)*; Henley & Savage/Corbis/Stock Market, *116 (center)*; Tom Pollack, *116 (right)*; Bettmann/Corbis, *117*; William Kurelek, *Prairie Childhood*, by permission of the Estate of William Kurelek, courtesy of the Isaacs Gallery of Toronto, *118*; Elizabeth Crews/Elizabeth Crews Photography, *120*; Rimma Gerlovina and Valeriy Gerlovin. *122*; Hampton University Museum, *124*; Mary Ellen Mark, *129*; Eastcott/Momatiuk/Woodfin Camp & Associates, *133*.

CHAPTER 6: Manu Sassoonian /Art Resource, N.Y., *138*; John Macionis, *139*; Jim Anderson/Woodfin Camp & Associates, *140*; AP/Wide World Photos, *141*; Richard Lord Enterprises, Inc., *142*; DiMaggio/Kalish/Corbis/Stock Market, *144*; David Cooper/Getty Images, Inc., *149 (top, left)*; Alan Weiner/Getty Images, Inc., *149 (top, center)*; Lynn McLaren/Index Stock Imagery, Inc., *149 (top, right)*; Guido Rossi/Getty Images, Inc., *149 (bottom, left)*; Richard Pan, *149 (bottom, center)*; Costa Manos/Magnum Photos, Inc., *149 (bottom, right)*; Paul Ekman, Ph.D. Professor of Psychology, University of California, San Francisco, *151 (left and right)*; Paul W. Liebhardt, *150 (left; center; right)*; Michael Newman/PhotoEdit, *154*; Jason Plotkin/*The York Dispatch*/AP/Wide World Photos, *157*; Angela Maynard/Getty Images, Inc./PhotoDisc, Inc., *153*; Myrleen Ferguson/PhotoEdit, *158*.

CHAPTER 7: The Bridgeman Art Library International Ltd, *162*; Nik Wheeler/Corbis, *163*; Galen Rowell/Peter Arnold, Inc., *164*; Jonathan Green Studios, Inc., *169*; Dan Habib/Impact Visuals Photo & Graphics, Inc., *170*; Cliché Bibliotheque nationale de France, Paris. From *The Horizon History of China* by the editors of Horizon Magazine, The Horizon Publishing Co., Inc., 551 5th Avenue, New York, N.Y. 10017. ©1969, *174*; Paul W. Liebhardt, *177*; The Metropolitan Museum of Art, *176*; Jose Luis Pelaez, Inc./Corbis/Stock Market, *179*; Michael S. Yamashita/Corbis, *180*; Gabe Palmer/Corbis/Stock Market, *182*; Saleh Rifai/AP/Wide World Photos, *184*.

CHAPTER 8: Noah's Ark Fine Art, *190*; Pat Sullivan/AP/Wide World Photos, *191*; SIPA Press, *193*; Cliff Owen/UPI/Corbis, *194*; Paul W. Liebhardt, *196*; Edward Gargan/New York Times Pictures, *199*; Stan Honda/Agence France-Presse, *200*; Andrew Lichtenstein/The Image Works, *201*; Danny Hellman, *203*; S. Liss/Corbis/Sygma, *205*; Rich Pedroncelli/AP/Wide World Photos, *207*; Paul Marcus/Studio SPM Inc., *209*; Washoe County, Nevada Police Department, *213*.

CHAPTER 9: Tate Gallery/Art Resource, N.Y., *220*; Kim D. Johnson/*The Sacramento Bee*, *221*; Andre Gallant/Getty Images, Inc., *222 (top, left)*; Pete Turner/Getty Images, Inc., *222 (top, center)*; Brun/Photo Researchers, Inc., *222 (top, right)*; Bruno Hadijh/Getty Images, Inc., *222 (bottom, left)*; Elliot Erwitt/Magnum Photos, Inc., *222 (bottom, center)*; George Holton/Photo Researchers, Inc., *222 (bottom, right)*; Thomas Friedmann/Photo Researchers, Inc., *223*; David McCoy/Rainbow, *225*; John Marshall Mantel/Corbis, *231*; Mark Peterson/Corbis/SABA Press Photos, Inc., *237*; AKG London Ltd., *239*.

CYBER.SCOPE PART II: T. Crosby/Getty Images, Inc., *244*; The Cartoon Bank, *245*.

CHAPTER 10: Paul Marcus/Studio SPM Inc., *246*; Illustration by Ken Marshall ©1992 from *Titanic: An Illustrated History*, a Viking Studio/Madison Press Book, *247*; Sebastiao Salgado/Contact Press Images Inc., *248*; Doranne Jacobson/International Images, *249*; Per-Anders Pettersson/Black Star, *251*; John Launois/Black Star, *253*; Francisco Conde/Impact Visuals Photo & Graphics, Inc., *254*; Bridgeman Art Library/London/SuperStock, Inc., *256*; Kevork Djansezian/AP/Wide World Photos, *258*; The Granger Collection, *260*; Doranne Jacobson/International Images, *262*; Ford Madox Brown (1821-93) *Work*. SuperStock, Inc., *265*.

NAME INDEX

Walczak, David, 421
Waldfogel, Jane, 336
Waldman, Steven, 480
Walker, Karen, 282, 480
Walker-Taylor, Yvonne, 42
Wall, Thomas F., 399, 473, 553
Wallace, Michael, 615-16
Wallace, Ruth A., 326, 328, 339, 343-44
Waller, Douglas, 456
Wallerstein, Immanuel, 315-16, 480
Wallerstein, Judith S., 429, 480, 482
Walmsley, Roy, 214-15
Walsh, Mary Williams, 394
Walsleben, Marjorie C., 529
Walton, John, 316, 429
Walton, Sam, 263
Warfield, David, 221
Warhol, Andy, 220
Waring, Elin, 202
Waring, Joan, 133
Warner, Barbara D., 197
Warner, R. Stephen, 510
Warner, W. Lloyd, 276-77
Warr, Mark, 197
Waskul, Dennis, 245
Waters, Malcolm, 641
Waters, Melissa S., 507
Watson, John B., 116, 122
Watson, John Keith, 507
Watson, Russell, 454
Watson, Thomas, 54
Wattenberg, Ben J., 574, 576
Watts, Duncan J., 170
Weber, A., 579
Weber, Adna Ferrin, 579
Weber, Marianne, 102
Weber, Max, 17, 32-34, 46, 89, 102-3, 106, 108-11, 113, 176-77, 185, 259-62, 268, 311, 419, 435-37, 459, 494-96, 515, 628, 632-33, 635, 639, 646
Webster, Murray, Jr., 141
Webster, Pamela S., 482
Weeks, John R., 500-501
Weicher, John C., 277
Weidenbaum, Murray, 427

Weinberg, Martin S., 483
Weinberg, Nancy, 171
Weiner, Norbert, 55
Weiner, Tim, 456
Weinreich, Max, 77
Weinrich, James D., 229
Weisberg, D. Kelley, 231, 235
Weisburd, David, 202
Weitzman, Lenore J., 10, 131, 283, 478, 480
Wellborn, Charles T., 503
Weller, Jack M., 601, 603, 606
Wellford, Charles, 201
Wells-Barnett, Ida, 368
Werner, Perla, 398
Wertheimer, Barbara Mayer, 411
Wesolowski, Wlodzimierz, 440
West, Elizabeth, 614
Western, Bruce, 421
Whalen, Jack, 613
Wheeler, Stanton, 202
Whelan, Christine B., 480
Whipple, Thomas W., 332
Whitaker, Mark, 452
White, Geoffrey M., 148
White, Jack E., 356
White, Lynn, 479
White, Ralph, 166
White, Walter, 604
Whitehead, Barbara Dafoe, 483
White-Means, Shelly, 558
Whitman, David, 292
Whittier, Nancy, 614
Wholstein, Ronald T., 603
Whorf, Benjamin Lee, 65
Whyte, William Foote, 44-45
Whyte, William H., Jr., 177
Wiarda, Frank D., 314
Wiatrowski, Michael A., 201
Wickham, DeWayne, 292
Widom, Cathy Spatz, 481
Widstrand, Carl, 592
Wiener, Anthony, 643
Wike, Richard S., 64
Wilcox, Clyde, 339, 513
Wilde, Marta L., 128
Wilde, Oscar, 155, 388
Wiles, P. J. D., 418
Willer, David, 170

Williams, Allen J., 444
Williams, Rhys H., 509
Williams, Richard A., 525
Williams, Robin, 618
Williams, Robin M., Jr., 69, 81, 398
Williamson, Jeffrey G., 263
Wilson, Barbara, 129
Wilson, Bryan, 503
Wilson, David, 585
Wilson, Edward O., 594
Wilson, James, 185
Wilson, James Q., 192
Wilson, Janet K., 200
Wilson, Margo, 192
Wilson, Thomas C., 583
Wilson, William Julius, 25, 33, 290-91, 370
Winfield, Idee, 171
Winfield-Laird, Idee, 252, 285
Winfrey, Oprah, 258-59
Wingert, Pat, 482
Winkler, Karen, 121
Winship, Christopher, 217
Winters, Rebecca, 335
Wirth, Louis, 583, 584, 597-98
Witkin, Gordon, 217
Witkin-Lanoil, Georgia, 116
Witt, G. Evans, 40
Wojtkiewicz, Roger A., 482
Wolf, Diane L., 34
Wolf, Naomi, 131, 332-33
Wolfe, David B., 388
Wolfgang, Marvin E., 209, 215
Wolfson, Adam, 401
Wolkomir, Michelle, 599
Wong, Buck, 371
Wood, Daniel B., 497
Wood, James L., 601
Woodberry, Robert D., 507
Woodhull, Victoria, 338
Woodman, Cousin, 449
Woodrum, Eric, 599
Woodward, Charlotte, 325
Woodward, Kenneth L., 128, 495, 505
Wooley, Orland W., 541
Wooley, Susan C., 541
Worden, Steven K., 614

Wordsworth, William, 60
Worsley, Peter, 317
Wren, Christopher S., 251
Wright, Erik Olin, 260
Wright, J., 210-11
Wright, James D., 196, 292, 480, 484
Wright, Quincy, 453
Wright, Richard A., 458
Wright, Robert, 171, 187
Wright, Stuart A., 613
Wu, Lawrence L., 482
Wyman, Bill, 466
Wyman, Stephen, 466
Wynter, Leon E., 406

Xie, Wen, 274

Yamagata, Hisashi, 337
Yang, Fenggang, 510
Yang, Yu, 547
Yankelovich, Daniel, 486
Yates, Ronald E., 392
Yeatts, Dale E., 182
Yeh, Kuang S., 337
Yeltsin, Boris, 255
Yeung, W. Jean, 133, 283, 288, 475, 482
Yinger, J. Milton, 363
Yinger, Richard E., 457
Yoder, Jan D., 479
Yoels, William C., 158-59, 531
Yudelman, Montague, 390

Zachary, G. Pascal, 245
Zafonte, Matthew, 427
Zald, Mayer N., 601, 613-16
Zangwill, Israel, 363
Zarycky, George, 417
Zeitlin, Irving M., 98
Zhang, Joshua, 196
Zhao, Dingxin, 614
Zhou, Min, 371
Zimbardo, Philip, 38-39, 48
Zimring, Franklin E., 217
Zuboff, Shoshana, 425
Zurcher, Louis A., 606, 614

SUBJECT INDEX

Abkhasians, 391
Aborigines, 90
Abortion, 239-41, 346, 443-44, 513, 576
Absolute monarchy, 438, 440
Absolute poverty, 286, 304-5
Academic standards, 266, 533-34
Achieved status, 140-41
Achievement, as value, 67
Acid rain, 592
Acquaintance rape (see Date rape)
Acquired immune deficiency syndrome (AIDS), 226, 235, 545, 550-52, 614-15
    HIV infection, global map, 551
    types of transmission as of 2000, 553
Acting crowds, 603
Active euthanasia, 553
Activity, value of, 67

Activity theory of aging, 397-98
Addictions, 68
Adolescence, 131
    identity development, 132
Adoption, by gay couples, 483
Adult education, 536
Adultery (see Extramarital sex)
Adulthood, 131
Advertising, gender role representation, 332-33
Affirmative action, 349, 378-79
Affluence (see Income; Wealth)
Afghanistan, 318, 328, 452, 453, 455, 457, 501
AFL-CIO (see American Federation of Labor-Congress of Industrial Organizations [AFL-CIO])
Africa, 73, 301, 304, 314, 319, 328, 334, 342, 518, 519, 591
    (see also global maps, specific countries)

and AIDS, 550, 551
colonization of, 315
African Americans (see also Race)
    affirmative action, 378-79
    and affluence, 47, 277
    and Afrocentrism, 76
    and aging, 394
    in cities, 584
    and civil rights movement, 364, 369, 494, 612, 614, 617, 618
    and crime, 209-10
    and development of sociology, 13
    and education, 3, 525, 526, 532
    elite, 41-43
    and family, 474, 476-77, 482
    family income, 275
    and feminism, 347

geographic distribution of, national map, 374
great women, 368
and health, 547-48, 552
and infant mortality, 548
intelligence debate, 360-61
Jim Crow, 369, 378, 612
in labor force, 418
life expectancy, 544-46
lynching of, 604
and mass media, 128
in medicine, 554
party identification, 445
in politics, 369-70
population, national map, 357
population growth, 357
and poverty, 209, 287, 476
and racism, 25, 41-43, 359
and religion, 508
residential patterns of affluent, 47

defined, 415
and democracy, 438
and deviance, 202
elements of, 415–16
federal government activities, 415–16
and gender stratification, 344, 345, 347
and health care, 553–55
Marx on, 97–98, 256, 259–60
and medicine, 560–61
and modernity, 633
and Protestantism, 494–95
and rationality, 103–5
relative advantages of, 418
and social change, 619, 626, 627
compared to socialism, 418, 438, 440
state capitalism, 418, 457
and urbanization, 585
welfare capitalism, 417, 457
Capitalist world economy, 315–16
Capitalists, defined, 97
Capital punishment
global map, 212
and retribution, 213–14
as social issue, 444
in U.S., national map, 216
Caregiving, 394
Case studies, 43
Caste system, 248–50
Casual crowds, 603
Category, 163
Catholic Church, 105, 312, 437, 500, 503, 506
and liberation theology, 495–96
schools of, 525
Catholics, 353, 355
and suicide, 3
Caucasian, 355
Cause and effect, 30–31
Cellular telephones, 54, 412, 442
Chad, 302, 328
Charisma, defined, 497
Charismatic authority, 436–37
Charter schools, 535
Chastity belt, 239
Chattel slavery, 307
Chechnya, 455
Chicago School, 583
Chicanos, 373, 375
Child abuse, 115, 117–18, 481
Child custody, 349, 479–80
Childhood, stage of, 129–31
Child labor, 79, 311, 410, 518–19
global map, 130
Child rearing, 473–74
and maternal employment, 336–37
Children (see also Family)
and cognitive development, 119–20
and development of self, 122–23
and divorce, 479–80
"hurried child" syndrome, 130–31
and moral development, 120–22
and poverty, 287–88, 305–7
in single-parent family, 482
and socialization (see Socialization)
street children, 305–7
Child slavery, 308
Child support, 479–80, 481
Child weddings, 471
Chile, 301, 302, 347, 440
Chinatowns, 363, 370

Chinese Americans, 360, 363, 370–71, 377
Chinese language, 66
Chosen Women, 513
Christianity, 92, 437, 492, 508
global map, 499
history and beliefs of, 499–500
women, status of, 494–95
Chromosomes, and sex differentiation, 222
Church
black, 508
defined, 496
electronic, 511, 513
Church of Jesus Christ of the Latter Day Saints (Mormons), 505, 506, 510
Cigarette smoking, 402, 548–49
Circumcision, male and female, 238
Cities (see also Urbanization)
evolution of, 10, 578–79
homeless in, 293
new shape of, 648
suburbs, 580
theories of urbanization, 582–84
U.S. growth of, 579–82
City-states, 437
Civil law, defined, 203
Civil religion, 508
Civil Rights Act of 1964, 379
Civil rights movement, 82, 141, 359, 364, 369, 494, 612, 614, 617, 618
Civil service examinations, first, 174
Civil War, 580, 612
Class conflict, 99–100
Class consciousness, 99–100
Class-society theory, 635–37
Class system, 250–56
Closed-end format, 40
Cockfighting, 198
Coercive organizations, 173
Cognitive development, 119–20
Cohabitation, 482–83
as family of affinity, 464
Cohort, defined, 133
Cold War, 457
Coleman report, 527
Collective behavior, 601–20 (see also Social movements)
crowds, 164, 603–6
defined, 601
fashions and fads, 609–10
mobs and riots, 603–4
panic and mass hysteria, 609
public opinion and propaganda, 608–9
rumor and gossip, 606–8
theories of, 604–6
Collective conscience, 108
Collective ownership, 416
Collectivities, 602–3
College
access to, 527–28
and African Americans, 369
areas of study and gender, 337–38
attendance, national map, 527
attendance and family income, 2, 3, 528
completion as personal merit, 528
cost of, 527–28
degrees, 521, 522
gender gap, 537
gender and later income, 528
and integration, 170
student activism, 618
student attitudes, 77

student passivity, 531–32
trends in bachelor's degrees, 522
College students, date rape, 237
Colombia, 211
Colonial cities, 579
Colonialism, 309, 315, 641
and genocide, 364
and slavery, 367–68
Command economy, 416
Common sense, versus scientific evidence, 27–28
Commonwealth of Independent States (see Russian Federation; Soviet Union)
Communications (see also Information Revolution)
advances and society, 103
global, 81
high-tech methods, 412, 442, 457
industrial era inventions, 94
organizational, 176
satellite, 54, 81, 442
Communism, 254
defined, 98, 417
and socialism, 417
Communitarian movement, 644–45
Community, loss of, 629, 630–31
Community policing, 217
Comparable worth policy, 336
Competition, and capitalism, 415
Competitive work teams, 182
Complementarity, and gender, 344
Computers (see also Information Revolution)
global map, 104
Concentric zone urban model, 585
Concept, 28
Concrete operational stage (Piaget), 120
Conflict (see also Social conflict)
and humor, 158–59
role, 143
of values, 69
Conflict subculture, 196
Conflict theory of prejudice, 361
Conformity
group, 166–67
versus deviance, 195
Confucianism, 11, 496, 507, 518
history and beliefs of, 504–5
Conglomerates, 426–27
Congo, Democratic Republic of the, 264, 302, 304, 440, 595
Conjugal family, 465
Consanguine family, 464
Conscience, 119, 200
Conservatism, and fundamentalism, 511, 513
Conservative politics, 444
Consolidated metropolitan statistical areas (CMSAs), 580–81
Conspicuous consumption, 278, 281, 609
Constitutional monarchy, 438
Contagion theory of crowd behavior, 604–5
Containment theory, 193
Contraception, 225, 312, 329, 346, 574, 577
global use of, 227
and poor, 307
"the pill," 225
Control, scientific, 31
Control group, 37

Control theory (Hirschi), 200–201
Controversy, and humor, 157
Conventional crowds, 603
Convergence theory of crowd behavior, 605
Conversion, religious, 497
Corporate crime, 203
Corporations, 425–29
agribusiness, 420
and competition, 427
conglomerates, 426–27
corporate welfare, 426
downsizing, 285–86, 291, 422
and global economy, 427–28
government regulation of, 429
multinational, 309, 316, 427–29, 442
sizes of, 426
women in, 424
Correlation of variables, 31–32
spurious, 31
Costa Rica, 586
Cottage industry, 410
Countercultures, 77, 94
Coup d'état, 450
Court system, 213
Courtship, 471–72
Covenant marriage, 480
Creationism, 512
Creative autonomy, of workers, 182
Credentialism, 528
Credit, and personal privacy, 186
Crime, 111, 206–11 (see also Violence)
against person, 206
components of, 206
defined, 191
Durkheim on, 107
and gender, 206, 208, 349
global perspective, 210–11
hate, 204
property, 206
prostitution, 232, 234–35
punishment, 214–15
and race and ethnicity, 209–10
rates in U.S., 208
and social class, 209
statistics, 206, 207
victimless, 207
white-collar, 202–3
Crime in the United States, 206
Criminal justice system, 211–15
defined, 192
Criminal law, defined, 203
Criminal recidivism, 215
Criminal subculture, 196
Critical sociology, 34–35
Croats, 454
Crowds, 164, 603–6
Crude birth rate, 570
Crude death rate, 570
Crusades, 493, 501
Cuba, 194, 263, 264, 315, 417, 438, 440
Cuban Americans, 375–76
Cults, 497–98
Cultural capital, 281
Cultural conventions, 326
Cultural diversity, 72–81, 169–70 (see also Ethnicity; Race; Social diversity)
counterculture, 77
and cultural change, 77–80
cultural relativism, 79–80
and deviance, 204–6
ethnocentrism, 79
multiculturalism, 75–76
subculture, 74
in workplace, 424–25

Egypt, 92, 93, 301, 321, 342, 347, 501, 585, 590–91
  population control and women, 577
Egypt, ancient, 224
El Salvador, 2, 302, 358
Elderly (*see also* Aging)
  in global population (2020), global map, 385
  as outsiders, 8
  population statistics for U.S., 385–86
  as share of population, national map, 387
Electronic church, 511, 513
Electronic mail, 56, 176, 442
  survey research, 40
Electronic town meetings, 458
Embarrassment, 152–53
Emergent-norm theory of crowd behavior, 606
Emigration, 571
Emotions, expression and culture, 148–49
Empirical evidence, 26
Empty nest, 474
Enclosure movement, 10
Endogamous marriage, 249, 465, 468
Energy consumption, 587
Energy sources, steam engine, 410
English language, 66, 76, 81, 153–55, 355, 367
Enlightenment, 214
Environment, organizational, 175
Environment (*see* Natural environment)
Environmental deficit, 587, 595
Environmental movement, strategies of, 595
Environmental racism, 594–95
Equal opportunity, 67, 521
Equal Rights Amendment (ERA), 345–46
Equality, value of, 271
Eros, 118–19
Eskimo, 229
Espionage, 211
Estate system, 252
Estonia, 301, 419
Ethics
  and death, 399–401, 403, 552–53
  and health, 399–401, 552–53
  and reproductive technology, 484
  and research, 36
Ethiopia, 2, 302, 317, 321, 440, 543
  gross domestic product (GDP), 304
Ethnicity (*see also* specific categories of people)
  categories, 356
  defined, 355
  and Information Revolution, 407
  minority-majority population, national map, 357
  and poverty, 287
  and religion, 507–8
  and social mobility, 283
  and social stratification, 275–76
Ethnic jokes, 158–59
Ethnic villages, 363, 376, 377
Ethnocentrism, 79
Ethnographies, 43
Ethnomethodology, 145–46
Eurocentrism, 76

Euthanasia, 400–401, 553
Evolution, 83, 257
  creationism issue, 512
  sociocultural, 90–96, 262
Exogamy, 465
Experiment, 36–39
  goal of, 36
Experimental group, 37
Expressions, facial, 148–49
Expressive crowds, 603
Expressive leadership, 165–66
Expressive traits, 344
Extended family, 464
Extinction, plants and animals, 594
Extramarital sex, 228, 473
Eye contact, in communication, 150

Facial expressions, 148–49
Facsimile (fax) machines, 54, 412
Factory system, 10, 54, 410, 420
Fads, 610
Faith, religious, 492
False consciousness, 98
Family
  African American, 209, 275, 476–77, 482
  and aging, 474
  alternative forms, 481–84
  Asian American, 210, 482
  and authority, 436
  basic concepts, 463–64
  blended, 480
  and caregiving, 394
  and child rearing, 336–37, 473–74
  defined, 463
  and divorce, 463, 478–80, 485, 486
  female-headed, 287, 289, 375, 476–77, 482
  and gender, 477–78
  and gender socialization, 330–31
  in global perspective, 464–66
  homeless families, 292
  incest taboo, 224
  and industrialization, 94
  and Information Revolution, 567
  in later life, 474
  in modern society, 11
  and new reproductive technology, 484
  patterns of descent, 465–66
  and race and ethnicity, 476–77
  recent trends in, 463
  residential patterns, 465
  single-parent, 209, 275, 287, 289, 482
  size, 473, 474
  and social class, 474–75
  social class and experiences, 281–82
  social-conflict analysis of, 469–70
  social-exchange analysis of, 470
  and socialization, 467
  stages of life, 471–74
  structural-functional analysis of, 467–69
  in Sweden, 466–67, 483
  symbolic-interaction analysis of, 470
  traditional, 486–87
  in twenty-first century, 484–85
  violence in, 340, 481
Family of affinity, 464
Family and Medical Leave Act, 474
Family of orientation, 464

Family of procreation, 464
Family unit, 464
"Family values" agenda, 226, 444, 474
Fascism, 440
Fashions, 609–10
Fecundity, 570
Federal Bureau of Investigation (FBI), crime statistics, 206, 207
"Female advantage," 179–80
Female circumcision, 238
Female genital mutilation, 340, 341–42
Female-headed families, 287, 289, 375, 476–77, 482
Female infanticide, 465
Feminine traits, 327, 330 (*see also* Gender)
Feminism, 345–348, 641 (*see also* Women's movement)
  basic concepts, 345–46
  defined, 345
  forms of, 346–47
  opposition to, 347–48
  and religion, 495
Feminist research, 34
Feminization of poverty, 287, 289
Fertility, 570, 576–78
Feudalism, 98, 253
Fieldwork, 43–45
Fifteenth Amendment, 369, 446
Fiji, 541
Filipino Americans, 370, 373, 377
Financial exchanges, 301
Finland, 126, 328
First estate, 252
First World, 299–300
Flexibility, organizational, 182–83, 185
Flirting, 144
Folkways, as norm, 70
Food production, 312–13, 316
Foot-binding, 330
Force, versus authority, 435
Foreign aid, 314
Formal communications, and bureaucracy, 175
Formal operational stage (Piaget), 120
Formal organizations (*see also* Bureaucracy)
  future view, 185
  and gender, 179–80
  Japanese, 180–81
  and personal privacy, 186–87
  and race, 178, 179
  compared to small groups, 175
  types of, 173–75
France, 71, 232, 295, 442, 455, 557
  gross domestic product (GDP), 304
Freedom
  and capitalism, 418
  culture as, 85
  economic (capitalism versus socialism), 418
  political, global map, 439
  and socialization, 135
  value of, 68
  versus social responsibility, 644–45
Freedom fighters, 452, 453
Freedom Summer, 617
Free enterprise, as value, 68
Free will, 1
French Revolution, 11, 450, 612
Function, social, 107 (*see also* Structural-functional paradigm)

Functional illiteracy, 533–34
Fundamentalism, religious, 318, 501, 510–11, 513
Funerals, 82

Gambling, 193, 198
Games
  and gender, 331
  and learning, 123
"Gay gene," 229
Gay people (*see also* Homosexuality; Lesbians)
  and AIDS, 550–52, 614–15
  couples, 483, 485
  gay rights movement, 231, 628
  and hate crimes, 204, 205
  homophobia, 231
  in military, 69, 329
  as outsiders, 8
  prostitution by, 235
  sexual orientation theories, 229–30
  in U.S. population, 230
Gay rights movement, 231, 628
GDP (*see* Gross domestic product [GDP])
Gemeinschaft, 582, 630–31, 634, 638
Gender (*see also* Feminism; Men; Women)
  and aging, 386, 392–93, 394
  and athletic performance, 326, 327
  and caregiving, 394
  and child rearing, 336–37
  and college degrees, 337–38, 528
  and complementarity, 344
  and crime, 208, 349
  and cultural variables, 325–30
  defined, 325
  and deviance, 204–5
  and discrimination, 337–38
  and divorce, 479–80
  and double standard, 35, 225, 226
  and education, 331, 337–38, 521, 524, 527
  equality, global view, 328
  extramarital sex, 228
  and eye contact, 152
  and family, 331, 477–78
  feminine traits, 327, 330
  and formal organization, 179–80
  global comparisons, 326–27
  and health, 546
  and income, 283–84, 336–37, 528
  and inequality, 325–30
  and infanticide, 465
  and Information Revolution, 407
  and intelligence, 326
  Japan, stratification, 253
  and language, 153–55
  and leadership, 165
  and life expectancy, 326, 349, 384
  and marriage, 477–78
  masculine traits, 327, 328, 330, 547
  in mass media, 332–33
  Mead's study, 326–27
  and military, 339
  and moral development, 121–22, 331
  and networks, 171
  and occupations, 274, 283, 335
  in organizations, 274
  and patriarchy, 328–30, 469

Impersonality, 105
  and bureaucracy, 175
Impression management, 147
Incarceration, 214–15
Incest taboo, 224, 236, 467–68
Inclusive education, 536
Income
  affluent minorities, national
    map, 47
  African Americans, 275, 283,
    369
  and aging, 394
  Asian Americans, 275, 370
  and college attendance, 3,
    527–28
  of college graduates, 528, 529
  disparity, global view, 273
  and education, 532
  and gender, 283–84, 336–37,
    528
  global, distribution of, 300
  global map, 264
  and health, 281, 548
  and health care, 558
  Hispanic Americans, 275, 283,
    375
  Kuznets curve, 263–65
  per capita U.S., national map,
    289
  and political apathy, 448
  and social inequality, 272
  and social mobility, 283
  and social worth, 258
  U.S. family (1950–2000), 285
  U.S. family (1980–2000), 283
  U.S. family (2000), 272–73
  and values, 281
Independent variable, 30, 36–37
India, 210, 303, 308, 316, 317,
  321, 347, 439, 473, 595
  caste system in, 248–49
  education in, 518–19
  infant mortality, 578
  marriage in, 471
  and nuclear weapons, 455
  poverty in, 310
  religion in, 493, 500, 503
Indians, American (see Native
  Americans)
Individualism, 61, 68, 181, 312,
  442, 478–79
Individuality, social context, 3–5
Individualization, 629
Individual liberty, 11
Individual rights, 11, 68, 438
Indonesia, 301, 455, 500
Inductive logical thought, 47–48
Industrialism, defined, 93
Industrialization (see also Work)
  and aging, 390
  and education, 518, 520
  and energy consumption, 587
  and energy sources, 93–94, 410
  and family, 472, 473
  and fashion, 609
  and growth of cities, 579
  and health, 545
  and modernization, 629
  and natural environment, 587
  and pollution, 592–94
  and population, 575–76
  and religion, 498
  and social change, 619
  and social stratification, 263
Industrial Revolution, 10, 54, 94,
  103, 252, 300, 311
  innovations of, 410
Industrial society (see also
  Industrialization)
  characteristics of, 93–94,
  96–97

Inequality (see Social-conflict
  paradigm; Social stratification)
Inertia
  bureaucratic, 178
  cultural, 311–12
Infanticide, 398
  and gender, 465
Infant mortality, 548
  defined, 571
  rates (2000), global view, 570
Infant mortality rate, 287
Infectious diseases, 385, 543–44,
  563, 578, 592
Infidelity, 473
Information Revolution, 54–57,
  95 (see also Internet)
  and age stratification, 407
  and cultural change, 245
  and culture, 72
  and the economy, 410–12, 566
  and education, 536–37
  and family, 567
  and gender, 407
  and global interconnection, 7
  and global stratification, 407
  and high-income countries, 301
  Internet access across U.S.,
    national map, 56
  and medicine and health, 567
  online democracy, 458
  and politics, 458, 566–67
  and presentation of self, 245
  privacy issues, 186–87
  and race and ethnicity, 407
  and religion, 509, 511
  and social change, 627, 648–49
  and social institutions, 566–67
  and social movements, 648–49
  and social research, 56–57
  and social stratification, 406–7
  and socialization, 244–45
  theoretical analysis of, 55–56,
    109
  and virtual culture, 72
  and war, 456
  and work, 425
Informed consent, 36
Infrastructure, 98
Ingroups, 168
Inheritance, 256, 469
Initiative versus guilt, 124
Inner city, problems of, 291
Innovation, deviance as, 195
Instincts, defined, 62
Institutional discrimination, 362
Institutional prejudice, 362
Institutional sexism, 328
Institutions
  social, 566–67
  total, 133–35, 173, 215
Instrumental leadership, 165–66
Instrumental traits, 344
Insurance, health, 558
Integration
  cultural, 77
  social, 3–4, 523
Intellectuals, and revolution, 450
Intelligence
  and culture, 63
  and gender, 326
  The Bell Curve debate,
    266–67, 360–61
Intelligent organizations, 185
Interaction, symbolic (see Social
  interaction; Symbolic-
  interaction paradigm)
Interdependence, functional, 109
Intergenerational social mobility,
  282
Interlocking directorate, 427

Internet, 56–57 (see also
  Information Revolution)
  access to, 407
  cyber.scopes, 54–57, 244–45,
    406–7, 566–67, 648–49
  global network, 171
  religion on, 511, 513
  for research, 45–46, 56–57
  service, national map, 56
Interpretive sociology, 34
Interracial marriage, 249, 363
Interviews, 41–43
Intragenerational social mobility,
  282
Intravenous drug use, 552
Invention
  and cultural change, 78
  and social change, 627
Invisible hand, 428–29
In vitro fertilization, 484
Iran, 194, 204, 304, 318, 455,
  501, 518
Iraq, 193, 318, 451, 455, 457
Irish Americans, 363, 376
Iron law of oligarchy, 177, 618
Iroquois Indians, 465
Islam, 92, 234, 311, 491, 507
  Balkan conflict, 454
  fundamentalist, 318, 501
  global map of, 499
  history and beliefs of, 498–99
  Middle East conflict, 493
  polygyny, 465
  state church, 496
  women's status, 309, 334, 494,
    495
Israel, 6, 71, 300, 455, 550
  kibbutzim, 326
  Middle East conflict, 493
Issei, 372
Italian Americans, 361, 363, 376
Italy, 417

Japan, 6, 71, 79, 126, 173, 210,
  232, 255, 295, 300, 312, 317,
  347, 354, 413, 418, 427, 442,
  483, 504, 550
  aging in, 390
  culture of, 73
  economy in, 6
  education in, 253, 520
  formal organizations in, 180–81
  gross domestic product (GDP),
    304
  health care in, 557
  medicine, 559
  recycling in, 590
  social stratification in, 252–54
Japanese Americans, 356, 363,
  371–73, 377
Jehovah's Witnesses, 441, 497
Jen, 504
Jericho, 578
Jews, 276, 353, 355, 356,
  376–77, 491
  anti-Semitism, 501–2, 507
  genocide of, 364, 502
  and suicide, 3
Jim Crow laws, 369, 378, 612
Job projections (to 2010),
  national map, 430
Jokes, 155–58 (see also Humor)
Judaism, 92, 505, 507 (see also
  Jews)
  history of beliefs of, 501–3
  and patriarchy, 495–96
Junk mail, 186
Juvenile delinquency, 192

Kaiapo of Brazil, 640
Karma, 504
Kaska Indians, 90

Key informant, 45
Kibbutzim, 326–27
Killing fields, 365
Kinship, 90, 94 (see also Family)
  defined, 463–64
  descent patterns, 465–66
Korean Americans, 363, 370, 373
Korean War, 373
Ku Klux Klan, 612, 619
Kumbh Mela, 503
Kuwait, 440
Kuznets curve, 263–65
Kwashiorkor, 543

Labeling theory, 197, 201, 205
Labor, division of, 109, 344,
  631–32
Labor force (see also Work)
  changing, 333–35
  child labor, global map, 130
  diversity of, 423–24
  participation by sex, race, and
    ethnicity, 419
  in U.S., national map, 419
  women in, 151, 333–35, 410,
    419, 422, 424
Labor unions, 260, 420–21
  and corporate structure, 181
Laissez-faire economy, 415
Laissez-faire leadership, 166, 175
Land mines, 455
Landfills, 589
Language, 64–66
  and cultural transmission,
    64–66, 67
  cyber-symbols, 57
  defined, 65
  diversity across U.S., national
    map, 77
  and gender, 153–55
  global maps, 66
  and military, 145
  and primates, 65
  and social class, 252
Lasers, weaponry, 456
Latchkey children, 474
Latent functions, 14–15
  of schooling, 523
Latin America, 6, 234, 304, 317,
  334, 439, 495–496, 518, 519,
  577 (see also specific
  countries)
Latinos (see Hispanic Americans
  (Latinos))
Latvia, 419
Leadership (see also Authority)
  group, 165–66
  types of, 165–66
Lesbians (see also Gay people;
  Homosexuality)
  couples, 483
  in U.S. population, 230
Liberal feminism, 346
Liberal politics, 444
Liberation theology, 495–96
Libya, 193, 455, 457, 591
Life course
  and family, 471–74
  and socialization, 128–33
Life expectancy, 71, 111,
  384–86, 391, 543
  defined, 571
  and gender, 326, 349, 474
  global map, 389
  increasing, 384–85, 563
  and social change, 626
  in U.S., national map, 546
  for U.S children born in 2000,
    549
Limits to growth thesis, 588

Literacy, 321
  and service worker, 412
Lithuania, 419, 523
  gross domestic product (GDP), 304
Living, standard of, global map, 319
Living wills, 400, 553
Lobbyists, 445
Localized collectivities, 602
Logic of growth thesis, 588
Logical thought, inductive and deductive, 47–48
Looking-glass self, 122
Love, romantic, 472, 479
Lowell factory system, 411
Lower-class, 280
  British, 252
Lower-upper class, 278
Low-income countries, 302–303
  (see also individual topics; specific countries)
  death, median age, global map, 306
  economic development in, 6, 7, 302–3
  gross domestic product in, 6, 304
  health in, 543–45
  and modernization theory, 311
  urban growth in, 586, 595
Low-income earners, 284
Luddites, 245
Lutherans, 505, 506
Lying, detection of, 150, 151
Lynching, 369, 603–4

McCulture, 644
"McDonaldization," 163, 183–85
Machismo, 476
Macro-level orientation, 16–18
Magnet schools, 535
Mainstreaming in schools, 535–36
Majority, minority interactions, 363–65
Malaysia, 272, 301, 304, 567
Malnutrition, 305, 321, 543
Malthusian theory, 574–75, 596
Management
  and race, sex, and ethnicity, 178
  scientific management, 178–79, 182
Manifest functions, 14
Manufacturing, 10
  decline of, 285, 292–93
  and industrialization, 410
Marginality, social, 8
Marital rape, 481
Marriage (see also Family)
  arranged, 471
  average age of, 284
  covenant marriage, 480
  defined, 464
  divorce, 111, 463, 478–80
  and divorce, 486
  endogamous, 249
  endogamous and exogamous, 465
  extramarital sex, 228
  and gender, 477–78
  ideal and real, 472–73
  interracial, 249, 363, 477
  patterns of, 465
  and religion, 493
  remarriage, 480
  same-sex, 483
  servile forms of, 308
  sexual activity in, 472–73
  social class and family, 281–82
  types, global map, 468

Marxism
  on capitalism, 97–98, 256, 259–60
  communist society, view of, 417
  on culture and society, 82
  elements of, 96–102
  on gender inequality, 344–45
  on modernity, 633
  political-economy model, 449
  on religion, 493
  on social change, 627–28
  on social class, 254, 256, 259–61
  and socialist feminism, 347
Masculine traits, 327, 328, 330, 547 (see also Gender)
Mass behavior, 603–10
Mass consumption, 312
Mass hysteria, 609
Mass media (see also Television)
  advertising, 332–33
  and gender, 332–33
  minorities, portrayal of, 128
  national map, 127
  and religion, 511, 513
  and sexuality, 129
  and socialization, 126–28
  and violence, 128–29
Mass production, 312
  and industrialization, 410
Mass-society theory, 613, 617, 633–35, 637–38
Master status
  defined, 141
  race as, 357
  stigma as, 198
Material culture, 61
Materialism, 67, 82, 98
Matriarchy, defined, 328
Matrilineal descent, 466
Matrilocality, 465
Mauritania, 309
"Me" (G. H. Mead), 123–24
Mean, 29
Measurement, 28
Mecca, 501
Mechanical solidarity, 108, 583, 631, 638
Media (see Mass media)
Median, 29
Medicaid, 558
Medical care, in socialist societies, 438
Medicalization of deviance, 199
Medicare, 558
Medicine, 551–556 (see also Health)
  availability of physicians, global map, 544
  in capitalist societies, 557, 560–61
  holistic, 555, 556
  and Information Revolution, 567
  as politics, 561, 563
  scientific medicine, 554, 561
  social-conflict analysis of, 560–61
  in socialist societies, 555–57
  structural-functional analysis of, 558–60
  symbolic-interaction analysis of, 560
  in twenty-first century, 563
  in U.S., 557–58
Megalopolis, 580–81
Melanesians of New Guinea, 238
Melting pot, 75, 363
Men (see also Gender; individual topics)
  athletic performance, 326, 327
  as crime victims, 349

extramarital sex, 228
  and gender differences, 325–26
  and housework, 336
  and intelligence, 326
  and life expectancy, 326
  life expectancy, national map, 546
  male rape, 235
  masculine traits, 327, 328, 330
  masculinity and health, 547
  and parenting, 485
  patriarchy, 328–30
  premarital sex, 226–27
  rights of, 349
  sex characteristics of, 223
  and social mobility, 283
Men's rights movement, 349
Mental illness, and labeling, 199
Mercy killing, 400–401, 553
Meritocracy, 250–51
  defined, 250
Metaphysical stage of history, 12
Methodists, 506
Metropolis, 580
Metropolitan statistical areas (MSAs), 580–81
Mexican Americans, 375, 377
Mexico, 6, 73, 264, 304, 312, 316, 358, 427, 439, 473, 504, 595
  age-sex population pyramid, 573
  street children, 306
Micro-level orientation, 16–18
Middle adulthood, 131
Middle Ages (see also Agrarian societies)
  cities in, 10–11, 578–79
  religion in, 493
  view of crime, 214
Middle class, 278–79
  British, 252
Middle-class slide, 285
Middle East, 342, 353–54
  religious conflict, 493
  water shortage, 590–91
Middle-income countries, 301–2
  (see also individual topics)
  death, median age, global map, 306
  economic development in, 7, 301–2
  gross domestic product in, 6, 304
Middletown study, 449
Migration
  defined, 571
  and global culture, 81
  and human traits, 354
  and social change, 628
Militarism, costs and causes of, 454–55
Military
  gays in, 69, 239
  and gender, 339
  language, 145
Military-industrial complex, 455
Militia counterculture, 77
Minimum wage, 292
  immigrant workers, 358
Minority
  characteristics of, 356–57
  defined, 339
  elderly as, 396
  majority interactions, 363–65
  women as, 339–40
Minority-majority
  national map, 357
  population trends, 584
Miscegenation, 363
Mixed marriages, 477
Mobs, 603–4
Mode, 29

Modernity, 629–41
  defined, 626
  and individual, 637–39
  mass society, 633–35, 637–38
  postmodernity, 626, 641–42
  and progress, 639–41
  social-conflict theory of, 635–37
  structural-functional theory of, 633–35
Modernization
  dimensions of, 629–30
  stages of, 312
Modernization theory of development, 429, 575–76, 642–45
  elements of, 311–14, 318
Modesty, and culture, 224
Moksha, 503
Moldavia, 353
Monarchy, 437–38
Monastery of Christ in the Desert, 511
Money, 93 (see also Income)
Mongoloid (Asians), 355
Monoculture, 73
Monogamy, 462, 465, 468
Monopoly, 427, 429
Monotheism, 500
Montgomery bus boycott, 364
Moral development, 120–22
  and gender, 331
Mores, as norm, 70
Mormons, 505, 506, 510
Morocco, 5, 496
Moro reflex, 116
Mortality (see also Death rate)
  defined, 570
  drop in poor countries, 574–75
Multiculturalism, 75–77, 611
  defined, 63, 75
  language diversity, national map, 77
  proponents and critics of, 76
Multinational corporations, 309, 317, 427–29, 442
Multiracial, as Census Bureau category, 355
Mundugumor of New Guinea, 327
Muslims (see Islam)
Mutually assured destruction (MAD), 455–56
Myanmar (Burma), 504

Nation, defined, 63
National Organization for Women (NOW), 618
National political surveys, 40
National Rifle Association (NRA), 445
Nation-states, 437
Native Americans, 355, 356, 357, 365–66, 578
  citizenship of, 366, 377
  social standing (2000), 366
Nativist movements, 377
Natural disasters, 299, 301
Natural environment, 586–96
  acid rain, 592
  air pollution, 593
  declining biodiversity, 594
  deficit in, 587
  defined, 586
  deforestation, 586
  ecologically sustainable culture, 595
  and energy consumption, 587
  global dimension, 586
  global warming, 593–94
  and industrialization, 96
  limits to growth, 588

logic of growth, 588
  and population growth,
    584–86, 596
  rain forests, 586, 593–94
  and recycling, 590, 595
  and solid waste, 589–90
  and technology, 587
  water pollution, 592
  water supply, 590–92
Natural selection, 83
Nature, versus nurture, 115–17
Navajo Indians, 224
Nazi Germany, 365, 440, 452,
    502, 613
Near poor, 286
Negroid, 355
Neocolonialism, 309
Neolocality, 465
Neo-Luddites, 245
Neo-Malthusians, 589, 596
Netherlands, 338, 438, 521, 534
  euthanasia, 400–401, 553
Networks, 170–71 (see also
    Internet)
New age spirituality, 510
New Deal, 429, 443
New Guinea, 229, 238
  Mead's gender studies, 326–27
New information technology (see
    Information Revolution)
New reproductive technology,
    484
New social movements theory,
    616, 617
Newspaper reading in U.S.,
    national map, 127
New Testament, 389, 492,
    494–95
New Zealand, 210, 214, 300
Nicaragua, 263, 314, 518
Niger, 308, 312, 328
Nigeria, 272, 316, 342
Nineteenth Amendment, 446
Nirvana, 504
Nisei, 372
Nonconformity, and deviance,
    191
Nongovernmental organizations
    (NGOs), 442
Nonmaterial culture, 61
Nonverbal communication,
    148–50
Normative organizations, 173
Norms, 69–70
  and deviance, 191, 193
  types of, 70
North Korea, 417, 440, 457
Northern Ireland, 353
  religious conflict, 493
Norway, 301, 328, 338, 347, 438,
    504, 557
Nuclear family, 464–65
Nuclear weapons, 96, 455, 457
  arms reduction, 457
  nuclear proliferation, 455
Nurture, versus nature, 115–17
Nutrition
  malnutrition, 543
  malnutrition in poor countries,
    305, 321

Obedience to authority, 166–67
Objectivity, and research, 32–33
Occupational prestige, 274
Occupational specialization, 94,
    105, 175, 410
Occupations (see also Work)
  and gender, 274, 283, 335
Oklahoma City bombing, 77
Old age (see Aging)
Old-age dependency ratio, 386

Old-boy networks, 170
Old Testament, 491
Oligarchy, 177–78
Oligopoly, 427
Open-ended format, 40
Operationalizing a variable, 29
Opportunity, as value, 67
Optimism, 111
Oral cultural tradition, 65
Organic solidarity, 108, 583, 631
Organizational environment,
    175–76
Organizations (see also Formal
    organizations)
  expansion of large-scale, 105
Organized crime, 203–4
Other-directedness, 638
Outgroups, 168
Overgeneralization, 35

Pacific Islanders, 357
Pakistan, 473, 500
  and nuclear weapons, 455, 457
Palestinians, 457
Panama, 255, 318
Panic, 609
Paradigms, sociological, 14–19
  social-conflict paradigm,
    15–17, 19
  structural-functional paradigm,
    14–15, 19
  symbolic interaction paradigm,
    17–19
Paraprofessionals, 422
Parochial schools, 525
Participant observation, 43–45,
    48
Pastoralism, 91–92, 96–97, 263,
    390
Patient rights movement, 559
Patriarchy, 234, 342, 345, 641
  defined, 436
  and education, 520
  and family, 469
  and religion, 494–95, 501
  and sexism, 328–30
Patrilineal descent, 465
Patrilocality, 465
Peace, approaches to, 454–57
Pearl Harbor, 167, 372, 451
Peer group
  and gender socialization, 331
  and socialization, 126
Pentagon attack, 194, 451, 452,
    453, 457, 602
Pentecostals, 513
People's Republic of China, 2,
    94, 99, 173, 234, 264, 300,
    440, 455, 457, 550
  economy in, 417
  gross domestic product (GDP),
    304
  health care in, 555–56
  population of, 6
  religion in, 504
Perestroika, 254, 614
Performances
  embarrassment and tact,
    152–53
  and gender, 151–52
  and idealization, 152
  and presentation of self,
    147–48
Persian Gulf War, women in, 339
Personal computers, global map,
    104
Personal freedom, 418
  and social responsibility,
    644–45
Personality
  authoritarian, 359–60

charismatic, 497
coping with aging, 392
and culture, 61
defined, 115
and deviance, 192–93
Freudian model of, 119
and society, 108
Type A, 328, 547
Personality disorders, 119
Personal orientation, of primary
    groups, 165
Personal space
  and culture, 37, 79
  defined, 152
  and gender, 152
Peru, 224
Pessimism, 111
  national map, 284
Philippines, 211, 299, 303, 308,
    315, 318, 373, 473, 595
Physical appearance
  and criminality, 192
  and culture, 60
Physical attraction, and
    courtship, 470
Physicians
  availability, global map, 544
  role of, 147–48, 559–60
Pink-collar occupations, 335
Placebo, 37
Plant biodiversity, 594
Play stage (G. H. Mead), 123
Plea bargaining, 213
Pluralism, 363, 366
Pluralist model of power, 448
Poland, 214, 419, 534, 614
Police, 211, 213
  community police, 217
Polish Americans, 361
Political action committees
    (PACs), 445–46
Political change, and economic
    development, 10–11
Political economy
  defined, 438
  urban, 582
Political revolution, 450–51
Political spectrum, 443–45
Political state, 437
Political surveys, 40
Politics, 435–59
  and African Americans,
    369–70, 445
  and authority, 435–37
  and critical sociology, 34–35
  defined, 435
  and economic issues, 443–44
  and gender, 338–39
  in global perspective, 437–42
  global system, 442
  and Hispanic Americans, 447
  and Information Revolution,
    458, 566–67
  Marxist political-economy
    model, 449
  medicine as, 561, 563
  and organizational
    environment, 175
  party identification, 281, 445
  political freedom, global map,
    439
  political spectrum, 443–45
  and revolution, 450–51
  and social class, 281
  and social issues, 444
  and special-interest groups,
    445
  systems of, 437–42
  and technology, 458
  and terrorism, 450–51
  theoretical analysis of, 448–50

voter apathy, 435, 446–47
  and war and peace, 457
Polls, 40
Pollution (see also Natural
    environment)
  air, 593
  water, 592
Polyandry, 465
Polygamy, 465, 468
Polygyny, 463, 465
Polytheism, 500
Popular culture, 73
Population (see also Demography)
  aging, 384–98
  in agrarian societies, 93
  composition of, 573–74
  control, 312
  demographic transition theory,
    575–76
  demography, 569–74
  doubling time, 573
  gay people in, 230
  in global perspective, 570, 572
  growth, 321, 571–73, 596
  growth, global map, 572
  growth, and global poverty,
    308
  internal migration, U.S.
    national map, 571
  Malthusian theory, 574–75,
    596
  and natural environment,
    584–86, 596
  neo- versus anti-Malthusians,
    596
  and social change, 628–29
  in survey research, 39
  theories, history of, 574–76
  in twenty-first century, 596
Pornography, 232, 342–43
  as power issue, 239
  and sexual violence, 343
Portugal, 521
Positivism, 12, 28
Post-denomination society, 510
Postindustrial economy, 410–12,
    419–25
  and social institutions, 566–67
Postindustrial societies,
    characteristics of, 94–97
Postindustrialism, defined, 95
Postmodernity
  defined, 626, 641
  themes of, 641–42
Poverty, 95, 286–95
  absolute poverty, 286, 304–5
  and African Americans, 287,
    394
  and aging, 286–87, 394
  and Asian Americans, 370
  as cause of death, 305
  and children, 287, 305–7
  and children, national map, 288
  culture of, 290
  feminization of, 287, 289
  and gender, 287, 289, 307, 482
  global, 303–10
  and health, 543–45, 548
  and Hispanic Americans, 287
  homelessness, 292–93
  and India, 310
  of low-income countries, 6, 7
  public opinion on, 295
  and race and ethnicity, 287, 394
  rate, U.S. (1960–2000), 286
  rates by age, in U.S., 394
  relative poverty, 286, 304–5
  urban and rural, 289
  versus modernization, 312
  views on, 290–92

and women, 482
  working poor, 290, 292
Poverty line, 286
Poverty threshold, 286
Power (see also Politics)
  defined, 435
  and deviance, 201
  and gender, 343–44
  and global relationships, 309
  and groups, 168
  and language, 153–55
  and personal space, 152
  and pornography, 239
  and rape, 235
  and sexual violence, 340
  and social inequality, 273
  of society, 448–49
  and wealth, 273–74
Power-elite model, 448
Powerlessness, modernity and, 639
Practicality, value of, 67
Practical learning, 522
Preconventional level of moral development, 120
Predestination, 103–4, 494–95
Preindustrial society (see Agrarian societies; Horticultural societies; Hunting and gathering societies)
Prejudice, 357–61
  defined, 357–58
  and discrimination, 362
  ethnocentrism, 79
  theories of, 359–61
Premarital sex, 226–27
Preoperational stage (Piaget), 119–20
Prescriptive norms, 69–70
Presentation of self, 147–48
  and Information Revolution, 245
Prestige, occupational, 274
Pretesting, 40
Primary deviance, 197
Primary economic sector, 412
Primary groups, 164–65
Primary labor market, 420
Primary sex characteristics, 223
Primates, 62–63, 65, 117
Primogeniture, 252
Prisons, 214–15
  incarceration rates, 214
  and resocialization, 133–35
  violence in, 38–39, 48
Privacy
  and bureaucracy, 186–87
  and information technology, 186–87
Private schools, 525–26
Pro-choice, 240–41
Profane, defined, 491
Professions, 421–22
Profit, and capitalism, 415
Pro-life, 240–41
Progress
  and modernity, 639–41
  as value, 67–68
Progressive education, 522
Prohibition, 203
Projective labeling, 198
Proletarians, 97, 99, 259
Promise Keepers, 513, 611
Propaganda, 609
Property crimes, 206
Property ownership
  and capitalism, 415
  inheritance, 469
Proposition 187, 377
Proscriptive norms, 69
Proselytize, 497

Prostitution, 233–35
  functions of, 236–37
  global map, 234
  risk of arrest, 238
  sexual slavery, 308
Protest crowds, 603
Protestant Reformation, 103, 311–12, 500
Protestants, 367, 505
  and capitalism, 494–95
  and patriarchy, 495
  and suicide, 3, 13
  work ethic, 367, 495, 625
Psychological changes in aging, 387–88
Psychosomatic disorders, 560
Public broadcasting, support for, national map, 608
Public opinion, 608–9
Public policy, and sociology, 10
Public schools, 521
  rating in U.S.(2001), 531
  versus private schools, 525–26
Puerto Ricans, 375, 476 (see also Hispanic Americans (Latinos))
Puerto Rico, 312, 315
Punishment, for crime, 214–15
Purchasing power parities, 304
Puritans, 224, 491
  sociological investigation of, 47–48
  witchcraft trials, 195
Pygmies, 90
Pyramids, 92

Q'ero, 59, 61, 69
Quakerism, sociological investigation of, 47–48
Qualitative research, 44
Quality of life, global view, 304
Quantitative research, 44
Queer theory, 239
Questionnaires, 39–40
Quid pro quo sexual harassment, 342
Qur'an (Koran), 491, 494, 500–501

Race, 353–79
  as caste, 250–51
  classification by, 355
  and crime, 209–10
  defined, 354
  and discrimination, 20, 361–62
  Du Bois on, 16
  and family, 475–77
  and formal organizations, 178, 179
  and hate crimes, 204
  and health, 546–48, 552
  and Information Revolution, 407
  and intelligence, 360–61
  majority/minority interactions, 363–65
  in organizations, 179–80
  and poverty, 287
  and prejudice, 357–61
  and religion, 507–8
  as social construction, 354–55
  and social mobility, 283
  and social stratification, 275–76
  and sports, 19–20
  and suicide rates, 3–4
  typology, 355
  and work, 418
Race consciousness, 361
Racism, 25, 41–43, 68
  and African Americans, 359
  environmental, 594–95
Radical feminism, 347
Rain forests, 586, 593–94

Random sampling, 39
Rape, 235–37, 341
  date, 235–37
  defined, 235
  male rape, 235
  marital, 481
  and pornography, 232
Rationality
  defined, 102
  of social organization, 102–7
Rationalization of society, 103, 174, 185, 632–33
Rational-legal authority, 436, 438
Real culture, 70
Reality, and humor, 155–59
Rebellion, and deviance, 196
Recidivism, criminal, 215
Recycling, 590, 595
Red tape, 177
Redemptive social movements, 611
Reference groups, 167
Reflexes, 116
Reformative social movements, 611
Reformatories, 214
Rehabilitation, criminals, 214
Reincarnation, 503
Relative deprivation, 612
Relative poverty, 286, 304–5, 305
Relativism, cultural, 79–80
Reliability, of measurement, 29–30
Religion, 491–513
  in agrarian societies, 93
  agrarian societies, 93
  basic concepts of, 491–92
  Buddhism, global map, 502
  Christianity, global map, 499
  civil, 508
  defined, 491
  eastern compared to western, 505
  electronic church, 511
  and ethnicity, 355–56
  fundamentalism, 510–11, 513
  Hinduism, global map, 502
  in history, 498
  horticultural societies, 92
  and Information Revolution, 511, 513
  Islam, global map, 499
  membership, national map, 506
  and patriarchy, 494–95, 501
  and prostitution, 234
  Puritan Boston and Quaker Philadelphia, 47–48
  and science, 512
  and secularization, 508
  and social change, 494–96
  social-conflict analysis of, 493–94
  and social stratification, 276, 507–8
  compared to spirituality, 510
  structural-functional analysis of, 492–93
  symbolic-interaction analysis of, 493
  in twenty-first century, 513
  in U.S., 505–13
  variation in U.S., 355
  world, 499–505
Religiosity, 30, 506–7
  forms of, 506
Remarriage, 480
Renaissance, 12
Replication of research, 33
Representative democracy, 458
Repression, 119

Reproduction, 83–84
  incest taboo, 467–68
  sex determination, 222
Reproductive rights, 346
Reproductive technology, 484
Research
  bias in, 34, 39
  and ethics, 36
  feminist, 34
  and gender, 35–36, 121
  and human behavior, 33
  Internet sources, 45–46
  methods (see Sociological investigation)
  and new information technology, 56–57
  objectivity in, 32–33
  and politics, 34–35
  summary of methods, 48
Reservations, 366
Residential patterns
  of affluent minorities, 47
  and marriage, 465
  in U.S., national map, 628
Resocialization, of prison inmate, 133–35
Resource-mobilization theory, 614–15, 617
Retirement, 132, 393–94
Retreatism
  and deviance, 196
  retreatist subculture, 196
Retreatists, 202
Retribution, 213–14
Retrospective labeling, 198
Reverse discrimination, 379
Revolution
  Marxist, 101, 260–61
  political, 450–51
  as social movement, 611
  urban, 578–79, 586
Revolutionary War, 450
"Right to die" debate, 399–401, 553
Rights, of individual, 11, 68, 438
Riots, 603–4
Ritual, defined, 491
Ritualism
  bureaucratic, 177
  and deviance, 196
RJR-Nabisco, 426
"Roaring Twenties," 225
Rock-and-roll, 107, 108, 194
Role, 141–43
  defined, 141
Role conflict, 142–43
Role exit, 143
Role models, 141
Role set, 142
Role strain, 143
Role-taking, 122
Roman Empire, 93, 500, 578
Romania, 419
Romantic love, 472, 479
Routinization of charisma, 437
Rules and regulations, and bureaucracy, 174
Rumor, 606–8
Rural areas, population trend, 581–82
Rural life (see Gemeinschaft; Mechanical solidarity)
Russia, 173, 214, 301, 302, 453, 550
Russian Federation, 255, 302, 304
  health care in, 556–57
Russian Revolution (1917), 254, 450
Rwanda, 314, 365, 543

SINGLE PC LICENSE AGREEMENT AND LIMITED WARRANTY

READ THIS LICENSE CAREFULLY BEFORE OPENING THIS PACKAGE. BY OPENING THIS PACKAGE, YOU ARE AGREEING TO THE TERMS AND CONDITIONS OF THIS LICENSE. IF YOU DO NOT AGREE, DO NOT OPEN THE PACKAGE. PROMPTLY RETURN THE UNOPENED PACKAGE AND ALL ACCOMPANYING ITEMS TO THE PLACE YOU OBTAINED THEM.

1.   GRANT OF LICENSE and OWNERSHIP: The enclosed computer programs ("Software") are licensed, not sold, to you by Prentice-Hall, Inc. ("We" or the "Company") and in consideration of your purchase or adoption of the accompanying Company textbooks and/or other materials, and your agreement to these terms. We reserve any rights not granted to you. You own only the disk(s) but we and/or our licensors own the Software itself. This license allows you to use and display your copy of the Software on a single computer (i.e., with a single CPU) at a single location for <u>academic</u> use only, so long as you comply with the terms of this Agreement. You may make one copy for backup, or transfer your copy to another CPU, provided that the Software is usable on only one computer.

2.   RESTRICTIONS: You may <u>not</u> transfer or distribute the Software or documentation to anyone else. Except for backup, you may not copy the documentation or the Software. You may <u>not</u> network the Software or otherwise use it on more than one computer or computer terminal at the same time. You may <u>not</u> reverse engineer, disassemble, decompile, modify, adapt, translate, or create derivative works based on the Software or the Documentation. You may be held legally responsible for any copying or copyright infringement which is caused by your failure to abide by the terms of these restrictions.

3.   TERMINATION: This license is effective until terminated. This license will terminate automatically without notice from the Company if you fail to comply with any provisions or limitations of this license. Upon termination, you shall destroy the Documentation and all copies of the Software. All provisions of this Agreement as to limitation and disclaimer of warranties, limitation of liability, remedies or damages, and our ownership rights shall survive termination.

4.   LIMITED WARRANTY AND DISCLAIMER OF WARRANTY: Company warrants that for a period of 60 days from the date you purchase this SOFTWARE (or purchase or adopt the accompanying textbook), the Software, when properly installed and used in accordance with the Documentation, will operate in substantial conformity with the description of the Software set forth in the Documentation, and that for a period of 30 days the disk(s) on which the Software is delivered shall be free from defects in materials and workmanship under normal use. The Company does <u>not</u> warrant that the Software will meet your requirements or that the operation of the Software will be uninterrupted or error-free. Your only remedy and the Company's only obligation under these limited warranties is, at the Company's option, return of the disk for a refund of any amounts paid for it by you or replacement of the disk. THIS LIMITED WARRANTY IS THE ONLY WARRANTY PROVIDED BY THE COMPANY AND ITS LICENSORS, AND THE COMPANY AND ITS LICENSORS DISCLAIM ALL OTHER WARRANTIES, EXPRESSED OR IMPLIED, INCLUDING WITHOUT LIMITATION, THE IMPLIED WARRANTIES OF MERCHANTABILITY AND FITNESS FOR A PARTICULAR PURPOSE. THE COMPANY DOES NOT WARRANT, GUARANTEE, OR MAKE ANY REPRESENTATION REGARDING THE ACCURACY, RELIABILITY, CURRENTNESS, USE, OR RESULTS OF USE, OF THE SOFTWARE.

5.   LIMITATION OF REMEDIES AND DAMAGES: IN NO EVENT, SHALL THE COMPANY OR ITS EMPLOYEES, AGENTS, LICENSORS, OR CONTRACTORS BE LIABLE FOR ANY INCIDENTAL, INDIRECT, SPECIAL, OR CONSEQUENTIAL DAMAGES ARISING OUT OF OR IN CONNECTION WITH THIS LICENSE OR THE SOFTWARE, INCLUDING LOSS OF USE, LOSS OF DATA, LOSS OF INCOME OR PROFIT, OR OTHER LOSSES, SUSTAINED AS A RESULT OF INJURY TO ANY PERSON, OR LOSS OF OR DAMAGE TO PROPERTY, OR CLAIMS OF THIRD PARTIES, EVEN IF THE COMPANY OR AN AUTHORIZED REPRESENTATIVE OF THE COMPANY HAS BEEN ADVISED OF THE POSSIBILITY OF SUCH DAMAGES. IN NO EVENT SHALL THE LIABILITY OF THE COMPANY FOR DAMAGES WITH RESPECT TO THE SOFTWARE EXCEED THE AMOUNTS ACTUALLY PAID BY YOU, IF ANY, FOR THE SOFTWARE OR THE ACCOMPANYING TEXTBOOK. BECAUSE SOME JURISDICTIONS DO NOT ALLOW THE LIMITATION OF LIABILITY IN CERTAIN CIRCUMSTANCES, THE ABOVE LIMITATIONS MAY NOT ALWAYS APPLY TO YOU.

6.   GENERAL: THIS AGREEMENT SHALL BE CONSTRUED IN ACCORDANCE WITH THE LAWS OF THE UNITED STATES OF AMERICA AND THE STATE OF NEW YORK, APPLICABLE TO CONTRACTS MADE IN NEW YORK, AND SHALL BENEFIT THE COMPANY, ITS AFFILIATES AND ASSIGNEES. THIS AGREEMENT IS THE COMPLETE AND EXCLUSIVE STATEMENT OF THE AGREEMENT BETWEEN YOU AND THE COMPANY AND SUPERSEDES ALL PROPOSALS OR PRIOR AGREEMENTS, ORAL, OR WRITTEN, AND ANY OTHER COMMUNICATIONS BETWEEN YOU AND THE COMPANY OR ANY REPRESENTATIVE OF THE COMPANY RELATING TO THE SUBJECT MATTER OF THIS AGREEMENT. If you are a U.S. Government user, this Software is licensed with "restricted rights" as set forth in subparagraphs (a)-(d) of the Commercial Computer-Restricted Rights clause at FAR 52.227-19 or in subparagraphs (c)(1)(ii) of the Rights in Technical Data and Computer Software clause at DFARS 252.227-7013, and similar clauses, as applicable.

Should you have any questions concerning this agreement or if you wish to contact the Company for any reason, please contact in writing: Senior Media Editor, Social Sciences, HSS, Prentice Hall, One Lake Street, Upper Saddle River, NJ 07458.

SYSTEM REQUIREMENTS
MACINTOSH: minimum 68040/33MHz, System 8.0 or above, 12mb RAM (16mb recommended), 1mb free HD space, 8x CD-ROM, 640X480 screen resolution, color monitor (thousands of colors required). QuickTime 4.0 installed from CD.

PC: minimum 486/DX25, Windows 95/98 (minimum 16mb RAM), 1mb free HD space, 8X CD-ROM, SVGA monitor, thousands of colors, sound and video cards required. QuickTime 4.0 installed from CD.